1001 Crystals

THE COMPLETE BOOK OF CRYSTALS FOR EVERY PURPOSE

CASSANDRA EASON

STERLING ETHOS
New York

Thank you to Sacha Grigg Tejani, www.silver-dove.net,
for her expertise, advice, and crystal wisdom.

STERLING ETHOS
New York

An Imprint of Sterling Publishing Co., Inc.

ISBN 978-1-4549-4574-1
978-1-4549-4575-8 (e-book)

For information about custom editions, special sales, and
premium purchases, please contact
specialsales@unionsquareandco.com

Printed in China

2 4 6 8 10 9 7 5 3 1

unionsquareandco.com

Anniversary Crystals and Gemstones list on pages 32–33 is an official list
of the American Gem Trade Association. Reproduced from
The Complete Crystal Handbook by Cassandra Eason, Sterling US (2010).

With thanks to Charles Reynolds at Charlies Rock Shop, 1929 Shop, Merton Abbey Mills, Watermill Way, London
SW19 2RD, for his expert advice and provision of many unusual minerals for this book.

Illustrations : Carolyn M. Casey
Cover design by Gina Bonanno and Melissa Farris
Interior design by Melissa Farris

Contents

Introduction

1001 Crystals is the culmination of more than forty years of my personal research into the mythology, traditional uses, healing, and everyday properties of crystals as I have traveled around the world. It draws, too, on my own constantly evolving, hands-on work in crystal healing, magick, and divination, plus the knowledge other crystal experts have shared with me.

   This book contains twice as many crystals as my most extensive earlier crystal books, but in no way replaces previous books I have written about crystals. Rather, it suggests additional and sometimes alternative ways of using crystals, which I have discovered since writing those earlier crystal books. Some of the new crystals I have described in *1,001 Crystals* are rare or relatively recently discovered, while others can be purchased for a few dollars. All are obtainable online or from good specialty mineral stores. I have included all my crystal favorites, too, those perennial stones that form the core of crystal wisdom through the ages.

How to Build Your Crystal Collection

However many or few crystals you have in your collection, crystals spread happiness and harmony in the home; heal people, animals, and places; bring fertility and prosperity; protect children and pets; and can be empowered as lucky charms, money-bringers, or protective amulets. They bring and preserve love and reconciliation; attract success in the workplace; guard against jealousy and spite from rivals, unpleasant neighbors, or colleagues; and protect us from danger as we go about our daily lives. All these—and many more uses—the individual crystal entries will reveal.

Be alert as you travel for crystals indigenous to a particular location you visit, which carry home with you the energies of the land. Look also on hillsides, ocean shores, and riverbanks for fossils or glints of crystals hidden in a seemingly ordinary stone—for when cracked open, they will reveal their gleaming hidden treasure. Explore country markets where people sell crystals they have dug up and polished. Go rummaging or fossil hunting, especially with an expert. Often, the crystals bought cheaply from a localized source or found for free, especially in their natural state within a matrix of rock, have a pure power their more embellished sisters and brothers lack.

Making Crystals Part of Your World

◆ Keep your crystals in a special place, perhaps in a bowl on a table reserved for that purpose, the delicate ones in velvet bags, with candles, growing flowers and fragrances.

◆ Take time to sit in your special crystal place, playing soft background music, holding different crystals in turn by candlelight, soft sunlight, or moonlight. Light beautiful incense and candles, and make your crystal time a sanctuary from the world, alone or as a unifier for your friends and family.

◆ Meditate or let your crystals take you on astral or waking dream journeys. Tell stories about them to your children. I have included many of the myths that bring the crystals to life.

◆ Pick a crystal daily by touch, asking a question if you wish. Hold it and let it reveal its special message, through your sensitive palm and finger energy centers that are connected to your heart chakra energy center.

◆ Allow images and words to flow through your mind or take them in as impressions.

◆ Set crystals around your home, in your workspace, and in the glove compartment of your vehicle, or carry them with you for luck or protection.

You don't need to be a crystal expert to benefit from crystals. Crystals are millions of years old, sometimes billions. If we trust them, they will guide and teach us how to move them to promote healing and let us share their wisdom. That is why children naturally relate to crystals because they allow their natural psyche to make the connection.

About This Book

Included in the book are ways of using crystals for healing, to enrich family and work life, for spiritual and magickal purposes as well as sections on identifying crystals instantly by color; cleansing and empowering them; and creating crystal grids or layouts for health, wealth, and happiness. You will also discover wedding anniversary crystals; those for children and pets; and those offering protection against ill-wishing, curses, attack, accidents, burglaries, and paranormal threats.

Crystals in Your Life

Above all, crystals are a reminder of how amazing nature is. For each crystal is a powerhouse, containing the ancient magickal elements and physical substances—Earth, Air, Fire, and Water—mixed, mingled, refined through the millennia into something greater than what it started as. Because of this almost magickal process, we can derive wisdom, knowledge, power, and healing, not from the physical composition of the crystal, but from the essence or energy field it radiates. Sometimes the stone was hurled from a meteor or cast up from what was once an ocean bed. Now found in a desert, the mineral may have been formed from a fossilized sea creature that lived at the dawning of life on Earth.

  So, while I hope this book will be a guide through the crystalline world, above all, tap into your very own crystalline connection. For crystal knowledge is constantly evolving and each one of us can make that unique link that awakens in us our inner spark.

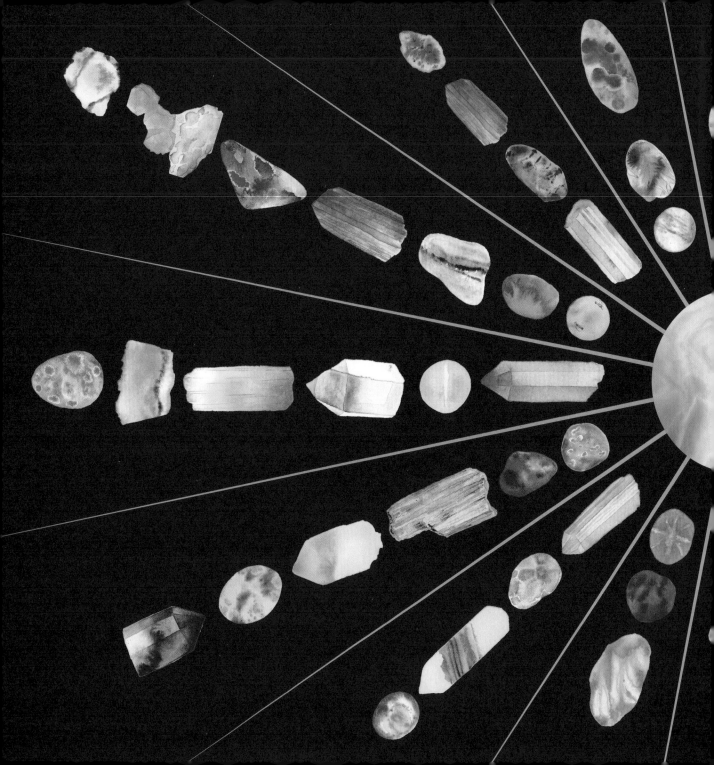

Crystals A *to* Z

Abalone Shell

COLORS: Iridescent green-blue or purple pearl contained within a convex oval brown or grayish shell
CRYSTAL TYPE: Shell, from a group of marine mollusks called haliotidae; also used as an organic gem (see also Paua Shell, page 339)
ZODIAC SIGN: Cancer (June 22–July 22)
CANDLE COLOR: Silver

PHYSICAL: Addresses high blood pressure, palpitations, vertigo, headaches, vision problems, psychosomatic conditions, indigestion (especially from hurried eating).
EMOTIONAL: Eases panic attacks; peace in crises, especially after heartbreak in love; restores self-esteem after negative comments about appearance.
HOME: Calms anger and rivalries within the family or from extended family members.
WORKPLACE: Defuses workplace tensions, dramas and over-competitiveness; works especially well for artists, illustrators, color therapists, and fantasy fiction writers.
CHILDREN: Hyperactive children and those affected by overstimulation; especially useful for teens teased because of physical blemishes or scars.
ANIMALS: Benefits tropical fish and koi.
PROTECTION: Guards against cynicism, disillusionment, and bitterness.

MAGICKAL AND PSYCHIC USES
For smudging ceremonies, burning cedar, sagebrush leaves, or sweetgrass coils in the shell; shamanic travel to undersea worlds, links with water spirits.

SPECIAL PROPERTIES
Releases creativity to transform unpromising situations into opportunities.

MYTHOLOGY AND HISTORY
Abalone has been used for food, adornment, healing, and ritual since time immemorial, especially in oceanic cultures. For example, on the northwestern coast of America, where once Abalone was traded as currency, it is associated with rites of passage for girls and women; the Sunrise Ceremony marks a girl's passage into womanhood among the Navajo and Apache nations, honoring White Painted Woman who survived the Great Flood in an Abalone shell.

Abundance Quartz

COLORS: Usually clear, colorless quartz, but can appear in other quartzes, including amethyst and citrine, itself a stone of abundance
CRYSTAL TYPE: Often long quartz crystal, with more than nine smaller crystals clustered around the base, silicon dioxide
ZODIAC SIGN: Sagittarius (November 23–December 21)
CANDLE COLOR: White

PHYSICAL: Promotes fertility, especially if a couple has one child but seems unable to conceive more; helps control excess weight, cholesterol.
EMOTIONAL: Addresses fears of poverty that lead to hoarding and unnecessary economies; counters shopping addiction.
HOME: Attracts abundance and prosperity. Place in the wealth corner of a home or a room. Boosts plant growth.
WORKPLACE: Encourages teamwork and collective efforts, such as if you are leading a project and need to get others on board; leads to good returns on investments.
CHILDREN: Heads off accusations of favoritism, especially in a large family.
ANIMALS: Promotes the well-being of pets interbred with exotic wild species.
PROTECTION: Guards against excesses and unnecessary extravagances.

MAGICKAL AND PSYCHIC USES
Abundance Quartz can be programmed for increase and manifestation; a focus for priest/priestess-led ceremonies and seasonal celebrations.

SPECIAL PROPERTIES
For luxury activities, fine dining and cordon bleu cookery, glamping, sports requiring a heavy financial outlay, vacations to exotic locales.

MYTHOLOGY AND HISTORY
The crystal of the pure life force to stir home, workplace, individuals, and teams into positive action; encourages decluttering the home, workplace, and the mind. Found in the Himalayas, Abundance Quartz represents regeneration and the ability to soar like the mountains.

Acasta Gneiss

COLORS: Brown, gray, black, white, pink in flowing bands of color
CRYSTAL TYPE: Composed mostly of quartz and feldspar during the earliest eon in Earth's history
ZODIAC SIGN: Aquarius (January 21–February 18)
CANDLE COLOR: Gray

PHYSICAL: Addresses aging problems, eczema, psoriasis, rosacea, hereditary conditions.
EMOTIONAL: Assuages fears of mortality and the dying process.
HOME: Enables people to put down roots in a new building; helps explore family history.
WORKPLACE: Aids people working beyond conventional retirement age, particularly geologists, mineralogists, paleontologists, and historians.
CHILDREN: Viewed as a treasure given on the first adult birthday.
ANIMALS: Promotes the study of cryptozoology and inexplicable life forms.
PROTECTION: Guards against regrets for not fulfilling your destiny.

MAGICKAL AND PSYCHIC USES
Promotes visions of ancient lives prehumanity; the age of some Mars rock is like rocks on the Acasta Gneiss, forming an extraterrestrial link.

SPECIAL PROPERTIES
A rarity and a collector's item, which some believe should not be marketed. However, it could be argued that Acasta Gneiss's unique antiquity, healing, and metaphysical powers should be more widely shared.

MYTHOLOGY AND HISTORY
Acasta Gneiss, which is approximately four billion years old, is the oldest exposed rock on the planet's surface. It's found only on an island 180 miles north of the town of Yellowknife in Canada's Northwest Territories and named after the Acasta River. The outcrop was first discovered in the 1980s, reached only by float plane. A four-ton boulder of Acasta Gneiss is displayed outside the National Museum of the American Indian in Washington, D.C.

Achroite or Colorless Tourmaline

COLOR: Clear, occasionally with a spot of color
CRYSTAL TYPE: Complex silicate of boron and aluminum, of the elbaite or fluor-elbaite family; the rarest of tourmalines
ZODIAC SIGN: Pisces (February 19–March 20)
CANDLE COLOR: Silver

PHYSICAL: Restores balance after trauma or prolonged illness; relieves chronic headaches, throat constrictions, physical blockages; aligns the body.
EMOTIONAL: Addresses lack of confidence, naivete, inability to tackle practical problems.
HOME: Encourages the acquisition of another language if living overseas or with a partner who speaks another language; quiets dominant family members.
WORKPLACE: Promotes clarity when speaking in meetings on- and offline or giving lectures; if constantly under pressure with deadlines and targets.
CHILDREN: Addresses speech difficulties; fears of speaking or reading aloud in class.
ANIMALS: Establishes that you are the alpha of the pack.
PROTECTION: Aids in knowing when you are being deceived.

MAGICKAL AND PSYCHIC USES
Enables automatic writing, channeling angels, guides, and ancestors; psychic artistry; natural wands to banish negativity, cleanse the aura, and find necessary resources.

SPECIAL PROPERTIES
For leadership and attracting positive interest at work or in love; developing unrealized talents at the right time.

MYTHOLOGY AND HISTORY
Tourmaline comes from the Singhalese word *turamali*, meaning "colored or mixed stone," because of its variety of colors. Colorless Tourmaline represents the synthesis of all the colors; different legends tell how tourmaline fell from the rainbow to Earth. Achroite amplifies the effects of other crystals, especially tourmalines, increasing the luck-bringing properties of your zodiac stone. This powerful stone should be worn only for short periods.

Actinolite

COLORS: Light to dark green, grayish green to black

CRYSTAL TYPE: Hydrous calcium magnesium iron silicate; may be found in quartz

ZODIAC SIGN: Scorpio (October 24–November 22)

CANDLE COLOR: Green

PHYSICAL: Assists in building cells, connective tissues; regenerates the body; removes toxins from liver, kidneys, all filtering body organs; alleviates hives, eczema, acne, rosacea, especially stress-related disorders.

EMOTIONAL: In lighter shades, counteracts isolation and alienation; makes social encounters less daunting.

HOME: Protects against external attack, vandalism, or burglary in dangerous areas, and aggressive neighbors.

WORKPLACE: Darker shades guard against factions, cliques, and divisions, open and hidden; helps with fitting into a new workplace.

CHILDREN: Helps children make friends at school and social events.

ANIMALS: Makes dogs friendlier to other pets.

PROTECTION: All-purpose shield as green or actinolite in quartz; for blending into unfamiliar lands and cultures; for avoiding unwittingly offending local customs.

MAGICKAL AND PSYCHIC USES

A dream crystal for past-life memories and ancient worlds; recalling predictive and healing sleep messages.

SPECIAL PROPERTIES

Hold a darker actinolite as an antipanic stone at work or when traveling; in the home to absorb worries of the day.

MYTHOLOGY AND HISTORY

Called the *ray stone* because it can appear as needles, its energies radiate as connections with others and the cosmos. Globally, each piece cumulatively promotes unity among all humankind, spreading goodwill between different faiths and political systems.

Aegirine

COLORS: Black, dark green, or brownish black

CRYSTAL TYPE: Sodium iron silicate, often as striated rods

ZODIAC SIGN: Pisces (February 19–March 20)

CANDLE COLOR: Dark green

PHYSICAL: Strengthens the immune system, promotes self-healing; increases the potency of other crystals; alleviates sleep disturbances; boosts energy.

EMOTIONAL: Improves poor body image if teased during childhood or adolescence; soothes after relationship breakup; keeps you from feeling overwhelmed by life; alleviates addictions.

HOME: Prevents family members from being led astray; encourages taking a sabbatical or time-out.

WORKPLACE: Helps in maintaining your identity if under threat; gives an unenthusiastic team a new sense of purpose; helps women facing sexism, especially those returning to work after maternity leave; prevents burnout among medical staff.

CHILDREN: Motivates lethargic teenagers; protects younger family members who are backpacking or taking a gap year overseas.

ANIMALS: Gives new life to overly domesticated pets.

PROTECTION: Guards against psychological or psychic attack caused by jealousy.

MAGICKAL AND PSYCHIC USES

As a magick wand to call what you need and repel what you do not; enhances reiki and other energy transference systems; promotes aura reading to see others without illusion.

SPECIAL PROPERTIES

Changes your lifestyle if it goes against your principles; helps you accept what cannot be changed for now without lowering your personal standards.

MYTHOLOGY AND HISTORY

Aegirine is named after the Norse sea god Aegir, since it was first found close to the sea in Norway. Its blade shape reflects the sword of truth, carried by heroes and heroines through the ages. This crystal offers power to women striving against multiple inequalities, such as agism and ethnicity.

Afghanite

COLORS: Shades of blue, from bright to dark midnight blue, can be contained within the same crystal; white or colorless

CRYSTAL TYPE: Hydrous silicate of sodium, calcium, and potassium, with chloride, carbonate, and sulfate; sometimes as elongated prisms or large crystals embedded in a calcite or marble matrix or smaller crystals encrusting the matrix

ZODIAC SIGN: Gemini (May 22–June 21)

CANDLE COLOR: Bright blue

PHYSICAL: Strengthens the throat, the thymus, the immune system, the brain, the bones; alleviates insomnia.

EMOTIONAL: Overcomes panic attacks. obsessions, over-reactions; useful in group therapy.

HOME: Helps families talk about feelings and express affection and praise.

WORKPLACE: Inspires analytical thinking, combining intuition with fast assimilation of facts; promotes productive brainstorming, networking, meetings, and conferences; especially useful for salespersons, advertisers, and publicity or press officers.

CHILDREN: Helps children to share and to become team players.

ANIMALS: Tempers greedy animals who constantly demand treats.

PROTECTION: Guards against internet scams, trolling, and negative social media communication.

MAGICKAL AND PSYCHIC USES

Promotes astral travel, meditation; puts you in touch with ancient past lives and interdimensional connections; helps access the Akashic records; increases telepathy.

SPECIAL PROPERTIES

The ultimate crystal of clear, persuasive communication of ideas in the workplace, on the internet through blogs and forums, for more loving relationships and understanding your own feelings.

MYTHOLOGY AND HISTORY

Named after the place it was first discovered in Badakshan Province, Afghanistan, Afghanite acts as a psychic radar, guiding you to hidden information, even if you're not sure what you're looking for.

Agate Slices

COLORS: All the natural colors of banded agate, but also injection-dyed in a variety of bright colors.

CRYSTAL TYPE: Most agates form as geodes or cavities in volcanic rock. Agate slices are thinly cut and polished segments of these, often containing a crystallized (frequently quartz) center.

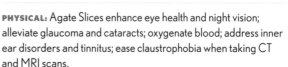

ZODIAC SIGN: Gemini (May 22–June 21)

CANDLE COLOR: According to color of the slice

PHYSICAL: Agate Slices enhance eye health and night vision; alleviate glaucoma and cataracts; oxygenate blood; address inner ear disorders and tinnitus; ease claustrophobia when taking CT and MRI scans.

EMOTIONAL: Calm you when life is spinning out of control, and you're unable to see beyond an immediate crisis.

HOME: Set in windows to catch sunlight and create rainbows to keep the life force, optimism, and health flowing.

WORKPLACE: Agate Slices, set where they catch the light, replace critical or apathetic attitudes with cooperation and cheerfulness.

CHILDREN: Stimulate imaginative play if hung in playrooms; enable glimpses of the fey, set outdoors.

ANIMALS: Soothe restless animals left at home alone.

PROTECTION: Placed in windows, Agate Slices repel psychic attack or ill-wishing coming your way.

MAGICKAL AND PSYCHIC USES

A dark-colored, highly polished Agate Slice, held up to candlelight, forms a dark magick mirror to view spirit guardians and wise ancestors.

SPECIAL PROPERTIES

Set beneath cups, bowls, and plates, Agate Slices energize the contents and make any difficult people using the utensils feel and speak more positively.

MYTHOLOGY AND HISTORY

As bookends, thick Agate Slices encourage the family to read actual books as well as online materials. Keep crystals to be used for healing or magick on top of an Agate Slice to constantly cleanse and recharge. Place Agate Slices at the four directions in a room where you carry out rituals or healings.

Agatized Coral

COLORS: White, pink, brown, gray, black, golden yellow, and red; often multicolored with small flower-like patterns; lustrous

CRYSTAL TYPE: When silica in ocean water hardens, lime-based corals are replaced with agate, chalcedony

ZODIAC SIGN: Cancer (June 22–July 22)

CANDLE COLOR: Cream

PHYSICAL: Alleviates emphysema, asthma, bronchitis, allergies, brittle bones, osteoporosis; enhances eye health, iridology, Eustachian tubes, lymphatic glands; addresses unsteadiness in later age.

EMOTIONAL: Eases personality disorders, overreactions, uncontrolled temper, gambling, drinking, overreliance on sex or psychic phone lines.

HOME: Addresses dysfunctional family or love relationships or, after divorce, altered living arrangements.

WORKPLACE: Promotes team building and cooperation, while discouraging infighting; helps fiction writers, as well as film, television, and radio producers of creative documentaries to preserve integrity; useful for ecologists and marine biologists.

CHILDREN: Protects against falls; eases acute shyness; deters teenagers from playing overly loud music.

ANIMALS: Reduces sensitivity to noise and crowded places.

PROTECTION: Shields therapists, counselors, and those who help others with problems against absorbing their pain and brings them peace.

MAGICKAL AND PSYCHIC USES

Connects with the divine inner core, unchanging through different lifetimes; awareness of the interdependence of life in all times and places.

SPECIAL PROPERTIES

The detective crystal, unraveling mysteries and secrets of those behaving furtively; increases intuition so you can understand hidden motives and assess trustworthiness in others.

MYTHOLOGY AND HISTORY

Agatized fossil corals occur in many parts of the world and may be up to 395 million years old. The long fossilization process results in forming a *pseudomorph*, replacing one mineral with another without losing its original form. It is illegal in several countries to harvest Agatized Coral; it is possible, however, to find ecologically sustainable coral.

Agni Magnetite

COLORS: Dark charcoal gray–black to smoky translucence when polished

CRYSTAL TYPE: A rare high-energy tektite

ZODIAC SIGN: Scorpio (October 24–November 22)

CANDLE COLOR: Gray

PHYSICAL: Increases energy levels, kick-starts the metabolism, and a sluggish immune system; alleviates autoimmune conditions; useful before major operations, intensive-care unit (ICU) treatment and where the prognosis is not good; promotes minor health miracles and the will to live and recover.

EMOTIONAL: Addresses lack of connection with life and people, extreme lethargy, and unwillingness to tackle problems; motivates those who have lost the will to live; banishes suicidal thoughts; prevents self-harm.

HOME: Brings assistance when an unscrupulous property owner refuses to carry out essential repairs; helps obtain the right accommodations in an area of high demand.

WORKPLACE: Inspires leadership for innovative projects and, if necessary, breaking away from accepted opinion.

CHILDREN: For those who talk of extraterrestrial or UFO dreams and experiences, and fear abduction.

ANIMALS: Cultivates telepathy with pets.

PROTECTION: Absorbs energies that are not from the light and all bad earthly intentions; prevents squandering gifts on unworthwhile causes or projects.

MAGICKAL AND PSYCHIC USES

For Star Souls and star wisdom; the sudden emergence of proof of psychic powers, especially clairvoyance; ability to see ghosts; enhanced healing powers.

SPECIAL PROPERTIES

For discovering or rediscovering a dormant talent and making it an increasingly important strand of life, whether for pleasure or as a new career.

MYTHOLOGY AND HISTORY

Agni Magnetite has recently been discovered on the isle of Java, Indonesia, created by a meteorite that crash-landed. It is named after the Sanskrit words *agni mani*, meaning "pearl of the divine fire," because its smoky translucence is like looking through a dark flame.

Agrellite

COLORS: White, pearly, also grayish-white, grayish-brown, and greenish-white
CRYSTAL TYPE: Sodium calcium silicate, an inosilicate; striated
ZODIAC SIGN: Sagittarius (November 23–December 21)
CANDLE COLOR: White

PHYSICAL: Helps heal fractures, bruises, Rapid Sequence Intubation (RSI), endocrine system; strengthens immune system and minimizes side effects after radiation and chemotherapy; alleviates infections; balances brain waves during waking and sleep.
EMOTIONAL: Minimizes the need to control others' lives or conversely hand over decisions to others; addresses repressed emotions that cause self-sabotage; counters anorexia, bulimia.
HOME: For minimizing quarrels, tantrums, and silent sulking within the home.
WORKPLACE: For relieving sick-building syndrome; keeps personalities and personal feelings out of the workplace if some colleagues act unprofessionally.
CHILDREN: Constrains an older sibling who orders younger children around; for relieving teenage moodiness and angst.
ANIMALS: For a pet who believes they are head of the household.
PROTECTION: Guards against anger, jealousy, and ill-wishing, both from others against you and your own negative feelings.

MAGICKAL AND PSYCHIC USES
For diagnosis of illnesses, either psychically or with the help of spirit guides; psychic surgery; radionics using electromagnetic waves over distances to heal a patient.
SPECIAL PROPERTIES
Overcomes writer's block; encourages writers to finish their work and send it for publication, rather than constantly rewriting.
MYTHOLOGY AND HISTORY
Originally found in 1973 in the Kipawa mine in Quebec, Canada, along with Eudialyte, Agrellite was named after the late Cambridge scholar, highly esteemed mineralogist, and collector, Stewart Olaf Agrell. Agrellite displays pink fluorescence under ultraviolet light.

Ajo Blue Calcite

COLORS: Soft blue with milky striations; can be medium blue, shines bluish green if held up to the light, sometimes with visible darker blue spots of ajoite
CRYSTAL TYPE: Calcite, calcium carbonate as an inclusion with ajoite, plus sometimes with the addition of another copper-based mineral, such as gem silica
ZODIAC SIGN: Pisces (February 19–March 20)
CANDLE COLOR: Pale blue

PHYSICAL: For gentle healing after invasive or prolonged treatment; alleviates backache, headache, arthritis, rheumatism, constrictions in throat.
EMOTIONAL: Eases compulsions and obsessions; relieves the need for overwork because of fears of failure or being found lacking.
HOME: Keeps the peace if some family members constantly provoke one another; for clearing energies left by sickness or disruptive visitors.
WORKPLACE: For a workplace where achievement is all; for negotiating better work conditions; for defusing challenges by colleagues or managers.
CHILDREN: Empowers those who cannot express their feelings when they are emotionally hurt, but react inappropriately or hold their sorrow inside.
ANIMALS: For small, timid pets in petting zoos or day-care facilities.
PROTECTION: Guards against those who deliberately stir up bad memories.

MAGICKAL AND PSYCHIC USES
For angelic and spirit guide communication; for work with genies or djinns in wish magick; for healers to bring peace to troubled clients without absorbing their pain.
SPECIAL PROPERTIES
For driving tests or any examinations with the need to instantly react if nerves are a major factor; called the happiness stone because it makes worries melt away.
MYTHOLOGY AND HISTORY
Found in Ajo, Arizona, close to where ajoite was discovered, Ajo Blue Calcite is gentler than ordinary Blue Calcite; it combines the watery associations of Blue Calcite with the spiritual energies of ajoite and the power of the desert; Ajo Blue Calcite protects all who travel by water, and travelers in remote places.

Ajoite

COLORS: Blue, blue-green, and turquoise

CRYSTAL TYPE: Copper silicate mineral often found as an inclusion in white quartz, with Plancheite (page 363), Papagoite (page 336), and Shattuckite (page 431)

ZODIAC SIGN: Virgo (August 24–September 22)

CANDLE COLOR: Turquoise

PHYSICAL Alleviates rheumatoid arthritis, motor neurone disease, muscular dystrophy, anemia, blood disorders, brain chemical imbalances, hormone imbalances, premenstrual syndrome (PMS), postnatal depression and menopausal mood swings; inspires minor miracles; boosts physical vitality.

EMOTIONAL: Gently releases deep emotional wounds; for victim support programs, intensive psychotherapy, and confronting in court perpetrators of sexual abuse or domestic violence.

HOME: Encourages peaceful settlements in divorce cases, relating to finances and custody arrangements, especially if you still share the family home.

WORKPLACE: For high standards of performance; for investigative journalists, helping those abandoned by society; for those engaged in children's broadcasting and writing; civil rights workers and lawyers.

CHILDREN: for those unfairly blamed or victimized at home or school.

ANIMALS: For the smallest or weakest of the litter.

PROTECTION: Shields against jealousy toward a partner by relatives you must frequently see.

MAGICKAL AND PSYCHIC USES

Attracts kindred spirits; aids in connecting through dreams and meditation with an ancestral spirit guide; enhances the effects of herbal medicine, including flower and tree essences and essential oils; overcomes bad karma; helps rediscover gifts from Lemuria and Atlantis; promotes automatic writing.

SPECIAL PROPERTIES

Expressing creativity through Earth-based and natural materials; for furthering environmental causes where there is opposition or scorn.

MYTHOLOGY AND HISTORY

Ajoite, known as the "stone of the Earth Mother Goddess," brings connection with the divine feminine, female angels, and the anima in men, and assists in resolving gender fluidity questions.

Ajoite with Shattuckite

COLORS: Blue-green/turquoise (Ajoite) and deep or turquoise blue (Shattuckite), creating a combined vivid blue

CRYSTAL TYPE: Both copper silicates; can, on occasion, be found together in quartz, polished, or tumbled

ZODIAC SIGN: Pisces (February 19–March 20)

CANDLE COLOR: Blue

PHYSICAL: Addresses bowel and intestinal blockages and growths; irregular bowel movements linked to stress and stress-based incontinence.

EMOTIONAL: For men who saw their mothers being abused by their fathers; for both sexes brought up in a strict religion or cult, for whom leaving led to a loss of family connections.

HOME: Creates a happy, harmonious home under difficult circumstances; helpful if you frequently move as a result of your own or a partner's career.

WORKPLACE: Unmasks a thief or computer hacker in your business; for working in investigative legal work.

CHILDREN: For those under seven who have vivid recall of a previous life and may become distressed that they cannot return.

ANIMALS: Helps spirit animals—who died in the home before you moved in and are seeking their owners—to move on peacefully.

PROTECTION: Guards against spirit possession or intrusion during séances.

MAGICKAL AND PSYCHIC USES

Helps oracles using tarot cards and crystals; promotes prophecy, developing mediumship, and discovering your spirit guide to connect you with the deceased.

SPECIAL PROPERTIES

Gives access to and confirmation of personal spiritual insights if you are new to psychic work or have been told all your life that your spiritual awareness is just imagination.

MYTHOLOGY AND HISTORY

A remarkable combination of two powerful spiritual crystals; the original Messina mine in South Africa, where the minerals were found in quartz, no longer exists, although stones are still available and can be found in Arizona. A stone of generous giving and in return receiving the bounty of life; offers physical and spiritual abundance.

Alabandite or Alabandine

COLORS: Black, gray, dark brown

CRYSTAL TYPE: A rare manganese sulfide that can be quite rough and sharp; sold alternatively as a glossy tumbled stone—best used for healing and metaphysical purposes in that form; can appear in jewelry, though less commonly

ZODIAC SIGN: Pisces (February 19–March 20)

CANDLE COLOR: Purple

PHYSICAL: Alleviates dyspraxia, inner ear problems, vertigo, compromised mobility, chronic conditions that can flare up without warning; relieves pain from accidents caused by rushing around; addresses low pulse, blood pressure issues, and lack of temperature control.

EMOTIONAL: Calms a whirling, chaotic mind that flits from one idea and one task to another; awakens awareness of the needs and opinions of others.

HOME: Creates time and stillness for doing nothing or enjoying quiet conversations, instead of filling every moment with background noise and activity.

WORKPLACE: For reorganizing an inefficient schedule or over-management and not enough production.

CHILDREN: Keeps you in a relaxing space, so that not only children but any disorganized adults, who are constantly late and losing or forgetting essential items for the day ahead, will benefit from the flowing energies.

ANIMALS: For calming hyperactive pets, including screeching birds and horses who try to take control of inexperienced riders.

PROTECTION: Guards against trying to do everything and ending up achieving nothing.

MAGICKAL AND PSYCHIC USES

By way of psychic defense, shields against curses, hexes, ill-wishing, and malevolent spirits or elementals, called up in amateur rituals or seances not properly closed down; for meditation in a noisy setting.

SPECIAL PROPERTIES

A light in the darkness stone; for all activities where grace and coordination are needed.

MYTHOLOGY AND HISTORY

Originally found in mines in Alabanda, Turkey, in the 1700s, but now mainly from Peru and Romania; used for repairing relationships where the other party will not listen or has preassigned blame.

Alabaster

COLORS: Milky white; minerals may tint it red, brown, or yellow

CRYSTAL TYPE: Soft gypsum, hydrous calcium sulfate, fine-grained, related to Selenite

ZODIAC SIGN: Pisces (February 19–March 20)

CANDLE COLOR: White

PHYSICAL: Aids in digestion, swallowing, headaches, heart issues; increases effectiveness of treatments; offers pain relief for those with chronic conditions or those affected by temperature or dampness.

EMOTIONAL: Avoids helplessness after an unwelcome change or loss; promotes anger management; eases free-floating anxiety.

HOME: For smooth house moves, to transfer good memories to the new home and bring good fortune; attracts a serene domestic atmosphere; prevents holding on to old grudges.

WORKPLACE: Attracts whatever resources are needed at the right time; enhances craftsperson skills, especially in sculpture and pottery.

CHILDREN: Helps avoid becoming distressed by mistakes; keeps babies and children safe; reduces prolonged crying.

ANIMALS: Calms pets who constantly fight or show aggression.

PROTECTION: Draws away all that is harmful.

MAGICKAL AND PSYCHIC USES

As deity statues, Alabaster activates divine blessings; power animal artifacts in Alabaster call forth desired strengths; empowers crystals and plants resting on an Alabaster slab.

SPECIAL PROPERTIES

For staying unaffected if working or being forced to regularly meet a perpetrator of harm or malice.

MYTHOLOGY AND HISTORY

Alabaster has been used for carvings and ornaments for more than two thousand years, notably by the Etruscans, whose culture flourished around 800 BCE in central and northern Italy. Alabaster is created from evaporated inland seas, so it brings the sacred into everyday life.

Albite

COLORS: Usually white, but also blue, yellow, orange, or brown; can be pearly and occasionally iridescent
CRYSTAL TYPE: Feldspar, sodium aluminum silicate, sometimes with the sodium partly replaced by potassium or calcium
ZODIAC SIGN: Cancer (June 22–July 22)
CANDLE COLOR: Silver

PHYSICAL: Eases stomach upset, stomach ulcers, heartburn, nausea during travel or pregnancy, eye issues, narrowing of veins or arteries; cleanses the blood; addresses menstrual difficulties and irregularities; promotes fertility.
EMOTIONAL: Eases postnatal depression; difficulty bonding with a baby after a traumatic birth or with a constantly crying infant; mood swings.
HOME: Helps in locating precious items you have mislaid; calling a missing pet home; for the flow of love and goodwill within the home.
WORKPLACE: Counteracts agism; finds employment or re-employment for older workers affected by redundancy or job loss; useful in speculation, dealing in stocks and takeover negotiations.
CHILDREN: For happy and uneventful travel with children, especially on long-haul flights.
ANIMALS: Aids in relocating a pet on a house move with minimal disruption.
PROTECTION: Guards against overwork, workaholic tendencies and potential burnout.

MAGICKAL AND PSYCHIC USES
For full moon rituals, when Albite is at its most powerful; fertility spells; a wish crystal effective on the crescent moon; promotes intergalactic dreams and waking visions.
SPECIAL PROPERTIES
For happy and safe overseas vacations; buying a second home in another part of the world or another state; brings a sense of adventure, particularly for older travelers.
MYTHOLOGY AND HISTORY
Albite is named after the Latin *albus*, meaning "white," because of its pure whiteness. Albite is a stone of balance, both emotionally and in lifestyle, between work, home, and leisure.

Alexandrite

COLORS: Rich deep to transparent green in natural light, changing color to ruby red in artificial light
CRYSTAL TYPE: The rare and expensive natural gem and synthetically grown ones in the laboratory share the same composition and properties; a rare form of color-changing Chrysoberyl (page 121)
ZODIAC SIGNS: Scorpio (October 24–November 22) and Gemini (May 22–June 21)
CANDLE COLOR: Red and green

PHYSICAL: Promotes healthy spleen, pancreas, male reproductive system, central nervous system and brain, especially connected with aging; alleviates inner ear problems, motion sickness.
EMOTIONAL: For grief after bereavement, estrangement, and partings.
HOME: Encourages happy family outings; unites a busy family.
WORKPLACE: Reduces flare-ups; encourages initiative; lessens workaholic tendencies, perfectionism, and dogmatic attitudes.
CHILDREN: Eases anguish after the death of a family member or a beloved pet; insulates against distressing media news.
ANIMALS: Not used for animals.
PROTECTION: Prevents healers from becoming overloaded by clients' troubles.

MAGICKAL AND PSYCHIC USES
Develops innate clairvoyant and divinatory powers; for love spells; meditation, past-life therapy, astral travel; enhances flower and gem essences, especially at full moon.
SPECIAL PROPERTIES
Lucky, especially in games of chance; vibrates to indicate good risks or investments; relates strongest to one owner.
MYTHOLOGY AND HISTORY
Called *emerald by day, ruby by night,* Alexandrite was first discovered in the Ural Mountains in Russia the day Tsar Alexander II came of age. Because he freed the serfs, it is considered a stone of freedom; Alexandrite protects against jealousy, green brings luck, and red lasting love.

Almandine Garnet

COLOR: Wine, purple-red, brownish, or pinkish red. Precious garnet refers to deep red, transparent Almandine
CRYSTAL TYPE: Iron aluminum silicate, the most common form of garnet
ZODIAC SIGN: Capricorn (December 22–January 20)
CANDLE COLOR: Red

PHYSICAL: Alleviates the pain of childbirth, wounds, menstruation; promotes circulation; addresses hemophilia, gallstones, fertility issues, sexual potency, libido; offers resistance against viruses.
EMOTIONAL: Eases the grief after losing a partner or a child; counters overindulgence to relieve stress; releases frozen feelings.
HOME: Almandine tumble-stones overcome inhibitions against expressing praise, thanks, or pleasure.
WORKPLACE: Defuses an emotionally or sexually charged environment; modernizes out-of-date or rigid practices; overcomes writers' block.
CHILDREN: Keeps children safe while swimming or when near water.
ANIMALS: For pets reluctant to be left home alone.
PROTECTION: Guards against resentment preventing progress, and against theft of possessions, ideas, or credit.

MAGICKAL AND PSYCHIC USES
In Eastern European legend, protects against vampires; shields against emotional vampires, mind control, and spirit possession.
SPECIAL PROPERTIES
Increases commitment in reticent lovers; kindles slow burning, lasting passion; revives an ailing sex life; deters a partner from seeking an affair or flirting online.
Alerts you if someone in your working or social world is draining your energy.
MYTHOLOGY AND HISTORY
The Roman historian, Pliny the Elder (23–79 CE), reported that Almandine was mined in Alabanda in Asia Minor, after which it was named. Crusaders wore Almandine rings as talismans to light the way home. In myth, a garnet illuminated Noah's Ark day and night. Almandine garnets were used in church and temple windows in medieval times.

Alurgite

COLORS: Red with purple tones, shimmering; when found with viridine, can form a purple-pink matrix with green (viridine)
CRYSTAL TYPE: Potassium magnesium muscovite, a form of mica; viridine (a form of andalusite); Alurgite can be made into cabochons
ZODIAC SIGN: Libra (September 23–October 23)
CANDLE COLOR: Purple

PHYSICAL: Addresses food allergies; fat, lactose, and wheat intolerance; sensitivity to smoke; digestive disorders caused or made worse by stress; body elimination systems adversely affected by anxiety.
EMOTIONAL: Alleviates the sense of being trapped by voices in your head from the past or maybe older living relatives who still diminish you; banishes judgmental attitudes toward those considered inferior.
HOME: Makes your home welcoming and homey, using creativity even if you cannot afford the expensive improvements and renovations you would like.
WORKPLACE: Raises your profile so that your enterprise is valued; creates organization out of chaos; overcomes nerves.
CHILDREN: For those who too readily accept the views of others and go along with bad influences.
ANIMALS: Enables pets who are descended from nondomestic animals to become home-based.
PROTECTION: Guards against those who criticize or try to diminish your confidence.

MAGICKAL AND PSYCHIC USES
Aids in overcoming past-life fears and fears of being punished in this life; mediumship for self and others to make peace with or let go of relatives who died with unresolved issues.
SPECIAL PROPERTIES
For improving your self-image if you lack confidence so you will shine socially; being a success at parties or conferences with people you do not know.
MYTHOLOGY AND HISTORY
A collector's stone, found in Piedmont, Italy, it is fragile as pure Alurgite; a stone for coming out of the shadows of self-doubt and negative programming from those who diminished your self-esteem for their own agenda.

Amazonite

COLORS: Blue-green or turquoise, often with white lines
CRYSTAL TYPE: Feldspar
ZODIAC SIGN: Virgo (August 24–September 22)
CANDLE COLOR: Turquoise

PHYSICAL: Alleviates sexual disorders, hair loss, acne, osteoarthritis, tooth decay, osteoporosis, upper spine issues, breast issues, issues affecting the throat and the thyroid; promotes overall health.
EMOTIONAL: For women who love too much; reduces self-neglect in women; transforms free-floating anger into positive action.
HOME: Blocks electromagnetic stress from microwaves, electrical goods, and cell phones; also from negative Earth energies flowing beneath the property.
WORKPLACE: Prevents unethical practices and foils those who risk other people's money; helps with being in the right place at the right time; attracts new business.
CHILDREN: Encourages children and teens to care for possessions and keep their rooms tidy.
ANIMALS: For horse competitions and pet shows; housetraining young pets.
PROTECTION: Guards against people invading your personal boundaries, workplace, neighborhood or psychically.

MAGICKAL AND PSYCHIC USES
Brings clairvoyant vision of water and Earth spirits; promotes weather magick, animal magick, telepathy, prosperity spells.
SPECIAL PROPERTIES
Attracts good luck in speculation, especially gambling, winning competitions and lotteries; keep three Amazonite crystals in a green bag with dried basil and mint.
MYTHOLOGY AND HISTORY
A stone of courage, Amazonite is named after the semimythical Amazon women warriors who may have led a matriarchal society, in Asia Minor, from about 1000–600 BCE. They were first mentioned by Homer, the ancient Greek eighth-century BCE poet. Amazonite gives women courage to overcome domestic abuse and unfair workplace prejudice; it also protects beautiful places from destruction.

Amber

COLORS: Translucent, yellow, golden orange, brown; often containing fossilized insects or plants
CRYSTAL TYPE: Organic gem from fossilized resin from coniferous trees that lived more than thirty million years ago
ZODIAC SIGN: Leo (July 23–August 23)
CANDLE COLOR: Gold, orange, or yellow

PHYSICAL: Promotes fertility; eases childbirth; alleviates gallstones; stimulates self-healing; improves short-term memory, sore throats, inner ear infections, digestion; helps to achieve long life.
EMOTIONAL: Increases self-esteem; banishes food-related addictions, depression, anxiety, seasonal affective disorder.
HOME: Brings prosperity, health, good luck; dispels restlessness.
WORKPLACE: For promotion and long-term career advancement; guards against modern technological pollution, such as computer rays.
CHILDREN: Relieves self-consciousness, pressure by image-conscious peers; anxiety-related speech problems.
ANIMALS: For pets disturbed by noise or sudden movements; for older pets living with young animals.
PROTECTION: Guards against physical danger, psychological and psychic attack; musters the courage to overcome fears.

MAGICKAL AND PSYCHIC USES
A gateway to past-life recall, ancient wisdom, ancestral roots, and astral travel; used with Jet (page 259) as God and Goddess in Wicca and fertility rituals.
SPECIAL PROPERTIES
Associated with the Baltic, source of much Amber, and Scandinavia, as the tears of Freyja, the Norse love Goddess; attracts passionate love and enhances radiance.
MYTHOLOGY AND HISTORY
Found in Paleolithic graves, Amber is said in China and the rest of Asia to contain the souls of many tigers and the power of many suns. Ancient Greeks believed Amber was formed from rays of the setting sun upon the sea.

Amblygonite

COLOR: White, clear, pale green, lilac, pink, and yellow; prized as clear mint aqua in gem form
CRYSTAL TYPE: Phosphate, includes other minerals, especially lithium, aluminum, and fluoride
ZODIAC SIGN: Taurus (April 21–May 21)
CANDLE COLOR: White

PHYSICAL: Boosts the immune system; relieves headaches, psychosomatic illnesses, IBS, digestive issues, adverse reactions to chemicals, vision problems; addresses genetic issues, autoimmune conditions, mobility.
EMOTIONAL: Eases oversensitivity to the frantic pace of modern life; removes and avoids negative emotions; assuages spontaneous anger; seeks the purpose of existence after life crises.
HOME: Helps in dealing calmly but firmly with confrontational neighbors, aids in ending a relationship peacefully if there must still be regular contact.
WORKPLACE: Eases intense pressure to meet deadlines; helps in avoiding burnout; especially useful for poets, artists, actors, dancers, and musicians; promotes confident speech making.
CHILDREN: For older teens/students panicking about examinations; addresses hyperactivity, Asperger's syndrome, and ADHD diagnosed in the late teens or the early twenties.
ANIMALS: For wildlife in areas where natural habitats are under threat.
PROTECTION: Shields from cravings for alcohol, food, prescription and recreational drugs, and smoking; guards against personal and others' obsessions.

MAGICKAL AND PSYCHIC USES
Increases clairvoyance, predictive powers, and clairaudience; encourages persistence with complex healing methods.
SPECIAL PROPERTIES
For speculation, gambling, lotteries, and raffles; resolving conflicting demands hindering completing necessary tasks. Helps resolve an irritating matter if you are losing patience.
MYTHOLOGY AND HISTORY
Amblygonite is used in jewelry for love later in life or rekindling love after difficulty. Set on a grid on plans of shopping malls, work, spiritual and educational premises, theaters, or sports stadiums to encourage the pleasurable free flow of personalities and avoid conflict.

Amegreen

COLORS: Mauve/purple and green, often merging, occasionally with white chevron-like banding
CRYSTAL TYPE: Amethyst, prasiolite (natural green amethyst), and white quartz
ZODIAC SIGN: Pisces (February 19–March 20)
CANDLE COLOR: Purple

PHYSICAL: Addresses hearing issues; ear infections; sleep disorders, such as narcolepsy, snoring, and sleep apnea; heart issues; aids in recovery from injury, accident, or trauma; relieves imbalances.
EMOTIONAL: For those who love too much and give too much and believe others will change, despite evidence to the contrary.
HOME: A natural money magnet for home and home-based money-generating enterprises.
WORKPLACE: For working in or starting businesses in the spiritual arts, helping those rejected by society without becoming overwhelmed by clients' troubles.
CHILDREN: Useful in keeping teens from getting into trouble when influenced by stronger personalities.
ANIMALS: Aids in the conservation of endangered, indigenous wildlife.
PROTECTION: Repels psychic or psychological attack and emotional vampires; returns negativity to sender.

MAGICKAL AND PSYCHIC USES
Adds power to empowerments and spells, especially in candle magick; enhances natural magick, connection with Earth and Air spirits, guardian angels and guides; for vision quests and pilgrimages to sacred sites, money magick.
SPECIAL PROPERTIES
Continuously cleanses the aura and chakras; awakens innate healing powers through love and compassion.
MYTHOLOGY AND HISTORY
A crystal of small miracles when nothing seems to be working; considered to reflect the violet healing flame of the ascended master St. Germain. For dealing with rigid, authoritarian attitudes and those who override others' opinions or exert undue influence over those less forceful.

Amesite

COLORS: Lavender to intense purple with the presence of chromium, in this form called chromium amesite; also, more commonly, colorless, pink, or green
CRYSTAL TYPE: Phyllosilicate, kaolinite-serpentine
ZODIAC SIGNS: Capricorn December 22–January 20) and Libra (September 23–October 23)
CANDLE COLOR: Purple

PHYSICAL: Alleviates rosacea, acne, eczema, moles, warts, sun damage, nausea, gastroenteritis, heartburn; boosts energy and stamina; encourages weight management, especially as chromium amesite; addresses physical imbalances, Alzheimer's disease, diabetes.
EMOTIONAL: Defuses excessive anger; helps stop foul language, whether deliberate or caused by Tourette's.
HOME: Turns luck around; balances personal and professional demands with family who need extra care.
WORKPLACE: For night workers, who need to remain alert during late shifts and need to have peaceful daytime sleep; prompts spontaneous readjustment of the sleep-waking cycle on days off.
CHILDREN: Useful for older teenagers who frequently fight with peers or challenge authority; helps parents cope with a sleepless infant.
ANIMALS: For pets aggressive toward other animals during exercise.
PROTECTION: Guards against emotional vampires and vulnerable people who constantly demand attention, but whom you cannot easily abandon.

MAGICKAL AND PSYCHIC USES
As a good luck charm, Amesite accumulates energies over time; chooses winning lottery numbers or helps you win at other seemingly random games of chance; expands awareness that there is more beyond this lifetime and universe; angel communication; past-life learning without trauma.

SPECIAL PROPERTIES
For day-by-day recovery from any major illness or reversal.

MYTHOLOGY AND HISTORY
Amesite changes color and becomes more intensely colored in artificial lighting. It combines intellect and logic with emotion and intuition, animus and anima, and makes the spiritual world more accessible in everyday life.

Amethyst

COLOR: Pale lilac, lavender, deep purple
CRYSTAL TYPE: Crystallized quartz; the purple comes from manganese during formation
ZODIAC SIGN: Aquarius (January 21–February 18)
CANDLE COLOR: Purple

PHYSICAL: Called the all-healer and nature's tranquilizer, Amethyst heals people, animals, and plants; balances the system; alleviates stomach and gallbladder issues; headaches, including migraines; eye strain; diabetes; calms hormones; eases puberty.
EMOTIONAL: Relieves bipolar disorder, mood swings, insomnia, alcohol and food addictions, mental clutter, stress.
HOME: Soothes anger and impatience, calming drama kings and queens; removes negative Earth energies beneath the home.
WORKPLACE: Prevents trivial conflicts from escalating in a hyperactive workplace with unrealistic deadlines.
CHILDREN: Eases nightmares, night terrors, and sleepwalking; counters bullies; for hyperactive, Indigo, and children on the autism spectrum.
ANIMALS: Gently energizes a sick or old pet; calms excessive barking and birds squawking; deters fleas.
PROTECTION: Shields against hostile ghosts and psychic attack through the third eye.

MAGICKAL AND PSYCHIC USES
Promotes meditation, clairvoyance, clairaudience; offers access to past worlds and psychic dreaming; as a pendulum for health decisions or ghost hunting.

SPECIAL PROPERTIES
Recharges other crystals; attracts luck; preserves fidelity; calls back lost love; draws new love.

MYTHOLOGY AND HISTORY
Amethyst is associated with St. Valentine and faithful lovers. The Greeks and Romans believed it was effective against drunkenness when made into goblets—*amethustos* means "not to be drunk." Legend has it that a beautiful maiden, Amethysta, attracted the unwelcome attention of Bacchus, God of wine. The Goddess Diana transformed Amethysta into a crystal, saying that henceforward all would be restrained in her presence.

Amethyst Aura

COLORS: Shimmering electric blue and purple or with softer sparkling lavender radiance
CRYSTAL TYPE: Amethyst bonded with platinum and sometimes silver
ZODIAC SIGN: Pisces (February 19–March 20)
CANDLE COLOR: Purple

PHYSICAL: As an enhanced version of Amethyst, which is used as an all-around healing crystal, Amethyst Aura is especially powerful in alleviating side effects of invasive treatments for rare illnesses; for small miracles and remissions where the prognosis is not good; as a master healer that gives a major infusion of the life force; brings a peaceful passing.
EMOTIONAL: Addresses addictions centered around danger, artificial stimulants, and excesses.
HOME: Restores light and joy to a home by releasing blocked Earth energies; encourages spirits resistant—even by a skillful medium—to being moved on to follow the rainbow light.
WORKPLACE: Useful when unforeseen childcare crises or the urgent needs of elderly relatives leave you exhausted; elicits a sympathetic response by employers and more flexible hours until the problems can be resolved.
CHILDREN: For those who are sick or hospitalized for prolonged periods; for restoring spontaneous joy and laughter to children who have been let down.
ANIMALS: Helps an extremely sick pet to let go of life.
PROTECTION: Guards against criminal activity and physical dangers.

MAGICKAL AND PSYCHIC USES
For communicating with the fey and nature spirits; past-life recall that explains and removes present-life trauma; angelic communication; for the ability to see spirits in haunted places; bolsters psychic artistry for recording auras so weaknesses or overactivity can be balanced.
SPECIAL PROPERTIES
Amethyst Aura acts like radar to call the right love or bring new opportunities after hurt, betrayal, or loss.
MYTHOLOGY AND HISTORY
Amethyst Aura is a transformative, alchemical stone, combining the healing of amethyst with proactive, outward-seeking platinum and sometimes loving, intuitive silver; brings a sense of magick and wonder to illuminate the most mundane situation.

Amethyst Herkimer

COLORS: Lilac, purple; may be brownish purple, depending on the proportions of the two minerals.
CRYSTAL TYPE: Quartz combination, silicate dioxide with impurities.
ZODIAC SIGN: Pisces (February 19–March 20)
CANDLE COLOR: Purple

PHYSICAL: A dual-acting crystal, joining gentle healing and removal of sickness or pain with new healthy growth and vitality; protects against side effects of chemotherapy, radiation, and other invasive treatments.
EMOTIONAL: Alleviates past-life and early present-life traumas that manifest as physical weaknesses or seemingly irrational fears.
HOME: Removes electromagnetic stress or out-of-balance Earth energies beneath the home; protects against electromagnetic pollution.
WORKPLACE: Keeps overenthusiasm and unrealistic ideas in check without stifling initiative; for making a spiritual or therapy business more viable.
CHILDREN: Gentler for children than pure Herkimer Diamond (page 241); lifts unhappiness when a best friend has deserted them.
ANIMALS: For a pet who's restless at night and disturbs the household.
PROTECTION: Guards against emotional vampires; acts as a powerful shield for the soul during healing.

MAGICKAL AND PSYCHIC USES
For bringing together in the present world forgotten or abandoned strengths and talents from past worlds; associated with the violet healing flame, the ascended master St. Germain, and the archangel Zadkiel; enhances telepathy.
SPECIAL PROPERTIES
Stimulates creativity as tangible results, rather than remaining as unexpressed good ideas.
MYTHOLOGY AND HISTORY
Dynamic, proactive Herkimer energies blend with healing, calming Amethyst to offer the required energies at any time; a transformative, high-vibration stone, refining what is redundant or self-destructive and replacing it with the freedom to follow new directions.

Ametrine

COLORS: Combination of transparent purple and sparkling yellow
CRYSTAL TYPE: Quartz containing amethyst and citrine naturally within the same crystal
ZODIAC SIGN: Gemini (May 22–June 21)
CANDLE COLOR: Yellow or purple

PHYSICAL: Replaces physical trauma with healing energies; minimizes side effects of invasive treatments, including transplants and transfusions; boosts immunity against colds and flu.
EMOTIONAL: Reduces cravings for cigarettes and unhealthy eating; relieves the urge to self-harm or engage in emotional self-sabotage.
HOME: Eases tensions if family or community oppose relationships involving different ethnicities, religions, or same-sex, transgender, or gender-fluid partnerships.
WORKPLACE: Reduces workaholic tendencies, especially among the self-employed; smoothes the way back to work after a lengthy absence; balances caring for family with a career.
CHILDREN: Enlivens teenagers while keeping them out of trouble.
ANIMALS: For transitioning from puppyhood to adult animal; aids in avoiding excess boisterousness or aggression.
PROTECTION: Shields against psychic attack during spiritual or healing work.

MAGICKAL AND PSYCHIC USES
Connects with angels, spirit guides, and power animals; grounds during astral projection; manifests wishes; a charm for lottery, games of chance, and moneymaking.

SPECIAL PROPERTIES
Ametrine's two-in-one blending combines sun and moon power, generating go-getting without excesses.

MYTHOLOGY AND HISTORY
Ametrines were given as tribute to the Spanish queen during the 1600s by a Spanish conquistador. He received the remote Ametrine mine in southeastern Bolivia as a dowry on marrying Princess Anahi of the Ayoreo people, native to Gran Chaco in South America. The mine was rediscovered in the 1960s and is still the only natural source of this crystal.

Ammolite

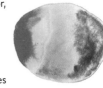

COLORS: Iridescent opal-like play of color, mostly green and red; may appear as purple, blue, and gold
CRYSTAL TYPE: An incredibly rare, organic gem, formed from mineralized ammonites, usually in a matrix, sometimes with surface fractures
ZODIAC SIGN: Leo (July 23–August 23)
CANDLE COLOR: Gold

PHYSICAL: Promotes fertility if you're having difficulty conceiving; protects the fetus during pregnancy, and safeguards mother and baby during labor; detoxifies and energizes the whole system.
EMOTIONAL: Unlocks and releases deeply buried sorrows.
HOME: Revives enthusiasm if your family never does anything together.
WORKPLACE: Popularly called psychic caffeine, for multitasking under pressure.
CHILDREN: For Crystal Children with rainbow auras, born to bring peace.
ANIMALS: For helper and rescue animals.
PROTECTION: Guards against temptation to stray in an established relationship.

MAGICKAL AND PSYCHIC USES
Fills auras and chakras with rainbow light; encourages astral travel in dreams; used in Goddess, puberty, birthing, and croning rites; helpful in rebirthing; manifests small miracles.

SPECIAL PROPERTIES
Incorporated recently into feng shui, Ammolite concentrates cosmic power in its coils, enhancing life-force flow through the body, and radiating enlightenment, wealth, health, and good fortune.

MYTHOLOGY AND HISTORY
Found mainly along the Bearpaw sedimentary rock formation, extending from Alberta to Saskatchewan in Canada and south to Montana in the USA. Indigenous people in Alberta call Ammolite *iniskim*, or "buffalo stone," because it resembles buffalo horns and was believed to draw buffalo to the hunters.

Ammonite, Serpent or Snakestone

COLORS: Brown, gray, or fawn, sometimes with iridescent colors

CRYSTAL TYPE: Fossilized sea creatures, about 435 million years ago, living in the spiral shell now the Ammonite fossil

ZODIAC SIGN: Cancer (June 22–July 22)

CANDLE COLOR: Brown or gray

PHYSICAL: Preserves strength in older people; addresses genetically transmitted diseases, cramps, erectile dysfunction, infertility, childbirth pain.

EMOTIONAL: Releases childhood dependence on parents' approval.

HOME: Attracts health, wealth, unity, happiness.

WORKPLACE: Builds businesses from small beginnings; promotes successful family ventures.

CHILDREN: For babies who are old souls; soothes infants after birth trauma.

ANIMALS: Useful for psychically attuned animals.

PROTECTION: Powerful against deception, disaster, evil, and danger.

MAGICKAL AND PSYCHIC USES
Encourages prophetic dreams, dreams of ancient lands such as Atlantis; enhances rituals with labyrinths, sacred spirals, and dragon rituals.

SPECIAL PROPERTIES
Symbol of rebirth after major loss; helps overcome problems rooted in earlier lives; charm for safe travel.

MYTHOLOGY AND HISTORY
Belief in the luck-bringing, protective powers of Ammonites is found throughout all ages and lands from Aboriginal Australia to Native North America and India, called there the stone of Vishnu. Named by ancient Egyptians after the ram-headed creator god Amun, Ammonites in Whitby, northeast England, were regarded as snakes, driven over the cliffs by the Celtic Christian St. Hilda in 657, most likely referring to the demise of druidesses unwilling to convert.

Amphibole or Angel Phantom Quartz

COLORS: Milky white, with several streaks of orange, red-brown, white, yellow, occasionally pink coloring the quartz

CRYSTAL TYPE: Quartz, containing fibrous amphibole minerals, such as Actinolite (page 12), with inner phantoms or shadow crystals

ZODIAC SIGNS: Aquarius (January 21–February 18) and Pisces (February 19–March 20)

CANDLE COLOR: White

PHYSICAL: Addresses issues with glands, tear ducts, arteries, veins, scars, burns, blisters, sunburn, cholesterol, blurred vision.

EMOTIONAL: Counters abuse, keeping you from feeling that you are to blame for the abuse and prompting you to move from the abuser; alleviates stress-related insomnia.

HOME: Creates sanctuary and self-time in a busy household; deters gossiping neighbors and visitors from overstaying their welcome; brings domestic peace.

WORKPLACE: For personal ventures, projects, inventions, self- or electronic publishing, spiritual one-person businesses; minimizes unnecessary meetings, mail, and conference calls.

CHILDREN: Encourages a shy, talented child to perform in public.

ANIMALS: For small pets who enjoy hiding or burrowing.

PROTECTION: Guards against hidden enemies and false friends.

MAGICKAL AND PSYCHIC USES
For pilgrimages to ancient misty places to encounter guardians of the place; secret love rituals; meditation to connect with the higher self; lucid dreaming.

SPECIAL PROPERTIES
For communication with angels, especially your guardian angel and spirit guides through clairaudience, dreams, and automatic writing; brings spirituality into everyday life.

MYTHOLOGY AND HISTORY
Amphibole Quartz is called "angel quartz" because its inclusions have a wispy angel-like appearance, resembling angel wings; gives a sense of being enfolded in soft angel wings.

Analcime

COLORS: Colorless, gray, tan, green, pink, yellow, or white
CRYSTAL TYPE: Zeolite, with a very mild electromagnetic charge if rubbed very hard
ZODIAC SIGN: Libra (September 23–October 23)
CANDLE COLOR: White

PHYSICAL: Alleviates muscle weakness, diabetes, water retention, lack of coordination; promotes the function of the pancreas; detoxifies; balances the natural electrical impulses within the body.
EMOTIONAL: Eases long-standing addictions, fears, or phobias that are part of a lifestyle that was set perhaps as early as childhood; lessens eccentricity.
HOME: If working creatively in a home-based setting, ensures that you have your own time and space, rather than fitting your work around the demands and needs of others.
WORKPLACE: For team building and teamwork; persuading others to try new approaches if the established ways are no longer working; overcoming objections by those who will never change; establishing rapport among competitive colleagues.
CHILDREN: Helps younger children to play games with others and to take turns; for children worried about popularity.
ANIMALS: Enables you to keep a small herd of donkeys, goats, or alpacas as a hobby, rather than commercially.
PROTECTION: Guards against a controlling partner, parent, or adult child who seeks to take away independence or choice.

MAGICKAL AND PSYCHIC USES
Promotes meditation while moving, dancing, walking, or doing gentle exercise; connects with the divine source of light, God, or Goddess through prayer, chanting, and private study of or translating sacred texts.

SPECIAL PROPERTIES
For unity in a relationship threatened by outside interference; maintaining fidelity in long-distance love.

MYTHOLOGY AND HISTORY
Traditionally, the stone of clear thinking, alertness, and focus to see unsought change in terms of new opportunities and advantages, rather than setbacks; inspires new ways of living communally with like-minded people or influencing an existing spiritual community to become more open to a fresh approach, combining individuality with mutual support.

Anandalite or Aurora Quartz

COLORS: Clear, sparkling with surface rainbows; can be lavender, gray, or yellow
CRYSTAL TYPE: Silicon dioxide with rhodium
ZODIAC SIGN: Pisces (February 19–March 20)
CANDLE COLOR: White

PHYSICAL: Revives energies, kick-starts self-healing and whole-body healing, especially central nervous system or autoimmune conditions; for serious illnesses and small miracles.
EMOTIONAL: Restores faith in humanity and higher purposes after disillusionment, depression, post-traumatic stress disorder, severe anxiety.
HOME: In the center of the home spreads rainbows that absorb and replace negativity from outside or within.
WORKPLACE: Helps in fulfilling major dreams and ambitions; for all who dedicate their lives to others; for homemakers and caregivers of young children, the sick, those with physical challenges, or the elderly.
CHILDREN: Maintains a sense of wonder and magickal belief in faeries and Santa Claus.
ANIMALS: Aids in adopting badly abused pets; for animal sanctuaries.
PROTECTION: Guards against cynics, conspiracy theorists, and all who take away hope or belief in goodness.

MAGICKAL AND PSYCHIC USES
Anandalite is Sanskrit for "divine bliss." Gives access to higher states of spiritual bliss, ecstasy, and peak experiences in meditation.

SPECIAL PROPERTIES
Derives healing from and through your angels and prayer. Offers protection during astral travel.

MYTHOLOGY AND HISTORY
Named after the Aurora Borealis and Aurora, Goddess of the dawn; also called Iris Quartz after Iris, angel of the rainbow. Though sometimes known as Rainbow Quartz (page 390), Aurora Quartz has rainbows on the surface, whereas conventional Rainbow Quartz has rainbow inclusions.

Anatase

COLOR: Yellow, green/yellow, blue, brown, or black
CRYSTAL TYPE: Titanium dioxide; can be found with other titanium minerals or with quartz
ZODIAC SIGN: Scorpio (October 24–November 22)
CANDLE COLOR: Yellow

PHYSICAL: Alleviates sinus conditions, memory loss, metabolic issues, psychosomatic illnesses, tics and stuttering, and conditions involving bones, skin, and teeth; counters allergies, especially to medicines.
EMOTIONAL: Eases stress, helps overcome chronic indecisiveness and the inability to face setbacks; for those who always try to please others,
HOME: For family conferences, establishing new ground rules and settling disputes.
WORKPLACE: Overcomes undermining and criticism by rivals; for clear, concise emails and presentations; especially valuable for researchers, policy makers and legislators, politicians, and judges.
CHILDREN: Promotes confidence among children who are self-conscious about speaking in class or at social gatherings.
ANIMALS: For pets bullied by animals they meet outdoors.
PROTECTION: Guards against corruption or hidden agendas when dealing with matters of justice or officialdom.

MAGICKAL AND PSYCHIC USES
For guiding you to whatever is lost or mislaid; use either by programming a pendulum with it or holding it directly in your dominant hand; for discovering the truth behind people's words.

SPECIAL PROPERTIES
The crystal of decisiveness and decision making in every aspect of life; for overcoming hesitation when planning a change of career or lifestyle.

MYTHOLOGY AND HISTORY
The wise communicator crystal, both within oneself and with others; for making a difference in your community or globally; the crystal of altruistic leadership, potential Nobel Peace Prize winners, or international peace ambassadors.

Ancestralite

COLORS: Silver, dark gray or deep red, banded, often with metallic sparkles
CRYSTAL TYPE: Martite, a variety of Hematite changed (pseudomorphed) under increased oxygen activity
ZODIAC SIGN: Capricorn (December 22–January 20)
CANDLE COLOR: Gray

PHYSICAL: For discovering underlying causes of illness; dealing positively with hereditary conditions; addressing blood disorders and aging/memory issues.
EMOTIONAL: For leaving earlier traumas behind, releasing guilt and buried conflicts that manifest as psychosomatic conditions.
HOME: If you are the family scapegoat—whatever your age— empowers you to reject this role.
WORKPLACE: If you're always racing to meet deadlines, slows you down so you don't miss important details or make mistakes, so you're actually performing more efficiently.
CHILDREN: Aids in overcoming sibling rivalry and blatant favoritism of one child by a parent or grandparent.
ANIMALS: For strengthening the runt of the litter and deflecting bullying.
PROTECTION: Guards against constantly choosing toxic people or self-destructive situations.

MAGICKAL AND PSYCHIC USES
For past-life recall, connection with family ancestors, shedding unwanted burdens from past worlds.

SPECIAL PROPERTIES
For discovering your family tree, especially missing links or family secrets; for adopted children to find birth families.

MYTHOLOGY AND HISTORY
Originally found in the Minas Gerais region of Brazil, Ancestralite is a relatively recent discovery. Nevertheless, it's one of the earliest minerals formed deep within the Earth, taking millions of years to come to the surface.

Andalusite

COLOR: Pleochroic, showing in this case three different colors or more when viewed from different angles and different lights (best seen when faceted as a gem); colors include orange-brown, pinkish brown, yellowish brown, yellowish green, red, colorless, and orange

CRYSTAL TYPE: Aluminum silicate

ZODIAC SIGN: Virgo (August 24–September 22)

CANDLE COLOR: Green

PHYSICAL: Alleviates conditions that fluctuate according to weather or season; conditions involving connective tissue; tics and involuntary movements; HIV; water retention.

EMOTIONAL: Eases the pain of deep, unresolved wounds from childhood incest, sexual abuse, physical cruelty; addresses the emotional wounds of domestic violence.

HOME: Helps when sharing a house or apartment if others do not take responsibility for chores or pay their way; counters those who manipulate family by playing the martyr.

WORKPLACE: Integrates information and people whose viewpoints differ widely; helps in discovering your true vocation.

CHILDREN: Useful in dealing with those who play fast and loose with the truth; teens who conceal their social life.

ANIMALS: For a cat who visits several homes to be fed.

PROTECTION: Guards against those who mask hostility under smiles.

MAGICKAL AND PSYCHIC USES

For scrying with the changing colors; dowsing for hidden information and choices, using as a pendant or wand as a pendulum; countering the evil eye.

SPECIAL PROPERTIES

For dealing amicably but firmly with an ex-partner if you share business interests or have joint custody.

MYTHOLOGY AND HISTORY

Andalusite is best known in its gray or black variety with a clay cross, called chiastolite or fairy wish stone. The polished, faceted form is proactive in replacing depression, anxiety, doubts, phobias, and fears with courage and confidence.

Andean Pink Opal

COLORS: Pink, pastel-colored with pearl-like sheen; swirling colors, including cream, white, and lavender

CRYSTAL TYPE: Hydrated silicon dioxide, a common opal, displaying no iridescence or fire

ZODIAC SIGN: Taurus (April 21–May 21)

CANDLE COLOR: Pink

PHYSICAL: Heals all who are vulnerable; addresses skin irritation, eyesight issues, heart conditions, Parkinson's disease, digestive distress, anemia, liver damage caused by alcohol abuse, low blood sugar, diabetes, low libido, infertility.

EMOTIONAL: For codependent relationships and neediness; detachment from life and emotions after a relationship breakup.

HOME: The crystal of sociability, for happy parties and outings; enables you to have fun on family outings, even on rainy days.

WORKPLACE: Allows therapeutic and people-centered businesses to avoid being drained by clients, combining altruism with financial viability.

CHILDREN: For hypersensitive children overwhelmed by noise and rough-and-tumble play; for a child separated from parents temporarily or longer term.

ANIMALS: Encourages timid animals, rescued after having experienced cruelty, to trust again.

PROTECTION: Guards against dishonesty hiding behind flattering words and false promises.

MAGICKAL AND PSYCHIC USES

Some contain an eye shape, said to be the "eye of deities," left on Earth to bring harmony; offers enhanced clairvoyant vision as well as guarding against the evil eye.

SPECIAL PROPERTIES

For attracting and increasing love and passion; identifying lovers not free to commit or leading double lives; honest speaking from the heart.

MYTHOLOGY AND HISTORY

Found only in the Andes. Like Blue Andean Opal, Pink Andean Opal is sacred to Aztecs, Incas, and Pachamama, the Peruvian Earth mother.

Andradite Garnet

COLORS: Dark yellow, yellow, olive or emerald-green, gray, black, brownish red

CRYSTAL TYPE: Calcium iron silicate, a group of garnet minerals with common properties; andradite can be found mixed with Grossular Garnet (page 231)

ZODIAC SIGN: Aquarius (January 21–February 18)

CANDLE COLOR: Burgundy or indigo

PHYSICAL: Increases strength and stamina; addresses slow metabolism, circulatory conditions, digestive issues, arthritis, concerns regarding the male reproductive system.

EMOTIONAL: Helps ease overreliance on the approval of others for decisions and lifestyle.

HOME: Andradite Garnet grows within its host rock, rather than as freestanding crystals, and can often be found on a matrix; brings a sense of security to the home.

WORKPLACE: For working alone, whether from home or within an organization; for online marketing.

CHILDREN: Prevents nightmares and disturbing paranormal influences.

ANIMALS: Provides a safe, quiet space for sick animals.

PROTECTION: Guards against mind control and the use of status or coercion to exert sexual power.

MAGICKAL AND PSYCHIC USES
Insulates against curses, hexes, ill-wishing, jinxes, and low-vibration spirits; black Andradite offers a shield against psychic attack.

SPECIAL PROPERTIES
Andradite in all forms attracts your cosmic twin, especially if you have been unlucky in love; traditionally used as an aphrodisiac or applied directly to the male's genitals to increase potency.

MYTHOLOGY AND HISTORY
Andradite has three gem varieties—Yellow Topazolite (page 479), Emerald-Green Demantoid (page 158), and Black Melanite (page 298), but the colors hold true for all Andradite. Yellow Andradite is the most active for matters of the mind, willpower, versatility, and creativity; green for expansion and emotions; black, protective and grounding; the reddish-brown mineral is a practical earthing and antispook stone.

Angel Aura Quartz, Pearl Aura, Opal Aura, or Rainbow Aura

COLORS: Rainbow and iridescent with pearly silvery sheen

CRYSTAL TYPE: Quartz crystal bonded with platinum and silver

ZODIAC SIGNS: Cancer (June 22–July 22) and Leo (July 23–August 23)

CANDLE COLOR: Rainbow colors combined in a single candle

PHYSICAL: An all-healer, especially helpful for autism, Asperger's syndrome, and Tourette's; for morning sickness.

EMOTIONAL: Calms anxiety, panic attacks and phobias; cleanses and seals the aura.

HOME: Attracts and enhances love and romance; especially good if you are planning to settle in a home of your own with a partner.

WORKPLACE: Assists in working cooperatively, brainstorming new ideas, and expanding your own career prospects.

CHILDREN: Enables children who are different to be valued for their gifts and not their perceived difficulties.

ANIMALS: Too powerful for smaller or young animals; good for animals who enter competitions or are trained for specific purposes.

PROTECTION: Guards against constantly choosing the wrong people with whom to socialize—particularly those who will try to charm you with lies and deceit.

MAGICKAL AND PSYCHIC USES
For connection with angels; for reiki healing and energy therapies.

SPECIAL PROPERTIES
An alchemist's stone where the energy of the quartz is bonded with the transformational powers of precious metals to create a crystal greater than and different from the separate minerals. Each angel aura contains the energies of its own angel.

MYTHOLOGY AND HISTORY
Considered a connector with Star People; for access to the Akashic records, the past, present and future of individuals and humankind.

Angelinite

COLORS: White and shimmering
CRYSTAL TYPE: Silicon dioxide, quartz, and calcium carbonate, sometimes with trace elements
ZODIAC SIGN: Leo (July 23–August 23)
CANDLE COLOR: Gold

PHYSICAL: Protects from the side effects of invasive or prolonged treatments; addresses bone thinning, white cell problems, and deep-seated conditions hard to reach even with major surgery; alleviates skin problems, vision loss.
EMOTIONAL: For deep depression; postnatal depression; intense grief, self-neglect, or self-harm; suicidal thoughts.
HOME: After bad news, restores hope, unites the family, and points to solutions.
WORKPLACE: For surviving in a hostile, purely profit-driven workplace until you can move on; for starting an ethically sourced business.
CHILDREN: Enables children to become more aware of their guardian angel.
ANIMALS: For exceptionally patient pets, protective of small children.
PROTECTION: Guards against fears of evil spirits and those who summon demons from dubious internet sites to attack rivals.

MAGICKAL AND PSYCHIC USES
Heals with light and the power of the angels; aids in receiving teaching and wisdom from archangels and healing guides from ancient traditions, using bibliomancy/stichomancy; discovering your gatekeeper and guide if you're learning mediumship.

SPECIAL PROPERTIES
For creating a shield of light around the aura and those who are vulnerable; for spreading happiness and optimism in your daily life.

MYTHOLOGY AND HISTORY
Recently found in Vermont, and so named because it resembles the shimmering of angel wings, Angelinite is not to be confused with Blue Angelite. A very powerful stone, so sometimes it's wise to balance it with Black Tourmaline (page 67).

Angelite

COLORS: Pale, medium or celestial blue; bluish-white or gray-lilac, occasionally with red flecks
CRYSTAL TYPE: Anhydrite sulfate, often veined with white wing markings (see also Anhydrite, page 31)
ZODIAC SIGNS: Libra (September 23–October 23) and Aquarius (January 21–February 18)
CANDLE COLOR: Pale blue

PHYSICAL: Addresses issues involving the throat, thyroid, glandular fever, cosmetic surgery, sunburn, fluid balance, bone density, shoulders.
EMOTIONAL: Eases communication difficulties, especially Tourette's syndrome; binge eating and weight issues; after divorce, betrayal, or bereavement.
HOME: For moving to a new home, especially if you are reluctant to do so.
WORKPLACE: Promotes equality in the workplace where there is a lack of facilities for those needing extra physical support; for musicians, tour guides, speech therapist.
CHILDREN: Counters fear of the dark or ghosts; for intellectually, physically, or emotionally challenged children needing the right education; enhances skills in mathematics.
ANIMALS: For the well-being of domestic and wild birds; guides deceased pets to the Rainbow Bridge.
PROTECTION: When psychologically disturbed or desperately unhappy individuals impulsively lash out.

MAGICKAL AND PSYCHIC USES
Promotes sound-healing; messages and healing from angels, clairaudience, mediumship, sacred chant, astrology; telepathy, prophecy.

SPECIAL PROPERTIES
The stone of peace and kindness, strengthening prisoners and people living under harsh political or religious regimes or whose lifestyle or background differs from convention.

MYTHOLOGY AND HISTORY
Angelite was reputedly a healing stone in Peru more than a thousand years ago; named Angelite when rediscovered in 1989, so becoming the stone of angels; avoid getting it wet.

Angel Wing Blue Anhydrite

COLORS: From pale to celestial blue

CRYSTAL TYPE: Unusual form of Anhydrite, linked with Angelite (page 30), calcium sulfate

ZODIAC SIGN: Libra (September 23–October 23)

CANDLE COLOR: Blue

PHYSICAL: Addresses issues involving the throat, voice, thyroid gland, reconstructive or cosmetic surgery (especially facial), sunburn, blood pressure, fluid imbalance, hormones in puberty, pregnancy, and menopause.

EMOTIONAL: Eases obsession with moneymaking to the exclusion of life quality; alleviates the constant need to refer to spiritual experts; encourages forgiveness of self or others for past mistakes.

HOME: Brings the blessings of the house angels; mellows abrasive relatives and visitors.

WORKPLACE: For spiritual fairs and healing festivals to discourage competitiveness and factions among exhibitors and keep healing spaces pure.

CHILDREN: Brings the protection of guardian angels.

ANIMALS: For feeling the presence of deceased pets.

PROTECTION: Filters negativity from the personal energy field.

MAGICKAL AND PSYCHIC USES

For communicating with angels, spirit guides, archangels, and ascended masters; removes spirit entities and cuts psychic and psychological hooks and cords if they're held like a blade; useful for meditation and psychic dreaming.

SPECIAL PROPERTIES

Stills whirling thoughts when you're trying to sleep, if you live or work with loud chattering people, endure continual background music, or travel through noisy and crowded streets.

MYTHOLOGY AND HISTORY

From Mexico, Angel Wing Blue Anhydrite shares Angelite properties. However, whereas Angelite from Peru has a smooth formation, Angel Wing grows in fan-shaped clusters resembling angel wings or frozen waterfalls.

Anhydrite

COLORS: White, colorless gray, purple, blue (see also Angel Wing Blue Anhydrite, and Angelite, page 30), yellow, pink, orange-red, red

CRYSTAL TYPE: Anhydrous calcium sulfate

ZODIAC SIGN: Virgo (August 24–September 22)

CANDLE COLOR: White

PHYSICAL: An all-purpose healer; addresses incontinence in adults and nocturnal bladder control in older children; eases conditions involving the throat, water retention, swellings, knee operations, weight control, heart enlargement, the lower intestinal tract, stamina; promotes end-of-life care.

EMOTIONAL: Encourages moving on from an overidealized past; banishes constant worry about the future.

HOME: Helps in downsizing or leaving the family home or homeland, and overcoming long-standing household issues.

WORKPLACE: Resolves employer or employment conflicts; promotes multitasking, splitting time between two jobs, career and family, or job and a talent.

CHILDREN: For teens in a multicultural community, helps to balance both worlds; enables young people to speak confidently in unfamiliar settings.

ANIMALS: Prevents fights between pets jostling for top place.

PROTECTION: Guards against being pulled in different directions in relationships or by workplace factions; those who deceive with a double life.

MAGICKAL AND PSYCHIC USES

A tracker crystal, Anhydrite draws the right people, opportunities, and information; for learning formal spirituality and releasing past-life trauma.

SPECIAL PROPERTIES

Promotes religious, cultural, ethnic, age, and gender equality and tolerance.

MYTHOLOGY AND HISTORY

Anhydrite is formed by the evaporation of water in gypsum, gradually changing into Anhydrite, where large volumes of seawater have dehydrated. When exposed to water Anhydrite reverts to gypsum. Because of its potential changeability, Anhydrite helps in learning customs and language in an unfamiliar country or culture; for adapting to drastic climate changes on travels.

Anniversary Crystals and Gemstones

1ST ANNIVERSARY*	GOLD JEWELRY
2ND ANNIVERSARY	GARNET
3RD ANNIVERSARY	CULTURED OR NATURAL PEARLS
4TH ANNIVERSARY	BLUE TOPAZ
5TH ANNIVERSARY	SAPPHIRE
6TH ANNIVERSARY	AMETHYST
7TH ANNIVERSARY	ONYX
8TH ANNIVERSARY	TOURMALINE
9TH ANNIVERSARY	LAPIS LAZULI
10TH ANNIVERSARY	DIAMOND JEWELRY
11TH ANNIVERSARY	TURQUOISE
12TH ANNIVERSARY	JADE
13TH ANNIVERSARY	CITRINE
14TH ANNIVERSARY	OPAL
15TH ANNIVERSARY	RUBY
16TH ANNIVERSARY	PERIDOT
17TH ANNIVERSARY	WATCHES
18TH ANNIVERSARY	CAT'S EYE
19TH ANNIVERSARY	AQUAMARINE

20TH ANNIVERSARY	EMERALD
21ST ANNIVERSARY	IOLITE
22ND ANNIVERSARY	SPINEL
23RD ANNIVERSARY	IMPERIAL TOPAZ
24TH ANNIVERSARY	TANZANITE
25TH ANNIVERSARY	SILVER JUBILEE
30TH ANNIVERSARY	CULTURED/NATURAL PEARL JUBILEE
35TH ANNIVERSARY	EMERALD
40TH ANNIVERSARY	RUBY
45TH ANNIVERSARY	SAPPHIRE
50TH ANNIVERSARY	GOLDEN JUBILEE
55TH ANNIVERSARY	ALEXANDRITE
60TH ANNIVERSARY	DIAMOND
65TH ANNIVERSARY**	BLUE OR STAR SAPPHIRE
70TH ANNIVERSARY**	PLATINUM
75TH ANNIVERSARY**	DIAMOND OR SAPPHIRE JUBILEE
80TH ANNIVERSARY**	RUBY JUBILEE
85TH ANNIVERSARY**	DIAMOND JUBILEE

*Though there are traditional associations of particular gems and crystals with wedding anniversaries, you may use a crystal or gem that has particular significance for you both or choose a stone associated with the zodiac sign in which the wedding occurred. These are listed under the individual crystal entries.
**There is less agreement about the later anniversaries.

Ankerite

COLOR: Pale buff, colorless, white, gray, yellow or yellowish to reddish-brown, often fluorescent

CRYSTAL TYPE: Calcium carbonate with varying amounts of iron, magnesium, and manganese

ZODIAC SIGN: Aquarius (January 21–February 18)

CANDLE COLOR: Yellow

PHYSICAL: Addresses age-related disorders, degeneration of cellular structures, iron assimilation; for fitness and memory training programs later in life.

EMOTIONAL: Promotes understanding of the reasons for present sorrow, rather than blaming the past; for sufferers of and those living with obsessive-compulsive disorder (OCD) and hyperactivity.

HOME: If you're seeking good-quality assistance, whether you are finding coping harder or caring for an elderly family member.

WORKPLACE: Encourages original thought and action for solo ventures, based on inventions or filling gaps in the market; starting a business later in life.

CHILDREN: Offers help for those who are dyslexic or find academic work challenging.

ANIMALS: For the runt of the litter or an unlovely animal looking to be cherished.

PROTECTION: Guards against regrets for what has not been achieved; prevents aura energy leakages.

MAGICKAL AND PSYCHIC USES

Promotes meditation, deep spiritual healing, automatic writing to connect with more evolved guides and to understand ancient teachings; develops mediumship.

SPECIAL PROPERTIES

For charitable endeavors in the community or globally; striving to make a difference in the world.

MYTHOLOGY AND HISTORY

The ultimate energy spiral for achieving a heightened state of spiritual bliss through meditation, prayer, contemplation, or relaxation; encourages the deep slow theta waves generally only experienced while falling asleep or dreaming; a powerful entrée to directed waking trance states; good for people who find it hard to relax.

Anorthosite

COLORS: Gray, dark gray and black; shimmers in different colors

CRYSTAL TYPE: Predominantly plagioclase feldspar, laboradite; may contain other minerals, including the rare Anorthite and sometimes form part of meteorites

ZODIAC SIGN: Scorpio (October 24–November 22)

CANDLE COLOR: Gray

PHYSICAL: Alleviates problems with the brain, especially a brain bleed after an accident; promotes recovery after a stroke or a heart attack; addresses night vision, vertigo.

EMOTIONAL: Eases the pull of addictions, linked with or made worse by lifestyle, and the attraction of those who offer instant excitement and risk taking.

HOME: For living in harmony with the cycles of the moon and the natural seasons; improving lifestyle satisfaction.

WORKPLACE: Makes you recognize the merit of a major career change, initially not welcomed but offering a full-time contract.

CHILDREN: For obtaining the right resources, learning environment, and teaching for a child with learning challenges.

ANIMALS: Enables the study of cryptozoology and the twilight zone on the other side of this world, where spirit creatures live and wander in and out of our world.

PROTECTION: Guards against encountering extraterrestrials who are potentially hostile during dreams.

MAGICKAL AND PSYCHIC USES

Enhances moon magick; full moon rituals; astrology, especially interpreting birth charts; star rituals; called the mystery stone that unlocks secrets of ancient wisdom.

SPECIAL PROPERTIES

A stone for traveling long haul and adjusting to different time zones; for increasing confidence in personal creativity.

MYTHOLOGY AND HISTORY

Found in Finland and a number of other sites, including Lake Minnesota and the Appalachian Mountains in the United States and eastern Canada; also called Northosite; discovered on the Highlands of the moon in a white form; when the outer moon melted and cooled, feldspar floated upward to form the outer lunar crust. Therefore, Anorthosite has a direct otherworldly connection that opens the door to access other dimensions and galaxies.

Apache Gold

COLOR: Brown or black and gold; shiny, metallic

CRYSTAL TYPE: Pyrite with Steatite (page 363) or Chalcopyrite with Quartz (page 112), and black chlorite schist (see also Healer's Gold, page 237)

ZODIAC SIGN: Aries (March 21–April 20)

CANDLE COLOR: Gold

PHYSICAL: Alleviates issues with the bowels, ears, teeth, jaw, bones, the alimentary canal; wheat and dairy intolerances, allergies caused by additives; improves appetite; promotes absorption of nutrients; protects healers during healing; aids magnetic healing.

EMOTIONAL: Stimulates coping strategies for developing a more positive outlook on life and people.

HOME: Brings money and good fortune, protects against resources draining away; encourages stay-at-home family members to have more fun.

WORKPLACE: Overcomes inertia; for young people seeking employment; for workers of all ages fighting redundancy or early retirement.

CHILDREN: Enables psychic children to avoid frightening paranormal experiences.

ANIMALS: For those disturbed by deceased pets whose spirits return home.

PROTECTION: Guards against ill-intentioned false friends and mischievous trickster low-level spirits.

MAGICKAL AND PSYCHIC USES

Promotes Earth healing; working with medicine wheels, labyrinths, shamanism, and indigenous forms of spirituality; shamanic astral traveling; channeling benign ghosts, family ancestors, and spirit guide teachers.

SPECIAL PROPERTIES

For prosperity through working single-mindedly toward goals; making the right impression by clearly and concisely demonstrating your competence.

MYTHOLOGY AND HISTORY

Found in Jerome, Arizona, a stone of the sun and fire, Apache Gold brings joy and abundance into your life in the way most needed. A ceremonial stone of Native North Americans; buried in ceremony as tribute to the Earth Mother.

Apache Tear

COLOR: Dark, smoky grayish brown

CRYSTAL TYPE: Rounded pebbles of obsidian, mainly black or dark-colored volcanic glass, usually composed of rhyolite

ZODIAC SIGN: Capricorn (December 22–January 20)

CANDLE COLOR: Gray

PHYSICAL: Eases muscle spasms, blockages in the lower body; helps eliminate toxins; aids in absorption of vitamins C and D; alleviates the pain and swelling of bites, boils, abscesses, and stings.

EMOTIONAL: Releases blocked feelings, unresolved hurts, bitterness, and regrets; helps you refuse unreasonable demands.

HOME: A luck-bringer; transforms negativity entering the home into harmony.

WORKPLACE: Absorbs negative vibes; ensures that opportunities aren't missed; promotes accurate analysis of facts and figures.

CHILDREN: Overcomes fear of darkness; heals grief after family loss or loss of a beloved pet.

ANIMALS: For neglected, ill-treated animals.

PROTECTION: Lowers your profile in lonely or dangerous places; shields against human snakes and venomous words.

MAGICKAL AND PSYCHIC USES

For vision quests, pilgrimages, smudging, and incense rituals; used in Native North American traditions.

SPECIAL PROPERTIES

Apache Tear, becoming darker in sorrow, offers light at the end of the tunnel, revealing future happiness when held to the light; removes self-limiting fears.

MYTHOLOGY AND HISTORY

Apache Tear is named after an incident in Arizona in the 1870s when the US cavalry attacked seventy-five Pinal Apaches. Only twenty-five survived and rode their horses off the mountain to their deaths, rather than be captured. The women of the lost warriors wept at its base for a moon month; the Great Spirit pressed their tears into the rocks; Apache Tear brings protection from sorrow, for the Apache women cried on your behalf.

Apophyllite

COLORS: Usually colorless or white, sometimes containing sparkling rainbows or mother of pearl–like sheen; other colors include pale green and pale pink because of the presence of other minerals

CRYSTAL TYPE: Potassium-calcium fluoride-silicate mineral, a phyllosilicate

ZODIAC SIGN: Gemini (May 22–June 21)

CANDLE COLOR: White or pearly

PHYSICAL: Eases asthma, cystic fibrosis, hay fever, emphysema, eczema; regulates heartbeat and pulse.

EMOTIONAL: For living on others' terms; helps you refuse unreasonable demands.

HOME: An ongoing space cleanser; heals fractured relationships caused by outside interference or divided loyalties; for successful saving.

WORKPLACE: Promotes efficiency and accuracy; useful for personnel involved in financial services, processing data, historical research; good for job shares and returning to work after an absence.

CHILDREN: For memory and concentration when facing major examinations or assessments.

ANIMALS: Calms horses and all who work with them.

PROTECTION: Clears negative thought patterns in self and others.

MAGICKAL AND PSYCHIC USES

In Crystal Reiki, transmits healing energies; identifies personal angels, guides, and power animals; as a cluster, draws negative energies from other crystals; enhances past-life recall of talents and languages. Pyramid-shaped apophyllite is imbued with added healing energy.

SPECIAL PROPERTIES

For saving for major purchases and wise use of resources; long-term financial commitments, such as house purchasing, starting or adding to a family; learning languages later in life.

MYTHOLOGY AND HISTORY

Discovered at the beginning of the nineteenth century, Apophyllite was considered a gift from Mother Earth to counteract the more materialistic attitudes of the Victorian Industrial Revolution.

Apricot Agate

COLORS: Pinkish apricot; usually banded with brown and gray lines if a natural stone

CRYSTAL TYPE: Natural chalcedony quartz; can be dyed gray agate

ZODIAC SIGN: Taurus (April 21–May 21)

CANDLE COLOR: Pink

PHYSICAL: Absorbs necessary nutrients; helps you heal following cosmetic surgery and reconstructive operations after an accident, illness, or to correct birth problems; promotes healthy blood circulation in the veins and arteries.

EMOTIONAL: Calms fears of losing looks and youthfulness; eliminates the need for romance and love, rather than focusing on the real person offering devotion; stabilizes your relationships.

HOME: Helps fashion a beautiful home, even on a budget; for creating a productive garden or a small plant, herb, or flower enterprise using local markets and customers.

WORKPLACE: Aids in resolving crises and troubleshooting formally or because of a reputation for trustworthiness; gives confidence to teach hard-won expertise to younger colleagues.

CHILDREN: Strengthens the bond between parents and children if a parent works long hours; helps to prevent minor accidents.

ANIMALS: For horse dressage conditions and pet shows where the animals' appearance and docility are crucial.

PROTECTION: Guards against self-sabotage that ensures plans will end badly.

MAGICKAL AND PSYCHIC USES

Promotes deep meditation; mindfulness; cognitive behavioral therapy, based around past-life fears as well as present-life experiences.

SPECIAL PROPERTIES

For finding love whatever your age; experiencing fulfilling sex in the golden years; for successfully conceiving a child if living alone or with a partner of the same sex who will co-parent with you.

MYTHOLOGY AND HISTORY

In its natural form apricot agate was used by Roman soldiers to give strength, endurance, and victory in battle; in modern times, it guides you to crafting an organized response to danger and difficulties, rather than succumbing to panic or anger; a stone of tactical victory.

Aqua Aura

COLORS: Electric or sky blue, with iridescent rainbows

CRYSTAL TYPE: Clear crystal quartz, bonded with molten gold

ZODIAC SIGN: Aquarius (January 21–February 18)

CANDLE COLOR: Bright blue

PHYSICAL: Boosts the immune system; alleviates genetic disorders, cerebral palsy, fevers; promotes resistance to new strains of viruses; eases symptoms of prolonged chemotherapy and radiation or surgical interventions.

EMOTIONAL: Clears secrecy and taboos; in crystal healing layouts, it empowers and integrates other crystals; relieves incoherence and shyness.

HOME: A feel-good stone; encourages the expression of affection and praise.

WORKPLACE: For perseverance in manifesting dreams; for the travel industry, pharmaceutical research, and thinking outside the box.

CHILDREN: Eases symptoms of autism and Asperger's in teenagers; promotes happy reunions between adopted children and their birth parents; encourages long-term fostering.

ANIMALS: To send strength to cruelly treated animals or endangered species.

PROTECTION: Guards against psychic and psychological attack, mind games, vicious tongues, and corrupting influences; shields against harmful rays, pollution, and toxicity.

MAGICKAL AND PSYCHIC USES

An Aqua Aura pendulum can channel automatic writing from angels and guides; increases psychic powers; a talisman for love and romance; ascension magick; environmental rituals.

SPECIAL PROPERTIES

An alchemical stone, Aqua Aura offers, through bonding precious metal and pure crystal, the power for life transformations, great and small.

MYTHOLOGY AND HISTORY

The crystal of the Age of Aquarius, Aqua Aura combines ancient wisdom with the limitless energy of the new spiritually focused era, sweeping aside any and every external or self-imposed restriction to offer a new worldview.

Aqua Lemuria

COLORS: Pale green or blue/green; glassy and very clear with small bubbles inside (see also Emra Lemuria, page 175)

CRYSTAL TYPE: Created from volcanic ash; resembling obsidian, natural volcanic glass; some believe Aqua Lemuria, or the Water of Lemuria, was created by the Lemurians themselves millennia ago, the ancient civilization that spread indigenous and nature-based spirituality throughout the world to preserve it from the Great Flood

ZODIAC SIGN: Libra (September 23–October 23)

CANDLE COLOR: Pale blue

PHYSICAL: Addresses fluid imbalances and retention; diabetes; hormonal ebbs and flows in puberty; lack of a menstrual cycle.

EMOTIONAL: Diminishes concern for material resources and instant results; opens blocked emotions; awakens awareness beyond the immediate; eases mood swings.

HOME: Continuously cleanses the home of what is redundant or destructive and blocked energies.

WORKPLACE: Addresses difficult negotiations or sensitive matters that must be resolved without causing lasting offense.

CHILDREN: Aids in overcoming fears of water and swimming if a frightening incident occurred when the child was younger or in a past world.

ANIMALS: For persuading an older animal to adopt a new animal of a different species, if the little one was separated from the mother too young.

PROTECTION: Guards against harsh or tactless words spoken in anger.

MAGICKAL AND PSYCHIC USES

Visions and dreams of old Lemuria before the flood when wisdom was stored in crystals; crystal healing.

SPECIAL PROPERTIES

For clearing a home after the death of a relative so sentimental treasures are shared and quarrels over what is of monetary value and property inheritance disputes are avoided.

MYTHOLOGY AND HISTORY

A stone from the mountains of Sumatra in Indonesia, an area associated with Lemurian wisdom; makes ancestral connections wherever you live in the world; creates a new settled family after remarriage.

Aquamarine

COLORS: Clear light blue, blue-green, or aqua
CRYSTAL TYPE: Beryllium, aluminum silicate
ZODIAC SIGN: Pisces (February 19–March 20)
CANDLE COLOR: Aqua

PHYSICAL: Eases conditions involving the throat, teeth, fluid retention, the lymph glands, the bladder; alleviates colds and upper respiratory difficulties, body and mouth odor, sunburn, fevers, motion sickness.

EMOTIONAL: Calms panic attacks during air or sea travel; counters fear of dental treatment and injections; promotes anger management.

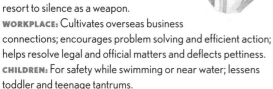

HOME: For clear communication with taciturn family members or those who resort to silence as a weapon.

WORKPLACE: Cultivates overseas business connections; encourages problem solving and efficient action; helps resolve legal and official matters and deflects pettiness.

CHILDREN: For safety while swimming or near water; lessens toddler and teenage tantrums.

ANIMALS: Useful for tropical and freshwater fish in tanks or ponds, plus whales, dolphins, and endangered ocean species.

PROTECTION: While traveling overseas or on boats; from deceit in love.

MAGICKAL AND PSYCHIC USES

For remote healing, clairvoyance, and remote viewing, meditation, dreams and spontaneous recall of Atlantis, Lemuria, and lands lost beneath the waves; making wishes on each seventh wave.

SPECIAL PROPERTIES

A stone of natural justice through compromise and negotiations; favorably resolving legal, official, and neighborhood disputes; uncovers false testimony.

MYTHOLOGY AND HISTORY

Aquamarine was dedicated to sea goddesses, including the Greek love Goddess Aphrodite; a love talisman for first or young love and a pledge of fidelity. The stone of mermaids used by sailors as an amulet to protect during storms and bring them home safely.

Aquatine Lemurian Calcite

COLORS: Deep blue or bluish green
CRYSTAL TYPE: Calcium carbonate
ZODIAC SIGN: Pisces (February 19–March 20)
CANDLE COLOR: Blue

PHYSICAL: Alleviates back pain and spinal problems, burns and skin inflammation, osteoporosis, dental issues, epilepsy, congenital problems such as cerebral palsy.

EMOTIONAL: Eases extreme stress and anxiety about the future that keeps you from enjoying the present.

HOME: Calms uptight family members and creates more fun and spontaneity if routines and timetables fill every moment.

WORKPLACE: For workaholics and those driven by a desire for perfection in self and others; keeps you from exclusively aiming for the top, at the expense of relationships.

CHILDREN: Helps children overcome a fear of water; for those pressured to succeed academically if talents lie elsewhere.

ANIMALS: Enables telepathic communication with whales and dolphins.

PROTECTION: Guards against self-sabotage by expecting misfortune.

MAGICKAL AND PSYCHIC USES

Awakens collective planetary memories of the ancient world of Lemurian wisdom and other more recent personal incarnations; promotes personal healing; however, most effective when dolphin or whale sounds are played.

SPECIAL PROPERTIES

For girls entering puberty, women during pregnancy and perimenopause, to flow with the energies and listen to bodily signals and feelings.

MYTHOLOGY AND HISTORY

Found only in one remote area of Argentina, Aquatine Lemurian Calcite is also sometimes called Blue Argentinian Calcite. This crystal enables those new to spirituality to tune into magickal worlds in their own way through spending quiet time by water, using the waves or river ripples to bring on a natural meditative state.

Aragonite Star Clusters or Sputniks

COLORS: Almost always orange or golden brown as a sputnik

CRYSTAL TYPE: Calcium carbonate; a special form of Aragonite with radiating arms (see Brown Aragonite, page 94, and Orange Aragonite, page 327), resembling the shape of the original *Sputnik*, the first satellite to orbit the Earth, launched on October 4, 1957 by the USSR

ZODIAC SIGN: Capricorn (December 22–January 20)

CANDLE COLOR: Orange

PHYSICAL: Eases the pain of wounds, cuts, bites, scar tissue, growths, adhesions from previous surgery; promotes recovery.

EMOTIONAL: Boosts tolerance for stress; helps overcome impatience, the inability to cede control, worries about the past and the future while neglecting the present.

HOME: Continuously radiates light in all directions through the home right up to the boundaries; accumulates money.

WORKPLACE: Counters sick-building syndrome, where there are frequent absences and stress-related conditions.

CHILDREN: For Star Soul Children; those who dream or talk about extraterrestrials.

ANIMALS: Encourages birds and small wildlife to come into the garden.

PROTECTION: Guards against spite, vicious words.

MAGICKAL AND PSYCHIC USES

Both names *Aragonite Star Cluster* and *Sputnik* create a powerful connection with extraterrestrial beings and other galaxies; for students and practitioners of astrology and astronomy; aids in healing past-life trauma.

SPECIAL PROPERTIES

The stone of Earth conservation and healing; clears blocked subterranean ley energy lines beneath the Earth and sluggish negative energies.

MYTHOLOGY AND HISTORY

Discovered in 1790 in Aragon, Spain, it draws together people with different viewpoints and draws attention to spiritual and practical matters.

Arfvedsonite

COLORS: Black, bluish-black, or gray-green, and banded with glassy shine

CRYSTAL TYPE: Sodium amphibole

ZODIAC SIGN: Gemini (May 22–June 21)

CANDLE COLOR: Silver

PHYSICAL: Removes energy blocks, assisting in the free flow of all fluids; for finding new remedies when existing ones aren't working.

EMOTIONAL: Prevents nightmares and brings understanding of dreams to heal unresolved worries; for overcoming phobias and bad habits.

HOME: Helps the family to communicate feelings and talk through problems.

WORKPLACE: For positive recognition as a potential high flyer; for increased productivity.

CHILDREN: Relieves teenage angst, counters excess secrecy, anxiety, and depression.

ANIMALS: Helps animals to adjust after moving to a new home.

PROTECTION: Protects against negative thoughts and self-destructive tendencies.

MAGICKAL AND PSYCHIC USES

For foretelling the future during meditation; to manifest what you most want; for astral travel while sleeping.

SPECIAL PROPERTIES

Unraveling mysteries and what is not yet known; for detectives, investigators, researchers, and scientists trying to find new cures.

MYTHOLOGY AND HISTORY

Named after its discoverer, the Swedish chemist Johan August Arfwedson in 1823, who also discovered lithium. Found in Canada, Denmark, Russia, Greenland, Norway, South Africa, and the USA, it traditionally guides you to the love of your life; if carried when proposing, it will bring a yes.

Arkimer Diamond

COLORS: Colorless, shining without the need for polishing
CRYSTAL TYPE: The Arkansas version of the New York Herkimer quartz, diamond-shaped, pointed at both ends, and stubby in the middle; distinct horizontal lines around the crystal body without black seeds
ZODIAC SIGN: Sagittarius (November 23–December 21)
CANDLE COLOR: White

PHYSICAL: Prevents burnout as a result of carrying too many burdens with lack of support; counters susceptibility to recurring viruses or infections not fully cleared.
EMOTIONAL: Eases unwillingness to reveal true motives or feelings; keeps you from expecting swift and extra repayment.
HOME: Fills every space with radiating light and warmth, even in winter; enables you to see financial rewards after losing hope in a home-based business.
WORKPLACE: Prompts research and double-checking facts and figures that promise instant results for a possibly risky investment.
CHILDREN: Gentler than Herkimer Diamonds (page 241), a study crystal if a teen gets easily distracted; generates a love of history and tradition.
ANIMALS: Promotes the conservation of ancient breeds, especially native to your area.
PROTECTION: Guards against deception and those who dazzle with apparent transparency to falsely gain trust.

MAGICKAL AND PSYCHIC USES
Receives and transmits communication with angels, guides, and ancestors clairaudiently and through automatic writing, meditation, signs, and omens.
SPECIAL PROPERTIES
Encourages listening to what is being said, not second-guessing what is expected or words from the past; promotes meaningful face-to-face communication between lovers and telepathic links with soul twins over distance.
MYTHOLOGY AND HISTORY
Found in the Mount Ida and Hot Springs areas of Arkansas, an increasingly popular version of the better-known Herkimer; combines spiritual links with protection in daily life and the ability to recognize the truth in any situation.

Ascension Stone Pairs

COLORS: Gray/brown/greenish, sparkling
CRYSTAL TYPE: Marcasite nodules; iron sulfide concretions made of Jurassic organic matter that has fossilized and become pyritized
ZODIAC SIGN: Aquarius (January 21–February 18)
CANDLE COLOR: Gold

PHYSICAL: If using one, hold it in your dominant hand, just an inch or two above the skin or gently touching the skin and moving it over a place of pain or discomfort. If using two, hold one in each hand and pass them both over the area most needing relief. Removes pain and infuses you with energy and health.
EMOTIONAL: Alleviates PTSD; counters a total loss of faith in humanity and promotes an appreciation for the innate goodness of the world.
HOME: Ascension Stones open possibilities if you wish to live in a more spiritually focused way, avoiding excessive materialism.
WORKPLACE: For those who want to make a difference, whether by working in one of the caring professions or in charity.
CHILDREN: Aids in teaching children to be charitable to those in need; lessening their obsession with designer labels.
ANIMALS: For returning endangered species to the wild.
PROTECTION: Shields the aura against psychic attack and hostile entities.

MAGICKAL AND PSYCHIC USES
Used by Reiki practitioners to connect their guides with those of clients who may sense extra hands healing them; for receiving guidance from higher planes.
SPECIAL PROPERTIES
Generally sold in pairs, one will possess yin/female energies with a smoother texture on the surface; the yang/male stone has a rough, protruding external pattern. If buying just one, choose whichever one you prefer.
MYTHOLOGY AND HISTORY
Though several crystals are called Ascension Stones because they offer access to higher spiritual levels, these marcasite balls are found only along the Jurassic coast of Dorset, England. There are different kinds of stone concretions. If you are a mineral collector or professional healer, you may build up a collection of different healing concretions.

Ashburton Agate or Wyloo Agate

COLORS: Browns and grays, often with white pathways across the stones, representing, some say, a map of the song lines of the Indigenous people who guided them between sacred places; can be bluish with pale blue, gray, or brown pathways

CRYSTAL TYPE: Silicon dioxide; frequently marked with pores, striations, and indentations; beautiful as a tumbled stone.

ZODIAC SIGN: Libra (September 23–October 23)

CANDLE COLOR: Blue or gray

PHYSICAL: Alleviates conjunctivitis, gastritis, stomach ulcers, boils, and abscesses; soothes bladder infections and weakness, especially after childbirth or a hysterectomy; eases thrush and STDs, issues involving the uterus, recovery from ectopic pregnancy.

EMOTIONAL: Keeps you from changing love partners at the slightest provocation or boredom.

HOME: For backpacking with younger family members, or older travelers visiting remote areas to guide them home.

WORKPLACE: Cultivates a professional, task-focused atmosphere if workers treat the office like a social club.

CHILDREN: Restores stability if children witness frequent arguments.

ANIMALS: For cats who frequently stray or run away.

PROTECTION: Guards against domestic abuse.

MAGICKAL AND PSYCHIC USES

Promotes meditation and scrying to astrally follow the pathways on the agate through wild bushland; for dreams and visions of ancient Australian rock art and secret ceremonies.

SPECIAL PROPERTIES

Encourages remaining faithful if a relationship is stagnant.

MYTHOLOGY AND HISTORY

Found near the Ashburton River and Wyloo Station in Ashburton Shire in Western Australia; an amulet to both descendants of the settlers and the Indigenous people to strengthen the protection of Mother Earth. The dolomite host rocks are 2 billion years old, though a major Earth shift caused the agates to be created about 900 million years ago.

Astaraline

COLORS: White, pale gray with pale pink areas or yellow streaks, sparkling with small points of light

CRYSTAL TYPE: Combination of muscovite, quartz, and cronstedtite

ZODIAC SIGN: Leo (July 23–August 23)

CANDLE COLOR: Gold

PHYSICAL: Addresses blood sugar imbalances, psychosomatic conditions, seasonal affective disorder; enhances the effectiveness of light, heat, and laser therapies; aids in recovery from surgery for cataracts, glaucoma; promotes self-healing.

EMOTIONAL: Counters seeing or fearing the worst in every situation; demanding perfection in self and others.

HOME: Resolves problems with neighbors, who don't maintain their property, without resorting to litigation.

WORKPLACE: For creating your own private workspace in a crowded or noisy open-plan office; for raising the level of communication if coworkers make suggestive remarks or act inappropriately.

CHILDREN: To bring light to those you encounter who have known sadness or abuse.

ANIMALS: For reading your pet's aura energy field to assess the pet's health and well-being.

PROTECTION: Surrounds you in radiance to prevent any harm from coming near.

MAGICKAL AND PSYCHIC USES

For connection with Beings of Light, with our own Star Soul if we believe we originated elsewhere; relieving past-life trauma and present-day illnesses; for clairvoyance, prophetic visions; healing with light.

SPECIAL PROPERTIES

A crystal of illumination, filling body, mind, and soul with light to enrich daily life and allow spiritual ascension to higher awareness levels.

MYTHOLOGY AND HISTORY

A gentle crystal, allowing each person to explore their own spiritual potential at their own pace and to the level that is right; bringing awareness that there is more than this world and present life.

Astronomite

COLORS: Dark chocolate brown, sometimes gray, with cream and orange-pink spheres over the surface

CRYSTAL TYPE: The rarest of all siltstones, with high iron content that is created through volcanic activity and reacts with the clay host material to form the spheres

ZODIAC SIGN: Pisces (February 19–March 20)

CANDLE COLOR: Orange

PHYSICAL: Alleviates migraines, visual distortions; oversensitivity to noise; for accessing clinical trials of hopeful treatments.

EMOTIONAL: Helps overcome self-imposed restrictions brought on by fear of change; counters obsession with gurus.

HOME: Transforms misfortune into good luck; bolsters loving relationships.

WORKPLACE: A problem solver, offering solutions to seemingly insoluble problems and long-standing obstacles; when used with even a small Kimberley diamond from its home area, Astronomite offers brilliant insights and lateral thinking during brainstorming.

CHILDREN: For Star Soul Children; those who have problems focusing their attention or remaining still.

ANIMALS: Encourages astral travel or dreams about animals that became extinct millennia ago, especially mythical creatures.

PROTECTION: Removes effects of negative thoughts and actions by others without ever needing cleansing or empowering.

MAGICKAL AND PSYCHIC USES

For intuitive astrology; connection with beings from other galaxies; accessing ancient wisdom through focusing on a particular sphere in the stone; psychic healing.

SPECIAL PROPERTIES

Astronomite gives strength and courage to initiate necessary endings and reach for beginnings when hesitation saps energy.

MYTHOLOGY AND HISTORY

Astronomites are from western Australia's Kimberley Ranges, close to the source of the Kimberley diamonds, sometimes called Kimberley moonstones. Formed 670 million years ago, discovered in 2002 by Johan Pas; Astronomite offers light at the end of the darkest tunnel.

Astrophyllite

COLORS: Golden yellow, bronze, red, brown, greenish brown or golden brown, with a metallic or pearly sheen

CRYSTAL TYPE: Rare titanium mineral, associated with feldspar, mica, and titanite

ZODIAC SIGN: Pisces (February 19–March 20)

CANDLE COLOR: Gold or silver

PHYSICAL: Alleviates reproductive, fertility, menstrual, and menopausal problems; migraines, oversensitivity to noise, light, chemical irritants, food allergies.

EMOTIONAL: Addresses sexual dysfunctions, caused by fears and inhibitions.

HOME: Keeps you from trying too hard to make others happy at the expense of your peace of mind.

WORKPLACE: For practitioners of nursing, medicine, hypnotherapy, psychology, or social care; massage, Reiki, acupuncture, acupressure, shiatsu, and reflexology.

CHILDREN: Helps youngsters deal with and positively channel negative emotions.

ANIMALS: Desensitizes horses and dogs to excessive noise and traffic.

PROTECTION: Shields from harmful rays from technological devices and electromagnetic pollution.

MAGICKAL AND PSYCHIC USES

For Star Souls; extraterrestrial dreams and experiences; astrology, out-of-body travel.

SPECIAL PROPERTIES

Enhances fidelity and trust in marriage and love commitments.

MYTHOLOGY AND HISTORY

Astrophyllite is derived from the Greek words meaning "star" and "leaf" because of its shape and shimmering color; counteracts bad astrological alignments in personal charts; discovered in 1854 and found in a few remote locations, including Colorado; Quebec, Canada, and on Laven Island, Norway.

Atlantisite

COLORS: Green (Serpentine, page 428) with inclusions of pink to purple (Stichtite, page 459), sometimes with brown or orange

CRYSTAL TYPE: Combination of Stichtite and Serpentine

ZODIAC SIGN: Pisces (February 19–March 20)

CANDLE COLOR: Purple

PHYSICAL: Alleviates issues involving the heart, lungs, digestion, stomach acidity, kidneys, diabetes, hypoglycemia, menstrual pain, hernias, skin complaints, pain from teeth or gums; contributes to long life.

EMOTIONAL: Addresses insecurity; lack of awareness of boundaries in social and relationship interactions; victim mentality.

HOME: To create a sanctuary of calm and harmony in a busy household; for those who live alone, from necessity not choice, to prevent loneliness.

WORKPLACE: To avoid being pressured by unrealistic demands for haste, leading to mistakes; to prevent impulsive words, later regretted; for office get-togethers where excessive alcohol may lead to unwise behavior.

CHILDREN: Atlantisite calms overexcited children or teenagers at a party or sleepover; benefits hyperactive children.

ANIMALS: For overly boisterous adolescent dogs.

PROTECTION: If your home or workplace was built on a site where tragedies, massacres, or sorrows occurred.

MAGICKAL AND PSYCHIC USES
Associated with the lost wisdom of Atlantis, Atlantisite is an ancient wisdom stone offering access to knowledge of different times and places through genetic memory.

SPECIAL PROPERTIES
The crystal of inner fire to activate the kundalini energy in the base of your spine for an instant power surge to succeed, shine, or fill yourself with courage and strength.

MYTHOLOGY AND HISTORY
Recently discovered in Zeeman, Tasmania, Atlantisite is often called Tasmanite. A guardian stone surrounding self and loved ones in a circle of light; Atlantisite attracts lasting love.

Augelite

COLORS: Colorless, white or pale yellow, blue, pink or green, sometimes bright green; usually found in a matrix

CRYSTAL TYPE: Aluminum phosphate hydroxide

ZODIAC SIGN: Virgo (August 24–September 22)

CANDLE COLOR: Green or yellow

PHYSICAL: Promotes circulation; addresses blood cell disorders, balance issues, obesity, food intolerances, digestive issues, and concerns regarding muscles, tendons, ligaments, mobility.

EMOTIONAL: Reduces victim mentality or the drive to offload blame; aids in anger management; counters insomnia.

HOME: For family gatherings where certain members cause arguments, stir up rivalries, or manipulate others.

WORKPLACE: Useful for those who work in law, including handling contracts, real estate, property development, or rehabilitation of prisoners, especially young offenders.

CHILDREN: For stepchildren resistant to a new parent; for an only child to avoid jealousy at a new arrival.

ANIMALS: Aids in introducing new animals or a baby to existing pets.

PROTECTION: Guards against nightmares and intrusion by unfriendly ghosts. poltergeists, succubi, and incubi during sleep.

MAGICKAL AND PSYCHIC USES
Connection with angelic sources of healing when dealing with distressed clients; for safe mediumship to avoid disruption by mischievous spirits; for reiki attunement; give to a teen whom you suspect is dabbling in Ouija boards or plays at summoning demons using rituals from dubious internet sites.

SPECIAL PROPERTIES
For love relationships, to resolve divided loyalties caused by two different families coming together or hostile ex-partners and relatives.

MYTHOLOGY AND HISTORY
In the mythical land of Faerûn in in Dungeons and Dragons, colorless Augelite reduces the power of magick spells and injury through magickal means. In ancient Greek, *Augelite* means "shining stone" because of its lustrous sheen.

Augite

COLORS: Greenish black to black, sometimes with gray-green streaks, dark green, brown, brownish green, purple, occasionally purplish brown

CRYSTAL TYPE: Silicate, pyroxene; contains calcium, magnesium, iron, titanium, and aluminum

ZODIAC SIGN: Capricorn (December 22–January 20)

CANDLE COLOR: Dark green

PHYSICAL: Addresses calcium deficiency, dental issues, bone fractures, osteoporosis; serious bowel disorders, requiring ileostomy or colostomy; tracheotomy.

EMOTIONAL: Alleviates fear of change in routine or going to different places; agoraphobia.

HOME: For smooth moves to a new home, transferring happy memories and leaving sorrow behind.

WORKPLACE: Brings prosperity; enables the entrepreneur to be in the right place at the right time.

CHILDREN: For children who have unusual likes and dislikes, usually relating to food.; for autistic children and teens with Asperger's in stressful situations.

ANIMALS: For pets who panic if transported by car or plane.

PROTECTION: Guards against those who would oppress or intimidate.

MAGICKAL AND PSYCHIC USES

For making the transition between the everyday and the world of spirit if the conscious mind and logic make it hard to transition.

SPECIAL PROPERTIES

The comparatively rare Augite is a useful addition to a crystal collection at a time when you feel ready for changes or know they are inevitable.

MYTHOLOGY AND HISTORY

Brown Augite is powerful if others cause complications or confusion because of their desire to keep you predictable and available. Black Augite is dynamic, removing redundant guilt or responsibility and translating plans into action if the change is painful. Green Augite emphasizes growth through change. Purple Augite is for spiritual awakening and may offer unexpected proof of the psychic world.

Aura Agate

COLORS: Aura Agate appears in various colors—blue, purple, orange, red, and cream—according to the kind of agate and the bonding metals; always shimmering, sparkling

CRYSTAL TYPE: Natural agate, frequently drusy; electroplated to give a rainbow shimmer

ZODIAC SIGN: Pisces (February 19–March 20)

CANDLE COLOR: Purple

PHYSICAL: Addresses vision issues, migraines, neurological disorders; promotes remission in chronic or degenerative conditions, fertility, pregnancy, and childbirth if previous problems or trauma.

EMOTIONAL: Helps overcome hopelessness; mood swings; pessimism.

HOME: For bringing light into the home at any time of the day or year; for creating harmony and unity.

WORKPLACE: For dark, dull workplaces; where there is inertia or lack of cooperation.

CHILDREN: Promises the happily-ever-after ending of the fairy tales; a wish crystal.

ANIMALS: For connecting with deceased pets at the Rainbow Bridge where they are said to wait for their owners.

PROTECTION: Offers security against frightening spirits, poltergeists, and those who sow chaos and fear.

MAGICKAL AND PSYCHIC USES

For cleansing, healing, strengthening, and protecting the aura; color healing, divination, and rituals.

SPECIAL PROPERTIES

Gentler than aura quartzes, Aura Agates are protective for beginners to spirituality to make a connection with guardian angels and increase psychic awareness.

MYTHOLOGY AND HISTORY

Rarer than aura quartz, Aura Agates have quite different energies, offering calm but vibrancy when the agate is covered with various metals and so transformed. Blue Aura Agate, for example, is bonded with gold, so adding qualities of prosperity, health, success, and the pure life force. Another example is Aura Flower Agate, created when platinum, silver, and gold are bonded to Flower Agate (page 190), transforming it with brilliant rainbows to bring new stability and regrowth in times of hardship.

Auralite 23

COLORS: Various shades of purple, transparent with shimmering inclusions or a translucent assortment of purple, gray, clear, orange, red, usually with purple amethyst or yellow citrine predominating.

CRYSTAL TYPE: A chevron form of amethyst, containing as many as thirty-five different elements.

ZODIAC SIGN: Scorpio (October 24–November 22)

CANDLE COLOR: Purple

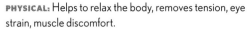

PHYSICAL: Helps to relax the body, removes tension, eye strain, muscle discomfort.

EMOTIONAL: Activates our chakra inner energy centers to gently energize with a sense of well-being.

HOME: Integrates a family where there are new stepparents and children in the mix.

WORKPLACE: Aids in adapting to a constantly changing situation or demands.

CHILDREN: For older children who are disturbed by psychic experiences.

ANIMALS: Too powerful for small animals; good for working horses that are subject to noise or crowds.

PROTECTION: Forms a barrier of defense against aggression or intimidation.

MAGICKAL AND PSYCHIC USES

Increases psychic sensitivity, assists with deep meditation, lucid dreaming (knowing you are dreaming while asleep), communicating with angels.

SPECIAL PROPERTIES

Because so many elements and minerals are in its composition, Auralite 23 is an alchemist's stone of transformation, whose combined minerals are more powerful than their individual forms.

MYTHOLOGY AND HISTORY

Called the stone of awakening, crystals of Auralite 23 are between 1.2 billion and 2 billion years old. Meteorites caused metallic ores to become part of the crystal formation. Found in Thunder Bay in northwestern Ontario, Canada.

Autumn Leaf Jasper

COLORS: Golden and light brown, mottled brick or rust red, and avocado green mixed together, resembling leaves in autumn

CRYSTAL TYPE: Silicate, chalcedony, quartz; also as tumbled stones.

ZODIAC SIGN: Capricorn (December 22–January 20)

CANDLE COLOR: Brown

PHYSICAL: Speeds all kinds of healing; helps with conditions occurring in the later years; reverses or slows physical deterioration; alleviates stress headaches; addresses thyroid, skin, and gastric problems related to fat, wheat, and lactose intolerance.

EMOTIONAL: Helps overcome a premature sense of aging and a sense that life is over in terms of opportunities; counters the tendency to abandon what could still be salvaged.

HOME: Enhances all longer-term self-improvement plans, especially in the second half of life, whether planning a long-term fitness and better nutrition regimen, taking a course of study, or pursuing a new major interest.

WORKPLACE: For assessments, profiling as the basis for advance planning; temporarily putting to one side ideas and projects that have not worked.

CHILDREN: Cultivates an awareness of the seasons anywhere in the world; for learning from the older generations.

ANIMALS: Gives older pets a new lease on life.

PROTECTION: Guards against evil that gradually seeps into life and is no longer challenged.

MAGICKAL AND PSYCHIC USES

For autumn equinox rituals; reconciliation spells; wise woman and wise man ceremonies; binding and banishing magick.

SPECIAL PROPERTIES

Encourages assessment and reassessment of the life path to determine where extra effort is needed, what should lie fallow and what should be abandoned and replaced.

MYTHOLOGY AND HISTORY

Found in the Atlas Mountains of Morocco, as well as in India, Madagascar, and South Africa, Autumn Leaf Jasper is a symbol of reconciling what has not been achieved and maybe is not achievable with the infinite possibilities ahead in the second half of life; rekindling a relationship that has become buried under parental responsibilities.

Autumn or Rainbow Hickoryite

COLORS: Tans and browns, with bands of reddish-brown, pink and yellow tones

CRYSTAL TYPE: Rhyolite, containing feldspar and quartz

ZODIAC SIGN: Sagittarius (November 23–December 21)

CANDLE COLOR: Orange

PHYSICAL: Eases the pain of infected insect bites and diseases caught from insect bites; wasp and bee stings; skin abrasions, eczema, dermatitis; sunburn; burns and scalds.

EMOTIONAL: Helps you cope with problems accepting becoming older; counters agoraphobia.

HOME: Aids in creating a home filled with color, laughter, and music; for buying an unusual property; for going back to nature.

WORKPLACE: Sparks creativity, especially for interior design, fabrics, and fashion; helpful in developing original approaches, innovation, and inspiration in working life.

CHILDREN: Opens the way to imaginative and creative experiences if excessive time spent on devices.

ANIMALS: For pets who stray too far too frequently.

PROTECTION: Guards against fears of exploring new activities and lifestyles.

MAGICKAL AND PSYCHIC USES

Connects with Indigenous sacred sites and learning Indigenous wisdom; group visualizations of shared past worlds; color rituals and therapy; autumn equinox ceremonies; empowering food with magickal incantations.

SPECIAL PROPERTIES

Stimulates a sense of adventure for vacation travel, new activities, and a broadening of horizons.

MYTHOLOGY AND HISTORY

Found near Rodeo, Durango State, Mexico, and southwest Utah, it is fashioned by Native Americans into beautiful jewelry and artifacts; a lucky talisman for finding unexpected treasure.

Avalonite

COLORS: Peach with white and green banding, sometimes mottled with black

CRYSTAL TYPE: A unique form of zoisite, containing a number of minerals, including feldspar, hornblende, mica, calcium, silica (see also Thulite, page 473)

ZODIAC SIGN: Pisces (February 19–March 20)

CANDLE COLOR: Coral

PHYSICAL: Eases the pain of hormones, PMS, dysmenorrhoa (period pain), endometriosis, related to anxiety, menopause; bonds mother and baby after traumatic birthing.

EMOTIONAL: Helps in overcoming fears of betrayal in love or of failing in life; alleviates loneliness, codependency, eating disorders, substance or alcohol abuse.

HOME: Brings color and beauty to a run-down neighborhood or less-than-ideal domestic circumstances.

WORKPLACE: Stimulates creativity among writers of fantasy fiction and sci-fi, animators, fantasy artists, and illustrators.

CHILDREN: Connects with elves and fairies; for children bewildered by the fast, noisy world.

ANIMALS: Increases telepathy between owner and pet; for helper dogs who must be alert to danger.

PROTECTION: Transforms negativity and discouragement into determination to succeed.

MAGICKAL AND PSYCHIC USES

Accesses mystical and mythological worlds, such as the Avalon Grail tradition, Atlantis, and Lemuria in dreams, automatic writing, and visions; promotes spirit artistry; encourages shamanic journeying to encounter magickal creatures, including unicorns and the phoenix; for Star people; accessing the Akashic records.

SPECIAL PROPERTIES

Replaces anxieties and doubts with certainty and laughter; brings spirituality into everyday life.

MYTHOLOGY AND HISTORY

Discovered in 1996 in one location in eastern Washington State, Avalonite is a stone offered by Mother Earth to cure modern ills; reawakens ancient cosmic memories through our inner wise man or woman.

Avalon Stone

COLORS: Black and brown, occasionally with white inclusions

CRYSTAL TYPE: Limestone and mudstone layers created during the later Triassic and early Jurassic period, approximately 195 million to 200 million years ago

ZODIAC SIGN: Pisces (February 19–March 20)

CANDLE COLOR: White

PHYSICAL: Alleviates pain in the feet, ankles, knees; long-term back injuries; bowel irregularities and irritable bowel syndrome (IBS) made worse by stress.

EMOTIONAL: Helps overcome deep insecurity; denial of emotions; fears of darkness, always seeing the worst in people and situations.

HOME: If your home is built on powerful Earth energies, such as ley lines, slows down hyperactivity and eases restlessness.

WORKPLACE: For new beginnings after redundancy or company closure; for night and shift workers.

CHILDREN: Keep in a teen's bedroom if they are experiencing troublesome premonitions or paranormal visitations.

ANIMALS: For pets spooked by a deceased animal who is always around the home.

PROTECTION: Shields against the discovery of secrets best left in your past; against those who would discredit you.

MAGICKAL AND PSYCHIC USES
Goddess rituals, grail ceremonies, seasonal celebrations, dowsing, Earth energy healing.

SPECIAL PROPERTIES
Avalon Stone enhances creativity both for pleasure and fulfilling ambitions to write or illustrate fantasy literature; encourages the exploration of the myths and legends of your own area.

MYTHOLOGY AND HISTORY
Avalon Stone (not to be confused with Avalonite, page 45) is found in the area around Glastonbury in Somerset, UK, with its many Arthurian and grail legend associations. The St. Michael and St. Mary ley energy lines pass through Glastonbury Tor. Avalon Stone activates our inner energy lines for experiencing and transmitting healing and joy.

Axinite

COLORS: Brown; sometimes purple/violet, brownish red or blue

CRYSTAL TYPE: Calcium aluminum borosilicate; Axinite is the name for a series of minerals. The most commonly used in crystal work is ferro-axinite

ZODIAC SIGN: Capricorn (December 22–January 20)

CANDLE COLOR: Brown

PHYSICAL: Addresses issues involving the adrenal glands; useful after an accident where there are multiple fractures or major organ damage; eases pain in the feet, ankles, legs, knees, hips; alleviates sensory and motor disorders.

EMOTIONAL: Helps overcome procrastination about improving health and fitness; counters the drive to conceal truth even when not necessary.

HOME: Encourages you to make the best of life changes that cause domestic disruption; improves memory.

WORKPLACE: Bolsters stamina if you work long or irregular hours or have a physically demanding job; if you're in a new position, overcomes resentment among established staff resistant to change.

CHILDREN: Helps an only child to make friends; aids in finding the right childcare, after-school programs, and vacation clubs.

ANIMALS: For preventing dogs from chasing after other pets or farm animals when on walks.

PROTECTION: Guards against those who manipulate facts.

MAGICKAL AND PSYCHIC USES
For joining a healing circle or psychic development group; for astral travel in trance to gain access to the Akashic records of our lives; provides focus if you're easily distracted during meditation.

SPECIAL PROPERTIES
Gives access to knowledge you have not consciously learned; speeds legal delays; reveals liars.

MYTHOLOGY AND HISTORY
Axinite's blade-like wedge shape resembles an axe, hence the name; Axinite has the power to cut through obstacles or doubts and is used in psychic surgery. A travel crystal to minimize the effects of jet lag and climate differences.

Azeztulite

COLOR: White or colorless
CRYSTAL TYPE: An unusual type of milky quartz, waxy with inclusions of microscopic water bubbles
ZODIAC SIGN: Aquarius (January 21–February 18)
CANDLE COLOR: White

PHYSICAL: Alleviates symptoms of multiple sclerosis, Parkinson's, and motor neurone disease; addresses cell disorders, tumors, physical blockages, tissue inflammation.
EMOTIONAL: Counters deep-seated emotional blockages and trauma; for all who feel different or alienated from life; for enlightenment in every aspect of life.
HOME: Offers hope and comfort to chronically ill or vulnerable family members.
WORKPLACE: Aids in finding your place in a large, impersonal company; overcoming a bad start in life to become successful.
CHILDREN: For Star Souls.
ANIMALS: Identifies pets that have been with you in many lifetimes.
PROTECTION: Spirals away negativity and neutral energies.

MAGICKAL AND PSYCHIC USES
Facilitates contact with archangels, Beings of Light, and extraterrestrial worlds, evolved teachers from ancient civilizations; promotes trance and profound meditative states, clairvoyant moving images of the future.

SPECIAL PROPERTIES
Azeztulite, one of the highest vibrational minerals, positively affects almost every illness, sorrow, or imbalance, guides to the right sources of help with minimal intrusive effects. Each stone has its own unique nature; use gradually to avoid disorientation.

MYTHOLOGY AND HISTORY
Azeztulite, originally discovered in the North Carolina mountains, was linked by the mystic Naisha Ahsian with the wisdom of Azez Star beings, believed to have revealed Azeztulite for all who wish to work with what she called the nameless light, offering access to healing and wisdom from many sources.

Azulicite

COLORS: Blue gray to blue green, iridescent like moonstone
CRYSTAL TYPE: Feldspar, a variety of sandine; in its original state coated in limonite and chlorite
ZODIAC SIGN: Libra (September 23–October 23)
CANDLE COLOR: Blue

PHYSICAL: Addresses pain and imbalances in the optic nerves, digestive tract, liver, stomach lining; regulates irregular or malfunctioning brain waves.
EMOTIONAL: Eases the pain of being or feeling marginalized because of a learning, speech, hearing, or communication disability; aids in refusing to discuss or deal with relationship difficulties.
HOME: For spring cleaning any time of the year and clearing unwanted clutter or material things that hold bad memories.
WORKPLACE: Aids in retrieving missing computer data and locating mislaid files; keeping up with the latest information to stay ahead of trends and ambitious colleagues; promotes efficient data processing.
CHILDREN: For those who are teased for not having the latest devices or designer fashions; helps them understand their true value.
ANIMALS: Aids in resisting pressure from children to buy unsuitable pets because of media hype.
PROTECTION: Guards against words that wound, control, and manipulate.

MAGICKAL AND PSYCHIC USES
Connecting with benign entities from other dimensions and clear recall of the communication; for receiving signs a deceased relative is watching over you.

SPECIAL PROPERTIES
A crystal of purity, associated with the white universal light, that brings clarity to the intentions of others and detachment from cliques, factions, and rivalries; encourages praise rather than criticism.

MYTHOLOGY AND HISTORY
A stone of breaking through communication barriers and misunderstandings, from romance to fair and impartial community, religious, or political negotiations; beware of deception.

Azumar

COLORS: Whitish blue, turquoise or robin's egg blue
CRYSTAL TYPE: Quartz, kaolinite, and trace minerals, including stibnite, which produces the bright blue shade
ZODIAC SIGN: Pisces (February 19–March 20)
CANDLE COLOR: Turquoise

PHYSICAL: Contributes to the free flow of all fluids and the balanced flow of hormones; eases puberty in both sexes, plus menstruation, conception, pregnancy, childbirth, perimenopause, and menopause; alleviates problems in the circulation and nervous system; promotes whole-body healing.
EMOTIONAL: Addresses free-floating anger, high stress levels often without cause; counters rigid attitudes and inability to adapt to circumstances or people who are different.
HOME: For organizing neighborhood and community events.
WORKPLACE: Helps transform outworn patterns of workplace practice; for all who work with or near water or any water-based therapies, such as essential oils and flower essences.
CHILDREN: Brings peace where there is rivalry between siblings and stepsiblings.
ANIMALS: For remaining unaffected by fierce rivalry at animal shows and competitions.
PROTECTION: Breaks negative obsessions and spirit attachments.

MAGICK AND PSYCHIC USES

Cultivates prophecy, reading oracles and omens; telepathy with dolphins and whales; opens the door to momentary bliss and connection with the whole universe.

SPECIAL PROPERTIES

Azumar, an especially high-vibration stone, transforms beginners to spirituality; spontaneously connects us with the community of humankind to discover that we have more similarities than differences.

MYTHOLOGY AND HISTORY

Discovered in Arizona in 2013, Azumar is another gift from Mother Earth to remind us of the importance of respecting the land and seas and awakening our innate psychic gifts. The name *Azumar* is taken from *azure*, for the blue of the sky and *mare*, the sea, uniting the elements and enabling ongoing personal, professional, and spiritual growth.

Azurite

COLOR: Bright blue, usually mixed with dark blue within the same crystal
CRYSTAL TYPE: Copper carbonate with high copper content; occasionally has a copper sheen
ZODIAC SIGN: Sagittarius (November 23–December 21)
CANDLE COLOR: Bright blue

PHYSICAL: Addresses issues involving the spine, ribs, circulation, blood oxygenation, aging; detoxifies; increases life-force flow.
EMOTIONAL: Overcomes the need for approval from others, bullying by family or friends; eases chronic worry.
HOME: Reduces tensions between different generations, especially those sharing a home; promotes harmonious stepfamily relationships; for happiness, health, and fulfillment in the middle and later years of life.
WORKPLACE: Enhances long-term career plans, leadership, careers in government, museums, libraries, universities, colleges, and counseling; brings prosperity.
CHILDREN: Aids in communicating with an unborn child; encourages study in older children and college students.
ANIMALS: Benefits aging animals and long-living species, such as tortoises or parrots.
PROTECTION: Guards against prejudice, judgmental attitudes, and narrow-mindedness.

MAGICKAL AND PSYCHIC USES

Sacred sound through music, sound healing with instruments and voice; prosperity rituals; prophetic dreams, visions of other dimensions, communication with spirit guides; past lives in ancient Egypt and Atlantis.

SPECIAL PROPERTIES

A stone of health, happiness, and fulfillment in the middle and later years; for mature students (those over fifty), who are traveling and relocating overseas; for older people living alone to maintain independence.

MYTHOLOGY AND HISTORY

The ancient Chinese called Azurite the stone of heaven, considering it an opener of celestial gateways. In ancient Egypt, Azurite was so sacred that only priests knew its secrets. US trance medium and visionary Edgar Cayce used Azurite to enter a trance state.

Azurite-Malachite

COLORS: An amalgam of rich and dark blue and dark green within the same stone; the exact color depends on the proportions

CRYSTAL TYPE: A combination stone of Azurite (page 48) and Malachite (page 288), alkaline copper carbonate, creating new amplified properties through their intermingling

ZODIAC SIGN: Gemini (May 22–June 21)

CANDLE COLOR: Turquoise

PHYSICAL: Oxygenates the blood, speeds the healing of fractures or torn muscles; promotes mobility; addresses issues involving the throat, teeth, gallbladder.

EMOTIONAL: Helps overcome narcissism; obsession with appearance; phobias; fears of disease.

HOME: Guards against harmful rays, chemical pollution, and toxic neighbors.

WORKPLACE: Associated with business; attracts prosperity and good fortune.

CHILDREN: A gift for a mother after the birth of her first child to celebrate entering a new stage of her life and to keep her strong and loving through good times and bad.

ANIMALS: Keep Azurite-Malachite with a photo of a beloved deceased pet as a reminder of the love that was shared.

PROTECTION: Guards against remaining tangled and tangling others in old self-destructive patterns.

MAGICKAL AND PSYCHIC USES

For rebirthing; healing with sacred sound; chanting, drumming, singing bowls; used in rituals against ill-wishing and spite; called the stone of heaven for bringing the celestial world closer to the daily world if there has been doubt or despair about the meaning of life.

SPECIAL PROPERTIES

An ideal travel crystal if travel results in a life change, or the beginning of a long vacation or relocation overseas for work.

MYTHOLOGY AND HISTORY

Also called Azurmalachite, Azurite-Malachite, which is found growing together in copper deposits, brings not romance, ideal lovers, or perpetually happy families, but realistic relationships and acknowledgment of the imperfections of self and others; if you have gone from one relationship to another, now may be the time to establish your own independent identity, rather than rushing to affirm it through another.

Babingtonite

COLOR: Black, brown, greenish brown, or dark green

CRYSTAL TYPE: A slightly magnetic calcium iron silicate, often with manganese, in which iron has replaced aluminum

ZODIAC SIGN: Aquarius (January 21–February 18)

CANDLE COLOR: Dark green

PHYSICAL: Alleviates issues with the throat, taste buds, cleft palate, thyroid, heart, veins, stuttering, recurring illness where a cause cannot be found.

EMOTIONAL: Removes obstacles from present and past lives; brings closure to a relationship going nowhere or destructive situation; overcomes tendencies to repeat past mistakes.

HOME: Draws family peacefully home at the end of the day

WORKPLACE: For resisting pressure to join a family firm or follow a traditional family profession.

CHILDREN: Eases communication difficulties; helps Indigo children who find the world confusing.

ANIMALS: For therapy animals who help those with severe physical or emotional challenges.

PROTECTION: Shields from self-defeating thoughts and toxic people who trigger memories of past failures.

MAGICKAL AND PSYCHIC USES

An ascension stone connecting divine with inner light, building on lessons from previous lifetimes, and overcoming karmic blocks; for light workers and Star souls; links with angels and ascended masters; used in Reiki.

SPECIAL PROPERTIES

To distinguish between what is actually being said and redundant critical voices in the mind.

MYTHOLOGY AND HISTORY

This rare, brittle mineral, found in cavities of volcanic rock, often with pale or white zeolites, is the state mineral of Massachusetts, one of its major sources; a stone to keep throughout life to guide your soul purpose and destiny.

Bamboo Leaf Jasper

COLORS: Earthy mixed colors—yellow, light to dark brown, tan, reddish or orange, as dark or mottled green, resembling elongated bamboo leaves; the swirling design is reminiscent of bamboo on a plantation swaying in the wind; reflective inclusions on the surface

CRYSTAL TYPE: Mix of sandstone in a silica matrix; chalcedony, also as tumbled stones, cabochons, and jewelry

ZODIAC SIGN: Virgo (August 24–September 22)

CANDLE COLOR: Green or brown

PHYSICAL: Stabilizes fluctuating blood pressure, heart, and pulse rates; restores growth to cells, damaged tissues, and internal organs; for long and healthy life.

EMOTIONAL: Addresses addictions, compulsions, obsessions; immature behavior.

HOME: Like the bamboo plant, Bamboo Leaf Jasper is considered very lucky; in many cultures the plant is tied with red or gold ribbon and kept in the kitchen to incubate good fortune.

WORKPLACE: Helps avoid overwork and burnout; roots out dishonesty and petty thievery; promotes rapid advancement through the current career structure.

CHILDREN: For those disturbed by noise, chaos, and disrupted routine.

ANIMALS: To help the runt of the litter thrive or the one who was separated from the mother too early.

PROTECTION: Keeps healers from becoming overwhelmed by others' sickness and sorrow.

MAGICKAL AND PSYCHIC USES
Brings connection with a new spirit guide for the next stage of your life; promotes the growth of psychic and healing abilities; recalls ancient wisdom in dreams.

SPECIAL PROPERTIES
Bamboo is one of the four plant "noble ones" of China, portrayed in art as four gentlemen, bamboo symbolizing long life, vitality, and blameless conduct; the others are plum blossom, chrysanthemum, and orchid.

MYTHOLOGY AND HISTORY
Bamboo Leaf Jasper is like the bamboo plant, connected in feng shui with the East and the Green Dragon, the element wood, and growth in every aspect of life. (See also Petrified Bamboo Agate, page 347.)

Banded Agate

COLORS: Though many agates are banded, Banded Agate popularly refers to natural Earth colors, predominantly gray, black, or brown, with concentric colored bands in cream or orange/red

CRYSTAL TYPE: Chalcedony, the banding formed from silica solution deposited into old veins and cracks in the rock

ZODIAC SIGN: Capricorn (December 22–January 20)

CANDLE COLOR: Brown

PHYSICAL: Brown Banded Agates for bones, arthritis: black Banded Agates for colon issues, gastroenteritis, IBS, and problems with the pancreas; gray Banded Agates for fatigue without an obvious cause; offers shielding from X-rays and prolonged medical intervention.

EMOTIONAL: Soothes after severe illness or accident; unrealistic or unrequited love; for those continually needing to improve their body through cosmetic surgery, excessive exercise, or weight loss.

HOME: Counteracts excess consumerism; enables the return of money owed; promotes satisfactory settlement of inheritance or property disputes.

WORKPLACE: Stabilizes a volatile atmosphere caused by strong personalities; counters sick-building syndrome; balances full-time employment with a separate business.

CHILDREN: Helps infants learning to walk; prevents stumbling if older children are always rushing.

ANIMALS: For health and protection of herds and flocks.

PROTECTION: Guards against assuming too many responsibilities; prevents you from absorbing others' sorrows.

MAGICKAL AND PSYCHIC USES
For overpowerful Earth energies beneath the home; guards against poltergeist activity or frightening paranormal activity.

SPECIAL PROPERTIES
A slow, ongoing release of good fortune and health; winning competitions; good property deals; stamina; harmonizing opposition in communities and globally.

MYTHOLOGY AND HISTORY
Called the Earth rainbow, muted Banded Agates have been made into artifacts in many cultures and as protective amulets dating back five thousand years; especially in earthy shades for calming storms and making the wearer invisible.

Banded Onyx

COLORS: The most common variety has a black base and a white upper layer; some have two or more colors, with straight parallel bands, orange, red, and white; honey and white; brown or green

CRYSTAL TYPE: Quartz, chalcedony; can be heat treated to enhance colors

ZODIAC SIGN: Libra (September 23–October 23)

CANDLE COLOR: Green

PHYSICAL: Addresses illnesses affecting balance, diabetes, Bell's palsy; restores movement to limbs after a stroke or injury; enhances success of in-vitro fertilization (IVF).

EMOTIONAL: Counters bipolar disorder, split personality, mood swings, seeing everything as black or white.

HOME: Calms drama kings or queens; helps those working from home while caring for a family.

WORKPLACE: Deters gossip, time-wasting, and inappropriate flirting; promotes multitasking.

CHILDREN: Prevents squabbling over who is the favorite; balances rules with self-regulation.

ANIMALS: Keeps pets from fighting over who is the alpha.

PROTECTION: Guards against being constantly pressured to choose between partner, parents, and children.

MAGICKAL AND PSYCHIC USES

Boosts the effectiveness of fertility spells for twins; complements feng shui, *I Ching*, tai chi; helps develop the sixth sense; used as power animal statues.

SPECIAL PROPERTIES

Balances inner and outer self; promotes logic and intuition.

MYTHOLOGY AND HISTORY

In 77 CE, the Roman philosopher Pliny the Elder named onyx from the Greek word for nail or claw, since the first onyx found—yellow with white banding—resembled a fingernail. Through the ages, Banded Onyx was engraved into images of deities for courage and protection. Honey, black, and white onyx was said to bring beautiful children and promised wealth if engraved with the image of Apollo and Artemis.

Barnacle Quartz

COLORS: Varies with type of quartz, usually clear

CRYSTAL TYPE: A crystal covered or partially covered with smaller crystals; can occur in other quartzes; small crystals can be a different crystal from the host or a larger mother crystal

ZODIAC SIGN: Gemini (May 22–June 21)

CANDLE COLOR: White

PHYSICAL: Said to protect against highly contagious diseases or epidemics; guards against rapidly spreading parasites, such as head lice and impetigo, skin tags, warts, moles, shingles, illnesses with rashes; promotes fertility; addresses irregular cell or bone growth.

EMOTIONAL: Useful after bereavement, especially a later miscarriage, sudden infant death syndrome, death of a child at any age or a life partner; overdependence issues.

HOME: Unites the family after a crisis; brings together the extended family.

WORKPLACE: For hospitality, public or community service; encourages cooperation in the workplace.

CHILDREN: Where parents or stepparents start a second or new family later in life, so older children feel included.

ANIMALS: For the adoption of an orphaned animal by a mother animal not necessarily of the same species.

PROTECTION: Guards against emotional vampires or spirit parasites who seek to possess; resolves disputes over inheritance; keeps baggage safe while traveling.

MAGICKAL AND PSYCHIC USES

For understanding past-life connections with family and partner; for discovering the source of bad karma.

SPECIAL PROPERTIES

Reprioritizes activities, people, and lifestyle so you spend time with those you value.

MYTHOLOGY AND HISTORY

The crystal of togetherness, where you take the lead, whether organizing fund-raising for charity, a community project, or sports- or social-related activities.

Basalt

COLOR: Gray to black, occasionally dark red, brown, or green, according to mineral impurities or weathering; black as basinite

CRYSTAL TYPE: Fine-grained, igneous, glassy, volcanic rock, produced under conditions of intense heat; includes soda-lime feldspar with pyroxene, plagioclase, iron ore, biotite, heulandite, and olivine; called basinite in very fine-grained form

ZODIAC SIGN: Aries (March 21–April 20)

CANDLE COLOR: Red

PHYSICAL: Enhances the function of the reproductive system; promotes fertility; builds muscles; useful in hot stone massage therapy; restores strength after debilitating illness or life-changing injuries.

EMOTIONAL: Reduces self-destructive habits and addictions by changing ingrained patterns; absorbs anger.

HOME: For structural rebuilding after damage from storms or other causes; brings stability to a temporary home.

WORKPLACE: Aids with physically challenging work; as basinite for creativity, turning an interest into a viable business.

CHILDREN: For those easily deterred by minor setbacks.

ANIMALS: Strengthens pets injured in traffic accidents.

PROTECTION: Guards against physical threats or intimidation by bullying neighbors or neighborhood gangs.

MAGICKAL AND PSYCHIC USES

Especially, but not exclusively, as basinite for shamanic healing, transforming illness with white light; for reintegrating a scattered identity through astral travel.

SPECIAL PROPERTIES

Gives strength to persevere through difficult times and bounce back stronger than before; offers courage to act upon rather than merely talk about needed change.

MYTHOLOGY AND HISTORY

Traditionally, Basalt promises that what is of worth and lasting in our lives and relationships will not fail; not to be confused with Black Jasper (page 61).

Bauxite

COLOR: Brown, pink to dark red or reddish-brown, if high in iron oxides; yellowish-white or gray; often mixed colors

CRYSTAL TYPE: As concretions and earthy masses in sedimentary rocks; a product of rock weathering, containing a mixture of hydrous aluminum oxides, silica, silt, iron hydroxides and clay

ZODIAC SIGN: Capricorn (December 22–January 20)

CANDLE COLOR: Brown

PHYSICAL: Addresses issues involving body acidity, hair, nails, digestion, throat, long-distance vision, stamina; promotes potassium and iron absorption.

EMOTIONAL: Useful for anger management; dissipates accumulated resentment.

HOME: Enables living amicably in shared accommodations while retaining your personal space; brings happiness and peace to any dwelling.

WORKPLACE: Aids in organizing a separate business within a community or collective setting; combines the best of traditional medicine, such as TCM, or Westernized practices with homeopathy, holistic therapies, and herbalism.

CHILDREN: For wise young souls; connects children with innate wisdom as past-life glimpses.

ANIMALS: Helpful in petting zoos or urban farms, where animals receive excessive attention.

PROTECTION: Shields from negative reactions of others due to resentment of achievements or lifestyle.

MAGICKAL AND PSYCHIC USES

Promotes meditation to connect with higher self; past-world memories in later life to understand karmic lessons; rituals using metals; fire magick.

SPECIAL PROPERTIES

Initially slow to give results, with perseverance Bauxite spontaneously clarifies future directions. A major source of aluminum, Bauxite is increasingly prized when cut and polished as a personal healing and magickal stone and as jewelry.

MYTHOLOGY AND HISTORY

Connects with healing Earth energies of ancient and Indigenous cultures; for amplifying self-healing and inner repositories of power.

Bay of Stoer Suevite

COLORS: Red to brownish red with black

CRYSTAL TYPE: Fragmented rock, melted sandstone with tektite inclusions, suevite being the impacted rock associated with meteorite landing areas

ZODIAC SIGN: Aries (March 21–April 20)

CANDLE COLOR: Red

PHYSICAL: Relieves acute pain; promotes recovery from physical shock and trauma, fractures, or damaged internal organs after a traffic accident or fall; protects during emergency surgery or treatments.

EMOTIONAL: Helps overcome fears of the unfamiliar and moving beyond the comfort zone; enables you to express emotions without losing control.

HOME: Guards against fire and storm damage, and kitchen accidents; for protecting the home and possessions in a high crime area.

WORKPLACE: For seeking new opportunities and new challenges within your existing workplace or profession; breaking through barriers to advancement.

CHILDREN: For children who are afraid of monsters; insulates young teens from viewing unsuitable material on television or social media when they're away from you.

ANIMALS: Keeps pets safe when exploring areas where there have been reported sightings of otherworldly creatures.

PROTECTION: While traveling to remote places or lands where there have been reported trouble spots.

MAGICKAL AND PSYCHIC USES

In connection with Celtic wisdom; druidry; UFO sightings; contact with Star People and Beings of Light from other galaxies; Earth energy rituals.

SPECIAL PROPERTIES

The stone of the adventurer and pioneer, both in physical travel and pushing back the boundaries of possibility in daily life.

MYTHOLOGY AND HISTORY

Some 1.2 billion years ago a meteorite hit the area around Stoer Bay in northwest Scotland, near where this suevite is found. The combination of local rock and celestial meteorite generates powerful energies from the land, connected in this case with the old Celtic world. Many believe the stellar input awakens the spirits of the land and the old culture.

Benitoite

COLORS: Blue, purplish blue, colorless, pink, white, sometimes partially colored, fluorescent

CRYSTAL TYPE: Cyclosilicate/barium titanium silicate

ZODIAC SIGN: Sagittarius (November 23–December 21)

CANDLE COLOR: Blue

PHYSICAL: Addresses issues involving mobility, the throat, degenerative eye conditions, night vision, cosmetic surgery or treatment, reconstructive surgery, burns, blood pressure, fevers, skin inflammation, scarring.

EMOTIONAL: Improves body image, if rejected because of appearance or physical impairment; helps overcome the inability to talk about sensitive topics.

HOME: Makes every day, however unpromising, happy.

WORKPLACE: Breaks through career barriers; promotes original plans and inventions; useful for those working in competitive or extreme sports, including wilderness guides, fitness instructors, team coaches; yoga and tai chi teachers, masseurs, chiropractors, reflexologists.

CHILDREN: For nightmares concerning monsters or giants; helps overcome fear of shadows in corners at night.

ANIMALS: For those who disturb owners' sleep.

PROTECTION: Guards against danger while pursuing adventurous activities and in remote places.

MAGICKAL AND PSYCHIC USES

Enhances astral travel abilities and extraterrestrial contacts; promotes clairvoyance and remote viewing; offers release from redundant karmic patterns; lighter-colored crystals used for stronger telepathic communication, especially with a lover.

SPECIAL PROPERTIES

For travel to unusual or far-off lands, activity and extreme-sport vacations; reveals untapped creative talents for pleasure or commercially.

MYTHOLOGY AND HISTORY

Benitoite, the official stone of California, was originally thought to be blue sapphire when discovered in the headwaters of the San Benito River, California. It is an extremely rare mineral, worth seeking. Though gem quality is only found in the San Benito mine, non-gem quality from other locations is equally effective for healing and magick.

Beryllonite

COLORS: Colorless, white, peach, yellow

CRYSTAL TYPE: Sodium, beryllium phosphate; good used as tumbled stones; occasionally faceted; some have a cat's-eye formation, striations; may form twins; can be shining and lustrous

ZODIAC SIGN: Gemini (May 22–June 21)

CANDLE COLOR: White

PHYSICAL: Enhances fertility and the function of reproductive organs; alleviates PMS, perimenopause; helps identify the root cause of an illness and facilitates finding the best remedy or practitioner.

EMOTIONAL: Counters irrational dislike of certain people; addresses phobia about personal appearance, especially after teasing in adolescence or rejection by a first love; helps overcome reluctance to seek help for depression.

HOME: Encourages you to reprioritize your life and delegate more when chores, family responsibilities, and work commitments overwhelm you.

WORKPLACE: Counters the tendency to be overly modest about your abilities and achievements; enables you to deal calmly and professionally with jealous or spiteful colleagues.

CHILDREN: Helps teens see options for future study, apprenticeships, or careers if an educational establishment reinforces stereotypes, deterring girls from historically male-oriented professions and vice versa.

ANIMALS: Helpful for pets who are overly mistrustful of strangers.

PROTECTION: Guards against fears of inadequacy that hold you back in life.

MAGICKAL AND PSYCHIC USES

Promotes closer connection with angels and spirit guides; psychic visions, vivid and sometimes prophetic dreams; clairvoyance; empowers other crystals as the center of a healing layout.

SPECIAL PROPERTIES

Makes time and effort for an existing relationship if you rarely spend time together except talking about finances, the home, and family; recaptures the joy of when you first met.

MYTHOLOGY AND HISTORY

High-quality Beryllonite is generally found in Maine, USA, also in Canada, Brazil, Finland, and Africa; cat's eye can come from Afghanistan. A stone of enlightenment when the answers to problems become instantly clear.

Beta Quartz

COLORS: Beige to bronze-brown, dull gray; may be pinkish

CRYSTAL TYPE: Beta Quartz forms six-sided pyramids as one crystal, a paramorph, changing its structure but not its chemical composition during creation

ZODIAC SIGN: Gemini (May 22–June 21)

CANDLE COLOR: Gray

PHYSICAL: Alleviates pain in the bones and cells; protects against the worst effects of highly infectious diseases and those who come in contact with sufferers; remedies conditions that start in the brain and affect the body's ability to function properly.

EMOTIONAL: Overcomes limits that have been imposed on what is possible in terms of progress in addressing physical or emotional challenges.

HOME: Helps gain the necessary financial allowances and practical support if officialdom is slow or resistant to fulfilling their obligations.

WORKPLACE: For high marks in professional examinations or oral assessments; aids in obtaining approval for a project nearing completion.

CHILDREN: Helps those discouraged by teachers or their environment from aiming high.

ANIMALS: For increasing telepathic communication between you and your pets.

PROTECTION: Guards against encountering or being defeated by those who opposed you in past worlds.

MAGICKAL AND PSYCHIC USES

Dowsing and divining for answers; finding hidden treasure, lost objects, and subterranean water; psychic dreaming.

SPECIAL PROPERTIES

Contains and releases the universal life force in pure form to expand your limits.

MYTHOLOGY AND HISTORY

A rare crystal, Beta Quartz is the next level or a super quartz of yet-unrevealed opportunity; found in silica-rich volcanic rocks, such as rhyolite, embedded in a quartz matrix or forming the matrix; may appear within different quartzes, such as clear quartz, Amethyst (page 22), or Smoky Quartz (page 445), or a mixture; mined in Monteriggioni in Siena, Toscana.

Biggs Jasper

COLORS: From beige to dark brown; rare blue Biggs Jasper also occurs with shades of blue, cream, lavender, reddish-brown, and pink.

CRYSTAL TYPE: A variety of picture jasper, microcrystalline quartz, some say the most beautiful form of picture jasper; in shell or layered patterns; prized also as a gemstone.

ZODIAC SIGN: Leo (July 23–August 23)

CANDLE COLOR: Gold

PHYSICAL: Acts as an antiinflammatory; addresses issues involving the intestines, kidneys, skin rashes, eczema, dermatitis, rosacea, scars slow to heal; helps remedy conditions caused and made worse by human environmental intrusion.

EMOTIONAL: Keeps you from living in a random, chaotic way, not learning from experiences or mistakes; helps overcome agoraphobia; puts you back in touch with family traditions.

HOME: Cleanses Earth energies around the premises.

WORKPLACE: For humanitarian and planetary endeavors.

CHILDREN: Prompts children to appreciate books and films of heroes of the past and the present day.

ANIMALS: Creates suitable habitats for urban wildlife.

PROTECTION: Guards against environmental and electromagnetic pollution.

MAGICKAL AND PSYCHIC USES

Enables you to follow the mountain trails pictured in the stones to older worlds and as gateways to mysterious lands through meditation and visualization; enhances rituals for world peace and climate change rites.

SPECIAL PROPERTIES

To bring home closer, especially if grown up among hills or wild landscape.

MYTHOLOGY AND HISTORY

Native North Americans had known about Biggs Jasper for centuries and used it for ritual, healing, arrowheads, and tools. The crystal was rediscovered around 1960, first at the bottom of a creek near Biggs Junction, Oregon, and later during roadwork in the American Pacific Northwest in the same area.

Biotite Mica or Black Mica

COLORS: Red-brown, brown, green, more commonly black; shiny metallic luster; tiny biotite crystals may resemble sparkling gold flakes

CRYSTAL TYPE: A form of mica, potassium iron magnesium aluminum silicate hydroxide fluoride. (See also Biotite or Birthing Stone, page 56); iron rich and sometimes referred to as "iron mica"; can form large shiny plates or books made up of numerous layers

ZODIAC SIGN: Capricorn (December 22–January 20)

CANDLE COLOR: Brown

PHYSICAL: Addresses conditions involving the skin, bone marrow, cosmetic or reconstructive surgery; releases toxins; addresses deteriorating vision; reverses temporary loss of language skills.

EMOTIONAL: Counters loss of true self and identity; living others' expectations and dreams; inability to accept blame in any situation.

HOME: The ultimate year-round spring-cleaning stone; aids in selling unwanted items or donating them to charity.

WORKPLACE: The organized crystal if colleagues are chaotic; for organizing data, delegating if you do everything yourself.

CHILDREN: Encourages children to be tidy and avoid morning dashes to get ready for school; introduces a routine for doing chores.

ANIMALS: Establishes boundaries if pets have taken over the home.

PROTECTION: Guards against inability to move away from circular thinking; stops negative atmospheres from penetrating your aura.

MAGICKAL AND PSYCHIC USES

Confers powerful protection against any low-vibration spirits during astral travel to the past and other realms; promotes clairvoyance and remote viewing.

SPECIAL PROPERTIES

A stone that lifts the veils of both illusion and self-doubt to reveal your true self so you no longer worry about how others perceive you.

MYTHOLOGY AND HISTORY

A crystal that helps you take pride in your individuality and show confidence in your own ideas and opinions if you are a people pleaser or are naturally indecisive; removes anxieties about making mistakes; strengthens the ability to kindly but firmly resist those who have ordered your life.

Biotite or Birthing Stone

COLORS: Black, brown, gray, or dark green, with metallic sheen
CRYSTAL TYPE: Phyllo or sheet silicate from the mica family, forming lenses and expanding outward when heated by the sun
ZODIAC SIGNS: Capricorn (December 22–January 20) and Scorpio (October 24–November 22)
CANDLE COLOR: White

PHYSICAL: Addresses issues with vision, kidney stones, digestion and bile duct; counters cellular disorders, rheumatism, sciatica; eases childbirth; enhances acupuncture, acupressure, shiatsu, and reflexology.
EMOTIONAL: Restores connection with the essential self; brings a sense of perspective.
HOME: For spring cleaning, clearing clutter, or feng shui.
WORKPLACE: Helps avoid financial mistakes before audits, filing tax returns, and balancing books; promotes divergent thinking.
CHILDREN: Assists naturally untidy, disorganized children and teens to organize their life.
ANIMALS: For obedience training in young animals.
PROTECTION: Guards against all who confuse, conceal, or falsify information.

MAGICKAL AND PSYCHIC USES
Enhances past-life therapy, rebirthing; promotes visions of the future and other dimensions.

SPECIAL PROPERTIES
For giving birth safely and easily, whether at home or in a high-tech hospital delivery room; promotes confident public speaking.

MYTHOLOGY AND HISTORY
The original birthing stones date to the formation of the mountains of northern Portugal, when summer heat causes the rocks to expand, and biotic lenses swell up and burst forth spontaneously from the rocks. Hence, they are associated with childbirth. Used as a fertility and childbirth charm, Portuguese Parideira or rock delivering stones have an outer Biotite layer and a potassium feldspar inner layer. However, any Biotite lens can be used in the same way.

Bird's Eye Rhyolite

COLORS: A mix of gold/yellow, brown, red, cream, pink, and black and gray/white spheres, usually with brown, orange, or red background
CRYSTAL TYPE: Iron oxides, quartz, and feldspar; similar to granite but with smaller grains; igneous rock formed by molten magma from volcanic eruption; spheres resemble birds' eyes on the crystal; can be found as tumbled stones, cabochons, and jewelry that are best for healing and magick
ZODIAC SIGN: Aquarius (January 21–February 18)
CANDLE COLOR: White

PHYSICAL: Bolsters eyes in every respect, as well as circulation, digestion; addresses gynecological problems; helps assimilate the right minerals; offers resistance to illness.
EMOTIONAL: Aids in overcoming reclusiveness and unwillingness to share feelings, doubts, or to seek help or advice; eases superiority complex.
HOME: Helps avoid online, telephone, or face-to-face scams; eases the move to a larger home or one with more space in and around it.
WORKPLACE: Gives an overview of any decision or situation where there are conflicting factors; allows you to rise above pettiness.
CHILDREN: Encourages them to value their own talents and not feel they must compete with siblings or peers.
ANIMALS: Promotes the conservation of wild birds in urban settings and gardens.
PROTECTION: Guards against deceit or concealment.

MAGICKAL AND PSYCHIC USES
Aids in dowsing for accurate decisions among a series of options or versions of the truth; shamanic flight via the world tree or on the back of a spirit eagle; astral travel.

SPECIAL PROPERTIES
Extends current abilities and performance to new heights and awareness of what is possible by stepping outside the boxes.

MYTHOLOGY AND HISTORY
Mined mainly in Chihuahua, in northern Mexico, in a valley without vegetation, Bird's Eye Rholite is the stone of refusing to give up under difficult circumstances; listening to what is actually being said and not substituting words in the head from the past that prejudge and misjudge the response.

Bismuth

COLORS: Silver white, with multicolored iridescent hues and metallic luster; in natural state usually a white crystalline soft metal with a pink to red tinge and multicolored tarnish

CRYSTAL TYPE: Mostly grown in the laboratory to form step-like structure; in its rarer natural state, a heavy base metal

ZODIAC SIGNS: Leo (July 23–August 23) and Aquarius (January 21–February 18)

CANDLE COLOR: Gold

PHYSICAL: Enhances new treatments for chronic conditions; encourages spontaneous remission; relieves chronic fatigue syndrome.

EMOTIONAL: Assists people hospitalized for a long time to settle back into the community.

HOME: Ensures a calm move to a new house and transfers the happy experiences to the new home.

WORKPLACE: Aids in organizing group projects or events, coaching sports teams, and teaching languages to a diverse group of students.

CHILDREN: Helps children who have been in state institutions to settle into foster homes or with adoptive parents.

ANIMALS: For companion animal obedience classes or training horses.

PROTECTION: Relieves a sense of isolation and loneliness.

MAGICKAL AND PSYCHIC USES

For astral projection or mind travel, using its rainbow stairway–like formation; for shamanic journeying.

SPECIAL PROPERTIES

Aids in manifestation and transformation, color therapy, and aura balancing.

MYTHOLOGY AND HISTORY

First discovered by Claude Geoffrey Junine in 1753. The Incas used Bismuth with copper and tin to create a bronze alloy to make their knives. Found naturally in small quantities in Bolivia, the UK, Germany, and the USA.

Black Amber

COLORS: Black, usually with dark red or brown shining through, if held to the light

CRYSTAL TYPE: Very dark natural amber or fossilized tree resin, mixed with tree matter.

ZODIAC SIGN: Scorpio (October 24–November 22)

CANDLE COLOR: Dark red or brown

PHYSICAL: Alleviates issues involving the stomach, bowels, pancreas, spleen, gallbladder; remedies fungal infections; addresses side effects of radiation and energy blockages.

EMOTIONAL: Eases depression, grief, fears of being cursed.

HOME: Counters negative energy if you live in a haunted house, feel under attack by a malevolent deceased relative, or live near an Indigenous burial ground.

WORKPLACE: Prevents rivals from hacking into your computer to read private messages; for keeping financial or career negotiations private from the overly curious.

CHILDREN: For teens who have frightened themselves calling up spirits or demons.

ANIMALS: Useful if a rival has been ill-wishing your show or competition animal.

PROTECTION: Guards against psychic and emotional vampires and psychic attack.

MAGICKAL AND PSYCHIC USES

Meditation, night magick, removing psychic hooks from the aura, Black Madonna rituals, dark mirror scrying; reflecting back curses and the evil eye.

SPECIAL PROPERTIES

For secretly building up your finances if you know attempts to save would be sabotaged; for privacy when sharing a home with relative strangers or have open office work facilities.

MYTHOLOGY AND HISTORY

A special form of amber, whether naturally dark or with plant material added; alter ego of solar golden amber and associated with the moon and women's mysteries; alternating black and gold amber makes a magickal necklace for Wiccans that constantly clears the aura.

Black Amethyst

COLORS: Appears black; may be very dark purple-black or with a violet tone in the black

CRYSTAL TYPE: Silicon dioxide with hematite inclusions and a high iron content within its matrix; can be found as tumbled stones

ZODIAC SIGN: Capricorn (December 22–January 20)

CANDLE COLOR: Dark purple

PHYSICAL: Relieves migraines; offers pain relief; addresses memory issues, blood clotting, inflammation, menstrual difficulties, complications of hysterectomy, perimenopause—especially early onset—and menopause.

EMOTIONAL: Counters deep despair; grief after bereavement; unresolved childhood rejection; overwhelming cravings.

HOME: For relaxation and quiet sleep if your life is hectic and your mind constantly whirling.

WORKPLACE: Provides a peaceful mind space if you are continually interrupted by other workers or unnecessary phone calls; for night workers with stressful jobs, such as medicine or security work, to switch off at the end of the shift; helps to regulate body clock.

CHILDREN: For essential study, especially math, science, and technology.

ANIMALS: Calms boisterous pets who knock down items and jump up at people.

PROTECTION: Resists cravings if trying to stop a bad habit.

MAGICKAL AND PSYCHIC USES

Increases psychic powers and, at the same time, provides protection against malevolent spirits encountered during astral travel or those who seek to manipulate or possess you in mediumship; casts a boundary around the aura so that mediums, clairvoyants, healers, and empaths will not be drained by the pain and sorrow of others.

SPECIAL PROPERTIES

If a bad habit is becoming an obsession, Black Amethyst restores moderation; for example, if gambling.

MYTHOLOGY AND HISTORY

Mainly found in Uruguay and Brazil as clusters; in India, Black Amethyst is mixed with white quartz and may have visible red hematite inclusions; a stone combining the will to win with common sense and limits.

Black Azeztulite

COLORS: Black with traces of white and gray

CRYSTAL TYPE: White quartz and black calcite found only in Vermont, USA, the calcite unusually rich in magnesium

ZODIAC SIGN: Scorpio (October 24–November 22)

CANDLE COLOR: Purple

PHYSICAL: Strengthens the autoimmune system; shields against the harmful side effects of chemotherapy, radiation, and surgery.

EMOTIONAL: Counters a sense of hopelessness; when dabbling with the occult, prevents low-life spirits from attaching themselves.

HOME: The "light in the darkness" crystal if there has been major misfortune, financial problems, health issues.

WORKPLACE: For total transformation of your working practices and lifestyle if work has become a chore; presents unexpected opportunities and offers.

CHILDREN: Keep in the home if you have Star Seed Children or very psychic teens whose paranormal experiences sometimes frighten them.

ANIMALS: Banishes restless animal spirits seeking their former owners who may have moved on.

PROTECTION: Removes psychic parasites and spirit attachments as well as curses.

MAGICKAL AND PSYCHIC USES

Together with red (fire) azeztulite and white azeztulite, the three colors form the basis of alchemical exploration to find the philosopher's stone of immortality; Black Azeztulite is especially powerful during the new moon and eclipses.

SPECIAL PROPERTIES

A reminder of our inner divine nature as part of the creative process; Black Azeztulite is empowered, like all Azeztulite (page 47), by the Azez Star Beings to bring healing and wisdom.

MYTHOLOGY AND HISTORY

Black Azeztulite reflects the color at its richest and most fertile and creative, like the ancient Egyptian black land or fertile land along the banks of the Nile that they called *kemet*; casts doubts and fears into the black hole formed by the midnight sun in the center of our galaxy, enabling surrender to personal and spiritual transformation.

Black Botryoidal Agate

COLORS: Dark brown to black, may be banded; black caused by manganese in nearby host rock

CRYSTAL TYPE: Forming bubbles or grape-like agate-chalcedony crystals on the same cluster, sometimes called Blackberry Agate

ZODIAC SIGN: Scorpio (October 24–November 22)

CANDLE COLOR: Purple

PHYSICAL: Relieves pain diagnosis and newly discovered treatment of unusual conditions or those resistant to existing medication; back, intestines; addresses dizzy spells; opens blocked arteries; useful in treating growths where surgery is risky because of proximity to major organs.

EMOTIONAL: Dispels belief in ongoing accumulating misfortune; overcomes the inability to see beyond problems; helps you grapple with debt due to unwise spending habits or addictions.

HOME: Draws the family together after grief, loss, or sorrow; absorbs negativity that enters the home if a family member has had a bad day.

WORKPLACE: Offers freedom from distractions where precision and total concentration is needed; for physicians, surgeons, dentists, pharmacists, nurses, therapists, and all who administer remedies.

CHILDREN: For those reluctant to start a new school, whether because of a natural age transition or due to relocation.

ANIMALS: For moving pets to a new home where a long journey is involved, perhaps by air freight.

PROTECTION: against hostile spirits trying to dominate a séance.

MAGICKAL AND PSYCHIC USES

Increases dowsing abilities, Earth healing rituals; clairaudience, especially assisted by the sounds of nature.

SPECIAL PROPERTIES

Called the doctor's stone by some crystal practitioners because of its ability to identify by touch the root of a problem and send healing, sometimes before the condition has fully developed.

MYTHOLOGY AND HISTORY

A sacred stone to the Indigenous people of Medicine Bow in south-eastern Wyoming and millions of years old, cast up in swamps near Medicine Bow during the rainy season; also found in Montana, Idaho, Turkey, and Bulgaria.

Black Coral

COLORS: Black or dark brown

CRYSTAL TYPE: Organic, branching calcareous skeletons of sea creatures that can be highly polished as tumbled stones or jewelry

ZODIAC SIGN: Scorpio (October 24–November 22)

CANDLE COLOR: Deep purple

PHYSICAL: Relieves pain relief; acute illnesses; fevers; infections; bowels; spine and spinal fluid, bones; male potency.

EMOTIONAL: If a partner dies in the early years of marriage; also assists parents who are grieving for a child who has passed on.

HOME: Protects residents and brings luck; placed over the front door inside the entrance to keep negative vibes from entering.

WORKPLACE: A stone of diplomacy and delicate negotiations, behind-the-scenes discussions; resolves individual grievances without recourse to legal remedies.

CHILDREN: For teens who constantly quarrel or end up in fights with peers and at odds with teachers.

ANIMALS: Calms dogs who growl at other animals during exercise; cats who regularly come home with injuries.

PROTECTION: Guards against bad weather, particularly hurricanes, typhoons, high winds, floods, and tsunamis.

MAGICKAL AND PSYCHIC USES

Integral to ocean rituals and divination; traditionally called king coral, this crystal was worn only by kings believed to be divinely chosen and with healing powers; in the modern world, Black Coral enhances wisdom and healing abilities.

SPECIAL PROPERTIES

Absorbs negativity and replaces it with serenity; takes away fears and specters of the night.

MYTHOLOGY AND HISTORY

Coral has been crafted as jewelry and crystals for thousands of years. It is still being harvested in Hawaii, where it is the official gemstone; however, it is illegal in several lands to harvest Black Coral; yet it is possible to find ecologically sustainable coral.

Black Diamond

COLORS: Black and sparkling

CRYSTAL TYPE: Diamond, graphite, and amorphous carbon; high amounts of graphite clusters as inclusions make the diamond appear black

ZODIAC SIGN: Scorpio (October 24–November 22)

CANDLE COLOR: Purple

PHYSICAL: Relieves pain; absorbs and reduces toxicity after invasive treatments, such as x-rays or chemotherapy, or strong medicines.

EMOTIONAL: For ongoing deep depression and suicidal thoughts, where help is refused; for those dabbling in demonology.

HOME: A stone of rich dark soil, Black Diamonds represent the slow, continuing growth of financial resources, especially those built up through generations.

WORKPLACE: For careers that take many years to reach the highest echelons, but offer lasting rewards; for the wise investment of business assets.

CHILDREN: Eases the suffering of anyone who has lost a child, whether through a custody battle, abduction by the other parent, or bereavement.

ANIMALS: For all birds and animals of the night and the safety of cats who roam in darkness.

PROTECTION: Guards against poltergeists, paranormal sexual predators and curses, and hexes that are generational.

MAGICKAL AND PSYCHIC USES

Night magick; full, waning, and dark of the moon rituals; for shadow scrying and scrying with dark crystal spheres and darkened water.

SPECIAL PROPERTIES

For lasting deep love after years of waiting to be together; finding a new love after a bereavement; keeping a family secret.

MYTHOLOGY AND HISTORY

In India, Black Diamonds acquired a reputation as cursed, because a large rare one was placed by worshippers in the eye of the statue of Brahma in his shrine near Pondicherry. The diamond was stolen and those who acquired it met untimely ends. A counter tale from Italy says that if lovers are having difficulties in their relationship, a Black Diamond will absorb all sorrow and ill will.

Black Jade

COLORS: Black, colored with dark minerals, such as black hornblende, graphite, and iron oxide

CRYSTAL TYPE: Jadeite Jade (page 258) and Nephrite Jade (page 315)

ZODIAC SIGN: Capricorn (December 22–January 20)

CANDLE COLOR: Indigo

PHYSICAL: Alleviates issues with the reproductive system, bowels, constipation, IBS, celiac disease, illnesses in older people, feet, legs, hip or knee replacement operations, kidney stones, bile duct, gallstones.

EMOTIONAL: Helps overcome fear of losing independence in the later years and that it is too late to pursue dreams.

HOME: As a guardian stone, provides a dwelling for protective spirits of the land and home.

WORKPLACE: For resisting domineering and controlling employers, managers, and colleagues; thwarts the designs of unscrupulous workplace rivals.

CHILDREN: Counters bullying; put next to a photo of the child being bullied.

ANIMALS: For draft horses and all heavy horses; prevents horses from becoming lame.

PROTECTION: Dims the evil eye of envy; guards against being psychically drained by emotional vampires.

MAGICKAL AND PSYCHIC USES

In the ancient world, black was the color of fertility and rebirth; enhances safe pregnancy and delivery rituals for a healthy child if there have been earlier miscarriages.

SPECIAL PROPERTIES

Absorbs into and preserves secure money in your life; promotes independent living by attracting the right resources and adaptations to home, workplace, and while traveling.

MYTHOLOGY AND HISTORY

Throughout time, black jade has been regarded as guardian against the powers of paranormal evil and human malice. It deflects anger and violence from dangerous people and situations.

Black Jasper

COLORS: Black, grayish or bluish black, occasionally with small white inclusions

CRYSTAL TYPE: Silicate, microcrystalline quartz, a rarer form of jasper

ZODIAC SIGN: Scorpio (October 24–November 22)

CANDLE COLOR: Dark blue

PHYSICAL: Alleviates pain; addresses issues with hip and knee replacement, feet, tissue deterioration, stomach ailments, kidneys, spleen, bladder, liver.

EMOTIONAL: Reduces susceptibility to sales talk, and the temptation to take the easy path.

HOME: Encourages positive results in disputes involving legal cases or challenges by neighbors over boundaries or noise; protects against domestic accidents.

WORKPLACE: For those working in hazardous fields, including detectives, insurance investigators, and welfare claims assessors; deters bullies.

CHILDREN: Guards against the risks of potentially dangerous activities by teenagers; offers protection while riding motorcycles or as novice car drivers.

ANIMALS: Protects pedigreed or exotic pets from being stolen or straying.

PROTECTION: Guards against injustice by corrupt officialdom or those misusing power, as well as internet scams and online romance scams.

MAGICKAL AND PSYCHIC USES

As a scrying stone, Black Jasper reveals what is hidden; in meditation it brings prophetic visions; used in Wicca to absorb negativity during rituals.

SPECIAL PROPERTIES

Black Jasper acts as a touchstone, said to show the purity of gold; potent where the value of an item or offer, or the trustworthiness of a person, is questionable.

MYTHOLOGY AND HISTORY

In medieval times Black Jasper was reputed to help great leaders win cities and fleets of ships. Black Jasper assists in making a supreme physical and mental effort after difficulty or obstacles.

Black Moonstone

COLORS: Black with silvery gray or blue flashes; white, gray, brown, peach, or tan striations

CRYSTAL TYPE: Plagioclase feldspar, glowing gently, seemingly from inside, called the Schiller effect

ZODIAC SIGN: Cancer (June 22–July 22)

CANDLE COLOR: Silver

PHYSICAL: Alleviates female reproductive problems, hormonal imbalances, PMS, menopause; promotes healthy pregnancy later in life.

EMOTIONAL: Eases the pain of relationship breakups and family traumas; aids in dealing with family secrets.

HOME: Keeps you from pressuring yourself to uphold impossible standards of domestic perfection.

WORKPLACE: Protects against cliques and factions interfering with impartial decision making.

CHILDREN: Addresses learning disabilities; clumsiness; fear of the dark.

ANIMALS: Creates space around injured or traumatized animals so they can rest.

PROTECTION: Reduces sensitivity to effects of electronic waves, especially in a high-tech office or near a radio tower; for nighttime travel.

MAGICKAL AND PSYCHIC USES

For rituals on the dark of the moon before the visible crescent; meditation; connecting with spirit guides; working with our shadow self.

SPECIAL PROPERTIES

Associated with the mystical Black Madonna statues brought to Europe by Crusaders and with Divine Feminine initiation mysteries.

MYTHOLOGY AND HISTORY

Only found in Madagascar; Black Moonstone specifically helps with mothering issues, including new mothers struggling to bond, single parents, anyone who was badly mothered or suffered maternal loss in childhood; at any age with a difficult mother.

Black Obsidian

COLORS: Black and gleaming (see also Apache Tear, page 34, and Gold Sheen Obsidian, page 212)

CRYSTAL TYPE: Volcanic glass/magma, formed when lava hardens so fast that no crystalline structures are created

ZODIAC SIGN: Scorpio (October 24–November 22)

CANDLE COLOR: Burgundy

PHYSICAL: Relieves pain; addresses issues involving circulation, arteries, stomach, bowels, arthritis, rheumatism, cramps; detoxifies.

EMOTIONAL: Reduces shock after accident, operation, or trauma; for survivors of rape and incest, those with phobias, acute anxiety, obsessive-compulsive disorder.

HOME: Counters the tendency of family members to slam doors and shout or rush like whirlwinds; reduces effects of drama kings and queens; prevents friends and neighbors from monopolizing your time with problems.

WORKPLACE: Improves efficiency and smooth running of an operation; promotes concentration in a disruptive work environment; for working or traveling at night.

CHILDREN: Enables autistic children to cope better with changes and disruption to daily routine; for restless, overly impulsive tots to teens.

ANIMALS: Desensitizes pets to traffic noise and being touched; for older animals in a boisterous household.

PROTECTION: Absorbs hostility; protects against others taking advantage and those who would deceive.

MAGICKAL AND PSYCHIC USES

For prophecy, labyrinth meditation; rituals for the Black Madonna, the Earth Mother form of the Virgin Mary; ancient Egyptian Goddess magick.

SPECIAL PROPERTIES

A personal stone, kept by one person throughout their life.

MYTHOLOGY AND HISTORY

Highly polished Black Obsidian was used by the Mayans for magick mirrors; the sixteenth-century astrologer Dr. John Dee had a similar mirror called his shew-stone for revealing the future. Obsidian is called the wizard stone in traditional magick.

Black Onyx

COLOR: Naturally black through iron and carbon in its formation or heat treated to change from gray to black. (See also Banded Onyx, page 51.)

CRYSTAL TYPE: Chalcedony

ZODIAC SIGN: Capricorn (December 22–January 20)

CANDLE COLOR: White

PHYSICAL: Promotes cellular regeneration; alleviates issues involving the ears, balance, teeth, bones, bone marrow, blood, soft tissue, feet, bites and stings; reduces nausea.

EMOTIONAL: Counters addiction to sex phone lines, internet pornography, and dubious influences masquerading as friends.

HOME: Protects the home and family after dark; keeps family members safe while working or traveling at night; brings order out of chaos.

WORKPLACE: For confidently refuting unfair criticism by someone with a personal vendetta; protects against hostility and psychic attacks; lowers sexual temperature if experiencing frequent inappropriate remarks or behavior.

CHILDREN: Prevents nightmares; aids concentration if a child is easily distracted.

ANIMALS: For cats roaming the neighborhood at night and animals in barns or stables after dark.

PROTECTION: Guards against black magick, curses, hexes, the evil eye, and mind control.

MAGICKAL AND PSYCHIC USES

Associated with wizards and sorcerers, Black Onyx brings psychic invisibility in circumstances of potential danger; as black scrying mirrors, connects with ancestors and spirit guides.

SPECIAL PROPERTIES

Reduces overdependency on you by others; letting go of activities, relationships, and friendships that no longer fulfill; releases unrequited or lost love that blocks new love.

MYTHOLOGY AND HISTORY

Popular as prayer beads, rosaries, and worry beads since Black Onyx absorbs sorrow and fears; antidote to frantic modern life; brings a practical, pragmatic approach to achieving goals and determination to succeed.

Black Opal

COLORS: Black Opal has a deep body tone, from dark gray to jet black; darker shades of blue or green, within which shine brilliant flashes of red, orange, green, blue, and purple

CRYSTAL TYPE: Hydrated silicon dioxide, with carbon and iron oxide trace elements

ZODIAC SIGN: Scorpio (October 24–November 22)

CANDLE COLOR: Red

PHYSICAL: Absorbs pain; relieves illness, chronic bone problems; alleviates disease deep within the body; counteracts side effects from radiation, laser treatments, or chemotherapy.

EMOTIONAL: Counters the inability to embrace one's own shadow side or accept others as less than perfect; overcomes the need for constant stimulation and excitement; addresses weight issues.

HOME: Helps a grandparent handle caregiving for grandchildren.

WORKPLACE: For starting a new career or business later in life; aids in becoming recognized as an authority in your area of expertise.

CHILDREN: Eases childhood fear of darkness.

ANIMALS: Assists pets with poor eyesight; useful for guide dogs for visually impaired people.

PROTECTION: Repels black magick and earthly and paranormal evil.

MAGICKAL AND PSYCHIC USES

A power stone, used throughout magickal history by wizards, witches, magicians, and, more recently, in Wiccan rituals as a God stone (a Precious White Opal is the Goddess stone); brings good fortune.

SPECIAL PROPERTIES

For happiness in middle and later years; for adventure, travel, and rediscovering a major talent after or instead of retirement.

MYTHOLOGY AND HISTORY

The earliest opals, about six thousand years old, have been found in a cave in Kenya. Australian Black Opals are the most valuable type, found mainly at Lightning Ridge in northern New South Wales, Australia. In 2008 the Black Opal was made the official gem of New South Wales, Australia.

Black or Shooting Star Kyanite

COLOR: Steel-gray or black, often with metallic sheen

CRYSTAL TYPE: Aluminum rich silicate, as blades or fans

ZODIAC SIGN: Aquarius (January 21–February 18)

CANDLE COLOR: Silver

PHYSICAL: Alleviates issues involving the adrenal glands, blood pressure, vocal cords, bone marrow, neurological disorders, visual disturbances, successful surgery.

EMOTIONAL: Eases regrets and anger over what cannot be resolved; counters irrational fear of ghosts.

HOME: Blades facing outward deflect stress entering the home; keeps vehicles and possessions safe.

WORKPLACE: Separates work relationships from personal relationships in order to avoid potential problems.

CHILDREN: Calms fears of malevolent invisible friends.

ANIMALS: Protects pets if there is a spate of pet thefts in your neighborhood.

PROTECTION: While undergoing reiki attunement, Wiccan initiations, and sacred dedications; helps you steer clear of exploitative ashrams and power-hungry spiritual organizations; guards against the evil eye; for driving away harm and danger.

MAGICKAL AND PSYCHIC USES

As a magick wand to draw what you wish and banish what is destructive; for dream recall and astral travel in sleep; increases clairvoyance; promotes extraterrestrial links; for Star Souls.

SPECIAL PROPERTIES

Called the itch's broom because it sweeps away harm; in its fan shape, cleanses the aura and clears rooms of negative energies, earthly and paranormal.

MYTHOLOGY AND HISTORY

Especially when shining, Black or Shooting Star Kyanite brings celestial energies into daily life; one myth says Archangel Michael cuts the cords of unwise attachments and energy vampires with Black Kyanite, opening the way to beneficial links that support but do not bind.

Black Pearl

COLOR: Black or dark-colored, lustrous
CRYSTAL TYPE: Organic (see Pearl, page 342)
ZODIAC SIGN: Scorpio (October 24–November 22)
CANDLE COLOR: Silver

PHYSICAL: Alleviates infections, emphysema, negative impact of secondary smoke; relieves symptoms of early-onset menopause, perimenopause, and menopause.
EMOTIONAL: As women move into the wise woman phase, promotes sensuality and sexuality in midlife and later years.
HOME: Attracts abundance and good luck; guards against flooding and other issues caused by water; encourages happy grandmother/grandchildren interactions.
WORKPLACE: For businesswomen establishing second careers, counteracts sexism and agism combined; prevents setbacks in business due to unfair competition and "glass-ceiling" cultures.
CHILDREN: Comforts children after their first loss; insulates against bad news in the media.
ANIMALS: For rituals to clean up polluted seas and waterways.
PROTECTION: Guards against psychic attacks, paranormal and earthly ill-wishers.

MAGICKAL AND PSYCHIC USES
Channeling wisdom from the Crone or Grandmother Goddess, scrying by silver candlelight; magick during the waning and dark moon.

SPECIAL PROPERTIES
For women in their middle and later years to maximize health, wisdom, and experience and not regret the passing of time.

MYTHOLOGY AND HISTORY
Chinese myth tells that the full moon produced dew from discarded dreams that fell into the sea. The oysters came to the surface, opening their shells and the dewdrops became pearls. Black Pearls are sad thoughts transformed into beauty by the Moon Mother. Natural (not cultured) Black Pearls occur rarely. Cultured Tahitian pearls from warm South Seas are grown in black-lipped oysters, the only pearls to have a black hue; some black pearls are irradiated or dyed.

Black Phantom Quartz

COLORS: Can be black all the way through, sometimes with sparkles. The darkness of the crystal depends on the size of the inner Black Phantom
CRYSTAL TYPE: Silicon dioxide, usually clear quartz, inside which a phantom or shadow quartz crystal appears
ZODIAC SIGN: Scorpio (October 24–November 22)
CANDLE COLOR: White

PHYSICAL: regrowth of bones after fractures; torn ligaments and muscles, tumors deep in the body and secondary tumors; transplants, implants, and transfusions.
EMOTIONAL: Counters withdrawal within the self after trauma or loss; unwillingness to physically and emotionally care for self.
HOME: Addresses structural issues and renovations; serves as a luck-bringing house guardian.
WORKPLACE: Gives ideas a practical foundation; enables you to start a business after bankruptcy or unemployment.
CHILDREN: A protective crystal for those who fear the dark, noises at night, and ghosts.
ANIMALS: Helps frail, old, or sick pets to walk more steadily.
PROTECTION: Deflects ill-wishing, curses, hexes, jinxes, and the evil eye.

MAGICKAL AND PSYCHIC USES
The ultimate yin/yang crystal for balancing energies within the home, workplace, and self; neutralizes negative Earth energies beneath buildings.

SPECIAL PROPERTIES
Brings recognition of those who have traveled through time with us, especially soul twins and close soul family.

MYTHOLOGY AND HISTORY
Black Phantom Quartz banishes negative paranormal spirits and energies from your home while welcoming benign deceased relatives as guardians; prevents people from dwelling on old grievances time and again or quarreling over unresolvable issues.

Black Shamanic Calcite

COLORS: Brownish black, may contain white
CRYSTAL TYPE: Calcite containing a high proportion of carbon, also barite, zircon, marcasite, pyrite, quartz, and strontianite; sometimes features small spiral shell fossil inclusions
ZODIAC SIGN: Scorpio (October 24–November 22)
CANDLE COLOR: White

PHYSICAL: Relieves chronic pain; alleviates side effects of chemotherapy, radiation, or invasive surgery; helps heal bowel obstructions and diseases.
EMOTIONAL: Counters excessive fears of accidents, potential disasters, or attacks that stand in the way of everyday freedom; eases obsessions with hauntings and paranormal evil.
HOME: Works as a guardian stone to provide shelter for the land and house guardians who protect your home.
WORKPLACE: Guards against unfriendly ghosts in a building where they lurk, if you must work late or remain there alone at night; makes you feel welcome in a business run exclusively as a family concern.
CHILDREN: Helps teens who have been dabbling in Ouija boards or online demonology stay safe.
ANIMALS: Protects companion animals if there have been a lot of pet thefts in your area.
PROTECTION: Creates a powerful force field to repel external psychic attack.

MAGICKAL AND PSYCHIC USES
For spiritual cleansing; astral travel and shamanic journeying; deep meditation; automatic writing; clairvoyance, clairaudience, mediumship.

SPECIAL PROPERTIES
A highly protective and grounding stone for those new to psychic work during healing or spiritual exploration; at the same time, Black Shamanic Calcite opens channels to wise guides and spirit helpers.
MYTHOLOGY AND HISTORY
Traditionally used for healing, connection with ancestors, and astral travel by Native North American shamans in the Colorado mountains where the stone is found.

Black Spinel

COLORS: Black, glassy, dense, also golden to dark brown
CRYSTAL TYPE: Magnesium aluminum oxide or magnesium aluminate
ZODIAC SIGN: Scorpio (October 24–November 22)
CANDLE COLOR: White

PHYSICAL: Addresses poor circulation in lower limbs, chronic exhaustion; alleviates endometriosis, cysts, polyps, womb infections, bladder problems, prostate issues, intestinal distress, lymph node issues; may be helpful with growth treatments.
EMOTIONAL: Defuses sudden inappropriate anger, suppressed rage over unresolved injustices.
HOME: Helps cultivate a mutually beneficial relationship when adult children return to live at home to avoid slipping back into parent/child roles; aids in resolving inheritance disputes.
WORKPLACE: Focuses your attention on issues at hand if a company is losing money or in danger of closing; avoids sacrificing self for a lost cause; concentrates your creativity and energy to meet deadlines.
CHILDREN: For encountering birth parents for the first time as a teenager or young adult.
ANIMALS: Comforts a pet grieving for an owner or mate.
PROTECTION: Reflects back ill-wishing and curses; prevents mind manipulation.

MAGICKAL AND PSYCHIC USES
Defensive and banishing magick; connects with spirit guides and ancestors; blocks spirit possession after a séance; counters demons; helps recall the contract made before present life.
SPECIAL PROPERTIES
Aids in rebuilding after loss, separation, or natural disaster, better than before.
MYTHOLOGY AND HISTORY
Spinel, as well as being a mineral occurring naturally in many different colors, is the collective name for a group of metal oxide minerals, including Franklinite (page 193). For civilized interactions, if a relationship cannot be completely severed because of shared children or business interests; an alternative to Jet (page 259) for mourning jewelry.

Black Star Diopside

COLORS: Dark brown to dark greenish black, black with a four-rayed star, most visible when cut and polished in dome-shaped cabochons
CRYSTAL TYPE: Pyroxene, calcium magnesium silicate
ZODIAC SIGN: Pisces (February 19–March 20)
CANDLE COLOR: Dark green

PHYSICAL: Alleviates pain from slipped discs, and issues involving the spine, back of neck, muscles, bowels, constipation, kidneys, fluid blockages, chronic pain, prostate, hernia, knees, feet; promotes circulation; useful after heart operations or heart attacks.
EMOTIONAL: Eases blocked emotions; inability to cry, especially in men; deep-seated fears and phobias from childhood.
HOME: Offers comfort if your partner or family are emotionally repressed.
WORKPLACE: Combines creativity with sound business sense; brings lucky breaks to hasten success; for recognition in your area of expertise.
CHILDREN: Counteracts tantrums in toddlers, teens, and adults who never quite grew up.
ANIMALS: To settle after a home move or prolonged veterinarian treatment; for unneutered male animals to minimize aggression.
PROTECTION: Guards against fear of darkness and ghosts.

MAGICKAL AND PSYCHIC USES
The star in Black Star Diopside acts as a gateway to other dimensions; for star and wish magick under a starry sky; connects with Earth elementals, Earth healing rituals; strengthens dowsing accuracy.

SPECIAL PROPERTIES
Black Star Diopside encourages overly cautious partners and older relatives to visit new places and try new activities and cuisine.

MYTHOLOGY AND HISTORY
Black Star Diopside is called the Black Star of India after its main source. It is the only crystal to produce a four- instead of a six-rayed white star. Tumbled Black Star Diopside stones have identical properties to the finest gem.

Black Strongstone

COLORS: Black or dark gray
CRYSTAL TYPE: Black quartz pebbles found along the ocean shores of Mexico, smoothed underwater through many years; as jewelry as well as naturally tumbled stone
ZODIAC SIGN: Scorpio (October 24–November 22)
CANDLE COLOR: Gray

PHYSICAL: Addresses issues involving the feet, ankles, lower limbs and back, pain, circulation, bowels and bodily elimination processes; boosts strength and survival instincts after a prolonged illness, major surgery, or necessary invasive treatments.
EMOTIONAL: For those who do not learn or benefit from life's trials, but waste their lives regretting what has been lost or never can be.
HOME: Fills the home with continually refreshing life energies; guides you to the ocean or back to oceanside living or long vacations if that is your dream.
WORKPLACE: Keeps barbed words, spite, and gossip from disturbing your harmony or affecting your focus; infuses you with courage to resist unfair treatment and seek redress.
CHILDREN: Helps with teaching children what information can be shared with the world and what should be kept within the family.
ANIMALS: For cats who secretly divide their time between two homes for double home comforts.
PROTECTION: Guards against the effects of psychic attack because of Black Strongstone's smooth surface on which negativity cannot get a toehold.

MAGICKAL AND PSYCHIC USES
Absorbs the power of the oceans; for tidal magick; as the water symbol on a crystal-based magickal altar; for visions during meditation of underwater kingdoms, both mythical and those lost through the millennia by the encroaching tides.

SPECIAL PROPERTIES
For hidden plans and undetected liaisons where there would be opposition or prejudice.

MYTHOLOGY AND HISTORY
A name coined by crystal expert and author Robert Simmons and rapidly adopted by lovers and collectors of beautiful stones. Black Strongstone is powerful because the round black pebbles are tumbled smooth without human intervention and so are true children of the sea.

Black Tourmaline or Schorl

COLOR: Black

CRYSTAL TYPE: Aluminum borosilicate mixed with iron, magnesium, or other metals

ZODIAC SIGN: Scorpio (October 24–November 22)

CANDLE COLOR: Deep purple

PHYSICAL: Alleviates arthritis, plus issues involving the bowels, constipation, IBS, celiac disease; strengthens the immune system; addresses problems with the heart, lower back, legs, ankles, feet; relieves muscle pain and pain in other areas; helps minimize scar tissue; promotes skeletal alignment.

EMOTIONAL: For panic attacks, especially of enclosed spaces, fears of dentists, doctors, injections, and medical procedures; counters suicidal thoughts, self-harm, drug abuse.

HOME: Deters complaining neighbors and family members, who expect you to fix their lives, from bothering you.

WORKPLACE: Guards against harmful electromagnetic energies; for sick-building syndrome where there are a lot of unexplained minor illnesses; for chiropractors, physiotherapists, acupuncturists, and kinesiologists.

CHILDREN: Discourages whining in toddlers and teens alike.

ANIMALS: Calms down howling dogs and yowling cats.

PROTECTION: Deflects back negative energies from people and spirits, especially succubi, incubi, and poltergeists; for psychic, psychological, and physical protection.

MAGICKAL AND PSYCHIC USES

Shamanic ritual and traveling between realms, meditation, scrying; eight Black Tourmalines used as a defensive circle for protection and purification rituals; for safely receiving messages from higher beings.

SPECIAL PROPERTIES

Offers all-round protection from environmental pollution, spite, ill-wishing, curses, hexes, emotional vampires, mind games, and physical attack.

MYTHOLOGY AND HISTORY

A stone associated with the Roman God Saturn, God of time, and also the planet Saturn, Schorl was once used by magicians to offer them protection against Earth demons when they were casting spells; brings grounding if feeling *spaced out* after healing or meditation.

Black Tourmaline with Mica

COLORS: Varies between gold/silver/white with black and black with silvery/gold specks

CRYSTAL TYPE: Mica (shiny white) with tourmaline (black) inclusions or (black) tourmaline or schorl with glittery mica inclusions or coating from a few specks to almost completely covered; sodium iron cyclosilicate

ZODIAC SIGN: Scorpio (October 24–November 22)

CANDLE COLOR: Gold

PHYSICAL: Keeps rogue cells from reproducing; addresses spine misalignment and injuries; minimizes allergies to environmental pollutants and additives to food; prevents nightmares.

EMOTIONAL: Counters unwise attraction to bad influences, risk taking, and being too trusting with exciting new people and offers.

HOME: Protects vehicles, possessions, and homes against theft, attack, and natural disasters.

WORKPLACE: In high-tech, fast-moving workplaces, for protection against harmful electronic energies.

CHILDREN: For reducing obsessions in older teens who spend hours on their devices.

ANIMALS: Useful in stables or larger animal stalls to prevent threat or attack.

PROTECTION: Shields against malevolent paranormal energies, curses, and hexes; the mica transforms less benign energy into light.

MAGICKAL AND PSYCHIC USES

The ultimate psychic defense combination as background protection for magickal ritual, séances, ghost hunting, and spirit rescue while welcoming benign entities and guardians.

SPECIAL PROPERTIES

The combination of light-bringing mica and protective black tourmaline repels what is harmful, attracts what is needed.

MYTHOLOGY AND HISTORY

Muscovite, the form of mica most often present in this crystal, is associated with sacred buildings; black tourmaline or schorl was traditionally considered protective against Earth demons; together they provide the ultimate spiritual tool for magickal exploration both astrally and in the spirit world through mediumship.

Blades of Light

COLORS: Very clear inside and colorless, striations on all faces except terminations; formations include long lasers with sloping sides; can contain Lemurian seeds with tiny quartz growths on one side (see Lemurian or Inca Jade, page 275)
CRYSTAL TYPE: Quartz, silicon dioxide
ZODIAC SIGN: Aquarius (January 21–February 18)
CANDLE COLOR: White

PHYSICAL: Helps defend against highly infectious viruses and diseases, believed to protect those who mine the mineral as well as those suffering from infections; addresses issues involving vision and hearing, including tinnitus.
EMOTIONAL: Counters indecisiveness; for those who live in a fantasy world of future fame, fortune, and celebrity without taking any steps toward achievement.
HOME: For welcoming the ancestors into the home, especially if you live far from your roots or family secrets cast a cloud over past connections.
WORKPLACE: Aids in getting to the truth about conflicting information or uncertainty involving speculation and investment; helps in making major decisions about your future if you are pressured to follow others' agendas.
CHILDREN: For those with communication difficulties; for Star Souls who find everyday living confusing.
ANIMALS: Comforts loyal pets who are always there for you.
PROTECTION: Guards against all black magick, curses, hexes, and those who use mind manipulation to deceive.

MAGICKAL AND PSYCHIC USES
A light-bringer, especially in the form of a laser, Blades of Light can be used as a wand to manifest what is most needed and for psychic surgery to remove areas of dis-ease, discomfort, or spirit attachments.

SPECIAL PROPERTIES
The clarity of Blades of Light cuts through doubts, indecision, hesitation, or deception.

MYTHOLOGY AND HISTORY
Found in Colombia; as a pyramid, Blades of Light connect with ancient Egyptian, Mayan, Inca, and Aztec wisdom; enhances telepathy and clairvoyance.

Blizzard Stone

COLORS: Black with flecks of white; can be mistaken visually for Snowflake Obsidian (page 446)
CRYSTAL TYPE: Combination of chlorite, serpentine, muscovite, pyroxene, hercynite, magnetite, and white feldspar, with black serpentine as matrix for white calcium rich feldspar
ZODIAC SIGN: Capricorn (December 22–January 20)
CANDLE COLOR: White

PHYSICAL: Alleviates symptoms of menopause, especially hot flashes; helps remedy infections, bruises, sprains, chemical and electrical imbalances, migraines, broken bones; offers pain relief; counters adverse effects of radiation therapy.
EMOTIONAL: Empowers you to resist being drawn to the wrong kind of person; helps overcome OCD, unreasonable anger, constant pessimism.
HOME: Integrates new family members with divided loyalties; for overly controlling partners worrying about finances and safety; reduces overdependence by others.
WORKPLACE: For a home office with technological equipment intruding on domestic space; promotes online marketing; useful for those installing and maintaining computers or electronic equipment.
CHILDREN: Counters fear of thunderstorms; balances the need to learn from experience with parental protection.
ANIMALS: Helps heal larger animals and those who mainly spend time outdoors.
PROTECTION: Guards against bad weather and floods, living near telephone poles, industrial waste sites, and pylons.

MAGICKAL AND PSYCHIC USES
A magnetic crystal to manifest what or whom you most want; enhances weather magick; learning from past-life mistakes where independence versus control issues recur.

SPECIAL PROPERTIES
For tough love with addicted family members, adult children reluctant to support themselves financially, and over-dependent partners.

MYTHOLOGY AND HISTORY
Blizzard Stone is also called Gabbro, an igneous rock that cools slowly deep in the Earth. As the name *blizzard* suggests, it will offer support through life's battles.

Blood of Isis

COLORS: Bright red; may be smoky
CRYSTAL TYPE: Rare gem form of carnelian, colored by iron oxide
ZODIAC SIGN: Leo (July 23–August 23)
CANDLE COLOR: Red

PHYSICAL: Addresses issues involving blood, female reproduction, menstrual flow, nosebleeds, worries about conception and early miscarriage; relieves pain.
EMOTIONAL: For parents devastated when children leave home; counters emotional effects of menopause, marking the end of fertility; alleviates grief over infertility, and after stillbirth or sudden infant death syndrome (SIDS); helps overcome fear of blood.
HOME: For reconciliation after a quarrel or jealous outburst.
WORKPLACE: Helps dispel stereotypes in predominantly male or female workplaces; encourages creativity as well as logic.
CHILDREN: For mothers having trouble allowing a child with a physical or emotional challenge to take risks.
ANIMALS: Promotes successful breeding programs among endangered species.
PROTECTION: Guards against the dark night of the soul.

MAGICKAL AND PSYCHIC USES
For Goddess rituals linked with the ancient Egyptian Mother Isis; for men and women exploring their inner goddess; enhances fertility rituals; promotes using cord, ribbon, or string to make your knots.

SPECIAL PROPERTIES
Especially potent during a blood moon, when the moon turns red during a full lunar eclipse; the Blood of Isis represents the surging life force.

MYTHOLOGY AND HISTORY
Originally found around the Red Sea, where it was worn as an amulet from ancient Egyptian times representing the fertilizing blood of Isis, this crystal offers renewal and protection to land and people in this world and in the afterlife. In 1253, King Alphonso of Spain produced his lapidary based on ancient Arabic texts, describing the Blood of Isis as the stone of sleep because it induced deep trances.

Blue Andean Opal

COLORS: Soft blue, often with a pearl-like sheen
CRYSTAL TYPE: Hydrated silicon dioxide, displaying no iridescence, unlike precious opals
ZODIAC SIGN: Libra (September 23–October 23)
CANDLE COLOR: Pale blue

PHYSICAL: Relieves depression, exhaustion, and ME/chronic fatigue syndrome; promotes absorption of essential nutrients; for tranquil pregnancy and childbirth.
EMOTIONAL: For healthy weight loss and overcoming eating disorders, especially among young people teased by peers about their weight or appearance.
HOME: Cleanses the home after negative visitors or quarrels.
WORKPLACE: Overcomes reticence in speaking at meetings, in public, or in job interviews; inspires fledgling authors.
CHILDREN: In the immediate days after childbirth, promotes parent-child bonding, especially if the birth was traumatic.
ANIMALS: For small or young animals in a home where there are children or a lot of noise.
PROTECTION: Defends those forced into conformity at any early age by family, community, or religion; for escaping the influence of cults.

MAGICKAL AND PSYCHIC USES
Powerful for Mother Earth rituals, especially against climate change and pollution; traditionally used in ceremonies to bring rain.

SPECIAL PROPERTIES
For past-life connections—whether actual or symbolic—through meditation, to explain present-world fears and phobias; a love stone, given to pledge commitment and fidelity.

MYTHOLOGY AND HISTORY
The national stone of Peru, sacred to Pachamama, the Peruvian Earth mother, and considered one of her gifts to humanity.

Blue Apatite

COLORS: Blue—light, bright, or dark blue; sometimes different blues within the same crystal, indigo, occasionally white-veined (see also Green Apatite, page 218)

CRYSTAL TYPE: Complex phosphate of calcium, chlorine, and fluorine, phosphate present in teeth and bones as hydroxyapatite

ZODIAC SIGNS: Gemini (May 22–June 21) and Libra (September 23–October 23)

CANDLE COLOR: Medium blue

PHYSICAL: Addresses issues involving teeth, gums, bones, cartilage; relieves pain; alleviates chronic illnesses; helps boost appetite.

EMOTIONAL: Controls food cravings and obsessions; for healthy weight maintenance; overcomes fears of dentists; prevents stress overload.

HOME: Reduces irritability among family members; encourages relaxation; helps in negotiating debt repayment.

WORKPLACE: Overcomes unemployment, redundancy, forced early retirement, or unfair dismissal; promotes steady business expansion; useful for youth workers, career advisers, business consultants, account or investment managers.

CHILDREN: Soothes teething babies if Blue Apatite is near a crib.

ANIMALS: For healthy breeding programs, especially among endangered species; increases psychic communication with pets and wildlife.

PROTECTION: Guards against emotional blackmail.

MAGICKAL AND PSYCHIC USES

Tunes into the future through increased synchronicity, signs, symbols, and omens; promotes claircognizance, psychically sensing spirits, and sixth sense in everyday life.

SPECIAL PROPERTIES

Improves memory and concentration, for long-term study and career; clears confusion and procrastination; enhances creativity.

MYTHOLOGY AND HISTORY

Blue Apatite closely connects human and animal kingdoms; the crystal is present in elephant tusks; associated with animal conservation and protection of habitats, including urban wildlife.

Blue Aragonite

COLORS: Pale turquoise or dark blue, caused by inclusion of copper; may be lustrous; sometimes dyed

CRYSTAL TYPE: Calcium carbonate

ZODIAC SIGN: Pisces (February 19–March 20)

CANDLE COLOR: Pale blue

PHYSICAL: Alleviates colds, flu, and viruses affecting throat or lungs, as well as stress-related illnesses, Reynaud's disease, muscle spasms.

EMOTIONAL: Eases grief because of bereavement or the breakup of a significant relationship; helps to express feelings of love, sympathy, need, or sorrow.

HOME: Encourages the creation of a comfortable home without unnecessary expenditure by revamping or repairing rather than replacing old items.

WORKPLACE: Promotes financial stability in business and wise investment; helps cultivate the ability to empathize with and communicate positively with different people and situations; prevents burnout.

CHILDREN: Counters acute shyness in class or with peers.

ANIMALS: For overly timid pets who tremble or cry when strangers visit.

PROTECTION: Guards against the indiscriminate outflow of resources and good fortune in the home, workplace, and life.

MAGICKAL AND PSYCHIC USES

Strengthens communication with guardian angels; makes psychic readings more accurate by tuning intuitively into what a client is feeling deep down; increases the flow of reiki energy.

SPECIAL PROPERTIES

Allows a soul twin to find you when the time is right, rather than constantly searching; helps in communicating heart to heart with a partner in a second or subsequent relationship to avoid becoming trapped in redundant reactions because of past relationships.

MYTHOLOGY AND HISTORY

First discovered under the blue skies of Aragon in Spain, Blue Aragonite makes you feel at home in the world and able to find your unique place.

Blue Aventurine

COLORS: Pale to medium blue, also dark blue; dumortierite inclusions provide the blue color
CRYSTAL TYPE: Microcrystalline quartz, containing mica that gives aventurine a metallic, iridescent glint
ZODIAC SIGNS: Libra (September 23–October 23) and Sagittarius (November 23–December 21)
CANDLE COLOR: Blue

PHYSICAL: Alleviates issues involving sinuses, vision, ears, headaches, allergies, colds, coughs, lungs, growth problems in children; keeps blood flowing through the arteries and veins; helps eliminate toxins in the body.
EMOTIONAL: Banishes bitterness or resentment, causing self-defeating behavior; helps dispel an illogical belief in having an unlucky or cursed life that causes thoughts of self-harming.
HOME: Guards against intruders, dangerous strangers, and scams involving building work.
WORKPLACE: Aids in obtaining leadership positions if relatively young or inexperienced; brings luck and the right conditions for success in job applications.
CHILDREN: Keeps children safe from accidents and from wandering off during journeys and vacations; calms them if they panic when taking tests.
ANIMALS: Prevents pets from straying or being stolen.
PROTECTION: While traveling, guards against mishaps, disruptions, delays, and lost luggage or documents.

MAGICKAL AND PSYCHIC USES
Traditionally, a stone of the Native North American medicine wheel, Blue Aventurine brings awareness of unseen protective spiritual guardians, clairvoyance, clairaudience.
SPECIAL PROPERTIES
Combines skill with good luck for passing driving tests, winning sports competitions, excelling at auditions and performances.
MYTHOLOGY AND HISTORY
Blue Aventurine brings or restores a desire for adventure at any age; for the fulfillment of travel plans, learning new languages, or studying overseas.

Blue Barite or Baryte

COLORS: Pale to deeper blue (see also Golden Barite or Baryte, page 205)
CRYSTAL TYPE: Barium sulfate, soft
ZODIAC SIGNS: Libra (September 23–October 23) and Aquarius (January 21–February 18)
CANDLE COLOR: Blue

PHYSICAL: Regulates blood pressure; lowers fever; addresses throat issues; relieves pain; useful after radiation and chemotherapy; eases shock following an accident or surgery; enhances brain and memory; valuable for mother and baby after a protracted birth or surgical intervention during childbirth.
EMOTIONAL: Allows expression of blocked emotions positively; overcomes fears of confrontation; for post-traumatic stress disorder.
HOME: Helps settle disagreements between partners or family members without saying something you may regret.
WORKPLACE: Aids in selling ideas and products, and presenting yourself in a favorable light; useful for politicians, travel representatives, team coaches, lifestyle mentors.
CHILDREN: Teaches children to make wise decisions.
ANIMALS: Keeps dogs from barking and cats from yowling excessively.
PROTECTION: Guards against false words.

MAGICKAL AND PSYCHIC USES
For clairaudience, sound healing, trance mediumship, shamanic drumming; inspires Earth and ozone layer healing, psychic dreams; aids in encountering higher teacher guides and increasing meaningful coincidences or synchronicity.
SPECIAL PROPERTIES
The "speaker's stone," for lectures, presentations, workplace meetings, seminars, interviews.
MYTHOLOGY AND HISTORY
Blue Barite encourages environmental self-sufficiency through organic gardening, solar heating, moving to a rural location and growing your own food, starting your own environmentally friendly business; for permaculture, ethical farming, and sourcing of food; for long-distance journeys at any age

Blue Calcite

COLOR: From pale to medium blue, sometimes with white veins; resembles blue ice in unpolished form

CRYSTAL TYPE: Calcium carbonate

ZODIAC SIGN: Pisces (February 19–March 20)

CANDLE COLOR: Pale blue

PHYSICAL: Alleviates neuralgia, sore throat, hormonal headaches, hot flashes, inflamed internal organs, rashes, high temperatures, high blood pressure, burns, scalds, toothache; promotes absorption of calcium for teeth and bones.

EMOTIONAL: Prevents burnout among workaholics and those with a frantic lifestyle; calms anxiety and clears the way for positive communication.

HOME: Protects the home from intruders and thieves when traveling with smartphones, tablets, and laptops; continuously cleanses rooms and possessions, ideal when moving from home to a furnished accommodation.

WORKPLACE: Slows down a hyperactive workplace; promotes negotiations to soften opposing views; for mediators, equal-opportunity employment officers, and crime prevention officers.

CHILDREN: Soothes teething or colicky babies; aids in learning to swim.

ANIMALS: Calms oversensitive pets who snap at strangers.

PROTECTION: Avoids miscommunication and the spread of false information.

MAGICKAL AND PSYCHIC USES

Connects with water spirits; promotes meditation, telepathy with loved ones far away to warn of potential danger; encourages dream journeying.

SPECIAL PROPERTIES

Calms nerves before a special event, such as a wedding, examination, interview, or driving test, especially if speaking or writing is involved.

MYTHOLOGY AND HISTORY

Blue Calcite is associated with clear, positive, and wise communication at every level, from prayer, resolving differences in relationships with nonconfrontational words, and defusing community tensions over racial or religious differences to sending positive, measured texts and emails, even when provoked.

Blue Celestite or Celestine

COLOR: Pale to medium blue (see also Orange Celestite or Celestine, page 328)

CRYSTAL TYPE: Strontium ore/sulfate, resembling ice crystal, containing holes

ZODIAC SIGN: Libra (September 23–October 23)

CANDLE COLOR: Pale blue

PHYSICAL: Addresses issues involving the thyroid, eyes, ears, throat, mouth, headaches, speech, brain imbalances, intestinal parasites and infections, fevers, high blood pressure related to lifestyle stresses; eases hyperventilation.

EMOTIONAL: Alleviates acute anxiety, obsessions, insomnia caused by worry, agoraphobia, fears of travel, crowds, speaking or eating in public, blushing, nervous tics; aids in releasing grudges from the past.

HOME: Encourages family members to listen to one another; for welcoming new family members of all ages.

WORKPLACE: Aids in responding calmly and assertively to being shouted down and petty bullying; counters stage fright and loss of voice for singers and actors.

CHILDREN: Protects children and teens from schoolyard bullying.

ANIMALS: Encourages abused rescue pets to trust again.

PROTECTION: At new-age festivals or psychic fairs protects against jealousy from fellow exhibitors and from unscrupulous practitioners.

MAGICKAL AND PSYCHIC USES

Promotes angelic communication from guardian angels, angel reiki, and the assistance of healing angels; encourages prayer and mindfulness; the inner caves, holes, and pathways of celestite clusters offer access to past worlds and other dimensions.

SPECIAL PROPERTIES

Flowing with life rather than fighting the inevitable; bringing spirituality into the everyday world.

MYTHOLOGY AND HISTORY

Blue Celestite/Celestine was created it is said by angel song from the celestial choirs, and each piece contains an angelic essence.

Blue Chalcedony

COLOR: Soft blues, sometimes banded
CRYSTAL TYPE: Cryptocrystalline quartz
ZODIAC SIGN: Libra (September 23–October 23)
CANDLE COLOR: Pale blue

PHYSICAL: Prevents sinus or eye fluid pressure from building up; counters bloating, plant allergies causing respiratory problems: promotes lung healing after quitting smoking, chronic hoarseness, early onset Alzheimer's; eases childhood infections; useful for lactation.
EMOTIONAL: Eases obsessive-compulsive disorder, Tourette's syndrome, autism and Asperger's, bipolar disorder.
HOME: At family reunions, Blue Chalcedony minimizes sibling rivalries, favorites, and factions.
WORKPLACE: Aids in learning foreign languages, codes and other technical information, new computer systems and software; overcomes fears of technology.
CHILDREN: Addresses situations when children are unfairly blamed for trouble they did not cause; encourages serious children to become playful.
ANIMALS: Helpful in becoming a professional animal trainer or whisperer.
PROTECTION: From excess worry by mothers and mothers-to-be.

MAGICKAL AND PSYCHIC USES
Enables telepathic communication with essences of plants, animals, devas, Earth guardians, and other dimensional life forms; intra-utero communication.
SPECIAL PROPERTIES
Blue Chalcedony used for safe, harmonious travel by sea; calms nervous flyers; promotes peacemaking to mend outworn quarrels.
MYTHOLOGY AND HISTORY
In ancient Egypt, Blue Chalcedony was carved into scarab amulets as a symbol of rebirth. It was sacred to the Greco-Roman Huntress Moon Goddess Diana. Among Native Americans, Blue Chalcedony was made into arrowhead amulets to bring good fortune and protection. In the thirteenth and fourteenth centuries, Blue Chalcedony was engraved with the image of a standing man with raised hand to bring good luck in legal matters.

Blue Coral

COLORS: Light to medium blue with white spots or smudges
CRYSTAL TYPE: Organic, branching calcareous skeletons of sea creatures
ZODIAC SIGN: Pisces (February 19–March 20)
CANDLE COLOR: Blue

PHYSICAL: Promotes fertility; addresses issues involving eyesight, throat, mucous membranes, glands, skin and bone grafts, rashes, acne, rosacea, eczema, dermatitis; eases the pain of swollen scar tissue, burns, scalds; regulates high blood pressure.
EMOTIONAL: During or after the menopausal years, alleviates women's fears of lack of desirability; for the male midlife crisis.
HOME: Combines material comfort and financial security with awareness of the spiritual world; for mothers who try to be all things to all people.
WORKPLACE: Infuses tact and diplomacy in a volatile work situation; for diplomats, embassy staff, negotiators, and anyone in service industries or a call center where endless politeness and patience are essential.
CHILDREN: Counters fears of water, swimming, and drowning, possibly prompted by a past-life memory; in the home, protects small children from water-related hazards, such as baths, pools, and ponds.
ANIMALS: For fish in aquariums, particularly tropical ones.
PROTECTION: Guards against losing data from an electronic device due to a virus or major system crash.

MAGICKAL AND PSYCHIC USES
For meditation with dolphin sounds; dolphin healing; ocean rituals on the incoming and outgoing tide; shell divination.
SPECIAL PROPERTIES
Problem-free travel by or over water; for safety in water sports, including sailing and swimming; enhances the ability to flow with life and let go of irritations and others' pettiness.
MYTHOLOGY AND HISTORY
Blue Coral is sacred to Diwata ng Dagat, the Goddess of the Sea and marine life in the Philippines. The taking of Blue Coral from the seabed is now banned in most countries; however, it is possible to find ecologically sustainable coral.

Blue Fluorite

COLORS: Blue, pale to dark blue; clear and glassy
CRYSTAL TYPE: Halide, calcium fluoride
ZODIAC SIGN: Aquarius (January 21–February 18)
CANDLE COLOR: Deep blue or purple

PHYSICAL: Valuable in speech therapy after an accident, brain trauma or illness, for Alzheimer's and different forms of dementia, eye irritation, inflammation of the inner ear and throat.
EMOTIONAL: Useful when unrealistic expectations and illusion blur everyday living.
HOME: Prevents tactless visiting relatives from upsetting you or the family.
WORKPLACE: Aids in replying clearly and with authority to those who blind you with jargon and supposedly superior knowledge.
CHILDREN: For those on the autism spectrum as well as those with Asperger's syndrome and Tourette's; for shy children and those with speech difficulties.
ANIMALS: Makes an old, confused, or nearsighted pet feel safe.
PROTECTION: Guards against frauds when you are in an online chat room or on a dating site.

MAGICKAL AND PSYCHIC USES
Increases clairvoyance in cloud scrying, using cloud formations for answers; helps to see angels in the sky.

SPECIAL PROPERTIES
Blue Fluorite is said to cloud over if someone is telling an untruth.

MYTHOLOGY AND HISTORY
Blue Fluorite is rare and highly prized. Fluorite has been used in amulets and artifacts since ancient Egyptian and Roman times. Indigenous fluorite carvings have been uncovered in fields and burial sites of southern Illinois–western Kentucky, dating from 900 CE onward.

Blue-Green Azeztulite

COLORS: Soft blue-green of the sea in all her moods and tides
CRYSTAL TYPE: Silicon dioxide with copper silicate inclusions
ZODIAC SIGN: Libra (September 23–October 23)
CANDLE COLOR: Turquoise

PHYSICAL: Relieves illnesses caused or made worse by an unhealthy lifestyle, high stress levels and repressed feelings; addresses issues involving the heart, throat constrictions, and choking when eating; promotes whole-body self-healing.
EMOTIONAL: Alleviates fixations on past injustices or bad habits acquired earlier in life that cause dependence.
HOME: Brings nature into the home in the form of an indoor green area, however small, centered around your Blue-Green Azeztulite, where the energies flow freely, even in a high-rise apartment.
WORKPLACE: Marks the psychic and psychological boundaries of your workspace with plants and your Blue-Green Azezulite, especially if there is artificial lighting for much of the day.
CHILDREN: Encourages children to express their feelings, both positive and challenging, through talking and creative outlets, rather than storing up anger leading to sudden outbursts of temper.
ANIMALS: Champions the end of intensive farming methods and animals used for entertainment or kept in confined and unnatural habitats.
PROTECTION: Guards against those who sulk and use the power ploy of silence if offended.

MAGICKAL AND PSYCHIC USES
Integral to Earth rituals; aids in dowsing for subterranean energy lines and water; communication with Earth devas at ancient and Indigenous sites; smudging, medicine wheel, and labyrinth ceremonies.

SPECIAL PROPERTIES
Breaks through the need to maintain a constant calm, coping image of perfection and to accept the self and others with all their imperfections.

MYTHOLOGY AND HISTORY
Discovered in the American Pacific Northwest.
Like all azeztulite, the blue-green variety is linked to the wisdom of Azez Star Beings, especially those with affinities to the Earth devas/angels who oversee the blueprint of nature and our need to find our place in the natural world.

Blue Halite

COLORS: Blue and indigo (see also Pink Halite, page 356), color due to minor impurities of potassium
CRYSTAL TYPE: Halide, sodium chloride
ZODIAC SIGN: Pisces (February 19–March 20)
CANDLE COLOR: Blue

PHYSICAL: Addresses issues involving the thyroid, thalamus, and thymus; aids in the absorption of iodine; alleviates heat exhaustion, sunstroke; useful in detoxing; relieves insomnia.
EMOTIONAL: Counters unwillingness to maintain a new health or fitness regimen; helps overcome fears of abandonment, mood swings, unresolved childhood trauma.
HOME: For insecure rentals and short-term leases; resolves debt problems; creates an oasis of calm in a hectic home.
WORKPLACE: Acts as an ongoing cleanser of stress, technological pollution, noise, and daily crises; increases efficiency by reducing pressure.
CHILDREN: Aids in making the right educational choices for children; helps teens consider the best study or training opportunities, not based on social considerations; aids in avoiding bad influences.
ANIMALS: Bury a crystal with a deceased pet to calm your pet as it crosses the Rainbow Bridge; calms barking dogs and yowling cats.
PROTECTION: Guards against financial and reputation loss due to false accusations.

MAGICKAL AND PSYCHIC USES
Triggers past connections at ancient sites or when contacting deceased ancestors; overcomes fear of ghosts if you are naturally psychic. Keep Blue Halite near other crystals or spiritual artifacts to continuously cleanse and empower them; increases spiritual powers.

SPECIAL PROPERTIES
Unexpectedly attracts what is beautiful or valuable into your life.

MYTHOLOGY AND HISTORY
Formed through evaporation of seawater from oceans that existed millions of years ago, carrying within it memories of a world before people walked the Earth, blue or indigo halite is exceedingly rare; dissolving in water like all halite, it is very fragile.

Blue Howlite

COLORS: Turquoise or bright blue; may have veins
CRYSTAL TYPE: Dyed white howlite, silicate, calcium borosilicate hydroxide
ZODIAC SIGN: Sagittarius (November 23–December 21)
CANDLE COLOR: Blue

PHYSICAL: Alleviates issues with the back, spine, neck, bones, teeth, gums, and recurring throat and tonsil infections; confers strength to recover from a long illness; eases memory problems caused by aging.
EMOTIONAL: Eases selfishness and self-absorption, anger if crossed or frustrated; inspires those who have given up on life because of continual setbacks.
HOME: To sell a house swiftly and profitably, set a single white howlite over the lintel of the door to the main living area and six Blue Howlites on different window ledges; useful for mothers of premature babies, sick or disabled children who need continuing care.
WORKPLACE: Gives direction to young people leaving school without any clear idea of a future career; for career advisers, trainers, and life coaches; aids in improving qualifications while holding down a job.
CHILDREN: For twins, triplets, or children close in age to benefit from sibling unity without losing their separate identities.
ANIMALS: Benefits mothers of large litters.
PROTECTION: Guards against those who patronize or diminish your expertise.

MAGICKAL AND PSYCHIC USES
A dream crystal for peaceful sleep, happy dreams, dream healing; promotes vivid dream recall.

SPECIAL PROPERTIES
A crystal of restoration for profit; helps renovate properties, antique furniture, vehicles, or artifacts obtained from yard sales.

MYTHOLOGY AND HISTORY
Often used as a substitute for turquoise with gentler ongoing strength, especially for girls and women seeking advancement in a world still dominated by the locker room mentality.

Blue Goldstone

COLOR: Medium to dark blue with gold sparkles

CRYSTAL TYPE: Glass with copper inclusions, cobalt providing the blue

ZODIAC SIGN: Sagittarius (November 23–December 21)

CANDLE COLOR: Gold

PHYSICAL: Alleviates headaches, epilepsy, visual disturbances, night and tunnel vision, glaucoma; useful after surgery or intensive chemotherapy; counteracts allergies due to pet hair or dust mites.

EMOTIONAL: Counters criticism or discouragement from a childhood in which creativity and initiative were stifled; aids in avoiding repeating destructive patterns and relationships.

HOME: Accumulates luck and opportunities as a Blue Goldstone angel or sacred statue.

WORKPLACE: Brings fame and fortune; leads to successful auditions, and talent and reality shows; for amateur performers turning professional; promotes valuable media appearances; strengthens scientific skills.

CHILDREN: Helps overcome fears of darkness; settling at night away from home.

ANIMALS: For all wild creatures of the night.

PROTECTION: Guards against unrealistic desires preventing action; drives away specters of the night and alien nightmares.

MAGICKAL AND PSYCHIC USES

In modern magick, Blue Goldstone is associated with Nut, the ancient Egyptian sky goddess, who arched over the whole world covered with stars; ancient Egyptian magick, star rituals; ufology; connects with star guardians; promotes telepathy.

SPECIAL PROPERTIES

A traveler's stone for long-distance vacations and working overseas; tuning into time zones on long flights.

MYTHOLOGY AND HISTORY

For gifts in astrology or astronomy. According to legend, only one Italian monk in each generation possessed the magick formula to empower Blue Goldstone; when the last monk alive despaired of humanity, he carried the secret with him, saying that those possessing Blue Goldstone must find the spiritual gold within.

Blue John

COLORS: Dark blue/blue purple and yellow banded, sometimes with bands of gray and red

CRYSTAL TYPE: Very rare, banded form of Blue Fluorite (page 74)

ZODIAC SIGN: Aquarius (January 21–February 18)

CANDLE COLOR: Dark yellow

PHYSICAL: Stimulates the immune system; alleviates colds, flu, bronchitis, shingles; useful for older children whose bedwetting has emotional origins.

EMOTIONAL: Assuages rifts in twin-soul love, where wounds from past relationships—in this or earlier lifetimes—cause misunderstandings.

HOME: For all who care for sick, disabled, or elderly relatives at home.

WORKPLACE: Brings precision to detailed or complex tasks to keep from making mistakes.

CHILDREN: For gifted children whose talents aren't recognized.

ANIMALS: Helps badly abused rescue animals regain trust.

PROTECTION: Keeps a spirit of adventure while guarding against the dangers of travel.

MAGICKAL AND PSYCHIC USES

A stone of prophecy linked to the early sixteenth-century prophetess, Old Mother Shipton, who lived in a cave near Knaresborough, Yorkshire, in northern England. Blue John still conjures up prophetic visions, inspired, it is said, by Mother Shipton herself.

SPECIAL PROPERTIES

Reveals in meditation the Akashic records to identify not fixed fate, but future potential and past-world insights.

MYTHOLOGY AND HISTORY

Found only at one location near Castleton in Derbyshire, England, first mined by the Romans, Blue John has at least fourteen banded or veined varieties.

Blue Kyanite

COLORS: Medium blue, blue green, bright blue, striated, sometimes streaked with black or white (see also Black or Shooting Star Kyanite, page 63; Green Kyanite, page 223; and Indigo Kyanite, page 253)
CRYSTAL TYPE: Aluminum silicate, flat mica-like layers, often sold as blades
ZODIAC SIGN: Pisces (February 19–March 20)
CANDLE COLOR: Medium blue

PHYSICAL: Promotes cell health from womb to old age; bolsters throat, neurological, muscular, and genitourinary systems, plus adrenal and parathyroid glands; enhances mobility; aids in recovery from strokes.
EMOTIONAL: Helps in breaking free from emotional blackmail, possessiveness, mind games, codependency, and self-imposed guilt.
HOME: Strengthens family and friendship networks.
WORKPLACE: Boosts creativity, especially for singers, dancers, composers, writers, painters, sculptors, and craftspeople.
CHILDREN: For shy children to be invited for playdates and parties; integrating children who have communication difficulties.
ANIMALS: Comforts small animals frequently disturbed in petting zoos or kindergartens.
PROTECTION: Dissipates negativity, hostility, and spite.

MAGICKAL AND PSYCHIC USES
Used in blade form as a magick wand; flicks away malevolence; promotes Earth regeneration; enhances past-life recall of interconnected lives, revealing the source of present-day fears; cleanses other crystals of negativity; inspires healing dreams.
SPECIAL PROPERTIES
For communication skills in public speaking, whether lecturing, addressing a group, leading a seminar or team meeting, answering questions, or improvising; for engaging in successful media interviews.
MYTHOLOGY AND HISTORY
Forms a link between other kingdoms—animals, birds, plants, fish, insects, crystal, and angelic; helps in finding your right path if you are off course; a good luck talisman, handed on when it has brought you luck.

Blue Lace Agate

COLOR: Pale blue, sometimes periwinkle with white lace threads, though occasionally blue, gray, or brown threads
CRYSTAL TYPE: Agate, banded chalcedony, cryptocrystalline quartz
ZODIAC SIGN: Aquarius (January 21–February 18)
CANDLE COLOR: Pale blue

PHYSICAL: Alleviates issues involving the throat, thyroid, ears, high blood pressure, skin allergies, bones, fevers; prevents burnout in healers.
EMOTIONAL: Addresses stress, postnatal depression; feeling overwhelmed by parenting or caring for an elderly or sick relative.
HOME: Avoids confrontations at family gatherings; protects against noisy neighbors and those who won't stop talking.
WORKPLACE: Enables you to address a meeting, seminar, or conference with calm coherent words; helps deal with stage fright if you're performing creatively.
CHILDREN: Helps overcome shyness in children or those with speech difficulties; for patience with challenging toddlers or teens.
ANIMALS: For pets who become overly excited in company.
PROTECTION: Shields against angry people, sarcasm, and unfair criticism

MAGICKAL AND PSYCHIC USES
Enhances clairaudience, guardian angel communication, meditation, trance mediumship; useful in rituals for relatives in the armed forces serving in hazardous environments; valuable in goddess spirituality.
SPECIAL PROPERTIES
For speaking the truth with kindness; communicating your needs in relationships, at work, or with family who won't listen; refusing unreasonable demands.
MYTHOLOGY AND HISTORY
Blue Lace Agate is called the mother's stone, linked with the Virgin Mary, an icon of mothers, motherhood, and men who find vulnerability hard to express. In pre-Christian times in Scandinavia and Denmark, Blue Lace Agate was dedicated to Nerthus, the Earth Mother.

Blue Lace Onyx or Blue Scheelite

COLORS: Dark cream, gold, and yellow within pale blue

CRYSTAL TYPE: Mixture of scheelite, calcite, and blue dolomite

ZODIAC SIGN: Cancer (June 22–July 22)

CANDLE COLOR: Bright blue

PHYSICAL: Restores depleted energies; alleviates issues relating to skin, allergies, sinusitis, bones, teeth, mineral absorption (especially calcium), reproductive system; addresses throat, nerves, and muscles, especially in lower back.

EMOTIONAL: Relieves the "dark night of the soul," encouraging positive resolution.

HOME: Detoxifies the atmosphere; makes the home feel bright and light in every way.

WORKPLACE: Reassures dreamers whose grandiose plans do not materialize; improves memory.

CHILDREN: Energizes unenthusiastic, lazy children, and lethargic teenagers.

ANIMALS: For overweight pets who hate exercise.

PROTECTION: Grounds energies if you have ghosts or overfast Earth energies in the home or workplace.

MAGICKAL AND PSYCHIC USES

Promotes astral travel, connection with spirit guides and angels; enhances undeveloped psychic abilities, meditation if you cannot settle.

SPECIAL PROPERTIES

This "half-full" rather than "half-empty" stone encourages an optimistic view of life; helps you to see good in everyone.

MYTHOLOGY AND HISTORY

Blue Lace Onyx does not contain lapis or onyx but retains the original name. An alchemist's stone of transformation, the best is found in Turkey. A perfect balance of anima and animus enables each of us to value ourselves and to celebrate diversity of ethnicity and religion and gender.

Blue Mist Quartz

COLORS: Clear with pale blue but, if held to the light or light is shone on it, the blue mist deepens and increases from the center to the tip

CRYSTAL TYPE: Crystal quartz with inclusions of different minerals, said to cause the inner blue (see "Mythology and History" below)

ZODIAC SIGN: Libra (September 23–October 23)

CANDLE COLOR: Pale blue

PHYSICAL: Relieves pain; addresses hormonal imbalances and fertility issues; boosts libido; alleviates heart disorders and irregularities.

EMOTIONAL: FOSTERS illusions of elevated mystical powers without any effort made in preparation or learning.

HOME: Continually circulates health, healing, and harmony; attracts abundance.

WORKPLACE: Aids in launching new business ventures or creative projects, especially in economically challenging times.

CHILDREN: For those who hide or hold back in the presence of people they do not know well; for Indigo Children teased by peers to learn strategies to avoid inappropriate retaliation.

ANIMALS: Protects rain-forest creatures threatened by deforestation.

PROTECTION: Guards against secrets kept from you, affecting your life.

MAGICKAL AND PSYCHIC USES

Forges connection with archangels, Beings of Light, Star People, and ascended masters; releases the healing blue light of Michael, archangel of the sun.

SPECIAL PROPERTIES

Some crystal experts consider Blue Mist Quartz as possessing Lemurian qualities to release ancient wisdom stored within the crystal; regardless, every Blue Mist or similar Blue Smoke Quartz offers access to far-off worlds.

MYTHOLOGY AND HISTORY

Blue Mist Quartz is mined in the Colombian Andes, created 100 million years ago. Limonite is sometimes found at the crystal base, adding a yellowish tint. The first Blue Mist Quartz was discovered by an avocado farmer on his land in Santander, Colombia and is one of the new Mother Earth crystals revealed to heal modern ills.

Blue Moonstone

COLOR: Shimmering pale blue
CRYSTAL TYPE: Feldspar
ZODIAC SIGN: Cancer (June 22–July 22)
CANDLE COLOR: Silver

PHYSICAL: Addresses issues involving the lymphatic system, throat, sinuses, fluid retention, bladder weakness, and bedwetting in older children, teens, and adults; counters insomnia, sleep apnea, travel sickness; slows the aging process.
EMOTIONAL: Helps overcome the inability to relax after the day or switch off at night; for women who live through their family or partner.
HOME: Aids those caring for infants, or sick or elderly relatives, where sleep is frequently disturbed; calms drama kings or queens.
WORKPLACE: For night workers or those who travel at night for their work; those involved in shift work in health-care settings.
CHILDREN: SOOTHES fears of the dark, night terrors; helps persuade a young child to sleep alone.
ANIMALS: For cats roaming at night; pets settling in a new home after a move.
PROTECTION: Guards against poltergeists, phantoms of the night; fears being alone at home at night.

MAGICKAL AND PSYCHIC USES
A lucky talisman for wishing on a blue moon; waning moon magick to banish misfortune, pain, or sorrow; sea rituals; for woman's magick.
SPECIAL PROPERTIES
For secret love or lovers parted by distance or circumstances as a token that love will endure.
MYTHOLOGY AND HISTORY
The most rare and precious Blue Moonstones are, according to myth, from Indian crystallized moonbeams, washed up on the shore on the night of the blue moon. In parts of Asia, it is told that the sea casts the finest Blue Moonstones when the sun and moon are in particular alignment once every twenty-one years. Considered the stone of safety for the traveler.

Blue Muscovite

COLORS: Medium to rich cobalt or dark blue, sometimes with white muscovite, the blue caused by the presence of more manganese than iron
CRYSTAL TYPE: Mica (potassium aluminum silicate hydroxide); the only time blue mica has been found
ZODIAC SIGN: Libra (September 23–October 23)
CANDLE COLOR: Blue

PHYSICAL: Alleviates stress-related conditions; promotes muscle repair and strengthening; addresses eye infections, sore throat, issues involving tonsils, and losing your voice, especially before an important meeting.
EMOTIONAL: Counters indecisiveness, the tendency to create problems rather than solving them.
HOME: Encourages planning the everyday organization of the home in a structured fashion to avoid chaos and confusion and so everyone does their share; keeps you from taking sides, especially if two people continually seek your attention as audience and referee.
WORKPLACE: Promotes problem solving and troubleshooting.
CHILDREN: Helps in dealing with those who know what you are thinking or are going to say in advance.
ANIMALS: Encourages pets who wait by the door five minutes before you come home even if there is not a regular time.
PROTECTION: Helps to warn you instinctively when people are lying, especially in matters of money and justice.

MAGICKAL AND PSYCHIC USES
Connects with divine sources of wisdom, especially wise ancestors and teacher angels, to guide you in addressing both important matters and everyday dilemmas, using channeled or automatic writing; promotes clairvoyance; boosts telepathy between partners and family members.
SPECIAL PROPERTIES
Aids in learning to trust your instincts rather than listening to others who may have their own agenda.
MYTHOLOGY AND HISTORY
Also called Lithian Muscovite or Australian Lapis Blue, Blue Muscovite was discovered in 2004 by miners in Yilgarn, Western Australia. Blue Muscovite makes it easier to connect with the divine part of our inner or spiritual self that we carry through different lifetimes.

Blue Obsidian

COLORS: In natural form, pale to medium blue; bright cobalt blues are usually made in the laboratory or dyed
CRYSTAL TYPE: Volcanic glass, high in silica
ZODIAC SIGN: Aquarius (January 21–February 18)
CANDLE COLOR: Blue

PHYSICAL: Alleviates issues involving the circulatory system, prostate, high blood pressure, irregular heartbeat, eyes, ears, nose, rhinitis; mitigates symptoms of Alzheimer's disease.
EMOTIONAL: Assuages severe agitation at the slightest crisis; helps in managing schizophrenia, paranoia, and multiple personality disorder; aids in overcoming extreme gullibility.
HOME: For speaking calmly but firmly to overcome toxic atmospheres caused by ex-partners with whom you must negotiate, vulnerable but acidic relatives for whom you care, and ever-complaining neighbors.
WORKPLACE: Boosts confidence to seek recognition for your ideas and work if your efforts are frequently overlooked; for public speaking from meetings to lectures if you are unfamiliar with or uncertain about talking to an audience; prevents incoherence and stammering due to nerves.
CHILDREN: For younger children who initially are slower to talk.
ANIMALS: Helps in managing pets who challenge you as leader of the pack.
PROTECTION: Guards against those who seek to deceive or make unjust accusations.

MAGICKAL AND PSYCHIC USES
Enhances telepathy, tarot reading, crystal ball reading, especially as a natural Blue Obsidian sphere.
SPECIAL PROPERTIES
For learning new languages and communicating confidently with people for whom your new language is their first language.
MYTHOLOGY AND HISTORY
Mined in the Atlas Mountains in Morocco, Blue Obsidian is formed when gas bubbles become trapped in the cooling lava; beautiful and more reasonably priced as tumbled stones, Blue Obsidian clears the way so you understand your own and others' intentions.

Blue Quartz

COLORS: Pale to medium blue in natural form
CRYSTAL TYPE: As natural, formed by inclusion of tiny blue rutile (as needles), tourmaline, zoisite, or other blue minerals
ZODIAC SIGN: Libra (September 23–October 23)
CANDLE COLOR: Blue

PHYSICAL: Promotes immunity; addresses issues involving the thyroid, throat, endocrine system, spleen, hay fever, sinuses, fevers, heat stroke, sunburn, burns.
EMOTIONAL: Counters the tendency to internalize negative feelings through excess food or alcohol, or unconsciously manifesting them psychosomatically; helps calm a troubled mind that never switches off.
HOME: For a noisy household where everyone talks at once; for harmonious mealtimes whether with others or alone.
WORKPLACE: Aids in striving for excellence in career and creativity, especially musical careers; helps in dealing with stubborn people, clients, and colleagues.
CHILDREN: Calms those with attention deficit/hyperactivity disorder; counters risk taking; connects with children's innate spiritual nature.
ANIMALS: Helps in managing nervous pets whose behavior is unpredictable.
PROTECTION: Keeps you from being overwhelmed by other people's problems.

MAGICKAL AND PSYCHIC USES
Promotes sound healing with voice; enhances the effects of prayer beads, mantras, chants, and sacred music; encourages mediumship, clairaudience, channeling from angels and guides.
SPECIAL PROPERTIES
A stone for music lovers. All Blue Quartz brings order to chaos and clarity to muddled thinking; for sorting bank accounts, tax filings, and official paperwork.
MYTHOLOGY AND HISTORY
Quartz containing blue mineral inclusions appears blue as a result of what is called *Rayleigh scattering*, submicroscopic inclusions that scatter blue light. Some clear Blue Quartz is artificially dyed rock crystal; Siberian quartz is laboratory-regrown quartz with added cobalt turning bright blue, said to induce visionary insights.

Blue Sapphire

COLORS: Pale to midnight blue; cornflower blue, known as Kashmir, is the most valuable

CRYSTAL TYPE: Corundum (aluminum oxide); non-gem-quality Sapphires share healing and magickal properties with the gem

ZODIAC SIGN: Libra (September 23–October 23)

CANDLE COLOR: Blue

PHYSICAL: Addresses issues involving the thyroid, blood, dementia, degenerative diseases, hearing, eyesight, fevers, swollen glands, nausea, speech problems.

EMOTIONAL: Curbs an inability to express emotions; encourages trusting after betrayal.

HOME: Eases necessary changes; counterbalances cynicism among disaffected family members.

WORKPLACE: Useful in contract and pay negotiations, plus other official matters; inspires loyalty between colleagues; discourages fraud and industrial espionage.

CHILDREN: For discontented teens swayed by materialism; connecting with the family guardian angel.

ANIMALS: For captive birds to have space to fly.

PROTECTION: Guards against impulsive judgments and actions; for resisting temptation if one partner works away.

MAGICKAL AND PSYCHIC USES
Channeling healing from angels and spirit guides; angel Reiki; sound healing through sacred chants; clairvoyance, clairaudience, and prophecy.

SPECIAL PROPERTIES
For purity of intention and action in relationships and business; love at first sight; lasting commitment (frequently chosen for engagement rings); speedy resolution of legal matters.

MYTHOLOGY AND HISTORY
Abraham was said in Judeo-Christian tradition to have worn a magnificent sapphire around his neck, which, when he died, rose to the sun. King Solomon's magickal ring was Sapphire Blue, symbolizing wisdom. The ancient Greeks called sapphire the jewel of the sun god Apollo. The blue stone was worn when consulting Apollo's Oracle at Delphi; used in medieval times when signing treaties.

Blue Scapolite

COLORS: Pale to rich blue, sometimes with pyrite specks, also lavender (see Purple Scapolite, page 379)

CRYSTAL TYPE: Sodium calcium aluminum silicate

ZODIAC SIGN: Libra (September 23–October 23)

CANDLE COLOR: Blue

PHYSICAL: Eases blood flow in veins and arteries, particularly in neck and head; regulates high blood pressure; counters circulation overload.

EMOTIONAL: Helps avoid total burnout; keeps you from offloading blame and responsibility for bad choices or unavoidable disaster onto others; counteracts panic attacks.

HOME: Prepares teens for living independently, taking more responsibility for the household, and organizing their own finances.

WORKPLACE: Helps build expertise and qualifications that take many years and a great deal of study for management and supervisory positions.

CHILDREN: Enables teens to develop a study plan for successful college admission; from an early age helps youngsters learn to clean up after themselves.

ANIMALS: Fosters obedience in dogs; prepares horses to take part in competitions.

PROTECTION: Guards against those who discourage others by flaunting their seeming expertise and superiority.

MAGICKAL AND PSYCHIC USES
For bibliomancy or stichomancy where messages are sought from angels and guides by turning seemingly at random to a page in a sacred book and applying the words.

SPECIAL PROPERTIES
Cultivates successful partnerships and joint enterprises in business or pooling resources with family for a major purchase.

MYTHOLOGY AND HISTORY
Blue Scapolite is the crystal of the calm approach to crises and challenges, enabling you to take extra time and muster extra effort to master facts and figures so you can speak with authority.

Blue Selenite

COLORS: Pale to medium blue; may occasionally be found brighter in natural state
CRYSTAL TYPE: Gypsum with impurities
ZODIAC SIGN: Cancer (June 22–July 22)
CANDLE COLOR: Blue

PHYSICAL: Addresses issues involving hormones, fertility, pregnancy, childbirth, breastfeeding, psychosomatic illnesses, rare conditions (especially those that are hereditary); alleviates epilepsy.
EMOTIONAL: Controls the inability to still the mind from old conversations and rerunning the events of the day; minimizes mood swings, bipolar condition, paranoia.
HOME: Repels malign energies, keeps far-away family members safe and brings them home.
WORKPLACE: For business dealings to gain success while preserving ethics; aids in discriminating between what is achievable and what is merely wishful thinking.
CHILDREN: Helps dreamy imaginative children to develop their gifts in tangible ways; protects teens from exciting but undesirable influences and temptation.
ANIMALS: For burrowing and nesting animals and birds living in a domestic setting.
PROTECTION: GUARDS against hidden injustices and secret gossip.

MAGICKAL AND PSYCHIC USES
For wish magick on the blue moon, sea magick, spells to call a soul twin.
SPECIAL PROPERTIES
Often called the crystal of light, Blue Selenite is associated with harmonious partnerships in love, family, friendship, and business.
MYTHOLOGY AND HISTORY
As the blue moon crystal, Blue Selenite will call forth, especially on the blue moon at the end of the month, unexpected opportunities and good fortune. Named after Selene, ancient Greek goddess of the full moon, Blue Selenite is the most proactive of the selenites, combining the intuitive power of the moon with clarity to make informed decisions.

Blue Spinel

COLORS: Medium blue, brighter blues colored by cobalt, darker blue, blue-gray to blue-violet by the presence of iron
CRYSTAL TYPE: Magnesium aluminum oxide or magnesium aluminate
ZODIAC SIGN: Sagittarius (November 23–December 21)
CANDLE COLOR: Bright blue

PHYSICAL: Alleviates issues involving high blood pressure, skin, hair, spine, healthy weight loss, eyesight, ears, fevers, throat constrictions, loss of voice, teeth, gums, memory, energy, stamina; counters lack of libido.
EMOTIONAL: Eases the feeling of being sidelined or abandoned; helps if previous attempts to change bad habits failed; addresses claustrophobia, PTSD, acute anxiety.
HOME: Helps fulfill a desire in later years to relocate, travel, or find new love; encourages communication between generations.
WORKPLACE: Aids in careers for which it takes many years to gain professional qualifications; propels promotion within a traditional career path; prevents inappropriate sexual behavior.
CHILDREN: For teens struggling with a necessary academic course; aids in resisting bad but enticing influences, despite the temptation.
ANIMALS: Useful for birds of prey and falconers.
PROTECTION: Guards against falling into a rut in relationships or life in general.

MAGICKAL AND PSYCHIC USES
Enhances healing, money, and examination spells; brings good luck and money; strengthens clairaudience.
SPECIAL PROPERTIES
For new beginnings and opportunities, especially powerful on the first day of the week or month, seasonal change points, and New Year's Day; for safe and pleasurable air travel, flying lessons, or air-related extreme sports.
MYTHOLOGY AND HISTORY
In Asia, Blue Spinels, like other rainbow-colored spinels, are said to be jewels falling from fading rainbows. This crystal promises lasting love, fidelity, and increased or renewed passion.

Blue Topaz

COLOR: Light blue, often natural to deep blue with green tints; darker and brighter shades tend to be heat-treated colorless or gray topaz

CRYSTAL TYPE: Aluminum silicate fluoride hydroxide

ZODIAC SIGN: Libra (September 23–October 23)

CANDLE COLOR: Blue

PHYSICAL: Prolongs youthfulness and alertness in older people; addresses issues involving metabolism, thyroid, throat, eyes, ears, nasal passages, menopause.

EMOTIONAL: Controls anger when you're deliberately provoked; alleviates panic attacks.

HOME: Gives courage to leave an abusive situation or report domestic abuse; defuses sarcasm and unnecessary provocation among family members.

WORKPLACE: Promotes leadership, authoritative non-confrontational communication if there is suppressed hostility; offers growing prosperity through promotion or business; for artists, writers, poets, publishers, editors, litigators, lawyers, and mediators.

CHILDREN: For those who have problems with authority and respond angrily.

ANIMALS: Helps in training impulsive dogs and horses; protects wild bird habitats and caged birds confined in small spaces.

PROTECTION: Guards against nightmares, psychic attack, and unfriendly spirits; keeps you from succumbing to unwise temptation to stray from a mundane but stable relationship.

MAGICKAL AND PSYCHIC USES

For prayer connecting with saints and divinity, meditation, increasing clairaudience.

SPECIAL PROPERTIES

Helps in achieving justice through official channels, unbiased tribunals, and David-versus-Goliath cases.

MYTHOLOGY AND HISTORY

Heat-treated and natural Blue Topaz have the same healing and metaphysical properties. Blue Topaz, like golden, was traditionally used in tips of divining wands to find precious metals. Blue Topaz was associated with Jupiter, both in the classical world and in Hindu astrology as a stone of justice, a role common also in pre-Christianized Mexico.

Blue Tourmaline or Indicolite

COLORS: Medium to dark blue; incredibly rare, and very expensive; Paraiba Tourmaline or Cuprite Elbaite is neon blue

CRYSTAL TYPE: Aluminum boron silicate; Paraiba Tourmaline contains copper

ZODIAC SIGN: Libra (September 23–October 23)

CANDLE COLOR: Blue

PHYSICAL: Eases blood flow through pulmonary arteries; alleviates issues involving the neck, thyroid, pituitary gland, throat, esophagus, eyes, ears, kidneys, bladder, fluid balance in the body, sinusitis.

EMOTIONAL: Counters insomnia, nightmares; addresses unresolved childhood trauma or abuse; helps in coming to terms with suppressed emotions and memories from the past.

HOME: Counterbalances controlling or single-minded family members and those obsessed with routine.

WORKPLACE: Helps in resolving complaints and compensation claims; aids in regaining enthusiasm for your work.

CHILDREN: Especially in lighter blue to encourage a child or teen to be patient.

ANIMALS: For wise animals of any age who alert owners to danger.

PROTECTION: While carrying out healing or spiritual work to ensure only light and goodness surrounds you; Paraiba Tourmaline creates a psychic force field to repel psychic or psychological intrusion.

MAGICKAL AND PSYCHIC USES

Increases the power of ritual; enhances psychic vision, clairaudience, clairsentience, claircognizance; for psychic dreams and vivid dream recall.

SPECIAL PROPERTIES

Blue Tourmaline, especially in deeper shades, opens the channels to higher realms and healing guides, helping a healer discover and understand the cause of the illness.

MYTHOLOGY AND HISTORY

Blue Tourmaline is the stone of fidelity and encourages open, honest, loving communication between a couple to resolve any difficulties, rather than walking away.

Blue Zircon

COLOR: Light pastel to deep intense blue

CRYSTAL TYPE: Zirconium silicate, with inner fire, caused by light entering the gemstone and separating into a prism of rainbow colors

ZODIAC SIGN: Sagittarius (November 23–December 21)

CANDLE COLOR: Blue

PHYSICAL: Alleviates breathing allergies due to airborne pollen or dust mites; addresses issues relating to the optical nerve, cataracts, stress-related voice loss; dissolves blood clots; promotes healing in women over fifty; counters long-term memory loss due to trauma or accident.

EMOTIONAL: Works after betrayal by someone deeply trusted.

HOME: Attracts blessings from ancestral spirits; offers aid in researching family origins; for emigration to a new land.

WORKPLACE: Deeper Blue Zircon aids in tracking inheritances, custodians, and guides at old sites and buildings; enables successful completion of long-term contracts overseas.

CHILDREN: Teaches the value of family traditions.

ANIMALS: Encourages the preservation of rare breeds.

PROTECTION: A traveler's crystal useful on long journeys, especially to countries where there has been unrest.

MAGICKAL AND PSYCHIC USES

A good luck talisman, Blue Zircon acts as a radar, becoming paler in the presence of an unreliable person or potential hazard; connects with divinity through prayer and sacred chants.

SPECIAL PROPERTIES

Though Blue Zircon is often heat-treated from brown zircon, it has the same qualities as natural blue; assists in studying history, old languages, archaeology, ancient wisdom, and traditional medicine; for mature students also working or caring for family.

MYTHOLOGY AND HISTORY

The Roman historian and naturalist Pliny the Elder compared Blue Zircon's color to hyacinth flowers; Blue Zircon is now called starlite. It was beloved by Victorians in large ornate natural zircon rings and brooches.

Boekenhout Jasper or Spirit Quartz Jasper

COLORS: Depending on the mix and proportions of jasper and quartz, colors may be predominantly white, purple, brown, orange, reddish, yellow, or a mixture

CRYSTAL TYPE: Combination of spirit quartz and jasper (see Spirit or Cactus Quartz, page 253)

ZODIAC SIGN: Aquarius (January 21–February 18)

CANDLE COLOR: Purple

PHYSICAL: Heals through white light wherever needed; alleviates malaria, yellow fever, mosquito and tick-borne diseases; bolsters the digestive system, mobility, blood sugar.

EMOTIONAL: Helps overcome fear of losing control, inability to ask for help, tobacco addiction if previous attempts to quit have failed.

HOME: Increases income while reducing financial drains; sheds light on family history where there are mysteries.

WORKPLACE: Promotes concentration in a noisy, chaotic workplace, or when studying and working; aids in turning professional in sports, learning new languages.

CHILDREN: For those reluctant to join physical activities; addresses dyslexia, dyspraxia, attention deficit disorders.

ANIMALS: Forges telepathic links with pets, developing their sixth sense warning of danger.

PROTECTION: Prevents intrusion on privacy.

MAGICKAL AND PSYCHIC USES

Associated with Lemurian wisdom; draws to us those who have shared past lives with us; helps identify totem animals.

SPECIAL PROPERTIES

Boekenhout Jasper or Spirit Quartz Jasper creates a grand formation where merging minerals generate extra properties; propels romance into lasting love.

MYTHOLOGY AND HISTORY

Named after the area of South Africa where it is found, Boekenhout Jasper forms the foundation upon which Spirit Quartz, usually amethyst, citrine, or clear quartz, has grown, rarely all three; jasper may alternatively replace part of the quartz, leaving the outline of the quartz crystal. In some cases quartz crystals remain as patterns within the jasper.

Boji Stone

COLOR: Gray/brown, black, sparkling as though sprinkled with gold; occasionally rainbow sheen

CRYSTAL TYPE: Palladium and pyrite stone disks or buttons in layers or platelets. Patented Boji Stones from Colorado have a certificate of authenticity; used in male/female pairs. Smooth round Boji Stones are female; slightly heavier male stones are angular, crystalline, with pointed uneven surfaces. Androgynous stones combine both features

ZODIAC SIGN: Scorpio (October 24–November 22)

CANDLE COLOR: Gold

PHYSICAL: Relieves pain; female stones heal older people and chronic conditions; male stones address more acute illnesses; aids in cell and tissue regeneration; unlocks energy blockages; promotes planetary healing.

EMOTIONAL: After stress or trauma, calms and energizes; rainbow boji restores well-being.

HOME: Use a pair to feng shui your home, first moving them close to release their energy force.

WORKPLACE: Creates focused concentrated space in a noisy home workspace or a frantic workplace.

CHILDREN: Not directly; rebalances children's rooms after trauma.

ANIMALS: In your home before collecting a rescue center pet.

PROTECTION: Acts as a barrier against psychic or emotional vampires.

MAGICKAL AND PSYCHIC USES
For past lives, astral travel, shamanism; placing the female stone below your feet and the male stone above your head makes golden auras, signifying deep wisdom and inner peace; enhances acupressure, acupuncture; connects with plant energies.

SPECIAL PROPERTIES
Balances body, mind, and spirit, with a stone in each hand, hold androgynous boji in the nondominant hand.

MYTHOLOGY AND HISTORY
Shamanic stones have been familiar to Native North Americans for hundreds of years; akin to the philosopher's stone in alchemy, revealing spiritual gold and self-healing powers.

Boli Stone

COLORS: Clear, bright white, brown, blackish-brown, or gray; may display rainbows within the crystal; glassy and smooth; the amount of included pyrite determines the darkness of the color

CRYSTAL TYPE: Calcium carbonate, calcite containing pyrite, spherical or flat

ZODIAC SIGN: Aquarius (January 21–February 18)

CANDLE COLOR: White

PHYSICAL: For whole body healing; used in laser and light therapies; raises serotonin levels; reestablishes or creates new neural pathways following brain injuries and diseases; for small miracles where the prognosis is not good.

EMOTIONAL: Eases inner turmoil; counters a tendency to blame others for whatever goes wrong; helps you get over a victim mentality.

HOME: For moving to a new location where the climate or lifestyle is completely different; for moving to a home in an area of natural beauty to live a more authentic life.

WORKPLACE: Aids in finding a job that brings fulfillment as well as financial advantage or using every opportunity to create and innovate to make work more satisfying for you; for careers in travel.

CHILDREN: Gives those who lack a sense of danger a more cautious outlook.

ANIMALS: For pets who wander off.

PROTECTION: Guards against being swept up by the chaos and dramas of others.

MAGICKAL AND PSYCHIC USES
Sometimes called Isis calcite after the ancient Egyptian goddess because of its powerful goddess energies; brings out the female divinity within men as well as women.

SPECIAL PROPERTIES
Increases positive communication and harmony with people in all places and from whatever culture or background; a powerful stone for rituals and world peace movements.

MYTHOLOGY AND HISTORY
Naturally polished by the soft desert sand and the winds, Boli Stones were first discovered in 2008 in a remote area in the Rub al Khali desert in Saudi Arabia. They are thought to be as old as the Earth and, like her, formed instantaneously, so they contain instant spiritual transformation powers.

Bolivianite

COLORS: A mixture of bluish-teal, purple, green, yellow, orange, brown, and white

CRYSTAL TYPE: A combination of serpentine and fluorite with some stichtite included, similar to the makeup of Atlantisite (page 42) and sometimes called Bolivian atlantisite

ZODIAC SIGN: Libra (September 23–October 23)

CANDLE COLOR: Blue

PHYSICAL: Alleviates colds, flu—especially new strains—bronchitis, pleurisy, pneumonia, emphysema, the effects of secondary smoking; an antiviral.

EMOTIONAL: Keeps you from being drained by an emotional vampire; counters postnatal depression and nicotine cravings.

HOME: Kick-starts the day after a session of yoga, tai chi, meditation, or some morning family exercise.

WORKPLACE: Avoids taking on the problems of colleagues and clients; for long and short-term career plans that involve action and selling your abilities to those with influence.

CHILDREN: Encourages those who are very shy to find a special friend; keeps them from being teased by assertive children.

ANIMALS: Helps timid small pets to become more accustomed to being handled, and teaches children to be gentle with them.

PROTECTION: Guards against psychic manipulation by those who gain what they want through attracting sympathy and feigning victimhood.

MAGICKAL AND PSYCHIC USES

Provides safe boundaries for empathic, shamanic, mediumistic, and healing work to close sessions and return to the everyday world without bringing back free-floating, unresolved energies or distressed spirits.

SPECIAL PROPERTIES

Manifests what you most need and want, prosperity, career, success, love, health, travel; gives you the confidence to reach out and the power to attract the right opportunities.

MYTHOLOGY AND HISTORY

Bolivianite is a newly known mineral, discovered in 2018 in Peru. The name has caused some confusion because Ametrine (page 24), the mix of citrine and amethyst, was originally called bolivianite when discovered in Bolivia. The new Bolivianite brings new energies and perspectives.

Bornite on Silver

COLORS: Iridescent (bornite) and silver

CRYSTAL TYPE: Bornite, copper sulfide, often cubic; either mixed with silver or on crystalline silver leaf; a collector's or display piece rather than jewelry or tumbled

ZODIAC SIGN: Cancer (June 22–July 22)

CANDLE COLOR: Silver

PHYSICAL: Promotes regrowth of healthy cells after a bone marrow transplant; regulates potassium levels; reduces calcification; bolsters fertility by regularizing monthly cycle; encourages fertility in older people; enables successful freezing/implantation of eggs and sperm.

EMOTIONAL: For men and women stereotyped in childhood into conventional gender roles; counters lack of nurturing in childhood that has later caused overcompensation, usually expressed in caring for others.

HOME: Attracts ongoing money and resources; helps older family members to safely live independently.

WORKPLACE: Cultivates an atmosphere where mentoring and being mentored are the norm; supports buddy programs in the workplace; for nondisruptive office romances.

CHILDREN: Aids in welcoming a new baby to the home or as a christening or naming gift; for fostering or adopting a child.

ANIMALS: For those waiting for a guide or therapy dog, to hasten the process.

PROTECTION: Guards against phantoms of the night; deflecting malicious intent if set near the front door.

MAGICKAL AND PSYCHIC USES

A magick mirror stone for scrying to connect with spirit guides for mediumship or contacting beloved ancestors; strengthens the silver cord between the physical and the spirit body.

SPECIAL PROPERTIES

An alchemical stone, where the silver representing Lady Luna or Moon is combined with another alchemical substance; brings transformation and the coming together of needs and desires.

MYTHOLOGY AND HISTORY

Found mainly in the San Martin mine, in Zacatecas, Mexico. A combination of the silver of the moon and the copper of Venus, so this crystal joins the love and mother goddesses and has a strong feminine and mystical energy.

Bornite or Peacock Ore

COLOR: Coppery red, or red-brown metallic tarnishing to iridescent blue, purple, turquoise, yellow, and red, in air, hence its folk name

CRYSTAL TYPE: Copper iron sulfide from many different types of copper deposits (see also Chalcopyrite, page 112); also called peacock copper

ZODIAC SIGN: Aquarius (January 21–February 18)

CANDLE COLOR: Red

PHYSICAL: Promotes healthy cells and cellular structure; alleviates fevers, convulsions; enhances adrenaline flow, metabolism; counters infections; encourages circulation in lower parts of the body; regulates potassium levels; reduces calcification.

EMOTIONAL: Diminishes flight-or-fight reaction; prevents overreliance on the approval of others.

HOME: A mood lifter, making daily events into special occasions.

WORKPLACE: Activates inner radar to identify potential adversaries; aids in standing out positively at auditions or interviews; separates logic from emotional reactions.

CHILDREN: For rainy days and alleviating grumpiness when plans go wrong.

ANIMALS: For colorful or exotic pets and wildfowl.

PROTECTION: Deflects negative energy, both psychological and psychic; offers insight into how to avoid future attacks.

MAGICKAL AND PSYCHIC USES
Aids in seeing benign ghosts in old houses and seeking ancestral family protection from deceased relatives; welcomes land guardians; for energy-balancing modalities such as Reiki, acupressure, shiatsu, and reflexology.

SPECIAL PROPERTIES
Helps in experiencing and radiating happiness; brings confidence in new situations.

MYTHOLOGY AND HISTORY
Said to have been formed during the alchemical process for the philosopher's stone that would transform other metals into gold and give immortality; Bornite was described as a magickal metallic peacock, forged in fire.

Botryoidal Hematite

COLORS: Silver, metallic-gray, black, bluish, red, reddish-brown; iridescent as specular rainbow hematite

CRYSTAL TYPE: Iron oxide, grape-like masses; in rarer red kind called kidney ore, resembling kidneys

ZODIAC SIGN: Aries (March 21–April 20)

CANDLE COLOR: Silver

PHYSICAL: Promotes circulation, absorption of iron; alleviates issues related to the kidneys, major surgery, transplants, blood transfusions; addresses hemorrhoids, hernia, prostate, male genitalia, growths.

EMOTIONAL: Helps overcome fear of crowds; soothes men who hate their body because they are small or physically weak.

HOME: For making like-minded friends if you are in a minority in your community; surrounds homes with a protective invisible wall against disasters.

WORKPLACE: Botryoidal Hematite draws customers from overseas, particularly to manufacturing or craft-based businesses; useful for networking.

CHILDREN: Encourages boys or teenagers in an all-female environment or with controlling male role models to get in touch with their positive masculine qualities.

ANIMALS: Facilitates acceptance of new pets by existing animals in the home.

PROTECTION: Guards against riots, terrorism, street and neighborhood gangs.

MAGICKAL AND PSYCHIC USES
Useful in fire and candle magick, defensive rituals, spells for attracting money.

SPECIAL PROPERTIES
Hematite feels heavier than many other crystals due to the compact metallic composition, especially in its Botryoidal forms (see Hematite, page 238). Encourages bonding through sports and physical activities.

MYTHOLOGY AND HISTORY
An old folk belief held that kidney ore and large clumps of red hematite were formed from the blood of soldiers who had died in battle and chose to remain together, even in death. Being magnetic, Hematite should not be worn by anyone with a pacemaker or any other implant.

Botswana Agate

COLOR: Pink, cream, and gray bands, occasionally with apricot
CRYSTAL TYPE: Chalcedony
ZODIAC SIGN: Gemini (May 22–June 21)
CANDLE COLOR: Pink

PHYSICAL: Promotes blood oxygenation; addresses issues involving the heart, sexual dysfunction, stomach, immune system, skin, eyes; treats underlying causes, rather than symptoms.
EMOTIONAL: Aids in quitting smoking; releases repressed emotions and desires; relieves depression; eases agoraphobia and panic attacks; removes psychological blocks to fertility; helps overcome insomnia.
HOME: Offers practical solutions when things go wrong, rather than assigning blame; maintains stability during unstable periods; deters intrusive neighbors.
WORKPLACE: Transforms creative ideas into reality; useful for those who work in emergency services.
CHILDREN: Encourages sensitive children and teens to find like-minded friends; prevents sleepwalking and night terrors.
ANIMALS: Enables successful animal breeding.
PROTECTION: Guards home and family from accidents, fire, and natural disasters. Botswana Agates with the eye formation shield against jealousy and psychic dreams of living or deceased foes.

MAGICKAL AND PSYCHIC USES
Works as a lucky charm, if there is an eye formation, for games of chance and competitions; keeps away unfriendly ghosts if you live near a ley line, ghost path, or on land where a tragedy occurred.

SPECIAL PROPERTIES
Aids in finding the right partner online through a dating site; makes blind dates and chance meetings go smoothly; cultivates a sense of adventure leading to travel; promotes safety while traveling.

MYTHOLOGY AND HISTORY
Named after the part of Africa where it was discovered, Botswana Agate is called the sunset stone because it retains comforting sunlight for dark times; traditionally used in African fertility ceremonies to encourage conception of strong healthy offspring.

Boulder Opal

COLOR: Opalescent and brown
CRYSTAL TYPE: Hydrated silicon dioxide, precious opal formed in veins and patches within brown ironstone boulders; when opal is mixed through ironstone, it is called matrix opal
ZODIAC SIGNS: Cancer (June 22–July 22) and Capricorn (December 22–January 20)
CANDLE COLOR: White

PHYSICAL: Alleviates skin lesions, wounds, burns, eyesight, bone calcification, veins, arteries, aging problems, Parkinson's disease; addresses bowel issues, such as IBS, wheat and dairy intolerance.
EMOTIONAL: Restores reality to those who live in dreams, without destroying imagination.
HOME: For putting down roots without sacrificing adventurousness; prevents homesickness.
WORKPLACE: Promotes vision and perseverance during protracted study, training, or slow progress.
CHILDREN: Offers the ultimate fairy treasure for disillusioned children.
ANIMALS: Reassures traumatized animals; for brightly colored birds and fish.
PROTECTION: Guards against those who destroy hope.

MAGICKAL AND PSYCHIC USES
A stone associated with Indigenous rites of passage among Australian Aboriginals; earth rituals; connection with subterranean earth spirits; past lives linked to Indigenous cultures.

SPECIAL PROPERTIES
A gift for key birthdays or difficult times, helps practical people recognize their spirituality and those who are spiritually minded to succeed financially in alternative therapies or running new-age stores or centers.

MYTHOLOGY AND HISTORY
Found only in Queensland, Australia, at major opal fields, such as Winton, dinosaur capital of Australia, and Quilpie, where there is a magnificent opal church altar; called the earth rainbow because Boulder Opal blends loveliness with lasting foundations, a reminder of hidden beauty in the most mundane situations.

Boulder Turquoise

COLORS: Shades of teal blue or turquoise set in black or brown

CRYSTAL TYPE: Turquoise forming veins running through jasper (black) or limonite (brown) rock

ZODIAC SIGN: Sagittarius (November 23–December 21)

CANDLE COLOR: Turquoise

PHYSICAL: Called the *stone of life*, for chronic conditions especially connected with the lungs; alleviates illnesses whose causes are hard to determine; addresses lupus, Lyme disease, Weil's disease, toxoplasmosis; guards against illnesses brought on by ticks and external parasites.

EMOTIONAL: Aids in retrieving lost connections with your roots; keeps you from pretending to be someone you are not; prevents you from constantly pursuing new moneymaking schemes without first checking their reliability.

HOME: Helps in acquiring financial security through wise property or land investment; preserving the original structure of a home during renovations or repairs.

WORKPLACE: A warrior stone tempered by its matrix, for gaining authority and respect through high ethics and hard work; for discovering, developing, and mentoring talented newcomers; for women aiming for the top while maintaining family commitments.

CHILDREN: For children with a hidden gift that may be overlooked.

ANIMALS: For guiding a lost pet home.

PROTECTION: Guards against fears while traveling by air; provides safety from hidden enemies and rivals; protects against black magick.

MAGICKAL AND PSYCHIC USES

For unexpected good fortune or a sudden windfall; dowsing for buried treasure and minerals; Earth and climate change rituals.

SPECIAL PROPERTIES

Often considered true turquoise, since turquoise veins are the most natural form of turquoise found in the Earth, Boulder Turquoise confers the power to aim high.

MYTHOLOGY AND HISTORY

The Navajo nation has long prized turquoise as a sacred stone and for adornments. Changing Woman, the Navajo goddess who is responsible for the revolving seasons, wears turquoise and lives in a turquoise home on the West horizon. The main Boulder Turquoise mine, located in northeast Nevada, was discovered in the 1970s by a Shoshone shepherd who saw a vein of turquoise on the hillside.

Bowenite or New Jade

COLOR: Pale to medium green; resembles polished jade

CRYSTAL TYPE: Variety of antigorite, hard serpentine (see also Greenstone or Pounamu, page 228)

ZODIAC SIGNS: Cancer (June 22–July 22) and Aquarius (January 21–February 18)

CANDLE COLOR: Pale green

PHYSICAL: Addresses issues involving the heart, cholesterol, blood sugar; hormonal swings in pregnancy; lactation; hair, scalp, alopecia; skin, nails; fertility, especially where medical intervention is needed.

EMOTIONAL: Alleviates childhood traumas blighting adulthood; counters fears of heights, darkness, elevators, and unfamiliar places; provides freedom from a destructive person or habit; addresses free-floating anxiety and depression.

HOME: Attracts abundance; smooths the way for buying and selling houses where there is legal delay; cleanses a new home of previous owners' energies.

WORKPLACE: Aids in dealing with intimidation or discrimination through official channels; helps in avoiding overwork.

CHILDREN: Encourages independence at every age.

ANIMALS: For pets who hate exercise and those who have lost their joie de vivre.

PROTECTION: Creates a shield against destructive people and self-sabotage; transforms bad health or business situations.

MAGICKAL AND PSYCHIC USES

A love amulet that dispels outside interference or romantic rivals; enhances rituals to attract true love, turn friendship into love, and increase commitment; aids in finding answers in dreams; increases psychic powers.

SPECIAL PROPERTIES

The crystal of showing tough love to friends, family, and neighbors who take advantage.

MYTHOLOGY AND HISTORY

Bowenite was popular in the Russian imperial court. Fabergé created a Bowenite clock to mark the birth of Tsar Nicholas and adorned ornamental eggs with Bowenite. The state mineral of Rhode Island.

Brandberg Amethyst

COLORS: A mixture of purple, brown, gray, or yellow; may contain a phantom crystal within (a crystal that stopped growing)

CRYSTAL TYPE: A combination of amethyst and smoky and clear quartz; generates powers greater than its separate components

ZODIAC SIGN: Pisces (February 19–March 20)

CANDLE COLOR: Deep purple

PHYSICAL: Increases recovery from illness or injury; restores energy; relieves headaches and insomnia; considered helpful after invasive treatment.

EMOTIONAL: For healing a broken heart, opening the way to new love, especially if the previous relationship was unfinished, past-life business.

HOME: Aids in relaxing if you have overly high standards of cleanliness and tidiness.

WORKPLACE: Guards against fears of failure; suggests creative solutions to problems.

CHILDREN: Overcomes fears of alien attack or abduction in very imaginative children.

ANIMALS: For healing animals using Reiki, crystals, and natural remedies.

PROTECTION: An amulet against psychic or paranormal attack, curses, hexes, and jinxes.

MAGICKAL AND PSYCHIC USES

For shamanic soul retrieval, restoring fractured parts of a person's psyche after trauma.

SPECIAL PROPERTIES

Heals war-torn places, the aftermath of natural disasters, and polluted land.

MYTHOLOGY AND HISTORY

Brandberg Amethyst crystals are found only near the Goboboseb Mountains, in Namibia, the world's oldest desert, in Africa. The mountain is sacred to Indigenous people of Damaraland as *the* "mountain of the gods." The area has more than 48,000 ancient rock paintings.

Brandberg Enhydro Quartz

COLORS: Can be clear, smoky quartz, smoky amethyst, or amethyst, usually with enhydros clearly visible

CRYSTAL TYPE: Quartz, silicon dioxide; as single or double terminations, twin crystals or clusters, occasionally shaped as a crystal sphere with the enhydro in the middle; may contain a phantom crystal

ZODIAC SIGN: Aquarius (January 21–February 18)

CANDLE COLOR: Purple

PHYSICAL: Addresses fluid retention, hormonal imbalances, the aftereffects of gynecological surgery, especially post-hysterectomy; promotes conception and fertility if clear quartz.

EMOTIONAL: Helps overcome the inability to empathize with others and family patterns regarding alcohol or drug abuse.

HOME: For amicably resolving inheritance disputes, where the sale or transfer of property proves a sticking point.

WORKPLACE: Aids in discovering and dealing with hidden agendas and factions; helps resolve personality clashes in a family business.

CHILDREN: Calms very spiritual children who sometimes find the world too noisy and chaotic.

ANIMALS: For pets with naturally healing, soothing energies; for animal Reiki.

PROTECTION: Guards against ancient curses passed down through the generations, whether actual or feared.

MAGICKAL AND PSYCHIC USES

Dual clairvoyance and clairaudience capabilities; moving the crystal enables you to hear messages from the water and, at the same time, see images in the crystal; shows you past lives linked with water, especially if there are inexplicable fears of drowning.

SPECIAL PROPERTIES

The crystal of resolving relationship issues if there are long-standing recurring grievances; encourages a couple to present a united front when others are fomenting divisions.

MYTHOLOGY AND HISTORY

The most magickal of all enhydros, containing the mystical ancient wisdom of the inner water formed millions of years ago, symbolic of the primal sea; combined with its location, near the Goboboseb Mountains in Namibia, the world's oldest desert in Africa, mountains sacred to Indigenous people of Damaraland, this is the ultimate wish crystal when a small miracle is needed.

Braunite

COLORS: Silver-gray, brownish black, metallic
CRYSTAL TYPE: Manganese silicate
ZODIAC SIGN: Capricorn (December 22–January 20)
CANDLE COLOR: Silver

PHYSICAL: Alleviates issues involving the lungs (including emphysema), chest, breasts; stabilizes heart and pulse; gives strength for the body to fight a debilitating condition; addresses anemia and blood cell deficiencies or mutations; reduces signs of skin aging.

EMOTIONAL: Counters the inability or unwillingness to accept the seriousness of an addiction; diminishes the tendency to play helpless or the victim to avoid shouldering blame for mistakes.

HOME: Enables you to raise the money to buy a home or land; for auctions or private sales where there is room for bargaining; helps in recognizing the conversion potential in a derelict or run-down building.

WORKPLACE: Braunite brings stability in uncertain times and deters colleagues who try to destabilize the workplace; for patience and perseverance.

CHILDREN: For children who find it hard to complete homework or projects.

ANIMALS: Promotes the training of dogs and horses if they are slow to learn.

PROTECTION: Guards against others who sabotage your efforts for happiness or success.

MAGICKAL AND PSYCHIC USES

During guided fantasies and visualizations, explores reasons for present fears and talents from past worlds.

SPECIAL PROPERTIES

Braunite encourages gradual repayment of debt and wise budgeting or, if solvent, steady savings.

MYTHOLOGY AND HISTORY

Braunite reveals hazards ahead so you can develop coping strategies and win as you proceed step by step; brings freedom, not by walking away from an unhappy relationship or situation but by offering solid workable alternatives.

Brazilianite

COLORS: Green, yellow, yellow-green, colorless
CRYSTAL TYPE: Sodium aluminum phosphate, sometimes striated
ZODIAC SIGN: Capricorn (December 22–January 20)
CANDLE COLOR: Dark yellow

PHYSICAL: Alleviates issues involving circulation, heart irregularities; counters heatstroke, sunburn, skin rashes caused by heat or allergies; addresses glands, bladder, kidneys, cystitis; aids in stopping bedwetting at any age; relieves concerns about the bile duct, spleen, nausea, travel sickness.

EMOTIONAL: Diminishes overreliance on the approval of others; overcomes codependency involving control by oppressor and sacrifice by the oppressed who may periodically change roles.

HOME: Pushes family members to help with chores; heads off pointless confrontations by refusing to be affected by subtle emotional pressure or feigned helplessness.

WORKPLACE: Provides the motivation and focus to succeed in your chosen area of expertise by working longer and harder than others; for aspiring writers, artists, and others involved in creative ventures to refuse to take no for an answer; for writers' block.

CHILDREN: For parents who find it hard to say no or impose rules on strong-willed teenagers; for older children or teenagers who are unfairly blamed for everything.

ANIMALS: Teaches pets firmly but kindly that you are the leader of the pack.

PROTECTION: Guards against intrusion of your boundaries with constant demands on your time.

MAGICKAL AND PSYCHIC USES

For accessing the wisdom of Atlantis; connecting with evolved Air spirits such as sylphs on hills and mountains; making peace with your past lives through fulfilling your uncompleted destiny in the present life.

SPECIAL PROPERTIES

For taking a risk on love, rather than holding back because you doubt your own self-worth.

MYTHOLOGY AND HISTORY

First discovered in Brazil and later in New Hampshire, Brazilianite is a stone of tuning into the sanctity of the homeland and the current location, if different; for formally celebrating or mourning key anniversaries.

Brecciated Jasper

COLOR: Dark or brick reds, patterned with brown, black, and beige swirls and/or clear crystal inclusions

CRYSTAL TYPE: Quartz red jasper and hematite, in which healed fractures in the jasper are replaced by other minerals (see also Poppy Jasper, page 366)

ZODIAC SIGN: Scorpio (October 24–November 22)

CANDLE COLOR: Red

PHYSICAL: Alleviates allergies to animals, digestive issues, eczema, psoriasis, rosacea, acne, fractures, scars; detoxifies the system.

EMOTIONAL: Overcomes fears after sexual abuse or a bad sexual experience or relationship; if life is chaotic and lateness a constant issue.

HOME: Guard against hostile, disruptive neighbors; prevents accidents with precious china, glassware, or other delicate objects.

WORKPLACE: Reduces fears of failing under pressure; mitigates writer's block; aids in working with animals or birds; enhances management skills.

CHILDREN: To prevent nightmares and sleepwalking.

ANIMALS: Supplements conventional treatment for old or chronically ill pets with natural remedies.

PROTECTION: Keeps you from becoming overwhelmed by negative thoughts that magnify problems out of proportion.

MAGICKAL AND PSYCHIC USES

Cuts cords of psychic manipulation or emotional vampirism; cleanses the aura; improves dream recall.

SPECIAL PROPERTIES

Offers strength and stamina over long periods when a burst of energy is needed, such as in endurance sports; resolves crises in a practical way as they occur.

MYTHOLOGY AND HISTORY

Brecciated Jasper was traditionally used to dispel drought by casting it into water. A crystal of happiness and confidence, a reminder to enjoy every day, rather than yearning for unattainable change.

Bridge Quartz

COLORS: Depends on quartz; usually in clear quartz

CRYSTAL TYPE: A smaller quartz crystal, penetrating and located partially within, partially outside a larger quartz crystal

ZODIAC SIGN: Gemini (May 22–June 21)

CANDLE COLOR: White

PHYSICAL: Strengthens connections between nerves, brain, and the body; addresses communication disorders, fractures, torn muscles and tendons; helps in recovery from heart surgery, pacemaker implants, transplants.

EMOTIONAL: Assuages hurts after rejection at an early age; for adoptees whose birth parent is reluctant to allow contact or give details.

HOME: Bridges the gap with new family members acquired through remarriage; keeps the peace in parent and teenager conflicts or with disapproving in-laws.

WORKPLACE: Useful for public relations and major publicity campaigns, teaching, or interpreting languages.

CHILDREN: Comforts those with invisible friends or who live in their own worlds of imagination.

ANIMALS: For a new pet to be accepted after the death of one of an established animal pairing.

PROTECTION: Guards against prejudice, bias, and hostility toward those who diverge from cultural norms.

MAGICKAL AND PSYCHIC USES

Bolsters connections with other dimensions, past worlds, angels, guides, and ancestors; empowers other crystals for healing.

SPECIAL PROPERTIES

Aids in establishing friendships in a multicultural area, or while working or relocating overseas; for keeping in touch with traveling family members.

MYTHOLOGY AND HISTORY

Some crystal practitioners regard Bridge Quartz as a master or major teaching and healing crystal; an inner-child crystal, Bridge Quartz restores spontaneity and joy if childhood or recent years have been traumatic.

Brochantite

COLORS: Emerald green, different shades of green, blackish-green

CRYSTAL TYPE: Sulfate formed in oxidation zone of copper deposits; closely linked with other copper minerals, such as Azurite and Malachite; best used as a tumbled stone

ZODIAC SIGN: Libra (September 23–October 23)

CANDLE COLOR: Green

PHYSICAL: Addresses issues relating to fluid retention, bladder, kidneys, spleen, pancreas, prostate, blood; alleviates asthma, emphysema, and other chronic lung conditions.

EMOTIONAL: Counters a preoccupation with material things; helps overcome a tendency not to share or give time or resources to others.

HOME: Enables you to focus on tasks that need to be done, such as making repairs or sorting through paperwork, when others say they will handle those jobs but constantly delay.

WORKPLACE: Aids in maintaining a courteous demeanor when dealing with problem customers in public service careers, such as call centers; for work travel if this proves exhausting.

CHILDREN: Teaches children tactics to keep a low profile at school, college, or socially if they're always in trouble.

ANIMALS: Keeps pets entering shows or competitions from feeling overwhelmed.

PROTECTION: The crystal loses its brightness if someone is not telling the truth or you are about the make an unwise decision.

MAGICKAL AND PSYCHIC USES

For empowerments and protective mantras when you do not have time for a ritual; protects a healer from absorbing the pain or sorrow of a client.

SPECIAL PROPERTIES

Found as twin crystals, Brochantite attracts like-minded people in love or friendship; for love expressed through deeds rather than romantic words.

MYTHOLOGY AND HISTORY

Brochantite was named after the eminent French mineralogist Brochant de Villiers in 1824, most famous for his involvement in the creation of the geological map of France. Also occasionally found as a gem, Brochantite, like its namesake, is a practical, hardworking stone for those behind the scenes who make life run smoothly for others.

Bronzite

COLORS: Brown, black, or greenish with golden bronze metallic patterns, gleaming if containing pyrite glints

CRYSTAL TYPE: Silicate of magnesium and iron rich pyroxene (see Augite, page 43, and Enstatite, page 176); can be found in meteorites

ZODIAC SIGN: Capricorn (December 22–January 20)

CANDLE COLOR: Golden brown

PHYSICAL: Counters anemia, red blood cell disorders; promotes absorption of necessary minerals, blood clotting; maintains energy levels in physically tiring jobs or lifestyle; resists infections.

EMOTIONAL: Overcomes indecisiveness, lack of self-confidence; rectifies past injustices and eases hurt.

HOME: For harmonious family life, if toddler tantrums, moody teenagers, uncooperative stepfamilies, or divisive intergenerational conflict abound.

WORKPLACE: Useful for customer service and hospitality workers dealing courteously with unreasonable complaints; for miners and all who work underground.

CHILDREN: Encourages children (and adults) who are consistently late or slow getting ready to get a move on.

ANIMALS: For churlish pets or those determined to be at the top of the pecking order.

PROTECTION: Shields against critical, rude, or abrasive attacks; reflects negativity back to its source.

MAGICKAL AND PSYCHIC USES

Rituals for Mother Earth; attracts blessings from Earth spirits guarding subterranean treasures, such as gnomes and dwarfs; promotes money magick; enables scrying by candlelight on the surface of Bronzite.

SPECIAL PROPERTIES

A fast money-bringer; also preserves longer-term prosperity; for creative ventures online and through direct sales.

MYTHOLOGY AND HISTORY

Worn powdered by the Romans for clear thinking, Bronzite represents the peaceful warrior, promoting self-confidence, certainty in decision making and acting on decisions, commanding respect from others, successful campaigning for equality and establishing your personal space and lifestyle.

Brookite

COLOR: Black, brown, reddish-brown, gray, occasionally white, metallic to diamond-like luster
CRYSTAL TYPE: Titanium oxide
ZODIAC SIGN: Aquarius (January 21–February 18)
CANDLE COLOR: Silver

PHYSICAL: Alleviates debilitating conditions; promotes circulation; counters infrequent ovulation or low sperm count; aids in recovering strength after illness, surgery, or injury; helps regenerate major organs.
EMOTIONAL HEALING: Overcomes lethargy and apathy; aids in understanding what caused a bad situation, so you avoid repeating self-destructive patterns.
HOME: Invites the blessings of guardian spirits of the home and land.
WORKPLACE: Useful for imaginative ventures; helps in retraining for new fields after your job has been eliminated or in a weakening market; aids in following a spiritual career.
CHILDREN: For a teen trying to obtain an internship, to become a military cadet, or secure a place in college.
ANIMALS: For pets unwilling to exercise.
PROTECTION: Guards against harmful electromagnetic energies; resists temptations to make money at the cost of life quality.

A high-vibration crystal for contacting spirit guides, guardian angels, wise spirit teachers; facilitates meditation; develops psychic powers; cultivates extraterrestrial encounters; discovers crop circles; enhances the power of other crystals; promotes astral travel.

SPECIAL PROPERTIES

For overcoming difficult situations, such as bereavement, abandonment, life-changing illness, or major financial loss.

MYTHOLOGY AND HISTORY

Considered an ascension stone offering clarity of life purpose and growing awareness of higher realms of experience it is possible to attain; leads to a change in priorities, where being is more important than achieving and the inner world as vital as the outer; using small pieces of Brookite is incredibly powerful.

Brown Aragonite

COLORS: Brown, golden to reddish-brown; may contain creamy lattice markings, especially if calcite is present
CRYSTAL TYPE: Dimorphous calcium carbonate, can form *Sputnik*-shaped hexagonal clusters with interpenetrating crystals or stalactite-like crystals
ZODIAC SIGN: Capricorn (December 22–January 20)
CANDLE COLOR: Golden brown

PHYSICAL: Alleviates issues stemming from bone fractures, dislocation, spine, slipped disc, bowel diseases, IBS, celiac disease, chronic fatigue syndrome, cramps, diabetes, eczema, psoriasis, moles, and discoloration of skin.
EMOTIONAL: Helps overcome fears of water and drowning; counters the need for constant reassurance and company; works to release old wrongs.
HOME: Brown Aragonite clusters draw the family together in everyday life; for improvements in the house and garden.
WORKPLACE: Keeps meetings on track and focused on practical solutions, rather than point-scoring; for the revival of traditional crafts involving natural fabrics, materials, and pigments.
CHILDREN: Creates a secure home environment if children are unsettled at school, college, or socially.
ANIMALS: For animals and birds living wild in cities, such as foxes, possums, and hawks.
PROTECTION: Guards against becoming spooked when camping in the wilderness or near water where there have been drownings.

MAGICKAL AND PSYCHIC USES

For Earth rituals, herbs and tree wisdom; gardening by natural cycles; a shield against psychic or psychological attack while sleeping.

SPECIAL PROPERTIES

For multitasking if there are not enough hours in the day or others are panicking and wanting everything completed instantly.

MYTHOLOGY AND HISTORY

Brown Aragonite is softer and more practically focused than yellow or orange aragonite. It offers cohesion to disorganized groups, teams, or campaigns. Brown Aragonite clusters unite other crystal energies where stability is needed.

Brown Diamond

COLORS: From light brown to deep chocolate; shades identified commercially as chocolate, champagne, and cognac; sparkling

CRYSTAL TYPE: Carbon; Brown Diamond mainly receives its color from nitrogen; the more nitrogen, the deeper the color

ZODIAC SIGN: Leo (July 23–August 23)

CANDLE COLOR: Gold

PHYSICAL: Relieves pain; addresses issues involving the feet and legs, bowels (including IBS), allergies to fur and feathers; eases concerns relating to the large intestine; for aging issues, slowing growths; alleviating chronic conditions.

EMOTIONAL: Counters an obsession with owning the best of everything, regardless of the consequences; for panic attacks; helps overcome overattachment to your physical home and obsessive tidiness.

HOME: Promotes long-term financial stability through property development, especially the renovation of older buildings; saving and wise investment.

WORKPLACE: For gaining a permanent contract if your position is only temporary; learning new skills or starting a business in later years.

CHILDREN: Kept with a photo to reduce hyperactivity and adverse reactions to overstimulation.

ANIMALS: Preserves woodland habitats, natural hedgerows, and riverbanks.

PROTECTION: Guards against oversensitivity to the presence of and attacks by restless spirits in haunted places or at scenes of ancient conflict.

MAGICKAL AND PSYCHIC USES

For finding what is lost or has been stolen; for money rituals to reduce debt and gain long-term financial security.

SPECIAL PROPERTIES

A diamond for secure, mature love in the later years; a gift for mothers or grandmothers who feel unappreciated.

MYTHOLOGY AND HISTORY

Brown Diamonds, the most easily available diamonds, were first made famous and a desirable possession when the Argyle mine in Australia gave one of the Brown Diamonds the exotic name, "champagne diamond"; thereafter, its association with celebrations and affluence grew.

Brown Jade

COLORS: Varying shades of brown

CRYSTAL TYPE: Jadeite Jade (sodium aluminum silicate) (page 258), also nephrite jade calcium (magnesium silicate) (page 315)

ZODIAC SIGN: Capricorn (December 22–January 20)

CANDLE COLOR: Golden brown

PHYSICAL: Alleviates issues involving the bones and joints, especially the hips and knees; eases arthritis; relieves issues relating to the bowels, including IBS and celiac disease; addresses pigmentation problems; soothes foot pain and fungal infections.

EMOTIONAL: Curbs an obsession with work to the exclusion of relationships and leisure; counters rigid attitudes and ultra-conservatism.

HOME: Attracts the slow accumulation of money; encourages healthy garden growth, especially of vegetables; keeps you from going deeply in debt.

WORKPLACE: Useful for starting any agricultural or horticultural business, especially organic; encourages living off the land; promotes working with crafts or manufacturing.

CHILDREN: Prompts fastidious children to get muddy or dirty.

ANIMALS: Maintains peace and privacy in petting zoos and city farms or schools.

PROTECTION: Guards against dogma, cults, and religions with overly strict rules that stifle choice and independent thought.

MAGICKAL AND PSYCHIC USES

Dowsing for ley lines and Earth energies using a pointed Brown Jade; psychically removes negative or blocked Earth flow from beneath the home.

SPECIAL PROPERTIES

For farms or homesteads that have been in a family for generations to help new partners of adult children adjust to rural life, if it is unfamiliar.

MYTHOLOGY AND HISTORY

The most down to earth of the jades, Brown Jade brings security and stability to home, relationships, and workplace; favors any property matters, especially do-it-yourself building projects or major renovations.

Brown Jasper

COLORS: Chocolate brown, taupe, varying shades of yellow brown to golden to reddish-brown

CRYSTAL TYPE: Silicate, microcrystalline quartz, often with mineral or organic inclusions

ZODIAC SIGN: Capricorn (December 22–January 20)

CANDLE COLOR: Golden brown

PHYSICAL: Alleviates issues involving the bowels, including constipation, gastroenteritis, irritable bowel syndrome, celiac disease, Crohn's; eases wheat and dairy allergies; addresses prostate issues.

EMOTIONAL: Calms chronic worriers (a natural worry stone); helps in quitting smoking; minimizes panic attacks.

HOME: Aids in carrying out DIY projects, home renovation, and car maintenance; promotes organizing family events.

WORKPLACE: Eases stress overload in frantic workplaces where technology dominates; for established businesses to prosper; offers extra stamina for meeting urgent deadlines.

CHILDREN: For those who panic about doing anything unfamiliar; useful at transition points in education.

ANIMALS: Aids animals with chronic illness, especially in later life; restores natural instincts to a pet living in a city apartment.

PROTECTION: Clears away negative entities, frightening extraterrestrial beings and hostile otherworldly presences.

MAGICKAL AND PSYCHIC USES

Like Gary Green Jasper (page 197), traditionally a rain-bringer and cloud-burster; for learning the Indigenous spirituality of the area in which you live, as well as Earth rituals, divination, and healing.

SPECIAL PROPERTIES

For buying, selling, or renting a home; renovating property to sell or rent out; consolidating debt.

MYTHOLOGY AND HISTORY

One of the traditionally used jaspers, in ancient Egypt Brown Jasper was called Egyptian marble and used for amulets, ritual vessels, and jewelry; also carved into arrowheads in Native North American and other Indigenous societies as a luck-bringer and for protection.

Brown Obsidian

COLORS: Medium to dark brown, tan

CRYSTAL TYPE: Volcanic glass; hematite or limonite (iron oxide) color the obsidian brown

ZODIAC SIGN: Capricorn (December 22–January 20)

CANDLE COLOR: Golden brown

PHYSICAL: Alleviates pain in the feet, legs, and spine; promotes mobility and steadiness walking, especially in much older people; counters irregular bowel movements; addresses issues caused by aging.

EMOTIONAL: Aids in continuing an estrangement despite the other party seeking reconciliation; keeps you from borrowing money that will be hard to repay.

HOME: A stone that counters the tendency to go into debt, and brings stability to chaotic finances; prompts you to seek the advice of an older relative or friend about a dilemma.

WORKPLACE: Helps in overcoming a potentially difficult business situation by acting decisively; though unpopular, your actions will ensure business survival.

CHILDREN: Teaches children to budget and save for what they really want if their peers instantly get everything they ask for.

ANIMALS: Eases the burden of a pet who has suffered a life-changing injury or has a chronic condition.

PROTECTION: Guards against accidents, one's own careless actions, and others' thoughtlessness.

MAGICKAL AND PSYCHIC USES

For collective past-life work with close friends, a partner, or family members to explore earlier connections and create collective visions of a shared future; as a magick mirror to see spirit guides.

SPECIAL PROPERTIES

Pointed Brown Obsidian is used by shamans to bring the cause of pain or suffering to the surface of the body and transform it into white light.

MYTHOLOGY AND HISTORY

Can be effectively used in labyrinths or magick circles to welcome the ancestors on traditional family occasions or seasonal celebrations.

Brown Topaz

COLORS: Golden to smoky brown and clear
CRYSTAL TYPE: Aluminum fluorine silicate
ZODIAC SIGN: Capricorn (December 22–January 20)
CANDLE COLOR: Golden brown

PHYSICAL: Strengthens fertility; alleviates problems with the back, hips, knees, ankles, and feet; addresses bowel disorders and irregularities; eases stress-related conditions.
EMOTIONAL: Counters excessive timidity, mistrust of people, agoraphobia, OCD; mitigates an obsession with saving money even at the cost of comfort.
HOME: Aids in beginning or adding to a family; preserves friendships that have existed for years.
WORKPLACE: Helps in starting a business; for those who work on the land, in conservation, or with animals.
CHILDREN: For children who are afraid of getting dirty or worry excessively about germs.
ANIMALS: Champions major animal rescue initiatives, especially of endangered species; aids in setting up an animal sanctuary.
PROTECTION: Guards against emotional disturbance and disruption by those who resent your stable life.

MAGICKAL AND PSYCHIC USES
For seeing Earth spirits and the fey on seasonal change points; each Brown Topaz is thought to contain a guardian spirit, a belief dating from ancient Greek times; for lasting love and fidelity rituals.

SPECIAL PROPERTIES
Called the Earth gem, Brown Topaz acts as an automatic radar so you can sense when you are moving off track.

MYTHOLOGY AND HISTORY
The homeliest, most easily obtainable and underregarded natural gem of the topaz family, Brown Topaz possesses the beauty of autumn and of nature at her loveliest.

Brown Zircon

COLOR: Golden brown, sometimes heat-treated to produce other colors (see Colorless or Clear Zircon [in purest form, page 133], Blue Zircon [page 84], Yellow Zircon [page 511], Green Zircon [page 230], and Red Zircon [page 404])
CRYSTAL TYPE: Zirconium silicate/neosilicate
ZODIAC SIGNS: Leo (July 23–August 23) and Capricorn (December 22–January 20)
CANDLE COLOR: Brown

PHYSICAL: Addresses concerns involving the pituitary and pineal gland, bowels, IBS, celiac disease, constipation; alleviates prostate issues; counters insomnia; helps overcome irregular or scanty menstruation; for older mothers giving birth.
EMOTIONAL: Restores faith in love after betrayal or loss.
HOME: For anyone caring for a parent or disabled relative; brings a permanent home to those in temporary lodgings.
WORKPLACE: Gives stamina and focus for an urgent short-term goal; aids in making a good impression in a new workplace.
CHILDREN: Helps infants learning to walk and older children seeking to increase agility.
ANIMALS: Promotes animal healing, particularly in dogs and horses; prevents inflammation from fleas, mites, and ticks.
PROTECTION: Guards against liars, thieves, jealousy, violence, accidents, fire, and extreme weather; said to glow red with approaching storms.

MAGICKAL AND PSYCHIC USES
Increases telepathy; helps in accessing Akashic records through meditation; for safe return of lost or stolen property.

SPECIAL PROPERTIES
Reduces commuting stresses and hazards during late-night journeys; enables successful vacations and business trips.

MYTHOLOGY AND HISTORY
Golden-Brown Zircon, like orange and red, was called jacinth by the Romans; according to the Roman writer Camillus Leonardus, zircon increased ingenuity, glory, and wealth. It was worn against the Black Death during the fourteenth century and the Great Plague of London in 1665. A Brown Zircon becoming redder may indicate hidden bad temper.

Brucite

COLOR: White, colorless, pale green, gray or blue, yellow, and red in manganese-bearing varieties

CRYSTAL TYPE: Magnesium hydroxide, a minor ore of magnesium metal and a source of magnesia

ZODIAC SIGN: Leo (July 23–August 23)

CANDLE COLOR: White

PHYSICAL: For blocked or out-of-balance areas of the body, whole-body healing; addresses issues involving cholesterol, migraines, gallbladder, heartburn, stomach acidity, magnesium deficiency, the cardiovascular system, constipation.

EMOTIONAL: Removes self-defeating thoughts and behavior after disappointments and disillusion; aids in overcoming an inferiority complex.

HOME: For those who always put others first; brings plans to fruition for domestic and life improvements.

WORKPLACE: Unblocks delays in the supply chain and production line in a business; makes motivational group interactions productive; cultivates personal progress, if necessary by challenging the status quo.

CHILDREN: Encourages persistence in difficult tasks; promotes independence in overreliant children.

ANIMALS: Reenergizes an elderly pet while they sleep.

PROTECTION: Guards against voices from the past warning of inadequacy; removes negativity from the atmosphere.

MAGICKAL AND PSYCHIC USES

Enhances tarot, runes, astrology, and palmistry; for remote healing; clears the aura by drawing cosmic light.

SPECIAL PROPERTIES

Initiates plans and projects and sees them through to successful completion without being diverted by others' doubts and lack of enthusiasm.

MYTHOLOGY AND HISTORY

Brucite is slowly growing in popularity as healers and crystal practitioners appreciate the light-bringing properties of this easily obtainable stone. A positive energy flame for making the seemingly unworkable feasible through clear planning and communication.

Bryozoan Fossils

COLORS: Blue-gray, gray, browns, black with various markings

CRYSTAL TYPE: Bryozoa Fossils are remarkable because they consist of at least 6,000 living water species as well as up to 17,800 fossil types, found in ancient rock from old seas. Each Bryozoan Fossil contains thousands of bryozoans

ZODIAC SIGN: Capricorn (December 22–January 20)

CANDLE COLOR: Gray

PHYSICAL: Repairs cells and regrows tissues; strengthens connectivity after organ transplants or heart valve replacements and bypasses; counters excess water retention.

EMOTIONAL: Comforts after loss or separation from parents at an early age, being fostered or put into institutional care as a child; counters intense dislike of communal activities or communal living.

HOME: Creates a calm, harmonious home if certain family members are drama kings or queens, or if living space is overcrowded.

WORKPLACE: For joining an established company with an in-house promotion structure; useful for those working in the rescue or security services or going to college where communal living is the norm.

CHILDREN: Calms an only child, away from home for the first time at summer camp.

ANIMALS: Helps in learning to work in teams or pairs.

PROTECTION: GUARDS against undertaking too many activities at once.

MAGICKAL AND PSYCHIC USES

For joining or establishing covens, druidic orders, and healing circles; for medicine wheel and labyrinth ceremonies where energies create a collective mystical experience.

SPECIAL PROPERTIES

Because Bryozoa Fossils span past and present, a transition stone for building on past experience to fashion the future; learning the wisdom of the ancestors and our root culture.

MYTHOLOGY AND HISTORY

Bryozoan Fossils may have originated some 500 million years ago. Since living bryozoa are natural filters and creators of a healthy marine environment, these fossils are a reminder of the need to look to the past for cures for modern ills.

Bustamite

COLORS: Pale pink, deep pink, raspberry, red, and brownish red; may include black

CRYSTAL TYPE: Manganese calcium silicate, sometimes found with purple sugilite (page 380); related to Rhodonite (page 407)

ZODIAC SIGN: Taurus (April 21–May 21)

CANDLE COLOR: Pink

PHYSICAL: Addresses issues involving the heart (especially irregular heartbeat), hardening of arteries, circulation; counters calcium deficiency; alleviates problems with the legs and feet, circulation, fluid retention, pancreas. prostate, pituitary gland, sexual dysfunction.

EMOTIONAL: Helps you escape a destructive or abusive situation because of guilt or loving too much; overcomes disconnection from life and people.

HOME: Makes a home or therapy space warm and welcoming; if you travel or relocate often, Bustamite enables you to put down roots, even in temporary accommodations.

WORKPLACE: For holistic practitioners and energy transference therapists; endocrinologists, orthopedic and pediatric physicians, and surgeons concerned with growth and physical development.

CHILDREN: Eases issues involving children who are much taller or shorter than their peers or who have temporary or permanent growth issues.

ANIMALS: For a physically weak puppy or kitten separated from the mother too young, abandoned at birth, or reared in a breeding farm.

PROTECTION: Guards against unsociable or unapproachable people at work and interfering relatives.

MAGICKAL AND PSYCHIC USES

Encourages positive healing experiences for nervous patients; shields the healer from taking on the troubles of the patient.

SPECIAL PROPERTIES

Brings the blessings of the Earth Mother on weddings, handfastings, baby-naming ceremonies, natural burials, and at seasonal celebrations.

MYTHOLOGY AND HISTORY

A happiness stone through making connections with others and enjoying every day without worrying about past or future. Bustamite increases love in new relationships.

Bustamite with Rhodonite

COLORS: Light pinkish brown, peach, yellow to a red/brown (bustamite), similar in color but less intense red than rhodonite; rhodonite occurring in pale pink to a deep red; together they may be orangey pink with black manganese-included dendrites or veins due to manganese dioxide in both minerals

CRYSTAL TYPE: Close cousins, but two distinct minerals, though often found growing together; bustamite is calcium manganese silicate, rhodonite manganese silicate, so they produce a harmonious blend (see also Bustamite with Sugilite, page 100)

ZODIAC SIGN: Libra (September 23–October 23)

CANDLE COLOR: Salmon pink

PHYSICAL: Addresses issues involving the pineal gland, heart rhythm problems, and congested lungs; synchronizes pancreas, liver, and spleen; promotes skin elasticity; relieves pain.

EMOTIONAL: Overcomes the inability to give or receive love for its own sake and not as a bargaining chip; eliminates codependency.

HOME: A crystal for fun and laughter; for spontaneous outings.

WORKPLACE: Encourages role-playing, team building.

CHILDREN: Calms those who worry about getting muddy, dirty, or wet; prompts indoor-based children to explore the great outdoors.

ANIMALS: Enables grooming if pets hate being washed or brushed; soothes those with a vet phobia.

PROTECTION: Guards against those who cast doubts in every situation, emphasizing the cons and never the pros.

MAGICKAL AND PSYCHIC USES

For Reiki and other energy-touch therapies; shamanic soul retrieval; a charm for love and happiness, so you will always laugh, not cry.

SPECIAL PROPERTIES

Emphasizes love and the people involved, rather than worrying about incurring the expense of lavish displays of material wealth.

MYTHOLOGY AND HISTORY

Combined as one stone in some mines in South Africa, the United States, and Brazil; strengthens determination to follow your heart in love if approval of others is withheld and living by your dreams and not others' dictates.

Bustamite with Sugilite

COLORS: Purple dark or bright, purplish red (sugilite) with peach/dark pink, reddish-brown/black (bustamite); usually with patches and/or bands of purple, depending on the mineral proportions of the crystal

CRYSTAL TYPE: Potassium sodium iron manganese aluminum lithium silicate (sugilite); manganese calcium silicate (bustamite, which is also found with Rhodonite [page 407])

ZODIAC SIGN: Scorpio (October 24–November 22)

CANDLE COLOR: Indigo

PHYSICAL: Alleviates problems concerning the heart (especially irregular heartbeat) and hardening of the arteries; addresses constipation and digestion, made worse by stress.

EMOTIONAL: Helps overcome the inability to escape from flashbacks to childhood abuse, PTSD memories, or other major trauma; strengthens the resolve to walk away from abuse.

HOME: For cleansing homes with unhappy memories or where there has been sickness, financial loss, or misfortune; counteracting overly heavy Earth energies or those where spirits of the place relive former tragedies that occurred there.

WORKPLACE: Generates a new start in a new venue, where a previous building caused problems; for office romances or running a business with someone who is also a love partner, to maintain professionalism.

CHILDREN: Desensitizes very psychic children from premonitions of disasters they cannot prevent and unfriendly spirits.

ANIMALS: For pets troubled by deceased pets who have remained in the home.

PROTECTION: Psychically removes the self from potentially hostile situations, making you unnoticeable until the danger has passed.

MAGICKAL AND PSYCHIC USES

For ceremonies to celebrate the unity of Earth and sky on solar and lunar festivals, Wiccan, pagan and druidic initiations, deep meditation.

SPECIAL PROPERTIES

Removes energy blocks from people, environments, situations, and artifacts that have sad memories or were acquired under less-than-ideal circumstances.

MYTHOLOGY AND HISTORY

These crystals have remarkably similar energies and blend to balance spiritual and everyday experiences; for organizing classes in spiritual development, healing, and mediumship.

Cacholong Opal

COLORS: Milky to creamy tones; smooth as porcelain

CRYSTAL TYPE: A common opal, often mistaken for agate; also popular as tumbled stones and in jewelry; very porous and for that reason may be infused to hold perfume

ZODIAC SIGN: Cancer (June 22–July 22)

CANDLE COLOR: White

PHYSICAL: Promotes skin and hair health, manual dexterity if you're naturally clumsy; strengthens eyesight; alleviates chronic headaches; stimulates fertility.

EMOTIONAL: For those who are too inhibited to express their feelings and desires; helps overcome lessons from childhood to stay in the background and not reveal knowledge for fear of *showing off*.

HOME: Attracts wealth and a happy, unified family life; generates optimism in the most pessimistic family member.

WORKPLACE: Prompts the emergence of creative gifts never before recognized; enables you to know instinctively whom you can trust in business.

CHILDREN: For those with their head in the clouds who find recalling facts and figures hard; enhances exceptional artistic talents at a young age.

ANIMALS: Creates a special memorial for a beloved pet in a place with happy memories for you both.

PROTECTION: Guards against malicious spells, curses, and those who practice destructive magick.

MAGICKAL AND PSYCHIC USES

For mystical and magickal gifts of manifestation; shamanic healing; astral travel on spirit bird flight; intuitive awareness.

SPECIAL PROPERTIES

A Valentine's romance stone, said to attract a true love if worn on St Valentine's Day; maintains fidelity.

MYTHOLOGY AND HISTORY

Also known as "kascholong," much Cacholong Opal comes from Russia and means "beautiful stone"; also found in Austria, the Czech Republic, Mongolia, and Uzbekistan, and named after the Cach River (now the Kashkadarja River) in Uzbekistan. Cacholong Opal is part of many Russian carvings and artifacts, dating from the mid- to late 1800s, a number of which are displayed in the Hermitage Museum in St. Petersburg; it continues to appear in cameos and jewelry today.

Cacoxenite

COLORS: Golden, yellow, yellowish brown, reddish yellow, brown, greenish yellow

CRYSTAL TYPE: Cacoxenite usually forms within a host crystal, commonly amethyst, smoky quartz, or clear quartz and is a major mineral in the super seven crystal; iron aluminum phosphate

ZODIAC SIGN: Sagittarius (November 23–December 21)

CANDLE COLOR: Yellow

PHYSICAL: Addresses cell disorders; regulates thyroid function; straightens out hormonal imbalances; alleviates parasites, growths, warts; enhances fertility treatments.

EMOTIONAL: Useful when conventional treatments or panaceas are ineffective because stress and anxiety are rooted in lifestyle issues and negative attitudes.

HOME: For happy relaxed mealtimes; minimizes problems and differences among family members.

WORKPLACE: For cooperation rather than rivalry, and compromise not confrontation; prompts totally original ideas and innovative, inspirational solutions to long-standing problems.

CHILDREN: Diminishes sibling rivalry and issues with cliques in the schoolyard.

ANIMALS: For pets who are overpossessive about their owners.

PROTECTION: Prevents intrusion by unfriendly neighbors or visitors who outstay their welcome; removes spirit attachments.

MAGICKAL AND PSYCHIC USES

Striving for and reaching higher levels of spiritual awareness in daily life; for moon magick on the crescent and full moon; channeling higher guides; enhanced ESP.

SPECIAL PROPERTIES

Cacoxenite takes on subtly different energies, according to its host crystal. In quartz it is far more active, dynamic, and fast-acting; in gentle, soothing amethyst, harmonizing; in Super Seven, offering infinite possibilities; and in smoky quartz it reveals light at the end of the tunnel.

MYTHOLOGY AND HISTORY

Associated with ancient Eastern European ceremonies to honor the Earth. The inner gold of Cacoxenite within its host crystal is a reminder that everyone has an inner divine spark and creative potential.

Californite

COLORS: Apple to lime green; may have bright green chromium inclusions

CRYSTAL TYPE: Cryptocrystalline, calcium aluminum iron silicate hydroxide, a green variety of Vesuvianite or Idocrase (page 493); generally mottled

ZODIAC SIGN: Virgo (August 24–September 22)

CANDLE COLOR: Green

PHYSICAL: Acts as a pain reliever and anesthetic; removes toxins and harmful bacteria; cultivates good bacteria within the body.

EMOTIONAL: Counters fears of impending loss and misfortune, particularly in finances.

HOME: Encourages and develops relationships, friendships, and mutual respect among groups or communities; enables you to live peacefully in communal or community settings.

WORKPLACE: Creates buddy and mentor groups in a large, impersonal organization; helps ensure the safety of police, security, and rescue services.

CHILDREN: Enables them to thrive in a noisy, crowded educational environment.

ANIMALS: Fosters the health and well-being of a litter.

PROTECTION: Guards against sudden disruptive change that cannot be turned to your advantage.

MAGICKAL AND PSYCHIC USES

Sends trapped spirits to the light; releases bad karma from past worlds; prompts visions of future worlds in meditation, astral travel, and dreams.

SPECIAL PROPERTIES

The stone of wealth when it's most needed; promotes both ingenious moneymaking ideas and focused petitions to angels, calling for a promise to share any abundance received.

MYTHOLOGY AND HISTORY

Sometimes called American jade and mistaken for jade; discovered in the early 1900s during the expansion of the Western Pacific Railroad, in the foothills of the Sierra Nevada mountains at Feather River Canyon; a stone of pioneers that empowers persistence and a sense that life is an adventure to be explored.

Camouflage Jasper

COLORS: Olive green and white, black/dark gray and white mottled, would blend in with dense vegetation; occasionally olive and dark pink

CRYSTAL TYPE: Chalcedony, containing hematite; mainly sold as a tumbled stone or jewelry

ZODIAC SIGN: Scorpio (October 24–November 22)

CANDLE COLOR: Gray

PHYSICAL: Clears up skin blemishes; alleviates illnesses mimicking others or hard to detect or diagnose; promotes fertility where a reason cannot be discovered for failure to conceive; addresses issues involving the liver, spleen, pancreas, gallbladder; aids in recovery from surgery to repair organs deep in the body.

EMOTIONAL: Counters the need to meddle in the lives of loved ones; alleviates problems with stalkers, anonymous mail, and phone calls; curbs internet trolling.

HOME: Enables you to find personal sanctuary, space, and time in a busy home schedule or shared home; for subtly changing behavior in others that is disruptive; prompts secretly saving and accumulating money if others would squander it.

WORKPLACE: Allows you to blend into an established workplace if newcomers are made to feel unwelcome; counters industrial espionage, phone or computer hacking, or those who would steal ideas or credit.

CHILDREN: Calms those who unwittingly cause disruption or do not know when to tone down their words or behavior.

ANIMALS: For cats who visit different neighborhood homes to be fed.

PROTECTION: Guards against those who eavesdrop on others' conversations or pry into private correspondence.

MAGICKAL AND PSYCHIC USES

For night magick; spells on the waning moon for binding and banishing; scrying in dark mirrors (see Obsidian Mirrors, page 320) to connect with ancestors and wise guides.

SPECIAL PROPERTIES

The stone of mystery when love cannot be revealed and secrets must be kept; for uncovering the double lives of others if this adversely affects you.

MYTHOLOGY AND HISTORY

Camouflage Jasper lets you bounce back stronger than before after a setback caused by being too trusting financially; the stone for personal success, abundance, and prosperity.

Campbellite

COLORS: Mixture of colors; especially blues, turquoise, red, orange, white; sometimes with glints of copper; metallic

CRYSTAL TYPE: Calcite, copper, cuprite, chrysocolla, malachite, tenorite, and turquoise; can be polished and cut into cabochons or jewelry

ZODIAC SIGN: Libra (September 23–October 23)

CANDLE COLOR: Blue

PHYSICAL: Increases the body's power of the energy field; enhances the effectiveness of energy and light therapies, including radionics; clears energy blockages; straightens out malfunctioning neural signals; controls fevers and regulates body temperature.

EMOTIONAL: For those resistant to spiritual healing, touch therapies, or in-depth counseling.

HOME: Fills the home with the white light of healing and reconciliation of conflict.

WORKPLACE: When logic, expertise, and common sense fail to solve a problem, use your intuition; prompts you to trust your instincts to start a new business.

CHILDREN: Promotes relaxation if there is a new baby or the addition of a foster child to the family or a young relative staying long term; brings acceptance and kindness between children in teams, social groups, and in playgrounds with unfamiliar peers.

ANIMALS: Place Campbellite with a photo of a missing pet to call them home.

PROTECTION: Warns by vibrating if a hazard or ill-wishing person is nearby.

MAGICKAL AND PSYCHIC USES

Gives healers an intuitive awareness of the true source of a problem; increases the power of other crystals if placed on top of them; enhances telepathic links between a potential love match and also through mediumship with departed loved ones.

SPECIAL PROPERTIES

Enables you to dowse for what is missing by visualizing the lost item or even a lost pet in the mind's eye while holding the stone.

MYTHOLOGY AND HISTORY

Originally from the now-closed Bisbee Mine in Arizona; though rare, Campbellite is still obtainable especially as jewelry; named by the miners who worked in the Campbell shaft where it was found.

Cancrinite

COLORS: Yellow, orange, pink, purple, white, or blue-green; may be pearly
CRYSTAL TYPE: Felspathoid, sodium calcium aluminum silicate carbonate
ZODIAC SIGN: Aries (March 21–April 20)
CANDLE COLOR: Yellow

PHYSICAL: Alleviates issues involving the neck, throat, congestion, pneumonia, bronchitis, emphysema, blockages in the bowels and intestines, kidney stones, bladder, connective tissues.
EMOTIONAL: Mends fractured relationships; dispels the deleterious effects of parental absence or neglect in childhood; helps overcome addictions.
HOME: A home blessing stone in all its colors, especially orange and yellow; makes any social occasion harmonious; encourages stimulating communication with a minimum of drama or tantrums.
WORKPLACE: Turns a meeting or application in your favor if the outcome is uncertain; raises your profile so your efforts and skills are appreciated.
CHILDREN: Ensures that negative parenting patterns are not passed on to the next generation.
ANIMALS: Keeps you from succumbing to children's pleas for a pet for which you know you will have to care.
PROTECTION: Casts a golden shield of light around you against danger and malice.

As a focus for remote viewing, seeing far-distant people, places, and events not yet manifest; meeting deceased mentors on the spirit plane during sleep.
SPECIAL PROPERTIES
For drawing up viable plans in every aspect of life, and sticking to them.
MYTHOLOGY AND HISTORY
Cancrinite, first discovered in the Ural Mountains of Russia in 1839, was named after Count Egor Frantsevich Kankrin, Russian minister of finance. Cancrinite symbolizes strength, willpower, and creating order out of chaos.

Candle Quartz

COLORS: White, off-white, cloudy; may have brown, pink, gray, golden-cream inclusions and inner phantoms
CRYSTAL TYPE: Quartz with small terminations and etchings all around the sides and base, resembling a candle with melting, dripping wax
ZODIAC SIGN: Leo (July 23–August 23)
CANDLE COLOR: Natural beeswax or cream

PHYSICAL: Eases headaches and resultant vision issues; assists in the processing of carbohydrates and fats.
EMOTIONAL: Counters repression of unresolved emotions, inability to see hope for the future.
HOME: Attracts abundance; a focal point for the guardian protecting the home.
WORKPLACE: For small workshops or one-person companies if business is slow; ensures safety driving at night.
CHILDREN: Helps parents avoid reproducing unloving patterns from their own childhood.
ANIMALS: Cultivates awareness of pets previously known in past worlds.
PROTECTION: Especially surrounded by candles, drives away sickness, misfortune, and frightening ghosts.

MAGICKAL AND PSYCHIC USES
As repositories of ancient wisdom, aids in accessing Akashic records; for traveling through its inner pathways to past worlds; offers insight into karmic patterns.
SPECIAL PROPERTIES
For fame and fortune where talents remained undeveloped because of fear of failure; a "light in the darkness" crystal.
MYTHOLOGY AND HISTORY
Candle Quartz is given different names, including "Artemis crystal," after the Greek goddess of the hunt, a long point-shaped quartz like a candle, bringing independence. It is also called celestial quartz, offering connection with divinity through prayer and meditation. Most intriguing with pink and gold cream inclusions, named strawberry Atlantean love stars, with Atlantean energies, mythologically a love token from Atlantis.

Cantera or Mexican Fire Opal

COLORS: Bright red to orange, partly caused by iron oxide

CRYSTAL TYPE: A fire opal with or without play of color, sometimes cut within its rhyolite matrix and lighter in weight than many opals; may contain one or more crystals, including goethite, limonite, hematite, and white chalcedony

ZODIAC SIGN: Aries (March 21–April 20)

CANDLE COLOR: Red

PHYSICAL: Alleviates problems with the eyes, abdomen, lower spine, genitals, potency, fertility, sexual desire.

EMOTIONAL: Addresses past or ongoing abusive relationships; counters the tendency to be taken in by superficiality.

HOME: Cleanses the home of lingering quarrels, misfortune, sickness, or doubts; fosters loving relationships with friends and family.

WORKPLACE: Useful for all artistic endeavors involving color; aids in taking center stage at work.

CHILDREN: Keep overnight with the clothes children will wear the following day so they will radiate confidence and attract friends.

ANIMALS: Before introducing a new pet to the home if the previous one passed on, to retain the happy memories.

PROTECTION: Guards against those who cloud your aura energy field with negative vibes.

MAGICKAL AND PSYCHIC USES

A good-luck charm; for fire and candle magick.

SPECIAL PROPERTIES

Cantera Opal brings self-confidence to those who are shy or whose self-esteem has been shaken.

MYTHOLOGY AND HISTORY

Cantera Opa is found in quarries at Magdalena, Querétaro. Once prized by the Aztecs, opal was sacred to Quetzalcoatl, the feathered or rainbow serpent. The original mines were lost during the Spanish conquest and opal mining was not rediscovered until the early 1800s in Querétaro, more than a hundred miles northwest of Mexico City.

Caribbean Calcite

COLORS: Blue and green, may be bright blue with pale brown and white

CRYSTAL TYPE: Blue and green calcite growing together, with brown-white bands of aragonite beneath; calcite and aragonite are closely related, cave-grown crystals

ZODIAC SIGN: Sagittarius (November 23–December 21)

CANDLE COLOR: Bright blue

PHYSICAL: Relieves headaches, stomach upset, and muscle pain, caused or made worse by stress; alleviates IBS and celiac disease, lactose intolerance, and food allergies.

EMOTIONAL: ASSUAGES fears about the future; calms constant anxiety about friends and family that may spill over as interference; keeps you from emotionally blocking yourself from enjoying life.

HOME: Encourages you to buy a fun travel trailer or a second home near the ocean or river; fosters plans for a long vacation or living on the road or in a boat for a while.

WORKPLACE: For new businesses involving activities and water sports; aids in finding a job that involves travel.

CHILDREN: For teens ready to go backpacking out of state or travel the world; for educational exchange visits.

ANIMALS: Aids in training dogs to return when called so they can enjoy freedom in open spaces.

PROTECTION: Guards against negative spells, black magick, curses, hexes, and ill-wishing from earthly sources.

MAGICKAL AND PSYCHIC USES

For clearing the mind and creating a relaxed state if you find it hard to focus during meditation; cleanses the aura field.

SPECIAL PROPERTIES

This dual-opening crystal first removes fears and energy drains, then seeks opportunities and adventures.

MYTHOLOGY AND HISTORY

Though named Caribbean Calcite, it actually comes from Pakistan and was discovered in 2019. This unusually proactive calcite, combined with reaching-for-freedom aragonite, opens opportunities for new ventures from which you have held back.

Carnelian

COLOR: Orange, orange-pink, red, red-brown
CRYSTAL TYPE: Chalcedony
ZODIAC SIGN: Leo (July 23–August 23)
CANDLE COLOR: Orange

PHYSICAL: Addresses issues involving fertility, IVF, artificial insemination, vaginismus, impotence, PMS, menstruation, menopause, gallstones, liver, spleen, pancreas, exhaustion, blood, heart, plant-related or dust-mite allergies.
EMOTIONAL: Aids in overcoming sexual anxieties; counters bingeing, bulimia, anorexia, codependency, jealousy, possessiveness, midlife crises; promotes anger management.
HOME: Keeps awareness of being a couple during parenthood; aids in buying and selling items and property on and offline; protects the home from fire, storms, and accidents during renovations.
WORKPLACE: Encourages major ambitions and leadership; helps mothers launching a home-based business; supports analytical, accurate, and ethical journalism and broadcasting; enables moneymaking through independent ventures.
CHILDREN: Keeps faith with a challenging child; boosts the confidence of teenagers teased about their appearance.
ANIMALS: Stimulates appetite in a lethargic pet; aids in training horses; helps overcome aggressiveness in a rescue animal.
PROTECTION: Repels anger, fear, envy, mind manipulation.

MAGICKAL AND PSYCHIC USES
For soul twin rituals, calling love through time; prosperity rituals; sex magick to kindle or restore passion; fire magick; clears other stones.

SPECIAL PROPERTIES
Promotes fertility and creativity in every way, from conceiving a child to shining in the performing arts, particularly acting and singing; defines personal space.

MYTHOLOGY AND HISTORY
Ancient Egyptians considered Carnelian setting sun rays. Also called the fertile blood of mother goddess Isis, Carnelians were shaped into protective amulets for life and the afterlife. Carnelians were etched in Roman times with the head of a lion or a great leader for courage. Engraved Carnelians were worn by medieval magicians to avoid enchantment.

Carpet Rock

COLORS: Brown, rust; may have colored bands
CRYSTAL TYPE: Found in triangular shapes, a pseudo-fossil; iron that has created shapes and patterns in oxidized sandstone
ZODIAC SIGN: Capricorn (December 22–January 20)
CANDLE COLOR: Golden brown

PHYSICAL: Promotes oxygenation of blood; addresses blood cell problems, limbs, joint mobility, knees, hips, osteoporosis, issues of aging.
EMOTIONAL: Helps overcome fears of aging and dependence on others; keeps you from feeling downtrodden or being bullied by the demands and opinions of others.
HOME: Brings stability to a newly built home, lacking character.
WORKPLACE: Helps recognize the experience and knowledge of older working people; aids in starting a new career after retirement.
CHILDREN: Gives children a sense of history; for valuing the memories of older relatives.
ANIMALS: For the care of long-living species, such as parrots and tortoises; for creating a quiet sanctuary for a very old pet.
PROTECTION: Guards against being pressured by younger relatives to give up your home if you are not ready to do so.

MAGICKAL AND PSYCHIC USES
For recall of ancient life-forms; because Carpet Rocks have existed through so many ages, they serve as a portal into personal past worlds; fosters divination from the pages of sacred books.

SPECIAL PROPERTIES
When combed gently across the brow, Carpet Rock removes unwanted thoughts. Works well with Brandberg Amethyst (page 90) and Aegirine (page 12).

MYTHOLOGY AND HISTORY
Carpet Rocks are found only at Petit Jean State Park in Arkansas, created by the effects of the rising Ouachita Mountains, in western Arkansas, around 290 million and 245 million years ago.

Cassiterite in Quartz

COLORS: Black, brown, shiny or silvery, and metallic (cassiterite) within white or yellowish quartz, the amount of black depending on the cassiterite content; occasionally red, yellow, or gray
CRYSTAL TYPE: Tin oxide, combined with quartz and silicon dioxide
ZODIAC SIGN: Sagittarius (November 23–December 21)
CANDLE COLOR: White

PHYSICAL: Mitigates deep-seated growths hidden behind or within major organs; addresses tooth decay, obesity, fungal infections, issues involving the reproductive system.
EMOTIONAL: For overcoming compulsions and addictions where despair has caused relapse; alleviates eating disorders that can swing from feast to famine.
HOME: Encourages a move to provide more room or better neighborhood facilities; resolves emerging problems, such as dampness, termite infestation, or settling.
WORKPLACE: Avoids wasting time and energy on projects that will not materialize; a go-for-the-top crystal.
CHILDREN: Sheds light on problematic aspects of mathematics or necessary rote learning.
ANIMALS: Bury a small piece with a deceased pet to guide their way home if their spirit wants to return.
PROTECTION: Eases the passing of those afraid of death, through the light of the quartz; reflects back ill will to a sender.

MAGICKAL AND PSYCHIC USES

In shamanism, protected by Beings of Light to visit other realms; for mediumship and discovering your personal protective spirit guide surrounding you with light; for initiation into covens, druidry or magick circles.

SPECIAL PROPERTIES

A light-in-the-darkness combination stone, suggesting a solution or way out of any dilemma.

MYTHOLOGY AND HISTORY

Found in USA, Peru, Mexico, Spain, England, Russia, the Czech Republic, and Australia. Some practitioners prefer Cassiterite, also called tinstone, enclosed in quartz as a tumbled stone for ease of handling. Cassiterite in Quartz also appears with shiny black crystals on a clear quartz or pale-yellow matrix.

Cassiterite or Tinstone

COLORS: Black, brown, shiny or silvery, and metallic, occasionally red, yellow, or gray
CRYSTAL TYPE: Tin oxide/tin ore
ZODIAC SIGN: Sagittarius (November 23–December 21)
CANDLE COLOR: Deep blue or silver

PHYSICAL: Alleviates symptoms of perimenopause and menopause, obesity, eating disorders, compulsions, hormonal imbalances.
EMOTIONAL: Prevents dissatisfaction with your own life compared with others'; calms free-floating fears of sickness and dying.
HOME: For carrying out home repairs, instead of just talking about them.
WORKPLACE: Promotes successful business advertising and publicity; helps you get recognized for advancement.
CHILDREN: Aids in overcoming difficulties with calculations and logical tasks.
ANIMALS: Helps older abandoned or abused pets to settle.
PROTECTION: Guards you while traveling, during extreme sports, and in hazardous occupations; returns negativity to sender.

MAGICKAL AND PSYCHIC USES

For astrologers, numerologists, and making connections with the departed.

SPECIAL PROPERTIES

Eases end-of-life transitions for the dying person and family; assuages the pain of rejection by family, in love, or, for adoptees, by birth families.

MYTHOLOGY AND HISTORY

Rare in gem quality, cassiterite deposits are found in many lands, including USA, Peru, Mexico, Spain, England, Russia, the Czech Republic and Australia. Tin is the metal of the god and planet Jupiter and associated with truth, justice, career advancement, faithful love, and prosperity.

Cataclasite or Impact Quartz

COLORS: Black, brown, and tan as veins in brecciated creamy quartz

CRYSTAL TYPE: Quartz bedrock, shattered by meteoric impact, the cracks filled by other Earth materials

ZODIAC SIGN: Aries (March 21–April 20)

CANDLE COLOR: Cream

PHYSICAL: Addresses issues involving digestion, long-term unhealthy eating, self-healing, fractures, multiple injuries after an accident, eczema, dermatitis.

EMOTIONAL: Helps overcome fear of letting go of control; eases post-traumatic stress disorder; helps in recovering after sudden physical trauma, such as a traffic accident or a violent attack.

HOME: Alleviates custody battles that have brought together sometimes unwilling family members.

WORKPLACE: Helps those who find it hard to delegate; embraces changes in working practices, new methods, sources, and resources.

CHILDREN: Enables children to form their own opinions and not be swept along by the crowd.

ANIMALS: Cultivates harmony where different species or ages share a home.

PROTECTION: Guards against any who seek to create trouble between a couple or family.

MAGICKAL AND PSYCHIC USES

For tantra; peak or ecstatic spiritual experiences and visions of divinity; blending different spiritual disciplines in a holistic spiritual practice.

SPECIAL PROPERTIES

Gives courage to leave your comfort zone; transforms old emotional patterns leading to the same situation time and time again; for remarriage and new relationships to avoid unfair comparisons with the past.

MYTHOLOGY AND HISTORY

Cataclasite, also known as impact quartz or cataclosite, is formed when shattered quartz is fused back whole in new, more beautiful patterns by intense meteoric heat and pressure. Therefore, the rock offers users power to rebuild even stronger after a catastrophe, with the benefit of acquired wisdom and experience.

Cathedral Quartz

COLORS: Varies according to quartz

CRYSTAL TYPE: Quercetin, resembling a cathedral or temple due to the stepped or layered effect, with smaller rooms or spires attached to the main structure and one main spire; can be in citrine, amethyst, clear quartz, or other variations

ZODIAC SIGN: Aquarius (January 21–February 18)

CANDLE COLOR: According to quartz

PHYSICAL: Relieves pain; enhances life-force energy, where prognosis is not hopeful; eases whiplash fractures.

EMOTIONAL: Keeps you from being locked in a cycle of self-hatred and despair; helps counter mind control by strict religious or cultural organizations.

HOME: Creates a spiritual sanctuary, whether living in one room in a shared apartment or in a busy family home.

WORKPLACE: For expanding a business; for traditional spiritual or religious training to become a professional practitioner.

CHILDREN: Comforts children confronting death or serious family illness.

ANIMALS: Soothes departed beloved pets waiting at the Rainbow Bridge in the afterlife for their owners.

PROTECTION: Guards against rivals or competitors who use unethical means.

MAGICKAL AND PSYCHIC USES

Cathedral Quartz offers access to the wisdom of humankind for prayer and chanting; musters the courage to embark on pilgrimages to sacred sites.

SPECIAL PROPERTIES

Cathedral Quartz can be programmed for any healing or metaphysical purpose, and to amplify the power of any other crystals.

MYTHOLOGY AND HISTORY

Cathedral Quartz is also known as Atlantean temple quartz because it is said to connect with the wisdom of Atlantis; also called Babylon or Babel quartz.

Cat's Eye or Cymophane

COLORS: Varies according to type, always a moving eye formation; as chrysoberyl, yellowish green, darker orange, or yellowish brown; translucent

CRYSTAL TYPE: Officially, only chrysoberyl is called cat's eye, due to it having the sharpest of any cat's eye gemstone. However, this crystal, along with grayish-green quartz cat's eye, also lays claim to the name

ZODIAC SIGNS: Leo (July 23–August 23) or Pisces (February 19–March 20)

CANDLE COLOR: Gold

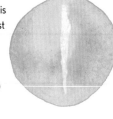

PHYSICAL: Enhances vision and night vision; alleviates coughs, headaches, hemorrhoids; promotes hair and skin health, mobility; regulates cholesterol and blood sugar fluctuations.

EMOTIONAL: Aids in overcoming self-esteem issues, teasing, and peer pressure.

HOME: Attracts abundance and good fortune; protects against jealous neighbors and intruders.

WORKPLACE: For recovery after business loss; alerts you to workplace opportunities and pitfalls; protects you while working or traveling at night.

CHILDREN: Traditionally kept in nurseries to protect babies from harm.

ANIMALS: Enhances; telepathy with any cat; feline safety after dark.

PROTECTION: Guards against envy, accidents through carelessness and nighttime driving hazards.

MAGICKAL AND PSYCHIC USES

For prosperity spells; extraterrestrial communication; warns of hidden enemies by changes in brightness, mood fluctuations in self and others.

SPECIAL PROPERTIES

Lowers visibility in confrontational situations; for retrieving missing possessions; assesses odds in speculation and gambling.

MYTHOLOGY AND HISTORY

From early times, especially in Asia and the Near and Middle East, Cat's Eye was believed to protect against disease and the evil eye, and attract fabulous wealth; also used by medieval archers as thumb rings for acute vision, particularly at twilight. Wearing the same Cat's Eye over years increases its power and good fortune.

Cavansite

COLORS: Bright or aqua blue; may be pearly

CRYSTAL TYPE: Calcium vanadium phyllosilicate, small needle-like, sometimes rosettes, balls, or attached to a zeolite-like white stilbite

ZODIAC SIGNS: Aquarius (January 21–February 18) and Libra (September 23–October 23)

CANDLE COLOR: Bright blue or turquoise

PHYSICAL: Promotes lasting remission in severe illnesses; assists those physically challenged, particularly as a result of speech disorders; relieves pain through endorphin release; addresses issues involving the eyes and metabolism.

EMOTIONAL: Aids in overcoming family tragedy or bereavement, especially if locked in a guilt or blame cycle.

HOME: Clears homes of negative energies from previous owners or lingering ghosts; absorbs tension from outside the home.

WORKPLACE: For conventional and complementary therapists working with clients' severe physical or emotional difficulties; useful for end-of-life care.

CHILDREN: Protects against social exclusion of children who are different in any way; encourages musical gifts.

ANIMALS: For loving unlovable animals.

PROTECTION: Guards against others' negative attitudes dragging you down.

MAGICKAL AND PSYCHIC USES

Tunes into the healing universal energy field; heightens the power of healing prayers; enhances sacred chants and sacred forms, circles, labyrinths, mandalas, medicine wheels, and crystal grids; clears blocked psychic energies.

SPECIAL PROPERTIES

Brings strength and stamina to all in need, from athletics to working long hours caring for others.

MYTHOLOGY AND HISTORY

Found in Poona, India, in 1988, seen as an antidote to twenty-first-century problems; rare but small pieces are incredibly powerful; also discovered in Oregon.

Cave Pearls

COLORS: Light brown, cream, white, orange, glossy when polished by moving water; Cave Pearls need to be wrapped when not in use unless specially treated in jewelry, as they can become rough when exposed to air for too long

CRYSTAL TYPE: Small pearl-like structures, usually 0.5-1 inch (1-2 cm) in diameter, though they can be up to 6 inches (15 cm), growing in limestone caves; a grain of sand or rock fragments rotate in a pool of water on the cave floor and in the process the nucleus becomes coated with calcium salts in calcium-rich water, forming a pearl

ZODIAC SIGN: Cancer (June 22–July 22)

CANDLE COLOR: Silver

PHYSICAL: For fertility and a healthy pregnancy, especially if you have experienced previous difficulties; strengthens bones and promotes the assimilation of calcium; regrows healthy cells and bones; remedies skin abrasions.

EMOTIONAL: Counters extreme introspection; enables you to see beyond superficial appearances to discover a person's true worth.

HOME: For searching through attics, basements, and junk sales for old treasures in need of restoration.

WORKPLACE: Aids in working with mining, minerals, cables, pipes, and excavations of all kinds; helps those pursuing a career in mineralogy; useful in rechecking paperwork.

CHILDREN: Encourages them to slow down if they are impulsive.

ANIMALS: For safe habitats for burrowing animals and nocturnal creatures.

PROTECTION: Guards against a quick fix and superficial solutions.

MAGICKAL AND PSYCHIC USES
Dowsing for subterranean treasure; dragon and cave rituals; prophecy; Earth blessings; wish magick.

SPECIAL PROPERTIES
The Cave of the Marbles in Mexico and Carlsbad Caverns in New Mexico have abundant supplies of Cave Pearls along their pathways; up to 200 million pearls lie deep on the cave floor in the Cave of the Marbles.

MYTHOLOGY AND HISTORY
It is illegal to remove the pearls from the Cave of the Marbles and Carlsbad Caves, but the caves can still be visited; a number of older Cave Pearls remain on the market, some made into jewelry.

Celadonite

COLORS: Shades of green, including gray green, bluish-green, and lime green

CRYSTAL TYPE: Silicate of iron, magnesium, and potassium, mica; obtainable as tumbled stones, frequently in quartz or as a phantom within quartz

ZODIAC SIGN: Virgo (August 24–September 22)

CANDLE COLOR: Green

PHYSICAL: Oxygenates the blood, bringing optimal health; manages heart failure and heart regeneration; for gentle healing where patients are vulnerable.

EMOTIONAL: Helps overcome the feeling of being unworthy to receive life's blessings; prevents self-sabotage at the point of success.

HOME: For beginning a home-based art, crafts, photographic, horticultural, or culinary business.

WORKPLACE: Enables you to seek promotion or a raise; aids in successfully applying for loans or grants.

CHILDREN: Encourages children to play with sand, wood, water, and clay, and enjoy natural surroundings as their playground.

ANIMALS: For unhealthy pets who are fed a human diet and snacks.

PROTECTION: GUARDS against refraining from seizing available opportunities.

MAGICKAL AND PSYCHIC USES
Manifesting what is most needed and desired; psychic artistry; connection with healing spirit guides and Earth spirits.

SPECIAL PROPERTIES
For artists who work with natural pigments and materials and craftspeople who shape wood, clay, and fabrics; for learning Indigenous arts.

MYTHOLOGY AND HISTORY
Named from the French word *celadon* for "sea green." Together with glauconite, it is most famous as the major component of the green earth pigment, first used by the Romans on wall paintings; later green earth in medieval paintings formed the undercoat to create the flesh tones of faces underneath pink; for example, in the *Annunciation* painting by the early fourteenth-century artist Duccio, now only the greenish tinge remains.

Celestobarite

COLORS: Salmon pink, pink/orange usually with gray/blue banding
CRYSTAL TYPE: Combines barium and strontium sulfates, mixing celestite and barite; fibrous
ZODIAC SIGN: Pisces (February 19–March 20)
CANDLE COLOR: Pink

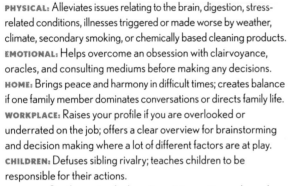

PHYSICAL: Alleviates issues relating to the brain, digestion, stress-related conditions, illnesses triggered or made worse by weather, climate, secondary smoking, or chemically based cleaning products.
EMOTIONAL: Helps overcome an obsession with clairvoyance, oracles, and consulting mediums before making any decisions.
HOME: Brings peace and harmony in difficult times; creates balance if one family member dominates conversations or directs family life.
WORKPLACE: Raises your profile if you are overlooked or underrated on the job; offers a clear overview for brainstorming and decision making where a lot of different factors are at play.
CHILDREN: Defuses sibling rivalry; teaches children to be responsible for their actions.
ANIMALS: Soothes pets who have to go into a cattery, a kennel, or a new home.
PROTECTION: Aids in developing an evolved intuitive awareness of potential disasters or setbacks; shields against paranormal dangers.

MAGICKAL AND PSYCHIC USES
Trance meditation and safe shamanic journeying; guidance from angels, guides, and power animals; ability to foresee the future to make informed decisions.
SPECIAL PROPERTIES
For accepting inevitable change, using strengths from the past and present to determine the best future path.
MYTHOLOGY AND HISTORY
The salmon pink–hued crystals foster altruism and encourage seeking the greatest good in every situation. Blue Celestobarite furthers oracular work through tarot and other divinatory tools to reveal answers to seemingly insoluble questions and opens many doorways into the past and other dimensions through dreams and visions.

Chabazite

COLORS: Colorless, white, cream, brown, green, pink, red, both pinkish and brick red, yellow; glassy and transparent
CRYSTAL TYPE: Zeolite, a collector's item; often twinned
ZODIAC SIGN: Capricorn (December 22–January 20)
CANDLE COLOR: White

PHYSICAL: Straightens out hormone imbalances; helps overcome obesity caused by comfort eating; regulates under- and overactive thyroid; relieves pain in torn or sore muscles; eases pain of fractures.
EMOTIONAL: Addresses an addictive personality; aids in living and thinking less chaotically; helps overcome the feeling of being alone, even surrounded by company.
HOME: Helps in dealing politely but firmly with unreasonably noisy neighbors; sets up quiet corners and creates a mini-sanctuary if you share a home; aids in planning family vacations.
WORKPLACE: Promotes concentration in a noisy workplace or one with constant interruptions; enables a multitasker to identify and focus single-mindedly on an immediate priority.
CHILDREN: Helps dreamers who find structured study hard or irrelevant focus on the task at hand; for twins to include others in their special world and language.
ANIMALS: Aids in getting overweight pets to adopt a healthier diet and do more exercise.
PROTECTION: Guards against those who deliberately cause disruption and distractions; ensures safety while undertaking mountain and rock climbing off the beaten track.

MAGICKAL AND PSYCHIC USES
Chaos magick; meditation in environments where it is hard to get peace; connecting with Earth devas and mountain spirits, and absorbing their freedom.
SPECIAL PROPERTIES
A stone for releasing anger creatively and in a controlled manner to right a wrong or an injustice, rather than repressing it or expressing it inappropriately at the wrong time.
MYTHOLOGY AND HISTORY
Chabazite is found near the Old Man of Storr pinnacle on the Isle of Skye, Scotland, though it is also found in other locations such as Brazil. According to Gaelic legend, the Old Man was a giant and, when he died, his thumb remained petrified aboveground forming the pinnacle and a reminder he is still guarding his island.

Chalcedony Gastropod

COLORS: Pale yellow, creams, neutral, gray, brown, blue, pink with often sparkling inner chalcedony

CRYSTAL TYPE: The gastropod fossil is replaced by chalcedony microcrystalline quartz; the fossil, usually found in spiral shells, is preserved in layers of chalcedony

ZODIAC SIGN: Pisces (February 19–March 20)

CANDLE COLOR: White

PHYSICAL: Eases twisted muscles or intestines; unblocks frozen limbs; relieves blockages within the body; useful for conditions caused or made worse by aging; a powerful reenergizer if in spiral form.

EMOTIONAL: Helps overcome the tendency to conceal your true self; keeps you from projecting an image of wealth or status to impress others; assuages fears of aging, including losing faculties and looks.

HOME: Enables a newly built home or an apartment in a soulless apartment block to connect with the ancient land guardians; aids in adapting to a new lifestyle in a different environment.

WORKPLACE: Changes the energies when taking over business premises where there have been a series of failures; helps in embarking on a long course.

CHILDREN: Brings history to life; teaches children to recycle.

ANIMALS: For relocating a country pet to the city or vice versa.

PROTECTION: Guards against missing clues from past events and unconsciously repeating counterproductive patterns.

MAGICKAL AND PSYCHIC USES

Connecting with ancient wisdom and the ability to gain knowledge from past worlds through meditation and spending time in ancient places.

SPECIAL PROPERTIES

The ability to evolve through the years, rather than trying to stop time; for those entering their wise man/wise woman phase.

MYTHOLOGY AND HISTORY

Gastropods were originally sea snails; 75,000 species still exist; they're related to whelks, limpets, and other small sea creatures. There are 15,000 known fossilized sea snails that inhabited the oceans more than 500 million years ago, toward the end of the Cambrian period; a talisman for moving to the next stage, especially if not asked for.

Chalcedony Stalagmites and Stalactites

COLORS: Vary according to the crystal but, as chalcedony, white, sometimes with tiny druzy sparkling crystals coating the tube; blue, orange, and black

CRYSTAL TYPE: Chalcedony stalagmites/stalactites may appear in clusters of stalactites/stalagmites on a base, single and elongated, or as hollow tubes; may also be found as calcite; chalcedony is a microcrystalline quartz

ZODIAC SIGN: Capricorn (December 22–January 20)

CANDLE COLOR: White

PHYSICAL: Alleviates issues involving the throat, nasal passages, all channels, blood and fluid flow within the body, digestive tract; addresses concerns with the fallopian tubes and ovaries.

EMOTIONAL: Enables the expression of repressed emotions; helps overcome suffering as a result of discrimination.

HOME: In the cluster form, encourages family time together without electronic devices; for clearing stagnant life-force chi from the home, using the hollow tube version.

WORKPLACE: Brings participants together for online meetings and conferences; for starting a business that will take many years to grow.

CHILDREN: Encourages youngsters to play musical instruments.

ANIMALS: For the well-being of the runt of the litter or a malnourished animal.

PROTECTION: Guards against rejecting trusted friends and faithful love in favor of instant gratification.

MAGICKAL AND PSYCHIC USES

The hollow forms enable you to speak through to send messages to those far away and to higher realms; for sacred music, chants, and dance.

SPECIAL PROPERTIES

Stalagmites/stalactites grow in caves, the stalactite growing downward, the stalagmite upward, so if you have both kinds they form a column.

MYTHOLOGY AND HISTORY

Stalactites and stalagmites take between several hundreds of years and a million years to grow and, if broken off, will take more than a mortal lifetime to start regrowth. Therefore, it is important that any sold have broken away naturally.

Chalcopyrite with Quartz

COLORS: As tumbled stones, brassy gold, sometimes with a slight green or iridescent tint. In its natural form it has a gold, blue, green, and purple sheen (more colorful than its sister bornite)

CRYSTAL TYPE: Copper pyrite, commonly found in sulfide deposits in ore-forming environments; best used for healing as a tumbled stone, especially when it is contained within quartz

ZODIAC SIGN: Taurus (April 21–May 21)

CANDLE COLOR: Green

PHYSICAL: Addresses brain disorders, genetic problems, infectious diseases, fevers, inflammation, hair loss or brittleness, arthritis, and rheumatism (especially in women).

EMOTIONAL: Counters poor self-image, fear of failure; helps overcome the tendency to remain unnoticed in social situations, group activities, or meetings.

HOME: For starting a fitness regimen, including participation in sports where prolonged stamina is crucial; promotes healthy nutrition.

WORKPLACE: Encourages gradual growth in business or promotion prospects and resulting prosperity; enhances careers in fashion, beauty, hairdressing, the media, or sales, where charisma is an advantage.

CHILDREN: Keep with a photo of the child with siblings or on a happy family outing to counteract loneliness at school and socially.

ANIMALS: For pets who are attached only to their owner.

PROTECTION: Guards against those who use love for sexual exploitation or financial gain.

MAGICKAL AND PSYCHIC USES

Aids in finding lost objects using a pointed stone; color rituals, divination, and aura reading; a talisman to attract good fortune.

SPECIAL PROPERTIES

Enhances the power of energy transference therapies, such as shiatsu, acupressure, acupuncture, the Bowen technique, Reiki, and reflexology.

MYTHOLOGY AND HISTORY

Used in some Indigenous cultures in rituals to bring rain, Chalcopyrite with Quartz is also a stone of fire; traditionally, it was believed to warm travelers in lonely places by generating heat in the body when placed inside outer garments. The stone of mystical experiences, Chalcopyrite with Quartz bolsters an instinctive understanding of the past and strengthens spiritual connection with personal ancestors.

Chalk

COLORS: White and powdery; very fragile

CRYSTAL TYPE: Calcium carbonate, sedimentary rock, a form of limestone created from calcite; soft and fine-grained

ZODIAC SIGN: Virgo (August 24–September 22)

CANDLE COLOR: White

PHYSICAL: Promotes fertility; removes toxicity; alleviates issues involving digestion, calcification of bones, heart valve and arterial stenosis, skin irritation.

EMOTIONAL: Counteracts a lack of courage and determination to stand up for your beliefs; keeps others from writing on your wall of destiny.

HOME: Develops strategies to deal with undesired changes, including financial restrictions that involve adapting to a new, more budget-conscious lifestyle.

WORKPLACE: Enables you to hold on to your job when there are anticipated redundancies or threats of closure; for gaining a permanent position if you are a temporary employee.

CHILDREN: For learning to handle precious artifacts with care.

ANIMALS: For overindulged pets to become fitter.

PROTECTION: Guards against losing what is valued, whether a relationship or a valued possession.

MAGICKAL AND PSYCHIC USES

A sacred substance; sacred buildings were frequently built on chalk foundations; chalk gives information of the distant past and visions of temples and rituals with priests and priestesses.

SPECIAL PROPERTIES

Because Chalk so easily washes or wipes off a surface, it can be used for writing what should be removed, for example the word *debt*, rubbed out and replaced with, in this case, *solvency*.

MYTHOLOGY AND HISTORY

In southern England, large Chalk figures are etched into chalk downlands, especially in Wiltshire, Southwest England. Though some are more than two thousand years old, dating back to the Celts, they are still the focus of pagan seasonal rituals to restore fertility to the polluted earth—and to individuals seeking to conceive a child. More recently, Chalk images are being used as a celebration of human courage; for example, the Chalk regimental badges on the hillside near Dorchester in Dorset.

Champagne Aura Quartz

COLORS: Soft but sparkling pale smoky gold, metallic; the color of bubbling champagne
CRYSTAL TYPE: Clear quartz, bombarded with gold and iron or iron oxide or with vaporized gold and indium
ZODIAC SIGN: Taurus (April 21–May 21)
CANDLE COLOR: Green

PHYSICAL: Calls down higher spiritual energies and kick-starts the body's own immunity; addresses all autoimmune problems and cellular disorders of the nervous system.
EMOTIONAL: Helps overcome the feeling that you're a victim of fate; curbs alcohol abuse involving social or business drinking that is spiraling out of control.
HOME: A Champagne Aura cluster acts as a center for spiritual harmony in the busiest of households; creates a sacred space to welcome the protective household guardian or domestic angel.
WORKPLACE: A small cluster in your workspace creates a calm atmosphere and a barrier of protection around you, especially if your job involves resolving complaints and conflicts.
CHILDREN: Keeps excitement at birthday parties and major social events at a manageable level.
ANIMALS: For purebred pets who want to be domestic not show animals.
PROTECTION: A protective crystal against negative spirit energies and essences in the home.

MAGICKAL AND PSYCHIC USES
For the removal of malevolent spirits unintentionally summoned by an inexperienced medium during a séance or through a ouija board, that refuse to depart; assists practitioners who developed psychic blocks; also, for those new to spiritual work or healing who doubt their gifts.
SPECIAL PROPERTIES
Keep Champagne Aura in your business to consolidate achievements or if you work for a company to exceed targets.
MYTHOLOGY AND HISTORY
A stone with a powerful energy field that encloses the human aura from attack, but also expands the aura during meditation and visualization to merge with the energies of higher realms and beings.

Channeling Quartz

COLORS: Clear quartz, varies according to the color of the quartz; may appear in amethyst, citrine or other quartzes
CRYSTAL TYPE: Quartz with seven edges surrounding the largest sloping face; the facet directly at the back of this side will form a triangle
ZODIAC SIGN: Pisces (February 19–March 20)
CANDLE COLOR: White

PHYSICAL: Enhances whole-body healing; even a small channeling quartz amplifies the power of any other crystals; directs healing to where the energy is most needed.
EMOTIONAL: Keeps self-destructive thoughts and actions at bay; counters a tendency to refuse to listen to your own intuition.
HOME: Brings harmony to the home that flows through every room and may be commented on by visitors. To resolve disputes by having each family member hold a Channeling Quartz crystal and speaking in turn while the others remain silent.
WORKPLACE: Brings professionalism into the workplace if some colleagues treat work like a social club; useful for speaking out calmly but firmly against any sexually inappropriate behavior.
CHILDREN: Enables Star Children and those with complete rainbow auras to hear angels and nature spirits with messages.
ANIMALS: For pets providing company and comfort for older or disabled people.
PROTECTION: Guards against voices in the head predicting doom and evil.

MAGICKAL AND PSYCHIC USES
For automatic writing while holding the Channeling Quartz in the nondominant hand to receive messages from angels, guides, and ancestors.
SPECIAL PROPERTIES
Your Channeling Quartz crystal may connect you with one personal angel or guide who will act as a gatekeeper for your spiritual explorations and help you channel mediumship, oracles, and predictions.
MYTHOLOGY AND HISTORY
Channeling Quartz is considered a master or teaching crystal that will help the owner to evolve spiritually. First and foremost, they are powerful receivers of wisdom from higher sources and from ancient worlds.

Charlevoix

COLORS: Soft gray or beige with a honeycomb pattern of small squarish shapes

CRYSTAL TYPE: Fossils of a coral that lived in warm, shallow seas in colonies from the Ordovician to the Permian Age, a period dating back 251–450 million years ago; hand-collected and found beautifully polished by the waters

ZODIAC SIGN: Scorpio (October 24–November 22)

CANDLE COLOR: Cream

PHYSICAL: Curbs infections and infectious diseases, especially childhood illnesses in adulthood; counters cell mutation; alleviates chronic fatigue syndrome seemingly without a cause.

EMOTIONAL: Reduces regrets over lost or abandoned relationships in the past that prevent settling into new ones; feeling overshadowed by colleagues, friends, or siblings.

HOME: Offers unexpected assistance if repossession is threatened or a lease is not being renewed; aids in making the best of career relocation by self or partner where there seem few advantages.

WORKPLACE: Helps you find a personal niche and role in a large organization; enables you to avoid doing the jobs of others, as well as your own, when staff leave the company.

CHILDREN: Aids in fitting into a new school or location and becoming part of the new community activities.

ANIMALS: For pets rehoused because of owner's illness or death.

PROTECTION: Guards against intrusion by unrelated spirits pretending to be relatives when you are making contact with deceased family members.

MAGICKAL AND PSYCHIC USES

Dowsing for hidden treasure or lost items, using a Charlevoix pendant; for spells to sell and buy property swiftly and profitably.

SPECIAL PROPERTIES

For an unexpected reunion with a childhood friend or sweetheart; for travel overseas or acquiring a vacation home near water.

MYTHOLOGY AND HISTORY

Also called favorite or honeycomb coral, Charlevoix is a close cousin of the better-known Petoskey Stone (page 346), often found together along the shores of Lake Superior; a different fossil species from Petoskey, Charlevoix is distinguished by small, tightly packed, irregular rows of empty hexagons, each one housing a tiny coral polyp.

Charoite

COLOR: Swirling purple, lilac, and violet and/or lavender; marble-like, may include black and white

CRYSTAL TYPE: Phyllo or sheet silicate, sometimes with inclusions of quartz and manganese

ZODIAC SIGN: Pisces (February 19–March 20)

CANDLE COLOR: Lilac

PHYSICAL: Alleviates cramps, headaches, visual disturbances, liver and pancreatic damage; regulates blood pressure and heart rate.

EMOTIONAL: Enables you to let go of self-limiting beliefs; counters sleepwalking or talking; curbs overwhelming fears of ill health and mortality; assuages acute loneliness.

HOME: For caring for sick or elderly relatives and family who cannot manage alone.

WORKPLACE: Aids in adapting to new working practices after a takeover or the introduction of technology; inspires accuracy and precision.

CHILDREN: Eases communication, social, and behavioral difficulties; helps overcome homesickness in children in residential care or with foster parents.

ANIMALS: Comforts whose owner has died or moved away.

PROTECTION: Blocks premonitions of unavoidable disasters; replaces bad dreams with peaceful sleep.

MAGICKAL AND PSYCHIC USES

UFO sightings; *seeing* alien or mythical animals; strengthens telepathy with family or friends far away, even if you have no idea of their location.

SPECIAL PROPERTIES

Smooths the way into a new life stage, whether chosen or imposed by circumstances, involving starting over in an unfamiliar location, particularly alone.

MYTHOLOGY AND HISTORY

Charoite is called the stone of courage in exile because it is found only near the Chara or Charo River area of Siberia that was once a place to which political prisoners were taken; gives strength to start over after a major setback.

Charoite with Tinkasite

COLORS: Lavender to shades of purple, mingled with swirling yellow gold

CRYSTAL TYPE: Charoite and tinkasite, titanium, sodium, potassium, and silicon; also as tumbled stones and jewelry; may also include green or black Aegirine (page 12)

ZODIAC SIGN: Pisces (February 19–March 20)

CANDLE COLOR: Purple

PHYSICAL: Alleviates infections, bacterial and viral conditions; regulates blood circulation, high blood pressure, atrial fibrillation.

EMOTIONAL: Banishes continual mental chatter from your head, repetitive songs that will not leave the mind, and overthinking.

HOME: Makes time and space for yourself in a busy life if you have a lot of people to care for or many outside commitments; for making a temporary home more homey.

WORKPLACE: For family-based or -run businesses, to promote unity and prevent personal quarrels or control issues from blocking professionalism; aids in overcoming personality clashes in the workplace.

CHILDREN: Encloses those on the autistic spectrum in a private oasis of calm when surrounded by noise and chaos.

ANIMALS: Desensitizes easily startled dogs and horses.

PROTECTION: Clears the aura energy field and the chakra energy centers of psychic debris accumulated from difficult experiences and hostile people.

MAGICKAL AND PSYCHIC USES

Lucid dreams and visions; astral travel in meditation to view the Akashic records, containing all knowledge of past, present, and future; psychic defense.

SPECIAL PROPERTIES

A crystal that clears the decks of inner clutter relating to former injustices that cannot be resolved but rankle years later; tackles family quarrels that can be put right given compromise and forgiveness.

MYTHOLOGY AND HISTORY

Before Charoite was officially identified during the 1940s, Charoite alone or the stone mix was boiled in tea by Indigenous people to drive away evil and cultivate family unity. Not recommended in modern mineralogy because of potential direct risks of toxicity by this crystal in water elixirs, but the properties remain the same.

Cherry Hummingbird Quartz or Red Tanzurine

COLORS: Bright or deeper red, colored by an intense infusion of red lepidolite

CRYSTAL TYPE: Quartz with lepidolite

ZODIAC SIGN: Leo (July 23–August 23)

CANDLE COLOR: Gold

PHYSICAL: Promotes fertility by overcoming psychological blocks or menstrual irregularities; boosts libido; counters allergies to food, fur, or feathers; kick-starts a sluggish metabolism and immune system.

EMOTIONAL: Musters the courage to confront domestic violence, past or ongoing; helps overcome fears of confrontation that cause repressed anger to suddenly flare in a seemingly unrelated situation.

HOME: Addresses situations where the life force is blocked and family members alternate between inertia and temper tantrums.

WORKPLACE: Revives interest in a project of great personal significance; counters inappropriate sexual innuendos or behavior that makes professionalism hard to maintain.

CHILDREN: For those who become easily upset by teasing; for adolescents who believe they have found their lifetime love without considering the consequences.

ANIMALS: Aids in controlling unpredictable pets.

PROTECTION: Guards against emotional domination by bullies who intimidate with ridicule.

MAGICKAL AND PSYCHIC USES

Sex magick; fertility spells; fire rituals, psychic defense; an amulet for safety from attack, accident, or theft of possessions while traveling.

SPECIAL PROPERTIES

For beginning and sticking to a fitness regimen; brings abundance; increases radiance, charisma, and positive reactions from others if you doubt yourself.

MYTHOLOGY AND HISTORY

Sometimes called Red Tanzurine to distinguish it from the more readily available Cherry Quartz that is often modified in color. This is naturally colored. Red Tanzurine is a balancing stone, increasing passion for life and love where there is inertia or stagnation; equally effective against excesses, such as bad temper or violence.

Cherry Opal

COLORS: Orange red to pink red

CRYSTAL TYPE: Clear, gelatinous, hydrated silica; raw in a matrix or tumbled

ZODIAC SIGN: Gemini (May 22–June 21)

CANDLE COLOR: Red

PHYSICAL: Alleviates headaches, PMS, menopause, muscle stiffness and pain, sluggish pulse, prostate issues, colitis, chronic constipation; addresses blood disorders and purifies the blood and kidneys; eases childbirth.

EMOTIONAL: Counters loss of willpower to tackle obstacles; prompts the ability to show loyalty in times of temptation or when relationships are going through a bad phase.

HOME: For setting up a home-based studio or craft workshop; prioritizing your own work time and space if you are combining working from home or study with family.

WORKPLACE: Propels financial advancement; calls forth promotion opportunities; aids in taking practical steps toward achieving your ambitions.

CHILDREN: For women giving birth for the first time who may suffer from irrational fears; for nervous mothers of newborns if they're subject to unwanted advice to trust their maternal instincts.

ANIMALS: Enables a temperamental pet to become more secure, even in unfamiliar surroundings.

PROTECTION: Guards against self-doubt about your talents or worthiness to receive love and admiration.

MAGICKAL AND PSYCHIC USES

Clairvoyance, clairsentience, sex magick; healing the inner child through deep meditation; rebirthing; parent and infant telepathy to know instinctively when a young child is in need of help or comfort.

SPECIAL PROPERTIES

For the awakening or reawakening of passion, especially in the middle or golden years, if this is a new relationship or there has been a period of celibacy or preoccupation with family and work needs in an existing marriage.

MYTHOLOGY AND HISTORY

Found in Ethiopia, where it is also called red opal; some sold as jewelry is synthetically produced; a precious opal as Mexican Cherry Fire Opal (see Fire Opal, page 187). A stone of immense security in your achievements and place in the world.

Cherry Quartz

COLORS: Cherry or more muted red, orangey, and pink hues, distributed through naturally found stones and in dyeing of clear quartz; flashes of color

CRYSTAL TYPE: Cinnabar (mercury sulfide), which is toxic, contained safely within reconstituted and melted quartz; silicon dioxide

ZODIAC SIGN: Aries (March 21–April 20)

CANDLE COLOR: Red

PHYSICAL: Purifies blood; enhances circulation; counters anemia; promotes healthy weight loss and maintenance, fertility, mobility; relieves pain in joints and muscles.

EMOTIONAL: Eliminates repressed anger and resentment that create psychosomatic problems; banishes the desire for wealth through improbable get-rich-quick schemes or unrealistic plans.

HOME: Aids in managing and reducing debt; brings light to dark areas of the home; stirs sluggish Earth energies to replace lethargy with enthusiasm.

WORKPLACE: Cinnabar, itself called the merchant's stone, amplified within quartz as Cherry Quartz, encourages moneymaking through enterprise.

CHILDREN: Keep with paperwork of children's bank accounts to encourage wise saving and spending habits.

ANIMALS: Place Cherry Quartz together with a photo of the pet when you are away to maintain the psychic link.

PROTECTION: Guards against hidden toxicity in the environment and within people, concealed jealousy, and spite.

MAGICKAL AND PSYCHIC USES

A rocket to the stars; breaks through barriers of doubt and fear to connect with other dimensions and worlds; for shamanic journeying and travel in dreams.

SPECIAL PROPERTIES

For taking up new hobbies, sports, and travel; for fitness regimens, yoga, and spiritual energy movement.

MYTHOLOGY AND HISTORY

The crystal to set in motion any plans and dreams; used by writers, artists, and all creators to express ideas and test them in the marketplace; for reviving passion.

Chert

COLORS: Gray, black, brown, red, orange, white, yellow, blue, green; glassy, smooth to touch; colored by other minerals, organic matter, or clay

CRYSTAL TYPE: Hard compact sedimentary rock, mainly very small quartz crystals, the mineral form of silicon dioxide

ZODIAC SIGN: Capricorn (December 22–January 20)

CANDLE COLOR: Cream

PHYSICAL: Alleviates allergies, chemical imbalances, memory loss, excess fatty deposits around organs, psychosomatic conditions, hypochondria, insomnia.

EMOTIONAL: Addresses misplaced anger, constant irritability, mood swings, excesses such as feast and famine dieting.

HOME: Introduces good humor and tolerance to the home, if there are unnecessary confrontations or flare-ups.

WORKPLACE: Cultivates the ability to remember facts and juggle priorities under pressure; aids in recalling names and relevant details of clients and contacts to make a good impression.

CHILDREN: For those who constantly forget or lose possessions; promotes peaceful sleep and happy dreams.

ANIMALS: For dogs and cats who wander and become lost.

PROTECTION: Guards against those with inflated egos making you feel inferior; insulates against others' gloom.

MAGICKAL AND PSYCHIC USES

Finding whatever is lost; recalling distant past-life memories; tumbled Chert, as a worry stone, absorbs anxiety and fears.

SPECIAL PROPERTIES

A stone of total honesty, cutting through flattery or insincerity; encourages common sense when others initiate impossible schemes.

MYTHOLOGY AND HISTORY

Chert was used ceremonially by Algonquin Native Americans as a channel for spirits, totem animals, and guides; used for making incredibly sharp tools more than a million years ago; also found as Indiana hornstone and banded Australian ribbon stone.

Chevron Amethyst

COLOR: Lavender or purple and white chevron patterns; also called dogstooth amethyst

CRYSTAL TYPE: Crystallized quartz; the purple comes from manganese during formation

ZODIAC SIGN: Aquarius (January 21–February 18)

CANDLE COLOR: Purple

PHYSICAL: Regulates imbalances of nervous system; addresses degenerative conditions, tics, migraines with visual disturbances, hearing issues, immunity; alleviates problems in the respiratory tract; counteracts viruses.

EMOTIONAL: Mitigates symptoms of Tourette's syndrome, bipolar disorder, schizophrenia; diminishes alcohol cravings, food imbalances involving swings between bingeing and fasting; helps overcome fears in pregnancy for the unborn child.

HOME: For fun parties and gatherings without antisocial behavior; spreads freshness throughout the home.

WORKPLACE: Chevrons with more white counteract lethargy; those with more purple lessen overcompetitiveness; promote wise choices in speculation.

CHILDREN: Counters oversensitivity to stimuli of any kind.

ANIMALS: Calms lively pets in apartments if neighbors complain.

PROTECTION: Prevents impulsiveness and impatience from sabotaging success; the dual color repels and dispels negativity.

MAGICKAL AND PSYCHIC USES

For astral travel, guided meditation; useful for prayer, mantras, and deep meditation; whole-self healing by both soothing pain and illness and reenergizing.

SPECIAL PROPERTIES

The ultimate dual crystal, synthesizing proactive and steadying vibrations in the right proportions, according to need and situation; replaces addictions or bad habits with positive life choices and prevents their return.

MYTHOLOGY AND HISTORY

Chevron Amethyst, called the breath of life, contains both the violet healing flame of the ascended master St. Germain and Archangel Michael's protective and empowering white light, so it harmonizes body, mind, and spirit.

Chiastolite or the Cross Stone

COLORS: Usually gray or brown with black or brown inclusions

CRYSTAL TYPE: Andalusite, containing brown or black clay or graphite, creating the characteristic cross

ZODIAC SIGN: Capricorn (December 22–January 20)

CANDLE COLOR: Brown

PHYSICAL: Alleviates rheumatism, nerve and muscle weakness; promotes mobility; helps those who are seriously ill; strengthens teeth and bones; for breastfeeding mothers.

EMOTIONAL: Prevents the repetition of destructive patterns, such as always choosing an unfaithful partner.

HOME: Place this crystal in the center of your home for health, harmony, abundance, and luck.

WORKPLACE: Aids in making wise choices at a career crossroads; leads to finding fulfillment in work.

CHILDREN: For quarreling or overcompetitive children; defuses accusations of favoritism.

ANIMALS: Minimizes fighting for top position; useful for large animals, particularly horses and donkeys.

PROTECTION: Repels the evil eye of envy and ill-wishing against emotional and psychic vampires.

MAGICKAL AND PSYCHIC USES

A bridge between dimensions, learning mediumship, spirit rescue, investigating hauntings; guards against spirit and emotional possession.

SPECIAL PROPERTIES

A symbol of safe travel, especially to international danger zones; guards against infections and viruses while traveling.

MYTHOLOGY AND HISTORY

Chiastolite comes from China, Spain, Australia, Russia, Canada, and the USA. Called the fairy cross because it's believed to be a gift from nature essences; worn as an amulet by sixteenth-century pilgrims returning from the Spanish Santiago de Compostela pilgrimage trail.

Childrenite

COLORS: Sparkling brown, yellowish brown to golden yellow or orange; glassy with small crystals when gem-quality; may be more opaque in larger crystals

CRYSTAL TYPE: Hydrated phosphate with iron, manganese, and aluminum; sometimes found growing with its sister Eosphorite (page 177) and/or on a feldspar or quartz matrix; may be twinned or occasionally double-terminated

ZODIAC SIGN: Gemini (May 22–June 21)

CANDLE COLOR: Orange

PHYSICAL: For health checks and daily care of body in nutrition, exercise, and stress levels; addresses high blood pressure, racing heart, and pulse made worse by surges of anger.

EMOTIONAL: Enables you to control fury; calms impulsive people who act or speak and only afterwards consider the wisdom and timing of their words or deeds.

HOME: Brings harmony, tact, and unity to social gatherings where there are personality clashes or unresolved grievances.

WORKPLACE: Aids in making major decisions in business; generates new ideas to increase the customer base.

CHILDREN: Keep Childrenite in a home where interactions between siblings and parents are volatile to lower the temperature of exchanges and model reasoned discussions.

ANIMALS: Place Childrenite near the bed of a dog who snaps and snarls at other pets, while exercising.

PROTECTION: Guards against sacrificing individuality for approval.

MAGICKAL AND PSYCHIC USES

For clearing redundant and often unrecognized karma from past worlds; adapts conventional healing and magickal techniques to work for you.

SPECIAL PROPERTIES

Overcomes relationship crises through perseverance and compromise; maintains a united front where there is outside interference or a temptation to stray.

MYTHOLOGY AND HISTORY

Childrenite is a collector's item, but it is possible to find reasonably priced pieces for healing and magick, especially in a quartz matrix; most famously mined in Tavistock in Devon, Southwest England, and Linópolis in Brazil, where it is sometimes found growing with Brazilianite (page 91).

Chinese Red Quartz

COLOR: Naturally red-tinted throughout
CRYSTAL TYPE: Silicon dioxide with particulate (minute separate particles) of hematite/iron oxide throughout (see Tangerine Quartz, page 468, and Red Phantom Quartz, page 400)
ZODIAC SIGN: Aries (March 21–April 20)
CANDLE COLOR: Red

PHYSICAL: Aids in recovery from blood transfusions, organ transplants, heart valve replacement; alleviates issues involving the thyroid, thymus, infertility, chronic fatigue, muscle weakness.
EMOTIONAL: Counters the inability to open the heart to love or forgiveness; helps in managing depression; helps overcome the fear of strong emotions in self and others.
HOME: Breaks up stagnant chi that causes inertia and slows the accumulation of health and wealth.
WORKPLACE: Prompts a major turnaround in business; useful for all physically arduous jobs; channels rivalries into team effort.
CHILDREN: For persevering in the performing arts or sports to get the right breaks.
ANIMALS: VALUABLE for horses who compete in racing or show-jumping.
PROTECTION: Guards against uncontrolled anger, bullying and intimidation; overcoming domestic abuse.

MAGICKAL AND PSYCHIC USES
Heals past-life trauma involving fears of change or confrontation; for feng shui and I Ching; enhances the power in other crystals; dragon rituals; fire and candle magick.
SPECIAL PROPERTIES
A proactive crystal, combining the energy and transformative powers of quartz with the determination and perseverance of hematite, perfectly blended to make almost anything possible; for those who are not advantaged, striving for and reaching the top.
MYTHOLOGY AND HISTORY
This distinctive red quartz is found only in China, especially in the Jiangxi and Sichuan regions; contains energies of air and water dragons.

Chinese Writing Rock or Stone

COLOR: Black or dark gray-green with white inclusions, which, when grouped, together resemble Chinese characters
CRYSTAL TYPE: Form of basalt, also called porphyry/porphyrite (an igneous rock), which has inclusions of plagioclase feldspar
ZODIAC SIGN: Scorpio (October 24–November 22)
CANDLE COLOR: White

PHYSICAL: Alleviates issues involving the eyes, spine, legs, protein deficiency, hereditary conditions, tropical diseases, carpal tunnel syndrome, hand muscles and arthritis, whole-body healing, disorientation.
EMOTIONAL: Aids in taking responsibility for actions; balances mood swings; helps overcome fear of failure and self-consciousness in social situations; counters the inability to express feelings.
HOME: AIDS IN restoring an old property and furniture; fosters a love of antiques and books.
WORKPLACE: Formulates clear strategies if others are indecisive; for authors, scriptwriters, linguists, translators, graphologists.
CHILDREN: For children with dyslexia or who find formal learning difficult.
ANIMALS: Boosts confidence of big pets with timid personalities.
PROTECTION: Guards against dark-night-of-the soul moments.

MAGICKAL AND PSYCHIC USES
Interprets wisdom psychically from ancient sacred texts and Akashic records; creates dreams to answer questions or meet deceased ancestors; for feng shui, automatic writing, I Ching.
SPECIAL PROPERTIES
Embraces new responsibilities at work, financially, and in relationship and family; manifests original creative impetus.
MYTHOLOGY AND HISTORY
Chinese Writing Rock or Stone is found, not surprisingly, in the Yangtse River Valley in the Hunan region of China and also in Auburn in the Californian foothills of the Sierra Nevada. A yin-yang stone, it balances intuition and logic, establishing a balanced path between dynamic action and spiritual growth, making life exciting but secure.

Chocolate or Brown Calcite

COLORS: Dark brown, often with light brown or tan stripes or banding; resembles cocoa beans; as brown calcite, it can be reddish-brown and semitranslucent

CRYSTAL TYPE: Calcium carbonate, usually sold as tumbled stones or jewelry

ZODIAC SIGN: Pisces (February 19–March 20)

CANDLE COLOR: Golden brown

PHYSICAL: Alleviates issues involving arthritis, rheumatism, bone weakness, bowels; minimizes IBS, celiac disease; promotes absorption of necessary nutrients, minerals, and vitamins.

EMOTIONAL: Helps overcome the inability to relax and have fun; keeps you from repeating the same mistakes and not learning from them.

HOME: Preserves a steady stream of income.

WORKPLACE: Aids in setting up a repair, construction, or renovation business; starts any venture small and building up step-by-step; promotes successful apprenticeships.

CHILDREN: Teaches children to make their own fun; for emotional and physical security at a new school or college.

ANIMALS: For home-loving pets with active owners, to foster compromise.

PROTECTION: Guards against toxic people and situations; cleanses rooms, workplaces, land, altars, and sacred spaces.

MAGICKAL AND PSYCHIC USES

Recall of past-life memories to explain and overcome present-day fears, phobias, and rediscover forgotten talents from old worlds.

SPECIAL PROPERTIES

A stone of reassurance in uncertain times that all will turn out well; valuable whenever you are experiencing free-floating anxiety or panic; introduces spontaneous fun and leisure into a workaholic schedule or fixed routine.

MYTHOLOGY AND HISTORY

The stone of practical manifestation of what is desired in everyday life by combining empowerments with practical actions; increases chances to save for a major purpose; aids in reducing a seemingly impossible mountain of debt through negotiations and realistic repayments.

Chondrite

COLORS: Dull gray, brown, or black on the outside; if cut and polished, the chondrite will be sparkling for beautiful jewelry and polished pieces

CRYSTAL TYPE: Stony meteorites, contain silicates, mainly pyroxene and olivine with small amounts of plagioclase feldspar; carbonaceous Chondrites, the most basic type, are rich in water, sulfur, and organic materials

ZODIAC SIGN: Aquarius (January 21–February 18)

CANDLE COLOR: Gray

PHYSICAL: Promotes absent or distance healing; calms inflammation within the body; aids in recovery from a multiple-injury crash; life-changing conditions.

EMOTIONAL: Counters feeling out of synchronicity with the world; always looking back to the past.

HOME: A lucky talisman for health, prosperity, and happiness; protects against fires and natural disasters.

WORKPLACE: Enables you to wait for the right moment to display your knowledge and expertise; for working with accuracy as well as speed.

CHILDREN: Viewed as a family treasure; empowers children who never ask questions or give an opinion.

ANIMALS: Calms pets who are spooked by the presence of entities.

PROTECTION: Guards against the physical dangers of the modern world, especially connected with explosions or extremist attacks.

MAGICKAL AND PSYCHIC USES

Chondrites tune into the psychic wavelengths of extraterrestrials and UFOs through meditation and astral travel.

SPECIAL PROPERTIES

The heat generated on impact within the Chondrite releases energy and impetus for those all-or-nothing moments when an instant impression or an off-the-clock reaction is needed.

MYTHOLOGY AND HISTORY

Chondrites, small spherical meteorites, are unchanged since the solar system was formed and are different from any rocks on Earth. They may date back 4.6 million years and are the most numerous. Meteorites take on the energies of the impact location. A Chondrite fall, like the one in Russia in December 1922, will feel subtly different from the meteorite that landed in Australia in 1969.

Chrysanthemum or Flower Stone

COLORS: Black or brown and white

CRYSTAL TYPE: Metamorphic rock with flashes of pale, andalusite crystals, whose patterns resemble chrysanthemums or multipetaled flowers

ZODIAC SIGN: Aquarius (January 21–February 18)

CANDLE COLOR: White

PHYSICAL: Promotes fertility, especially under difficult conditions; addresses issues involving fibroids, endometriosis, pregnancy, childbirth, cystitis, absorption of nutrients, skin, eyes, bones; removes toxins.

EMOTIONAL: Reopens trust and prompts emotional growth after abuse or trauma; brings joy to those who have given up hope.

HOME: Aids in making a change in living arrangements or leaving a comfort zone; for beautiful indoor plants.

WORKPLACE: Useful when working overseas in a hostile environment or in a security job where there is opposition or resentment for your role; helps in overcoming career problems.

CHILDREN: Promotes healthy growth through childhood and puberty; inspires children with medical, physical, or emotional challenges (also adults) to overcome those obstacles.

ANIMALS: Soothes animals separated too early from their mothers.

PROTECTION: Guards against anyone interfering in love or dividing lovers.

MAGICKAL AND PSYCHIC USES

For light trance/meditation time travel, frequently to ancient worlds; manifests seemingly impossible dreams; harmonizes with the moon and planetary rhythms; enhances flower psychometry.

SPECIAL PROPERTIES

Aids in finding love later in life, particularly after caring for a relative or pursuing a career dedicated to others.

MYTHOLOGY AND HISTORY

Traditionally called the stone of wealth and honor in China, Chrysanthemum figures in Chinese legends of lovers who refused to be parted; after they died, the man turned into a rock, the woman into a chrysanthemum, and they were united in the stone; promises everlasting love, happiness, luck, and abundance.

Chrysoberyl

COLORS: Clear yellow, honey, yellowy green, or brown

CRYSTAL TYPE: Aluminum oxide containing beryllium (see also Alexandrite, page 18, and Cat's Eye, page 108)

ZODIAC SIGNS: Gemini (May 22–June 21) or Leo (July 23–August 23)

CANDLE COLOR: Yellow or gold

PHYSICAL: Counters exhaustion; alleviates diarrhea, IBS, celiac disease, stomach ulcers, food allergies and intolerances, chest infections, resistance to illness; promotes gentle weight loss; enhances healing with other crystals or alternative remedies.

EMOTIONAL: Inspires those excessively influenced by the opinions and values of others to trust and express their own beliefs.

HOME: Brings reason and compromise if family members are constantly arguing.

WORKPLACE: For good ethics, if there is dishonesty or corruption at any level.

CHILDREN: Teaches children to be honest and kind toward others who are less fortunate.

ANIMALS: Increases telepathic communication with cats, dogs, or horses.

PROTECTION: Prevents psychological or psychic manipulation; guards against accidents and natural disasters.

MAGICKAL AND PSYCHIC USES

Enhances visions during mirror rituals or divination; useful in prosperity rituals; traditionally, in love magick, attracts a wealthy partner.

SPECIAL PROPERTIES

For organization and success of community or charity events, parties, handfasting, weddings, baby namings or christenings, especially if you anticipate interference by difficult guests.

MYTHOLOGY AND HISTORY

Yellow Chrysoberyl, discovered in Brazil in the seventeenth century, became associated with great leaders, especially in Spain and Portugal. Chrysoberyl, especially yellow, attracts prosperity, overcoming fears of financial loss and deprivation of what is most valued.

Chlorastrolite or Turtle Stone

COLORS: Bluish-green to dark green semiprecious patterned stone, resembling the shell of a turtle or terrapin; shimmering when moved in different directions in polished state; forms small but beautiful cabochons and jewelry

CRYSTAL TYPE: Hydrated calcium magnesium silicate hydroxide, related to the zoisite-epidote family; Chlorastrolite is a variety of pumpellyite

ZODIAC SIGN: Leo (July 23–August 23)

CANDLE COLOR: Blue

PHYSICAL: Alleviates conditions caused or made worse by smoking, travel sickness, skin disorders.

EMOTIONAL: Dissipates repressed anger that can manifest in physical conditions; controls automatic negative reactions to certain people.

HOME: For restoring old furniture, vehicles, or a property to reveal its true beauty; to embrace new opportunities.

WORKPLACE: Aids in starting a new job after a period of unemployment, sick or maternity/paternity leave; helps develop a particular skill to gain a much-cherished position.

CHILDREN: For Star Children who hide their talents because they feel different and want to fit in with their peers.

ANIMALS: Useful for marine and freshwater turtles, terrapins, and land-based tortoises.

PROTECTION: To repel the evil eye of envy.

MAGICKAL AND PSYCHIC USES

Astrology; communicating with other galaxies; recognizing fellow Star Souls in everyday life; water magick.

SPECIAL PROPERTIES

Helps overcome fear of water and swimming, especially if linked with past-life drowning; offers protection while traveling.

MYTHOLOGY AND HISTORY

Made the state gem of Michigan in 1973; also called Isle Royale greenstone after the area where the bluish-green version is found in the Isle Royale area of Lake Superior; whether the stones are found in basalt nodules or as small, rounded, patterned pebbles where the basalt has washed away.

Chlorite Phantom Quartz

COLORS: Pale green, watery; can tint the whole crystal; clear white with pale green inner ghost; the greenness depends on the amount of chlorite

CRYSTAL TYPE: Quartz crystal with a chlorite phantom or faint crystal outline within (see also Phantom Quartz, page 348)

ZODIAC SIGN: Virgo (August 24–September 22)

CANDLE COLOR: Green

PHYSICAL: Strengthens underfunctioning organs; regulates low blood sugar; addresses bladder issues; reduces side effects of radiation and chemotherapy.

EMOTIONAL: Counters self-destructive behavior, self-harm; dispels bitterness accumulated over many years.

HOME: Protects the home and attracts wealth and luck; brings the countryside into city homes.

WORKPLACE: For moving forward if workplace practices are out of date or there are established factions; helps newcomers feel welcome.

CHILDREN: Useful for those who live and go to school near busy roads; enables you to see nature spirits in urban parks and yards.

ANIMALS: For pets who exercise mainly in city streets.

PROTECTION: Guards against fears of healing treatments, and medical and dental appointments.

MAGICKAL AND PSYCHIC USES

Earth rituals, connection with Earth, Tree and Air spirits; for psychic surgery; empowers herbs, essential oils, homeopathic remedies, and plant essences before healing.

SPECIAL PROPERTIES

Reduces overprotectiveness by parents as teens seek independence and begin to engage in romantic relationships.

MYTHOLOGY AND HISTORY

Chlorite Phantoms are formed within clear quartz when green chlorite attaches itself as a coating around quartz during its early development. In myths of many cultures, Chlorite Phantom Quartz has formed a natural home for fairies, Earth spirits, and home guardians.

Chohua Jasper

COLORS: White, gray, silver with red, brown, maroon, or blue splashes; often predominantly gray and brown
CRYSTAL TYPE: Chalcedony, silicon dioxide
ZODIAC SIGN: Aries (March 21–April 20)
CANDLE COLOR: Red

PHYSICAL: Alleviates issues relating to the heart, oxygenation of the blood, veins, arteries, bypass operations, stents, and pacemakers; awakens the root energy, the kundalini power to vitalize or revitalize the whole system; for convalescing after an energy-depleting illness or intensive treatment.
EMOTIONAL: Keeps from turning trivial setbacks into major dramas; helps overcome a reluctance to take risks, out of fear of disappointment.
HOME: Enables you to display and use family treasures instead of saving them for special occasions; aids in collecting family stories and legends to record for the present and future generations.
WORKPLACE: Turns ideas, plans, and visions into successful projects; gives you the courage to undertake leadership roles; creates solid financial results and returns in creative businesses.
CHILDREN: A happiness and fun crystal for children.
ANIMALS: For city and apartment pets to connect with nature; for wildlife that has adapted to city habitats.
PROTECTION: Guards against those who would damage your reputation or blame you for their mistakes.

MAGICKAL AND PSYCHIC USES
Dragon rituals; fire magick; candle magick; communicating with fire spirits and devas; genii wishes; manifestation of desires; for overcoming blocks in yoga, tai chi, qi gong, and kung fu, and allowing the energies to flow.
SPECIAL PROPERTIES
A very active jasper, this crystal brings order out of chaos, clarity out of confusion, and awareness of opportunities and prosperity that had not been seen but were always there.
MYTHOLOGY AND HISTORY
Found only on the Lijing River, in China, a Chinese luck-bringing crystal, associated with healing pearls dropped to the ground as the dragons fight or mate in the spring; also the fire dragon of pure power, guardian of treasure from greedy humans who are in charge of your finances.

Chrysocolla

COLORS: Mixed blue and bluish-greens, turquoise; intense colors
CRYSTAL TYPE: Hydrated copper silicate (see also Gem Silica, page 199)
ZODIAC SIGN: Taurus (April 21–May 21)
CANDLE COLOR: Turquoise

PHYSICAL: For female-specific problems, especially relating to puberty, hormones, reproduction, and menopause; addresses issues relating to the hips, arthritis, rheumatism, fetal health, thyroid, hypertension, diabetes (particularly type 2), lungs.
EMOTIONAL: Helps men to express vulnerability; aids in recovery from domestic violence, incest, and sexual abuse.
HOME: Shields against obstructive neighbors; enables you to feel safe if you're living alone; helps in recovery after burglary; reduces petty squabbles.
WORKPLACE: Counters ageism directed toward women, especially in media or publicity careers; promotes businesses run by and for women.
CHILDREN: Encourages love of music; fosters loving relationships with grandparents far away.
ANIMALS: For older, pregnant animals or those who endured previous birth trauma.
PROTECTION: Returns on- and offline malice so perpetrators feel the pain; deters partners from straying.

MAGICKAL AND PSYCHIC USES
Rituals to heal the planet; wise woman rituals; psychic dreams; a stone of Venus for love and romance rituals; prayerfulness.
SPECIAL PROPERTIES
For older women expressing wisdom through writing, painting, music, crafts, or spirituality; for grandmothers and great-grandmothers to balance caring with independence.
MYTHOLOGY AND HISTORY
Chrysocolla dates back to ancient Greece and Rome and was a talisman of Cleopatra; a Native American crystal for encouraging peace between nations; the stone of musicians and singers, professional and for pleasure, and, if desired, success in reality or talent shows; in the modern world the color of Earth seen from space, so it represents a united world.

Citrine

COLOR: Natural Citrine is transparent pale to golden yellow or honey-brown; artificially heat-treated Citrine is brighter than natural, and sparkling yellow-orange

CRYSTAL TYPE: Natural Citrine is quartz-heated in the Earth; artificially heat-treated Citrine is derived from amethyst or smoky quartz

ZODIAC SIGN: Gemini (May 22–June 21)

CANDLE COLOR: Lemon

PHYSICAL: Alleviates issues relating to the liver, spleen, gallbladder, pancreas, digestion; enhances short-term memory; addresses migraines and skin allergies related to food and chemical intolerance, fibromyalgia, motion sickness, morning sickness during pregnancy.

EMOTIONAL: Reduces self-destructive behavior, overwork, overspending, gambling, depression, and phobias.

HOME: Brightens dark, unfriendly rooms, caused by negative Earth energies; aids in balancing the family budget.

WORKPLACE: Useful for those involved in sales, technology, science, medicine, sports and fitness, media (especially investigative journalism), research, clairvoyant pursuits.

CHILDREN: For reluctant students; children with speech or communication difficulties; enuresis in older children.

ANIMALS: Valuable for pets of lonely owners; for settling pets in new homes.

PROTECTION: Stops human snakes; protects travelers.

MAGICKAL AND PSYCHIC USES
Believed by some to transmit ancient Atlantean solar healing; for prosperity rituals, automatic writing, creative visualization to manifest a goal; banishes poltergeists and unfriendly spirits.

SPECIAL PROPERTIES
Speculation, entrepreneurial ventures, and investments; called the merchant's stone, it's often placed in cash registers.

MYTHOLOGY AND HISTORY
Called the sun stone, Citrine holds sunlight, never absorbing negativity. The stone of swift-moving Mercury, the Roman messenger, Citrine brings travel opportunities, new experiences, new information, and changing perspectives; attracts good love, protecting against love cheats.

Citrine Aura Quartz

COLORS: Yellow to golden; may have rainbows

CRYSTAL TYPE: Citrine bonded with silver or sometimes silver, gold, and platinum

ZODIAC SIGN: Gemini (May 22–June 21)

CANDLE COLOR: Gold

PHYSICAL: Promotes fertility if your biological clock is running out; addresses hormonal imbalances, headaches (including migraines), visual and auditory disturbances, PMS; regulates excess testosterone or estrogen.

EMOTIONAL: Eases phobias, especially concerning cleanliness or becoming ill if there is a flu or viral epidemic; banishes envy of others; assuages gender-issue uncertainties.

HOME: Automatically balances the yin and yang if these are causing either inertia and depression or overactivity and restlessness, to ensure the harmonious flow of the life force; automatically cleanses the home (needs no cleansing itself) if you move into a house with a negative history.

WORKPLACE: As an enhanced version of Citrine, which is called the merchant's stone, Citrine Aura Quartz attracts money; silver, gold, and platinum are all natural wealth-bringers.

CHILDREN: For those at a disadvantage—physically, emotionally, or educationally; for teens struggling with maintaining friends on social media.

ANIMALS: Helps overcome mistrust among rescue pets who have been mistreated.

PROTECTION: Containing pure dawn sunlight, Citrine Aura Quartz guards against those who would deceive, spread falsehoods.

MAGICKAL AND PSYCHIC USES
As silver is the metal of the moon and Citrine (also gold, if included) a stone of the sun, and platinum a metal of what is lasting, Citrine Aura Quartz brings the manifestation of wishes when sun and moon are in the sky at the same time.

SPECIAL PROPERTIES
Combines logic with intuition for wise decision making.

MYTHOLOGY AND HISTORY
Citrine Aura Quartz is also called aura citrine or, when bonded with silver, gold, and platinum, angel aura citrine; for travel or relocation overseas; also for finding a treasure at an auction or sale or receiving one as a gift.

Citrine Smoky Quartz

COLORS: Gray and translucent with golden sparkles; the amount of gold color depends on the proportion of citrine to smoky quartz

CRYSTAL TYPE: Citrine and smoky quartz combined in the same crystal

ZODIAC SIGN: Gemini (May 22–June 21)

CANDLE COLOR: Gray

PHYSICAL: Relieves pain from deep-seated or chronic conditions; promotes energy, self-healing; useful when conventional treatments are debilitating; for end-of-life care.

EMOTIONAL: Helps overcome fears of the dark and enclosed spaces, such as elevators or crowds, where fears cause inaction.

HOME: Valuable when three or more generations or adult children and parents share a house.

WORKPLACE: For making wise investments and long-range financial or business decisions; for shift and night workers' body-clock readjustment.

CHILDREN: Calms those who are easily frightened in unfamiliar settings or spooked by strange noises at night.

ANIMALS: For pets without a sense of danger.

PROTECTION: Guards against repeating old mistakes in new situations.

MAGICKAL AND PSYCHIC USES

For safe mediumship and ghost investigations; helps a client to feel a deceased relative's presence; aids in leaving past-life experiences of loss or poverty behind, replacing them with abundance energies.

SPECIAL PROPERTIES

For opening new social and relationship opportunities; like other citrines, it does not need cleansing.

MYTHOLOGY AND HISTORY

Citrine is clear quartz, heated naturally in the Earth, occurring in the same environment as smoky quartz and blending to form something greater than the separate crystals; may form a citrine phantom within the smoky quartz; an alchemist's stone, balancing protection with power.

Clear Crystal Quartz

COLORS: Transparent and glassy, sparkles in the sun; many variations in color

CRYSTAL TYPE: Silicon dioxide, appearing in many forms from a single point to a teaching or Master Crystal, such as the Isis Quartz (page 257). Its natural formation is six-sided or -faceted

ZODIAC SIGN: Leo (July 23–August 23)

CANDLE COLOR: Gold

PHYSICAL: Heals and energizes the whole body, and wherever it is directed for contact and remote healing.

EMOTIONAL: Counters deep sorrow, a sense of hopelessness, depression, and lack of faith in yourself, humanity, and higher powers.

HOME: A Clear Crystal Quartz sphere or pyramid in the center of the home continually filters light and the life force through every room.

WORKPLACE: Clear Crystal Quartz transforms sarcastic or critical words into appreciation and gossip into friendly conversation.

CHILDREN: The stone of Michael, archangel of the sun, traditionally a gift for a newborn child, kept throughout life as a talisman.

ANIMALS: Placed under a pet bed, makes an older animal more energetic.

PROTECTION: Creates a shield of light to deflect paranormal harm and those with ill intent.

MAGICKAL AND PSYCHIC USES

Amplifies psychic, magickal, and healing powers and the power of prayer; calls guardian angels and spirit guides; increases telepathy and, as a pendulum, aids in making decisions.

SPECIAL PROPERTIES

The stone of health, wealth, and happiness, Clear Crystal Quartz absorbs energy from sunlight; the life force from flowers, trees, and plants; and from angels and the cosmos, releasing it into your rainbow aura energy field and inner chakra power centers.

MYTHOLOGY AND HISTORY

According to myth, Hercules dropped the clear crystal of truth from Mount Olympus and it shattered into millions of pieces. That is the reason a person using a crystal for scrying can never lie (see Crystal Spheres, page 147).

Clear Danburite

COLOR: Colorless, sparkling when polished (see also Pink Danburite, page 355, and Yellow or Agni Gold Danburite, page 510)
CRYSTAL TYPE: Calcium boron silicate
ZODIAC SIGN: Leo (July 23–August 23)
CANDLE COLOR: White

PHYSICAL: Gentler than Clear Crystal Quartz for healing sick children, older people, or anyone with preexisting conditions if illness is acute; alleviates energy blockages, Ménière's disease, inoperable conditions, chronic pain; aids in end-of-life care.
EMOTIONAL: Brings persistence where walking away is not an option.
HOME: For successful celebrations from a child's birthday to a housewarming or business entertaining.
WORKPLACE: A stone of clear intellect; encourages thinking on your feet for appearing knowledgeable when you have not had time to prepare.
CHILDREN: Protects children from online sexual predators.
ANIMALS: Prevents jealousy by pets toward newcomers, animal or human.
PROTECTION: Deters time wasters, fantasists, scammers, and less benign contacts on the internet or telephone.

MAGICKAL AND PSYCHIC USES
A source of cosmic light; occasionally contains a Buddha image within, so it creates a portal to enhanced spiritual awareness; promotes visions of guardian angels; guides inexperienced healers to transmit divine light.

SPECIAL PROPERTIES
Draws like-minded people and potential partners at singles or social events, and at online friendship and dating sites.

MYTHOLOGY AND HISTORY
Considered a crystal cast up by Mother Earth in the late 1830s to enlighten the harsh industrial age. A betrothal stone for those of more modest financial means, who are rich in love.

Clear or Colorless Calcite

COLOR: Clear, colorless
CRYSTAL TYPE: Calcium carbonate (see also Optical Calcite or Iceland Spar, page 326)
ZODIAC SIGN: Aquarius (January 21–February 18)
CANDLE COLOR: White

PHYSICAL: A whole-body healer; addresses bone calcification, intestines, skin disorders, warts, migraines, childhood growth disorders; strengthens eyesight; speeds metabolism; aids in healthy weight loss.
EMOTIONAL: Alleviates obsessive-compulsive disorder, Tourette's syndrome, tics, self-harm; keeps you from continually gravitating toward people who cause distress.
HOME: A powerful energy cleanser for cold or dark dwellings, especially when moving into a property that has remained empty or where previously there was sorrow, illness, or misfortune.
WORKPLACE: Aids in making a good impression at a new workplace; changes routines that no longer work with minimal disruption; reduces unnecessary competition, especially in or from middle management.
CHILDREN: Soothes restless children at night; encourages successful studying before examinations if a teen appears not to have made an effort.
ANIMALS: Cools pets in excessively hot weather.
PROTECTION: Guards against black magick, unfriendly spirits, and those intending physical or psychological harm, as well as scams or hidden deception.

MAGICKAL AND PSYCHIC USES
Amplifies the healing properties of other crystals; assists in finding what is lost; for ongoing cleansing of therapy rooms; ensures that divination remains uplifting when dealing with resistant clients.

SPECIAL PROPERTIES
A crystal of light, especially for remote healing; brings healing from angels and guides.

MYTHOLOGY AND HISTORY
Calcite is one of the most common and diverse minerals, with over three hundred calcite forms; colorless or white is the purest. Known as a crystal of truth, spoken with kindness, Clear Calcite cuts through harmful illusion.

Clear or White Aragonite

COLORS: White or clear in its purest form

CRYSTAL TYPE: Calcium carbonate, forms hexagonal-shaped or stalactite-like crystals (see also Orange Aragonite, page 327, and Yellow Aragonite, page 507)

ZODIAC SIGN: Capricorn (December 22–January 20)

CANDLE COLOR: White

PHYSICAL: Alleviates issues stemming from bone fractures, dislocation, osteoporosis, slipped disc, teeth, fevers, inflammation, hair, chronic exhaustion, cramps, diabetes, eczema, rosacea, psoriasis.

EMOTIONAL: Keeps you from remaining locked in past loss or injustice; reveals family secrets that haunt the present.

HOME: Slows individuals rushing in and out, grazing, and communicating via cell phone.

WORKPLACE: Keeps decision making open at social gatherings or clubs, rather than being secretive; makes collective enterprises, where there may be differing extreme viewpoints, productive.

CHILDREN: As a miniature angel, draws the protection of the child's guardian angel.

ANIMALS: For kittens and puppies separated from their mother.

PROTECTION: Radiates a shield of light around those living alone or in unsafe areas; removes negativity from any situation.

MAGICKAL AND PSYCHIC USES

Protects against psychological or psychic attack while sleeping; cleanses and energizes other crystals; fills the energy system with light that can be channeled into healing.

SPECIAL PROPERTIES

Also known as cave calcite, Clear or White Calcite encourages care of the environment through practical efforts, including Earth- and climate-healing rituals.

MYTHOLOGY AND HISTORY

Much gentler than clear quartz, Clear Aragonite initiates changes where people are emotionally sensitive or set in their ways. Aragonite increases generosity in the workplace, family, and community, not only in money, but in time, resources, ideas, and praise.

Cleavelandite

COLORS: Creamy white, white, clear

CRYSTAL TYPE: Silicate, plagioclase feldspar; a bladed form of albite that forms snowflake patterns as clusters; can often be found interspersed with or as a matrix of such crystals as smoky quartz, apatite, tourmaline, mica, lepidolite, and amazonite

ZODIAC SIGN: Libra (September 23–October 23)

CANDLE COLOR: White

PHYSICAL: Alleviates brain malfunctions involving blood vessels, tremors, dyspraxia, epilepsy; promotes gentle recovery after time in intensive care or an induced coma; useful following life-changing illnesses or accidents.

EMOTIONAL: Minimizes a superiority complex, excluding those who are regarded as less academic or of lower status.

HOME: A bringing-together stone, particularly where there are twinned crystals, of two families on remarriage, especially step-grandparents, so no one feels left out or resentful.

WORKPLACE: For working positively through major career changes due to closure, takeover, or downsizing.

CHILDREN: Keep in the home to convince a child of their value and unique gifts if they are excluded socially by peers or underrated academically by teachers.

ANIMALS: Aids in accepting that a pet bought for showing, competing, or breeding is happiest as a domestic animal and not destined for greatness.

PROTECTION: Guards against dissatisfaction with life as it is.

MAGICKAL AND PSYCHIC USES

For coming to terms with a near-death encounter, an intense religious awakening, or a life-changing spiritual experience; spending time in an ashram, a Buddhist temple, or spiritual retreat.

SPECIAL PROPERTIES

Cleavelandite restores a sense of contentment if family members, a partner, or close friends are restless or going through a period of transition; eases midlife crises in both sexes, encouraging positive changes in lifestyle within existing relationships rather than beyond them.

MYTHOLOGY AND HISTORY

Cleavelandite guides journeying, whether on a vision quest, a spiritual pilgrimage, or exploration of places untouched by time, incorporating long-distance or long-term travel.

Clinohumite

COLORS: Orange, honey, light yellow, brown-yellow, reddish-brown; bright as a tumbled stone or faceted; more common in non-gem variety

CRYSTAL TYPE: Silicate and oxide layers; magnesium silicate

ZODIAC SIGN: Sagittarius (November 23–December 21)

CANDLE COLOR: Orange

PHYSICAL: Alleviates issues involving the liver, pancreas, kidneys, gall and kidney stones, stomach disorders made worse by stress, IBS; strengthens eyes and night vision; improves artery health; aids in recovery from bypass surgery.

EMOTIONAL: Counters lack of confidence in self that causes over-reliance on others.

HOME: In yellow and orange, a stone that spreads happiness on the coldest, darkest day; repels the toxicity of hostile neighbors.

WORKPLACE: For stressful jobs involving long hours of detail and routine that lead to careless mistakes.

CHILDREN: For teens reluctant to study for a long-term future; as an amulet of protection for babies and small children.

ANIMALS: Protects prize or show animals from being stolen.

PROTECTION: Guards against attacks of any kind at night.

MAGICKAL AND PSYCHIC USES

For clairvoyance, remote viewing of absent people and scenes over long distances, spontaneous accurate predictions; enhances intuition.

SPECIAL PROPERTIES

For beginning a new gentle fitness regimen and nutritional plan; Clinohumite takes away misfortune and fears of being jinxed that can cause accidents or anxiety.

MYTHOLOGY AND HISTORY

Clinohumite was first discovered in 1876 in limestone blocks that had erupted from Mount Vesuvius in Italy. Legend holds that yellow Clinohumite stones are pieces of the sun that were ripped off when it was defending the inhabitants of the Pamir Mountains in Tajikistan against nomads during a nighttime battle in a place now called Fire Mountain; considered a lucky charm in the region for births and weddings, and placed in cradles and tombs for protection.

Clinozoisite

COLORS: Golden brown to coffee-colored; also colorless, yellow, pink to rose red, and green; colors will be mixed in the stone; may be transparent or translucent

CRYSTAL TYPE: Calcium aluminum, sorosilicate; member of the Epidote family (page 178); contains small quantities of iron; also sold as tumbled stones or in jewelry

ZODIAC SIGN: Cancer (June 22–July 22)

CANDLE COLOR: Pink

PHYSICAL: Aids recovery after illness, surgery, or necessary radiation therapy; works as a detoxifier; alleviates issues involving the heart, lungs, pancreas, gallbladder, liver, spleen, stress-related stomach upset and conditions caused by overly rich or fatty foods; mitigates lactose intolerance.

EMOTIONAL: Eases heartbreak and heartache; promotes forgiveness of self or others for mistakes; counters repressing positive as well as negative emotions.

HOME: For bonding in families during times of crisis or when new members enter through remarriage; creating friendships in communal residential settings.

WORKPLACE: Reveals who is loyal and reliable and who has their own secret agenda; for alliances with coworkers to tackle workplace inadequacies.

CHILDREN: For children hurt by the disappearance of a parent from their lives, when the parent refuses to maintain contact.

ANIMALS: Soothes pets who find it hard to share an owner's attention.

PROTECTION: Removes unwanted entities and earthly stalkers or those obsessed with the minutiae of another person's life.

MAGICKAL AND PSYCHIC USES

Psychic defense during astral travel or while communicating with spirits in a séance; increases telepathy with children, partners, and parents.

SPECIAL PROPERTIES

Enhances self-love and self-respect rather than trying to be what others expect; boosts love and sexual magnetism with a partner or attracting the right person who will return loyalty and devotion.

MYTHOLOGY AND HISTORY

A stone associated with cooperation and collective interests, rather than going it alone; for natural introverts, it helps make a positive impression in interviews and appraisals.

Cloud Agate

COLOR: Gray, bluish-gray, blue, light gray, off-white, with gray, white, or black cloud-like markings or blurry, misty, patchy inclusions

CRYSTAL TYPE: Chalcedony, cryptocrystalline quartz

ZODIAC SIGN: Gemini (May 22–June 21)

CANDLE COLOR: Gray

PHYSICAL: Relieves recurring headaches, migraines causing visual disturbances, dizziness, hearing issues, fevers, chronic pain, blocked or narrowed arteries; addresses issues involving the bone marrow; promotes recovery following invasive treatment or surgery.

EMOTIONAL: Soothes acute anxiety; counters the inability to switch off, workaholic tendencies, and OCD.

HOME: Insulates against noisy neighbors, overly loud social settings, or a family for whom everything is full volume.

WORKPLACE: Guards against computer hackers, intrusive colleagues; for working in public service industries, high-profile careers; valuable in jobs where unobtrusiveness is essential, such as surveillance or security.

CHILDREN: Helps older children keep their rooms and possessions safe from younger siblings; for overactive children.

ANIMALS: For secretive or nocturnal animals, and protection of their habitats.

PROTECTION: Guards against psychic intrusion, mind control, and spirit possession.

MAGICKAL AND PSYCHIC USES

Weather magick for bringing rain; cloud divination; candlelight scrying in dark spheres; connecting with guardians and ancestors through dark mirrors.

SPECIAL PROPERTIES

Prevents falls by small children, older people, or those with mobility or balance problems; prevents accidents with sharp implements or tools.

MYTHOLOGY AND HISTORY

Once believed to bring physical invisibility, in modern times used to lower psychological profile in danger. A stone associated with necessary secrecy, twin Cloud Agates are a natural talisman of secret love between two people, one kept by each person.

Cobalt Aura

COLOR: Brilliant shades of metallic royal blue, violet, and gold, mixed together

CRYSTAL TYPE: Molecules of pure cobalt bonded by a natural electric charge to clear quartz

ZODIAC SIGN: Sagittarius (November 23–December 21)

CANDLE COLOR: Bright blue

PHYSICAL: Addresses cellular disorders; boosts the immune system; for those unresponsive to treatment or exhausted by prolonged medical intervention; complements the work of enzymes, myelin sheath, glucose processing.

EMOTIONAL: Alleviates claustrophobia, agoraphobia, phobias keeping you from working or socializing outside the home, fear of elevators.

HOME: Brings family together in shared activities if technology causes isolation.

WORKPLACE: For participating in and organizing creative exhibitions; removes self-limiting blocks; for culinary endeavors, especially competitions or writing cookbooks, and for restaurant owners; makes an impersonal workplace more welcoming.

CHILDREN: Encourages those with exceptional artistic talents who find everyday life hard.

ANIMALS: For rainbow-colored birds, chameleons, brightly colored frogs, butterflies, and dragonflies.

PROTECTION: Guards against negative entities and specters of the night.

MAGICKAL AND PSYCHIC USES

Increases natural clairvoyance; for working in a healing center, festival, or expo to keep your space cleansed of negative energies from visitors passing too close; promotes alchemy and transformation magick; aids in discovering hidden magickal places.

SPECIAL PROPERTIES

For building a dream home or redecorating and renovating to transform your living space, whether a tiny city apartment or a huge rural property.

MYTHOLOGY AND HISTORY

An alchemist stone, where bonded cobalt and quartz create a more powerful crystal than the separate components; the smallest piece is equally potent for healing, empowerment, and protection.

Cobaltoan Calcite

COLORS: Magenta, but may be rose, salmon, or paler pink (see also Mangano Calcite or Manganoan Calcite, page 291)

CRYSTAL TYPE: Calcium carbonate, containing cobalt, the amount of cobalt determining the richness of the pink

ZODIAC SIGN: Taurus (April 21–May 21)

CANDLE COLOR: Bright pink

PHYSICAL: Alleviates heart problems, especially in babies, children, and young people; addresses issues involving puberty, menstrual problems and irregularities; for teenage mothers; aids in recovery from hysterectomy.

EMOTIONAL: Counters fear of letting down your guard and showing emotion; counters lack of self-love and care while pouring devotion into others; mitigates eating disorders.

HOME: Creates a loving home; calms overactive Earth energies, causing restlessness in certain rooms.

WORKPLACE: For those who create healing artifacts; enhances therapeutic careers relieving the pain of abuse and suffering of others without absorbing that pain or overempathizing.

CHILDREN: After a divorce, reassures a child who feels pressured by splitting time between two homes; for fostering and adopting children.

ANIMALS: Persuades a pet to welcome a young animal into the family.

PROTECTION: Guards against becoming a martyr for others and then resenting when they are not grateful.

MAGICKAL AND PSYCHIC USES

For distance healing, fertility rituals if conception is not occurring in a new relationship; calls a soul twin later in life.

SPECIAL PROPERTIES

Under its name as the "Aphrodite stone," dedicated to the ancient Greek love goddess Aphrodite, Cobaltoan Calcite is a powerful talisman for calling both new and restored love. Enables you to sever ties with someone overreliant on your fixing their problems.

MYTHOLOGY AND HISTORY

Also called cobaltian, cobalt or cobalto calcite, big sister of soft pink mangano calcite; brings tough love to remove dependency in those who go from one guru to another seeking answers to situations only they can resolve.

Code Keeper of Freedom, Root or Mother of Lemuria

COLORS: Clear inside with etchings and markings on the surface, regarded by some as codes to ancient wisdom

CRYSTAL TYPE: Quartz, silicon dioxide

ZODIAC SIGN: Aquarius (January 21–February 18)

CANDLE COLOR: White

PHYSICAL: Clears up confusion after a major operation or prolonged anesthetic; addresses memory loss; promotes whole-body, mind, and soul healing; alleviates symptoms of Parkinson's, multiple sclerosis, motor neurone disease, Huntington's chorea.

EMOTIONAL: Counters brainwashing by extreme cults, communities, or religions with rigid rules and prohibitions; keeps you from blindly accepting and following the opinions of others.

HOME: Prompts younger family members to show respect and regard for your knowledge and experience.

WORKPLACE: Promotes humanitarian projects, charity work, Doctors Without Borders (*Médecins Sans Frontières*), overseas aid, volunteer and paid work.

CHILDREN: For Star Children and very old souls.

ANIMALS: For pets that return to life in different forms.

PROTECTION: Guards against being pressured to act against principles and conform to a repressive situation.

MAGICKAL AND PSYCHIC USES

For ascending to higher spiritual levels to access the higher self, wise archangels, teacher guides and ascended masters.

SPECIAL PROPERTIES

The Code Keeper of Freedom enables those who use it to discover or rediscover their true soul purpose.

MYTHOLOGY AND HISTORY

The Code Keeper of Freedom was recently discovered in Minas Gerais, Brazil. Often called the Root of Lemuria or the Mother of Lemuria because Lemurian seed crystals grow on top of it, it is said to be the key to the knowledge of Old Lemuria (see Lemurian Seed Crystal, page 275); empowers other crystals.

Coffee or Coffee Bean Jasper

COLORS: Also called mocha coffee jasper, brown and cream in bands or swirls resembling cream being stirred into coffee; may contain splashes of rust-black or gray

CRYSTAL TYPE: Microcrystalline quartz, chalcedony

ZODIAC SIGN: Virgo (August 24–September 22)

CANDLE COLOR: Brown

PHYSICAL: Counters intolerance of caffeine and artificial stimulants or additives in food and drink; purifies and oxygenates blood; regulates and balances insulin production; promotes fertility for natural conception, IVF, and artificial insemination.

EMOTIONAL: Alleviates panic attacks and free-floating fears not triggered by an actual cause; aids in quitting smoking; reduces the psychological effects of prolonged physical inactivity.

HOME: For tea and coffee afternoons to get to know neighbors better; for potluck suppers and wine-and-cheese gatherings to widen your local friendship group and raise money for charity.

WORKPLACE: If you encounter an actual or psychological toxicity, Coffee Jasper acts as a shield; prompts you to take regular breaks, both screen breaks and time away from the workspace.

CHILDREN: Helps children who feel they are unlucky or are always overlooked for privileges and praise to brighten their aura energies so they attract positive reactions and increased visibility.

ANIMALS: Protects pets from unfriendly neighbors and visitors.

PROTECTION: Guards against unfriendly ghosts and restless spirits.

MAGICKAL AND PSYCHIC USES

Tea leaf, coffee ground, and wine dreg divination; Earth rituals; herbs in water scrying; natural magick.

SPECIAL PROPERTIES

Attracts fortunate coincidences; in love, psychically calls the person you most want to notice you.

MYTHOLOGY AND HISTORY

Used in societies for thousands of years, including ancient Egypt for carving amulets and ritual artifacts and as protective arrowhead charms among Native Americans; found in Australia, Canada, Egypt, India, and China, where it is more of a siltstone; a dual-action stone, removing what is unhelpful and replacing it with new energies and opportunities.

Colemanite

COLORS: Milky white, white with shades of yellow and gray; may be colorless and brilliant or pearly

CRYSTAL TYPE: Hydrated calcium borate hydroxide, fluorescent and with a mild electrical charge under change in temperature

ZODIAC SIGN: Gemini (May 22–June 21)

CANDLE COLOR: White

PHYSICAL: Addresses issues involving the gynecological system and female fertility; promotes circulation; acts as a detoxifier; alleviates major acute conditions; increases energy to the heart and lungs; heightens the power of acupressure.

EMOTIONAL: For compensatory excesses and overindulgence; aids in surviving dark times when the natural desire is to give up.

HOME: Strengthens patience and tolerance with vulnerable but challenging family members.

WORKPLACE: Encourages thinking outside the box; for brainstorming sessions; makes the workplace environmentally friendly.

CHILDREN: Kept in a play or therapy room, encourages withdrawn or solitary children to interact more with their peers.

ANIMALS: Reassures and comforts overworked or abused animals in animal sanctuaries.

PROTECTION: Prevents psychic intrusion or mind manipulation by others.

MAGICKAL AND PSYCHIC USES

For dowsing, especially finding minerals or water in unfamiliar locations; discovering answers with a pendulum; connecting with the higher self and divinity through automatic writing or trance meditation.

SPECIAL PROPERTIES

Linked with studying and practicing the arts, as well as holistic and herbal medicine; has intense energies so do not use Colemanite in healing for prolonged periods, but this crystal is ideal for a sudden infusion of healing or for the power to release an energy block.

MYTHOLOGY AND HISTORY

Often used with the similar mineral Tunellite as a pair to remove unwanted emotional or psychic attachments that cause a return to a destructive situation or relationship.

Colombianite

COLORS: Lavender-gray, smoky gray; if held to the light, Colombianite reflects smoky or yellowish light

CRYSTAL TYPE: Tektite, created by the fall of a large meteorite five million years ago

ZODIAC SIGN: Scorpio (October 24–November 22)

CANDLE COLOR: Silver

PHYSICAL: Promotes whole-body healing; healing through prayer; for brain disorders; eases the passing to the next world.

EMOTIONAL: Counters fear of being condemned to misfortune because of inherited karma; loss of faith in religion, people, and life.

HOME: Aids in finding the right home or making your existing home perfect for you.

WORKPLACE: For all careers involving helping humanity; for starting your own spiritual sanctuary or school of healing.

CHILDREN: Helps Star Seed, Indigo, or Crystal Children, who may be misunderstood, to develop coping strategies for everyday living.

ANIMALS: For connecting with spirit totem animals from ancient cultures, which may have been with you in many lifetimes.

PROTECTION: Guards against predatory spirits, black magick, and the evil eye.

MAGICKAL AND PSYCHIC USES

Predictions, prophecy, communication with extraterrestrials, mystical visions; alchemy; initiation into Wicca, druidry, and the priesthood of other faiths.

SPECIAL PROPERTIES

Reinforces awareness that we are spiritual beings in a physical body; prompts enlightenment in whatever way is most desired or needed.

MYTHOLOGY AND HISTORY

With gentler energies than the magickal Cintamani (or Chintamani) stone, Colombianite is found only in Colombia and Peru and is sacred to the Colombian Indigenous people of the Muisca nation (also called *Chibcha*). Their civilization, which dates back to 1500 BCE, was famed for gifts in crafting gold and was associated with the mystical El Dorado. Colombianite is called by them *Piedra Rayo*, "lightning stone" or the "stone of light." It promises light at the end of any tunnel; reveals a seemingly impossible way ahead; enables you to live according to your own beliefs.

Color-Changing Sapphire

COLORS: Generally blue in natural light, changing to light purple or deep violet in electric light or candlelight

CRYSTAL TYPE: Corundum; impurities such as chromium and vanadium cause the color change

ZODIAC SIGN: Sagittarius (November 23–December 21)

CANDLE COLOR: Violet

PHYSICAL: Alleviates epilepsy, ear infections, communication difficulties in a progressive illness; addresses gender issues.

EMOTIONAL: Works if you're unresponsive to psychiatric or psychological intervention or pharmaceutical treatment for depression or personality disorders.

HOME: For redecorating or refurbishing your home the way you like it; introducing your family to nutritional and fitness regimens.

WORKPLACE: Helpful in juggling two part-time jobs or when you're in transition between careers and have to manage both; for jobs requiring a more public and visible role.

CHILDREN: Keep Color-Changing Sapphire with a photograph of a special needs child as a reminder that their talents, not their limitations, will triumph.

ANIMALS: For adopting a former therapy or show animal as a pet.

PROTECTION: Guards against those who use charm to defraud or deceive.

MAGICKAL AND PSYCHIC USES

If you practice the psychic arts, aids in healing or mediumship in the evenings and weekends while pursuing a conventional daytime career.

SPECIAL PROPERTIES

The chameleon of the sapphires, for changing your image and the way people view you; encourages new activities and new interests.

MYTHOLOGY AND HISTORY

The stone of seizing the best of both worlds, incorporating a freer more fulfilling lifestyle without walking away from what is good; as a love token in same-sex marriages or formal commitments.

Colored Crackle Quartz

COLORS: A variety of dyed bright colors, including purple, pink, red, orange, green, and yellow (see Fire and Ice Quartz, page 187, which is usually but not always clear crackle quartz)
CRYSTAL TYPE: Natural quartz, fractured by heating and cooling under pressure to create fissures and sparkles; brittle
ZODIAC SIGN: Aries (March 21–April 20)
CANDLE COLOR: White

PHYSICAL: Strengthens heart, lungs, and immune system; alleviates fractures, brittle bones, osteoporosis; promotes overall health and stamina.
EMOTIONAL: Counters depression, a sense of disillusionment with people and life, belief in ill fortune or curses blighting every endeavor.
HOME: A bowl filled with Colored Crackle Quartz in all the rainbow colors, placed in the center of the home, draws health, abundance, fun, laughter, and good fortune.
WORKPLACE: For artists, interior designers, and children's artists, writers, and illustrators; protects against plagiarism and jealous rivals.
CHILDREN: Often the first crystal chosen because of the bright colors; ideal for storytelling about crystal fairies.
ANIMALS: Green and blue Crackle Quartz helps maintain health in pets.
PROTECTION: Purple or red Crackle Quartz guards against earthly aggression and unfriendly spooks; all colors of this crystal repel evil.

MAGICKAL AND PSYCHIC USES
Green for good fortune, blue for career advancement, purple for increasing spiritual gifts, red for success and power, orange for independence, yellow for money; purple or blue Crackle Quartz for yoga or any energy therapy. Pick one each morning with your eyes closed to tune in to the required energies of the day ahead.
SPECIAL PROPERTIES
A crystal of pure life force, Crackle Quartz in all its colors successfully speeds new beginnings.
MYTHOLOGY AND HISTORY
The rainbow crystals allow your inner child to come out and play, and bring hope no matter how daunting the task.

Colorless or Clear Zircon

COLORS: Colorless with brilliant flashes of multicolored light, giving it inner fire
CRYSTAL TYPE: Zirconium silicate, the purest form of zircon
ZODIAC SIGN: Leo (July 23–August 23)
CANDLE COLOR: White

PHYSICAL: Aids in preventing infection from superbugs such as MRSA, *c. Clostridium difficile*; assists in alleviating the symptoms of diabetes.
EMOTIONAL: Dispels the dark night of the soul; dissipates fears of possession by evil spirits after dabbling in the occult or curses on family or land from past generations.
HOME: Clears the home of unfriendly ghosts, blocked Earth energies, and any misfortune, lingering sickness, or sorrow from recent events.
WORKPLACE: Promotes prosperity through being in the right place at the right time and meeting the right people; enables you to rapidly gain a good reputation.
CHILDREN: Brings happiness into your life with children, whether through giving birth, stepparenting, adoption, fostering, or becoming involved with youngsters professionally.
ANIMALS: For a pet who picks up one illness or infection after another.
PROTECTION: Guards against racism, sexism, ageism, homophobic tendencies, and all prejudice against fellow humans.

MAGICKAL AND PSYCHIC USES
A crystal of pure light for removing hexes and curses—recent and from earlier generations; heals land where nothing grows.
SPECIAL PROPERTIES
A beautiful and less expensive substitute for diamonds for betrothals as a symbol of lasting love; beware of being sold artificially made cubic zirconia.
MYTHOLOGY AND HISTORY
A stone for getting a lucky break in any of the creative or performing arts if you have encountered closed doors; for writers to find the right publisher or outlet; for a way into your desired media profession.

Conch or Nassau Pearl

COLORS: Usually pink but can be white, beige, yellow, brown, or golden

CRYSTAL TYPE: Calcareous concretion; oval; produced by the queen conch, a large sea snail prized for its meat

ZODIAC SIGN: Cancer (June 22–July 22)

CANDLE COLOR: Silver

PHYSICAL: Alleviates issues relating to the breasts, ovaries, fertility, skin, hormones, fluid imbalances, PMS, scars.

EMOTIONAL: Helps overcome a poor self-image and the tendency to wait for the perfect moment or ideal opportunity.

HOME: Draws the family safely home at night; for discovering secrets, especially concerning addictions.

WORKPLACE: For beauticians; therapists helping those who self-harm or have eating disorders.

CHILDREN: A special gift at birth and at key milestones, made into jewelry or a talisman on the 18th birthday.

ANIMALS: For endangered marine life, clear oceans, and rivers.

PROTECTION: Guards against fears of drowning, swimming, sailing, or traveling by sea.

MAGICKAL AND PSYCHIC USES

Foretelling the future within the pearl; clairaudience using a conch shell to receive messages from water spirits.

SPECIAL PROPERTIES

The only pearls created with no human intervention, when an irritant such as a piece of broken shell enters the conch naturally; very rare—only about 1 in 10,000–15,000 conch shells contains pearls; no longer permitted to be caught in some areas.

MYTHOLOGY AND HISTORY

Ix Chel, the Mayan moon and conch shell goddess, loved the sun god, but all the other gods were jealous and pursued her; she was hidden within a giant conch shell in the sea until reunited with her love. It is said that whoever gives or receives a conch pearl will love forever; found in the Caribbean.

Conglomerate Stone

COLORS: Variety of vivid colors, depending on the composition of stones within

CRYSTAL TYPE: Used frequently as a tumbled stone, a palm stone, or in jewelry; a conglomerate stone, as the name suggests, which varies in its composition; a sedimentary rock containing round pebbles, greater than two millimeters in diameter, sometimes chert or limestone; formed naturally where smoothed, broken-off fragments of rock accumulate, the spaces filled with sand, silt or clay particles, often cemented in a matrix of calcite or quartz

ZODIAC SIGN: Aquarius (January 21–February 18)

CANDLE COLOR: Green

PHYSICAL: Speeds healing of fractures; alleviates issues involving connective tissues, cells; boosts energy and vitality.

EMOTIONAL: Helps overcome claustrophobia; extreme dislike of social gatherings.

HOME: Strengthens family and friendship bonds; encourages reunions between the generations.

WORKPLACE: For those in leadership positions; promotes team building and successful merging of different departments or companies.

CHILDREN: Encourages them to become team players.

ANIMALS: For successful breeding programs, both for profit and in the world of conservation.

PROTECTION: Guards against loneliness or exclusion by cliques.

MAGICKAL AND PSYCHIC USES

Strengthens links with ancestors, both those recently deceased and more distant relatives with whom you have an affinity.

SPECIAL PROPERTIES

Since the pebbles within Conglomerate Stone are naturally water-smoothed and broken fragments of older rocks, cemented together, this is a stone for reconciliation in love, and remarriage after being divorced.

MYTHOLOGY AND HISTORY

Since the minerals your Conglomerate Stone contains are largely unknown, this crystal represents taking a chance, knowing you will be provided with the necessary resources. Conglomerate pebbles are tumbled through running water or waves, to give them their signature rounded shape; a stone of adaptability to the current needs and wisdom through experience.

Connemara Marble

COLORS: Rich to pale green; may contain gray and brown
CRYSTAL TYPE: Calcite marble with large quantities of
serpentine; also diopside and chlorite (all
green) and calcite with dolomite (white)
ZODIAC SIGN: Virgo (August 24–
September 22)
CANDLE COLOR: Green

PHYSICAL: Addresses issues relating to bone marrow,
bone strength, back weaknesses; defends against viruses and
bacteria that are slow to clear or return; alleviates indigestion and
high blood pressure.
EMOTIONAL: Counters an obsession to own whatever is new or
high-end designer-made; fears of natural aging.
HOME: Connects with ancestral lines overseas, whatever your
root culture; useful for returning to live in an area where you spent
your childhood or happy years.
WORKPLACE: For practicing traditional crafts and setting up a craft
workshop or community; finding a meaningful role in a family
business where you can develop your own ideas.
CHILDREN: Often presented to parents of newborn babes as a
talisman through life for health, wealth, and good fortune.
ANIMALS: Revives and maintains ancient breeds or those
indigenous to the area where you live or work.
PROTECTION: Guards against ageism, forced redundancy, or early
retirement if that's not what you want.

MAGICKAL AND PSYCHIC USES
Using the Celtic Ogham tree stave divination method, knot
magick; Earth energies at ancient sites and on ley or fey paths,
especially in Ireland; connection with the fey, especially the little
people of Ireland, and leprechauns.
SPECIAL PROPERTIES
Each piece is uniquely patterned; a marble for all who have
Gaelic or Celtic ancestry, however distant.
MYTHOLOGY AND HISTORY
Called the gemstone of Ireland and crafted into beautiful jewelry
and artifacts, and as tumbled stones, Connemara Marble is found
only in Connemara, County Galway, in the West of Ireland. It is
900 million years old. The Blarney stone is made of Connemara
Marble, and so is associated with wishes.

Cookeite

COLORS: Pale blue, pink, yellow, green, purple, brown
CRYSTAL TYPE: Chlorite and lithium; tabular crystals that are rare;
may be found included in quartz that is more manageable for
healing and magick; can be a coating on pink tourmaline
ZODIAC SIGN: Libra (September 23–October 23)
CANDLE COLOR: Blue

PHYSICAL: Helps overcome plant and fur allergies; alleviates
muscle spasms and locking; relieves insomnia and sleep apnea;
addresses issues involving the small intestine and absorption
of nutrients.
EMOTIONAL: Counters tactlessness, speaking before thinking;
eases panic attacks and fears of the unknown.
HOME: Keeps away hostile or distressed spirits and cleanses the
atmosphere if you have moved into premises where previously
there had been unhappiness, divorce, bereavement, or violence.
WORKPLACE: Increases sales; aids in solving a problem that has
eluded a solution by reexamining all the data.
CHILDREN: Creates the right atmosphere for home study in a noisy
or crowded house; for those with a school phobia.
ANIMALS: For pets oversensitive to outside stimuli.
PROTECTION: A powerful shield and block against psychic attack
and all who intend harm physically and psychologically.

MAGICKAL AND PSYCHIC USES
For ceremonies and celebrations to draw participants together, even
if they're strangers, and ensure the magickal flow among them.
SPECIAL PROPERTIES
When found with or within quartz, Cookeite is amplified
in its protective powers; if family mealtimes are chaotic
or confrontational, encourages a lively but positive and
unhurried atmosphere.
MYTHOLOGY AND HISTORY
A prosperity stone that draws in financial opportunities, especially
in business. A stone of positive communication and community
to emphasize similarities, rather than differences. Cookeite
was discovered in 1866 and is named after Josiah Parsons
Cooke Jr., a Harvard University scientist known for his work in the
measurement of atomic weights. Cookeite is sometimes found as
the blue inclusions in blue smoke or Blue Mist Quartz (page 78)
recently discovered in Colombia.

Copal

COLORS: Yellow to golden, red to brown

CRYSTAL TYPE: Oxygenated resinous hydrocarbon; resin collected from living tropical trees, found in soil beneath trees or mined if buried; buried Copal tends to take a more solid form. Copal is younger amber, less than 100,000 years old

ZODIAC SIGN: Aries (March 21–April 20)

CANDLE COLOR: Red

PHYSICAL: Promotes fertility; eases childbirth; alleviates issues relating to the heart, diminished energy, kidneys, bladder, stomach, dermatitis, impetigo, deeper causes of illness; aids in recovery after surgery.

EMOTIONAL: Counters undesirable influences, addictions, depression, anxiety, fears of the supernatural after a negative psychic experience.

HOME: Brings blessings of the ancestors, especially around Halloween; cleanses rooms, artifacts, and crystals.

WORKPLACE: Leads to fulfillment of major ambitions; useful for fieldwork in charitable organizations; valuable for teachers of mediumship, magick, druidry, energy therapies, meditation, or yoga.

CHILDREN: Encourages old souls, and Indigo and Star Children to reveal their abilities with crystals from an early age.

ANIMALS: For working with magickal animals, such as the phoenix, thunderbird, and unicorn.

PROTECTION: As Copal nuggets, jewelry, or incense, guards against bad atmospheres, malevolent spirits, and the evil eye.

MAGICKAL AND PSYCHIC USES

Because Copal melts at a lower temperature than amber, it's often burned as sacred incense on charcoal; brings on altered states of consciousness; draws assistance from the spirits for healing.

SPECIAL PROPERTIES

Connects with ancient formal rituals, evoking memories of priestess/priestly traditions, temples, and ceremonies.

MYTHOLOGY AND HISTORY

Among the Aztecs in the early 1500s, Copal was burned on braziers carved with the image of Chalchiuhtlicue, goddess of water and fertility; it was also sacred to her rain-god husband, Tlaloc. Fossil Copal from London blue clay is called copalite or Highgate resin.

Copper

COLORS: Burnished golden-reddish bronze

CRYSTAL TYPE: Metal nuggets or dendritic leaf-like formations

ZODIAC SIGN: Taurus (April 21–May 21)

CANDLE COLOR: Green

PHYSICAL: Alleviates circulation issues, infected wounds, rheumatism, arthritis, stiffness and swelling of hands and feet, exhaustion, motion sickness; promotes fertility, healthy weight loss; boosts libido, particularly in women.

EMOTIONAL: Helps overcome disconnection with people, constantly seeking new experiences, and risk-taking.

HOME: Copper nuggets attract money and good luck; Copper ornaments insulate against storm, fire, and flood, and attract good friends and neighbors.

WORKPLACE: Keeps business opportunities flowing your way; prevents office romances from interfering with professionalism; motivates lethargic employees or colleagues; persuades difficult clients to accept your advice.

CHILDREN: Prevents car sickness; helps youngsters learn the value of money.

ANIMALS: Settles restless pets; eases their way when moving to a new home.

PROTECTION: Guards against jealous romantic rivals.

MAGICKAL AND PSYCHIC USES

Activates instinctive radar to find lost items or pets; Copper angle rods locate subterranean minerals or water; useful as a magick wand; promotes fertility and enhances love spells; energizes other crystals; boosts telepathy.

SPECIAL PROPERTIES

Calls love at first sight and lasting love. Copper is sacred to love goddesses, the Greek Aphrodite and the Roman goddess Venus; the metal most commonly associated with the planet Venus; a Copper ring on the heart finger attracts love at any age.

MYTHOLOGY AND HISTORY

The Keweenaw Peninsula in Michigan is the world's largest source of Copper; Copper artifacts were made here by Indigenous people seven thousand years ago. Neolithic people adopted Copper as a substitute for stone by 8000 BCE. Copper leaves are a traditional good luck charm.

Copperlite

COLORS: Deep black/very dark red with squarish flecks and copper/bronze-colored flashes

CRYSTAL TYPE: Black galaxy granite; contains ferrous-rich bronzite

ZODIAC SIGN: Capricorn (December 22–January 20)

CANDLE COLOR: Dark red

PHYSICAL: Balances blood sugar; aids digestion, circulation, fertility; counters motion sickness, stiffness and swelling of hands and feet, especially due to fluid retention.

EMOTIONAL: Kindles difficult or nonexistent relationships with fathers and other older male relatives; keeps you from repeating past mistakes in new situations; banishes irrational jealousy.

HOME: A stone to infuse the home with the right amount of life force, when needed, to balance enthusiasm and stability, activity and quiet times.

WORKPLACE: Cultivates prosperity through investment, networking, and seeking new sources of income that may not at first seem obvious; keeps you from taking personal problems to work and work problems home.

CHILDREN: For teens who have difficulties with authority figures; for finding suitable employment during your vacation.

ANIMALS: Helps older, less mobile pets to create their own pace of life and find a quiet place to rest.

PROTECTION: Breaks negative karmic connections; guards against present and future mind manipulation.

MAGICKAL AND PSYCHIC USES

Money and speculation/gambling spells; understanding fears and phobias from past worlds and so overcoming them; for psychic shielding against malign spirits and earthly ill-wishers.

SPECIAL PROPERTIES

A stone with strong animus properties that benefits both sexes who want to become more assertive and take more initiative; counters bullying or unfair criticism or discouraging voices lingering from the past.

MYTHOLOGY AND HISTORY

This rare stone from India is often mistaken for Greenland nuumite and is also called coppernite, or, more commonly, Indian nuumite. Indian nuumite works more gradually than the Greenland form (many say Greenland has the true nuumite). The Indian version lets old sorrows and grievances flow away and brings a period of stability.

Coprolite

COLORS: Mottled brown, bluish-gray, beige; may have flecks of red

CRYSTAL TYPE: Fossilized animal feces, usually from dinosaurs, where the original form has been replaced by minerals, such as silicate and calcium carbonate

ZODIAC SIGN: Capricorn (December 22–January 20)

CANDLE COLOR: Brown

PHYSICAL: Promotes digestion; eliminates toxins from the body; aids in assimilation of nutrients; addresses issues relating to OCD, skeletal misalignment, IBS, celiac disease, lactose intolerance, irregular bowel movements.

EMOTIONAL: Counters an unwillingness to spend money and hoarding old or unwanted items.

HOME: Encourages moving on from the old to the new, whether a new house location or lifestyle; for spring cleaning any time of the year.

WORKPLACE: Cuts through unnecessary jargon, doublespeak, and seeming expertise not based on knowledge; clears up the mistakes of others.

CHILDREN: Aids in overcoming fear of monsters, ghosts, demons, and nighttime dream foes; helps if children tend to give up too easily.

ANIMALS: For pets slow to become litter-trained or who spray the home when a new pet arrives.

PROTECTION: GUARDS against evil entities and psychic attack generated by our own fears.

MAGICKAL AND PSYCHIC USES

Past-life regression; banishing magick; meditation to connect with plants, animals, and scenes from ancient times; as an amulet against harm and a money-attracting charm.

SPECIAL PROPERTIES

For overcoming seemingly insurmountable challenges. Choose the Coprolite from the kind of creature you most need for strength, whether a sea creature or a plant or a meat-eating dinosaur for fierce defense or fighting for what you want; Coprolite may contain small bones, sinews, fish scales, seeds.

MYTHOLOGY AND HISTORY

First discovered by the British fossil collector Mary Anning in the early 1800s along the Jurassic Coast around Lyme Regis, Dorset, Coprolite may be found all around the world in sedimentary deposits. Makes beautiful jewelry when polished, though not the most romantic gift.

Cordierite

COLORS: Medium to dark blue, greenish, yellowish, gray, brown, or colorless

CRYSTAL TYPE: Non-gem version of Iolite Sunstone (page 255); magnesium aluminum silicate, almost always containing iron, with etches, striated, or as waterworn pebbles

ZODIAC SIGN: Libra (September 23–October 23)

CANDLE COLOR: Blue

PHYSICAL: Counters deteriorating vision through age, cataracts, or glaucoma; addresses issues involving the ears, sinuses, nails; alleviates hirsutism and excess testosterone in women and hormone imbalances in both sexes; aids in recovery from liver transplants.

EMOTIONAL: Helps in managing OCD and being ruled by the clock; keeps you from approaching situations from a negative perspective and infecting others with gloom.

HOME: A crystal for eliminating debt, making necessary economies, and negotiating with creditors.

WORKPLACE: Assesses odds in horse racing and professional gambling, using formulas and/or computer projections, combined with intuition.

CHILDREN: For psychic teenagers and children whose paranormal experiences interfere with sleep and everyday life; for codependent twins or triplets.

ANIMALS: Keeps deceased pets from making their presence known around their former homes; helps a resident spirit animal move on.

PROTECTION: Fills the aura with light; transforms pessimism into hope and clear solutions.

MAGICKAL AND PSYCHIC USES

For goddess rituals; channels emerging psychic awareness if you're afraid of spontaneous premonitions.

SPECIAL PROPERTIES

Helps gentle men, from macho families or workplaces, who are expected to hide emotion; for women to express power without being overly assertive.

MYTHOLOGY AND HISTORY

Non-gem Cordierite is not as instantly beautiful as its gem sister Iolite Sunstone but has softer, slower energies, merging spirituality with practical living; relaxes the hold of a controlling partner; for peacefully ending an unhappy, long-term relationship.

Coromandel Stonewood

COLORS: Rich brown, sometimes flecked with gray, black, or red

CRYSTAL TYPE: Petrified wood, silicon dioxide, pseudomorph of the original wood with jasper or chalcedony replacing or altering the original wood

ZODIAC SIGN: Capricorn (December 22–January 20)

CANDLE COLOR: Golden brown

PHYSICAL: Promotes longevity; counters calcification buildup in the body, stenosis of the heart valves, gallstones, premature skin aging.

EMOTIONAL: Helps overcome fears of aging and memory loss; obsession with death.

HOME: Restores stability to a home if there have been too many rapid changes; a house-blessing stone.

WORKPLACE: Bolsters established or multigenerational businesses; revives traditional crafts using natural materials, such as stone or wood.

CHILDREN: For old soul children who find the world too fast.

ANIMALS: Preserves rare breeds.

PROTECTION: Guards against free-floating anxiety and fears of things that may never come to pass.

MAGICKAL AND PSYCHIC USES

The expert mineralogist Robert Simmons, who first researched Coromandel Stonewood as well as other sacred stones such as Vortexite (page 498), considers this crystal to contain the memories and wisdom of the Old Ones of Lemuria.

SPECIAL PROPERTIES

A stone of the sacred Earth, for preservation or restoration of ancient natural sites of power, long-established woodlands, and the reintroduction of almost extinct species.

MYTHOLOGY AND HISTORY

Coromandel Stonewood is more than 170 million years old, dating from when New Zealand was still part of the vast supercontinent of Gondwana. The Coromandel Peninsula on the East Coast of New Zealand's North Island is considered one of the major Earth energy vortices and is today the location for many spiritual activities.

Cotham Marble

COLORS: Gray, blue, yellow, brown, and cream, in polished or tumbled-stone form, resembling an open rural landscape
CRYSTAL TYPE: Colonies of fossilized algae in limestone, known as Mary Ellen Stromatolite Jasper (page 296), may contain distinct shell-like fossils
ZODIAC SIGN: Capricorn (December 22–January 20)
CANDLE COLOR: Brown

PHYSICAL: Alleviates allergies caused by pollen; addresses pigmentosa, aging issues, and reduction in mobility; helps overcome a reluctance to accept a diagnosis that does not feel right but prompts you to seek a second opinion or use internet research (consulting "Dr. Google") for new approaches; aids in exploring natural remedies.
EMOTIONAL: Counters agoraphobia, resistance to making necessary changes, and fear of losing your youthful looks, prompting excessive cosmetic treatments.
HOME: For reorganizing and adding an extension to the home; moving to an area where you have always wanted to live.
WORKPLACE: Propels career advancement, especially if you have hit an impasse or you are being unfairly blocked for promotion.
CHILDREN: For artists who lack confidence or encouragement to express original ideas; for fostering a love of plants and gardening.
ANIMALS: Calls home a missing pet.
PROTECTION: Guards against being ruled by others' demands.

MAGICKAL AND PSYCHIC USES
Enables astral travel to other lands and dimensions through the stone; for encountering tree spirits and guardians of the land, even in a city; encourages druidry and rituals at ancient Indigenous sites.

SPECIAL PROPERTIES
A stone that opens horizons for a less restrictive lifestyle, prompting days, weekends, or vacations where nature is untamed.

MYTHOLOGY AND HISTORY
Cotham, or "landscape marble," is found in an extensive area around Bristol in Southwest England and is about 220 million years old.

Covellite

COLOR: Indigo or midnight blue to almost black, with blue metallic iridescence
CRYSTAL TYPE: Copper sulfide, sometimes with iron; a minor copper ore
ZODIAC SIGN: Sagittarius (November 23–December 21)
CANDLE COLOR: Dark blue

PHYSICAL: Alleviates issues involving the ears, eyes, throat, sinuses, mouth, jaw, face, and electrical flow from natural elements within cells; addresses arthritis, rheumatism, toxicity from environmental pollution; counteracts unwelcome side effects of necessary medical treatment.
EMOTIONAL: Helps overcome the tendency to fantasize about fame, fortune, and celebrity status; counters overindulgence; eliminates fear of accepting responsibility.
HOME: For home and natural births; education based on Montessori, Steiner, or other child-centered methods.
WORKPLACE: Promotes clear communication in writing and speaking; for authors and artists; brings objectivity when personalities intrude on good practice.
CHILDREN: When life has disappointed children, this crystal helps them regain hope and the determination to succeed.
ANIMALS: For recovery of a good quality of life in sick or injured pets.
PROTECTION: Guards against unfounded jealousy, possessiveness, and insecurity needing constant reassurance from others.

MAGICKAL AND PSYCHIC USES
Past lives and past-life recall, vision quests and pilgrimages, clairvoyance, astral travel, meditation and guided fantasies to experience Atlantis; identification of spirit guides; rebirthing; for mediums and healers to combine knowledge with natural intuitive flow.

SPECIAL PROPERTIES
A crystal of small miracles, turning dreams into reality, through earthly effort combined with divine intervention.

MYTHOLOGY AND HISTORY
Covellite, also called covelline, is the crystal of constantly flowing energies to unite with infinite possibility.

Cowrie Shell

COLORS: Smooth, porcelain-like shine, colorful patterns; yellow for prosperity; striped or spotted brown and white tiger cowrie for protection and lucky white associated with astrology and divine blessings

CRYSTAL TYPE: Organic, shells of small to large marine sea snails, marine gastropod mollusks; rounded with a long, narrow, slit-like opening, toothed at the edges; found in warm seas

ZODIAC SIGN: Pisces (February 19–March 20)

CANDLE COLOR: Yellow

PHYSICAL: Promotes conception; alleviates issues involving the vulva, womb, ovaries, pregnancy, hormone imbalance, childbirth, inner ear, hearing, spine, nervous system.

EMOTIONAL: Counters infertility, miscarriages, gambling addiction, obsession with money.

HOME: Draws abundance; blesses mothers, grandmothers, great-grandmothers, and other female nurturers.

WORKPLACE: Once a traditional form of currency in lands surrounded by warm seas, Cowrie Shells attract prosperity to business ventures; for collective and artistic enterprises.

CHILDREN: Encourages learning; helps students applying for scholarships and internships.

ANIMALS: For breeding rare, valuable animals.

PROTECTION: Keeps away envy and malice.

MAGICKAL AND PSYCHIC USES

Traditionally used in divination in India, West and East Africa, and in African-American religions, such as Santeria and Candomblé; enhances rituals for fertility and manifesting wealth, tidal water spells, full moon rites.

SPECIAL PROPERTIES

Cowrie Shells contain triple energies for wealth, protection, and fertility; awaken innate powers of oracular wisdom for predicting the future.

MYTHOLOGY AND HISTORY

In ancient Egypt and other warm oceanic lands, Cowrie Shells have been used for guarding women right through life, especially during pregnancy and childbirth; worn in ancient Egypt as a girdle; under the protection of ocean goddesses, such as Yemaya.

Cradle of Humankind

COLORS: Medium to light gray

CRYSTAL TYPE: Agate/limestone/chert

ZODIAC SIGN: Capricorn (December 22–January 20)

CANDLE COLOR: Gray

PHYSICAL: Beneficial in healing and strengthening bones and the skeletal structure.

EMOTIONAL: If you've been hurt, slowly helps you to overcome guilt, sorrow, shame, and pain, and start over.

HOME: Offers a sense of deeper belonging if you're living far from home or feel alienated from your community.

WORKPLACE: Improves the ability to take in a lot of information and see the interconnections.

CHILDREN: Brings a feeling of security during a period when a lot of changes are occurring.

ANIMALS: Gives very old animals a sense of stability, especially in a noisy household.

PROTECTION: Protects against those who stir up prejudice and dissension.

MAGICKAL AND PSYCHIC USES

For past-life regression work and an instinctive understanding of ancient forms of healing.

SPECIAL PROPERTIES

Connects with our personal ancestors and what the psychotherapist Carl Jung called the collective unconscious—the wisdom and knowledge of all times and places.

MYTHOLOGY AND HISTORY

The Cradle of Humankind stone comes from caves in Magaliesberg, South Africa, a world heritage site, where the oldest hominid fossils are found, dating back as far as 3.5 million years ago.

Crazy Lace Agate

COLORS: Mixed rust red, orange, gray, brown, yellow ocher, cream, white, with fine crisscross lines and patterns, resembling lace or spiderwebs

CRYSTAL TYPE: Microcrystalline quartz, infused with aluminum and iron

ZODIAC SIGN: Aquarius (January 21–February 18)

CANDLE COLOR: Red

PHYSICAL: Alleviates eczema, acne, and issues relating to eyesight, heart, arteries, pancreas, blood circulation; helps recover from surgery for hernia and varicose veins.

EMOTIONAL: Overcomes fear of insects; increases self-esteem; reduces emotionally based food issues; removes redundant attachments.

HOME: Spreads happiness at parties held at home; promotes a bride's happiness in her new home; encourages creativity in interior design or redecorating.

WORKPLACE: Cultivates networking to improve communication; dampens bad temper; for comedians, comedy writers, wedding and party planners, dancers, choreographers.

CHILDREN: Assuages fears of children afraid of clowns, mimes, or people in disguise; keeps teens from being attached to smartphones.

ANIMALS: For animals unfriendly toward children.

PROTECTION: Guards against becoming entangled in other people's negativity, deception, and efforts to control; protects against travel accidents.

MAGICKAL AND PSYCHIC USES

Encourages ghost hunting or exploring old places for past-world visions and spirits without being spooked; for knot magick and binding people against harming you; repels curses and black magick.

SPECIAL PROPERTIES

Called the laughter stone, Crazy Lace Agate is associated with Mexican fiestas and dancing; for spontaneity if your relationship or life has lost its magick.

MYTHOLOGY AND HISTORY

Also called Mexican agate, an instant energy stone, for marathons, sports competitions, and whenever you need extra physical stamina; avoid using it late at night or in the bedroom, except for kindling passion.

Creedite

COLORS: Usually orange-red; also colorless, white, or purple

CRYSTAL TYPE: Hydrated calcium aluminum sulfate hydroxide fluoride; found in fluorite-bearing hydrothermal mineral deposits

ZODIAC SIGN: Virgo (August 24–September 22)

CANDLE COLOR: White

PHYSICAL: Detoxifies the blood; addresses issues involving the nerve endings, nerve malfunctioning, Bell's palsy, chemical and electrical imbalances in the body and brain, the immune system; aids in recovery from microsurgery; enhances the effects of new techniques and medication; counteracts lingering viruses.

EMOTIONAL: Speeds recovery from chronic depression; overcomes inability to take responsibility for life; for overburdened parents with challenging children.

HOME: For moving to a new home without regrets; helps reluctant adult children transition toward independent living.

WORKPLACE: Use Creedite clusters for rapid results if staff members lack initiative; for craftspeople fulfilling orders without sacrificing creativity; orange Creedite brings success when you're striking out on your own.

CHILDREN: Calms children afraid of changes in routine.

ANIMALS: For pets reluctant to leave the fireside.

PROTECTION: Guards against staying in an unsatisfactory relationship because of fears of loneliness.

MAGICKAL AND PSYCHIC USES

A portal for astral travel; aids in understanding sacred ancient texts; accesses the wisdom of angels, guides, the Akashic records, and your evolved self; purple Creedite incorporates formal spiritual learning, especially regarding crystals, into daily life.

SPECIAL PROPERTIES

Colorless Creedite curbs procrastination when you need to make changes to bring lasting good results.

MYTHOLOGY AND HISTORY

A rare mineral, orange (sometimes containing clear or white crystals) often form *Sputnik*-like clusters, other colors may form small crystals covering part or the whole host mineral; Creedite clusters offer concentrated energy for putting plans into action fast.

Crinoids or Sea Lilies

COLORS: May be brightly colored, especially when polished; often soft layers of pink, brown, and gray tints

CRYSTAL TYPE: Crinoids are an aquatic animal fossil, resembling a flower on a thick stem

ZODIAC SIGN: Capricorn (December 22–January 20)

CANDLE COLOR: Indigo

PHYSICAL: For skeletal and genetic issues; for the health of older people.

EMOTIONAL: Soothes you after bereavement or moving away from your roots.

HOME: Attracts abundance and welcome to visitors and family alike.

WORKPLACE: Useful where traditional crafts are practiced, for workers in conservation, museums, history, or archaeology.

CHILDREN: For children disturbed by news of disasters or when a family member has died.

ANIMALS: Helps elderly animals maintain a good quality of life.

PROTECTION: Guards against spite and those who drip emotional poison.

MAGICKAL AND PSYCHIC USES

For connection with ancient worlds, repositories of ancient wisdom, especially Lemuria and Atlantis.

SPECIAL PROPERTIES

A sacred talisman, traditionally found in Northeast England, called St. Cuthbert's Beads after the seventh-century Northumbrian saint; still occasionally made into rosary beads.

MYTHOLOGY AND HISTORY

The oldest Crinoids date back 245–570 million years ago, found widely in the UK, Europe, and the USA. In Malta, legend has it that they fell from clouds during thunderstorms.

Crop Circle Stones

COLORS: Brown, tan, off-white, reddish-brown, or a mixture

CRYSTAL TYPE: Flint in unusual formations; found within crop circles, as well as near sacred circles, such as ancient stone rings, labyrinths, or medicine wheels

ZODIAC SIGN: Virgo (August 24–September 22)

CANDLE COLOR: Green

PHYSICAL: Promotes the free flow of blood and fluids through the body; alleviates issues involving the nervous system; counters dizziness and inner-ear problems, visual disorientation.

EMOTIONAL: Enhances connection with the Earth; keeps you from demanding certainties in every situation.

HOME: Helps in seeing the potential in a beautifully located but totally run-down property; creates a home-based spiritual sanctuary.

WORKPLACE: Establishes a unique business where there is a gap in the market; for making long-term future financial projections.

CHILDREN: Soothes children who do not feel at home in the world.

ANIMALS: Eases encounters in dreams and visions with otherworldly cryptozoological creatures.

PROTECTION: Guards against spirits wandering in from the shadow worlds.

MAGICKAL AND PSYCHIC USES

For working with or creating your own crop circles (cut in grass), labyrinths, or stone circles; linking with ancient guardians of the land.

SPECIAL PROPERTIES

Contains the energies of the circle in or near which it is found; stimulates trance mediumship.

MYTHOLOGY AND HISTORY

The majority of crop circles are found in England, usually within Wiltshire, and have also been reported in the United States, Russia, Germany, Australia, Japan, and Israel. Crop circles, formed in flattened areas of grain, seemingly are messages from extraterrestrial beings and crafted as a way for humans to cease pollution.

Cross Quartz

COLORS: Varies according to quartz, often clear quartz, citrine, smoky, or amethyst

CRYSTAL TYPE: Cross Quartz is formed by one crystal growing at right angles or close to right angles to another; may be a traditional upright cross or X-shaped

ZODIAC SIGN: Gemini (May 22–June 21)

CANDLE COLOR: Gold

PHYSICAL: Addresses hereditary conditions, viruses, and superbugs, such as C. difficile (a germ that causes inflammation of the colon).

EMOTIONAL: Lifts burdens that should have been shed long ago; counters the inability to make even the simplest decision.

HOME: For those living on the site of former prisons, mental hospitals, sweatshops, orphanages, or warehouses where workers or inmates suffered poor conditions.

WORKPLACE: Aids in conflict resolution; helps when considering a major career change; for love partners working together.

CHILDREN: For psychic children and teens who have negative experiences with spirits or premonitions of disasters.

ANIMALS: Protects a successful show or competition animal threatened by jealous owners of other animals in the competition.

PROTECTION: Guards against evil spirits, curses, hexes, and earthly ill-wishing.

MAGICKAL AND PSYCHIC USES

For spiritual experience both of divinity within us all and the source of light; for prayer and contemplation.

SPECIAL PROPERTIES

For wise decision making when you are at a crossroads in your life.

MYTHOLOGY AND HISTORY

Besides its religious significance, the equal-armed cross is an ancient magickal symbol. The four arms of the vertical cross represent the four directions, the four seasons, and the four ancient elements, Earth, Air, Fire, and Water. The X formation is a heraldic and protective symbol.

Crystal Amulets, Talismans, and Charms

COLORS: Whatever crystal contains the desired power or choose it by color; for example, green for luck (see Crystals and Colors, page 520)

CRYSTAL TYPE: An amulet is a crystal storing protection, released over months and years. A talisman is a crystal empowered for a specific purpose and time frame. A charm holds ongoing blessings, each carried, kept in a small bag, or worn as jewelry

ZODIAC SIGN: Pisces (February 19–March 20)

CANDLE COLOR: According to the crystal(s) used

PHYSICAL: As crystal elixirs most safely made by an indirect method of empowering the water (page 145), for massage over different energy centers (see Crystals and Chakras, page 147), or in a healing layout chosen according to the healing properties of each.

EMOTIONAL: As for physical healing, carried in an appropriately colored charm or amulet bag of three, seven, or nine crystals, the same or different crystals (see Crystal Grids of Layouts, page 524).

HOME: Set a bowl of crystals in the center of the home, the zodiac crystals of each family member, present or absent, plus individual crystals for health, happiness, protection, home and family security.

WORKPLACE: Keep business success crystals mixed with harmony and protection crystals in a dish in your workspace.

CHILDREN: Crystals may be given to teens, put in a safe place in the bedroom, or sewn into the lining of a coat.

ANIMALS: Earth-colored crystals under a pet bed bring health.

PROTECTION: Use crystal arrows to repel harm, especially at night.

MAGICKAL AND PSYCHIC USES

Empower any chosen crystal by drawing over it in the air in incense smoke a single word for what you desire.

SPECIAL PROPERTIES

For extra power, sprinkle around your crystal a clockwise circle of salt, spirals of incense smoke, a lighted candle, and a circle of water drops, using the four magickal elements while chanting the purpose of the amulet or charm.

MYTHOLOGY AND HISTORY

Amulets, animal parts or representations of animals made on tusks or bones, date back 32,000 years. Amulets of hieroglyphs in the ancient Egyptian world were etched on crystals and gems for the living and those in the afterlife.

Crystal Angels

COLORS: According to the angel

CRYSTAL TYPE: Crystal Angels come in many crystal kinds and sizes—carved, polished, and usually featureless

ZODIAC SIGN: All signs

CANDLE COLOR: According to angel

PHYSICAL: Promotes healing involving prayer and angels, and when the cause of an illness cannot be discovered or the patient is not responding; aids in recovery from major surgery.

EMOTIONAL: Revives faith in people and life.

HOME: Buy a zodiac angel for a newborn baby or as a birthday gift to bring good fortune.

WORKPLACE: Wear a Crystal Angel pendant or keep a small angel in a pouch in your workspace to protect you from malice.

CHILDREN: Place a small opalite or rainbow quartz angel for Muriel, angel of happy dreams, in the bedroom to prevent nightmares and stem fears of the dark.

ANIMALS: For very old or sick animals. Choose Hariel, angel of pets, whose crystal is any brown agate or jasper.

PROTECTION: A black obsidian angel repels all harm—earthly and paranormal—from the home or when traveling.

MAGICKAL AND PSYCHIC USES

For safe magickal rituals, set four Crystal Angels as your guardians in the four main directions: bloodstone or hematite for Uriel in the north, citrine for Raphael in the east, clear quartz for Michael in the south, and moonstone in the west for Gabriel.

SPECIAL PROPERTIES

The seven main archangels are each associated with particular crystals and days of the week: Michael, archangel of the sun (Sunday), Clear Quartz; Gabriel, archangel of the moon (Monday), Moonstone; Camael or Samael, archangel of Mars and courage (Tuesday), Red Jasper; Raphael, archangel of Mercury and healing (Wednesday), Yellow Citrine; Sachiel, archangel of Jupiter, justice, and prosperity (Thursday), Turquoise; Anael, archangel of Venus and love (Friday), Green Jade; Cassiel, archangel of boundaries and security (Saturday), Purple Amethyst.

MYTHOLOGY AND HISTORY

To make an angel place, purchase a medium-sized clear Michael Crystal Angel and set it on a small table in the center of your main room. Add fresh flowers and regularly light a white candle and floral incense.

Crystal Clusters

COLORS: Varies with the crystal; Clear Quartz is the most common and dynamic

CRYSTAL TYPE: Crystals that have grown together on a matrix, forming separate crystal points; a cluster may contain more than one crystal type

ZODIAC SIGN: Libra (September 23–October 23)

CANDLE COLOR: Gold

PHYSICAL: All clusters align body and mind, righting imbalances; address conditions that attack different parts of the body; combine conventional with complementary medicine and lifestyle improvements; bolster central nervous system.

EMOTIONAL: For isolation, even in company; for those who are stifled by a possessive lover or family.

HOME: Promotes family reunions; increases neighborhood connections in an unfamiliar area.

WORKPLACE: Makes an impersonal workplace friendlier; enhances networking during workplace social events, team-building exercises, and harmonious office parties.

CHILDREN: Encourages shy children to make friends.

ANIMALS: Valuable for those living in herds.

PROTECTION: Prevents cliques, gossip, and factions.

MAGICKAL AND PSYCHIC USES

An Amethyst or Clear Quartz Cluster cleanses and energizes other crystals; any cluster may serve as the central focus for a coven, healing circle, or psychic development group; draws individuals' guides into the circle.

SPECIAL PROPERTIES

Though having properties relating to their crystal composition, every cluster brings compatible people together in friendship, online forums, social media sites, and charitable enterprises.

MYTHOLOGY AND HISTORY

Some cluster formations have additional powers. For inspiration for writers, artists, and musicians, use a nine-crystal muse cluster—nine similar crystals, named after the nine muses of ancient Greece; a sprouting cluster, with crystals pointing different ways, stimulates fresh ideas.

Crystal Elixirs

Crystal-infused elixirs are empowered water that has been filled with the power of crystals.

They are not physical remedies, since they alter the energies of the water, not its mineralogical properties. The infused water acts as vehicle for vibrations of the crystal, which interacts with the person's own energy field.

Elixirs can be used in everyday life as well as for healing. You can drink them; use them in cooking; splash them on chakras or pulse points; add them to bathwater; use them to massage aching limbs; place them in washing machines; sprinkle them around rooms, offices, equipment, or artifacts; use them to water plants; or put them in pet bowls.

An elixir calms, energizes, fills you with confidence, and protects you, according to the crystal used.

You can cover all needs with two very safe crystal elixirs, with crystals directly in the water: Clear Quartz, beloved by the Celts, for all energizing purposes and Purple Amethyst for balancing, soothing, and relieving pain.

Making Crystal Elixirs

There are two main methods of making crystal elixirs. The first involves direct contact between crystal and water, using tumbled stones, where a crystal contains no toxic components, even in small quantities.

Some people use only the second, indirect method, which is just as effective.

Apply the nondirect method where a crystal is porous or raw (unpolished or not contained within quartz); is metallic; contains lead, sulfur, phosphate, aluminum, or asbestos or may flake or crumble in water even if it's not toxic (see the section on toxic crystals, page 526).

Whichever method you use, choose a crystal that contains the properties you most need, whether for healing, protection, or empowerment.

DIRECT-INFUSION METHOD

One small, rounded crystal, the size of an average coin, will infuse a normal-sized glass or individual bottle of water up to 1 cup (250 ml).

Of course, you can use more than one crystal of the same kind or a combination of different crystals to add different properties you need, increasing the water proportionately, on average up to four crystals in a larger, sealable jug per 1 quart (1 liter).

1. First wash the crystal or crystals under running water.
2. Next, place the crystal/s in the intended elixir using a spoon or tongs.
3. As you add the crystal/s to the water, name the purpose(s) of the elixir, asking that the elixir be created for the greatest good and with the purest purpose.
4. Seek the help of your special angels or spirit guides or the angel of crystal waters, Assiel.
5. Cover the container.
6. Leave the covered water and crystals in the refrigerator all night.
7. In the morning remove the crystal(s).
8. Unless you have made a glass of crystal elixir to drink immediately, pour the water into suitable containers.

Crystal waters keep their full power for about twenty-four hours, or three days in the refrigerator.

INDIRECT METHOD OF MAKING CRYSTAL ELIXIRS

The second method involves floating the crystal(s) in a container on the surface of a bowl of water if you have any doubts about a crystal's toxicity or firmness.

1. Half-fill a large glass bowl, again about 1 cup (250 ml) per crystal, but since this is a spiritual process the quantities are not set in stone.
2. Place the crystal(s)/gem(s) in a sealable waterproof small, glass container (such as an old makeup jar with a screw-top lid or a wide stoppered test tube).
3. Hold the container over the water, dedicating the crystal(s)/gem(s) to the highest good, stating the purpose of the elixir as in the direct-infusion method.
4. Float the sealed container in the water in the bowl.
5. Cover the bowl or put fine mesh across so it cannot become polluted.
6. Leave the bowl for a full 24 hours indoors near a window. Fill bottles or containers with the water and use as needed.

Crystal Pendulums

COLORS: Any color, depending on the crystal from which the pendulum is crafted

CRYSTAL TYPE: Clear Quartz or any hard mineral or metal; tapered at the end, barrel-shaped or triangular, on a chain or cord

ZODIAC SIGN: Capricorn (December 22–January 20)

CANDLE COLOR: Gold

PHYSICAL: An all-purpose healing tool, slowly passed over the front of your body (front and back for others), head to foot, in spirals: first counterclockwise to remove stress and energy blockages and then clockwise to energize and harmonize.

EMOTIONAL: Releases blockages caused by repressed feelings or fears; calms overactivity brought on by obsessions.

HOME: If you have lost something, go where you last had it and start walking. The pendulum will swing clockwise if you are on track, but if it swings counterclockwise, you are offtrack.

WORKPLACE: To decide among options, write them all down; hold the pendulum over each option in turn. The pendulum will vibrate and pull down over the best choice.

CHILDREN: Hide objects around the home and garden to be found with the pendulum.

ANIMALS: Follow the trail of a missing pet by attaching a hair from the pet brush to the pendulum.

PROTECTION: Make counterclockwise spirals around you to act as a spirit trap for malevolent ghosts, curses, and ill-wishes.

MAGICKAL AND PSYCHIC USES

As an external tangible expression of inner intuition; program your pendulum by swinging it gently clockwise and naming that as the positive response and counterclockwise for a *no*.

SPECIAL PROPERTIES

Hold the pendulum over one food at a time that you suspect may cause allergies. You will experience coldness in your fingers or counterclockwise spiraling over problem substances.

MYTHOLOGY AND HISTORY

Pendulum dowsing dates back to the second millennium BC. Use your pendulum to detect the presence of a ghost or finding subterranean minerals or water; suspend the pendulum over a map to discover the best location for a holiday or new home.

Crystal Skulls

COLORS: Varies according to the skull

CRYSTAL TYPE: Usually Clear Quartz, but created in different stones, especially forms of Agate, Amethyst, Citrine, Jasper, or Smoky Quartz

ZODIAC SIGN: Scorpio (October 24–November 22)

CANDLE COLOR: Indigo

PHYSICAL: Focuses light and power for whole-body healing; alleviates migraines and other headaches, sinuses, brain disorders.

EMOTIONAL: Helps overcome fears of confronting mortality and aging.

HOME: Acts as a channel for receiving and transmitting Earth and cosmic power.

WORKPLACE: The Celts considered the head as the center of the soul and intelligence; if you are unhappy at work, placing a small skull in the workspace infuses you with the determination to triumph.

CHILDREN: For older teens who have lost a relative, as a reminder that love goes on.

ANIMALS: Keep a Crystal Skull with the urn of a deceased pet's ashes or to mark the burial place.

PROTECTION: Guards against ill-wishing and mind manipulation.

MAGICKAL AND PSYCHIC USES

Ancient Mesoamerican Crystal Skulls hold keys to past wisdom and the future of humankind. Modern Crystal Skulls, by transference, give knowledge of past and future lives and visions of Mayan and Aztec worlds.

SPECIAL PROPERTIES

In medieval times, a *memento mori* (Latin for "remember you must die"), a tiny, jeweled skull, was carried as a reminder that earthly life is finite and to make the most of every opportunity.

MYTHOLOGY AND HISTORY

There are a number of apparently ancient Crystal Skulls in existence that have caused much dispute as to their authenticity. The most famous was in the possession of the Mitchell-Hedges family until recently, believed to be old Mayan, though no evidence has been found as to how it was carved or with what tools. A Mayan legend tells of thirteen sacred Crystal Skulls, hidden in different places, considered imperative to be brought together before December 21, 2012, the end of the Mayan calendar, though we have no idea if this happened.

Crystal Spheres

COLORS: Depends on the crystal, from clear to darker opaque

CRYSTAL TYPE: Clear Quartz with lines and markings within; spheres are also made of many crystals, the most popular being Amethyst, Citrine, Rose, and Smoky Quartz

ZODIAC SIGN: Leo (July 23–August 23)

CANDLE COLOR: Gold

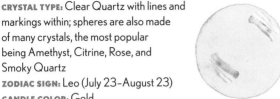

PHYSICAL: All spheres are healing for all purposes; the more sparkling the crystal the more intense the energies. Clear Quartz is transformative, Citrine gently energizing, Amethyst balancing, Rose Quartz soothing, and Smoky Quartz used for gradual recovery.

EMOTIONAL: Helps overcome the tendency to live in your own head and believe in a totally fixed destiny.

HOME: A Clear Crystal Quartz sphere, placed near the center of the home, draws in continuing good health and abundance.

WORKPLACE: A clear sphere attracts success, money, and new orders to a business.

CHILDREN: The ultimate wish crystal.

ANIMALS: Calls the right buyers for animals you have bred; for success in competition.

PROTECTION: Absorbs all that is disharmonious and transforms it into light.

MAGICKAL AND PSYCHIC USES

Clear Quartz spheres are the best for gazing within and seeing images in the inner lines and markings. For a translucent ball or one with a gleaming opaque pattern, use candlelight to cast shadow images on the surface. Seek three different images—past, present, and future—one after the other, or use three spheres—Smoky Quartz for past, Citrine for present, and Clear Quartz for future for visions of angels, guides, and ancestors within the sphere.

SPECIAL PROPERTIES

From ancient China has come the tradition of the sphere reflecting power from the sun to spread good fortune throughout the home and workplace.

MYTHOLOGY AND HISTORY

Because crystal balls are perfect spheres, they have no beginning and no end and reflect in miniature the cosmos, and act as a bridge between human and spiritual realms.

Crystals and Chakras

CHAKRA POWER

This section summarizes which crystals listed in the book will best heal, protect, and empower each chakra or energy center in the body and the functions it governs.

The chakra crystals can be identified by their color, so, for example, Red Jasper is a root crystal. I have also listed some crystals I know work well for each chakra in the table, pages 150–152.

Chakras are the driving force of our inner energy system, made up of seven main energy centers, controlling different parts of the body and mind, and the energy channels that link them. Chakras are not solid organs, like the liver or spleen, but are concentrated centers of constantly moving energy.

They are part of our inner spiritual body, described as "whirling rainbow vortices of energy" that empower the aura, the rainbow energy field around us that also receives and transmits the life force between ourselves and the world (see also Crystals and Colors, Blue through Black, page 520, and Crystals and Colors, White through Green, page 522). You can heal any blocked or overactive chakras with small, round or oval chakra crystals by holding the appropriate chakra crystal on the relevant chakra area.

The body will take the required amount of healing from each chakra crystal through its chakra, as needed.

CHAKRA 1: THE ROOT OR BASE

CRYSTAL COLORS: Red, brown, gray, and black.

This root center is located in the perineum, between the anus and genitals and the small of the back.

This chakra connects with the golden brown or black Earth star chakra, an additional chakra in and beneath the soles of our feet (not included in Figure 1).

Other chakras related to the root chakra are gray or brown and are found in the knees.

For the Earth star chakra around the ankles, sides of the feet, and the soles of the feet, use T weighed down by life; counteracts the tendency toward self-limitation.

See table, page 152, for physical properties connected with the root chakra, together with the Earth star and the knee chakras.

CHAKRA 2: THE SACRAL OR HARA

Located just below the navel, and, in women, below the womb and the reproductive system. It is a chakra especially sensitive to stress and imbalance.

See table, page 151, for physical properties connected with the Sacral or Hara chakra.

CHAKRA 3: THE SOLAR PLEXUS

CRYSTAL COLOR: Yellow.

Located around the center of the upper stomach, just below the rib cage.

See table, page 151, for physical properties connected with the solar plexus chakra and crystals to use in healing.

CHAKRA 4: THE HEART

CRYSTAL COLORS: Green and pink (pink usually in the center of the chakra).

You will find the heart chakra in the center of the chest and between the breasts in a woman.

It is the center where the higher cosmic energies and the rising Earth energies meet, merge, and are transmitted as healing powers via the hands and arms of the healer.

A minor but significant chakra associated with the heart chakra is the turquoise thymus or etheric heart chakra in the upper chest, which governs altruism, selflessness, sensitivity, and inner peace. The thymus chakra is situated in the center of the upper chest between the chest and the base of the throat.

See table, page 151, for which crystals to use and physical properties connected with the heart chakra.

CHAKRA 5: THE THROAT

CRYSTAL COLORS: Sky or light blue.

This chakra is centered around the throat and the Adam's apple.

Just above this chakra, at the base of the brain at the back of your neck, is the minor brain-stem chakra. This is deeper blue, merging to indigo, and is concerned with dreams and unconscious wisdom, past-life recall, and especially prophetic dreams.

See table, page 150, for which crystals to use and physical properties connected with the throat chakra and brain-stem chakra.

CHAKRA 6: THE BROW OR THIRD EYE

CRYSTAL COLOR: Indigo (bluish purple). Some people see this chakra color as different shades of purple and also tinged with silver. It is close to the outermost crown chakra that shines violet or rich purple, going into white and gold.

See table, page 150, for which crystals to use and physical properties connected with the brow or third-eye chakra.

CHAKRA 7: THE CROWN

CRYSTAL COLORS: Violet, rich purple, merging into pure white and gold.

The crown is at the very top of your head and the soul star begins about half an arm's length above the head and brings in spiritual energy from the cosmos via our crown chakra that we use in universal energy healing.

See table, page 150, for which crystals to use and the chakra physical properties associated with the Crown chakra.

CRYSTALS AND CLEANSING

Crystals, with the exception of a few listed throughout the book—notably, Citrine, Kyanite, and Apophyllite—benefit from regular cleansing.

They should be cleansed when you first buy them and then afterward to empower and program them for your own purposes. Then, they should be cleansed after any healing or divinatory sessions.

Protective amulet crystals, kept around the home or workplace, should be cleansed weekly, as should charms to attract good fortune, health, or love. You will soon learn when your crystal is not as powerful as usual.

MOTHER EARTH: Wrap a crystal, or more than one, in cloth; bury it in a marked place for twenty-four hours. This works best for unpolished, natural stones.

Set delicate crystals/gems on a dish resting on the soil of growing herbs.

WATER: Wash under running water most tumbled stones, except fragile ones like Selenite or metallic gems, such as Lapis or Turquoise.

Raw crystals, or those that are soft, porous, even slightly toxic, or coated, and fluorites are not suitable for immersion.

Instead, sprinkle circles of water droplets (use water in which Amethyst or Clear Quartz has been soaked) in counterclockwise circles.

AMETHYST: Amethyst cleanses any other crystal. Use a small amethyst geode, resting individual crystals on the flat part of the geode. Alternatively, make a circle of crystals around a large unpolished piece of Amethyst. In either case, leave the crystal there for twenty-four hours.

USING FRAGRANCE: For any crystal or gem, circle a sagebrush or cedar smudge stick or lemongrass, pine, juniper, or lavender incense stick in counterclockwise spirals in the air over crystals to be cleansed for three or four minutes. Let the incense burn through.

USING SOUND: Over the crystals, ring either a hand bell or Tibetan bells nine times, or strike a small singing bowl for about a minute. Repeat twice more.

LIGHT: Sunlight is the best cleanser for vibrant, richly colored, or sparkling crystals and gems, like Topaz or Diamond, from dawn or whenever you wake up until noon. All soft-hued, cloudy, or delicate crystals, like Rose Quartz, Selenite, or gems respond to full moonlight from moonrise to set. Cleanse any crystal on the full moon.

SALT: Though salt is a traditional cleansing method, it is also physically abrasive. Rather than immersing crystals in salt, make three counterclockwise circles of salt around the crystals. Leave the crystals within the salt circles for about twelve hours.

Alternatively, rest the crystals in a ceramic or glass dish or plate on top of a large bowl of salt, or wrap your crystals in cloth and set in the center of packed salt for heavy cleansing.

USING A CRYSTAL PENDULUM: Pass a Clear Quartz or Amethyst pendulum over a large crystal or circle of small ones in slow, counterclockwise circles nine times.

USING BREATH: Blow softly on crystals three times, as you hold them, picturing any darkness or heaviness fading.

CRYSTALS AND COLORS: BLUE THROUGH BLACK

Color is one of the easiest ways to identify the best crystal for any purpose. If a crystal is vibrant or sparkling, it releases more active energies than a softer hue. Hold two crystals of the same color in different hands; for example, a soft-blue Lace Agate and a rich gold and blue Lapis Lazuli to feel the different sensations.

CRYSTALS AND COLORS: WHITE THROUGH GREEN

Color is one of the easiest ways to choose a crystal for a particular purpose for healing, empowerment, or protection if you do not have time to search the book or you are choosing from your personal collection of special crystals (see also Crystals and Colors: Blue through Black, page 520). I would suggest you keep one of each of the main colors in a bowl.

I have listed popular crystals for each color.

CRYSTALS AND CHAKRAS

CHAKRA	CRYSTAL COLORS	USES	CRYSTALS	CHAKRA PHYSICAL PROPERTIES
7 SOUL STAR About half an arm's length above the head	Clear and sparkling, like crystal quartz Gold/silver/white	Contains the unchanging divine spark of our evolved or higher spiritual self, connection with Divinity	Diamond, White Sapphire or substitute Clear Crystal Quartz or Herkimer Diamond; any gold/silver/white stones	
7 CROWN Center of top of skull	Violet, rich purple, merging into pure white and gold	The spiritual self, the mind, body, and spirit united	Clear Quartz Crystal, Clear Aragonite, Danburite, Clear White Calcite and Clear Fluorite, Herkimer Diamond, Sugilite, Imperial Topaz, Clear Zircon; any rich purple or clear stones	Brain, skull, immune system, general health, long life, mind/body/spirit integration
6 BROW OR THIRD-EYE CHAKRA Middle of forehead	Indigo (bluish purple); some people see this chakra color as different shades of purple and also tinged with silver	The psychic self, connection with angels and guides, clairvoyance	Amethyst, Lapis Lazuli, Sodalite, Purple Fluorite, any of the aura crystals; for example, Aqua Aura, Opal Aura or Titanium Aura; any dark blue/purple stones	Eyes, ears, sinuses, pituitary gland, face; both hemispheres of the brain, radiating into the central cavity of the brain
5 BRAIN-STEM CHAKRA At the base of the skull, but, in crystal layouts, this will be healed by the throat and brow chakra crystals	Deep blue to indigo	Dreams and unconscious wisdom	Sodalite, Bornite, Blue Goldstone, Kunzite, Turitella Agate and all fossils; any indigo stone	
5 THROAT CHAKRA Over and through the throat	Light or sky blue	Communication; bridge to the outer world, listening and talking, external vision	Angelite, Aquamarine, Blue Chalcedony, Ametrine, Blue Lace Agate, Blue Quartz, Celestite, Lapis Lazuli (also the brow chakra), Kyanite, Turquoise, and Blue Sapphire; any light or rich blue stones	Neck, voice mechanism, bronchial passages, lungs, jaw, mouth, neck, nape of the neck, passages running to the ears

(continued)

CHAKRA	CRYSTAL COLORS	USES	CRYSTALS	CHAKRA PHYSICAL PROPERTIES
4 HEART CHAKRA Center of the chest or middle of the breasts, not to be confused with the actual heart muscle	Green or pink	Compassion, self-love, loving relationships, healing	Amazonite, Green Aventurine, Chrysoprase, Emerald, Jade, Rose Quartz, Pink or Green Opals; any green or pink stones	Upper back, rib cage, chest, lymph glands, skin, circulatory system, lower lungs, abdominal cavity
4 THYMUS Situated between the heart and the throat chakras in the upper chest	Turquoise	Altruism, selflessness, inner peace	Chrysocolla, Bornite, or Turquoise; any turquoise or iridescent stones	
4 HAND, PALM, AND FINGERTIPS Can be healed through the heart chakra	Silver or misty white	Transmission of healing energies	Rainbow Quartz, Rainbow Moonstone or Rainbow Obsidian, or Blue Moonstone; any silver or misty white stones, or use any master healing crystals	Central to hands-on healing. Hold pair of any round or oval rainbow crystal, such as Rainbow Quartz or Rainbow Moonstone, one in each hand
3 SOLAR PLEXUS The bottom of the rib cage, the upper stomach	Yellow	The integration of all experiences—good and bad—willpower, identity, the timeline of your life	Citrine, Lemon Chrysoprase, Yellow Jasper, Sunstone, Golden Topaz; any yellow/ gold stones	Digestion, liver, spleen, gallbladder, stomach and small intestine, abdomen, lower back, autonomic nerve system and its metabolism
2 SACRAL OR HARA Over the belly button	Orange and silver	Desire and needs for satisfaction, dependence versus independence; gut instinct, location of your inner self and inner child	Amber, Orange Aragonite, Carnelian, Chalcopyrite, Orange Calcite, Moonstone, Mookaite, Pearl, Selenite, Snow Quartz, White or Rainbow Opal; any Fluorite except purple; any Tourmaline except black Any orange stones	Abdomen, lower back, genitals, well-being of blood and all other bodily fluids, hormones, menstrual and menopausal problems, reproductive system, fertility, sperm production, kidneys, bladder

(continued)

CRYSTALS AND CHAKRAS

CHAKRA	CRYSTAL COLORS	USES	CRYSTALS	CHAKRA PHYSICAL PROPERTIES
1 ROOT OR BASE CHAKRA At the base of the spine, between the legs	Red	Survival, material needs to work and have a home, physical strength, health and stamina, stability	Red Tiger's Eye or Ox Eye, Red Aventurine, Garnet, Jet, Ruby and Red Jasper; any red stones	Together with Earth star and knee chakras, governs the legs, feet, skeleton (including teeth, bones, joints), bowels, arms, prostate, cell structure
1 KNEES	Gray and brown	Hidden emotions, grief, maybe from much earlier in life, uncertainty	Gray Smoky Quartz, Black Tourmaline, Mahogany Obsidian or Apache Tear; any gray or brown stones	Healing may not always be needed
1 EARTH STAR	Golden brown or black	Your Earth self, what is essential to you, your ancestors and roots; grounding	Golden tiger's eye, any brown or sandy patterned or banded Agate, and Snowflake Obsidian; any black or golden-brown stones	Ankles, sides and soles of feet, can be healed through the Root chakra

CRYSTAL COLORS

CRYSTAL COLOR	USES	HEALING	SUGGESTED CRYSTALS
BLUE	Leadership, justice, career advancement, promotion, authority, marriage, partnerships of all kinds, prosperity, business expansion, peace	Thyroid gland, throat, fevers, inflammation, teeth; childhood rashes, cuts, bruises, scalds, burns; high blood pressure, vision problems, communication disorders	Chrysocolla, Turquoise, Lapis Lazuli, Andean Opal, Sodalite, Blue Topaz, Angelite, Celestine, Kyanite, Blue Lace Agate
PURPLE	Spirituality, imagination, dreams, psychic powers, intuition, teaching, counseling, healing from higher sources such as angels, energy healing like Reiki, banishing past sorrow or present troublesome influences; psychic protection	Headaches (including migraines), ears, hair, sinusitis, childbirth, addictions, neuroses, phobias, nerve endings and connections, allergies to chemicals and modern living, hyperactivity, insomnia	Amethyst, Charoite, Lepidolite, Purple Fluorite, Chevron Amethyst, Kunzite, Sugilite
PINK	Reconciliation, happy family relationships, friendship, kindness, children and teenagers, girls entering puberty, young or new love, trust after betrayal	Glands, ears, PMS, skin, ulcers, psychosomatic and stress-induced illnesses, insomnia, nightmares; family ills, babies, children; abuse and self-hatred	Rose Quartz, Mangano and Pink Calcite, Andean Opal, Rhodonite, Rhodochrosite, Pink Chalcedony
BROWN	Practical matters, security, gradual accumulation of money, learning new skills in later years; home, property, financial institutions, officialdom (also blue), older people, animals, finding what is lost or stolen, perseverance, patience	Feet, legs, bowels, hernia, anus, prostate, chronic conditions, relief of chronic pain; growths, degenerative conditions in old age, panic attacks	Golden Tiger's Eye, Petrified Wood, Jasper, Banded Agate, Desert Rose, Chiastolite, Zircon
GRAY	Compromise, adaptability, ability to merge into the background, neutralizing unfriendly energies, negotiations, keeping secrets, shielding from psychic attack	Lesions, wounds, burns, tissue and nerve connections, obsessions and acute anxiety, persistent pain	Smoky Quartz, Hematite, Laboradite, Iron Pyrites, Banded Agate, Cat's Eye
BLACK	Transformation, peaceful endings, grief; banishing sorrow, guilt, and destructive influences; acceptance of what cannot be changed, working within restrictions, blocking a negative or harmful force; psychic protection	Pain relief, constipation, IBS, side effects of invasive treatments such as radiation or chemotherapy	Obsidian, Snowflake Obsidian, Jet, Tourmaline, Onyx, Apache Tear, Obsidian Arrows

CRYSTAL COLORS

CRYSTAL COLOR	USES	HEALING	SUGGESTED CRYSTALS
WHITE OR COLORLESS	Originality, new beginnings, developing talents, ambitions, innovations, good health, contact with angels and spirit guides; can be substituted for any other color	Whole-body healing, integration of mind/body/soul, neurological disorders, autoimmune system; acute pain relief	Aragonite, Clear and Optical Calcite, Fluorite, Herkimer Diamond, Crystal Quartz, Topaz
WHITE CLOUDY (translucent) or **OPAQUE** (solid color)	Nurturing; slower new beginnings, unfolding potential; protection against negativity; for mothers and babies; granting wishes, calling love from the past or from afar	Hormones, fluid balance, fertility, pregnancy; gradual recovery from illness, depression, or exhaustion; bone marrow, cells	Calcite, Chalcedony, Howlite, Magnesite, Milky or Snow Quartz, Moonstone, Selenite
RED	Movement, courage, positive change, strength, action, determination, assertiveness, power, sexual passion, male potency, taking the initiative, competitiveness, protecting loved ones, overcoming obstacles	Energy, muscles, low blood pressure, poor circulation, anemia; feet, hands, skeleton, reproductive organs	Aventurine, Blood or Fire Agate, Garnet, Jasper, Mahogany Obsidian, Poppy Jasper, Ruby, Red Tiger's Eye
ORANGE	Confidence, joy, creativity, female fertility (also red), abundance, independence; self-esteem and self-image, happiness, self-employment	Ovaries, intestines, pulse rate, kidneys, bladder, menstruation, menopause, food allergies, arthritis, rheumatism, immune system, food-related addictions	Amber, Aragonite, Peach Aventurine, Calcite, Carnelian, Mookaite
YELLOW	Logic, memory, determination, concentration, study, examinations, tests, new technology, clear communication (also blue); job changes, moneymaking ventures, speculation, conventional healing, repelling envy, malice, spite, deception	Lymphatic system, metabolism, blood sugar (also green and blue), digestion, liver, gallbladder, pancreas, spleen, nervous system, eczema, skin problems, nausea	Yellow and Honey Calcite, Citrine, Lemon Chrysoprase, Jade, Jasper, Mookaite, Golden Topaz
GREEN	Love, fidelity, commitment, beauty, horticulture, environment; healing through nature, crystal healing, gradual growth in every way, health, wealth, brings luck, helps win competitions	Heart, lungs, respiratory system, infections and viruses, especially colds and influenza (also blue), pollen and fur allergies, addictions and obsessions (also blue)	Amazonite, Aventurine, Calcite, Chrysoprase, Fluorite, Jade, Nephrite And Jadeite, Malachite, Serpentine, Tree Agate

Crystal Wands

COLORS: Depends on the crystal used

CRYSTAL TYPE: Solid narrow pieces of crystal, shaped into a wand, rounded at one end and more pointed at the other; alternatively, wood, crystal, or metal wands, especially Copper, in which a crystal is inserted in one or both ends, often Clear Quartz at the projecting (energy-releasing) point and a rounder Amethyst at the base

ZODIAC SIGN: Pisces (February 19–March 20)

CANDLE COLOR: Silver or gold

PHYSICAL: A powerful healing tool, especially Clear Quartz, for infusing pure life-force energy, Amethyst for balancing and taking away pain, and Rose Quartz for gentle healing.

EMOTIONAL: Defuses extreme emotional tension; helps overcome difficulty in giving or receiving love, praise, or approval.

HOME: Creates protective spirals around a photograph of the family or valuables, including absent family members.

WORKPLACE: Point the wand alternately outward and inward to draw new customers and attract business.

CHILDREN: For making wishes on birthdays, Christmas, and other special occasions.

ANIMALS: Draw a circle of light around an image of your pet on your smartphone if you will be coming home.

PROTECTION: Point the wand outward, facing the bedroom door, to repel nightmares, fears of the dark, and spooks.

MAGICKAL AND PSYCHIC USES

Releases power into the cosmos after a ritual; cuts negative ties with destructive people or entities by making a downward slashing movement.

SPECIAL PROPERTIES

Wands represent the Fire element in magick and are one of the four sacred tools and treasures associated with the Holy Grail quest.

MYTHOLOGY AND HISTORY

Crystal wands are a powerful way to direct the powers of specific crystals in healing or to attract success, love, and happiness with a clockwise movement; counterclockwise to banish illlness and bad luck. Circling your wand over a lucky charm will activate it.

Cuprite

COLOR: Red, brownish-red, crimson or blackish, depending on mineral impurities; also called red or ruby copper

CRYSTAL TYPE: Copper oxide, one of the highest-yielding copper ores

ZODIAC SIGN: Taurus (April 21–May 21)

CANDLE COLOR: Red

PHYSICAL: A natural energizer; addresses issues involving the bladder, kidneys, thymus, heart, blood; relieves cystitis, arthritis, rheumatism, cramps, altitude sickness, PMS, menstrual problems, menopause; strengthens muscles after pregnancy and childbirth.

EMOTIONAL: Prevents excessive worrying by mothers over children of any age; for those not nurtured by their mothers as children or whose mothers died young; for overharsh fathering.

HOME: Cuprite placed at the four corners of your home attracts ongoing prosperity; helps stepfathers unfamiliar with children or grappling with divided loyalties to bond.

WORKPLACE: For domineering employers or managers; in a small business, boosts confidence in dealing with autocratic officials.

CHILDREN: If children are bullied because of their accent, background, ethnicity, or poverty.

ANIMALS: For overprotective pet mothers.

PROTECTION: Guards against fears of pain, illness, and mortality.

MAGICKAL AND PSYCHIC USES

Represents the Divine Feminine; for fertility rituals, twin souls, single-sex or gender-fluid relationship rites, all-female covens, rites of passage, especially passing over.

SPECIAL PROPERTIES

The woman's stone, minimizing inequality and prejudice toward women in male-dominated professions; for women in traditional communities caught between cultures.

MYTHOLOGY AND HISTORY

Sacred to the Norse Earth mother Nerthus, Cuprite was buried in corners of fields after harvest so that the crops might be reborn. Exchanged as tokens where love must be secret.

Cynthia Stone or Leopard Skin Serpentine

COLORS: Olive to lime green with black spots and markings, resembling leopard skin in color and texture

CRYSTAL TYPE: Serpentine (green) with magnetite (black); magnesium in silicate hydroxide

ZODIAC SIGN: Sagittarius (November 23–December 21)

CANDLE COLOR: Green

PHYSICAL: Detoxifies; eradicates internal and external parasites, especially head lice in children; addresses calcium and magnesium deficiency, hypoglycemia, diabetes, and issues involving the thyroid and pancreas; alleviates shingles.

EMOTIONAL: For excessive timidity; counters the tendency to allow others to dictate the future for you; banishes irrational fears expressed as nightmares of wild animals and being eaten alive.

HOME: Guards home, possessions, yourself, and loved ones from harm, attack, and threats.

WORKPLACE: For physically hazardous jobs; for engaging in formal and informal negotiations if there are conflicts.

CHILDREN: Helps overcome phobias about snakes, spiders, and crawling insects.

ANIMALS: For the conservation of wild fierce cats, such as leopards and jaguars.

PROTECTION: Ensures safety while traveling from attack, accidents, theft, terrorism, and loss of documents or luggage.

MAGICKAL AND PSYCHIC USES

A psychically magnetic crystal to draw toward you what is desired, whether money, success, love, or fertility; shamanic trance travel on the back of a leopard or another fierce steed to retrieve lost power in previous lifetimes.

SPECIAL PROPERTIES

For spending time in the wilderness or planning an out-of-town relocation; for conservation of beautiful places under threat.

MYTHOLOGY AND HISTORY

Leopard-skin Serpentine, by its association with the leopard, is a power icon for self-empowerment, uniqueness, and making personal fortune and destiny. The leopard in Egypt was sacred to Osiris, god of rebirth. Leopards are also associated with creation in Africa, where Osiris was considered a ruler of the earth.

Dalmatian or Dalmation Jasper

COLORS: Pale gray, cream or beige-brown with dark spots, brown, black, or orange resembling the dalmatian dog after which it was named

CRYSTAL TYPE: Silicate, microcrystalline quartz, with organic matter or minerals as inclusions, black tourmaline, dravite, iron oxide, or arfvedsonite

ZODIAC SIGN: Virgo (August 24–September 22)

CANDLE COLOR: Brown

PHYSICAL: Boosts immunity; acts as a detoxifier; addresses issues involving the muscles, bowels (including IBS and constipation), skin, allergic rashes, sprains in athletes.

EMOTIONAL: Counters the sense that life is a burden and day-to-day survival difficult; roots out the tendency to smoke.

HOME: Strengthens and increases family bonds; enables family members to have fun; bolsters long-term marriages and friendships.

WORKPLACE: Fosters team effort and cooperation for setting up a new business or a solo venture.

CHILDREN: Protects from nightmares about monsters.

ANIMALS: Increases telepathic communication with pets.

PROTECTION: Counters cynicism and skepticism from bad-tempered relatives and colleagues; protects against false friends and financial scams, especially concerning animal purchases.

MAGICKAL AND PSYCHIC USES

By magickal transference, connects with canine-like power animals, such as wolves; increases dowsing abilities to find missing items and pets.

SPECIAL PROPERTIES

A slow-acting crystal that gradually builds up healing and protection; does not absorb negativity, but transforms it.

MYTHOLOGY AND HISTORY

The unusual appearance of this Mexican stone was Mother Nature's clue to its connections with healing animals and for veterinarians practicing alternative healing.

Darwin Glass or Darwinite

COLORS: Light to dark green, white, black
CRYSTAL TYPE: Darwin Glass is a natural glass, a tektite from Tasmania, the island that is the most southerly part of Australia; twisted masses, fragments, or chunks
ZODIAC SIGN: Aries (March 21–April 20)
CANDLE COLOR: Green

PHYSICAL: Addresses issues involving the brain and the autoimmune system; acts as a catalyst for other forms of healing and the self-healing system.
EMOTIONAL: Counters fear of the unknown, obsession with the negative aspects of the paranormal, and conspiracy theories about alien encounters.
HOME: Protects your family from storms, lightning, and fire; brings family members with outlandish plans down to Earth.
WORKPLACE: Offers success, good fortune, and profit to any commercial venture; for introducing and having accepted original ideas that will change working practice.
CHILDREN: Takes away fears of the dark, unfriendly aliens.
ANIMALS: Restores the freshness of nature to the lives of city pets.
PROTECTION: Guards against those who bombard you with emotions, false sentiment, and guilt trips.

MAGICKAL AND PSYCHIC USES
Promotes deep meditation and astral dreams of extraterrestrial encounters; connects you with the healing you most need in the way you most need it.
SPECIAL PROPERTIES
Each kind of tektite relates not only to the origins of its meteorite, but the land in which it may have been buried for hundreds of thousands of years; the pure energies of Tasmania and its relative proximity to the Antarctic give Darwin Glass a clarity to cut to the heart of any matter, inspiring exploration off the beaten track and giving new life to any situation or relationship.
MYTHOLOGY AND HISTORY
Darwin Glass is named after Mount Darwin in the West Coast Mountain range, near Queenstown, and was later called Darwin Crater, as this was probably the original meteorite impact crater and source of the glass. Darwin Glass is made up of parts of the Earth's crust, melted when an iron meteorite crashed there about 816,000 years ago.

Datolite

COLOR: White, colorless, sometimes with a green tinge; green, yellow, gray, brown, pink-red, red
CRYSTAL TYPE: Calcium boron silicate hydroxide
ZODIAC SIGN: Aquarius (January 21–February 18)
CANDLE COLOR: White

PHYSICAL: Alleviates diabetes, hypoglycemia, memory loss, degenerative brain conditions (especially early onset), genetic conditions, tics, stammering, excessive blushing.
EMOTIONAL: Prevents a return to bad habits after treatment for addiction; counteracts excessive dependence on others for company, approval, and advice.
HOME: Brings order to chaos to avoid misplacing possessions or being late.
WORKPLACE: Aids in understanding and memorizing complicated data; for clear expression in presentations or oral examinations, particularly languages; encourages lateral problem solving.
CHILDREN: Helps a child recall happy memories when a family member dies; assists in preparing for exams without stress.
ANIMALS: For training a lovable but easily distracted pet.
PROTECTION: A radar warning of danger before it appears; guards against becoming overwhelmed by life's demands.

MAGICKAL AND PSYCHIC USES
Offers access to ancient spiritual wisdom, past lives, and connection with angels and guides; encourages intuitive interpretation of tarot cards, runes, or astrology charts, where wisdom is blocked; helps in seeing auras. Green Datolite links with nature essences.
SPECIAL PROPERTIES
Yellow or white Datolite cultivates strategic thinking in competitions, such as chess, war games, or billiards and rapid, accurate, mind-eye-body coordination in ping-pong, tennis, soccer, baseball, and other ball games.
MYTHOLOGY AND HISTORY
Datolite, a stone that opens the door to the universe, encourages adventure, both in faraway places and for intellectual and spiritual exploration; enables you to think outside the box and to avoid self-defeating limitations.

Demantoid Garnet

COLORS: Deep emerald green (the rarest and most precious), shades of green from light and bluish- or yellowish-green to brownish-golden; brilliant, fiery

CRYSTAL TYPE: An andradite garnet, calcium iron silicate; the intense green is caused by chromium

ZODIAC SIGN: Aquarius (January 21–February 18)

CANDLE COLOR: Bright green

PHYSICAL: Alleviates issues relating to eyesight, resistance to viruses and infections, recurring colds, bronchitis, pneumonia, septicemia, blood sugar, heart, arteries, internal parasites, thyroid, Hodgkin's lymphoma, secondary tumors.

EMOTIONAL: Counters isolation and detachment in those not given a chance to form loving bonds in childhood.

HOME: Diminishes insecurity and need for reassurance.

WORKPLACE: A magnet for success in hospitality and child-centered services or products; promotes harmonious business relations with a love partner or close family members.

CHILDREN: Restores a sense of security if there has been fierce quarreling or a dramatic breakup by parents.

ANIMALS: For amicable arrangements where both of a separating couple claim ownership of a beloved pet.

PROTECTION: Guards against a partner straying.

MAGICKAL AND PSYCHIC USES

Demantoid Garnets have been used for hundreds of years in shamanistic healing and spiritual traditions by Native Americans, Mayans, Aztecs, and African healers. Hold one in your dominant hand as you send love and blessings to the unwell.

SPECIAL PROPERTIES

A pledge between love partners that nothing will ever come between them; a betrothal ring for couples in their middle years and beyond.

MYTHOLOGY AND HISTORY

Emerald-green Demantoid was used by Peter Carl Fabergé, the Russian jeweler, in his jeweled eggs, made for European royalty in the late 1880s and early 1900s. Non-gem Demantoid has the same properties as gem-quality stones.

Dendritic Limestone

COLORS: Black dendrites or fern-like inclusions in white or creamy limestone, sometimes with a slightly darker limestone background

CRYSTAL TYPE: Limestone with iron and manganese oxide inclusions, often in small slabs

ZODIAC SIGN: Virgo (August 24–September 22)

CANDLE COLOR: Green

PHYSICAL: Promotes circulation of blood and other bodily fluids through veins and arteries; slows or stops growths of all kinds, especially on the skin; addresses excess body and facial hair, internal parasites, fungi, and skin-burrowing bugs.

EMOTIONAL: Counters a negative and/or distorted perception of your body image, agoraphobia.

HOME: Aids in catching up with old friends and restoring contact with people with whom you have lost touch.

WORKPLACE: At stressful moments, gaze for a few minutes into the dendritic slab to clear the mind of problems and conflicting demands.

CHILDREN: For sharing, at bedtime, tales of magickal lands and fey forests; developing their talents in imaginative art.

ANIMALS: Connects pets living in city apartments with the natural world.

PROTECTION: Guards against working 24/7 indoors.

MAGICKAL AND PSYCHIC USES

If meditation is hard when the mind is racing, Dendritic Limestone lets your mind go blank; allows pictures to appear in the dendrites totally spontaneously. Through your Dendritic Limestone, you'll forge spontaneous connections with tree spirits and essences of the Earth, even in an urban park, to flow, heal, and restore.

SPECIAL PROPERTIES

An excellent focus for setting up an internet blog or online interest groups to join with genuine like-minded people.

MYTHOLOGY AND HISTORY

The third of the dendrites (see also Dendritic or Tree Agate, page 159, and Dendritic Quartz, page 159); one of Mother Nature's wonders, every specimen of Dendritic Limestone is unique.

Dendritic or Tree Agate

COLORS: White with feathery green veins

CRYSTAL TYPE: Chalcedony with dendrite inclusions of iron and manganese

ZODIAC SIGNS: Virgo (August 24–September 22) and Gemini (May 22–June 21)

CANDLE COLOR: Pale green or white

PHYSICAL: Clears energy blockages; alleviates fluid retention, pain, vein and capillary problems, neuralgia, and osteoporosis.

EMOTIONAL: Lessens mood swings; helps adults overcome childhood trauma and create their own happy family.

HOME: Encourages absent family members to keep in touch; as the gardener's crystal, energizes potted plants, balcony gardens, and outdoor spaces.

WORKPLACE: Promotes networking; aids in working with forests, wildlife, horticulture, websites, and internet connectivity.

CHILDREN: Encourages going outdoors if obsessed with electronic devices.

ANIMALS: Reconnects aviary and cage birds with nature.

PROTECTION: Guards against people attaching to emotional or psychic hooks; ensures safe air travel.

MAGICKAL AND PSYCHIC USES

Works with Celtic tree staves and druidry; connects with tree and nature spirits; facilitates rituals to prevent deforestation and destruction of rain forests.

SPECIAL PROPERTIES

Heals counter geopathic stress, if you have blocked or harsh Earth energies beneath your home; for exploring family trees and connecting with birth families.

MYTHOLOGY AND HISTORY

Dendrite, the Greek name for a tree, is associated with the ancient Greek dryads—woodland spirits; the crystal was buried in fields by the ancient Greeks and in India to ensure a good harvest. Traditionally, Dendritic or Tree Agate brings growth of money and good luck, reconnection with former friends and lovers.

Dendritic Quartz

COLORS: Usually clear, with fern- or plant-like black, brown, yellow, or red inclusions; clarity varies according to the amount of the inclusion; some quartz may be yellowish or smoky

CRYSTAL TYPE: Silicon dioxide, containing manganese oxide, iron, hematite, and sometimes pyrolusite dendrites

ZODIAC SIGN: Gemini (May 22–June 21)

CANDLE COLOR: Pale yellow

PHYSICAL: Promotes blood circulation and blood oxygenation through veins, arteries, small capillaries, and orifices in the body; strengthens nerve connections and endings; ensures easy pregnancy and childbirth, including a healthy placenta and fetal growth.

EMOTIONAL: Counters codependency in a needy relationship.

HOME: If plants fail to thrive, place Dendritic Quartz in the soil to kick-start growth; for encouraging connections between extended family members reluctant to meet for gatherings.

WORKPLACE: Good for new businesses to get a foothold in the market, for partnerships and mergers.

CHILDREN: Increases children's sociability if they are shy with strangers or do not like being left at day care or going to school.

ANIMALS: Ensures adoption of a strong, healthy animal.

PROTECTION: Guards against being bound with guilt.

MAGICKAL AND PSYCHIC USES

A crystal associated with goddess spirituality, especially goddesses of the moon and the forests and with seasonal celebrations; Earth healing; working with and making tree essences and oils.

SPECIAL PROPERTIES

Brings the rapid growth of abundance, prosperity, health, and happiness and untangles obstacles.

MYTHOLOGY AND HISTORY

Dendritic Quartz is different from Dendritic Agate in that Dendritic Agate has a milky, opaque background to the dendrites and represents slower growth; by contrast, Dendritic Quartz is more shimmery, iridescent, and transparent, used more frequently for jewelry and with proactive, fast-moving energies for faster life growth. Both dendrite crystals, plus the third in the trio—solid Dendritic Limestone—make a wonderful triple play to draw opportunity and a good social life.

Desert Rose

COLORS: Pale brown, rough texture with glints of silver, white, or pearl

CRYSTAL TYPE: Gypsum with brown sand inclusions, forming in desert places in rose-like clusters; separate crystals resemble nuts

ZODIAC SIGNS: Scorpio (October 24–November 22) and Capricorn (December 22–January 20)

CANDLE COLOR: Light brown

PHYSICAL: Resolves viral infections, especially those affecting the skin; alleviates skin growths, blemishes, eczema, chronic fatigue, issues involving the prostate and testes, motion sickness, stress-related stomach disorders.

EMOTIONAL: Assuages grief; addresses abuse, panic attacks, phobias (especially claustrophobia); restores confidence after accident, illness, or emotional breakdown.

HOME: Promotes family unity; attracts unexpected money; protects against troublesome outsiders or family members.

WORKPLACE: Aids in developing expertise if advancement is slow; assists with study, training, or retraining; defuses an unstable or hostile workplace.

CHILDREN: Helps reticent children express their talents; enables those who are different to value their unique potential.

ANIMALS: For elderly or sick pets; animals grieving for their mate.

PROTECTION: Guards against isolation and helplessness during trauma; shields against sexual harassment.

MAGICKAL AND PSYCHIC USES

For fire, star, and storm magick; accessing past lives; contacting angels, devas, and fire spirits; a love charm.

SPECIAL PROPERTIES

Aids in relocating to warmer climes or adopting a different lifestyle, especially in later years; resolves disputes involving issues relating to taxes, compensation, insurance payouts, or inheritance.

MYTHOLOGY AND HISTORY

According to myth, Desert Roses were formed by sand struck by lightning as solidified fire, a gift from deities and desert spirits. The stone of inner gold, if life has passed you by, Desert Rose promises fulfillment at any age.

Devalite

COLORS: Apple-green/yellow (serpentine) mixed with black and gray as a band

CRYSTAL TYPE: Metamorphic rock, a mixture of serpentine and augite; semiprecious; also found as tumbled stones and jewelry

ZODIAC SIGN: Pisces (February 19–March 20)

CANDLE COLOR: Green

PHYSICAL: Resolves issues involving the lungs; alleviates plant, fur, feather, and pollen allergies; addresses conditions first apparent in childhood or puberty; mitigates heart irregularities; counters an unhealthy lifestyle that leads to or worsens minor illnesses and causes lack of vitality.

EMOTIONAL: Transforms poor body image, distorted view of weight and outer appearance that can lead to anorexia, bulimia, and unnecessary beauty treatments or cosmetic surgery.

HOME: Enables greenery and plants indoors and out to flourish.

WORKPLACE: A breath of fresh air to rethink and rework practices that are unproductive.

CHILDREN: Encourages children to be kind to those less fortunate and to animals; rewards honesty.

ANIMALS: For fund-raising for animal charities, volunteering at rescue centers, or training future therapy dogs.

PROTECTION: GUARDS against taking to heart rejections or put-downs.

MAGICKAL AND PSYCHIC USES

Named for its strong abilities to bring awareness of devas, Earth energies, and nature spirits; useful in working with medicine wheels, labyrinths, circle dancing, feng shui, Wiccan ritual, and all forms of natural magick.

SPECIAL PROPERTIES

Brings a new awareness of and interest in natural forms of healing, making herbal remedies, healthy nutrition.

MYTHOLOGY AND HISTORY

Found in the Tonto Forest in Arizona, a stone linked with the land and sacred Earth ceremonies; encourages outdoor living during weekends and vacations spent in nature, exploring ancient energy tracks and the sites along them; propels you to collect your own set of natural stones for meditation and ritual.

Devic Temple Quartz

COLORS: Usually colorless (quartz) but can appear in other color quartzes, such as brown or gray (smoky) or purple (amethyst)

CRYSTAL TYPE: Quartz with inclusions, characterized by inner mirrors, fractures, rainbows and fairy frost-like wisps and veils; may also appear in a Dow Crystal (page 165), called a temple heart Dow; or a terminated quartz containing a white, gray, or green phantom

ZODIAC SIGN: Leo (July 23–August 23)

CANDLE COLOR: Gold

PHYSICAL: Promotes healing through light and prayer; whole-self healing to align body with mind and spiritual well-being.

EMOTIONAL: Keeps you from feeling alienated from life and others; curbs a tendency to work 24/7 without deriving satisfaction from your efforts.

HOME: If you obtain a rare Devic Heart Temple with its three seven-sided faces, alternating with three triangular faces, your home will radiate sanctity and welcome to all who enter.

WORKPLACE: Aids in maintaining integrity and a sense of perspective in a high-pressure or high-flying career.

CHILDREN: Sends angelic healing to a sick child or one who finds communication and daily life difficult.

ANIMALS: For therapy, guide, and guard dogs.

PROTECTION: Accesses the essence of the deva of light within the crystal to guard against all harm.

MAGICKAL AND PSYCHIC USES

One of the most powerful master teacher crystals, Devic Temple crystals offer visions of priests and priestesses in ancient temples in meditation, dreams, or waking visions; you may identify with one of the old worlds.

SPECIAL PROPERTIES

Devic Temples resemble inner temples with steps or ledges and often the face or figure of a deva—an evolved being, akin to a nature angel—who has chosen to protect the owner of the crystal. Crystal expert Melody describes rare quartz crystals with a seated Buddha inside.

MYTHOLOGY AND HISTORY

Your personal Devic Temple will reveal different insights according to your changing needs; the inner guardian remains the same and becomes clearer over time.

Diamond

COLOR: Usually clear with dazzling rainbows; also yellow, brown, green, blue, pink, purple, and black containing numerous black inclusions

CRYSTAL TYPE: Carbon, diamond being the hardest mineral

ZODIAC SIGN: Aries (March 21–April 20)

CANDLE COLOR: Gold

PHYSICAL: A master healer, diamond amplifies other crystals in healing layouts; balances right and left hemispheres; promotes female fertility; helps overcome sexual dysfunction in both sexes.

EMOTIONAL: Alleviates anxiety, neuroses, depression; if your diamond becomes cloudy, you are overloaded; counters loss of identity and self-worth.

HOME: Brings sunshine, even in winter.

WORKPLACE: Aids in processing new skills and information quickly; cultivates fame and fortune through exceptional performances and successful auditions.

CHILDREN: Diamond chips in a sealed jar encourage imaginative play.

ANIMALS: For attaining best-of-breed awards.

PROTECTION: Guards against venomous people, false friends, and love rivals.

MAGICKAL AND PSYCHIC USES

For contacting angels and devas; for silent prayer; counteracts negative astrological predictions.

SPECIAL PROPERTIES

Non-gem diamonds have the same powers as gem-quality stones. Jewel of the sixtieth wedding anniversary, representing strengthening love through the years.

MYTHOLOGY AND HISTORY

In Greek mythology, diamonds were considered fragments of stars or deity tears. Cupid's arrows were reputedly tipped with diamonds. A stolen diamond is said to bring bad luck to all who subsequently own it. For example, the blue Hope diamond, which was stolen from a statue in India, now in the Smithsonian Museum in Washington. But diamonds are not unlucky; rather, they reflect the owner's tendencies toward good or bad. Diamond is the state stone of Arkansas.

Dianite or Blue Jade

COLORS: Creamy blue, light bluish-green, occasionally with veins of azure

CRYSTAL TYPE: Jadeite, one of two jade minerals, sodium aluminum silicate with mineral inclusions

ZODIAC SIGN: Libra (September 23–October 23)

CANDLE COLOR: Blue

PHYSICAL: Alleviates pain from arthritis, asthma, headaches, stress-related conditions, tinnitus; assists in sound healing and laser treatment.

EMOTIONAL: Helps you cope if you're overwhelmed or overburdened by responsibilities; addresses insomnia and sleep disturbances; counters post-traumatic stress disorder.

HOME: Promotes harmony if three or more generations share a home.

WORKPLACE: Eases tensions if colleagues or management turn tasks into a three-part drama; aids in working from home if you have children.

CHILDREN: Calms hyperactivity; mitigates issues involving eyes, ears, adenoids, and tonsils; enables Indigo Children to make friends.

ANIMALS: Allows for treatment of birds, marine life, and any other creatures that don't like being handled.

PROTECTION: Guards against extremism, emotional blackmail, or attempted coercion; prevents those who lie about you from being believed.

MAGICKAL AND PSYCHIC USES
Enhances mediumship, clairaudience, and clairvoyance.

SPECIAL PROPERTIES
The crystal of truth, Dianite provides strength not to be pressured to suppress what you know to be right.

MYTHOLOGY AND HISTORY
Dianite or Blue Jade is named in memory of Diana, Princess of Wales. Very rare, found in Siberia. A stone that helps if you struggle with Reiki or another spiritual art to open yourself to the innate wisdom rather than formal learning.

Diaspore

COLORS: Red, green, yellow, white, whitish-gray, greenish-gray, brown, colorless; pink, purple, or lilac with a pearly luster

CRYSTAL TYPE: Aluminum oxide hydroxide; an incredibly rare and expensive, color-changing, gem-quality Diaspore, called Csarite or Zultanite, is used in jewelry

ZODIAC SIGN: Pisces (February 19–March 20)

CANDLE COLOR: Pink or yellow

PHYSICAL: Alleviates memory loss; encourages healthy weight loss; eases water retention; promotes acid/alkaline balance; addresses Parkinson's and other neurological conditions.

EMOTIONAL: Counters fears of aging and becoming dependent on others; mitigates constant worrying.

HOME: Helps create a spiritual lifestyle and home, especially if children are being bribed by an ex-partner.

WORKPLACE: For rapidly memorizing information and new techniques; for generating written reports, presentations, and articles.

CHILDREN: Enables those with attention issues, who do not fit into the educational system, to succeed in extracurricular activities.

ANIMALS: Helps pets losing their faculties to compensate by using other their senses.

PROTECTION: Guards against those who change their persona depending on who is present.

MAGICKAL AND PSYCHIC USES
For vivid astral dreams, astral travel, past-life dreams, and clear dream recall; as a high-vibration crystal, Diaspore opens other realms in trance meditation and visualization.

SPECIAL PROPERTIES
Enables older people to come to grips with new technology, such as smartphones, and a workplace where machines rule.

MYTHOLOGY AND HISTORY
Diaspore, Diaspor, or Diasporite displays pleochroism, changing color according to the way it is held, viewed, or under varying lighting, strengthening the ability to see situations from different perspectives.

Dinosaur Bone

COLOR: Agatized as brown to black with splashes of red, blue, and bright yellow; occasionally yellow-gold and red; brown, gray, white, or black, if natural

CRYSTAL TYPE: Agatized dinosaur bone is fossilized bone in which cellular structure has been replaced with quartz, leaving the bone structure intact; also as natural fossilized bone

ZODIAC SIGN: Capricorn (December 22–January 20)

CANDLE COLOR: Gray

PHYSICAL: Alleviates osteoporosis, fractures, conditions involving the bone marrow, fever, genetic issues, hereditary conditions, chronic pain; promotes fertility; useful in end-of-life care.

EMOTIONAL: Counters fears of aging and panic attacks; aids in coping after the death of a partner or child, or the end of a long-standing relationship.

HOME: Kept in a new or renovated home for good fortune and to prevent structural problems; guards family unity against troublesome newcomers.

WORKPLACE: Aids in breaking into established markets and working with younger, competitive colleagues; fosters team building; for caregivers of older people.

CHILDREN: Helps in coping with grief after the death of a grandparent or great-grandparent.

ANIMALS: For elderly pets living with children or young animals.

PROTECTION: Guards against intergenerational conflicts, especially sharing a home; deflects negativity from past-life adversaries.

MAGICKAL AND PSYCHIC USES

Forges connection with ancient worlds; enables spontaneous past-life recall and safe mind travel; protects against negative entities.

SPECIAL PROPERTIES

Helps in stepping back from a frantically paced world and redefining lifestyle priorities.

MYTHOLOGY AND HISTORY

Dinosaurs first appeared on Earth about 230 million years ago. Even the smallest dinosaur bone releases millions of years of history and wisdom.

Dioptase

COLORS: Emerald, turquoise, or deep rich green

CRYSTAL TYPE: Hydrated copper silicate

ZODIAC SIGN: Taurus (April 21–May 21)

CANDLE COLOR: Turquoise

PHYSICAL: Alleviates issues involving the cardiovascular and central nervous systems, heart, blood pressure, angina, stress-related stomach problems, arthritis, irritable bowel syndrome, motion sickness, varicose veins; counters the effects of being HIV-positive.

EMOTIONAL: Reduces disregard of personal health and fitness; heals scars of childhood neglect or abuse by teaching self-love.

HOME: For mending family quarrels and uniting stepfamilies and different generations.

WORKPLACE: Aids in returning to work after absence or long-term unemployment; restores confidence after major career setbacks or injustice that cannot be put right.

CHILDREN: Teaches children to be more tolerant and to compromise.

ANIMALS: For small and vulnerable pets in a household of lively children.

PROTECTION: Shields healers and counselors from absorbing patients' illnesses or troubles.

MAGICKAL AND PSYCHIC USES

For abundance rituals; spells to attract love, increase commitment, or promote reconciliation; rituals for healing hatred between and within nations and softening prejudice; releasing old karma.

SPECIAL PROPERTIES

For living in the moment; encourages enjoyment of beautiful possessions instead of hoarding them, planning a vacation, relocation or career change now, not waiting for the ideal moment.

MYTHOLOGY AND HISTORY

Called the copper emerald, Dioptase is dedicated to Venus; a stone of realistic expectations in love—not giving up at the first imperfection, not waiting for an ideal that may not exist, yearning for a lover who will never return or commit, or expecting a partner to fix your life.

Dolomite

COLOR: Pink, beige with pink hue, milky white, colorless, reddish-white, brownish-white, yellowish-white, gray; pearly (see also Green Dolomite, page 222)

CRYSTAL TYPE: Calcium magnesium carbonate

ZODIAC SIGN: Taurus (April 21–May 21)

CANDLE COLOR: White

PHYSICAL: Strengthens bones, teeth, skin, muscles; addresses PMS, menopause, female reproductive problems, genitourinary issues, asthma, emphysema, kidney stones, lung oxygenation, heart, circulation, resistance to illness.

EMOTIONAL: Keeps you from wasting energy on useless causes; alleviates feelings of isolation; promotes healthy weight loss where there are image problems; helps overcome fears and phobias.

HOME: Attracts sufficient resources to the home; counteracts jealousy between family members, a new partner, and stepchildren or parents who resent an adult child's partner.

WORKPLACE: Fosters original creative ventures; aids in finding favor for innovative proposals; directs energies if you become sidetracked.

CHILDREN: Boosts confidence in delicate children and those with challenging intellectual or emotional issues; for premature babies and after difficult births.

ANIMALS: FOR pets separated from their mother too early.

PROTECTION: A stone of moderation, Dolomite guards against excesses in self and others.

MAGICKAL AND PSYCHIC USES

A stone of small miracles, for manifesting wishes through visualization; useful in energy layouts during sleep or healing; for Earth-healing rituals.

SPECIAL PROPERTIES

The charitable crystal, Dolomite attracts resources for voluntary initiatives and fund-raising; supports caregivers of aging or sick relatives.

MYTHOLOGY AND HISTORY

Discovered in the late 1790s in the Swiss Alps by the explorer, Dolomieu, the crystal is said in local folklore to be the stored treasure of gnomes. Though used industrially and pharmaceutically, Dolomite is increasingly regarded as a vital metaphysical and healing stone.

Double-Terminated Quartz

COLORS: Varies according to the quartz; clear quartz points are most powerful

CRYSTAL TYPE: Quartz of different kinds; double-terminated crystals have points at both ends

ZODIAC SIGN: Pisces (February 19–March 20)

CANDLE COLOR: White

PHYSICAL: Healing energy travels inward and outward from both ends: one end to remove pain, negativity, and sickness and the other for energizing, empowering, and harmonizing.

EMOTIONAL: For a person switched off emotionally; cultivates an ability to empathize or identify with others.

HOME: Singly or in a circle around the inside of the house, protects precious possessions, home, and family; prevents vandalism or carjacking.

WORKPLACE: For networking via computer, phone, or directly; casts an aura of exclusion around smartphones, tablets, and computers for privacy and to deter hacking and scams.

CHILDREN: Keep with the photo of a child for safety outside the home and to bring them safely home.

ANIMALS: To call a lost pet home.

PROTECTION: Returns earthly ill-wishing and paranormal attacks to their source.

MAGICKAL AND PSYCHIC USES

Double-terminated crystals grow freely in clay and can be directed to telepathically call an absent person and link with other dimensions, guides, and ancestors; for psychic dreaming and astral travel during sleep.

SPECIAL PROPERTIES

As a crystal of connection, Double-Terminated Quartz can be used to attract a specific love, strengthen commitment, and foster reconciliation.

MYTHOLOGY AND HISTORY

Naturally formed Double-Terminated Quartz is far more effective for healing, protection, and empowerments than those specially carved.

Dow Crystal

COLORS: Usually clear quartz, but may appear as other transparent quartzes
CRYSTAL TYPE: Crystal quartz with three seven-sided faces, each opposite a three-sided one, in alternate three- and seven-sided faces; may contain other features such as a record keeper (page 392) or Lemurian Seed Crystal (page 275)
ZODIAC SIGN: Aquarius (January 21–February 18)
CANDLE COLOR: White

PHYSICAL: Radiates healing to wherever energy is most needed or for absent healing; amplifies and refines self-healing powers.
EMOTIONAL: Counters overidentification with the problems and sorrows of others, and living through the achievements and lives of partners and children.
HOME: Continuously clears the home of stagnation, misfortune.
WORKPLACE: Aids in succeeding on your own merits if others rely on status or nepotism to advance.
CHILDREN: For children worried about achieving anything less than perfection.
ANIMALS: For pets who heal people by their loving energies.
PROTECTION: Acts as a gatekeeper during meditation, séances, and rituals to keep away unhelpful spirits.

MAGICKAL AND PSYCHIC USES
Promotes past-life recall of the timeline of earlier lives; one of the most powerful crystals for accessing higher spiritual beings and realms during meditation.
SPECIAL PROPERTIES
A rare crystal, but one that will act as a safe portal to the spiritual world, growing in power as your connection with it increases.
MYTHOLOGY AND HISTORY
Dow Crystals combine the transmitting and receiving aspects of other quartz crystals to create a third energy, sometimes called transchanneling, associated with triple divine powers: the triple goddesses of maiden, mother, and wise woman, the male equivalent triplicate, the Christian trinity, or the alchemical King Sol, Queen Luna, and the Divine Child; a powerful master healer and teacher crystal; the sacred number seven represents the seven main chakras and aura levels, the seven archangels, and the seven traditional planets.

Dragon's Blood Jasper

COLOR: Olive to darker green with red throughout
CRYSTAL TYPE: Mixture of green epidote and red piemontite
ZODIAC SIGN: Leo (July 23–August 23)
CANDLE COLOR: Red

PHYSICAL: Promotes recovery from illness, especially colds, flu, and other viruses; addresses issues involving blood pressure, arthritis, cramps, heart, fertility, libido, multiple sclerosis; alleviates back pain; aids in recovery from spleen and stomach maladies.
EMOTIONAL: Helps in overcoming trauma and PTSD; keeps you from clinging to outworn ways of living, and fears of unfamiliar people and places.
HOME: For successfully relocating and finding the right home, even if you're unwilling to move.
WORKPLACE: Aids in completing long-term projects; boosts stamina for hard physical tasks or working long hours; for all engaged in punishing training schedules.
CHILDREN: Helps parents understand their children better; encourages perseverance in difficult tasks.
ANIMALS: Helps pets to settle in a new home or with new owners.
PROTECTION: Guards against violence, terrorism, mugging, and hidden enemies.

MAGICKAL AND PSYCHIC USES
A seer stone to reveal past worlds, especially through meditation; opens future pathways based on the continuing soul journey.
SPECIAL PROPERTIES
Strengthens courage and inner dragon power to achieve major goals—especially creatively; helps in facing life changes involving leaving the comfort zone; cultivates wealth through hidden talents.
MYTHOLOGY AND HISTORY
Dragon's Blood Jasper is found in western Australia, site of many dinosaur remains and recently in South Africa. In Australia, where large goannas and dragon lizards roam, dreamtime legend tells of the Wati Kutjara lizard men, traveling through the western desert, singing animals, plants, and landscapes into being.

Dravite or Brown Tourmaline

COLORS: Golden brown to dark brown

CRYSTAL TYPE: Aluminum boron silicate

ZODIAC SIGNS: Virgo (August 24–September 22) and Scorpio (October 24–November 22)

CANDLE COLOR: Golden brown

PHYSICAL: Purifies the blood; alleviates pain in hip and other joint replacements, legs, feet, ankles; offers overall pain relief; addresses Crohn's disease, IBS, scars, ulcers, wounds; energizes when you have to keep going.

EMOTIONAL: Aids in accepting your faults and failures, overcoming bad habits (including self-abuse and addictions); comforts during bereavement.

HOME: Prevents long-standing family rivalries or overreactions, marring happy family gatherings; absorbs negative energies.

WORKPLACE: For relaxed and successful conferences; useful for all who create beauty with their hands; grounds people with unrealistic ideas or targets.

CHILDREN: Helps children accept and control negative emotions; for those with a short attention span.

ANIMALS: For horses, donkeys, and farm animals; preserves woodland wildlife.

PROTECTION: Guards against disliking those with characteristics you deny in yourself.

MAGICKAL AND PSYCHIC USES

Said to be the fallen leaves from trees in fairyland/the elf kingdoms, offering fey visions, connection with devas; for nature rituals and druidry.

SPECIAL PROPERTIES

Aids in amicably resolving inheritance and property disputes; for a fruitful, happy retirement; for long-term study where much needs to be memorized.

MYTHOLOGY AND HISTORY

A gardener's and land crystal; for landscape, environmental, and habitat conservation; dowsing for ley lines and balancing earth energies; a lucky charm to bring happiness or fulfillment of a dream or project within six months.

Druze

COLORS: Druze usually resembles sparkling white sugar crystals, sprinkled over the surface of a host stone; can also be purple, green, pink, blue, red/orange, brown, gray, or white, depending on the minerals that have formed the druze

CRYSTAL TYPE: Druze is a cluster of tiny, usually quartz, crystals covering the surface of a larger body of a crystal, the host including azurite, agate (often colorless druze within a geode), chrysocolla, danburite, dolomite, garnet, and quartz; Druze may not stay connected to its matrix but form a separate mini-cluster; sparkling; often used in jewelry

ZODIAC SIGN: Cancer (June 22–July 22)

CANDLE COLOR: Silver

PHYSICAL: Keeps you safe during pandemics and epidemics; counters infectious diseases among children that can also affect adults; alleviates shingles and skin eruptions.

EMOTIONAL: Helps overcome fear of potential disasters, even without reason, and a sense that everyone else is having a good time but you are always excluded.

HOME: Brings money in slowly but regularly and prevents major unexpected outlays.

WORKPLACE: For covering up mistakes until you can make things right; for neutralizing negative sha, or poison arrows, when applying feng shui to the workplace and restoring chi flow.

CHILDREN: A Yuletide crystal as a centerpiece for a snow scene display; set on a photo of your child to counter stage fright.

ANIMALS: Enables all in a large litter to thrive.

PROTECTION: Guards against becoming swept away by majority views with which you disagree.

MAGICKAL AND PSYCHIC USES

For spiritual workshops, group meditations, visualizations, and collective past-life work with those who feel they have been together before.

SPECIAL PROPERTIES

Often called stardust and considered a magickal crystal for wishes coming true, especially clear Druze, whatever its host rock.

MYTHOLOGY AND HISTORY

Druze is formed over a million years or more as silica dissolved in groundwater in porous rock, evaporating as tiny crystals on the surfaces or cavities of those rocks.

Dulcote Agate or Potato Stone

COLORS: Brown when as a nodule, lined with red, pink, and cream agate; swirls if broken open

CRYSTAL TYPE: Jasper-agate nodules resemble a potato when whole, with crystalline eyes breaking through the rind; may contain calcite, clear quartz, citrine, amethyst, or other minerals

ZODIAC SIGN: Capricorn (December 22–January 20)

CANDLE COLOR: Brown

PHYSICAL: Alleviates issues involving the liver, kidney stones, gallstones, IBS, Crohn's disease, stomach ulcers, buildup of fatty deposits; addresses blocked arteries, lung congestion.

EMOTIONAL: For those living in the past; counters the inability to accept that a particular love is over.

HOME: Aids in finding hidden treasure in attics, garage sales, online auctions, or estate sales.

WORKPLACE: Leads to opportunities to further your career; for careers involving many years of education and apprenticeship.

CHILDREN: Promotes stable health among children and teens throughout their growing years; allows their unique gifts to evolve.

ANIMALS: Enables a young animal who is not thriving to gain strength.

PROTECTION: Brings safety while traveling; guards against theft.

MAGICKAL AND PSYCHIC USES

Contains fey energies; breaks negative spells and ill-wishing; for earth rituals at Indigenous places of power.

SPECIAL PROPERTIES

A stone of hidden treasures, including looking for and discovering unexpected qualities in someone you had dismissed as dull; aids in recalling and planning an exciting adventure you had put aside. The Potato Stone is a reminder that we all still have an inner child ready to reemerge.

MYTHOLOGY AND HISTORY

From the Mendip Hills in Somerset, UK; in myth, Potato Stone was considered a Celtic druid icon to bring protection during travel; believed to have been taken by the Celts from Somerset to the ancient Neolithic Rollright Stones circle in Oxfordshire to be empowered by the stones.

Dumortierite

COLORS: Deep blue to violet, with black inclusions; can be pinkish-brown

CRYSTAL TYPE: Borosilicate, translucent to opaque

ZODIAC SIGNS: Leo (July 23–August 23) and Aquarius (January 21–February 18)

CANDLE COLOR: Dark blue or violet

PHYSICAL: Alleviates issues relating to ligaments, tendons, throat, thyroid, hidden causes of illnesses, nausea, seasickness, upset stomach, fever.

EMOTIONAL: Useful for anger management and anger management therapy.

HOME: For selling a home, when there's little interest or low offers.

WORKPLACE: Boosts efficiency and organization if others' chaos interferes with your output.

CHILDREN: Promotes mathematical and language skills, and retention of knowledge.

ANIMALS: Calms boisterous dogs, and horses who hate traffic or are hard to train.

PROTECTION: Guards crisis and frontline workers from trauma.

MAGICKAL AND PSYCHIC USES

Unconsciously clears unresolved past-life experiences hindering present life; for past-life shamanic and meditative experiences.

SPECIAL PROPERTIES

Calls a soul mate; twin crystals, one for each person, preserve soul connection when you're far apart; brings closeness to angels and divinity in sacred buildings and sites.

MYTHOLOGY AND HISTORY

Not discovered until the end of the 1800s, named after its discoverer, the French paleontologist Eugene Dumortier, Dumortierite has become associated with the planet Uranus because both initiate positive change in unexpected ways; found in eastern France, Brazil, Namibia, as well as Colorado, Nevada, and Washington State.

Eclogite

COLORS: Green, often with red and white

CRYSTAL TYPE: Combines red garnet, omphacite (green diopside and jadeite), and quartz, plus almadine, kyanite, zoisite and dolomite

ZODIAC SIGN: Sagittarius (November 23–December 21)

CANDLE COLOR: Red

PHYSICAL: Counters sexual dysfunction and loss of libido; relieves the pain of childbirth and PMS; believed to promote white blood cell health.

EMOTIONAL: Comforts you from past sorrows, so you feel safe to love again.

HOME: Promotes understanding between generations sharing a home.

WORKPLACE: For overcoming self-doubt when applying for a new post or a promotion.

CHILDREN: Assists fearful children starting school or joining a new activity.

ANIMALS: Helps a new pet settle into a home where there are other animals.

PROTECTION: Activates your internal radar to become aware of danger or deceit.

MAGICKAL AND PSYCHIC USES

For past-life dreams and astral or soul traveling during sleep; to magickally manifest wishes.

SPECIAL PROPERTIES

Brings forgiveness of others and yourself if you got it wrong; for starting again with a clean slate.

MYTHOLOGY AND HISTORY

Up to 650 million years old, the most ancient deposits are in Brazil and Mali; also in Europe and the USA; called the Christmas crystal because of its festive colors.

Edenite

COLORS: Dark green translucent; dull gray, greenish-gray, black or brown; rarely white, tan, or yellow

CRYSTAL TYPE: Amphibole, sodium calcium magnesium iron aluminum silicate hydroxide

ZODIAC SIGN: Pisces (February 19–March 20)

CANDLE COLOR: Green

PHYSICAL: Counters muscle weakness and spasms, heart irregularities, heart attack; addresses kidney stones, calcification of bones, nerve fibers; promotes mobility and digestion.

EMOTIONAL: Helps you come to terms with a secret about your birth or deception by your partner; aids in starting a new life after threats.

HOME: For peacefully resolving family grievances, where tensions escalate between parents and children or if there is sibling rivalry.

WORKPLACE: Aids in dealing with unfair dismissals, sexism, ageism, or prejudice without pursuing litigation; for hostage and kidnap negotiations.

CHILDREN: Helps if a school or college is unwilling to intervene in bullying situations.

ANIMALS: For small pets who attack larger animals.

PROTECTION: Guards against those who exercise undue physical or mind control.

MAGICKAL AND PSYCHIC USES

Use Green Edenite for mediumship, both professionally and to contact ancestors; develops claircognizance, psychic knowing; connects with angels.

SPECIAL PROPERTIES

For tracing long-lost relatives overseas; finding missing pieces in your family history.

MYTHOLOGY AND HISTORY

Like other amphiboles (see Amphibole or Angel Phantom Quartz, page 25), Edenite connects the everyday and spiritual worlds. Edenite is the name of an individual mineral, as well as a group name for similar Edenite-related minerals. While Edenite has not received the attention of other new age healing minerals, it is prized by collectors for safe and meaningful spiritual exploration.

Edinburgh Cobblestones

COLORS: Gray, brown, black; set as jewelry in sterling silver

CRYSTAL TYPE: Basalt and granite cobblestones made into jewelry by Edinburgh miner and retailer Two Skies, which was gifted the old stones with the rebuilding of the Rose Street area in Edinburgh, originally set with the cobblestones in 1767

ZODIAC SIGN: Scorpio (October 24–November 22)

CANDLE COLOR: Indigo

PHYSICAL: Repairs muscles; helps with mobility and issues of aging; restores strength after debilitating illness, major surgery, or life-changing injuries.

EMOTIONAL: Resolves unfinished business from the past; quiets voices in the head that remind you of past failures or mistakes.

HOME: Gives a sense of tradition to a newly built home or new suburbs if they lack character; for those of Celtic origin to link with their roots.

WORKPLACE: Aids in developing an interest in historical fiction into a paying part-time or even full-time career; working with established crafts, traditional trades, or in buildings of historic interest.

CHILDREN: A way into appreciating history for teens but not for the psychically sensitive.

ANIMALS: An amulet against spirits that spook pets.

PROTECTION: Guards against hauntings and fears of hauntings.

MAGICKAL AND PSYCHIC USES

Walking in the shoes of the past in meditation, visualization, and automatic writing/psychic artistry, not only of those who lived in the Georgian part of town, but Old Edinburgh, which dates back thousands of years.

SPECIAL PROPERTIES

One of the most exciting links to the past and your personal ancestors, since many footsteps were imprinted on the cobblestones.

MYTHOLOGY AND HISTORY

Edinburgh is one of the most haunted cities in the world, as many of the ancient buildings still stand or were buried under rebuilding after being abandoned to plague in 1645. The area was sealed after the plague and not built over for one hundred years; these cobblestones, though not in the immediate area, provide a psychokinetic link to hauntings, not only for Celtic descendants or those visiting Edinburgh, but by psychic transference to any places where restless spirits walk.

Eilat, Eliat, or King Solomon Stone

COLOR: Green-blue, turquoise, swirling deep green with blue; bright lustrous colors

CRYSTAL TYPE: Mixture of azurite, chrysocolla, malachite, turquoise, and other secondary copper minerals, sometimes with silver and copper inclusions

ZODIAC SIGN: Sagittarius (November 23–December 21)

CANDLE COLOR: Turquoise

PHYSICAL: Alleviates issues involving the throat, sinuses, lungs, mouth, fever, inflammation, bones, tissues, arthritis, wrists, knees, elbows; for color therapy.

EMOTIONAL: For valuing yourself rather than fitting others' expectations; for overcoming the trauma of sexual abuse and/or incest.

HOME: Encourages respect and care for older generations within a family, especially those frail or losing their memory.

WORKPLACE: Enables older people to be valued for their wisdom and experience in a youth-oriented world; for linguists, singers, writers, communicators, legal professionals, academics, archaeologists, historians, religious leaders, spiritual gurus.

CHILDREN: For those at boarding school, in residential or foster care, or have migrated to a new land, to connect with home.

ANIMALS: Maintains good health for older pets and those with a long natural life span, such as parrots and tortoises.

PROTECTION: Guards against loneliness if you're far from home.

MAGICKAL AND PSYCHIC USES

For formal magickal rituals, past lives to ancient worlds, psychic visions; strengthens telepathic links between lovers.

SPECIAL PROPERTIES

For journeys along sacred or pilgrimage trails, to ancient cities or lands; for spiritually focused handfasting and weddings.

MYTHOLOGY AND HISTORY

Associated with King Solomon and his copper mines near Eilat in Israel, Eilat is the national stone of Israel. It brings deeper understanding of ancient literature, sacred texts, and old complex languages.

Elephant Skin Jasper

COLORS: Reddish-brown, dark brown, golden yellow, or tan, with light brown and black lines running through it

CRYSTAL TYPE: Silicate, microcrystalline quartz, with mineral or organic inclusions of fossilized shells, bones, and vegetation

ZODIAC SIGN: Capricorn (December 22–January 20)

CANDLE COLOR: Orange

PHYSICAL: Alleviates asthma, bronchitis, eczema, adhesions of internal scar tissue; promotes fertility, especially with a gap in conception after a first or subsequent child; eases pregnancy and childbirth; counters amnesia after an accident.

EMOTIONAL: Helps overcome lack of self-love and lack of self-esteem; living in the fast lane leading to burnout; fears of the unknown; loneliness.

HOME: Protects buildings from age-related deterioration and neglect by the property owner; brings luck and prosperity if enclosed in the wall of new construction; encourages family unity.

WORKPLACE: Cultivates success through business travel and international online networking; helps with long-term ventures and apprenticeships.

CHILDREN: For gifted children who feel isolated; teens demanding instant gratification.

ANIMALS: Protects elephants and rhinoceroses from illegal poaching.

PROTECTION: Keeps you safe while traveling, especially during long-distance driving.

MAGICKAL AND PSYCHIC USES

For Reiki; animal communication and healing; graphology (evaluation of personality characteristics by studying handwriting); studying contemplative religions.

SPECIAL PROPERTIES

Worn as a bracelet or necklace, different shades of Elephant Skin Jasper draw together its powers—increased memory, strength, prophecy, and writing skills—reflected in its names: Elephant Skin, Miriam (the prophetess) Stone, and the Calligraphy Stone.

MYTHOLOGY AND HISTORY

From the Himalayas, stone of Ganesha, the elephant-headed god of wisdom, travel, happiness in love and prosperity.

Elestial Angel Calcite

COLORS: White, colorless or off-white with a wrinkled surface resembling white moldavite, though it is not moldavite

CRYSTAL TYPE: Calcium carbonate, with tiny fissures over the face and body of the layered or highly etched surface (see Elestial Quartz, page 25)

ZODIAC SIGN: Pisces (February 19–March 20)

CANDLE COLOR: White

PHYSICAL: Alleviates headaches, epilepsy and petit mal seizures, skin growths, vertigo; addresses issues involving the visual cortex; helps the body to fight illness.

EMOTIONAL: Counters fear of flying, drug-related burnout, living only for the present moment.

HOME: Aids in adapting a home and creating a new fulfilling lifestyle after a life-changing incident in the family; helps in creating a memory table with photos and mementoes.

WORKPLACE: Promotes equal opportunities, resources, and support in employment for those who are psychologically, physically or emotionally challenged.

CHILDREN: Gives children an awareness of the protection of their guardian angel; for those naturally gifted in music, especially those with communication disorders.

ANIMALS: For being blessed with an old-soul pet.

PROTECTION: Guards against spirits summoned in séances or by a ouija board, who promise rewards that rarely materialize.

MAGICKAL AND PSYCHIC USES

Cultivates the power to hear the music of the spheres, the songs of the angels, and the harmonies of the planets; angelic communication for experienced practitioners and those new to spirituality.

SPECIAL PROPERTIES

Elestial Angel Calcite is believed to reawaken parts of the mind associated with the preliterate, instinctive psychic awareness of the hidden and evolved realms with which we once freely mingled.

MYTHOLOGY AND HISTORY

Found in the sand dunes in the Mojave Desert near the Colorado River in western Arizona, the stone comes from sacred land; Elestial Angel Calcite can yield insights through meditation, dreams, and waking visions of its inherited memories of the dawn of humanity.

Elestial Quartz

COLORS: Depends on the composition of the mixture of crystals; characteristically gives a smoky effect
CRYSTAL TYPE: Quartz based, usually a combination of two crystals growing with natural terminations over the body and face of a layered elestial; clear, smoky (common), citrine, amethyst, occasionally rose quartz or ametrine
ZODIAC SIGN: Leo (July 23–August 23)
CANDLE COLOR: Gold

PHYSICAL: Addresses issues involving the pineal gland, pituitary gland, brain disorders, vertigo, bones, scoliosis, connective nerves and tissues; mitigates effects of x-rays and other forms of radiation therapy.
EMOTIONAL: Helps overcome limitations imposed by the criticism and prohibitions of others; alleviates schizophrenia, bipolar disorder.
HOME: As the centerpiece of any home, brings harmony, light, and blessings on all within.
WORKPLACE: Puts the human factor back into an impersonal or highly competitive workplace.
CHILDREN: For children afraid of surgical treatment or seeing a physician.
ANIMALS: Aids in deciding whether to proceed with invasive veterinary tests or prolonged treatment with an uncertain outcome.
PROTECTION: Guards against psychic or psychological intrusion by others.

MAGICKAL AND PSYCHIC USES
A high-vibration crystal for contact with spirit guides and ascended masters; sacred geometry; soul-to-soul communication with a partner through the crystal to recall shared previous lives.
MYTHOLOGY AND HISTORY
First discovered in Africa, Elestial Quartz crystals often have etchings on the faces, believed to hold keys to ancient wisdom, activated by touch. Used in Indigenous ceremonies from South America and North America to Africa to call ancestors.

Emerald

COLORS: Bluish-green to pure green, with not-too-dark vivid color saturation
CRYSTAL TYPE: Beryl; gem and non-gem share similar healing and magickal properties
ZODIAC SIGN: Taurus (April 21–May 21)
CANDLE COLOR: Bright green

PHYSICAL: Alleviates issues involving the eyes, sinuses, angina, rheumatism, diabetes, epilepsy, lymph nodes, skin inflammation, viruses, infections, kidneys, insect bites, PMS, menopause, respiratory complaints; promotes fertility, youthfulness, and ease in childbirth; traditionally a poison antidote.
EMOTIONAL: Helps overcome fears of aging and recurring nightmares.
HOME: Creates happiness at home; guards against false friends, neighborhood gossip, and divisions between couples.
WORKPLACE: Prompts prosperity and success; smooths the way for older women changing career or returning to work midlife.
CHILDREN: In tumbled stones form, Emerald restores confidence in teenagers teased about their weight or because parents cannot afford designer goods.
ANIMALS: For aristocratic dogs and cats.
PROTECTION: Guards against domestic violence; musters courage among women in communities where they are considered inferior; binds nighttime psychic attacks and paranormal evil.

MAGICKAL AND PSYCHIC USES
For bibliomancy—psychically identifying relevant information from the Bible or stichomancy, using other sacred literature.
SPECIAL PROPERTIES
Encourages lasting, faithful love and friendship, and successful court hearings and legal disputes involving dishonesty; a talisman for women in later life to find true love.
MYTHOLOGY AND HISTORY
Besides symbolizing eternal life, passion, and beauty, Emeralds were linked with wisdom by the ancient Egyptians who considered them a gift from Thoth, god of learning. An early Christian bishop, Andreas of Caesarea, declared Emeralds the stone of St. John the apostle, possessing power to release penitents from sin.

Emerald Hummingbird Quartz or Green Tanzurine

COLORS: Medium to emerald-green, due to the dense inclusion of green fuchsite within the quartz

CRYSTAL TYPE: Quartz with fuchsite

ZODIAC SIGN: Aries (March 21–April 20)

CANDLE COLOR: Green

PHYSICAL: Relieves pain; addresses hard-to-treat illnesses or those slow to respond to treatment; alleviates asthma; eases plant allergies; ensures safe childbirth.

EMOTIONAL: Counters arrested emotional development due to trauma, mood swings, unwillingness to try new experiences or to leave mistakes by self and others in the past.

HOME: Brings the life force into the home; restores laughter, good humor, and optimism.

WORKPLACE: Makes anything seem possible; overcomes conflict situations and permanently irritable colleagues or hard to please managers; encourages self-growth.

CHILDREN: In the home, Green Tanzurine brings the day to a natural close; prevents insomnia, nightmares and night terrors.

ANIMALS: For shielding the runt of the litter from bullying siblings.

PROTECTION: against taking on too much and giving too much to others; for safe travel.

MAGICKAL AND PSYCHIC USES

Connects with the ancestors, especially ones distant in time; for natural magick, making natural remedies.

SPECIAL PROPERTIES

Green Tanzurine assists all new beginnings, whether a new relationship, an addition to the family, or starting again in a relationship where there was separation.

MYTHOLOGY AND HISTORY

Recently discovered, like Cherry Hummingbird Quartz or Red Tanzurine (page 115), by Jonathan Bartky on Masai tribal land in northern Tanzania, the crystal has become associated with the brightly colored hummingbird of the Americas. Although the smallest of birds, it is believed to always speak the truth with courage, and its versatility in flight mirrors green hummingbird quartz qualities; acts as an amulet at times when the odds seem overwhelming.

Emerald Quartz or Emerald in Quartz

COLORS: Emerald Quartz is a bright emerald color throughout; in Emerald in Quartz, the natural emerald may be seen within clear quartz

CRYSTAL TYPE: Two different stones but with remarkably similar properties. Emerald Quartz contains chromium, while Emerald in Quartz is a beryl emerald on a quartz matrix. Sometimes rough emeralds are included in the category of Emerald in Quartz

ZODIAC SIGN: Taurus (April 21–May 21)

CANDLE COLOR: Emerald

PHYSICAL: Counters heart irregularities and atherosclerosis; eases stress-related conditions; relieves pain and exhaustion made worse by insomnia; for resisting infections and viruses, especially recurring ones; addresses issues involving the eyes, kidneys, bladder; promotes fertility and eases pregnancy.

EMOTIONAL: Helps overcome the inability to express or accept love without doubting the motive, fear of infidelity in a good relationship because of past betrayal.

HOME: Increases family harmony, especially among siblings.

WORKPLACE: Brings business success through persuasiveness and the ability to anticipate potential new markets.

CHILDREN: For chaotic teenagers to bring order to their lives.

ANIMALS: Enables pets to tolerate noise and strangers.

PROTECTION: As a warning against the presence of an unreliable person or a risky situation, especially Emerald in Quartz where the stone may become paler.

MAGICKAL AND PSYCHIC USES

For manifesting your heart's desire; twin-soul rituals; spells for commitment and fidelity if a partner is tempted to stray by an unscrupulous rival.

SPECIAL PROPERTIES

Both crystals attract good luck and financial gain, and are powerful for gradual and lasting growth through maximizing opportunities.

MYTHOLOGY AND HISTORY

Emerald Quartz translated into Sanskrit means "green growing things," so both stones represent emotional security, profit in property, especially a bargain on the first step on the ladder, health, and matters of love and fidelity.

Empowering Crystals

Directly after cleansing a crystal, you can empower it for a specific purpose or ongoing energies if it is an amulet or charm. There may be other times—for example, the day before an examination, a driving test, or a special date—you wish to enhance the good-fortune energies of a particular crystal or piece of jewelry (see page 148, "Cleansing Crystals"). You can empower crystals before a healing or divinatory session, cleansing, and reempowering them between sessions.

USING NATURE

Natural sources of energy, like the sun and moon, fill crystals with energy and healing light as they are cleansing them. Full moonlight or Midsummer or Solstice Eve, from sunset to sunrise, are sufficiently gentle to both cleanse and allow natural energies to empower any crystals.

Places of beauty—a lakeside, rock formation, a forest, a sacred site, a tree in a local park, flowers or herbs on your balcony or in your garden—act a focus of natural power. Set your crystals on top of a flat rock or on the grass, sand, or earth close to your chosen focus; leave the crystals for ten or fifteen minutes to absorb the life-force energies from the natural world.

WITH FRAGRANCE AND LIGHT

Leave an individual crystal or a circle of crystals surrounding a lighted white, gold, or, best of all, a beeswax candle. Let the candle burn away. If crystals need special power for a specific occasion or after you have cleansed them with incense smoke or smudge (see page 151), make slow spiral smoke circles over the crystals clockwise nine times, picturing desired results as you do. Let the incense burn through.

USING YOUR PERSONAL ENERGIES

We used a similar method empowering your jewelry. For a crystal point, gently stroke it from the base to the tip and down again to the base and up again to create a rhythmic movement.

For a round or oval crystal hold it in your nondominant hand and with the index finger of the other hand make spirals on the crystal surface until you connect with its innate rhythm, like a gentle throbbing.

If you have a number of small crystals, place them in a circle; move the palms of your hands above and over them, palms down and fingers together, the right hand in clockwise circles and the left hand counterclockwise at the same time for a minute or two, asking the purpose as a soft chant.

At the same time, picture light pouring golden from the cosmos, red and gold from the Earth, and rich green from nature into your crystal or crystal circle.

Ask that the chosen crystal(s) be used for the *"greatest good"* and invite the angels or guides you work with you to assist you with whatever is most desired or needed *"at the time and in the way that is most appropriate."*

USING A PENDULUM

Directly after cleansing your crystal(s) with your pendulum by making counterclockwise circles (page 151), circle the pendulum nine times slowly clockwise over the crystal(s), asking your guardian angel and any guides to infuse your crystals with light, power, and healing.

Empath Wounded Warrior Quartz

COLORS: Depends on the type of quartz, from clear to yellow, purple, or black

CRYSTAL TYPE: A quartz crystal that has been damaged by humans or a natural process and may have cracks, marks on the sides or point, or missing pieces; it can appear in any quartz crystal

ZODIAC SIGN: Cancer (June 22–July 22)

CANDLE COLOR: Silver

PHYSICAL: Aids in recovery from accidents; counters life-limiting conditions; useful in cosmetic surgery and reconstructive surgery; promotes the speedy healing of wounds.

EMOTIONAL: For anyone with scars or life-changing injuries or appearance after an accident or severe illness; eases post-traumatic stress disorder.

HOME: For adapting your lifestyle if you have lost your home, your job, or your relationship; for showing sympathy with a family member who has caused their own problems.

WORKPLACE: Prompts you to obtain the right facilities and resources to cope in the workplace, if you're physically, emotionally, or intellectually challenged.

CHILDREN: Assuages those who have spent long periods in hospital or undergoing prolonged treatment.

ANIMALS: For nursing an injured creature back to health.

PROTECTION: Guards against lack of support in times of need.

MAGICKAL AND PSYCHIC USES

Enhances angelic communication, shamanic travel for soul retrieval; for prayer, chanting, and ritual to seek blessings and alleviate burdens; collective healing rituals for a sick or injured member of a coven or spiritual group.

SPECIAL PROPERTIES

For courage in adversity; starting from where you are and building an authentic, fulfilling life by calling on your inner warrior to overcome doubt and fear.

MYTHOLOGY AND HISTORY

Empath Warrior crystals have come through their own trials; though wounded, they have survived, and have great strength and healing powers to offer positive solutions to all in distress for whom the way ahead is not clear. They teach not to be influenced by external appearance, wealth, or charisma.

Empowerite

COLORS: Black, brown with white or cream banding

CRYSTAL TYPE: High silicate form of chert

ZODIAC SIGN: Virgo (August 24–September 22)

CANDLE COLOR: Green

PHYSICAL: Alleviates issues involving the gallbladder, pancreas, liver, hands, feet, shoulders; for convalescing after illness or injury.

EMOTIONAL: Helps overcome the feeling that you're not at home in your body or your life, and constantly feeling unable to deal with practical issues or make decisions.

HOME: For high-rise living or in a major urban development; for the creation of city gardens and farms.

WORKPLACE: Enables you to focus on necessary tasks when there are a lot of distractions; for fitness instructors; those who work with soil, clay, minerals, agriculture, horticulture, in construction or manufacturing.

CHILDREN: Calms hyperactive children and those with ADHD; for those who are naturally clumsy.

ANIMALS: For farm animals, especially rare breeds and those being raised on organic farms.

PROTECTION: Guards against becoming overwhelmed by the demands of others.

MAGICKAL AND PSYCHIC USES

For Earth and Earth-healing rituals; dowsing with a forked wooden rod for what is lost and subterranean water; in a healing layout, Empowerite provides strength and stability where a prognosis is uncertain.

SPECIAL PROPERTIES

The stone of Mother Earth, as its name suggests Empowerite is very empowering for practical, tangible achievement and for courage to stand up for your rights.

MYTHOLOGY AND HISTORY

A recent discovery, hidden in the forests of New Zealand for millions of years, in swampy ground, Empowerite may contain fossils; it promises the unfolding of your powers in the years ahead.

Emra Lemuria

COLORS: A green version of Aqua Lemuria, sometimes very clear; like Aqua Lemuria, contains gas bubbles

CRYSTAL TYPE: Created from volcanic ash; resembling obsidian, natural volcanic glass; however, one theory holds that Emra and Aqua Lemuria were stones created by the Lemurians themselves millennia ago; the Emra carried the knowledge of the Earth and the Aqua the knowledge of the sea, surviving the Great Flood

ZODIAC SIGN: Virgo (August 24–September 22)

CANDLE COLOR: Green

PHYSICAL: Increases the effectiveness of all plant-based remedies and traditional healing methods, such as Ayurveda and traditional Chinese medicine; enhances hydrotherapy; mitigates plant, pollen, feather, and fur allergies.

EMOTIONAL: Eases agoraphobia; keeps you from spending 24/7 plugged into technological devices or watching television.

HOME: For beautiful and healthy gardens and conservatories; encourages birds and wildlife to come into your garden.

WORKPLACE: Prompts you to add plants and crystals to the workplace environment and your personal workspace to keep energies circulating, to avoid inertia, and to bring on prosperity.

CHILDREN: Encourages children of all ages to plant fruits and vegetables and to explore the wilderness.

ANIMALS: Aids in healing pets using touch therapies, Reiki, crystals, and alternative remedies and supplements.

PROTECTION: Guards against those who replace green spaces with industrialization and urbanization.

MAGICKAL AND PSYCHIC USES

Prompts connection with nature spirits, Earth and forest devas; for Wicca, druidry, paganism, and nature spiritualities.

SPECIAL PROPERTIES

Coming from the mountains of Sumatra, like its sister Aqua Lemuria, it is believed the Emra stones contain the wisdom of the submerged continent once between Australia and India; each programmed to reveal to its owner, through dreams, visions, and meditation the secrets they individually need to know.

MYTHOLOGY AND HISTORY

The hidden treasure crystal, Emra means "jewel" in Hindi and "gem" in the Gaelic language; links humans in an unbroken circle with crystals, stones, plants, trees, animals, and birds.

Enhydro or Water Agate

COLORS: Cloudy white, also in other colored agates, such as red, gray, deep brown, black, or blue

CRYSTAL TYPE: Outer casing of chalcedony within which is sealed a cavity filled with water. You can hear the water moving if you shake the stone; the water is visible when the crystal is held to bright light (see also Enhydro Quartz, page 176).

ZODIAC SIGN: Cancer (June 22–July 22)

CANDLE COLOR: White

PHYSICAL: Detoxifies the liver; regulates fluid and hormone imbalances; the waters within the crystal tune into and reflect a woman's monthly energy and hormonal ebbs and flows.

EMOTIONAL: Assuages after extreme trauma; alleviates postnatal depression, midlife crises in either sex, fear of water.

HOME: Aids in locating missing correspondence on the computer or necessary official papers, evidence, deeds, and warranties.

WORKPLACE: During negotiations, disputes, and tribunals, helps pick up the hidden agenda and underlying tempo; for those in counseling, psychology, therapy work, or social work.

CHILDREN: For teenage girls and boys and those approaching puberty, when raging hormones may clash with older female relatives' mood swings or a midlife crisis.

ANIMALS: For frustrated pets in heat.

PROTECTION: Guards against being misled.

MAGICKAL AND PSYCHIC USES

Enhances telepathy, especially with people overseas, as well as clairvoyance and remote viewing; aids in reconnecting with spirit guides.

SPECIAL PROPERTIES

Gentler and more stable than Enhydro Quartz, for resolving delicate situations or negotiations.

MYTHOLOGY AND HISTORY

Representing the waters of the womb of the Earth Mother, Enhydro Agate is the stone of Iemanja, the Yoruba/Africa Caribbean sea goddess, a stone of both fertility and abundance. The water within the agate may be millions of years old and offers access to ancient wisdom and underwater worlds.

Enhydro Quartz

COLOR: Takes the color of the host quartz

CRYSTAL TYPE: Quartz with moving bubbles of water or occasionally plant oil trapped millions of years earlier, still totally pure; Enhydros are also found in Agate (page 13) and chalcedony

ZODIAC SIGN: Pisces (February 19–March 20)

CANDLE COLOR: White

PHYSICAL: Regulates fluid imbalances, hormones; pinpoints foreign objects trapped in your body; alleviates stomach acidity, chronic flatulence, blisters, abscesses, hydrocephalus; eases pregnancy, especially if you're carrying twins or other multiples; useful for tests and treatments for an in-utero infant.

EMOTIONAL: Counters the tendency to cling to old grievances and guilt; helps overcome self-destructive patterns acquired in childhood.

HOME: Establishes boundaries—physical and psychological—with difficult neighbors, family members, or friends.

WORKPLACE: Aids in knowing whether colleagues and clients are being truthful; for insurance assessors, benefits and tax fraud investigators, decision makers in welfare or custody cases.

CHILDREN: For adopted children searching for their roots.

ANIMALS: Useful in calling old-soul pets to return.

PROTECTION: Guards against fears of aging and mortality.

MAGICKAL AND PSYCHIC USES

A seer stone for accessing past, present, and future; aids in exploring ancient wisdom and lost worlds; enhances other crystals' powers; taps psychically into the unspoken needs and feelings of others.

SPECIAL PROPERTIES

A personal evolution crystal to fulfill your potential at every life stage and understand your soul purpose.

MYTHOLOGY AND HISTORY

Associated with the three sisters of Fate in different cultures, the ancient energies of Enhydro, combined with proactive quartz, enable past wisdom to guide the right steps for future action and understanding our place in the scheme of life.

Enstatite

COLOR: Green, yellowish, colorless, white, gray, brown, black; green-brown in rare gem-quality

CRYSTAL TYPE: Pyroxene, magnesium silicate, sometimes found with diopside, with diamonds in South Africa or in stony meteorites (see also Bronzite, page 93)

ZODIAC SIGN: Aries (March 21–April 20)

CANDLE COLOR: Dark green

PHYSICAL: Alleviates anemia, short-term memory loss, brain degeneration with age, exhaustion; boosts recovery for slow-healing wounds; strengthens muscles (including the heart muscle); counteracts male sexual dysfunction; promotes assimilation of iron.

EMOTIONAL: Helps overcome fear of being alone, resulting in unsatisfactory relationships or entering new ones to fill an inner void.

HOME: Establishes boundaries between work and home if you have a home-based business or office.

WORKPLACE: Avoids intrigues and politicking, particularly by authority figures who play favorites or create an excessively competitive atmosphere.

CHILDREN: Prevents sibling rivalry.

ANIMALS: For horse shows and horse racing, canine competitions, and sheepdog trials.

PROTECTION: Guards against those who would discredit you, especially when found with diopside; aids in winning legal disputes or sidestepping unhelpful officials.

MAGICKAL AND PSYCHIC USES

Encourages you to follow a spiritual or religious path where learning is supplemented by spontaneously recalling ancient wisdom; Enstatite from meteor sites prompts communication with advanced civilizations.

SPECIAL PROPERTIES

The winner's crystal, especially Enstatite from diamond sources, for competitions, lottery, gaming; helps in succeeding in any area of life where there is unfair competition.

MYTHOLOGY AND HISTORY

The stone of chivalry, altruism, and justice, Enstatite bolsters courage to stand up for the vulnerable, fight against corruption, and resist temptation to resort to unethical means.

Eosphorite

COLORS: Colorless, pale pink, pale yellow, light to dark brown, reddish-brown, orange, black; the pinkish-orange shades may be found faceted

CRYSTAL TYPE: Hydrated manganese iron aluminum phosphate hydroxide, almost always with inclusions; sometimes on a rose quartz matrix; may form rosettes

ZODIAC SIGN: Leo (July 23–August 23)

CANDLE COLOR: Gold

PHYSICAL: Useful in recovery on the cellular level; for genetic counseling; motivates you to take time out for yourself.

EMOTIONAL: Counters unnecessary and sometimes unwanted self-sacrifice; dissipates an inferiority complex or the victim syndrome.

HOME: Encourages caregivers, whether of children or elderly relatives, to make time for their own needs; for overcoming the empty-nest syndrome.

WORKPLACE: For the confidence to carve out your own niche or position in the workplace if the ideal post does not exist.

CHILDREN: For teens with a poor self-image to love themselves as they are and value their unique gifts, rather than comparing themselves with celebrities; to guard against online trolling.

ANIMALS: Ensures that pets who are patient with small children are not overwhelmed by too much attention.

PROTECTION: Guards against those who try to persuade you that you are selfish for refusing unreasonable demands.

MAGICKAL AND PSYCHIC USES

For revisiting the source of bad karma in meditation, past-life regression, or dreams, as a way to leave it behind.

SPECIAL PROPERTIES

A stone that puts you center stage in your own life and aids in shedding unnecessary burdens; for the freedom to step back from family peacekeeping duties.

MYTHOLOGY AND HISTORY

Derived from the Greek *eosphoros,* which means "dawn bearing," this refers to the pink color of the original Eosphorite, first found in 1878 in Fairfield County, Connecticut; after heartbreak or heartache in its pink/orange shades, Eosphorite forms a reconciliatory love token.

Epididymite

COLORS: Usually white or colorless; may be purple, violet, yellow, gray, green, or light blue

CRYSTAL TYPE: Sodium beryllium silicate; may be included in quartz or on a matrix of aegirine or smoky quartz

ZODIAC SIGN: Aquarius (January 21–February 18)

CANDLE COLOR: Purple

PHYSICAL: Protects against contagious diseases, especially when people are living or working in close proximity; alleviates skin conditions like eczema.

EMOTIONAL: For those who call up the deceased, demanding favors, or dabble in magick, spirits, or demons without any form of psychic protection; for obsessions with ghost hunting, haunted houses, and online incantations.

HOME: Keeps you safe if you move into a home haunted by unfriendly presences, because of bad events that occurred there or being too close to where energy lines cross.

WORKPLACE: For mediums, healers, priests and priestesses, professional exorcists and all seeking to guide distressed spirits to the light.

CHILDREN: Keep this crystal high in a young child's room as insulation from nightmares about ghosts or monsters disturbing their sleep and teenagers who have scared themselves with demonology.

ANIMALS: Calms psychic pets who bark or yowl at every unearthly vibe.

PROTECTION: Guards against attacks on the aura, especially psychic attacks.

MAGICKAL AND PSYCHIC USES

For psychic protection against low-level spirits while conducting magick rituals or mediumship; enhances psychic abilities.

SPECIAL PROPERTIES

Called a stone of ascension, Epididymite connects with the higher self and the higher dimensions; some people use a grounding crystal with it at first, such as black tourmaline or an earthy agate.

MYTHOLOGY AND HISTORY

First discovered in 1893 on the island Aro in Norway, Epididymite is a rare mineral but much prized if you are professionally developing your spiritual and healing powers or need to channel your psychic gifts if they are random and disturbing.

Epidote

COLORS: Olive green or pale to dark green; can also be yellowish- or brownish-green, brown to black

CRYSTAL TYPE: Calcium iron aluminosilicate (See also Epidote Quartz or Dream Quartz)

ZODIAC SIGN: Gemini (May 22–June 21)

CANDLE COLOR: Green

PHYSICAL: Alleviates issues relating to the liver, gallbladder, skin, recovery after illness or surgery (including heart-valve operations), dehydration, fluid imbalances, brain disorders, cystic fibrosis, thyroid; addresses heart irregularities.

EMOTIONAL: Helps overcome agoraphobia, fears of travel, being trapped in a cycle of negative thinking and self-defeating behavior, overeating, martyrdom, self-pity.

HOME: Brings good health and energy into the home, encouraging a healthy lifestyle; filters out stress introduced from the outside world.

WORKPLACE: Cultivates awareness of hidden agendas as well as unexplored opportunities; boosts confidence to apply for promotion if your professional progress has stalled.

CHILDREN: For encouraging children enamored of fads to try new foods.

ANIMALS: For overindulged pets who expect human privileges.

PROTECTION: Guards against attracting misfortune through fears of being jinxed or cursed.

MAGICKAL AND PSYCHIC USES

A manifestation crystal, Epidote brings the best results if you're focusing on positive goals, such as prosperity, career success, travel, or love; enhances the power of other crystals.

SPECIAL PROPERTIES

Epidote brings to everyone the qualities they most need once negative thinking is eradicated.

MYTHOLOGY AND HISTORY

Epidote has gained a reputation as the stone that awakens users both to their own potential and to the wonders of the world and nature. According to crystal folklore, one special Epidote crystal not yet discovered will make the invisible world of nature spirits visible to all humans with good hearts.

Epidote Quartz or Dream Quartz

COLOR: Light green to bluish-green, sometimes with darker markings

CRYSTAL TYPE: Clear quartz with epidote inclusions, as a green shadowy inner crystal or epidote filling the quartz; epidote and quartz also grow together with quartz as the matrix

ZODIAC SIGN: Pisces (February 19–March 20)

CANDLE COLOR: Green

PHYSICAL: Amplifies the healing powers of plants and crystals; alleviates issues involving the cardiovascular system, asthma, thyroid, obesity, autoimmune disorders, glandular fever, Hodgkin's disease, fluid retention, recurring viruses and infections, internal parasites.

EMOTIONAL: Quiets past negative inner voices; rejects unfair criticism and sarcasm.

HOME: For living alone after separation or from loss of a partner.

WORKPLACE: Manifests the fulfillment of major ambitions through perseverance, study, and good luck; after downsizing or retirement, assists in developing a new creative career or business venture.

CHILDREN: Prevents teens from being influenced by undesirable friends.

ANIMALS: Deters pets from ingesting harmful substances outdoors.

PROTECTION: Shields from malicious entities during sleep and astral travel, and energy vampires.

MAGICKAL AND PSYCHIC USES

Channels angels, spirit guides, and devas; enhances deep meditation, prophetic dreams, encounters with deceased relatives in dreams.

SPECIAL PROPERTIES

For peaceful sleep, driving away insomnia and nightmares; brings vivid dream recall and answers to questions in dreams; promotes lucid dreaming; useful for past-life dreams and dream travel.

MYTHOLOGY AND HISTORY

Epidote in Quartz combines proactive quartz with magickal epidote, bringing closer possibility and actuality and the manifestation of desires. A radar to increase awareness of the right opportunities and people, harmful influences, and dead ends.

Etched Quartz

COLORS: Usually clear, but can be found in almost any quartz, sometimes as a mosaic pattern

CRYSTAL TYPE: Etched markings can appear on most quartzes, caused originally by water during the growth cycle or mineral inclusions that dissolved away in formation

ZODIAC SIGN: Aquarius (January 21–February 18)

CANDLE COLOR: White

PHYSICAL: Promotes traditional forms of healing such as Ayurveda, traditional Chinese medicine, herbal and plant healing, and homeopathy; counters reactions to chemical pollutants.

EMOTIONAL: Mitigates the inability to read warning signs, even if you previously encountered them; a throwaway attitude to anything that breaks or is not the latest design.

HOME: For living in and restoring a home with a history; collecting small family treasures for a memory box.

WORKPLACE: Aids in following or reviving traditional methods.

CHILDREN: Enables those who are hyperactive to slow down.

ANIMALS: Restores natural instincts to pets who have lost their sense of what is safe when roaming.

PROTECTION: Guards against the 24/7 frantic pace of the modern world.

MAGICKAL AND PSYCHIC USES

Enhances visions of ancient worlds, higher beings, and their messages contained within etched markings; a doorway to ancient Egypt if hieroglyph-like markings are visible, Lemuria, Atlantis, Star realms, and the wisdom of lost worlds.

SPECIAL PROPERTIES

It is said an etched quartz will come into our life when we most need its wisdom.

MYTHOLOGY AND HISTORY

The significance of the etchings on the quartz will vary according to where it is found. For example, evolight quartz, discovered in 2016 in Sichuan Province, China, has distinctive etchings across the termination faces. Evolight contains the wisdom of the sages who made the area their home through the centuries, as well as the sanctity of the mountains that have been in existence for millions of years; similarly Etched Quartz from the Kullu Valley, Himachal Pradesh, India carries its own sacred connections.

Ethiopian Precious Fire Opal

COLORS: Vivid play of color, especially green and purple, flashing from a body color—usually orange or red, but sometimes brown, white, or yellow; its body colors, flickering streaks, and opalescence qualify it both as a precious and fire opal

CRYSTAL TYPE: From stratified volcanic rocks, opalized rhyolitic ignimbrite (igneous rock) on a base of clay

ZODIAC SIGN: Cancer (June 22–July 22)

CANDLE COLOR: Silver

PHYSICAL: Promotes gentle weight loss, gain, or maintenance, as needed; addresses skin complaints, such as rosacea, made worse by stress, plus skin inflammation, rashes, and sunburn.

EMOTIONAL: Counters poor self-image, distorted body image; helps overcome a tendency for anorexia, bulimia, feasting, and fasting; mitigates self-harm; keeps you from being inhibited by fear of failure.

HOME: Enables you to enjoy your own company.

WORKPLACE: For those who make others feel valuable just as they are, not wanting because they fall short of what the media deems as perfection.

CHILDREN: Gives self-confidence to teens teased about their appearance; counters social awkwardness.

ANIMALS: For meditation on magickal animals to bring desired qualities and strengths.

PROTECTION: Strengthens the silver cord that is said to hold our etheric body safely to the physical form during astral travel.

MAGICKAL AND PSYCHIC USES

Connects with Earth and Fire spirits; especially magickal Fire elements from different lands; sharpens visions of the future.

SPECIAL PROPERTIES

Removes negative or redundant karma and fears from past worlds to ensure new beginnings.

MYTHOLOGY AND HISTORY

Different kinds of opals have been discovered in Ethiopia as well as the precious fire opal that is often called Welo or Wollo opal, after Wollo Province in northern Ethiopia, where it was discovered in 2008. However, Ethiopian opals were known to Indigenous people in times past and opal tools have been discovered in Africa dating back as early as 4000 BCE.

Euclase

COLOR: Light pale, sapphire, or aquamarine blue, blue-green, light green, yellowish, white, colorless

CRYSTAL TYPE: Beryllium aluminum hydroxide silicate, rare form of Datolite (see page 157)

ZODIAC SIGN: Libra (September 23–October 23)

CANDLE COLOR: Blue

PHYSICAL: Relieves the pain of arthritis, muscle cramps, inflammation, blood vessel constrictions, sinus headaches; alleviates issues involving speech, eyes, difficulties swallowing; promotes a healthier lifestyle; works as an antiseptic and antibacterial agent.

EMOTIONAL: Counters unhealthy lifestyle patterns, self-destructive and self-defeating behavior; overcomes blockages keeping you from expressing to significant others feelings and needs, often a family trait.

HOME: Brings joy into any home through simple pleasures and finding something good about each day.

WORKPLACE: For mathematics, geometric calculations, and fields where precision and detail are essential; for architects, designers, landscape gardeners, town planners, and graphic designers.

CHILDREN: Boosts the confidence of young people leaving home for the first time; for adult children unwilling to leave the nest.

ANIMALS: Keeps pedigreed animals from becoming oversensitive to everyday life.

PROTECTION: Guards against negative thoughts and becoming weighed down by doubts and fears that prevent you from taking positive action.

MAGICKAL AND PSYCHIC USES

Connects with energies of sacred sites, labyrinths, cathedrals, temples, and ancient roads; leave negative karma behind through past-life healing.

SPECIAL PROPERTIES

For satisfaction through creative ventures and activities; seeing and seizing opportunities others miss; a stone of justice through honest communication.

MYTHOLOGY AND HISTORY

Traditionally the stone of happiness and limitless possibility if life seems restricted; a "thinking and acting outside the box" crystal at any age or stage to find an ideal solution fast.

Eudialyte

COLOR: Pink-red, red, brownish red, red-violet, green, or yellow, sometimes with black (tourmaline) and white inclusions

CRYSTAL TYPE: Cyclosilicate, minor ore of zirconium, within coarse-grained host rock, often containing calcium, cerium, iron, manganese, sodium, and yttrium in its structure; may contain up to forty-six different chemical elements

ZODIAC SIGN: Taurus (April 21–May 21)

CANDLE COLOR: Pink or red

PHYSICAL: Alleviates issues involving the eyes (especially the optic nerves), the pancreas, thyroid, blood, cells, skin, heart, bones; promotes self-healing, vitality; counters the inability to tolerate certain foods or chemicals.

EMOTIONAL: Reduces obsessive-compulsive disorder; encourages self-love; lowers the drive for achievement no matter what the cost.

HOME: After a family crisis when a member's behavior has shaken the family structure.

WORKPLACE: Bolsters self-belief to make the right decisions if power-hungry colleagues unsettle you; aids in finding your right life path; unblocks creativity.

CHILDREN: For teens in love with love; helps move beyond obsession with celebrities; encourages you to foster or adopt abused children.

ANIMALS: Calls power animals, rather than actual ones.

PROTECTION: Keeps away pessimistic people and self-defeating thoughts; guards against psychic attack.

MAGICKAL AND PSYCHIC USES

Clairaudience, especially messages from ancestors, angels, or spirit guides; telepathy; feng shui.

SPECIAL PROPERTIES

Resolves jealousy in love, whether by or of a partner or ex-partner; helps you overcome a constant fear of betrayal; aids in ending a love going nowhere.

MYTHOLOGY AND HISTORY

The stone of attaining one's heart's desire; recognizing and finding one's soul mate and members of the soul family; resolving problems experienced in past worlds with them.

Extra-Terminated Quartz or Extraterrestrial Crystal

COLORS: Usually clear; varies according to the type of quartz

CRYSTAL TYPE: Can appear in any quartz, especially smoky, citrine, and amethyst, with a single termination at the tip and multiple terminations at the base; occasionally one or more terminations extend from the sides

ZODIAC SIGN: Aquarius (January 21–February 18)

CANDLE COLOR: White

PHYSICAL: The base can be directed to draw out pain or illness and return it to the Earth and the tip to send energy and health to self or others by transformation of cosmic power; offers both contact (direct) or remote healing.

EMOTIONAL: Keeps you from being pulled in different ways based on loyalty.

HOME: Amplifies and radiates love in all directions if you have a large or extended family and many friends.

WORKPLACE: Aids in multitasking; if you work from home, enables you to divide your time so people who assume you are free to socialize do not disrupt your schedule.

CHILDREN: For Star Seed Children or those fascinated by astronomy; for space-mad teens who sometimes scare themselves.

ANIMALS: Heals a sick or exhausted pet with the dual energies of the Earth and the higher realms.

PROTECTION: Guards against allowing others to denigrate your beliefs about the possibilities of other worlds.

MAGICKAL AND PSYCHIC USES

For communication with extraterrestrials; astral travel to other galaxies; increasing awareness of intuitive astrology.

SPECIAL PROPERTIES

Absorbs the universal life force through the single termination; amplifies and simultaneously diffuses it through the base into your life and the lives of those to whom you are close.

MYTHOLOGY AND HISTORY

Whether you regard the quartz as an extra-terminated crystal or an intergalactic ET or both, it is particularly powerful for healing and magick because it draws upward the power of the Earth Mother and, at the same time, it draws downward cosmic and angelic energies.

Eye of the Storm or Bahia Jasper

COLORS: Earthy colors, such as deep green, brown, cream, pink, gray, and russet; each stone patterned differently

CRYSTAL TYPE: Mixture of jasper and agate

ZODIAC SIGN: Libra (September 23–October 23)

CANDLE COLOR: Blue

PHYSICAL: Addresses issues involving the kidneys, genetic conditions, toxins, DNA, absorption of nutrients; reduces side effects of chemotherapy, enhances regrowth of healthy cells; HRT; melanomas.

EMOTIONAL: For panic attacks and automatic flight or fight responses; drama kings and queens for whom the slightest setback is a three-act tragedy.

HOME: Protects against hurricanes and cyclones, storms and tornadoes; avoiding taking sides in family rivalries.

WORKPLACE: remaining focused when pressurized into unrealistic targets; for fair rewards for effort if the workplace uses nepotism for promotion.

CHILDREN: For staying calm when a toddler throws a major tantrum in public; standing firm against teenage dramas.

ANIMALS: For horses to remain untroubled by sudden noises.

PROTECTION: against those who use threats or fury to intimidate.

MAGICKAL AND PSYCHIC USES

Chaos magick; weather rituals; meditation when you cannot find a quiet space to work; retaining magickal power for gradual release; Buddhist chants; singing bowls.

SPECIAL PROPERTIES

The stone of remaining true to yourself and your beliefs, whatever the pressures to act otherwise.

MYTHOLOGY AND HISTORY

In the center of a hurricane or cyclone is the eye where it is totally calm, the point around which the hurricane rotates. This stone comes from Bahia in Brazil. Sometimes you might detect a faint center to your stone; also known as "Judy's stone" after the late crystal expert Judy Hall.

Faden Quartz

COLOR: Clear with milky, feather-like, white lines or threads within the crystal

CRYSTAL TYPE: Silicon dioxide; clear crystal quartz. Lines are close to the center, perpendicular to the apex, either straight or curving

ZODIAC SIGN: Aries (March 21–April 20)

CANDLE COLOR: White

PHYSICAL: A mender crystal, for bones, cartilage, sports injuries, broken blood vessels; generates self-healing and the will to recover.

EMOTIONAL: Mends broken hearts, following loss, betrayal, and shattered dreams.

HOME: For single-parent families without support; enhances house renovations and decorating.

WORKPLACE: For online marketing and sales; all who fix problems on- and offline or repair what is broken, from vehicles to technology.

CHILDREN: Teaches them to care for possessions; keeps them from being influenced by ads for the latest gadgets.

ANIMALS: For older pets with mobility problems.

PROTECTION: Repairs the aura if it's weakened by negative atmospheres and people; for safe air travel; removes fear of flying.

MAGICKAL AND PSYCHIC USES

Telepathy, safe astral travel, automatic writing, sacred chant; Earth healing; exploring past and future lives.

SPECIAL PROPERTIES

For connection and communication—spoken, written, and telepathic—between people and with other dimensions; the feather-like thread connects with guardian angels; for mending relationships; for online dating.

MYTHOLOGY AND HISTORY

Faden Quartz is called the *self-healer,* symbol of wounded heroes and heroines through the ages who went on to victory. The line in the quartz is created when the Earth moves during the crystal's formation, causing a crack; once stabilized the crystal joins again.

Fairy Frost

COLORS: Colorless with inner white wisps and veils that resemble frost

CRYSTAL TYPE: Quartz with inclusions of air, water bubbles, or gas, with fractures and swirls caused by the trapped air

ZODIAC SIGN: Cancer (June 22–July 22)

CANDLE COLOR: Silver

PHYSICAL: For all forms of natural healing, including herbal remedies, flower oils and essences, homeopathy, naturopathy, traditional Chinese medicine and Ayurveda; for an unexpected improvement or remission.

EMOTIONAL: Helps overcome a tendency to be cynical, over-logical, and focus solely on duty, materialism, and obligation; counters workaholism.

HOME: Makes a fey center with fairy frost and small fairy statues in or outdoors among greenery to keep energies fresh and attract health, wealth, and good fortune.

WORKPLACE: For writers, illustrators, and researchers into mythology, fantasy, and the unseen world of nature; useful in an overserious office of big egos that ignore the needs of workers.

CHILDREN: Keeps magick alive for children.

ANIMALS: Makes very psychic pets on a rural property acceptable to local nature spirits.

PROTECTION: Guards against losing awareness of possibility and the inexplicable in logical terms.

MAGICKAL AND PSYCHIC USES

For contact with the fey at any age, and wish magick, especially on the full moon when the moonlight shines through the crystal.

SPECIAL PROPERTIES

Some believe each fairy frost, fairy dust, and devic temple is blessed by a guardian fey and contains its essence, revealed especially on Fridays, the day of the fairies, the full moon, and May Eve and Halloween.

MYTHOLOGY AND HISTORY

Though Fairy Frost is present in Devic Temple Crystals, it is not itself a Devic Temple Crystal. Fairy dust has similar properties to Fairy Frost; however, the markings are on the outside in fairy dust as tiny crystals that sparkle in light, like a light dusting of ice.

Fairy Opal

COLORS: Blue or sometimes rainbow colors, heat-treated or altered with nontoxic additives so the porous, sandstone matrix becomes dark and the opal colors shine within it

CRYSTAL TYPE: Tiny pieces of precious opal scattered throughout the porous sandstone; opals in the area only grow within the sandstone

ZODIAC SIGN: Cancer (June 22–July 22)

CANDLE COLOR: Silver

PHYSICAL: Remedies issues involving fractures, teeth, nails, mobility, night vision, migraines, neurological disorders; promotes fertility, pregnancy, and childbirth.

EMOTIONAL: Counters extreme cynicism and sarcasm as the common response to communication by others; thwarts scattered energies where interest is rapidly lost and causes are instantly abandoned.

HOME: Creates a color-filled home; encourages hosting impromptu potluck evenings and weekends for family, friends, neighbors, and colleagues, so your home is filled with laughter.

WORKPLACE: For success in writing, illustrating, and animating stories about talking animals, nature spirits, and fantasy creatures; for improving your chances of gaining employment.

CHILDREN: Encourages belief in magick while children are still young; teaches children to forgive siblings and peers.

ANIMALS: Aids in welcoming a stray or rescue pet into your home, rather than buying one; for communication with your pet.

PROTECTION: Guards against becoming overwhelmed by bad news in the media and on social media; against those who pretend to be what they are not.

MAGICKAL AND PSYCHIC USES

For fey magick and connection with Indigenous and traditional fairies, rainbow rituals, color magick, and divination.

SPECIAL PROPERTIES

A stone of transformation if life is stagnant or has lost its magick; Fairy Opal jewelry continuously spreads good humor and optimism throughout the gloomiest workplace and home.

MYTHOLOGY AND HISTORY

Found only in Queensland, Australia, opalized sandstone is called Fairy Opal or treasure because the tiny pieces of opal shimmer against the dark background, especially when held to the light.

Fairy Stone Calcite

COLORS: Gray, off-white, tan, brown, beige

CRYSTAL TYPE: Calcium carbonate, fine-grained clay sand mixed with limestone cement; in formation, the front smooth, the back irregular containing organisms fossilized millions of years ago

ZODIAC SIGN: Virgo (August 24–September 22)

CANDLE COLOR: Brown

PHYSICAL: Reduces fever; alleviates arthritis, effects of radiation and/or chemotherapy, cellular damage; addresses wounds; promotes health in the eighties, nineties, and beyond; reverses calcification.

EMOTIONAL: Helps overcome recurring addictions and bad habits, especially smoking; mitigates fight-or-flight reactions and excessive defense mechanisms.

HOME: Brings good fortune and abundance; welcomes the house guardians; calms you after a stressful day.

WORKPLACE: For original ideas; aids in standing out from the crowd for promotion and success; helps avoid plagiarism.

CHILDREN: Enables you to assume a parenting role later in life through remarriage, fostering, or adoption; prevents nightmares.

ANIMALS: For animal conservation, especially preserving local habitats.

PROTECTION: Guards against personal insecurity and jealousy souring present relationships because of past hurt; shields the aura during ritual and divination.

MAGICKAL AND PSYCHIC USES

Connects you with nature beings and fey; enhances goddess rituals; strengthens Earth energies at ancient sites; guards against psychic attack.

SPECIAL PROPERTIES

Described as natural sculptures or goddess stones because of their resemblance to the rounded paleolithic goddess of Willendorf statues; softens overassertive, domineering attitudes; each stone believed to contain a helper spirit.

MYTHOLOGY AND HISTORY

Found mainly in northern Quebec in ancient glacier deposits. The Algonquin nation used the stones for good fortune, as love tokens, to protect homes, for good hunting and fishing, and to keep away all evil.

Falcon, Hawk, or Blue Tiger's Eye

COLORS: Blue, blue-gray, blue-green; iridescent when held to the light

CRYSTAL TYPE: Unoxidized form of tiger's eye, where blue crocidolite is replaced by quartz, not iron oxide, retaining its blue color

ZODIAC SIGN: Sagittarius (November 23–December 21)

CANDLE COLOR: Blue

PHYSICAL: Alleviates issues involving eyesight, vertigo, sinuses, throat, neck; eases motion sickness when flying; mitigates the effects of prolonged radiation or chemotherapy.

EMOTIONAL: Eases hypochondria, chronic pessimism, fear of enclosed or high spaces.

HOME: Attracts prosperity in the southeastern wealth corner.

WORKPLACE: Ensures successful promotion interviews or when asking for increased salary; assists with relocation, especially overseas.

CHILDREN: Helps older teens going backpacking, or traveling out-of-state or overseas.

ANIMALS: Attracts wild birds to gardens; promotes the well-being of aviary birds, conservation of endangered birds of prey.

PROTECTION: Guards against fears of flying; protects air travelers; shields you from physical harm.

MAGICKAL AND PSYCHIC USES

Clairvoyance and remote viewing; visions during meditation; astral travel; totem spirit birds; bird divination.

SPECIAL PROPERTIES

Shields against the evil eye of jealousy, curses, hexes, jinxes, and ill-wishing, reflecting back malice to its source; reveals others' lies.

MYTHOLOGY AND HISTORY

The hawk, a bird that in legend flies closest to the sun, appears on medicine wheels, often representing the South. In Celtic mythology, Merlin shape-shifted into a hawk to travel swiftly. In ancient Egypt the sky god Horus, the falcon or hawk-headed god, enfolded the Pharaoh in his protective wings. The hawk/falcon also represented part of the spirit released after death.

Faulted Agate

COLORS: Varies according to the location

CRYSTAL TYPE: Agates whose bands are disrupted along fault lines by Earth movement or nearby Earth tremors, recemented with calcite or chalcedony in a slightly different position; sometimes hard to spot but other times obvious; may have been smoothed by waters; sometimes found in veins along fault lines or rock cracks

ZODIAC SIGN: Gemini (May 22–June 21)

CANDLE COLOR: Red

PHYSICAL: For fractures, bone splintering, and reconstructive, cosmetic, or implant surgery; aids in recovery from heart-bypass operations, reconnecting veins that have become blocked, ulcerative colitis.

EMOTIONAL: Helps overcome an unwillingness to embrace necessary changes after a loss or setback; counters feeling out of tune with the world.

HOME: Aids in making renovations after natural disasters; restores what can be fixed in practical and emotional terms, rather than throwing away what is broken.

WORKPLACE: Finds a new way of working after a takeover; helps in starting a different business after a forced sale.

CHILDREN: Eases the way for those uprooted or unsettled for any reason; comforts those who do not quite fit in at school; enables successful fostering and adoption.

ANIMALS: Aids in nursing a pet back to health.

PROTECTION: Guards against those who resist any change or movement from the comfort zone.

MAGICKAL AND PSYCHIC USES

Chaos magick; leaving behind old karma through past-life exploration; dowsing for treasures and intuitively piecing together different finds to uncover a secret from old worlds.

SPECIAL PROPERTIES

A reminder that after sometimes inevitable changes, better patterns of living can be created, given wisdom gained from experience and adaptability.

MYTHOLOGY AND HISTORY

Found in coastal Cornwall, Scotland, the United States, including Wyoming, and in Mexico; sometimes the center of the agate has collapsed, another clue to this remarkable collector's piece; sometimes made into cabochons and jewelry.

Feather Pyrite

COLORS: Silvery gold with black feather patterns

CRYSTAL TYPE: Iron sulfide; metallic; feathery vein-like patterns on pyrite, usually sold highly polished or cut into cabochons; often a collector's piece

ZODIAC SIGN: Aries (March 21–April 20)

CANDLE COLOR: Gold

PHYSICAL: Promotes healthy blood circulation; eases fur and feather allergies; helps overcome impotence.

EMOTIONAL: Counters unrealistic plans and ideas that do not materialize; curbs the tendency to abandon long-term ventures or relationships in favor of short-term satisfaction.

HOME: Helps people come together in harmony and well-being as a result of joining hands to weather difficult times.

WORKPLACE: Aids in achieving your ambitions in the face of opposition or daunting odds; a lucky stone for opening doors to opportunity; for new businesses taking off financially.

CHILDREN: Enables children to learn to respect wildlife and grow up protecting creatures in distress or danger.

ANIMALS: Helps give aviary and cage birds sufficient space and freedom to fly; prevents threatened wild bird species from losing their habitats.

PROTECTION: Guards against those whose words deceive.

MAGICKAL AND PSYCHIC USES

Aids in accessing messages from deceased relatives and more distant ancestors; smudging with feather fans; spirit flight and shape-shifting; prosperity spells.

SPECIAL PROPERTIES

Overcomes fear of flying; creates a protective web around the aura and chakra energy centers to tangle up any negativity sent deliberately or by unconscious ill-wishing.

MYTHOLOGY AND HISTORY

Found only in the East Harz Mountains in Niedersachsen in Lower Saxony in Germany. Feathers are sacred to the rituals of many lands from ancient Egypt, Greece, and Rome and the Norse world to Native North America, among the Australian Aboriginals and New Zealand Maori people; Feather Pyrite is believed to increase the power of the individual bird species; since birds are considered to be messengers of the deities and the form the freed soul takes after death.

Fenster or Window Quartz

COLORS: Clear

CRYSTAL TYPE: Quartz; with transparent windows in the sides of the crystal where sunken areas are framed by raised parts like windows

ZODIAC SIGN: Cancer (June 22–July 22)

CANDLE COLOR: Silver

PHYSICAL: Enhances eyesight, left- and right-brain hemisphere connection; aids in finding new treatments for existing conditions, focusing a window on a painful spot or source of trouble.

EMOTIONAL: Relieves OCD, obsessions, and addictions rooted in childhood; counters excessive concern with the lives of others.

HOME: Enables you to step back from a family member who is damaging family life and finances with an addiction or antisocial behavior for which they refuse to seek treatment.

WORKPLACE: Valuable when accuracy and attention to detail are essential; detects hidden intrigue in the workplace and the motives of others they conceal behind smiles.

CHILDREN: For storytelling through the different windows.

ANIMALS: Calms pets traumatized by early cruelty or abandonment.

PROTECTION: Guards against the false images others project to gain financial advantage or emotional or psychic control.

MAGICKAL AND PSYCHIC USES

Often called the "window to the soul," the windows open to other worlds, including past lives, early years in this lifetime, as well as other dimensions; finding access to your first incarnation on Earth to identify any unfulfilled karmic tasks.

SPECIAL PROPERTIES

Locates missing animals, objects, and people with whom you have lost touch; aids in connecting with an old love via social media or a reunion at your former school or college.

MYTHOLOGY AND HISTORY

Fenster is German for "window." Fenster Quartz has a skeletal appearance with windows inside the main crystal, which is often double terminated; also found on a clear quartz crystal as a diamond window or an extra seventh face, between and lower than the six main faces.

Ferberite

COLORS: Black, reddish-brown, black-brown; may be glassy or slightly metallic

CRYSTAL TYPE: Sulfate, iron tungstate with high iron content, slightly magnetic, minor ore of tungsten

ZODIAC SIGN: Capricorn (December 22–January 20)

CANDLE COLOR: Gray

PHYSICAL: Bolsters physical strength, recovery after illness; alleviates blood disorders, especially anemia and sickle cell disease; addresses arthritis, muscle pain, abscesses, bladder weakness, incontinence caused by stress; regulates bodily fluids.

EMOTIONAL: Mitigates obsessive-compulsive disorder, fear of showing emotions; keeps you from making unwise attachments or obsessing about old loves.

HOME: Brings back fun and laughter into the home after a sad period; aids in starting again after repossession or an unwelcome sale due to divorce or financial loss.

WORKPLACE: For business and manufacturing ventures; starting a consultancy; brainstorming; valuable for rescue and emergency service personnel and paramedics.

CHILDREN: Kept with a photo in their absence, helps children have fun at summer schools or vacation activities if they are nervous about being away from home; for adult children to find a home of their own.

ANIMALS: For animals in the last stages of their life.

PROTECTION: Guards against those who would deceive or lead astray.

MAGICKAL AND PSYCHIC USES

Pendulum dowsing; banishing with white light malevolent spirits claiming kinship, royal, or celebrity connections through ouija board sessions.

SPECIAL PROPERTIES

Brings freedom into your life if you feel obligated by outworn burdens; enables you to say no; frees you from restrictive beliefs; an anticult stone.

MYTHOLOGY AND HISTORY

Crystal of the trader, especially sole traders, for adapting to changing market and economic demands; for attracting new orders at markets and festivals.

Fire Agate

COLOR: Brownish-red, with small glints and flashes of red, yellow, and orange resembling fire

CRYSTAL TYPE: An iridescent form of red agate with plated crystals of iron or thin layers of limonite over layers of chalcedony; also with goethite inclusions

ZODIAC SIGN: Aries (March 21–April 20)

CANDLE COLOR: Scarlet

PHYSICAL: Promotes vitality, sexual libido; addresses issues involving the stomach and circulation; burns away fever, lingering illnesses, viruses, and infections; alleviates menopausal hot flushes; strengthens night vision.

EMOTIONAL: Reduces cravings, self-destructive thoughts, and addictive behavior; aids in recovery from emotional exhaustion.

HOME: Protects home and family against intruders, those threatening harm, and unscrupulous debt collectors.

WORKPLACE: Helps you achieve major ambitions, where instant action or response is required.

CHILDREN: For teens bullied on social media or threatened by a gang.

ANIMALS: Motivates a pet who has lost the will to live.

PROTECTION: Creates a shield reflecting ill-wishing and harm back to the source.

MAGICKAL AND PSYCHIC USES

Fire magick; connecting with fire elementals and fire spirits; protective magick.

SPECIAL PROPERTIES

A power crystal to overcome any obstacles or danger and achieve any goal, however seemingly impossible.

MYTHOLOGY AND HISTORY

Fire Agate was used in alchemy because it was believed to contain the essence of fire. In many traditions it is sacred to fire deities such as Agni, the Hindu god of fire; encourages high standards in self and others; brings passion in every area of life.

Fire and Ice Quartz

COLORS: Clear with many sparkling inclusions and rainbows

CRYSTAL TYPE: Naturally formed quartz or crackle quartz; natural quartz crushed under great pressure to yield the numerous jagged inner inclusions

ZODIAC SIGN: Aries (March 21–April 20)

CANDLE COLOR: White

PHYSICAL: Addresses intense visual disturbances, migraines, arrhythmia, major trauma following an accident or bad fall, especially to the spleen.

EMOTIONAL: Aids in recovery from severe trauma, shock, PTSD, split personality, feeling or being torn by conflicting loyalties.

HOME: Brings the home and family back together after a split or crisis.

WORKPLACE: For working on several different sites belonging to the same company; freelancing in different workplaces.

CHILDREN: The ultimate fey crystal, especially the sphere, for those whose belief about Santa Claus, the tooth fairy, and the world of fey has been crushed.

ANIMALS: After a lost pet has returned home and will not settle.

PROTECTION: Guards against those who would sabotage new beginnings.

MAGICKAL AND PSYCHIC USES

Rune divination and magick, rituals for the changing seasons, mediumship to connect with wise ancestors.

SPECIAL PROPERTIES

Clears confusion and doubt; transforms a seemingly impossible situation through a flash of inspiration that offers a new positive perspective.

MYTHOLOGY AND HISTORY

Ice is the fifth element in the Norse tradition. It fused with the cosmic fires of Muspelheim to create life. So, Fire and Ice Quartz contains a huge amount of generated energy for transformation, whether within a tumbled crystal, sphere or pyramid.

Fire Opal

COLOR: Red to bright orange or yellow background, glowing; Fire Opal has flickering red streaks

CRYSTAL TYPE: Hydrated silicon dioxide, a distinctive type of opal, defined by color; considered a Precious White Opal (page 369) if it displays iridescent flashes

ZODIAC SIGN: Aries (March 21–April 20)

CANDLE COLOR: Red

PHYSICAL: Alleviates issues involving the intestines, abdomen, kidneys, lower spine, eyesight, central nervous system, genitals, potency, fertility, sexual desire; illnesses diminishing life quality; blood disorders.

EMOTIONAL: Counters the effects of sexual abuse, incest, domestic violence, and rape trauma.

HOME: Helps you adjust to living solo after leaving a destructive relationship if loneliness or poverty tempts you to return.

WORKPLACE: Attracts money and customers to businesses; aids in fast-tracking a career; useful in hazardous jobs or where instant decision making is needed.

CHILDREN: Encourages independence in teens unduly influenced by their peers.

ANIMALS: Bolsters campaigns against animal neglect and cruelty in less charismatic species.

PROTECTION: For resisting guilt or financially induced parental control at any age.

MAGICKAL AND PSYCHIC USES

Sex magick; working with the four elements and fire spirits; candle magick; acupuncture, acupressure.

SPECIAL PROPERTIES

The most active of opals, Fire Opal gives courage to resist if you are experiencing family or community opposition to your lover.

MYTHOLOGY AND HISTORY

Fire Opal is considered in Mexico, its main source, to be born of fire, because it comes from the depths of ancient volcanoes. Fire Opal was called by the Aztecs the bird of paradise stone, after their feathered serpent creator god Quetzalcoatl, and was found in burial chambers. Fire Opals offer power to explorers, conquerors, and great leaders.

Fiskenaesset Ruby

COLORS: From rose red to pigeon-blood red; may be silver-black; called Pink Sapphire (page 359) when pale pink

CRYSTAL TYPE: Corundum containing an unusually large quantity of chromium; found in a matrix

ZODIAC SIGN: Aries (March 21–April 20)

CANDLE COLOR: Red

PHYSICAL: Boosts strength and vitality; eases restricted blood flow; promotes fertility, sexual potency, reproductive system health in men and women; addresses issues involving the lymph nodes.

EMOTIONAL: Helps overcome codependency, overpossessiveness by parents toward children of any age, frozen emotions, and expression of feelings after rejection.

HOME: Attracts wealth, ensures the free flow of chi, the life force; maintains the heart of the home so that returning family members feel the love after an absence.

WORKPLACE: Generates leadership opportunities; aids in developing a passion into a moneymaker.

CHILDREN: Comforts a child whose mother is in hospital, working far from home temporarily, or no longer living with the child.

ANIMALS: For animal mothers after a traumatic birth of their young.

PROTECTION: Guards against psychic and emotional vampirism and psychic attacks.

MAGICKAL AND PSYCHIC USES

Induces a deep meditative trance for communication with the spirit world. Like all rubies, Fiskenaesset Ruby darkens when in the presence of danger; healing the soul of past-life trauma.

SPECIAL PROPERTIES

This ruby shields against giving too much and doing too much for others, leaving yourself exhausted.

MYTHOLOGY AND HISTORY

Said to be among the oldest gems on the planet, buried under ice for between 2.9 billion and 3.1 billion years, Fiskenaesset Ruby has been mined only in Greenland and, unusually for rubies, extracted from rock very recently. One of the few consolations of global warming, since it has now appeared as a new Earth treasure. However, the rubies may have been known to Indigenous hunters for centuries. A stone of increasing love between two people without sacrificing their identity.

Flame Aura Black Kyanite

COLORS: Colors vary through gold, blue, rainbow, but always shimmering; may resemble flashing flames

CRYSTAL TYPE: Striated black kyanite fan, bonded and covered permanently with titanium; the fan shape distinguishes it from other titanium auras, providing the underlying strength and courage of black kyanite

ZODIAC SIGN: Pisces (February 19–March 20)

CANDLE COLOR: Gold or rainbow stripes

PHYSICAL: Unblocks energies and the natural flow of hormones, blood, and fluids throughout the body; alleviates issues involving the adrenal glands, vocal cords, bone marrow; addresses neurological disorders.

EMOTIONAL: Those who leave themselves open without discrimination to people who flatter to mislead; helps overcome fear of ghosts and spirit possession.

HOME: A powerful home defense, propped upright, so the fan acts as a shield; balances the yin-yang energies and enables the clear flow of chi throughout the property or your part of the property.

WORKPLACE: Enables calm thought, decision making, and reactions where others are panicking; creative brainstorming.

CHILDREN: The ultimate bedtime magick wand, under supervision, to drive away fears of the night.

ANIMALS: Keep with a picture of a pet who wanders in the night, to cast the rainbow aura of protection to guide the animal safely home.

PROTECTION: Guards against malicious, low-vibration spirits who try to intrude on mediumship and seances.

MAGICKAL AND PSYCHIC USES

For newcomers to psychic work and those more experienced whose energies are blocked or not progressing; connects with guardian angels and spirit guides.

SPECIAL PROPERTIES

The crystal of moving energies, the fan is used to remove what is harmful and destructive and cleanse the aura with an outward sweep and inward to call what is most desired from the cosmos; the defensive form of Titanium Aura Quartz (page 478).

MYTHOLOGY AND HISTORY

Used in cutting psychic and psychological cords, in cases where this will cause pain to either or both people, but necessary to remove codependency.

Flamingo Jasper

COLORS: Pink with black veins
CRYSTAL TYPE: Jasper, chalcedony
ZODIAC SIGN: Taurus (April 21–May 21)
CANDLE COLOR: Pink

PHYSICAL: Alleviates skin irritation or breathing problems caused by allergies to feathers or fur; eases digestion that is adversely affected by eating the wrong foods or by food intolerances.
EMOTIONAL: Helps overcome obsession with physical appearance and valuing people for their possessions and status.
HOME: Protects against electromagnetic pollution from electronic devices and nearby telephone poles and high-tension wires.
WORKPLACE: Promotes working cooperatively as part of a team; for conferences and meetings so you will be noticed in a positive light.
CHILDREN: For encouraging children to value themselves as they are and not envy others; for those who find crowded schoolyards or playgrounds daunting.
ANIMALS: Aids in the conservation of water birds where habitats are threatened.
PROTECTION: Keeps you from adopting the opinions of others for the sake of approval.

MAGICKAL AND PSYCHIC USES
Feather magick, water rituals; sacred dance; working with bird totems; seasonal group celebrations; participating in healing festivals.
SPECIAL PROPERTIES
For travel with a partner, family, friends, or for work; for organizing successful community events.
MYTHOLOGY AND HISTORY
Flocks of flamingos can be very extensive in number; Flamingo Jasper is therefore associated with sociability and group or collective, rather than solitary, activities. Because flamingos absorb their color from the food they eat, the strength of the jasper of which Flamingo Jasper is composed enables us to absorb what is needed in terms of fitting into work and social situations without losing our individuality.

Flint

COLOR: Gray, smoky-brown, brown/beige, white, tan, black, sometimes with bands and swirls; glassy when polished
CRYSTAL TYPE: Chalcedony, cryptocrystalline sedimentary rock
ZODIAC SIGN: Aries (March 21–April 20)
CANDLE COLOR: Silver

PHYSICAL: Addresses concerns regarding the liver, kidney stones and gallstones, digestion, cardiopulmonary conditions, skin disorders, pain, calcification; aging issues.
EMOTIONAL: Helps overcome acute shyness, the need to break unwise attachments, bad habits or destructive relationships with parents or elderly relatives.
HOME: Brings abundance; calms drama kings, queens, princes, and princesses.
WORKPLACE: Aids in making your own fortune; intuitively guides you to opportunity and needed resources.
CHILDREN: Helps children feel safe at night; comforts children with separation anxiety.
ANIMALS: For very old animals in their sleeping place.
PROTECTION: Shields against unfriendly ghosts attached to home or land.

MAGICKAL AND PSYCHIC USES
Telepathy with loved ones and cosmic sources; people and aura reading skills; as arrows for psychic surgery; Mother Earth and fire rituals.
SPECIAL PROPERTIES
Helps in managing money if you have debt; stems the flow of more money leaving than entering or a family member draining resources; deters shopaholics; three Flint arrows attract money.
MYTHOLOGY AND HISTORY
For thousands of years, Flint created sparks to light fires, so it was considered magickal. In Scandinavia larger pieces of Flint were traditionally kept at home, believed to contain protective spirits. Flint arrowheads were called "elf shot," after medieval country dwellers found prehistoric flint tools and arrowheads in plowed fields, believing they were dropped by fairies. Flint arrows are said to grant a single fey wish.

Flower Agate or Cherry Blossom Agate

COLORS: Semitranslucent pink, plus other subtle shades, with pale pink flowers on surface
CRYSTAL TYPE: Chalcedony/cryptocrystalline quartz; close relative of plume agate
ZODIAC SIGN: Taurus (April 21–May 21)
CANDLE COLOR: Pink

PHYSICAL: Aids in convalescing; alleviates skin complaints, scars, allergies, and intolerances, especially hay fever.
EMOTIONAL: Soothes fears and phobias, especially claustrophobia or agoraphobia.
HOME: Encourages a beautiful garden, even if you only have a window box.
WORKPLACE: For flower growers, florists, flower arrangers, horticulturists, gardeners, all who paint wildlife and nature or work in the beauty industry.
CHILDREN: For children who find it hard to express their emotions.
ANIMALS: After a prolonged illness, surgery, or with chronic conditions, revives energy and well-being.
PROTECTION: After an accident, attack, or trauma, restores self-belief and encourages a slow return to life.

MAGICKAL AND PSYCHIC USES
Flower Agate brings connection with plant devas; for therapeutically making and using floral oils and flower essences.
SPECIAL PROPERTIES
Said to release the power of the crystal, which has in its pattern both the seeds (the orbicular swirls) and flowers (the plumes) to allow any enterprise or relationship to evolve.
MYTHOLOGY AND HISTORY
Quite rare and recently discovered in Madagascar; associated with all flower goddesses, including Flora, the Roman goddess of flowers, whose festival, Floralia, lasted from April 26 to May 3.

Flower Amethyst

COLORS: From colorless to lilac to deep purple, with the color intensity increasing the closer it moves to the center of the crystal
CRYSTAL TYPE: Quartz cluster in the shape of an opening flower, illuminated by quartz with iron naturally created during formation
ZODIAC SIGN: Aquarius (January 21–February 18)
CANDLE COLOR: Purple

PHYSICAL: Alleviates issues relating to cosmetic and reconstructive surgery, female gynecological problems, frigidity, male impotence.
EMOTIONAL: Helps overcome poor body image; obsession with appearance; sexual inhibitions.
HOME: Brings beauty and harmony into the home no matter how challenging the external environment; attracts house blessings and ongoing good fortune.
WORKPLACE: Valuable for beauty and fashion businesses; media work where physical appearance or age is a determining factor; for horticultural businesses, artists of flowers and plants; wedding planners.
CHILDREN: For Indigo Children to find understanding and to learn to cope with a fast, often confusing world of double standards.
ANIMALS: Enables you to choose a physically unlovely pet from a rescue center.
PROTECTION: Guards against those who deliberately create disharmony and chaos; shields you from harmful energies emitted by handheld devices.

MAGICKAL AND PSYCHIC USES
For sacred sexuality and Holy Grail rituals; Buddhist chants, singing bowls, flower healing, telepathy across great earthly distances, and communication with and guidance from healing Beings of Light in other dimensions.
SPECIAL PROPERTIES
Yin and yang balancing within self, relationships, and the environment; understanding your life's purpose.
MYTHOLOGY AND HISTORY
A rare and incredibly beautiful form of amethyst that spreads harmony, beauty, and healing wherever it is placed in your home or workplace; enhances radiance while you sleep; promotes self-awareness and self-love.

Fluorapatite or Fluoroapatite

COLOR: Colorless in its purest form, frequently green; also blue, purple, pink, yellow, or brown

CRYSTAL TYPE: Fluorinated calcium phosphate, a major component of apatite

ZODIAC SIGN: Pisces (February 19–March 20)

CANDLE COLOR: Olive green

PHYSICAL: Addresses issues involving the teeth, gums, osteoporosis, HIV, fluid and blood sugar imbalances, nausea, IBS, high blood pressure, menopause, kidney stones, gallstones; strengthens response to dialysis, transfusions.

EMOTIONAL: Restores willpower and confidence to those made a scapegoat; for achieving healthy weight when eating is a psychological issue.

HOME: Enables you to trust your natural instincts as a first-time parent, stepparent, or with a new partner, rather than striving for impossible ideals.

WORKPLACE: Aids in adapting to management changes, takeovers, unfamiliar technology or new working practices.

CHILDREN: Helps reticent children become team members; for those constantly worrying about mistakes.

ANIMALS: For pets dominated or intimidated by other animals.

PROTECTION: Shields against those who seek to control others' thoughts.

MAGICKAL AND PSYCHIC USES

Manifestation rituals, especially for humanitarian purposes; for yoga, tai chi, feng shui; bringing chakras and auras into harmony; for psychic practitioners with blocked energies.

SPECIAL PROPERTIES

For uniting groups socially or professionally; organizing charity events, pilgrimages, sightseeing tours, or conventions.

MYTHOLOGY AND HISTORY

Fluorapatite enhances power in other crystals, especially in crystal layouts; found in sharks' teeth; occurs as small, often green, glassy crystals in igneous rocks, magnetite deposits, high-temperature hydrothermal veins (replacing original minerals in rocks) and metamorphic rocks (undergoing changes in formation). This makes Fluorapatite a catalyst for change, always for the highest purpose.

Fortification Agate

COLORS: Gray and white; red-and-gold banding, blacks, browns, whites, creams, beige, tans, beige, or orange bandings

CRYSTAL TYPE: Concentric bands give an inner holly leaf agate shape, often with a colorless hollow quartz center; the bands form a distinctive castle or fortress when the agate is looked down on or propped up; also as tumbled stones, cabochons, or jewelry

ZODIAC SIGN: Scorpio (October 24–November 22)

CANDLE COLOR: Purple

PHYSICAL: Promotes blood circulation; alleviates atherosclerosis, constrictions at the throat, ear blockages, dizzy spells, concerns about aging; strengthens the spleen.

EMOTIONAL: Eases excessive defensiveness, obsessive concern with privacy and being spied on, extreme isolation if you refuse friendship or other assistance.

HOME: Helps overcome threats of eviction or repossession; aids in finding a home where you have outdoor space.

WORKPLACE: Valuable for painstaking, time-consuming work, demanding precision and attention to detail; helps you retain your independence if rival businesses are trying to take over your company or close you down.

CHILDREN: For stories of magickal castles, dragons, and enchanted lands; for reassuring children who are afraid at night.

ANIMALS: Keeps pets off furniture and beds if they are causing damage.

PROTECTION: Prevents intrusion by overzealous officials and curious neighbors who watch your every move.

MAGICKAL AND PSYCHIC USES

Psychic protection; binding and banishing with blessings unfriendly family ghosts or restless spirits.

SPECIAL PROPERTIES

If you have moved around a lot, enables you to find a place where you can settle and build up security, instead of living out of a suitcase.

MYTHOLOGY AND HISTORY

Fortification agate is a generic name for stones whose bands are arranged at sharp angles. It is commonly found in Scotland and Mexico; if you feel intruded upon or under siege, Fortification Agate creates strong boundaries around your home and your workspace and keeps you safe when you travel.

Fossilized or Petrified Wood

COLORS: Brown, gray, red, fawn; often banded, including white

CRYSTAL TYPE: Wood from fossilized trees where wood is replaced by a mineral, usually quartz or agate, to assume the shape of the original tree

ZODIAC SIGN: Virgo (August 24–September 22)

CANDLE COLOR: Brown

PHYSICAL: Alleviates pain and other symptoms of progressive or chronic illnesses or those difficult to diagnose or treat; eases mobility, aging; addresses issues involving the spine, hips, skeletal alignment, hair, skin growths, and plant allergies, including hay fever.

EMOTIONAL: Releases unresolved karma or inherited family quarrels or grudges; resolves tensions if a relative dies without making peace.

HOME: Useful for old buildings, those with structural problems, and those undergoing renovations, including conversions of barns or warehouses into dwellings.

WORKPLACE: Counteracts ageism; for librarians, historians, archaeologists, researchers of ancient religions, environmentalists; aids in establishing a new career or moneymaking endeavor after retirement.

CHILDREN: Teaches youngsters to value family traditions and nature; inculcates patience.

ANIMALS: For older animals and pets who have lost a connection with the outdoors.

PROTECTION: Shields healers against clients' pain and sorrows; guards against mischievous spirits during astral travel.

MAGICKAL AND PSYCHIC USES
Planetary rituals, natural magick, ley lines, dowsing with hazel rods; channeling knowledge from traditions such as Native North America or druidry; connecting with Indigenous spirit guides, wise ancestors, and deceased relatives; for accessing past lives.

SPECIAL PROPERTIES
A stone of transformation after major setbacks; aids in researching family roots and missing links.

MYTHOLOGY AND HISTORY
Legends abound of forests turned to stone by witches or wizards, waiting for reawakening by Merlin or a good fairy breaking the curse; official gem of Washington State.

Fossil Pinecone

COLORS: Tan, brown, black

CRYSTAL TYPE: Organic, ancient pinecone, fossilized with a mineral such as quartz or jasper filling empty cellular spaces, so the pinecone patterns remain

ZODIAC SIGN: Capricorn (December 22–January 20)

CANDLE COLOR: Brown

PHYSICAL: Alleviates issues involving the pineal gland, veins, arteries, osteoporosis; addresses age-related conditions, care of the elderly; eases the effects of life-changing accidents or illnesses; enables fertility, long life.

EMOTIONAL: For lingering dark moods; unwarranted guilt; dissatisfaction, no matter how much you achieve or possess; helps overcome a tendency to remain in the past.

HOME: Cleanses the home of bad memories; clears spirit energies from past tragedies on the land, maybe centuries earlier.

WORKPLACE: Promotes financial gain through long-term investments; useful for careers involving extended training; valuable for archeologists, anthropologists, conservationists of ancient woodlands.

CHILDREN: Discourages young children from developing strong dislikes and fads.

ANIMALS: For rare breeds; forest creatures living in the wild.

PROTECTION: Guards against the manipulation of others.

MAGICKAL AND PSYCHIC USES
Recalls ancient wisdom from early worlds not your own; past lives; future lives, prophecy, psychometry for filling in gaps in family history.

SPECIAL PROPERTIES
Establishing a happy family or circle of friends, where newcomers drastically change the structure; overcoming prejudice against anyone who is different.

MYTHOLOGY AND HISTORY
The oldest Fossil Pinecone in the world—130 million years old—comes from the Yorkshire Coast, UK. Pinecones were symbols of fertility and eternal life by ancient Egyptians, Romans, Greeks, and Assyrians. According to Celtic myth, Merlin climbed the sacred pine of Barenton in the magickal Breton Forest Broceliande, where he awaited the return of the Golden Age.

Franklinite

COLOR: Black, brown-black, metallic with reddish-brown streaks
CRYSTAL TYPE: Oxide/zinc manganese iron oxide
ZODIAC SIGN: Gemini (May 22–June 21)
CANDLE COLOR: Dark brown

PHYSICAL: Promotes hair growth; strengthens vision, male reproductive system; alleviates colds, flu, and lung viruses; leads to new treatments for hard-to-cure illnesses.
EMOTIONAL: Offers sudden insight into hidden causes of emotional problems; clears illusions clouding judgment; rebuilds relationships by confronting unresolved issues.
HOME: Prevents money from going out faster than it's coming in.
WORKPLACE: For creative or artistic work, where imagination plays an important role; for inventors, negotiators, and nonprofit debt-consolidation managers.
CHILDREN: Encourages outspoken children to learn tact and when to say nothing.
ANIMALS: For overly boisterous animals in social situations.
PROTECTION: Signals an early warning of impending events that need attention.

MAGICKAL AND PSYCHIC USES
Franklinite's magnetic charge magickally attracts what is most wanted and repels what is redundant or destructive; for adapting formal spiritual techniques that may seem obscure or irrelevant; trance work; spiritual massage.

SPECIAL PROPERTIES
For diplomacy with difficult people and situations within the family, the workplace, the community, and more widely; softens sarcasm and inappropriate humor.

MYTHOLOGY AND HISTORY
Named by a French geologist in 1819 in honor of US scientist Benjamin Franklin, and mined at Franklin, New Jersey, Franklinite is well known for its plentiful and unusual minerals. The crystal played an important role in the industrialization of New Jersey and has transferred that grounding power to the world of healing.

Frondelite

COLORS: Brown, yellow-brown, orange-brown, greenish-brown, greenish-black, black or pinkish-bronze, exhibiting pleochroism, displaying two or three different colors when viewed from different angles
CRYSTAL TYPE: Hydroxyl phosphate of iron and manganese, where manganese predominates iron
ZODIAC SIGN: Scorpio (October 24–November 22)
CANDLE COLOR: Brown

PHYSICAL: Eases the pain of repetitive motion injuries, such as carpal tunnel syndrome; alleviates issues involving the ears, nose, rhinitis, sinusitis, seasonal allergies, catching one cold after another; bolsters a suppressed immune system after invasive treatment; helps ease the symptoms of HIV.
EMOTIONAL: Counters excessive fear of dirt and disease, terror of crawling insects, a propensity to return to a past or a past love that is falsely recalled as perfect.
HOME: Promotes fair division of chores among family members; aids in cleaning out clutter.
WORKPLACE: Brings order out of chaos if your business suffers from inefficient employees, supply-chain delays, or unreliable contractors or freelancers working from home.
CHILDREN: Encourages children and teens to keep their room tidy and be more responsible for their possessions.
ANIMALS: For training pets slow to respond to instructions.
PROTECTION: Removes and shields against ill-wishing and spirit implants or attachments from previous lives.

MAGICKAL AND PSYCHIC USES
Forms a bridge with other worlds; blocks false messages from malicious spirits during ouija board sessions or séances that seek to mislead; aligns the chakra energy centers of the body and balances the aura energy field, without ever needing cleansing.

SPECIAL PROPERTIES
For creating successful systems for role playing or gaming and seeing patterns behind seemingly random results.

MYTHOLOGY AND HISTORY
A very integrating stone, Frondelite brings and holds together home, workplace, and relationships. For all whose lives inevitably involve variables not 100 percent under their control, Frondelite is the glue that allows reasoned choices to be made.

Fuchsite

COLOR: Emerald-green; sometimes glittering green with golden highlights

CRYSTAL TYPE: A chromium rich variety of muscovite-mica (see Blue Muscovite, page 79)

ZODIAC SIGN: Libra (September 23–October 23)

CANDLE COLOR: Emerald

PHYSICAL: Relieves deep-seated or long-lasting physical conditions; alleviates issues involving the larynx, throat, arteries, circulation, carpel tunnel syndrome, spine, immune system, inflammation, eczema, skin allergies, snoring, sleep apnea, healthy weight loss.

EMOTIONAL: Reduces reliance on stimulants and placebos; helps overcome a tendency to sacrifice yourself needlessly for others.

HOME: Brings beauty, even in unsatisfactory or temporary accommodations; restores fun to family life; balances conflicting domestic schedules.

WORKPLACE: For inspired brainstorming; diplomacy when facing flare-ups or rivalries; encourages teamwork; aids in organizing and implementing targets and timetables.

CHILDREN: Teaches children to value possessions; encourages overserious children to laugh.

ANIMALS: For exotic birds away from their natural habitat; wildlife conservation.

PROTECTION: Guards against those making unreasonable demands or manipulating others by inducing guilt.

MAGICKAL AND PSYCHIC USES
Astral projection, connection with angels, fairies, dragon energies, and nature spirits; herbalism, flower and tree essences and essential oils; Earth energies and Earth healing.

SPECIAL PROPERTIES
Energizes other crystals in healing layouts; the self-healer's stone, Fuchsite assists with spontaneous recovery from illness, exhaustion, or helplessness.

MYTHOLOGY AND HISTORY
Because of its shimmer, Fuchsite was considered a gift from the Earth spirits, the Virgin Mary, or Iemanjá, the sea goddess, in its homeland of Brazil. Called the fairy crystal because it scatters green sparkles and flecks of gold if rubbed, Fuchsite is a wish and luck-bringing crystal.

Fulgurite

COLOR: Pale or smoky gray, fawn-brown, also shiny black; occasionally white

CRYSTAL TYPE: Lightning fused quartz sand. As lightning strikes the Earth, it melts quartz sand into a glass cylinder, forming a tube

ZODIAC SIGNS: Virgo (August 24–September 22) and Gemini (May 22–June 21)

CANDLE COLOR: Gray

PHYSICAL: Addresses issues involving the ears, nose, and throat; alleviates dizziness, and disorders of the colon and digestive tract; promotes cellular regeneration; strengthens electromagnetics in the body; counteracts illness resistant to treatment or leading to gradual deterioration; associated with miracles.

EMOTIONAL: Motivates you to seek help when life seems hopeless as a result of illness, disability, depression, or trauma.

HOME: Gives courage to leave an abusive situation; for totally restoring a run-down property.

WORKPLACE: Enables you to find the right person or resources quickly; useful for inventors, as well as fantasy, science-fiction, or children's fiction authors; valuable for anyone in a career rut.

CHILDREN: For gifted teens with high IQs who don't fit into conventional roles; for children who dream of UFOs or are scared by psychic experiences.

ANIMALS: Supports pets who save their owners from disaster or assist the severely physically challenged.

PROTECTION: Shields those imprisoned by strict community beliefs; an anticult and indoctrination crystal.

MAGICKAL AND PSYCHIC USES
Calls extraterrestrials and Beings of Light; connects Star People with their origins; enhances storm and fire magick, manifestation rituals, prayer, access to past lives, clairaudience, clairvoyance, kabbalistic ritual.

SPECIAL PROPERTIES
Because of its instant intense formation, Fulgurite enables all-or-nothing change; an aphrodisiac.

MYTHOLOGY AND HISTORY
The name *Fulgurite* comes from Latin, meaning *"lightning"*; Fulgurite was once believed to be a gift from the fire deities, containing fire. The tube formation acts as a transmitter for amplifying prayer or psychic powers.

Future Time Link or Timeline Quartz

COLORS: Generally colorless, but may be found in other clear quartzes; especially citrine and smoky quartz

CRYSTAL TYPE: One of two closely related master timeline quartzes (see also Past Time Link Quartz, page 338). Future Timeline Quartz crystal has a forward-slanting, diamond-shaped, seventh window below the other six faces, in the shape of a parallelogram, leaning to one side; may contain a Phantom Quartz

ZODIAC SIGN: Sagittarius (November 23–December 21)

CANDLE COLOR: Gold

PHYSICAL: Promotes health through good nutrition and exercise.

EMOTIONAL: Helps overcome a tendency to repeat self-destructive patterns with new people and situations, and worrying obsessively about potential serious illness and mortality.

HOME: For purchasing a new house, or building one in a new area.

WORKPLACE: Aids in starting or breathing new life into a business in premises that have been abandoned or neglected or where a previous concern went bankrupt; helps you learn new skills.

CHILDREN: Encourages reticent children, and those susceptible to fads, to try new foods and activities.

ANIMALS: Helps a new pet settle in after the disappearance or death of a former one.

PROTECTION: Guards against fears of leaving your comfort zone and taking a risk on new ventures.

MAGICKAL AND PSYCHIC USES

For predictions, prophecy, and divination; directing meditation and astral travel to future lives to see how lifetime patterns may need changing in the present world to avoid repeating karma in the next life; empowers divinatory crystals with Future Timeline Quartz to explore alternatives through fortune telling.

SPECIAL PROPERTIES

Psychically connects with an unborn child before conception and in the womb so that after birth the crystal will be soothing and bonding for infant and parents.

MYTHOLOGY AND HISTORY

The natural alter ego of the Past Time Link crystal. If possible, buy both past and future crystals so you can create a psychic timeline from past worlds as far into the future as you wish.

Gaia Stone or Helenite

COLOR: Emerald green, lustrous; also blue, orange, or red

CRYSTAL TYPE: Human-enhanced stone, created by heating chromium-rich ash from the Mount St. Helens 1980 volcanic eruption in the USA; colored by aluminum, iron, chromium, titanium, and copper present in the ash

ZODIAC SIGN: Taurus (April 21–May 21)

CANDLE COLOR: Green

PHYSICAL: Alleviates illnesses caused or worsened by modern pollution, additives, chemicals, or harmful rays; enhances natural remedies, including homeopathy.

EMOTIONAL: Helps overcome heartbreak; mends fractured relationships; counters the inability to accept kindness or help.

HOME: Generates more harmonious living between different generations and viewpoints.

WORKPLACE: Resolves rivalries in a family business; aids in receiving fair compensation when an accident or work injury damages the quality of your life.

CHILDREN: An excellent background stone for a psychic child.

ANIMALS: Calls a lost pet home.

PROTECTION: Removes negative energy from rooms and buildings.

MAGICKAL AND PSYCHIC USES

Increases connection with nature and fire spirits; healing for the Earth.

SPECIAL PROPERTIES

Called "soul of the Earth," Gaia Stone encourages conserving Earth's resources and reversing climate change.

MYTHOLOGY AND HISTORY

The glittering green stone was originally formed by the heat of acetylene torches used by salvagers melting volcanic ash, while recovering equipment after the blast. Gaia Stone is named after Gaia, Greek Earth mother, whose name has come to symbolize the twentieth-century ecological principle of Earth as a biological self-regulating mechanism. The stone reminds you if people harm the Earth, they damage their life support system—but that out of tragedy can come blessings.

Galaxyite

COLOR: Dark green or gray green with milky inclusions that, when held to the light, flash opalescent, resembling planets and stars

CRYSTAL TYPE: Micro-labradorite crystals in feldspar

ZODIAC SIGN: Sagittarius (November 23–December 21)

CANDLE COLOR: Dark green

PHYSICAL: Addresses issues involving the brain, blood vessels, vision, migraines, PMS, menstruation, motion sickness; counters the adverse effects of radiation therapy; amplifies the power of other crystals in a healing layout.

EMOTIONAL: Eases stress-induced illnesses; helps overcome disillusionment or feeling weighed down by life; counteracts the tendency toward self-limitation.

HOME: Offers practical and emotional support for those who are disabled, disadvantaged, or isolated at home and feel forgotten.

WORKPLACE: Fosters original ideas and inventions; useful for astronomers, pilots, airplane crew members and mechanics, science-fiction and fantasy writers, computer software and game designers, high technology and aeronautical research; parapsychologists.

CHILDREN: Calms fears of children who talk about seeing UFOs or extraterrestrials; for security when parents cannot be with them.

ANIMALS: For psychic pets aware of spirit animals in the home.

PROTECTION: Shields against ill-wishing and negative entities at night and frightening psychic dreams.

MAGICKAL AND PSYCHIC USES

Interpreting astrology intuitively; connecting with personal constellations and planets; astral travel and extraterrestrial communication; cleanses, energizes, and mends the aura.

SPECIAL PROPERTIES

The connector crystal, for making and strengthening friendship, love, work relationships, and globally and cosmically through the collective experience of humanity, past, present, and future.

MYTHOLOGY AND HISTORY

Galaxyite was discovered in 1995 in Quebec, Canada. According to myth, it was revealed by the angels to help humans cope with modern life.

Garnet in Limestone

COLORS: Red or orange-red within white or grayish-white

CRYSTAL TYPE: Spessartine garnet stones (manganese aluminum silicate) contained within limestone (calcium carbonate)

ZODIAC SIGNS: Aries (March 21–April 20) and Cancer (June 22–July 22)

CANDLE COLOR: Red

PHYSICAL: Promotes self-healing; strengthens efficiency of natural remedies; increases libido; addresses issues involving the small intestine, lactose intolerance, calcium deficiency.

EMOTIONAL: Counters a lack of nurturing by your parents when you were young, so you're constantly seeking a substitute in adulthood; helps overcome an obsession with an unavailable person.

HOME: For neutralizing overly active Earth energies beneath the home; placed in the center of a crystal layout or grid of crystals, it casts protective boundaries around the home and land; keep one in the car to guard against aggressive motorists, theft, and carjacking.

WORKPLACE: Defends you if factions in the workplace are pulling you in different directions; shields against emotional vampires who drain your energies through constantly seeking sympathy for their feigned helplessness while you do the work.

CHILDREN: Eases the fears of children afraid of monsters in the night; protects teens who have been dabbling in the occult or with sexually explicit adult material online.

ANIMALS: For rearing a rejected litter.

PROTECTION: GUARDS against those who use sex to try to break up a couple; place this crystal near the bed to guard against nightmares and poltergeists.

MAGICKAL AND PSYCHIC USES

As a pendulum for dowsing the relative merits of different herbal remedies, oils, and crystals; for the manifestation of wishes; easing the passing of a loved one.

SPECIAL PROPERTIES

Garnet in Limestone increases sexual passion with a caring, committed partner if a relationship has become dull.

MYTHOLOGY AND HISTORY

Garnet in Limestone combines passionate garnet energies with stable grounding limestone to realize what is most needed or desired in tangible terms; brings financial success and acclaim in marketing talents.

Gary Green Jasper or Larsonite

COLORS: Teal blue to lime green and a mix of green shades in between; orange and pale to brighter yellow

CRYSTAL TYPE: Petrified bog wood; also sold as tumbled stones, cabochons, and jewelry

ZODIAC SIGN: Capricorn (December 22–January 20)

CANDLE COLOR: Green

PHYSICAL: Alleviates skin blemishes and signs of aging on the skin; helps recover from hysterectomy and other gynecological surgery; addresses prostate issues.

EMOTIONAL: Counters impatience while waiting for the results of actions or requests; eases fears of aging.

HOME: Creates an indoor or outdoor garden; planting larsonite in the soil encourages healthy growth.

WORKPLACE: Helps to achieve promotion and recognition as a result of patience and perseverance; counters ageism.

CHILDREN: For taking city children into nature, and encouraging them to grow plants and seeds.

ANIMALS: Helps wean pets to a more nature-based diet.

PROTECTION: Guards against breakage of precious items and personal accidents.

MAGICKAL AND PSYCHIC USES

Herb and tree magick and divination; nature-based spiritualities, such as Wicca, paganism and druidry; healing with herbs and making natural remedies.

SPECIAL PROPERTIES

The stone of welcoming the wise man and woman years as a time for planning the desired future, and stepping back from excessive financial pressures and demands for practical support from children and grandchildren.

MYTHOLOGY AND HISTORY

Named after Gary McIntosh and Ray Larson who first mined it near McDermitt, on the Nevada/Oregon border (also called McDermitt jasper); only found in this region in a petrified swamp in what was once a volcanic hotspot, so filling the stone with dynamic energies.

Gaspeite or Allura

COLOR: Light to apple, bright, or lime green; may contain brown host rock

CRYSTAL TYPE: Nickel magnesium iron carbonate

ZODIAC SIGN: Taurus (April 21–May 21)

CANDLE COLOR: Green

PHYSICAL: Addresses issues involving the heart, gallbladder; alleviates symptoms of bronchitis and cystic fibrosis; offers relief from viruses—especially those causing flu and colds—plus plant and pollen allergies; promotes blood oxygenation, healthy weight loss, speech and sensory organs.

EMOTIONAL: Helps hoarders to clear out emotional and physical clutter.

HOME: To put down roots after a major home or location move while maintaining old ties.

WORKPLACE: Strikes the right balance of work, leisure, and family; counteracts workaholic tendencies.

CHILDREN: For children who find it hard to let go of grievances or injustices.

ANIMALS: Helps large dogs adapt to life in the city.

PROTECTION: Guards against financial loss in business or losing precious items or money through carelessness or theft.

MAGICKAL AND PSYCHIC USES

Increases the effectiveness of crystal and herbal healing and homeopathy; for Earth energy rituals, palmistry, psychometry, touch therapies; attracts to you what you most need when you need it.

SPECIAL PROPERTIES

Holding a flat Gaspeite palm stone restores equilibrium, reducing unavoidable stress; Gaspeite is an amulet for spontaneous long and short travel in a motor home or camping.

MYTHOLOGY AND HISTORY

A sacred stone, called Allura by the Aboriginal people of western Australia, one of Gaspeite's two main geological sources; used for healing and to bring visions of the Dreamtime. The other source is the Gaspe Peninsula in Quebec, Canada, after which it is named.

Gateway Quartz

COLORS: Varies with the kind of quartz
CRYSTAL TYPE: Quartz, often clear, distinguished by a clear cup-like indentation or opening from the side or face of the crystal into the interior
ZODIAC SIGN: Aquarius (January 21–February 18)
CANDLE COLOR: White

PHYSICAL: Aids in discovering innovative treatments for resistant conditions; alleviates blockages in veins and arteries; creates new neural pathways, replacing damaged ones; rebuilds cells and bones; helps recover mobility.
EMOTIONAL: Helps overcome long-standing psychological and personality disorders, in addition to fears and phobias inhibiting daily living.
HOME: Placed near the front door, filters incoming energies so only health, abundance, and harmony enter.
WORKPLACE: Opens previously closed career doorways; builds bridges between individuals, in the workplace and the community; for border security officers, and those working in the construction industry and transportation links.
CHILDREN: Counteracts bullying, abuse, or family trauma.
ANIMALS: Aids in recovery after life-changing injuries.
PROTECTION: Guards against those causing hidden divisions and those summoning ancient demons not easily banished.

MAGICKAL AND PSYCHIC USES

A single drop of water or flower essence, poured into the crystal's indentation on a full moon night as an offering to the Moon Mother, will open the right doorways, enabling you to access angelic, past, or future worlds, as well as other galaxies and guides who have been with you through many lifetimes.

SPECIAL PROPERTIES

For natural milestones and rites of passage.

MYTHOLOGY AND HISTORY

Gateway Quartz is a powerful Master Crystal (page 297), offering whatever experiences most needed at a particular time. Each gateway has a protective doorkeeper.

Gehlenite

COLOR: Yellow-brown, brown, green-gray, colorless
CRYSTAL TYPE: Calcium aluminum silicate, melilite group
ZODIAC SIGN: Gemini (May 22–June 21)
CANDLE COLOR: Yellow

PHYSICAL: Strengthens bones, brain connections, cardiovascular system, coccyx, spleen, pancreas; addresses fractures, osteoporosis, tumors, chemical and electrical imbalances, and issues relating to the jaw, teeth especially bruxism (tooth grinding) in adults and children.
EMOTIONAL: Helps the real you emerge; counters fear of open spaces.
HOME: Useful for fixing and mending, especially if you're new to these skills; for all outdoor activities and wilderness vacations; for creating a welcoming atmosphere.
WORKPLACE: Valuable for craftspeople with wood, metal, or natural fabrics; gardeners and horticulturists, farmers, plumbers, builders; for starting up or running practical or construction businesses.
CHILDREN: For apprentices learning hands-on trades; for children who are naturally clumsy.
ANIMALS: For all rescue and therapy animals.
PROTECTION: Guards against the effects of agoraphobia; abusive family members and workmates who use you as a verbal punching bag.

MAGICKAL AND PSYCHIC USES

Enhances Earth energies and rituals, chanting, circle dancing, drumming to link with the rhythms of the Earth; promotes climate healing, manifestation of needs through visualization, foresight.

SPECIAL PROPERTIES

For those who are not naturally nurturing to develop good parenting skills; brings out caring skills and patience with a sick or confused relative; helps an immature partner to grow up and take responsibility.

MYTHOLOGY AND HISTORY

Gehlenite is a Mother Earth crystal that connects with nature, even in the center of a city, and encourages wildlife areas and reintroducing natural flora and fauna to urban green spaces; creates a beautiful garden inside or outdoors, no matter how confined the space; a natural happiness-bringer.

Gel Lithium Silica

COLORS: Pale to bright to darker magenta; sparkles

CRYSTAL TYPE: A richly colored form of lepidolite, potassium lithium aluminum silicate, with the color coming from the high amount of lithium within

ZODIAC SIGN: Taurus (April 21–May 21)

CANDLE COLOR: Bright pink

PHYSICAL: Alleviates severe stress that causes or makes illnesses worse, such as heart disease, high blood pressure, or intestinal troubles; enhances the effectiveness of conventional or herbal antidepressants or anxiety medication.

EMOTIONAL: Helps sever an attachment to a previous relationship that cannot be revived; overcomes a tendency to wait for a perfect love to come along to keep from taking risks.

HOME: For coming to agreement in divorce cases where children and property are central; finding the right living accommodations for frail elderly relatives.

WORKPLACE: Maintains personal equilibrium if domineering or oversensitive colleagues or managers are constantly creating dramas that interfere with the smooth running of the company.

CHILDREN: Protects a child from being bullied or teased by a particular peer or social group to achieve, if not friendship, a cessation of unpleasant words, social media trolling, or threatening text messages.

ANIMALS: Stops pets from continually fighting.

PROTECTION: Guards against severe anxiety that keeps you from trying new activities, exploring new places, or engaging in social events.

MAGICKAL AND PSYCHIC USES
For channeling, prayer, sacred song, singing bowls, circle dancing, and sound healing; enhances goddess rituals.

SPECIAL PROPERTIES
A crystal of pure yin to counteract people and situations that are overly yang; for gentle men forced into emotionless roles in childhood.

MYTHOLOGY AND HISTORY
Found in a remote mine in New Mexico, Gel Lithium Silica can be tumbled and included with other minerals, such as fluorite, calcite, or with white beryl, Smoky Quartz, and Blue Apatite; a stone for bringing calm to a chaotic life.

Gem Silica

COLORS: Bright blue, bluish-green; clearer, more richly colored, and translucent than ordinary chrysocolla

CRYSTAL TYPE: Gem Silica is gem-quality chrysocolla, agatized in chalcedony quartz (see Chrysocolla, page 123)

ZODIAC SIGN: Aquarius (January 21–February 18)

CANDLE COLOR: Bright blue

PHYSICAL: Addresses issues involving the respiratory system, childbirth and the weeks afterwards, fevers, menopausal problems, hormone replacement therapy (HRT), hysterectomy, Tourette's syndrome (especially in young women), diabetes.

EMOTIONAL: Counters unwillingness or inability to communicate, using silence and sulking as a weapon.

HOME: Promotes harmony, peace, and well-being.

WORKPLACE: For reinventing your professional image; appearing outwardly confident until your inner self-esteem catches up.

CHILDREN: Strengthens your belief in your own mothering or fathering skills, particularly for a first baby.

ANIMALS: For setting up a cattery or pet hotel.

PROTECTION: Guards against those who twist words to confuse.

MAGICKAL AND PSYCHIC USES
Gem Silica is a crystal of the goddess; set it in the center of a healing crystal layout for absent healing; promotes sound and voice healing, mediumship, channeling others' guides and ancestors in a trance state.

SPECIAL PROPERTIES
A natural prosperity-bringer; restores fortunes after loss or setbacks, whether rebuilding your credit rating, restarting a business, or reentering the property market; for learning sign language.

MYTHOLOGY AND HISTORY
Gem Silica, also known as chrysocolla chalcedony or gem silica chrysocolla, is harder than ordinary chrysocolla because of the quartz and can be made into jewelry or carved more easily. Sometimes other copper minerals, as well as chrysocolla, are embedded in it, such as malachite. A very rare form, called quattro silica, has shattuckite, malachite, and dioptase as inclusions. Gem Silica is a natural home or workplace filter for pollutants.

Generator or Projector Quartz

COLOR: Depends on type of quartz

CRYSTAL TYPE: A natural quartz point, usually and most powerfully as clear quartz in which six equal-sized sides join sharply to form the terminating apex

ZODIAC SIGN: Sagittarius (November 23–December 21)

CANDLE COLOR: White

PHYSICAL: Addresses issues arising from surgery, laser treatment, light therapies, radiation therapy, dentistry, conditions requiring regular injections, inoculations; relieves acute pain, symptoms of appendicitis.

EMOTIONAL: Transforms depression, exhaustion, and disconnection into passion for life.

HOME: Removes disharmonious subterranean Earth energies; dissipates effects of lingering sickness, sorrow, or anger.

WORKPLACE: For completing urgent tasks, working under pressure, meeting deadlines; advertising, publicity, or selling; making your mark.

CHILDREN: Sends love to a child if they are staying away from home and homesick.

ANIMALS: Assuages cruelly treated animals or those in poorly maintained zoos.

PROTECTION: Disperses evil from whatever source.

MAGICKAL AND PSYCHIC USES
A magic wand for drawing circles of light around yourself; for making a magickal group; as the center of a healing circle to radiate energies wherever they're most needed.

SPECIAL PROPERTIES
A Master Crystal and healer, Generator Quartz creates and projects light, realigning what is out of balance in individuals, groups, homes, workplaces, and the Earth herself.

MYTHOLOGY AND HISTORY
Clear Generator Quartz possesses animus/yang energies and cloudy anima/yin; if yours contains both, use the cloudy end to absorb, remove, and clear to project and infuse. Generator Quartz amplifies the collective power of any healing crystal layout.

Genesis Stone

COLORS: Orange, black, dark gray, red-brown, and golden-yellow bands, from very thin into widening layers

CRYSTAL TYPE: Hematite, magnetite, and jasper in this 1.8–2.5-billion-year-old stone; may be naturally polished smooth over many millenia; best in polished form for healing and magick

ZODIAC SIGN: Capricorn (December 22–January 20)

CANDLE COLOR: Golden brown

PHYSICAL: Aids in recovery from long illnesses and preventing recurrence; alleviates chronic conditions, problems of aging.

EMOTIONAL: Counters the tendency to seek a quick fix for every problem; deters disregard for the vulnerable.

HOME: Cleanses the home of lingering quarrels, illness, misfortune, and blocked subterranean energies.

WORKPLACE: Promotes long-term career plans in the same company; aids in surviving and riding out economic downturns.

CHILDREN: For old souls; as a family treasure to help children understand the time scale of the Earth if they dismiss anything that is not brand-new or high-tech.

ANIMALS: When buying a new pup, kitten, or pony, helps to recognize an animal who has been with you in former worlds.

PROTECTION: Guards against energy vampires.

MAGICKAL AND PSYCHIC USES
Increases or awakens channeling powers; removes spirits who have not moved on or who were called up in ouija board sessions and refused to leave.

SPECIAL PROPERTIES
A stone of immense stability in uncertain times.

MYTHOLOGY AND HISTORY

Also called banded ironstone, Genesis Stone is found in the desert areas of the southwest United States, so named because of its great antiquity. It is a sacred Native North American stone associated with the elements, particularly Fire, Wind, Storm, and Water; as such, it offers staying power in troubling times—whether your relationship is rocky or you're undergoing financial stress. Genesis Stone reassures you that, with patience and perseverance, life will improve.

Geodes

COLORS: Depends on the kind of inner crystal, but usually gray, brown, or black outside

CRYSTAL TYPE: Hollow, crystal-lined, globe-like cavities found in sedimentary rocks, such as limestone, dolomite, or volcanic rocks, containing tiny or sometimes larger crystals, clear quartz, amethyst, or needle-like Goethite (see also Thunder Egg, page 473)

ZODIAC SIGN: Cancer (June 22–July 22)

CANDLE COLOR: According to crystal

PHYSICAL: Alleviates migraines, malfunctioning of or injuries to the brain, skull, head and neck; dissipates blood clots; promotes fertility; enables you to carry a baby to full term after having had miscarriages.

EMOTIONAL: Addresses deep-rooted problems when the person is in denial; for those who feel bound to secrecy as victims of abuse, incest, or whose families are involved in crime.

HOME: An amethyst Geode replaces anger, resentment, pressure, and anxiety with gentleness and kind words.

WORKPLACE: Acts as an antitheft device in a business; Citrine or Clear Quartz Geodes attract new customers.

CHILDREN: Works as a fairy castle and a source for interactive storytelling.

ANIMALS: If placed in a garden, encourages nocturnal creatures, especially shy ones.

PROTECTION: An agate geode shields against hostile visitors, phone calls or emails.

MAGICKAL AND PSYCHIC USES

In meditation or visualization, a larger cave-like Geode offers access to other realms, especially magickal or fantasy ones; useful for crystal healing and applying them to a painful part of the body.

SPECIAL PROPERTIES

Matching Geodes, where the two halves are kept together, strengthen love if one or both lovers are frequently absent.

MYTHOLOGY AND HISTORY

According to legend, Geode eggs were laid by magickal birds; for example, the North America Indian Thunderbird, whose flashing eyes and huge wings brought the rain and storms. Geodes offer insight into whatever is hidden, whether a person's true nature, good or bad, hidden talents, or secret motives.

Gibeon Meteorite

COLOR: Brown or gray, with crystalline patterns, formed on inner surfaces over millions of years of cooling

CRYSTAL TYPE: Magnetic space rock, 4 billion years old, alloyed with 90 percent iron content, 8 percent nickel and smaller amounts of cobalt and phosphorus, plus other mineral traces

ZODIAC SIGN: All signs

CANDLE COLOR: Gold

PHYSICAL: Alleviates blood disorders, acute pain, mineral deficiencies; addresses wounds, epilepsy, modern germs resistant to antibiotics; responds to issues involving the bowels, degenerative conditions in older people, seasonal affective disorder.

EMOTIONAL: For all who have suffered physical, emotional, or sexual abuse or neglect in residential care or foster homes.

HOME: Guards the home against fire, storm, hurricane, and flood.

WORKPLACE: Helps you complete projects despite obstacles; aids in achieving a lifetime career ambition; promotes intuitive decision making though others advise caution.

CHILDREN: Protects against fears of becoming lost, abducted, or abandoned.

ANIMALS: Useful in the conservation of endangered species.

PROTECTION: Guards against intimidation by powerful, corrupt organizations or faceless officialdom.

MAGICKAL AND PSYCHIC USES

A good luck charm; connects with ancient wisdom and intergalactic energies.

SPECIAL PROPERTIES

Enables successful property acquisition and development if vested interests oppose it; helps you succeed at a talent you may have doubted.

MYTHOLOGY AND HISTORY

Though Gibeon Meteorite was officially discovered in 1838 in Namibia by Captain James Alexander, fragments were polished and sharpened by Kalahari Desert people as arrowheads and spearheads for thousands of years. This meteorite, from broken asteroid fragments or an exploded star, carries warrior courage; the twisted and distorted patterns formed as it exploded, makes it one of the most powerful meteorites against seemingly immovable opposition.

Ginger Quartz

COLORS: Brownish-red to pinkish-ginger (hematite and micro-pyrite), coloring the whole clear crystal
CRYSTAL TYPE: Quartz with included hematite and micro-pyrite
ZODIAC SIGN: Aries (March 21–April 20)
CANDLE COLOR: Red

PHYSICAL: Alleviates motion sickness, morning sickness in pregnancy, lack of libido, low pulse and blood pressure, coughs, colds, indigestion, tendon and muscle strain; promotes fitness in physical activities, such as dancing, aerobics, Zumba.
EMOTIONAL: Helps overcome fear of poverty and homelessness, the inability to relate love and sex; keeps you from making inappropriate sexual innuendos.
HOME: Bury Ginger Quartz in a thriving ginger plant in the home to attract ongoing prosperity, health, and good fortune.
WORKPLACE: For rapidly growing prosperity in new businesses.
CHILDREN: Comforts small children who need extra nurturing.
ANIMALS: Aids in training animals for competitions.
PROTECTION: GUARDS against malevolent spirits in the home, during rituals, or healing; repels rivals in love who use unfair tactics.

MAGICKAL AND PSYCHIC USES
A gambling charm; useful as an aphrodisiac; for sex magick.

SPECIAL PROPERTIES
Considered lucky in the horse and dog racing world for successful bets, wins as an owner or trainer, and at other sporting events where skill of participants enables predictions to be made.

MYTHOLOGY AND HISTORY
Ginger plant has been known for over five thousand years, originating in Southeast Asia; first mentioned in written records by the sage Confucius who lived between 475 BCE and 221 BCE. Ginger's magickal and healing powers have been transferred by association in amulet or talisman form to the crystal; Ginger Quartz is one of the fastest acting anti–motion sickness charms against fears of flying (see Crystal Amulets, Talismans, and Charms, page 143).

Girasol Quartz

COLORS: Cloudy and colorless, with a translucent glow that may appear blue; can be pale pink or even pale gold, described as light passing through a veil
CRYSTAL TYPE: Silicon dioxide. A variety of quartz with a milky sheen, can appear opalescent due to the inclusion of microscopic water droplets caught within the quartz during formation
ZODIAC SIGN: Cancer (June 22–July 22)
CANDLE COLOR: Silver

PHYSICAL: Alleviates blurred vision, headaches, dizziness, balance problems due to inner ear infection, pain, diabetes, physical exhaustion.
EMOTIONAL: Helps overcome fears, phobias (including claustrophobia), and acute sensitivity to noise, crowds, and pollution.
HOME: Creates television- and technology-free time to relax and talk; brings balance to tempestuous love.
WORKPLACE: Calms a workplace that creates the impression of frantic activity; for practitioners of talk therapies.
CHILDREN: For teenagers confused by their sexuality or gender issues.
ANIMALS: Calms pets who are afraid of storms.
PROTECTION: Guards against those who seek to dominate through rank and status.

MAGICKAL AND PSYCHIC USES
Reiki, reflexology, yoga, tai chi, Bowen therapy, crystal healing, energy transference.

SPECIAL PROPERTIES
The crystal that combines the clarity of thought, words, and actions of quartz with the gentleness of girasol to speak the truth with kindness and compassion.

MYTHOLOGY AND HISTORY
Girasol Quartz has associations with Blodeuwedd, white goddess of the Celts, who inspires writers, musicians, and all who create; Girasol Quartz releases innate creativity through writing, music, or any artistic endeavor, whether for pleasure or professionally.

Glacial, Etched, or Ice Quartz

COLORS: White, fissured, and etched
CRYSTAL TYPE: Silicon dioxide
ZODIAC SIGN: Cancer (June 22–July 22)
CANDLE COLOR: White

PHYSICAL: Addresses immobility of joints, frozen shoulder, arthritis, Raynaud's disease, ganglia, inability to regulate body temperature, fevers.
EMOTIONAL: Dispels fears of loneliness and being abandoned; helps overcome codependency, victim mentality, and the inability to stick with a relationship or career.
HOME: For gently but persistently encouraging adult children to leave the nest if they have returned after college and show no signs of moving on.
WORKPLACE: For intricate work, where patience and attention to detail are needed; for starting an independent business.
CHILDREN: Encourages children to become more independent if they're unwilling to leave a parent to attend kindergarten, elementary school, or stay with relatives or friends.
ANIMALS: Calms a restless pet who needs to be constantly on the move when outdoors.
PROTECTION: Guards against making hasty, unwise decisions if there are delays.

MAGICKAL AND PSYCHIC USES
Meditation, if concentration is hard; Reiki; the crystal's etchings hold secrets of ancient wisdom; for gently removing redundant karmic debts and blocks.

SPECIAL PROPERTIES
For knowing when the time is right to act and when to wait, but not postponing actions indefinitely as the chances will disappear.

MYTHOLOGY AND HISTORY
A gentler form of Nirvana or Himalayan Ice Quartz (page 317), formed and etched in the glaciers of Pakistan; a stone that encourages independence if an adult child is using emotional blackmail; allows each one to maintain separate interests and identity within an intense love match.

Glendonite

COLORS: Light medium-red or cinnamon brown
CRYSTAL TYPE: Ancient mineral formed when hydrous calcium carbonate of ikaite loses its water and is transformed into the calcium carbonate mineral calcite; adopts the crystal form of ikaite instead of its own form when replacing the ikaite; retains the star- or flower-like cluster of transformed ikaite
ZODIAC SIGN: Pisces (February 19–March 20)
CANDLE COLOR: Brown

PHYSICAL: Alleviates headaches, insomnia; strengthens bones, teeth, white blood cells, kidneys, intestines; promotes regrowth of neural pathways after brain injury or disease, including Alzheimer's.
EMOTIONAL: Aids in overcoming inherited patterns of behavior from past generations; mitigates old family feuds.
HOME: Creates a happy home and family life; helps discover family history.
WORKPLACE: Transforms a failing business; enables you to learn new skills for modern life.
CHILDREN: Comforts very old souls; prompts past-life recall until the age of seven.
ANIMALS: Champions lizards, tortoises, and descendants of ancient life-forms.
PROTECTION: Guards against clinging to a destructive relationship.

MAGICKAL AND PSYCHIC USES
Connects with past worlds where life came from the waters; aids in walking between worlds in meditation and astral travel; promotes inner stillness.

SPECIAL PROPERTIES
The stone of transformation in mid- to later life; thaws emotions for reconciliation; develops forgotten talents.

MYTHOLOGY AND HISTORY
First found in 1840 at Glendon in the Hunter Valley, New South Wales, Australia, Glendonite may date as far back as 285–270 million years ago, formed under Ice Age conditions on ancient seabeds, then transformed as the seas warmed. Glendonite offers clues to scientists about ancient climatic conditions and the worldwide floods, often called Noah's Flood.

Gobi Eye Agate

COLORS: Usually brown or reddish-brown, especially with the distinctive raised eye; may also be blue, yellow, or orange; may have creamy agate within

CRYSTAL TYPE: A combination of agate and chalcedony, both quartz, found just below the surface of the desert; raised multilayered eye in relief, like a carving on each stone

ZODIAC SIGN: Capricorn (December 22–January 20)

CANDLE COLOR: Golden brown

PHYSICAL: Addresses eye problems (including color blindness and floaters); aids in recovery from scans, x-rays, and angioplasty; promotes healthy pregnancy to full term.

EMOTIONAL: Counters a tendency to keep secrets and practice subterfuge; helps overcome envy of what others have.

HOME: Guards the home by day and night from thieves, vandals, unfriendly visitors, and neighbors; encourages health and abundance in every corner.

WORKPLACE: A charm to attract good fortune and prosperity to a business; shields you from rivals and those who resent your success.

CHILDREN: Keep this crystal high in the baby's nursery to deter all who are jealous, ill-wishing, and intent on doing harm.

ANIMALS: Place in barns with larger animals who may be stolen or injured; take to animal shows and competitions to protect from other entrants' unscrupulous tactics.

PROTECTION: Guards against the evil eye; reflects back negative energies, intrusion, and excessive curiosity.

MAGICKAL AND PSYCHIC USES

Sand and stone divination; defensive magick; dowsing for what is lost or has been returned to the wrong place.

SPECIAL PROPERTIES

Naturally smoothed by being tumbled by the desert sands, Gobi Eye Agate is infused with the power of the winds, the storms, and the sun.

MYTHOLOGY AND HISTORY

Traditionally a shamanic stone, prized by the nomads of Inner Mongolia and Northern China to protect against evil spirits and ill-wishing; found in the remote Gobi Desert after years of apparently disappearing; still worn as beads, pendants, and bracelets for good luck and protection; also called Gobi Desert Agate.

Goethite

COLORS: Black-brown, brownish-red, orangish- or yellowish-brown

CRYSTAL TYPE: Iron hydroxide

ZODIAC SIGN: Aries (March 21–April 20)

CANDLE COLOR: Gold or golden brown

PHYSICAL: Addresses issues involving the ears, nose, throat, esophagus; oxygenates the blood; bolsters the bone marrow; restores strength; alleviates absent or scant menstruation, anemia.

EMOTIONAL: Balances care for others with self-care; comforts in times of bereavement or intense loss.

HOME: Aids in working from home with a young family, and home study if there are many interruptions.

WORKPLACE: Helps cope with a takeover, introduction of radical new technology, or rationalization affecting your role; aids writers with creative blocks.

CHILDREN: Grounds children upset by everyday problems.

ANIMALS: Reconnects urban pets to the Earth.

PROTECTION: Guards against adverse effects of seismic waves, earthquakes, and landslides.

MAGICKAL AND PSYCHIC USES

Strengthens dowsing abilities at ancient sites and ley lines; channels clairaudient angelic messages; for Mother Earth rituals.

SPECIAL PROPERTIES

Lifts gloom and hopelessness; encourages creativity for pleasure; after completing training, graduation, or apprenticeship, overcomes the "What next?" feeling.

MYTHOLOGY AND HISTORY

Goethite is the source of color for ochre, a pigment found from prehistoric times in cave paintings such as Lascaux, France, making Goethite a channel for preliterate wisdom; from Australia, Germany, the Czech Republic, France, England, Canada, and the USA. A Mother Earth crystal for healing the earth and connecting Earth religions, druidry, Wicca, or shamanism with the twenty-first century.

Gold

COLOR: Metallic yellow and gleaming
CRYSTAL TYPE: Native element/precious metal
ZODIAC SIGN: Leo (July 23–August 23)
CANDLE COLOR: Gold

PHYSICAL: A master healer, benefits almost every condition; amplifies the effects of other crystals and metals; addresses arthritis, as well as issues involving the heart, spine, circulation, nervous system, digestion.
EMOTIONAL: Reduces negative thoughts and harmful actions.
HOME: Brings and preserves prosperity.
WORKPLACE: Encourages ambition; aids in gaining promotion, having successful auditions, and winning fame and fortune.
CHILDREN: Fosters parental authority over rebellious teenagers; promotes talents in the performing arts; counters autism, dyslexia.
ANIMALS: For beautiful show pets.
PROTECTION: Beseeches Archangel Michael to cut cords with destructive but alluring attractions.

MAGICKAL AND PSYCHIC USES
Gold is the metal of the sun, powerful, especially at noon and midsummer; a traditional offering to deities for wealth; with silver in alchemy for the union of moon and sun.
SPECIAL PROPERTIES
Gold rings for fidelity, marriage, and protection from jealous rivals; for the unattached, offers confidence to approach a desired partner and fight for love.
MYTHOLOGY AND HISTORY
Associated in many lands and ages with immortality and enduring wealth; ancient Egyptians believed the skin of deities was gold. Tutankhamen was given a gold mask after death and his mummy set in three gold coffins. El Dorado, the legendary city of gold in Colombia, represents untold wealth and a mystical quest. The legendary city was linked with initiation rites, whereby a newly created chief from Muisca society, covered in gold dust, plunged into a sacred lake offering golden treasures to the deities. In Ireland there is reputedly a pot of gold at the end of the rainbow.

Golden Barite

COLOR: Yellow to golden and golden brown
CRYSTAL TYPE: Barium sulfate, soft
ZODIAC SIGN: Leo (July 23–August 23)
CANDLE COLOR: Gold

PHYSICAL: Eases stress-related stomach disorders, spleen, liver, gallstones, IBS; after prolonged radiation or chemotherapy, offers whole-body energy; provides resistance to winter chills, infections, and viruses any time of the year; addresses tropical diseases.
EMOTIONAL: Counters addictions, obsessions, cravings (especially food-related), rooted in poor self-image.
HOME: Makes money go further in times of major expenditures or unexpected shortfalls.
WORKPLACE: For brainstorming solutions fast when time is short; setting up a workers' cooperative; franchising.
CHILDREN: Comforts those who constantly worry about not pleasing others; aids young people finding it hard to leave a loving family of origin.
ANIMALS: For establishing an animal sanctuary.
PROTECTION: Guards against those with big egos and opinions who do nothing but talk.

MAGICKAL AND PSYCHIC USES
Used by Native Americans to shape-shift into animal form; for connecting with totem animals; solstice celebrations; dream recall and creative problem solving in sleep.
SPECIAL PROPERTIES
Brings appreciation of blessings and happiness in life now, rather than dreaming of tomorrow; boosts confidence to achieve whatever you want if you believe in yourself.
MYTHOLOGY AND HISTORY
The sunshine stone of self-love, self-confidence, and self-esteem, radiating power to live by your own rules while still loving others and being loved. A rare gem form of Golden Barite is found in Colorado.

Golden Beryl

COLOR: Canary to golden yellow, seldom with inclusions

CRYSTAL TYPE: Beryl, ring silicate, also called heliodor, especially in its yellow-green variety

ZODIAC SIGN: Sagittarius (November 23–December 21)

CANDLE COLOR: Gold

PHYSICAL: Alleviates issues involving the heart, liver, stomach, spleen, pancreas, gallstones, motion sickness, diarrhea, seasonal affective disorder, and chronic fatigue syndrome.

EMOTIONAL: Golden Beryl restores confidence and well-being; relieves eating disorders; banishes fear.

HOME: Brings happiness to pessimistic family members; promotes health, abundance, and family unity no matter what outside pressures or influences are brought to bear.

WORKPLACE: Assists in understanding and recalling new information and techniques; during difficult times in business or threatened takeover or redundancies, maximizes opportunities, encouraging proactive responses.

CHILDREN: Encourages reluctant students to apply themselves; valuable as a naming day or christening gift, symbolizing intellect, protection, and a cheerful nature.

ANIMALS: For an animal who has lost its mate or human companion.

PROTECTION: Shields against emotional blackmail, unfriendly ghosts, and poltergeists.

MAGICKAL AND PSYCHIC USES
A seer stone for uncovering secrets and hidden intentions; scrying the future.

SPECIAL PROPERTIES
The crystal of joy and infinite possibilities; offers fame and fortune in return for monumental effort and unwavering faith.

MYTHOLOGY AND HISTORY
Crystal balls were traditionally made of Golden Beryl. John Dee, Queen Elizabeth I's astrologer, foretold the coming of the Spanish Armada invasion in his beryl sphere. A talisman for married or committed couples to maintain or restore joy and passion; it is said if you wear Golden Beryl, you'll never lack admirers.

Golden Black Seraphinite, Serafinite, or Serafina

COLORS: Dark, rich brown with golden or cream, shimmery streaks; some crystals are more golden

CRYSTAL TYPE: Rare variety of *clinochlore*, magnesium iron aluminum silicate hydroxide; the gold is due to the presence of extra iron; feather-like inclusions

ZODIAC SIGN: Leo (July 23–August 23)

CANDLE COLOR: Gold

PHYSICAL: A whole-body healer, this crystal detoxifies, aids in achieving weight loss; promotes circulation, nervous system, and connectivity between brain and motor functions, addresses hypoglycemia, diabetes, colds, and chronic coughs; alleviates side effects of necessary medication.

EMOTIONAL: Counters excessive nervous energy, inability to settle; helps overcome obsession with unattainable love, and an inability to empathize with others.

HOME: Floods the home with light and beauty; invites the presence of the guardian angel of the home.

WORKPLACE: For those in the caring professions to show compassion and patience with difficult and resistant clients.

CHILDREN: Protects psychic children with angelic light if they are frightened of their experiences.

ANIMALS: Lets an old or sick pet go with blessings and peaceful passing.

PROTECTION: Traditionally worn against snakebite; guards against vicious words, spite, and lies.

MAGICKAL AND PSYCHIC USES
The stone of the angels, for connecting with your guardian angel and archangels; tantra; yoga; tai chi; ignites your inner fire.

SPECIAL PROPERTIES
Golden Black Seraphinite, with its angelic inner feathers, awakens spiritual powers in those previously unaware of the divinity within us all.

MYTHOLOGY AND HISTORY
Called the guiding stone, to lead you to the right places, time, and people, and draw to you what you most need.

Golden Coracalcite

COLORS: Gold, soft yellow, or white

CRYSTAL TYPE: Fusion of fossilized coral with calcite, occurring on or around skeletal coral formations

ZODIAC SIGN: Pisces (February 19–March 20)

CANDLE COLOR: Gold

PHYSICAL: Creates new neural pathways after illness or invasive surgery; strengthens bones, connective tissues, nerve endings; promotes fertility among older couples; ensures successful organ transplants.

EMOTIONAL: Helps accept that an ex-partner has moved on; helps you stop clinging to a destructive love.

HOME: For bringing or restoring light to a home plagued by misfortune or sickness; for creating beautiful water features inside or outdoors.

WORKPLACE: Enables a long-existing business, which isn't thriving, to adopt innovative ideas and new personnel; revives traditional trades and crafts.

CHILDREN: Helps insecure foster children to settle into a new home while maintaining a connection with their birth family.

ANIMALS: For tropical fish and turtles to thrive.

PROTECTION: Guards against being stifled by convention and traditions that have been part of your life for many years.

MAGICKAL AND PSYCHIC USES

Enhances the power of other crystals; increases instinctive understanding and spontaneously receiving the benefits of their deeper qualities.

SPECIAL PROPERTIES

Golden Coracalcite manifests what is most needed in our lives at the right time, rather than that for which we are not ready.

MYTHOLOGY AND HISTORY

Found in the Caribbean, Golden Coracalcite combines the qualities of coral, calcite, and fossils, tiny shells that may sometimes be seen within coracalcite to tap into spiritual wisdom.

Golden Enhydro Herkimer

COLORS: Clear with gold (oil bubbles) and black (seeds) within

CRYSTAL TYPE: Forms as Herkimer diamonds, quartz, and silicon dioxide with impurities, containing tiny cavities filled with pure golden oil; the stone is also known as petroleum quartz

ZODIAC SIGN: Pisces (February 19–March 20)

CANDLE COLOR: Gold

PHYSICAL: Useful for those considering sex-change surgery (enhances medication and successful surgery); alleviates cell damage; aids in organ removal because of serious illness or for lifesaving surgery, as well as colostomies and ileostomies; promotes remission and a small miracle when the prognosis is poor.

EMOTIONAL: Counters gender confusion when family, friends, or the community condemn your choice; keeps you from demanding external support for every setback.

HOME: Dispels geopathic stress and overly harsh Earth energies beneath the home that cause restlessness and minor accidents.

WORKPLACE: For sick-building syndrome where there are a lot of absences due to stress-related illnesses and minor viruses.

CHILDREN: A wonder of nature, this crystal offers help to children when it's kept with the family treasures.

ANIMALS: For badly injured or abused rescue pets who need one-on-one care.

PROTECTION: Removes spirit implants and diminishes the power of those who seek to manipulate the minds of others.

MAGICKAL AND PSYCHIC USES

For rituals and meditation with sacred spirals, mandalas, and labyrinths; past-life healing of old wounds and betrayals to clear the energy field of redundant psychic debris.

SPECIAL PROPERTIES

When ultraviolet light shines on the crystal, the oil adopts a bright bluish-green-yellowish fluorescence; its illuminated inner treasures encourage the manifestation of as-yet-undeveloped gifts.

MYTHOLOGY AND HISTORY

A stone from the Hindu Kush Mountains in the sacred Himalayas, Golden Enhydro Herkimer contains golden liquid as the oil that is millions of years old, black bitumen seeds, and the solid and methane gas bubbles for the air; unites within the single crystal Earth, sea and sky in a dynamic combination of body (seeds), mind (gas), and spirit (liquid) for a sense of wholeness.

Golden Feldspar

COLORS: Golden, tan, or clear; shiny, glittering luster
CRYSTAL TYPE: Silicate/aluminosilicate
ZODIAC SIGN: Leo (July 23–August 23)
CANDLE COLOR: Gold

PHYSICAL: Regenerates cells, tissues, and organs, particularly following liver damage; strengthens you pre- and postsurgery; prevents scarring; counters melanomas, sun damage to body or skin, torn muscles; regulates menstrual cycles; increases fertility in both sexes.
EMOTIONAL: Helps overcome pessimism, extreme reactions not triggered by external events.
HOME: On dark, dull days, when everything seems to be going wrong, Golden Feldspar restores light and optimism; suggests solutions preventing the same problems from recurring.
WORKPLACE: Unburdens you if you're feeling weighed down by responsibility for major decisions or managing large sums of money; boosts brainstorming.
CHILDREN: Encourages communication and successful therapy with children seriously withdrawn because of abuse or traumatic experiences; stirs lethargic teenagers to play outdoors.
ANIMALS: For pets bullied by other animals.
PROTECTION: Guards against perpetually gloomy people, continual minor illnesses, and sudden depression striking even when things are going well.

MAGICKAL AND PSYCHIC USES

A component of moon rock, Golden Feldspar increases intergalactic communication; brings harmony with the moon cycles; useful if a couple is trying to conceive a baby.

SPECIAL PROPERTIES

Golden Feldspar is the vacation crystal, whether a short break or a major adventure with friends, family, or striking out alone; encourages you to take up outdoor activities.

MYTHOLOGY AND HISTORY

Feldspar is a major component of most igneous rocks, molten rock deep under the Earth that has cooled. As well as feldspar's innate Earth, Fire, and cosmic energies, this is a stone of total optimism.

Golden Healer Quartz

COLORS: Yellow to golden because of golden iron minerals just below the surface or as inclusions
CRYSTAL TYPE: Silicon oxide
ZODIAC SIGN: Leo (July 23–August 23)
CANDLE COLOR: Gold

PHYSICAL: Removes blockages, rebalancing body, mind, and spirit; brings hope to a gloomy prognosis, chronic illness, or ongoing pain.
EMOTIONAL: Overcomes self-defeating or destructive patterns; counters depression and PTSD after serious abuse.
HOME: Brings light and warmth to a dark, cold home; transforms sadness to happiness; distances you from ongoing family squabbles.
WORKPLACE: Brings fulfillment and financial success through ethical dealings and worthwhile projects; for aid workers and healers in conventional medicine and alternative therapies.
CHILDREN: Helps children facing physical or emotional challenges and those with debilitating conditions.
ANIMALS: For pets acting as helpers to owners.
PROTECTION: Protects against dark nights of the soul when everything seems hopeless.

MAGICKAL AND PSYCHIC USES

For receiving wisdom from higher spiritual sources, ascended masters, saints, Beings of Light, devas, and your own higher consciousness.

SPECIAL PROPERTIES

The ultimate master healer, empowering crystal layouts and healing work of any kind; cleanses the aura and chakras by drawing light from the cosmos and the Earth.

MYTHOLOGY AND HISTORY

Golden Healer Quartz is sometimes associated with Chiron, the wounded healer, the comet named after the ancient Greek centaur who healed and taught; represents our own deepest wounds, which we must first identify and heal in order to heal others. Golden Healer Quartz is becoming increasingly popular in counterbalancing the ills of and those caused by modern living.

Golden Labradorite

COLORS: Transparent gold or champagne-colored
CRYSTAL TYPE: Plagioclase feldspar (tectosilicate)
ZODIAC SIGN: Leo (July 23–August 23)
CANDLE COLOR: Gold

PHYSICAL: Alleviates issues involving digestion, gallbladder, spleen, incontinence, detoxification, metabolism, whole-body healing, life-threatening and life-changing conditions, seasonal affective disorder, lack of vitamin D.
EMOTIONAL: Helps resolve unfinished business, including absent family members of whom there is no news, an unexplained suicide or murder, overdependence on counseling or therapy.
HOME: An ongoing energizer for joint family plans, such as several generations sharing property or vacationing together.
WORKPLACE: A confidence booster to avoid being overlooked or having your opinions disregarded; for a permanently dark, cold building.
CHILDREN: Assists children struggling to play imaginatively or outdoors.
ANIMALS: For golden Labradors as therapy dogs, especially for the visually impaired.
PROTECTION: For cutting ties with emotional and psychic vampires; guards against fears of abandoning a stifling life path.

MAGICKAL AND PSYCHIC USES
Attracts what is most desired; brings good luck in lotteries, raffles, and competitions; mends holes in the aura and suffuses it with light; solar, solstice, and equinox magick.

SPECIAL PROPERTIES
Called the stone of liquid gold for bringing prosperity, success, and spiritual gold as enhanced psychic and healing abilities.

MYTHOLOGY AND HISTORY
Also known as Bytownite and Oregon Sunstone, Golden Labradorite is ruled by Michael, archangel of the sun, and other solar angels, such as Gurid, a midsummer angel with a halo of flowers; for experiencing joy and infinite possibility any time of the year or climate.

Golden or Imperial Topaz

COLOR: Golden to orange-yellow, caused by chromium impurities. Imperial topaz is most prized
CRYSTAL TYPE: Silicate mineral of aluminum and fluorine
ZODIAC SIGN: Sagittarius (November 23–December 21)
CANDLE COLOR: Bright yellow

PHYSICAL: Addresses issues involving metabolism, colds, coughs, epilepsy, allergies caused by pollutants, gallbladder, digestion, arthritis, rheumatism, motion sickness.
EMOTIONAL: Counters lack of motivation, weight loss through reducing feast and famine yo-yo dieting, inflated ego, nervous exhaustion, stress-related insomnia.
HOME: Imperial Topaz protects against fire, lightning, burglary, and accidents.
WORKPLACE: For money, success, and fame in careers in the media, theater, or writing; attracts business sponsors.
CHILDREN: Helps overcome fears of darkness and nighttime noises.
ANIMALS: For breeding healthy pedigreed animals.
PROTECTION: Guards against hostile neighbors, workplace intrigues, and jealousy in friendship.

MAGICKAL AND PSYCHIC USES
Prosperity rituals; a money and love charm; astral travel; confers invisibility when a low profile is needed.

SPECIAL PROPERTIES
Imperial or Golden Topaz continuously recharges energy, like a magnet attracting business, friendship, advantage, soul love (traditionally a wealthy lover), and improving existing relationships and contacts.

MYTHOLOGY AND HISTORY
A stone of royalty and master magicians, the finest Golden Topaz was found on Serpent Isle in the Red Sea from ancient Egyptian times, harvested only at night when gems shone brilliantly. The ancient Egyptians thought Golden Topaz contained the golden rays of the sun god Ra. Romans believed it protected against poison and changed color when danger or a liar was near.

Golden or Yellow Onyx

COLORS: Golden or yellow, single color; glowing
CRYSTAL TYPE: Natural, sometimes dyed to enhance color; also as jewelry and tumbled, polished stones; chalcedony, microcrystalline quartz; the yellow caused by iron oxide
ZODIAC SIGN: Leo (July 23–August 23)
CANDLE COLOR: Gold

PHYSICAL: Addresses wounds slow to heal, gallstones and gallbladder issues, digestion, effective processing of fat; strengthens spine and lumbar regions; reverses short-term memory loss, light sensitivity.
EMOTIONAL: Helps overcome chronic worry and fears of disaster, even when everything is going well; enables you to stop holding on to redundant attachments and memories.
HOME: Aids in finishing long-overdue repairs and renovations, uncompleted paperwork.
WORKPLACE: Guides when to speak and when to hold back, when to act and when not to; aids in persisting with a project that is meeting resistance.
CHILDREN: Encourages children to persevere with difficult tasks.
ANIMALS: For dogs and horses slow to respond to training.
PROTECTION: Keeps you safe while commuting; during short-haul or frequent air travel; counters spite and jealousy.

MAGICKAL AND PSYCHIC USES
A good luck charm, especially in relation to speculation, investments, gambling, and moneymaking schemes.
SPECIAL PROPERTIES
A stone of physical strength, stamina, and willpower; ideal for marathons, endurance sports, or organizing charity fun runs and other community activities.
MYTHOLOGY AND HISTORY
Golden Onyx is sourced in India as gleaming polished jewelry; yellow is found in Chile, Mexico, Australia, Italy, and in Arizona; beloved by shamans from ancient India to the Aztecs as representing sun deities and so powerful for healing and to bring gold; used in modern times in ornaments and buildings; for example, the Hôtel de la Païva in Paris and the new Mariinsky Theater Second Stage in St. Petersburg. The practical larger-scale uses of this healing stone radiate the joy-bringing qualities of yellow and gold onyx into daily life.

Golden Rutilated Quartz

COLORS: Clear quartz, occasionally smoky with golden needles within (see also Red Rutilated Quartz, page 401)
CRYSTAL TYPE: Silicon dioxide with titanium oxide rutiles
ZODIAC SIGN: Leo (July 23–August 23)
CANDLE COLOR: Gold

PHYSICAL: Alleviates issues stemming from bronchitis and asthma, as well as progressive illnesses or problems brought on by aging; strengthens brain cells, blood vessels, veins, hair, bone marrow; addresses issues with transfusions, chronic conditions, impotence, infertility.
EMOTIONAL: For bipolar and personality disorders; enhances self-love in people told they are ugly or sexually undesirable.
HOME: Shields those living in or near town centers, near busy highways or heavy industry.
WORKPLACE: Counters ageism; for late starters; aids in retraining in the middle years.
CHILDREN: Eases loneliness for a child without siblings; helps resolve family crises; aids in developing alternative talents if children don't excel in academics.
ANIMALS: Enables you to love physically unlovely pets.
PROTECTION: Believed to contain a protective guardian spirit, an amulet against dark moods, fears, danger, and hostile ghosts.

MAGICKAL AND PSYCHIC USES
For anyone who has dabbled in black magick or ouija boards; connects with divinity and angels; for alchemy, the search for spiritual gold, grail quests; claircognizance, the sixth sense; manifesting wishes.
SPECIAL PROPERTIES
Increases sexual desire, especially in older people; eases midlife crises; solves seemingly insoluble problems; helps remediate places affected by pollution; encourages you to try unexpressed creative crafts and performing arts.
MYTHOLOGY AND HISTORY
In ancient times, gold within quartz was believed to be crystallized sunlight or the gold of slain dragons; called angel hair or the golden hair of the Roman love goddess Venus or the Norse goddesses of beauty, Freya and Sif, preserved by Earth spirits.

Golden Scapolite

COLORS: Pale gold, gold to yellow, to yellowish green; also white, Blue Scapolite (page 81) and Purple Scapolite (page 379)
CRYSTAL TYPE: Sodium calcium aluminum silicate. *Wernerite* is the old name still used to describe the mineral
ZODIAC SIGN: Taurus (April 21–May 21)
CANDLE COLOR: Gold

PHYSICAL: Alleviates issues stemming from cataracts, glaucoma, arthritis, absorption of calcium, severe PMS; addresses gallstones, liver, spleen, veins, arteries, endometriosis, Alzheimer's disease and dementia (especially early-onset).
EMOTIONAL: Helps overcome self-destructive patterns, self-sabotage, postnatal depression, the tendency to hold onto past hurt.
HOME: For pleasurable and drama-free family events, whether Christmas, anniversaries, or weddings; attracts contentment with life as it is.
WORKPLACE: For counselors, psychotherapists, life coaches; promotes group therapy and team bonding; eases physical and emotional tensions if you are constantly bombarded by technology.
CHILDREN: Helps to acquire independence without rebellion or taking undue risks; improves memory and personal responsibility in children.
ANIMALS: Dispels pets' jealousy of the owner paying attention to other animals or children.
PROTECTION: Guards against psychic attack and any who undermine confidence.

MAGICKAL AND PSYCHIC USES
Rebirthing and regression therapy to resolve unacknowledged trauma; clairsentience, psychic knowing, clairaudience.
SPECIAL PROPERTIES
The happiness stone for releasing laughter and spreading happiness at work and home, personally and socially.
MYTHOLOGY AND HISTORY
The go-it-alone scapolite for people pleasers—to express their independence, not for selfish purposes, but for self-realization; the golden version of scapolite embraces infinite possibilities, even if you have previously tried to initiate change and have then fallen prey to inertia.

Golden Selenite

COLORS: Yellow, gold, amber
CRYSTAL TYPE: Gypsum, calcium sulfate dihydrate
ZODIAC SIGNS: Cancer (June 22–July 22) and Leo (July 23–August 23)
CANDLE COLOR: Gold

PHYSICAL: A powerful form of selenite for whole-body healing; addresses light sensitivity, SAD, cataracts, glaucoma, digestion, IBS, celiac disease, arthritis.
EMOTIONAL: Alleviates past and present trauma, acute anxiety about potential dangers to self and family (use golden fishtail or angel wing selenite resembling a fish tail or celestial wing), overcompensation with food, alcohol, or cigarettes, due to poor self-esteem.
HOME: Golden Selenite combines gentle sun and moonlight in dark rooms with sluggish energies to radiate warmth and well-being.
WORKPLACE: Cleanses a depressing workplace aura created by petty rivalries, cliques, or inertia.
CHILDREN: For children entering puberty late who are teased by peers.
ANIMALS: For golden fish in a tank to attract prosperity.
PROTECTION: Guards against critical and discouraging people who sap enthusiasm.

MAGICKAL AND PSYCHIC USES
Charges other crystals; for solar and lunar eclipses; rituals when the sun and moon are both in the sky.
SPECIAL PROPERTIES
Golden Selenite, especially in its twin form—sometimes called butterfly selenite—gives power to connect closely with spirit guides and guardian angels; for new beginnings and transformation.
MYTHOLOGY AND HISTORY
Sunset gold selenite is a recently discovered, amber-colored selenite from the Southwest United States, combining the energies of waning moon and sun the hour before sunset, for letting go of activities you no longer enjoy and people who drain your energies.

Gold-Included Quartz

COLORS: Pure gold within clear quartz; also found within other quartzes
CRYSTAL TYPE: Varies from flakes of gold to small gold nuggets within a quartz matrix; rare, especially in gem-quality
ZODIAC SIGN: Leo (July 23–August 23)
CANDLE COLOR: Gold

PHYSICAL: Gold amplifies quartz and quartz gold, removing toxins and acting as a whole self-healer and energizer, when united; promotes fertility in older couples or those with problems conceiving and carrying a baby to term; alleviates issues relating to heart failure, deep vein thrombosis, circulation, digestion.
EMOTIONAL: Counters unwise attraction to criminals or other dangerous people, as well as the desire for wealth to the exclusion of all else.
HOME: Fills the home with beauty, radiance, abundance, health, and happiness.
WORKPLACE: For investments; high-profile media work; finding fame and success in the second half of life.
CHILDREN: Aids in making a breakthrough with children locked within themselves.
ANIMALS: For magickal power guardians, such as the unicorn, phoenix, and dragon.
PROTECTION: Guards against malevolent spirits, poltergeists, and demons, especially those unwittingly invited while dabbling in the occult.

MAGICKAL AND PSYCHIC USES

For profound religious and spiritual experiences and peak experiences of momentary unity with the cosmos; alchemy; connection with archangels, especially Michael, archangel of the Sun; fire magick.

SPECIAL PROPERTIES

Gold-Included Quartz attracts rapid and lasting prosperity, especially through speculation.

MYTHOLOGY AND HISTORY

The ultimate alchemist stone of transformation, whether as small flakes or streaks in raw quartz or as finely crafted golden nuggets in quartz jewelry. The fire power of Gold-Included Quartz gives dynamism to break through any obstacles to success in the way most desired.

Gold Sheen Obsidian

COLORS: Dark brown to black with gold sheen
CRYSTAL TYPE: Volcanic silica glass (see also Silver Sheen Obsidian, page 440), created when gas bubbles are aligned along layers created as lava rapidly cools
ZODIAC SIGNS: Scorpio (October 24–November 22) and Sagittarius (November 23–December 21).
CANDLE COLOR: Gold

PHYSICAL: Alleviates issues with digestion, back, impotence (especially stress-related), genetic illnesses, neurological conditions, glaucoma, progressive eye problems, acute pain; aids in attaining the right weight.
EMOTIONAL: Helps overcome the tendency to live through others' joys and sorrows; helps to resolve issues stemming from abuse in childhood by a powerful or authority figure.
HOME: Clears stagnation, attracting health and happiness.
WORKPLACE: For business expansion; gets to the root of any problem; for diagnostic practitioners; deals with people with inflated egos.
CHILDREN: Casts protection around Indigo, Star, or Crystal Children.
ANIMALS: Connects with power animals, especially magickal ones.
PROTECTION: Reflects back harmful words; deters those obstructing your success and prosperity through jealousy.

MAGICKAL AND PSYCHIC USES

A Gold Sheen Obsidian sphere in candlelight creates a timeline from the past (including past lives), through present to future potentials; enhances shamanism, astral travel, psychic surgery, reiki healing; a magick mirror to connect with spirit teachers.

SPECIAL PROPERTIES

Kept with financial papers near a business computer, purse, or wallet, Gold Sheen Obsidian attracts fast money and longer-term prosperity.

MYTHOLOGY AND HISTORY

The fire of obsidian and gold sheen together manifest abundance, not just financially, but promote fulfillment of as-yet-undiscovered talents, self-confidence, and the power to make your own dreams come true.

Goshenite or Colorless Beryl

COLOR: Clear, colorless
CRYSTAL TYPE: Aluminum beryllium silicate; purest form of beryl
ZODIAC SIGN: Cancer (June 22–July 22)
CANDLE COLOR: White

PHYSICAL: Addresses vision issues, stress-related exhaustion; strengthens leg and arm muscles; counters dust-mite and pollen allergies, infections and viruses attacking immune system, acute PMS; regulates body fluids, hormones; offers accurate medical diagnoses.

EMOTIONAL: Alleviates mood swings, postnatal depression, bipolar disorder.

HOME: The crystal of honesty, Goshenite deters gossiping neighbors, and family and friends who take liberties with the truth.

WORKPLACE: Speeds lazy or incompetent colleagues; deters stealing or fraud; promotes mathematical and analytical skills.

CHILDREN: For overly imaginative children, who frighten themselves with their own fantasies.

ANIMALS: For pets with failing eyesight to heighten other senses.

PROTECTION: Guards against those who would slander or libel to hide their own misdemeanors.

MAGICKAL AND PSYCHIC USES

Historically, one of the earliest crystal balls or spheres; a moon crystal most powerful at full moon; contacts female and moon angels; connects with higher spheres in dreams or meditation.

SPECIAL PROPERTIES

A crystal to enhance intuition to unmask a thief at work, discover if a lover is faithful, and discourage temptation; as a betrothal ring; for keeping secrets and protecting confidential information.

MYTHOLOGY AND HISTORY

Called the mother of crystals, Goshenite is associated with motherhood, especially mothers bringing up children alone; traditionally, a gift from mother to a daughter who has just given birth; used in ancient Greece as spectacles; aids in finding treasure at garage sales or prospecting for gold or gems.

Grandidierite

COLORS: Teal, turquoise, bluish-green to deep green or light yellow/colorless, the color due to traces of iron; the more iron, the bluer the shade
CRYSTAL TYPE: Magnesium aluminum borosilicate
ZODIAC SIGN: Leo (July 23–August 23)
CANDLE COLOR: Blue

PHYSICAL: Regulates heart rhythms; keeps pacemakers, stents, and heart bypasses working smoothly; strengthens blood circulation, breathing; alleviates throat issues.

EMOTIONAL: Counters an inability to plan or assess situations to prevent escalation, and difficulty in socializing.

HOME: To welcome absent family members home or new members into the family.

WORKPLACE: Promotes networking, teamwork; setting up a business with friends to establish a professional structure to keep personal issues from intruding.

CHILDREN: A gift for a special occasion, such as an eighteenth birthday (in which you legally attain adulthood), whether a small piece of jewelry or beautiful tumbled Grandidierite.

ANIMALS: Connects with noble power creatures, such as lions, unicorns, dolphins, or water and air dragons.

PROTECTION: Guards against confused thinking or being pressured into hasty decisions.

MAGICKAL AND PSYCHIC USES

For trance meditation and mediumship; rituals for prosperity; justice spells if a witness against you is dishonest or a judge is biased; cloud scrying; oracle cards.

SPECIAL PROPERTIES

The gem of generosity with resources, time, and emotions if a love partner comes from a family where nothing was openly expressed.

MYTHOLOGY AND HISTORY

First discovered in southern Madagascar in 1902. Rarer than diamonds, the world's third most expensive gemstone and among the ten rarest stones in the world, Grandidierite can be obtained in non-gem tumbled stone variety, making it more affordable and containing the same healing properties.

Granite

COLORS: Pink, gray, yellow-brown, black, white, red, green, and blue; often sparkling

CRYSTAL TYPE: Consists mainly of quartz and orthoclase (feldspar) with mica and sodium; can be found as tumbled stones and in jewelry

ZODIAC SIGN: Libra (September 23–October 23)

CANDLE COLOR: Pink

PHYSICAL: Alleviates pain from rheumatism, bone and muscle weakness (especially due to childhood illness); promotes balance, if mobility is a problem; counters cerebral palsy, dyspraxia, irregular ovulation, low sperm count, aging issues.

EMOTIONAL: Helps overcome fears of impermanence in love, sudden ill health, loss or lack of financial security; keeps you from unnecessary risk taking.

HOME: Removes toxic Earth energies beneath the home; encourages the free flow of chi.

WORKPLACE: Fosters cooperation between groups; for diplomacy if colleagues or employees take suggestions as personal attacks; for restoring stability after a hostile takeover.

CHILDREN: For those who live in a fantasy world and find everyday living hard.

ANIMALS: Helps easily startled pets become accustomed to noise and sudden movement.

PROTECTION: Guards against paranormal attack; skeptical people who trample on dreams.

MAGICKAL AND PSYCHIC USES

Connection with ancient Egypt, both personal past lives and memories of the ancient world; access to star wisdom and star lives; sound healing; creates a safe sacred space for magick rituals.

SPECIAL PROPERTIES

Encourages prosperity to naturally flow in and remain; relieves trauma and stressful events by offering practical solutions.

MYTHOLOGY AND HISTORY

Revered by the Mayans and Australian Aboriginals as a sacred and magickal stone. The granite area, north of Mount Magnet in western Australia, contains rock art nine thousand years old. Aswan pink Granite was used in ancient Egypt for creating obelisks, sacred to the sun god Ra, in temples and the pyramids.

Grape Agate

COLORS: Purple, from almost white to deep purple, occasionally including blue crystals as part of the cluster

CRYSTAL TYPE: Botryoidal chalcedony, small sphere-shaped crystals radiating outward from the center of the crystal to form a cluster that resembles a bunch of grapes (see also Black Botryoidal Agate, page 59), cryptocrystalline silica, intergrowth of quartz and moganite

ZODIAC SIGN: Pisces (February 19–March 20)

CANDLE COLOR: Purple

PHYSICAL: Dispels dyspraxia or excess clumsiness in children and adults; alleviates growths, warts, melanomas, verrucae; counters viruses or infections that spread rapidly through a community, such as a school or college.

EMOTIONAL: Helps overcome difficulty in maintaining relationships or seeing the point of view of others; banishes rigid thinking and intolerance of those who are different.

HOME: Valuable for family gatherings, welcoming home absent family members; for different generations sharing a home.

WORKPLACE: For establishing a collective, technological, or artisans' complex or commune; for noncontroversial office parties, outings, and team-building events.

CHILDREN: Encourages those with musical talents or a flair for the performing arts.

ANIMALS: For running a kennel, cattery, animal sanctuary, or stables where unrelated animals live together.

PROTECTION: Guards against cliques and excluding factions.

MAGICKAL AND PSYCHIC USES

Trance meditation, psychic dreaming; attracts nature spirits, especially during water scrying in rivers or lakes; scrying with wine or wine dregs.

SPECIAL PROPERTIES

For finding a new life path, new relationships, and seeking deeper meaning in life.

MYTHOLOGY AND HISTORY

Created in Indonesia through volcanic activity, Grape Agate or chalcedony is the stone of community and peace, whether building up connections within the neighborhood, seasonal celebrational events, particularly at the fall equinox in the northern hemisphere, or for cultivating world peace.

Graphic Amazonite

COLORS: Blue-green or turquoise, with black or gray lines or markings

CRYSTAL TYPE: A feldspar with smoky quartz and silicon dioxide inclusions that forms the lines through the stone; may also contain black tourmaline and small quantities of black mica; best as tumbled stones for healing and magick

ZODIAC SIGN: Gemini (May 22–June 21)

CANDLE COLOR: Turquoise

PHYSICAL: Addresses issues involving sexual disorders and genitourinary infections, hair loss, mastitis, osteoarthritis, osteoporosis, tooth decay and gum disease, maintaining overall health; relieves chronic pain.

EMOTIONAL: For those who love too much and unwisely when all hope is gone or stay with an abusive partner; counters self-harm.

HOME: Protects against electromagnetic energies from computers, cell phones, living near cell phone towers, pylons, industrial sites, or crowded roads; keeps bad temper, sarcasm, and hostility from entering the home from whatever source.

WORKPLACE: For aiming for the top while avoiding alienating those who would stand in your way; for remaining outwardly neutral in office gossip.

CHILDREN: Teaches children that there are alternative viewpoints and often two sides to every story.

ANIMALS: Protects cats who live near busy roads.

PROTECTION: Guards against sexism, ageism, and LGBTQ+ prejudices in the workplace and community.

MAGICKAL AND PSYCHIC USES

Rituals to turn debt into solvency; drains negative energies with the nondominant hand through the crystal into the Earth and replenishes through the dominant hand by drawing down cosmic energies with it.

SPECIAL PROPERTIES

Aids in remaining true to yourself and your principles, even if you are not immediately in a position to make changes.

MYTHOLOGY AND HISTORY

Found in Colorado and in Russia, this unique blend of minerals combines the protectiveness of smoky quartz with the courage and confidence of amazonite, which seems especially effective for women seeking to claim or reclaim their power and resist inequality and abuse.

Graphic Feldspar

COLORS: Black, gray, and brown translucent marbled inclusions (smoky quartz) in cream or tan stone (feldspar)

CRYSTAL TYPE: Feldspar and smoky quartz, growing together with layers of smoky quartz flowing through the feldspar matrix; also as tumbled stones, worry palm stones, and jewelry

ZODIAC SIGN: Capricorn (December 22–January 20)

CANDLE COLOR: Brown

PHYSICAL: A stone of alignment or realignment of chakra energy centers, meridian energy lines, spine, and skeletal structure, especially after an accident.

EMOTIONAL: Counters lack of trust in people after betrayal; tears down personal barriers that prevent meaningful communication even with family or a partner.

HOME: Clears negative energies from rooms, artifacts, and from social gatherings; aids in finding lost or misplaced items.

WORKPLACE: Helps figure out innovative ways of reaching goals; valuable in using tact, diplomacy, and persuasion to gain the cooperation of others.

CHILDREN: For gaining confidence at skills and socially at their own pace; finding new friends if there have been major breakups.

ANIMALS: To call a lost pet home and tune into their new location or sense through the stone where they are located.

PROTECTION: For safety during astral travel and when communicating with spirits.

MAGICKAL AND PSYCHIC USES

Linked to ancient Egyptian wisdom and pyramid healing; awareness of Star Soul energies with fellow Star Seed People on Earth and with the intergalactic realms; finding your star twin.

SPECIAL PROPERTIES

For writers and aspiring writers to express their thoughts, ideas, and inspiration, for pleasure and to share with the world through conventional publication or self-publication.

MYTHOLOGY AND HISTORY

Called Graphic Feldspar because the lines of included smoky quartz resemble writing; also known as zebradorite, since some interpret the markings as zebra-like stripes. It is found in Madagascar and the USA.

Graphite

COLOR: Black to silvery gray
CRYSTAL TYPE: Carbon, occurring in nature in pure form
ZODIAC SIGN: Capricorn (December 22–January 20)
CANDLE COLOR: Gray

PHYSICAL: Alleviates issues relating to the feet, legs, hearing, spine, bowels, nerve connections, Parkinson's disease, cataracts; promotes healthy weight loss (especially graphite included in quartz).
EMOTIONAL: Eases post-traumatic stress disorder worsened by disability or memory loss; aids in letting go of what is no longer needed or is destructive.
HOME: For budgeting if more money goes out than in; for deterring shopaholics.
WORKPLACE: Communicates expertise in online applications for jobs, a place in college, or promotion; for mathematicians, scientists, systems analysts, statisticians, software designers, surveyors, writers of manuals.
CHILDREN: Enhances skills in mathematics and deduction; suddenly uprooting from a familiar home or location.
ANIMALS: For training guide and therapy dogs.
PROTECTION: Guards against electrical faults at home or work, and against those who subtly undermine your confidence.

MAGICKAL AND PSYCHIC USES

Automatic writing to connect with ancestors; powerfully transmits healing energies.

SPECIAL PROPERTIES

Helps you live your own way if others have previously steered your life path; sharpens skills in Sudoku, quizzes, chess, or crosswords.

MYTHOLOGY AND HISTORY

Graphite and diamond are both carbon; Graphite much softer than its shining sister, the difference being the arrangement of carbon atoms. Graphite is best known in pencils and as an effective conductor of electricity. The first graphite pencils were used around 1560 when a storm uprooted a large tree in Borrowdale in the Lake District and graphite was discovered beneath its roots.

Grass Flower Jasper

COLORS: Browns, creams; may be swirled with gray, pink, and burgundy
CRYSTAL TYPE: Chalcedony; the more common, brown, subdued shades may contain chert
ZODIAC SIGN: Virgo (August 24–September 22)
CANDLE COLOR: Brown

PHYSICAL: Offers stability where mobility or balance is a problem; strengthens immunity; counters allergies prompted by pollen, fur, and feathers; salves cuts and wounds; promotes fertility.
EMOTIONAL: Dispels envy of others who appear more attractive, smarter, richer, or more charismatic; makes you less self-conscious about showing your abilities.
HOME: Balances the chi, the life force in the home; reduces tension at gatherings of extended family.
WORKPLACE: For successful internet business connections and online conferencing; knowing the right time to ask for a raise, promotion, or extra time off.
CHILDREN: Teaches children to not interrupt and to learn to take turns.
ANIMALS: For dealing with visitors who are terrified of or hate pets.
PROTECTION: Guards against dangerous situations, especially those where we may take unnecessary risks.

MAGICKAL AND PSYCHIC USES

Flower rituals, flower healing and psychometry with plants; communicating with garden and wildflower meadow spirits.

SPECIAL PROPERTIES

Encourages genuine friendships and lasting love online or vacation romances out of state or overseas.

MYTHOLOGY AND HISTORY

The crystal of hidden beauty and opportunity; if you wait for the right time and energies, Grass Flower Jasper will offer the recognition you deserve and spread your influence without ostentation or effort.

Gray Agate or the Stone of Secrets

COLORS: Different shades of gray, especially light gray, sometimes with bands
CRYSTAL TYPE: Chalcedony
ZODIAC SIGN: Scorpio (October 24–November 22)
CANDLE COLOR: Gray

PHYSICAL: Addresses smoke- and chemical-related allergies and illnesses, lung congestion, gastroenteritis, fatigue; reduces cravings.
EMOTIONAL: Helps overcome addictions, compulsions, and obsessions; fears of eating or talking in public; the tendency for impulsive words or behavior; inability to keep confidences.
HOME: For finding peace and quiet in a noisy household; when you must keep part of your life private.
WORKPLACE: Helps you avoid the overly curious who steal your ideas and take credit; if you are planning to move on but must keep your intentions quiet; for patenting an invention or the results of a project before declaring it publicly.
CHILDREN: Comforts psychic children who are teased by peers when they talk about their experiences.
ANIMALS: For children welcoming and loving a pet who is not the latest craze; calms hyperactive animals.
PROTECTION: Guards against threats while traveling at night by psychically lowering your profile.

MAGICKAL AND PSYCHIC USES
For night magick; astrology; to work undetected if your community disapproves of psychic work or magick; dowsing for what is missing or being concealed.

SPECIAL PROPERTIES
For love that cannot be revealed; for bringing contentment for life as it is now with the people, career, home, and lifestyle who are part of it and not wishing life away for what cannot be.

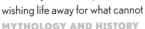

MYTHOLOGY AND HISTORY
The most mysterious of the agates. It is sometimes called the stone of secrets, since it has been used by magickians and witches in times past to shield their aura when they wish or need to be undetected, not only from the overly curious, but as they walk between worlds.

Gray Diamond

COLORS: Fancy-colored gray, very clear, from a faint tinge or light gray to darker shades, salt and pepper with white inclusions, or black flecks inside the stone
CRYSTAL TYPE: Diamond, carbon, fancy gray, the clearest kind colored by hydrogen or occasionally boron; often round
ZODIAC SIGN: Gemini (May 22–June 21)
CANDLE COLOR: Gray

PHYSICAL: Promotes balance, especially in older people; alleviates blood clots and strokes, narrowed blood vessels; reconnects nerves and tissues; relieves chronic pain; eases dementia; mitigates deteriorating eyesight.
EMOTIONAL: Helps you cope with great pressure from family to enter a marriage and produce descendants to keep the family name and/or business going; for obsessions that interfere with relaxation or sleep.
HOME: Brings good luck to the home and family; attracts what is needed and will confer a better quality of life, rather than what is desired.
WORKPLACE: Enables you to merge into the background in a new workplace until you understand existing alliances and rivalries; for negotiations between workers and management.
CHILDREN: For the family treasure box, to be brought out on special occasions; encourages children to compromise.
ANIMALS: To protect all silver or gray wild cats, rhinos, and elephants from poachers and threatened extinction.
PROTECTION: Guards against jealous love rivals and ex-partners.

MAGICKAL AND PSYCHIC USES
Lowers your profile in times of potential danger to create a virtual state of invisibility; to repel psychic attack and neutralize hostile energies.

SPECIAL PROPERTIES
For a love that must be kept secret; for pledges of fidelity if you're separated by distance or circumstances.

MYTHOLOGY AND HISTORY
Popular in betrothal rings with couples who want a low-profile engagement and wedding and are secure in their love without needing ostentation; for second or third marriages between older people.

Green Apatite

COLORS: Vibrant green, pale, olive, sea green, or deep green
CRYSTAL TYPE: Phosphate
ZODIAC SIGNS: Virgo (August 24–September 22) and Libra (September 23–October 23)
CANDLE COLOR: Green

PHYSICAL: Repairs brittle bones, osteoporosis, cells, growth problems in children, hypertension, heart valves; alleviates pain of heart attacks, jaw, teeth, kidneys, metabolism; promotes absorption of calcium; regulates glands, fluid imbalances; aids with gradual recuperation; addresses anorexia, bulimia.
EMOTIONAL: Helps overcome the inability to move on from love that did not last, dislike or fear of social contact, fears of poverty and scarcity.
HOME: For success in organic gardening, permaculture, and sustainability; encourages community spirit for local environmental issues.
WORKPLACE: Awakens or reawakens enthusiasm for a long-term project; refocuses coworkers or employees who spend too much time on personal emails, surfing the net, or phone calls, impacting your workload or business efficiency.
CHILDREN: Eases symptoms of autism, AHDD, hyperactivity, especially where diet is implicated; improves hand-eye coordination.
ANIMALS: Encourages animal healing, telepathic communication with pets; for psychic pets who warn of danger.
PROTECTION: Guards against those who are accident-prone or naturally clumsy.

MAGICKAL AND PSYCHIC USES
Telepathy with people far away and between parents and children of all ages; extraterrestrial contact; druidry and nature spirituality; for global predictions.

SPECIAL PROPERTIES
Good luck in driving tests, especially as a result of last-minute cancellations; balances heart and mind, logic and intuition; aids in accumulating money.

MYTHOLOGY AND HISTORY
Called the *bones of the earth*, Green Apatite brings healing through amplifying the effects of essential oils, herbs, and flower essences, increasing receptivity.

Green Apophyllite

COLORS: Light, medium, or rich forest green; may be clear as glass
CRYSTAL TYPE: Hydrated potassium calcium silicate; may have inclusions of or form clusters with Hydrated potassium calcium silicate; may have inclusions of or form clusters with Heulandite (page 242)
ZODIAC SIGN: Virgo (August 24–September 22)
CANDLE COLOR: Green

PHYSICAL: Promotes fertility; after surgery, helps to remove diseased parts of the body; addresses colostomies, heart and circulation issues, new fitness regimens.
EMOTIONAL: Helps overcome codependency; removes emotional baggage from previous relationships; discourages voices from the past.
HOME: Reorganizes domestic life to cut down on unnecessary waste and expenditure.
WORKPLACE: Relocates a business or career to an area with a better quality of life.
CHILDREN: Helps logical, practical parents enter a child's magickal world and fantasy games.
ANIMALS: Enables telepathic communication with pets and wild animals; animal whispering.
PROTECTION: Guards against unwanted attachments, both by possessive people and spirits.

MAGICKAL AND PSYCHIC USES
Encourages communication with plant essences and devas; empowers growing herbs for healing; opens energy portals in ancient hillsides and places with otherworld entrances, such as Glastonbury Tor in the UK.

SPECIAL PROPERTIES
A crystal that injects fun and spontaneity into relationships, where a couple are work- and achievement-oriented; for deciding whether to have children.

MYTHOLOGY AND HISTORY
Green Apophyllite was first discovered by a farmer in Poona in India. Associated with growth of health, prosperity, and self, it clears away anxieties, doubts, and living by others' rules, so you can reveal and love your true self.

Green Aventurine

COLORS: Light to dark or creamy green; usually translucent medium green

CRYSTAL TYPE: Oxide, quartz, containing mica, which gives it a metallic, iridescent glint

ZODIAC SIGNS: Virgo (August 24–September 22) and Taurus (April 21–May 21)

CANDLE COLOR: Mint green

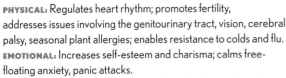

PHYSICAL: Regulates heart rhythm; promotes fertility, addresses issues involving the genitourinary tract, vision, cerebral palsy, seasonal plant allergies; enables resistance to colds and flu.

EMOTIONAL: Increases self-esteem and charisma; calms free-floating anxiety, panic attacks.

HOME: Sparkling Green Aventurine, placed in front of a garden gnome, attracts prosperity; encourages a flourishing garden.

WORKPLACE: Encourages moneymaking; an entrepreneurial crystal; for pursuing an untapped business opportunity.

CHILDREN: For clumsy, hyperactive, or accident-prone children; keeps teenagers safe while cycling, driving, or traveling.

ANIMALS: Calms large, boisterous pets, causing mayhem.

PROTECTION: Repels psychic and psychological intrusion.

MAGICKAL AND PSYCHIC USES

Conjures up psychic and predictive dreams; increases clairvoyance; when dowsing, brings connection with Earth energies, nature spirits, and devas; useful in Earth healing rituals, past-life recall, ascension magick.

SPECIAL PROPERTIES

The good luck crystal (especially three in a green bag) for games of chance or speculation; aids in finding love, especially in later years; helps discover what is relevant.

MYTHOLOGY AND HISTORY

In ancient Tibet, Green Aventurine, sometimes called the stone of heaven, was used for statue eyes to represent deities' all-seeing power; increases potency in tree essences, herbs, oils, and homeopathic remedies; also draws money if kept in cash boxes, tills, or near a computer.

Green Calcite

COLOR: Light to medium green, occasionally emerald or apple green; resembles water ice or sea-washed glass

CRYSTAL TYPE: Calcium carbonate

ZODIAC SIGN: Virgo (August 24–September 22)

CANDLE COLOR: Light green

PHYSICAL: Alleviates colds, flu, and chest infections, heart irregularities; addresses bypass, valve, and transplant surgery; helps slow growths in lungs, breasts, and lymph nodes; calms arthritis pain; offers healing wherever it's most needed in the body.

EMOTIONAL: Helps overcome obsessive behavior, overthinking, the inability to give or receive love; for relaxing patients during energy therapies; assuages the pain of divorce, loss, or bereavement.

HOME: Suffuses the home with calm; for fresh energies in city apartments; creates beautiful gardens; aids in preparing nutritious meals, even when you're in a hurry.

WORKPLACE: Reduces workaholic tendencies in high-stress careers; useful for those working with animals, plants, farming, natural energy, herbalism, crystals, mining, metallurgy, and rural hospitality businesses.

CHILDREN: Soothes hyperactive children; encourages generosity; helps solitary children overcome shyness.

ANIMALS: Cools longhaired or thickly coated pets; for animal Reiki.

PROTECTION: Guards against accidents and injuries in sports.

MAGICKAL AND PSYCHIC USES

For money rituals; as a charm to draw business, especially to new companies; for good luck, natural magick, druidry, connecting with nature spirits in quiet places.

SPECIAL PROPERTIES

For philanthropic projects, volunteering for charities, help lines, and community ventures.

MYTHOLOGY AND HISTORY

Green Calcite is the stone of small, benign, Earth spirits who live in woodlands or grassy fairy mounds near water, in societies from Scandinavia to Native North America where Green Calcite was gifted in ceremonies to share abundance.

Green Chert

COLORS: Pale to emerald green

CRYSTAL TYPE: Cryptocrystalline quartz stone, chert that has metamorphosed from fuchsite; contains chromium (see also Chert, page 117); often sold as a tumbled stone

ZODIAC SIGN: Virgo (August 24–September 22)

CANDLE COLOR: Green

PHYSICAL: Addresses issues involving the heart (especially irregular heartbeat), the immune system, pancreas, blood sugar balance, diabetes, elimination of waste products from the body, plant allergies.

EMOTIONAL: Counters the inability or unwillingness to move on from childhood trauma or neglect; for healers who have unresolved past trauma.

HOME: For initiating construction of a house or a major relocation that will take time and huge effort but be worth it in terms of life quality; spring cleaning any time of the year.

WORKPLACE: Aids in striving 100 percent for promotion, a new job, a total career change or a business of your own.

CHILDREN: Encourages children to save for what they want; helps teenagers find and stick with vacation and weekend work.

ANIMALS: For pets who prefer to live outdoors.

PROTECTION: Guards against being pressured to meet other people's expectations.

MAGICKAL AND PSYCHIC USES

Dowsing for fast, accurate answers, also for water and minerals; increases the power of healing sessions and the power of crystals and oils being used; for herbal healing.

SPECIAL PROPERTIES

Initiates and develops new relationships and friendships; helps start a pleasurable fitness and healthy eating regimen.

MYTHOLOGY AND HISTORY

A relatively new find in western Australia in the Pilbara region; different from Indiana green chert, which is more subtle in its color and energies, being light to dark green with distinctive banding.

Green Chrysoprase

COLORS: Bright apple green, mint green, or light green

CRYSTAL TYPE: Chalcedony; quartz with nickel traces

ZODIAC SIGN: Taurus (April 21–May 21)

CANDLE COLOR: Apple green

PHYSICAL: Resolves issues involving the ears, eyes, stomach acidity, heart, overactive nervous system, colds; detoxifies; reduces chronic medication side effects; promotes fertility if conception is slow after a first child.

EMOTIONAL: Counters compulsive or impulsive behavior; heals the wounded inner child; reduces codependency; works as an antidepressant.

HOME: Spring-cleans homes any time; brings abundance, health, happiness; confers a sense of space in cramped accommodations.

WORKPLACE: Encourages loyalty; offers viable options to failing ventures; for media, publicity, advertising, and fiction writers.

CHILDREN: For overweight children to eat healthily without becoming obsessed with food.

ANIMALS: Comforts those suffering from cold and damp.

PROTECTION: Creates a low profile in confrontational situations; shields against jealousy.

MAGICKAL AND PSYCHIC USES

Enhances herbal healing, oils, and essences; a money and fertility charm; creates insightful tarot readings.

SPECIAL PROPERTIES

A relationship stone, which offers renewal after setback, betrayal, or outside interference; encourages commitment and fidelity; mends a broken heart.

MYTHOLOGY AND HISTORY

Chrysoprase is said in folklore to have fallen from heavenly apple trees; recommended by the early twelfth-century mystic Hildegard von Bingen for turning anger into forgiveness. In Eastern Europe, chrysoprase was believed to help communication with lizards and other reptiles; a crystal connecting strongly with nature, nature spirits, and magickal animals.

Green Dalmatian Jasper

COLORS: Naturally colored pale or yellowy to medium green with black or green spots or white with green spots; commonly dyed as bright green with black spots

CRYSTAL TYPE: Silicate, microcrystalline quartz, with organic matter or minerals as inclusions; the black and green spots are tourmaline; may be found as tumbled stones and in natural form as jewelry

ZODIAC SIGN: Virgo (August 24–September 22)

CANDLE COLOR: Green

PHYSICAL: Purifies the blood; addresses plant, fur, and pollen allergies, experienced as breathing difficulties; counters bowel problems, such as IBS and constipation, made worse by an unhealthy diet; relieves lactose intolerance.

EMOTIONAL: Helps overcome dissatisfaction with life, envy of others who seem wealthier, happier, or with better relationships.

HOME: For cooking, gardening, reviving hobbies, walks, cycling, and swimming to make leisure time pleasurable, and to meet new people.

WORKPLACE: Makes the journey to work as enjoyable as possible; creates a natural workspace, however small, with crystals, plants, and small personal treasures.

CHILDREN: Encourages outdoor fun if children spend too much time on electronic devices; for summer vacations to learn self-sufficiency.

ANIMALS: For farm and rural dogs and cats who live mainly outdoors.

PROTECTION: Reflects back ill-wishing or jinxes.

MAGICKAL AND PSYCHIC USES

Defensive magick; anti-evil eye; natural magick; animal Reiki and healing; increases gifts with herbalism, plant oils, flower and tree essences.

SPECIAL PROPERTIES

A good luck and financial advantage crystal, to bring success in speculation, gambling, and moneymaking, and to guard against scams, especially online romance scams.

MYTHOLOGY AND HISTORY

The crystal that says the cup is half full, not half empty; makes you happy, even in small ways every day; promotes participation in or organizing of workplace and community fun runs, charity fund-raising, and outings.

Green Diopside

COLOR: Light green, greenish-brown to dark green, with glassy or pearly luster, also white, bright green as chromium-rich diopside

CRYSTAL TYPE: Calcium magnesium silicate, a pyroxene mineral

ZODIAC SIGN: Gemini (May 22–June 21)

CANDLE COLOR: Bright green

PHYSICAL: Alleviates stress headaches, blood pressure issues, degenerative conditions in older people, hand tremors, post-surgical complications; addresses concerns about menopause, heart, arteries, lungs affected by smoking or asbestos, emphysema, asthma.

EMOTIONAL: Counters eating disorders, addictions, obsessive behavior, overreliance on prescription drugs, painkillers, and recreational drugs.

HOME: For strength and patience caring for older relatives or family members with disabilities.

WORKPLACE: Aids in retraining after redundancy or a forced career change; for writers to remove writer's block and meet deadlines; for young people seeking a job or apprenticeship in areas of high unemployment.

CHILDREN: Helps overcome learning difficulties, dyslexia, and dyspraxia.

ANIMALS: Calms overly excitable pets.

PROTECTION: Removes unrecognized causes of addictions and obsessions.

MAGICKAL AND PSYCHIC USES

Meditation, scrying; developing automatic psychic radar to discover what is hidden, from information to unexpected treasure; cultivating psychic vision in darkness; chromium-rich diopside for Gaia rituals, Earth spirit and fey connections; strengthens psychic links with the plant, animal, and mineral kingdom.

SPECIAL PROPERTIES

For all formal learning; higher education courses for mature students; learning languages, passing driving tests.

MYTHOLOGY AND HISTORY

A crystal for awakening our inner spiritual nature to the hidden mysteries of the universe; green cat's eye with tiny rutile inclusions and darker Green Diopside containing a shimmering four-pointed star, manifest possibilities.

Green Dolomite

COLOR: Olive, variety of greens
CRYSTAL TYPE: Calcium carbonate with zinc coloring it green
ZODIAC SIGN: Virgo (August 24–September 22)
CANDLE COLOR: Green

PHYSICAL: Relieves symptoms of colds, influenza, bronchitis, pneumonia; closes up wounds; promotes immunity and memory; addresses issues involving the eyes, hair, skin, nails, teeth, bones, breasts, pregnancy, bed-wetting; regulates blood sugar, body temperature.
EMOTIONAL: Counters alcohol abuse, addictions, self-harm; helps overcome an obsession with media-induced beauty and the tendency for eating disorders.
HOME: Attracts like-minded friends in a new area; encourages a friendly atmosphere among neighbors; aids in establishing or joining community activities and campaigning for better local facilities.
WORKPLACE: Deters inappropriate flirting or sexual innuendos; deters sexual harassment where acceptance offers a route to promotion; obtains a voluntary aid position overseas, work or internship with a charity or international organization.
CHILDREN: Reduces fear of animals, especially large ones.
ANIMALS: For pets who are the sole companions of a homebound owner.
PROTECTION: Guards against those who try to break up a relationship.

MAGICKAL AND PSYCHIC USES
Sometimes called the crystal herb because it works well with plant medicines; empowers medicinal herbs, potions, plant oils and essences; attracts nature spirits into the garden.
SPECIAL PROPERTIES
Though Green Dolomite is rarer than pink or white, it has unique properties for promoting lasting faithful love if your partner works far away or is naturally flirtatious.
MYTHOLOGY AND HISTORY
Associated with treasure unclaimed by gnomes in the Swiss Alps, so it's a gift to humans, Green Dolomite is the stone of sharing resources, rather than hoarding, and encouraging generosity among financially overcautious relatives and friends.

Green Fluorite

COLORS: From deep to pale yellow-green
CRYSTAL TYPE: Halide, calcium fluoride; glassy, cube-like
ZODIAC SIGN: Pisces (February 19–March 20)
CANDLE COLOR: Green

PHYSICAL: Promotes the immune system, cell regeneration, energy, absorption of minerals for teeth and bones; addresses issues involving the throat, blood vessels, lungs, back, scar tissue, nausea, indigestion.
EMOTIONAL: Unblocks grief from unresolved past bereavement; counters eating disorders caused by negative body image.
HOME: Dissipates excess energies and encourages considerate behavior if there is constant noise and chaos; revives dying plants; enables decluttering.
WORKPLACE: For dispelling disharmonious energies from electrical equipment, air conditioning, and constant overhead lighting; brings freshness into high-rise or industrial complexes.
CHILDREN: Defends those traveling through traffic-polluted areas to school or playing in urban parks close to roads; encourages reluctant students to study.
ANIMALS: Attracts butterflies to the garden.
PROTECTION: Guards against constant worries that prevent sleep; shields from envy; darker green shades useful for safe travel.

MAGICKAL AND PSYCHIC USES
Draws nature spirits, especially water essences; as a wand, it empowers other crystals, herbs, essential oils, and flower essences; enhances outdoor meditation.
SPECIAL PROPERTIES
Green Fluorite creates order out of chaos; revives partnerships or cooperative ventures in relationships or work when you're going through a difficult period; clears rooms of negative vibes.
MYTHOLOGY AND HISTORY
Green, like other colored fluorites, was carved into vessels in China more than five hundred years ago and was substituted for jade. Green Fluorite in natural pyramid formations is believed to offer visions of Atlantis and other lands lost beneath the waves.

Green Goldstone

COLORS: Emerald to dark green with shimmering gold

CRYSTAL TYPE: Silica glass made from quartz sand, infused with chromium oxide

ZODIAC SIGN: Pisces (February 19–March 20)

CANDLE COLOR: Green

PHYSICAL: Stabilizes the heart; strengthens lungs, skin, hands; alleviates allergies to feathers, animal fur, and dust mites; relieves joint pain and helps overcome lack of mobility.

EMOTIONAL: Comforts you after heartbreak, when there seems no point in going on; for earlier damaging trauma that triggers extreme reactions to even minor setbacks.

HOME: For conversions (for example, barns or warehouses into homes), or adding space, such as conservatories and loft rooms in an existing home; for cultivating good relations with neighbors.

WORKPLACE: Prevents quarrels, rivalries, and unfair tactics in a competitive workplace; clears up misunderstandings caused by volatile personalities.

CHILDREN: Counters a tendency among teens to be overly anxious about tests or interviews and so defeat themselves in advance.

ANIMALS: For pets who become hyperactive when children play with them.

PROTECTION: Deters those who constantly play on your sympathies for financial support.

MAGICKAL AND PSYCHIC USES

A talisman for wealth, health, and happiness; attracts the presence of nature spirits.

SPECIAL PROPERTIES

A stone of the life force and steady growth, using what the twelfth-century German mystic Hildegard von Bingen called *veriditas,* the greening principle that brings all into necessary balance for growth.

MYTHOLOGY AND HISTORY

Vincenzo Miotti, the Italian astronomer, was granted the exclusive license by the Doge of Venice to create goldstone. Goldstone was traditionally revered as magickal because it was created by humans using the divine spark of creation within us all.

Green Kyanite

COLORS: Light, mossy, medium or dark green; striated; may look quite glassy with white, brown and yellow; may appear almost black when viewed from certain angles; sometimes Green Kyanite has a central blue core, so combining the two colors (see Blue Kyanite, page 77)

CRYSTAL TYPE: Aluminum silicate as elongated blades, also as tumbled stones and gems

ZODIAC SIGN: Virgo (August 24–September 22)

CANDLE COLOR: Green

PHYSICAL: Alleviates low blood sugar; high blood pressure, racing heart; promotes regrowth of cells and tissues; addresses illnesses made worse by stress; regulates serotonin levels.

EMOTIONAL: Counters an inability to forgive others, lack of compassion for the less fortunate; enables spiritual and personal growth.

HOME: For beautiful gardens inside and out; restores wilting plants; softens judgmental relatives or neighbors.

WORKPLACE: Translates thoughts into action; offers surges of energy for urgent work with fast-approaching deadlines.

CHILDREN: Encourages playing in nature, even in local parks; helps children develop at their own pace, regardless of what are considered official developmental milestones.

ANIMALS: For large pets in apartments or homes with restricted outdoor space.

PROTECTION: Rejects emotional manipulation; guards against plausible people who do not tell the truth.

MAGICKAL AND PSYCHIC USES

Prompts connection with local nature spirits and devas wherever you live; aids in healing the Earth and healing through Earth energies.

SPECIAL PROPERTIES

The reality check crystal, to cut through illusion and focus on what is possible, realistic, and attainable; alerts by its vibrations to the presence of any who are less than honest, as well as phone and online scams.

MYTHOLOGY AND HISTORY

A relatively rare kyanite, this crystal of the Earth is a crystal of peace, globally, in communities and among families; it also brings slow-growing but steady financial benefits.

Greenlandite

COLORS: Green, light to dark or bluish-green

CRYSTAL TYPE: Combination of quartzite, fine-grained quartz, and a large amount of green fuchsite, evenly spread throughout the rock, creating sparkles and metallic glow

ZODIAC SIGN: Taurus (April 21–May 21)

CANDLE COLOR: Green

PHYSICAL: Addresses issues involving the eyes, thymus, sinus headaches, emphysema, asbestosis, allergies, heart and arteriosclerosis, cholesterol, genitourinary system, skin, mobility.

EMOTIONAL: Helps overcome stammering and communication difficulties, inability to accept any blame for self-induced sorrows, heartache and heartbreak, neuroses.

HOME: Set in a grid formation throughout the house, relieves blocked Earth energies beneath the home.

WORKPLACE: Promotes leadership and dynamic action; absorbs harmful electromagnetic energies; counters sick-building syndrome.

CHILDREN: Guards against overexposure to and overuse of smartphones, tablets, and gaming machines.

ANIMALS: For pets sensitive to chemical products, noise, and traffic.

PROTECTION: Shields against psychic and emotional vampires.

MAGICKAL AND PSYCHIC USES

Cuts psychic cords, whether present-day or past-life karma; enhances contact with devas, automatic writing; alerts you to false friends and hidden enemies.

SPECIAL PROPERTIES

For protecting the ecosystem; past-life healing; restores equilibrium if life is going badly wrong.

MYTHOLOGY AND HISTORY

One of the oldest stones on Earth, Greenlandite is 3.8 billion years old and the most ancient gemstone. Traditionally, it adorns the Bishop of Greenland's cape. Greenlandite was officially discovered during the 1960s within a large iron deposit at Isukasia, near Nuuk, Greenland's capital, and is found only in Greenland. However, it has been long been part of Indigenous rituals for protection and to warn of approaching danger.

Green Moonstone

COLORS: Pale green or pale yellowish-green, obtaining its color from the presence of 6–7 percent nickel ore

CRYSTAL TYPE: Feldspar, opalescent form of orthoclase

ZODIAC SIGN: Pisces (February 19–March 20)

CANDLE COLOR: Green

PHYSICAL: Addresses issues relating to PMS, menstruation, pregnancy, postnatal depression, menopausal hot flushes, mood swings, breasts, breastfeeding; aids in mammograms, cervical smears, and any gynecological tests or biopsies.

EMOTIONAL: Helps overcome the tendency to live in your head, affected by random moods rather than external events; counters overthinking, fears about the future.

HOME: Calms family members for whom even the smallest crisis is magnified into a major disaster.

WORKPLACE: Establishes a vegan or vegetarian restaurant or specialty food store; for entering politics as an environmental activist.

CHILDREN: Soothes overactive children to prepare them for sleep; for girls approaching puberty who are embarrassed by their changing bodies.

ANIMALS: Helps rescued strays finding it hard to become domesticated.

PROTECTION: Guards against dangers of the night if you're staying in the wilderness or you live in a remote place; for repelling malevolent Earth spirits.

MAGICKAL AND PSYCHIC USES

For nature magick under the full moon; for lunar gardening; fertility spells on the full moon.

SPECIAL PROPERTIES

Aids psychic journaling to express feelings and insights via automatic writing, meditation, and psychic artistry, portraying guardian angels, guides, ancestors, and auras.

MYTHOLOGY AND HISTORY

Green Moonstone is the closest moonstone to the Earth element. It balances the anima/feminine side of men and women, so each person is comfortable within their own mind and skin.

Green Obsidian

COLORS: Glassy bottle green to creamy darker opaque green in its natural form

CRYSTAL TYPE: Obsidian with impurities in its darker green shades, of iron and magnesium; green is also caused when gas bubbles remain in the lava

ZODIAC SIGN: Scorpio (October 24–November 22)

CANDLE COLOR: Green

PHYSICAL: Alleviates asthma, hay fever, breathing difficulties, chronic pain, allergies, Alzheimer's disease, schizophrenia, and multiple personality disorder.

EMOTIONAL: Counters overreliance on therapies and counseling.

HOME: Assists in moving to a rural setting; encourages wildflowers and herbs in city gardens.

WORKPLACE: Green Obsidian, particularly green sheen, promotes international business connections; for long plane journeys, guards against jet lag during regular overseas or interstate travel; aids in working away from home for long periods.

CHILDREN: Curbs hesitancy in speaking in class or socially; helps develop talents in children with special needs.

ANIMALS: For urban farms; reintroduces city animals to wildlife areas and endangered species.

PROTECTION: Shields against negative Earth energies in buildings and negative spirits attached to land.

MAGICKAL AND PSYCHIC USES

Removes psychic hooks; enhances Reiki healing; heals cracked or broken crystals; brings connection with nature essences, plants, and trees; for tarot card reading and other forms of divination.

SPECIAL PROPERTIES

For learning new languages or working as a translator, addressing meetings or participating in the performing arts; counteracts those who refuse to allow others to have their say.

MYTHOLOGY AND HISTORY

Green Obsidian, also found as green sheen obsidian, with a greenish luster over the surface, is lucky in gambling, speculation, and successful risk assessment.

Green Onyx

COLORS: Single color, gleaming, from pale green to olive to emerald; often mistaken for emerald or jade

CRYSTAL TYPE: Natural, though some are dyed to enhance color; chalcedony, microcrystalline quartz; colored by copper and magnesium in the darker green shades, iron with copper make it light green

ZODIAC SIGN: Virgo (August 24–September 22)

CANDLE COLOR: Green

PHYSICAL: Addresses heart irregularities; alleviates lung infections during cold damp weather or caused by plant allergies, stomach ulcers; promotes fertility, male potency.

EMOTIONAL: Eases chronic anxiety brought on by doing too much too fast; counters dislike of physical contact even with family.

HOME: For the gradual growth of a home-based business; for home study combined with family; improves finances.

WORKPLACE: Curbs distractions, interruptions, and information overload when you're facing a deadline; aids in chairing meetings and Zoom calls if you're inexperienced.

CHILDREN: Connects with nature spirits; resolves anger issues where sensitive children are deliberately provoked by peers.

ANIMALS: Calms yowling cats and barking dogs.

PROTECTION: Guards against hostile words by others and self-sabotage.

MAGICKAL AND PSYCHIC USES

For plant wisdom and healing; psychometry, obtaining information through psychic touch; getting back in touch with spiritual powers.

SPECIAL PROPERTIES

For overcoming love difficulties or hesitancy in expressing feelings; for commitment and moving in together if you are ready for the next stage, but a partner is reluctant due to previous experiences; encourages the growth of passion.

MYTHOLOGY AND HISTORY

In ancient Greece, Green Onyx was highly prized for healing and in even earlier Neolithic times it was found as an amulet in burial sites as well as gemstones or highly polished crystals in jewelry; as tumbled stones, ideal carried as anti-worry amulets; Green Onyx is also popular for carved animal figurines.

Green Pernatty Selenite

COLOR: Light green, due to layers of iron sulfate/copper sulfides permeating growth bands of the crystals

CRYSTAL TYPE: A unique form of gypsum, usually found in clusters and needles (see also White Selenite, Blue Selenite, and Orange Selenite, pages 505, 82, and 331, respectively)

ZODIAC SIGN: Virgo (August 24–September 22)

CANDLE COLOR: Green

PHYSICAL: Strengthens the immune system; addresses plant allergies, arthritis, blood cleansing, water retention, skin, lactose intolerance, aging issues.

EMOTIONAL: Aids in expressing the true self without fear, shame, or repression.

HOME: For spring-cleaning clutter any time.

WORKPLACE: Attracts money and business to a workplace, if kept in cash registers or with computers used for finances.

CHILDREN: Teaches children to value money; encourages friendships if a child is shy.

ANIMALS: For homes where there are several kinds of pets.

PROTECTION: Guards against scams, con artists, and unwise investments.

MAGICKAL AND PSYCHIC USES

Earth healing rituals involving crystal layouts centered around Green Selenite.

SPECIAL PROPERTIES

For making new friendships and strengthening or renewing old ones; for befriending others in need, creating connections in neighborhood and community, especially with people whose lifestyles are different.

MYTHOLOGY AND HISTORY

Only found in the Pernatty Lagoon, in South Australia, formed by natural growth because of copper mining in the area probably due to runoff from copper-leaching activities; used in ceremonies by the Aboriginal people to transfer the energies of the land into their lives and walkabouts.

Green Petrified or Fossilized Wood

COLORS: Shades of green, caused by the trace mineral chromium, Green Calcite (page 219), or copper (as blue green)

CRYSTAL TYPE: Opalized or agatized fossil wood, a form of silicon dioxide (see also Fossilized or Petrified Wood, page 193)

ZODIAC SIGN: Capricorn (December 22–January 20)

CANDLE COLOR: Brown

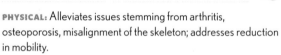

PHYSICAL: Alleviates issues stemming from arthritis, osteoporosis, misalignment of the skeleton; addresses reduction in mobility.

EMOTIONAL: Counters fear of aging and losing your looks; clears up unresolved family and ancestral grudges.

HOME: For preserving and restoring old houses, especially where there are structural issues; for amicable inheritance matters.

WORKPLACE: For all environmentally focused jobs and those where advancement takes many years.

CHILDREN: Creates new family traditions and customs in a small nuclear family if there are no older relatives remaining.

ANIMALS: Establishes a winning pedigree line in animal breeding.

PROTECTION: Guards against malevolent family ancestors.

MAGICKAL AND PSYCHIC USES

For traditional, folk, and natural magick; making herbal remedies from family recipes; for mediumship and connection with the newly deceased.

SPECIAL PROPERTIES

Keeps setbacks in perspective, and keeps you from being thrown off course by petty problems and unhelpful people.

MYTHOLOGY AND HISTORY

Petrified or fossilized wood, unlike ordinary fossils that tend to be an imprint or compression, is a three-dimensional form of the original organic material that has been replaced by minerals; represents long-lasting relationships through good and troubled times and working toward long-term future plans. Arizona Green Petrified Wood is one of the rarest and most prized green petrified woods, from the Winslow, Arizona area and is 200–220 million years old.

Green Ridge Quartz

COLORS: Though found in a variety of colors, all share the same underlying energies (see Crystals and Colors, page 520); includes light (amethyst), and clear, golden, cream, and orange (quartz)

CRYSTAL TYPE: Quartz; iron-staining or coated forms may appear in any color (choose one where the iron does not flake)

ZODIAC SIGN: Sagittarius (November 23–December 21)

CANDLE COLOR: Orange

PHYSICAL: Each color positively affects different inner energy centers (see Crystals and Chakras, page 147); two or three as a layout around the body speeds whole-body healing.

EMOTIONAL: Counters dislike of physical activities or the outdoors; helps overcome inertia and a lack of enthusiasm.

HOME: Iron-coated or stained crystals foster family unity; encourages new partners to be accepted by the family.

WORKPLACE: In the clearer colors, promotes joint ventures and interdepartmental cooperation; reduces resentment from existing workers or management toward those newly hired to shake things up and boost productivity.

CHILDREN: Keep Green Ridge Quartz on display in the home to encourage stepsiblings to become one family, particularly if non-resident parents are stirring up dissension.

ANIMALS: As clear pale amethyst quartz, helps pets settle in a new home after a major move.

PROTECTION: Cleanses the aura energy field of low-vibration entities who are disturbing sleep at night.

MAGICKAL AND PSYCHIC USES

In all its colors, but especially clear, orange, and amethyst, Green Ridge Quartz opens the gateway to the spiritual world and future knowledge and wisdom; creates personal and spiritual networks on every level.

SPECIAL PROPERTIES

For community and neighborhood harmony; organizing street parties, fetes, fun runs, and local activities.

MYTHOLOGY AND HISTORY

The Green Ridge area, in King County, Washington State, is known for its quartz, barite, chalcopyrite, and pyrite. Green Ridge Quartz is considered to have healing, magickal, and spiritual powers.

Green Sardonyx

COLORS: Medium to dark green markings on a white background or light green to dark green with bands of green or ivory

CRYSTAL TYPE: Microcrystalline quartz, a variety of onyx, layered with sard, a less common color of Sardonyx (page 419) and more muted than many of its sisters

ZODIAC SIGN: Virgo (August 24–September 22)

CANDLE COLOR: Green

PHYSICAL: Assuages inflammation of skin and breathing difficulties caused by plant allergies; alleviates fevers, mouth and throat infections, inner ear infections, issues involving teeth (especially wisdom teeth), postoperative complications, fluid imbalances, nausea.

EMOTIONAL: Counters the inability or unwillingness to control a bad temper, moodiness.

HOME: For beautiful gardens in a hot climate or unseasonably hot weather; for relocating to a property with space around it.

WORKPLACE: Increases prosperity, status, and opportunities by staying with the same company and advancing slowly within an established career structure.

CHILDREN: Aids in making friendships if a child is naturally solitary.

ANIMALS: Motivates inactive domesticated pets who are reluctant to exercise.

PROTECTION: Guards against the worst effects of stormy weather, tornadoes, floods, and earthquakes if you live on or close to a fault line.

MAGICKAL AND PSYCHIC USES

Communication with nature spirits; healing with plants; mindfulness; brings out the healing properties of other stones, plants, and essences; for druid and Wiccan Earth blessing ceremonies.

SPECIAL PROPERTIES

A crystal of good fortune to attract health, wealth, love, and happiness, especially after a streak of bad luck.

MYTHOLOGY AND HISTORY

The stone of happy marriage and committed relationships, minimizing conflicts within them; a stone of happiness through moderation in all things.

Green Stilbite

COLORS: Shades of green, especially dark, an unusual color for stilbite

CRYSTAL TYPE: Sodium calcium hydrous aluminum silicate, a member of the zeolite family; the green due to the inclusion of celadonite; often found in its peachier colors with Green Apophyllite (page 218)

ZODIAC SIGN: Virgo (August 24–September 22)

CANDLE COLOR: Green

PHYSICAL: For regrowth of tissue, muscle, and the mending of wounds; eases sore throat; alleviates plant, fur, and pollen allergies, manifest especially as skin inflammation and coughs; assuages lung congestion; addresses blood sugar imbalances, sunburn.

EMOTIONAL: Helps overcome fear of letting barriers down to express or receive love or spontaneity; counters dislike of others expressing emotions or vulnerability.

HOME: Creates a beautiful garden or indoor plant display; explores natural pigments and products when redecorating.

WORKPLACE: For direct marketing; setting up displays, exhibitions, publicity, and practical demonstrations to bring new business.

CHILDREN: Encourages children to participate in physical play, playground activities, and team sports.

ANIMALS: Develops a daily exercise routine that is pleasurable, rather than a duty.

PROTECTION: Guards against heartache and heartbreak.

MAGICKAL AND PSYCHIC USES

Spontaneous growth of psychic abilities; claircognizance or psychic knowledge based on what is sensed, rather than seen or heard; flower and herbal spells and remedies; psychic artistry and enhanced aura interpretation.

SPECIAL PROPERTIES

Creates for pleasure; learns new artistic skills or hands-on activities that will open new friendships and cultivate personal growth.

MYTHOLOGY AND HISTORY

Well worth finding, this upbeat, laid-back form of stilbite opens up a new growth cycle in the self to enjoy life and activities for their own sake; finding a like-minded partner or taking up new leisure activities with your current partner; a counterbalance for workaholics or those for whom activity must always have a purpose.

Greenstone or Pounamu

COLORS: Light green with cloud-like streaks, strong green, pearly whitish, all nephrite; olive-green to bluish-green

CRYSTAL TYPE: Mainly nephrite jade (pounamu), some bowenite or serpentine Greenstone pendants are worn on a leather thong, level with the two collarbones meeting or as a carving

ZODIAC SIGN: Virgo (August 24–September 22)

CANDLE COLOR: Green

PHYSICAL: A universal healer, enhances acupressure; counters food and lactose intolerance, plant allergies, infections, viruses; remedies issues involving the kidneys and bladder.

EMOTIONAL: Helps overcome overreliance on artificial stimulants, obsession with consumerism.

HOME: Hang a Greenstone *Manaia* pendant attached to a leather thong, or cord, just inside the front door of your home. *Manaia,* the Guardian, is a bird-like person with head in profile and represents sacred blessings on the home.

WORKPLACE: Wear a Greenstone fishhook pendant, called a *Hei-matau,* on a leather thong, or cord. Attracts successful business opportunities and prosperity; protects during travel overseas.

CHILDREN: *Koru,* the fern frond, signifies love between parent and child. Hang a greenstone *Koru* on a leather thong, or cord, on the wall behind your child's bed.

ANIMALS: Connects with dolphin healing.

PROTECTION: Greenstone dolphins and whales guard against harm.

MAGICKAL AND PSYCHIC USES

Collect different symbols according to need, asking permission of the Greenstone guardians; to improve luck, choose *Hei-Tiki,* representation of the first Maori who came from the stars, bringing love and fertility.

SPECIAL PROPERTIES

Greenstone is found only on the South Island of New Zealand. Any Greenstone becomes part of its owner.

MYTHOLOGY AND HISTORY

Greenstone has been used by Maoris for tools, weapons, ornaments, pendants, and earrings since reaching Aotearoa (New Zealand), Land of the Long White Cloud, only seven hundred years ago. The energies of Greenstone, like the land, transmit unspoiled power of nature and sea.

Green Talc

COLORS: Slightly luminous soft green; pearly luster; may be white or pale blue

CRYSTAL TYPE: Clay mineral, hydrated magnesium silicate (see also Soapstone or Steatite, page 447, a talc-schist)

ZODIAC SIGN: Virgo (August 24–September 22)

CANDLE COLOR: Green

PHYSICAL: Stimulates the life force; counters insomnia; promotes cell regeneration; addresses issues stemming from the liver, pancreas, kidneys, and spleen; regulates metabolism.

EMOTIONAL: Helps overcome rigid attitudes and repressed feelings, as well as acute anxiety.

HOME: Absorbs tensions from the outside world and the working world; a money magnet.

WORKPLACE: Because it is so delicate in pure talc form, assists with using tact and persuasion in dealing with difficult colleagues or employees; brings in money and business by subtle advertising.

CHILDREN: Keep this crystal high in a child's room or with a photo to prevent bad dreams and night terrors.

ANIMALS: Place Green Talc with a brochure of your local animal rescue center or a picture of your ideal breed of pet to attract a kind, gentle creature into your life.

PROTECTION: Guards against nightmares and negative sleep or presleep experiences with poltergeists, paranormal predators, and malevolent ghosts.

MAGICKAL AND PSYCHIC USES

Trance meditation; used in powder form for making magick herb and essential oil mixes to scatter on thresholds for protection.

SPECIAL PROPERTIES

A natural manifester of money; the white kind was used in prehistoric cave paintings, so talc, especially in lucky green, helps artists, writers, performers, and musicians to attract the right opportunities.

MYTHOLOGY AND HISTORY

The softest mineral on Earth, Green Talc has been used in ancient cultures, such as Egypt and India, where it was especially popular for relieving skin irritation; no longer currently used in baby powder in the United States because of counterclaims about its contents, but available in the UK; a rare form of crystallized Green Talc is found in Vermont.

Green Taralite

COLORS: Pale mint green to grayish green

CRYSTAL TYPE: Volcanic rock; form of andesite

ZODIAC SIGN: Virgo (August 24–September 22)

CANDLE COLOR: Green

PHYSICAL: Alleviates issues stemming from the heart, circulation, hormones, lungs, lymphatic system, liver, digestion; enhances light and laser therapies; leads to successful major organ transplants; useful in sex-reassignment surgery.

EMOTIONAL: Helps overcome problems with mothers, mothering, or motherhood; encourages understanding or empathy for others; for women raised to adopt a subservient role.

HOME: For supporting family members experiencing difficulties or behaving out of character.

WORKPLACE: Promotes happiness, well-being, and equality among workers; offers support to anyone who is struggling.

CHILDREN: Teaches them to show kindness toward those less fortunate.

ANIMALS: For all therapy and assistance dogs.

PROTECTION: Guards against those who spread gloom and cynicism.

MAGICKAL AND PSYCHIC USES

Contacting divinity beyond the self as well as within through chanting, meditation, and prayer.

SPECIAL PROPERTIES

Awakening in every woman her inner goddess and in men compassion for humanity and expression of their own sacred anima.

MYTHOLOGY AND HISTORY

The Goddess Green Tara is associated in Buddhism and Hinduism with compassion, actively changing life for the better; as a bodhisattva, she is dedicated to remain on Earth as long as there is suffering. Green Tara is a star goddess, a fierce protector of the vulnerable and Mother Earth; Green Taralite, found in New Zealand, carries Green Tara power since its qualities mirror Tara's gifts to comfort and uplift.

Green Tourmaline or Verdelite

COLORS: Green, green-blue, green-yellow, intense emerald green as chrome tourmaline

CRYSTAL TYPE: Aluminum boron silicate. The more expensive chrome tourmaline contains traces of chromium and vanadium

ZODIAC SIGNS: Virgo (August 24–September 22) and Libra (September 23–October 23)

CANDLE COLOR: Green

PHYSICAL: Promotes heart regeneration after a heart attack or major heart surgery; strengthens the male reproductive system; addresses blood sugar disorders, rashes, eczema, scars, birthmarks, as well as IBS and other chronic bowel diseases.

EMOTIONAL: Eases gender issues where there is prejudice or lack of support; helps overcome jealousy and envy; counters obsession with an unavailable partner or celebrity.

HOME: Aids either sex in breaking free from or standing up to a controlling male; helps elderly relatives maintain their independence while unobtrusively supporting them.

WORKPLACE: Attracts money and success in business ventures; for networking over the internet; assists in dealing with intimidating authority figures.

CHILDREN: Teaches children and teens to love nature; reduces the desire for material possessions; persuades them not to hold grudges.

ANIMALS: Enables city pets to maintain a connection with nature.

PROTECTION: Wards off negative energies, and emotional and psychic vampires.

MAGICKAL AND PSYCHIC USES

For herbal wisdom and healing; healing plants, Earth rituals and healing.

SPECIAL PROPERTIES

For athletes, men in particular, promotes stamina and endurance; for endurance sports and physical training sessions.

MYTHOLOGY AND HISTORY

A good luck crystal for increasing fortunes in the way most needed. Green Tourmaline awakens compassion toward difficult or socially challenged people.

Green Zircon

COLOR: Deep olive green, yellowish-green, brownish-green, sometimes cloudy. May be heat-treated to improve color quality

CRYSTAL TYPE: Zirconium silicate

ZODIAC SIGN: Virgo (August 24–September 22)

CANDLE COLOR: Green

PHYSICAL: Addresses cystic fibrosis, issues involving the heart (including pacemakers), nerve connectivity; alleviates allergies to wheat and other grains, plus pollen; restores normal body functioning after invasive treatment, such as transplants and transfusions.

EMOTIONAL: Reduces excessive emotional dependency on others, possessiveness, or disproportionate concern with the lives of others; helps overcome victim syndrome.

HOME: Encourages redecoration and renovation, especially if you are living somewhere less than ideal; creates a good social life if you have lost touch with former friends.

WORKPLACE: Cultivates prosperity through gradual, continuing growth of income; aids in winning a prestigious position; combines alternative and more conventional therapies professionally.

CHILDREN: For long-term fostering or adopting a child who has suffered neglect.

ANIMALS: Guides you to alternative remedies and natural nourishment for pets allergic to conventional products.

PROTECTION: Guards against theft, including loss of money and valuables, while traveling or in crowded places.

MAGICKAL AND PSYCHIC USES

Draws Earth and mountain spirits; natural healing and natural magick, using herbs, and flower and tree essences.

SPECIAL PROPERTIES

For winning money, games of chance, and being in the right place at the right time; attracts love; traditionally worn by those seeking a wealthy or beautiful partner, but in modern times to call a soul twin.

MYTHOLOGY AND HISTORY

The Kalpataru Divine Tree of Life, sacred in Hindu and Buddhist teachings, is described as having Green Zircons as its foliage.

Grossular or Grossularite Garnet

COLORS: Clear, white, pink, honey, gray, usually lemon to greenish-yellow, yellowish-green to mint green (see also green Tsavorite or Tsavolite [page 485] and orange Hessonite Garnet or Cinnamon Stone [page 241])

CRYSTAL TYPE: Calcium aluminum silicate; fire visible in lighter colors

ZODIAC SIGNS: Capricorn (December 22–January 20) and Aquarius (January 21–February 18)

CANDLE COLOR: Green

PHYSICAL: Promotes immunity, fertility; alleviates issues stemming from the heart and circulation, respiration, deep vein thrombosis; offers protection against infectious diseases, such as Norovirus, MRSA, C Difficile, and influenza.

EMOTIONAL: For relationships that swing between high and low, especially if this mimics the pattern in previous relationships.

HOME: Red or orange Grossular Garnet protects against abusive neighbors and physical threats.

WORKPLACE: Colorless Grossular Garnet is useful for receiving an overdue pay increase, for new business ventures, and for companies offering spiritual products or services, combining caring with financial viability.

CHILDREN: For teens experimenting with ouija boards; shields them if there are dangerous influences around.

ANIMALS: Protects pets from vicious animals and humans while outdoors.

PROTECTION: Shields you from harm if you're visiting or staying in a building or on land where past evil or tragedy occurred.

MAGICKAL AND PSYCHIC USES
Guards against poltergeists, psychic vampires, and nighttime paranormal sexual predators.

SPECIAL PROPERTIES
Grossular Garnet in any color enhances romance, boosting passion if lovemaking has become routine; assists successful pursuit of lawsuits.

MYTHOLOGY AND HISTORY
Grossular Garnet has the most varied color scheme of all the garnets. It is a talisman for acquiring wealth. The name *grossular* derives from the Roman and botanical term for gooseberry, *grossularia*, because of its resemblance to the color of the fruit.

Grounding Quartz

COLORS: Colorless and clear

CRYSTAL TYPE: Quartz crystal with one eight-sided face

ZODIAC SIGN: Taurus (April 21–May 21)

CANDLE COLOR: White

PHYSICAL: Minimizes damage to cells and organs after chemotherapy, radiation, prolonged steroid treatment, or other necessary ongoing treatments.

EMOTIONAL: Counters problems dealing with the practical aspects of life if you're living in a fantasy world.

HOME: Creates workable timetables and schedules in a busy home so everyone does their share; for people who begin every sentence with, *One day I will . . .* who never do.

WORKPLACE: Counterbalancing "idea" people, managers, and administrators with achievers; running esoteric businesses, including crystal or therapy stores.

CHILDREN: Helps those who are always late or seriously underestimate the time needed to complete tasks to meet deadlines.

ANIMALS: Assists exotic and expensive pets who find it difficult to thrive in an everyday setting.

PROTECTION: Guards against being persuaded to buy top-of-the-line goods when a modest version would serve just as well.

MAGICKAL AND PSYCHIC USES
To avoid paying extortionate amounts of money or signing up for long courses with gurus with big egos who spend all their time talking about themselves.

SPECIAL PROPERTIES
Other crystals, as well as quartz, have grounding powers to bring you back to the real world after a ritual or healing. Alternative grounding crystals include brown and gray agates, smoky quartz, petrified wood, jet, black tourmaline, or schor. However, Grounding Quartz is a multipurpose crystal, and will act as an anchor to the Earth no matter what the psychic, psychological, or physical adrenaline rush.

MYTHOLOGY AND HISTORY
On a practical level, Grounding Quartz enables you to deal with one matter at a time if you have a mountain of pressing jobs and do not know where to start; a grounding crystal for a gradual return to daily life after psychic work.

Growth Interference Quartz

COLORS: Clear quartz; may be dense and cloudy or slightly frosted

CRYSTAL TYPE: Growth Interference Quartz occurs when thin flat calcite crystals grow within quartz, then dissolve before crystallization is complete, leaving missing parts as if the quartz had been carved with a saw; alternatively, the crystal may manifest as squares or triangles

ZODIAC SIGN: Cancer (June 22–July 22)

CANDLE COLOR: Silver

PHYSICAL: Encourages successful artificial insemination or IVF with donor sperm or egg, ensures successful surgical interventions—including major ones, involving incisions—for pacemakers, stents, artificial heart valves, implants, and bone replacements.

EMOTIONAL: Helps overcome the inability to adapt to change, domination that has become codependency.

HOME: Shares a home with an estranged partner if you cannot afford to leave; for communal living with other families.

WORKPLACE: Aids in coping with a takeover when many familiar staff leave; helps you find another job after bankruptcy or forced closure.

CHILDREN: When a parent suddenly leaves home, refusing contact.

ANIMALS: Assists in finding missing pets.

PROTECTION: Helps in breaking away from a cult; alerts you to potential danger.

MAGICKAL AND PSYCHIC USES

For banishing harmful spirits called up during irresponsible magick; establishes connection with higher planes of existence.

SPECIAL PROPERTIES

For adapting to loss due to external circumstances, such as recession, pandemic, ill health, or accident.

MYTHOLOGY AND HISTORY

Found in Russia and Brazil, Growth Interference Quartz is seen in amethyst as Himalayan Ice Quartz (page 317). Calming calcite remains within the quartz, enabling wisdom from every experience to form new foundations.

Guangdong Tektite

COLOR: Black

CRYSTAL TYPE: Natural meteoric glass, named after the new location where it was discovered, Guangdong in China, often banana- or pen-shaped or oval

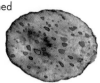

ZODIAC SIGN: Aquarius (January 21–February 18)

CANDLE COLOR: Dark brown

PHYSICAL: Strengthens autoimmune system; promotes fertility; protects against the harmful effects of radiation and chemotherapy.

EMOTIONAL: Eases strong repressed feelings that may emerge as an angry unprovoked outburst; counters the tendency to see only the negative side of life and people.

HOME: Guards against fires, floods, and storms; attracts good fortune and abundance to the home.

WORKPLACE: Aids in finding a new role after a major shake-up or takeover of a workplace; for introducing radical changes in your business.

CHILDREN: Protects children who are disturbed by dreams or fears of alien contact or abduction; for teens overly sensitive to bad news or scary movies.

ANIMALS: Guards the natural habitats of burrowing creatures.

PROTECTION: Shields against those who spread false rumors.

MAGICKAL AND PSYCHIC USES

Telepathy; connection with extraterrestrial beings; feng shui, the *I Ching*; to recognize those you have known in past worlds, especially your soul twin.

SPECIAL PROPERTIES

Considered a symbol of world peace, revealed by Mother Earth at a time peace is needed more than ever; Guangdong Tektite, like other Chinese-located tektites, is filled with the water dragon's healing and wealth-bringing powers.

MYTHOLOGY AND HISTORY

Guangdong is a coastal province in southern China. This newly discovered tektite site is considered part of the vast Australasian tektite strewn field, created when molten glass rained down from the sky during a meteor strike over parts of Southeast Asia, Australia, Antarctica, and into the neighboring ocean basins during the Pleistocene era, about 790,000 years ago.

Guardianite or Guardian Stone

COLORS: Black on gray-white background, intricately dotted and grainy

CRYSTAL TYPE: Aegirine, feldspar, nepheline, analcime, riebeckite-arfvedsonite, biotite, olivine, and apatite

ZODIAC SIGN: Gemini (May 22–June 21)

CANDLE COLOR: Gray

PHYSICAL: Mends a damaged energy field after major shock or trauma and so speeds physical healing; addresses illnesses caused or worsened by self-neglect; alleviates Menière's, neurological disorders.

EMOTIONAL: For those who fear being alone, especially at night; counters self-sabotage.

HOME: A source of the life force to continuously energize and harmonize the home.

WORKPLACE: As a pair of stones, offers financial security to a business if payments are slow.

CHILDREN: Gives children a sense of security at home if they are nervous when adults are out of sight.

ANIMALS: For temperamental pets and those bred from more exotic species.

PROTECTION: Guards against earthly intruders and entities summoned by dabbling with the occult.

MAGICKAL AND PSYCHIC USES

For connecting with Earth energies and Earth devas or angels; dowsing with a pointed Guardianite; crystal and stone divination and healing; as an altar stone.

SPECIAL PROPERTIES

Associated with the Azez Star People (see Azeztulite, page 47) and so with stellar and ancient wisdom; a stone that increases self-confidence and willpower.

MYTHOLOGY AND HISTORY

The original Guardian Stones were pairs of standing stones at the corners of stone enclosures around dolmen, especially in Scandinavia and parts of Germany. The Oregon Guardianite has continued the tradition as two small pillar stones, set on either side of the front door outside or just inside, to act as home and land guardians.

Gyrolite

COLORS: White, colorless, brown, occasionally green

CRYSTAL TYPE: Phyllosilicate, a rare sodium calcium silicate hydrate

ZODIAC SIGN: Virgo (August 24–September 22)

CANDLE COLOR: Brown

PHYSICAL: Aligns spine and skeleton; relieves osteoporosis and other sources of pain; alleviates genetic illnesses; enhances effects of acupuncture and acupressure, reflexology, shiatsu, and crystals, especially in layouts on or around the body; circulates the life force through the body.

EMOTIONAL: Counters excessive introspection and dislike of company; secrecy and denial of addictions.

HOME: For a family who finds it hard to express affection or praise.

WORKPLACE: Keeps you calm if schedules are hectic or clients, managers, or colleagues are overly demanding; enables you to project unruffled authority when negotiating with those who use charm or seeming reasonableness to mask ruthlessness to get their own way.

CHILDREN: Establishes and maintains rules or boundaries set for teenagers, even when you're under pressure to give in.

ANIMALS: For willful pets, who refuse to be trained.

PROTECTION: Provides safety when working with challenging people or potentially dangerous situations.

MAGICKAL AND PSYCHIC USES

A high-vibration stone of wisdom linked with Buddhism and ancient India; connects with ancient wisdom in recalling information without ever consciously learning it; for dancing and drumming, aided by spontaneous recall of old traditions.

SPECIAL PROPERTIES

For making and checking travel arrangements, timetables, and connections to ensure problem-free journeys; aids in overcoming extreme shyness and self-consciousness that lead others to undervalue your personal or professional capabilities.

MYTHOLOGY AND HISTORY

The awakener stone, Gyrolite encourages new activities or a different life path, which suddenly seems totally familiar, maybe first explored in past worlds.

Hackmanite

COLORS: Changes color from violet to grayish or greenish-white when exposed to sunlight, a process called *tenebrescence;* in darkness or short-wave ultraviolet light, it reverts to its original violet color

ZODIAC SIGN: Sagittarius (November 23–December 21)

CANDLE COLOR: Violet

PHYSICAL: Alleviates issues relating to bones, ligaments, hormones, metabolism, imbalances, insomnia, oversensitivity to electromagnetic waves and pollution.

EMOTIONAL: Counters overindulgence, abandonment at any stage of life that creates neediness or, conversely, total withdrawal.

HOME: Aids in finding an authentic home and lifestyle.

WORKPLACE: Helps retain your individuality in an impersonal organization; aids in resisting unethical practices; promotes clear thinking outside the box.

CHILDREN: For those who try to please everyone.

ANIMALS: Calms pets who become aggressive over food.

PROTECTION: Guards against those who display a false sense of superiority.

MAGICKAL AND PSYCHIC USES

For cutting cords with unwise emotional attachments and malicious paranormal entities during ouija board sessions or séances; prophetic and lucid dreaming involving astral travel; interpreting messages from guides and angels.

SPECIAL PROPERTIES

The ability to fit into any situation and environment without losing your core identity; opening to infinite possibility.

MYTHOLOGY AND HISTORY

Called the chameleon stone, Hackmanite represents the chance to integrate different aspects of yourself and your life; when mined, Hackmanite is pale to deep violet; in sunlight, it quickly fades to grayish or greenish white; in darkness or exposed to short-wave ultraviolet light, violet slowly returns; the reverse can occur in specimens mined in Afghanistan or Myanmar, where it appears colorless on mining and becomes pink-red to violet in sunlight.

Hambergite

COLORS: Colorless (the kind occasionally used for gems), white, gray, yellowish, colorless in luminous light; some semicolorless Hambergite is lightly tinted pink or purple; glass-like when polished but generally has inclusions even in the clearest form

CRYSTAL TYPE: Beryllium borate; sometimes displays a cat's-eye effect

ZODIAC SIGN: Taurus (April 21–May 21)

CANDLE COLOR: White

PHYSICAL: Counters low metabolism; enables you to reach the optimal weight; alleviates fluid retention, problems with vision (including glaucoma and the inability to adjust to light), racing pulse, chills, hypothermia.

EMOTIONAL: Helps overcome self-neglect while caring for others, excess eating as a security blanket against unhappiness, living a double life or living in ways that keep you from revealing your true self.

HOME: For not saving precious items or heirlooms for future inheritance, but encouraging their use in daily life.

WORKPLACE: Aids in remaining true to yourself in a workplace where minor dishonesty and lowering of standards are overlooked or encouraged.

CHILDREN: Teaches the difference between truth, fantasy, and lies; Hambergite is a lovely collectible for the family treasure box.

ANIMALS: For overweight pets who are given tidbits a little too often.

PROTECTION: Guards against being pressured to act in ways that make you feel uncomfortable.

MAGICKAL AND PSYCHIC USES

For channeling to reach new heights of spiritual awareness; for bliss by momentarily becoming one with the universe.

SPECIAL PROPERTIES

Builds your unique character so you fulfill your personal blueprint, destiny, and life purpose.

MYTHOLOGY AND HISTORY

The stone of integrity, Hambergite displays double refraction (unpolarized light, split in two, each ray traveling in a different direction). This acts as a reminder that there is always an option as to which path to take, though the choice may not be easy.

Hanksite

COLORS: White, colorless, yellow, gray, light green, light blue; varies according to the chemical and clay impurities during Hanksite's formation

CRYSTAL TYPE: Potassium sulfate, carbonate chloride

ZODIAC SIGN: Pisces (February 19–March 20)

CANDLE COLOR: White

PHYSICAL: Counters water retention, head colds, breathing difficulties made worse by excessive mucus.

EMOTIONAL: Assuages unresolved anger, jealousy, and resentment.

HOME: Aids in living in an environmentally friendly way and supporting green ventures.

WORKPLACE: A crystal of truth and justice; for successful compensation negotiations or dismissal of unfair claims.

CHILDREN: Makes younger people aware of ecological responsibility for their own piece of the Earth and to peacefully participate in young people's environmental causes.

ANIMALS: Revives almost-extinct species using DNA.

PROTECTION: Guards against trickery and lies; keeps you from being misled by charismatic people whose charm is used to gain financial advantage.

MAGICKAL AND PSYCHIC USES
Removes spirit attachments or harmful energies in your aura; cleanses other crystals, as well as any room at home or at work.

SPECIAL PROPERTIES
An altruistic stone for healing the planet, working against deforestation, the melting of the polar ice caps, for clean water worldwide, and to remedy the changing climate.

MYTHOLOGY AND HISTORY
Hanksite is formed in California's boron-rich salt lakes, where the water dries out, leaving minerals that combine and solidify; its concentrated salt makes Hanksite one of the most effective spiritual cleansing and purification crystals for everything from attitudes to artifacts; use to make a dream love real. Do not get the crystal wet, as Hanksite dissolves in water.

Harlequin, Fire Hematoid, or Ferruginous Quartz

COLORS: Tiny red stars or red clouds within quartz

CRYSTAL TYPE: Clear quartz with hematite inclusions, often at the base of a crystal point

ZODIAC SIGN: Aries (March 21–April 20)

CANDLE COLOR: Red

PHYSICAL: Alleviates blood disorders; assists with blood thinning, vertigo; strengthens liver, kidneys, and heart; addresses allergic skin rashes, acne, recurring infections, hemorrhoids, hernia.

EMOTIONAL: Increases self-esteem; encourages having fun; called the *dancing-for-joy* crystal.

HOME: Brings joy and laughter into the home; for impromptu family outings.

WORKPLACE: Transforms brilliant ideas into practical action; aids in obtaining necessary financial support for your business.

CHILDREN: For those with ADHD; makes solemn children smile.

ANIMALS: Encourages overly domesticated pets to enjoy exercise.

PROTECTION: Guards against fears and uncertainties imposed by others, or past failures.

MAGICKAL AND PSYCHIC USES
For soul retrieval, reclaiming the missing parts of yourself, using ritual or visualization; an alchemical stone to manifest spiritual gifts.

SPECIAL PROPERTIES
For trying out secret talents or dreams if you fear that others may laugh.

MYTHOLOGY AND HISTORY
Fine specimens of this crystal are found in Madagascar but, though relatively rare, may also occur worldwide; traditionally used by anyone needing to build up and maintain physical stamina and mental discipline, including those in the military, athletes, marathon and long-distance runners, weight lifters and bodybuilders, rock and mountain climbers.

Hausmmanite

COLORS: Brown, black, or silvery gray; metallic, lustrous

CRYSTAL TYPE: Complex manganese oxide, made up of many small pyramid crystals on a matrix, often with other minerals, such as andradite garnet

ZODIAC SIGN: Capricorn (December 22–January 20)

CANDLE COLOR: Brown

PHYSICAL: Speeds all healing, a property of both Hausmmanite and pyramids; counters bone thinning, hair loss, migraines, skin eruptions, burns, bites, bruises; unblocks blood vessels; promotes successful angioplasty and heart bypass surgery.

EMOTIONAL: Helps overcome an unwise attraction to destructive though charismatic people; keeps you from taking unnecessary risks; calms extreme frustration at inevitable delays.

HOME: For reorganization of the home, redecoration, or relocation; ensures security of home, vehicles, and possessions if there have been recent burglaries in the area.

WORKPLACE: As the stone of security, Hausmmanite brings a desired longer-term contract or permanent job offer while you're in a temporary situation.

CHILDREN: Enables you to do well at a new school or college, either because of problems at the previous one or a normal transition.

ANIMALS: Finds a new home for your pet if relocation requires it.

PROTECTION: Guards against unforeseen delays and diversions while traveling.

MAGICKAL AND PSYCHIC USES

In the center of crystal layouts for bringing yourself into alignment; trance meditation to link with universal energies and experience out-of-body bliss; for accessing past lives—whether personal or from the cosmic well of wisdom—of ancient Egypt and especially the pyramids and healing temples, whose knowledge you may bring back.

SPECIAL PROPERTIES

A crystal of manifestation to attract love, prosperity, the right home or career.

MYTHOLOGY AND HISTORY

Pyramids of all kinds, especially crystal ones, enhance clairvoyance and telepathy, reduce pain, and calm hyperactive adults and children; intuitively increases everyday awareness of the intentions of others and of situations just over the horizon needing advance preparation.

Healerite or Noble Serpentine

COLOR: Lime green

CRYSTAL TYPE: Magnesium silicate, a form of serpentine, soft and waxy, may contain up to sixteen different minerals, including olivine and talc

ZODIAC SIGN: Taurus (April 21–May 21)

CANDLE COLOR: Bright green

PHYSICAL: Aligns body; relieves back pain; counteracts exhaustion; alleviates complex conditions, secondary growths, or progressive illnesses that spread throughout the body from a primary source.

EMOTIONAL: Keeps you from feeling out of tune with people and life; helps overcome an obsession with past grievances, over-sensitivity to criticism.

HOME: Cultivates joy and health; enhances any form of hospitality; encourages relatives and friends—slow to contribute financially or practically—to be more generous.

WORKPLACE: For pooling ideas and sharing credit for results; persuades an employer to pay you what you are worth.

CHILDREN: Encourages children to share toys and possessions with siblings and visiting peers.

ANIMALS: Calms pets who become aggressive if anyone comes near their food.

PROTECTION: Guards against emotional and psychic vampires; spite and envy.

MAGICKAL AND PSYCHIC USES

For accessing and healing past-life trauma and unfinished karma; prosperity rituals and as a talisman for attracting good fortune and opportunities.

SPECIAL PROPERTIES

Heals and energizes the healer; within a therapeutic space, constantly directs the life force—at the intensity and toward the part of the body, mind, or spirit or all three—where healing is most needed.

MYTHOLOGY AND HISTORY

Recently discovered in a remote mountainous area in Washington State, Healerite is often called Noble Serpentine because of its power to realign and uplift body, mind, and soul.

Healer's Gold

COLORS: Black with gold and sometimes white inclusions or black and silver

CRYSTAL TYPE: Combination of pyrite (iron sulfide) and magnetite (iron oxide)

ZODIAC SIGN: Leo (July 23–August 23)

CANDLE COLOR: Gold

PHYSICAL: Addresses blood conditions; stabilizes hemoglobin levels; alleviates issues stemming from circulation, bowels, intestines, excess bleeding (from wounds, during menstruation, or after surgery), blood clots; relieves pain; promotes fertility.

EMOTIONAL: Counters excessive dependence on others and codependency; helps overcome the inability to put up barriers against emotional vampires because of the payoff of being needed.

HOME: Heals where neighborhood disputes have split a community; accepts newcomers after a controversial building scheme.

WORKPLACE: Restores the emphasis on spirituality in situations where factions have caused a breakaway movement in a spiritual organization.

CHILDREN: Sends healing to children caught up in a humanitarian disaster.

ANIMALS: For hero or heroine animals who save their owners or their young from danger.

PROTECTION: Guards against technological pollution at home, in the workplace, and in the neighborhood.

MAGICKAL AND PSYCHIC USES

In bead form for remote-healing prayers and chanting; enhances spiritual healing, especially crystals, Reiki, or traditional energy therapies.

SPECIAL PROPERTIES

Shields healers from becoming drained during intensive or prolonged healing sessions; protects patients from harmful effects of high-technology equipment or powerful drugs.

MYTHOLOGY AND HISTORY

Healer's Gold is often sold as Apache Gold, since it's remarkably similar in appearance to Apache Gold (page 34), though they are mineralogically different. In practice both are equally high-vibration healing stones for healers and those being healed. In addition, Healer's Gold is also a stone of lasting love and fidelity.

Hedenbergite

COLORS: Light green, medium to dark green, greenish-black, gray, or black; the clarity of the enclosing white depends on the density of the inclusion

CRYSTAL TYPE: Calcium magnesium silicate, usually found within clear quartz or occasionally amethyst; also called Seriphos Green Quartz in Hedenbergite (page 428); an iron-rich mineral, closely related to diopside

ZODIAC SIGN: Virgo (August 24–September 22)

CANDLE COLOR: Green

PHYSICAL: Remedies malfunctioning production of cells; alleviates fevers, infections, lung conditions made worse by smoking, osteoarthritis, osteoporosis.

EMOTIONAL: Counters the inability to empathize with others; helps overcome an unwillingness to move on from an unsatisfactory relationship, a past love, or a career going nowhere.

HOME: Smooths the way during regular house moves, because of your or a partner's job, to maintain continuity for the family.

WORKPLACE: For workplace changes that were not expected or wanted; for moving to a different department where you will need to acquire new expertise.

CHILDREN: Enables you to show patience with challenging teens at times of transition.

ANIMALS: For pets reluctant to exercise.

PROTECTION: Creates a psychic shield against emotional manipulation and psychic vampires.

MAGICKAL AND PSYCHIC USES

Earth healing; psychic defense; within amethyst for remote healing; for enhanced telepathy and psychic awareness when Hedenbergite is contained within clear quartz.

SPECIAL PROPERTIES

Attracts new friends, new love after loss or betrayal, and new opportunities in every area of life.

MYTHOLOGY AND HISTORY

Sometimes found in chondrite meteors, notably the Allende huge meteorite that fell over Chihuahua in Mexico in 1969, Hedenbergite is considered a powerful spiritual component in sacred Mongolian quartz. It enhances the power of other crystals for healing and magick when included in amethyst and offers courage for change when in clear quartz.

Heliotrope or Bloodstone

COLORS: Dark green with red or orange spots; sometimes includes white markings

CRYSTAL TYPE: A jasper variety of chalcedony

ZODIAC SIGN: Aries (March 21–April 20)

CANDLE COLOR: Red

PHYSICAL: Reduces back pain, nosebleeds, anemia; useful for circulation issues; for healthy bone marrow, alleviates menstrual issues and menopausal imbalances; eases labor pains.

EMOTIONAL: Addresses issues regarding mothering, whether from your own mother or as a mother yourself.

HOME: Resists interference from mothers, mothers-in-law, or grandmothers in your home and family.

WORKPLACE: Rejects attempts to set you up in unfair competition against other workers.

CHILDREN: For tough love if your teenager is wayward; for teenage pregnancy.

ANIMALS: Helps baby animals survive rejection after birth.

PROTECTION: Guards against all bullying, from physical attacks to subtle character assassination.

MAGICKAL AND PSYCHIC USES

Wizardry, alchemy, weather magick, mother goddess rituals, sex magick.

SPECIAL PROPERTIES

For sports training and competitions, professionally and for pleasure; good for legal matters; a natural aphrodisiac.

MYTHOLOGY AND HISTORY

Heliotrope means "turning with the sun." According to legend, it was once green jasper, stained red at the crucifixion when the blood of Christ fell on to it. Bloodstone is like seftonite, but comes mainly from India, not Africa. A lucky talisman for wealth and a healthy life.

Hematite

COLORS: Metallic gray, silver and shiny, also dark red or reddish-brown, with a red streak, leading to the belief that the stone bled

CRYSTAL TYPE: Iron oxide

ZODIAC SIGN: Aries (March 21–April 20)

CANDLE COLOR: Silver

PHYSICAL: Alleviates anemia, blood clots, circulation issues, fatigue, leg cramps, backache, motion sickness in airplanes, jet lag; draws out pain, fevers; excessive menstrual flow.

EMOTIONAL: Counters fears of blood, contagious illnesses, germs, flying insects, spiders.

HOME: As a magnetic stone, attracts money into the home; protects against fire and kitchen accidents.

WORKPLACE: Resists workplace bullying, unfair accusations, or pressure to quit; increases salary or helps you obtain a promotion.

CHILDREN: Aids in understanding mathematics, developing logic if impulsive; reduces clumsiness.

ANIMALS: For dogs who protect the home and family.

PROTECTION: Guards against on- and offline scams, and emotional blackmail.

MAGICKAL AND PSYCHIC USES

Scrying in reflective surface to foresee future and see spirit guides; spells to reflect hostility back to the sender; twin Hematite to attract lasting love.

SPECIAL PROPERTIES

Called the lawyer's stone, for successful outcomes in court cases, as well as disputes over wills, compensation, divorce, and taxes if you're representing yourself; assists in bringing your ambitions to fruition.

MYTHOLOGY AND HISTORY

In Neolithic times, bones were interred with powdered Hematite to represent the blood of Mother Earth; also symbolizes the warlike planet Mars. Roman soldiers rubbed red powder from the stone on their bodies to make them invulnerable. If you have a pacemaker, do not use Hematite. Hematite as permanent magnets may interfere with its function.

Hematoid Calcite

COLORS: Pink, pale orangey, red, or yellow-red if the hematite is an inclusion within the calcite; may be pink, yellow, clear, or red calcite growing on a darker hematite matrix or occasionally black shiny hematite crystals on clear calcite/quartz

CRYSTAL TYPE: Hematite (iron oxide), either included in the calcite (calcium carbonate) or calcite growing on the hematite; sometimes the hematite is within the quartz, covered or partly covered by calcite crystals

ZODIAC SIGN: Libra (September 23–October 23)

CANDLE COLOR: Pink

PHYSICAL: Oxygenates blood; counters forgetfulness, especially due to overload or stress.

EMOTIONAL: Helps overcome a victim mentality, sometimes expressed as excessive defensiveness; exploits weakness and elicits sympathy as a form of control.

HOME: Shields you from being affected by others' bad moods; resists the temptation to try to make everything right for family members.

WORKPLACE: Offers the right mix of assertiveness and tolerance of those with inflated egos.

CHILDREN: Identifies those who feign illness to avoid school.

ANIMALS: For new pets learning that they are not the alpha animal in the home.

PROTECTION: Guards against falling for hard-luck stories.

MAGICKAL AND PSYCHIC USES

Amplifies healing powers by relieving clients' deep-seated problems; connects with challenging spirits and teaching guides; links with a protective spiritual guardian or gatekeeper in mediumship or astral travel.

SPECIAL PROPERTIES

Offers psychic protection against those whom you must see regularly, but who are malicious yet physically or emotionally vulnerable; for asserting tough love in a relationship in which you are being taken for granted or exploited.

MYTHOLOGY AND HISTORY

This crystalline duo has many variations in color and appearance, most beautifully as a pink calcite flower with rose-colored points and hematite drusy; fiery and proactive Hematite with the gentle healing flowing calcite achieves results while maintaining inner harmony.

Hematoid Rose Quartz

COLORS: Pink with red inclusions or tinted red

CRYSTAL TYPE: Rose quartz (silicon dioxide with manganese impurities) and hematite (iron oxide)

ZODIAC SIGN: Taurus (April 21–May 21)

CANDLE COLOR: Pink

PHYSICAL: Strengthens the heart and circulation; promotes fertility, especially if a woman is planning to become a single mom or is in a same-sex relationship; alleviates excessive menstruation; aids in recovery from all gynecological surgery, including hysterectomy.

EMOTIONAL: Counters the inability to refuse any demands or emotional blackmail from family and friends; salves wounds from domestic abuse, whether present or from childhood.

HOME: Helps practice tough love with family members who are disrupting family harmony; for an urgent infusion of good luck.

WORKPLACE: Increases self-esteem if you are dealing with domineering employees who make others feel inadequate.

CHILDREN: For amicable custody and visitation arrangements so the children do not have to make a choice.

ANIMALS: Calms loving pets who are overexcited by visitors or children.

PROTECTION: Guards against using emotional blackmail to manipulate or pressure others.

MAGICKAL AND PSYCHIC USES

Fertility spells; money rituals; sacred sexuality; female mysteries and initiation ceremonies into goddess religions and all-female Wiccan covens.

SPECIAL PROPERTIES

If a controlling or manipulative mother has caused or is still causing angst and loss of self-confidence.

MYTHOLOGY AND HISTORY

Found in Madagascar, home of many unusual and sacred stones, the perfect mix of the fire of hematite and the love of the rose quartz; called sacred heart rose quartz by some crystal practitioners because the red hematite represents the love of the Virgin Mary and Mother deities such as the ancient Egyptian goddess Isis, who hid her child Horus in the rushes to save him from the threats of his uncle Set; a stone for both sexes who have made or are making sacrifices for their children out of pure love.

Hemimorphite or Buddha Stone

COLORS: Electric blue, green-blue, gray, brown, white, colorless

CRYSTAL TYPE: Silicate/sorosilicate (zinc silicate)

ZODIAC SIGN: Libra (September 23–October 23)

CANDLE COLOR: Bright blue

PHYSICAL: Alleviates hormonal headaches and PMS problems; promotes weight loss; speeds recovery after any invasive treatment.

EMOTIONAL: Breaks the influence of emotional vampires who drain your energies by imposing on you false obligations.

HOME: Keeps you from worrying when family members are away from you, especially your adult children.

WORKPLACE: For all situations where persuasion is central; for creating original software.

CHILDREN: Helps children value experiences and people over materialism.

ANIMALS: Diminishes aggression toward other animals.

PROTECTION: Guards against a destructive love who will never change or one that can never be.

MAGICKAL AND PSYCHIC USES

A lucky charm; good for meditation, yoga, and Asian religions; bolsters connections with spirit guides; useful for remote healing as a central focus for a healing group.

SPECIAL PROPERTIES

Called the Buddha Stone because it reduces anger, obsessions; encourages inner peace and a spiritual lifestyle.

MYTHOLOGY AND HISTORY

Found in New Mexico, Montana, Colorado, and Pennsylvania in the USA, Austria, Germany, Belgium, Australia, and many other countries. Hemimorphite (from the ancient Greek for "half-shape") crystallizes in two forms, a glassy clear or white-bladed crystal with different-shaped terminations at each end and a blue-green botryoidal, grape-like cluster.

Herderite

COLORS: White, colorless, golden brown, pale yellow, rose, pale green, or blue

CRYSTAL TYPE: Calcium beryllium phosphate

ZODIAC SIGN: Aries (March 21–April 20)

CANDLE COLOR: White

PHYSICAL: Alleviates issues stemming from the gallbladder, spleen, pancreas, migraines; aids in recovering acuity and memory after brain injury or trauma; offers a powerful energy infusion when needed.

EMOTIONAL: Counters conditions leading to erratic behavior or mood swings, such as bipolar disorder or schizophrenia.

HOME: Enables family members to evolve new ways of relating; helps avoid self-limiting patterns—the helpless child, the martyred mother, the scapegoat, etc.

WORKPLACE: Promotes leadership and team building, combining diplomacy with decisive direction; for major brainstorming and divergent thinking; for successful results in long-term training.

CHILDREN: Keep this crystal in the home for children away at boarding school or residential facilities to maintain connection.

ANIMALS: Ensures the safety and health of animals in flocks and herds or in conservation areas.

PROTECTION: Guards against becoming stuck in circular guilt and regrets after setback or rejection.

MAGICKAL AND PSYCHIC USES

For teachers of healing, psychic development, and mediumship; for esoteric students to connect with their personal guide; clairvoyance, clairaudience.

SPECIAL PROPERTIES

For study and complex research in medicine, technology, or mind sciences, broadly referred to as psychology; for overcoming frustration when people prove stubborn, uncooperative, or situations turn unnecessarily complicated.

MYTHOLOGY AND HISTORY

Herderite connects spontaneously to higher realms, for interdimensional astral travel and awareness of Light and Star Beings; breaks through limitations for a total understanding of problems and, almost simultaneously, long-term as well as immediate solutions.

Herkimer Diamond

COLORS: Colorless, sparkling, containing rainbow inclusions, water, air bubbles, or a black carbon inclusion

CRYSTAL TYPE: Clear quartz, double-terminated (pointed at both ends)

ZODIAC SIGNS: Aries (March 21–April 20) and Sagittarius (November 23–December 21)

CANDLE COLOR: White

PHYSICAL: Prevents physical exhaustion, burnout, potential infections, and viruses; replaces toxins with energy; enhances vision.

EMOTIONAL: Unrestricted growth of Herkimer Diamonds in soft mud brings freedom from restrictions, however caused.

HOME: Insulates the home from electromagnetic pollution, negative Earth energies, difficult neighbors; resolves quarrels; counters illness and misfortune.

WORKPLACE: Aids in learning new techniques fast; generates groundbreaking research; for teachers of alternative therapies; stabilizes business finances.

CHILDREN: Too powerful for youngsters, except to shield teens worried about extraterrestrial dreams or out-of-body experiences.

ANIMALS: Too powerful to use directly; hold one to guide a lost pet home.

PROTECTION: Vibrates if someone is lying or has bad intent.

MAGICKAL AND PSYCHIC USES

Conjures up vivid dreams, especially of other realms, and promotes accurate dream recall; ensures safe out-of-body experiences.

SPECIAL PROPERTIES

Each Herkimer Diamond is said to contain a guardian luck-bringing Earth spirit. Restrict time carrying or wearing Herkimer, as its other worldly energies may cause disorientation.

MYTHOLOGY AND HISTORY

True Herkimer Diamonds, only found in Herkimer, New York, were formed 500 million years ago, resembling diamonds in shape and brilliance; the double termination replaces what is redundant with new cosmic energies.

Hessonite Garnet or Cinnamon Stone

COLORS: Reddish-brown, orange from medium to dark brown-orange, due to iron and manganese inclusions

CRYSTAL TYPE: Calcium aluminum silicate, a variety of Grossular Garnet (page 231), natural, tumbled stone and faceted as a gem

ZODIAC SIGN: Capricorn (December 22–January 20)

CANDLE COLOR: Orange

PHYSICAL: Regulates and boosts the immune, metabolic, and hormonal systems, improving overall health and well-being.

EMOTIONAL: Helps those plagued by an inferiority or guilt complex, particularly one expressed by eating disorders.

HOME: If socializing is hard with strangers or large groups, counters the inability to make conversation.

WORKPLACE: The most creative garnet, Hessonite brings success in self-initiated businesses, based on an original idea or unfilled market niche.

CHILDREN: Comforts those who have lacked consistent mothering or been expected from childhood to parent younger siblings.

ANIMALS: For those separated from their mother too young.

PROTECTION: Guards against emotional and psychic manipulation and vampirism; shields you from spirit sexual predators.

MAGICKAL AND PSYCHIC USES

Highly valued in Vedic astrology, Hessonite opens the way for astrological abilities in any tradition and learning Ayurvedic healing.

SPECIAL PROPERTIES

Hessonite Garnet inspires artistic expression for pleasure as well as for professionally developing natural talents.

MYTHOLOGY AND HISTORY

According to Vedic astrologists, wearing a two-carat or larger Hessonite Garnet is said to bring wealth and success as well as promote long life. It is called the Cinnamon Stone because of its color and because it originated in the land of spices, Ceylon, now called as Sri Lanka. Hessonite has been in use since the times of ancient Rome and Greece, where it was carved into cameos.

Heulandite

COLOR: Brown, green, peach, or pink—sometimes so pale it appears white or colorless; also, gray, yellow, red; pearly luster
CRYSTAL TYPE: Zeolite containing barium, magnesium, potassium, and other minerals
ZODIAC SIGNS: Libra (September 23-October 23) and Sagittarius (November 23-December 21)
CANDLE COLOR: Golden brown

PHYSICAL: Alleviates pain and other issues in the knees, back, feet, nervous system, liver; counters breathlessness, side effects of viruses, toxins, water retention; bolsters memory; helps absorb nutrients; addresses food intolerances.
EMOTIONAL: Helps overcome addictions, especially those regarding food, alcohol, and drugs (including painkillers); useful in dealing with weight issues based on distorted self-image.
HOME: Makes you to feel at home if you live alone or have recently moved; deters intrusive neighbors.
WORKPLACE: Defuses potential conflict; leads to successful pay and contract negotiations; promotes international business.
CHILDREN: Encourages friendship between children of different ethnicities and religions, including children with physical or emotional challenges in mainstream activities.
ANIMALS: Helps volunteers and staff at rescue shelters with a constant flow of animals to make each animal feel welcome and cherished.
PROTECTION: Guards against sarcasm, spite, and criticism socially, at home, and at work.

MAGICKAL AND PSYCHIC USES
Visions and spontaneous memories of historical and spiritual root cultures; connects through meditation and astral travel with Lemuria, Atlantis, and ancient Egypt; encounters evolved spirit guides.
SPECIAL PROPERTIES
Heulandite clears repetition of karmic patterns; combine pale and green Heulandite to align body, mind, and spirit.
MYTHOLOGY AND HISTORY
The integrator crystal that brings compromise and tolerance between people of different backgrounds and persuasions; lighter colors focus more on the spiritual, stronger colors are more proactive, green and brown awaken a practical and nature-based bent; all Heulandite shares the same core properties.

Hiddenite or Green Kunzite

COLORS: Pale green to yellow-green or emerald (see also Pink Kunzite [page 357] and Lilac or Lavender Kunzite [page 279])
CRYSTAL TYPE: Aluminosilicate, a rare gem variety of spodumene
ZODIAC SIGN: Taurus (April 21-May 21)
CANDLE COLOR: Pale green

PHYSICAL: Healing on all levels; balances hemispheres of the brain; addresses hyperventilation, fluid imbalances; promotes fertility; alleviates issues relating to circulation, heart muscle, toothache.
EMOTIONAL: For loss of or parting from loved ones; after losing your home, job, or health.
HOME: Enables you to enjoy family life, rather than constantly responding to outside commitments.
WORKPLACE: Aids in finding fulfilling and lucrative employment; rekindles abandoned career dreams.
CHILDREN: Cultivates a sense of gratitude in children who demand material parity with their peers.
ANIMALS: Helps overcome panic at traffic, noise, storms, or while being handled.
PROTECTION: Shields against focusing on past grievances and failures.

MAGICKAL AND PSYCHIC USES
Called the evolution crystal because it awakens spiritual awareness of global responsibility for humankind and the planet; morphic resonance, the ability to experience telepathically wisdom acquired by others; manifesting money.
SPECIAL PROPERTIES
Enhances herbs, oils, homeopathy, energy touch therapies, and hydrotherapy; brings healing through love; deepens online love; attracts soul-twin love.
MYTHOLOGY AND HISTORY
Hiddenite was first discovered in 1879 in North Carolina. William Hidden, a mineralogist, had been commissioned to find platinum in the area, a reminder that we may think we know what we are looking for; what we find instead may be what we need. Hiddenite is used by healers to assist in diagnosis and psychic surgery.

Highland Marble

COLORS: Pistachio, lime or olive green, sometimes with white
CRYSTAL TYPE: A cousin of Skye Marble (page 443), but with its own unique energies; made into cabochons, jewelry, and artifacts, including Celtic cross pendants, also called Scottish greenstone; made of serpentine and metamorphosed limestone
ZODIAC SIGN: Pisces (February 19–March 20)
CANDLE COLOR: Green

PHYSICAL: Used by healers to remove the stresses and pollution of the modern world that cause or worsen many present-day illnesses; regulates fluid imbalances.
EMOTIONAL: Helps overcome a tendency not to go with the flow of life but rather demand guarantees; counters a disrespect for the environment and its creatures.
HOME: Attracts good fortune, abundance, and a sense of loyalty to one's roots and kin.
WORKPLACE: For working or relocating overseas; careers connected with water; returning to an area or business with family ties.
CHILDREN: For seeing the fey people, plus Earth and water spirits.
ANIMALS: Said to be protected against human cruelty by the fey.
PROTECTION: Traditionally used by fishermen for centuries for safety at sea, Highland Marble is still an amulet for safe travel especially overseas.

MAGICKAL AND PSYCHIC USES
Of special power to those of Celtic origin ancestrally or who have experienced past druidic lives or lives as tenants farming for the person who owns the land; for visions and dreams of the struggles of the Highland clans through the centuries.
SPECIAL PROPERTIES
Iona marble, which is of the same family, is the sacred stone of St. Columba, who introduced nature-based Celtic Christianity in 563 when he founded the monastery on Iona.
MYTHOLOGY AND HISTORY
Hand-mined and retrieved by divers from the company Two Skies, Highland marble is found in the Scottish Highlands and the West Coast islands; contains pure Celtic energies since it has been prized for hundreds of years as a talisman. Its history goes back 800 million years when limestone was formed under the Scottish seas, plant life died, settled on the seabed, releasing chlorophyll to join with the limestone to create this unique marble.

Hilutite or Hilulite

COLORS: Dark pink, brownish-red, orange; may have black or white inclusions and sparkles
CRYSTAL TYPE: Garnet, zircon, goethite, and quartz combined
ZODIAC SIGN: Aquarius (January 21–February 18)
CANDLE COLOR: Gold

PHYSICAL: Promotes circulation of the blood, balance if one part of the body or the brain is adversely affecting general health, mobility, and physical steadiness.
EMOTIONAL: Counters fear of sexual contact; helps overcome the tendency to use conflict and confrontation as a defense mechanism.
HOME: Cultivates mutual respect and consideration if one person always gives way to more dominant family members; for those living in unsafe areas.
WORKPLACE: Fosters reasoned negotiations where there are disputes or rigid attitudes; for all who work in conflict prevention and resolution.
CHILDREN: Aids in finding their place in the home and world if children or teens always feel alone.
ANIMALS: For telepathically wise pets who seem otherworldly.
PROTECTION: Guards against those who demand total conformity to the dogma of their cultural norms or faith.

MAGICKAL AND PSYCHIC USES
For manifesting desires; connecting with higher dimensions, not only in meditation or spiritual practice but for daily glimpses, guidance, and insights.
SPECIAL PROPERTIES
A crystal that reminds us that we are spiritual beings in a physical body and are responsible for the well-being of others who share the world with us.
MYTHOLOGY AND HISTORY
Hilutite or Hilulite was recently discovered in Sri Lanka. Its purpose is teaching us to value ourselves and others, but not for what we have or earn.

Holey or Hag Stones

COLORS: Brown, fawn, gray, white; with glassy flint called adder stones

CRYSTAL TYPE: Any stone with a natural hole caused by water or weathering, found on riverbanks and by the seashore

ZODIAC SIGNS: Virgo (August 24–September 22) and Capricorn (December 22–January 20)

CANDLE COLOR: Brown

PHYSICAL: Relieves pain, childhood ills, cramps, rheumatism; alleviates issues regarding bones, warts, stomach; promotes fertility, remote healing.

EMOTIONAL: Helps overcome fears of being cursed or inheriting family curses; curbs obsession with spirit messages.

HOME: Placed near the front door on a knotted red cord, these stones guard against burglary and natural disasters; on the bedpost, they repel nightmares and nocturnal psychic attack.

WORKPLACE: A holey stone, with three holes, brings luck; glassy adder stones offer justice.

CHILDREN: Over bedroom doors these stones shield youngsters from sleep disturbances; block malice toward teens via social media or unkind peers.

ANIMALS: In stables, barns, near sleeping places, Holey Stones safeguard farm animals, horses, and pets.

PROTECTION: Guard against paranormal harm, ill-wishing, and mind manipulation.

MAGICKAL AND PSYCHIC USES

Looking through the hole of a natural stone at midnight on a full moon reveals fairies, nature spirits, and benign ghosts; a pointed Holey Stone on a red cord forms a pendulum; most powerful around Halloween.

SPECIAL PROPERTIES

A small Holey Stone on a red cord tied with three knots, suspended with dried yarrow over the bed, promises lasting love; renew yarrow annually.

MYTHOLOGY AND HISTORY

Called odin stones in Scandinavia and the north of England, Holey Stones were considered a gateway to other dimensions; large ones set near the entrance of Neolithic burial chambers offered passage to the Otherworld.

Holly Blue Agate

COLORS: Blue, blue-lavender to rich pink-violet; may be banded

CRYSTAL TYPE: Chalcedony, cryptocrystalline quartz

ZODIAC SIGNS: Virgo (August 24–September 22) and Libra (September 23–October 23)

CANDLE COLOR: Blue

PHYSICAL: Alleviates stress-related headaches and pain in neck and upper spine, pregnancy nausea, motion sickness, fevers, high blood pressure.

EMOTIONAL: Helps overcome the inability to accept what cannot be restored; counters obsession with unattainable love.

HOME: For tranquil mealtimes and family discussions, especially concerning decisions that will affect the whole family.

WORKPLACE: Creates a peaceful space for working in an open-plan office; keeps you from becoming distracted by checking emails, text messages, or social media if this is affecting your concentration.

CHILDREN: Helps teens to accept reasonable boundaries in their social life.

ANIMALS: For large city dogs who need a lot of exercise.

PROTECTION: Guards against online predators, fraudulent declarations of love, and requests for help.

MAGICKAL AND PSYCHIC USES

Associated with the Air element, for rituals in high places; connects with Air spirits and devas.

SPECIAL PROPERTIES

Holly Blue Agate is associated with healing angels. Each piece has its own unique angelic connections to heal you and those you love.

MYTHOLOGY AND HISTORY

Though the purer blue shades of Holly Blue Agate are similar to Blue Lace Agate, or Ellensburg blue agate, Holly Blue Agate is more translucent and glowing when polished, as it has a far higher opal content. It is named after Holly Mountain in Arkansas where it was originally mined.

Honduras Matrix Opal

COLORS: Opaque, dark matrix (volcanic basalt) speckled with precious opal throughout; pinpricks of fire, with flashes of color throughout

CRYSTAL TYPE: A precious opal, formed in small spaces in basalt lava flows, distributed evenly in veins throughout its host rock; even more rare as a seam opal with milky white opal and dark matrix layers

ZODIAC SIGN: Cancer (June 22–July 22)

CANDLE COLOR: Silver

PHYSICAL: Identifies and salves hidden or deep-seated problems within the body; aids in diagnosis through electrocardiograms, ultrasounds, CT and MRI scans; promotes fertility, pregnancy; eases childbirth; alleviates issues stemming from veins and arteries, bowels, constipation, and IBS.

EMOTIONAL: Helps you cope with empty-nest syndrome, and adult children who involve parents in their relationships.

HOME: Because Honduras Matrix Opals are linked with local farming, their strong Earth and land-based energies provide a sense of security in the face of money or property worries.

WORKPLACE: Created from volcanic eruptions, Honduras Matrix Opals carry great stores of energy when a sudden input or extra effort is needed.

CHILDREN: A treasure to display, Honduras Matrix Opal encourages children not to accept the superficial but to explore deeper.

ANIMALS: Strengthens those with poor vision or mobility.

PROTECTION: Guards against slow undermining of confidence.

MAGICKAL AND PSYCHIC USES

Shamanic rituals especially at night; initiation ceremonies in Wicca, Druidry, and goddess spiritualities, where temporary sensory deprivation or coming from darkness to light is central.

SPECIAL PROPERTIES

For long-lasting love, known in the heart rather than expressed sentimentally, that grows through the years.

MYTHOLOGY AND HISTORY

Believed to be the oldest mined opal in the world; the kind with a black background is most valuable; lighter-colored basalt may be treated with sugar or smoke (should be marked TREATED HONDURAS MATRIX OPAL); Australian Andamooka opal matrix from South Australia is similar (see also Cantera Opal, page 104).

Honeycomb Amethyst

COLORS: Purple or occasionally green (amethyst) and pale yellow/white citrine/quartz (for the patterned lattice)

CRYSTAL TYPE: A very unusual silicon dioxide crystal; in its raw natural state, the amethyst has a citrine/quartz lattice resembling a honeycomb; often carved and faceted with purple lattice patterns on the front for jewelry

ZODIAC SIGN: Cancer (June 22–July 22)

CANDLE COLOR: Purple

PHYSICAL: Promotes cell health, muscle and tissue repair, rapid healing of wounds, fertility in older people; alleviates food allergies.

EMOTIONAL: Counters possessiveness, repressed anger, irritability, impatience.

HOME: For abundance, not just prosperity, manifest as happy family meals, evenings talking together, outings.

WORKPLACE: Ensures job satisfaction as well as success; improves productivity through team effort if workers are pulling in different directions.

CHILDREN: Impresses a work ethic on teenagers who expect their parents to support them 100 percent into adulthood.

ANIMALS: For older pets who are possessive about their owners.

PROTECTION: As an amulet for babies, children, the very old, or anyone vulnerable or chronically sick, to call on the guardianship of the ancestral grandmothers.

MAGICKAL AND PSYCHIC USES

Wise woman and croning rituals; finding possessions and animals that are lost; making telepathic connections with estranged or missing people.

SPECIAL PROPERTIES

Resisting mind games, psychological and psychic manipulation in the workplace and in relationships.

MYTHOLOGY AND HISTORY

As far back as 5000 BCE, the Queen Bee was used as an image to represent the Mother Goddess and the hive was likened to the womb of the Great Mother. The bee became regarded as an emissary of the Virgin Mary and her mother St. Anne. Since amethyst is also the special stone of St. Anne, as the grandmother of Jesus, Honeycomb Amethyst is a powerful protector and empowerer for grandmothers, great-grandmothers, and women entering their wise woman years. Honeycomb Amethyst is found in Africa.

Honey Opal

COLORS: Honey-colored, clear to resinous or glassy; resembles honey
CRYSTAL TYPE: Hydrated silicon dioxide, a common opal, though occasionally it may display play of color (see also Lemurian Golden Opal); beware cheap synthetics
ZODIAC SIGN: Taurus (April 21–May 21)
CANDLE COLOR: Honey-yellow, orange-brown

PHYSICAL: A whole-body healer; addresses issues involving the throat, colds, flu, congestion, digestion, liver, wounds, stings.
EMOTIONAL: Eases excessive defensiveness because of previous trauma, inability to give and receive love, mothering issues.
HOME: Attracts health, abundance, and new friends; creates harmonious mealtimes; promotes cyber-friendship and romance to meet genuine people with whom to connect in person.
WORKPLACE: Encourages you to be in the right place at the right time; for women's businesses, especially home-based.
CHILDREN: Protects babies and small children because the parents can telepathically anticipate distress or need.
ANIMALS: For psychic links with a pet so they come when you call them in your mind.
PROTECTION: Guards against spite, jealousy, lies, and gossip.

MAGICKAL AND PSYCHIC USES
For increased telepathy between parents and children of any age, partners and close friends; visualization and creative expression of other worlds where you once lived.

SPECIAL PROPERTIES
For winning competitions, quiz shows, and tests of ability and knowledge, rather than random chance, a quality shared with other golden yellow opals; pursuing part-time study or taking extra training to improve qualifications.

MYTHOLOGY AND HISTORY
Over the millennia, bees have been adopted as the icon of Rhea, the Greek Earth Mother; Demeter, the ancient Greek Grain Mother; Cybele, Great Mother of the Gods; Artemis, the Greek huntress, and her Greco-Roman counterpart, Diana; and Aphrodite, goddess of love. By association Honey Opal is a love token as well as one given to mothers on the birth of a baby.

Honey or Amber Calcite

COLORS: Golden honey, amber
CRYSTAL TYPE: Calcium carbonate
ZODIAC SIGN: Sagittarius (November 23–December 21)
CANDLE COLOR: Honey-yellow, orange-brown

PHYSICAL: Addresses issues involving the cells, skin, healthy growth in children, diabetes, blood sugar fluctuations, fertility, SAD, bites, stings, digestion, intestines, liver, gallbladder, pancreas, spleen, nausea, bed-wetting, stress-based incontinence, libido.
EMOTIONAL: After a hysterectomy, eases grief for lost fertility and feelings of undesirability in the face of early-onset menopause or menopause.
HOME: For happy, harmonious family parties and celebrations; pleasant mealtimes, especially if conflicts are caused by food fads or obsessions; helps flowers and herbs flourish, especially in poor soil.
WORKPLACE: Aids in overcoming disappointment if you've been passed over for promotion or increased salary; redoubles efforts to succeed next time; promotes networking, setting up websites, blogs, and web links; initiates projects.
CHILDREN: For adolescents with eating disorders or serious body-image problems; calms nerves before a test; encourages outdoor activities.
ANIMALS: Attracts bees, butterflies, and dragonflies to the garden.
PROTECTION: Guards against spiteful and wounding words, gossip, and online trolling.

MAGICKAL AND PSYCHIC USES
Goddess rituals for abundance; fertility and money spells; organizing or attending psychic and healing groups.

SPECIAL PROPERTIES
Draws prosperity, abundance, blessings, health, and well-being; helps you find love on dating sites and through social networking.

MYTHOLOGY AND HISTORY
A rare form, Honeycomb Calcite is found only in Utah, with long fibrous or tubular cells, resembling petrified honey. Honey and Honeycomb Calcite are associated in Christian tradition with the Virgin Mary and her mother Anne, who is the patroness of beekeepers.

Hornblende

COLORS: Dark green to black; may display pleochroism—different colors when viewed from different angles

CRYSTAL TYPE: A mixture of calcium-iron-magnesium silicate, aluminum-iron-magnesium silicate, and iron-magnesium silicate

ZODIAC SIGN: Scorpio (October 24–November 22)

CANDLE COLOR: Dark green

PHYSICAL: Alleviates issues stemming from the inner and middle ear, kidneys, small intestine, bladder infections, stress-based incontinence; enables absorption of necessary nutrients (particularly vitamins A and D, calcium, magnesium, iron) and maintenance of proper sodium levels.

EMOTIONAL: Counters overly judgmental and dismissive attitudes toward others you consider inferior; promotes perseverance.

HOME: For compromise and finding mutual agreement among family members, neighbors, and in cases of disputes over community development projects.

WORKPLACE: Inspires writers, artists, musical composers, and all who create; encourages you to complete and market your creations.

CHILDREN: Teaches children to be honest about their mistakes and misdeeds, and try to rectify them.

ANIMALS: Encourages pets who have been part of the family for many years to accept human or animal newcomers.

PROTECTION: Guards against giving up when the going gets hard.

MAGICKAL AND PSYCHIC USES

In meditation, evokes a sense of timelessness, momentary bliss, and unity with the cosmos; for psychic defense rituals and protection if set around the home and land.

SPECIAL PROPERTIES

A stone for attracting prosperity, especially through moneymaking ideas and being in the right place at the right time.

MYTHOLOGY AND HISTORY

Hornblende, also called amphibolite, dates back to Neolithic times; considered a sacred stone that has been part of traditional ceremonies in Africa and among the Australian Aboriginals and Native Americans for centuries. In recent times it has been incorporated into labyrinth meditation and natural magick as an offering to Mother Earth, both in collective and private rituals.

Hourglass Gypsum or Selenite

COLORS: Appears orange, orangey, or chocolate brown, enclosed in white, because of the inclusions

CRYSTAL TYPE: Hydrous calcium sulfate, a phantom selenite with inclusions of particles of sand, clay, or iron oxide deposited within the stone during its creation; double-terminated hourglass shape

ZODIAC SIGN: Gemini (May 22–June 21)

CANDLE COLOR: Orange

PHYSICAL: Removes toxins from the body; addresses issues involving the ovaries and womb; for freezing eggs for later IVF; useful after an ectopic pregnancy; for men with a low sperm count.

EMOTIONAL: Eases fears of mortality; counters a sense that your destiny is fixed and so fighting against difficult circumstances is pointless.

HOME: Reestablishes a stable home after major disruption; creates happy memories; welcomes new family members, especially relatives of new partners.

WORKPLACE: For those who cannot meet deadlines or stick to schedules; for multitasking; organizing conferences.

CHILDREN: Encourages children to maintain a routine and regular bedtimes.

ANIMALS: For lovable pets not amenable to training.

PROTECTION: Guards against those who sow chaos in your life for the sake of it.

MAGICKAL AND PSYCHIC USES

Astrology, ritual magick, manifesting what is needed and is of the highest good; bringing together different healing therapies and knowledge to create a spiritual system that can be taught to others.

SPECIAL PROPERTIES

A reminder that every day is precious and important; the mindfulness crystal to live in the here and now.

MYTHOLOGY AND HISTORY

Found only in the hourglass shape in the Oklahoma Great Salt Plains State Park in Alfalfa County; a variation as small white sand and gypsum opaque or transparent crystals are also mined in New Mexico. Often called the "As above, so below stone," the hourglass crystal links the earthly world with the movements and reflection of planets and the influences of higher realms.

Hubnerite

COLORS: Black, black/gray, reddish-brown, yellow/brown, brown/black; striated and with metallic luster

CRYSTAL TYPE: Manganese tungsten oxide, usually found growing with quartz, the best partner for healing and magick, as it amplifies Hubnerite's powers; bladed, sometimes completely enclosed in quartz at back; pyrite and augelite are also good attached partner crystals for Hubnerite

ZODIAC SIGN: Aries (March 21–April 20)

CANDLE COLOR: Red

PHYSICAL: Boosts energy and vitality; useful in treating anemia and red cell blood disorders, muscle weakness.

EMOTIONAL: For lack of enthusiasm for anything involving change or leaving the comfort zone even temporarily; self-imposed restrictions based on outmoded patterns of thinking.

HOME: Linking with Earth energies and the natural world in a city apartment or urban development; feeling secure and settled in a new home.

WORKPLACE: Promotes problem solving; helps you discover who is trustworthy and who has a personal agenda.

CHILDREN: Keep this crystal with luggage to calm youngsters if a family travels frequently or regularly relocates.

ANIMALS: For pets to adapt to two homes, with a shared-custody arrangement, following a divorce or separation.

PROTECTION: Guards against restrictions and unreasonable prohibitions by others.

MAGICKAL AND PSYCHIC USES

Channels automatic writing; enables deep trance meditation if this is usually difficult; increases psychic awareness.

SPECIAL PROPERTIES

For all endurance sports, marathons, aerobics, weights, and careers involving constant physical activity.

MYTHOLOGY AND HISTORY

Also known as huebernite and found occasionally as a gem in the Mundo Nuevo mine in Peru. Because Hubernite is created in geothermal vents, under great pressure that causes rapid development, it eases the effects of sudden unexpected change and offers adaptability to change course with minimum disruption.

Hyalite or Water Opal

COLORS: Colorless and glassy, transparent; sparkles when cut and polished

CRYSTAL TYPE: Hydrated silicon dioxide, common opal (no play of colors), though it can also be found as Precious White Opal (page 369)

ZODIAC SIGN: Cancer (June 22–July 22)

CANDLE COLOR: Silver

PHYSICAL: Addresses issues involving the bones, hands, teeth, vision, ovaries, womb, childbirth, PMS, and menopause; enhances the effects of laser surgery and light therapies.

EMOTIONAL: Helps overcome poor or distorted body image, as well as lack of social interaction due to self-consciousness about perceived imperfections.

HOME: Prompts extended family get-togethers, uniting the neighborhood and community for mutual benefit.

WORKPLACE: Fosters team building, coming together in cooperative or communal enterprises; deters those who use glamour, charisma, and flirting for advancement.

CHILDREN: Encourages children to take up interests, join clubs, or engage in outdoor activities.

ANIMALS: Persuades visitors to an animal rescue center to adopt less cute or cuddly creatures.

PROTECTION: Acts as a warning against misfortune and potential hazards.

MAGICKAL AND PSYCHIC USES

Scrying within the opal to connect with spirit realms and recall the life-path contract entered before birth; facilitates visions of the future.

SPECIAL PROPERTIES

A natural magnet for accumulating whatever is most needed; for collectors and treasure hunters to acquire desired artifacts at a bargain price.

MYTHOLOGY AND HISTORY

Hyalite forms botryoidal masses (covered in opal grape-like forms) as well as unusual shapes; some *electric* Hyalite may be fluorescent, turning intense green under low-grade UV and bright sunlight. Hyalite is also called Muller's Glass after its original discoverer, Franz-Joseph Müller von Reichenstein, an Austrian mineralogist.

Hyperstene or Orthopyroxene

COLORS: Deep brown, sometimes including green, gray, silvery-brown, bronze/black, or dark red metallic luster; strongly pleochroic (revealing colors from different angles and in different lights)

CRYSTAL TYPE: A member of the pyrozene family of magnesium iron silicate

ZODIAC SIGNS: Sagittarius (November 23–December 21) and Capricorn (December 22–January 20)

CANDLE COLOR: Silver

PHYSICAL: Reduces physical stress causing muscle tension; addresses blood disorders, issues involving the large intestine, prostate, ovaries, chronic fatigue syndrome; promotes absorption of nutrients.

EMOTIONAL: Helps overcomes intense shyness in company; quiets self-criticism and keeps you from feeling pressured to reach impossibly high standards from an overly critical childhood.

HOME: Discourages criticism and undermining of more vulnerable family members.

WORKPLACE: Useful for insurance adjustors, investigators, detectives; for setting up a business with a love partner.

CHILDREN: Calms frustration when children cannot perform tasks that are beyond their abilities.

ANIMALS: For snappish or unpredictable dogs and horses.

PROTECTION: Prevents misunderstandings in online relationships that may keep them from developing.

MAGICKAL AND PSYCHIC USES

Opens clairaudience and clairvoyance; aids meditation if relaxation is hard; heals during meditation.

SPECIAL PROPERTIES

For manifesting solutions to seemingly insoluble problems and attracting the necessary resources.

MYTHOLOGY AND HISTORY

The bad-hair-day crystal, Hyperstene makes things right when everything is going wrong. Found in igneous and metamorphic rocks, stony and iron meteorites, it produces major life changes; mined mainly in the USA and Canada.

Ibis Jasper

COLORS: Brownish-red with splashes of white and blue

CRYSTAL TYPE: Southern Madagascan brecciated jasper, recently discovered; stones broken apart by water or weather during formation, cemented together with chalcedony; usually sold as tumbled stones or jewelry

ZODIAC SIGN: Aries (March 21–April 20)

CANDLE COLOR: Red

PHYSICAL: Aids in recovery after trauma; relieves stress-related illnesses, energy blocks anywhere in the body, fractures, bone splintering, skin eruptions; enhances micro- and robotic surgery.

EMOTIONAL: Calms chaotic feelings that prevent the resolution of trauma; counters an overwhelming desire for perfection; keeps you from rejecting anything less than the most expensive, regardless of quality.

HOME: Repairs what is fixable rather than discarding it; renovates old furniture and property to its former glory; clears clutter.

WORKPLACE: For troubleshooting and organizing business accounts for official assessment; creates order out of chaos when taking over a disorganized business or department.

CHILDREN: Encourages untidy children to keep order.

ANIMALS: For training clumsy animals who cause chaos indoors.

PROTECTION: Keeps you from giving up on people or situations.

MAGICKAL AND PSYCHIC USES

Shamanic soul rescue; mediumship to send restless, earthbound spirits to the light; exploring past lives to understand present fears and leave behind old, outworn karma.

SPECIAL PROPERTIES

Brings reconciliation to broken relationships or seemingly unsalvageable situations, not to continue as before, but with new growth based on the acceptance of supposed imperfections.

MYTHOLOGY AND HISTORY

The colors and patterns of ibis resemble the Madagascan ibis, rather than the Egyptian black and white kind. The ibis species is historically linked with the ancient Egyptian ibis-headed god Thoth, deity of wisdom and god of mathematics, astronomy, and writing. So the stone is associated with wisdom and learning; also linked with the legendary golden phoenix of rebirth; therefore, it is a powerful new-beginning crystal.

Icicle Agate

COLORS: Brown agate inside with a white surface from Oregon; can also have lacy icicles or a white icicle shape with white/gray markings or drusy sparkling minerals, usually from Mexico

CRYSTAL TYPE: Chalcedony, silicon dioxide; pitted or bubbled areas of quartz borders; usually seen as tumbled stones and jewelry

ZODIAC SIGN: Capricorn (December 22–January 20)

CANDLE COLOR: White

PHYSICAL: Eases frozen shoulder or other joints; alleviates conditions made worse by cold weather or a sudden drop in body temperature; addresses chilblains, poor circulation.

EMOTIONAL: Helps overcome the inability to show, express, or feel emotions or empathy; counter an unwillingness to act on the spur of the moment.

HOME: Aids in grappling with problems with water supply and plumbing at cold times of the year; for politely but firmly dealing with delays.

WORKPLACE: For patience and perseverance if a promised promotion or pay raise does not materialize; in business, helps you pursue orders or supplies that are holding up production.

CHILDREN: Breaks through exclusion from peer friendship groups; prevents young children from falling and teens from taking unnecessary risks.

ANIMALS: For less mobile pets needing nurturing and peace.

PROTECTION: Guards against those who promise but never deliver; helps you deal with fears of losing your faculties.

MAGICKAL AND PSYCHIC USES

For reconciliation rituals; psychic surgery; with fire agate for balancing yang and yin in home or workplace; love rituals to speed a marriage proposal.

SPECIAL PROPERTIES

Icicles represent frozen water and the need to cautiously proceed, waiting for the right moment to speak or act.

MYTHOLOGY AND HISTORY

Icicle Agate encourages planning for the future; above all, seizing the chance to progress cautiously if there is a sudden opportunity, as if crossing a bridge of ice between two usually separated pieces of land where the way ahead is accessible only for a short time, until the ice melts.

Icicle Calcite

COLORS: Orange at the base and whitish yellow at the top; bicolor and opaque

CRYSTAL TYPE: Typified by finger icicle–like structure, calcium carbonate; a more proactive crystal and mineralogically different from Icicle Agate

ZODIAC SIGN: Capricorn (December 22–January 20)

CANDLE COLOR: Orange

PHYSICAL: Addresses illnesses involving multiple causes or parts of the body, frozen and immobile limbs and joints, intense fear of needles; ensures successful open-heart surgery.

EMOTIONAL: Counters destructive habits and attitudes in the family, acquired in childhood and passed down through the generations.

HOME: Cools in hot weather or if people are getting hot and bothered over a disagreement; cleanses the home of hyperactive, restless vibes.

WORKPLACE: Identifies and tactfully points out errors and miscalculations; finds the right outlet for a creation or innovative idea.

CHILDREN: Works as a magick wand at special times for making wishes come true; fosters awareness of the fey in younger children.

ANIMALS: For discovering individual characteristics in cold-blooded pets, and so increasing affection for them.

PROTECTION: Guards against refusal to act in a crisis that could be averted by intervention.

MAGICKAL AND PSYCHIC USES

As a wand for ritual and healing; in psychic surgery, the white tip is used to identify and remove problems and the orange to reenergize; creates a safe space around yourself and your altar by spiraling the wand in alternating counterclockwise and clockwise directions.

SPECIAL PROPERTIES

The crystal of melting ice, which speeds up matters that have been stuck or very slow in materializing.

MYTHOLOGY AND HISTORY

A crystal to point the way to the future by resolving unfinished personal issues from the past that affect the present; accepting that you may not be able to put right long-standing family generational issues, but may need to step back and create your own inner serenity.

Ilmenite or Manaccanite

COLORS: Dark gray, brown or black, metallic

CRYSTAL TYPE: Titanium iron oxide; found included in clear or smoky quartz, on a quartz matrix, or occasionally containing quartz; more commonly attached to magnetite or hematite

ZODIAC SIGN: Capricorn (December 22–January 20)

CANDLE COLOR: Gold

PHYSICAL: Useful in addressing new viruses or those resistant to treatment, autoimmune conditions; alleviates issues involving bones, tissues, muscles.

EMOTIONAL: Eases long-standing personality problems, recurring depression, telephone sex and porn addictions, a victim mentality.

HOME: Restores a home to its former glory or preserves its original character.

WORKPLACE: For working from home or living over the workplace; bringing a run-down business back to life; restoring antiques or broken items; helping people or animals rejected by society.

CHILDREN: Encourages you to persevere at a sport or in course of study if you have a tendency to give up at the first obstacle.

ANIMALS: For old, infirm pets and rescue animals scarred emotionally and physically.

PROTECTION: A barrier against people—from neighbors to employers—who try to undermine you.

MAGICKAL AND PSYCHIC USES

Defensive magick, especially when mixed with hematite; creates magickal boundaries around home, business premises, vehicle, or other valuable items.

SPECIAL PROPERTIES

Inspires determination, if you're physically or emotionally challenged, to obtain the necessary resources to improve your quality of life and realize your full potential; for starting again and winning after hitting rock bottom.

MYTHOLOGY AND HISTORY

The effects of Ilmenite are greatly amplified when mixed with quartz, whether for healing, protection, or power.

Imperial Jade

COLORS: Emerald green, translucent; color due to chromium

CRYSTAL TYPE: Silicate/inosilicate/pyroxene; jadeite

ZODIAC SIGN: Virgo (August 24–September 22)

CANDLE COLOR: Bright green

PHYSICAL: Promotes fertility, especially for those who want several children; addresses issues stemming from the kidneys, bladder, bed-wetting at any age, hips, legs, knees, ankles, heart, blood purification, high cholesterol, diabetes; strengthens hair, skin.

EMOTIONAL: Counters self-loathing that prevents a seriously overweight person from seeking help or staying on a diet; alleviates illnesses caused or made worse by overindulgence; eases fears of mortality.

HOME: As the richest color, imperial jade is the luckiest of the jades for drawing love, peace, beauty, harmony, and abundance.

WORKPLACE: Encourages leadership bids and success in senior positions; for multigenerational family businesses to promote unity.

CHILDREN: Protects small and physically or emotionally delicate children.

ANIMALS: For high-strung, aristocratic pets.

PROTECTION: Guards against the undermining effects of family members who criticize your childcare or marriage.

MAGICKAL AND PSYCHIC USES

Imperial Jade is the most powerful of the jades for manifestation; luckiest in the form of a charm or dragon statue, etched with the five traditional virtues of jade: charity, modesty, courage, justice, and wisdom.

SPECIAL PROPERTIES

An Imperial Jade green dragon symbolizes the Chinese element of Wood and the springtime, set in the east of the home for new beginnings.

MYTHOLOGY AND HISTORY

Beloved by the emperors of the later dynasties since the late 1700s, when jadeite became better known in China, emerald-green Imperial Jade is also found in Guatemala and is prized by the Maya for jewelry.

Imperial Porphyry

COLORS: Red, purple, purplish-red, pinkish-violet; purple is the most prized color by ancient emperors and royalty

CRYSTAL TYPE: Igneous rock formed from magma columns, with large embedded alkaline feldspar

ZODIAC SIGN: Leo (July 23–August 23)

CANDLE COLOR: Purple

PHYSICAL: Promotes fertility; artificial insemination or IVF with a chosen donor; long life.

EMOTIONAL: unwillingness to test self in any way if success is not certain.

HOME: Attracts prosperity, health, and a sense of well-being; for welcoming a birth child who was adopted or being welcomed into the birth family if you trace birth parents.

WORKPLACE: Aiming for the top in your chosen profession; for fame and fortune in the way most desired.

CHILDREN: Displayed in the family relaxing room; for children who lack confidence in their own abilities.

ANIMALS: aristocratic pets who love being pampered.

PROTECTION: against curses, hexes, psychic attack and hostile spirits.

MAGICKAL AND PSYCHIC USES

Even the smallest Imperial Porphyry chips in a vial pendant have the same power as a larger piece; visions in meditation, dreams, and daydreaming; a charm for safe birth and, it is said, an infant who will rise high in the world.

SPECIAL PROPERTIES

Considered the rarest stone in the world, found only north of Jabal al Dukhan (meaning: "Mountain of Smoke") in the eastern desert of Egypt and recently in Colorado; not easy to track but worth the search; ask for a certificate of authenticity.

MYTHOLOGY AND HISTORY

Imperial Porphyry was the stone of ancient Egyptian pharaohs, Roman and Byzantine emperors, and popes to adorn their buildings, and to be crafted into fabulous artifacts and tiles and sarcophagi as a sign of their high status. The birthing chambers of Byzantine empresses were lined with the stone to acknowledge the newborn infant's position as a rightful possessor of royal blood.

Indicolite Quartz

COLORS: Clear or milky white (quartz); medium to dark blue (indicolite); the blue color is due to a small amount of iron

CRYSTAL TYPE: Usually indicolite or blue tourmaline, aluminum boron silicate, is enclosed within the silicon dioxide quartz; may sometimes appear as needles or a slender blue wand growing from the quartz or attached to it

ZODIAC SIGN: Libra (September 23–October 23)

CANDLE COLOR: Blue

PHYSICAL: Alleviates recurring sore throats, stammering, Tourette's syndrome in adults as well as children, autism and Asperger's in people of all ages, insomnia; addresses issues involving the bladder and kidneys.

EMOTIONAL: Eases fear of speaking out or contradicting others.

HOME: Soothes home life if an impending court case, false accusation, or investigation by an official department is pending.

WORKPLACE: Aids in finding a career that inspires passion.

CHILDREN: Boosts self-esteem for a child who is overshadowed by a very talented or outgoing sibling.

ANIMALS: Reassures a resident pet if they're feeling excluded by the family when a cute kitten or puppy comes along.

PROTECTION: Guards against emotional blackmail or fears of actual blackmail if a mistake or infidelity has been uncovered.

MAGICKAL AND PSYCHIC USES

Communication with higher guides and archangels; traveling through different planes of existence.

SPECIAL PROPERTIES

Quartz amplifies the conciliatory powers of blue tourmaline; blue tourmaline, mingled with quartz, ensures that important matters will not be swept under the rug.

MYTHOLOGY AND HISTORY

This rare, beautiful crystal unifies different people, lifestyles, and opinions that together create far more powerful energies than as separate stones. Depending on the proportion of the mix, individual crystals have slightly different emphases, but whether bought by mail order, online, or in person, you always find the right Indicolite Quartz.

Indigo Gabbro or Mystical Merlinite

COLORS: Black and white or light indigo violet, with occasional flashes of light

CRYSTAL TYPE: Quartz, feldspar, multiple trace minerals, dark magmatic rock, formed when magma cools into crystalline formations

ZODIAC SIGN: Pisces (February 19–March 20)

CANDLE COLOR: Indigo

PHYSICAL: Strengthens cells, the immune system, alkaline balance, alignment of spine, arteries, circulation; eases menopause.

EMOTIONAL: Counters a tendency to see people as either angels or demons; enables you to deal with negative emotions.

HOME: Balances yin and yang in the home, so the life force flows steadily and freely.

WORKPLACE: Enables you to accept a less-than-ideal job or workplace situation, maximizing opportunities, rather than complaining.

CHILDREN: For Indigo Children and any who find life confusing or harsh.

ANIMALS: Empowers pets who heal their owners.

PROTECTION: Shields against electromagnetic pollution, and sensitivity to negative technological emissions.

MAGICKAL AND PSYCHIC USES

Ritual magick, Wicca, clairvoyance, clairaudience, clairsentience, recall of past-life wisdom, manifestation of wishes, communication with plant spirits.

SPECIAL PROPERTIES

The stone of bridging and balancing yin and yang, darkness and light, earthly and spiritual, optimism and realism.

MYTHOLOGY AND HISTORY

Found in Madagascar and Alaska, two contrasting lands, Mystical Merlinite is named after legendary magician Merlin who may have been a fifth-century druid. Walking between the everyday and spiritual worlds, darkness and light, like the stone, Merlin balanced his human side with the divine inner seed all possess.

Indigo Kyanite

COLORS: Indigo, sometimes a very dark blue, between blue and black

CRYSTAL TYPE: Aluminum silicate, flat-bladed crystals, may contain quartz and mica; polishes well into tumbled stones or as gems; one of the rarer forms of kyanite

ZODIAC SIGN: Scorpio (October 24–November 22)

CANDLE COLOR: Indigo

PHYSICAL: Recharges pineal gland; enhances the effectiveness of psychic surgery; leads to successful surgery or other treatment for the brain, head, neck, or ears; eases migraines; for cuts, splinters, and wounds slow to heal.

EMOTIONAL: Counters a tendency to always put self-interest first; eases divided loyalties between family and partner; keeps you from lying and covering your tracks as a habitual way of reacting.

HOME: Encourages family loyalty if this has been in question or tested; repairs relationships.

WORKPLACE: Fosters business success in cases when establishing rapport is important; for conflict resolution and negotiations to remove the personal agendas and self-interest of others.

CHILDREN: In tumbled form or as jewelry for Indigo Children to help them feel more at home on Earth.

ANIMALS: For therapy and guide dogs who act as eyes, ears, and hands for their owners.

PROTECTION: Cuts through cords of spirit attachments and manipulative people.

MAGICKAL AND PSYCHIC USES

Opens or develops psychic powers, especially clairaudience, clairvoyance, and telepathy; promotes lucid dreaming; pursues astral travel in meditation or dreams to ancient temples, priest and priestess rituals; connects with elementals.

SPECIAL PROPERTIES

Encourages perseverance if the going gets tough; when justice depends on a witness telling the truth.

MYTHOLOGY AND HISTORY

Teal-colored kyanite shares many spiritual powers with indigo. Indigo Kyanite is the most spiritually oriented of the kyanites; it allows the rekindling of old dreams and makes them possible; if spiritual experiences prove elusive, Indigo Kyanite cuts through barriers of doubt and allows visions and insights to emerge naturally.

Infinite Stone

COLOR: Pale to dark green, some with gray, brown, or black

CRYSTAL TYPE: Magnesium silicate, serpentine mixed with chrysotile, a variety of patterns, including dendritic

ZODIAC SIGNS: Aries (March 21–April 20) and Pisces (February 19–March 20)

CANDLE COLOR: Pale green

PHYSICAL: Relieves chronic pain, including pain in muscles, cells, gallstones, and kidney stones; alleviates stomachache, menstrual pain, nausea, sinus congestion and headaches, migraines, skin conditions; soothes you after facial, dental, or jaw surgery.

EMOTIONAL: Aids in overcoming fears of enclosed spaces and places, and reluctance to return to life after prolonged illness.

HOME: Helps you care for a terminally ill or severely disabled relative or partner; soothes insomniac children if you need to sleep; aids in finding lost objects.

WORKPLACE: For shifts involving irregular hours or overnights.

CHILDREN: Encourages enthusiasm for simple pleasures.

ANIMALS: Supports programs to return endangered species to the wild.

PROTECTION: Shields and repairs a torn aura; deflects spite from human snakes.

MAGICKAL AND PSYCHIC USES

Experiencing what American twentieth-century psychologist Abraham Maslow called a peak experience, becoming one momentarily with all creation; Reiki attunement; linking with archangels, Earth devas, waterfalls, mountain spirits, and ley energies.

SPECIAL PROPERTIES

The stone of infinite possibility, by integrating self on every level; spontaneously heals the past, resolves the present, so as to open a future without restrictions.

MYTHOLOGY AND HISTORY

Discovered in South Africa by US mineralogist and healer Steven Roseley, named by him because of its powerful healing spiritual powers. Paler green brings gradual inner change.

Iolite or Water Sapphire

COLORS: Pale blue-purple or violet-blue; transparent

CRYSTAL TYPE: Silicate/cyclosilicate of aluminum and magnesium; gem version of Cordierite (page 139)

ZODIAC SIGNS: Pisces (February 19–March 20) and Cancer (June 22–July 22)

CANDLE COLOR: Violet or lilac

PHYSICAL: Alleviates issues with vision, disorientation brought on by migraines, Ménière's disease, insomnia, nightmares; increases pain threshold; fosters weight loss.

EMOTIONAL: Relieves fears and effects of being jinxed or cursed; brings order to a chaotic lifestyle; reduces codependency.

HOME: Attracts good health; promotes happy family outings; aids in bonding with difficult in-laws or new family members; protects family members who are absent overseas.

WORKPLACE: Enables you to settle into a new workplace if management or colleagues are resistant; encourages brainstorming.

CHILDREN: Reduces sibling rivalry or hostility toward or from a stepparent.

ANIMALS: For visually impaired animals and guide dogs for visually impaired humans; for hard-to-love animals.

PROTECTION: Reduces pressure to consume alcohol in excess, leading to addiction.

MAGICKAL AND PSYCHIC USES

Increases psychic powers; for Wicca and natural magick; goddess rituals; astral travel; placed on the third eye for visions of Knights Templar mysteries, Arthurian grail legends.

SPECIAL PROPERTIES

Encourages creativity and performing; brings independence from pressures to join a family business.

MYTHOLOGY AND HISTORY

Iolite was called the Water Sapphire and Viking compass and used by Norse sailors in navigation. They used a thin, polarizing, iolite filter lens to discover the direction of the sun on cloudy days for accurate navigation. Iolite was sacred to Ran, Viking goddess of the sea, and her husband Aegir, god of the sea.

Iolite Sunstone

COLORS: Violet/blue, mingled with milky white and with a golden shimmer; radiates distinct colors at different angles and in different lights

CRYSTAL TYPE: Found in two forms, combined in one stone or more recently as one mineral growing with or on the other; a close cousin of Cordierite (page 139); makes beautiful tumbled stones and jewelry

ZODIAC SIGN: Pisces (February 19–March 20)

CANDLE COLOR: Violet

PHYSICAL: Alleviates issues stemming from the throat and vocal cords; addresses hydrocephalus, headaches, sensitivity to light and temperature extremes.

EMOTIONAL: Eases codependency; helps overcome fears of being overshadowed or outperformed by rivals.

HOME: For living in a vehicle or boat and traveling out of state or overseas; homeschooling children while traveling.

WORKPLACE: Called the vision stone or stone of foresight for creative ideas and insights in any kind of work.

CHILDREN: Stimulates imagination and encourages a love of reading and storytelling.

ANIMALS: For telepathy to reassure pets if you will be unexpectedly late coming home.

PROTECTION: Guards against psychic and psychological hooks of guilt and obligation.

MAGICKAL AND PSYCHIC USES

Increases awareness of the presence of your guardian angels and spirit guides in your everyday life; enhances psychic powers.

SPECIAL PROPERTIES

Identifies priorities and the power to manifest these as reality in your everyday world.

MYTHOLOGY AND HISTORY

Found in Tamil Nadu in India. However, both stones are also connected with the Norse world. The Vikings wore sunstone as an amulet while traveling and iolite served as a compass in navigation. Iolite Sunstone is found in Norway and is associated with the study of ancient Asian sacred texts and is believed to provide a deep understanding of and, in some cases, insight into alternative interpretations.

Iowaite

COLORS: Rich to deep purple when containing chromium; also honey yellow, greenish-white, and bluish-green

CRYSTAL TYPE: Member of the hydrotalcite group, containing oxygen, magnesium, iron, hydrogen and chlorine; waxy, brittle

ZODIAC SIGN: Aquarius (January 21–February 18)

CANDLE COLOR: Purple

PHYSICAL: As purple chromium Iowaite, its most powerful form, relieves intense headaches, sinusitis, chemical imbalances in the brain (such as low serotonin levels, causing depression).

EMOTIONAL: Helps overcome frustration, irritability, feeling as if you're at the hands of fate and overwhelmed by life.

HOME: For leaving work problems and unfinished tasks outside the front door.

WORKPLACE: Prevents the workplace from becoming a therapy room for colleagues or employees' problems.

CHILDREN: Keeps teens from overreacting to every setback; for teaching children to take care of pets and the home.

ANIMALS: For dogs who bark at the slightest noise or someone passing the house.

PROTECTION: Guards against being pressured into instant decisions or to cut corners to meet a deadline.

MAGICKAL AND PSYCHIC USES

Meditation, in its purple form associated with the purple flame of the ascended master St. Germain, so Iowaite links with wise spirit teachers, ascended masters, and archangels.

SPECIAL PROPERTIES

The feel-good crystal, chromium Iowaite especially, reduces anxiety and creates a calm, focused, harmonious approach to life.

MYTHOLOGY AND HISTORY

Named after Sioux County, Iowa, where it was first discovered, rich chromium purple Iowaite brings balance and a sense of well-being, the yellow brings financial stability, the greenish-white balanced health, and the bluish-green fairness in work and personal life.

Iron Meteorites

COLORS: Very dark red/brownish black

CRYSTAL TYPE: Made of 90–95 percent iron, with the remainder comprising nickel and trace amounts of heavy metals, including iridium, gallium, and sometimes gold

ZODIAC SIGN: Aries (March 21–April 20)

CANDLE COLOR: Red

PHYSICAL: Boosts red blood cells, circulation, physical strength, and mobility; offers protection against radiation and the side effects of radiation therapy; promotes recovery after prolonged illness.

EMOTIONAL: Eases fear of confrontation; counters a tendency to frequently change opinions and loyalties.

HOME: Considered a gift from the deities, since this was the first form of iron available to humans and it occasionally contained gold. Iron meteorite promotes successful speculation.

WORKPLACE: A powerful symbol if you want to reach the top, but are striving against nepotism and favoritism; for starting a job where newcomers are not made to feel welcome.

CHILDREN: Teaches children about the solar system.

ANIMALS: For pets who are afraid of sudden, loud noises, such as fireworks.

PROTECTION: Guards against bullying, intimidation, and threats at any age.

MAGICKAL AND PSYCHIC USES

Fire rituals; connection with extraterrestrial forces and star systems through meditation, dreams, and visions; for urgent money or physical security spells.

SPECIAL PROPERTIES

The meteorite is affected by the land where it falls, so each one will have additional properties; for example, in the case of the Canon Diablo meteorite in Arizona, this stone will have properties of the desert, including a strong sense of everything in its own time.

MYTHOLOGY AND HISTORY

Found as Gibeon Meteorites (page 201), as the Henbury iron meteorite of Central Australia, and the Sikhote-Alin iron meteorite in eastern Russia; Iron Meteorites are traditionally regarded as the fireballs of Mars, god of war; Iron Meteorites have great affinity with Earth, so they can endow users with the fiery qualities to resolve any dilemma and reinforce our identity.

Iron Pyrites or Fool's Gold

COLOR: Brassy gold as polished nuggets; darker gold-brown; some paler and silvery; often found on beaches as gold-like flakes embedded in black iron matrix

CRYSTAL TYPE: Iron sulfide

ZODIAC SIGN: Aries (March 21–April 20)

CANDLE COLOR: Silver or gold

PHYSICAL: Addresses colds, flu, viruses, digestion, bones, red blood cells, asthma, bronchitis, skin conditions, impotence, male infertility, debilitating conditions.

EMOTIONAL: Aids in resisting controlling people attempting to provoke a reaction.

HOME: Attracts abundance; deters unwise financial decisions; reduces debt; protects against scams.

WORKPLACE: For promotion, managing, or owning a successful business; generating wealth through personal enterprise.

CHILDREN: Improves teenagers' memory for tests.

ANIMALS: Heals skin problems; useful for reptiles, especially lizards.

PROTECTION: Shields medical personnel against disease during epidemics; an amulet when you're away from home.

MAGICKAL AND PSYCHIC USES

Polished pyrites are valuable as a scrying mirror, as in Mayan and Aztec tradition, for perceiving the future, guides, and ancestors; fire rituals; ceremonies to replenish Earth's minerals. connecting with UFOs and extraterrestrials.

SPECIAL PROPERTIES

Returns malice to sender; protects against physical danger, especially hazardous activities and environmental pollutants.

MYTHOLOGY AND HISTORY

Regarded from Paleolithic times as a magickal fire stone because it emits sparks when struck; associated with fiery Mars, pyrites were valued as amulets by the ancient Greeks, Incas, and many Indigenous people in the Americas. Iron Pyrites is called fool's gold because it is often mistaken for real gold and may be found close to it.

Isis Quartz

COLORS: Clear quartz; varies in other quartzes
CRYSTAL TYPE: Quartz with at least one five-sided face (normally as the front or main face); occasionally forms the tip of a single point
ZODIAC SIGN: Cancer (June 22–July 22)
CANDLE COLOR: White

PHYSICAL: Promotes fertility, conception, IVF, artificial insemination, pregnancy, childbirth; alleviates postnatal depression, PMS, menstrual disorders, menopause, issues with HRT, concerns with breasts; regulates hormones in either sex.
EMOTIONAL: Eases midlife crises in both sexes; counters self-neglect, self-harm; comforts those who lost their mother young or were inadequately mothered; helps overcome fears of being a bad parent.
HOME: Supports single parents; Isis, ancient Egyptian mother goddess after whom the crystal was named, was the first single-parent deity.
WORKPLACE: If you are continually sidelined or passed over for promotion; aids in running a business while caring for children.
CHILDREN: For temporary or long-term fostering.
ANIMALS: Stimulates kittens or puppies who are failing to thrive.
PROTECTION: GUARDS against mind manipulation and false gurus.

MAGICKAL AND PSYCHIC USES
For Wiccan, goddess, and spiritual groups, especially all-female ones; for men and women seeking the Divine Feminine; for initiation into Wicca, magickal groups, or as a solitary practitioner; for sacred geometry.
SPECIAL PROPERTIES
A gift for a first-time mother; takes back power from those who control, abuse, or destroy confidence; weakens hold of a brainwashing cult or coven.
MYTHOLOGY AND HISTORY
The gentlest Master Crystal (see page 297), Isis crystals are associated with Isis because five was a number sacred to her; for men to reconnect with their sensitive nature after a macho, all-male, or emotionally cold upbringing.

Isua Stone

COLOR: Alternating as gray, black, tan, and beige band
CRYSTAL TYPE: Contains fossilized layers of algae, iron, iron-based minerals, and sedimentary rock, such as chert, plus rare Earth elements
ZODIAC SIGN: Scorpio (October 24–November 22)
CANDLE COLOR: Gray

PHYSICAL: Counters aging and premature aging; alleviates blood disorders, blockages, immune system issues, inherited conditions; helps with DNA health and ancestry testing.
EMOTIONAL: For those who feel lost or alone because of relocation or inner loneliness; aids in recognizing and overcoming negative past-life patterns in current relationships.
HOME: Frees you from what is no longer necessary, whether possessions, habits, activities, or unnecessary expenditures to live authentically.
WORKPLACE: For intergenerational family crafts; helps resist pressure to join a family company.
CHILDREN: Useful for those who talk about past lives; fosters an interest in history.
ANIMALS: Supports tortoises, parrots, elephants, and any other naturally long-living species.
PROTECTION: Cuts destructive emotional or psychic cords, maintaining strong personal boundaries; removes ancient curses on family or land.

MAGICKAL AND PSYCHIC USES
For accessing the Akashic records and early preliterate incarnations; traveling astrally through time and space during meditation; for Star Souls.
SPECIAL PROPERTIES
For connecting with your family ancestry to understand what has shaped you through generations; a powerful stone, so crystal practitioners must gradually attune themselves to this powerful crystal.
MYTHOLOGY AND HISTORY
Only recently discovered near Nuuk, Greenland, where another ancient stone, Nuumite, is found (see Tugtupite with Nuumite, page 486). Isua Stone contains the first life-forms and is over 3.75 billion years old.

Jadeite Jade

COLORS: Green; also white, lilac, pink, brown, red, black, orange, and yellow

CRYSTAL TYPE: Sodium aluminum silicate/pyroxene; harder than Nephrite Jade (see page 315)

ZODIAC SIGNS: Pisces (February 19–March 20) and Libra (September 23–October 23)

CANDLE COLOR: Green

PHYSICAL: Alleviates issues stemming from the kidneys, bladder, eyes, hips, knees, bed-wetting, fluid retention, blood sugar, bronchitis, cystic fibrosis, endometriosis, PMS, pregnancy, hormones.

EMOTIONAL: Addresses psychosomatic conditions; low self-esteem, rooted in childhood.

HOME: The gardener's crystal for healthy plant growth; brings mealtime blessings; jade-infused water cleanses the home.

WORKPLACE: Deters bullying, sexual harassment, and abuse of power; for human resources, call center personnel, prison officers, armed forces peacekeepers.

CHILDREN: Calms teenagers displaying aggression toward parents, teachers, and caregivers.

ANIMALS: Encourages health and long life; for pets giving birth.

PROTECTION: Protects women during and after childbirth, newborn babies, the elderly, and the vulnerable in residential care.

MAGICKAL AND PSYCHIC USES

For good luck, money rituals, anti-drought spells; cuts destructive ties; lucid dreaming; repels malicious spirits in spirit rescue.

SPECIAL PROPERTIES

Protects the possessor; if Jadeite suddenly breaks, be extra vigilant.

MYTHOLOGY AND HISTORY

Jadeite was used in Neolithic times for tools and weapons. In Mesoamerica among Indigenous people of Mexico, and Central and South America, Jadeite was carved into deity masks as early as 800 BCE; also cast into wells as offerings to the water spirits. To the Aztecs, Jadeite was sacred to Xiuhtecuhtli, the god of fire. Jadeite was named *piedra de hijada* (hip stone) during the Spanish conquest of Central and South America because it healed painful joints.

Jeremejevite

COLORS: White, colorless, blue, pale to golden yellow, yellowish-brown, greenish, pale blue to blue-green; may be mistaken for beryl, especially the blue for aquamarine; rarely violet; may be beautifully clear as a gem with few inclusions

CRYSTAL TYPE: Aluminum borate, with varying fluoride and hydroxide ions; one of the ten rarest crystals in the world, but obtainable online; mainly gem-quality or polished

ZODIAC SIGN: Virgo (August 24–September 22)

CANDLE COLOR: Green or blue

PHYSICAL: Alleviates issues stemming from the colon, pituitary gland; counters indiscriminate cell reproduction, winter epidemics, frozen or swollen limbs, childhood growth issues.

EMOTIONAL: Helps overcome dieting issues and accumulation of debt.

HOME: Prompts you to explore garage sales for treasures.

WORKPLACE: For dealing with those with a superiority complex who lack expertise but treat others as inferior.

CHILDREN: This small stone teaches children that what is of value is what is beautiful and lasting, not the latest disposable consumer goods.

ANIMALS: Aids in choosing the right pet with the best temperament from a rescue organization.

PROTECTION: Guards against missing warning signs of potential hazards or unreliable people.

MAGICKAL AND PSYCHIC USES

Spontaneously develops the innate psychic gifts that may not have been explored or which were set aside in adulthood; seeing into the future.

SPECIAL PROPERTIES

Accepting yourself as you are now, where you are, and with whom you are—with all your talents and weaknesses—rather than dreaming life away in discontentment.

MYTHOLOGY AND HISTORY

In the gem form, Jeremejevite is very powerful for healing and magick. Discovered in Siberia in 1883 as single very small crystals or microscopic grains, by the 1970s larger-face table crystals were emerging from Namibia; also now from Germany and Myanmar.

Jet

COLORS: Black, very dark brown; lustrous

CRYSTAL TYPE: Organic; lignite, fossilized wood turned into a dense form of coal

ZODIAC SIGN: Capricorn (December 22–January 20)

CANDLE COLOR: Purple

PHYSICAL: Alleviates conditions involving the skin, bites, stings, teeth, migraines, colon or bowel irritation, colds, childbirth, swelling of lower body; addresses menstruation issues in older women.

EMOTIONAL: Curbs nightmares, hallucinations, depression, panic attacks; fears of mortality.

HOME: Deters negative vibes from entering; an anti-debt crystal; protects your family while traveling.

WORKPLACE: For new business ventures; stabilizes finances during hard times; protects older workers from ageism.

CHILDREN: Keeps harm from newborn babies; offers reassurance when a relative dies.

ANIMALS: Eases the passing of old or sick pets.

PROTECTION: Guards against physical violence, jealousy, evil spirits, psychic attack, and ill-wishing; an anti-vampire crystal.

MAGICKAL AND PSYCHIC USES

Jet represents divine energies in Wicca; often worn as alternating beads with goddess amber; a doorway to the past; increases psychic powers.

SPECIAL PROPERTIES

Associated with rites of passage, Jet amulets have been discovered in prehistoric burial chambers. Generally, Jet is worn by one person and on death buried with them.

MYTHOLOGY AND HISTORY

Jet is sacred to Cybele, mother of the gods in classical mythology. Used by Viking women in spindles to sew into their husbands' battle garments with magickal chants as a source of protection. Since the Bronze Age, Jet from Yorkshire has been formed into ornaments and jewelry. It was popularized by Queen Victoria after the death of her consort, Prince Albert, in 1861. Jet was carried by sailors' wives to keep their husbands safe at sea.

K2 or Raindrop Azurite

COLORS: Silvery gray with perfectly circular blue orbs

CRYSTAL TYPE: Granite (quartz, muscovite, biotite, and sodium plagioclase) hardened, with the azurite droplets occurring following the hardening of the primary stone

ZODIAC SIGN: Sagittarius (November 23–December 21)

CANDLE COLOR: Blue

PHYSICAL: Rebalances the body; removes toxins; counters breathing difficulties, hyperventilation, altitude sickness, apnea; for revealing underlying conditions; clears up skin blemishes.

EMOTIONAL: Calms troubled emotions and overreactions, fears of aging, terror of heights.

HOME: For city dwellers to explore rural peace.

WORKPLACE: Aids in brainstorming to shape new ideas into workable outcomes; for trainers and explorers of all adventure sports.

CHILDREN: Helps overcome temper tantrums in toddlers and teens.

ANIMALS: For pets who wander or run away when off the leash.

PROTECTION: Protects you from nightmares and specters of the night during sleep travel.

MAGICKAL AND PSYCHIC USES

Increases psychic abilities; opens the doorway to the higher self and evolved spiritual guides; can be programmed for any positive purpose; offers access to the Akashic records; aids in shamanic soul retrieval to collect the fragmented self; Reiki.

SPECIAL PROPERTIES

For harmonious meetings, assemblies large and small, peaceful protests, gatherings for celebrations, or to make communal decisions.

MYTHOLOGY AND HISTORY

K2 or Raindrop Azurite is found only in the snowy peaks of Chhogori, the second-highest mountain in the world, on the Pakistani side of the mountains that border China and Pakistan. This links within the stone the powers of Earth and the heavens; a high-vibration stone that opens spiritual and angelic pathways, even to the most inexperienced.

Kakortokite

COLORS: White with small black inclusions and raspberry grains in varying proportions

CRYSTAL TYPE: Albite spar (white), arfvedsonite (black), and eudialyte (raspberry)

ZODIAC SIGN: Aquarius (January 21–February 18)

CANDLE COLOR: Dark pink

PHYSICAL: For seasonal affective disorder; addresses optic nerves and conditions leading to loss of vision, exhaustion without obvious cause, food and lactose intolerance, pancreatitis.

EMOTIONAL: Helps curb the inability to accept your real self with all your strengths and faults, so you create an illusion; aids in severing ties with destructive people for fear of being alone.

HOME: For banishing resentment by one family member for another; promotes good humor.

WORKPLACE: A stone for overcoming major difficulties, either in a business or where a company is threatened with closure or redundancies and the atmosphere is toxic.

CHILDREN: Neutralizes a situation where siblings are jealous of one another or a parent or stepparent experiences jealousy of a child's relationship with the other partner.

ANIMALS: Pets that fight for the owner's attention, especially regarding food.

PROTECTION: Guards against ties both from past worlds and present redundant obligations.

MAGICKAL AND PSYCHIC USES

The flying stone for spontaneous out-of-body experiences and planned astral travel; for shamanic journeying to upper and lower worlds.

SPECIAL PROPERTIES

Fluoresces orange; for identifying soul family members who have traveled through other lifetimes with you.

MYTHOLOGY AND HISTORY

Found in Greenland, where remarkable rocks originate, Kakortokite is a high-vibration stone to lift you to a new level of spiritual understanding and an overview of your future life path.

Kambaba Jasper, Green Stromatolite, or Crocodile Rock

COLORS: Dark with green swirls and black circles, resembling crocodile skin

CRYSTAL TYPE: Sedimentary rock, microcrystalline quartz, containing stromatolites, fossilized blue and green algae, and other primeval microorganisms

ZODIAC SIGNS: Cancer (June 22–July 22) and Capricorn (December 22–January 20)

CANDLE COLOR: Green

PHYSICAL: Boosts immunity; cleanses internal and external parasites; alleviates issues relating to the teeth, jaw, neck, skull, plus stress-related illnesses; ensures healthy pregnancy.

EMOTIONAL: Calms chronic anxiety, fears of dentistry; brings peaceful sleep.

HOME: For budgeting to ease financial stress; brings fun and laughter.

WORKPLACE: Promotes moneymaking through established careers and businesses, especially family ones; a money charm.

CHILDREN: Comforts those rejected by family or peers, or suffering bereavement.

ANIMALS: For tropical fish, exotic pets needing warmth; for rescue animals.

PROTECTION: Guards against predatory human crocodiles; allows for safe adventure vacations or deep-sea diving.

MAGICKAL AND PSYCHIC USES

Connects to ancient spirits; repels paranormal attack; for séances or ouija boards; trance meditation.

SPECIAL PROPERTIES

Prevents unnecessary change; resists troublemakers in your life; attracts the right love.

MYTHOLOGY AND HISTORY

Kambaba Jasper, dating back three billion years, is found mainly in Madagascar and South Africa. From northern Madagascar comes the myth from Lake Antagnavo. An old man was thirsty. Only one woman would help; he warned her to leave with her children when rains began. That night the village became a lake and the inhabitants crocodiles; offerings are still made to the ancestral crocodiles.

Kammererite

COLORS: Red to rose or purple, the color varying according to the amount of chromium present
CRYSTAL TYPE: Part of the chlorite mineral group, a chromium-rich version of clinochlore
ZODIAC SIGN: Pisces (February 19–March 20)
CANDLE COLOR: Silver

PHYSICAL: Bolsters male reproductive system, especially addressing delayed ejaculation; promotes female fertility and ability to carry a baby to full term if there have been previous miscarriages.
EMOTIONAL: For rigid patterns of behaving and reacting because of a strict childhood or controlling partner; for those who have escaped from a cult.
HOME: Brings the blessings of house spirits, recorded in the folklore of many lands (for example, the Swedish Tomten or house elves); if tensions are running high use Kammererite in the center of a crystal layout.
WORKPLACE: Assists adaptation to changes within the workplace; preserves your integrity.
CHILDREN: For children starting at a new school or dividing time between separated parents' homes.
ANIMALS: For rescue pets previously chained up and never exercised.
PROTECTION: Guards against psychic attack and internet trolling by resentful people.

MAGICKAL AND PSYCHIC USES
Connects with angels; increases psychic awareness; enhances telepathy, clairvoyance; speeds healing.
SPECIAL PROPERTIES
Considered one of the most healing, spiritual-awakening stones, Kammererite is unique because it possesses within the same crystal detoxifying clinochlore and energy-balancing chromium.
MYTHOLOGY AND HISTORY
Mainly found in Scandinavia, Turkey, and the United States, Kammererite works simultaneously on every level of the self, as and where needed.

Kauri Gum or Kaurilite

COLORS: Golden to golden brown
CRYSTAL TYPE: Kauri Gum is the fossilized or semifossilized, amber-like resin from the ancient New Zealand kauri trees, which is transformed into Kaurilite over thousands of years
ZODIAC SIGN: Capricorn (December 22–January 20)
CANDLE COLOR: Orange

PHYSICAL: For a long healthy life; enhances all detox programs; alleviates blood disorders, especially those brought on by bacterial infections; oxygenates the blood; counters breathing difficulties; promotes self-healing; relieves issues involving the lymphatic system.
EMOTIONAL: Helps overcome the quest for lasting youth and beauty; keeps you from giving up at the first sign of difficulty.
HOME: For restoring old buildings and streets in the neighborhood to recapture a sense of tradition.
WORKPLACE: A symbol of natural quiet authority, ideal for those who wish to lead by example and persuasion; for a new career in the golden years.
CHILDREN: For those who are always in a hurry and so accident-prone.
ANIMALS: Helps older animals, whose owners have died, to find good homes.
PROTECTION: Guards against a throwaway attitude toward anything not brand-new.

MAGICKAL AND PSYCHIC USES
Increases prophecy and prediction; offers ongoing purification of sacred places in the home, altars, and workplaces; gives visions of tree spirits and Earth devas.
SPECIAL PROPERTIES
Kauri Gum releases a floral and pine-like fragrance when rubbed; assists in combining tradition with innovation because the kauri trees are among the oldest species still extant.
MYTHOLOGY AND HISTORY
Kauri trees have existed for over 150 million years and once covered much of New Zealand before deforestation by settlers. For decades, it was very popular commercially as resin, the fossilized resin is sacred to the Maoris who call it *kupia*, found on beaches or riverbanks, near the sites of former forests that have become sand dunes or scrubland; used in making pigment for the traditional Indigenous moko tattoos and sold as jewelry and beautiful artifacts.

Keyiapo Stone

COLOR: Golden

CRYSTAL TYPE: Iron pyrites/marcasite with quartz; cluster, rare but worth seeking

ZODIAC SIGN: Aries (March 21–April 20)

CANDLE COLOR: Gold

PHYSICAL: Alleviates issues relating to the male genitourinary system, impotence, prostate, as well as female fertility, scanty or irregular menstruation; addresses a condition if nothing else is relieving it; brings a daily infusion of energy.

EMOTIONAL: Increases self-worth; overcomes fears of being alone, providing the courage to leave a bad relationship.

HOME: The stone of gold, attracting and keeping abundance in the family; for encouraging joint family investments.

WORKPLACE: Attracts opportunities and success in independent enterprises; moneymaking from hobbies, inventions, and marketing currently unused skills.

CHILDREN: Stimulates gifted children in any area of life.

ANIMALS: For winning competitions, events, breeding, and shows involving animals.

PROTECTION: Guards against free-floating anxiety and internal fears that interfere with leisure and pleasure.

MAGICKAL AND PSYCHIC USES

Gives access to the Akashic records; the universal store of wisdom, past, present, and future; a good luck charm to turn fortunes around; enhances money spells; keeps you from having frightening paranormal dreams and unwelcome spirit presences around the home.

SPECIAL PROPERTIES

For attracting wealth through speculation and being in the right place at the right time; for competitions, lottery, and games where chance plays a major part.

MYTHOLOGY AND HISTORY

An alchemist's stone, enhancing every aspect of life materially and bringing joy, health, and contentment in present life and resources; for women wishing to conceive who suffer anxiety, to hold before lovemaking.

Key or Keyhole Quartz

COLORS: Clear quartz; appears in other colored quartz

CRYSTAL TYPE: Recognized by a three- or six-sided indentation or hole in the crystal, resembling a keyhole; on the crystal surface, with stepped indentations descending in size, forms an inverted apex within the crystal

ZODIAC SIGN: Aquarius (January 21–February 18)

CANDLE COLOR: White

PHYSICAL: Pinpoints hard-to-diagnose or rare conditions, hereditary illnesses; addresses narrowing of arteries, veins, and other pathways.

EMOTIONAL: For communication difficulties, nonverbal autism and Asperger's in adults and children; those locked in their minds after trauma.

HOME: Ensures privacy from intrusive neighbors, visitors outstaying their welcome, and overly curious relatives.

WORKPLACE: Helps ferret out hidden agendas, concealed truths, and complex information; evokes a response from elusive people.

CHILDREN: For those needing extra time to master new information.

ANIMALS: Preserves endangered species by re-creating natural habitats.

PROTECTION: Guards against those attempting to read your thoughts.

MAGICKAL AND PSYCHIC USES

Accesses the universal well of wisdom—past, present, and future—past lives that explain a mysterious condition, scar, or phobia.

SPECIAL PROPERTIES

A key to unlocking traditional healing powers, discovering previously inaccessible or forgotten knowledge; useful as a worry stone.

MYTHOLOGY AND HISTORY

If you are new to crystal work, begin with a key quartz and progress to a Gateway Quartz (page 198), where a deeper indentation forms an actual gateway; aids in finding missing links, lost possessions, animals, or a person who has disappeared off the radar.

Khutnohorite or Kutnohorite

COLORS: White, pale rose, pink, light to medium brown; bubbly and botryoidal or ribbed; can resemble a feather fan or flower

CRYSTAL TYPE: Calcium manganese carbonate with magnesium and iron, part of the dolomite family; very fragile

ZODIAC SIGN: Taurus (April 21-May 21)

CANDLE COLOR: Pink

PHYSICAL: Alleviates issues stemming from the bones, teeth, acid-alkali balance, fluid retention; reduces pain caused by or made worse by stress, especially headaches (including migraines).

EMOTIONAL: For men forced into an overtly macho role by their upbringing; curbs hypochondria; counters an inability to relax.

HOME: This crystal creates calm and promotes good humor.

WORKPLACE: Aids in concentration and focus in a highly competitive, achievement-oriented workplace without being affected by the general mayhem; memorizing and communicating complex or jargon-filled material in comprehensible terms.

CHILDREN: Keep this crystal with a photo of children who find it hard to fit in at school to help them feel good about themselves.

ANIMALS: For unlovely creatures with loving natures.

PROTECTION: Guards against trying to meet others' expectations at the expense of your own needs and desires.

MAGICKAL AND PSYCHIC USES

Flower magick and divination; sound healing, especially voice and sacred chants; soul retrieval and journeying.

SPECIAL PROPERTIES

Discovering your soul purpose and accepting and loving yourself just as you are, rather than trying to attain impossible ideals.

MYTHOLOGY AND HISTORY

Originally found in 1901 in Kutná Hora, Bohemia, after which it was named, Kutnohorite is the crystal of inclusion with tolerance of those who have different fixed beliefs; helps resolve gender issues if there have been pressures to conform; keeps you from allowing anyone to make you feel inferior because you have a different lifestyle or simply aren't concerned with making money.

Kieseltuff

COLORS: Gray, green, brown, dark brown, reddish-brown, dark cream, with rings around the stone that are often black

CRYSTAL TYPE: A form of chert, very hard silicified volcanic ash

ZODIAC SIGN: Aries (March 21–April 20)

CANDLE COLOR: Red

PHYSICAL: Useful for skin imperfections and sensitivity, oily skin, acne, burns, scalds.

EMOTIONAL: For those who live in a fantasy world and find it hard to admit the truth or reality of a situation.

HOME: Shields you from burglary, fire, and those who outstay their welcome or borrow and never return; for open communication to resolve family disagreements.

WORKPLACE: For clear communication at meetings, seminars, and conference speeches; aids in overcoming dishonesty and petty pilfering within a business; keeps you from trusting those who smile and secretly make trouble.

CHILDREN: Encourages children to be truthful; for teens who have shoplifted, whether caught or not.

ANIMALS: Enables you to love a pet you were deceptively sold who grows very large or is completely different from what was originally promised.

PROTECTION: Guards against those who would deceive online or through phone calls or face-to-face meetings; protects against paranormal intrusion.

MAGICKAL AND PSYCHIC USES

Enhances divinatory readings, channeling, and mediumship, bringing close connection with spirit guides who may be ancestors.

SPECIAL PROPERTIES

A stone of being true to yourself and living authentically, even if others disapprove or do not understand; for finding new, trustworthy friends.

MYTHOLOGY AND HISTORY

Kieseltuff means "pebble" or "stone of volcanic ash." Most of the massive Moai statues on Easter Island, built between 1400 and 1650 CE, are constructed of Kieseltuff, carved from the volcano Rano Raraku, using only stone tools. The Romans also used Kieseltuff, which was a common building material in Italy as well as Germany.

Killiecrankie Diamonds

COLORS: Mainly clear and colorless; may be glacial blue or pale straw

CRYSTAL TYPE: Topaz, mistaken for diamonds, washed up on the beaches in the gravels of Killiecrankie Bay and Mines Creek on remote Flinders Island off Tasmania, Australia. They were discovered in 1810 by New South Wales mineralogist, A.W.H. Humphrey. Gem-quality may be faceted

ZODIAC SIGN: Cancer (June 22–July 22)

CANDLE COLOR: White

PHYSICAL: Alleviates emphysema, asthma, colds, bronchitis, influenza; strengthens vision; soothes and heals chronic pain.

EMOTIONAL: Helps overcome a tendency to be unwilling to make an effort because you have a sense of entitlement; assists in learning not to accept people at face value.

HOME: Aids in cherishing lasting relationships and friendships in less rewarding times.

WORKPLACE: Keeps you from relying on first impressions of people and situations; reassesses and reworks existing methods and resources for hidden benefits, rather than abandoning them.

CHILDREN: Teaches children to develop longer-lasting friendships.

ANIMALS: For persevering with hard-to-train pets.

PROTECTION: Guards against accepting offers or purchases without checking their authenticity.

MAGICKAL AND PSYCHIC USES

Rituals along the shore edge to incorporate the tides; taking a cautious approach to gurus promising instant magickal powers.

SPECIAL PROPERTIES

Killiecrankie gems are filled with the power of both sea and land; whether bought from an island gemmologist or collected and hand-polished, the energies are healing, restorative, and pure.

MYTHOLOGY AND HISTORY

A verified story is told by young Tasmanian artist Geoff Middleton of two missing huge green diamonds/topaz. Last officially recorded for the Great London Exhibition of 1851, one of the green stones was stolen by a convict, enlisted to collect specimens. This first stone was hidden on the mountain, recovered briefly years later, but lost again with the death of the finder, a descendant of the original Indigenous guide, in a rockfall in the 1960s, which Middleton witnessed. The second is rumored to be Queen Victoria's Green Fire diamond pendant. Neither stone reached the 1851 Exhibition.

Kimberlite

COLORS: Dark gray with sparkling inclusions

CRYSTAL TYPE: Igneous rock containing minerals, including chrome diopside, diamonds, enstatite, pyrope garnet, ilmenite, olivine, and phlogopite. Most famous for the tiny diamonds found within

ZODIAC SIGN: Sagittarius November 23–December 21)

CANDLE COLOR: Gold

PHYSICAL: Roots out deep-seated problems within the body, including blockages in the intestines; ensures accurate MRI, CT, and ultrasound scans; alleviates hormone imbalances, skin eruptions.

EMOTIONAL: Keeps you from feeling overburdened, buried by responsibilities, and unappreciated; eases bipolar conditions.

HOME: Helps you identify and acquire hidden treasure from attics, garage sales, and estate sales.

WORKPLACE: For all investigators, from detectives to archeologists and documentary researchers; for gaining a place on reality television or whose gifts are recognized by a talent scout.

CHILDREN: Aids those who struggle with academic subjects to shine through their often-hidden creative talents.

ANIMALS: For a female who unexpectedly defies odds by producing a beautiful, show-winning offspring.

PROTECTION: Guards against those who pretend to be genuine but intend to defraud, as well as false loves on the internet who ask for money in order to be together.

MAGICKAL AND PSYCHIC USES

Cleanses and empowers other crystals; Mother Earth's gift, especially when containing diamonds, to manifest abundance through meditation and rituals.

SPECIAL PROPERTIES

For building up stamina and success for athletes; for fitness regimens.

MYTHOLOGY AND HISTORY

Found in the Kimberly region of South Africa, famed for its diamonds, the tiny diamonds become embedded in the Kimberlite as the volcanic rock formed deep within the Earth over millennia rises to the surface through subsequent volcanic eruptions. Diamonds continue to grow within Kimberlite, even after it is mined.

King Cobra Jasper

COLORS: Resembling a king cobra skin—brown, cream, tan, white, mottled, with orbs or spheres; may appear in brighter hues, but some of these are the similar cobra jasper

CRYSTAL TYPE: Volcanic rock, silicate

ZODIAC SIGN: Scorpio (October 24–November 22)

CANDLE COLOR: White

PHYSICAL: Alleviates issues associated with circulation, liver damage, stomach upsets, excessive sex drive, blood sugar issues, vertigo, pain in the lower spine, lack of vitality, skin problems, scant or painful menstruation.

EMOTIONAL: Helps overcome the inability to cope with change; curbs indiscriminate flight-or-fight reactions.

HOME: Enables you to reassert your authority if you have rebellious teenagers or cantankerous tots.

WORKPLACE: For those in counseling and therapy work to encourage clients to take a step back and become self-motivated; for making quick decisions where there is no time for discussion.

CHILDREN: Curbs fears of snakes or crawling insects.

ANIMALS: For keeping snakes, lizards, and exotic insects.

PROTECTION: Guards against venomous words and actions of those in authority.

MAGICKAL AND PSYCHIC USES

Defensive and banishing magic; goddess rituals, sacred dance; connecting with the primal kundalini, the serpent energy coiled around the spine, for a surge of focused power manifest in the way most needed; sex magick.

SPECIAL PROPERTIES

King Cobra Jasper increases alertness for opportunity and hazards.

MYTHOLOGY AND HISTORY

Found in India and across the Indian subcontinent and Southeast Asia, as well as the southern areas of East Asia and North Africa, the king cobra is revered, though feared. The cobra is associated with reincarnation. King Cobra Jasper, brings status, nobility of purpose, and positive recognition.

Kinoite

COLORS: Light to deeper blue, always pure color

CRYSTAL TYPE: Hydrated calcium copper silicate, often found in clusters, attached to or encrusted with other minerals, such as apophyllite or dioptase

ZODIAC SIGN: Pisces (February 19–March 20)

CANDLE COLOR: Light blue

PHYSICAL: Alleviates issues stemming from wounds, infections, bruises, bones, muscles, skin tags, moles, warts, growths, cysts, teeth, vocal cords, tonsils, adenoids, sinuses, HIV.

EMOTIONAL: Overcomes restrictive upbringing and negative life experiences; reduces tendency to magnify crises and imagined slights.

HOME: For starting over again after betrayal by a family member or partner.

WORKPLACE: Enables you to make the right long-term policy and business decisions; for clear communication in avoiding misunderstandings by negotiators, company lawyers, charity administrators and staff, and civil rights workers.

CHILDREN: Encourages honesty and kindness for those less fortunate; fosters participation in charity ventures.

ANIMALS: For unloved and unlovely pets.

PROTECTION: Guards against lies, false friends, flattery, and false love.

MAGICKAL AND PSYCHIC USES

For studying magickal alphabets and tracts in their original languages; for love spells; calling love known or unknown in dreams; clairaudience through meditation or angel channeling; psychic surgery.

SPECIAL PROPERTIES

A crystal of deep, peaceful sleep; assists with mobility or physically challenging conditions or progressive illness.

MYTHOLOGY AND HISTORY

Named after the seventeenth-century Jesuit explorer Eusebio Francisco Kino, Kinoite is found in only a few locations, the most famous Christmas Mine in Arizona. A stone of love goddesses in many cultures, it represents romance, fidelity, and the love of humanity.

Klinoptilolith or Clinoptilolite

COLORS: White, whitish-gray, chalky or pale green, with pinpricks on the surface; looks cherty

CRYSTAL TYPE: Zeolite, hydrated aluminosilicate

ZODIAC SIGN: Taurus (April 21–May 21)

CANDLE COLOR: White

PHYSICAL: Eases overactive stomach and bowels when stressed, side effects of chemotherapy, radiation, and invasive tests or treatment.

EMOTIONAL: Counters the urge to treat every new acquaintance instantly as a best friend; curbs an addiction to being the center of attention and shopaholic tendencies.

HOME: Absorbs pollutants if you live near high-tension wires, a cell phone tower, or a freeway.

WORKPLACE: Makes space and time for yourself, even in the most frantic day and workplace, to avoid stress overload.

CHILDREN: Enables you to ignore peer pressure to acquire the latest designer clothes and devices.

ANIMALS: Aids in training excitable dogs not to bark or jump up at visitors or strangers if they are on a walk.

PROTECTION: Counters the effects of toxic people, so you can ignore them.

MAGICKAL AND PSYCHIC USES

For removing entities and attachments, both paranormal and earthly, who have created hooks into the aura for mind control; for Reiki.

SPECIAL PROPERTIES

A rebalancing crystal for body, mind, home, workplace, and relationships to put everything in perspective and cultivate harmony.

MYTHOLOGY AND HISTORY

This relatively new crystal, found in Russia, Turkey, Mexico, and the USA, has the power to soak up toxicity and pollution. This power came from erupting volcano plumes traveling thousands of miles and landing on Earth to be absorbed in shallow marine basins. Over many years, this pure crystalline form evolved.

Kornerupine

COLORS: Clear brown, greenish-brown, pink, yellow, brown, colorless; rarely clear emerald

CRYSTAL TYPE: Magnesium aluminum iron borosilicate hydroxide; may be faceted as a gemstone; may display cat's eye or a star effect as a gem; found as tumbled stones and raw as well as gem-quality

ZODIAC SIGN: Gemini (May 22–June 21)

CANDLE COLOR: Green

PHYSICAL: Restorative to mind and body; discourages bad habits or an unhealthy lifestyle; strengthens connective tissues; curbs infections and bacteria, especially affecting the blood; complements end-of-life care.

EMOTIONAL: For those who self-harm, who have suicidal thoughts, and who find it hard to accept help.

HOME: Clears physical clutter, major house cleans; sorting and completing unfinished paperwork; likewise, logically dealing with accumulated worries, dismissing those that will never happen.

WORKPLACE: Helps teachers acquire an air of authority and confidence if they are new to the profession or have challenging students.

CHILDREN: For parents of toddlers or teens going through a very rebellious stage; for picky eaters.

ANIMALS: Quiets barking dogs and yowling cats.

PROTECTION: Guards against bad influences, including charlatan gurus, or those who would tempt you to act unwisely.

MAGICKAL AND PSYCHIC USES

Considered a very magickal stone for manifesting urgent needs; if you're overly reliant on fortune tellers or clairvoyant readings, develops trust in personal intuition and innate psychic powers to plan the future.

SPECIAL PROPERTIES

For alleviating midlife crises, and focusing on a happy life if the right love partner has not yet come along.

MYTHOLOGY AND HISTORY

Kornerupine was first discovered in 1884 in Greenland; it is also referred to as prismatine. Sometimes mistaken for emerald, all colors of Kornerupine display pleochroism, where different colors can be seen from different viewing angles. A crystal for challenging unfair legal or official practices.

Kundalini Quartz

COLORS: Rich gold/champagne-colored or brownish-yellow; clearest often in the center
CRYSTAL TYPE: Defined as relatively large natural pure citrine, hand-mined in a remote area in the Democratic Republic of the Congo; may contain some hematite or smoky quartz, but true Kundalini Quartz is never artificially treated
ZODIAC SIGN: Aries (March 21–April 20)
CANDLE COLOR: Yellow

PHYSICAL: Strengthens the reproductive system; promotes fertility; enhances libido; restores physical strength and stamina; stimulates circulation in legs, feet, and ankles; ensures successful heart bypass surgery.
EMOTIONAL: Keeps you from giving up at the first setback; counters an inability to transform ideas into practical action.
HOME: Generates abundance and a sense of well-being, plus material and emotional security; for initiating and carrying through home improvements if others procrastinate.
WORKPLACE: Brings practical results to creative ventures and an inflow of money, resources, and contacts through networking and face-to-face as well as online direct marketing.
CHILDREN: Enables delicate children or those who have been ill for a while to regain vitality and enthusiasm for life.
ANIMALS: Returns a pet to health after an accident or injury.
PROTECTION: Guards against those who use their position for corrupt purposes.

MAGICKAL AND PSYCHIC USES
Tantric sex; Earth energy and rituals; developing intuitive senses and claircognizance, the sixth sense of psychic knowing, the Scottish kenning.
SPECIAL PROPERTIES
Awakens the kundalini energy stored at the base of the spine to rise upward through all the chakra energy centers, unblocking and energizing them, to the crown of the head.
MYTHOLOGY AND HISTORY
A crystal for making a difference in every aspect of life, with the logic and focus to devise what is workable and the determination to put it into practice; brings passion in love and for life; a travel stone for those ready for adventure.

Labradorite

COLORS: Gray-green, dark gray, black or gray-white with flashes of blue, red, gold, orange, purple, and green iridescence
CRYSTAL TYPE: Plagioclase feldspar
ZODIAC SIGN: Scorpio (October 24–November 22)
CANDLE COLOR: Burgundy red

PHYSICAL: Bolsters the immune system, vision (especially at night); alleviates bronchitis, respiratory complaints, metabolism, colds, warts, skin and hair parasites, gout, rheumatism, issues concerning menstruation, high blood pressure.
EMOTIONAL: Counters stress; overcomes dependence on others' approval, plus prescription medicines, food, alcohol, or tobacco; slows an overactive mind at night.
HOME: Brings fun back into your home if you're in a rut.
WORKPLACE: Eases changes in management or work practices; for fiction writers, playwrights, and composers; promotes positive customer relations; valuable for part-time and temporary staff.
CHILDREN: Encourages imaginative play; reduces impulsivity in children and teenagers (as well as adults).
ANIMALS: For therapy and guard dogs, especially for the visually impaired.
PROTECTION: A reflective shield against negativity, suppressing negative thoughts and fears; prevents aura attack.

MAGICKAL AND PSYCHIC USES
Enhances clairvoyance and mediumship; reopens established mediums whose gifts are blocked; shamanic rituals; trance work.
SPECIAL PROPERTIES
Enables you to remain neutral if you're asked to take sides in family disputes or workplace conflict; aids in avoiding hostile crowd situations.

MYTHOLOGY AND HISTORY
Named after Labrador, in the easternmost Canadian province; associated with Indigenous magickal practices. Older Inuit people recount how an Inuit warrior struck labradorite with his spear and created the Northern Lights. Another legend tells the first labradorite fell from the fire of the ancestors in the Aurora Borealis.

Lakelandite

COLORS: Dark greenish-gray or purple with pale cream circular inclusions

CRYSTAL TYPE: Combination of basalt and bytownite, a calcium-rich plagioclase feldspar

ZODIAC SIGN: Capricorn (December 22–January 20)

CANDLE COLOR: Gray

PHYSICAL: Alleviates issues stemming from the kidneys, spleen, stomach, skin, reproductive system, waterborne viruses, premature aging, disorientation, weight loss where gain was due to trauma.

EMOTIONAL: Curbs depression, victim mentality, insomnia, nightmares, and sleep disturbances resulting from stress; promotes anger management.

HOME: Restores security when events have caused temporary instability in daily life.

WORKPLACE: For traditional workplaces that have been in the family for generations; for those teaching sailing or water sports on inland waters.

CHILDREN: Calms anxious children afraid of outdoor activities or getting dirty.

ANIMALS: Encourages retirement for mistreated donkeys and working horses.

PROTECTION: Guards against misfortune and accidents.

MAGICKAL AND PSYCHIC USES

Dream recall; incubating dreams to bring answers or healing; past-life recall and healing from ancient times; water and Earth rituals; empowers fossils and stones found deep in the Earth; connecting with ancient Earth guardians near water.

SPECIAL PROPERTIES

Brings order out of chaos and peace to conflict; enables wise decisions to be made under pressure and enables you to resist demands for instant answers.

MYTHOLOGY AND HISTORY

Formed 480 million years ago at Coldbeck Falls in the Lake District of Cumbria, England, Lakelandite's antiquity and connection with water enables major sorrow to gently flow away in its own time, rather than forcing new beginnings.

Lamprophyllite

COLORS: Golden yellow to deep brown; pearly

CRYSTAL TYPE: Titanium silicate; usually found as sprays, needles, or blades

ZODIAC SIGN: Pisces (February 19–March 20)

CANDLE COLOR: Yellow

PHYSICAL: Addresses frequent stomach upsets caused or made worse by stress; alleviates burns, scalds, skin inflammation; valuable for kidney infections and kidney stones; eases cystitis and genitourinary infections; reduces high cholesterol.

EMOTIONAL: Enables you to tolerate noise or crowds; counters dislike of eating in public and socializing outside the home.

HOME: Brings comfort in times of distress; offers insulation against excessive noise and boisterous behavior from younger family members or neighbors.

WORKPLACE: Aids in putting into practice ideas to improve efficiency, mastering new skills needed to keep pace with workplace changes; identifies when tact and discretion are needed.

CHILDREN: Especially in the star formation, a wonderful Christmas or yule centerpiece; a year-round display in the home for inspiring unimaginative, overly practical children to develop their creativity.

ANIMALS: Encourages sedentary pets to take more exercise.

PROTECTION: against unkind words and actions, whether intentional or caused by lack of tact.

MAGICKAL AND PSYCHIC USES

For prophecy during divination, premonitions and predictions; automatic writing and psychic artistry to draw auras, clients' angels, guides and ancestors who are surrounding them; trance meditation.

SPECIAL PROPERTIES

For those who would like to write and publish a book, especially channeled from angels or wise guides or their life or family ancestral story.

MYTHOLOGY AND HISTORY

Similar to Astrophyllite (page 41); also called pyrophyllite, Lamprophyllite is frequently purchased as a collector's piece, especially in its radiating star form; occasionally a gemstone or polished pebble, ideal for healing; brings radiance and unlimited potential to any person or setting. The star formations are found on the Sengischorr Mountain in Russia, usually in a matrix of eudialyte.

Lapis Lazuli or Lapis Lazula

COLORS: Rich medium to royal blue, purplish-blue, with gold flecks (pyrites)

CRYSTAL TYPE: Metamorphic rock, formed by multiple minerals, including lazurite, sodalite, calcite, and pyrite

ZODIAC SIGN: Libra (September 23–October 23)

CANDLE COLOR: Royal blue

PHYSICAL: Addresses issues relating to the endocrine system, nervous system, recurring headaches, migraines, ears, nasal passages, eyes, throat, vocal cords, thyroid, blood pressure.

EMOTIONAL: Aids in developing self-reliance and resistance to setbacks; curbs free-floating anxiety, depression, an inability to express your feelings.

HOME: Brings contentment and family loyalty; for overworked mothers.

WORKPLACE: Prompts promotion, leadership; inspires the trust of others; counters unfair dismissal, accident claims, or compensation; useful for writers, journalists, data analysts, psychologists, and psychotherapists.

CHILDREN: Valuable for gifted children; those with autism, Asperger's syndrome, Tourette's syndrome, or communication difficulties; cleft palate.

ANIMALS: For show or competition animals; for high-strung pets.

PROTECTION: Guards against envy and spite from rivals.

MAGICKAL AND PSYCHIC USES

Accessing Akashic records through meditation; ceremonial magick; ancient Egyptian rituals; astrology, ancient goddess traditions; night magick, for Star People; prophetic dreams.

SPECIAL PROPERTIES

For wealth, fame through creativity, auditions, online promotion, lucrative advertising blogs, reality television shows; useful before performances.

MYTHOLOGY AND HISTORY

Lapis was among the first gemstones used as jewelry. The Sumerians believed lapis contained the spirit of deities. The ancient Egyptians dedicated it to the star goddess Nut, considering it protective as an Eye of Horus amulet or powdered around the eyes. Michelangelo reputedly used lapis pigment in the Sistine Chapel frescoes. Lapis Lazuli is the stone of truth, justice, integrity, lasting love, and friendship.

Larimar or Pectolite

COLORS: Light, sky, or deep blue; occasionally turquoise; streaked with white and sometimes red spots

CRYSTAL TYPE: Pectolite, chain silicate of volcanic origin

ZODIAC SIGN: Pisces (February 19–March 20)

CANDLE COLOR: Silver

PHYSICAL: Addresses issues stemming from the thyroid, thymus, infections, fevers; ensures successful treatments involving heat, light, water, acupuncture, and acupressure; regulates chemical imbalances.

EMOTIONAL: Overcomes fear of doctors, hospitals, injections, and surgery; aids in managing anger issues; eases post-natal depression.

HOME: Heals disagreements between people with strong personalities.

WORKPLACE: Enables you to function effectively despite threatened job losses, while remaining alert to alternatives; for personnel working in call centers, customer service, public relations, and medicine.

CHILDREN: Eases communication and emotional difficulties.

ANIMALS: Calms pets frightened by other animals or terrified of veterinary treatment.

PROTECTION: Removes negative entities and spirits playing mind games.

MAGICKAL AND PSYCHIC USES

Amplifies dolphin healing energies through music based around dolphin or ocean sounds; cleansing/empowering other crystals or artifacts, telepathy, accessing Akashic wisdom; calling a past-life soul mate.

SPECIAL PROPERTIES

The stone of inner and outer peace, in people, places, or the world.

MYTHOLOGY AND HISTORY

Larimar is a variety of blue pectolite, found only in the Dominican Republic, created millions of years ago through volcanic activity. Larimar was first used as jewelry by Indigenous Tainos people; said to reflect the blue of Caribbean seas. Larimar is called the Atlantis stone because it is believed to channel wisdom from the lost continent.

Larvakite, Larvikite, or Norwegian Moonstone

COLORS: Black-gray, blue-gray, gray, with sheen or iridescent color flashes, often silvery blue, giving rise to its folk name, Norwegian moonstone

CRYSTAL TYPE: Iridescent variety of syenite, containing feldspar, pyroxene, mica, and amphibole

ZODIAC SIGN: Sagittarius (November 23–December 21)

CANDLE COLOR: Silver

PHYSICAL: Addresses issues relating to high blood pressure, brain stem, and after strokes, heart attack, and thrombosis; alleviates concerns with the lungs, PMS, menopausal hot flashes, skin, healthy weight loss.

EMOTIONAL: Counters excessive mood swings, triggered by pregnancy, PMS, or, perimenopause; eases intense love that clouds your judgment; promotes inner transformation.

HOME: Helps if you are struggling to combine learning with full-time work or caring for a family.

WORKPLACE: Keeps emotions and personalities from intruding on business; aids in achieving goals faster than anticipated; for teachers of children with learning or behavioral difficulties.

CHILDREN: Useful for hormonal teenagers; prevents overreaction to everyday frustrations.

ANIMALS: For pets finding training programs difficult.

PROTECTION: Counteracts overexposure to artificial stimulants, harsh lighting, and music; ensures safety while traveling.

MAGICKAL AND PSYCHIC USES

Reverses magick spells; returns hexes or curses; connections with deceased relatives, spirit guides, and past lives in sleep; recalling dream messages; healing dreams; links with urban nature spirits; meditation.

SPECIAL PROPERTIES

For putting plans into action where there has been procrastination; a worry stone to absorb anxiety; telling true friends from false.

MYTHOLOGY AND HISTORY

Larvikite, an igneous rock named after the town of Larvik, Norway, where it was first found, is the Norwegian national stone. Its mixture of ornamental, practical, and spiritual functions links everyday life with other dimensions.

Laser Quartz

COLORS: Usually clear quartz, often with inclusions or striated; may appear to look foggy inside

CRYSTAL TYPE: A long, slender, quartz, wand-like crystal with small faces at the termination. Wider at the base than at the tip; may have three-sided points at the top or a rounded point resembling a finger

ZODIAC SIGN: Aries (March 21–April 20)

CANDLE COLOR: Gold

PHYSICAL: Aids in recovering from surgery, laser or radiation treatment, cuts, wounds, lesions; offers pain relief and whole-body healing.

EMOTIONAL: Counters a tendency not to leave behind past sorrows; keeps you from clinging to destructive habits.

HOME: Protects home and precious items if you're going away, and laptops and smartphones you carry with you daily.

WORKPLACE: Directs (clockwise) and deflects (counterclockwise) energies where they're most needed for incisive decision making.

CHILDREN: As a wish wand for birthdays and special occasions; for Star Children.

ANIMALS: Enables pets to appear their best when competing in shows.

PROTECTION: Creates a personal exclusion zone of light around you against those who would do you harm.

MAGICKAL AND PSYCHIC USES

Associated with wands used for magick in ancient Lemuria and Atlantis and with temple priests and priestesses, wizards, and witches throughout history.

SPECIAL PROPERTIES

For cutting ties with destructive situations, or relationships going nowhere; removing unwanted spirit beings from your aura.

MYTHOLOGY AND HISTORY

Rare lightning-strike jagged markings, on the surface or included, amplify the powers of the laser quartz. A laser wand will empower other crystals; keep it with amethyst, rose quartz, or jade if the energies feel too intense.

Lava

COLORS: Brown, gray or black, also blue

CRYSTAL TYPE: Volcanic rock; if rough and pockmarked, contains animus energies and smoother, anima energies (see also Pumice Stone, page 375)

ZODIAC SIGN: Aries (March 21–April 20)

CANDLE COLOR: Red

PHYSICAL: Pointed lava draws out pain; alleviates chronic skin conditions, rashes, allergies; promotes fertility, energy resurgence; propels you to fight back when illness is life-limiting.

EMOTIONAL: Curbs lethargy, hopelessness, and destructive emotional attachments.

HOME: Protects your home from intruders, lightning, fires, accidents in the kitchen or involving electricity or gas; deters relatives who constantly cause quarrels.

WORKPLACE: Protects against hectoring bosses, cliques, gossip, and troublemakers; overcomes long-term unemployment; aids in getting a break toward the big time.

CHILDREN: Sends protection to children in war zones or refugee camps

ANIMALS: Helps those whose habitats are threatened by deforestation or industrialization.

PROTECTION: Shields against perpetually angry people, domestic violence, and those creating crises for attention.

MAGICKAL AND PSYCHIC USES

For candle, fire rituals, and fire elementals; wards off paranormal attack while asleep and nocturnal astral attacks from humans; a good luck charm.

SPECIAL PROPERTIES

Rapid positive transformation and manifestation of desires; for fame and fortune; revives passionate love and spontaneous lovemaking where anxiety is blocking desired conception.

MYTHOLOGY AND HISTORY

Lava is sacred to Pele, Hawaiian goddess of volcanoes. Once healing temples made of lava rock were dedicated to her and altars are still set up near lava streams; also carried by Native North Americans to give courage and strength.

Lavender Angelite

COLORS: Pale lavender; sometimes veined with white wing markings

CRYSTAL TYPE: Found in its raw state in a grainy matrix, but most useful as a tumbled stone; rare; anhydrite-sulfate, the purple is due to manganese

ZODIAC SIGN: Pisces (February 19–March 20)

CANDLE COLOR: Lavender

PHYSICAL: Alleviates chronic fatigue, immobile or painful muscles and joints, respiratory illness, bites and stings.

EMOTIONAL: Curbs constant fear of loss or attack, anger toward others perceived to invade your personal space; eases mood swings; counters free-floating anxiety that intensifies in any new situation.

HOME: A good luck stone to turn fortunes around; for buying a home with someone with whom you are not emotionally involved.

WORKPLACE: For making money in a people-centered, therapeutic, or healing business; working in a family or love partner enterprise, where one person tends to take control; aids in keeping an office affair secret.

CHILDREN: For teens who have dabbled with the occult or ouija boards, to free themselves from paranormal threats or spiteful peers who use amateur demonology to control them.

ANIMALS: Sends distressed spirit animals to the light.

PROTECTION: Guards against haunted places, poltergeists, ghostly sexual predators, and removes restless spirits from the home or workplace.

MAGICKAL AND PSYCHIC USES

For higher spiritual connections than even blue angelite, connecting with archangels, especially Archangel Zadkiel, angel of truth, spiritual powers, crystals, and herbs.

SPECIAL PROPERTIES

Both soothes and energizes as is most needed; a crystal that links with the higher self or unchanging soul that travels through many lifetimes and increases awareness of our personal divinity.

MYTHOLOGY AND HISTORY

Also known as lavender anhydrite, Lavender Angelite enhances celebrations on the seasonal change points, equinoxes, solstices, and full moons whether private, coven, healing group, or public gatherings; links with those who, through the centuries, have connected with the land and cosmos at energy shift points.

Lavender Jade

COLORS: Shades of lavender, including pale and pinkish lavender, the color due to manganese. Brighter shades may be dyed
CRYSTAL TYPE: Jadeite, sodium aluminum silicate
ZODIAC SIGN: Libra (September 23–October 23)
CANDLE COLOR: Lavender

PHYSICAL: Alleviates headaches, migraines, visual disturbances, neuralgia, toothache, heart pains, inflammation, issues involving the nervous system; counteracts cells that attack one another.
EMOTIONAL: Keeps you from being perpetually angry, irritable, cynical, or sarcastic; fends off panic attacks, fear of elevators.
HOME: Calls on your angels and guardians to take unfriendly spirits to the light, if you move into or stay in a haunted property.
WORKPLACE: Useful for working at healing festivals and psychic fairs to establish healing space boundaries.
CHILDREN: For children with ADHD, Tourette's, autism, or Asperger's to learn strategies to counteract excessive reactions.
ANIMALS: Valuable for overactive dogs who live in apartments.
PROTECTION: Guards against the evil thoughts of others directed at us.

MAGICKAL AND PSYCHIC USES
Prayer, sound healing; connection between inner divinity and the higher realms of spirit, channeled through automatic writing, dreams, or waking visions.
SPECIAL PROPERTIES
Lavender Jade guides you to the right teachers, mentors, and sources of reliable spiritual information.
MYTHOLOGY AND HISTORY
The most spiritual of the jade, Lavender Jade is associated with the energies of the angels and archangels, the violet spiritual flame of the ascended master St. Germain, and Kwan Yin, the Chinese and Tibetan Buddhist mother of compassion.

Lazulite

COLORS: Azure blue, dark, pale blue, or bluish-green
CRYSTAL TYPE: Hydrous magnesium aluminum phosphate; also as inclusions in quartz
ZODIAC SIGN: Libra (September 23–October 23)
CANDLE COLOR: Deep blue

PHYSICAL: Alleviates pain of burns, scalds, sunburn, bruises, teeth and gums (especially wisdom teeth), thyroid, lymph glands, liver, pineal gland, bones; counters food intolerances.
EMOTIONAL: Overcomes addictive patterns and compulsions; restores belief in people after childhood abuse or neglect; eases midlife crises.
HOME: For settling family disputes and preventing relatives from using favoritism; overcoming sibling rivalry at any age; keeping rebellious teenagers safe.
WORKPLACE: Bolsters your authority if you're constantly undermined by someone with less ability but higher status; for counselors, mediators, psychologists, psychotherapists, team leaders, life coaches, and human resources officers.
CHILDREN: Promotes healthy growth; mitigates communication disorders and hyperactivity exacerbated by additives.
ANIMALS: Eliminates negative behavior patterns in a rescue animal or a badly trained horse.
PROTECTION: Guards against unjust authority, officialdom, and religious intolerance.

MAGICKAL AND PSYCHIC USES
For peace rituals to influence world leaders; love spells for increasing commitment; as a channel for intuition.
SPECIAL PROPERTIES
Called the negotiator's stone, for a satisfactory outcome in legal or tax disputes, court cases, disciplinary hearings, pay-raise or working-condition discussions, trade-union meetings, discrimination arbitration; useful when entering politics and making leadership bids.
MYTHOLOGY AND HISTORY
According to legend, Lazulite, called the stone of heaven, was given to the world by King Solomon so that disagreements might be settled not by fighting but through compromise and mutual respect.

Lemon Calcite

COLORS: Lemon, though it may appear as other yellow shades (including with a green tinge); much more translucent and glowing than lemon chrysoprase, but not as clear as lemon quartz

CRYSTAL TYPE: Calcium carbonate, a recent discovery from Pakistan, already being shaped into tumbled stones, spheres, jewelry, and artifacts; when etched on the surface, Lemon Calcite enables rapid lateral thinking through access to ancient sources of wisdom

ZODIAC SIGN: Gemini (May 22–June 21)

CANDLE COLOR: Lemon yellow

PHYSICAL: Alleviates colds, coughs, sore throats; promotes healthy weight, especially if you tend to engage in rushed grazing.

EMOTIONAL: Helps overcome a tendency to hold on to resentment long after the event and after the perpetrator has gone from your life.

HOME: For health, wealth, the cleansing of lingering resentment or negativity after a hostile visitor or neighbor has gone or in the wake of any family quarrels.

WORKPLACE: Aids in avoiding being dragged into workplace pettiness and troublemaking; for increased logic, memory, focus, and concentration; swift and accurate decision making.

CHILDREN: Gives courage to those who are hesitant to make decisions or choices.

ANIMALS: For pets with a poor sense of direction, placed on a collar to guide them home.

PROTECTION: Guards against spite, jealousy, lies, and gossip.

MAGICKAL AND PSYCHIC USES
Removes hexes, curses, and jinxes; for magickal manifestation using the mind and words while focusing on the stone; a charm for success in tests, especially written driving tests or oral language examinations.

SPECIAL PROPERTIES
Avoiding tricksters and those who use hard luck stories to drain you of money, time, and resources.

MYTHOLOGY AND HISTORY
A stone for successful short-term vacations; like all lemon stones ruled by Mercury, Lemon Calcite enhances wise speculation, gambling, and games of chance involving rapid assessment and calculations.

Lemon or Citron Chrysoprase

COLORS: Lemon yellow to yellow-green, light-yellow with brown veining

CRYSTAL TYPE: Sometimes a yellow shade of green chrysoprase (chalcedony); often with inclusions of nickel-rich magnesite, magnesium carbonate

ZODIAC SIGN: Gemini (May 22–June 21)

CANDLE COLOR: Lemon yellow

PHYSICAL: Alleviates morning sickness during pregnancy, motion sickness, diarrhea, food-related headaches, issues involving the liver, cholesterol, bile duct; promotes healthy weight loss, visual acuity, fertility following contraception.

EMOTIONAL: Offers freedom from emotional blackmail, manipulation, and mind games.

HOME: Deters unfriendly neighbors; prevents family members from taking advantage of you.

WORKPLACE: Ferrets out a scheme if someone is plotting against you; for focused decision making.

CHILDREN: Reduces night terrors and sleepwalking in younger children; counteracts bad influences on teens.

ANIMALS: For pets jealous of a new human companion or animal.

PROTECTION: Guards against spite, envy, and deception, as well as urban hazards while traveling at night.

MAGICKAL AND PSYCHIC USES
Breaks ill-wishing and curses, by casting the stone into flowing water.

SPECIAL PROPERTIES
For tackling legal problems, delays in relocation, tax audits, compensation claims. For studying history, psychology, sociology, or philosophy to discover the meaning of life.

MYTHOLOGY AND HISTORY
Alexander the Great wore a chrysoprase on his belt for victory. Legend has it that while he was resting after an Egyptian battle, a cobra stung the stone, saving his life. The stone was lost, and he never won another major campaign. True Citron Chrysoprase (magnesite) is found in western Australia, an Indigenous stone of power and healing.

Lemon Quartz or Ouro Verde

COLORS: Pale yellow, lemon, golden, yellow-green

CRYSTAL TYPE: Silicon dioxide/quartz; occurring naturally, the yellow due to iron; many Lemon Quartz crystals are metamorphosis quartz treated by gamma radiation, a fast process that does not leave traces of radiation. Properties remain the same

ZODIAC SIGN: Gemini (May 22–June 21)

CANDLE COLOR: Lemon yellow

PHYSICAL: A detoxifier, addresses nausea, motion sickness, diabetes, lingering colds, fungal skin and nail infections, issues involving the bladder, bile duct, and memory; promotes healthy weight loss, convalescence.

EMOTIONAL: Aids in overcoming pessimism and self-defeating attitudes; reduces cravings for cigarettes; eases food-related issues involving binge and fasting.

HOME: Brings good fortune to the home and fresh-flowing energies to even a small apartment.

WORKPLACE: Prevents unprofessional friendships and office romances from interfering with efficiency.

CHILDREN: For coping calmly with tests and memorizing information if concentration is difficult.

ANIMALS: Enables therapy animals to ignore distractions.

PROTECTION: Shields against spite, gossip, envy, and human snakes.

MAGICKAL AND PSYCHIC USES

Repels psychic attack, curses, hexes, mind control, and psychic manipulation; for ghost investigations in unfamiliar settings or where there is known poltergeist activity.

SPECIAL PROPERTIES

Making successful instant decisions regarding investments and speculation; acquiring fast money in an emergency.

MYTHOLOGY AND HISTORY

Ouro Verde is Portuguese for "green-gold," after the color of the natural stone found only in the Bocarica Brazilian mine. Lemon Quartz acts faster than citrine for tests or interviews where you feel unprepared, and helps you resist flattery and unwise temptation.

Lemurian Golden Opal

COLORS: Golden yellow; not a precious opal so no play of colors

CRYSTAL TYPE: Hydrated silica

ZODIAC SIGN: Pisces (February 19–March 20)

CANDLE COLOR: Gold

PHYSICAL: Eases restricted flow of circulation; mends breaks in transmitting vital signals within the nervous system; addresses gallstones.

EMOTIONAL: Counters self-defeating thoughts and actions; helps overcome procrastination that keeps you from bringing plans to fruition.

HOME: Fills the home with radiance on the darkest and coldest days.

WORKPLACE: Gives you authority and leadership qualities whatever your current position; aids in making wise, calm decisions when others waver.

CHILDREN: For a love of crystals and instinctive crystal healing abilities from a relatively young age.

ANIMALS: Increases telepathy with pets.

PROTECTION: Guards against paranormal visitations who do not come from the light.

MAGICKAL AND PSYCHIC USES

Identifying and removing past-life issues; clairvoyance; lucid dreaming, dream recall, and astral travel to ancient lands, such as Lemuria, in sleep and trance meditation.

SPECIAL PROPERTIES

Brings connection with ancient Lemurian wisdom. Lemuria is believed to have existed fourteen thousand years ago, a source of the wisdom of indigenous people worldwide. Madagascar is the only source of golden opal, a land linked with the Lemurians. Legend has it that the holy people of the Lemurian culture had foreknowledge of the flood and stored information in crystals. These crystals were taken deep within the Earth; certain crystals such as Lemurian Golden Opal are especially powerful transmitters of this wisdom.

MYTHOLOGY AND HISTORY

Lemurian Golden Opal breaks down barriers between the human, animal, plant, and stone kingdoms, creating a sense of being one with all life-forms.

Lemurian or Inca Jade

COLORS: Dark green, gray, dark green with black, black, the proportion of each of its minerals determining its color; called shadow Lemurian jade in its gray/green shades and midnight Lemurian in the darker colors

CRYSTAL TYPE: Jadeite, pyrite, and quartz; fine pyrite lines or golden flecks distinguish this jade from black jade and identify it as Lemurian

ZODIAC SIGN: Virgo (August 24–September 22)

CANDLE COLOR: Dark Green

PHYSICAL: Alleviates heart failure and cardiac irregularities, illnesses or weakness associated with aging; strengthens bones and the immune system; promotes recovery from illnesses; enables effective management of chronic conditions; for end-of-life care and a peaceful passing.

EMOTIONAL: Curbs unfinished business that holds back progress; eases trauma after long-term abuse.

HOME: For developing self-sufficiency and use of natural forms of energy; creating a beautiful, environmentally sound indoor or outdoor garden.

WORKPLACE: Allows for survival through an economic downturn by finding new outlets and adapting skills.

CHILDREN: Helps children to appreciate what they have and not constantly crave new possessions.

ANIMALS: For city pets to maintain or regain a connection with nature.

PROTECTION: Darker shades of Lemurian quartz useful for cutting psychic cords with destructive people and intrusive spirits.

MAGICKAL AND PSYCHIC USES
For connection with the ancient wisdom and the world of the Incas; for Earth Mother rituals originally dedicated to the Andean Earth Mother Pachamama who regulated the seasons; enhances shamanism.

SPECIAL PROPERTIES
For safe travel to distant or remote places; connection soul to soul with a partner, however physically distant.

MYTHOLOGY AND HISTORY
Lemurian Jade is found only in one mine near Lima in Peru. It was sacred to the Incas, considered protective against attack, illness, and evil spirits. It brings closer harmony with nature, even in a city, and makes connection with our higher self easier.

Lemurian Seed Crystal

COLORS: Colorless, sometimes with a reddish glow or smoky; also pink

CRYSTAL TYPE: Frosted with horizontal striations on at least one side

ZODIAC SIGN: Aquarius (January 21–February 18)

CANDLE COLOR: White

PHYSICAL: Promotes whole-body healing; improves quality of life for those with severe, chronic, or degenerative conditions; relieves pain; bolsters the immune system; works small miracles, especially for those in comas.

EMOTIONAL: A light in the darkness; valuable for witnesses of murder, terrorism, or violent crimes; alleviates post-traumatic stress, past-life trauma.

HOME: Aids in caring for a chronically ill or disabled family member at home or if you are sick or disabled yourself.

WORKPLACE: For those working voluntarily or professionally for charity and peace organizations; teachers of spirituality, yoga, tai chi, qi gong, meditation; spiritual life coaches, anthropologists.

CHILDREN: Useful in a magick wand for special occasions to grant wishes.

ANIMALS: For pets who are old souls.

PROTECTION: Guards against those who denigrate spiritual beliefs.

MAGICKAL AND PSYCHIC USES
For visions of lost worlds and Indigenous spiritual traditions; past lives through inducing light meditative trances.

SPECIAL PROPERTIES
Each crystal connects with all other Lemurian crystals worldwide, linking Star People with their celestial home; helps access universal sources of wisdom.

MYTHOLOGY AND HISTORY
Lemurian Seed Crystals are associated with the legendary lost land of Lemuria, whose wisdom is regarded as the source of the spirituality of Indigenous peoples worldwide. Legend has it that the Lemurian holy people stored information in crystals to keep it safe in the face of the approaching great flood.

Leopardskin Jasper or Leopardskin Rhyolite

COLORS: Brown, gray, dark sandy with brown or black leopard-like spots

CRYSTAL TYPE: Silicate; rhyolite with glassy inclusions, formed by molten magma from a volcanic eruption

ZODIAC SIGNS: Gemini (May 22–June 21), Virgo (August 24–September 22), and Scorpio (October 24–November 22)

CANDLE COLOR: Yellow

PHYSICAL: Promotes fertility, pregnancy, postoperative recovery; addresses chronic health conditions, skin problems, bites, stings.

EMOTIONAL: Eases post-traumatic stress disorder, shock; increases pleasure during lovemaking; counters animal phobias.

HOME: Protects your family from outside threats and bad influences if you live in a dangerous or hostile area.

WORKPLACE: Cultivates innovative projects; fosters decisive action; enables you to assert authority, fight injustice, be in the right place at the right time.

CHILDREN: Strengthens links between animals and children; stops young children from teasing pets.

ANIMALS: Conserves endangered big cats; champions the fight against animal cruelty; enhances telepathic communication with pets.

PROTECTION: Lowers psychological and physical profile when confronted by danger.

MAGICKAL AND PSYCHIC USES

Connects with power totem animals; a shaman's stone for astral travel to other realms; four winds rituals for swift change.

SPECIAL PROPERTIES

Makes you feel younger and energetic; encourages spontaneity and breaking through stifling convention.

MYTHOLOGY AND HISTORY

Also called the jaguar stone, brings courage to shape life your way; overcomes opposition to love by family or community; found throughout the world including the USA, Central and South America, Australia, Africa, and Russia.

Lepidocrocite

COLORS: Yellow, red, brown, also deep red to black, sometimes scarlet

CRYSTAL TYPE: Iron oxide hydroxide; more commonly sold as tumbled stones within clear quartz or amethyst

ZODIAC SIGN: Sagittarius (November 23–December 21)

CANDLE COLOR: Red

PHYSICAL: Alleviates issues stemming from the iris, reproductive system, heart, lungs, blood (including excessive bleeding); eases side effects of conventional cancer treatment.

EMOTIONAL: Mitigates excessive hunger due to stress; boosts confidence after a serious illness, accident, or trauma.

HOME: Lepidocrocite included in quartz or amethyst or a small piece of the mineral in a pouch reduces aloof or unfriendly behavior by neighbors or parents in the schoolyard in a new area.

WORKPLACE: For stamina and alertness at work if you are sleep-deprived.

CHILDREN: Calms classroom hyperactivity, caused by uninspiring teaching.

ANIMALS: For unresponsive rescue animals.

PROTECTION: Drives away negative energies and entities.

MAGICKAL AND PSYCHIC USES

Lepidocrocite in quartz or amethyst increases communication with heavenly realms; helps Reiki therapists reach the source of a problem; removes blockages in rebirthing sessions and offers safe astral travel; included in clear quartz for accurately foretelling the future.

SPECIAL PROPERTIES

All Lepidocrocite can be programmed for any positive purpose; for building and maintaining love if a couple is having communication difficulties.

MYTHOLOGY AND HISTORY

Lepidocrocite included within quartz amplifies and speeds the effects of the mineral; amethyst softens and makes results more gradual. Lepidocrocite is also one of the seven minerals in the crystal Super Seven (page 466). It brings a sense of security at times of transition.

Lepidolite

COLORS: Lilac, lilac-gray, rose, purple; shimmering
CRYSTAL TYPE: Silicate; mica containing varying amounts of lithium
ZODIAC SIGN: Aquarius (January 21–February 18)
CANDLE COLOR: Lilac

PHYSICAL: Alleviates nerve-related disorders, irregular heartbeat, joint pain, cramps, aftereffects of anesthesia, PMS, hormonal imbalances, dementia, Alzheimer's, digestive issues.
EMOTIONAL: Counters overdependence on others for emotional well-being, stress-induced psychosomatic illnesses, long-standing weight issues, addictions, PTSD.
HOME: Overcomes obsessions about germs and lack of cleanliness, fears of letting children play outdoors or take risks.
WORKPLACE: Insulates you from constant chatter from colleagues, a loud public address system, or constantly piped-in music.
CHILDREN: For adult children who return home after college and show no signs of moving on; calms tantrums and hyperactivity.
ANIMALS: Comforts pets who bark or yowl constantly if left home alone.
PROTECTION: Guards against overwhelming fears of accident and mortality in self or loved ones.

MAGICKAL AND PSYCHIC USES
Each Lepidolite crystal is believed to have a keeper who offers protection to the owner of the stone; the right crystal will find you.
SPECIAL PROPERTIES
Lepidolite removes self-imposed obstacles and redundant voices of discouragement from the past, standing in the way of fulfilling your dreams.
MYTHOLOGY AND HISTORY
The feel-good stone to reduce anxiety and the sense that you're "running on empty," especially for women who try to do too much while remaining nurturing. Lepidolite offers instant relaxation. An Earth-calming stone as well, Lepidolite in a grid or layout adjusts disturbed Earth energies and subterranean ley lines.

Lepidolite in Quartz

COLORS: Depends on the color of the lepidolite and its proportion to the quartz; may be predominantly clear (quartz), white, pinkish-maroon, purple, lavender, dark violet, or pink, especially if there is also pink tourmaline included; silver flecks in the lepidolite
CRYSTAL TYPE: Lepidolite flakes or more solid inclusions within the quartz or lepidolite growing on the quartz, sometimes both at the same time; quartz as silicon dioxide and lepidolite, lithium aluminum mica
ZODIAC SIGN: Libra (September 23–October 23)
CANDLE COLOR: Purple

PHYSICAL: Promotes mobility and motor skills; counters dyspraxia; enhances acupuncture, acupressure; mitigates gradual loss of vision, aftereffects of anesthesia.
EMOTIONAL: Curbs eating disorders; boosts your ability to distinguish between fantasies and what is realistic, given effort.
HOME: For enjoying the home and leisure time more, even if that means leaving chores undone or enlisting help; for resisting children's ploys of playing one parent off against the other.
WORKPLACE: Makes rest areas more comfortable and relaxing; for avoiding pressure from others or yourself to work throughout the day.
CHILDREN: Placed in the bedroom of newborn babies, eases the transition into the world, especially if the birth was traumatic.
ANIMALS: Creates for a pet an undisturbed place inaccessible to children if the animal is becoming distressed by noise.
PROTECTION: Guards against energy leaking from or being drawn from the aura by others.

MAGICKAL AND PSYCHIC USES
Shamanism by traveling through the crystal; goddess rituals for men and women; manifesting wishes and dreams with the combined and heightened power of the stones.
SPECIAL PROPERTIES
A sleep crystal for beautiful dreams and a state of deep meditation during power naps or daydreams to give healing and restorative visions.
MYTHOLOGY AND HISTORY
From the Minas Gerais area of Brazil, Lepidolite in Quartz combines the proactive and energizing quartz with the feel-good, soothing lepidolite to create balance in every aspect of life.

Libyan Gold Tektite or Libyan Desert Glass

COLORS: Pale yellow, clear, milky or bubbly, sometimes with dark brown bands and swirls

CRYSTAL TYPE: Natural smooth glass, pure silica (98 percent), tektite

ZODIAC SIGN: Leo (July 23–August 23)

CANDLE COLOR: Gold or pale yellow

PHYSICAL: For whole-body healing, IBS, Crohn's disease, stomach and digestive issues.

EMOTIONAL: Aids in resisting energy vampires, plus medical and spiritual charlatans.

HOME: Brings luck and money; deters scammers, con artists, and rogues of every stripe.

WORKPLACE: Attracts new customers and increased profitability; builds up from small beginnings.

CHILDREN: Prevents misdiagnosis and unhelpful labeling of Indigo and Star Children.

ANIMALS: For lizards, tortoises, and reptiles to thrive.

PROTECTION: Shields all who are different from prejudice, abuse, and discrimination.

MAGICKAL AND PSYCHIC USES
Brings access to the Akashic records of past, present, and future, plus freedom from negative karmic patterns from past lives.

SPECIAL PROPERTIES
Contains the mystical healing golden ray; helps Star Souls feel at home in daily life.

MYTHOLOGY AND HISTORY
Over 28 million years old, its earliest recorded use was in ancient Egypt, carved into a scarab on the breastplate of Tutankhamen. Because of the inclusion in some pieces of extraterrestrial meteoric mineral iridium, Libyan glass may have been created by the airborne explosion of a comet or asteroid landing on Earth.

Lightning Stone

COLORS: Brown with yellowy white calcite, forming lightning patterns on a dark background

CRYSTAL TYPE: Septarian concretions, mineral clay cemented on to the iron mineral siderite (see also Septarian or Dragon Stone, page 426)

ZODIAC SIGN: Aries (March 21–April 20)

CANDLE COLOR: Red

PHYSICAL: Promotes successful surgery for acute conditions, sudden illness, visual disturbances, blood circulation, heart valves, acute pain, nearsightedness

EMOTIONAL: Keeps you from holding on to illness or weakness to escape the world, as well as unresolved grievances that sap your happiness.

HOME: For protection from storm damage, forest fires, or other major fires; keeps family members from constantly redecorating or renovating.

WORKPLACE: After a takeover, enables you to ride out changes and adapt without compromising your principles.

CHILDREN: Encourages you to release anger in a nondestructive way.

ANIMALS: For unpredictable pets who suddenly run off.

PROTECTION: Guards against people who constantly change their mind or alter arrangements at the last minute.

MAGICKAL AND PSYCHIC USES
Shamanism, fire and candle magick; the Kabbalah; defensive magick; connection to wisdom of other solar systems; studying ancient scripts.

SPECIAL PROPERTIES
Because of their association with lightning, Lightning Stones ease sudden change in career and personal life, especially if changes are unwelcome; helps you anticipate and prepare for changes in advance.

MYTHOLOGY AND HISTORY
Lightning Stones are balls of clay created fifty million years ago on the ocean bed from mineral mud and clay that became fractured and were filled by calcite brought by groundwater; mainly found on the beaches of Lake Michigan in the Allegan area; first noted in the eighteenth century, Lightning Stones were considered dinosaur eggs and sometimes called turtle stones.

Lilac or Lavender Kunzite

COLORS: Light purple, lilac, lavender, occasionally violet

CRYSTAL TYPE: Spodumene, deeply striated

ZODIAC SIGN: Pisces (February 19–March 20)

CANDLE COLOR: Lilac

PHYSICAL: Eases menopause; libido-reducing gynecological or psychological problems in older women; counters self-induced illnesses, faking illnesses for attention, Munchausen syndrome by proxy, memory loss; addresses issues involving the lungs and end-of-life care.

EMOTIONAL: Helps you to accept that a former partner will not return; mitigates obsessive love for an unattainable person; helps overcome a constant need for company; curbs symptoms of schizophrenia.

HOME: Aids in avoiding bringing work problems home or constantly checking work emails and texts while at home, on vacation, or while socializing.

WORKPLACE: Protects against unhealthy office electromagnetic energies; resists ongoing pressures to constantly be on call, even when you're off duty.

CHILDREN: Keeps children calm and well-behaved on car journeys, planes, and trains, especially with siblings.

ANIMALS: Comforts animals if you need to drive them to the veterinarian.

PROTECTION: Removes sad or restless spirits from the home.

MAGICKAL AND PSYCHIC USES

For wise woman rites of passage; peaceful passing over to the next life ceremonies; channeling protective spiritual guardians; Earth energies at ancient sites and sacred places.

SPECIAL PROPERTIES

The crystal of driving; reduces tensions and exhaustion of driving long distances and commuting; keeps everyone in the vehicle safe from accidents.

MYTHOLOGY AND HISTORY

Lilac Kunzite is more proactive than pink kunzite and a wise woman stone, whereas pink kunzite has maternal energies; attracts a partner in the later years who is open to life's adventures. A good anti-shopaholic stone.

Limb Cast

COLORS: Shades of brown, fawn, or golden; pink or green are considered especially valuable

CRYSTAL TYPE: Small limbs of trees, sometimes whole trees, covered by volcanic ash where the wood has been replaced by agate or opal while keeping the outer shape, rather than the cellular structure

ZODIAC SIGN: Capricorn (December 22–January 20)

CANDLE COLOR: Gold

PHYSICAL: Addresses bones (especially fractures or bone thinning), hip and knee replacements; for conditions caused or made worse by the aging process.

EMOTIONAL: Counters the inability to express feelings or show love due to childhood trauma; deflects emotional blackmail by elderly relatives using promises of future inheritance.

HOME: For taking on the long-term care of an older, sick, or disabled relative; for matters of inheritance where property is causing family dissension.

WORKPLACE: Transforms a business after major financial loss or economic downturn; breathes life into a project that has ground to a halt but still has potential.

CHILDREN: Establishes security at home if there are sudden changes; for close relationships with grandparents and great-grandparents.

ANIMALS: For very old, immobile pets.

PROTECTION: Small pieces carried as an amulet counteract hostile ancestral spirits or curses.

MAGICKAL AND PSYCHIC USES

For connection with ancient worlds; astral travel; deep meditation; for traditional spiritual learning, such as Chinese medicine or Buddhism.

SPECIAL PROPERTIES

A rock to put life into perspective and calmly consider long-term options in times of sudden crises.

MYTHOLOGY AND HISTORY

One of the most fascinating forms of fossilized wood, created as wood burns away after being covered by hot ash; the agate or opal leaves rock that retains the shape of the original tree limb. Limb Casts may date back to the Oligocene era, 23–34 million years ago, when mammals first roamed the Earth. Found mainly in Wyoming and Nevada.

Limonite

COLORS: Yellow, yellow-brown, red-brown, orange, often vivid colors

CRYSTAL TYPE: Hydrated iron oxide concretions, composed mainly of Goethite (page 204)

ZODIAC SIGN: Virgo (August 24–September 22)

CANDLE COLOR: Orange

PHYSICAL: Addresses concerns with the blood, lungs, liver, jaundice, IBS, chronic diarrhea; used in traditional Chinese medicine for issues involving the intestines, stomach, digestion.

EMOTIONAL: Helps overcome fears of potential disasters; soothes those adopted who know nothing about their birth roots or ethnicity.

HOME: Makes a comfortable welcoming home for one or many; aids in feeling at home in hotels or residential accommodations; helps you cope if you have an intrusive landlord or landlady, roommates, or neighbors.

WORKPLACE: Valuable when there are threats or rumors of redundancies, cutbacks, or a takeover; for artists and those who work with color.

CHILDREN: Aids in studying; useful for exploring family history, especially if ancestors come from overseas.

ANIMALS: For herds of animals living independently of humans; for exotic pets.

PROTECTION: Guards against physical, psychological, and psychic attack.

MAGICKAL AND PSYCHIC USES

Improves visionary skills; Earth-healing rituals and rites of passage; Limonite, no matter what its source, carries genetic memories of ancient Earth power.

SPECIAL PROPERTIES

For creative ventures for profit and pleasure, using natural materials and traditional tools; establishing a craft workshop community.

MYTHOLOGY AND HISTORY

Used as artist's pigment in ancient cave art among Australian Aboriginal and other Indigenous people worldwide; also used in murals in ancient Egypt; red-brown gives ochres, orange-brown siennas, and umbers browns. More recently Anthony Van Dyck, the early seventeenth-century portrait artist, used Limonite ochre and sienna.

Lion or Lionskin Stone

COLORS: Tan or brown with black markings, spots, streaks, and stripes, resembling the skin of a lion

CRYSTAL TYPE: Combines golden tiger eye and quartz within the same crystal

ZODIAC SIGN: Leo (July 23–August 23)

CANDLE COLOR: Gold

PHYSICAL: Boosts stamina and energy when you experience dips in blood sugar; strengthens legs, muscles, tendons, heart; counters breathlessness; stimulates fertility when overall health issues need to be addressed.

EMOTIONAL: For making grandiose plans, but never following through; curbs irrational fear of danger or the anger of others, which keeps you from taking action and seizing your freedom.

HOME: Promotes family loyalty and unity in times of division.

WORKPLACE: Cultivates leadership; aids in achieving ambitions and refusing to compromise your principles; for businesswomen to break through the glass ceiling.

CHILDREN: Helps children to deal with schoolyard bullying and teens to stand up to online trolling.

ANIMALS: For small dogs with the heart and courage of a lion(ess).

PROTECTION: Guards against hesitation to move beyond the comfort zone.

MAGICKAL AND PSYCHIC USES

For enhanced intuition of dangers and opportunities; dowsing for water and minerals; starting a psychic development or healing circle.

SPECIAL PROPERTIES

Attracts abundance through personal endeavor; for breaking free of restrictions; for justice if you're threatened by corrupt officials; for rapidly adapting to change.

MYTHOLOGY AND HISTORY

Lion or Lionskin Stone, also called lionskin quartz and lionskin jasper, was recently discovered in South Africa. In Western mythology, the lion is the king of the beasts. Lion goddesses were important in ancient Egypt and the Middle East. Ashtoreth or Astarte the Phoenician moon goddess and goddess of war, is depicted with a lioness's head, as is the fierce leonine warrior, sun and fire goddess Sekhmet, in ancient Egypt. Lion stone brings out the finest qualities and instills courage in all situations.

Lithium Light

COLORS: Whitish-gray/beige, yellow and/or pink, with many microcrystalline sparkles

CRYSTAL TYPE: A combination stone containing Lepidolite (page 277), quartz and cronstedtite, iron silicate; the Lepidolite contains a significant amount of lithium, hence the name Lithium Light

ZODIAC SIGN: Aquarius (January 21–February 18)

CANDLE COLOR: White

PHYSICAL: Alleviates psychosomatic conditions, panic attacks, and hyperventilation that mimic more serious conditions, digestive disorders and heartburn caused by stress and rushed eating.

EMOTIONAL: Counters mood swings, stress that manifests as or exacerbates physical illnesses, the inability to feel joy or hope.

HOME: For launching or expanding a massage or energy therapy business at home if it is necessary to extend or adapt the premises.

WORKPLACE: Aids in adapting workplace practices and making adjustments to hours and physical input after major surgery or illness.

CHILDREN: Keep this crystal in the home of parents or a single parent who works all the time if the child has to care for siblings and become independent relatively young.

ANIMALS: For a pet surrounded by an aura of light who tunes into the owner spiritually and offers healing.

PROTECTION: A light shield against psychic attack and psychic hooks by controlling humans and spirits who try to enter the aura energy field.

MAGICKAL AND PSYCHIC USES

For visions of higher realms, the dwelling place of wise teacher guides, archangels, and ascended masters who offer glimpses of before and after lives as reassurance that this world is not all there is.

SPECIAL PROPERTIES

Halts a frantic, frenetic life with the realization that you cannot do everything and be everything to everyone without suffering spiritual, emotional, and physical burnout.

MYTHOLOGY AND HISTORY

From the Colorado Rocky Mountains; Lithium Light provides moments of ecstasy and connection with the source of light and unity; the whole body is filled with light in these moments, occurring in a place of beauty and solitude or during deep meditation.

Lithium Quartz

COLORS: Soft magenta lavender-gray; occasionally clear

CRYSTAL TYPE: Clear quartz with inclusions of lithium; sometimes a phantom or shadowy lithium within the quartz

ZODIAC SIGN: Libra (September 23–October 23)

CANDLE COLOR: Lilac or gray

PHYSICAL: Balances serotonin levels; mitigates epilepsy, repetitive motion injury, muscle and tendon strains, atrophy in any part of the body, chemical imbalances, blood infections.

EMOTIONAL: Alleviates acute anxiety, depression, bipolar conditions, and panic attacks; strengthens conventional medication.

HOME: Brings order to a home with untidy or chaotic family members; promotes plant health.

WORKPLACE: Clears negative atmospheres; effective against cliques and exclusion in new workplaces.

CHILDREN: For children with anger management or hyperactivity issues.

ANIMALS: Consoles pets grieving for a deceased animal companion.

PROTECTION: Shields against unwanted apparitions, unfriendly spirits, poltergeists.

MAGICKAL AND PSYCHIC USES

Prayer, chanting, sound healing, a complete chakra balancer; connects with the higher self and with divinity and the divine spark within us all; for light workers.

SPECIAL PROPERTIES

Increases love and passion between two people in a long-standing relationship.

MYTHOLOGY AND HISTORY

Rare, from Minas Garais, Brazil, Lithium Quartz resonates with every note on the musical scale; enhances all musical activities, especially choirs, orchestras, spiritual and religious music; some Lithium Quartzes are record keepers, containing ancient wisdom; light-bringers.

Lizardite or Orthoantigorite

COLORS: Pale yellow-green, rich lime green, white; translucent

CRYSTAL TYPE: Magnesium silicate, a variation of serpentine; sometimes contains hematite

ZODIAC SIGN: Virgo (August 24–September 22)

CANDLE COLOR: Green

PHYSICAL: Alleviates issues stemming from the pancreas; regulates insulin balance; promotes absorption of minerals; helps overcome menstrual difficulties made worse by stress; enhances acupuncture and acupressure.

EMOTIONAL: Encourages women with problems concerning lovemaking and sexuality to love their bodies.

HOME: For plant health in indoor gardens, on balconies, and on patios.

WORKPLACE: Fosters negotiations; aids in putting old grudges aside to unite a team.

CHILDREN: Calms overly imaginative children. Avoid direct contact because serpentine may be toxic if ingested.

ANIMALS: Keep near a tank of lizards or other reptiles to aid them in maintaining optimal health.

PROTECTION: As jewelry, keeps spite and jealousy from seeping into your chakra energy centers and being absorbed by your aura.

MAGICKAL AND PSYCHIC USES

For dragon rituals; connecting nature essences and elementals; clearing the aura of stagnation and negative energies; meditation.

SPECIAL PROPERTIES

Links all the chakra inner energy centers of the body with the Earth to ground and restore your connection with the natural world.

MYTHOLOGY AND HISTORY

Discovered in Kenack Cove on the Lizard Peninsula, in Cornwall, in 1955; also found in Canada, southern Norway, Russia, and the USA; associated with regenerative powers of geckos and lizards to regrow tails; sparks regeneration in everyday life and past-life recall.

Lodalite, Dream Crystal, Inclusion or Landscape Quartz

COLORS: Clear with mixed color inclusions, usually with brownish tendrils within a domed quartz crystal, revealing forests, subterranean worlds, or magick landscapes

CRYSTAL TYPE: Quartz family (silicate) with mineral inclusions, such as chlorite and feldspar

ZODIAC SIGNS: All signs, especially Scorpio (October 24–November 22)

CANDLE COLOR: White, silver, or the predominant color of your Lodalite

PHYSICAL: Enhances all forms of healing by balancing and recharging the body's energies.

EMOTIONAL: Releases fears from early childhood; helps overcome fear commitment or intimacy in love.

HOME: Draws together family who spend excessive time using cell phones; makes the garden thrive.

WORKPLACE: Encourages creative and imaginative projects; facilitates original brainstorming.

CHILDREN: Counteracts overreliance on computers, gaming machines, and social media.

ANIMALS: For connecting with nature if your pet spends a lot of time indoors.

PROTECTION: Guards against malevolent spirits by catching them within the inner crystal web.

MAGICKAL AND PSYCHIC USES

Probably the best crystal for past-life recall and meditation; use before sleep for lucid dreaming (that is, knowing you are dreaming while you are dreaming).

SPECIAL PROPERTIES

Each Lodalite is unique; a wish crystal to manifest what you most want.

MYTHOLOGY AND HISTORY

Created a million years ago in the Minas Gerais area of Brazil, Lodalite was regarded as a shamanic stone, offered by the nature essences and elementals to give power and healing gifts to the possessor.

Lodestone or Magnetite

COLORS: Dark gray, black

CRYSTAL TYPE: Naturally magnetized iron oxide. Pointed Lodestones possess animus energies and square or rounded ones anima energies; usually used as a pair

ZODIAC SIGNS: Virgo (August 24–September 22), Libra (September 23–October 23), and Capricorn (December 22–January 20)

CANDLE COLOR: Red

PHYSICAL: Alleviates issues stemming from arthritis, rheumatism, muscle cramps, circulation, heartbeat, bowels, rectum, lower back, ankles, feet; relieves pain; a male/female pairing balances energies.

EMOTIONAL: One in each hand neutralizes feelings of helplessness and overdependence; downward-facing prevents panic.

HOME: A pair ensures stable finances; reduces effects of negative Earth energies beneath the home.

WORKPLACE: A pointed Lodestone facing the entry door attracts prosperity, new business; one facing a computer raises your online profile.

CHILDREN: Prevents similar-aged children from vying for favoritism.

ANIMALS: Useful in stables of donkeys or working horses.

PROTECTION: Pointed outward, and concealed in your dominant hand, Lodestone flicks away negativity as you speak and move your hand.

MAGICKAL AND PSYCHIC USES

In love spells, a pair attracts love, maintaining fidelity through hardship; two of the same work for a same-sex relationship; sex magick rites; the manifestation of wishes.

SPECIAL PROPERTIES

A pair beneath the mattress revives passion; promotes conception; anoint a male lodestone on a full moon with patchouli oil for potency.

MYTHOLOGY AND HISTORY

Lodestones were once used as compasses. Lodestone charms have almost universally been carried to attract luck (especially in gambling), money, and love to the bearer.

Lunar Quartz

COLORS: Gray merging into pink where gray predominates in both tumbled and raw stones

CRYSTAL TYPE: Combination of graphite, carbon (diamonds are also carbon), and rose quartz, silicon dioxide (see also Lunar Rose, page 284, which has different properties because of the different proportion of the crystal colors)

ZODIAC SIGN: Cancer (June 22–July 22)

CANDLE COLOR: Gray

PHYSICAL: Eases heart stenosis or blocked arteries, accelerated by stress and a frantic lifestyle; pinpoints hard-to-diagnose illnesses or those that have multiple symptoms.

EMOTIONAL: Comforts a relative or friend diagnosed with Alzheimer's disease, who is afraid and fears the future, especially with early-onset dementia; for feeling paralyzed about accumulated debt.

HOME: For making difficult but necessary decisions about elderly relatives who can no longer manage alone.

WORKPLACE: For those working in senior care; setting up a therapeutic or healing business that will be commercially viable without losing its spiritual aspect.

CHILDREN: Helps premature or low-birth-weight babies thrive.

ANIMALS: Gives you the courage to end the suffering of a beloved pet by letting them go.

PROTECTION: Guards against those who play on sympathy to borrow money they have no intention of repaying.

MAGICKAL AND PSYCHIC USES

A full moon crystal for channeling the power of the Moon Goddess, psychic artistry, automatic writing, clairvoyance, healing the deeply distressed, or easing the way of those ready to pass.

SPECIAL PROPERTIES

To send a written communication to ask for or offer forgiveness; for a lasting faithful love, even if short on romance.

MYTHOLOGY AND HISTORY

A very recent discovery, combining the creative grounding power of graphite with the healing, loving energies of rose quartz, so you can follow your heart but never lose touch with reality and practicality; helps you express your feelings and imagination in a way that has tangible results.

Lunar Rose

COLORS: Pink and cream or light gray, where pink predominates

CRYSTAL TYPE: Rose quartz combined with graphite; good for healing and magick as tumbled stones (see also Lunar Quartz, page 283, where gray graphite predominates over the rose quartz and the properties differ)

ZODIAC SIGNS: Leo (July 23–August 23) and Cancer (June 22–July 22)

CANDLE COLOR: Gold and silver

PHYSICAL: Alleviates women's hormonal, gynecological, and breast problems, including endometriosis, which makes everyday life hard while menstruating; for clear results of tests, scans, and biopsies; for those with a low pain threshold.

EMOTIONAL: For those who express sympathy for strangers' troubles yet rarely offer practical support to those close to them; for living with a partner who finds it hard to show affection.

HOME: Creates a quiet sanctuary in a busy or shared home or apartment; aids in learning to say no to unreasonable demands.

WORKPLACE: Helps you distance yourself from colleagues who make every challenge a major drama; if you work with people in crisis, teaches them to solve their own problems.

CHILDREN: For toddlers who are unsteady on their feet, and accident-prone older children and teens; encourages tough love if teens make their own problems and expect you to fix them.

ANIMALS: For pets whose loving nature outweighs their intelligence and constantly need rescuing.

PROTECTION: Guards against domestic accidents, electrical shorts, and dangers after dark.

MAGICKAL AND PSYCHIC USES

Rituals when the sun and moon are both in the sky; full moon rituals at moonrise; connecting with the immediate and more distant maternal ancestral line through automatic writing and psychometry.

SPECIAL PROPERTIES

Quartz is usually associated with the sun; moon quartz offers an ideal balance when used with clear crystal solar quartz to combine intuition with clarity of thought.

MYTHOLOGY AND HISTORY

Found in Namibia in recent years, Lunar Rose is a powerful gateway into the hidden realms of magick and women's mysteries.

Luxullianite

COLORS: Reddish-pink, black, and white

CRYSTAL TYPE: Granite, consisting of orthoclase feldspar (pink) with tourmaline needles (black) and quartz (white)

ZODIAC SIGN: Libra (September 23–October 23)

CANDLE COLOR: Deep pink

PHYSICAL: Addresses unpredictable illnesses whose effects may vary from day to day, fever alternating with shivering, hormonal swings, adverse reactions to chemical pollutants and electromagnetic waves; enhances effects of pacemakers; promotes recovery of older people after a debilitating illness or accident.

EMOTIONAL: Counters quick changes of opinions, friends, jobs, and lifestyle because contentment is elusive; helps overcome the need for drama to gain attention.

HOME: Creates a sense of security and stability, based on family love and unity; for older people intent on maintaining their independence in their own home.

WORKPLACE: Calms those with extreme viewpoints and personal prejudices if a meeting is getting heated; for stating your case logically and refusing to be distracted at a biased disciplinary hearing.

CHILDREN: Helps moody teenagers and temperamental tots gain a sense of perspective; for those seriously distressed by teasing.

ANIMALS: For overactive young animals living in a confined space.

PROTECTION: Guards against accepting changes simply made for the sake of change.

MAGICKAL AND PSYCHIC USES

Rituals for peace in the community; for psychic protection during and after magick, healing, and séances; removing poltergeists and out-of-control elementals released during a magick rite that was not properly concluded.

SPECIAL PROPERTIES

For organizing peaceful and orderly protests, neighborhood watch meetings, and petitions.

MYTHOLOGY AND HISTORY

Luxullianite is more than 280 million years old and is found only in the village of Luxulyan near St. Austell in Cornwall, UK, but this stone of quiet authority and calm leadership is well worth the search. The Duke of Wellington's stone coffin in St. Paul's Cathedral in London is made of Luxullianite.

Machu Picchu Stone

COLORS: Green through to creamy brown; varies according to the mineral composition
CRYSTAL TYPE: Includes rhodochrosite, merlinite, cuprite, calcite, and quartz, with landscape markings
ZODIAC SIGN: Pisces (February 19–March 20)
CANDLE COLOR: Green

PHYSICAL: Alleviates seasonal affective disorder, immobile limbs, breathing difficulties; promotes fertility.
EMOTIONAL: Counters fears of blood; curbs a tendency to sacrifice your life and needs for those of others; overcomes an unwillingness to relocate or change your lifestyle.
HOME: Helps overcome fears or threats of losing your home; encourages you to find your forever home.
WORKPLACE: For major projects whose results will last for many years; for persevering in what may seem pointless tasks.
CHILDREN: Endows children with a love of history and mythology.
ANIMALS: For all mountain creatures, especially large wild cats and the preservation of their habitats.
PROTECTION: Guards against fears of becoming lost or attacked in the wilderness or unfamiliar places.

MAGICKAL AND PSYCHIC USES
Solar celebrations on the changing seasons; Earth Mother rituals; astrology.
SPECIAL PROPERTIES
Machu Picchu Stones confer a sense of sacred connections with old worlds, with nature, and with ancient sites.
MYTHOLOGY AND HISTORY
Named after the ancient ruins of Machu Picchu, whose energies it contains, this is a stone of the sun that the Incas worshipped in the form of their solar deity Inti. Also linked with the Andean Earth and mountain goddess Pachamama, Inti's consort. Machu Picchu was built over five hundred years ago in the Peruvian Andes 7,900 feet above sea level. The Machu Picchu Stone is associated with the Temple of the Sun and the Intihuatana stone. Machu Picchu is one of the wonders of the world, and some believe it was built with the assistance of a more evolved extraterrestrial race, imbuing the stone with strong otherworldly energies.

Madeira Citrine

COLORS: Gold to golden orange, reddish-brown to brown; richly colored
CRYSTAL TYPE: Natural citrine, the most valuable kind, but also found in tumbled stones and rough grade as well as gems; quartz heated in the Earth, enriched in color by iron

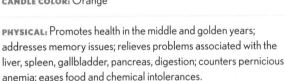

ZODIAC SIGN: Sagittarius (November 23–December 21)
CANDLE COLOR: Orange

PHYSICAL: Promotes health in the middle and golden years; addresses memory issues; relieves problems associated with the liver, spleen, gallbladder, pancreas, digestion; counters pernicious anemia; eases food and chemical intolerances.
EMOTIONAL: Curbs an unwillingness to share money or resources; helps overcome fear of poverty; counteracts personal overindulgence in rich food and wine.
HOME: Continually balances the yin and yang energies in the home, and of the people who live there.
WORKPLACE: For all successful business enterprises, especially commercial ventures and those involving speculation.
CHILDREN: Aids in working toward winning a scholarship or a prestigious internship.
ANIMALS: For breeding or acquiring a show winner or future champion.
PROTECTION: Guards against malice from a person in authority.

MAGICKAL AND PSYCHIC USES
Enhances money rituals in the center of your sacred space; at work, ensures the influx of abundance, energy, health.
SPECIAL PROPERTIES
For awakening sexuality and sensuality, especially from the middle years onward, in a new or developing relationship; for traveling in comfort without delays.
MYTHOLOGY AND HISTORY
Named after the color and richness of Madeira fortified wine, made on the Portuguese Madeira Islands, Madeira Citrine is mined in Brazil, once a Portuguese colony. Genuine natural Madeira Citrine encourages those who care for or spend money on others, but not themselves, to enjoy the good things in life.

Magnesite

COLORS: White, also marbled with gray, brown, yellow or tan, depending on included minerals

CRYSTAL TYPE: Magnesium carbonate from the calcite family, resembling porous unglazed porcelain, chewing gum, or a cauliflower floret; sometimes mistaken for howlite, though with different chemical composition

ZODIAC SIGN: Libra (September 23–October 23)

CANDLE COLOR: White

PHYSICAL: Alleviates issues stemming from the bones, teeth, PMS, menstrual cramps, body temperature, headaches, stomach acidity, cholesterol, angina, arteriosclerosis, body and mouth odor.

EMOTIONAL: Curbs codependency; reduces intolerance of others' lifestyles; eases chronic irritability; for exhausted mothers.

HOME: For sharing family mealtimes without electronic devices; not bringing work worries home.

WORKPLACE: Encourages multitasking when you're facing conflicting priorities; aids in clearing the mind and desk of clutter.

CHILDREN: Overcomes fear of animals and other children.

ANIMALS: For pets who hate being left home alone.

PROTECTION: Keeps you from practicing self-deception and denying painful emotional responses.

MAGICKAL AND PSYCHIC USES

For deep meditation, trance work, visions, and messages from higher realms, especially ascended masters; developing psychic powers; visualization to manifest wishes; the sound of silence beyond sound.

SPECIAL PROPERTIES

Promotes self-esteem and self-love; encourages you to offer unconditional love, rather than becoming disillusioned when loved ones prove less than perfect.

MYTHOLOGY AND HISTORY

In the folk tradition of different lands, Magnesite was considered a gift from the Earth Mother because it's the color of mother's milk. Though a physically unremarkable stone, often dyed blue as mock turquoise, it brings to daily life powerful spiritual awakening and awareness of the hidden world.

Magnifier Quartz

COLOR: Clear

CRYSTAL TYPE: Slender small quartz, silicon dioxide; varying shapes, but slender compared with length; inside an inner crisscross, lattice pattern, often single- or double-terminated

ZODIAC SIGN: Sagittarius (November 23–December 21)

CANDLE COLOR: Gold

PHYSICAL: Promotes fertility, and ensures an easy and swift birth; enhances the potency of medicines to improve health; ensures a healthy blood cell count.

EMOTIONAL: For those seriously in debt who have given up trying to extract themselves from the debt spiral; aids in overcoming loss of love.

HOME: Set Magnifier Quartz in a pot of coins to attract money; if selling a home, put a crystal on each indoor window ledge and around a printout of the advertisement for the listing to maximize viewings and offers.

WORKPLACE: Place one at each corner of a room with a printout of your résumé before applying for a job; carry them to interviews in a small bag to stand out from other candidates.

CHILDREN: If a child is lonely, surround a photo of the child having fun with Magnifiers to attract new friends; place with sports equipment the night before a game.

ANIMALS: Keep this crystal with a pet's health supplements for added vitality.

PROTECTION: Guards against financial loss or those who would denigrate your reputation.

MAGICKAL AND PSYCHIC USES

In rituals with the charm being empowered and another at each quadrant of the circle; with tarot cards, runes, or other divinatory tools to increase accuracy and rapport with clients.

SPECIAL PROPERTIES

Enhances the energies of everything from food inside refrigerators to work, therapy rooms, and vehicles.

MYTHOLOGY AND HISTORY

Discovered in Madagascar and so associated with the wisdom of old Lemuria, magnifier quartz either singly or in groups has become popular among healers worldwide to amplify or increase the power, magically or spiritually, of anything from vitamins to crystals. It also increases aura power.

Mahogany Obsidian

COLORS: Mahogany, brownish-red, or orange-brown with black spots; black with brownish spots

CRYSTAL TYPE: Volcanic glass that has started to crystallize, containing inclusions of magnetite or hematite

ZODIAC SIGN: Scorpio (October 24–November 22)

CANDLE COLOR: Burgundy

PHYSICAL: Addresses issues concerning circulation, teeth (especially wisdom teeth), gums, debilitating illness, deep skin healing, menopause, vaginismus, dust mites allergy, Reynaud's disease, carpel tunnel syndrome.

EMOTIONAL: Counters poor body image that hinders sexuality; aids in letting go of grievances that cannot be put right.

HOME: Shields your home from the risks of settling, erosion, kitchen accidents, dangers involving fire, gas, or electricity, plus natural disasters, such as floods, storm damage, and hurricanes.

WORKPLACE: For wise decision making under pressure; for those working in mining, explosives, electricity, nuclear energy, gas, or other fuel.

CHILDREN: Strengthens links with grandmothers and great-grandmothers, especially those involved in daily care.

ANIMALS: Helps older pets tolerate boisterous children or young animals.

PROTECTION: Guards against volatile people and situations.

MAGICKAL AND PSYCHIC USES

Earth energies, dowsing; past lives, fire and candle magic; cutting cords with destructive relationships or habits.

SPECIAL PROPERTIES

For older women to attract work opportunities if they're facing age or appearance discrimination; draws lasting love and sexual happiness in the later years.

MYTHOLOGY AND HISTORY

Mahogany Obsidian is often called the blood of Mother Earth and of Pele, Hawaiian goddess of volcanoes; also linked with wise women goddesses, such as the Viking Edda, the Celtic Cailleach, and the grandmother of Christ, St. Anne, and so with female ancestral traditions.

Mala Beads

COLORS: Depends on the kind of beads; white, cream, brown, red, yellow, gray, or a mixture of colors

CRYSTAL TYPE: Created in India from wood, seeds, crystals, sandalwood, or holy rudraksha seeds, said to be made from the tears of Lord Shiva; in Nepal, bone, bodhi, or lotus seeds

ZODIAC SIGN: Scorpio (October 24–November 22)

CANDLE COLOR: Indigo

PHYSICAL: Before any major treatment or surgery, prepares the body and mind; hold the largest (guru) bead against the source of pain for relief.

EMOTIONAL: Curbs the inability to switch off anxiety.

HOME: Find a quiet place indoors or outside to build up the daily energies through your chanting with Mala Beads whenever you need power or healing.

WORKPLACE: Chant silently with the beads to escape from noise or stress.

CHILDREN: Share with older children one of the many Gayatri or Ohm recordings or help them to create personal mantras with their personal Mala Beads when they get overly stressed.

ANIMALS: Send healing through your beads to a pet unresponsive to treatment.

PROTECTION: If you start to panic, touch each bead and recite silently a calming word 108 times.

MAGICKAL AND PSYCHIC USES

Incorporate into meditation and yoga by repeating mantras, prayers, or breaths 108 times, one for each bead.

SPECIAL PROPERTIES

Mala Beads have been adopted by people in all lands and spiritualities, including in India as early as the eighth century BCE. Some practitioners recite traditional Buddhist or Hindu chants, such as *Om Mani Padme Hum* or the *Gayatri* mantra 108 times.

MYTHOLOGY AND HISTORY

Mala Beads can be worn as necklaces with the full 108 beads and a tassel to mark the end of the sequence, as half malas of 54 beads or a wrist mala of 27 beads. The largest bead, the guru bead, marks the beginning and end of the sequence.

Malachite

COLORS: Emerald to grass green with black or pale green stripes, bands, swirls, or marbling
CRYSTAL TYPE: Copper carbonate hydroxide
ZODIAC SIGN: Scorpio (October 24–November 22)
CANDLE COLOR: Bright green

PHYSICAL: Alleviates asthma, toothache, gum infections, sinus issues, headaches with visual disturbances, PMS, endometriosis, painful menstruation, menopausal symptoms (especially hot flashes).
EMOTIONAL: Counters resistance to emotional blackmail; eases the pain of childhood emotional abuse; discourages possessive relationships and relationships with those who drain your energies.
HOME: Shields from excessive rays from freezers, refrigerators, microwaves, televisions, smartphones, tablets, laptops, home PCs, or gaming consoles; protects against interfering relatives or intrusive neighbors.
WORKPLACE: Cleanses techno-pollution and toxicity of noise and overly bright fluorescent lighting; for marketing and sales professionals, especially at conferences and trade shows.
CHILDREN: Reduces obsession with and excessive hours spent on social media and gaming; helpful with dyslexia.
ANIMALS: For pets who lack outdoor access; encourages telepathic communication with human companions.
PROTECTION: Overcomes fears of flying; shields from internet frauds, scams, social media attacks, internet trolls, vicious texts and email messages.

MAGICKAL AND PSYCHIC USES
Protective magick and travel spells, especially when traveling by air or commuting; amplifies wishes; enhances prosperity rituals.
SPECIAL PROPERTIES
Brings acceptance of yourself as you are; helps to start anew, breaking patterns of guilt, fear, and past failures.
MYTHOLOGY AND HISTORY
The stone of love goddesses, bringing lasting realistic rather than romantic love at any age or stage in life; a lucky charm for selling through online marketplaces and turning hobbies into moneymakers.

Malacolla

COLORS: Turquoise, sometimes rich green with banding of lighter and darker shades of bright green
CRYSTAL TYPE: Malachite, copper carbonate hydroxide with chrysocolla, hydrated copper silicate in varying proportions; may be on a matrix; most often used as a tumbled stone
ZODIAC SIGN: Sagittarius (November 23–December 21)
CANDLE COLOR: Turquoise

PHYSICAL: Mitigates recurring infections, blood disorders, menstrual problems affecting fertility, heart imbalances, stress incontinence; regulates blood sugar levels.
EMOTIONAL: Curbs a tendency to create drama over trivial matters as a way to block out the pain of deep emotional wounds, often involving past abuse.
HOME: Aids in resisting emotional pressures from a maternal figure who provides 24/7 support as a form of control over other family members.
WORKPLACE: Restores balance to a workplace where personalities and emotional outbursts interfere with professionalism.
CHILDREN: For those who find it hard to express their feelings of hurt or unhappiness; helps develop musical or performing talents.
ANIMALS: Calms pets who travel frequently with their human companions, especially overseas or by air.
PROTECTION: Returns all malice and psychic attacks, whether earthly or paranormal, to the sender.

MAGICKAL AND PSYCHIC USES
The stone of Gaia and goddess rituals; for labyrinth meditations; ley and Earth line energy dowsing, protection during spirit communication in séances and mediumship.
SPECIAL PROPERTIES
For a complete detoxification physically, emotionally, and spiritually; this high-vibration stone opens or reopens channels of psychic awareness to assist in wise daily decision making.
MYTHOLOGY AND HISTORY
The combination of two mutually supportive copper minerals creates a clear communication stone to understand what is in our best interests and to offer support to those we care for without becoming overwhelmed by their needs or overidentifying with their problems.

Maligano Jasper

COLORS: Varies in color; may include a mix of peachy or creamy tan, black, light and dark grays, red, blue, sand yellow, and orange, with grayish-silver agate filling cavities in the stone

CRYSTAL TYPE: A form of picture jasper with dendritic patterns, unique to its Indonesian location; as it was being formed, it was fractured and healed to yield the brecciated texture (cemented together in a fine matrix by other minerals)

ZODIAC SIGN: Sagittarius (November 23–December 21)

CANDLE COLOR: Orange

PHYSICAL: Alleviates illnesses made worse by chronic anxiety, fractures, scars, eczema, psoriasis, rosacea, acne.

EMOTIONAL: Curbs a tendency to hold on to parts of life and people no longer a positive influence, out of fear of change; counters bad habits that act as an anesthetic against life's pain.

HOME: Helps you start over in a new location or move in with a new partner; restores treasures you find at garage sales for pleasure or profit.

WORKPLACE: Eases your way when returning to work after maternity leave or a period of unemployment.

CHILDREN: For those temporarily or permanently excluded from education to be given the support they need.

ANIMALS: Aids in adopting an injured and abandoned pet.

PROTECTION: Guards against those who break promises or constantly postpone delivering what has been offered.

MAGICKAL AND PSYCHIC USES
The images on the stone, often viewed as rivers and forests, vary in the eyes of the questioner, depending upon what is being asked; rebirthing and recall of a previous life.

SPECIAL PROPERTIES
For walking vacations, orienteering, rock climbing. kayaking, canoeing, or wilderness retreats.

MYTHOLOGY AND HISTORY
Maligano Jasper was discovered in a small village on the island in Sulawesi, Indonesia, in 2012, having formed in ancient hot springs. Since then, it has become increasingly popular, especially in the USA. Because of its beautiful colors, Maligano Jasper is crafted into spheres, power statues, and jewelry as a charm to bring ongoing good fortune and well-being.

Mandarin Garnet

COLORS: Though Spessartine Garnets (page 450) do appear in different shades of orange, Mandarin Garnet orange is exceptionally sparkling, bright, translucent, or transparent, resembling a brilliant rising or setting sun

CRYSTAL TYPE: A spessartine garnet, manganese aluminum silicate, usually some of the manganese replaced by ferrous oxide

ZODIAC SIGN: Leo (July 23–August 23)

CANDLE COLOR: Orange

PHYSICAL: Promotes fertility when a couple have lost joy and spontaneity as a result of ovulation charts and tests; also, when they are older and are trying for a first baby.

EMOTIONAL: Curbs eating disorders, fears of food, extreme cravings during an addiction detox, and jealousy over others' love lives, physical attractiveness, or money.

HOME: Brings abundance in every way, plus happiness, confidence, and the chance to succeed in performances.

WORKPLACE: Helps avoid the fallout from overly intense office romances; unfair promotion, or extra privileges for family members, partners, or friends, especially in a smaller business.

CHILDREN: Encourages those who are gifted but lack confidence; for talent contests, competitions, auditions, modeling, dance, music, success in sports, gymnastics, or cheerleading.

ANIMALS: For a prizewinning dog or horse who is scared of crowds.

PROTECTION: Guards against love rivals and straying lovers.

MAGICKAL AND PSYCHIC USES
Earth, sand, stone, and bone divination; celebration of solar festivals, especially Midsummer; sunrise and sunset spells; sex magick; fire and candle magick.

SPECIAL PROPERTIES
For a rekindling of passion or a new love later in life; fosters independence in speech, thought, and actions at any age or stage.

MYTHOLOGY AND HISTORY
Discovered in a remote spot near the Kunene River along the border of Namibia and Angola in 1991. Brilliantly colored Spessartines were found in the southwest corner of Nigeria, in a mine in the riverbed, and in Tanzania in 2007. Unlike some garnets, the stone radiates spontaneous life, warmth, and joy.

Manganese with Sugilite

COLORS: Black with lesser amounts of purple; lavender or purple
CRYSTAL TYPE: Potassium sodium lithium iron manganese aluminum
ZODIAC SIGN: Pisces (February 19–March 20)
CANDLE COLOR: Purple

PHYSICAL: Eases tension headaches; addresses issues stemming from the pineal and pituitary glands; alleviates burns, scalds, inflamed skin and sunburn, adverse reactions to high temperatures, Parkinson's disease and other conditions where the brain malfunctions and affects the whole body.
EMOTIONAL: Helps curb alienation from others, acute loneliness, irrational prejudice against anyone with different views.
HOME: Promotes family activities, vacations, intergenerational living, communities, and cooperatives.
WORKPLACE: Keeps office romances or a business run by love partners within professional boundaries.
CHILDREN: Works with those for whom rote learning is hard and causes stress; eases pressures and brings out a more relaxed attitude; aids in finding the right help for dyslexia.
ANIMALS: Helps a rescue pet who has lost faith in humans.
PROTECTION: Guards against those who deliberately create disorder and chaos.

MAGICKAL AND PSYCHIC USES
Increases awareness of and trust in intuition among logical minds; aids in joining or starting a Wiccan coven, a druidic grove, a healing circle, a psychic development group, or organizing regular pagan moots on the full moons and seasonal festivals; enhances solitary or group initiations.

SPECIAL PROPERTIES
A powerful connector with angelic realms, angelology, psychic artistry to portray guardian angels surrounding others.

MYTHOLOGY AND HISTORY
Recently discovered in South Africa, Manganese with Sugilite, especially with black bands, absorbs pain, stress, disharmony; cleanses healing spaces, especially at festivals and shared premises.

Manganite

COLORS: Black or dark steel gray; may have a brilliant metallic luster if not weathered
CRYSTAL TYPE: Manganese-oxide hydroxide, once a major ore of manganese, often prismatic and striated; a close cousin of Pyrolusite (page 383)
ZODIAC SIGN: Libra (September 23–October 23)
CANDLE COLOR: Silver

PHYSICAL: Addresses issues relating to mucous membranes, enzymes, kidneys, bladder, water retention, blood circulation, high blood pressure, swellings, headaches, IBS, celiac disease; offers pain relief; eases diarrhea caused by anxiety.
EMOTIONAL: For those who love too much and feel responsible for the happiness of a partner, family members, friends, and even colleagues.
HOME: Fosters a balanced approach between keeping the home free of clutter and obsession with tidiness and germs that can, if unresolved, cause conflict with family members.
WORKPLACE: Encourages delegation if you or another member of the staff feel you must do everything yourself; place near the workspace of a personal assistant who discourages access to the boss.
CHILDREN: Near the sports or training equipment if a teen is obsessed with sports or fitness and wears themselves out or neglects other aspects of life.
ANIMALS: For a pet jealous of the attention of other humans or pets toward their human companion.
PROTECTION: Guards against being swayed by sentiment or emotion if controlled by a charismatic manipulator.

MAGICKAL AND PSYCHIC USES
Cutting ties with a destructive person, situation, or bad habit.

SPECIAL PROPERTIES
For team bonding exercises, managing, or captaining a sports team; organizing a seminar or workshop for opinionated people and believing in your own expertise.

MYTHOLOGY AND HISTORY
A stone of spontaneity to open relationships, friendships, or activities that have become routine and lost the ability to give you pleasure; relieves fertility issues caused by anxiety or too strong a focus on ovulation charts that has taken the joy out of lovemaking.

Mangano Calcite or Manganoan Calcite

COLORS: Pale pink, with white bands
CRYSTAL TYPE: Calcium carbonate with manganese
ZODIAC SIGN: Cancer (June 22–July 22)
CANDLE COLOR: Pale Pink

PHYSICAL: For prolonged illnesses and recovery after traffic accidents or physical assault; absorbs pain; eases pregnancy; helps premature babies thrive; aids in curing childhood illnesses.
EMOTIONAL: Promotes self-love; for those who have been inadequately mothered or whose mother died while they were young; counters postnatal depression; aids in bonding with a baby after a traumatic birth; for mothers, fathers, and grandparents who lose a child at any age.
HOME: Restores security after domestic crises; repairs damage after burglary or natural disaster, such as floods or storms.
WORKPLACE: Ensures that your ideas are taken seriously if you're working for a family business; for foster and adoptive parents, and all who help mothers, babies, and children, whether medically or in social settings.
CHILDREN: Helps young children overcome separation anxiety and fears of invisible friends.
ANIMALS: For pets separated early from their mothers.
PROTECTION: Guards against worries of being a less-than-perfect parent,

MAGICKAL AND PSYCHIC USES
Associated with fairies and gentle Earth spirit and mythical creatures, especially unicorns; Mother Goddess rituals; love spells for lost or unrequited love.
SPECIAL PROPERTIES
For mending estrangements with mothers, stepmothers, and grandmothers; for mothers or fathers separated from their children through custody disputes or adoption.
MYTHOLOGY AND HISTORY
Called the Reiki stone because it transmits universal life-force energy to wherever in the body it is most needed; Mangano Calcite, or Manganoan Calcite, shares healing attributes with other pink calcites.

Mango Quartz

COLORS: Clear at one end and golden yellow or mango colored at the other, resembling a strip of mango
CRYSTAL TYPE: Double-terminated points, quartz (clear) containing halloysite (yellow), an aluminosilicate clay mineral within the quartz, but not coating the crystal
ZODIAC SIGN: Gemini (May 22–June 21)
CANDLE COLOR: Yellow

PHYSICAL: Promotes digestion, absorption of minerals and nutrients, strength; helps overcome low levels of serotonin; counters insomnia.
EMOTIONAL: Aids in curbing reliance on additive-filled fast food for comfort; helps overcome a tendency to deny your true self, to have low self-esteem, and to engage in addictive behaviors.
HOME: Attracts abundance, health, and good fortune.
WORKPLACE: A feel-good crystal that attracts new business and prosperity; for winning prizes and recognition.
CHILDREN: Teaches children to share their toys, and keeps them from feeling resentment if a new baby arrives.
ANIMALS: For pets jealous of a new arrival—whether a new partner, a new baby, or a new animal.
PROTECTION: Absorbs and removes any inner toxicity.

MAGICKAL AND PSYCHIC USES
Intuitive astrology and planetary alignment to overcome potential chart misalignments; clairvoyance; celebrating the monthly full moon esbats (Wiccan lunar holy days).
SPECIAL PROPERTIES
The stone of shaping or re-creating your destiny on your own terms, not those dictated by others; confers the self-confidence to rewrite your personal rule book.
MYTHOLOGY AND HISTORY
Found only in Boyacá, Colombia, Mango Quartz was first discovered by Colombian strongman Don Victor Carranza during the early 1980s. He took all the Mango Quartz for himself, sealing the mine, and it only started to appear on the market in late 2020, a reminder of the need to share beauty and resources; also called corona quartz because the points are tipped with gold, like a coronet.

Mani de Lion or Lion's Paw Scallop Shell

COLORS: Soft purple, cream, peach, dark or bright orange, red, brown

CRYSTAL TYPE: Calcium carbonate, phylum Mollusca, may be hinged together; Lion's Paw has large ridges, creating a wider, larger shape than usual scallop shells; resembles a lion's paw.

ZODIAC SIGN: Cancer (June 22–July 22)

CANDLE COLOR: White

PHYSICAL: Regulates fluid imbalances, hormonal fluctuations, menstrual problems, low levels of iodine; promotes fertility; addresses issues associated with the teeth, calcification of bones and heart valves, foot and ankle injuries.

EMOTIONAL: Counters an inability to adapt to changes.

HOME: Aids in assuming a position of responsibility in community affairs; campaigning against developments that will damage the local environment.

WORKPLACE: Lion's Paw gives the courage to resist those who criticize whatever you do; for rising to a position of leadership.

CHILDREN: The kitten's paw, a small version of the Lion's Paw, helps children gain confidence.

ANIMALS: Lion's Paw protects pets out at night.

PROTECTION: Guards against trickery.

MAGICKAL AND PSYCHIC USES

Calling the lion or lioness as a power icon; defensive magick; sacred journeys and pilgrimages; seeking small miracles.

SPECIAL PROPERTIES

The scallop shell is associated with the apostle St. James, said to be buried in Santiago de Compostela in Galicia, Spain, still a famous pilgrimage route. Traditionally, pilgrims were given a scallop shell when they completed the pilgrimage; scallop shells mark the route, making all scallop shells an amulet for safety during travel.

MYTHOLOGY AND HISTORY

Though scallop shells are found worldwide, the finest specimens of Lion's Paw are found in Florida, bringing courage to tread a unique path through life.

Manifestation Quartz

COLORS: Varies according to the crystal type, often clear

CRYSTAL TYPE: One or more quartz crystals enclosed within another quartz, unlike a phantom where the inner crystal is a shadow

ZODIAC SIGN: Leo (July 23–August 23)

CANDLE COLOR: White

PHYSICAL: Provides effective diagnosis and treatment of illnesses, including tumors (especially deep-seated ones), with radiation and chemotherapy; complements IVF and other fertility interventions; eases pregnancy and childbirth; ushers in quality end-of-life care.

EMOTIONAL: Useful for bipolar and schizophrenic conditions; promotes psychological development arrested in childhood or teenage by trauma, abuse, or prolonged illness.

HOME: For establishing a new lifestyle and relocation after divorce, remarriage, bereavement, or in retirement.

WORKPLACE: Aids in relocating to a different branch of a company; building a franchise; working in horticulture or agriculture or achieving a self-sufficient lifestyle.

CHILDREN: Allows children to maintain a belief in Santa Claus and fairies.

ANIMALS: For those acting as eyes, ears, and providing mobility for their owner.

PROTECTION: Guards against pressures to conform outwardly when your heart says otherwise.

MAGICKAL AND PSYCHIC USES

Manifesting desires through ritual and mind power; astral travel through the inner doorway to other dimensions; connecting with angels; intuitive awareness of how a client needs healing; psychic surgery.

SPECIAL PROPERTIES

Launching a new business, successful inventions, and saleable creative ideas.

MYTHOLOGY AND HISTORY

Because the outer crystal is younger, the inner crystal holds the accumulated wisdom of ancient worlds; offers fulfillment, in the second half of life, of plans set aside by everyday living.

Manifest Light Quartz

COLORS: Clear or smoky (quartz) with floating, shimmering, silver-gray hematite inclusions
CRYSTAL TYPE: A unique form of hematite-included quartz (see also Harlequin, Fire Hematoid, or Ferruginous Quartz, page 235)
ZODIAC SIGN: Aquarius (January 21–February 18)
CANDLE COLOR: White

PHYSICAL: Used to stimulate the healing process of many common diseases such as influenza, and childhood illnesses such as chicken pox and measles as it harmonizes the aura's vibrational energies.
EMOTIONAL: Keeps you from being weighed down by material desires; counters an unwillingness to reach for the light at the end of the tunnel in bad times, while blaming fate.
HOME: Brings peace and hope to a home where there is ongoing sickness, a bereavement, or family estrangement.
WORKPLACE: Brightens an impersonal, competitive workplace; for sick-building syndrome, causing frequent absenteeism through minor illnesses and stress.
CHILDREN: A lovely family guardian crystal, illuminated by candles before bed.
ANIMALS: Comforts a pet who has lost a mate.
PROTECTION: Transforms negative words and actions into a positive response.

MAGICKAL AND PSYCHIC USES

For safe astral travel, aware that you can return any time; for remote healing to direct the light wherever it's needed while you constantly replenish your own energy via the strengthening hematite; amplifies the crystal's pure life-force through yoga, tai chi, qi gong, martial arts, and other energy-balancing modalities.

SPECIAL PROPERTIES

Manifests what is most yearned for by visualizing an image of what is most needed within the crystal several times a day; activates the inner hematite to bring the fulfilled desire into the everyday world.

MYTHOLOGY AND HISTORY

First named by the crystal expert Robert Simmons and found only in Brazil, Manifest Light Quartz, which is different from Manifestation Quartz (page 292), is an ideal crystal for spiritual practitioners to call the light into themselves.

Mani Stone

COLORS: Black and white, banded; may be patterned
CRYSTAL TYPE: Jasper
ZODIAC SIGN: Cancer (June 22–July 22)
CANDLE COLOR: White

PHYSICAL: Alleviates breathlessness, psychosomatic illnesses, high blood pressure made worse by stress.
EMOTIONAL: Encourages you to forgive or let go of grievances going back to childhood or even earlier generations.
HOME: For avoiding the blame game and focusing on addressing problems as they arise.
WORKPLACE: Counters a work environment where newcomers are automatically excluded; promotes equality at every level.
CHILDREN: Teaches children to admit their mistakes, make them right, and learn from the experience.
ANIMALS: For rescuing racehorses and greyhounds who have been harshly treated or are worn out.
PROTECTION: Guards against evil spirits and human predators.

MAGICKAL AND PSYCHIC USES

Another form of Mani Stones are stone prayer plates or rocks in Tibetan Buddhism, traditionally engraved with the six-syllable devotion *Om Mani Padme Hum*, commonly translated as "The jewel is in the lotus." Some people write the devotion in incense smoke in the air over the black and white Mani Jasper while chanting the mantra.

SPECIAL PROPERTIES

The stone of unconditional love, compassion, and kindness.

MYTHOLOGY AND HISTORY

The Mani Jasper is named after Mani, the third-century Persian mystic who founded the Manichean religion, which, for over a thousand years, was an influential faith. This is a stone for always striving toward the highest good in word and action.

Marble

COLORS: White in its purest form, takes color from mineral impurities, black, green, orange, red, yellow, brown, in many color combinations or patterned as a ruin or a landscape marble
CRYSTAL TYPE: Calcium carbonate, granular organic metamorphic rock derived from limestone or dolomite, formed over millions of years
ZODIAC SIGN: Cancer (June 22–July 22)
CANDLE COLOR: White

PHYSICAL: Alleviates issues stemming from the bone marrow, conjunctivitis, headaches, hormone imbalances, progressive illnesses; strengthens bones and teeth; mitigates the effects of viruses and bacterial infections; promotes fitness regimens.
EMOTIONAL: Aids in overcoming addictions, emotional stress, burnout, and restlessness.
HOME: Marble artifacts provide a calm oasis amid frantic activity.
WORKPLACE: Brings practicality and attention to detail to channel creativity into tangible results; counteracts panic, impossible deadlines, and constant drama.
CHILDREN: Counters hyperactivity and an unwillingness to complete tasks.
ANIMALS: For overactive pets in confined spaces.
PROTECTION: Shields you when pursuing physically, mentally, or spiritually a hazardous or unknown path.

MAGICKAL AND PSYCHIC USES

Connects with and channels celestial realms; meditation; psychic dreams, recall of past lives as priests or priestesses in ancient cultures.

SPECIAL PROPERTIES

Brings calm, patience, serenity, and acceptance of what cannot be changed; discourages random web surfing, boredom, and time wasting.

MYTHOLOGY AND HISTORY

Michelangelo, who created the marble statue of *David*, said, "Marble not yet carved can hold the form of every thought the greatest artist has." White marble, regarded as the symbol of purity and incorruptibility through time, appears as statues of deities in ancient Greece and Rome, sacred buildings, angels in Victorian churches, and as memorials.

Marcasite

COLORS: Metallic silver-gray to brassy gold; sparkling
CRYSTAL TYPE: Iron sulfide
ZODIAC SIGNS: Aries (March 21–April 20) and Leo (July 23–August 23)
CANDLE COLOR: Gold

PHYSICAL: Calms overactive calms those with high testosterone levels; eases childbirth, aftereffects of anesthetic; addresses stammering, blushing, tics, hyperventilation, memory issues; strengthens blood cells; stanches infections and viruses; alleviates disorientation and conditions deteriorating with age.
EMOTIONAL: Counters to urge to unnecessarily sacrifice your own happiness for others' needs; overcomes irrational fears of poverty and loss.
HOME: For relatives who feign illness to control family members; a happy family charm.
WORKPLACE: Brings organization to chaotic functioning; attracts wealth.
CHILDREN: For psychic children with invisible friends; increases intellectual abilities, especially for mathematics.
ANIMALS: Connects with deceased pets.
PROTECTION: Guards against jet lag; blocks psychic attack; keeps family members or partners from using anger as a means of control; empowers women in unequal situations.

MAGICKAL AND PSYCHIC USES

Lucid dreaming and dream astral travel; magick and magickal manifestation at every level, from mind power to spellcasting; opens psychic gateways; enhances clairvoyance.

SPECIAL PROPERTIES

Releasing inner fire to manifest what is needed and desired by radiating confidence, power, courage, and charisma; drawing the right opportunities at the right time in every aspect of life.

MYTHOLOGY AND HISTORY

Also called white pyrite, Marcasite was highly prized by Incas who wore it in jewelry and buried it as grave goods; they also created polished marcasite mirrors, probably for sun worship and to tell the future. Marcasite is found in ancient Native American medicine bundles, and was beloved as jewelry by Victorians.

Marialite

COLORS: White, yellow, honey-colored in gem-quality, green, pink, and brown

CRYSTAL TYPE: Sodium-rich form of scapolite, sodium aluminum chloro-silicate

ZODIAC SIGN: Aquarius (January 21–February 18)

CANDLE COLOR: Yellow

PHYSICAL: Addresses issues associated with the arteries and the eyes, including cataracts, glaucoma, iris problems; promotes postoperative recovery; alleviates varicose veins, incontinence caused by stress, muscle or bladder weakness, uterine prolapse.

EMOTIONAL: Aids in refusing to accept the scapegoat or victim role; curbs the tendency to adopt a preordained lifestyle out of family obligation, even though it causes you unhappiness.

HOME: For creating a loving atmosphere, whether you live alone or in a household of many; welcoming those who are lonely.

WORKPLACE: Helps pursue projects and ventures with a good chance of success and abandon those going nowhere.

CHILDREN: Preserves childhood innocence as long as possible and practical; teaches responsibility for those less fortunate.

ANIMALS: Revives rare pure breeds; for winning shows with pedigreed animals and for professional animal breeding.

PROTECTION: Guards against accepting the negative opinions of others.

MAGICKAL AND PSYCHIC USES
For prayers to the Virgin Mary, the Black Madonna, and Mother Goddesses; for goddess rituals; recalling and adapting prebirth contracts and destiny.

SPECIAL PROPERTIES
The stone of a chosen change in lifestyle, location, relationships, or friendships; for seeking new love, whether through a dating service, online, or by engaging in new activities.

MYTHOLOGY AND HISTORY
Named after the Virgin Mary, because of its gentle loving energies or after Maria Rosa Rath, wife of Von Rath who discovered Marialite in 1866 in the Phlegraean volcanic complex in Campania, Italy; a stone for striving to relieve poverty, hunger, inequality, and disadvantaged environments.

Mariposa Calcite or the Butterfly Stone

COLORS: Orange, yellow, honey, golden browns (calcite), red or pink (hematite); may have different-colored calcites within the same cluster

CRYSTAL TYPE: Calcium carbonate with hematite (iron oxide) inclusions and inner phantoms; in clusters in the shape of butterfly wings or resembling a complete butterfly; sometimes alternating layers of dogtooth calcite and hematite. Mariposa Calcite both fluoresces and phosphoresces

ZODIAC SIGN: Aquarius (January 21–February 18)

CANDLE COLOR: Green

PHYSICAL: Strengthens the immune system, metabolism, thyroid, adrenal and pituitary glands; for end-of-life care.

EMOTIONAL: fear of permanence, inability to settle or focus.

HOME: breaking with routine and leaving chores in favor of spontaneous outings and last-minute vacations; exchanging activities undertaken out of duty for ones that bring pleasure.

WORKPLACE: Brings success through your own efforts; prompts you to leave a restrictive organization for a more open-minded establishment.

CHILDREN: Eases the return to school after a long period of absence due to illness or homeschooling.

ANIMALS: For creating an area of the garden where butterflies, bees, moths, and lizards can flourish.

PROTECTION: Guards against whatever restricts or restrains you from progress, whether internal fears or others standing in your way.

MAGICKAL AND PSYCHIC USES
Rebirthing; connection with Air spirits, especially mountain swan-like sylphs; astral travel to other realms in waking visions, structured daydreaming, or lucid dreaming.

SPECIAL PROPERTIES
For transformations and makeovers of all kinds.

MYTHOLOGY AND HISTORY
Produced in the Mariposa Mine in Texas and in Chihuahua, Mexico, Butterfly Calcite—a special crystal for women starting over—has strong connections with the symbolism of the butterfly and is said to be a reminder to enjoy every moment of happiness. *Mariposa* is Spanish for "butterfly."

Mariposite

COLORS: Orange, yellow, honey, golden browns (calcite), red or pink (hematite); may have different-colored calcites within the same cluster

CRYSTAL TYPE: Calcium carbonate with hematite (iron oxide) inclusions and inner phantoms; in clusters in the shape of butterfly wings or resembling a complete butterfly; sometimes alternating layers of dogtooth calcite and hematite. Mariposa Calcite both fluoresces and phosphoresces

ZODIAC SIGN: Aquarius (January 21–February 18)

CANDLE COLOR: Green

PHYSICAL: Addresses chronic fatigue syndrome, HIV, suppressed growth or delayed development in childhood, issues relating to transplants; promotes self-healing; after brain damage, degeneration, or strokes, helps other parts of the brain to take over.

EMOTIONAL: Curbs fears and anxiety, magnified out of proportion, causing fight, flight, or panic reactions.

HOME: For renovations and restoration of property to increase sale value; a boundary stone against urban pollution.

WORKPLACE: Maximizes business potential by introducing innovations and more efficient working practices.

CHILDREN: Enables adjustment to a new home, location, or educational environment.

ANIMALS: For butterflies and wildlife areas in urban gardens; encourages nesting birds.

PROTECTION: Aids in resisting persuasion to part with money.

MAGICKAL AND PSYCHIC USES

For shadow scrying, shine a candle on the Mariposite surface; psychic dreaming; connecting with higher realms through meditating in nature.

SPECIAL PROPERTIES

Supporting difficult change, whether that involves economizing, quitting smoking or alcohol, or starting a fitness and diet regimen.

MYTHOLOGY AND HISTORY

Named after Mariposa County, California, where it was originally discovered. The rock was linked with the 1849 gold rush, where green and white rocks in streams or outcrops indicated they might contain gold. The County is named Mariposa (Spanish for butterfly) because of numerous butterflies in the area.

Mary Ellen Stromatolite Jasper

COLORS: Bright red, pink, white, yellow, and green, with black swirls

CRYSTAL TYPE: Jasper, microcrystalline quartz, built up over billions of years from colonies of blue and green algae and cyanobacteria as fossiliferous stromatolite and through oxidization of iron/hematite

ZODIAC SIGN: Capricorn (December 22–January 20)

CANDLE COLOR: Red

PHYSICAL: Alleviates bacterial infections, memory issues (especially those linked with aging), nausea (including morning sickness), impotence; promotes deep tissue and organ healing.

EMOTIONAL: Curbs fears of aging and mortality; mitigates issues with male relatives and partners that may date back to a controlling or absent father in childhood.

HOME: For buying or renting an older property and restoring it to its original beauty; for conversions of old industrial buildings into multigenerational dwellings; for love in later years.

WORKPLACE: Aids in focusing on the task in hand if you are facing a seemingly endless mountain of work; encourages the local community, especially schools, to get involved in a business.

CHILDREN: Helps find good substitute role models if fathers or grandfathers are absent.

PROTECTION: Guards against controlling older relatives.

MAGICKAL AND PSYCHIC USES

Shamanic travel, connection with prehuman worlds, deep meditation (especially recalling underwater worlds); mediumship.

SPECIAL PROPERTIES

Because oxygen was first released into the world by cyanobacteria, Mary Ellen Jasper, like other stromatolites, stimulates the free-flowing life force. If your current environment is stagnant, this crystal breathes fresh life into a long-standing relationship in which you've been taking each other for granted.

MYTHOLOGY AND HISTORY

Mary Ellen Stromatolite Jasper is named after the Mary Ellen Mine in Minnesota and is over two billion years old. A combination of the proactive energies of jasper, the strength and determination of iron, stabilized by the timelessness of stromatolite, it ensures that long-term ventures do not run out of steam midway.

Master Crystals

COLORS: Mainly colorless

CRYSTAL TYPE: Most often clear crystal quartz, with unusual markings or indentations, that make the crystal especially powerful as healer and teacher; may be other kinds of quartz, especially amethyst, citrine, rose quartz, and smoky quartz or gems such as ruby

ZODIAC SIGN: Leo (July 23–August 23). Individual Master Crystals may have their own star signs listed in separate entries

CANDLE COLOR: Gold

PHYSICAL: Any Master Crystal is a powerful all-purpose healer; helpful where the prognosis is uncertain or a patient is worn out from prolonged treatment.

EMOTIONAL: Alleviates deep-seated sorrow, anger, fear; opens up those who are closed to the love and support of others.

HOME: Avoids minor spills and accidents, and infusing the space with calm and enthusiasm, replacing lethargy and hyperactivity.

WORKPLACE: Even a small Master Crystal increases considerate behavior and courtesy without sacrificing efficiency or focus.

CHILDREN: Enables psychic children to overcome fears of experiences and connect with their angel guardian.

ANIMALS: Heals a chronically sick pet who's losing the will to live.

PROTECTION: Guards against all fear and danger.

MAGICKAL AND PSYCHIC USES

Empowers other crystals and healing remedies; set at the center of a crystal grid or layout (see page 524) or in the middle of an altar to purify, empower, and protect collective rituals and individual spells; each Master Crystal acts as a channel to past and future the longer you work with it.

SPECIAL PROPERTIES

Whatever their special focus, one particular Master Crystal may work for you for all purposes. Each opens doorways to higher spiritual planes and sources of healing.

MYTHOLOGY AND HISTORY

There is variation among crystal experts as to which are Master Crystals containing the power to fill the user with knowledge understanding on a deep level and enhance personal and collective healing powers. For a list of the most commonly accepted Master Crystals, see page 527.

Maw-Sit Sit

COLORS: Bright green with black to black-green veining; mottled

CRYSTAL TYPE: A stone composed mainly of three different minerals in different quantities—kosmochlor (a pyroxene), albite feldspar, and chromian jadeite

ZODIAC SIGN: Taurus (April 21–May 21)

CANDLE COLOR: Green

PHYSICAL: Alleviates issues stemming from the heart (especially heart failure, and blocked aorta and mitral valves), fevers, eczema, rosacea; strenthens cells; addresses cramps, female reproductive disorders, genitourinary infections.

EMOTIONAL: Helps you sever dysfunctional relationships; curbs overreliance on the approval or support of others; helps overcome consistent bad temper and depression.

HOME: A natural joy-bringer, lifts the atmosphere, filtering out gloom if a family member is depressed or constantly downbeat.

WORKPLACE: For prosperity through business success; advancing professionally after arduous training; moneymaking projects based on careful research.

CHILDREN: Builds up happy memories through family outings and activities; overwrites the past for children who have previously been in foster care.

ANIMALS: For stabilizing highly sensitive or neurotic pets.

PROTECTION: Creates a defensive aura against all forms of evil; guards against illness on vacations.

MAGICKAL AND PSYCHIC USES

Money magick, rituals for travel; to call soul-twin love; connection with devas of nature.

SPECIAL PROPERTIES

For pleasurable weekends away and short spontaneous vacations; for romance, passion, sexual pleasure.

MYTHOLOGY AND HISTORY

Maw Si Sit, found in the foothills of the Himalayas, was named after the nearby village in the northwest region of Burma, now Myanmar; identified in 1963 by the late Swiss geologist and gemologist, the late Dr. Edward Gubelin, Maw-Sit-Sit is a recent addition to spiritual work to bring happiness and optimism.

Medusa Stone or Gilalite in Quartz

COLORS: Varies from clear tinged blue with bluish-green or more blue inclusions, depending on the amount of gilalite

CRYSTAL TYPE: Quartz containing gilalite, a copper-based inclusion; the gilalite appears tendril-like or with rounder and more mushroom-shaped irregular (turquoise) spots inside

ZODIAC SIGN: Aquarius (January 21–February 18)

CANDLE COLOR: Turquoise

PHYSICAL: Promotes healthy circulation (especially through veins and arteries), vision, hearing; addresses illnesses that spread to different organs and parts of the body.

EMOTIONAL: Curbs fear of standing out from the crowd; banishes inner demons and repressed negative feelings.

HOME: Restores calm if you feel overwhelmed by responsibilities or work.

WORKPLACE: A crystal unique in appearance and energies, for prioritizing the most useful way of spending your time to gain maximum results.

CHILDREN: For those who are different in any way to value themselves for their uniqueness.

ANIMALS: Enables pets to adapt after sustaining life-changing injuries.

PROTECTION: Guards against those who would silence you.

MAGICKAL AND PSYCHIC USES

For increasing telepathic connections with those close to you and beings from other dimensions; promotes visualization.

SPECIAL PROPERTIES

For speaking clearly and authoritatively in the workplace and community so others take your opinions seriously.

MYTHOLOGY AND HISTORY

Also called Paraiba quartz, after the area in Brazil where it is mined, the name *Medusa* comes from the tendril jellyfish-like blue inclusions in the finest clear Medusa Stones. Medusa was one of the three Gorgon sisters—once beautiful goddesses. According to myth, the sky-worshipping Greeks feared powerful women, and Medusa was depicted as a hideous snake-haired hag, who turned gazers into stone. This is a powerful stone for water energies and the inflow of whatever is needed.

Melanite Garnet

COLORS: Black, dull to usually glossy, where titanium replaces some of the iron

CRYSTAL TYPE: Calcium iron silicate, a rare variety of Andradite Garnet (page 29)

ZODIAC SIGN: Capricorn (December 22–January 20)

CANDLE COLOR: Gray

PHYSICAL: Alleviates conditions relating to arthritis, bowels, testes, sexual dysfunction, prostate, hernia, stroke, heart, infections, melanomas; strengthens red blood cells; relieves pain; promotes absorption of necessary medication.

EMOTIONAL: For men who have experienced stern fathering or strict single-sex schooling and are unable to express love; curbs suicidal thoughts; counters lack of love from others.

HOME: Leads to practical organization if your partner or family members opt out of chores and home management.

WORKPLACE: For perseverance in a career with high unemployment; overcoming prejudice or discrimination in existing employment.

CHILDREN: Enables those who live with their head in the clouds to become more down-to-earth.

ANIMALS: Calms impulsive, unpredictable pets.

PROTECTION: Gleaming Melanite returns curses, hexes, and ill-wishing to their source; shields from psychic or psychological manipulation.

MAGICKAL AND PSYCHIC USES

Clears a safe spiritual space when working at psychic fairs or festivals; for healers to avoid absorbing clients' negative energies.

SPECIAL PROPERTIES

For peaceful transition to a relationship's next stage, whether moving in together, marrying, having a baby, overcoming infidelity, or agreeing to separate; brings compromise to custody or property disputes.

MYTHOLOGY AND HISTORY

Hindu tradition associated Melanite with the root or base chakra energy center; source of Earth power for practical endeavors, avoiding illusion, and ensuring a secure basis for a new project or relationship.

Melo Pearl

COLORS: Pale yellow, golden to intense orange or brown; usually totally spherical, with flame-like patterns flickering across the surface

CRYSTAL TYPE: Formed from calcite and aragonite; not iridescent, like oysters or mussels, but with a smooth porcelain luster

ZODIAC SIGNS: Cancer (June 22–July 22) and Leo (July 23–August 23)

CANDLE COLOR: Orange

PHYSICAL: Purifies and energizes the whole body; promotes fertility, pregnancy, and childbirth; boosts low pulse.

EMOTIONAL: Revives those who have lost sight of their dreams.

HOME: A single Melo Pearl brings joy and harmony.

WORKPLACE: Even as a screen saver on the computer, a reminder of the need to focus on whatever represents fulfillment.

CHILDREN: A special treasure, whether photographed in a museum, a jewelry exhibition, or perhaps an actual family treasure, for inspiring tales of dragons and exotic places.

ANIMALS: Works with dragon imagery in meditation, visualization, art, writing, or ritual for calling tangible success and fame.

PROTECTION: Guards against those who destroy beauty for profit.

MAGICKAL AND PSYCHIC USES

Melo Pearls were believed to be cast from dragons in the sky, a magickal symbol of wealth and nobility; traditionally in Asia a symbol of royalty, though they might not be worn even by emperors.

SPECIAL PROPERTIES

A lunar and solar symbol, combined with the power of the Earth and the seas, to bring inner and outer gifts to manifestation.

MYTHOLOGY AND HISTORY

Found in the South China Seas and also around Myanmar, Thailand, Vietnam, the Philippines, and Cambodia, Melo Pearls are rare collectors' items and cannot be cultured. Melo Pearls come from the melo melo snail, a marine gastropod from the Volutidae genus, known also as the Indian volute. They are handed down from one generation to the next, either as jewelry or as a single large pearl, symbolizing the inheritance of family traditions.

Merlinite

COLORS: Black and white, varying from dark gray to bluish-black and dark blue

CRYSTAL TYPE: Though various stones are called "merlinite," including dendritic opal, generally it is a psilomelane quartz combination from one mine in New Mexico, made up of black manganese oxide crystals, covered or layered with white quartz or a mixture of several different minerals, including manganese

ZODIAC SIGN: Scorpio (October 24–November 22)

CANDLE COLOR: Silver

PHYSICAL: Removes energy blockages; promotes deep healing, left- and right-brain hemisphere balance; strengthens the brain stem; speeds recovery from major surgical procedures.

EMOTIONAL: Salves deep wounds; encourages self-forgiveness; overcomes dark nights of the soul; balances anima/animus, goddess/god energies.

HOME: Finds the right accommodations in an expensive area or if there is high demand.

WORKPLACE: Musters courage and stamina to survive in a hostile work environment.

CHILDREN: Connects with benign nature spirits.

ANIMALS: For old soul pets, with you in many lifetimes.

PROTECTION: Breaks the hold of those who use magick, religion, or psychic powers to manipulate others, control their minds, or extort money from them.

MAGICKAL AND PSYCHIC USES

An offering in ceremonial magick and Earth healing; contact with spirit guides; automatic writing, astral dream travel, messages from deceased relatives; alchemy, shamanism, and wizardry.

SPECIAL PROPERTIES

The stone of attracting good fortune; developing your psychic radar for awareness of opportunities just over the horizon.

MYTHOLOGY AND HISTORY

Associated with magickal traditions, such as the Celtic druid wizard Merlin, Merlinite offers visions of ancient magickal worlds and reawakens past-life spiritual gifts.

Mesosiderite

COLORS: Grays and browns

CRYSTAL TYPE: A stony iron meteorite, where half is iron and nickel and the rest silicates; caused when two asteroids collide, so this stone is infused with incredible energy. In the crash, molten metal mixes together with solid fragments of silicate rocks, creating lumps or pebbles

ZODIAC SIGN: Aries (March 21–April 20)

CANDLE COLOR: Red

PHYSICAL: Leads to successful microsurgery to rejoin tissue or reattach body parts; useful for heart, liver, lung, and kidney transplants, as well as replacement heart valves, triple-bypass surgery, stents, and pacemakers.

EMOTIONAL: Helps overcome co-dependence and dependence issues; curbs an inability to let children grow up and become independent.

HOME: Merges two households after remarriage.

WORKPLACE: Enables two companies to forge a joint venture or launch a new partnership.

CHILDREN: For children reluctant to leave home and attend kindergarten, day care, or start school; for teenagers clashing with parents over imposed restrictions.

ANIMALS: Retrains a pet who suddenly begins to misbehave.

PROTECTION: Guards against feeling or being taken over by another person or spirit.

MAGICKAL AND PSYCHIC USES

For attraction and manifestation rituals, thanks to the magnetic properties of meteorites; fire magick; calling a soul twin, known or unknown, to appear in your life.

SPECIAL PROPERTIES

This meteorite is the ultimate unifier, whether it guides two people to come together in love, aids you in finding the perfect niche in life, or helps in joining forces in a successful property venture with a relative or partner, usually after initial difficulties.

MYTHOLOGY AND HISTORY

The most famous Mesosiderite fall was in 1879 in Estherville, Iowa, the largest meteorite to fall in North America. Other notable falls have occurred at Vaca Muerta in the Atacama Desert in Chile, and at Dong Ujimqin Qi in China in 1995.

Messina Quartz

COLORS: Clear quartz, colored by its inclusions; for example, strawberry pink if there are multiple pink hematite phantoms within; often hand-polished

CRYSTAL TYPE: Remarkable as a quartz that contains many different minerals, often more than one mineral in the same quartz, sometimes as multilayered phantoms; minerals include azurite, epidote malachite black, pink and red hematite, shattuckite, and, less commonly, papagoite and ajoite

ZODIAC SIGN: Aquarius (January 21–February 18)

CANDLE COLOR: White

PHYSICAL: A whole-body healer, amplified in strength by the enclosing quartz—ajoite for hormones, azurite for detoxifying, epidote for liver, hematite for red blood cell problems, malachite for headaches, papagoite for throat, and shattuckite for diabetes (see separate crystal entries for full list).

EMOTIONAL: Helps curb a tendency to constantly change interests.

HOME: Draws energies from the Earth, nature, and the cosmos to create a continuing flow of life force.

WORKPLACE: For coordinating a multifocused team or project involving different concurrent stages.

CHILDREN: Calms those who find it hard to settle into routine schoolwork because of an overactive mind.

ANIMALS: Messina is close to Timbavati, South Africa, which means "place where the sacred came from the stars"; the long-prophesied white lions came to the area in the 1970s, just after Messina Quartz attracted people's attention.

PROTECTION: Guards against missing what is of true worth and beauty.

MAGICKAL AND PSYCHIC USES

Connection with subterranean Earth spirits.

SPECIAL PROPERTIES

Messina Quartz carries the concentrated energies of what remains now in the ground and so will become more magickal through the years as it becomes even scarcer.

MYTHOLOGY AND HISTORY

The Messina region is home to what is believed to be the abandoned, mysterious kingdom of Mapungubwe, the place of the boiling stones, which survived up to about 1,000 years ago.

Meteorite

COLORS: Gray, black, brown-black, or red-brown on the outside; often silver-gray inside

CRYSTAL TYPE: Magnetic space rock, alloyed with nickel and iron

ZODIAC SIGNS: All signs

CANDLE COLOR: Silver

PHYSICAL: Eases muscle spasms, anemia, digestive issues; addresses illnesses difficult to diagnose or treat.

EMOTIONAL: Helps overcome bad habits or phobias after past failure; amplifies remote healing.

HOME: Meteorites near entrances protect against fire, storms, and tornadoes.

WORKPLACE: Breaks through rigid thinking, inspires new practices and international or online business ideas.

CHILDREN: Comforts Star Children and those who dream of or describe extraterrestrials or UFOs.

ANIMALS: For aristocratic, telepathic cats.

PROTECTION: Guards against unwise emotional attachments and temptations; deflects crises.

MAGICKAL AND PSYCHIC USES

For astrologers, cryptozoologists, and inventors; positive extraterrestrial encounters and connection with Beings of Light; protects against unfriendly alien encounters.

SPECIAL PROPERTIES

An amulet against international terrorism, hijacking, or violent crime; inspires major lifestyle changes.

MYTHOLOGY AND HISTORY

Most Meteorites originate in the asteroid belt between Mars and Jupiter. The most common small, spherical Meteorites—chondrite—are unchanged since the solar system was formed, being unlike any rocks on Earth. The ancient Egyptians had a hieroglyph for "heavenly metal" and capped some pyramids with meteorites. For thousands of years, Meteorites were considered signs from the gods and gifts to humankind, containing treasures—iron, olivine crystals, and occasionally diamonds. Signifying divine displeasure, Jupiter's thunderbolts may also have been Meteorites; meteor showers opportunely appeared over Ireland as St. Patrick was trying to persuade pagans about the might of God.

Mica

COLORS: Pearly with shimmer, pink, violet, gray, black, brown, green, purple, red, white, yellow

CRYSTAL TYPE: A group of minerals, phyllosilicates (sheet silicates); delicate

ZODIAC SIGN: Aquarius (January 21–February 18)

CANDLE COLOR: Silver

PHYSICAL: Strengthens arteries, liver, digestion, blood sugar; alleviates candida and sexually transmitted infections, colds, viruses, dehydration, insomnia, sleep apnea, fears of childbirth after a difficult previous birth; bolsters skin elasticity, stamina, memory, concentration.

EMOTIONAL: Curbs hysteria, binge eating, feast and famine dieting; keeps you from projecting your personal failings onto others.

HOME: Balances Earth energies beneath the home, whether too harsh or sluggish; protects you while living in an earthquake zone.

WORKPLACE: For mentoring and being mentored; prevents your own and others' personal problems from adversely affecting your professionalism; keeps you from taking work problems home.

CHILDREN: Guards teens against fears of ghosts, evil, and frightening premonitions.

ANIMALS: Protects against those who wish to harm others' pets; thwarts animal thieves.

PROTECTION: Shields you from becoming overwhelmed by life; guards against anger, spite, violence, theft, and neighborhood gangs.

MAGICKAL AND PSYCHIC USES

Clairvoyance, awareness of the fey; enhances healing crystal grids; aligns body, mind, and spirit; increases psychic powers.

SPECIAL PROPERTIES

Insulates you from excessive energy from phone towers, high-tension wires, electrical appliances, and technological devices.

MYTHOLOGY AND HISTORY

Mica was known in ancient Egypt, Greece, Rome, and the Aztec world. It is a generic name for a group of thirty-seven complex, hydrous, potassium-aluminum silicate minerals that differ in chemical composition. Some have strong individual characteristics and distinctive crystal names; for example, Biotite (page 55), Lepidolite (page 277), Fuchsite (page 194), and Muscovite (page 312), the most common form of mica.

Midnight Lace Obsidian

COLORS: Black with white/beige lace patterns on the surface; may have layers of black and clear stone
CRYSTAL TYPE: Volcanic glass, with patterning caused by the initial volcanic flow in its formation; may include traces of other obsidians, such as mahogany
ZODIAC SIGN: Scorpio (October 24–November 22)
CANDLE COLOR: White

PHYSICAL: Alleviates insomnia, inflammation of the joints, neuralgia, viruses, infections, allergic reactions to insecticides, overreliance on prescription drugs.
EMOTIONAL: Helps establish boundaries between yourself and others; keeps you from leading a double life in love or finances.
HOME: For tact and diplomacy in bringing together relatives or extended family at necessary celebrations.
WORKPLACE: Enhances investigative work, such as insurance or compensation claims; avoids plagiarism of ideas.
CHILDREN: For siblings who raid others' possessions; for those who take delight in reporting others' misdeeds.
ANIMALS: Aids in introducing pets to new family members, whether a partner, baby, or stepchildren.
PROTECTION: Guards against intrusion of privacy, both physically and of thoughts.

MAGICKAL AND PSYCHIC USES

Creating a shield of invisibility or low profile where there is potential danger; a powerful amulet against malicious intent.

SPECIAL PROPERTIES

The stone of secrecy for those who need to keep love or beliefs hidden or who require uninterrupted time to complete tasks.

MYTHOLOGY AND HISTORY

Midnight Lace Obsidian, recently discovered in the Caucasian Mountains of Armenia, is one of the new dynamic fire crystals offered by Mother Earth to spread reconciliation and communication between people; another luck-bringer.

Milarite

COLORS: Green, yellow, colorless, clear
CRYSTAL TYPE: Rare hydrated potassium, calcium, aluminum beryllium silicate; may be gem quality
ZODIAC SIGN: Virgo (August 24–September 22)
CANDLE COLOR: Green

PHYSICAL: Addresses excessive testosterone in either sex, diabetes, retinal problems, kidney dialysis, and transplants.
EMOTIONAL: Counters aggression and the desire to always control others; curbs the tendency to live an image and deny your true self.
HOME: Balances the yin and yang energies if some family members are overly confrontational; creates a loving sanctuary where all within feel valued and safe.
WORKPLACE: For an overly competitive workplace, where personal targets and bonus incentives cause disharmony.
CHILDREN: For nonacademic children in a school where high marks and rewards for achievement predominate.
ANIMALS: Aids in gently retiring a show, breeding, or competition animal if their performance is deteriorating.
PROTECTION: Valuable for ongoing cleansing of undesirable or harmful energies and influences.

MAGICKAL AND PSYCHIC USES

For beginners or those uncertain about astral travel to gain the assurance of the silver cord, enabling the mind to return to the body any time; scrying within the stone; messages may be seen as words in the mind, supplemented by subsequent automatic writing.

SPECIAL PROPERTIES

For learning to heal, especially using touch therapies or energy transference, by allowing compassion for the client to guide the process, rather than worrying about following specific techniques to the letter.

MYTHOLOGY AND HISTORY

From Brazil and the Alps, Mexico and New Hampshire, Milarite is the stone of expressing the true self without ego or concern for image; where an overtly macho culture in childhood has left men struggling to express their anima nature; for women executives in a male-dominated company to stand their ground without resorting to aggression.

Milky Opal

COLORS: Milky white to light gray and cloudy

CRYSTAL TYPE: Hydrated silicon dioxide; a fairly common opal, though the name is sometimes applied to milky white opalescent precious opal and those with light backgrounds

ZODIAC SIGN: Cancer (June 22–July 22)

CANDLE COLOR: Cream

PHYSICAL: Promotes conception, pregnancy, childbirth; addresses breast problems in women of any age; alleviates dementia, especially in women.

EMOTIONAL: Curbs fears of childbirth deterring a woman from trying for a baby; eases overwhelming fears during pregnancy and the early months of a baby's life.

HOME: For a family member whose memory is fading; for harmonious mealtimes.

WORKPLACE: For professions caring for babies and children; calms angry customers if you work in customer service or in a call center.

CHILDREN: Aids in dealing with foster children or stepchildren who test your patience; to ease a child into day care or his or her first school experience.

ANIMALS: For exotic aviary birds and tropical fish.

PROTECTION: Guards against an overly possessive mother figure.

MAGICKAL AND PSYCHIC USES

Traditionally believed to confer invisibility, Milky Opal creates a low profile in times of potential danger; for tantric sex, tai chi, sacred dance, yoga, prayer, and connecting with a guardian angel.

SPECIAL PROPERTIES

Traditionally, Milky Opal promotes fertility, buried beneath a willow, the mother tree or any fruit tree on full moon to conceive a child.

MYTHOLOGY AND HISTORY

Common opals have the same healing and magickal powers as iridescent precious opals, but their energies are slower-acting. Milky Opals have been called the milk drops of the Mother Goddess in a number of cultures and are an ideal gift for a new mother.

Mochi or Moqui Marbles

COLOR: Brownish-black, tan, lighter reddish-brown

CRYSTAL TYPE: Compacted sandstone in a shell of iron compounds, ranging from small marble to baseball size

ZODIAC SIGN: Capricorn (December 22–January 20)

CANDLE COLOR: Dark red.

PHYSICAL: Stimulates the life-force by addressing physical blockages or misalignments; counters unsteadiness, artery constrictions, osteoporosis; supports the immune system; strengthens cells.

EMOTIONAL: Curbs alienation and isolation from life after rejection; creates the right individual male/female energy mix if you're struggling with gender issues.

HOME: A Moqui Marble, placed inside the home on either side of the front door, deters fire, flood, lightning, unfriendly spirits, and intruders.

WORKPLACE: A pair of marbles psychically alerts you to trustworthiness or untrustworthiness when buying from a new supplier, investing, or trading; restores night workers' and shift workers' sleep patterns.

CHILDREN: For children who love unicorns and dragons.

ANIMALS: Establishes connections with magickal animals and creatures not found on Earth.

PROTECTION: Guards against those taking advantage of your generosity.

MAGICKAL AND PSYCHIC USES

Shamanic visionary, healing and magickal stones in Native North America; for trance states, extraterrestrial communication, ancient civilizations, and future worlds; Earth healing.

SPECIAL PROPERTIES

For healing and metaphysical purposes, use a large and a small one, one rounded and one disk-shaped.

MYTHOLOGY AND HISTORY

Mochi or Moqui Marbles, originally found in the southwestern United States, were discovered during archaeological excavations in other continents. According to Native North American Hopi myth, Moqui Marbles are the gaming stones of departed ancestors returning to play at sunset. Similar rocks have been found on Mars; the earthly forms inspire astronomers, astrologers, and ufologists.

Moldau Quartz

COLORS: White, gray, orange, rusty brown

CRYSTAL TYPE: Silicon dioxide, found in the Czech Republic, now referred to as Czechia, in close proximity to natural glass Moldavite, created by the impact of an asteroid almost fifteen million years ago; over time Moldau Quartz has absorbed the deep healing powers of Moldavite

ZODIAC SIGN: Aquarius (January 21–February 18)

CANDLE COLOR: White

PHYSICAL: Helps overcome general ill health, constantly feeling exhausted and below par without an obvious cause, reliance on numerous seemingly miracle cures.

EMOTIONAL: For clinging to unhealthy habits and addictions while paying lip service to therapy; being influenced by risk takers who appear exciting.

HOME: Aids in influencing wayward family members by example and practical assistance, rather than arguing or assigning blame; gradually creates the décor that for you constitutes beauty.

WORKPLACE: For absorbing knowledge through working in a chosen field, rather than studying the theory; for naturopaths.

CHILDREN: Insulates Star Children from acute sensitivity to earthly stimuli in their first or an early incarnation on Earth.

ANIMALS: For pets who react badly to the presence of other animals.

PROTECTION: Guards against bombardment by random premonitions and spirit contact.

MAGICKAL AND PSYCHIC USES

For beginners in magick, healing, and divination to gradually open their psychic powers; enhances Reiki, clairvoyance, and clairaudience.

SPECIAL PROPERTIES

Moldau Quartz awakens the inner divine spark and brings celestial energies into the everyday world; combines emotions, intuition, and logic to offer an overview of whatever is under consideration.

MYTHOLOGY AND HISTORY

Like Rosophia (page 410), Moldau Quartz is linked with Sophia, the ancient Greek goddess of wisdom, who became known as the angel Sophia and St. Sophia, beloved of the Russian Orthodox church.

Moldavite

COLORS: Deep bottle green; glassy

CRYSTAL TYPE: Silica-based tektite, natural glass, created by the impact of an asteroid almost fifteen million years ago

ZODIAC SIGNS: Scorpio (October 24–November 22) and Aquarius (January 21–February 18)

CANDLE COLOR: Deep green

PHYSICAL: Slows degeneration; stimulates regeneration of mind and body; promotes fertility; counters hair loss, and ills caused by the modern world; alleviates issues stemming from the eyes and the respiratory system; may make you feel disoriented.

EMOTIONAL: Rapidly brings chakra energy centers into harmony when shattered by trauma; reduces cravings for cigarettes.

HOME: Prevents loneliness if you live alone, whether by choice or necessity.

WORKPLACE: Brings satisfaction working from home or in a one-person business.

CHILDREN: Helps dreamy children manifest imagination creatively.

ANIMALS: For pets, especially cats, who have been with you before.

PROTECTION: Shields against negative spirit entities, undesirable influences, weaknesses leading to addictions.

MAGICKAL AND PSYCHIC USES

Brings connection with spirit guides, ascended masters; for Star Souls to link especially with the Sirius star system, or Pleiades, through lucid dreams and astral travel.

SPECIAL PROPERTIES

An amulet from Paleolithic times, a symbol of lasting love, traditionally given to brides; brings good fortune and manifests wishes.

MYTHOLOGY AND HISTORY

Called the holy grail crystal, Moldavite, in myth, adorned the grail cup, having fallen from Lucifer's crown when he was thrown from heaven. Found only in Czechia, formerly the Czech Republic, in the Moldau River Valley.

Molybdenite in Quartz

COLORS: Steel gray, bluish-silver, metallic (resembles graphite but lighter and bluer) within clear crystal

CRYSTAL TYPE: Sulfide, soft enough to leave a mark on paper; best used included in quartz, as it crumbles

ZODIAC SIGN: Scorpio (October 24–November 22)

CANDLE COLOR: White

PHYSICAL: Promotes strength and vitality by rebalancing the body; addresses teeth, jaw, and face problems; assists with long-term effects of mercury dental fillings.

EMOTIONAL: Curbs false-memory syndrome, which has damaged relationships, denying your true personality to fit with the expectations of others.

HOME: For keeping in a high place in the home near a skylight, attic, or air vent to draw upward and outward emotional debris, replacing it by constant circulation.

WORKPLACE: Organizes and harmonizes groups or teams, where there may have been initial differences in personality and aims.

CHILDREN: Aids in understanding children with communication difficulties and releasing their potential.

ANIMALS: For bringing out in a pet the ability to instinctively connect with you when you are not together.

PROTECTION: Guards against unhelpful people who may disguise their intentions.

MAGICKAL AND PSYCHIC USES

Merges the auras of two people for love or a group working together for ritual, healing, or collective past-life work; brings answers and healing in dreams.

SPECIAL PROPERTIES

Called the light in the darkness crystal for new beginnings and a new life, while preserving what is good about the past and present.

MYTHOLOGY AND HISTORY

Combined with quartz, the mystical powers of Molybdenite are given strength and focus; believed by some crystal experts to have been sent to Earth from a distant planet. The purpose, it is said, was so Lemurians might empower the transference of their knowledge into crystals and enable them to travel to other parts of the world to spread their wisdom.

Montebrasite

COLORS: Blue, clear/colorless, gray, pink, tan, white, yellow; often vibrant colors

CRYSTAL TYPE: Lithium phosphate, a variety of Amblygonite (page 21); faceted for jewelry, especially in clear form; good for healing and magick and as anti-worry amulets as tumbled stones

ZODIAC SIGN: Leo (July 23–August 23)

CANDLE COLOR: Gold

PHYSICAL: Alleviates fluid retention, heartburn, IBS, stomach ulcers, celiac disease, lactose intolerance, allergies to modern chemicals in swimming pools or added to water supplies or as additives to flavored drinking waters.

EMOTIONAL: Eases bipolar conditions, phobias, fear of germs, OCD, acute anxiety.

HOME: Aids in completing half-finished projects around the home and property; demanding definite dates and commitments from your partner or family members for vaguely suggested vacations or major plans.

WORKPLACE: Encourages honesty among colleagues or employees as turquoise blue or clear crystals; the presence of the crystal makes it hard for others to conceal facts.

CHILDREN: Keep this crystal with school reports or college assignments for those who find it hard to complete tasks.

ANIMALS: For pets who lose focus during a training session.

PROTECTION: Guards against specific fears, named as the stone is held.

MAGICKAL AND PSYCHIC USES

Traditionally placed on top of a written wish or need and left for seven days to bring strategies for its attainment and ultimately the manifestation of solutions.

SPECIAL PROPERTIES

To maintain a cheerful, encouraging disposition, especially with the yellow crystal, when friends, family, and colleagues are particularly challenging.

MYTHOLOGY AND HISTORY

Originally discovered in Montebras in the Creuse region of France in 1871 and also found in Pakistan, the USA, and Brazil; the crystal can be programmed as a talisman to block specific fears and carried to keep them from returning; brings happiness to family occasions, vacations, parties, or social gatherings.

Mookaite

COLORS: Mottled patches of yellow, orange, brown, beige and white, mauve and purple
CRYSTAL TYPE: Jasper (chalcedony quartz) and chert, sometimes with fossilized inclusions
ZODIAC SIGN: Virgo (August 24–September 22)
CANDLE COLOR: Orange

PHYSICAL: Slows down aging; speeds up wound healing; settles bodily imbalances, especially in the digestive tract.
EMOTIONAL: Often used in crystal elixirs to reduce stress that makes physical conditions worse (see page 527 for making elixirs).
HOME: For relocations and major renovations (guards against accidents).
WORKPLACE: Useful if colleagues or management are constantly procrastinating.
CHILDREN: Helps pregnant parents connect with their unborn child.
ANIMALS: Restores natural rhythms to overly domesticated pets.
PROTECTION: Increases awareness of potential dangers when traveling or during adventurous activities.

MAGICKAL AND PSYCHIC USES
An Australian Aboriginal earth rainbow stone, containing sacred Earth energies that have passed into general healing and magickal use.

SPECIAL PROPERTIES
Used in rituals or buried with blessings to heal the planet and to conserve Earth energy sites, whose energies have been adversely affected by insensitive land-management practices or tourism.

MYTHOLOGY AND HISTORY
From Mooka Creek, Western Australia—*Mooka* being Australian Aboriginal for "running waters"; dating from great antiquity, Mookaite is created from radiolarian, which are microscopic protozoa (one-celled creatures), whose skeletons form a hard silica shell over millennia in now-receded shallow seas.

Morella or Mooralla Smoky Quartz

COLORS: Dark gray to black, the darkest naturally occurring smoky quartz, irradiated in the Earth and not artificially
CRYSTAL TYPE: Silicon dioxide, often double-terminated or in clusters
ZODIAC SIGN: Scorpio (October 24–November 22)
CANDLE COLOR: Gray

PHYSICAL: Considered helpful against side effects of radiation, chemotherapy, or prolonged invasive treatment; alleviates chronic pain, especially in the lower half of the body; promotes successful hip and knee replacements; aids in elimination of toxins from adrenal glands, kidneys, and pancreas.
EMOTIONAL: Counters panic attacks, agoraphobia, compulsions, obsessions, and cravings; curbs hyperactivity in people of any age.
HOME: Guards against social media attacks or trolling; creates an aura of calm so evenings will be relaxed.
WORKPLACE: Absorbs gossip, jealousy, resentment; deters those who deliberately provoke disagreements keeps colleagues who are overly curious about your work practices from hacking into your devices.
CHILDREN: Place Morella with the photo of a child as a shield against all harm; for those spooked by fears of ghosts or monsters in their bedroom.
ANIMALS: For overly sensitive pets who are disturbed by loud noises, fireworks, storms, or sudden movements.
PROTECTION: Guards against those who speak or act maliciously in your absence; deflects curses, hexes, jinxes, and ill-wishing.

MAGICKAL AND PSYCHIC USES
Drives away poltergeists, malevolent or restless ghosts; cleanses property or land where tragedies or evil have occurred in earlier times, even hundreds of years before.

SPECIAL PROPERTIES
Very protective if you regularly use crowded commuter freeways or drive alone at night.

MYTHOLOGY AND HISTORY
Found only in Morella, Victoria, Australia, a sacred stone of Australian Indigenous ceremonies; contains within it the wisdom and Earth healing of the Indigenous world, wherever you live on the globe; brings a deep connection with your own ancestral lands.

Morganite or Pink Beryl

COLORS: Pink, rose-lilac, peach; colored by manganese and lithium; sometimes called pink emerald
CRYSTAL TYPE: Beryllium-aluminum silicate
ZODIAC SIGN: Taurus (April 21–May 21)
CANDLE COLOR: Pink

PHYSICAL: Alleviates issues stemming from the larynx, tongue, thyroid, burns and scalds, bruises, abrasions; counters breathing difficulties, heart palpitations; chronic fatigue syndrome, particularly in women; stress-related illnesses.
EMOTIONAL: Helps younger people overcome eating disorders; for all who have poor self-image or problems with sexuality or gender; releases redundant attachments.
HOME: For closed-minded family members to accept alternative viewpoints or lifestyles.
WORKPLACE: Propels self-employment and small businesses facing competition from larger organizations.
CHILDREN: Assists those lacking effective mothering, especially girls approaching puberty; eases loneliness; helps children to say thank-you.
ANIMALS: For animals abandoned at birth; pets taken too young from their mother.
PROTECTION: Aids in dealing with difficult, hostile, or disturbed people to maintain compassion without being intimidated.

MAGICKAL AND PSYCHIC USES
Forges connection with guardian angels and personal spirit guides; offers psychic protection in spooky places; enhances goddess rituals; contacts female ancestors, especially deceased mothers and grandmothers.

SPECIAL PROPERTIES
Attracts and keeps love, draws soul twins; enables a couple to express deep feelings; promotes romance; cultivates awareness of divine love, especially after loss.

MYTHOLOGY AND HISTORY
Named in honor of John Pierpoint Morgan, an American banker and philanthropist who was interested in magic and mineralogy, Morganite has been adopted as the stone of lawyers, bankers, and negotiators, as well as individuals facing legal battles regarding inheritances, compensation, or threats from official financial organizations, such as the IRS.

Morion Quartz

COLORS: Black or almost black
CRYSTAL TYPE: A form of smoky quartz, silicon dioxide mixed with organic impurities, naturally irradiated in the Earth
ZODIAC SIGN: Capricorn (December 22–January 20)
CANDLE COLOR: Gray

PHYSICAL: Balances unstable conditions; shields against harmful effects of radiation therapy; counters asbestosis, or lead or mercury poisoning; eases pain in the back, legs, and feet.
EMOTIONAL: Comforts after tragedy, attack, or serious abuse; mitigates panic attacks, self-destructive tendencies, self-harm.
HOME: Useful if you live on an Earth energy line, near a site of past tragedies or massacres, or previous homeowners who experienced major sorrow.
WORKPLACE: Promotes effective teamwork; enables you to see through deceitful people and offers; brings good luck in business deals.
CHILDREN: For angry teenagers who lash out physically, especially at parents; prevents nightmares.
ANIMALS: Helps a pet with an unpredictable temperament to become more reliable.
PROTECTION: Guards against malicious spirits called up in ouija boards, séances, or online demonic rituals.

MAGICKAL AND PSYCHIC USES
Increases psychic abilities; aids channeling while offering built-in protection; ensure safe shamanic journeying by night or in dreams.

SPECIAL PROPERTIES
Fosters reconciliation; encourages acceptance of faults in yourself and others if you have a tendency to put a lover on a pedestal and become rapidly disillusioned.

MYTHOLOGY AND HISTORY
Pliny the Elder, the first-century CE Roman natural historian, called an unidentified black crystal "momorion"; though rare, Morion is sought after by ghost hunters, shamans, and healers as a shield against low-life spirits masquerading as deities, angels, relatives, and famous people; keep in teenagers' rooms if they are dabbling in the occult.

Moroccan Seam Agate

COLORS: Vibrant shades of red, pink, orange, yellow, white, brown, green as Moroccan green skin seam agate, and gray and white with red as Moroccan ghost seam agate

CRYSTAL TYPE: Cryptocrystalline silica in colored bands, a semi-precious agate with plumes branching outwards

ZODIAC SIGN: Sagittarius (November 23–December 21)

CANDLE COLOR: Red

PHYSICAL: Promotes lactation; eases stomach upset; useful in treating issues associated with the uterus, fallopian tubes, labia, lesions.

EMOTIONAL: Curbs postnatal depression, problems parenting, especially among those who were inadequately mothered as children; helps overcome fear of flying.

HOME: For living overseas or in warm, sunny places; being part of a dual-faith household or adopting a partner's religion.

WORKPLACE: Builds up confidence in a new workplace.

CHILDREN: Aids in balancing a modern peer group way of life with a traditional lifestyle.

ANIMALS: For a mother animal to adopt an orphan of a different species.

PROTECTION: Guards travelers, their possessions, and their documents.

MAGICKAL AND PSYCHIC USES

A good luck talisman; banishes unfriendly spirits; for connecting with benign Mountain and Air spirits.

SPECIAL PROPERTIES

Because the Atlas Mountain ranges, where Moroccan Seam Agate is found, form the barrier between the arid Sahara and Morocco's milder coast, Moroccan Seam Agate is considered a transition stone for moving into happier times.

MYTHOLOGY AND HISTORY

Seam agate is found in many countries, though the Moroccan variety is considered one of the most beautiful and magickal stones. Other seam agates include bright blue tide agate from Indonesia, Lake Superior seam agate in Michigan, and Idaho seam agate.

Moss Agate

COLORS: Clear or milky white with green inclusions resembling moss or lichen; may appear dark green with bluish inclusions; occasionally has red spots

CRYSTAL TYPE: Quartz-based chalcedony with inclusions of manganese, iron oxide, or hornblende (see also Dendritic or Tree Agate, page 159)

ZODIAC SIGN: Virgo (August 24–September 22)

CANDLE COLOR: Dark green

PHYSICAL: An antiinflammatory, Moss Agate alleviates colds, flu, viruses, low blood sugar, dehydration, fungal and skin infections, progressive illnesses; supports the immune system; eases childbirth.

EMOTIONAL: Releases fears preventing new beginnings; counters withdrawal from life after illness, loss, or burnout.

HOME: Known as the gardener's crystal to make plants flourish; encourages savings, reverses outflow of money.

WORKPLACE: Promotes new business, gradual expansion, and growing prosperity; aids in balancing the books and completing necessary paperwork; useful for careers in finance, horticulture, agriculture, aromatherapy, and homeopathy.

CHILDREN: Attracts friends when you're starting a new school or relocating.

ANIMALS: Helps indoor pets maintain vitality and connection with nature.

PROTECTION: Filters impurities from the aura if you live or work in a polluted environment.

MAGICKAL AND PSYCHIC USES

Contact with fey energies and nature spirits; magickal gardening by the moon; enhances effectiveness of herbal remedies; tunes into cloud-bursting and weather control.

SPECIAL PROPERTIES

Brings new friendships with like-minded people, new love, or regrowth of love; twin moss agates represent faithful love; increases mental and physical speed.

MYTHOLOGY AND HISTORY

In ancient Rome, Moss Agate was a talisman for good fortune, blessings of the deities, and victory. In Native North America, Moss Agate was considered a rain-bringer.

Moss Aura and Apple Aura Quartz

COLORS: Apple Aura is bright green and Moss Aura a softer shimmery moss or yellow green with iridescent flashes and a slightly metallic sheen

CRYSTAL TYPE: Two separate but very similar aura quartzes, Apple Aura Quartz is mainly nickel-bonded to quartz and Moss Aura Quartz has less nickel and added platinum

ZODIAC SIGN: Aquarius (January 21–February 18)

CANDLE COLOR: Green

PHYSICAL: Detoxifies the body; offers immunity to pollutants; strengthens the spleen; promotes absorption of nutrients and conditions where processing food within the body is an issue.

EMOTIONAL: Helps overcome an inability to break free from destructive relationships or attachments that hold back progress.

HOME: Aids in creating boundaries, and starting a new life, if you are temporarily sharing a home with an ex-partner after a separation.

WORKPLACE: For taking over abandoned or run-down business premises and transforming them into productive workspaces; attracts abundance to a workplace that closed due to bankruptcy or retirement.

CHILDREN: Prevents children from being forced to choose in custody and visitation disputes.

ANIMALS: Fosters amicable agreement over the future of pets after a divorce.

PROTECTION: Guards against sacrificing your personal identity to please others.

MAGICKAL AND PSYCHIC USES

For Earth energy rituals, nature magick; for connecting with Earth spirits; Apple Aura Quartz works with tree spirits and essences.

SPECIAL PROPERTIES

Moss Aura Quartz has gentler, lighter energies than Apple Aura Quartz, but both offer fresh energies and the removal of stagnation from any home, workplace, or situation.

MYTHOLOGY AND HISTORY

As a rare transformation crystal, Apple Aura Quartz brings lasting gradual growth, and Moss Aura Quartz spiritual awareness.

Mother and Child Quartz

COLORS: Varies with the quartz, but often clear

CRYSTAL TYPE: Two quartz crystals, one small, attached to the side of a larger crystal, not joined at the base; resembles a mother carrying a small child; also called the dolphin crystal, if pictured as a mother and baby dolphin

ZODIAC SIGN: Pisces (February 19–March 20)

CANDLE COLOR: White

PHYSICAL: Promotes fertility, pregnancy, childbirth, lactation; alleviates brain disorders and damage, cerebral palsy, memory and cognition issues, hydrocephalus, fluid retention.

EMOTIONAL: Curbs postnatal depression and out-of-proportion fears about everyday dangers to children; helps overcome inadequate or absent mothering in your own childhood.

HOME: Valuable for single parents; for creating a fun-filled, happy home on a budget.

WORKPLACE: For mothers with employers unsympathetic toward working mothers in a family crisis; counters unspoken reluctance to promote mothers.

CHILDREN: Encourages children afraid to leave their mothers to attend day care or social events; for intellectually challenged children to maximize their potential.

ANIMALS: To protect dolphins, whales, and other intelligent sea creatures from exploitation in water parks.

PROTECTION: Guards against psychic and psychological manipulation in the name of love.

MAGICKAL AND PSYCHIC USES

Promotes telepathy between parents, children, siblings, and partners; healing by swimming with dolphins.

SPECIAL PROPERTIES

Restore fun, joys and playfulness to an individual, brought up to display a rigid, unemotional response to life and relationships.

MYTHOLOGY AND HISTORY

Both the image of the mother and baby and the mother and infant dolphin make this a very nurturing crystal. No matter how you see the crystal—mother or dolphin—it will spontaneously release your own innate self-healing powers.

Mother of Pearl

COLORS: White, cream, or brown; iridescent

CRYSTAL TYPE: Organic, usually the lining of oyster shells, created from nacre or calcium carbonate that forms the shell lining

ZODIAC SIGN: Cancer (June 22–July 22)

CANDLE COLOR: Silver

PHYSICAL: Alleviates issues stemming from sinuses, cells, skin allergies, fluid retention; promotes preconception health, fertility, pregnancy, childbirth; helps newborn babies thrive; encourages gentle weight loss.

EMOTIONAL: Counters overreliance on parenting figures in adulthood, feast or famine dieting, fears of childbirth.

HOME: Attracts beauty, harmony, and abundance; for single parents.

WORKPLACE: Aids in returning to work after maternity or paternity leave; unburdens parents who work from home.

CHILDREN: Protects against separation anxiety; guards babies from harm.

ANIMALS: For a puppy or kitten taken from their mother too early.

PROTECTION: Repels negative vibes and paranormal entities; safeguards travelers alone, overseas and at night.

MAGICKAL AND PSYCHIC USES

For wish magick, fertility spells; sea rituals; moon magick on the crescent, waxing, and full moon.

SPECIAL PROPERTIES

Helps overcome maternal loss or the death of a child at any age; breaks patterns of destructive mothering in adulthood.

MYTHOLOGY AND HISTORY

Mother of Pearl is sacred to sea mothers; for example, in Peru, Mama Cocha or Mother Sea, the whale goddess, was originally worshipped by the Incas. Mother of Pearl attracts wealth, health, and longevity. Mother of Pearl amulets in the form of totem animals and sea creatures have been created by coastal Indigenous people for centuries.

Mount Shasta Opal

COLORS: Blue in an off-white or white matrix; the opal may contain dendrites, giving it green, white, and black inclusions

CRYSTAL TYPE: Common opal without play of colors; hydrated silica with impurities

ZODIAC SIGN: Aries (March 21–April 20)

CANDLE COLOR: Blue or red

PHYSICAL: Addresses issues involving the throat, eyes, blood sugar swings; for a gentle ongoing infusion of healing and insulation from pain and physical shock.

EMOTIONAL: Comforts you in the face of deep trauma following physical attack, extreme violence, a major accident, or witnessing murder or terrorism.

HOME: Creates a private harmonious space when moving to a refuge, detox center, or temporary accommodation.

WORKPLACE: For athletes, and those practicing yoga, tai chi, qi gong, and all energy-movement modalities; for entering a religious or spiritual order.

CHILDREN: Supports Star Souls and Crystal Children with a perfect rainbow aura and very old souls.

ANIMALS: Promotes the energies of magickal animals, such as unicorns and dragons, whose essences are said to dwell within Mount Shasta.

PROTECTION: Guards against cynicism and skepticism by those who mock or denigrate your spirituality.

MAGICKAL AND PSYCHIC USES

Opens portals between dimensions to communicate with archangels, ascended masters, Star Beings, elementals, and higher spirit guides.

SPECIAL PROPERTIES

Mount Shasta Opal brings and stabilizes lasting relationships and marriage.

MYTHOLOGY AND HISTORY

Mount Shasta, one of seven main energy vortices, is linked with the ancient wisdom of Lemuria. It is at the southern end of the Cascade Mountain Range in Siskiyou County, California.

Mozarkite

COLORS: White, gray, or brown; sometimes containing patches and swirls of pink, red, purple, orange, green, gold, black, and yellow

CRYSTAL TYPE: Chert, microcrystalline quartz, with gray or milky chalcedony

ZODIAC SIGN: Aries (March 21–April 20)

CANDLE COLOR: Red

PHYSICAL: Helps overcome vertigo; addresses issues stemming from the kidneys, liver, throat, speech and vocal cords; for developing an exercise regimen; aids in discovering your own allergy triggers.

EMOTIONAL: Curbs fear of injections and dentistry; mitigates an inability or unwillingness to give up recreational drugs.

HOME: Use Mozarkite to discover the source of harmful Earth energies near your home; spontaneously neutralizes the harmful energies once you've identified them, replacing them with positive, regulated flow.

WORKPLACE: Inspires actors, singers, musicians, and creators in the performing arts to shine in auditions and when approaching production companies.

CHILDREN: Soothing if your child is a natural worrier; helps clumsy children to gain fine motor skills.

ANIMALS: For large pets who clumsily walk or run into furniture.

PROTECTION: Guards against fear, panic, and anxiety.

MAGICKAL AND PSYCHIC USES

Astrology; channeling messages from the spirit world and interpreting them for others; enhancing psychic abilities; astral travel through meditation.

SPECIAL PROPERTIES

Enables you to really listen and understand the deeper feelings of others, whether professionally or for family and friends; aids in becoming the wise man or woman of your community.

MYTHOLOGY AND HISTORY

The state stone of Missouri, Mozarkite is found mainly in west-central Missouri in residual dolomite soils and as pebbles and cobbles in streams. It was used by Native North Americans to make tools and weapons and was formed during the Ordovician age about 505 million years ago, being named after the Ozark Mountains.

Mtorolite, Mtorodite, or Matorolite

COLORS: Rich emerald green

CRYSTAL TYPE: Chromium-rich chalcedony

ZODIAC SIGN: Virgo (August 24–September 22)

CANDLE COLOR: Bright green

PHYSICAL: Enhances effectiveness of flower remedies and essences, herbs, naturopathy, and aroma oils.

EMOTIONAL: Calms complaints made worse by anxiety; prevents insomnia; relieves depression.

HOME: If you've got too much to do, heads off accidents caused by haste.

WORKPLACE: Relieves stress or panic if you are pressured by deadlines.

CHILDREN: Lifts the mood of naturally pessimistic children.

ANIMALS: Enables overly domesticated animals to reconnect with nature.

PROTECTION: Shields against negative, toxic people.

MAGICKAL AND PSYCHIC USES

In meditation Mtorolite brings visions of Earth spirits. A shamanic stone, linked with Lemuria, the semimythical land believed to have existed fourteen thousand years ago, whose ancient wisdom is said to be stored in crystals; a source of past lives if held.

SPECIAL PROPERTIES

Brings the ability to discover our true-life purpose; opens hearts to life and love again after betrayal.

MYTHOLOGY AND HISTORY

Mainly found in Zimbabwe, where it was rediscovered in the 1950s. Used by the Romans for jewelry and seals but disappeared in the second century CE; a sacred stone to the Indigenous people of western Australia; in Bolivia, Turkey, and the Balkans, prized for its Earth wisdom.

Multicolored Tourmaline or Elbaite

COLORS: Combinations of two or more shades of pink, green, clear, purple, blue, pink, orange, red, or yellow, generally in bands
CRYSTAL TYPE: Sodium lithium aluminum boron-silicate
ZODIAC SIGN: Libra (September 23–October 23)
CANDLE COLOR: Green

PHYSICAL: An integrator crystal, for any malfunctioning connections in the mind or body; alleviates illnesses when the brain causes problems with speech or movement.
EMOTIONAL: Addresses acute psychological problems, psychosis, hallucinations; eases distress; valuable for gender issues where there is lack of support.
HOME: If you seem to be a sanctuary for neighbors, friends, and every waif and stray, to draw your boundaries without appearing unsociable.
WORKPLACE: For multitasking, bringing together people with different skill bases in a single project; combining part-time jobs into a new career or business; for artistic people.
CHILDREN: Useful for youngsters when they are getting mixed messages from parents who are living apart or experiencing divided loyalties.
ANIMALS: For adopting a trustworthy, mixed-breed pet, if the animal's background is unknown or the animal is a stray.
PROTECTION: Guards against being overwhelmed by demands, deadlines, and irrelevant information.

MAGICKAL AND PSYCHIC USES
The crystal of beautiful psychic dreams and bringing answers in dreams; for experiencing past-world visions at ancient sites or places of worship.

SPECIAL PROPERTIES
Multicolored Tourmaline brings harmony between the mind, body, spirit, and soul; balances all aspects of the self, assisting in all forms of spiritual, emotional, and physical healing.

MYTHOLOGY AND HISTORY
The most colorful member of the tourmaline group of crystals, hence the traditional belief in different cultures that tourmalines fell from the rainbow.

Muscovite

COLORS: White, silver, yellow, green (deep green as fuchsite), pink, purple, brown, often white tinged with other colors; sparkly
CRYSTAL TYPE: Mica (potassium aluminum silicate hydroxide)
ZODIAC SIGNS: Sagittarius (November 23–December 21) and Leo (July 23–August 23)
CANDLE COLOR: White

PHYSICAL: Alleviates dyspraxia and general clumsiness, sleep disturbances; reduces hunger pangs during detox or diets.
EMOTIONAL: Brings loving connections in a new relationship after a breakup.
HOME: If you've had a run of bad luck at home or illness; assists positive change.
WORKPLACE: Fosters problem solving; aids in interviewing new staff and checking out new sources of materials; helps to win contracts and sales, especially to other countries.
CHILDREN: Promotes study skills, especially if teens have difficulty revising their work.
ANIMALS: For young animals, pining for their mother.
PROTECTION: Ensures safe air travel, especially long-distance.

MAGICKAL AND PSYCHIC USES
For learning spirituality and traditional healing techniques of other lands; connecting with spirit guides.

SPECIAL PROPERTIES
Vibrates if a person is lying or exaggerating; place the crystal by a computer for wise internet shopping; helps in learning languages and mastering technical material.

MYTHOLOGY AND HISTORY
Muscovite, originally used for window glass, especially in sacred buildings in Russia, is also found in Austria, the Czech Republic, New Mexico, Switzerland, the USA, and western Australia. Yellow Brazilian Muscovite, forming a five-pointed star, assists astrologers and astronomers.

Mystic Topaz

COLORS: Produces an array of shining rainbow colors, usually predominantly green or purple, bluish-green being the most common
CRYSTAL TYPE: Made with titanium vapor treatment on a colorless topaz
ZODIAC SIGN: Scorpio (October 24–November 22)
CANDLE COLOR: Purple

PHYSICAL: Alleviates issues stemming from the eyes, inner ear, glands, blockages in veins and arteries, irregular heartbeat, weakness after injury to the spinal column; promotes balance, virility.
EMOTIONAL: Helps overcome depression, pessimism, inability to forgive self or others for past hurts or wrongs; curbs a tendency to blame childhood and old love affairs for life's failures.
HOME: Also called fire topaz, Mystic Topaz casts a powerful rainbow aura around the home, filling it with light, love, and laughter.
WORKPLACE: Brings prosperity and good luck by attracting the right business associates, opportunities, and networks for profitable deals.
CHILDREN: Reduces nightmares, sleepwalking, sleep talking, and fears of the dark.
ANIMALS: For a seriously traumatized, totally unresponsive animal.
PROTECTION: Reduces visibility in hostile or potentially dangerous situations.

MAGICKAL AND PSYCHIC USES
Cleanses and strengthens the aura, replacing missing or pale colors and increasing confidence and charisma to find new friends, lasting love, and recognition.
SPECIAL PROPERTIES
The stone of forgiveness for wrongs done to you that weigh you down or, if too bad to forgive, to walk away with blessings; for bringing together diverse people with whom you feel soul affinity.
MYTHOLOGY AND HISTORY
Mystic Topaz, also called fire topaz, releases the white-light spectrum of its base, colorless topaz, into a moving rainbow to fill your future with promise of fulfillment.

Natrolite

COLORS: Usually white, also found as colorless, yellowy, or gray
CRYSTAL TYPE: Sodium aluminum silicate, a slender, vertically striated zeolite
ZODIAC SIGN: Pisces (February 19–March 20)
CANDLE COLOR: White

PHYSICAL: Addresses brain and nervous system disorders and neural pathways, particularly in degenerative conditions; alleviates chronic illnesses unresponsive to treatment or made worse by stress; counters fluid retention.
EMOTIONAL: Effective against self-harming, self-destructive behavior.
HOME: Absorbs toxins; cleanses negative atmospheres, especially those brought home after a bad day at work.
WORKPLACE: For pursuing a career that is of service to others as well as making money; for writers, especially those who write self-help books
CHILDREN: Comforts psychic children who are unsettled by paranormal experiences and powers; aids in overcoming fear of water.
ANIMALS: For connecting telepathically with pets when you are late coming home or must be away.
PROTECTION: Guards against negative energies, influences, and entities.

MAGICKAL AND PSYCHIC USE
Strengthens angelic and spirit guide connections; increases clairaudience and clairvoyance, astral travel to other dimensions; automatic writing.
SPECIAL PROPERTIES
Offers enlightenment and light-bulb moments when the purpose of your life becomes clear.
MYTHOLOGY AND HISTORY
Sometimes called pathway to the angels, Natrolite is found in Australia, Germany, India, Russia, the Czech Republic, and the USA. A powerful stone for creating a bridge between the spiritual and the everyday worlds.

Nebula Stone

COLORS: Dark green, almost black, with light green, swirling, nebula-like eye formations and white patterns

CRYSTAL TYPE: Igneous, containing aegirine, anorthoclase, acmite, arfvedsonite calcite, riebeckite, white quartz, and zircon

ZODIAC SIGN: Scorpio (October 24–November 22)

CANDLE COLOR: Deep green

PHYSICAL: Offers whole-body healing; addresses malfunctions of nervous and neurone systems; alleviates degenerative conditions, illnesses caused by chemicals and environmental pollution, kidney problems.

EMOTIONAL: For maintaining your position when people are pulling you in different directions.

HOME: Aids in settling in if you're sharing a house; offers comfort if you've moved away with a partner and miss your family.

WORKPLACE: Valuable for lawyers and all who professionally fight against injustice or in a peace movement.

CHILDREN: For children on the autism spectrum or with communication difficulties.

ANIMALS: Stimulates the protection of endangered species.

PROTECTION: In hard times, encourages you to be kind to yourself and seek help.

MAGICKAL AND PSYCHIC USES

Called the window into the cosmos; for meditation, feng shui, star wisdom, connection with extraterrestrial beings, and astrology.

SPECIAL PROPERTIES

The patterns on Nebula Stone resemble the night sky, reminding us of what we can achieve.

MYTHOLOGY AND HISTORY

Available only in one location, discovered by Karen and Ron Nurnberg in 1995 in a remote mountain area of Mexico; effective as large flat palm-stones for massage, in sweat lodges, Reiki, prayer, and chanting.

Needle Crystals

COLORS: Clear quartz

CRYSTAL TYPE: Very thin, needle-like quartz crystals, single-terminated, often found growing in clusters; most usually as groups of separate needles

ZODIAC SIGN: Scorpio (October 24–November 22)

CANDLE COLOR: White

PHYSICAL: Relieves pain; enhances psychic surgery; removes illness turning a single needle point outward, counterclockwise; infuses you with health and energy by turning a single needle point clockwise.

EMOTIONAL: Helps overcome fear of speaking your mind.

HOME: Place twelve needle crystals, evenly spaced, around the downstairs of the home, or the whole area if an apartment, with six pointed inward to draw light and energy, and six alternately pointed outward to keep away all harm.

WORKPLACE: Hide needles around your workspace, points facing inward to prevent intrusion, stem idle gossip, and pointing outward, they deter shoplifters.

CHILDREN: Attached to a dream catcher, point the crystals facing downward to drive away bad dreams.

ANIMALS: In stables and in barns, in groups of seven, prevent theft, rustling, or harm to the animals.

PROTECTION: Carry a bag of needle crystals when you are traveling or coming home alone at night, if you feel nervous.

MAGICKAL AND PSYCHIC USES

Associated with fey energies as elven swords or Cupid's or Venus arrows when found as needle-like golden rutiles within clear quartz; in a bowl to act as Singing Quartz (page 441); when rubbed within the bowl or gently shaken, provide answers to your questions.

SPECIAL PROPERTIES

Needle Crystals are considered master teachers and healers; a single one, used as a miniature wand, can be used for dowsing subtly over plants, crystals, and remedies to choose the best. Each needle is just as powerful as a much larger quartz.

MYTHOLOGY AND HISTORY

Every day, place Needle Crystals, one at a time, in a glass bowl of dried basil. Hold it up to the morning light, saying, "One, two, four, money gather by the score, arrows fly swift and do not wait, double, treble, don't hesitate." Each day add a new needle until the bowl is full, then start again leaving one in the bowl for luck.

Nellite

COLORS: Gleaming, golden brown with blue shining through or shimmering blue with gold metallic splashes and flashes, the color depending on the proportion of the minerals; choose more blue for dynamic change and gold for increasing advantage

CRYSTAL TYPE: Quartz silicate, a combination of golden tiger's eye and blue pietersite, the storm or tempest stone; mainly sold as a tumbled stone

ZODIAC SIGN: Leo (July 23–August 23)

CANDLE COLOR: Gold

PHYSICAL: Aids in recovery from sudden illnesses; alleviates shock after an accident or an unexpected loss; sharpens distance vision, night vision; eases side effects of inoculations; counters exhaustion.

EMOTIONAL: Curbs a tendency toward scattering your energies and focusing on too many commitments while completing none satisfactorily.

HOME: Stimulates a sudden infusion of money; brings moneymaking plans to fruition when all hope of success was lost.

WORKPLACE: Promotes inventions, innovations, and brainstorming to achieve personal success; encourages speculation that may lead to a new career.

CHILDREN: Encourages teens who resist conventional study and focus on individual enterprises; reduces the influence of peers.

ANIMALS: For moderating pets' predatory behavior, so they keep down the population of rodents, but do not trouble grazing animals.

PROTECTION: Guards against those who intimidate through menacing words, either face-to-face, by text, or on social media.

MAGICKAL AND PSYCHIC USES
Enhances money magick, shamanic healing; offers psychic defense of home, vehicles, and loved ones.

SPECIAL PROPERTIES
Boosts confidence, self-belief, and the ability to meet the right people at the right time in the right place to manifest dreams and desires in practical, achievable terms.

MYTHOLOGY AND HISTORY
Also called the honey stone, Nellite is sold mainly in tumbled stone form; recently found in South Africa and Namibia in relatively small quantities; encourages speaking out against unfairness.

Nephrite Jade

COLORS: Medium to dark green, creamy; also white or black

CRYSTAL TYPE: Calcium magnesium iron silicate, a variety of actinolite-tremolite (see also Jadeite Jade, page 258)

ZODIAC SIGNS: Taurus (April 21–May 21) and Pisces (February 19–March 20)

CANDLE COLOR: Green

PHYSICAL: Alleviates issues concerning the skin, hair, asthma, premature aging, hips, kidneys, cystitis, bed-wetting, inner ear, blood sugar, burns, scalds, motion sickness, fertility, especially later in life.

EMOTIONAL: For young or elderly people cared for away from family; fends off sexual abuse by a woman.

HOME: A Nephrite Jade Buddha brings good fortune, prosperity, and peace.

WORKPLACE: Increases prosperity; attracts new business; for producers and suppliers of goods and services for children and animals.

CHILDREN: Protects against tumbles, illness, and ill-wishing people.

ANIMALS: For older animals with mobility problems.

PROTECTION: Guards against accidents, financial loss, and psychic attack.

MAGICKAL AND PSYCHIC USES
Promotes Earth healing; attracts power animals, good luck; useful in soul-twin and prosperity rituals; an amulet for safe travel.

SPECIAL PROPERTIES
A symbol of faithful love; young men in China traditionally gave their betrothed a jade butterfly.

MYTHOLOGY AND HISTORY
Jade is the generic term for two different gems—nephrite and jadeite; experts only differentiated between them in the late 1800s. Jade was called the royal gem in ancient China as early as 3000 BCE and believed to contain chi, or life force. In China, where most pre-1800 jade was nephrite, jade burial suits were made for royalty during the Han Dynasty (206 BCE–220 CE) to preserve the body and grant eternal life to the spirit.

Neptunite

COLORS: Black, flashes of deep red, occasionally brownish-red, translucent to opaque

CRYSTAL TYPE: Silicate, prismatic; may have terminations (energy points) at both ends, often embedded in Natrolite (page 313) or Benitoite (page 53)

ZODIAC SIGN: Pisces (February 19–March 20)

CANDLE COLOR: Deep red

PHYSICAL: Curbs alcohol and substance abuse; strengthens gums, teeth, and bones; helps in absorption of vitamins and minerals; mitigates scars and wounds.

EMOTIONAL: Aids in finding balance between physical fitness and excessive exercise or health regimens.

HOME: For calm if you live with drama kings or queens.

WORKPLACE: Reveals hidden potential; brings intuitive solutions to problems; encourages team bonding.

CHILDREN: Assists parents in letting their teenagers become independent.

ANIMALS: Enables tropical, cold-water fish and frogs to thrive in aquariums or ponds.

PROTECTION: Protects against sudden flare-ups of anger, bullying, and violence.

MAGICKAL AND PSYCHIC USES

Connects with other dimensions, opens psychic powers; for ocean or moon rituals; cleanses a place or your personal aura of negativity.

SPECIAL PROPERTIES

The warrior crystal, offering courage to confront injustice and corruption, especially in major organizations; also good for successful marriage and commitment arrangements.

MYTHOLOGY AND HISTORY

Neptunite was named after Neptune, Roman god of the sea, and discovered in the early 1900s; mainly sourced in the Diablo Mountain Range near the San Benito River on the Central Coast of California, as well as in Russia and Canada.

Nguni Jasper

COLORS: Tan or beige with darker or rich chocolate brown spots or patterns; may contain yellowy and whitish-beige inclusions

CRYSTAL TYPE: Chalcedony

ZODIAC SIGN: Virgo (August 24–September 22)

CANDLE COLOR: Brown

PHYSICAL: Alleviates issues stemming from stomach upset, liver, gallbladder, pancreas, spleen, skin blemishes, feet, knees, legs; counters the effects of ticks.

EMOTIONAL: Curbs fears of spontaneity and changes in routine; helps overcome agoraphobia.

HOME: For building your own home; promotes self-sustainability and permaculture, organic gardening.

WORKPLACE: The stone of networking; for team building and collective ventures; enables you to weather difficult times in business.

CHILDREN: Addresses a situation in which children hate playing outside in all weather and worry about getting muddy or dirty.

ANIMALS: For setting up or volunteering for a pet rescue center or animal conservancy.

PROTECTION: Guards against evil spirits, malevolent nature elementals if camping or staying in the wilderness, and all danger outdoors.

MAGICKAL AND PSYCHIC USES

For Earth rituals; natural magick; divination with the sound of the wind in the trees or casting stones in water; healing with plants.

SPECIAL PROPERTIES

A stone for relaxing rules and obsessive control that may be holding you back from joy, laughter, and seeking adventure; for wilderness trips and alternative lifestyles.

MYTHOLOGY AND HISTORY

Found in South Africa, Nguni Jasper is so named because it resembles the markings on the Nguni cattle, naturally sociable animals that adapt to harsh environments. The Nguni people are traditionally cattle herders and, according to their oral tradition, originated from a mystical land called Embo in the Congo Basin of Central Africa. Nguni stones are a talisman for seeking abundance and connection with Mother Earth.

Nirvana or Himalayan Ice Quartz

COLORS: Pink, clear, white; sometimes tinged with purple or green

CRYSTAL TYPE: A Growth Interference Quartz (page 232), where the growth of calcite or other minerals within, during the quartz's formation, later dissolves, leaving the quartz with holes and irregular formations

ZODIAC SIGN: Aquarius (January 21–February 18)

CANDLE COLOR: Pink

PHYSICAL: Helps diagnose and ensure recovery from rare illnesses, autoimmune diseases, genetic or neurological malfunctions, inflammation, conditions rooted in past lives; mitigates birthmarks.

EMOTIONAL: Overcomes a feeling of being victimized, an inferiority complex, self-destructive behavior; curbs spending way beyond means.

HOME: For a major makeover of home and relationships.

WORKPLACE: Aids in rescuing a failing business; supports those who restore or fix what is broken or damaged.

CHILDREN: Prompts youngsters to experience magickal lands and fairies through holes or windows in the crystal.

ANIMALS: Aids in accessing totem creatures, such as unicorns, the phoenix, and the thunderbird.

PROTECTION: Shields you from becoming weighed down by responsibilities with no time for stillness and silence.

MAGICKAL AND PSYCHIC USES

Connected with the Great White Brotherhood, immortals residing in the Himalayas; studying theosophy, working with ascended masters; trance meditation to attain detachment, bliss, and the state called in Buddhism "nirvana"; promotes mindfulness.

SPECIAL PROPERTIES

A high-vibration crystal, bringing peace, wisdom, and enlightenment; reveals your destiny; removes old karma.

MYTHOLOGY AND HISTORY

Nirvana Quartz, also called Himalayan ice quartz, is found in the Himalayan Mountains of North India. Nirvana Quartz was revealed in 2006, after part of an 1,800-foot-high glacier melted, because of global warming; it was previously hidden under ice for thousands of years.

Noreena Jasper

COLORS: Brightly colored and patterned, white/gray, yellow/orange in red matrix

CRYSTAL TYPE: Silicified mudstone, contains cryptocrystalline quartz with clays, muscovite, and goethite, with metallic luster

ZODIAC SIGN: Scorpio (October 24–November 22)

CANDLE COLOR: Red

PHYSICAL: Promotes fertility; alleviates impotence, hemorrhages, toxins in body, intestinal issues (including IBS, celiac disease, chronic constipation).

EMOTIONAL: Counters fears of mortality and physical dependence on others in later life; curbs jealousy in love.

HOME: Protects the home, if set outside, against attacks of all kinds; gives courage to overcome domestic violence and leave a dangerous situation.

WORKPLACE: Brings official recognition of knowledge and achievement in the workplace and community; for geologists, fossickers, gem miners, and all prospectors.

CHILDREN: Provides safety for older teens and young adults while backpacking or on adventure vacations.

ANIMALS: Keeps accident-prone pets safe.

PROTECTION: Guards your personal energy field against psychic intrusion, curses, hexes, and jinxes.

MAGICKAL AND PSYCHIC USES

For connection with ancient ceremonies and rituals in sacred places; past-life healing where a former life was cut short; fire and candle rituals.

SPECIAL PROPERTIES

Brings freedom from self-imposed constraints and restrictions created by others, or just by unfortunate circumstances.

MYTHOLOGY AND HISTORY

Found in the Pilbara region of Western Australia, a stone sacred to the Aboriginal people of the region. Noreena Jasper may be up to 2,687 million years old. Called the eternal flame, Noreena Jasper embodies the universal idea of the ever-burning fire throughout history, from the eternal flame of ancient Greece, to the everlasting flame on war memorials. A crystal that self-generates energy and inspiration.

Novaculite

COLORS: White, grayish-black, cream, black

CRYSTAL TYPE: A variety of chert or flint, composed of microcrystalline quartz, with very high silica concentration

ZODIAC SIGNS: Capricorn (December 22–January 20) and Scorpio (October 24–November 22)

CANDLE COLOR: Gray or brown

PHYSICAL: Alleviates moles, warts, melanomas, skin tags, scar tissue; eases childbirth; used by psychic surgeons and in angel-inspired healing.

EMOTIONAL: Helps overcome obsessive-compulsive disorder, claustrophobia, agoraphobia, depression.

HOME: Aids in clearing clutter, doing major spring cleaning any time.

WORKPLACE: For successful buying and selling, making fast decisions, setting aside jealousy and pettiness.

CHILDREN: On social media, protects from you from predatory grooming, trolling, or nasty peer attacks.

ANIMALS: Breaks bad habits in adopted animals.

PROTECTION: Shields against those who drain your energies and control you through guilt.

MAGICKAL AND PSYCHIC USES

Use in cutting-the-cord rituals against curses, ill-wishing, destructive relationships, or bad luck.

SPECIAL PROPERTIES

The stone of common sense; for shopaholics and to avoid scams.

MYTHOLOGY AND HISTORY

The name *Novaculite* comes from the Latin word for "razor stone," because of its potential to be sharpened. Prehistoric Native Americans created weapons and tools from sharpened Novaculite. Good for learning ancient languages and studying early cultures to distinguish fact from fantasy. Found in Russia in the Ural Mountains, Brazil, Africa, and the USA.

Nunderite or Noondorite

COLORS: Green and tan/brown with green dots throughout

CRYSTAL TYPE: Silicate, mixture of andalusite quartz (brown) with epidote (green)

ZODIAC SIGN: Taurus (April 21–May 21)

CANDLE COLOR: Golden brown

PHYSICAL: Alleviates issues stemming from the heart, including open-heart surgery, arrhythmia; promotes memory function, stamina; addresses problems with the feet, legs, hips, skin.

EMOTIONAL: Keeps you from becoming trapped in a repetitive loop to the past; for refusing to acknowledge childhood memories and experiences, whether good or bad.

HOME: For finding your birth parents; for parents whose children have been taken far away by partners or custody arrangements are regularly broken; for grandparents who have lost touch with grandchildren through no fault of their own.

WORKPLACE: Enables you to merge into the background when necessary and keep a low profile when confrontations loom large.

CHILDREN: Helps children to understand the lives ancestors experienced to appreciate the benefits of the modern world.

ANIMALS: For sniffer dogs at airports or with security services.

PROTECTION: Guards against emotional vampirism and the presence of hooks and cords by manipulative people or spirits.

MAGICKAL AND PSYCHIC USES

Stone of the Earth Mother and Earth healing; for astral travel, particularly to earthy or watery landscapes and ancient worlds to see Indigenous people close to the land or sea.

SPECIAL PROPERTIES

The clandestine crystal of keeping secrets; for those wishing to separate different parts of their life and maintain a double relationship or life.

MYTHOLOGY AND HISTORY

A rare stone mined in the 1960s at Nundora Station near Broken Hill in New South Wales, Australia, but still available as tumbled stones, jewelry, and well worth seeking; the writers' crystal for investigative journalists, poets, authors, and people whose words will not be silenced even if unpopular or forbidden by a repressive regime.

Nuummite

COLORS: Black and white and gray and white, with bronze, gold, red, orange, yellow, green, blue, and purple flashes
CRYSTAL TYPE: Metamorphosed igneous rock, composed of anthophyllite and gedrite
ZODIAC SIGN: Scorpio (October 24–November 22)
CANDLE COLOR: Indigo or white

PHYSICAL: Alleviates exhaustion; promotes whole-body healing; counters infections that are slow to clear; addresses circulatory, blood, and body fluid issues; regulates insulin production.
EMOTIONAL: Cures you of a victim or scapegoat pattern that may have started in childhood and has been repeated in adult relationships.
HOME: Protects the home against natural disasters, intruders, and paranormal activity.
WORKPLACE: Enables you to get work permits, work overseas, and earn as you travel.
CHILDREN: Encourages children to play outdoors if they worry about getting dirty.
ANIMALS: Comforts exotic pets far from their natural habitat.
PROTECTION: Protects against psychic attack, malevolent spirits, curses, hexes, and ill-wishes; deflects all harm.

MAGICKAL AND PSYCHIC USES
The ultimate stone for magick, ritual, and gazing within it for psychic insights.
SPECIAL PROPERTIES
Contains wild natural energies, opening horizons of possibility for those trapped in a restrictive life.
MYTHOLOGY AND HISTORY
Known as the sorcerer's or magician's stone because it was prized by shamans, Nuummite is more than three billion years old. A rare crystal, it is found mainly in a very inaccessible area of Greenland.

Nzuri Moyo

COLORS: Mottled pink and green to green/gray
CRYSTAL TYPE: Epidote, clinozoisite, rhodonite, and copper
ZODIAC SIGN: Libra (September 23–October 23)
CANDLE COLOR: Pink

PHYSICAL: Eases pain, inflammation, swelling, joint problems; boosts the immune system; aids in detoxifying after overexposure to electronic devices.
EMOTIONAL: An antidote to heartbreak, heartache, and emotional trauma.
HOME: Encourages growth of plant life in gardens where nothing flourishes.
WORKPLACE: Helps you to put your heart and soul into important work if others are cynical or indifferent.
CHILDREN: Good for children without siblings or those with few friends.
ANIMALS: Helps young animals, separated from their mothers too early.
PROTECTION: Guards against those who exploit your compassionate nature.

MAGICKAL AND PSYCHIC USES
For those who become easily distracted during meditation; good for increasing telepathic connection between lovers and for soul-twin-calling rituals.
SPECIAL PROPERTIES
Brings acceptance of what or who cannot be changed, so it helps you avoid championing lost causes.
MYTHOLOGY AND HISTORY
From Namibia, Nzuri Moyo is a Swahili name that means "good heart," also called sacred heart. Relatively recently discovered by Alex Harcourt at his Namibian mine, it's said that new minerals appear in response to new needs. Maybe a heart stone is just what's needed right now.

Obsidian Arrows

COLOR: Black
CRYSTAL TYPE: Volcanic glass arrowheads carved from obsidian
ZODIAC SIGN: Sagittarius (November 23–December 21)
CANDLE COLOR: Red

PHYSICAL: Alleviates issues stemming from digestion, wounds, pleurisy, chronic coughs, impotence, male illnesses, gastroenteritis; relieves acute pain; promotes successful surgery.
EMOTIONAL: Counters a lack of direction and curbs a propensity to dabble in the dark arts; keeps you from telling lies, even when not necessary.
HOME: One Obsidian Arrow under the front doormat, pointing outward, repels harm; prevents spiteful words by family and visitors.
WORKPLACE: Seven arrows, pointing inward, attract business to a store; aids in finding employment in a competitive market; direct one arrow outward near a computer containing sensitive material to keep it from being hacked.
CHILDREN: Seven arrows, threaded on a dark cord, circling a photo, deters bullying.
ANIMALS: Place Obsidian Arrows over stables or barns to prevent theft or harm to the animals at night.
PROTECTION: Pointing outward in sevens around the bed guards against psychological and psychic attack and nightmares.

MAGICKAL AND PSYCHIC USES
The tip, melted in a candle flame, sets in motion any spell; attracts and banishes magick, cuts destructive psychic and emotional cords; used as a pendulum for making choices.

SPECIAL PROPERTIES
Helps find the right direction if you are making decisions based on others' expectations; helps you discover the truth.

MYTHOLOGY AND HISTORY
Obsidian Arrow heads date from Paleolithic times. Found from the late fifth millennium BCE in Mesopotamia; also in ancient Egypt, among Native North Americans in the northwest and western United States, and used by the Maya and Aztecs, as weapons for their razor sharpness and as magickal amulets of protection in battle and for healing wounds.

Obsidian Mirrors

COLORS: Deep black and highly polished; when light is reflected on the mirror it may become slightly transparent
CRYSTAL TYPE: Volcanic glass/magma; usually round or oval
ZODIAC SIGN: Scorpio (October 24–November 22)
CANDLE COLOR: White

PHYSICAL: As you gaze into it (scry) by full moon or candlelight, you will see in the mirror or your mind's eye your healing spirit guide, showing symbols that hold clues to the causes and remedies of an unspecified illness.
EMOTIONAL: If there seems no solution or way forward, Obsidian Mirrors offer a sense of being nurtured and the presence of a wise ancestor to offer consolation.
HOME: Holds the essence of family protectors and guardians of the home to bring blessings, security, and reassurance that all will be well.
WORKPLACE: A small dark mirror in a bag or pouch offers, if held within the pouch, courage, calm, and consolation if you feel excluded or unfairly treated.
CHILDREN: Keep a miniature mirror wrapped in dark silk with a child's photo, if the child is away from home, to keep them safe and reassured.
ANIMALS: Tape a picture of a missing pet to the back of the mirror to call them home.
PROTECTION: Facing outward, toward the front door, repels specters, threatening spirits, and earthly intruders at night.

MAGICKAL AND PSYCHIC USES
For creating gateways into other worlds and receiving answers to questions about unresolved past dilemmas, and the way forward.

SPECIAL PROPERTIES
For past-life visions helping you discover where and when you first encountered your spirit guides, reminders of long-forgotten talents.

MYTHOLOGY AND HISTORY
Ruined Central American Mayan temples sometimes contain dark transparent obsidian slabs on walls. The Incas of Peru in South America also consulted dark mirrors. The Aztecs dedicated Obsidian Mirrors to the sky god Tezcatlipoca and used them to foretell the future.

Ocean Jasper

COLORS: Multiple colors and patterns of green, red, orange, yellow, cream, pink, white, and brown, with orb-like inclusions; colored by different minerals

CRYSTAL TYPE: Ocean Jasper is a rare variety of Orbicular Jasper (page 331); some experts suggest it is chalcedony

ZODIAC SIGN: Cancer (June 22–July 22)

CANDLE COLOR: Silver

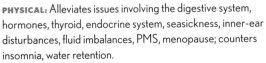

PHYSICAL: Alleviates issues involving the digestive system, hormones, thyroid, endocrine system, seasickness, inner-ear disturbances, fluid imbalances, PMS, menopause; counters insomnia, water retention.

EMOTIONAL: Releases pent-up anger; enables you to relax; curbs addictions that disrupt family life; keeps you from self-harm.

HOME: Calms bad temper in toddlers, teenagers, and midlife angst.

WORKPLACE: For temperamental employers and managers; for working for a family business where relationships intrude.

CHILDREN: Overcomes fears of water and swimming, especially if past-life-related.

ANIMALS: For cleansing the seas and preserving marine life.

PROTECTION: Keeps safe those who sail, go offshore fishing, or work on or with boats or water sports; for travelers by sea.

MAGICKAL AND PSYCHIC USES

Ocean Jasper guides visualizations to lands lost beneath the waves and the wisdom of Atlantis; an offering in water rituals; for meditation and scrying.

SPECIAL PROPERTIES

A powerful anti-worry and de-stress stone; for healers and therapists to restore depleted energy after troubled or resistant clients.

MYTHOLOGY AND HISTORY

The name *Ocean Jasper* is given only to orbicular jaspers collected at low tide along the shores of northwest Madagascar; called moon gems because of their resemblance to the moon's surface, combining Earth, sea, and lunar energies.

Ocho Geode

COLORS: Depends on contents of the geode, the enclosing matrix is generally gray, black, or brown, though it may be dyed

CRYSTAL TYPE: Miniature Ocho or Occo Geodes that are used separately or in twos, threes, sevens, and nines; cut and polished quartz in a hollow matrix with a center that contains drusy quartz, quartz, and chalcedony; may also be found as agates or banded chalcedony, containing embedded fossils and seashells (see Geodes, page 201)

ZODIAC SIGN: Sagittarius (November 23–December 21)

CANDLE COLOR: Gold

PHYSICAL: Though not often associated with healing, nine Ocho Geodes placed around the body or bed, bring the body into balance.

EMOTIONAL: Counters excessive secrecy and lies that there is no point in telling; curbs a gambling addiction.

HOME: Bowls of small ochos around the home attract money, health, family unity, and happiness.

WORKPLACE: Keeps a manager or senior colleague from constantly pulling rank and leaving all the humdrum work to you; for success in speculation, stocks, and shares.

CHILDREN: A bowl of different-colored, polished mini-geodes is an ideal treasure trove for older children.

ANIMALS: Keep three together or however many members of the family there are, including the pet, when a new family member arrives—whether human or animal—to avoid jealousy.

PROTECTION: An Ocho mini-Geode captures malevolent spirits; take one outside in the morning and shake it in order to rid it of the malevolent spirit.

MAGICKAL AND PSYCHIC USES

For good luck in gambling, games of chance, wagers, and competitions, where luck is a major factor.

SPECIAL PROPERTIES

As pairs, move them nearer for three nights until they are touching; bind together with red ribbon to attract your soul twin.

MYTHOLOGY AND HISTORY

The most famous Ocho miniature Geodes come from Brazil. Other cultures, such as Native North Americans and Aboriginal Australians, use mini-Thunder Eggs (page 473) in a similar way as protective amulets and to attract good things.

Odontolite or Bone Turquoise

COLORS: Turquoise, color caused by manganese and was naturally colored in the Earth by heat

CRYSTAL TYPE: Fossilized bone, especially from the teeth of mammoths, mastodons, dinosaurs, and other large prehistoric animals, the bone replaced almost entirely by Fluorapatite (page 191)

ZODIAC SIGN: Capricorn (December 22–January 20)

CANDLE COLOR: Turquoise

PHYSICAL: Promotes the health and long life of older people; for successful kidney, liver, heart, and lung transplants of human and animal organs, and mechanical implants, such as heart valves and pacemakers.

EMOTIONAL: Curbs fears of past problems returning, former illnesses, and people from the past who caused you unhappiness.

WORKPLACE: Encourages valuing older workers for their long experience.

CHILDREN: When Odontolite is viewed in museums or fossil collections, it awakens an awareness of the wonders of nature.

ANIMALS: For long-living pets to live out their natural span in peace.

PROTECTION: Guards against ghosts from the past who live on in the mind, and against falsehood masquerading as outstanding opportunities and offers.

MAGICKAL AND PSYCHIC USES

Transformation magick; past-life worlds in preliterate times; bibliomancy and stichomancy from ancient sacred books to answer present-day questions.

SPECIAL PROPERTIES

A talisman against all danger; gives safe visions of hauntings on the sites of old battlefields, massacres, gallows, and prisons without angry spirits attacking or trying to return with you.

MYTHOLOGY AND HISTORY

Incredibly rare and expensive; can be found as antique jewelry, in auctions among conventional turquoise, or occasionally still unearthed close to a copper mine; in the past, mistakenly confused with Vivianite (page 497) that was thought to give the bone its color.

Okenite

COLORS: Pearly white, colorless, occasionally yellow or pale blue

CRYSTAL TYPE: Silicate, a fibrous hydrothermal mineral lining the inside of basalt rocks and geodes

ZODIAC SIGNS: Sagittarius (November 23–December 21) and Virgo (August 24–September 22)

CANDLE COLOR: Pearly white

PHYSICAL: Alleviates issues relating to fever, the aging process, blood, nervous stomach disorders, upper-body circulation; eases lactation; addresses scalds, burns, inflammation.

EMOTIONAL: Enables self-forgiveness for past mistakes; restores eroded identity; eases grief and loneliness.

HOME: Softens tactless words by abrasive visitors or rejection by emotionally cold family members; prevents homesickness when absent.

WORKPLACE: Overcomes unfair failures and lack of deserved reward, strengthening your determination to succeed next time.

CHILDREN: Comforts youngsters and encourages them not to give up after doing badly on tests or not getting into a school or onto a team of their choice.

ANIMALS: For overly timid pets who run away from other animals or adults.

PROTECTION: Guards against simultaneous attacks from different directions.

MAGICKAL AND PSYCHIC USES

Offering direct access to the wisdom of planets and constellations through channeling planetary archangels and zodiac angels; recalling ancient wisdom; manifesting wishes; revisiting past lives to heal old karma.

SPECIAL PROPERTIES

Okenite overcomes obstacles through persistence and patience; surmounts immobility or restrictions caused by long illness, disability, or accident; aids in fighting for rights and resources for yourself or a loved one.

MYTHOLOGY AND HISTORY

Called the crystal snowball, resembling fuzzy, pliable, mini-snowballs, Okenite forms a bridge between earthly and cosmic energies in dreams, waking visions, and meditation. Because Okenite is delicate, buy one within its geode outer shell.

Oligoclase

COLORS: Colorless, white, cream, pale yellow, pink, brownish-red, gray, occasionally green
CRYSTAL TYPE: Silicate/plagioclase feldspar
ZODIAC SIGN: Gemini (May 22–June 21)
CANDLE COLOR: White

PHYSICAL: Alleviates mumps and other childhood illnesses in adulthood, glandular fever, tinnitus, abdomen, IBS, shingles, herpes, jaundice, and illnesses carried by insects, ticks, or vermin; addresses autoimmune problems.
EMOTIONAL: Releases suppressed anger, which manifests in excesses, self-harm, or obsessions.
HOME: For merging into one family stepchildren, step in-laws, and step-grandparents to overcome suspicion, possessiveness, and overidealizing previous relationships.
WORKPLACE: Oligoclase brings order to facts, figures, lists, schedules, meetings, agendas, and proposals.
CHILDREN: Teaches children to share time, attention, and possessions with siblings and visiting children.
ANIMALS: For an overly indulged pet to accept a new animal or baby in the home.
PROTECTION: Guards against giving energy to unworthy people or causes.

MAGICKAL AND PSYCHIC USES
Rituals when both sun and moon are in the sky; connecting with spirit guides and planetary beings at sunset or full moonlight.
SPECIAL PROPERTIES
A stone of justice to address unfair treatment, officially, legally, and personally; unmasks liars.
MYTHOLOGY AND HISTORY
Oligoclase is often mistaken for sunstone and moonstone, its close relatives. It has the same shimmer caused by light refracting back and forth between different crystal layers. Sunstone, moonstone and oligoclase together bring protection and attract good fortune. Particularly in its clear, gem form, Oligoclase combines solar and lunar powers, animus and outward-looking, the anima and intuitive qualities for balancing your life; also good for gender-fluid couples.

Olive Jade

COLORS: Olive green from light to dark olive
CRYSTAL TYPE: Nephrite, calcium magnesium iron silicate
ZODIAC SIGN: Virgo (August 24–September 22)
CANDLE COLOR: Green

PHYSICAL: Addresses issues relating to acne and other skin conditions, hair, bones, and joints (particularly hips), bacterial and viral infections, bladder, kidneys, cystitis, genitourinary problems; eases childbirth; counters motion sickness; alleviates childhood and adult ear infections, perforated eardrums.
EMOTIONAL: Mitigates frequent emotional meltdowns over relatively trivial matters, panic attacks, extreme phobic reaction when the trigger unexpectedly appears.
HOME: An Olive Jade Buddha statue or Kwan Yin, mother of compassion, kept with fragrant white flowers, brings continuing peace to the home and soothes temperamental people.
WORKPLACE: Dark olive green is an improving-fortunes charm if you are earning minimum wage or cannot get full-time or permanent work; enables you to obtain a more lucrative and permanent post.
CHILDREN: Calms temper tantrums that frighten the child as well as cause disruption.
ANIMALS: For neighborhood barking dogs, keep Olive Jade with a smartphone camera image of the offending animal.
PROTECTION: Guards against those who would cheat you out of money using charisma and false promises of fast returns.

MAGICKAL AND PSYCHIC USES
Meditation with olive beads, touching and repeating a mantra for each breath until deep relaxation is attained; for money magick.
SPECIAL PROPERTIES
A travel stone for exchange-student vacations, gap years, or sabbaticals involving travel overseas or exchanging homes with someone in another country for a vacation.
MYTHOLOGY AND HISTORY
The most peacemaking and peace-loving jade, Olive Jade is the stone of reconciliation after a quarrel with a lover, friend, or family member, particularly if you lost touch because of a disagreement; also good for calling back via social media or a reunion event a former love or someone you would have liked as a love.

Olivine

COLORS: Olive green to pale, yellowish- or brownish-green

CRYSTAL TYPE: Magnesium iron silicate; opaque sister of bottle green rarer gemstone form, Peridot (page 343)

ZODIAC SIGN: Virgo (August 24–September 22)

CANDLE COLOR: Olive or pale green

PHYSICAL: Alleviates asthma, allergies, bites, stings, vision problems, infections, and viruses connected with the respiratory system, nausea, morning sickness in pregnancy, jaundice.

EMOTIONAL: Allays fears of loss or misfortune that spoil present happiness.

HOME: A natural luck-bringer; set an Olivine for each family member around a lighted green candle Fridays at sunset to enhance luck.

WORKPLACE: To increase profits, put in store cash registers or next to credit card machines.

CHILDREN: Protects teens from online bullying and nasty texts from peers.

ANIMALS: On a collar, Olivine keeps pets safe outdoors and brings cats safely home after dark.

PROTECTION: Five Olivine crystals guard against spite, gossip, and jealousy.

MAGICKAL AND PSYCHIC USES

For money magick; put a pinch of sand each day in a pot with a lid for steady financial growth.

SPECIAL PROPERTIES

A token of fidelity; hang a green bag with seven Olivine crystals and dried yarrow over the marital bed; replace every seven years.

MYTHOLOGY AND HISTORY

Olivine, also called chrysolite in yellower forms, is found in stony iron meteorites and deep rock brought to the surface in volcanic activity. Olivine crystals are said to be the tears of the Hawaiian volcano goddess Pele.

Olmec Blue Jade

COLORS: From pale blue to bluish-green; also found occasionally in darker, more intense blue and a lighter also more intense variety; rare

CRYSTAL TYPE: Jadeite, colored by traces of titanium and iron

ZODIAC SIGN: Aquarius (January 21–February 18)

CANDLE COLOR: Blue

PHYSICAL: Regulates cardiac rhythms; addresses hereditary conditions, sensitivity to heat or sunlight, throat problems, inner-ear issues, sinus conditions, arthritis; strengthens bones.

EMOTIONAL: Curbs resentment against convention, authority, and officialdom; counters a tendency to cling to lost youth.

HOME: Aids in finding what is lost or misplaced; helps when inheriting a home or land that has been in the family for generations.

WORKPLACE: For leadership if you are young and others resent your authority; for research into ancient lost civilizations.

CHILDREN: Encourages very old souls who, from a young age, are fascinated by myths and legends.

ANIMALS: Useful for physically small pets with big personalities who overestimate their strength in relation to other animals.

PROTECTION: Guards against spirits attached to artifacts or ancient places.

MAGICKAL AND PSYCHIC USES

Formal rituals and ceremonies; connection with ancient wisdom and particularly vanished Mesoamerican worlds; shamanism using the jaguar as a power animal for astral travel.

SPECIAL PROPERTIES

For reviving or restoring disappearing crafts and folk traditions.

MYTHOLOGY AND HISTORY

Jadeite was the most sought-after stone in the oldest civilization in Mesoamerica, the Olmecs, that flourished from 1500 BCE to 400 BCE. The Olmecs created beautiful jade artifacts, including ceremonial axes and face masks resembling humans and jaguars, believed to be their ancestors.

Onyx Marble

COLORS: Varies according to mineral makeup; patterned brown, yellow, most often green, tan, orange, gold, ivory, white, or rarely pink; sold highly polished

CRYSTAL TYPE: Metamorphic rock, a very stable form of calcium carbonate, with large distinct crystals; often contains aragonite, calcite, and limestone; an alternately banded form of yellow and brown calcite and aragonite is sometimes also given the name onyx marble

ZODIAC SIGN: Cancer (June 22–July 22)

CANDLE COLOR: Depends on color of the Onyx Marble

PHYSICAL: Alleviates issues relating to skin, hair, eyes, teeth; promotes fertility; preserves youthfulness; valuable in detoxifying.

EMOTIONAL: Counters acute anxiety; enables you to see beyond self-imposed fears and limitations.

HOME: The West Azerbaijan cave mines in Iran produce pink onyx marble that can be polished as clear as a mirror; reflects love and kindness to every corner of the home.

WORKPLACE: For success and prosperity; helps you maintain high work ethics in a workplace where there may be petty dishonesty or concealment of truth; for long-term careers with a clear structure.

CHILDREN: Pink- or green-based Onyx Marble protects small children from harm, accidents, and falls.

ANIMALS: For delicate young animals who are not thriving.

PROTECTION: Reflects back to sender malice, ill-wishing, curses, and hexes.

MAGICKAL AND PSYCHIC USES

Recall of ancient worlds, temples, and ceremonies; highly polished as a magick mirror for visions of spirit guides and ancestors; initiation ceremonies, for example into Wicca or druidry.

SPECIAL PROPERTIES

Onyx Marble containing or predominantly in shades of green strengthens determination to start a new life path.

MYTHOLOGY AND HISTORY

Highly prized for its transparency. In ancient Egypt, transparent Onyx Marble was made into sacred oil and perfume bottles because of its purity. In Iran, it has traditionally been used in the tombs of eminent imams; called the stone of the inner warrior for inner courage and determination.

Oolitic Limestone

COLORS: Off white, cream, yellow, gray; may be different-colored from the connecting limestone

CRYSTAL TYPE: Oolite Limestone is a sedimentary rock made up of ooids, calcium carbonate (aragonite or calcite) eggs; larger spherical and older oolites are called pisolites. As a polished tumbled stone, Oolitic Limestone is a powerful healer

ZODIAC SIGN: Libra (September 23–October 23)

CANDLE COLOR: Cream

PHYSICAL: Promotes blood flow and blood oxygenation; alleviates abdominal disease; addresses issues stemming from nerves, muscles, intestines; enables fertility in later life, the successful freezing of maternal eggs.

EMOTIONAL: Counters workaholic tendencies; curbs negative patterning that may be passed on to future generations.

HOME: Brings the family together if members are preoccupied with outside interests and team activities.

WORKPLACE: Revives traditional businesses and crafts.

CHILDREN: For teens obsessed with social media to the detriment of direct communication.

ANIMALS: Helps you open or run a cattery, a kennel, or an animal sanctuary.

PROTECTION: Guards against abandoning existing relationships or lifestyle for the novelty of a temporary thrill.

MAGICKAL AND PSYCHIC USES

For connecting with ancient underwater worlds; collective magick and rituals. The pyramids of ancient Egypt, having been constructed from limestone, promote connection with ancient Egyptian mysteries.

SPECIAL PROPERTIES

Oolitic Limestone may contain small shell fossils and shell casts from the Jurassic Age, around which calcium carbonate forms.

MYTHOLOGY AND HISTORY

Also called the egg stone and the Hildegard stone after the twelfth-century mystic Hildegard von Bingen, who studied stones and plants and used oolites for healing; limestone cliffs, such as those on the Dorset Coast of Southwest England, contain many dinosaur fossils. A Mother Earth climate change stone to draw together people of different nations to preserve and restore the planet for future generations.

Opalite

COLORS: Milky white, opalescent with purple, orange, red, and green, with a blue sheen

CRYSTAL TYPE: Opalite is synthetic glass that, because of its iridescent beauty, has taken on both healing and magickal qualities

ZODIAC SIGN: Aquarius (January 21–February 18)

CANDLE COLOR: Silver

PHYSICAL: Alleviates emotional and spiritual traumas, manifest in physical conditions, such as digestive disorders and sexual dysfunction.

EMOTIONAL: Frees you from sexual, gender-related, or occupational stereotypes from childhood.

HOME: A feel-good crystal that promotes matchmaking between compatible friends or relatives.

WORKPLACE: Attracts business and financial success, especially in solo ventures.

CHILDREN: Comforts a young child afraid of the dark or suffering nightmares, as a crystal angel in the child's room.

ANIMALS: For timid pets rescued from abuse or abandonment.

PROTECTION: Transforms anger, jealousy, spite, and ill-wishing into positive emotions.

MAGICKAL AND PSYCHIC USES

A mood stone that, if held in the morning, reflects the current aura, mirroring the best approach for the day ahead—dynamic if the stone turns predominantly red, logical if blue, new beginnings if green, treading gently if purple; for wish magick.

SPECIAL PROPERTIES

For a first sexual experience; if sex was used for control in a previous relationship.

MYTHOLOGY AND HISTORY

The ancient Egyptians believed that human-created stones were far more powerful than natural gems because people could imitate the creator. Opalite, like manufactured Goldstones, has absorbed living energies; sometimes called Tiffany stone, which is a natural opalized fluorite.

Optical Calcite or Iceland Spar

COLORS: Colorless, water-like clear, sometimes with rainbows, occasionally pink

CRYSTAL TYPE: Calcium carbonate, displays an optical illusion called double refraction (see below); rhombic or squarish

ZODIAC SIGN: Leo (July 23–August 23)

CANDLE COLOR: White

PHYSICAL: A whole-body healer; promotes self-healing, clearing energy blockages and toxins; addresses vision, migraines; eases bipolar conditions.

EMOTIONAL: Curbs the tendency to cling to old sources of pain or wrongs, especially involving deception that led to financial loss or a former partner living a double life.

HOME: Enables you to work from home if you're dividing your time between business and family.

WORKPLACE: Useful for multitasking; if you work split shifts or travel to other time zones.

CHILDREN: For young children or gaming-obsessed teenagers spending too much time in fantasy.

ANIMALS: Fosters good relationships among pets who are siblings or mother/offspring.

PROTECTION: Guards against doublespeak, hidden meanings, and deception—both written and spoken.

MAGICKAL AND PSYCHIC USES

Doubles the intensity of spells, healing, and empowerments; adds to effectiveness of other crystals or natural remedies; complements prayer.

SPECIAL PROPERTIES

Opens doors of opportunity and good fortune; brings connection with a soul twin or brings two lovers closer.

MYTHOLOGY AND HISTORY

Optical Calcite, which is naturally doubly refractive, splits light rays in two, producing a double image. If you're looking at a straight line through an Optical Calcite, you see two wavy lines. Called fairy glass in Icelandic folklore, the double image was considered a trick of the fey. Danish physician Rasmus Bartholin of Copenhagen wrote about this phenomenon in 1669, turning existing optical theories on their heads.

Optical Selenite

COLORS: Clear, sometimes with tiny snowflake effects where the clear surface is dotted with splashes of cloudy white
CRYSTAL TYPE: Calcium sulfate dihydrate, layers of clear selenite, one on top of the other
ZODIAC SIGN: Cancer (June 22–July 22)
CANDLE COLOR: Silver

PHYSICAL: Strengthens eyesight; counters double vision; regulates hormones; promotes fertility (especially on full moon night); ensures successful diagnostic tests, including scans like MRI, and colonoscopy and endoscopy.
EMOTIONAL: Curbs a tendency to live in fantasy; eases fluctuating moods; keeps you from viewing life only from a personal perspective and acting in a way that benefits yourself to the detriment of others.
HOME: For large families with a wide age range so each family member feels valued as an individual; if adult siblings are hostile toward one another.
WORKPLACE: Protects you from unfair tactics by business rivals; enables fair interviews on merit, without nepotism or favoritism.
CHILDREN: Empowers those who find it hard to communicate; for psychic children who have clear visions of the future but are rarely believed.
ANIMALS: For guide dogs for the visually impaired.
PROTECTION: An ongoing shield of light against hostile people and places; removes disturbed and disturbing entities.

MAGICKAL AND PSYCHIC USES
Conjures up angelic visions by spanning the dimensions through scrying within the crystal or meditation; time travel; because it is flat, often used as an altar centerpiece on which to empower and cleanse other crystals and ritual items.

SPECIAL PROPERTIES
Selenite is a moonstone, but the clarity and layers within the crystal add the power of the sun and light for power and protection 24/7.

MYTHOLOGY AND HISTORY
Found in the USA, especially Utah and Idaho, and also Mexico. Optical Selenite is softer that Optical Calcite and adds the spiritual lunar energies. It becomes more powerful from the crescent to the full moon for increasing love, luck, and health.

Orange Aragonite

COLORS: Orange, orange-brown, brown
CRYSTAL TYPE: Dimorphous calcium carbonate, growing usually as twin crystals or in clusters, sometimes as stars
ZODIAC SIGN: Capricorn (December 22–January 20)
CANDLE COLOR: Orange

PHYSICAL: Alleviates issues stemming from the ovaries, prostate gland, central nervous system, unsettled stomach and irritability due to irregular meals, chronic fatigue, winter chills, chilblains, circulation, hair loss.
EMOTIONAL: Moderates obsessions and excesses, such as dieting, exercise, or binge eating.
HOME: For keeping track of time if family members are constantly late or find it hard to wake up; for family members who constantly put off tasks.
WORKPLACE: Aids in meeting deadlines, business networking, website marketing, advertising initiatives, organizing training seminars and conferences.
CHILDREN: For impatient children who interrupt or will not take turns; for calming turbulent teens and multigenerational tensions.
ANIMALS: Helps train animals, especially horses.
PROTECTION: Aragonite star clusters release and transform anger and negativity within the body instead of letting it fester.

MAGICKAL AND PSYCHIC USES
Useful in medicine wheel ceremonies, druidry, smudging, dowsing, Earth Mother rituals; neutralizes geopathic stress if you're living near an earthquake zone, former or current volcanic activity, or close to the sea; star clusters enhance wish spells.

SPECIAL PROPERTIES
Centers and focuses energies before healing; in crystal layouts, cultivates friendship between nations and calls home absent family or friends.

MYTHOLOGY AND HISTORY
Aragonite is found as a deposit in hot springs, cavities in volcanic rocks, caves, and mines, and as iridescent colors in abalone and mother of pearl shells; offered to the mothers of both Earth and sea.

Orange Calcite

COLORS: Pale orange through peach to bright orange

CRYSTAL TYPE: Calcium carbonate, resembles ice in its natural state

ZODIAC SIGN: Leo (July 23–August 23)

CANDLE COLOR: Bright orange

PHYSICAL: Useful in detoxifying; alleviates issues stemming from gallstones, liver, spleen, female hormones, painful muscles, kidneys, bladder; irritable bowel syndrome, chronic fatigue, sexual dysfunction, low fertility, urinary incontinence.

EMOTIONAL: Restores sexual desire after rejection; heals psychological scars after sexual attack; overcomes depression, dark thoughts, and low self-esteem; addresses food-related conditions, excessive exercising.

HOME: At family mealtimes, creates a peaceful but lively atmosphere; for congenial dinner parties and social occasions.

WORKPLACE: Enhances creativity; for hospitality workers, party planners, children's entertainers, those selling or manufacturing food.

CHILDREN: For easier toddler toilet training and older bed-wetting children; discourages teenage inertia.

ANIMALS: Curbs cats' tendency to spray and keep all pets from causing damage indoors; domesticates pet hens, ducks, and rabbits.

PROTECTION: Guards against people spreading doom, gloom, and draining enthusiasm.

MAGICKAL AND PSYCHIC USES

Sun magick on solstices; love rituals for love later in life, turning friendship into love or rekindling a past relationship; for divination if psychic energies are blocked; automatic writing for problem solving.

SPECIAL PROPERTIES

Called the happiness stone, for spontaneous outings and parties; use preconception, especially if prospective parents are older or have used prolonged artificial contraception.

MYTHOLOGY AND HISTORY

In folk tradition, Orange Calcite is considered a gift cast from the chariot of the sun goddess Saule as she rode across the skies on the winter solstice on December 21, promising light and joy returning.

Orange Celestite or Celestine

COLORS: Orange (see also Blue Celestite, page 72)

CRYSTAL TYPE: Strontium sulfate, like blue sometimes found in geodes

ZODIAC SIGN: Sagittarius (November 23–December 21)

CANDLE COLOR: Orange

PHYSICAL: A health- and energy-bringer; addresses issues relating to the gallbladder, liver, spleen, pancreas, frozen or cold limbs, hypothermia, food allergies.

EMOTIONAL: Curbs overdependence on food, alcohol, cigarettes, prescription medicines, or a person sapping your confidence.

HOME: Attracts health, well-being, abundance, and incoming financial resources; establishes a new happy home after unwillingly leaving a long-standing one.

WORKPLACE: For settling into a new cliquey workplace; establishes better work practices when the status quo is inefficient.

CHILDREN: Encourages clingy children to become more independent; for school phobias, fears about mortality after a family bereavement.

ANIMALS: Deters pets left home alone from yowling, barking, or being destructive.

PROTECTION: Guards against fires, explosions, and people controlling others with anger.

MAGICKAL AND PSYCHIC USES

Sensing ghosts and past visions in old buildings; awareness of fragrances from other ages; aromatherapy; aura reading; fire rituals, candle magick.

SPECIAL PROPERTIES

For life changes—large and small—whether a new home, job, or location; knowing instinctively the right approach in unfamiliar situations.

MYTHOLOGY AND HISTORY

In India, celestite powder was cast on ritual fires, causing bright red flames to flare in tribute to the fire god Agni. Celestite is used in fireworks and flares, but magickally orange is associated with fire spirits and elementals.

Orange Goldstone

COLORS: Bronzed orange with glittering gold sparkles

CRYSTAL TYPE: Glass with copper, smelted gypsum, feldspar, and copper salts

ZODIAC SIGN: Sagittarius (November 23–December 21)

CANDLE COLOR: Gold

PHYSICAL: Alleviates issues stemming from circulation, arthritis, inflammation, skin complaints due to food allergies, metabolism, bones, stomach disorders (especially those that are stress-related), dizziness.

EMOTIONAL: Helps overcome chronic self-consciousness that makes socializing, eating, or speaking in front of others embarrassing.

HOME: Aids in redecorating, extending, or renovating a house, barn, or warehouse; useful for flipping properties for fast profit.

WORKPLACE: For major moneymaking ventures, reaching the top of an organization, high-profile careers, far-reaching ambitions; stimulates creative inspirational energies.

CHILDREN: Encourages the making of wishes; works as treasure for imaginative games.

ANIMALS: Promotes good luck when a pet enters a competition.

PROTECTION: Guards against financial trickery or a love scam.

MAGICKAL AND PSYCHIC USES

For prosperity rituals; finding unexpected treasures at garage sales; as a lucky charm for competitions, games of chance, financial speculation, and lotteries; a radar if lost at night and technological aids fail.

SPECIAL PROPERTIES

Though not a natural crystal, the power of the added minerals creates a psychic power magnet.

MYTHOLOGY AND HISTORY

One explanation for Goldstone's origin suggests it was created by Italian monks in the sixteenth century, called monks' gold. Others claim it resulted from accidentally spilling copper dust and filings into molten glass at the Murano glass factory of the Miotti family in seventeenth-century Venice. A third theory links Goldstone to early experiments by alchemists to create the elusive philosopher's stone. Victorians wore Goldstone jewelry because of its glitter.

Orange Kyanite

COLORS: Orange to golden brown, due to small amount of manganese within the structure; may have black streaks

CRYSTAL TYPE: Aluminum silicate, in blades, though Orange Kyanite may be sold as tumbled stones or gems

ZODIAC SIGN: Sagittarius (November 23–December 21)

CANDLE COLOR: Orange

PHYSICAL: For fertility (especially if medical or surgical intervention or IVF are required), PMS, menstrual problems, endometriosis; alleviates bladder issues and nighttime bed-wetting in older children and teens.

EMOTIONAL: Curbs eating disorders linked with body image distortions, sexual dysfunction, loss or lack of libido; addresses unresolved sexual abuse.

HOME: Builds bridges with estranged or unsociable family members; creates happy memories through family celebrations.

WORKPLACE: Cultivates a happy workplace atmosphere; encourages team building and cooperative ventures.

CHILDREN: Enables reticent children to try new activities, lose their inhibitions, and have fun.

ANIMALS: Helps badly treated rescue pets learn to trust humans again.

PROTECTION: Guards against pessimistic people who cast a cloud over any signs of enthusiasm.

MAGICKAL AND PSYCHIC USES

Clairsentience; as a magick wand to call abundance and manifest wishes; fertility spells; travel rituals to make travel possible and ensure that it is a pleasurable experience without delays or complications; for pilgrimages to learn more about Indigenous cultures.

SPECIAL PROPERTIES

For creativity, especially writing, music, acting, and painting in the early stages; for impetus to persist and find the right people to help with sales.

MYTHOLOGY AND HISTORY

Recently discovered in Tanzania, Orange Kyanite opens the horizons for travel near and far, for learning new things, and for chronicling experiences in a blog, on social media, or in a travelogue; releases the inner child when life gets too serious.

Orange Natrolite

COLORS: Medium to bright orange, sometimes with brown or grayish patches, one of the rarer natrolite crystals

CRYSTAL TYPE: Zeolite with high sodium content; works best for healing and magick as a tumbled stone

ZODIAC SIGN: Sagittarius (November 23–December 21)

CANDLE COLOR: Orange

PHYSICAL: Promotes self-healing after illness, surgery, or an injury; strengthens the immune system; balances the organs of the body to avoid undue strain from one area; alleviates vision problems (including eye irritation and dry eyes), seasonal affective disorder, nightmares.

EMOTIONAL: Curbs inner insecurities of being disliked; keeps you from living superficially to avoid revealing your authentic self for fear of condemnation or ridicule.

HOME: A sunshine crystal all year round and in all weathers, bringing joy and spontaneous fun; if you are happy living alone but others pressure you to find a partner.

WORKPLACE: For working independently, even within an organization; keeps you from becoming an unofficial therapist, soother of egos, and dispute resolver.

CHILDREN: Aids those who are different, yet try to fit in with others.

ANIMALS: For a pet who tunes in to your moods the moment you walk through the door.

PROTECTION: Guards against staying in an unhappy relationship purely to avoid being alone.

MAGICKAL AND PSYCHIC USES

The crystal of the inner world and personal spiritual exploration; mindfulness; deep meditation; channeling your guardian angel through automatic writing; accessing angelic realms through dreams, waking visions, astral travel.

SPECIAL PROPERTIES

The crystal of physical withdrawal if you are burned-out, to find inner peace; to accept that being alone is not the same as being lonely.

MYTHOLOGY AND HISTORY

A stone of privacy, drawing boundaries if others, however beloved, want to share your every thought and waking moment; keeping a spiritual journal that may one day be published to guide others on their inner journey.

Orange River Quartz

COLORS: Orange, red, brown, pink, and golden, depending on the inclusions

CRYSTAL TYPE: Silicon dioxide with hematite patches or inclusions; also may contain other trace minerals, such as red phantom quartz and iron

ZODIAC SIGN: Aries (March 21–April 20)

CANDLE COLOR: Red

PHYSICAL: Restores red blood cell health; promotes blood oxygenation and free flow of fluids; useful in treating liver, spleen; strengthens fertility and health of reproductive organs.

EMOTIONAL: Keeps you from giving away your power, either in this or in a past life; helps overcome the victim syndrome, which may be a form of control.

HOME: After a major setback, or if you are living where you do not want to be, but must stay for now, to rekindle enthusiasm to make your surroundings beautiful and happier.

WORKPLACE: For seeing a new project through from beginning to completion; revives a potential moneymaker.

CHILDREN: Enables a child or teen who has been sick for a long time or has a chronic condition to regain strength.

ANIMALS: Aids in adopting an older pet in a young household.

PROTECTION: Guards against those who take energy deliberately or through overdependence.

MAGICKAL AND PSYCHIC USES

Flowing water rituals to wash away symbols of what is no longer wanted or to call from the water increased power or love; fierce psychic defense.

SPECIAL PROPERTIES

Orange River Quartz may appear in many forms, such as clusters, points, or even soul-twin or etched crystals, but all carry the power of the river to revive, restore, and regenerate.

MYTHOLOGY AND HISTORY

Found only in the area surrounding the Orange River, near Riemvasmaak, in the Northern Cape of South Africa; located just below the surface of the Earth; filled with flowing water and Earth energies; restores physical strength, and emotional and mental zest for living.

Orange Selenite

COLORS: Peach to deep orange, even red, caused by iron oxide inclusions

CRYSTAL TYPE: Fiber Gypsum, hydrous calcium sulfate (see also White, Green Pernatty, and Blue Selenite, pages 505, 226, and 82)

ZODIAC SIGN: Cancer (June 22–July 22)

CANDLE COLOR: Orange

PHYSICAL: Regulates hormone imbalances; alleviates endometriosis, PMS, issues with menstruation and menopause, bladder weakness, motion sickness, fluid retention, gallstones, and kidney stones; improves appetite.

EMOTIONAL: For food-related issues, such as bingeing, anorexia, or bulimia; curbs excessive anxiety to please.

HOME: Promotes harmonious, unhurried mealtimes in a busy household; attracts abundance and well-being; removes electromagnetic stress.

WORKPLACE: Enables working mothers to balance childcare needs with career; helps businesswomen feel secure at night in unfamiliar hotels; aids in selling creative items, beauty products, or homemade food at fairs and festivals.

CHILDREN: Curbs an attraction to food fads by fussy eaters; settles babies who wake up crying at night.

ANIMALS: For an older pet giving birth after previous failed litters.

PROTECTION: Shields you from harm while traveling at night or in spooky places during the waning moon.

MAGICKAL AND PSYCHIC USES

An Earth-healing crystal connecting waxing and full moonlight with Earth devas to energize the land; recalling past lives.

SPECIAL PROPERTIES

For women having difficulty conceiving who become overly anxious; eases pregnancy worries, fears of giving birth, bonding after a difficult birth, or temporary separation from baby after birth.

MYTHOLOGY AND HISTORY

Associated with the harvest moon, first full moon after the autumn equinox in the northern hemisphere, Orange Selenite manifests creativity and imagination in tangible form.

Orbicular Jasper

COLORS: Grays and blacks, browns, white, and creams; the overall color often determined by the predominant orb color

CRYSTAL TYPE: Chalcedony with its orb-like spheres or even cell formations, may contain agate bands or drusy quartz (see also Ocean Jasper, page 321)

ZODIAC SIGN: Gemini (May 22–June 21)

CANDLE COLOR: White

PHYSICAL: Strengthens white blood cells; promotes brain-cell regrowth after severe illness or accident, making new neural pathways to replace fatally damaged ones.

EMOTIONAL: Helps overcome paranoia, OCD, fixed patterns of behavior no longer relevant or appropriate.

HOME: For discovering distant relatives through genealogical or DNA searches; finally finishing lingering renovations or redecorations.

WORKPLACE: Aids in working in and for the community; networking within an international organization.

CHILDREN: Helps find a friendship group in a new school or neighborhood.

ANIMALS: Encourages patience training a dog who finds it hard to be on a leash.

PROTECTION: Guards against cliques, factions, and social exclusion, especially in new workplaces or neighborhoods.

MAGICKAL AND PSYCHIC USES

For sacred circle rituals, circle dancing, and sound healing, in the center of and bringing together the energies of crystal grid layouts.

SPECIAL PROPERTIES

For communal living, whether in a dorm at college, a shared apartment, with extended family, or in a commune.

MYTHOLOGY AND HISTORY

Often grouped together with the Madagascan Ocean Jasper, a form of orbicular jasper, Orbicular Jasper is in contrast to the water-based ocean form, a stone of the Earth. Mainly found in Morgan Hill, Santa Clara County, California. Draws together people of all nations and faiths in common causes connected with conservation and climate.

Orchid Calcite

COLORS: Bright orange with black/gray inclusions

CRYSTAL TYPE: A vibrant calcite often found growing with and containing black tourmaline; may also be bought as tumbled stones, jewelry, and polished points

ZODIAC SIGN: Sagittarius (November 23– December 21)

CANDLE COLOR: Orange

PHYSICAL: Bolsters the reproductive system in both sexes and addresses sexual difficulties; promotes fertility; enhances radiance; addresses issues relating to the skin, bladder, kidneys; alleviates PMS, menstrual problems, inflammation, fevers, stress-based incontinence, seasonal affective disorder; aids in absorbing nutrients from food.

EMOTIONAL: Curbs acute anxiety about speaking, eating, or wearing the right clothes in public; counters impulsive buying.

HOME: Aids in planning a special exotic vacation, setting long-term future goals, especially if you want to build your own home in a place of beauty.

WORKPLACE: A very upbeat crystal for getting personal desired results; for unusual careers and success in beauty, fashion, design, or the luxury end of the market; protects against unfair competition if establishing a business in these areas.

CHILDREN: Encourages children to express themselves artistically and creatively for pleasure and to be proud of their efforts.

ANIMALS: For pets who are disturbed by the full moon and by storms.

PROTECTION: Deeply protective against those who spread gloom and fears that come in the night.

MAGICKAL AND PSYCHIC USES

Love magick; fertility spells; remote healing; flower magick, oils, and floral essences; clairsentience; full moon rituals.

SPECIAL PROPERTIES

Called the birthing stone for easing early stages of labor and also initiating any creative project, moneymaking venture, or making the first move in a desired love affair.

MYTHOLOGY AND HISTORY

Like the orchid after which it is named, this calcite increases confidence in one's natural charisma and is associated with sensual pleasures, luxury, and acquiring wealth.

Orgonite

COLORS: An assortment of colors; may have spiritual designs, such as the tree of life or the ohm

CRYSTAL TYPE: Orgonite consists of resin, metals usually including copper coils or shavings, sometimes gold flakes and quartz, chosen in proportion to balance the bioenergy of the user or wearer, their sexual energy, chi or prana life force

ZODIAC SIGN: Aquarius (January 21–February 18)

CANDLE COLOR: Gold

PHYSICAL: Increases resistance to illnesses; alleviates chronic conditions, headaches, allergies due to chemical pollution or harmful rays from power lines and cell phone towers.

EMOTIONAL: For those overwhelmed by noise, rush, and pollution.

HOME: Orgonite (especially crystals containing copper coils) is said to clear land and home from surrounding and internal harmful electromagnetic forces; promotes plant growth.

WORKPLACE: If your workplace is disturbed by noisy air conditioning, fluorescent light, and the constant ringing of phones, separate Orgonite towers in the corners will purify and insulate the atmosphere.

CHILDREN: If going to their school or college involves traveling down traffic-filled roads or is near a freeway, set a small piece of Orgonite near their clean clothes overnight.

ANIMALS: Keep an Orgonite crystal near a leash or bridle when it's not in use if your pets exercise in busy or polluted areas.

PROTECTION: Guards against negative energies.

MAGICKAL AND PSYCHIC USES

Acupuncture, acupressure; qi gong, tai chi, yoga, energy-balancing modalities, crystal healing, meditation.

SPECIAL PROPERTIES

Orgonite pyramids are considered effective because the inherent power within the pyramid form (see Pyramids, page 382) magnifies the positive energy.

MYTHOLOGY AND HISTORY

Austrian psychiatrist Dr. Wilhelm Reich was the first to research orgone energy during the first half of the twentieth century. His theories are based on the belief that out-of-balance energy is absorbed into the Orgonite artifact by the metal-resin mix and recycled into health and harmony.

Orpheus Stone

COLORS: Layers of green (often celadonite), yellow, brown, and red (jasper) bands, colored by iron oxides; central chalcedony in green or blue (may be dendritic); the stone may also contain white

CRYSTAL TYPE: Chalcedony, celadonite, jasper, and iron oxides; sometimes called orpheus agate

ZODIAC SIGN: Taurus (April 21–May 21)

CANDLE COLOR: Green

PHYSICAL: Addresses breathing difficulties, vertigo, high-altitude problems, oxygenation of blood, plant allergies.

EMOTIONAL: Curbs an inability to grieve and move on; keeps you from wanting what cannot be attained or achieved to the detriment of what can.

HOME: For creating physical, emotional, and spiritual space in the home so energies can flow freely.

WORKPLACE: Aids in not being deterred by setbacks, accepting petty immovable rules in the workplace while finding subtle ways of expressing personal freedom and individuality.

CHILDREN: Introduces even young children to different kinds of music; makes music, singing, or dancing lessons fun.

ANIMALS: For animal whispering and animal healing.

PROTECTION: Guards against those who deceive with false promises.

MAGICKAL AND PSYCHIC USES

Sacred dance, chanting, mantras, and spoken or sung empowerments; sound healing; rituals to meet a soul twin later in life; prophecy.

SPECIAL PROPERTIES

Encourages all creative talents—especially musical, performing, and writing—to flourish, whether for pleasure or professionally.

MYTHOLOGY AND HISTORY

Found in the region of the Rhodope Mountains in Bulgaria and named after Orpheus the mythical ancient Greek musician and prophet, who was said to wear a colorful agate/jasper that acted as his inspirational muse. Orpheus is best known for trying to bring his wife Eurydice back from the Underworld after her death; but he turned to see if she was following, which the Underworld God Hades had forbidden and so she was lost.

Orthoceras

COLORS: Black and gray, black and white, green, smoky gray with pearl white; often highly polished

CRYSTAL TYPE: An ancient mollusc that lived in the seas between 485 million and 443 million years ago. The conical shell of this ancient ancestor of the modern-day squid is preserved in fossil form, usually in a black shale matrix

ZODIAC SIGN: Virgo (August 24–September 22)

CANDLE COLOR: White

PHYSICAL: Ensures a long, good-quality life; offers gradual chronic pain relief; alleviates digestive disorders, rheumatism; helps remove and protect against toxins; promotes spine and skeleton alignment.

EMOTIONAL: Aids when life seems hopeless; curbs a tendency to deny or fight the passage of time; helps counter the urge to refuse to deal with necessary routine tasks because you're becoming overwhelmed.

HOME: For staying within budget and time frames for longer-term home renovation projects, new construction, or major property conversions; balancing Earth energies within the home.

WORKPLACE: Insulates against electromagnetic energies and the draining effects of artificial lighting and air conditioning.

CHILDREN: Enables a child to learn from and benefit from mistakes; increases wonder at the natural world.

ANIMALS: For the conservation of marine creatures and coral reefs.

PROTECTION: Guards against neglect of the traditional and natural world.

MAGICKAL AND PSYCHIC USES

A matching pair of fossils acts as a telepathic link for a couple who are far apart; past-life regression either alone in meditation or directing a session for someone else.

SPECIAL PROPERTIES

The smooth polished surface of an individual orthoceras fossil may be used as a worry stone, held both to relieve fears about aging and illness in yourself or loved ones and letting go of old hurts.

MYTHOLOGY AND HISTORY

The ultimate antiageism stone, both in the workplace and socially (where the culture of youth predominates), in the media, and in family disregard for wisdom and experience.

Orthoclase

COLORS: Yellow, champagne, colorless, white, cream, gray, pinkish-red to red, occasionally green
CRYSTAL TYPE: Potassium feldspar
ZODIAC SIGN: Cancer (June 22–July 22)
CANDLE COLOR: Pale yellow

PHYSICAL: Alleviates issues stemming from the spine, teeth, lungs, vision, heart, transplants, end-of-life care.
EMOTIONAL: Valuable after sudden tragedy, attack, rape, or profound grief; allays fears of physically and mentally aging.
HOME: Brings peace in times of unsought domestic change; for harmoniously merging stepfamilies.
WORKPLACE: Aids in maintaining your identity in a conformist workplace; helps resolve disagreements through discussion, rather than denial or arbitrary decisions.
CHILDREN: For those unable to maintain friendships or constantly changing their likes and dislikes; for seriously traumatized children.
ANIMALS: Helps you come to terms with the loss of a pet.
PROTECTION: Guards against threats of violence; for those who live in dangerous locations or perilous times.

MAGICKAL AND PSYCHIC USES
For Earth-healing layouts on maps where there is major disaster, war, drought, or famine; clarifies messages from other dimensions; if UFO contact or cryptozoological experiences are disbelieved or denigrated; connecting with pyramid energies and ancient pyramid builders.

SPECIAL PROPERTIES
Found in many parts of the world, though not officially discovered until 1801; adopted in many cultures throughout the ages, including Native North American medicine men and women as a whole-body-healing stone.

MYTHOLOGY AND HISTORY
Orthoclase is found on Mars in large quantities and in lunar sand on the moon. The crystal helps those in the later years, especially if they're physically more limited, to maintain a youthful spirit.

Owyhee Opal

COLORS: Celestial to light blue with white mixed through; color may fade and the opal become more opaque with exposure to air and dehydration, unless as tumbled stone
CRYSTAL TYPE: Common opal without play of color; hydrated silica, high in silica and water content
ZODIAC SIGN: Libra (September 23–October 23)
CANDLE COLOR: Blue

PHYSICAL: Addresses the throat (especially bacterial and viral infections), sinuses, eyes, skin, seasonal virus epidemics, neurotransmitter conditions, inflammation, PMS; eases pregnancy and childbirth.
EMOTIONAL: Curbs acute shyness, stammering, Tourette's syndrome, inhibitions about revealing the true self because of fears of rejection, overeating as a form of comfort.
HOME: Helps if you constantly forget where you have left possessions or what you were doing if interrupted in the middle of a task.
WORKPLACE: For business meetings to understand the hidden agenda of others.
CHILDREN: Boosts confidence of those afraid to speak up in class or in unfamiliar social situations.
ANIMALS: For older pets who become easily confused.
PROTECTION: During psychic exploration, shields against harmful spirits or those masquerading as relatives, royalty, or deceased celebrities; guards against any psychic attack.

MAGICKAL AND PSYCHIC USES
Shamanic journeying, psychic dream work; two-way communication with higher guides and archangels; mediumship, especially directing earthbound spirits to the light.

SPECIAL PROPERTIES
Make for clear, confident, concise speech with authority but without arrogance in public speaking, acting, and teaching areas of expertise; for singers and mime artists.

MYTHOLOGY AND HISTORY
First found near the sacred Indian springs of Owyhee, Oregon in 2003 and still the only source, this rare opal releases ancient Indigenous wisdom and powerful Earth connection wherever you live in the world.

Painite

COLORS: Orange red and brownish-red (due to traces of chromium, vanadium, and iron); also deep ruby or garnet red; transparent, often with inclusions
CRYSTAL TYPE: Calcium, zirconium, boron, aluminum, titanium, and trace amounts of chromium, vanadium, and iron
ZODIAC SIGN: Aries (March 21–April 20)
CANDLE COLOR: Red

PHYSICAL: Relieves chronic pain; addresses heart conditions especially in women; promotes fertility; counters excessive menstruation; tempers early-onset menopause, perimenopause, and menopause; aids in recover from hysterectomy.
EMOTIONAL: Eases a troubled, circular-thinking mind that keeps you from moving forward.
HOME: Clears the mind and the home of clutter; for strong maternal influence in steering the family through difficult times.
WORKPLACE: Identifies targets and the steps necessary for success; for all women-owned businesses, especially in a male-dominated area of expertise.
CHILDREN: Discourages gender stereotypes in education, where boys are steered toward the sciences and technology and girls to the caring professions.
ANIMALS: Nurtures a maternal animal who is always brooding.
PROTECTION: Guards against dominant females at work or in the family who use caring as a weapon of control.

MAGICKAL AND PSYCHIC USES
Psychic protection against emotional and psychic vampires; fertility magick for an older couple.
SPECIAL PROPERTIES
A prosperity charm for making money by finding and collecting rare treasures and recognizing a hidden bargain that may need repair.
MYTHOLOGY AND HISTORY
Found in Myanmar, one of the world's rarest stones; originally only three known faceted gems were confirmed until the early 2000s. Since 2002 a new source in Magok, northern Myanmar, has increased the yield to several thousand. Some are gem-quality, many fragments and lower grade; these have the same healing and magickal properties as the finest gems; still incredibly rare and expensive in fine gem-quality.

Pallasite Meteorite

COLORS: Iron black or steel gray, containing yellowish-green to brighter green crystal chunks
CRYSTAL TYPE: Olivine or sometimes gem-quality peridot extraterrestrial gems embedded in an iron nickel matrix, with crystals and metal in approximately equal amounts
ZODIAC SIGN: Scorpio (October 24–November 22)
CANDLE COLOR: Green

PHYSICAL: Alleviates neurological conditions, degenerative disorders, self-induced illnesses brought on by an unhealthy lifestyle.
EMOTIONAL: Counters fear of the unknown and fear of people from different backgrounds and cultures; curbs an obsession with hoarding money and possessions.
HOME: For those who live their own way and are not afraid of challenging convention; for moving to the wilderness or permanently living in a nature-based commune.
WORKPLACE: Useful for astrophysicists, those involved in space research, mineralogists of rare stones, astronomers and astrologers.
CHILDREN: A welcome-to-the-world gift for a newborn to be shown on birthdays and given to the young adult on their eighteenth birthday.
ANIMALS: Aids in studying cryptozoology and mythical creatures that may once have lived.
PROTECTION: Guards against frightening experiences of alien abduction or mind control by extraterrestrials, when others do not believe in alien existence.

MAGICKAL AND PSYCHIC USES
For extraterrestrial experiences with wise beings from other dimensions, ufology, metal and gem magick; channeling other dimensions in psychic dreams.
SPECIAL PROPERTIES
Because of the speed Pallasites hurtled through space, they form a catalyst for total life changes; natural moneymakers.
MYTHOLOGY AND HISTORY
Considered the most beautiful of meteorites, Pallasites come from an extinct planet and are approximately 4.5 billion years old. Pallasites can be incredibly expensive. Some may be found more reasonably priced, but be sure to request a certificate of authenticity.

Palm or Worry Stones

COLORS: Vary according to the crystal

CRYSTAL TYPE: Large, flat, oval, smooth crystal in a wide variety, usually with a central indentation for the thumb

ZODIAC SIGN: Libra (September 23–October 23)

CANDLE COLOR: Depends on the stone

PHYSICAL: A natural endorphin, removing pain and tension if rubbed between thumb and index finger of your dominant hand or used directly on the point of discomfort for massage; alleviates all stress-related conditions; for specific healing refer to the properties of the crystal used.

EMOTIONAL: Curbs anxiety and panic attacks when a new situation arises.

HOME: A black Palm Stone set in earth in a planter outside the front or back door repels hostility.

WORKPLACE: To stop grazing at your workstation or going outside for excessive smoking breaks, massage your Palm Stone between thumb and index finger of your nondominant hand while continuing to work.

CHILDREN: Calms those who are frequently anxious but cannot express the cause of their worries.

ANIMALS: Rotate counterclockwise on or near the pet's fur to remove pain; clockwise to energize.

PROTECTION: Guards against fears of entering a crowded elevator or confined space.

MAGICKAL AND PSYCHIC USES

Choose a highly patterned Palm Stone, tracing the pattern until you enter a light trance. Have a basket of different crystal Worry Stones. When you feel troubled, take one without looking and just hold it.

SPECIAL PROPERTIES

Hold your Worry Stone prior to a dental or medical appointment, an examination, test, court case, or stressful meeting. It will ease your worry.

MYTHOLOGY AND HISTORY

For thousands of years, people have adopted a particular stone in times of crisis. Find a naturally smoothed stone with an indentation on the seashore or on a hillside. Wash it regularly to remove energies. Druids and druidesses etched mini-labyrinths on stones to become entranced.

Papagoite

COLORS: Sky blue or light to greenish-blue

CRYSTAL TYPE: Calcium copper aluminum silicate hydroxide; thin veins, crusts, and as snowball-like formations as a phantom or included in quartz

ZODIAC SIGN: Libra (September 23–October 23)

CANDLE COLOR: Blue

PHYSICAL: Addresses issues related to the throat, loss of voice or stuttering made worse by stress, confusion caused by brain overload, vision, muscles, IBS, lactose intolerance.

EMOTIONAL: Eases guilt at seeking pleasure after a strict upbringing; for major sexual hang-ups.

HOME: Strengthens relationships; cuts across differences and divisions.

WORKPLACE: Aids in developing friendships that extend beyond the workplace environment; for office romance.

CHILDREN: Brings happiness to children after a family loss or tragedy.

ANIMALS: Comforts severely abused pets who have lost hope.

PROTECTION: Shields against shadow spirits and those with lower vibrations, called inadvertently by fooling with spirit contact.

MAGICKAL AND PSYCHIC USES

Brings euphoria during meditation; raises vibrations to communicate with higher self and evolved spirits and guides; Ajoite and Papagoite together bring the wisdom of Earth and sky.

SPECIAL PROPERTIES

Said to bring your heart's desire and to generate pleasure and joy once you let go of inhibitions and limitations.

MYTHOLOGY AND HISTORY

Though rare and expensive, Papagoite in quartz is incredibly beautiful for any crystal collection and healing work and for spiritually and emotionally uplifting yourself, your home, your workplace, and your family. It is named in honor of the Native North American people, the Papago.

Papagoite in Ajoite

COLORS: Both papagoite and ajoite blue, can form bright blue together, the amount of blue depending on the clear quartz surrounding them

CRYSTAL TYPE: Though rare, both papagoite and ajoite are found together in quartz, from the now-extinct source of the mine at Messina, South Africa; ajoite is copper silicate and papagoite calcium copper aluminum silicate hydroxide

ZODIAC SIGN: Aquarius (January 21–February 18)

CANDLE COLOR: Blue

PHYSICAL: Returns the body to a state of health after a period of poor nutrition, lack of exercise, and bad habits.

EMOTIONAL: For minds closed to the possibility of anything beyond the material world; those who lack principles.

HOME: Brings the home into balance; protects in an area where there are gangs, street violence, and vandalism.

WORKPLACE: Creates an ethical workplace or workspace if there is bad practice; establishes a financially viable spiritual business.

CHILDREN: For children with complete rainbow auras who have come to bring peace to the world.

ANIMALS: For pets who are alert to the presence of good and bad spirits.

PROTECTION: Guards against spirit and earthly attachments if psychic protection was not used during magickal work.

MAGICKAL AND PSYCHIC USES
Smudging rituals where Father Sky and Mother Earth form directions; connection with archangels, ascended masters, and the essential higher soul.

SPECIAL PROPERTIES
Ajoite transforms negative energies—both surrounding and within—into positive feelings and papagoite, said to give momentary awareness of the Garden of Eden before the Fall, adds the happiness factor.

MYTHOLOGY AND HISTORY
Papagoite is often called grandfather or father of heavenly wisdom and ajoite is sometimes called mother or grandmother of earthly knowledge. Here both energies combine; if in quartz doubling the power. A stone for exploring spirituality when you have many earthly commitments.

Papaya Quartz

COLORS: Pinkish-orange, tends to be either mainly pink or mainly orange

CRYSTAL TYPE: Resembles a cross between Ruby and Pink Sapphire; clear with brilliant light shining through it

ZODIAC SIGN: Sagittarius (November 23–December 21)

CANDLE COLOR: Orange

PHYSICAL: Promotes fertility, both through natural conception and with IVF; clears blockages in the body; aids in healing following cosmetic surgery and Botox treatments.

EMOTIONAL: Counters the drive to claim status and expertise you don't have; releases emotional blockages causing difficulties with sex and commitment.

HOME: Makes the home a welcoming place for gatherings for family, friends, and neighbors; for returning to live in a family home after college, while saving for a deposit on a home of your own, or after a marital breakup, when grandchildren also move in.

WORKPLACE: Called the stone of royalty and status, especially in orange, for rising high in your career.

CHILDREN: Encourages you to tell stories and show photos of your childhood and those of your ancestors to your children.

ANIMALS: Helps you manage when inheriting a family pet after a death in the family or a relative has moved away; aids in gaining custody of an animal after a divorce.

PROTECTION: Guards against deception, lies, and stealing, whether regarding your reputation or your possessions.

MAGICKAL AND PSYCHIC USES
Sunrise and sunset rituals; abundance and prosperity spells; rituals to ensure that love will remain true.

SPECIAL PROPERTIES
Papaya Quartz is said to be viewed at its best just after sunrise or just before sunset to transmit fresh energies for the day ahead and bring evening calm.

MYTHOLOGY AND HISTORY
Found in Madagascar, Papaya Quartz is named after the tropical fruit called the "fruit of the angels" by Christopher Columbus; rarely, it is found as papaya amphibole quartz with its shadowy pink or orange inclusions (see Amphibole or Angel Phantom Quartz, page 25) to provide direct access to angelic energies.

Pargasite

COLORS: Mainly apple to lime to emerald-green, also shades of brown, greenish-brown, dark green, light yellow or black

CRYSTAL TYPE: Magnesium calcium iron aluminum sodium, an Amphibole and a cousin of Hornblende (see pages 25 and 247), often in a matrix such as granite; may be faceted

ZODIAC SIGN: Virgo (August 24–September 22)

CANDLE COLOR: Green

PHYSICAL: Addresses heart conditions made worse by stress, racing pulse, lung and breathing difficulties, hyperventilation, psychosomatic illnesses.

EMOTIONAL: Counters high stress levels, panic attacks, lack of self-esteem, closed heart and mind after betrayal or trauma, hypochondria.

HOME: After a major emotional setback, finds reconciliation, extends forgiveness for what was said and done.

WORKPLACE: Gives you the confidence to set up your own business if that is your dream, and to successfully apply for loans, grants, and necessary training to work for yourself.

CHILDREN: Encourages talents to increase self-esteem if a child is not conventionally academic.

ANIMALS: Empowers pets who are always last to eat at the food bowl and bullied by other animals.

PROTECTION: Guards against those who constantly bring up former injustices or words spoken in anger.

MAGICKAL AND PSYCHIC USES

Past-life healing to leave unhappiness and bad karma behind; a good luck charm, especially in green; encountering higher-nature spirits; empowering herbs and essences for healing.

SPECIAL PROPERTIES

Working regularly with this crystal can lead to a reassessment of life, major or minor, and shedding outworn activities and friends who no longer bring happiness.

MYTHOLOGY AND HISTORY

Pargasite is named after Pargas in Finland, where it was discovered in 1814 by Count Fabian Gotthard von Steinheil; more recently, Vietnam has become a major source of the stone, where the stones are in a white marble matrix, sometimes with red spinel enclosed for extra power.

Past-Time Link or Timeline Quartz

COLORS: Generally colorless but can be found in other clear quartzes; especially citrine and smoky quartz

CRYSTAL TYPE: Past-Time Link or Timeline Quartz crystals have a backward-slanting, diamond-shaped seventh window below the other six faces in the shape of a parallelogram, facing left; may be found with a phantom

ZODIAC SIGN: Cancer (June 22–July 22)

CANDLE COLOR: Silver

PHYSICAL: Past-Time Quartz helps prevent the recurrence of previous illnesses, seasonal allergies, or flare-ups of existing conditions that are now under control.

EMOTIONAL: Counters the inability to let go of a destructive relationship when a partner returns, promising to change, but lapses after a week or two.

HOME: Aids in returning to an earlier or a childhood home or home area by choice if relatives are helping financially.

WORKPLACE: Revives and teaches an ancient craft; for profitable demonstrations in communal workshop premises, a museum, or folklore center.

CHILDREN: Teaches children about their root culture and more distant history, traveling to areas where the family once lived.

ANIMALS: Persuades the family to adopt an older, rescue pet.

PROTECTION: Guards against those who constantly refer to past mistakes in quarrels.

MAGICKAL AND PSYCHIC USES

For past-life exploration to understand and overcome present-day fears and phobias; psychometry; psychic touch (psychometry) of family artifacts or personal treasures of clients to answer questions about current dilemmas linked to the past.

SPECIAL PROPERTIES

For taking what is of value to be learned from the past and leaving behind outmoded ways of reacting and living.

MYTHOLOGY AND HISTORY

The alter ego of the Future Time-Link or Timeline Quartz, both master healers and teachers, that together bring awareness of what has been unconsciously inherited from family attitudes and consciously determining what values should be passed on to future generations.

Paua Shell

COLORS: Deep blue, green, or purple, occasionally with crimson, pink, or gold; iridescent when polished

CRYSTAL TYPE: Organic; sea opal shell, from the Abalone Shell family (page 10), found only in New Zealand's southern coastal waters, but sold worldwide

ZODIAC SIGN: Cancer (June 22–July 22)

CANDLE COLOR: Silver

PHYSICAL: Encourages fertility; alleviates issues stemming from the breasts, uterus, ovaries, rashes, cholesterol, blood pressure, heart valves; eliminates water retention; regulates hormones.

EMOTIONAL: For mothers after a traumatic birth, maternal separation after birth, postnatal depression.

HOME: Promotes healthy growth of exotic indoor plants.

WORKPLACE: Brightens an uninspiring, impersonal environment; integrates workers communicating via online conferencing.

CHILDREN: Brings magick and laughter to children old before their years.

ANIMALS: For pets with depressed owners.

PROTECTION: Traditionally inlaid as eyes in mystical Maori carvings in wood and Greenstone (page 228) Paua Shell jewelry reflects back harm and prevents you from taking unwise actions.

MAGICKAL AND PSYCHIC USES

Each Paua Shell has unique markings; induces light trance in meditation; rainbow wish magick, sea rituals, water divination.

SPECIAL PROPERTIES

The rainbow stone of inner beauty and radiance, brings happiness, hope, love, good fortune, and fertility.

MYTHOLOGY AND HISTORY

Iridescent Paua Shell, the most colorful of shells, is used by Maori people as adornment and in ceremonies. According to legend, Paua Shell was created by Tanangaroa, god of the sea, from the many colors of nature. For respectful wearers, it offers far-reaching certainty of the right path ahead.

Peach Aventurine

COLORS: Soft peach or glowing orange caused by goethite, hematite, and pyrite

CRYSTAL TYPE: Microcrystalline quartz, containing mica, giving aventurine its metallic, iridescent glint.

ZODIAC SIGN: Taurus (April 21–May 21)

CANDLE COLOR: Peach

PHYSICAL: Alleviates issues involving the genitourinary and reproductive systems, lungs, heart, adrenal glands; eases skin problems (such as acne, rosacea, dermatitis, eczema, hives, birthmarks); counters nausea in pregnancy and motion sickness.

EMOTIONAL: Curbs chronic worry about potential disasters to yourself and loved ones, obsessive-compulsive disorder, fear of heights and elevators.

HOME: Brings order to a chaotic shared home; creates comfort if you spend many nights in soulless motels.

WORKPLACE: Aids in forging a career in the beauty or fashion industries or making others feel attractive; for dermatologists; for raising your profile at work.

CHILDREN: For teenagers worried about skin blemishes and weight issues; attracts friends to shy children.

ANIMALS: Calms pets frightened of unfamiliar humans.

PROTECTION: As a space clearer to keep your home free from frustrations brought from work; shields you from putting yourself in danger while driving by overreacting to others' inconsiderate behavior.

MAGICKAL AND PSYCHIC USES

Gentle Reiki and energy-balancing modalities for children, animals, pregnant women, and those who are emotionally vulnerable.

SPECIAL PROPERTIES

For success in creative ventures, writing, art, or talent shows; brings lucky breaks and determination to persevere.

MYTHOLOGY AND HISTORY

Like all aventurine associated with the Chinese goddess of compassion Kuan Yin, Peach Aventurine brings tolerance and empathy, as well as enhancing self-love. The more sparkling mica that is present in the crystal, the more Peach Aventurine brings you closer to attaining your heart's desire.

Peach Moonstone

COLORS: A distinctive shade of moonstone, combining orange and pink, joining love and strength (see also Pink Moonstone, page 357), colored by its high level of aluminum; glows from within

CRYSTAL TYPE: Potassium aluminum silicate feldspar

ZODIAC SIGN: Taurus (April 21–May 21)

CANDLE COLOR: Peach

PHYSICAL: From Roman times, an amulet for fertility, safe and healthy pregnancy and childbirth; promotes female gynecological health from puberty to the wise woman; strengthens skin health, libido; regulates hormones; antiaging.

EMOTIONAL: Curbs dislike of your body, fears of sexuality, especially in women.

HOME: A powerful moonstone for making your home life personally fulfilling as well as keeping others happy; for personal makeovers not to conform with media ideals of beauty but to become happy in your own skin.

WORKPLACE: For women in a strongly male-biased workplace or work culture to avoid getting caught up in aggressiveness and competition.

CHILDREN: Encourages teens to develop a good self-image, based on their abilities and personality and not just appearance.

ANIMALS: Keeps physically beautiful or exotic pets from being stolen or wandering off at night.

PROTECTION: Offers safety while traveling at night and overseas.

MAGICKAL AND PSYCHIC USES

Tantric sex; full moon rituals; clairvoyance, especially gazing into water lit by moonlight; manifestation magick.

SPECIAL PROPERTIES

A charm for lasting love, fidelity, and commitment, adopted in India centuries ago; awareness of sensual pleasures and of occasionally indulging yourself as you do others; not a selfish crystal, but one of self-awareness.

MYTHOLOGY AND HISTORY

According to Chinese mythology, peaches were eaten by the Eight Immortals and represent long and healthy life; this meaning has become attached to the Peach Moonstone. Fossilized remains of a peach tree date back 2.6 million years in China; for allowing men to express their gentler nature, especially if this was discouraged in childhood; helping children to avoid sexual stereotyping.

Peach Quartz

COLOR: Peach, the color caused by the presence of hematite

CRYSTAL TYPE: Quartz with hematite inclusions

ZODIAC SIGN: Sagittarius (November 23–December 21)

CANDLE COLOR: Orange

PHYSICAL: Alleviates physical and energy blockages, coughs, gastroenteritis, gastritis, perspiration, internal parasites; addresses issues involving the lungs, blood pressure, skin, cosmetic and reconstructive surgery, fertility, vitality.

EMOTIONAL: Helps combat lack of self-esteem and poor self-image, difficulty in expressing emotions, a tendency to surrender control to others.

HOME: Creates a beautiful sanctuary, whether a shared city apartment or a rural idyll.

WORKPLACE: Encourages patience and stamina in dealing with clients for all in public positions, from government officials to hospitality staff, caregivers, and call center workers.

CHILDREN: Boosts confidence among teenagers teased about their weight or appearance to value themselves as they are.

ANIMALS: For large animals easily intimidated by smaller creatures.

PROTECTION: Guards against others making you feel helpless or inadequate.

MAGICKAL AND PSYCHIC USES

For empowering crystal grids; meditation, magickal rituals, tarot reading, awakening the divinity within everyone.

SPECIAL PROPERTIES

Achieving your dreams by opening doorways and giving impetus to strive when the going gets hard; for a passionate, caring sex life if you have children or there are distractions that keep you from spending time focusing on your partner.

MYTHOLOGY AND HISTORY

From Brazil and Madagascar, a talisman of good luck, power, and success in every aspect of life and the determination to achieve them; enhances the true self, rather than emulating or trying to gain the approval of others.

Peanut Obsidian

COLORS: Black, red, orange, with shimmering spheres

CRYSTAL TYPE: Variety of perlite, volcanic glass with a high water content; with red feldspar spheres, stained red over an extended period by a hematite coating

ZODIAC SIGN: Aries (March 21–April 20)

CANDLE COLOR: Orange

PHYSICAL: Lowers cholesterol; addresses gallstones; promotes absorption and healthy conversion of body fat; relieves pain; regulates blood sugar; fosters fertility where eggs are irregularly released; ensures successful IVF and artificial insemination.

EMOTIONAL: Curbs self-destructive tendencies; keeps you from constantly voicing petty complaints and feeling dissatisfaction, so you never have peace of mind.

HOME: Draws financial advantage to the home and family; ensures harmonious gatherings with friends, colleagues, neighbors, and family, so the home becomes a welcoming social hub for impromptu events.

WORKPLACE: Gives creative ideas a practical, workable basis—especially useful for patenting new ideas; for making jewelry with gems and crystals for individual orders.

CHILDREN: For those who have been hurt by teasing or unfair criticism.

ANIMALS: Aids in collecting waifs and strays, and caring for them or rehousing them.

PROTECTION: Wards off evil spirits at old sites or in haunted homes.

MAGICKAL AND PSYCHIC USES

A stone of manifesting dearly held desires, where there is a sense of urgency; fire magick; fertility magick; defensive against the evil eye of envy.

SPECIAL PROPERTIES

Said to make the user more charismatic and attractive to others, especially if there is one person you wish attract; polishes into beautiful jewelry and cabochons.

MYTHOLOGY AND HISTORY

Peanut Obsidian is found only in Alamos, Sonora, Mexico where it was discovered during the 1960s by Alberto Maas. It is so named because its inclusions resemble peanuts; enriches the soul and makes a deep connection with the Earth even in the city.

Peanut Wood

COLORS: Dark brown to black, with white, tan, or cream-color markings

CRYSTAL TYPE: Jasper, petrified or fossilized wood in which organic matter is replaced by agate, wood gradually becoming stone; markings are egg-shaped, the size of a peanut and so named; may contain opal or be of gem quality

ZODIAC SIGN: Virgo (August 24–September 22)

CANDLE COLOR: White

PHYSICAL: Alleviates symptoms of perimenopause, menopause, issues with aging; promotes long life; counters calcification of bones; addresses the feet, ankles, and knee and hip replacements.

EMOTIONAL: Allays the fear of losing your youth and attractiveness with the passing years.

HOME: During crises, Peanut Wood jasper offers strength and calm so solutions can be found and well-being restored.

WORKPLACE: For business success and leadership opportunities; hidden talents emerging from the middle years onward.

CHILDREN: Ensures safety near water or while swimming; for non-academic children developing creative talents; teenagers whose hormones are causing extreme mood swings.

ANIMALS: Enables the changing of bad habits acquired with a previous owner or as a stray.

PROTECTION: Guards against the petty jealousies of others.

MAGICKAL AND PSYCHIC USES

Past-life recall; visions during meditation and astral travel to pre-human worlds when seas covered much of the Earth.

SPECIAL PROPERTIES

A stone of gentle transformation from one life stage to another; fosters stability of finances through wise budgeting.

MYTHOLOGY AND HISTORY

Called the stone of the Earth, unlike other petrified woods, many conifers in Western Australia were carried after their death as driftwood into the shallow salty sea covering much of Australia during the Cretaceous period; the driftwood was attacked by small marine clams, called *teredo*, about 70 million years ago, which created boreholes in it, later filled with sediment; that became agate/jasper; most famously it is mined by hand in the Kennedy Ranges near Western Australia's Gascoyne Junction.

Pearl

COLORS: White, gray, cream, pink/peach, blue, Black Pearl (page 64); iridescent

CRYSTAL TYPE: Organic, product of the pearl oyster, from salt water, fresh water, or cultured commercially

ZODIAC SIGN: Cancer (June 22–July 22)

CANDLE COLOR: Silver

PHYSICAL: Addresses skin issues, nausea; regulates fluid imbalances, hormones; alleviates PMS; promotes fertility; eases childbirth; useful for treating soft organs and tissue injuries, growths.

EMOTIONAL: Counters stress overload, burnout; eases the transition for adolescents struggling with puberty.

HOME: Encourages family loyalty and traditions.

WORKPLACE: Valuable for sole proprietors and owners of small businesses, plus midwives, obstetricians, gynecologists, doulas; useful for women returning to work after maternity leave.

CHILDREN: Collect a pearl every birthday to be given to a child on the eighteenth birthday; a jar of pearls in a newborn baby's room offers the protection of Archangel Gabriel.

ANIMALS: For animal mothers who previously failed to rear litters; calms overly boisterous pets.

PROTECTION: Guards against sorrow, especially in love; pearls were given to a new bride to ensure that she would never cry during her marriage.

MAGICKAL AND PSYCHIC USES

Bringers of good fortune and prosperity; breaks psychic, psychological holds and deflects deliberate psychic attack; best owned by one person, though a lovely gift.

SPECIAL PROPERTIES

Pearls, especially white or cream, represent truth, loyalty, and lasting fidelity in love; pearls borrowed from a happy couple transfer joy to bride and groom at their wedding.

MYTHOLOGY AND HISTORY

In ancient China, pearls fell from the sky when weather dragons fought. In India, the god Vishnu plucked the finest pearls from the ocean for his daughter Pandaia's wedding. Ancient Greeks regarded pearls as tears of the deities and in Christianity angels weep pearls for humanity.

Pecos Diamond

COLORS: Orange to light to deep peach, iron providing the color

CRYSTAL TYPE: Quartz, similar to but not the same as rose quartz; usually double or multiterminated; formed inside gypsum that crumbles away leaving the Pecos Diamond; larger crystals may absorb the color of the gypsum and so vary in hue

ZODIAC SIGN: Taurus (April 21–May 21)

CANDLE COLOR: Peach

PHYSICAL: Promotes fertility through spontaneous lovemaking if ovulation charts are causing undue anxiety.

EMOTIONAL: For those who never laugh or smile, either because of current circumstances or earlier trauma.

HOME: Enhances parties, celebrations, happy vacations, and spontaneous outings; rights the work/home balance.

WORKPLACE: Helps in launching new ideas or pushing through existing ones that have hit an impasse.

CHILDREN: Makes it possible for children to enjoy childhood fun if they have grown up too quickly because of family responsibilities.

ANIMALS: Trains destructive puppies while preserving their playfulness.

PROTECTION: Guards against being affected by self-doubt, irrational fears, and free-floating anxiety. and ignoring intuition when new, slightly risky opportunities arise.

MAGICKAL AND PSYCHIC USES

Defense against malevolent magick, curses, hexes, and jinxes; fertility magick, sacred sex rites; solar magick at seasonal change points.

SPECIAL PROPERTIES

A stone that brings happiness to relationships, emphasizes similarities and minimizes differences in any social setting; assists in adopting new fun activities.

MYTHOLOGY AND HISTORY

Found in the Pecos Valley in the southeastern region of New Mexico, Pecos Diamonds, newly emerged from gypsum, are described when the sun shines as a glittering pathway of light; hence the name *diamond*, especially when clear, colorless ones occasionally appear. A stone that enhances sexual desire in established relationships and sends out love signals to a soul twin who has just appeared in your life.

Pentagonite

COLORS: Bright or aqua blue, the blue being caused by the presence of vanadium

CRYSTAL TYPE: Hydrous calcium vanadium oxide silicate; a form of cavansite, but more needle-like; said to vibrate at a greater spiritually evolved level; usually on a matrix, for example, white albite

ZODIAC SIGN: Sagittarius (November 23–December 21)

CANDLE COLOR: Bright blue

PHYSICAL: Addresses inner-ear complaints, tinnitus, issues involving the throat; for end-of-life care.

EMOTIONAL: Curbs self-destructive behavior, lack of respect for others, impulsive overreactions.

HOME: An integrating crystal, drawing together in unity all present and absent; encourages loyalty and fends off negative outside influences.

WORKPLACE: For clear and focused thought if you need to make executive decisions fast; a stone of integrity, cutting through doublespeak, flattery, and half-truths.

CHILDREN: Keep a tumbled stone in a safe place in the child's room to banish fears of monsters and scary creatures.

ANIMALS: For pets easily spooked by sudden noises or movements.

PROTECTION: Guards against scattered energies.

MAGICKAL AND PSYCHIC USES

Wiccan rituals and golden dawn ceremonies because of its association with the magickal five-pointed pentagram star, an amulet against paranormal harm.

SPECIAL PROPERTIES

A wealth- and abundance-attracting stone, both in material and spiritual terms; connects with universal energies during meditation or out-of-body moments gazing at the stars, to feel total weightlessness, lack of awareness of the everyday world, and momentary unity with the cosmos.

MYTHOLOGY AND HISTORY

Named after the Greek word *pente*, meaning "five," Pentagonite has an esoteric link with the magickal defensive and power-attracting pentagram (it is sometimes called the pentagram stone). Pentagonite is found in the United States and India.

Peridot

COLORS: Bright olive or bottle-green; transparent

CRYSTAL TYPE: Silicate/nesosilicate, gem form of olivine, formed in molten rock brought to the surface by earthquakes or volcanic activity

ZODIAC SIGN: Libra (September 23–October 23)

CANDLE COLOR: Bright green

PHYSICAL: Increases effectiveness of medications and treatment; alleviates the allergic reaction to stings and bites; eases all digestive disorders; addresses issues relating to the breasts, vision; for delayed or slow labor.

EMOTIONAL: Relieves insecurity and overpossessiveness linked to a previous relationship betrayal.

HOME: Finds what is lost; attracts good fortune.

WORKPLACE: For bartering, sales, and auctions, plus property negotiations and speculation.

CHILDREN: Guards against night terrors, sleepwalking, and nightmares.

ANIMALS: Guides clumsy or nearsighted animals.

PROTECTION: Shields against shopaholic tendencies, debt through extravagance or overgenerosity.

MAGICKAL AND PSYCHIC USES

Charm against sorcery, negative magick, and evil spirits; attracts true love from afar, in modern days through websites; enhances Reiki; makes nature beings visible.

SPECIAL PROPERTIES

Called the evening emerald, peridot calms addictions, phobias, fears (especially those associated with obsessive-compulsive disorder) and Tourette's syndrome.

MYTHOLOGY AND HISTORY

Rarely, Peridot has extraterrestrial origins, found in meteorites formed 4.5 billion years ago, from solar system beginnings. An ancient source of Peridot is Zagbargad Island off the coast of Egypt. Peridot was prized by pharaohs to protect them from envy, hidden enemies, and to prevent potential threats from the ruling priesthood.

Peridot with Magnetite and Chromite

COLORS: Olive, apple, or bottle-green, glassy (peridot), sometimes on a silvery, brown, black matrix (magnetite); chromite, black to brown may be greenish

CRYSTAL TYPE: Magnetite (iron oxide) (see Lodestone, page 283); Peridot (neosilicate) and chromite (iron chromium oxide, a member of the spinel family)

ZODIAC SIGN: Virgo (August 24–September 22)

CANDLE COLOR: Green

PHYSICAL: Increases effectiveness of medications and treatment.

EMOTIONAL: Curbs insecurity, overpossessiveness; counters a tendency to attract friends who may be unreliable.

HOME: As a display piece near the center of the home, draws the family together in unity and prevents divisions.

WORKPLACE: A career booster to attract opportunities within the workplace and to be approached by other companies for promotion.

CHILDREN: Keep the crystal in a safe place in the home to minimize sibling rivalries and potential conflicts between stepparents and stepchildren.

ANIMALS: For jealous pets or new family members resentful toward a long-established pet.

PROTECTION: Repels entities from attaching to the aura and malevolent elementals remaining after a magick ritual.

MAGICKAL AND PSYCHIC USES

For extraterrestrial connections and messages; UFO sightings and dreams; star magick; an amulet against sorcery.

SPECIAL PROPERTIES

A stone of increase and growth; peridot brings wealth and commitment, magnetite acts as a psychic and physical magnet for what is desired or needed; chromite, which is not always present, in the triplicate, brings ingenuity and original ways of achieving goals.

MYTHOLOGY AND HISTORY

A collector's piece; remarkable in that it combines the strengths of three complementary minerals to create a power greater than the three of them separately. Magnetite and chromite are found in meteors, as occasionally is peridot, making this a powerful, otherworldly, triple crystal and an icon for star souls.

Peridotite

COLORS: Bright to darker green or yellow with black specks

CRYSTAL TYPE: Olivine pyroxene, coarse-grained igneous rock, rich in magnesium and iron; may also contain chromite, garnet, and plagioclase

ZODIAC SIGN: Aries (March 21–April 20)

CANDLE COLOR: Green

PHYSICAL: Alleviates infections that appear as a wound that will not heal or becomes inflamed; strengthens a compromised immune system; counters adverse effects of food additives and chemicals; addresses asthma, allergies, and viruses connected with the respiratory system.

EMOTIONAL: Curbs an inability to forgive yourself or others for mistakes; deters you from making unwise attachments to those who use charisma and flattery to drain energy or resources.

HOME: A natural luck-bringer in small, ongoing ways; aids in searching the attic for forgotten or unrealized treasure or yard sales for bargains; for renovations and refurbishment.

WORKPLACE: A stone of action if there is unfairness or malpractice at work; for pursuing compensation and unfair dismissal claims, even against large corporations.

CHILDREN: Promotes the conception and safe delivery of strong, healthy, and courageous children if a pregnancy is causing undue anxiety.

ANIMALS: For pets who hide when unfamiliar visitors are present.

PROTECTION: Removes cords and attachments, both spirit and earthly, from present and earlier lives.

MAGICKAL AND PSYCHIC USES

The stone of meditating among wild nature; for herbs, herbalism. and empowering these with healing; Earth healing; working with crystals and stones found in their natural state on seashores, riverbanks, or hillsides, and those Indigenous to the home area of the finder.

SPECIAL PROPERTIES

A stone for acquiring financial stability in the long term by revising budgeting and starting a savings plan, however modest.

MYTHOLOGY AND HISTORY

Peridotite is the dominant rock in the upper part of Earth's mantle; a stone for hands-on spontaneous empowerments, blessings, and incantations, rather than formal ritual; restores a sense of security.

Petalite

COLORS: Colorless, white, pale gray, pink
CRYSTAL TYPE: Lithium aluminum silicate
ZODIAC SIGN: Aquarius (January 21–February 18)
CANDLE COLOR: White

PHYSICAL: Alleviates allergies, rashes, stomach upset, tense muscles, neck and back pain, dyspraxia (clumsiness), issues involving the gallbladder, chronic fatigue syndrome, symptoms of being HIV positive and having AIDS.
EMOTIONAL: For family therapy and healing where problems go back generations; unfinished business with the deceased.
HOME: Creates order in a chaotic household, especially if everyone is always late.
WORKPLACE: Prevents burnout if you are a workaholic and never switch off.
CHILDREN: For those who find the world noisy and unpredictable; for those with ADHD, accident-prone children, and those who are targets of bullying.
ANIMALS: Enables animals to safely tolerate boisterous toddlers or teens.
PROTECTION: Guards against psychic and psychological attack and mind control; neutralizes negative energy.

MAGICKAL AND PSYCHIC USES
A gateway between realms, to encounter angels, ascended masters, spirit guides, ancestors, and power animals; manifests what you most need.
SPECIAL PROPERTIES
For a peaceful vacation, to leave your working world and domestic worries behind.
MYTHOLOGY AND HISTORY
In Scandinavian legend, Petalite is called the crystal of the light elves, allowing mortals glimpses of them. Petalite is traditionally a talisman against black magick. Places where it is found include USA, Canada, Brazil, Sweden, Namibia, and Russia. Petalite at its finest resembles sparkling, diamond-like stones.

Petalite with Black Tourmaline

COLORS: Colorless or white (petalite) with black inclusions (tourmaline)
CRYSTAL TYPE: Lithium aluminum silicate (Petalite), aluminum borosilicate mixed with iron, magnesium, or other metals (Black Tourmaline, page 67)
ZODIAC SIGN: Scorpio (October 24–November 22)
CANDLE COLOR: White

PHYSICAL: Addresses arthritis, bowel issues (including IBS and celiac disease); relieves pain; alleviates concerns with the lower back, legs, ankles, feet, muscles, scar tissue; skin eruptions, warts.
EMOTIONAL: Counters claustrophobia, and phobias and fears going back to unresolved childhood issues.
HOME: Balances the yin and yang energies within the home to ensure the free flow of chi; creates a bubble of angelic light, surrounded by a protective dark shield around the home.
WORKPLACE: Promotes equal opportunities in the workplace.
CHILDREN: For those who are unfairly blamed at school for defending themselves against bullies who hide their aggression; for Asperger's and autistic children who are teased into over-reaction.
ANIMALS: Improves the profile of big dogs who are gentle.
PROTECTION: Guards against mind games and manipulation in the name of caring.

MAGICKAL AND PSYCHIC USES
Feng shui, Daoism, tai chi, yoga, and all Asian energy transformation systems; for communicating safely with the spirit realms.
SPECIAL PROPERTIES
Dual-protective-crystal energies actively guard against psychological attack, corruption, and implied threats that cannot be proven; allow light and benign spiritual presences to draw close to your everyday world to bring joy and inspiration.
MYTHOLOGY AND HISTORY
A stone for walking and talking with the angels while keeping your feet safely on the ground; defensive if you suspect relatives in another part of the state or world are casting black magick spells on you or your family.

Petalite with Lepidolite

COLORS: Pink (petalite) blended with lilac (lepidolite) to create a soft purplish-pink or pink and lilac mix; may be iridescent

CRYSTAL TYPE: Lepidolite (silicate; mica containing varying amounts of lithium) and petalite (lithium aluminum silicate); makes beautiful tumbled stones and jewelry

ZODIAC SIGN: Taurus (April 21–May 21)

CANDLE COLOR: Lilac

PHYSICAL: For first-time mothers-to-be, especially if the pregnancy was unexpected after a family seemed complete or for parents who will be helping their pregnant teenager; for heart problems in younger people.

EMOTIONAL: Allays overwhelming fears of potential disasters, especially to the family; curbs fears of abandonment by a partner, even if that's not likely.

HOME: Brings peace and relaxation if you have weathered illness or a period of worry; introduces harmonious unhurried mealtimes.

WORKPLACE: Aids in taking proper meal and screen breaks to refresh your energies; encourages workaholics (maybe yourself) to slow down and prioritize so work does not become almost impossible to switch off.

CHILDREN: Boosts confidence among timid children who find the schoolyard terrifying.

ANIMALS: For very small pets in a noisy and boisterous household.

PROTECTION: Guards against hurtful remarks and sarcasm.

MAGICKAL AND PSYCHIC USES

Transmits the pink healing ray of Archangel Chamuel, who is the angel of love for the devotion of a soul-twin family; angel of humanity and charity as well; for clairvoyance and clairaudience.

SPECIAL PROPERTIES

Two crystals of harmony that together create a feel-good factor and the right home/work balance; brings or increases love based on mutual care and respect.

MYTHOLOGY AND HISTORY

A stone for removing unnecessary stress through trying to be all things to all people; prompts you to step back to explore solitary pursuits and quiet times at work and home so that you can tune into your spiritual nature and listen to your growing intuition.

Petoskey Stone

COLORS: Taupe, tan, browns, or grays, with intricate hexagonal or eye patterns when polished; in rare cases, pale pink when iron ore becomes part of fossilization

CRYSTAL TYPE: Organic, fossilized coral, calcite, pebble-shaped

ZODIAC SIGN: Cancer (June 22–July 22)

CANDLE COLOR: Brown

PHYSICAL: Alleviates infections and infectious diseases (especially childhood illnesses in adulthood); address issues stemming from the eyes, HIV, chronic fatigue syndrome, lungs, fluid levels, growths, cell mutation, genetic illnesses, menstruation, tooth grinding.

EMOTIONAL: Repels pressure to change your beliefs or behavior when family or community disapproves; resolves unfinished business.

HOME: Aids in researching family origins; connecting with overseas family.

WORKPLACE: Encourages promotion, successful creative endeavors, professional restoration and renovation, archaeological investigation, writing historical fiction or drama; for medical researchers.

CHILDREN: Makes unobservant children aware of potential hazards.

ANIMALS: Protects cats who go out at night from harm.

PROTECTION: Guards against malevolent spirits channeling misleading information or masquerading as relatives in séances; blocks visions of unpreventable disasters.

MAGICKAL AND PSYCHIC USES

Clairvoyance; intuition about people's intentions; protects against the eye of envy, especially hidden malice.

SPECIAL PROPERTIES

Aids you in traveling solo, adopting a more adventurous lifestyle.

MYTHOLOGY AND HISTORY

Petoskey is the state stone of Michigan, where much fossilized coral is found along Lake Michigan and Lake Huron. Named after the son of a nineteenth-century Frenchman who married a Native North American chieftainess, called Pet-o-Sega, meaning "rising sun" or "rising dawn." Petoskey's ancient origins and watery energies date from a coral colony 350 million years ago, when warm inland seas covered Michigan.

Petrified Bamboo Agate or Agatized Bamboo

COLORS: Especially from Indonesia, blue, purple, and pink to orange; red, yellow, and white have recently been uncovered; China has more neutral colors

CRYSTAL TYPE: The bamboo has been replaced over millions of years with agate, following the death of the inner organic material; in some specimens, a distinct, hollow, tube-like structure, covered in agate, appears, but in others it takes on a less definite amorphous shape, often white, in which the molecules of bamboo are still visible

ZODIAC SIGN: Capricorn (December 22–January 20)

CANDLE COLOR: Brown

PHYSICAL: Counters illnesses and natural decline in the later years, early-onset dementia; promotes regenerative fitness programs; enhances quality of life and end-of-life care.

EMOTIONAL: Curbs a propensity to hold on to what is no longer needed, in the form of hoarding, and as old hurts or attitudes no longer relevant to present-day life and relationships.

HOME: Encourages the whole family, and not just one member, to take responsibility for caring for older family members.

WORKPLACE: Respects the wisdom, authority, and experience of older workers; assesses new methods and technology.

CHILDREN: As bamboo is the fastest-growing plant on the planet, a family treasure kept with growing bamboo demonstrates the effects of time.

ANIMALS: Mends pets with chronic skin complaints.

PROTECTION: Absorbs and transforms psychic and psychological attacks.

MAGICKAL AND PSYCHIC USES

For aura cleansing and balancing; exploring herbal remedies and traditional healing methods, such as Ayurveda.

SPECIAL PROPERTIES

Standing back and allowing others, especially young adults, to make their own mistakes and judgments that may seem unwise, but where it is not your place to control their destiny.

MYTHOLOGY AND HISTORY

The earliest fossilized bamboo dates from the later Miocene period in Yuhan, southwest China, between 11 million and 3 million years ago. A find of agate tubes of varying colors was recently uncovered in a remote area of Java near the Marapi volcano.

Petrified Palm

COLORS: Golden with fossilized black dots or inner rods; red, brown, orange

CRYSTAL TYPE: Transformed into chalcedony with the original form and structure of the wood preserved; may be up to 20 million years old

ZODIAC SIGNS: Scorpio (October 24–November 22) and Sagittarius (November 23–December 21)

CANDLE COLOR: Gold

PHYSICAL: Alleviates issues of aging, adverse responses to intense heat or cold, fluid imbalances (causing swellings of legs, feet, and ankles), eustachian tube dysfunction, light sensitivity.

EMOTIONAL: Eases chaotic emotions; keeps you from giving up when the way ahead involves effort; counters a tendency to live through the achievements of others.

HOME: For attracting money, good fortune, and welcoming family members home who have been absent for a while.

WORKPLACE: Encourages quick reactions to sudden changes or those seeking to unfairly shift blame.

CHILDREN: Teaches children to respond to emergencies and practice simple first aid; for those afraid of doctors or dentists.

ANIMALS: Comforts pets traumatized by a traffic accident or a fight.

PROTECTION: Guards against harmful paranormal influences and absorbing negative emotions during healing, meditation, and magickal ritual.

MAGICKAL AND PSYCHIC USES

Time travel, full moon ceremonies, visions of Middle Eastern and biblical worlds where palm trees grow, plus past lives.

SPECIAL PROPERTIES

For adventure activities, such as skydiving, rock and mountain climbing; for triumph and tangible rewards after a long, hard endeavor.

MYTHOLOGY AND HISTORY

The state stone of Texas and the fossil of Louisiana, Petrified Palm is associated with Ophiuchus, sometimes considered the thirteenth planet between Scorpio and Sagittarius, the serpent/healing staff bearer associated with the Greco-Roman healer god Aesculapius and so with healing and restoration to wholeness of mind, body, and soul.

Phantom Quartz

COLORS: Depends on the composition of the inner crystal; true phantom or ghost quartz contains a whitish or pale-gray ethereal crystal (see Black Phantom Quartz, page 64, and Chlorite Phantom Quartz, page 122)
CRYSTAL TYPE: Usually clear quartz, in which the shadow crystal is enclosed
ZODIAC SIGN: Aquarius (January 21–February 18)
CANDLE COLOR: Gray

PHYSICAL: Aids in treating illnesses using diagnostic scans, radiation treatment, microsurgery; helps pinpoint the source of illnesses with uncertain causes; alleviates psychosomatic conditions, deep vein thrombosis, flare-ups of earlier illnesses.
EMOTIONAL: Releases buried trauma from present or past worlds, for talking therapies such as psychotherapy and hypnosis; keeps destructive patterns from recurring.
HOME: A silver phantom, with sparkling crystals around the inner phantom, attracts good fortune, health, and wealth.
WORKPLACE: Aids in maintaining a low profile in confrontational situations; for investigators, researchers into complex diseases, microbiologists.
CHILDREN: Connects parents with the unborn child; protects children from night fears.
ANIMALS: Attracts nocturnal wildlife to gardens.
PROTECTION: Hides necessary secrets and secret love.

MAGICKAL AND PSYCHIC USES

For ghost investigations; connecting with recently deceased relations; a gateway for meditation, psychic dreams, astral travel, and past lives; each phantom is said to contain an angel or fairy.

SPECIAL PROPERTIES

Reveals to healers root causes; for psychic surgery.

MYTHOLOGY AND HISTORY

A phantom is caused by a pause in a crystal's growth lasting thousands of years, leaving a partial or complete phantom within the crystal after growth continues. Sometimes quartz encloses a different crystal type or a different crystal grows around quartz that stopped growing. Use white for major transformation; restorative if circumstances restrict desired changes.

Phenacite or Phenakite

COLORS: Milky to clear white, also tinted yellow, pink, or brown
CRYSTAL TYPE: Rare beryllium silicate
ZODIAC SIGN: Aquarius (January 21–February 18)
CANDLE COLOR: White

PHYSICAL: Alleviates nerve damage, brain imbalances, genetic disorders, autoimmune diseases, HIV, issues relating to the eyes (especially optic nerves); promotes whole-body healing; restorative after chemical or surgical intervention or radiation treatment.
EMOTIONAL: Brings powerful insights to problems; opens receptivity to counseling or psychotherapy; counters addiction; distinguishes freeloaders from true friends.
HOME: Overcomes family feuds and grudges, especially going back generations; for neighborhood and community ventures.
WORKPLACE: Aids in turning hobbies or talents into a second career (especially after retirement), or becoming a professional healer, clairvoyant, or medium.
CHILDREN: Assists teenagers subjected to violence or influenced by gangs or aggressive peers.
ANIMALS: For poorly trained guard dogs to reduce aggression.
PROTECTION: Guards against psychic attack, curses, and hexes.

MAGICKAL AND PSYCHIC USES

A high-vibration crystal, connection with guardian angels, archangels, and spirit guides; opens doorways into other dimensions, enhances clairvoyance; a gift for handfasting and traditional marriage ceremonies; lucid dreaming; Reiki attunement; psychokinesis.

SPECIAL PROPERTIES

Phenacite aids life changes, including leaving home, marriage or remarriage, major relocation, retirement; discovering a more fulfilling lifestyle.

MYTHOLOGY AND HISTORY

A light in the darkness crystal; if faceted, Phenacite resembles a diamond, but with more spiritually focused energies, aptly named after the ancient Greek word *phenas* for "false diamond"; increases telepathy between soul twins; deepens self-awareness to discover the true self and life path at any age or stage of life.

Philippinites or Rizalites

COLORS: Black or dark gray

CRYSTAL TYPE: Philippine tektites, often spherical or spheroid shapes, unusually have finer, smoother, and smaller surface texture than tektites from other places and shine more brightly; tektite is natural glass, created from the heat of meteorite impact with the Earth

ZODIAC SIGN: Scorpio (October 24–November 22)

CANDLE COLOR: Purple

PHYSICAL: Placed on a point of pain or the source of a problem, Philippine tektites are said to lift out discomfort or dis-ease and transform it into light, rather than absorbing it within the tektite; strengthens the autoimmune system; alleviates recurring tropical diseases, caused by parasites or mosquitoes.

EMOTIONAL: Eases major shock or trauma that has resulted in total withdrawal into the yourself; counters an unwillingness to seek treatment or follow healing regimens.

HOME: Protects the home from natural disasters; for family members who have returned home to live after an accident, unemployment, or a relationship breakup.

WORKPLACE: For relocating to a hot climate; boosts stamina if major projects involve overtime or taking work home.

CHILDREN: For Star Children and those fascinated by astronomy.

ANIMALS: Keeps pets from fighting after frequently receiving bites or cuts.

PROTECTION: Creates spiraling light to repel attacks on physical or psychic energy.

MAGICKAL AND PSYCHIC USES

One of the most effective tektites for psychic surgery, Philippine tektite's effect is described as swirling energies around the client and healer.

SPECIAL PROPERTIES

In addition to its host material, Philippine tektite has absorbed the tropical and rain-forest energies of the land and so regenerates as it heals.

MYTHOLOGY AND HISTORY

Philippine tektites are sometimes called Rizalites after the Philippine province Rizal, where they were first discovered in 1926. Their formation dates back to a meteor impact about 710,000 years ago. They have since been discovered as Iron Age grave goods in the form of amulets and charms.

Phlogopite

COLORS: Browns, pale yellow, or reddish-brown, with a pearly luster; may include stars of rutile or tourmaline; sometimes displays a copper-like reflection

CRYSTAL TYPE: Magnesium mica sheet silicate (phyllosilicate) with biotite; may appear as scattered crystals within a magnesium-rich limestone

ZODIAC SIGN: Aquarius (January 21–February 18)

CANDLE COLOR: Golden brown

PHYSICAL: Relieves back pain; alleviates issues involving the bile duct, tooth enamel; strengthens bones; addresses astigmatism, near- and farsightedness.

EMOTIONAL: Curbs flashes of uncontrolled anger at minor trigger points; keeps you from being unable to back down or compromise.

HOME: Insulates against excessive energy from cell phone towers, power lines, electrical appliances, and technological devices; restores the heart of the home if family members are communicating with people outside the home on their devices and ignoring those within.

WORKPLACE: Aids in retaining information needed for meetings, presentations, and promotion interviews or examinations.

CHILDREN: For those who constantly lose or break their possessions and whose bedrooms are total chaos.

ANIMALS: Calms unpredictable, impulsive, but lovable pets.

PROTECTION: Guards against the duplicity of those who show only their surface layer; for those who chip away at your confidence.

MAGICKAL AND PSYCHIC USES

Used in sacred ceremonies, magick rituals, medicine wheel rites, and smudging ceremonies to unite the powers of Earth, Air, Fire, and Water with Father Sky above and Mother Earth beneath; for channeling teacher guardians and angels.

SPECIAL PROPERTIES

Enables you to ask for what you want and need in love, a committed relationship, or a close friendship.

MYTHOLOGY AND HISTORY

Phlogopite is a stone of taking over the reins of life, rather than allowing fate or others—however well meaning—to dictate future direction; especially valuable if people around you are pressuring you to pursue a path that they consider best for you instead of what you want.

Phosphosiderite

COLORS: Deep purple, lilac, lavender, purple to reddish-violet
CRYSTAL TYPE: Iron phosphate
ZODIAC SIGN: Cancer (June 22–July 22)
CANDLE COLOR: Purple

PHYSICAL: Promotes whole-body healing, wherever it's most needed; alleviates issues stemming from the abdomen, thyroid, adrenal glands, skin, hair, colds, flu and viruses affecting respiration, aging worries.
EMOTIONAL: Counters creative burnout; releases negative emotions from the past; eases deep-seated stress causing psychosomatic conditions; curbs an inferiority complex, insomnia, and nightmares.
HOME: Ensures that personal needs do not get lost in caring for family and home.
WORKPLACE: For artists and all creators to allow inspiration to flow from the heart; avoids overthinking that blocks spontaneous words or images.
CHILDREN: Useful for angry teenagers or those teased by siblings and peers.
ANIMALS: Calms nervous pets who fear change of routine.
PROTECTION: Guards against those who keep you in their grip through guilt and obligation; shields you from emotional vampires, curses, and hexes.

MAGICKAL AND PSYCHIC USES
Meditation, clairaudience; opening to higher dimensions and evolved spiritual teachers, angels, and ancestors.
SPECIAL PROPERTIES
Restores integration to the whole self if fragmented or torn in different directions; mends a fractured aura, guarding it from further damage.
MYTHOLOGY AND HISTORY
Phosphosiderite, a rare stone, is sometimes called *La Rosa Voca* ("pink rock") in its rose-colored form, which is especially connected with committed love and the discovery and deepening of soul-twin relationships, recognized from past worlds.

Picasso Jasper, Marble, or Stone

COLORS: Mixture of black, brown, gray, rust, and cream in abstract patterns
CRYSTAL TYPE: Metamorphic limestone, crystallized dolomite, or calcium magnesium carbonate, undergoing numerous changes during formation
ZODIAC SIGNS: Taurus (April 21–May 21) and Virgo (August 24–September 22)
CANDLE COLOR: Light brown

PHYSICAL: Strengthens arteries, vision, bowels, colon, intestines, feet, legs; alleviates Parkinson's disease, multiple sclerosis, carpel tunnel syndrome; boosts sex drive; encourages weight loss; eases toxicity.
EMOTIONAL: Counters anxiety, stress and troubling thoughts; for those who have given up on people and life; a mood-lifter.
HOME: For parties, outings, and celebrations to integrate unsociable family members.
WORKPLACE: Aids in breaking into the market with creative ventures, especially painting, textiles, sculpture, web design, and photography; promotes effective online meetings and networking.
CHILDREN: Teaches children to play well with others.
ANIMALS: Helps breed healthy, well-adjusted animals.
PROTECTION: For safety in crowds in unfamiliar places.

MAGICKAL AND PSYCHIC USES
For group meditation and visualization; discovering your spiritual path; linking with angels, guides, star, and planetary beings, trance mediumship, astral travel.
SPECIAL PROPERTIES
Reconnecting with old friends via the internet, school and college reunions; attracting new friends, maybe rekindling first romance; a joy-bringer.
MYTHOLOGY AND HISTORY
The metamorphic formation of Picasso Jasper leaves a map of its journey through time, in an array of subtle colors with the abstract quality of the works of the Spanish painter Pablo Picasso, after whom it was named. Picasso Jasper is a reminder to enjoy life to the fullest and find the right work/life balance.

Picture Jasper

COLORS: Sandy, tan, golden, or brown due to high iron content, with color bands, veins, and flowing patterns

CRYSTAL TYPE: Silicate, microcrystalline quartz (see also Picasso Jasper); resembles a miniature landscape seen from above

ZODIAC SIGN: Capricorn (December 22–January 20)

CANDLE COLOR: Brown

PHYSICAL: For easing childbirth; addresses issues relating to skin disorders and allergies caused by chemicals or additives, intestines, IBS, constipation, hernia, prostate, hips, knees, feet, lumbago, kidneys, immune system.

EMOTIONAL: Eases repressed fears, sorrows, and grief from childhood; fends off unrealistic expectations of others; keeps you from craving cigarettes and comfort eating.

HOME: Helps overcome homesickness and adjust to a new lifestyle if you and/or your partner are from different lands.

WORKPLACE: Useful for overcoming creative blocks in writing or other artistic endeavors; those who work with wind farms or solar power.

CHILDREN: For taking children overseas for the first time.

ANIMALS: Valuable for exotic breeds, where domestic and wild animals are mixed.

PROTECTION: Guards against hazards in remote places or becoming lost when technology fails.

MAGICKAL AND PSYCHIC USES
Shows landscapes and pathways for astral flight journeying to earlier civilizations, such as ancient Egypt.

SPECIAL PROPERTIES
For traveling overseas or out of state on prolonged vacations, treks across the wilderness, becoming part of a local community if you're away from home.

MYTHOLOGY AND HISTORY
The stone of psychic artistry, drawing auras, spirit guides, angels, and deceased relatives visible around others. Picture Jasper offers access to the global energy web via a local ancient site or subterranean energy track.

Piedmontite

COLORS: Deep red, red violet, red brown, interspersed with off white/gray

CRYSTAL TYPE: Sorosilicate, manganese-rich variety of epidote (see also Dragon's Blood Jasper, page 165), lustrous with crystalline veins (red) running through a quartz matrix (white/gray), the amount of red depending on the proportion of quartz to piedmontite

ZODIAC SIGN: Aries (March 21–April 20)

CANDLE COLOR: Dark red

PHYSICAL: Alleviates issues stemming from the heart, liver, small intestine, kidneys, thyroid; promotes fertility; helps overcome impotence, premature ejaculation, vaginismus; boosts metabolism; addresses brain irregularities and loss of memory.

EMOTIONAL: Banishes the effects of incest when you were a child and into adulthood; counters an addiction to pornography.

HOME: Encourages family members who waste food or buy far more than their needs to develop more responsible habits.

WORKPLACE: Deters inappropriate flirting, sexual harassment, or those offering sexual favors in return for promotion or special privileges.

CHILDREN: Useful for those who become easily embarrassed.

ANIMALS: For action to ensure animal welfare.

PROTECTION: Guards against making impulsive decisions.

MAGICKAL AND PSYCHIC USES
Calling a person telepathically to contact you.

SPECIAL PROPERTIES
For establishing or reviving a sexual relationship based on love and mutual respect as well as passion; if a previously loving partner refuses to make love or discuss the reasons; lovemaking after a long period of celibacy.

MYTHOLOGY AND HISTORY
Found in New Mexico, the quartz matrix strengthens the qualities of the Piedmontite; some being entirely included in quartz, some mainly displaying red sometimes polished into beautiful jewelry. The brighter and more prominent the red, the more joy and pleasure in life will be spontaneously felt and expressed.

Pietersite, Tempest, or Storm Crystal

COLORS: Combination of blue-black, blue, gold, golden brown

CRYSTAL TYPE: Quartz, silicon dioxide, variation of the less proactive tiger eye, and hawk's/falcon's eye, forming chaotic patterning and coloring, partly due to golden swirls of crocidolite

ZODIAC SIGNS: Leo (July 23–August 23) and Sagittarius (November 23–December 21)

CANDLE COLOR: Gold

PHYSICAL: Stimulates the pituitary gland and growth hormones; alleviates bronchitis and respiratory complaints worsened by weather or altitude; addresses eye infections, distance vision and night vision; regulates body temperature in extreme heat or cold.

EMOTIONAL: Reduces cravings when you're overcoming addictions.

HOME: Protects your home from storm damage and natural disasters.

WORKPLACE: Guards against interruption and trivia when you're concentrating.

CHILDREN: For teens who lose possessions and resist routine.

ANIMALS: Banishes fear of storms.

PROTECTION: Shields against adverse technological effects; for safe driving in bad weather.

MAGICKAL AND PSYCHIC USES

Said to contain the power of storms, offering power to manifest change; for weather rituals; clairvoyance, and precognition.

SPECIAL PROPERTIES

Combines wisdom with the desire for knowledge and truth; for researchers, scientists, philosophers, gurus, investigators; for discovering new treatments, vaccines, and cures.

MYTHOLOGY AND HISTORY

Named after Sid Pieters, who discovered it in Namibia in 1962; also mined in Henan Province, China. Pietersite works to shake the world out of a passion for materialism and a sense of spiritual inertia.

Pink Amethyst

COLORS: Pale pink, pale lavender/lilac-tinted pink

CRYSTAL TYPE: Quartz, colored by manganese and hematite during formation

ZODIAC SIGN: Taurus (April 21–May 21)

CANDLE COLOR: Palest pink

PHYSICAL: A whole-body healer, especially for those who are physically vulnerable; makes any conventional treatment more effective.

EMOTIONAL: For quitting bad habits and addictions, and overcoming fears and phobias with deep roots in childhood.

HOME: For kindness in a competitive, volatile family.

WORKPLACE: Increases tolerance for difficult colleagues or managers.

CHILDREN: Helps sensitive children to mix with their classmates.

ANIMALS: Persuades high-strung, pregnant animals to accept their young.

PROTECTION: Guards against negativity from troubled people and restless spirits.

MAGICKAL AND PSYCHIC USES

Brings happy, lucid dreams, in which you know you are dreaming.

SPECIAL PROPERTIES

Attracts spiritual, gentle love; increases self-esteem for the person you are now.

MYTHOLOGY AND HISTORY

Pink Amethyst, recently discovered in Patagonia, is linked with purple calafate berries. The berries, like the crystal, are symbols of love that can never be parted but will always return.

Pink Apatite

COLORS: From pale to rose and vivid pink

CRYSTAL TYPE: Complex phosphate of calcium, chlorine, and fluorine; the gentlest of the apatites

ZODIAC SIGN: Taurus (April 21–May 21)

CANDLE COLOR: Pink

PHYSICAL: Alleviates growth and teething issues in babies and children; addresses issues relating to teeth, wisdom teeth, gums; eases the transition to puberty and menopause.

EMOTIONAL: Counters weight-related disorders, hypochondria, Munchausen's syndrome by proxy; low self-esteem; postnatal depression that stands in the way mother-baby bonding.

HOME: Pink Apatite soothes the bustle and noise of family life and creates time and space for quality interactions; defuses sibling rivalry.

WORKPLACE: For a mentoring or buddy system for new entrants or younger colleagues; makes an impersonal work setting friendlier.

CHILDREN: Calms hyperactive children and creates an oasis of tranquility and routine for those with autism, even in the busiest home; keeps teens safe from inappropriate online and offline activities.

ANIMALS: Conserves animals with tusks or horns from poaching or the destruction of their habitat.

PROTECTION: Guards against voices from the past encouraging self-defeat.

MAGICKAL AND PSYCHIC USES

For powerfully increased maternal and paternal instincts with offspring, no matter what the age or how far apart you are.

SPECIAL PROPERTIES

The stone of the growth of trust after betrayal or a major emotional breakup; for tough love where a partner or family member is being unreasonable.

MYTHOLOGY AND HISTORY

Rare facet-grade Pink Apatite has recently been found in La Marian Mine at Boyacá, Colombia, and in Pakistan, Afghanistan, and Brazil; it may also be obtained as tumbled stones. Apatite's name comes from the Greek word *apatao*, which means "to deceive," because over many centuries gem apatite in different colors has been mistaken and sometimes substituted in place of other more expensive gems. Apate, one of the spirits released from Pandora's box in ancient Greek mythology, was the goddess of deceit, fraud, and trickery.

Pink Aragonite

COLORS: Pale pink in natural form, resembles coral; may be fluorescent

CRYSTAL TYPE: Calcium carbonate; found also as tumbled stones and in jewelry, especially presented as a gift after a woman has given birth

ZODIAC SIGN: Taurus (April 21–May 21)

CANDLE COLOR: Pink

PHYSICAL: Alleviates colds, coughs, influenza, lung infections caused by bacterial infections or viruses, vitamin and mineral deficiency; for the health, bonding, and well-being of mothers and babies after a prolonged or traumatic birth or if they were temporarily separated afterward.

EMOTIONAL: Curbs scattered energies; useful for those who find it hard to give or receive generosity, presents, or praise; counters a negative or distorted body image.

HOME: Calms domestic dramas; enables you to calmly ignore critical relatives, friends, or neighbors, pointing out your mistakes or oversights.

WORKPLACE: If you do more than your fair share of work and do not receive appreciation or tangible reward.

CHILDREN: Helps children to adapt to routines when they begin school or change educational settings; for establishing regular bedtimes and sleeping through the night.

ANIMALS: For a retired guide, therapy, guard, or racing dog to adapt to everyday domesticity.

PROTECTION: Guards against being smothered in the name of caring by a maternal or paternal figure at home or at work.

MAGICKAL AND PSYCHIC USES

Traditional meditation from the Hindu or Buddhist traditions; chanting; mantras; working with mandalas, sacred geometric drawings.

SPECIAL PROPERTIES

Avoids the blame game if others try to offload their failures or inadequacies on you, a scapegoating pattern that may have come from childhood or even been inherited at birth.

MYTHOLOGY AND HISTORY

Found in Brazil, Pink Aragonite dispels unwarranted fears of infidelity or lack of love in a partner, rooted in earlier relationship betrayals and insecurities in one or both partners; teaches mutual trust.

Pink Chalcedony

COLORS: Varying shades of pink, often creamy pink (see also Blue Chalcedony, page 73, and White Chalcedony, page 501), the pink caused by manganese or ferrous oxide impurities

CRYSTAL TYPE: Cryptocrystalline quartz

ZODIAC SIGN: Pisces (February 19–March 20)

CANDLE COLOR: Pink

PHYSICAL: Addresses issues involving the skin, breasts, heart, baby and childhood illnesses (especially rashes), pregnancy, postnatal problems and depression, psychosomatic conditions, fears of aging.

EMOTIONAL: Relieves shock and trauma; eases obsessive-compulsive disorder, fear of germs, neglect or abandonment in early childhood; for young girls reaching early puberty.

HOME: For dealing with challenging relatives; helps parents-to-be and new parents adjust to their new life; brings warmth and hominess to soulless homes.

WORKPLACE: Heals bitterness, rifts, and jealousy caused by unfair promotion or reorganization; for historians, storytellers, therapists, writers, midwives, obstetricians, social housing or service workers.

CHILDREN: Protects babies in the early days of life; for children unsettled by the arrival of a new baby, divorce, or foster, step- or adoptive children with conflicting loyalties.

ANIMALS: For baby or orphaned animals who are not thriving.

PROTECTION: Shields against heartache and heartbreak, and against emotional vampires who prey on any physical weakness.

MAGICKAL AND PSYCHIC USES

Increases telepathic communication between parents-to-be and the infant in utero; for goddess rituals and connection with the female aspect of God; entry into womanhood rites.

MYTHOLOGY AND HISTORY

Sacred in Native North American spirituality, a universal stone promoting the brotherhood and sisterhood of humankind; for releasing or rediscovering your inner child and connecting with the wonders of nature.

Pink Coral

COLORS: From pale to magenta pink; may sometimes be dyed in brighter shades

CRYSTAL TYPE: Organic, branching, calcareous skeletons of sea creatures

ZODIAC SIGN: Pisces (February 19–March 20)

CANDLE COLOR: Pink

PHYSICAL: Alleviates menstrual difficulties, especially in younger women who want a baby; promotes fertility when conception is slow after a first child; addresses issues relating to the breasts, heart problems in women; for illnesses and infections in babies and children.

EMOTIONAL: Offers strength to teenage mothers-to-be who have no network of support; for an adoptive mother whose adopted child returns to the birth mother.

HOME: For single parents, and especially lone fathers, providing a nurturing environment for children; for finding a female role model/mentor in an all-male household.

WORKPLACE: Aids in obtaining the right childcare facilities to continue a promising career.

CHILDREN: Pink Coral is especially soothing for babies and young children; teething rings of red, white, or pink coral were traditionally given in a number of cultures to protect babies from harm and still are treasured as family heirlooms.

ANIMALS: For nervous overly defensive nursing pets who have not produced a litter before.

PROTECTION: Guards against unkindness within families at any age.

MAGICKAL AND PSYCHIC USES

For psychic defense against those who are physically vulnerable or old, but practice malicious spells and hexes; fertility magick; protective magick for babies and children against the evil eye.

SPECIAL PROPERTIES

Calms teenage girls who are struggling with puberty; hide Pink Coral in a teenage boy's rooms if he has become aggressive.

MYTHOLOGY AND HISTORY

Pink Coral is associated with the sacred tree of the first Mother Goddess on which she grew all the creatures of the sea. It is illegal in several countries to harvest Pink Coral; it is possible, however, to seek ecologically sustainable coral. Coral has been used for thousands of years in jewelry and for healing. All of us need to question if and how far the use of coral is still viable.

Pink Danburite

COLORS: Very pale pink, like clear glass, gentler and rarer sister of colorless danburite

CRYSTAL TYPE: Calcium borosilicate

ZODIAC SIGNS: Taurus (April 21–May 21) and Aquarius (January 21–February 18)

CANDLE COLOR: Deep pink

PHYSICAL: Strengthens the heart, heart-valve replacements, bypasses, muscles; alleviates allergies or illnesses caused or made worse by chemicals, pollutants, and harmful rays.

EMOTIONAL: Addresses trauma after accident, attack, abuse, divorce, or bereavement.

HOME: Fills a home with love, healing if you still live in the marital home after a divorce or bereavement.

WORKPLACE: For workers who deal with crises and traumas daily.

CHILDREN: Comforts children who are delicate physically, grieving, or traumatized.

ANIMALS: For very ill small creatures and injured wild birds.

PROTECTION: Protects you from manipulation by others in the name of love.

MAGICKAL AND PSYCHIC USES

Healing powers from angelic sources; effective in healing layouts, Reiki, reflexology, kinesiology, meditation.

SPECIAL PROPERTIES

Discovered during the Industrial Revolution, insulates against a materialistic way of life; restores direct, loving contact, rather than via social media.

MYTHOLOGY AND HISTORY

Named after Danbury, Connecticut, where it was first found; gem-quality stones come mainly from Mexico; the ultimate crystal of the heart for those abandoned by society or anyone who is lonely.

Pink Diamond

COLORS: Pale pastel pink to bright intense pink as natural; may be recolored diamonds. Pink diamonds often come with a secondary hue, purple-pink, orange-pink, or brownish

CRYSTAL TYPE: Carbon, the pink coloring due to grain or fiber lines, irregularities during formation

ZODIAC SIGN: Taurus (April 21–May 21)

CANDLE COLOR: Pink

PHYSICAL: Alleviates issues stemming from the breasts, fertility, pregnancy, childbirth, heart, circulation, hormone-related headaches.

EMOTIONAL: Eases rejection in childhood, in favor of a sibling, which continues into adulthood.

HOME: Aids in restoring an old building to its former glory.

WORKPLACE: For creative enterprises; jewelry designers; interior designers.

CHILDREN: Helps overcome fears of childbirth and coping with motherhood later in life or as a young teenager.

ANIMALS: For anticipated birth complications.

PROTECTION: Guards against fears of betrayal, creating problems where none exist.

MAGICKAL AND PSYCHIC USES

Rituals for romance and happily-ever-afters; female rites of passage.

SPECIAL PROPERTIES

Brings reconciliation after a major breakup or betrayal.

MYTHOLOGY AND HISTORY

Ninety percent of Pink Diamonds come from the Argyle Diamond Mine in Western Australia; it is among the rarest of diamonds; only 0.01 percent of all diamonds in the world are pink. The world's largest cut diamond is the pale pink Daria-i-Noor, weighing 186 carats, currently part of the Iranian crown jewels in Tehran. Queen Elizabeth II was given a Pink Diamond brooch as a wedding gift by Canadian geologist Dr. John Williamson in November 1947, which she wore at the wedding of the Prince of Wales and Princess Diana.

Pink Halite

COLORS: Pink/peach, deep pink to orange; pink caused by algae growing within the mineral, orange caused by hematite inclusions
CRYSTAL TYPE: Sodium chloride, halide
ZODIAC SIGNS: Cancer (June 22–July 22) and Pisces (February 19–March 20)
CANDLE COLOR: Pink

PHYSICAL: Aids in recovery from heart-valve stenosis, heart surgery, cardiac arrhythmia, heart failure, allergies causing breathing difficulties, water retention, chemical imbalances; pink or orange halite, carved into lamps, are natural air ionizers to induce health and well-being.
EMOTIONAL: Helps release old attachments and emotions that have outlived their purpose; aids in accepting that a love is unattainable.
HOME: Restores the heart of the home if a move was caused by financial or emotional loss.
WORKPLACE: Fosters persuasion and a personal approach in negotiations; for clear decision making.
CHILDREN: For moody teens and those who lack self-esteem.
ANIMALS: Keeps pets from constantly picking up minor infections or parasites.
PROTECTION: Guards against taking unfair criticism, sarcasm, or spite to heart.

MAGICKAL AND PSYCHIC USES
Acupressure and acupuncture; clearing the aura; rituals for wealth, love, and healing, Earth energies; cleanses other crystals.
SPECIAL PROPERTIES
For surviving loss or setbacks and starting again, without self-blame.
MYTHOLOGY AND HISTORY
Halite is a fast-growing crystal; some specimens can be less than a year old. It can also be found as deposits in ancient bedrock, from evaporated seas or salt lakes. Some halite is accumulated over millions of years in salt caverns; traditionally, halite clusters enclosing treasures were cast into salt lakes as offerings.

Pink Howlite

COLORS: Vibrant pink, color-enhanced, because of its porous nature white howlite absorbs dye well; has black veins
CRYSTAL TYPE: Howlite, calcium borosilicate hydroxide
ZODIAC SIGN: Taurus (April 21–May 21)
CANDLE COLOR: Pink

PHYSICAL: Aids in breast reconstruction after mastectomy or for cosmetic reasons; useful in cosmetic enhancements and removal of unwanted tattoos and blemishes that cause self-consciousness and negative remarks from others.
EMOTIONAL: Curbs uncontrolled anger and domestic violence toward and by both sexes.
HOME: For reasoned responses when deliberately provoked by family members or neighbors.
WORKPLACE: Counters workaholic tendencies, especially among women who feel or need to prove that motherhood has not affected their ability to strive for the top; for beauty-enhancing businesses.
CHILDREN: Helps show by example that happiness comes through sharing simple pleasures.
ANIMALS: For caring for small animals.
PROTECTION: Deflects deliberate unkindness and others' attempts to wound your self-esteem by drawing attention to your supposed inadequacies.

MAGICKAL AND PSYCHIC USES
For men and women to connect with loving female icons, such as Kwan Yin; Mother Goddesses, Mother Mary, the Black Madonna, or female angels; to allow women to express their unique qualities in a competitive world.
SPECIAL PROPERTIES
Eases a desire for perfectionism in every aspect of life and harshly judging yourself.
MYTHOLOGY AND HISTORY
Called the imitation stone, because it is often used as a substitute for more expensive stones, in this case pink sugilite; dyed Pink Howlite combines the physical, mental, emotional, and psychic strengths of undyed howlite with joy-bringing fuchsia pink.

Pink Kunzite

COLORS: Varying pink shades (see also Lilac or Lavender Kunzite, page 279)

CRYSTAL TYPE: Spodumene with manganese creating pink; may have deep striations

ZODIAC SIGN: Taurus (April 21–May 21)

CANDLE COLOR: Pink

PHYSICAL: Addresses hormone-linked migraines, female reproductive issues, PMS, menstruation, pregnancy; relieves problems stemming from circulation, heart, neuralgia, epilepsy; alleviates skin rashes from chemical allergies, psychosomatic conditions; curbs anesthetic aftereffects.

EMOTIONAL: Counters postnatal depression, panic attacks, phobias linked with low self-esteem; helps young or first-time mothers needing mothering themselves.

HOME: Fosters patience after sleepless nights with a new baby or a chronically ill or confused relative.

WORKPLACE: Useful if a manager or employer displays personal prejudices or uses sexual harassment to exert power; calms interview or evaluation nerves.

CHILDREN: Eases babies toward life outside the womb after a prolonged or traumatic birth.

ANIMALS: For animal mothers indifferent toward their young.

PROTECTION: Guards against fears and doubts offloaded by others; deflects dangerous driving or aggression by other drivers.

MAGICKAL AND PSYCHIC USES
For Mother Goddess and Earth-healing rituals; angelic communication; for Star Souls; shards of kunzite hung where the wind catches them create healing sound.

SPECIAL PROPERTIES
The woman's stone for every stage of life, from puberty through female rites of passage; for struggling single parents; for finding the right love partner after a relationship breakup.

MYTHOLOGY AND HISTORY
A relatively recently discovered stone, from the early twentieth century. Under the Gaia principle, Mother Earth reveals crystals needed to heal new ills created by humans. Kunzite's color varies according to the angle from which it is viewed, called "pleochroism" or "multicoloredness."

Pink Moonstone

COLORS: Various shades of pink—translucent to opaque

CRYSTAL TYPE: Member of the feldspar family of potassium aluminum silicates

ZODIAC SIGN: Cancer (June 22–July 22)

CANDLE COLOR: Rose pink or silver

PHYSICAL: For reproductive disorders, enhances fertility in women by helping to bring menstrual cycles in alignment with the moon; for relieving fluid retention and food allergies, especially dairy and wheat intolerances.

EMOTIONAL: Curbs eating disorders and body-image problems, separating food from emotional and spiritual needs.

HOME: A dish of Pink Moonstones encourages peaceful times if the home is noisy or chaotic.

WORKPLACE: Wear Pink Moonstone on your right-hand side for clear communication, on the left for creativity.

CHILDREN: Prevents nightmares and sleepwalking.

ANIMALS: Protects young animals from accidentally escaping and straying at night.

PROTECTION: Guards against emotional abuse of the vulnerable and those who are too trusting.

MAGICKAL AND PSYCHIC USES
Brings clairvoyant powers to the fore, especially around full moon. Hold the crystal to moonlight and see images on the shimmering surface of a translucent Pink Moonstone.

SPECIAL PROPERTIES
Most powerful around the full moon of April, called by some Native American nations the "pink moon"; good for dancers and those with poor coordination.

MYTHOLOGY AND HISTORY
Found in India, Pink Moonstone, like all moonstones is a sacred stone, believed to be formed from moonbeams.

Pink Moss Agate

COLORS: Medium to salmon to orangey pink with plant-like inclusions in black or occasionally brown or red

CRYSTAL TYPE: Quartz-based chalcedony with inclusions of manganese, iron oxide, or hornblende

ZODIAC SIGN: Taurus (April 21–May 21)

CANDLE COLOR: Pink

PHYSICAL: Alleviates issues involving the fallopian tubes, uterus, breasts, pregnancy, and childbirth; especially helpful for single mothers or those whose own mother has passed on; eases blood flow through veins and arteries; strengthens neural pathways or promotes growth of new ones after a stroke; valuable in treating children's heart conditions.

EMOTIONAL: Reduces a sense of isolation, extreme shyness, inability to forgive; keeps you from holding on to bad childhood memories; useful in dealing with difficulties in nurturing children or those who are vulnerable.

HOME: Encourages the growth of flowers; for tolerance between family members of one another's faults; for harmonious meals.

WORKPLACE: Aids in setting up a mentoring or buddy system at work; for midwives, community health nurses, family therapists, and counselors in domestic abuse shelters.

CHILDREN: Fends off personality clashes between a particular child and a parent; addresses rebellious children.

ANIMALS: For a pet who becomes jealous of another animal's litter.

PROTECTION: Guards against mind manipulation through guilt, sentiment, and possessiveness in the name of caring.

MAGICKAL AND PSYCHIC USES

For fey magick, especially flower fairies; flower magick and healing; fragrance magick using oils, flower waters and floral incense; for baby blessings.

SPECIAL PROPERTIES

The stone of forgiveness, both self-forgiveness for what cannot be put right and of those who have caused hurt by acting thoughtlessly; for tough love when necessary.

MYTHOLOGY AND HISTORY

A gentler, more personally focused version of green or greenish-blue Moss Agate (page 308); encourages face-to-face meetings, friendship groups, and setting up mutual aid groups.

Pink or Rose Agate

COLORS: Pink; some are tinted or dyed to yield a brighter magenta shade; undyed Pink Agate is gentle in color (see also Botswana Agate, page 88); may be rose-colored as regency Rose Agate

CRYSTAL TYPE: Microcrystalline quartz, chalcedony; smooth and waxy, may contain small clear crystals inside (see Geodes, page 201) and have visible bands. Regency Rose Agate is a transparent to translucent silicate agate

ZODIAC SIGN: Libra (September 23–October 23)

CANDLE COLOR: Pink

PHYSICAL: Stems hair loss, PMS, heart problems (especially heart-valve stenosis); strengthens eyes, blood vessels, skin, uterus; alleviates varicose veins; stimulates weight loss.

EMOTIONAL: Counters resignation to the inevitability of a destructive situation; transforms a distorted self-image.

HOME: Brings stability to a home if circumstances are not ideal; Pink Agates with crystals inside attract unexpected financial resources.

WORKPLACE: For couples, families, or close friends to preserve goodwill when running a business together.

CHILDREN: Promotes warm, loving relationships between parents and children of all ages.

ANIMALS: Encourages a pet to allow family near her kittens or puppies.

PROTECTION: Guards against deliberate belittling and hurtful comments.

MAGICKAL AND PSYCHIC USES

Goddess rituals; female rites of passage from the onset of puberty to passing on.

SPECIAL PROPERTIES

Restores love and passion to a couple weighed down by the responsibility of work, family, and finances.

MYTHOLOGY AND HISTORY

Regency rose was traditionally carried by miners and prospectors for good luck. Rose Agate with a rose-pink center in a white or yellow agate is a protective form of pink agate against the evil eye of envy.

Pink Sapphire

COLORS: From light pink to intense magenta

CRYSTAL TYPE: Corundum, aluminum oxide, typically containing traces of iron, titanium, vanadium, and chromium; the amount of chromium present determines the intensity of color

ZODIAC SIGN: Taurus (April 21–May 21)

CANDLE COLOR: Pink

PHYSICAL: Eases puberty and early-onset puberty, especially for girls; alleviates issues involving the breasts, endometriosis, heart, circulation.

EMOTIONAL: Counters the propensity to seek perfect romance and idealized love at the expense of a real relationship; for obsessions with celebrity lifestyles.

HOME: Aids in arranging an engagement, marriage, or handfasting if family is planning an elaborate celebration and the couple is reluctant; for moving in with a partner for the first time.

WORKPLACE: Helps businesswomen and female entrepreneurs to overcome gender-based bias and maintain their integrity.

CHILDREN: Valuable for first love; for a teenage pregnancy; encourages girls to train for traditionally male professions.

ANIMALS: For a mother giving birth to her first litter far too young.

PROTECTION: Keeps you strong when you cannot leave a difficult or disturbing situation.

MAGICKAL AND PSYCHIC USES

Acts as a magnet to draw the right love and friendship; telepathy between love partners; for reconciliation during an impasse.

SPECIAL PROPERTIES

A stone to attract beautiful artifacts into your life; the motivation to strive only for what is of true worth.

MYTHOLOGY AND HISTORY

In Asian lore, Pink Sapphires are associated with the sacred lotus. The rarest sapphires—pink-orange sapphires, discovered in Sri Lanka—are called padparadscha. In Sinhalese, *Padma radschen* means "aquatic lotus blossom" because the flower has a similar pink-orange hue. Princess Eugenie of the UK was given a blush-colored padparadscha engagement ring, surrounded by smaller diamonds, by her fiancé in 2018.

Pink Spinel

COLORS: From pale to bright pink shades, including a magenta pink, sparkling. The paler the pink the gentler its properties

CRYSTAL TYPE: Magnesium aluminum oxide

ZODIAC SIGN: Taurus (April 21–May 21)

CANDLE COLOR: Pink

PHYSICAL: Promotes preconception health; alleviates chronic tiredness and debilitating conditions, such as chronic fatigue syndrome; relieves pain; addresses endometriosis, issues involving the breasts; valuable for mammograms, biopsies, cervical smears.

EMOTIONAL: Curbs acute anxiety, phobias, and obsessions, especially those connected with childhood trauma; helps overcome fear of pregnancy and childbirth, as well as post-natal depression.

HOME: Encourages introverted family members to express themselves in family discussions, rather than just agreeing.

WORKPLACE: Aids in making money through creative careers, such as publishing, media, design, event planning; for interior design and the creation of lovely gardens.

CHILDREN: Counters school phobia, fears of the mother dying; for young teenage mothers-to-be if they feel they need support.

ANIMALS: For timid, nocturnal pets or those who have been roughly handled.

PROTECTION: Guards against having your opinions ignored.

MAGICKAL AND PSYCHIC USES

For love and fertility magick; for blessing ceremonies such as naming, christenings, or handfasting; a crystal for finding a first love or for calling back your first love.

SPECIAL PROPERTIES

A love token if a couple works or live far from each other and can rarely meet; for a secret love if there is major family or religious opposition; for finding romance or encouraging romance in a down-to-earth partner.

MYTHOLOGY AND HISTORY

Pink Spinel is often mistaken for Pink Sapphire. In 2007, workers found a giant spinel in a farmer's field in Mahenge, Tanzania, displaying the vibrant pink now called Mahenge spinel; often considered one of the most beautiful finds of the modern age, a gift of beauty and love from Mother Earth.

Pink Starburst Quartz

COLORS: Pale pink and transparent; may have a lilac tinge or even appear as pale amethyst

CRYSTAL TYPE: Unlike rose quartz, which grows in large masses without faces, Pink Starburst Quartz forms distinct crystals, seen best in galaxy-like clusters; has inner five-point small stars that reflect the light and sparkle in the sun (see also Star Hollandite Quartz, page 455)

ZODIAC SIGN: Pisces (February 19–March 20)

CANDLE COLOR: Pink

PHYSICAL: Promotes fertility, if you had given up hope; dissolves pain and eases the source of distress.

EMOTIONAL: Helps resist temptation to engage in a secret love that cannot be revealed without hurting others; keeps you from being emotionally manipulated by an older, physically dependent relative.

HOME: For a happy, loving home to which different generations return regularly and willingly; for teens embarrassed about revealing intimate problems.

WORKPLACE: This gentle form of starburst quartz brings rapid fulfillment in career, not just profit.

CHILDREN: For fostering children who have been abused or mistreated; for newborn babies with wise old souls.

ANIMALS: Aids in animal rescue and sanctuary work.

PROTECTION: Guards against those who delay plans and deny living for and in the present.

MAGICKAL AND PSYCHIC USES

Clairvoyance, clairaudience, remote healing, especially for the young, the old, animals, and the vulnerable; goddess rituals.

SPECIAL PROPERTIES

To find lasting love or to become aware that someone you've taken for granted *is* the one; for awakening passionate love, familial love, deep friendship, and love of humanity.

MYTHOLOGY AND HISTORY

Found in Morocco, a gentler but no less powerful form of clear starburst, Pink Starburst Quartz, named after the astronomical term for rapid star formation, inspires those who want to make a difference to the world.

Pink Sugilite

COLORS: Pale pink to lavender to magenta/fuchsia, sometimes streaked with black manganese

CRYSTAL TYPE: Potassium sodium lithium iron manganese aluminum silicate

ZODIAC SIGN: Taurus (April 21–May 21)

CANDLE COLOR: Pink

PHYSICAL: Alleviates headaches (especially when containing black manganese streaks); relieves pain, burns, inflamed skin or organs.

EMOTIONAL: Addresses Asperger's syndrome, autism, and personality disorders where empathy and reading social signals are a problem; for those who take on the troubles and pain of others; counters a sense of hopelessness.

HOME: A feel-good crystal that prevents one family member from being unfairly scapegoated for all the problems in the family.

WORKPLACE: Enables those involved in social or psychological care of vulnerable people to show empathy without becoming overwhelmed.

CHILDREN: Eases dyslexia, dyspraxia, learning difficulties; for older teens rejected by birth parents they have traced; for sensitive children who find social interactions daunting.

ANIMALS: For timid pets who fear other animals and visitors; keeps stronger animals from victimizing the runt of the litter.

PROTECTION: As a shield of light against self-doubt, hostility, and jealousy from others.

MAGICKAL AND PSYCHIC USES

For past-life recall of earlier childhoods that may explain current fears or phobias; calling a soul twin, if known but not acknowledged by the other person.

SPECIAL PROPERTIES

A powerful love crystal, especially in more vibrant pink; for avoiding unrealistic expectations in relationships while encouraging loyalty in good times and bad.

MYTHOLOGY AND HISTORY

Pink Sugilite, also called lavulite, is a self-help crystal where professional assistance has failed; counteracts the tendency to seek temporary comfort in food, gambling, or out-of-control spending.

Pink Sunstone

COLORS: Pinkish-yellow; may include white or flecks of black; Pink Sunstone often grows with yellowy-orange sunstones

CRYSTAL TYPE: Plagioclase feldspar, with a hematite infusion creating the pink

ZODIAC SIGN: Taurus (April 21–May 21)

CANDLE COLOR: Pink

PHYSICAL: Alleviates low blood count, blood sugar fluctuations; gentler than orange sunstone for gradually restoring health, strength, and recovery for children, teenagers, new mothers.

EMOTIONAL: Counters frequent depressed moods; curbs a tendency to seek support from others, rather than tackling issues yourself; keeps you from acting helpless and as the victim, while drawing strength from others.

HOME: Works like an early morning sunrise, filling the home with optimism for each new day; acts like a soft sunset letting all anger, resentment, and quarrels go before sleep.

WORKPLACE: For successfully fulfilling a day's work that seems impossible, by adopting a calm, measured approach.

CHILDREN: Encourages children to try new activities and approach peers they would like to know better.

ANIMALS: For nocturnal animals, both pets and wildlife.

PROTECTION: Guards against physical and emotional energy drains by clingy people and demands on your time.

MAGICKAL AND PSYCHIC USES

A charm for good luck after loss or setback; clairvoyant visions in dreams; astral travel and meditation; your future life path and your next incarnation.

SPECIAL PROPERTIES

A stone of love after loss or betrayal to allow trust to regrow slowly whether trying again in a relationship or redeveloping self-confidence.

MYTHOLOGY AND HISTORY

Associated with sunset goddesses, such as the ancient Egyptian Mother Goddess Hathor, goddess of marriage, women, music, dance, fertility, and protection, whose special hour is the hour before sunset or the Greco-Roman Venus, the evening star, at her brightest minutes after the sun goes down.

Pink Topaz

COLORS: Light to vibrant pink (natural and very rare, pink caused by the presence of chromium); heat-treated in varying shades of pink

CRYSTAL TYPE: Aluminum silicate fluoride hydroxide

ZODIAC SIGN: Taurus (April 21–May 21)

CANDLE COLOR: Pink

PHYSICAL: Addresses issues involving the breasts, ovaries, early-onset puberty, or menopause; enhances the effects of HRT; alleviates inflammation, fever, insomnia, asthma, hemorrhages, heart palpitations, hearing difficulties; promotes fertility and fertility treatments.

EMOTIONAL: Counters a tendency to love the wrong person too much; curbs unrequited love that is blocking future relationships.

HOME: Establishes a home-based crafts industry, artist's studio, or self-sustaining enterprise.

WORKPLACE: Aids in working with family or a love partner in business.

CHILDREN: For a teen heartbroken by the end of a first love.

ANIMALS: Consoles a pet who has lost a lifetime mate.

PROTECTION: Awakens awareness of falsehoods and illusions in others; shields against injuries and mishaps.

MAGICKAL AND PSYCHIC USES

For prayer, religious and formal spiritual ceremonies; guards against evil and those dabbling in demonic rites online.

SPECIAL PROPERTIES

For good luck in love, a love token for deepening affection; prompts self-love and self-esteem; keeps you from rushing from one broken commitment to another because of loneliness.

MYTHOLOGY AND HISTORY

Like red, natural Pink Topaz is one of the most valuable stones; it's found in Brazil, Russia, and Pakistan. The first artificial Pink Topaz was created in 1750 when a Parisian jeweler discovered that more widely available yellow topaz turns pink if exposed to moderate heat. The largest known Pink Topaz is an oval-shaped gemstone of more than 75 carats from Russia.

Pinolith or Pinolite

COLORS: Black/gray and white with pinecone patterns

CRYSTAL TYPE: A metamorphic rock that is mixture of dolomite, graphite, and magnesite

ZODIAC SIGN: Cancer (June 22–July 22)

CANDLE COLOR: White

PHYSICAL: Alleviates stress-related stomach upset, IBS, issues involving the female reproductive organs (including PMS), muscle cramps, angina, racing heart, high cholesterol, gallbladder pain, kidney stones, foot problems, tooth and gum disorders.

EMOTIONAL: Curbs self-deception; keeps you from sabotaging your personal happiness through fear of letting others get close; counters phobias about dentistry and invasion of personal space during medical examinations or treatment.

HOME: For finding and making a forever home after disruptive moves; for example, military families, or where work has taken the family to numerous posts overseas.

WORKPLACE: Overcomes prejudice and exclusion of talented individuals who do not conform to the company agenda.

CHILDREN: Allows children to develop at their own pace without comparison with their peers.

ANIMALS: For pets who are patient with babies and children.

PROTECTION: Prevents inner conflicts and self-doubts.

MAGICKAL AND PSYCHIC USES

Pinolith enhances clairvoyance, spontaneous psychic visions for deep meditation; helpful for letting go of logic and doubts and allowing psychic wisdom to flow.

SPECIAL PROPERTIES

Helps you be supportive, without being dragged down, if a partner is struggling with depression, bipolar disorder, or an addiction.

MYTHOLOGY AND HISTORY

Pinolith or Pinolite is also called the pine stone. It is prized as an ornamental stone, especially in church architecture, in jewelry, and as smooth tumbled stones for bringing calm in the midst of chaos. It was used in the construction of St. Stephen's Cathedral in Vienna in 1641. Pinolith is found in Austria and northeastern Spain.

Pipestone or Catlinite

COLORS: Deep red, light pink, brick to blood red; may display smaller lighter spots

CRYSTAL TYPE: Solidified, soft, clay-like mineral, a form of argillite, in a matrix of Sioux quartzite; smooth, easily carved, and polished

ZODIAC SIGN: Pisces (February 19–March 20)

CANDLE COLOR: White

PHYSICAL: Addresses issues stemming from the lungs, legs, feet, spine, and body, mind and spirit alignment; promotes sound healing; enhances fitness programs.

EMOTIONAL: Resolves underlying causes of resentment, rather than projecting negativity onto trivial matters.

HOME: Creates an oasis of calm, however small.

WORKPLACE: Keeps you from making unwise decisions; for military and security personnel, athletes, sports coaches, those in physically hazardous jobs or places.

CHILDREN: Counters an obsession with material possessions.

ANIMALS: Aids in reconnecting urban pets with nature.

PROTECTION: Guards against shopaholic tendencies and incurring unnecessary debt; deflects psychic attack.

MAGICKAL AND PSYCHIC USES

Meditation, Native American spirituality, exploring spiritual roots of personal ancestors; manifesting abundance; for those who experience Native American past lives.

SPECIAL PROPERTIES

For recognizing the interconnectedness of life, uniting plants, people, animals, and stones; prayer and ritual in everyday life.

MYTHOLOGY AND HISTORY

Pipestone has been shaped into sacred pipes, ritual objects for ceremonies, totems, and as amulets for protection for hundreds of years by Native North Americans, especially among the Plains nations. Among the Sioux, the Lakota recount that White Buffalo Calf Woman brought the gift of the pipe to form a bridge between the people and Great Spirit. The best-quality Pipestone is found in southwestern Minnesota.

Pistachio Calcite or Sea Green Calcite

COLORS: Bright lime, bluish, aqua, or pale green; may have bands of yellow, and pale and darker green

CRYSTAL TYPE: Calcium carbonate, the green caused by chromium infiltrating during crystallization

ZODIAC SIGN: Pisces (February 19–March 20)

CANDLE COLOR: Green

PHYSICAL: Addresses issues concerning the heart, circulation, blood clots, arthritis, adrenal glands, muscles; heals with visualized blue-green light.

EMOTIONAL: Counters fear of social situations, eating and talking in public; keeps you from holding on to resentment and taking criticism to heart.

HOME: Boosts tolerance of the weaknesses of others; creates quiet times for listening if family members tend to shout one another down.

WORKPLACE: Persuades a business partner that it is time to ease up when they will not admit they are struggling; for workaholics; for fair hearings.

CHILDREN: Teaches younger children patience and the need to take turns.

ANIMALS: For dogs who race ahead or pull at the leash during exercise.

PROTECTION: Guards against the intrusive thoughts of others; deflects hostile paranormal or earthly energies.

MAGICKAL AND PSYCHIC USES

Connects with spirits of fresh water and oceans; empowers healing oils and essences; meditation to bring mind, body, and spirit into alignment.

SPECIAL PROPERTIES

A stone for encouraging peace in the home, workplace, community, and globally.

MYTHOLOGY AND HISTORY

Found in Pakistan and Afghanistan, Pistachio Calcite brings acceptance of life, as it is named after the soft, green, nutmeat inside a pistachio nut; it shields against harsh, insensitive people and situations that shake your equilibrium; a crystal of personal privacy.

Plancheite

COLORS: Light blue to bluish-green, with a silky luster

CRYSTAL TYPE: Hydrated copper silicate, often confused with Shattuckite (page 431)

ZODIAC SIGN: Leo (July 23–August 23)

CANDLE COLOR: Turquoise

PHYSICAL: Promotes blood coagulation; addresses issues relating to the tonsils, throat complaints; relieves pain and lack of mobility in joints and bones; counters loss of short-term memory.

EMOTIONAL: Comforts in the face of intense grief; curbs incoherence, stuttering, stammering, and blushing when you're required to speak in front of group of people professionally or socially.

HOME: For redesigning and redecorating your home, even on a budget.

WORKPLACE: Enables knowledgeable, authoritative, public speaking, whether you're a teacher, in the field of law, selling ideas, or defending yourself against a complaint.

CHILDREN: Keeps you from being intimidated by authorities, if they are being unfairly critical of your child, at meetings about your child or at back to school nights.

ANIMALS: For overly timid small animals who hate being handled.

PROTECTION: Guards against false friends and lovers, especially internet romance scammers.

MAGICKAL AND PSYCHIC USES

For automatic writing, divination, and astrology, recalling knowledge of the solar system.

SPECIAL PROPERTIES

For fame and fortune through increasing your public profile and meticulous preparation for auditions and presentations.

MYTHOLOGY AND HISTORY

A stone traditionally associated with power and authority, and therefore potent in dealing with aggressive people in your life who try to shout you down; enables you to speak unhesitatingly under pressure with calmness and accuracy; if threatened by a bully using physical strength, Plancheite enables you to walk away safely and claim your rights.

Platinum

COLORS: Silver-gray to white-gray, white when polished
CRYSTAL TYPE: Element, metal
ZODIAC SIGN: Aquarius (January 21–February 18)
CANDLE COLOR: Silver

PHYSICAL: Alleviates problems stemming from the testes, ovaries, endocrine system, genetic and cellular issues, lungs, malignancies; aids in twin or multiple births; mitigates the effects of toxins; eases prolonged invasive treatments; helps in combating rare illnesses; enhances remote healing.
EMOTIONAL: Counters unusual phobias; helps overcome resistance to counseling.
HOME: A tiny piece in the wall of a newly built or renovated home brings lasting health and wealth.
WORKPLACE: Platinum flakes or grains in a jar attract prosperity and good results from small beginnings; for a highly competitive job market.
CHILDREN: Helpful when a child is born to older parents after years of trying.
ANIMALS: For pets regarded as precious children.
PROTECTION: Returns ill will and curses to the sender.

MAGICKAL AND PSYCHIC USES
Aids in healing the environment; protects against frightening extraterrestrial encounters or dreams and nocturnal paranormal sexual attacks; helps dowsers seeking archaeological treasures or underground water.
SPECIAL PROPERTIES
Platinum is a symbol of incorruptible love, for soul twins or lovers parted by distance or opposition.
MYTHOLOGY AND HISTORY
Platinum in nature contains iron, copper, and sometimes gold or iridium. Some Platinum originated in meteorites. Indigenous people mined Platinum in Colombia, South America, for hundreds of years. Sixteenth-century Spanish conquistadors considered Platinum inferior silver; not until 1751 was Platinum recognized as an element. Platinum was viewed as a precious metal in Russia in the nineteenth century. Widespread trading of Platinum coins and bars began in the 1970s. The US mint launched a Platinum American eagle coin in 1977.

Platinum Obsidian

COLORS: Black with silver-gray, platinum-colored bands
CRYSTAL TYPE: Banded obsidian with iron oxide and aluminum oxide impurities
ZODIAC SIGN: Scorpio (October 24–November 22)
CANDLE COLOR: Silver

PHYSICAL: For radiotherapy, chemotherapy, laser treatment, biopsies, deep organ or tissue surgery; mitigates migraines, macular degeneration, cataracts, glaucoma, night-vision problems, tinnitus; addresses misfiring neurons.
EMOTIONAL: Eases intense grief; curbs unbalanced emotions, causing an overreaction toward trivial matters.
HOME: Guards against lightning strikes and storm damage, tornadoes, and fires caused by faulty wiring or carelessness; binds vicious tongues of neighbors or visiting relatives.
WORKPLACE: Platinum Obsidian fire focuses on making wealth through creative inspiration; useful in working with metals, chemicals, electricity, fossil fuels, nuclear power, or gases.
CHILDREN: Protective if children are afraid of the dark or of ghosts.
ANIMALS: For pets overly sensitive to spirit presences during late-night walks.
PROTECTION: Guards against becoming overwhelmed by rekindled emotions best left in the past.

MAGICKAL AND PSYCHIC USES
Shamanic healing to remove affliction from an affected part of the body by psychic surgery; prophecy, spellcasting, wizardry; witchcraft; chanting and incantations of power; extraterrestrial contact.
SPECIAL PROPERTIES
A stone especially effective during the waning moon or meteor showers for taking away pain or starting a detox program when cravings are intense.
MYTHOLOGY AND HISTORY
From Mexico, Platinum Obsidian represents the night and the moon, tapping into our innate hidden psychic nature, where answers hidden during the day are revealed as flashes of inspiration or visions; a stone for keeping secrets, especially love that cannot be revealed.

Plum Blossom Jasper

COLORS: Dark blue or black with pink or red, blossom-like sprays over the surface, the colors depending on the kind of Plum Blossom stone

CRYSTAL TYPE: *Plum Blossom* refers to the patterns on the stone and is mainly found in jasper, which is chalcedony, microcrystalline quartz; may also be found as a pattern less frequently on tourmaline, aluminum boron silicate

ZODIAC SIGN: Taurus (April 21–May 21)

CANDLE COLOR: Pink

PHYSICAL: Eases early-onset puberty in girls; promotes fertility, especially if conception is slow or medical intervention is needed; useful in cosmetic surgery to hold back the aging process; addresses skin issues and plant allergies; relieves stress.

EMOTIONAL: Counters an overemphasis on the need for a perfect appearance, immaculate home, and successful career; curbs a propensity for intolerance of human frailty; helps overcome OCD.

HOME: For a new fitness and healthy eating regimen; valuable for physical and fashion makeovers; protects the home against harsh weather, especially out of season.

WORKPLACE: For dealing with sensitive issues or colleagues who take constructive advice as criticism.

CHILDREN: Helps teens counteract image problems and eating disorders.

ANIMALS: Useful in animal grooming.

PROTECTION: Shields from physical harm, threats, and intimidation.

MAGICKAL AND PSYCHIC USES

Flower oils and essences; flower psychometry; love and fertility rituals; fragrance magick; psychic protection.

SPECIAL PROPERTIES

A good luck charm in times of adversity and inevitable but feared change; for a gradual turnaround in fortune; promotes good results with prolonged steady use.

MYTHOLOGY AND HISTORY

Plum blossom symbolizes the spirit of Chinese culture, perseverance, maintaining dignity in hard times, courage, and self-improvement; the same qualities have come to represent Plum Blossom Jasper. It is also a stone of transition, as plum blossom appears on the trees between the end of winter and the beginning of spring, promising that the leaves and fruit will return in abundance.

Pollucite

COLORS: Cloudy white, colorless in some gems; also less frequently as blue, gray, peach, pink, or violet

CRYSTAL TYPE: Zeolite; as a tumbled stone best for healing and magick; increasingly available in gem-quality

ZODIAC SIGN: Gemini (May 22–June 21)

CANDLE COLOR: White

PHYSICAL: Radiates the complete rainbow aura around it and so can synthesize healing in every chakra energy center and the aura, as and where needed; useful in end-of-life care and easing the passing.

EMOTIONAL: Counters intense grief, heartbreak through loss or betrayal; helps banish a sarcastic or disapproving persona to mask your own sense of inferiority.

HOME: Counteracts toxicity in the atmosphere, such as acid rain or living near a landfill site, and those who sour the atmosphere with discouraging words.

WORKPLACE: Gives you an aura of authority and makes others respect and listen if you are often overlooked.

CHILDREN: Keep Pollucite with a photo of your child if they are on the fringes and do not get picked for teams or invited to parties; promotes closeness between siblings and individuality in twins.

ANIMALS: For a physically large and strong pet with the heart of a mouse.

PROTECTION: Keeps you safe those if you travel by sea or work with, on, in, or close to water.

MAGICKAL AND PSYCHIC USES

Personal mediumship with relatives or close friends who have passed on; deep meditation to create a momentary state of bliss.

SPECIAL PROPERTIES

Encourages unity within the extended family, the community, and efforts toward world peace.

MYTHOLOGY AND HISTORY

Named after the heavenly twins of the Zodiac, Castor and Pollux, who were taken into the heavens as the constellation Gemini because they could not bear to be parted in death, though Pollux was immortal. The stones Pollucite and Castorite, now called Petalite (page 345), are frequently found growing together and may combine in the gem form of Pollucite.

Polychrome or Desert Jasper

COLORS: Brown, red, tan, rust, grays, greens, and sand colors; may be mottled

CRYSTAL TYPE: Microgranular quartz/ chalcedony with iron

ZODIAC SIGN: Leo (July 23–August 23)

CANDLE COLOR: Orange

PHYSICAL: Alleviates issues stemming from digestion, bowels, celiac and Crohn's disease, IBS (especially made worse by stress), lactose intolerance, gastroenteritis, chronic constipation, skin complaints (such as dermatitis, acne, and eczema); boosts libido.

EMOTIONAL: Counters misplaced anger; eases obsession with a cause to the point where you ignore any moral restraints.

HOME: Offers a sense of stability in temporary accommodations or if you are fighting eviction or repossession.

WORKPLACE: Aids in innovative projects or self-funded ventures, regaining enthusiasm for your career.

CHILDREN: Motivates children to adopt new interests or dedicate more time to a talent; cheers up permanently sullen teens.

ANIMALS: For pets who are lethargic.

PROTECTION: Deflects negative energies and repels the evil eye.

MAGICKAL AND PSYCHIC USES

Powerful Earth energies for dowsing; lucky for prosperity; enhances a telepathic connection with animals, plants, crystals, and stones to receive their strength and wisdom.

SPECIAL PROPERTIES

The stone of passion and fire, Polychrome Jasper encourages the expression of the true self in reaching out for what or who is most desired, or in reviving a mundane relationship with passion.

MYTHOLOGY AND HISTORY

From Madagascar, Polychrome (which means "many-colored") Jasper is dug straight from the Earth and so it's not shaken by drilling. The ultimate psychic, physical, and emotional injection of initiative, rooted in firm foundations, combines dynamic Fire with stabilizing Earth, enabling the smooth transition of ideas into reality and restlessness into practical achievement.

Poppy Jasper

COLORS: Brick-red with shades of brown or black; also with golden yellows, cream, or white in a single stone, with dark red, poppy-like spots

CRYSTAL TYPE: Silicate, microcrystalline quartz with mineral or organic inclusions, variation of Brecciated Jasper (page 92)

ZODIAC SIGN: Aries (March 21–April 20)

CANDLE COLOR: Red

PHYSICAL: Regulates adrenaline; eases prolonged or delayed childbirth; counters plant, pollen, and animal fur allergies; useful in treating blood disorders.

EMOTIONAL: Alleviates post-traumatic stress disorder, caffeine addiction, extreme anxiety, obsession with diet, fitness, and exercise.

HOME: For growing beautiful plants and wildflowers, energizing cut flowers.

WORKPLACE: Increases business through proactive marketing and high-profile publicity; boosts opportunities to travel.

CHILDREN: Encourages children to grow flowers and vegetables and care for wildlife.

ANIMALS: Useful when traveling with pets; enhances mind-to-mind communication with all animals.

PROTECTION: Guards against indifference and inefficiency when seeking resources for disability; traditionally protective against snake and spider bites.

MAGICKAL AND PSYCHIC USES

Healing with flower oils and essences, flower psychometry, connecting with the flower fey; tuning into the pulse of the world at ancient sites through Poppy Jasper's link with world chakras, the energy vortices that occur at sacred places.

SPECIAL PROPERTIES

The wake-up call and get-up-and-go stone to offer an instant adrenaline boost, plus stamina and enthusiasm to start the day.

MYTHOLOGY AND HISTORY

Because of the association of poppies with international war remembrance and peace, Poppy Jasper is a symbol of reconciliation within families and between nations, ethnic groups, and religions.

Porcelainite or Porcellanite

COLORS: White, resembling unglazed porcelain as tumbled stones

CRYSTAL TYPE: Silicate, glass-like clay, containing calcareous matter

ZODIAC SIGN: Virgo (August 24–September 22)

CANDLE COLOR: White

PHYSICAL: Addresses bone fractures and thinning, issues with teeth, gingivitis, lactose intolerance, scars and nevus growths, warts, moles, verrucae, internal adhesions.

EMOTIONAL: Counters a tendency among those who were not nurtured in childhood to seek substitute parents in adulthood among friends and colleagues; helps allay a fear of independent decision making or taking action.

HOME: Keeps you from becoming overwhelmed if yours is a young family or you have multiple generations living together who require your undivided attention.

WORKPLACE: Calms industrial strife, overly assertive individuals and unnecessary rivalry and competition; for a first job if you feel insecure in a well-established office or work environment.

CHILDREN: Soothes restless infants and children with sleep disturbances.

ANIMALS: Comforts orphaned young animals.

PROTECTION: Guards against falling for hard luck stories and emotional manipulation.

MAGICKAL AND PSYCHIC USES

For ritual magick, alchemy, metal magick, feng shui; making magickal brews, potions, and healing lotions; herb lore and wisdom.

SPECIAL PROPERTIES

For decluttering the home, freeing up personal space at work, clearing redundant emotional pressures and commitments to make room for choice and freedom from obligation due to habit or guilt.

MYTHOLOGY AND HISTORY

Associated with alchemy, Porcelainite, also spelled Porcellanite, was traditionally used in medieval times for creating crucibles, called the Hessian crucible after the German town where they were made; used for melting gold, silver, and other precious metals and with the legendary quest to create the philosopher's stone, elixir of life; said to turn base metals into gold; also called mullite because Porcelainite was first identified officially in 1924 on the Isle of Mull in Scotland; also found in Poland, the Czech Republic, and Northern Ireland.

Poudretteite

COLORS: Colorless to pale pink

CRYSTAL TYPE: One of the rarest gems in the world, though it is possible to find small pieces on the internet, sold sandwiched between clear quartz that has the same properties (ask for a certificate of authenticity); potassium, sodium, boron, and silicon

ZODIAC SIGN: Taurus (April 21–May 21)

CANDLE COLOR: Pink

PHYSICAL: Aids in exploring new treatments and identifying new practitioners if current remedies or intervention are not working.

EMOTIONAL: Curbs a desire for what is instantly available and replaceable; keeps you from valuing life and people only for their material worth.

HOME: Use images or slivers of Poudretteite between quartz as a reminder that life can be special; enables you to make memories each day.

WORKPLACE: Represents, even as a screen saver, what is attainable and not settling for what is simply on offer.

CHILDREN: Teaches children the value of rarity in any aspect of life.

ANIMALS: For dreams of mystical totem guide creatures, such as dragons, thunderbirds, unicorns, and the golden phoenix, usually heralding a happy event.

PROTECTION: Guards against accepting second best in life or in love.

MAGICKAL AND PSYCHIC USES

A mystical stone, for wishes granted and visions of other worlds. Work with a fragment sandwiched between quartz, a photograph, or holding at sensitive palm energy center chakras; the Smithsonian Institute possesses a pale pink 9.41-carat gem in the National Gem Collection.

SPECIAL PROPERTIES

A reminder of what is precious in life that need not be possessed and hoarded to give pleasure but carried in the imagination to inspire.

MYTHOLOGY AND HISTORY

Seven small Poudretteites were discovered in a quarry owned by the Poudrette family in 1965 in Mont Saint-Hilarie, Quebec, Canada. Officially recognized as a new mineral in 1986; in 2000 the first gem-quality Poudretteite was identified in Mogok, Myanmar. It is estimated that fewer than fifty of the actual gems have been identified.

Powellite

COLORS: White, colorless, yellow, gray, brown, blue-black; pearly

CRYSTAL TYPE: Calcium molybdenite, a pseudomorph retaining the outer shape of molybdenite, but replaced by Powellite; may form pyramids

ZODIAC SIGN: Sagittarius (November 23–December 21)

CANDLE COLOR: White

PHYSICAL: Reduces fatty deposits around vital organs; promotes healthy weight loss; counters autism, intolerance to chemicals and additives; helps identify illness manifested as symptoms in a different part of the body; enhances holistic healing.

EMOTIONAL: Keeps you from feeling out of step with those close to you; helps temper paranoia about the intentions of others.

HOME: Encourages family members to help around the house; for joint savings for a major family vacation or purchase.

WORKPLACE: Widens your range of expertise; helps persuade others through presentations, publicity, or direct sales talk; boosts staying power for long-term projects or training.

CHILDREN: Useful for those entering puberty, especially if early or delayed; for those who never finish a task.

ANIMALS: Valuable for adolescent animals, testing their limits.

PROTECTION: Guards against those who scam or cheat using charm, financially or in love.

MAGICKAL AND PSYCHIC USES

Trance meditation; pyramid healing; bringing spiritual practices into the everyday world; singing-bowl healing; establishing a psychic or healing group.

SPECIAL PROPERTIES

For overcoming physical limitations by fighting for necessary resources and practical help; the stone of artists and authors to explore new techniques and markets.

MYTHOLOGY AND HISTORY

First discovered in Idaho by American geologist John Wesley Powell in the 1800s; a new rich source has recently been found in India. The humanitarian crystal for all charitable ventures, whether local or global.

Prairie Tanzanite

COLORS: Delicately blended pink, cream, white, and purple

CRYSTAL TYPE: Zoisite within jade

ZODIAC SIGN: Pisces (February 19–March 20)

CANDLE COLOR: Pink

PHYSICAL: Eases psychosomatic and stress-induced conditions; alleviates ongoing chronic illnesses (first experienced in childhood), pain from hip and knee replacements, delayed or scant menstruation; for gentle alternative therapies if you experience adverse reactions to pharmaceutical treatments; calms panic before medical tests, dentistry, or surgery.

EMOTIONAL: Curbs acute anxiety, and a feeling of spiritual and emotional alienation from others.

HOME: Helps family members to express their worries and fears without fear of judgment.

WORKPLACE: Establishes more honest, open communication when people hide behind roles and status.

CHILDREN: For sensitive Star Souls or Indigo Children who overreact to the rough and tumble of peer interactions.

ANIMALS: For small, timid pets who dislike being handled.

PROTECTION: Guards against fear of confrontation or disapproval.

MAGICKAL AND PSYCHIC USES

For in-depth tarot and divinatory readings; for prayer, meditation, chanting, study of sacred texts; for automatic writing and bibliomancy/stichomancy, to receive wise answers and explain repressed fears that may be rooted in childhood or earlier lives.

SPECIAL PROPERTIES

For unraveling complex parental and adult child issues, especially when the adult child marries or wants to move to a new location.

MYTHOLOGY AND HISTORY

A relatively new find in the jade area of Wyoming, combining the gentleness of jade with the creative inspiration and problem-solving aspects of zoisite. A stone for smoothing out extreme reactions to life's setbacks, allowing measured responses. Prairie Tanzanite creates a calmer, kinder atmosphere and, as a result, a more effective approach to life.

Prasiolite or Vermarine

COLORS: Olive, pale, celery green or yellow green

CRYSTAL TYPE: Silicon dioxide, naturally though rarely found as green quartz; most Prasiolite is heat-treated amethyst, so it is popularly called green amethyst

ZODIAC SIGN: Virgo (August 24–September 22)

CANDLE COLOR: Green

PHYSICAL: Promotes self-healing, fertility, and fertility treatment if slightly older; addresses wounds, immunity, endocrine glands, cellular disorders, burns, scalds, eczema, stomach acid, tumors.

EMOTIONAL: Alleviates constant anger, mood swings, and irritability: counters extreme dieting and excessive exercise regimens; eliminates the need for artificial stimulants.

HOME: Reverses financial bad luck or money worries by attracting money and opportunities.

WORKPLACE: Aids in meeting deadlines, motivating a team, balancing dedication to the job with your personal life; for part-time and home workers to be valued; helps you accumulate wealth through fame.

CHILDREN: Teaches children to have fun playing outdoors with natural resources; encourages self-reliance.

ANIMALS: For overweight and overly indulged pets.

PROTECTION: Shields you from malice and toxic people; curbs self-defeating thoughts.

MAGICKAL AND PSYCHIC USES

For connection with totem animals through outdoor meditation or visualization; goddess rituals; Earth spirits, elementals, and beings from other galaxies.

SPECIAL PROPERTIES

A natural luck- and money-bringer; for love when you had given up hope, employment if there are few available positions, healing when the prognosis is not good; brings out unique talents.

MYTHOLOGY AND HISTORY

Natural and heat-treated Prasiolite have the same properties, acting as a bridge between body, mind, and spirit; releases the inner child; encourages fun that does not rely on money or simulated theme park–like thrills.

Precious White Opal

COLORS: Milky white with a spectrum of colors; Precious White Opals with a light background and rainbow fire, are also called white opals. Some white opals do not have opalescence (see, for example, Milky Opal, page 303)

CRYSTAL TYPE: Hydrated silicon dioxide

ZODIAC SIGN: Cancer (June 22–July 22)

CANDLE COLOR: White

PHYSICAL: Balances left and right hemispheres of the brain; regulates biorhythms, fluid levels, and hormones; alleviates issues involving the central nervous system, nausea, vision, infant-feeding difficulties, menstrual problems during puberty, vaginismus, erectile dysfunction.

EMOTIONAL: Counters fear of sex; curbs food-related disorders, postnatal depression; helps overcome failure to bond with an infant.

HOME: For parents experiencing empty-nest syndrome

WORKPLACE: Helps writers, artists, dancers, musicians, and actors to get a break their chosen field.

CHILDREN: Aids in winning admission to a theater or art school, dancing academy or music conservatory.

ANIMALS: For overly sexual pubescent pets.

PROTECTION: Guards against online grooming or sexual exploitation by an older person.

MAGICKAL AND PSYCHIC USES

For connecting with the ancient wisdom of yoga, tai chi, and other spiritual movement arts; communicating with guardian angels.

SPECIAL PROPERTIES

A symbol of lasting love if open commitment is not possible; for sensuality and erotic pleasure; returning to the dating scene after a relationship breakup.

MYTHOLOGY AND HISTORY

Roman naturalist and historian Pliny the Elder described how Mark Antony so coveted a valuable opal owned by Senator Nonius that he banished the senator for refusing to part with it. Called the happy opal, Precious White Opal is found almost exclusively in the Australian desert town of Coober Pedy, opal capital of the world.

Prehnite

COLORS: Pale or mint green, yellowy- or brownish-green, with inclusions or shadow crystals within

CRYSTAL TYPE: Silicate; broken surfaces shine like mother of pearl, often attached to cavities or veins of basaltic rocks

ZODIAC SIGN: Virgo (August 24–September 22)

CANDLE COLOR: Pale or mint green

PHYSICAL: Prompts regeneration after illness; boosts stamina when you cannot rest; detoxifies; promotes efficient metabolism; balances meridians within body; relieves pain; promotes remote healing.

EMOTIONAL: Helps if you worry about your health; aids in expressing negative feelings calmly.

HOME: For decluttering your home; if you have an untidy family.

WORKPLACE: Useful if you do more than your share without appreciation.

CHILDREN: Transforms the family dynamic if your family expects 24/7 room service; counteracts hyperactivity and nightmares.

ANIMALS: Promotes successful animal behavior training.

PROTECTION: Protects your home during absences; kept with portable electronic equipment, such as laptops, the crystal deters thieves.

MAGICKAL AND PSYCHIC USES

A dream crystal bringing prophetic dreams and lucid dreaming: called the prophecy stone, useful with tarot cards and other divinatory methods.

SPECIAL PROPERTIES

Brings unconditional love, when loved ones are difficult; overcomes bad childhood memories.

MYTHOLOGY AND HISTORY

Named after Major Hendrik von Prehn, who discovered it at the end of the eighteenth century in South Africa; found in Australia, Canada, Mali, and Tanzania; used for prophecy by Indigenous South African medicine men and women; restores strength to burned-out healers; connects with nature essences and land guardians.

Prehnite with Epidote

COLORS: Green (epidote), mixed with green prehnite, sometimes included as yellowy- or brownish-green or darker green; a mixture of greens or apple green as tumbled stones, ideal for healing and magick; also used as jewelry

CRYSTAL TYPE: Silicate as prehnite with broken surfaces shining like mother of pearl; epidote is also a silicate mineral, a perfect blend, mirroring and enhancing the others' predominantly spiritual qualities

ZODIAC SIGN: Pisces (February 19–March 20)

CANDLE COLOR: Green

PHYSICAL: Removes toxins; strengthens the bladder, kidneys, immune system; restores strength and health after illness.

EMOTIONAL: Counters a propensity to hoard possessions and money because of fears of poverty or loss, however unlikely.

HOME: Aids in preventing you from buying expensive devices that will rarely be used, collecting experiences and memories instead.

WORKPLACE: Aids in refusing unreasonable demands; working toward your ideal job; deciding to focus on quality time outside the working environment.

CHILDREN: Protects psychic children from frightening dreams.

ANIMALS: Increases telepathy with pets.

PROTECTION: Guards against vaguely distressing premonitions of disaster that cannot be identified to offer warnings or send healing if not preventable.

MAGICKAL AND PSYCHIC USES

Because both stones are strongly otherworldly, Prehnite with Epidote opens direct channels to spiritual guardians and star realms; awakens personal divinatory powers, especially with tarot cards, crystal spheres, and visions of ancestors and personal guides in dark mirrors; a powerful crystal combination for experienced mediums.

SPECIAL PROPERTIES

Heals the healer and insulates spiritual practitioners from overly identifying with clients' troubles.

MYTHOLOGY AND HISTORY

Prehnite was a prophecy stone among medicine men and women in South Africa; epidote, the dream stone, brings prophetic dreams; together they offer amplified prophetic insights.

Prehnite with Flowers

COLORS: Pale or mint green, yellow- or brownish-green, with white crystalline flowers that can occasionally take on the main prehnite color

CRYSTAL TYPE: Prehnite with radiating, flower-like clusters or bud formations on the surface of the crystal; the flower formations are also prehnite, pseudomorphs or replacement of a crystal displaying a radiating structure with usually white prehnite

ZODIAC SIGN: Virgo (August 24–September 22)

CANDLE COLOR: Green

PHYSICAL: Curbs plant allergies; useful for regeneration after an illness or an accident; aids in acceptance by the body of organ transplants—natural and artificial; promotes fertility.

EMOTIONAL: Counters a tendency to look back to lost love or love that never could be requited; alleviates post-traumatic stress disorder.

HOME: Helps when moving into a new home or relationship that needs adjustments in lifestyles; keeps you from making comparisons with the past, especially if your home was previously occupied by your partner with an ex.

WORKPLACE: For working outdoors in horticulture or as a florist, arranging weddings and special occasions, to instinctively fit the wedding flowers to the personality of the couple.

CHILDREN: Brings the flower fey into the garden or home.

ANIMALS: Develops pets' natural instincts for safe or harmful substances, especially if there has been a spate of animal poisonings in the area.

PROTECTION: Guards against returning to a former lover whom you know has not changed and giving up a new blossoming relationship.

MAGICKAL AND PSYCHIC USES
Spells to attract love and romance; communicating with nature spirits even in the city; for aromatherapy and flower essences.

SPECIAL PROPERTIES
Given to a lover on an engagement, handfasting, marriage, or anniversary present, instead of flowers, as a token of love that will not fade.

MYTHOLOGY AND HISTORY
Prehnite with Flowers is often called flower sun jade, and is only found at Wave Hill in Australia's Northern Territory. Though rare, it is worth acquiring as a symbol of love and fidelity.

Preseli Bluestone or Stonehenge Bluestone

COLORS: May be green or greenish-gray when polished

CRYSTAL TYPE: Mottled dolerite containing feldspar and augite, with inclusions of tiny flecks of yellow or white minerals, such as flint, white quartz, or white chalk

ZODIAC SIGN: Capricorn (December 22–January 20)

CANDLE COLOR: Moss green

PHYSICAL: Enhances vibrational healing and Earth-based remedies, such as herbs, for energy-based therapies, especially kinesiology.

EMOTIONAL: Two equal-sized pieces, one in each hand, boost self-esteem if others make you doubt yourself.

HOME: Helps family members value traditions and older relatives.

WORKPLACE: A piece placed on either side of your workspace keeps you from becoming unsettled by dominant, confrontational people.

CHILDREN: Grounds children who exaggerate or deviate from the truth.

ANIMALS: Connects urban animals to the Earth.

PROTECTION: Hold in your dominate hand if you suspect others are not telling the truth.

MAGICKAL AND PSYCHIC USES
Linked with Celtic druidic magick and wisdom; promotes past-life recall and connection with distant ancestors, Earth wisdom, sacred sites, geomancy, and dowsing abilities.

SPECIAL PROPERTIES
Aids time travel, especially in dreams, to ancient mythological worlds, such as Atlantis.

MYTHOLOGY AND HISTORY
From the Preseli Mountains in Wales, megalithic Stonehenge is made from bluestone. The Preseli Mountains are believed to contain doors to the Celtic otherworld, with the fey and Merlin.

Preseli Snow Quartz

COLORS: Opaque white, created by small cavity inclusions containing carbon dioxide (see also Snow Quartz, page 447)

CRYSTAL TYPE: Rare, recently found source of Snow Quartz, sometimes containing Preseli golden healer quartz, golden iron oxide coatings within the crystal; also attached to Preseli Bluestone

ZODIAC SIGN: Cancer (June 22–July 22)

CANDLE COLOR: Silver

PHYSICAL: Enhances traditional medicine when modern treatments fail; eases frozen, immobile joints and limbs; alleviates fluctuating blood pressure and body temperature; promotes healing with plants.

EMOTIONAL: Counters cynicism; keeps you from accumulating debt by acquiring the latest material goods; curbs addiction to slot machines; mitigates childish tantrums in adulthood.

HOME: Brings gentle reconciliation after separation or estrangement.

WORKPLACE: Conserves sites of beauty, museums of industrial and domestic life; aids in practicing traditional crafts.

CHILDREN: Connects children with family history; instills a love of nature.

ANIMALS: For revival of rare breeds; organic farming.

PROTECTION: Guards against pressure to change for change's sake.

MAGICKAL AND PSYCHIC USES

Enhances planetary alignments; activates Earth energies between sacred places; Arthurian and grail wisdom; full moon rituals; a doorway in the Preseli Mountains to Annwn, the Celtic otherworld of light.

SPECIAL PROPERTIES

Aids in adopting a more self-sufficient lifestyle; embracing nature spirituality; especially powerful for those with Celtic ancestry.

MYTHOLOGY AND HISTORY

The Preseli Mountains, sacred since prehistoric times, are the source of the Preseli Bluestone, said to have been transported magickally by Merlin to Stonehenge, a place of ancient stones, including the druidic initiation dolmen at Pentre Ifan. Preseli snow quartz combines Earth and lunar energies; offers access to ancient magickal worlds.

Printstone

COLORS: Ochre, tan-brown, brown-violet, in regular semicircular and linear bands and patterns on the stone

CRYSTAL TYPE: Siltstone/claystone, containing quartz with bands of iron; a composition between silt and shale, also found as tumbled stones and cabochons

ZODIAC SIGN: Taurus (April 21–May 21)

CANDLE COLOR: Golden brown

PHYSICAL: Eases muscle tension and boosts strength; propels digestion and elimination of waste products from the body.

EMOTIONAL: Counters perfectionism, obsessions (especially those associated with OCD); keeps you from refusing to accept anything but the best.

FOR THE HOME: For making the best purchasing decisions.

WORKPLACE: Aids in becoming single-minded in pursuit of a goal, banishing distractions, irrelevant factors, and doubts; ensures that you spend extra time and effort on details.

CHILDREN: Helps youngsters avoid becoming easily distracted from study or completing homework; for teens who get buried under mountains of details and lose focus on project or tasks.

ANIMALS: For fussy pets who hate getting wet or dirty.

PROTECTION: Guards against continual distractions if family, friends, or neighbors assume you are always available.

MAGICKAL AND PSYCHIC USES

Printstone has become associated with festivals for the return of light and solstice festivals in midwinter; learning formal systems of magick and ritual, including Wicca, druidry, Ásatrú (Norse magick).

SPECIAL PROPERTIES

A stone to guide awareness of the lessons still to be learned in this lifetime and the overall destiny to be followed, not having to repeat in future lives what has not been learned.

MYTHOLOGY AND HISTORY

Found in the Hamersley Ranges in the Pilbara region of Western Australia, Printstone is so named because the regular design looks as if it has been printed. A stone that says the answers are all there if the immediate goal is pinpointed first.

Psilomelane

COLORS: Lustrous black or blue-black with bands of metallic gray

CRYSTAL TYPE: Manganese oxide

ZODIAC SIGN: Sagittarius (November 23–December 21)

CANDLE COLOR: Gray

PHYSICAL: Addresses an erratic digestive system, heartbeat, and circulation; alleviates pneumonia, fluid in the lungs, ineffective carbohydrate conversion, blood sugar fluctuations; skin inflammation; regulates fluid levels; promotes health in older people and eases the natural aging process.

EMOTIONAL: Curbs an inability to express love or positive emotions; enables you to let go of negative experiences; counters a tendency to blame others without self-examination.

HOME: Keeps you from acting as a one-person service industry for running the home.

WORKPLACE: Allows you to cut back on unnecessary expenditures in your business, offering lower prices and special offers to attract more customers.

CHILDREN: Controls impulsive behavior; for those who are accident-prone.

ANIMALS: Aids in recovery after abuse that occurred before rescue or if a pet has been lost and badly frightened since returning home.

PROTECTION: Guards against evil entities and malevolent elemental spirits, summoned during careless magickal ritual and not returned to their element afterward.

MAGICKAL AND PSYCHIC USES

Protects against energy vampires, earthly and from the spirit world; creates trance states for directed mind travel and remote viewing to a prechosen destination.

SPECIAL PROPERTIES

A stone of good fortune and wealth acquired gradually by careful strategies, increasing savings, avoiding loopholes for money draining out of your life.

MYTHOLOGY AND HISTORY

Though the name *Psilomelane* is used for a group of six or more minerals, including Romanechite, this opaque, black, shiny manganese oxide form is used for healing and metaphysical purposes, as well as jewelry.

Puddingstone or Pudding Stone

COLORS: Often brightly colored, sometimes in paler matrix

CRYSTAL TYPE: Conglomerate stone, containing pebbles of minerals including jasper, sandstone, chert, and quartz

ZODIAC SIGN: Gemini (May 22–June 21)

CANDLE COLOR: Yellow

PHYSICAL: Alleviates skin allergies, multiple illnesses or ones that attack different parts of the body simultaneously, growths and lesions, progressive illnesses, chemical imbalances, unhealthy gut bacteria; relieves pain.

EMOTIONAL: Helps overcome multiple personalities, schizophrenia, bipolar disorder.

HOME: Blends different age groups and personalities when two families come together; aids in making friends in a new environment or country.

WORKPLACE: For imagination and original ideas in creative arts or brainstorming new approaches; promotes team building where a variety of skills are needed; keeps progress on track if you're distracted.

CHILDREN: Encourages children with a single interest to participate in other activities; for fun children's parties.

ANIMALS: For pets of mixed heritage; mating two related breeds.

PROTECTION: Shields you from cliques and factions.

MAGICKAL AND PSYCHIC USES

Recalling dreams in meditation; accessing other worlds in dreams and astral travel; associated with the four directions, four elements, and four winds uniting to create a greater magickal energy.

SPECIAL PROPERTIES

Resolving unfair treatment by negotiation, rather than litigation; strengthening love against troublemakers.

MYTHOLOGY AND HISTORY

Puddingstone is found as water-worn pebbles or river gravel, cemented by a mineral deposit filling in the spaces, forming solid rock; it was created during an Ice Age. English settlers in South Dakota in the 1840s named them because they resembled a fruit-filled pudding they cooked.

Pumice Stone

COLORS: Fawn to light gray or tan, occasionally black if containing iron and magnesium

CRYSTAL TYPE: Igneous rock formed as lava rapidly cools and gas bubbles trapped in molten rock; may be glassy between holes

ZODIAC SIGN: Aries (March 21–April 20)

CANDLE COLOR: Gray

PHYSICAL: Relieves pain during labor; alleviates menstrual and stomach cramps, edema, weight loss, muscle soreness, issues of the heart and cells, plus skin complaints, scar tissue, degenerative conditions.

EMOTIONAL: Counters repressed emotional baggage causing repeated self-destructive patterns; offers insight to avoid repeating experiences karmically.

HOME: Lighter-colored Pumice in the center of the home attracts good fortune; a darker one near the door absorbs negative vibes.

WORKPLACE: Aids in launching new ventures and businesses; promotes advancement in an existing career; works well for those in careers involving electricity, gas, the water supply, solar and nuclear power.

CHILDREN: For fears of water and swimming.

ANIMALS: Helps timid pets overcome fear of other animals.

PROTECTION: Guards against, fire, flood, Earth tremors, and natural disasters.

MAGICKAL AND PSYCHIC USES

Wishes fulfilled or sorrows banished by whispering them into the holes and floating Pumice away; a guardian stone for home or workplace; rituals to enhance beauty.

SPECIAL PROPERTIES

Insulates against abrasive people, sarcasm, and criticism that reduce your confidence, especially by people you must see regularly; to cleanse the Pumice of negativity, wash it weekly until it crumbles.

MYTHOLOGY AND HISTORY

Considered magickal because it floats and it was born of fire because of its dynamic generation, Pumice cleanses spirit, body, and mind, and enhances radiance, inspiration, and confidence.

Purple and Violet Halite

COLORS: From lilac to deep purple and violet, the color caused by defects in the crystal lattice

CRYSTAL TYPE: Sodium chloride, composed of rock salt, called halide

ZODIAC SIGN: Aquarius (January 21–February 18)

CANDLE COLOR: Violet

PHYSICAL: Dissolves pain and blockages anywhere in the body; helps overcome psychological blocks and unconscious reluctance to get back to life that may slow down recovery; alleviates issues involving the lymph glands, underactive thyroid, inability to absorb iodine.

EMOTIONAL: Counters a resignation to any misfortune or setbacks as malign fate, rather than devising strategies to resolve difficulties; keeps you from passing on to children unconscious fears and attitudes of blaming others when life goes wrong.

HOME: Placed above the lintel of the front door (you need only a small piece), Purple Halite gives the home the sanctity of an ashram, whether you live alone or with many other people.

WORKPLACE: Aids in choosing job satisfaction and personal fulfillment over aiming for the top and earning a high salary.

CHILDREN: For helping an older child or teen create a memory capsule with small treasures from their childhood; avoids constant demands for designer goods.

ANIMALS: Bury a small piece, wrapped in silk, in the resting place of a deceased pet to ease their passing to the afterlife.

PROTECTION: Guards against shopaholic tendencies and excesses.

MAGICKAL AND PSYCHIC USES

Darker shades of Purple Halite are considered profound dream crystals to open the way to spiritual realms; for spontaneous clairvoyance and enhanced psychic powers.

SPECIAL PROPERTIES

The stone of pilgrimages, sacred quests studying alternative and comparative religions, and for prayer and chanting to flow with the cosmos and merge momentarily with the source of light or your chosen deity.

MYTHOLOGY AND HISTORY

Purple Halite, like other halites (see Blue Halite and Pink Halite, pages 75 and 356); dissolves if it becomes wet; a symbol therefore of conserving and preserving resources, of saving rather than squandering money.

Purple Angeline

COLORS: Medium to deep purple, with gold inclusions

CRYSTAL TYPE: A combination of amethyst and smoky quartz, both crystallized quartz and cacoxenite, iron aluminum phosphate, three main components of the famed Super Seven crystal (page 467); also tumbled stones

ZODIAC SIGN: Pisces (February 19–March 20)

CANDLE COLOR: Purple

PHYSICAL: A whole-body healer, Purple Angeline balances the system, relieves pain, and encourages self-healing; protects against allergies and illnesses caused by modern pollutants.

EMOTIONAL: Curbs dysfunctional reactions to everyday family life and relationships, linked with an unhappy childhood or past-life traumas.

HOME: Creates a harmonious, relaxed atmosphere where work troubles are left at the front door.

WORKPLACE: Opens unexpected opportunities for advancement, increased status, and recognition of gifts without causing jealousy, resentment, or rivalry.

CHILDREN: Aids in making friends with children from different backgrounds and cultures; helpful toward those with physical, emotional, and learning challenges.

ANIMALS: For a pet who protects family members who are different or have practical difficulties with daily living.

PROTECTION: Guards against energy draining from the aura energy field due to entity attack or human energy vampires.

MAGICKAL AND PSYCHIC USES

Psychic protection during spirit communication; ability to connect with ancient cultures and spiritual faiths through meditation, visualization, and ritual.

SPECIAL PROPERTIES

Gentler than Super Seven for those who are new to the spiritual world or who have turned away because of earlier bad psychic experiences.

MYTHOLOGY AND HISTORY

Found in Brazil, this super three crystal combines protection, balance in every aspect of life, plus awareness that with faith and effort almost anything is achievable; brings unity and cooperation within the home, workplace, community, or while working for equality and world peace.

Purple Anhydrite

COLORS: Purple, from silvery lilac to dark purple; gleaming

CRYSTAL TYPE: Anhydrous calcium sulfate, created as the result of the loss of water in rock, forming mineral gypsum

ZODIAC SIGN: Pisces (February 19–March 20)

CANDLE COLOR: Purple

PHYSICAL: Regulates fluid imbalances and counters water retention; promotes weight control; alleviates issues involving headaches (including migraines), sinuses, throat constrictions (especially those caused or made worse by stress), perimenopause and menopause; allays concerns about aging.

EMOTIONAL: Keeps you from remaining trapped by past losses and betrayal in this and previous lives; counters a tendency to self-sabotage your achievements at the point of success.

HOME: Helps the family to restore love and trust after betrayal or lack of loyalty by a family member; calls the household guardians if you live alone and feel nervous at night.

WORKPLACE: Restores confidence if you're returning to work after burnout or psychological trauma; creates a personally uplifting workspace in an impersonal organization.

CHILDREN: Calls extra protection from a child's guardian angel and benign ancestors if the child is distressed or worried by life.

ANIMALS: Aids in becoming aware of the love and presence of a recently departed pet around the home.

PROTECTION: Guards against false gurus who demand large amounts of money for prolonged teaching.

MAGICKAL AND PSYCHIC USES

For beginners to psychic work to awaken to their powers; mediumship and, if you have not already, discovering your spirit guide gatekeeper who will keep you safe; psychic artistry.

SPECIAL PROPERTIES

Purple Anhydrite (and other anhydrites) should be kept dry to prevent them from gradually turning back into gypsum.

MYTHOLOGY AND HISTORY

One of the rarest forms of anhydrite; sometimes called purple angelite or purple moonstone because of its shimmer. A gentle birthing stone if you know you will be having a caesarean or after a birth when intervention was necessary, to restore the wonder of a new infant and assist with bonding.

Purple Fluorite

COLORS: Violet, lavender, or lilac; clear
CRYSTAL TYPE: Halide/calcium fluoride
ZODIAC SIGN: Pisces (February 19–March 20)
CANDLE COLOR: Purple

PHYSICAL: Alleviates tension headaches and issues stemming from the bones, bone marrow, ears, sinuses, fluid retention, respiratory tract, throat; resists colds, viruses, and infections; addresses shingles, stress-related illnesses, childhood illnesses in later years.
EMOTIONAL: Helps overcome addictions, obsessions, the inability to face reality, PTSD; stills a whirling mind.
HOME: Ensures the smooth running of a household in the midst of distractions; curbs spending if there are financial constraints; reduces free-floating tensions.
WORKPLACE: Promotes financial success in spiritual businesses; for self-help writers, psychic artists, religious and spiritual teachers, healers.
CHILDREN: For hyperactive or ADHD children and those whose ideas race ahead of life; for Indigo Children isolated from others.
ANIMALS: Encourages dogs and horses to perform well in dog or horse shows; calms pets' bad reactions to visitors, new environments, or noise.
PROTECTION: Guards against hostile ghosts, poltergeists, and spirits called up in ouija boards; allays fears of elevators.

MAGICKAL AND PSYCHIC USES
Dreamwork and astral dream travel, past-life recall, connecting with angels and higher spiritual beings who reveal ancient mysteries; pyramid healing and meditation.
SPECIAL PROPERTIES
For inspiring written assignments, course materials, and presentations; memorizing facts for tests; creating a good impression at interviews; relaxing during medical scans, tests, or treatment.
MYTHOLOGY AND HISTORY
In ancient China, Purple Fluorite offered protection from evil spirits. In folklore, each Purple Fluorite crystal is considered more protective and powerful the longer it is used.

Purple Goldstone

COLORS: Dark purple to deep violet shades; may sparkle more silver than gold
CRYSTAL TYPE: Purple goldstone, silicate glass with manganese inclusions that cause the sparkles
ZODIAC SIGN: Pisces (February 19–March 20)
CANDLE COLOR: Purple

PHYSICAL: A whole-body healer; alleviates progressive illnesses that affect different parts of the body, multiple sclerosis.
EMOTIONAL: Curbs a progressive illness that affects the life and prognosis of yourself or loved ones; counters a loss of faith.
HOME: Useful if neighbors or friends have an affluent lifestyle and make you feel lacking.
WORKPLACE: For religious and spiritual training and vocations; for spiritual life coaches and writers of spiritual literature.
CHILDREN: Teaches children to value what they have; enables psychic children not to fear their gifts.
ANIMALS: For old-soul animals.
PROTECTION: Guards against cults and religious fanaticism that divide families.

MAGICKAL AND PSYCHIC USES
For staying in or joining a religious community or ashram; for faith healing using prayer.
SPECIAL PROPERTIES
Purple Goldstone connects with the divine spark within us and the divinity of the creator/creatrix or source of light and so is the most spiritual of the goldstones.
MYTHOLOGY AND HISTORY
Purple Goldstone is mythologically linked with the quest for the philosopher's stone, for long life and health, and some believe it could turn ordinary metals into gold. According to the Treatise of Hermes Trismegistus, credited as being the first alchemist, this fruition is described as the "Son" (created by the union of King Sol and Queen Luna) and is invested with the red garment.

Purple Howlite

COLORS: From lavender to medium purple to bright violet

CRYSTAL TYPE: Dyed white howlite, calcium borosilicate hydroxide

ZODIAC SIGN: Pisces (February 19–March 20)

CANDLE COLOR: Purple

PHYSICAL: Alleviates migraines and headaches triggered by stress or food allergies, insomnia, sinus problems, rhinitis, hearing problems.

EMOTIONAL: Keeps you from living in a world of dreams while opting out of life's practicalities and expecting others to pick up the pieces; curbs a tendency to plan new projects that never materialize.

HOME: Opens the energies of a family member who is cynical or skeptical about spiritual matters or is conventionally religious and condemns your beliefs.

WORKPLACE: Aids in starting a spiritual business while following a conventional career with the aim of eventually becoming self-supporting in the spiritual world.

CHILDREN: Helps psychic children when they are teased about their experiences by peers or have their experiences dismissed as fantasies by other family members; for coping with a child's frightening invisible friend.

ANIMALS: For pets disturbed by the spirits of deceased animals who have returned to the home.

PROTECTION: Guards against spirits summoned by ouija boards or unprotected séances.

MAGICKAL AND PSYCHIC USES

For connecting with personal guardian angels and kindly deceased grandparents or ancestors in dreams or through meditation; psychometry; obtaining information from old or family items about the original owners.

SPECIAL PROPERTIES

Alerts your instincts to recognize false gurus, ego-inspired teachers, and those who charge too much for prolonged therapies.

MYTHOLOGY AND HISTORY

Purple Howlite represents bringing the spiritual and everyday worlds closer together; uses psychic and healing powers to improve others' lives.

Purple or Violet Sapphire

COLORS: Pale amethyst, lavender, pinkish-purple, purple, and violet; colored purple by vanadium, a natural stone, though it is sometimes heated to distribute the color more evenly; transparent or pearly

CRYSTAL TYPE: Corundum, an aluminum oxide

ZODIAC SIGN: Aquarius (January 21–February 18)

CANDLE COLOR: Purple

PHYSICAL: Addresses colds, influenza, viruses, heart health, veins and arteries in the brain; promotes a healthy lifestyle.

EMOTIONAL: Helps those who are easily spooked but have an obsession with the paranormal and contacting spirits; counters excessive worry.

HOME: Purple Sapphire overcomes pettiness, laziness, and small-mindedness if you are sharing accommodations with others.

WORKPLACE: A stone of gaining status and leadership opportunities; for prosperity in business.

CHILDREN: For storytelling of real-life heroes, heroines, magickal lands, and noble deeds.

ANIMALS: Aids in breeding pedigreed animals with good temperaments.

PROTECTION: Guards against betrayal in love and false promises.

MAGICKAL AND PSYCHIC USES

A stone of priests and priestesses, for recalling ancient formal magickal rituals; prayer; mantras; ability to tap into future destiny through scrying and deep-trance meditation.

SPECIAL PROPERTIES

The most spiritual of the sapphires and also a stone that encourages all artistic endeavors; living authentically in the middle and golden years.

MYTHOLOGY AND HISTORY

Also called plum sapphire, Purple Sapphire is associated with the violet flower and the Virgin Mary, said to have sprung up in the place where the Archangel Gabriel appeared to Mary. There is also the legend of a Delhi Purple Sapphire, looted from the Temple of Indra, god of war, during the Indian rebellion against the British East India Company in 1857. It was said that those who took ownership of the stone through the years suffered misfortune—financial and personal—because, as it had been stolen, it was cursed.

Purple Sage Agate

COLORS: Purple, bluish-gray, with black patterns, lines, and dendritic (tree-like) formations

CRYSTAL TYPE: Silicon dioxide. microcrystalline quartz, chalcedony

ZODIAC SIGN: Virgo (August 24–September 22)

CANDLE COLOR: Purple

PHYSICAL: Alleviates issues relating to emphysema, the reproductive system, debilitating conditions, throat, brain, tension headaches, visual disturbances.

EMOTIONAL: Keeps you from returning to addictions previously overcome; jettisons emotional baggage affecting new relationships; counters insomnia due to constant worrying in circles; banishes self-destructive guilt and blame for what could not have been changed.

HOME: For completing unfinished tasks, repairs, and renovations to move on or enjoy your present surroundings.

WORKPLACE: Increases creativity with color or design; enhances analytical skills; for networking, greater productivity; attracts the right people and opportunities.

CHILDREN: Protects children and teens from bad influences.

ANIMALS: Aids in breeding strong, healthy, pedigreed pets.

PROTECTION: Guards against being manipulated by false obligation or flattery; shields you from psychic attack by spirits masquerading as benign.

MAGICKAL AND PSYCHIC USES

Smudging ceremonies, medicine wheel rituals, past-life healing; Purple Sage Agates are sometimes linked with the violet flame of the ascended master St. Germain; labyrinth meditation.

SPECIAL PROPERTIES

Enhances self-love and accepting that your values may not be the values of others; being true to yourself, no matter what the cost.

MYTHOLOGY AND HISTORY

In mythology, agates were said to contain the wisdom of old souls; Purple Sage Agate is sacred, offering connection with the circle of life and taking away fears of mortality and isolation within the self; Purple Sage Agates were prized by Indigenous people as protective amulets.

Purple Sagenite

COLORS: Dense purple, so the rutiles appear solid inside

CRYSTAL TYPE: A form of rutilated agate containing lithium within

ZODIAC SIGN: Scorpio (October 24–November 22)

CANDLE COLOR: Purple

PHYSICAL: Promotes cell regeneration; slows the aging process; increases immunity to viruses and epidemics; reassures older first-time mothers during pregnancy.

EMOTIONAL: Curbs depression, mood swings, acute loneliness because of a sense of being different; counters an awareness of time passing.

HOME: Lifts the mood of the home if you or your family bring work troubles home; at family gatherings, cheers cantankerous relatives.

WORKPLACE: Valuable in using your experience and authority to resolve difficult workplace situations; for older workers to have their knowledge valued.

CHILDREN: For closer relationships with grandparents, great-grandparents, and the senior generation.

ANIMALS: Encourages older animal mothers or those who adopt orphaned animals of the same or different species.

PROTECTION: Shields and cleanses sacred spaces used for rituals.

MAGICKAL AND PSYCHIC USES

For shamanic healing and soul retrieval; the stone of the wise woman, Purple Sagenite is an appropriate gift at a croning ceremony; contains the violet ray of healing; increases the spiritual light generated during smudging.

SPECIAL PROPERTIES

Associated with love and called Cupid's arrows or love's arrows, Purple Sagenite especially calls a soul twin or strengthens a soul-twin relationship; if there have been difficulties or love is unrequited.

MYTHOLOGY AND HISTORY

Found in Madagascar and Brazil, Purple Sagenite is worth seeking; a stone for personal contemplation and meditation and to make time for the inner self, especially if you act as a cheerleader for a sometimes ungrateful world; for spiritual retreats and time alone in nature to rediscover the core person you have always been and to return to life refreshed.

Purple Scapolite

COLORS: Purple from pale lavender to intense violet; when cut and polished all scapolite has a vitreous luster

CRYSTAL TYPE: Sodium calcium aluminum silicate

ZODIAC SIGN: Aquarius (January 21–February 18)

CANDLE COLOR: Violet

PHYSICAL: Eases anaphylactic shock, problems triggered by aging, degenerative conditions linked with the malfunctioning of the brain and nervous system.

EMOTIONAL: Curbs an inability to forgive yourself or others for past mistakes or omissions; allays a desire for revenge out of proportion to the wrong.

HOME: Balances the chi energies.

WORKPLACE: For beginning work in new-age or crystal stores, healing or psychic festivals if your presence is resented by established practitioners; for setting up a spiritual website and social media presence.

CHILDREN: For increasing maternal and paternal instincts with children from newborn babies to adults living far away.

ANIMALS: Strengthens telepathic links with pets to anticipate your homecoming.

PROTECTION: Shields against angry spirits where a tragedy, massacre, or major accident occurred years before.

MAGICKAL AND PSYCHIC USES

A high-vibration stone that opens the way to communication with angels, guides, and ancestors; feng shui; covens, psychic development, and healing circles.

SPECIAL PROPERTIES

Cat's eye formations can be found in Purple Scapolite (also occasionally in Blue Scapolite, page 81); protective against the evil eye.

MYTHOLOGY AND HISTORY

The jewel in the scapolite crown and most magickal, an intensely violet 76.9-carat scapolite from Burma is on display in the Smithsonian Institute in Washington, DC.

Purple Smithsonite

COLORS: From lavender pink to lavender violet or lilac

CRYSTAL TYPE: Zinc carbonate (see Smithsonite entry, page 444, for additional properties); a form of calcite, a minor ore of zinc, often found growing naturally with hemimorphite; sold as tumbled stones and in natural form covered with botryoidal bubbles; shiny

ZODIAC SIGN: Pisces (February 19–March 20)

CANDLE COLOR: Purple

PHYSICAL: Addresses slow heartbeat, low blood pressure, weak pulse; alleviates sinus issues, stress headaches made worse by noise and overly bright artificial lighting, problems with scalp and hair; relieves pain.

EMOTIONAL: Curbs claustrophobia; keeps you from excessively using drugs—recreational and/or prescription—and alcohol as an anesthetic to mask emotional pain.

HOME: Aids in contacting friends and family members, with whom you have lost touch or who live far away, either on social media or by going to school or college reunions.

WORKPLACE: Maintains quality in work, even if pressured to work fast and cut corners; helps refuse to sacrifice ethics.

CHILDREN: Allays fears of being abandoned or parents dying and leaving the child alone; for Indigo Children to make sense of what is sometimes an irrational world.

ANIMALS: For gentle, spiritual animals who seem to have healing powers themselves.

PROTECTION: Guards against those who present illusion as fact for personal gain.

MAGICKAL AND PSYCHIC USES

The most spiritual of the smithsonites; any of the purple shades bring closeness to your guardian angel; opens the channels to innate psychic powers.

SPECIAL PROPERTIES

For developing imagination in the form of storytelling and all innovative forms of the arts.

MYTHOLOGY AND HISTORY

Associated with the compassionate goddess Kwan Yin and with Osiris, father and underworld god of the ancient Egyptians, who promised immortality to all, not just pharaohs and nobles, if their hearts were pure. Purple Smithsonite also resonates with Saga, Norse goddess of wisdom, who released the gift of storytelling to the world.

Purple Spinel

COLORS: Purple from light to dark or red violet, including lavender

CRYSTAL TYPE: Magnesium aluminum oxide, often found in natural form, glassy, beryllium creating the purple

ZODIAC SIGN: Scorpio (October 24–November 22)

CANDLE COLOR: Purple

PHYSICAL: A whole-body healer; relieves deep-seated pain; alleviates epilepsy, migraines, hardening of the arteries, hydrocephalus, Parkinson's disease, motor neurone disease, circulatory problems in legs; strengthens skin and hair.

EMOTIONAL: Counters isolation and alienation from others; eases your mind in the face of intense psychic or religious experiences when no one takes them seriously.

HOME: Encourages independence in older relatives; creates a sense of space and personal boundaries if the home is crowded.

WORKPLACE: Darker Purple Spinel keeps coworkers and management from foisting on you extra work and responsibilities; aids in launching a successful spiritual business, developing paranormal media projects.

CHILDREN: Deflects frightening psychic experiences.

ANIMALS: For a pet disturbed by deceased animal spirits around the home.

PROTECTION: Guards against earthly hostility and paranormal threats, reflecting back ill-wishes to the sender.

MAGICKAL AND PSYCHIC USES

For attending or setting up a mediumship circle or ghost investigations; receiving spontaneous messages from others' deceased relatives; astral travel and recall of experiences.

SPECIAL PROPERTIES

Overcomes practical difficulties caused by physical or psychological challenges, through lack of the right resources and support in the workplace or community.

MYTHOLOGY AND HISTORY

Purple Spinel combines spirituality with determination to maintain your ethics and beliefs if you work with cynical, materialistic people or those in your community or family who try to make you conform. Purple Spinel reassures older people who find modern living bewildering.

Purple Sugilite or Luvulite

COLORS: Purple, lilac to violet with black, white, orange, brown, or, less frequently, blue markings (see also Pink Sugilite, page 360)

CRYSTAL TYPE: Cyclosilicate, potassium sodium lithium iron manganese aluminum silicate

ZODIAC SIGNS: Aquarius (January 21–February 18) and Gemini (May 22–June 21)

CANDLE COLOR: Violet

PHYSICAL: A regulator crystal, directing energy wherever it's needed; realigns the body; strengthens pineal, pituitary, and adrenal glands; alleviates headaches, influenza.

EMOTIONAL: Dispels angry, jealous, and irrational feelings; curbs nervous disorders, hypochondria.

HOME: An anti-guilt crystal if relatives make you feel inadequate; counteracts bad influences and bribery by and on family members; for unsupported single parents.

WORKPLACE: Assists you in maintaining your equilibrium in a situation where profit, targets, and rivalry predominate; establishes an eco-friendly business.

CHILDREN: Helps teenagers resist peer pressure and designer goods advertising; eases dyslexia and autism.

ANIMALS: For telepathic and aristocratic cats.

PROTECTION: Guards against self-doubt, unfriendly entities, and spirit possession during spirit rescue.

MAGICKAL AND PSYCHIC USES

Rituals restoring ecological balance and increasing compassion among world leaders; meditation, channeling angels and ascended masters, especially St. Germain and Archangel Zadkiel, keeper of the violet flame; every sugilite is believed to be programmed to release spirituality.

SPECIAL PROPERTIES

A love stone for meeting a known or unknown lover in dreams; to strengthen existing love; deters rivals; enhances sacred sexuality.

MYTHOLOGY AND HISTORY

Discovered in Japan in 1944, considered a gift from Mother Earth to heal modern problems; linked with the Age of Aquarius and a more compassionate worldview.

Purple Topaz

COLORS: Light violet to deep purple

CRYSTAL TYPE: A rare form of imperial topaz; takes its color from the inclusion of chromium; Purple Topaz is sometimes produced in a laboratory but can be found naturally

ZODIAC SIGN: Pisces (February 19–March 20)

CANDLE COLOR: Purple

PHYSICAL: Alleviates illnesses due to unwise lifestyle choices; relieves pain and aftereffects of injections and tattoos; eases autoimmune conditions.

EMOTIONAL: Keeps you from repeating old patterns, dreaming life away, and not dealing with practical necessities; moderates schizophrenia and personality disorders.

HOME: Brings blessings on the home in the way most needed.

WORKPLACE: Promotes astute decision making to avoid making mistakes or wrong judgments and to intuitively access future trends to stay ahead.

CHILDREN: For naïve teens rebelling without the common sense to avoid trouble; for autistic children to obtain the necessary resources to develop their unique gifts.

ANIMALS: For fussy, picky, spoiled pets.

PROTECTION: Guards against attracting the wrong people into your life, especially in love.

MAGICKAL AND PSYCHIC USES

Purple Topaz attracts luck and abundance; for sending prayers to others for healing; clairaudience; connecting telepathically with a yet-unknown future love, either clairaudiently or in dreams; like other topaz, Purple Topaz increases in power with the moon, reaching its full energies on full moon night.

MYTHOLOGY AND HISTORY

The topaz of spiritual as well as actual wealth, like golden imperial topaz, Purple Topaz has been a stone of royalty and nobility through the ages; opens the pathway to higher spiritual teachers, archangels, and ascended masters.

Purple Tourmaline

COLORS: Pale purple, lavender, deep violet; coloring from combining pink manganese and blue iron

CRYSTAL TYPE: Silicate, sometimes called siberite in paler shades

ZODIAC SIGN: Pisces (February 19–March 20)

CANDLE COLOR: Purple

PHYSICAL: Counters the effects of modern pollutants; alleviates issues relating to the pineal gland, thyroid, headaches (including migraines), chronic fatigue, Alzheimer's, epilepsy, poor coordination, neurological dysfunctions, heart.

EMOTIONAL: Curbs obsessive-compulsive disorder, flight-or-fight reactions, self-destructiveness, self-harm; supports conventional antidepressants.

HOME: Keeps energies balanced, welcoming health and happiness, and barring stress from external sources.

WORKPLACE: Promotes fiction writers (especially books for children), poets, musicians, dream analysts, psychic life coaches, holistic healing or clairvoyant businesses; useful for rigorous testing in parapsychology.

CHILDREN: Counters delayed physical development in early years, dyslexia, dyspraxia, excessive parental fears of children catching germs or suffering accidents.

ANIMALS: For young pets hard to housetrain.

PROTECTION: Protects against mind manipulation and entities attaching to the aura.

MAGICKAL AND PSYCHIC USES

Connects with the violet flame of the ascended master St. Germain; nature devas; aromatherapy, flower essences, sound therapies (using chanting, Tibetan bells, or singing bowls).

SPECIAL PROPERTIES

Encourages an imaginative lifestyle, exploring nature rather than simulated experiences or passive entertainment, buying a motor home or a vacation home.

MYTHOLOGY AND HISTORY

Purple Tourmaline has been used in magick and healing for centuries, since it holds an electrical and magnetic charge. It also changes form, appearing transparent when viewed from the side, and almost opaque when viewed down the long axis from either end. A love token to strengthen bonds weakened by opposition.

Purpurite

COLORS: From deep red to purple, metallic luster
CRYSTAL TYPE: Manganese phosphate
ZODIAC SIGN: Virgo (August 24–September 22)
CANDLE COLOR: Purple

PHYSICAL: Cures wounds, bruises, excessive bleeding; addresses issues involving the pulse, high blood pressure, blood circulation and oxygenation, heart palpitations; alleviates sunburn, adverse effects of radiation; promotes brain functioning; tempers acidity in stomach or urine.
EMOTIONAL: Helps overcome victim and martyr complexes, panic attacks, self-defeating thoughts.
HOME: Attracts prosperity or returning prosperity after a reversal due to bad luck or illness.
WORKPLACE: Strengthens leadership, entrepreneurial abilities, and financial acumen; encourages the self-employed to make wise business decisions; aids in adapting skills to a new career at any age.
CHILDREN: Comforts those made to feel different because of physical or emotional challenges.
ANIMALS: For an older person whose pet has died to adjust to a new animal companion.
PROTECTION: Guards against frightening psychic experiences; clears the aura of malevolent spirit energies and psychic attacks; an anti-poltergeist stone.

MAGICKAL AND PSYCHIC USES
Enhances crystal healing, channels random psychic powers into healing, clairvoyance, and mediumship.
SPECIAL PROPERTIES
For confident and clear public speaking so others listen when there is likely to be automatic opposition or heckling.
MYTHOLOGY AND HISTORY
Purpurite is formed by the alteration of lithiophilite into a pseudomorph, a mineral with the shape of one mineral but a different chemistry and structure. Often some lithiophilite remains in the Purpurite. This creates a powerful psychological and psychic tool for adapting to change in a positive way and opening the way to new love and friendships by leaving behind bad memories.

Pyramids

COLORS: From clear, often with inner markings or pathways to opaque Pyramids, sometimes engraved with Egyptian hieroglyphs
CRYSTAL TYPE: Varies according to the crystal; some Pyramids are naturally formed; for example, apophyllite, clear quartz, or amethyst; others are carved (see also Orgonite, page 332)
ZODIAC SIGN: Leo (July 23–August 23)
CANDLE COLOR: Gold

PHYSICAL: A whole-body healer, particularly in the squat shape of the ancient pyramid of King Cheops at Giza near Cairo, built around 2500 BCE; transparent Pyramids energize and are good for remote healing and absorbing pain, sickness, and sorrow.
EMOTIONAL: Counters obsessions and phobias, some from past worlds; allays inner turmoil when one worry replaces another.
HOME: A crystal Pyramid in the center of the home continually diffuses health, healing, and tranquility; calms sibling and intergenerational squabbling.
WORKPLACE: Keeps a small Pyramid in your workspace; support the base with your nondominant hand and draw strength through your cupped dominant hand over the point.
CHILDREN: An amethyst Pyramid in the bedroom reduces night terrors and brings beautiful dreams.
ANIMALS: For pets who fear being left alone.
PROTECTION: A smoky quartz Pyramid near the front door keeps earthly and paranormal harm from entering.

MAGICKAL AND PSYCHIC USES
The Cheops Pyramid induces strong psychic powers that exist even in miniature versions; hold or meditate with a Pyramid to increase clairvoyance, telepathy, astral travel, prophecy, and healing.
SPECIAL PROPERTIES
Experiments have shown that contact with pyramid shapes increases the slower brain-wave patterns associated with deeper dream states; have one at your side when relaxing.
MYTHOLOGY AND HISTORY
The Pyramid was believed to represent the first mound of earth that rose from the primal waters of creation in ancient Egypt. Keep a small squat Pyramid with your fruit and vegetables, near your main drinking water source and next to milk in the fridge for extra freshness.

Pyrite Suns

COLORS: A metallic luster, brass gold to yellow

CRYSTAL TYPE: Iron sulfide (see Iron Pyrites or Fool's Gold, page 256), disk-shaped mineral concretions of pyrite with smaller amounts of marcasite; varying in size from a small coin to a large plate

ZODIAC SIGN: Aries (March 21–April 20)

CANDLE COLOR: Gold

PHYSICAL: Removes pain, especially in the back; mitigates male infertility and erectile dysfunction; counters viruses, colds, coughs; strengthens bones.

EMOTIONAL: Allays fears of being cursed or jinxed; curbs an obsession with gambling and buying unnecessary material possessions; keeps you from valuing people only in terms of their wealth.

HOME: Attracts money and good fortune, and prevents it draining out.

WORKPLACE: Increases memory to ensure recall of necessary facts for presentations or interviews; useful for financial institutions involving stocks and shares.

CHILDREN: Buy one at a child's birth and add one for each birthday; give them to the teen at eighteen as a talisman so they will never lack money.

ANIMALS: Keep with entry forms or printouts of competition entries or proof of pedigree to attract success.

PROTECTION: Guards against debt, unwise gambling, and losing all your money.

MAGICKAL AND PSYCHIC USES

A talisman for attracting more money than anticipated or unexpected money; for games of chance where the main factor is luck; speculation where there are unknown factors.

SPECIAL PROPERTIES

Draws your talents to the notice of those who can advance your position; for talent contests, reality shows, and auditions where you need to instantly shine and remain memorable.

MYTHOLOGY AND HISTORY

Also called miners' dollars, larger Pyrite Suns are found only in Sparta in Illinois, in rocks about 300 million years old, 200–250 feet below ground on the roof of coal mines; Pyrite Suns offer expansion of horizons, whether travel, career advancement, or accumulation of money.

Pyrolusite

COLORS: Dark steel gray, lighter gray, black, bluish; may have fern-like dendrites on the surface

CRYSTAL TYPE: Manganese dioxide, best used as a tumbled stone; belongs to the rutile mineral family

ZODIAC SIGN: Libra (September 23–October 23).

CANDLE COLOR: Gray

PHYSICAL: Alleviates blurred vision, astigmatism, bronchitis, fluid on the lungs, lack of libido, sluggish metabolism; addresses issues relating to the feet, ankles, torn muscles.

EMOTIONAL: Keeps you from being manipulated by the mind games of others; curbs conflicting emotions and rapidly changing opinions according to the latest popular theories.

HOME: Prevents intrusion by troublesome and complaining neighbors and uninvited sales phone calls; for an effective non-intrusive neighborhood watch organization, if official security is ineffective or absent; for weddings, christenings, naming ceremonies, and family or school reunions.

WORKPLACE: Clears up misunderstandings, mixed messages and trouble stirred up for the sake of mischief-making; aids in working independently with an organization or starting your own business.

CHILDREN: Valuable when children have problems dealing with authority, especially teenagers excluded from education because of their unwillingness to follow rules.

ANIMALS: For training classes if dogs will not come when called.

PROTECTION: Guards against psychic attack by low-level spirits from dubious occult sites; repels curses and hexes.

MAGICKAL AND PSYCHIC USES

Keeps the aura clear from unwanted attachments, earthly and paranormal; ritual magick; Wicca; for initiation ceremonies.

SPECIAL PROPERTIES

As a charm for immense good fortune relating to specific needs and wishes.

MYTHOLOGY AND HISTORY

A stone of transformation and transfer of energies, traditionally used by magickal practitioners for manifestation and banishing spells; also believed to drive away Earth demons. Manganese dioxide was used in cave paintings in ancient Europe, so this stone furthers traditional arts, including natural pigments and material from the Earth.

Pyromangite

COLORS: Deep pink or pinkish-red to red
CRYSTAL TYPE: Manganese silicate, rich in manganese
ZODIAC SIGN: Taurus (April 21–May 21)
CANDLE COLOR: Pink

PHYSICAL: Promotes fertility where inability to conceive is causing relationship issues; combats heart stenosis, lack of oxygenation in blood; aids in successful angioplasty, heart bypass, and pacemaker implantation.
EMOTIONAL: Addresses unresolved business in love from past worlds or earlier in the present lifetime; counters a tendency not to let adult children lead their own lives.
HOME: Creates a special place with mementos of family who have passed to keep their memory alive; for welcoming protective house and land guardians.
WORKPLACE: Curbs unrequited love for a colleague or boss that interferes with business interactions; aids in persuading colleagues or managers to adopt more modern and efficient ways of working.
CHILDREN: Comforts those who never knew their grandparents, especially their grandmothers.
ANIMALS: Helps older animal mothers struggling to cope with a litter.
PROTECTION: Guards against giving mixed messages to a former love to whom you still feel attraction.

MAGICKAL AND PSYCHIC USES
Mediumship to connect with deceased relatives; for magick rituals to welcome the ancestors into the circle and seek their wisdom and healing.

SPECIAL PROPERTIES
A powerful female energy, bringing loving connections and resolving issues with female relatives; assists men dominated by matriarchs who have problems expressing their anima side.

MYTHOLOGY AND HISTORY
Pyromangite is similar in appearance to rhodonite but with a different crystalline form, internal structure, and less iron, and is far more intense in energies for cutting through relationship issues.

Pyrope Garnet

COLORS: Bright red, resembling rubies, darker to violet-red in larger stones, almost always without inclusions
CRYSTAL TYPE: A magnesium aluminum garnet, often found with iron-rich Almandine Garnet (page 19)
ZODIAC SIGN: Capricorn (December 22–January 20)
CANDLE COLOR: Red

PHYSICAL: Boosts libido; alleviates issues stemming from reproductive disorders, exhaustion, blood, circulation, heart, low blood sugar, influenza, nosebleeds, recurring viruses.
EMOTIONAL: Restores the will to live; phobias about blood.
HOME: Removes emotional and financial parasites.
WORKPLACE: Keeps you from missing deadlines or targets; aids in maintaining a high-powered job without sacrificing your quality of life; helps you fulfill lifetime ambitions.
CHILDREN: For inert teenagers who live online or in their heads.
ANIMALS: Protects fierce creatures from trophy or bounty hunters.
PROTECTION: Guards against becoming obsessed with a new passion or interest.

MAGICKAL AND PSYCHIC USES
For defensive magick against curses, hexes, emotional vampires, and mind control; sex magick; fire rituals, shamanism.

SPECIAL PROPERTIES
For courage, willpower, and single-mindedness to overcome obstacles; inventiveness.

MYTHOLOGY AND HISTORY
Each of the ten kinds of garnet possesses unique qualities. Pyrope Garnet, the most proactive, was called by the Dutch philosopher Erasmus "living fire." Bohemia, now part of the Czech Republic, is famous for Pyrope Garnets as big as hen eggs. In the eighteenth and nineteenth centuries, bohemian garnets were made into ornate jewelry for European society beauties. Pyrope bullets were used in battle slings in Asia because of their hardness and blood-like color. Non-gem pyrope shares the powers of the gem.

Pyrophyllite or Pencil Stone

COLORS: White, apple-green, grayish-green, brownish-green, yellowish

CRYSTAL TYPE: Phyllosilicate, aluminum silicate hydroxide, with silver or yellow fan-like structures throughout; belongs to the talc family

ZODIAC SIGN: Gemini (May 22–June 21)

CANDLE COLOR: White

PHYSICAL: Calms overactive adrenal glands, stomach disorders, chronic indigestion, heartburn; eases constrictions and blockages.

EMOTIONAL: Keeps you from living by other people's rules through guilt or obligation; counters codependence, low self-esteem.

HOME: Balances yin and yang energies in the home if the atmosphere is overactive and assertive, or lethargic and emotional.

WORKPLACE: Transforms innovative ideas into practical manifestation within a creative profession; aids in launching a creative side hustle to progress into a full-time business.

CHILDREN: Comforts those who are clingy and reluctant to go to kindergarten or to visit other children's homes without an accompanying parent; useful for those who are distressed by loud voices or others' quarrels.

ANIMALS: Deters a neighbor's continually barking dogs, if Pyrophyllite is set in a safe place near an adjoining wall.

PROTECTION: Guards against those who shout, bluster, and threaten to get their way.

MAGICKAL AND PSYCHIC USES

Communication with stellar beings and spirit guides through channeling, automatic writing, psychic artistry, clairaudience, dreams, and astral travel.

SPECIAL PROPERTIES

Severs ties with those who are destructive or controlling and with old, redundant ways of living; increases sexual confidence after a bad relationship, if it is a first sexual encounter or after a long period without a partner, especially later in life.

MYTHOLOGY AND HISTORY

Also called the pencil stone because it is the crystal of enhancing the power of automatic writing and, if you're a beginner, opening the way through a benign guide or the archangel of writing, the shimmering Metatron; boosts success in writing and having published books, screenplays for TV series, or articles in journals.

Quantum Quattro Silica

COLORS: Bright, medium, or royal blue; deep to light green, gray, and brown

CRYSTAL TYPE: Combining shattuckite, dioptase, malachite, and chrysocolla within a smoky quartz matrix

ZODIAC SIGN: Sagittarius (November 23–December 21)

CANDLE COLOR: Turquoise

PHYSICAL: Alleviates cardiovascular conditions, misalignment of body, issues involving the digestive tract.

EMOTIONAL: Counters unwise attachments, codependence, fascination with evil, self-harm, fear of sex.

HOME: Brings a sense of well-being after a difficult period; for caregivers who make too many sacrifices for an ungrateful relative.

WORKPLACE: For making the quantum leap, the sudden breakthrough when a business takes off or seemingly insurmountable obstacles are overcome with a change of personnel.

CHILDREN: Offers incredibly gifted children the opportunities they need.

ANIMALS: For rearing a show-winning or champion breeding animal after an unpromising beginning.

PROTECTION: Guards against lower-vibration spirits called up in séances or magick and not returned to their realms.

MAGICKAL AND PSYCHIC USES

A Master Crystal (page 297), Quantum Quattro Silica cuts cords with past-life attachments and present obsessions with a lover who will never change; brings the self into alignment with the soul purpose.

SPECIAL PROPERTIES

Quantum Quattro Silica is considered especially effective in sunlight for an infusion of energy, for emotional ills, and to relieve pain.

MYTHOLOGY AND HISTORY

Discovered in Namibia in 1996; regarded as a stone of the coming new millennium by bringing together five different minerals as a transformational force for human and Earth healing.

Que Sera

COLORS: Blue, pink, and, rarely, greenish clasts (fragments) in fine-grained dark brown matrix

CRYSTAL TYPE: A conglomerate including quartz, calcite, potassium feldspar, kaolinite, iron oxide, magnetite, clinozoisite, and leucozene

ZODIAC SIGNS: Sagittarius (November 23–December 21) and Aquarius (January 21–February 18)

CANDLE COLOR: Blue

PHYSICAL: Addresses the adrenal glands, deep-cell healing, immune system, seasonal affective disorder, viruses affecting multiple organs, whole-body healing.

EMOTIONAL: Allays fears and phobias (especially rare ones), a sense of feeling powerless; helps you learn to say no.

HOME: Brings health, happiness, and love.

WORKPLACE: For team building, especially with distinctive creative personalities; for inventions; useful for researchers developing new treatments and vaccines.

CHILDREN: For children with school phobia, who are frequently absent with minor illnesses.

ANIMALS: For a special therapy animal or one who has been with you in many lifetimes.

PROTECTION: Shields against electromagnetic energy and Wi-Fi rays from technological equipment.

MAGICKAL AND PSYCHIC USES
Clairaudience and sound healing, sacred chants; kinesiology; healing guides from ancient cultures; accessing the Akashic records.

SPECIAL PROPERTIES
An alchemist stone, synthesizing the higher and earthly self and all chakra energy centers; for miracles, for peace between nations and religions.

MYTHOLOGY AND HISTORY
Named by the US crystal expert Melody after the Spanish title of the 1956 song made famous by Doris Day, meaning "what will be will be," so trust in the future. Some claim if you sing the words the crystal vibrates along with it.

Rainbow Fluorite

COLORS: Multiple bands of varying fluorite hues that may intermingle, especially green, purple, yellow/gold, clear and blue; sometimes flecks of pyrite

CRYSTAL TYPE: Calcium fluoride

ZODIAC SIGN: Pisces (February 19–March 20)

CANDLE COLOR: Gold

PHYSICAL: Promotes cell regeneration and repair after mutation; addresses DNA-related degenerative conditions, osteoporosis, psychosomatic illness, self-injury as a cry for help.

EMOTIONAL: Curbs an inability to set aside old quarrels, grudges, and injustices; keeps you from rejecting support or medication; allays fear of dentists.

HOME: Brings reconciliation after quarrels and acceptance of different viewpoints; aids in redecorating the home and creating a beautiful indoor or outdoor garden.

WORKPLACE: Useful for professional artists, fabric designers, those who create tapestries and work in interior design; valuable for those performing in theatrical spectaculars, professional magicians, storytellers, illustrators, and writers of fantasy fiction.

CHILDREN: The ultimate magick treasure; for abused children to regain trust; for Indigo Children; encourages painting and drawing.

ANIMALS: For exotic birds and tropical fish.

PROTECTION: Shields the aura when surrounded by toxic people or atmospheres; repels psychic attack; cuts cords with spiritual or psychological attachment.

MAGICKAL AND PSYCHIC USES
Connection with devas, higher nature spirits; wishes when a rainbow appears; cleansing, healing, and empowering the aura; exploring shamanic magickal lands through meditation or fantasy.

SPECIAL PROPERTIES
The mixture of colors creates an energy greater than separate fluorites; grants small miracles; forges unity of mind, body, and soul.

MYTHOLOGY AND HISTORY
In China for centuries Rainbow Fluorite was shaped into vessels to bring wealth and health; for free clear thinking without the need of approval from others.

Rainbow Garnet

COLORS: Iridescent, dark red or orangey-brown with a range of rainbow colors that change as the gem moves, some displaying a full spectrum of colors

CRYSTAL TYPE: An unusual form of Andradite Garnet or Grossular Garnet

ZODIAC SIGN: Aries (March 21–April 20)

CANDLE COLOR: Red

PHYSICAL: Mitigates blood disorders, anemia, and red blood cell problems; eases headaches caused by PMS; promotes fertility.

EMOTIONAL: Allays fears of the unknown; transforms a damaged inner child who has turned away from spontaneity and rigidly follows the rules of life.

HOME: Encourages optimism; for redecorating the home and creating a colorful garden.

WORKPLACE: Empowers those in the entertainment field, especially comedy; for a career involving a flow of new people and projects.

CHILDREN: Aids youngsters who have taken on responsibility for a sick parent or younger siblings.

ANIMALS: For brightly colored birds and exotic species.

PROTECTION: Guards against those who constantly remind us of old injustices they have endured.

MAGICKAL AND PSYCHIC USES

A wish crystal, especially when there is a rainbow in the sky; the rainbow disappears in the presence of someone who is a threat; fills your aura with color if you are tired or unwell.

SPECIAL PROPERTIES

For encouraging kindness in abrasive impatient people; for buying or renting a motor home for vacations.

MYTHOLOGY AND HISTORY

Rainbow Garnet was first found in 1934 in the Adelaide mining district, in Nevada, and since then in Mexico and Japan, where production has now stopped. A remarkable gem, combining possibility with the steady moneymaking nature of other garnets, so opening the way to hidden sources of profitability.

Rainbow Lattice Sunstone

COLORS: Displays small, yellow to deep orange (hematite), highly reflective small inclusions; giving an overall sunshine glow and iridescence; the inclusions joined by black lattice patterns with a magnetic sheen (magnetite)

CRYSTAL TYPE: Feldspar consisting of 75 percent orthoclase and 25 percent albite, the name *sunstone* referring to its glowing appearance, rather than the mineral composition

ZODIAC SIGN: Leo (July 23–August 23)

CANDLE COLOR: Gold

PHYSICAL: Eases blood flow through veins, arteries, and neural pathways; mitigates seasonal affective disorder; aids in healing with light and color therapies; alleviates vision problems.

EMOTIONAL: Curbs self-limitation, cynicism; keeps you from dampening the enthusiasm of others.

HOME: Makes a welcoming sanctuary for the wider family, friends, neighbors, colleagues, and lonely acquaintances, attracting blessings threefold back into your life.

WORKPLACE: Fosters leadership opportunities, having your efforts recognized and rewarded.

CHILDREN: A magickal stone for the family treasure box, to be shared at special family times; as a special star on the yule tree.

ANIMALS: For the return of a deceased pet in a new body.

PROTECTION: Guards against exploitation of gifts by those who deny you due credit for your efforts.

MAGICKAL AND PSYCHIC USES

A stone of sun and moon power combined, of the alchemical Queen Luna and King Sol, creating a magickal space where manifestation can occur.

SPECIAL PROPERTIES

A magickal stone that psychically tunes into the ley energies of the Western world, the ancient tracks in Chaco Canyon in New Mexico set down by the ancient Anasazi people in the USA and Australian Aboriginal song energy lines.

MYTHOLOGY AND HISTORY

Found in one small remote area at Harts Range, in Australia's Northern Territory; first discovered in the Utnerrengatye (Rainbow Caterpillar) mine as a commercial stone in 1985; much earlier as a sacred stone by the Eastern Arrernte Indigenous people on whose land the stone is found.

Rainbow Moonstone

COLORS: Milky white with rainbow sheen/flashes
CRYSTAL TYPE: Opalescent feldspar
ZODIAC SIGN: Cancer (June 22–July 22)
CANDLE COLOR: Silver

PHYSICAL: Regulates hormonal and menstrual cycles; promotes fertility; aids in recovery after breast, uterine, and ovary operations or sterilization; boosts low resistance to illness.
EMOTIONAL: Mitigates the effects of early trauma; counters addictive habits, self-harm, or suicidal tendencies.
HOME: For safety when living in remote or rural areas; encourages healthy plant growth.
WORKPLACE: Aids in adjusting your body clock if you're working shifts or regularly traveling across time zones; keeps you from experiencing jealousy from colleagues if you're conducting a romantic relationship in the workplace.
CHILDREN: Addresses speech problems and learning difficulties, plus nightmares; allays fears of the dark and ghosts.
ANIMALS: Attracts butterflies, moths, and dragonflies to gardens.
PROTECTION: Strengthens aura against any who would deceive; prevents earthly ill-wishing or paranormal harm entering your dreams; protects against incubus and succubus.

MAGICKAL AND PSYCHIC USES
A wish crystal and good luck talisman; calling a dream lover on the astral plane; romance spells; full moon magick; communication with higher self and evolved guides; accurate predictions.

SPECIAL PROPERTIES
A gentle stone for all who are or feel alone, lost, or vulnerable to bring hope by attracting the right people and opportunities to transform your life; prevents jet lag.

MYTHOLOGY AND HISTORY
Believed in classical times by the Roman philosopher Pliny the Elder, to absorb moonlight and starlight, Rainbow Moonstone is the original mood stone, increasing in translucence or becoming dull in response to the mood of the owner.

Rainbow Myanite

COLORS: Golden orange, with deep yellow coating and iridescent rainbows
CRYSTAL TYPE: Quartz, the iridescence caused by goethite or hematite inclusions within the coating
ZODIAC SIGN: Leo (July 23–August 23)
CANDLE COLOR: Gold

PHYSICAL: Alleviates neurological conditions affecting the whole body; aids in success with investigative surgery, angiograms, MRIs, and CT scans, biopsies; whole-body healing; reverses unhealthy lifestyles; addresses hereditary conditions.
EMOTIONAL: Keeps you from being locked in behavior and thinking dating back through generations, and believing a family or family land is cursed.
HOME: Brings peace to a home where emotions run high or there are intense rivalries.
WORKPLACE: Ensures positive, welcoming, and pleasant stays for owners or managers of hotels, motels, or bed-and-breakfasts.
CHILDREN: Empowers Star or Crystal Children with complete rainbow auras, born wise and with evolved psychic powers.
ANIMALS: For the passing of a beloved pet, believed to wait at the Rainbow Bridge for their owners.
PROTECTION: Casts a rainbow shield around the aura.

MAGICKAL AND PSYCHIC USES
In its blade form, cuts destructive cords, attachments, and hooks with possessive people or emotional vampires.

SPECIAL PROPERTIES
A more intensely colored and powerful version of Golden Healer Quartz (page 208), brings safe and happy travel, especially on business.

MYTHOLOGY AND HISTORY
Found only in one mine in the foothills of the Cascade Mountains in eastern Washington State, Rainbow Myanite was discovered in 2011. Rainbow Myanite is seen as a pathway between the Earth and the heavens.

Rainbow Obsidian and Peacock or Velvet Sheen Obsidian

COLORS: Rainbow Obsidian is black with a blue sheen or green-black with flashes of purple, red, and blue, characterized by the rainbow shimmer of light. Peacock Obsidian appears black until it is polished and held in bright light when swirling green, red, blue, violet, and orange appear and disappear as if fingers are run against the grain of velvet.

CRYSTAL TYPE: Volcanic glass, its shimmering rainbow sheen caused by trapped water bubbles as the magma cooled; best used as a tumbled stone

ZODIAC SIGN: Aries (March 21–April 20)

CANDLE COLOR: Red

PHYSICAL: Addresses vision problems, especially cataracts, tunnel and night vision; alleviates deep vein problems.

EMOTIONAL: Keeps you from creating a false image of your achievements and status to impress others.

HOME: A stone of forgiveness because the rainbow signified the start of the new world after the Flood, a reminder after betrayal to let bitterness go.

WORKPLACE: Rainbow and Peacock Obsidian turn around bad fortune in career or business; for a second creative career.

CHILDREN: Comforts those who fear the dark; calms teens nervous being home alone at night.

ANIMALS: Promotes appreciation of pets who are not visually appealing but have lovely natures.

PROTECTION: Offers a psychic shield against paranormal harm.

MAGICKAL AND PSYCHIC USES

Cutting psychic cords with a destructive ex-partner who has made it clear they no longer want you but stops you from moving on; dark mirror magick to contact ancestors and spirit guides.

SPECIAL PROPERTIES

Keeps you from becoming overwhelmed by spiritual teachings and learning instead to trust intuitive awareness.

MYTHOLOGY AND HISTORY

Rainbow Obsidian is very similar to Peacock Obsidian or Velvet Obsidian and they share energies. Peacock Obsidian's colors form swirls, and Rainbow Obsidian's colors form layers.

Rainbow Opal

COLORS: The most brilliant of the precious opals, whose rainbow, play of color (an optical effect resulting in flashes of colored light or flashing iridescence), is seen in curved bands resembling a rainbow

CRYSTAL TYPE: Hydrated silicon dioxide

ZODIAC SIGN: Cancer (June 22–July 22)

CANDLE COLOR: Silver

PHYSICAL: Alleviates issues stemming from vision, migraines, neurological disorders, pain, skin, infections; promotes minor miracles in chronic or degenerative conditions, fertility, pregnancy, and healthy childbirth.

EMOTIONAL: Counters distress, hopelessness, helplessness; difficulty following social norms.

HOME: The happiest opal, radiating good humor and gently energizing the home.

WORKPLACE: For injecting enthusiasm into routine tasks; for call center staff answering complaints; for fantasy writers and artists.

CHILDREN: Useful for those who have a complete rainbow aura but may find it hard to communicate with peers.

ANIMALS: For pets who have departed this life but can be sensed around the home.

PROTECTION: Guards against cynicism, sarcasm, and pessimism.

MAGICKAL AND PSYCHIC USES

A wish stone, especially with a rainbow in the sky; opens psychic pathways last experienced in childhood, mind travel.

SPECIAL PROPERTIES

Rainbow Opal is the stone of happy dreams, if you or a child sleep badly or suffer from recurring nightmares.

MYTHOLOGY AND HISTORY

Rainbow Opals are the most prized precious opal categorized as white opals, black opals, and fire opals. Over 90 percent of precious opals come from Australia and opal is Australia's national gemstone.

Rainbow Quartz

COLORS: Light, refracted by the prismatic effect of inner fractures, divides and forms rainbow colors within the crystal
CRYSTAL TYPE: Silicate/tectosilicate, clear quartz with inner markings and cracks
ZODIAC SIGN: Leo (July 23–August 23)
CANDLE COLOR: White

PHYSICAL: Alleviates issues involving the bladder, cystitis, bowel disorders, exhaustion, menstrual difficulties, seasonal affective disorder, lack of serotonin, blood oxygenation, blood sugar levels.
EMOTIONAL: Curbs disillusionment with love, career, family, or life; inability to forgive and move on.
HOME: The happiness crystal, Rainbow Quartz spreads joy, health, and harmony throughout the home.
WORKPLACE: Transforms a bad atmosphere; a personal insulation for troubleshooters, trade union representatives, counselors, crisis center or social workers.
CHILDREN: Encourages those who are different in any way to appreciate themselves and be appreciated for their special gifts.
ANIMALS: Works with the energies of magickal creatures, such as the phoenix and unicorns; uplifts an animal who has lost the will to live.
PROTECTION: Guards against those who spread gloom and despair.

MAGICKAL AND PSYCHIC USES
More magickal than a flawless clear quartz, Rainbow Quartz spheres reveal within divinatory images of the future.
SPECIAL PROPERTIES
Reconciliation in love after a bad quarrel or betrayal; for finding the right partner.
MYTHOLOGY AND HISTORY
Rainbow Quartz combines the dynamic, energizing power of clear quartz with gentler rainbow energies associated with reconciliation, healing, and promises of a better tomorrow. The Hindu goddess Maya Shakti created the colors of the rainbow behind her seven rainbow veils and laughed with the pleasure of sharing their beauty with humanity.

Rainforest Jasper

COLORS: Mossy, green, with brown, tan, yellow, and white
CRYSTAL TYPE: Rhyolite lava, may contain quartz, feldspar, and other minerals
ZODIAC SIGN: Virgo (August 24–September 22)
CANDLE COLOR: Green

PHYSICAL: Eases colds, influenza, viral epidemics, infections; promotes healthy blood circulation, blood sugar levels; counters environmental pollution from cell phone towers, power lines, and chemicals in the air and water.
EMOTIONAL: Keeps you from being out of tune with your natural needs, manifested in overeating, smoking, excessive alcohol, and a diet of fast food; curbs an unwillingness to engage in gentle exercise.
HOME: Creates a beautiful indoor or outdoor garden; for buying a home with acreage for self-sustainability.
WORKPLACE: For outdoor occupations, environmentally focused careers, including botany; supports organizations working toward alleviating climate change and promoting conservation.
CHILDREN: Encourages children to play in forests, parks, and open spaces, using the natural materials they find on hand.
ANIMALS: For wildlife habitats, especially in rainforests, and the preservation of indigenous creatures; for pets who have lost their normal vitality.
PROTECTION: Guards against deforestation that destroys the lungs of the Earth.

MAGICKAL AND PSYCHIC USES
For natural magick, contact with Earth, forest, and tree mother spirits, druidry, and nature-based religions.
SPECIAL PROPERTIES
For learning about herbal healing and wisdom, tree and flower essences, or recalling knowledge from earlier worlds.
MYTHOLOGY AND HISTORY
Green Rainforest Jasper is found in Western Australia, where there are one thousand pockets of dry rainforest supporting numerous plant species, many that cannot be seen anywhere else; the stone will give inner visions of the wise Aboriginal grandmothers of countless generations to those who respect the old traditions.

Rathbunite

COLORS: Reddish-brown, yellow, orange, white, and gray jasper mixed as curving, curling stripes throughout the stone
CRYSTAL TYPE: Jasper, microcrystalline quartz
ZODIAC SIGN: Leo (July 23–August 23)
CANDLE COLOR: Gold

PHYSICAL: Boosts the immune system and metabolism; eases stress-induced illnesses; keeps you from pushing physical endurance beyond your limits out of pride or stubbornness when it may be time to ease off.
EMOTIONAL: Curbs an inability to relax and have fun; counters pessimism and seeing the worst in others; mitigates the effects of gnawing injustices and wrongs from the past.
HOME: Fosters a happy home, spontaneous celebrations, picnics, outings, vacations with friends and family; aids in acquiring a motor home or vacation home in the wilderness.
WORKPLACE: Brings thoughts and ideas together in those who have brilliant concepts but find it hard to carry a project through to completion; for those working in leisure centers or theme parks, as entertainers, magicians, clowns event planners.
CHILDREN: Boosts confidence in solemn or acutely shy children who find it hard to join in play.
ANIMALS: For good-natured pets who instantly cheer you up when you are sad or anxious.
PROTECTION: Guards against unenthusiastic people who spread gloom and doom on any innovations or suggested activities.

MAGICKAL AND PSYCHIC USES
Earth energy rituals; sand healing and divination; developing and trusting your sixth sense; manifesting wishes, needs, and desires.
SPECIAL PROPERTIES
Rathbunite replaces excessive feelings of guilt, duty, and workaholic tendencies with time for pleasure, relaxation, and leisure.
MYTHOLOGY AND HISTORY
Often called the laughter stone or crystal of the never-ending smile, Rathbunite was discovered in Arizona and so is a stone of the sacred land, containing its timeless warmth and the belief that all shall one day be well. Rathbunite enables you to overcome feelings of selfishness if you make yourself happy, rather than focusing entirely on the needs of others.

Raw or Rough Colombian Emerald

COLORS: Greens from pale to dark, lacks the sparkle of gem emerald but retains its powers
CRYSTAL TYPE: Beryl with trace amounts of chromium md vanadium making it green
ZODIAC SIGN: Taurus (April 21–May 21)
CANDLE COLOR: Green

PHYSICAL: Alleviates issues involving the eyes, sinuses, angina; traditionally used as an antidote to poison; promotes fertility.
EMOTIONAL: Works against those who are serially unfaithful or who tempt those in relationships to stray.
HOME: For building or renovating a home in a location you like, rather than an area that would be more practical.
WORKPLACE: Aids in winning legal battles if there are ruthless threats by rivals or intimidating officialdom.
CHILDREN: Helps teenage girls, obsessed with their appearance, to realize that superficial beauty is not as important as a loving heart.
ANIMALS: Teaches children to love a less than aesthetically pleasing pet, rather than the latest craze.
PROTECTION: Guards against temptation to risk a long-term relationship for short-term thrills.

MAGICKAL AND PSYCHIC USES
Spells to attract a soul twin.
SPECIAL PROPERTIES
Raw Emerald possesses all the qualities of gem emerald in a very direct active form; a powerful connection to your psychic gifts if you are new to psychic work.
MYTHOLOGY AND HISTORY
A totally unpolished emerald of less monetary value than a gem and therefore more affordable, especially as a tumbled stone. From Colombia in South America comes the legend of the immortal woman Fura and Tena her husband, created to populate the Earth. To keep their eternal youth, they had to be faithful to each other. But Fura was not, one of the reasons emeralds are said to fade if there is infidelity, so they grew older and died. The creator turned them into two mountains and Fura's tears became emeralds.

Receiver Quartz

COLORS: Generally clear, but its qualities can be present in other colored quartzes, such as gray/brown (smoky quartz)

CRYSTAL TYPE: Quartz crystal with a broad upward-sloping face at the tip

ZODIAC SIGN: Cancer (June 22–July 22)

CANDLE COLOR: Silver

PHYSICAL: Promotes successful blood transfusions, the body's acceptance of transplants and implants, receptivity to treatments both conventional and alternative.

EMOTIONAL: Helps overcome preconceived ideas and prejudices, an unwillingness to listen to advice or warnings.

HOME: Aids in learning to listen to what is actually being said, rather than overwriting the present with voices from the past.

WORKPLACE: Cultivates receptivity to new ideas and ways of working; tactfully bypasses those who dominate meetings.

CHILDREN: Useful for those who find it hard to concentrate and listen at school and home.

ANIMALS: For pets who do not come when they are called.

PROTECTION: Guards against being bombarded with conflicting opinions and information.

MAGICKAL AND PSYCHIC USES

Meditation and relaxation without conscious effort or techniques; listening to the voices of angels and spirit guides through clairaudience, transmitted through your own inner voice or automatic writing.

SPECIAL PROPERTIES

Occasionally, a Receiver crystal may also be a generator with one face sloping more than the other five. This builds up the life force and acts as a personal repository of physical health and spiritual wisdom, especially messages received from higher realms or the higher self or soul essence that travels with us through different incarnations.

MYTHOLOGY AND HISTORY

A stone for those who are always giving to others time, resources, gifts, practical help, a listening ear, and money, but find it hard to ask for or accept help for themselves; for stepping back and considering all the facts before making an irrevocable decision.

Record Keeper Quartz

COLOR: Clear; may have faint inclusions forming pathways to the inner doorway(s)

CRYSTAL TYPE: Quartz, occasionally found in rubies, indicated by a perfect triangle or several triangles on one or more sloping faces of the crystal (usually the largest)

ZODIAC SIGN: Aquarius (January 21–February 18)

CANDLE COLOR: White

PHYSICAL: A personal crystal, offering healing when it's most needed; aids in adjusting unhealthy lifestyle patterns.

EMOTIONAL: Promotes a positive approach to problems, even if you cannot eradicate difficulties.

HOME: For a less pressured lifestyle; discourages excessive technological communication among family.

WORKPLACE: Propels you to abandon a lucrative, meaningless career to follow a dream.

CHILDREN: Encourages Star, Indigo, and Crystal Children to understand their uniqueness.

ANIMALS: Connects with your protective power animal from many lifetimes.

PROTECTION: Eases worries about mortality, particularly if you're responsible for children.

MAGICKAL AND PSYCHIC USES

For accessing the Akashic records of humankind in all times, places, past, and future; knowledge of Atlanteans and Lemurians, considered descendants of the original Record Keepers.

SPECIAL PROPERTIES

Felt as an indentation, most visible when held to the light; fill the Record Keeper with happy memories, a repository for future generations.

MYTHOLOGY AND HISTORY

Place the triangle against your third eye, center of your brow, closing your eyes; alternatively rub your thumbprint, non-dominant hand, from top to bottom of the triangle, allowing visions, words, and impressions to answer questions you never knew needed answering.

Red Amethyst

COLORS: May be red throughout, red-tipped purple amethyst, or red on the outside of an inner purple amethyst

CRYSTAL TYPE: Amethyst, hematite, iron, sometimes smoky quartz

ZODIAC SIGN: Gemini (May 22–June 21)

CANDLE COLOR: Red

PHYSICAL: Stabilizes and energizes; promotes blood circulation; alleviates motion sickness, debilitating pain constantly draining energy, menorrhagia (menstrual bleeding that lasts more than seven days), muscle strain after intense exercise.

EMOTIONAL: Curbs strong cravings for food, alcohol, tobacco, or drugs; addresses ongoing insomnia due to whirling thoughts; counters fatigue and nausea, caused by medical or surgical intervention, between treatments; keeps you from becoming overly sensitive to the approval of others.

HOME: Balances chi if there are drama kings and queens in the family.

WORKPLACE: Eases debt issues and creates a steady source of income; promotes successful business travel.

CHILDREN: For those veering between hyperactivity and inertia; for peaceably regulating time teens spend online.

ANIMALS: Calms overly boisterous pets in a confined living space.

PROTECTION: Deters hidden enemies masking malice beneath affability; counters unfair legal or official action.

MAGICKAL AND PSYCHIC USES

A talisman for breaking stagnation in luck; for wealth-generating rituals; sending trapped spirits to the light.

SPECIAL PROPERTIES

The intermingling of proactive hematite and balancing amethyst creates energy greater than the separate minerals; offers a safe base to act courageously; attracts and strengthens passion and lasting love.

MYTHOLOGY AND HISTORY

Red Amethyst occurs naturally beneath the Earth's surface as hematite and iron seep into purple amethyst. Rare, with the largest source in Ontario, Canada, similar red aura amethyst is found in the Amazon where amethyst clusters are naturally coated with iron oxide.

Red and Gold Himalayan Azeztulite

COLORS: May be found as separate red and gold crystals, but often combined within the same stone, doubling the power

CRYSTAL TYPE: Quartz, gold being recently found in the same North Indian mineral deposit as red

ZODIAC SIGN: Leo (July 23–August 23)

CANDLE COLOR: Gold

PHYSICAL: Red Azeztulite is a powerful source of prana (life force), for blood, especially circulation, immune system, and cell health; both colors boost libido.

EMOTIONAL: For those who have given up on life and people who have suffered major trauma or betrayal; counters self-harm; red enhances healing after sexual abuse.

HOME: Aids in exploring alternative, freer lifestyles for vacations, or a more permanent spiritually based lifestyle.

WORKPLACE: Encourages you to take a chance on a long-desired vocation; for artistry using vivid colors as well as metalwork.

CHILDREN: Allows children to remain children, experiencing the magick of childhood.

ANIMALS: For the conservation of lions, tigers, leopards, and all fierce wild creatures.

PROTECTION: Guards against those who cast doubt and cynicism on your dreams.

MAGICKAL AND PSYCHIC USES

For sacred sex rituals, fire magick, alchemy, celebrating the equinoxes and solstices.

SPECIAL PROPERTIES

Both colors bring peak experiences, moments of bliss, feeling totally at one with the universe.

MYTHOLOGY AND HISTORY

According to Hinduism, the Himalayas are the abode of Shiva and are personified as Himavat, god of the mountains and of snow. Red and Gold Himalayan Azeztulite carries the sacred powers of the mountains, giving direct connections to the divinity within us.

Red Aventurine

COLORS: Red or orangey-red (see also Peach Aventurine, page 339)

CRYSTAL TYPE: Microcrystalline quartz, containing inclusions of hematite, goethite, or iron mica to give it color and metallic, iridescent glint

ZODIAC SIGN: Aries (March 21–April 20)

CANDLE COLOR: Deep or bright red

PHYSICAL: Stabilizes cholesterol levels; alleviates eczema, dermatitis, rosacea, skin fungi, side effects of radiotherapy, low blood pressure, erratic pulse, irregular heartbeat, fibromyalgia, hernia pain, and issues involving the lower back and the urinary tract; speeds recovery from illness; promotes fertility.

EMOTIONAL: Awakens good humor, happiness, and optimism in pessimistic people; increases libido, sexual magnetism; restores fun to lovemaking.

HOME: Useful for fair distribution of chores; for happy family parties and social events where there may be challenges.

WORKPLACE: Fosters ambition without ruthlessness; aids in maintaining impetus and energy if you work long hours or shifts that cause irregular sleep patterns.

CHILDREN: Encourages play and study choices without stereotyping; for children who find having fun hard.

ANIMALS: Inspires overweight, lazy pets to enjoy exercise and be less greedy.

PROTECTION: Guards against theft, fire, storms (especially lightning storms), and traffic accidents.

MAGICKAL AND PSYCHIC USES

Fertility rituals; in red charm bags for urgent infusions of money or promotion with spices added to the bag.

SPECIAL PROPERTIES

For overcoming long-term weight problems or fluctuations to maintain a healthy weight; said to speed metabolism and burn fat.

MYTHOLOGY AND HISTORY

The talisman of the Mississippi paddleboat poker players; carried by some Native North Americans to survive long forced treks to reservations. One of the luckiest crystals when odds are against you winning or succeeding.

Red Beryl or Bixbite

COLORS: Red to pinkish- or raspberry-red, its color coming from trace amounts of manganese

CRYSTAL TYPE: Beryllium aluminum silicate; sometimes called the red emerald

ZODIAC SIGN: Aries (March 21–April 20)

CANDLE COLOR: Red

PHYSICAL: Alleviates issues involving the mouth, throat, thyroid, heart, liver, lungs, pancreas, stomach; addresses chronic illnesses, chilblains, and winter chills (especially in older people), Raynaud's disease; restores strength; promotes fertility.

EMOTIONAL: Enables you to love and trust again after heartache, heartbreak, or betrayal; rekindles sexual desire after a bad experience or abusive relationship; breaks a cycle of codependence.

HOME: Eases family coldness when there is disapproval of a partner; for welcoming a new stepparent into the family.

WORKPLACE: Strengthens family businesses or small companies that specialize in personalized service.

CHILDREN: Fosters amicable custody arrangements after divorce.

ANIMALS: For breeding high-strung or pedigreed animals.

PROTECTION: Guards against psychic and psychological vampires and all who manipulate or deceive through charm and persuasion; an antiscam gem.

MAGICKAL AND PSYCHIC USES

Rituals for calling a known or an as-yet-unknown soul twin; for sex rites; candle magick; attracting fire spirits.

SPECIAL PROPERTIES

For lasting love and to maintain a relationship through bad times or after infidelity, choose Red Beryl as a betrothal ring for a subsequent marriage or love in later years.

MYTHOLOGY AND HISTORY

Rarest of all beryls, gem-quality Bixbite is found only in the Ruby Violet Mine in the WahWah mountains of Utah. However, non-gem-quality has the same healing and magickal properties.

Red Bushman Quartz or Bushman Red Cascading Quartz

COLORS: White with red/orange or orange/brown coating

CRYSTAL TYPE: Quartz with a coating of tiny limonite or hematite crystals, often cascading downward, making the crystal dual-colored top and bottom

ZODIAC SIGN: Aries (March 21–April 20)

CANDLE COLOR: Red

PHYSICAL: Strengthens blood vessels, blood circulation, muscles; counters anemia; promotes fertility; curbs impotence; mitigates physical growth problems.

EMOTIONAL: Alleviates lethargy; enables you to accept help that requires personal effort; keeps you from lapsing back into addictions.

HOME: Helps if you feel unsettled in a new home or area.

WORKPLACE: Fosters creative solutions; for teachers to inspire students who can't see the point in study.

CHILDREN: Sends strength to children who have a life-threatening illness or a degenerative condition.

ANIMALS: For mountain rescue dogs.

PROTECTION: Offers a shield against aggression, intimidation, and violence.

MAGICKAL AND PSYCHIC USES

Linked with the Virgin Mary; a repository of the ancient wisdom of all people in all times through its roots back to the Indigenous South African San people.

SPECIAL PROPERTIES

For successful legal outcomes through diligent research, especially combined with smoky quartz.

MYTHOLOGY AND HISTORY

Bushman Quartz is also found in its cascading non-red form as milky or less frequently clear quartz. Like Tsesit or Tsesite (page 485) it is associated with the San people, who are believed to date back sixty thousand years, famed for their prolific rock art. Bushman Quartz is found in what is now Namibia. The first Dutch settlers in 1652 called the San people Bushmen or *Boschjesmans*.

Red Chalcedony

COLORS: A variety of reds from more subdued to a brilliant red

CRYSTAL TYPE: Fine-grained form of quartz, milky and translucent, often found as a geode or tumbled stone (see also the mineralogically harder, larger-grained semiprecious Carnelian, page 105, also a chalcedony)

ZODIAC SIGN: Aries (March 21–April 20)

CANDLE COLOR: Red

PHYSICAL: Strengthens blood circulation, blood clotting, blood pressure; eases blood flow through veins and arteries; alleviates anemia and Raynaud's disease; promotes fertility if ovulation is irregular or after an ectopic pregnancy.

EMOTIONAL: Curbs addictions linked with physical gratification; counters an unwillingness to persist if small obstacles or setbacks occur.

HOME: Fills the home with color, laughter, and fun to generate abundance and attract good fortune; teaches a new, emotionally inhibited partner to express warmth, generosity, and to share.

WORKPLACE: Aids in going it alone to develop a business or bring to fruition a creative dream; helps you recognize the right time is to speak and act and the right time to wait or remain silent if colleagues are volatile or perpetually irritable or there is a manager whose moods change by the hour.

CHILDREN: Comforts children who are afraid of the dark.

ANIMALS: Calms overly excitable pets who bark incessantly at the least provocation.

PROTECTION: Guards against those who hoard resources and hold back affection as a weapon.

MAGICKAL AND PSYCHIC USES

Fire and candle rituals; genie wishes; fertility rites; sex magick; telepathy over distance; psychic defense against malevolent spirits.

SPECIAL PROPERTIES

For lawsuits where your reputation is at stake; if there is pressure for witnesses to change their statements or recant their testimony.

MYTHOLOGY AND HISTORY

A stone beloved in Native American giveaway ceremonies, where resources are ceremonially shared; represents giving freely without seeking reward but knowing under cosmic law that generosity will be returned threefold.

Red Coral

COLORS: Red, red-orange

CRYSTAL TYPE: Organic, branching calcareous skeletons of sea creatures (see also environmentally friendly Red Horn Coral, page 397)

ZODIAC SIGN: Aries (March 21–April 20)

CANDLE COLOR: Red

PHYSICAL: Addresses issues relating to infections, blood cells, bone marrow, blockages in circulation, impotence; promotes fertility, the health of a pregnant woman and her unborn child.

EMOTIONAL: Helps overcome compulsions and obsessions; curbs unwise passions; allays fear of taking chances on love after previous betrayals.

HOME: Attracts wealth and good fortune after a period of hardship or debt; restores warmth to family relationships.

WORKPLACE: Aids in determining your goals for the day ahead; staying or getting back on track if you encounter frequent interruptions.

CHILDREN: Prevents falls and accidents for toddlers learning to walk and on play equipment.

ANIMALS: Keeps cats safe if they're roaming away from home.

PROTECTION: Said to temporarily lose color if danger or a potentially harmful person is present, as a way to warn you.

MAGICKAL AND PSYCHIC USES

For psychic defense against black magick spells, curses, hexes, and ill-wishing.

SPECIAL PROPERTIES

Red Coral brings courage and confidence to firmly but coolly confront spiteful neighbors and local gossips; for women living in a community or working in a profession where women are not respected.

MYTHOLOGY AND HISTORY

Sacred to love goddesses in different ages and cultures, including Venus and Oshun, deity of the Yoruba people of southwestern Nigeria and in Santería and Candomblé called Orisha of the spring waters. The ancient Egyptians believed coral contained the blood of the deities and therefore was an amulet for the deceased on their journey to the afterlife.

Red Feldspar with Phenacite

COLORS: Red (feldspar) with clear white inclusions (phenacite); tiny mineral inclusions of hematite creating the red coloring

CRYSTAL TYPE: Silicate/aluminosilicate (feldspar) and beryllium silicate (phenacite)

ZODIAC SIGN: Aries (March 21–April 20)

CANDLE COLOR: Red

PHYSICAL: Repatterns the whole system, including the etheric spiritual body; eases neural pathways; addresses issues involving the head and neck, including the two hemispheres of the brain.

EMOTIONAL: Keeps you from blaming childhood experiences for present failures or inability to thrive in adulthood.

HOME: Deters unwanted and often uninvited visitors who outstay their welcome.

WORKPLACE: The stone of action, impetus, and incentive to inject new life, light, and enthusiasm into the workplace, whether you own a business or you're a team leader.

CHILDREN: Useful for those who try to shift blame for mistakes or bad behavior onto others and deny all responsibility for wrongdoing.

ANIMALS: For pets who never grow out of destructive habits.

PROTECTION: Guards against unwelcome entities called up in amateur unprotected séances and attempted spirit rescue.

MAGICKAL AND PSYCHIC USES

For prophetic dreams; fire and candle magick; exploring the red ray of wisdom ruled by Archangel Uriel; defensive magick.

SPECIAL PROPERTIES

A major life changer, demanding courage to take risks and promising infinite possibilities for those who do; not taking yourself too seriously spiritually but introducing fun and laughter when mistakes occur in coven rituals, psychic development, and healing groups.

MYTHOLOGY AND HISTORY

A stone found in Russia, Zimbabwe, the United States, and Brazil; a stone thought of as high-vibration, it brings spirituality to the everyday world; keeps you from being intimidated by ego-driven gurus and teachers who consider themselves way above their students.

Red Fox Agate or Crater Agate

COLORS: Filled with deep red, the exterior walls are smoky black or occasionally blue, with inclusions of fine red lines

CRYSTAL TYPE: Hollow geode filled with pillowy, bubbled, botryoidal hematite, contained within smoky agate/chalcedony walls

ZODIAC SIGN: Aries (March 21–April 20)

CANDLE COLOR: Red

PHYSICAL: Alleviates blood disorders, anemia, hemorrhages; aids in recovery from deep-seated organ or tissue surgery.

EMOTIONAL: Keeps you from hiding behind others if there is controversy, acting helpless to avoid carrying out difficult tasks.

HOME: Aids in repairing structural damage or weaknesses in your home; for creating a home from an industrial building or barn; protects the home from fire.

WORKPLACE: The warrior crystal for success if you suspect colleagues or management are secretly working against you; for protection against aggressive colleagues.

CHILDREN: Useful for those who are afraid to answer questions in class or volunteer for activities they would enjoy.

ANIMALS: For unpredictable pets who may suddenly snap, bite, or scratch.

PROTECTION: Guards against hidden enemies and behind-the-scenes machinations.

MAGICKAL AND PSYCHIC USES

Fertility rituals; empowers other crystals; fierce defensive magick; love rituals to attract someone who never notices you.

SPECIAL PROPERTIES

The outermost layer is UV-reactive, and, under fluorescent lighting, turns lime green; for discovering deep love and passion with someone you thought was just a friend.

MYTHOLOGY AND HISTORY

A rare agate geode from a remote area of Patagonia near petrified-wood fields. The name *Red Fox Agate* comes from the red-furred Patagonian fox, called the Culpeo fox. The alternative name, *Crater Agate*, refers to a nearby ancient volcano.

Red Horn Coral

COLORS: Red; also cream, tan, blue, black, and gray

CRYSTAL TYPE: Calcium carbonate; extinct rugose (wrinkled) corals, resembling the branches or roots of a tree or a stag's antler; the coral was replaced by minerals over millions of years; horn coral may have cup shapes at the top

ZODIAC SIGN: Scorpio (October 24–November 22)

CANDLE COLOR: Red

PHYSICAL: For girls approaching puberty, alleviates PMS, excessive menstruation, and endometriosis; promotes fertility; addresses osteoporosis, brittle bones, carpal tunnel syndrome.

EMOTIONAL: If your income has dried up, keeps you from giving up and expecting others to bail them out, rather than looking for a replacement income source; curbs a tendency to hoard beautiful artifacts "for company" and never using them.

HOME: Prompts gentle souls to muster the courage to be assertive with troublesome neighbors or family.

WORKPLACE: Attracts money from sources that seemed unprofitable; for business connected with water sports, clean-water projects, and the conservation of marine and freshwater life.

CHILDREN: Protective against falls, stumbles, and accidents if a child is naturally clumsy.

ANIMALS: Enables you to discover totem creatures, especially whales and dolphins.

PROTECTION: Guards against malevolent influences, earthly and paranormal; traditionally protective of brides, babies, and children.

MAGICKAL AND PSYCHIC USES

A shamanic good luck charm, sacred to the goddess; fertility rituals, sex magick to restore passion; learning traditional spirituality.

SPECIAL PROPERTIES

Sometimes called a dragon's tooth, where it is fang-shaped, gives courage to resist those who intimidate or threaten your livelihood, family, or home.

MYTHOLOGY AND HISTORY

Red Horn Coral can be found in Riley's Canyon in northeastern Utah. It is created when the coral has been replaced by red chalcedony and iron. The ancient Greeks believed red coral was formed from the severed head of Medusa, the sea monster who turned any who gazed on her to stone and so is fiercely protective.

Red Howlite

COLORS: From brick to cherry red to brighter red
CRYSTAL TYPE: Dyed white howlite, calcium borosilicate hydroxide
ZODIAC SIGN: Aries (March 21–April 20)
CANDLE COLOR: Red

PHYSICAL: Eases burns, scalds, severe skin inflammation and irritation; for medical tests, including CT, ultrasound, and MRI scans.
EMOTIONAL: Curbs extreme reactions of joy, anger, or sorrow, not merited by a situation; deflects resentment that has been simmering for years.
HOME: Guards against accidents (especially with fire, gas, or electricity), kitchen hazards, and falls.
WORKPLACE: For impartial negotiations, if there is a lot of emotion involved; for achieving business success through effort and single-mindedness, without undue pressure exerted by those with overly ambitious goals; for exposing dishonesty.
CHILDREN: Teaches children or teens anger-management strategies; reduces tensions during custody disputes.
ANIMALS: For show animals to follow instructions and ignore distractions.
PROTECTION: As a shield against angry spirits in the home and workplace; for hidden foes who take revenge by devious means.

MAGICKAL AND PSYCHIC USES
For safe fire magick if you are working with volatile people; psychic insulation if you are attempting unfamiliar reading techniques; for objectivity in tarot when reading for those you know.

SPECIAL PROPERTIES
Acts as a brake on overreaction, impulsive words or actions; for channeling feelings of injustice or resentment into a focused, calm response.

MYTHOLOGY AND HISTORY
Much less assertive than some red stones, such as Red Jasper (page 399), Red Howlite represents quiet determination and persistence to win without resorting to anger or threats.

Red Jade

COLORS: Medium red, bright to orangey-red
CRYSTAL TYPE: Jadeite, sodium aluminum silicate
ZODIAC SIGN: Aries (March 21–April 20)
CANDLE COLOR: Red

PHYSICAL: For major surgery, with potential heavy blood loss; addresses problems with stitches; stanches hemorrhaging before, during, or immediately after childbirth; prevents traffic accidents; alleviates menorrhagia (menstrual bleeding that lasts more than seven days).
EMOTIONAL: Counters misdirected or uncontrolled anger; curbs sex and pornography addictions.
HOME: Promotes the circulation of chi around a home where the atmosphere is stagnant; for neighbors who resist newcomers.
WORKPLACE: Aids in dealing with hidden prejudice and inequalities by those who reinterpret the rules to support their own bias; for women subtly passed over for promotion.
CHILDREN: Encourages timid children to try new experiences.
ANIMALS: Keeps pets from reacting badly to noise and sudden movement; for snappish, unpredictable animals.
PROTECTION: Guards against apparently helpless souls who seek sympathy while secretly causing trouble.

MAGICKAL AND PSYCHIC USES
Sex magick; ritual magick, fire rituals, and divination; prompts luck for games of chance.

SPECIAL PROPERTIES
The life-force and warrior crystal, especially good for empowering women; for studying and practicing martial arts.

MYTHOLOGY AND HISTORY
The stone of dragon firepower for wealth, health, longevity, and success. The most proactive and luckiest of the jades for stamina, passion for life and love; restores the will to powerfully start over again after financial loss or ruin.

Red Jasper

COLORS: Bright red to reddish-brown, sometimes with black lines (see also Brecciated and Poppy Jasper, pages 92 and 366)
CRYSTAL TYPE: Chalcedony, microcrystalline quartz; red due to high iron content
ZODIAC SIGN: Aries (March 21–April 20)
CANDLE COLOR: Red

PHYSICAL: Promotes strength, fitness, fertility and successful fertility treatments, circulation, healthy menstruation, easy childbirth; alleviates arthritis, cold weather ills, anemia, rheumatism, heart issues.
EMOTIONAL: Gives courage to resist domestic abuse; aids in coping with illnesses with an uncertain outcome.
HOME: Protects against aggressive neighbors or living in a dangerous neighborhood.
WORKPLACE: Boosts recognition in the performing arts; for drama, dance, and art therapists.
CHILDREN: For successful single parenting; shields children from schoolyard bullies.
ANIMALS: Encourages timid animals to defend themselves; for endangered fierce creatures.
PROTECTION: Returns negativity to the source; protects against physical and psychic attack, traffic accidents, and aggressive drivers.

MAGICKAL AND PSYCHIC USES
Connects with Earth spirits, Earth energies, ley lines, and sacred sites; sex magick; a charm for good fortune.
SPECIAL PROPERTIES
Increases passion in love; boosts stamina when competing in endurance sports, such as marathons.
MYTHOLOGY AND HISTORY
According to Norse and Anglo-Saxon myth, the hilt of the magickal sword of Siegfried the dragon slayer was inlaid with Red Jasper. Among some Native North American nations, Red Jasper is called the blood of the Earth mother; in ancient Egypt, the stone was linked with the fertilizing blood of Mother Isis, the first single-parent deity; Mark Anthony supposedly used a Red Jasper seal ring for marking letters to Cleopatra.

Red Malachite

COLORS: Creamy red or terra-cotta, with Malachite-like patterns; may contain brown, orange, and fawn; often sold as tumbled stones
CRYSTAL TYPE: Banded jasper, silicon dioxide, chalcedony quartz
ZODIAC SIGN: Aries (March 21–April 20)
CANDLE COLOR: Red

PHYSICAL: Alleviates blood disorders, overly rapid heartbeat and pulse, issues with circulation, legs, and feet (especially vein blockages or varicose veins); promotes optic nerve health; addresses cataracts.
EMOTIONAL: Keeps you from unwise obsessions in love, repeating the same mistakes and blaming others for your misfortune.
HOME: As a grid layout, either indoors or out, Red Malachite crystals create a protective boundary if you live in an area where there are many break-ins or you have hostile neighbors.
WORKPLACE: For exuding calm authority when others are panicking or having a meltdown; taking a courageous step in financing a new venture or refinancing an ailing business.
CHILDREN: Name a Red Malachite stone for each child; carry them with you to send protection to your children while they are away.
ANIMALS: According to an ancient Russian superstition, whoever drinks from a malachite goblet will have the power to understand the language of animals; in modern terms, Red Malachite, like green malachite, increases telepathy with pets.
PROTECTION: Guards against the evil eye of jealousy.

MAGICKAL AND PSYCHIC USES
Called the firestone in some traditions; for urgent money spells; creates aura boundaries to keep away all who would disrupt or destabilize your life; for cleansing and empowering sacred places; a Joan of Arc symbol, especially for female power rituals to resist bullying or abuse.
SPECIAL PROPERTIES
Like green malachite, Red Malachite amplifies an instinctive sense of potential danger and unreliable people.
MYTHOLOGY AND HISTORY
A gateway crystal, used in the construction of Aztec temple gateways and, it has been conjectured, in Atlantis; opens pathways and opportunities to new beginnings and spiritually enables moving to higher levels of awareness.

Red Mica Quartz

COLORS: Clear with a rose-red or pink-red sheen as a coating on the quartz crystal or as inclusions; the color depends on the proportion of red mica to quartz

CRYSTAL TYPE: Quartz silicon dioxide (quartz), mica (phyllosilicates)

ZODIAC SIGN: Aries (March 21–April 20)

CANDLE COLOR: Red

PHYSICAL: Promotes healthy weight level and maintenance, reducing cravings for unhealthy foods; boosts low levels of vital minerals and vitamins; addresses anemia.

EMOTIONAL: Curbs ineffective anger about petty or irrelevant causes; keeps you from being overly defensive and picking needless fights.

HOME: Insulates you against excessive energy from cell phone towers, power lines, electrical appliances, and devices.

WORKPLACE: For a thorough workplace shakeup if you have shielded others from the consequences of their indifference and kept the workplace running single-handedly for too long.

CHILDREN: Helps children develop a sense of humor if they find jokes and pranks upsetting and confusing.

ANIMALS: Encourages older pets to tolerate younger ones.

PROTECTION: Guards against those who use anger and shouting others down to get their own way.

MAGICKAL AND PSYCHIC USES

Fire magick; creating crystal boundaries against noisy or hostile neighbors along adjoining walls or fences; defensive magick; reducing psychic visibility in potentially dangerous situations.

SPECIAL PROPERTIES

For crusades and campaigns to protect the vulnerable and oppressed; quartz brings the impetus to act, not just talk about what needs doing; red mica gives the confidence to initiate and lead practical, immediate relief efforts and fund-raising, involving high-profile feats of endurance and stamina.

MYTHOLOGY AND HISTORY

Red mica and quartz are a powerful combination of crystals for controlled, persistent assertiveness, focused power, and determination not to back down if a cause is just; brings or restores passion in love relationships; turns an all-consuming interest into a career for which your expertise and opinions break new ground.

Red Phantom Quartz

COLORS: Bright or orangey-red, often sparkling and coloring the whole inner crystal

CRYSTAL TYPE: Clear quartz in which the phantom is enclosed, containing limonite and hematite (both iron oxides) and sometimes kaolinite (see also Phantom Quartz, page 348)

ZODIAC SIGN: Aries (March 21–April 20)

CANDLE COLOR: Red

PHYSICAL: Alleviates chronic lack of energy, blood and circulation disorders, internal bleeding, stomach ulcers, viruses manifesting as rashes and fever, inflammation, hearing issues.

EMOTIONAL: Curbs repressed anger, a sense of powerlessness created by bullying or harsh criticism in childhood, especially in women; counters addictions, especially for cigarettes and food.

HOME: Aids in resisting and escaping from domestic abuse; keeps teens from physically attacking and verbally abusing their parents.

WORKPLACE: Brings confidence in a first job, internship, or apprenticeship or when returning after a career break, sabbatical, or leave of absence.

CHILDREN: For those not reaching their potential; guards against bullies and being overlooked in the educational system.

ANIMALS: Enables guard dogs to show gentleness with owners.

PROTECTION: Shields you from fears or threats of violence and intimidation; provides safety for those in the military or security services.

MAGICKAL AND PSYCHIC USES

Past-world healing, especially of injustice, bloodshed, or life cut short in battle; removes negative spirits who seek to attach to the aura.

SPECIAL PROPERTIES

Increases passion in love, for a talent, or for a good cause.

MYTHOLOGY AND HISTORY

A double-energy crystal, linking the higher self and realms with the grounded, thrusting, upward energy from the Earth. Red Phantom Quartz is created when an iron oxide mineral coats a quartz crystal point during formation.

Red Pietersite

COLORS: Red, red-gold, brownish-red, rust, golden yellow; swirling bands; gleaming

CRYSTAL TYPE: Microcrystalline silicon dioxide; contains more golden or Red Tiger's Eye or Ox Eye (see page 403) than the blue-gold version of Pietersite, which consists of proportionally more blue hawk eye

ZODIAC SIGN: Aries (March 21–April 20)

CANDLE COLOR: Red

PHYSICAL: Alleviates anemia, sexual dysfunction in men; regulates blood pressure; increases strength, vitality; bolsters eyesight, night vision; boosts libido in both sexes.

EMOTIONAL: For midlife crises in both sexes; for men with uncontrolled anger issues (often worn as male jewelry as a counterbalance).

HOME: Brings stability to the home if there are underlying tensions or simmering resentments; aids in standing up to a domestic bully.

WORKPLACE: Counters inequality in the workplace—open and more subtle—including sexism, ageism, homophobia, or racism.

CHILDREN: Teaches young children right from wrong.

ANIMALS: Offers extra care and protection around aggressive neighborhood animals.

PROTECTION: Guards against physical and psychic attack; surrounds the user and loved ones with the fierce protection of the Archangels of Mars.

MAGICKAL AND PSYCHIC USES

Money spells; fire rituals; candle magick, psychic defense; sex rites.

SPECIAL PROPERTIES

It may be possible to obtain red, gold, and blue in the same crystal; combining the qualities of the blue, said to hold the keys to the kingdom, both in terms of material success and spiritually, with the dynamism of red to overcome all obstacles.

MYTHOLOGY AND HISTORY

Where the blue gold version is called storm or tempest stone, this even more powerful red version is often referred to as the chaos stone; enables dramatic positive changes, often involving a step into the unknown. Found only in Namibia in Africa and Henan Province in China.

Red Rutilated Quartz

COLORS: Clear with red rutiles or needles inside that, if sufficiently numerous, will color the quartz red

CRYSTAL TYPE: Quartz with rutiles of titanium dioxide; the high quantity of iron oxide makes the rutiles red

ZODIAC SIGN: Aries (March 21–April 20)

CANDLE COLOR: Red

PHYSICAL: Promotes fertility; alleviates endometriosis, impotence, premature ejaculation; regulates the blood cell count; eases blood flow through the veins and arteries; addresses issues involving the heart, including heart-valve stenosis.

EMOTIONAL: Allays excessive fears of danger, especially fears of fire or enclosed spaces; eases flight-or-fight response to any crisis.

HOME: Protects against fire and accidents, particularly in the kitchen or during renovations.

WORKPLACE: For physically arduous and hazardous work connected with fuel, rescue services, and long-distance and endurance sports.

CHILDREN: Counters bullies when a school refuses to take complaints seriously.

ANIMALS: Comforts a new pet if a dog or cat attacks them, and resolves the confrontation.

PROTECTION: Guards against dangers of physical attack while traveling or in crowded public places.

MAGICKAL AND PSYCHIC USES

Fire magick, sacred sex rituals; shamanic healing and soul retrieval; for opening psychic channels.

SPECIAL PROPERTIES

For optimism, courage, and confidence to face any confrontation or conflict head-on without aggression; standing up for principles and justice.

MYTHOLOGY AND HISTORY

The combination of proactive quartz and piercing red rutiles creates a power greater than the separate crystals to break through barriers and remove limits to ambitions; associated with warrior gods and goddesses, including the Norse Freyr, the nature god who brought back the sun at midwinter and red-haired Freyja, whose battle maidens chose the worthy from the battlefield to live in her heavenly halls.

Red Snowflake Obsidian

COLORS: Red, black, and white snowflake patterns; may have red circles mixing with the white; shiny when tumbled

CRYSTAL TYPE: Volcanic glass with impurities mingling with the colors

ZODIAC SIGN: Aries (March 21–April 20)

CANDLE COLOR: Silver

PHYSICAL: Promotes regrowth of healthy blood cells after blood issues, recovery from a stroke; creates new neural pathways after a stroke; eases stiffening of limbs and joints; addresses issues with the spleen.

EMOTIONAL: Enables you to stick to rehabilitation programs; addresses domestic abuse (whether the abuser or abused), unacknowledged childhood incest.

HOME: For tough love when one family member's addiction or undesirable friends are affecting home life.

WORKPLACE: Helps when you are left to deal with a business failure; for reliable debt management if you have fallen prey to loan sharks.

CHILDREN: Offers a fresh start for children excluded from school.

ANIMALS: For dogs who resist training.

PROTECTION: Absorbs energies that may harm the physical body.

MAGICKAL AND PSYCHIC USES

For fierce defensive magick; fire rituals; channeling kundalini Earth energy for major transformations and healing.

SPECIAL PROPERTIES

The snowflake aspect introduces kindness, altruism, recognition of the needs of others, and similarities rather than differences in different cultures and faiths; for all involved in humanitarian causes.

MYTHOLOGY AND HISTORY

A powerful alchemical stone that combines the fierce protection of black obsidian with the creative regeneration of red obsidian and the gently optimistic snowflake; disperses anger and brings new beginnings; the combined energies create a dynamism greater than and different from the separate components.

Red Spinel

COLOR: Rich red; sparkling

CRYSTAL TYPE: Magnesium aluminum oxide; choose natural rather than artificial spinel

ZODIAC SIGN: Leo (July 23–August 23)

CANDLE COLOR: Bright red

PHYSICAL: Alleviates debilitating conditions, pain, mobility issues, impotence, and vaginismus; addresses concern involving the blood; promotes self-healing; boosts libido.

EMOTIONAL: Counteracts people who disregard your opinions; aids in moving from the shadow of a dominant family; curbs panic attacks; valuable when sex is used for control.

HOME: Protects against domestic fires and accidents; for women who choose to become pregnant without a permanent partner.

WORKPLACE: Attracts support from those able to propel career advancement; boosts your profile at among hiring professionals and at job interviews; for those working with fire, such as chefs, rescue workers, or those in physically hazardous jobs.

CHILDREN: For single-parent and LGBTQ+ families.

ANIMALS: Helps breed valuable but reluctant animals.

PROTECTION: Repels negative influences; protective against physical attack and wartime action, particularly among women in combat.

MAGICKAL AND PSYCHIC USES

Red candle spells to increase courage and prosperity; sex magick; working with fire elementals.

SPECIAL PROPERTIES

For love under difficulties because of commitments, such as a preexisting relationship; stepchildren; family, religious, or community opposition; or a long-distance relationship.

MYTHOLOGY AND HISTORY

Red Spinel is often mistaken for ruby. The Black Prince's Ruby in the British imperial state crown is Red Spinel. Henry V wore it on his helmet at Agincourt (the helmet saved his life from an axe blow); persistence without aggression in combating unfair divorce settlements, engaging in custody battles, or fighting unjust dismissal.

Red Tiger's Eye or Ox Eye

COLOR: Gleaming red, with dark to light banding

CRYSTAL TYPE: Oxide, quartz, chatoyant, reflecting iridescent light from its banded surface

ZODIAC SIGN: Aries (March 21–April 20)

CANDLE COLOR: Deep red

PHYSICAL: Alleviates issues stemming from anemia, sexual dysfunction and potency in men, menstruation; addresses eyesight, night vision; promotes strength, vitality, libido in both sexes; aids in recovery after major surgery.

EMOTIONAL: Eases psychosomatic conditions, depression, anger-management issues (especially in men); helps those surviving domestic abuse.

HOME: Guards against intruders and threats from ex-partners, debt collectors, and law enforcement officers.

WORKPLACE: Fends off inappropriate sexual remarks or conduct; for hospital workers, surgeons, metalworkers, security and armed forces personnel, long-distance drivers.

CHILDREN: Shields teens against drug abuse; deters schoolyard bullying and social media trolling; curbs toddler and teen tantrums.

ANIMALS: Protects cats from cat haters.

PROTECTION: Repels the evil eye of envy; guards against attack and accidents during nighttime traveling.

MAGICKAL AND PSYCHIC USES

A charm for money, good luck, and power; fire rituals and scrying, tantra, sex magick.

SPECIAL PROPERTIES

For women fighting sexism or trying to break into a male-dominated profession; for turning a passionate interest into a career.

MYTHOLOGY AND HISTORY

Red Tiger's Eye traditionally gives the wearer courage and invulnerability. It is associated with fire deities, such as Hephaestus, Greek god of fire and metalwork, and Agni, Hindu god of fire. Red Tiger's Eye occurs naturally when the golden-brown variety is exposed to heat by fire or lightning while in the Earth; most is artificially heat-treated, which does not affect healing or magickal qualities.

Redwood Opal

COLORS: Cream, tan, browns, and rust-colored swirls; beautiful as jewelry when polished or as tumbled stone talismans; not naturally iridescent

CRYSTAL TYPE: Opalized redwood, petrified wood from an ancient extinct redwood forest in Mexico; similar in color and banded formation to living redwood now found mainly in northern California

ZODIAC SIGN: Aries (March 21–April 20)

CANDLE COLOR: Red

PHYSICAL: Aids in recovery of physical strength after illness, surgery, or an accident; promotes long life; addresses growth issues in children, loss of libido, fertility if the passion has been replaced by ovulation charts.

EMOTIONAL: Helps overcome sexual frigidity in both sexes; allays concerns about rejection by friends, family, and community in a continuing search for the perfect family and life companion.

HOME: Creates a home in an imperfect environment; revives passion in a relationship if you work long hours, have small children, or your partner spends too much leisure time with friends.

WORKPLACE: Supports ambitious plans and aiming for the top; makes for successful networking.

CHILDREN: Helps children who are physically small to overcome feelings of inferiority.

ANIMALS: For small dogs with the heart of a lion.

PROTECTION: Guards against putting self-imposed limitations to change or leaving your comfort zone.

MAGICKAL AND PSYCHIC USES

Sex magick; tree rituals; connection with tree spirits and forest devas; druidry, Wicca, and all forms of natural magick.

SPECIAL PROPERTIES

The stone of breaking through obstacles that may have proven troublesome for years; grieving for whom or what is lost but moving slowly forward to the future.

MYTHOLOGY AND HISTORY

The Redwood Opal was first discovered in Mexico in 2011. Redwoods are the largest trees in the world, with interlinking supportive roots; Redwood Opal reflects the same sense of community and support for others, and offers great physical and emotional strength for group ventures.

Red Zircon

COLORS: Rich red, red-orange, red-violet, and darker red
CRYSTAL TYPE: Zirconium silicate
ZODIAC SIGN: Sagittarius (November 23–December 21)
CANDLE COLOR: Red

PHYSICAL: Protects against blood cell problems, blood clots, blood disorders, blocked circulation; for emergency operations, hemorrhages, hemophilia; addresses irregular or scant menstruation.
EMOTIONAL: Curbs inner turmoil that prevents relaxation and sleep; allays fear of blood, surgery, and injections; fends off the inability to deal with your own or others' anger.
HOME: Shields you from lightning strikes, fire, accidents in the kitchen involving sharp utensils; for a favorable response to planning applications.
WORKPLACE: For salespersons, telemarketing staff, performers, and broadcasters, press and publicity officers, spokespersons, speechwriters, or lecturers.
CHILDREN: Calms toddlers who panic or hold their breath when they become furious.
ANIMALS: For protecting children against fierce dogs encountered in the street or in neighboring gardens.
PROTECTION: Guards against evil spirits, nightmares, and enchantment by those who use mind manipulation to create an aura of irresistibility.

MAGICKAL AND PSYCHIC USES

For defensive magick; binding those who would harm you or loved ones; knot magick; fire rituals; sex magick.

SPECIAL PROPERTIES

Red Zircon is an antitheft crystal, when kept with precious possessions or jewelry; deters burglary, mugging.

MYTHOLOGY AND HISTORY

Red Zircon was traditionally called jacinth or hyacinth. In Greek mythology, the youth Hyacinthus was accidentally killed because of Apollo the sun god and Zephyrus the west wind's rivalry over his love. Apollo transformed the blood of the slain youth into the hyacinth flower, so Red Zircon represents needless jealousy. Red Zircon loses its sheen after you've been spending time with a particular person who is draining you.

Revelation Stone

COLORS: Red, yellow, brown, green, or black, or a mixture
CRYSTAL TYPE: Jasper, microcrystalline quartz
ZODIAC SIGN: Aquarius (January 21–February 18)
CANDLE COLOR: Purple

PHYSICAL: Counters memory loss with aging, Alzheimer's, amnesia due to a head accident; frees up blockages in brain and heart; promotes the discovery of new cures for seemingly untreatable conditions.
EMOTIONAL: Helps overcome false memory syndrome; allays irrational fears of the future and what is unknown.
HOME: Helpful when moving into or remaining in a dwelling owned by a recently deceased relative; for encouraging existing family to act respectfully toward any inheritance.
WORKPLACE: Useful for speculation, staying ahead of trends, making business decisions when all the facts are not yet known.
CHILDREN: When a beloved grandparent or great-grandparent passes on, aids children in connecting with the good memories and enduring love.
ANIMALS: Comforts a heartbroken pet whose owner has died.
PROTECTION: Guards against holding on to situations and relationships that have run their course.

MAGICKAL AND PSYCHIC USES

Enhances psychic abilities and the accuracy of divinatory readers, mediums, channelers, and healers; for personal contact with the deceased and family ancestors; for prophetic visions of future life patterns, rather than fixed events in the future or past lives; recalling early childhood and prebirth experiences; shamanic travel.

SPECIAL PROPERTIES

Increases intuition by acting as a psychic radar to alert you to opportunities and hazards before they occur; instinctively knowing whom to trust.

MYTHOLOGY AND HISTORY

Found by the sea, in mountains, and inland in New Zealand, Revelation Stone is named after the Book of Revelations where it was foretold that jasper would form the walls of the New Jerusalem; combines functioning effectively in the world without fear while seeking this life's higher purpose.

Reverse Orange Phantom Quartz

COLORS: Orange and white

CRYSTAL TYPE: Crystal quartz fused with carnelian; quartz and carnelian form the outside of the crystal and the clear quartz can be seen inside

ZODIAC SIGN: Aries (March 21–April 20)

CANDLE COLOR: Orange

PHYSICAL: Alleviates blood disorders, heart blockages in valves or arteries; promotes successful open-heart surgery and major surgical procedures involving heart-lung machines; salves deep wounds slow to heal; stanches internal bleeding; addresses autism, Asperger's.

EMOTIONAL: Counters repressed envy; curbs suppression of your identity in excessive nurturing of others; assists men dominated by their mothers.

HOME: Introduces spontaneity to an overly tidy home and strict routine.

WORKPLACE: Aids in leaving a safe job to pursue a dream.

CHILDREN: Brings out talents and potential if a child's future is planned from an early age.

ANIMALS: For search-and-rescue dogs.

PROTECTION: Guards against stifling ingenuity and adventure for the sake of a peaceful life, resisting financial incentives by relatives to sacrifice your independence.

MAGICKAL AND PSYCHIC USES

Medical intuitive clairvoyance; clairaudience as a strong inner voice; trance meditation.

SPECIAL PROPERTIES

For fertility issues, where a couple is older or there have been failed IVF attempts or unsuccessful medical intervention.

MYTHOLOGY AND HISTORY

Reverse Phantoms are quite rare. Together with Reverse Orange Phantom Quartz from Colorado and Arkansas, you may find a snowy Reverse Phantom with a layer of milky quartz coating, a clear crystal quartz inner point, and a thin layer of clear quartz sealing it. This contains the dynamic, anything-is-possible energies ready to be released, bringing out talents in a way that will benefit yourself, your loved ones, and humanity, and combine freedom with sharing.

Rhodazez or Pink Azeztulite

COLORS: Salmon pink to tan, orangey-pink, vibrant

CRYSTAL TYPE: Combining the elements of rhodochrosite and azeztulite

ZODIAC SIGN: Taurus (April 21–May 21).

CANDLE COLOR: Pink

PHYSICAL: Alleviates heart problems (especially after the loss of a partner or child), asthma; makes for successful conception after an ectopic pregnancy or where ova release is irregular; for conception with IVF.

EMOTIONAL: Keeps you from clinging to beliefs instilled in childhood about being unworthy of love, less attractive, or less smart than siblings.

HOME: Attracts benign protective and luck-bringing spirits, house and land guardians, and loving deceased relatives.

WORKPLACE: For all in the caring professions to keep from being overwhelmed by others' problems; enables those in crime detection or those dealing daily with suffering and death not to become desensitized.

CHILDREN: Connects with their guardian angels; for seeing or sensing the presence of a deceased relative without fear.

ANIMALS: For pets who know precisely when an owner is coming home; helps anticipate and warn of danger to pets.

PROTECTION: Guards against those who seek to manipulate.

MAGICKAL AND PSYCHIC USES

For soul retrieval; connection between healer and client; for powerful divinatory readings for others by linking heart to heart.

SPECIAL PROPERTIES

For reconciliation where quarrels were caused by divided loyalties; unites a couple against those who would come between them.

MYTHOLOGY AND HISTORY

Pink Azeztulite connects with the wisdom of the ancient Azez Star Beings; offers teaching from the Azez healers and fills the body with light to bring serenity and compassion.

Rhodizite

COLORS: Yellow, grayish, greenish, white, colorless, frequently in a matrix, occasionally rose pink
CRYSTAL TYPE: Beryllium aluminum borate, tiny twelve-faced crystals with glassy luster; often used in threes or sevens
ZODIAC SIGN: Leo (July 23–August 23)
CANDLE COLOR: Yellow

PHYSICAL: Clears blockages, cells, neural pathways; alleviates headaches, effects of strokes; aids with end-of-life care.
EMOTIONAL: Keeps you from overidealizing your parents in adult life; curbs a tendency to reject partners who do not meet your ideals; allays fears of mortality.
HOME: Attracts what is most needed; restores connection with estranged family members.
WORKPLACE: Boosts confidence to advance career; helps ace interviews after a period of unemployment or facing fierce competition.
CHILDREN: Promotes the safe return of a child taken overseas or out of state by a noncustodial parent without permission.
ANIMALS: Aids in finding the right pet, where and when that's least expected.
PROTECTION: Places a dual-purpose defense and empowering aura of gold around individuals; cuts intrusive psychic cords.

MAGICKAL AND PSYCHIC USES
Astral travel; finding crop circles; a Master Crystal (page 297), cleansing and empowering other crystals; for medical intuitive abilities, clairaudience, telepathy, clairvoyance, remote viewing, visions of other realms, trance meditation.
SPECIAL PROPERTIES
Even the smallest crystal radiates high spiritual vibrations; transmits the power of the sun as a source of healing energy.
MYTHOLOGY AND HISTORY
Rhodizite was discovered by Gustav Rose, a father of mineralogy in 1834 in the Russian Ural Mountains; named after *rhodizein*, Greek for "rose-colored," because it colors the flame of a blowpipe red; traditionally associated with cloudbursts, bringing rain.

Rhodochrosite

COLORS: Rose pink with white or paler pink banding; may vary from lighter pink to almost red
CRYSTAL TYPE: Manganese carbonate
ZODIAC SIGN: Sagittarius (November 23–December 21)
CANDLE COLOR: Bright pink

PHYSICAL: Promotes healthy circulation, heart, blood pressure; alleviates asthma, stress-related migraines; enables successful IVF and artificial insemination; restores fertility cycles after prolonged use of artificial contraception; counters anorexia, bulimia, and feast-famine weight control.
EMOTIONAL: Helps overcome love betrayal; moderates unreasonable jealousy or possessiveness; assists the expression of love toward others without fear of rejection.
HOME: Makes new family members and neighbors feel welcome; revives family traditions, including celebrating the lives of ancestors.
WORKPLACE: Establishes friendly professional interactions in an emotionally or sexually charged atmosphere.
CHILDREN: Encourages youngster to make friends when starting kindergarten, a new school, or college; for foster and adoptive children, and challenging stepchildren.
ANIMALS: For successfully mating animals.
PROTECTION: Guards against love rivals and those who seek to cause division, whether family members, ex-partners, or community.

MAGICKAL AND PSYCHIC USES
Enhances Reiki and other energy-balancing modalities; rituals for soul-twin love; a charm for living together; sex magick; making love potions.
SPECIAL PROPERTIES
Rhodochrosite increases telepathic links between you, your family, and animals; helps new mothers to trust their maternal instincts; calls back lost love, an estranged family member, or a missing pet.
MYTHOLOGY AND HISTORY
Rhodochrosite is called the Inca rose because Native Americans who lived in the Andes believe the crystal contained the blood of ancestral great rulers; a power stone for asserting personal needs and desires for those who always put others first.

Rhodolite

COLORS: Rose-colored form of garnet, lighter and with more purple than other garnets; sparkling

CRYSTAL TYPE: Magnesium aluminum silicate with manganese, chromium, and iron silicate

ZODIAC SIGN: Taurus (April 21–May 21)

CANDLE COLOR: Dark pink

PHYSICAL: Alleviates erectile problems; for young men experiencing their first sexual encounter; for menopausal women to explore their sexual freedom; addresses issues involving the breasts and prostate.

EMOTIONAL: Curbs a tendency to try to keep natural aging at bay through excessive cosmetic surgery, Botox, and crash diets; counters the effects of sexual abuse, body shaming.

HOME: Fosters peace when a new partner to parent or adult child is breaking into an existing, tightly knit, parent/child bond.

WORKPLACE: Helps you resolve crises not of your making without diminishing others' self-esteem.

CHILDREN: Aids in learning to share love if sibling rivalry is strong or one divorced parent competes for a child's affection through bribery.

ANIMALS: For a long-established pet to overcome jealousy of a new partner or baby sharing the bed.

PROTECTION: Guards against you or a partner being tempted to be unfaithful with someone intent on splitting you up; a shield against harm.

MAGICKAL AND PSYCHIC USES

For love spells and sex magick; manifesting your wishes in the way most desired; healing.

SPECIAL PROPERTIES

For a newly married older couple to rediscover passion after years of celibacy; removes inhibitions about revealing your body.

MYTHOLOGY AND HISTORY

The name *Rhodolite* comes from the Greek word *rhodizein*, meaning "rose-colored"; Rhodolite, like the rose, symbolizes all kinds of love: *eros*, passion; *philos*, love for family and friends; and *agape*, love of all humanity.

Rhodonite

COLORS: Pink, rose, or salmon pink, with black patches and veins (manganese oxide); occasionally red or red-brown

CRYSTAL TYPE: Manganese silicate; may contain significant amounts of iron, magnesium, and calcium

ZODIAC SIGN: Aries (March 21–April 20)

CANDLE COLOR: Pink

PHYSICAL: Alleviates stings, allergic reactions, wounds, scar tissue, birthmarks, ulcers, autoimmune conditions, emphysema, chronic lung problems, issues relating to the heart; war-related and land-mine injuries.

EMOTIONAL: Restores equilibrium after an abusive relationship; keeps you from pursuing an unrequited love.

HOME: Heals family bitterness, resentment; aids in accepting that a long-standing family rift cannot be mended.

WORKPLACE: For maintaining self-esteem when colleagues or employers undermine you; for peacekeepers, armed forces personnel, and aid workers in war zones, plus musicians, singers, service industry personnel; harmonizes sleep rhythms if you're working shifts.

CHILDREN: Useful for those with anger issues; keeps youngsters safe from predators while online; enables children with Down syndrome or cerebral palsy to maximize their potential.

ANIMALS: For inseparable pets; making lizards, snakes, and other cold-blooded creatures more responsive.

PROTECTION: Guards against stalkers and overly persistent suitors.

MAGICKAL AND PSYCHIC USES

Feng shui balancing of yin and yang energies in the home and workplace; becoming aware of potential fraud and unreliable people.

SPECIAL PROPERTIES

Finding the right lasting love; ending unsatisfactory relationships peacefully and going on to other love.

MYTHOLOGY AND HISTORY

The fire of Rhodonite is tempered by loving Venus and stabilizing Earth, reducing the power of possessive or controlling love and codependency. For this reason, it is often called the burning rose (*rhodon* is Greek for "rose").

Rhyolite

COLORS: Greens, browns, gray, tan, pink, speckled, patchy, or with web-like markings; also plain or banded

CRYSTAL TYPE: Igneous rock containing feldspar and quartz, formed by molten magma from volcanic eruption (see also Rainforest, Leopardskin, and Orbicular Jaspers (page 390, 276, and 331)

ZODIAC SIGN: Gemini (May 22–June 21)

CANDLE COLOR: Green

PHYSICAL: Boosts stamina; alleviates infections, colds, flu, skin allergies; strengthens arteries; promotes absorption of B vitamins.

EMOTIONAL: Salves your heart after emotional breakdown or burnout; counters rejection, whether because of workplace ageism or being replaced by a younger lover.

HOME: Encourages the family to live a healthier lifestyle and take up outdoor activities together.

WORKPLACE: Helps if business is slow or business plans are not materializing; for permanent or full-time employment; turning unsought change to your advantage.

CHILDREN: Strengthens bonds with animals.

ANIMALS: Increases telepathy with cats; conserves habitats of wild cats.

PROTECTION: Guards against constantly reliving the past and worrying about the future.

MAGICKAL AND PSYCHIC USES

Drawing strength from spirit totem creatures; working with elementals; meditating on surface crystal pathways to reach other lands and dimensions.

SPECIAL PROPERTIES

Inspires older people to develop creativity, travel, or study, especially after retirement; rekindles love after a breakup or later in life after losing touch.

MYTHOLOGY AND HISTORY

Rhyolite is said to contain hidden treasure, as it can form the outer casing of Oregon blue opal, representing talents becoming moneymakers or second careers; encourages the realization of long-held dreams.

Richterite

COLORS: Brown, red, pinkish-red, yellow, gray-brown, pale to dark green, blue, bluish-gray

CRYSTAL TYPE: Complex sodium calcium magnesium silicate with iron; may also be found as gem-quality or tumbled stones

ZODIAC SIGN: Sagittarius (November 23–December 21)

CANDLE COLOR: Brown

PHYSICAL: Addresses issues involving the kidneys, kidney transplants, mineral balance, circulation, glands (particularly thyroid); alleviates glandular fever, pain.

EMOTIONAL: Counters PTSD; impulsive fight-or-flight reactions to crises; curbs an inability to consider alternatives beyond the chosen path.

HOME: Aids in knowing the right time to speak or act or when to remain silent during domestic disputes.

WORKPLACE: Defuses potential conflict among fellow workers or aimed at you; keeps everyone calm if there is uncertainty over takeovers or redundancies.

CHILDREN: Helps avoid self-defeating behavior caused by fear of failure.

ANIMALS: For taking as a pet one who has been retired from racing, was involved in intensive security force investigations, or overused for breeding.

PROTECTION: Guards against panicking in a crisis and making matters worse.

MAGICKAL AND PSYCHIC USES

Astral travel, accessing the Akashic records through deep meditation to discover the next optimal stages on your life path; for meaningful meditation if you have problems focusing or finding time and space to be undisturbed.

SPECIAL PROPERTIES

Increases status, recognition, and advancement socially and in your career; assists in moving love on to commitment if a lover is reticent.

MYTHOLOGY AND HISTORY

A stone of transformation, especially if it is yellow, though all colors of Richterite bring the power to listen to the wise inner self when doors appear to be closing or a conflict is becoming unbearable; by helping you step back, avoid taking sides, or keep from being pressure into making decisions before you are ready, Richterite offers the space to put yourself and your needs center stage.

Rose Aura Quartz

COLORS: Raspberry-pink, metallic sheen (see also Ruby Aura Quartz, often favored by older women, page 413)

CRYSTAL TYPE: Layers of platinum, plus sometimes silver and gold, fused to the surface of a quartz crystal

ZODIAC SIGN: Taurus (April 21–May 21)

CANDLE COLOR: Deep pink

PHYSICAL: Addresses heart issues, acute teenage illnesses, onset of puberty in girls, early menstrual difficulties, teenage pregnancy without a network of support, bacterial and fungal infections; alleviates issues stemming from the endocrine system, sciatica, frequent colds, lingering viruses, recurring childhood stomach bugs or head lice.

EMOTIONAL: Keeps younger women from being obsessed with dieting, exercise, and a perfect body image, because of media, or teasing about obesity.

HOME: Prevents outflowing money; for good health and good fortune; attracts what is lasting.

WORKPLACE: Helps writers of romantic fiction, plus those working with fragrances, beauty products, services, modeling, hairstyling, and fashion.

CHILDREN: For girls lacking maternal support to guide them into womanhood.

ANIMALS: Assists a young mother having a first litter.

PROTECTION: Shields against overspending.

MAGICKAL AND PSYCHIC USES

Love magick; binds emotional vampires and love rivals sending curses; cleanses inherited artifacts or jewelry with sad memories.

SPECIAL PROPERTIES

Transformation in love, bringing lasting faithful love, strengthening commitment, calling back lost love through telepathy between lovers; moving on from destructive love.

MYTHOLOGY AND HISTORY

Bonded or fused quartzes are created by a modern version of alchemy when quartz is heated to extremely high temperatures and the purified metal added in a vacuum, permanently fusing it to the surface of the quartz; aids with the continuance of the happiness of your wedding day, handfasting, and honeymoon.

Rose Quartz

COLORS: Clear to translucent pale to deep pink; ice-like chunks if unpolished

CRYSTAL TYPE: Quartz, silicon dioxide with manganese impurities

ZODIAC SIGN: Taurus (April 21–May 21)

CANDLE COLOR: Pale pink

PHYSICAL: Alleviates issues involving the heart, circulation, skin, hair, scars, puberty, menstruation, fertility, infants and children, breasts, hyperventilation, postnatal depression.

EMOTIONAL: Salves emotional wounds, grief, stress, abuse; helps overcome image problems linked to eating disorders among young women; addresses trust issues.

HOME: Brings peace; protects one family member from being unfairly blamed for family problems.

WORKPLACE: Shields against intrusion, gossip, factions, excessive competition; useful for those working in beauty, fashion, interior design, life coaching.

CHILDREN: Eases the transition from childhood to puberty; counters teasing over physical appearance.

ANIMALS: For pregnant and nursing mothers; reduces aggressiveness.

PROTECTION: Guards against nightmares and fear of the dark.

MAGICKAL AND PSYCHIC USES

Rituals for first or new love and reconciliation; fertility rites; a soul-twin charm; spells enhancing beauty and radiance; for world peace and abused women everywhere.

SPECIAL PROPERTIES

A mothering crystal, if you have lost your own mother or suffered inadequate mothering; women who fear labor or are having difficulty loving a new infant.

MYTHOLOGY AND HISTORY

Stone of beauty found as face masks in ancient Egyptian tombs. In Greek mythology, Adonis, Aphrodite's lover, was attacked by the jealous warrior god Ares, disguised as a boar. Aphrodite cut herself on a briar bush, trying to save Adonis, their mingling blood staining the white stones. Zeus restored Adonis to Aphrodite for half of each year, making Rose Quartz a symbol of reconciliation in love.

Rosette Chalcedony

COLORS: Colors vary, but often pale blue, gray-blue, blue and white, orange and pink

CRYSTAL TYPE: Cryptocrystalline quartz, distinguished by petals radiating outward from within the center of the chalcedony, resembling a rose; occasionally as in a new variety from India, small petals all over the outside; often drusy

ZODIAC SIGN: Libra (September 23–October 23)

CANDLE COLOR: Pale blue

PHYSICAL: Addresses growths, nevi, warts, verrucae, late-onset puberty in both sexes, loss of hair after chemotherapy or due to stress; promotes full-term healthy pregnancy and easy birth; for children with growth problems or who are slow to reach developmental milestones.

EMOTIONAL: Allays fears of sexuality; helps overcome an unwillingness to grow up and take responsibility at whatever age; keeps you from needing to win first prize in any competition.

HOME: Aids in becoming the hub of the community, school events, social arrangements, and family gatherings as your confidence grows.

WORKPLACE: Increases your reputation and authority, leading to enhanced pay, promotion, and leadership opportunities.

CHILDREN: Encourages children to grow plants and care for animals; calms those who are nervous competing, for fear of failure.

ANIMALS: For natural remedies if conventional medication is not effective.

PROTECTION: Guards against fears of saying or making the wrong moves.

MAGICKAL AND PSYCHIC USES

For flower magick, flower oils, perfume and flower essence magick; joining a psychic, magick, or healing group.

SPECIAL PROPERTIES

For major new beginnings, transitions, or stages in your life, from conceiving a child, starting new study options, career advancement.

MYTHOLOGY AND HISTORY

The more vibrant the color of your Rosette Chalcedony, the more confident you become in revealing your true self and speaking what you know to be the truth, but with kindness; brings unexpected success in competitions and games of chance.

Rosophia

COLORS: Salmon-pink to red-orange, containing white or black inclusions

CRYSTAL TYPE: A variety of azeztulite also called azezulite, containing feldspar, quartz, and particles of biotite

ZODIAC SIGN: Taurus (April 21–May 21)

CANDLE COLOR: Pink

PHYSICAL: Alleviates heart issues (especially irregularities made worse by stress), including heart failure, poor circulation; boosts the autoimmune system; promotes fertility, particularly in would-be older parents.

EMOTIONAL: Curbs a feeling of being unloved, as well as lack of self-esteem, heartache, and heartbreak.

HOME: Creates a sanctuary or ashram space in the noisiest home or shared apartment.

WORKPLACE: For long-term study, research, and writing books that inform and guide; for following the heart in a career that brings fulfillment and is for the good of humanity.

CHILDREN: Offers support to infants who are born wise and always remain the heart and peacemakers of the family.

ANIMALS: Valuable for pets who are old souls or familiars who have been with you in many lifetimes.

PROTECTION: Guards against reacting to triggers from childhood, present or past worlds, or those foretelling the inevitability of failure.

MAGICKAL AND PSYCHIC USES

Prayer, chanting, sacred dance; energy therapies using hands or crystals; assists with pyramid healing and meditation.

SPECIAL PROPERTIES

A heaven to Earth stone for connecting with Earth energies, ley lines, and the guardians of ancient sites; guides you to the right healing circle, faith, or philosophy. Unexpected proof that your intuitive powers are spontaneously growing.

MYTHOLOGY AND HISTORY

Rosophia, or the Rose of Sophia, is the name given to this gemstone, discovered as recently as the early 2000s in New Mexico and the Rocky Mountains of Colorado. Sophia was the ancient Greek goddess of wisdom, associated in modern spirituality with the Divine Feminine.

Royal Plume or Purple Jasper

COLORS: Shades of purple with plume-like markings

CRYSTAL TYPE: Silicate, microcrystalline quartz, often with organic matter or other minerals as inclusions

ZODIAC SIGNS: Scorpio (October 24–November 22) and Sagittarius (November 23–December 21).

CANDLE COLOR: Purple

PHYSICAL: Alleviates migraines, sinus issues, epilepsy, Parkinson's disease, memory loss (particularly in aging), visual disturbances, concerns with the pituitary gland and the central nervous system, type 2 diabetes, rheumatism.

EMOTIONAL: Prevents indecision and confusion in making proper choices; for personality disorders and emotional vulnerability.

HOME: For single-parent households, where a noncustodial parent undermines authority.

WORKPLACE: Aids in deputizing in a senior position if there is resentment, team building; for interviewers, recruitment officers, and others who evaluate workplace performance.

CHILDREN: Useful for free spirits struggling with school rules.

ANIMALS: For pets bullied by those higher in the pecking order.

PROTECTION: If you're working overseas in a country with a repressive regime, guards against those who conceal incompetence behind rank or seniority.

MAGICKAL AND PSYCHIC USES

Connecting with archangels, ascended masters, and saints; studying formal spirituality, such as druidry, Wicca or Ástarú; mediumship or ancient healing training.

SPECIAL PROPERTIES

A stone of leadership, uniting others for a common purpose.

MYTHOLOGY AND HISTORY

A stone traditionally associated with wise power and authority; for all striving to reach the top in a discriminatory environment against unfair odds; those en route from rags to riches, obscurity to fame; facing down bullies and those who judge others by class, gender, or wealth.

Rubellite in Lepidolite

COLORS: Red and lilac-gray, rose and purple, mixed

CRYSTAL TYPE: Rubellite, also called red tourmaline, is lithium-rich crystalline silicate; lepidolite, a type of mica, contains varying amounts of lithium

ZODIAC SIGN: Libra (September 23–October 23)

CANDLE COLOR: Deep pink

PHYSICAL: Eases heart attacks and artery blockages; alleviates issues stemming from the spleen, liver, pancreas, reproductive system in both sexes, stress-related illnesses, HIV, epilepsy, Alzheimer's, sciatica; boosts libido.

EMOTIONAL: Curbs mood swings, bipolar condition, lack of trust and openness with others; keeps you from constantly needing proof of love and fidelity.

HOME: Creates a welcoming atmosphere; softens the tongues of abrasive neighbors or relatives.

WORKPLACE: Creates a calm environment where you can concentrate; brings inspiration and creativity to a less than ideal workplace where management skills are lacking.

CHILDREN: Reassures children who are overwhelmed by noisy classrooms and playgrounds.

ANIMALS: Offers a quiet place for older animals away from the rough and tumble of family life.

PROTECTION: Guards against harmful rays from computers, phones, faxes, and external electronic energies, such as those emitted by cell phone towers or power lines.

MAGICKAL AND PSYCHIC USES

For keeping a healing, counseling, or divinatory space sacred and enclosed if you're working at a festival or sharing space with other practitioners.

SPECIAL PROPERTIES

Helps you to attract the right love and good friendships.

MYTHOLOGY AND HISTORY

The combination of these two minerals creates a powerful healing and balancing tool for maintaining the right yin/yang mix in the home, workplace, and socially, so everyone feels comfortable; the take-a-step-back-and-breathe crystal if you are being pressured for deadlines or decisions.

Rubellite or Red Tourmaline

COLORS: Red to red-violet or pinkish-red
CRYSTAL TYPE: Lithium-rich crystalline silicate
ZODIAC SIGN: Scorpio (October 24–November 22)
CANDLE COLOR: Red

PHYSICAL: Bolsters heart, energy, spleen, liver, circulation; alleviates anemia, chills, coughs, sore muscles, back; restores libido; energizes you if you're exhausted.
EMOTIONAL: Enables men to express their anima if repressed by harsh or macho fathering; for women reclaiming power if pressured into the "little woman" stereotype.
HOME: For dealing tactfully but firmly with domineering or interfering relatives.
WORKPLACE: Deflects challenges to your authority and expertise; helps overcome hidden discrimination, no matter what the cause.
CHILDREN: Counters unfair pressure on children living in two households, forced to choose; enhances study and learning.
ANIMALS: For kittens or puppies taken from their mother too early.
PROTECTION: Guards against overpossessiveness or subtle undermining that reinforces former childhood dependency.

MAGICKAL AND PSYCHIC USES

A love crystal/gem for attracting a soul twin, passionate love, fidelity, sex magick; prevents a partner from straying; restores lost love; promotes prosperity magick.

SPECIAL PROPERTIES

Rubellite is pyroelectric, creating a voltage at different temperatures; insulates against all shock and harmful electromagnetic fields; for translating intentions into action.

MYTHOLOGY AND HISTORY

Only clear bright red is considered by some gemologists true Rubellite. Indeed, the International Colored Gemstone Association defines true Rubellite as red gems that shine just as intensely in artificial light as in daylight; resembles ruby but rivals it in transmitting the pulse of the life force. However, less expensive reddish-pink to violet-red tourmaline shares similar healing and magickal properties. Peter the Great, the czar of Russia, in the late 1600s commissioned ruby jewelry, which in fact was Rubellite.

Ruby

COLORS: From deep to light red, most valuable as deep red with a slightly blue tinge, called pigeon's blood
CRYSTAL TYPE: Corundum, aluminum oxide silicate
ZODIAC SIGNS: Capricorn (December 22–January 20) and Sagittarius (November 23–December 21)
CANDLE COLOR: Red

PHYSICAL: Addresses issues involving the blood, heart, impotence, menstruation, endometriosis, fibromyalgia, hysterectomy, early-onset menopause, pregnancy in older women; counters the effects of excessive caffeine and other stimulants.
EMOTIONAL: Aids in escaping from a violent partner; for older women whose mature beauty and wisdom are denigrated; controls weight loss linked with emotions.
HOME: Protects home and possessions against fire, storms, and intruders; guards against predators while traveling at night.
WORKPLACE: For ongoing prosperity; raising awareness of leadership potential; dispute resolution.
CHILDREN: Protects infants in the womb.
ANIMALS: A tumbled stone for first-time older pet mothers.
PROTECTION: Guards against psychic and psychological attack. Rubies reputedly grow darker in the presence of a false friend, faithless lover, or liar.

MAGICKAL AND PSYCHIC USES

Sex magick to generate passion; rituals to deter a lover from straying; prophetic dreaming.

SPECIAL PROPERTIES

For women's fertility, especially at full moon; lasting fidelity and commitment. Ruby in gem and natural form share healing and magickal properties.

MYTHOLOGY AND HISTORY

According to legend, whoever owns a Ruby will attract more precious stones (and so increasing wealth). In India, Ruby is believed to be part of the spear of Lord Krishna; some opaque ones with triangles on the surface are considered Record Keepers, holding wisdom from Lemuria and ancient India.

Ruby Aura Quartz or Blood Aura Quartz

COLORS: Deep fuchsia, scarlet, or ruby red, with a metallic sheen

CRYSTAL TYPE: Clear quartz fused with platinum and gold or silver, differing from Rose Aura Quartz (page 409) by a slightly different bonding process that creates an altered alchemical mix

ZODIAC SIGN: Aries (March 21–April 20)

CANDLE COLOR: Ruby red

PHYSICAL: Alleviates issues with early-onset menopause, menorrhagia (menstrual periods with abnormally heavy or prolonged bleeding), hot flashes, endocrine system, sciatica.

EMOTIONAL: Mitigates the aftereffects of violence and/or mental or sexual abuse (especially in childhood); curbs sexual extremes from addiction to sex to total frigidity.

HOME: Creates a warm, welcoming atmosphere, whether you live alone or with a large family; useful if a new partner moves in and adult children object.

WORKPLACE: Discourages sexual harassment and sexual innuendos, as well as the use of flirting or sexual favors to gain promotion.

CHILDREN: Soothes young children who become upset when their mother goes out.

ANIMALS: Prevents antisocial behavior, such as spraying or ripping furniture.

PROTECTION: Guards against energy leakages from the aura, caused by emotional vampirism.

MAGICKAL AND PSYCHIC USES

For mediumship; sex magick, tantra; psychic dreaming about other realms.

SPECIAL PROPERTIES

Ruby Aura attracts lasting love and brings nurturing into your life if you have always cared for others; for passion and eroticism from the middle years onward; protects against a flirtatious partner's temptation to stray.

MYTHOLOGY AND HISTORY

The big sister and more dynamic form of Rose Aura Quartz, often preferred by older women or those planning major life changes.

Ruby in Kyanite

COLORS: Deep red and blue; sometimes teal or darker blue in varying proportions melting together

CRYSTAL TYPE: Corundum (ruby) and aluminum silicate (kyanite)

ZODIAC SIGN: Pisces (February 19–March 20)

CANDLE COLOR: Red

PHYSICAL: Addresses issues involving the heart, muscles, throat constrictions, cell disorders, circulation, hormones, blood pressure, pressure within the eyes; maintains balanced health.

EMOTIONAL: Counters bipolar disorder, extreme mood swings, post-traumatic stress disorder; works against cravings for nicotine and caffeine.

HOME: In the form of spheres, eggs, or as statues of deities, attracts good fortune and protection.

WORKPLACE: Working out of town for long periods or frequently changing locations; for professional caregivers and counselors to avoid overdependency by client on caregiver.

CHILDREN: For those who misread social signals or act inappropriately; encourages necessary routine learning.

ANIMALS: Calms pets overly reliant on their owners.

PROTECTION: Guards against social vampires who at first meeting take over; prevents psychic attack.

MAGICKAL AND PSYCHIC USES

As a massage wand to guide inexperienced healers to a problem's source and the right treatment; promotes lucid dreaming, finding answers in dreams, directed astral travel in sleep and meditation.

SPECIAL PROPERTIES

For fears of commitment in love; where one partner is unwilling to have children; feeling at ease in unfamiliar social situations.

MYTHOLOGY AND HISTORY

An alchemist's stone found in southern India, occasionally joined to Ruby in Fuchsite, combining yang and yin; ruby offers power, wealth, and love and kyanite keeps negativity from entering the stone, directing the right path for ruby energies. Together they release what is not of worth and allow manifestation of what is most desired.

Ruby in Moonstone

COLORS: Red or pink, depending on the proportions of ruby to moonstone

CRYSTAL TYPE: Corundum, aluminum oxide silicate (ruby) and feldspar (moonstone)

ZODIAC SIGNS: Aries (March 21–April 20) and Cancer (June 22–July 22)

CANDLE COLOR: Red

PHYSICAL: Regulates hormones; promotes fertility where age is a limiting factor; alleviates endometriosis, fibromyalgia; for successful IVF, for pregnancy in the middle years.

EMOTIONAL: Soothes intense grief; enables you to move on after a loss; allows for reconciliation if a mother or another person in a caring role died without making peace.

HOME: Restores trust when there has been infidelity in a long-lasting relationship.

WORKPLACE: For women returning to work after maternity leave, a career break, or illness to reestablish their confidence.

CHILDREN: A comfort stone if a child is temporarily or permanently separated from the main caregiver; for protection of the fetus within the womb.

ANIMALS: Keep near a pet who has lost their mate.

PROTECTION: Guards against hostile spirits at night; promotes safety for night workers while traveling to and from work.

MAGICKAL AND PSYCHIC USES

Mediumship to connect with deceased relatives; for full-moon romance, love, and fertility rituals; for female rites of passage from puberty to wise woman.

SPECIAL PROPERTIES

For protection of a secret love where a couple takes risks to meet despite opposition; for a new passionate relationship after years of celibacy.

MYTHOLOGY AND HISTORY

Ruby in Moonstone is sometimes also found with biotite, the stone of the life force that adds immediacy and a proactive element to the other combined crystals. Moonstone and ruby are love stones, and together they deepen commitment and fidelity in a romance going nowhere; the stone brings easier expression of love in relationships for a man who has been taught to conceal his feelings.

Ruby in Zoisite or Anyolite

COLORS: Green with dark pink to red inclusions

CRYSTAL TYPE: Epidote (calcium aluminum silicate) with ruby (corundum) inclusions and hornblende (black) patches

ZODIAC SIGNS: Aries (March 21–April 20) and Taurus (April 21–May 21)

CANDLE COLOR: Red or green

PHYSICAL: Alleviates reproductive disorders, fibroids; promotes fertility; useful after miscarriage, hysterectomy, or early menopause; mitigates side effects of chemotherapy and radiotherapy; eases racing pulse and heartbeat; protects against viruses and bacterial infections.

EMOTIONAL: Consoles you during bereavement; resolves dilemmas concerning single-sex, transgender, gender-fluid, and bisexual relationships; calms mood swings.

HOME: For men running the home and handling childcare full time; changes the status quo if one partner is controlling; transforms negative energies into positive.

WORKPLACE: Aids in meeting targets and deadlines; helps transform a workplace where women are underrepresented in top jobs or encounter hidden prejudice in manual work or frontline in rescue or armed services; deflects inappropriate sexual advances.

CHILDREN: Keeps youngster from stereotyping; assists them in following necessary rules without becoming crushed.

ANIMALS: For training older or rescue animals.

PROTECTION: Guards against returning to lack of self-care or bad habits that led to problems.

MAGICKAL AND PSYCHIC USES

Sacred sex rites and tantra, Kabbalistic learning and practice; creating magickal mind journeys; interdimensional astral travel.

SPECIAL PROPERTIES

Restores passion and commitment if a partner loses interest or is a serial flirt; aids in becoming part of the local scene while traveling.

MYTHOLOGY AND HISTORY

Stone of the undiluted life force, Ruby in Zoisite mingles alchemical fire with earth, combining focused power with freedom to allow life to unfold.

Ruin Marble

COLORS: Various shades of yellows and browns; also contains gray, reddish, blue, and black

CRYSTAL TYPE: Limestone rock, calcium carbonate, where iron and manganese oxide dispersed through the stone in creation, making light and dark patterns resembling a ruined city or landscape

ZODIAC SIGN: Capricorn (December 22–January 20)

CANDLE COLOR: Yellow

PHYSICAL: Addresses issues relating to the respiratory tract, veins and arteries, large intestine; strengthens connective tissues; alleviates osteoporosis, declining mobility and memory in the later years; enhances naturopathy and homeopathy.

EMOTIONAL: Curbs an unwillingness to return to life after a broken relationship or monetary loss; enables you to adapt to living in a new location.

HOME: Aids in restoring a run-down house to its former glory; persuading an older relative they may need more assisted care.

WORKPLACE: For starting over in a business that went bankrupt or was closed by the previous owner; for all who work in archaeology.

CHILDREN: Inspires children to take an interest in history by taking them to old buildings or ancient sites.

ANIMALS: For adopting a very old pet no one else wants.

PROTECTION: Being careful of rivals whose jealousy seeks to wreck your career, business, or relationship.

MAGICKAL AND PSYCHIC USES

Through meditation or scrying, Ruin Marble offers psychic visons of ancient civilizations and sometimes recalls past lives there; for traveling ancient pilgrimage trails and exploring leys between sacred sites.

SPECIAL PROPERTIES

Encourages a sense of community, emphasizing similarities rather than differences in multiethnic areas; for encouraging those living far from home to maintain their roots and traditions.

MYTHOLOGY AND HISTORY

Found mainly in Florence, Italy, Ruin Marble as jewelry is a symbol of fidelity and unity in times of division, because many ancient civilizations lasted for thousands of years and left a legacy to future worlds.

Russian Rainbow Pyrites

COLORS: Metallic, darker gray/black with a drusy covering of miniature minerals on the surface, shimmering with rainbow colors, including gold, green, rose pink, and blue

CRYSTAL TYPE: Iron sulfide

ZODIAC SIGN: Aries (March 21–April 20)

CANDLE COLOR: Gold

PHYSICAL: Relieves migraines, autoimmune diseases, genetic conditions, colds, influenza, viruses attacking multiple organs, anemia, sickle cell disease, lupus, Weil's disease, chronic fatigue.

EMOTIONAL: For adults with Asperger's syndrome to develop strategies at work and socially; counters extreme introversion.

HOME: An amulet for young travelers embarking on adventures; to lighten a social gathering where there are factions and potential flashpoints.

WORKPLACE: Promotes prosperity through original business ventures; success in individual sporting events or extreme sports.

CHILDREN: A magick crystal for bedtime stories. Be careful that little ones do not handle it for safety reasons.

ANIMALS: Keep this crystal with competition entries and medals for show animals.

PROTECTION: Reflects back paranormal attacks and ill-wishing.

MAGICKAL AND PSYCHIC USES

For ghost investigations in haunted buildings to attract benign spirits and protect against hostile entities; rituals to manifest abundance.

SPECIAL PROPERTIES

For performing arts and reality television shows, talent contests, televised quiz or game shows; professional cheerleading, circus acts, acrobatics, or juggling.

MYTHOLOGY AND HISTORY

Russian Rainbow Pyrite, discovered relatively recently near Ulyanovsk, on the Volga River in Russia—its only location—is a good luck stone; potent for making wishes when a rainbow or double rainbow is in the sky.

Rutilated Topaz

COLORS: Usually colorless with golden to brownish-yellow threads; may appear in other colored topaz

CRYSTAL TYPE: Hydrous aluminum silicate, containing needles of limonite or sometimes goethite

ZODIAC SIGN: Sagittarius (November 23–December 21)

CANDLE COLOR: Gold

PHYSICAL: Promotes healthy digestion, metabolism, skin; counters internal parasites; reduces side effects of stomach stapling, gastric bands, and operations to assist weight loss; curbs lack of taste and smell.

EMOTIONAL: Counters anorexia, bulimia, plus a tendency to wait for the ideal love, the perfect job, or opportunity, and therefore achieve nothing.

HOME: Aids in acquiring a beautiful artifact or piece of furniture you have long desired; useful in redecorating or renovating a home.

WORKPLACE: Puts business plans and ideas into practice; develops talents that have been set aside.

CHILDREN: Enables the artistic or creative child to develop their gifts; for winning a place at art college, music or theater school, or a sports academy.

ANIMALS: Helps to see the potential in an animal undervalued by others.

PROTECTION: Prevents intrusion from earthly sources or mischievous spirits disturbing your peace.

MAGICKAL AND PSYCHIC USES

A crystal of divine light, Rutilated Topaz reveals the hidden spiritual world all around; assists manifestation of what is needed or desired; for scrying to seek specific past lives, answer questions, or visit specified realms.

SPECIAL PROPERTIES

The redder and denser the inner threads, the more power Rutilated Topaz gives to survive any setback and emerge victorious.

MYTHOLOGY AND HISTORY

A stone of enchantment and limits imposed only by the extent of the imagination; brings an appreciation of good food, good company, music, flowers, literature.

Sacred Sigil Quartz

COLORS: Colors vary, but most are orange or colorless, with natural etchings on the sides and faces

CRYSTAL TYPE: Feldspar packed with hematite (see also Graphic Feldspar, page 215), famed for runic markings; clear quartz where natural markings represent recognizable sigils or symbols

ZODIAC SIGN: Sagittarius (November 23–December 21)

CANDLE COLOR: Gold

PHYSICAL: Links with the universal well of healing and wise guides from the past who bring strength; useful in exploring traditional remedies from ancient cultures to supplement conventional treatments.

EMOTIONAL: For living only in the here and now.

HOME: Enriches even a new home with a sense of tradition and connectedness with the past.

WORKPLACE: Enables you to see the whole picture if solutions elude you; offers stability in a new or ultra-technological company.

CHILDREN: Allows children to tell you stories about the crystal.

ANIMALS: For old-soul animals who have been with you before.

PROTECTION: Guards against feeling rootless or alienated from life.

MAGICKAL AND PSYCHIC USES

Each sigil symbol or set of symbols acts as a gateway to universal wisdom and will carry you back, not only to its own world in meditation or visions, but to other relevant ancient cultures with wisdom for you.

SPECIAL PROPERTIES

The sigil stone you buy, even apparently randomly, links you to a specific relevant past culture; as you allow messages to unfold through holding the stone, you will understand the significance of your choice.

MYTHOLOGY AND HISTORY

There may be a single symbol or several on the crystal, leading you to the wisdom of a particular culture; you may need to do detective work with a symbol book, initially to identify the specific symbol(s) on your chosen sigil crystal if they're unfamiliar. Handcrafted crystal rune or chakra symbol sets are an initial entry point for working with crystal sigils.

Saffordite or Cintamani Stone

COLORS: Black or brown, but in sunlight lavender/gray and under a flashlight beam turns orange

CRYSTAL TYPE: It is still disputed whether this is a tektite from a meteor, as considered likely, weathered obsidian, or natural volcanic glass; washed by rivers during their thirty-million-year existence

ZODIAC SIGN: Scorpio (October 24–November 22)

CANDLE COLOR: Purple

PHYSICAL: For whole-body self-healing, and autoimmune conditions and diseases where the body attacks itself.

EMOTIONAL: Allays fears of mortality and dying helpless and in pain; counters an obsession with gurus, new religions, and different healing therapies.

HOME: Brings good fortune and blessings to the home; if you live in an area of high UFO sightings, increases safe connection.

WORKPLACE: For those who work to live, not live to work; for sci-fi and fantasy writers.

CHILDREN: Helps children to understand and not fear relatives with dementia.

ANIMALS: For working spiritually with power animals, especially magickal ones or those long extinct.

PROTECTION: Guards against fears that we are no more than our physical body.

MAGICKAL AND PSYCHIC USES

Associated with the qualities of the semilegendary cintamani stone, said to be the original philosopher's stone or Holy Grail; often used as a personal good luck talisman.

SPECIAL PROPERTIES

Believed to manifest what is most desired; forms the anima to the animus of Moldavite.

MYTHOLOGY AND HISTORY

A mystery stone found in the Arizona desert, Saffordite has been credited by some practitioners as having profound spiritual powers and extraterrestrial energies. In fact, descriptions of the original Cintamani stone, which no one in the modern world has yet found, come from the Hindu tradition associated with Vishnu and Ganesha.

Sanda Rosa Azeztulite

COLORS: White with green/black, pink, red, its shade depending on proportions of included minerals, sparkling

CRYSTAL TYPE: Quartz with green/black mica and red/pink spessartine almandine garnet inclusions; found only in North Carolina

ZODIAC SIGN: Leo (July 23–August 23)

CANDLE COLOR: White

PHYSICAL: Promotes multidimensional healing; alleviates issues concerning the heart, malignancies, digestion; enhances light, laser, and heat treatments.

EMOTIONAL: Eases anxiety, depression, phobias (especially claustrophobia and agoraphobia); prevents inner conflicts from manifesting as or worsening physical conditions.

HOME: Brings light into the home in positive daily encounters; for naturally dark or gloomy houses.

WORKPLACE: Useful in companies where business progress is limited by personal agendas; encourages united, mutually beneficial goals.

CHILDREN: Encourages positive psychic experiences and connection with guardian angels.

ANIMALS: For unpredictable pets to settle into a domestic routine.

PROTECTION: Guards against attacks from paranormal entities and malicious people who create a sense of fragmentation and inner confusion.

MAGICKAL AND PSYCHIC USES

Meditation, psychic dreaming, remote viewing, all forms of divination, connection with higher spiritual beings; expressing spirituality in the here and now.

SPECIAL PROPERTIES

Restores a sense and expression of the authentic self if life has necessitated living by others' rules and standards.

MYTHOLOGY AND HISTORY

Like white Azeztulite, said to originate from extraterrestrial Star Beings, there are more than a dozen different varieties, each with different powers according to mineral inclusions. All bring illumination in the way most needed. Some people collect their favorites for healing or divination (see Pink Azeztulite, page 405).

Sand Calcite

COLORS: Tan/brown; lighter brown

CRYSTAL TYPE: Calcite, crystals consisting of 40 percent calcite and 60 percent sand, with inclusions; double-terminated, elongated, mainly quartz, chert, and quartzite with lesser amounts of feldspar, siltstone, shale, and other minerals; may be twinned or in clusters

ZODIAC SIGN: Virgo (August 24–September 22)

CANDLE COLOR: Green

PHYSICAL: Alleviates dry skin, viral infections (especially on skin), skin growths, scars, eczema, dermatitis, pigmentation problems, chronic fatigue, prostate issues, Alzheimer's.

EMOTIONAL: Helps overcome confusion, a perpetually sharp tongue, belief in illusions; curbs deception; mitigates anger that can flare if thwarted or denied; eases claustrophobia.

HOME: For outdoor crystal grids or layouts if you live in a geologically unstable area or one at risk of flooding or forest fires.

WORKPLACE: Useful if workplace conditions are substandard and employers are unwilling to invest in improvements.

CHILDREN: For toddler and teen tantrums, infant breath-holding, or sulking at any age as a power ploy.

ANIMALS: For pets who are aggressive toward other animals.

PROTECTION: Guards against anger and creating dramas to control a person or a situation.

MAGICKAL AND PSYCHIC USES

Lucid dreaming; dream recall; visions of Indigenous ceremonies, both those of the Native North American culture and your own root ancestry; for sand healing and divination.

SPECIAL PROPERTIES

Finding support from the neighborhood or wider community for unwelcome changes that will spoil local green places and damage the environment with mining, fracking, or commercial exploitation of the land.

MYTHOLOGY AND HISTORY

Found in Jurassic rocks, many Sand Calcites are located in Rattlesnake Butte in Jackson County, in southwestern South Dakota. Sand Calcite has been commercially known since the 1800s and has been part of the Indigenous tradition for centuries.

Sandstone

COLORS: Creamy-white, tan, rusty brown; when found mixed with quartz, also pink and peach

CRYSTAL TYPE: Hardened, coarse-grained, sedimentary rock composed of sand-sized grains of mineral, rock, or organic material; occasionally fossilized; most useful for healing and magick in its polished form or as the Indian kind mixed with quartz, called phenomenite

ZODIAC SIGN: Gemini (May 22–June 21)

CANDLE COLOR: Yellow

PHYSICAL: Addresses wounds, fractures, misalignment of the spine, fluid imbalances, allergic rashes, deteriorating eyesight, glaucoma, alopecia (hair loss); strengthens nails.

EMOTIONAL: Helps overcome claustrophobia (especially in elevators and crowds), mood swings, thoughts clouded by memories and future worries that keep you from clear decision making.

HOME: Softens the words of tactless, abrasive family members, visitors, and neighbors; for family parties, outings, celebrations, plus joint vacations with friends or family.

WORKPLACE: Guards against cliques and factions where newcomers are made to feel unwelcome.

CHILDREN: Teaches children to enjoy team sports, even if their team does not win; for defusing toddler and teen tantrums.

ANIMALS: For opening or taking over a rescue center or animal sanctuary.

PROTECTION: Shields you from deceit, lies, trickery, and face-to-face, phone, or internet scams.

MAGICKAL AND PSYCHIC USES

For visions and past lives in ancient Egypt or hot sandy places; divination with sand and stones.

SPECIAL PROPERTIES

For budgeting and saving; selling unwanted goods at a yard or community sale; fund-raising to improve local facilities.

MYTHOLOGY AND HISTORY

Sandstone is the most common rock found worldwide. Shaped through millennia by the combined forces of earth, air, fire, and water, Sandstone may represent the Earth element in magick and act as a symbol of unity in the workplace, love relationships, family or friendship group loyalties.

Sardonyx

COLORS: Varied range of patterns and colors, red-brown, yellow, and white bands

CRYSTAL TYPE: Microcrystalline quartz, a variety of onyx, layered with sard or carnelian

ZODIAC SIGN: Capricorn (December 22–January 20)

CANDLE COLOR: White

PHYSICAL: Strengthens metabolism, spine, bowels, prostate, bladder, feet, legs; eases the flow of bodily fluids, menstruation; counters impotence, sterility, blockages, HIV.

EMOTIONAL: Mitigates stress, sadness, anxiety, an unwillingness to make necessary life changes.

HOME: Resolves legal matters, especially those concerning domestic disputes, inheritance, or property.

WORKPLACE: Encourages honesty and hard work; attracts good fortune; for processing new information; for apprentices, training or retraining, internships; aids in finding good employment.

CHILDREN: Fosters a desire to study if peers are discouraging.

ANIMALS: For finding lost pets.

PROTECTION: Musters the courage to stand your ground against intimidation; promotes safety while traveling.

MAGICKAL AND PSYCHIC USES

Fire and candle magick; Earth rituals; a Sardonyx talisman traditionally brings lasting love within the year.

SPECIAL PROPERTIES

For commitment and marriage; mends marital quarrels and divisions between parents and adult children, especially over a love partner. Sardonyx rings bring fidelity if you and your love are often apart; attracts new friends.

MYTHOLOGY AND HISTORY

From classical times, Sardonyx was carved into cameos, mosaics, statues, or artifacts, associated with the god Mars and hero Hercules, and, in Christian times, with martyred saints. Sardonyx gems were fixed in gold on the shoulders of the high priest of the Israelites to support the sacred breastplate.

Satin Spar

COLORS: White, glowing with pearly opalescence and bands of moving white light that resemble satin

CRYSTAL TYPE: Fibrous gypsum, close sister of White Selenite (page 505), calcium sulfate hydroxide

ZODIAC SIGN: Cancer (June 22–July 22)

CANDLE COLOR: Silver

PHYSICAL: Alleviates PMS, irregular menstrual cycles, migraines, visual disturbances; helps scar tissue fade; speeds recovery after surgery (especially gynecology and cesareans); eases osteoporosis, skin; fertility.

EMOTIONAL: Curbs an inability to relax or switch off; counters an obsession with fitness and exercise; mitigates burnout; salves the scars of inadequate or absent mothering.

HOME: For single parents to create a nurturing environment; for homes where there is no mother or grandmother figure.

WORKPLACE: An antidote to a harsh, noisy workspace, where production is more important than people.

CHILDREN: For those afraid of the dark; psychic children who see spirits everywhere.

ANIMALS: Keeps cats safe who wander at night.

PROTECTION: Guards against phantoms of the night, sexual predator spirits, and homes built on old cemeteries or places of former sorrow.

MAGICKAL AND PSYCHIC USES

Fertility spells on full moon night; a wish crystal also on the night of the full moon.

SPECIAL PROPERTIES

Attracts ongoing good fortune, love, money, travel opportunities, and abundance.

MYTHOLOGY AND HISTORY

In ancient Greece Satin Spar was believed to have been part of the Moon Goddess's robe, discarded after she has danced at full moon. Satin Spar will cleanse and reempower a tarot pack or spiritual artifacts, especially in moonlight, and also program other crystals for specific healing and magickal purposes.

Saturn Chalcedony

COLORS: Green and white stripes or bands with different shades of green

CRYSTAL TYPE: Silicon dioxide

ZODIAC SIGN: Capricorn (December 22–January 20)

CANDLE COLOR: Green

PHYSICAL: Alleviates problems with aging, including loss of memory; promotes oxygenation of the blood, efficient processing of fat; addresses issues involving vision, mobility, and unsteadiness walking or on stairs; filters impurities through the body.

EMOTIONAL: Counters extreme introversion and unsociability; curbs lack of generosity with money and resources; helps overcome a sole focus on future security and neglecting present needs and pleasures.

HOME: A lucky charm for all property matters, including buying and selling; attracts prosperity through safe ventures and proven investments.

WORKPLACE: Exercises caution if a new business or employment offer involves risks but great rewards.

CHILDREN: For good relationships with grandparents and great-grandparents whom they do not see very often; encourages kindness to animals and those in need.

ANIMALS: Gives an unsociable pet space and privacy.

PROTECTION: Guards against intrusion by those who would control your life.

MAGICKAL AND PSYCHIC USES

For finding lost objects; protective magick; creating magickal boundaries around the home, possessions, and vehicles; strengthens maternal instinct and telepathy between parent and child.

SPECIAL PROPERTIES

An anti-debt crystal if you have been given bad advice or are being unreasonably pressured for payments.

MYTHOLOGY AND HISTORY

Saturn, the Roman god of fate and agriculture, was said to have ruled over a golden age of peace and plenty after he was dethroned by his son Jupiter. Saturn Chalcedony reflects the saturnine qualities of caution with money, wise property dealings, and establishing boundaries and good fortune.

Satyaloka Azezulite or Azeztulite

COLORS: Clear or translucent, also in rose and yellow

CRYSTAL TYPE: A special form of clear quartz from the Satyaloka Mountain region of southern India

ZODIAC SIGN: Leo (July 23–August 23)

CANDLE COLOR: Gold

PHYSICAL: Eases chronic sickness; offers small miracles in the face of life-limiting conditions; alleviates cellular disorders.

EMOTIONAL: Curbs extreme cynicism, narcissism, inability to empathize with others.

HOME: Restores peace to the home after major trauma or loss; creates a sanctuary if you are living somewhere you dislike.

WORKPLACE: Counteracts a materialistic workplace, where employees' needs are disregarded; aids in pursuing religious or spiritual studies.

CHILDREN: Helps youngsters gain strength if they are very sick or hospitalized.

ANIMALS: For mourning a beloved pet who has passed on if others are unsympathetic.

PROTECTION: Guards against a sense of malevolence in your home or land so restless spirits will go to the light.

MAGICKAL AND PSYCHIC USES

For peak experiences to become one momentarily with the universe and divine bliss; awakens the body of spiritual light within everyone.

SPECIAL PROPERTIES

Awakens spiritual practices for everyday life; brings out the best in yourself and others; for staying or living in a religious or spiritual community.

MYTHOLOGY AND HISTORY

Gathered and blessed by the monks at the Satya Loka—which means the "place of truth"—a monastery in southern India, said to be one of the most spiritually evolved places on Earth. The monks endow the crystal with higher dimensional and mountain energies; the crystal is also sold as satyaloka quartz and carries the same white-light energies.

Satya Mani

COLORS: Transparent to clear or slightly milky

CRYSTAL TYPE: Satya Mani is a quartz from the Satya Loka Mountain region of southern India, close to where the sacred Satyaloka Azeztulite is found, and belongs to the same family

ZODIAC SIGN: Aquarius (January 21–February 18)

CANDLE COLOR: Silver

PHYSICAL: Promotes soft-tissue healing; helps if malfunctioning of the brain is causing deterioration in the whole body.

EMOTIONAL: Counters attachment to fantasies and illusions that can cause self-deception.

HOME: Brings gentleness and compassion to a home where there is continual one-upmanship among strong-minded individuals.

WORKPLACE: In cases where logic and structured thinking have failed, restores the intuitive inspiration that comes straight from the heart and cuts through seemingly unresolvable problems.

CHILDREN: For old souls, Indigo Children, Crystal Children, with their complete rainbow auras and Star Seeds.

ANIMALS: For mountain rescue dogs.

PROTECTION: Guards against those who would lie or deceive.

MAGICKAL AND PSYCHIC USES

For manifestation of what will bring the highest good; for connection with archangels and ascended masters.

SPECIAL PROPERTIES

Satya Mani means "pearl or gem of truth," and so offers instant awareness of what is true if others conceal facts; reveals in a flash of inspiration the right path where spiritual, rather than material, values offer a fulfilling life.

MYTHOLOGY AND HISTORY

Satya Mani is associated with the goddess of compassion Kuan or Kwan Yin and the Azez Star Beings; works well in a triplicate with Satyaloka Azeztulite (page 420) and Nirvana or Himalayan Ice Quartz (page 317) for major healing needs or crises.

Saussurite

COLORS: Grayish-green, emerald-green within an off-white or gray base; the number of microscopic minerals within making it appear mottled

CRYSTAL TYPE: Mineral aggregate, formed by the alteration of calcium or sodium-bearing plagioclase feldspar through natural heat; includes albite, chlorite, epidote, scapolite, and zoisite

ZODIAC SIGN: Aquarius (January 21–February 18)

CANDLE COLOR: Green

PHYSICAL: Eases atrial fibrillation, hypertension, racing pulse, hyperventilation during panic attacks, all conditions caused or made worse by stress.

EMOTIONAL: Counters pessimism and a refusal to consider alternatives or personal change because you believe the world is out of step with you.

HOME: For major makeovers of yourself and your home, redecoration and refurbishment in a new home.

WORKPLACE: Calms a manager or colleagues who constantly panic over trivialities.

CHILDREN: Connects children with their guardian angel if they fear the dark or are reluctant to sleep in their own room.

ANIMALS: Reassures pets who hate being left alone, by using the owner's telepathic energies when they're apart.

PROTECTION: Guards against terrifying paranormal dreams.

MAGICKAL AND PSYCHIC USES

Contacts angels and teacher guides, revealing their messages through meditation and automatic writing; for allowing natural psychic powers to find expression.

SPECIAL PROPERTIES

As an anxiety-relieving tumbled stone, held during a phone call or a collective zoom meeting with unfamiliar people or if you feel under scrutiny.

MYTHOLOGY AND HISTORY

Much prized for sculptures and artifacts, Saussurite was first discovered in the 1760s on the slopes of Mont Blanc by Swiss geologist and mountaineer Horace Benedict de Saussure, who believed it was jade. Saussurite opens limitless possibilities previously unthought of or dismissed as unachievable.

Scepter or Scepter Quartz

COLORS: Varies with the kind of quartz, but may be different-colored quartzes at termination and base

CRYSTAL TYPE: Natural, often clear quartz point in which the terminating end has grown, as a second-generation crystal, disproportionally large compared with the main crystal rod; if the base is larger, it is called a reverse scepter quartz (see also Reverse Orange Phantom Quartz, page 405)

ZODIAC SIGN: Leo (July 23–August 23)

CANDLE COLOR: White

PHYSICAL: Addresses issues involving male genitalia, fertility, fallopian tubes, skin growths, visible tumors, lesions, scar tissue, blockages.

EMOTIONAL: Counters a need to dominate others because of innate insecurity; keeps you from hiding behind status and authority; curbs psycho-sexual problems.

HOME: Aids in holding your own with domineering relatives.

WORKPLACE: For teachers of disruptive children, professions that involve people management, or the restoration of order.

CHILDREN: Encourages a young person who wants to be a reality TV star, model, or athlete to study for tests or pursue an alternative career.

ANIMALS: For older pets struggling with boisterous children or lively young animals.

PROTECTION: A pair of scepters, either in a cross pattern or side by side, if one is a reversed scepter, replaces harm with positive energies.

MAGICKAL AND PSYCHIC USES

Increases powers of other crystals; a fertility and potency talisman because of its phallic shape.

SPECIAL PROPERTIES

Directs power or healing via the tip for absent as well as contact healing; a reverse Scepter Quartz recycles the healing power through the healer.

MYTHOLOGY AND HISTORY

Scepter wands may have been the first ritual, healing, and ceremonial tools carried by a priest or priestess to bring fertility to Earth, animals, and people.

Schalenblende

COLORS: Intricate patterns of alternating cream, yellow/gold, brown, and metallic gray or silver layers; undulating appearance

CRYSTAL TYPE: Zinc iron sulfide, combining several compacted metal ores, sphalerite (see page 450), wurzite, galena, possibly containing elemental silver, and metallic gray/black Marcasite (see page 294)

ZODIAC SIGN: Capricorn (December 22–January 20)

CANDLE COLOR: Silver

PHYSICAL: Speeds wound recovery; alleviates diabetes; promotes the immune system, brain and red blood cell regeneration, and sense of smell, taste, and vision; useful for the prostate gland, genitalia, preconception health and fertility.

EMOTIONAL: Eases pent-up frustrations that cloud rational thinking; aids in permanently leaving a destructive relationship or situation.

HOME: For property matters, including buying, selling or renovation; attracts good luck; for happy parties.

WORKPLACE: Protects computers and other devices against new viruses, hacking, unpleasant emails, nuisance callers, and malicious texts; for alternative ideas and brainstorming; for wedding planners and conference and event organizers.

CHILDREN: Shields against social media bullying and online predators; for joining clubs.

ANIMALS: Helps if you travel with or relocate pets.

PROTECTION: Guards against stalkers; dispels negative energies in a neighborhood or community.

MAGICKAL AND PSYCHIC USES

A fertility charm; banishing and binding magick; shamanism; safe travel through spiritual realms; establishing spiritual or healing groups.

SPECIAL PROPERTIES

A stone of peace with those potentially hostile; brings the right people together at the right time.

MYTHOLOGY AND HISTORY

According to folklore, Schalenblende was a protective talisman in Celtic times. Schalenblende Polen, an amalgam of zinc, sphalerite, galena, and marcasite in a single boulder, found in Poland, is regarded as especially magickal and healing.

Scheelite

COLORS: Yellow or golden, orange, green-gray, brown, white

CRYSTAL TYPE: Sulfate, calcium tungstate

ZODIAC SIGN: Libra (September 23–October 23)

CANDLE COLOR: Gold

PHYSICAL: Balances male and female hormones and reproductive systems; addresses excessive facial and body hair in women; alleviates issues involving the lower back, legs, hips, circulation in the lower body and extremities.

EMOTIONAL: Promotes anger management; curbs excessive timidity and anxiety about life's dangers; mitigates domestic violence in both sexes.

HOME: Valuable in all-male or single-parent households dominated by adolescent boys; for multitasking if you work from home or have too many commitments.

WORKPLACE: Counteracts sexism, ageism, racism, gender issues, and prejudice; for maintaining a calm demeanor during official assessments or investigations.

CHILDREN: For ADHD and hyperactivity, especially if manifest as aggression; reduces potential violence in young females and criminal influences on teenagers of both sexes.

ANIMALS: Calms overly boisterous pets or those who scratch or bite.

PROTECTION: Alerts the mind to potential and approaching danger.

MAGICKAL AND PSYCHIC USES

Meditation and moving meditation, especially for beginners, or if you encounter many distractions; trance mediumship; shamanic or trance dance; shape-shifting; ghost-hunting; dowsing with copper or hazel rods; astral travel to a prechosen destination.

SPECIAL PROPERTIES

The stone of punctuality if keeping track of time, schedules, and deadlines are an issue, and for completing tasks.

MYTHOLOGY AND HISTORY

As a major tungsten ore, Scheelite raises thought patterns, opening the mind to psychic awareness in everyday life and activating and harmonizing all the chakras, the body's invisible energy centers; adds intuitive awareness to logic and common sense for multidimensional, informed decision making.

Scolecite

COLORS: Colorless, white or yellow, often silky; may be pink, red, or green if other trace minerals are present

CRYSTAL TYPE: Zeolite, hydrated calcium silicate

ZODIAC SIGN: Capricorn (December 22–January 20)

CANDLE COLOR: White

PHYSICAL: Alleviates issues stemming from the liver, spleen, lower digestive system, heart, eyes, brain chemistry, blood-related disorders, circulation; for weight loss regimens; promotes spinal alignment, mobility.

EMOTIONAL: Releases past mistakes; curbs anxiety, stress, fear of being alone; eases panic attacks in crowded places; keeps you from self-imposed restrictions.

HOME: Increases positive communication between different generations; aids in sharing responsibilities and chores if one person does it all.

WORKPLACE: Fosters cohesion in projects and meetings without feeling the need to please everyone; delegating to avoid over-commitment.

CHILDREN: For introverted children who find school life too intense.

ANIMALS: Calms pets in petting zoos or kindergartens.

PROTECTION: Banishes overanalysis of the day past and the day ahead that interferes with sleep.

MAGICKAL AND PSYCHIC USES

A high-vibration crystal for communication with evolved spirits, extraterrestrial beings, and ancient civilizations; meditation, lucid dreaming, and encountering a dream lover; talking with deceased family members in sleep.

SPECIAL PROPERTIES

Brings soothing yin energies if life is too yang and fraught; manifests inner calmness as a relaxed outer attitude.

MYTHOLOGY AND HISTORY

Unique clusters of prismatic, needle-like points radiating outward or crisscrossing like crystal sculptures (needles can be seen in tumbled stones); an ideal wand. Cohesive Scolecite concentrates absent healing energies in group work or set in the middle of a healing crystal layout.

Scottish Lewisian Gneiss

COLORS: Black and white, gray, pink, and green

CRYSTAL TYPE: One of the oldest rocks in the world, three billion years old; contains epidote, feldspar, quartz, and sometimes magnetite and garnet; may be formed into beautiful cabochons and polished stones for jewelry as well as collectors' pieces of the ancient rock.

ZODIAC SIGN: Capricorn (December 22–January 20)

CANDLE COLOR: Gray

PHYSICAL: Addresses recurring or slow-to-clear infections, gastric problems, nausea, morning sickness.

EMOTIONAL: Counters overdependence on parents as an adult or constantly seeking parent substitutes if parents have passed away.

HOME: Aids in nurturing the self if you always care for others; introduces fun and unstructured time in a rigid schedule.

WORKPLACE: Keeps you from being panicked by rumors of future redundancies, but being alert to alternative opportunities elsewhere.

CHILDREN: Encourages playing outdoors in nature without the need for elaborate toys.

ANIMALS: For an old-soul pet who unmistakably finds you as a new kitten, puppy, or foal.

PROTECTION: Guards against those who insist that everything must remain exactly as it is and obsessive hoarders.

MAGICKAL AND PSYCHIC USES
Natural magick, druidry, Wicca, and nature-based spirituality; increased claircognizance, psychic knowing, intuitive awareness.

SPECIAL PROPERTIES
Called the stone of hope, bringing the belief that all shall be well, given patience and perseverance, reflecting the enduring faith of the people and land of the ancient stone throughout the millennia.

MYTHOLOGY AND HISTORY
The Lewisian Gneiss extends through the Isles of Lewis, Harris, and North Highlands in Scotland. A stone treasured by the clans of Scotland for thousands of years, believed to contain the essence of the courage and determination of the untamed land in each piece. Megaliths, such as the Callanish stone circle on the Isle of Lewis, were created from the rock and, if visited, reveal visions of the years of triumphs and suffering.

Sedona Stone

COLORS: Reddish-gray to orange

CRYSTAL TYPE: Sandstone concretions with a high level of quartz

ZODIAC SIGN: Aries (March 21–April 20)

CANDLE COLOR: Orange

PHYSICAL: Revitalizes the whole body; infuses the mind, body, and spirit with strength, alertness, and stamina; for conditions that are hard to diagnose and treat; for hope if there is none.

EMOTIONAL: Counters disconnection from life and relationships, disillusionment, indecisiveness.

HOME: Removes stagnant Earth energies beneath your home that may have been reflected in tiredness, lack of initiative, and failure of plans to materialize.

WORKPLACE: For careers involving prolonged physical or mental activity to avoid burnout; for spiritual businesses to prosper.

CHILDREN: Teaches psychic children of any age not to fear their gifts.

ANIMALS: For connecting with your totem animals.

PROTECTION: Guards against those who drain emotional, physical, or psychic energy.

MAGICKAL AND PSYCHIC USES
Spontaneously increases psychic powers; psychic dreaming; past worlds, especially of Indigenous cultures; for Native North American rituals; Earth healing.

SPECIAL PROPERTIES
Sedona Stones both empower and harmonize body, mind, and soul, and allow the psyche to apply the wisdom channeled from higher planes.

MYTHOLOGY AND HISTORY
Sedona Stones or Sedonalite contain the power of Sedona vortex energies within them wherever in the world they are used. Sedona in Arizona has four major swirling vortices of power at Airport Mesa, Cathedral Rock, Bell Rock, and Boynton Canyon; each radiates its own unique healing Earth and sky energies that constantly fill the stones.

Seer Stones

COLORS: Vary according to the quartz

CRYSTAL TYPE: Seer Stones, tumbled naturally by river water, are found as clear quartz, smoky quartz, rose quartz, citrine, or amethyst, with a reflective clear polished flat surface and frosty white sides

ZODIAC SIGN: Pisces (February 19–March 20)

CANDLE COLOR: Silver

PHYSICAL: Addresses fluid imbalances, hormones, water retention, incontinence, nighttime bed-wetting in children, bladder, kidneys, blood circulation, hemophilia.

EMOTIONAL: Keeps you from oversentimentality; curbs an addiction to fortune tellers and messages from the spirit world.

HOME: A selection of different Seer Stones ensures sensitive communication between generations.

WORKPLACE: For psychic investigators, parapsychologists, cryptozoologists, and all who professionally research the unknown.

CHILDREN: Ensures peaceful dreams, especially as rose quartz.

ANIMALS: For the conservation of water creatures in rivers, oceans, and reefs.

PROTECTION: Reflects back ill-wishing, curses, hexes, and hauntings.

MAGICKAL AND PSYCHIC USES

Offers access to ancient wisdom and cultures; may be programmed to tune into a specific age or culture, especially as amethyst and smoky quartz stones; following the timeline of personal past, present, and future, especially as clear quartz Seer Stones.

SPECIAL PROPERTIES

As citrine or clear quartz, Seer Stones are believed to enable lovers to communicate telepathically over long distances.

MYTHOLOGY AND HISTORY

Natural Seer Stones are tumbled in the Ema River in southern Brazil; also named Ema's Eggs, after the river and because their uncut white shell resembles an egg. When these frosted stones are cut, and one end polished by a lapidarist, their windows reveal other worlds.

Seftonite, Vulcan, or African Bloodstone

COLORS: Mossy or gray-green with large red patches, lighter in color, with more red than Indian heliotrope or bloodstone

CRYSTAL TYPE: A jasper variety of chalcedony; occasionally contains pyrites

ZODIAC SIGN: Aries (March 21–April 20)

CANDLE COLOR: Red

PHYSICAL: Fights infections, blood disorders (especially iron deficiency), bladder problems; cleanses the body of toxins; eases cramps; good for the heart.

EMOTIONAL: For counteracting irritability, free-floating anger, and impatience.

HOME: Gives power and strength to walk away from or seek help for domestic abuse.

WORKPLACE: Enhances and focuses creativity; gives talents tangible expression for all who work in or teach the arts.

CHILDREN: Calms children easily angered or distressed when frustrated or provoked.

ANIMALS: Reduces tendencies for fighting other animals.

PROTECTION: Guards against evil people and negative entities, deflecting negativity into the Earth.

MAGICKAL AND PSYCHIC USES

For candle and fire magick, divination, clairvoyance, significant dreams.

SPECIAL PROPERTIES

Brings connection with ancestors; in times of crisis, acts as a radar, steering you away from potential danger or confrontation.

MYTHOLOGY AND HISTORY

Named after the Roman blacksmith and fire god Vulcan African, Seftonite has faster-releasing energies than traditional bloodstone.

Self-Healed Quartz

COLORS: Depends on the kind of quartz

CRYSTAL TYPE: Quartz crystal, often clear, where the crystal broke off from its matrix or cluster during formation but continued to grow in the Earth with new terminations or regrew to complete the original structure; found also in smoky quartz, amethyst, and citrine

ZODIAC SIGN: Virgo (August 24–September 22)

CANDLE COLOR: White

PHYSICAL: Triggers the innate self-healing system; addresses fractures, growth problems, transplants, implants, transfusions, IVF; promotes regrowth of hair after chemotherapy; enables body reconstruction after accident or disease.

EMOTIONAL: Counters overdependence on psychotherapy or counseling; curbs addictions when substituted substances or other addicts hinder progress.

HOME: Aids in avoiding major breakages and breakdowns; repairing a house after flood, fire, or settling.

WORKPLACE: Fosters self-employment, entrepreneurial enterprises; helps in retraining after job loss; promotes equal opportunities for physically challenged workers.

CHILDREN: For those teased because of physical or emotional challenges.

ANIMALS: Comforts pets who have lost a limb, eyesight, or hearing.

PROTECTION: Earthquake quartz—broken off from its cluster by seismic disturbance—that repairs itself internally, guards against earthquake, fire, flood, and tornado.

MAGICKAL AND PSYCHIC USES

Transfers healing powers to other broken or damaged crystals; healing self and clients by allowing them to hold a Self-Healed Crystal.

SPECIAL PROPERTIES

A starting-over-again crystal after loss, illness, or betrayal.

MYTHOLOGY AND HISTORY

Whatever form or degree the Self-Healed Crystal manifests, and those completely healed internally are considered Master Crystals, a reminder that beauty can lie in imperfection and overcoming problems brings wisdom and compassion.

Septarian or Dragon Stone

COLORS: Mainly pale to rich brown with pale yellow or brown and/or brown/red and gray

CRYSTAL TYPE: Bentonite clay or marl concretions, cemented by silica, carbonates or iron oxide; veins and concentric cracks of aragonite and/or calcite, forming a circular web pattern within an outer shell

ZODIAC SIGN: Taurus (April 21–May 21)

CANDLE COLOR: Yellow

PHYSICAL: Strengthens the immune system; alleviates issues stemming from muscle spasms, pain, teeth, skin lesions, eczema, hair, nails, feet, ankles, nerve connections and endings, cleft palate, seasonal affective disorder.

EMOTIONAL: Protects against being overly influenced by stronger personalities; balancing being stuck in the past and not learning from it.

HOME: Aids in getting to know your neighbors and community in a new area; finding privacy in a crowded household.

WORKPLACE: Helps you pace yourself when facing multiple demands; promotes networking, online business contacts; fosters public speaking, teaching, and lecturing.

CHILDREN: Teaches children to become team players and take turns.

ANIMALS: For harmonizing numerous household pets; comforts reptiles away from their natural habitat.

PROTECTION: Shields against nightmares, psychic attack, and unjust lawsuits.

MAGICKAL AND PSYCHIC USES

As polished spheres for meditation, divination, and scrying; safe ghost hunting and séances; dragon and fire rituals.

SPECIAL PROPERTIES

Finding your voice and authority if no one listens to you or takes your views seriously; communicating via social media without compromising privacy.

MYTHOLOGY AND HISTORY

Each Septarian, which is unique, resembles dragon scales. In myth, this crystal was considered the remains of baby dragon eggs from which they had hatched. Septarians formed around sixty million years ago and contain ancient wisdom of lost seas.

Serandite

COLORS: Pale pink, salmon pink, rose, orange, brown, or colorless

CRYSTAL TYPE: Hydrous silicate of manganese, calcium, and sodium; part of the calcium silicate wollastonite family

ZODIAC SIGN: Libra (September 23–October 23)

CANDLE COLOR: White

PHYSICAL: Strengthens bone density; promotes absorption of sufficient manganese and calcium in the diet; mitigates health problems made worse by excessive salt, consumption of fast foods, and preservatives.

EMOTIONAL: Soothes you after the breakup of a relationship; enables you to let an ex-partner go; counters an inability to reach out to others; eases hypersensitivity.

HOME: Valuable when new family members move into an existing living space; for curbing excessive materialism.

WORKPLACE: For professional musicians, performers, producers, and composers, and those working toward professional status.

CHILDREN: Reduces temper tantrums in toddlers, teens, and adults who never quite grew up; encourages harmonious play when placed safely in playrooms.

ANIMALS: For a pet who starts attacking another household pet, seemingly without reason.

PROTECTION: Guards against the jealousy of others who may seek to spoil the happiness you have, especially love rivals.

MAGICKAL AND PSYCHIC USES

Removes negative entities from your home, workplace, and energy field by sending them to the light.

SPECIAL PROPERTIES

The stone of harmony, Serandite strengthens or restores harmonious relationships in romance, the workplace, and socially.

MYTHOLOGY AND HISTORY

Serandite was discovered in 1931 at Mont Saint-Hilaire in Quebec, itself a source of beautiful crystals. Since then, it has also been found elsewhere, including in Brazil, Guinea, Namibia, Australia, and Italy.

Seraphinite or Clinochlore

COLORS: Deep green with silvery white streaks

CRYSTAL TYPE: Silicate/chlorite

ZODIAC SIGN: Taurus (April 21–May 21)

CANDLE COLOR: Deep green or silver

PHYSICAL: Cleanses the body of toxins; rejuvenates cells; promotes self-healing; guards against the recurrence of illness.

EMOTIONAL: Curbs eating disorders and tendencies to engage in excessive exercise or dieting.

HOME: Showers unconditional but tough love on an antisocial family member.

WORKPLACE: Brings peace and harmony to a workplace where there are frequent absences due to stress.

CHILDREN: A Seraphinite crystal angel or crystal egg offers the protection of their guardian angel while they sleep.

ANIMALS: For animals who are nervous around strangers or in unfamiliar places.

PROTECTION: A protective stone for all forms of travel; shields service personnel on active duty anywhere.

MAGICKAL AND PSYCHIC USES

For astral travel to the realms of angels and nature spirits; channels healing energies from the angels, especially through Reiki.

SPECIAL PROPERTIES

Brings direct contact with your guardian angel and the archangels.

MYTHOLOGY AND HISTORY

Seraphinite is called the angel stone because of its shimmering silvery white angel-wing appearance, caused by mica inclusions. It comes from Russia, giving it associations with St. Sophia, much beloved in the Russian Orthodox Church.

Seriphos Green Quartz

COLORS: From pale through to darker green, colored by hedenbergite mineral inclusions
CRYSTAL TYPE: Silicon dioxide
ZODIAC SIGN: Virgo (August 24–September 22)
CANDLE COLOR: Green

PHYSICAL: Alleviates issues stemming from the eyes, speech, communication, heart, heart surgery and transplants, bones, lungs, plant allergies, sunburn.
EMOTIONAL: Counters constant worrying, burnout, over-identification with others' troubles, a chaotic personality.
HOME: For a better quality of life, increasing outdoor pursuits, downsizing, moving to an island, working from home in the countryside or near the ocean; attracts blessings and abundance; encourages spring cleaning at any time.
WORKPLACE: Useful for outdoor workers, those working in agriculture, horticulture, water sports and swimming coaching or competing; counteracts a stressful, noisy workplace; aids in learning nature-based therapies; promotes organizational skills.
CHILDREN: Allays fears of water and swimming.
ANIMALS: Conserves marine life and the waters they inhabit.
PROTECTION: Guards against paranormal evil, after using ouija boards, online demonology, or black magick.

MAGICKAL AND PSYCHIC USES
Strengthens herbal healing, homeopathy, essential oils, crystals and flower remedies; connects with nature spirits and devas; removes psychic and psychological hooks; cultivates outdoor meditation; useful for angel Reiki, telepathy, psychic surgery.

SPECIAL PROPERTIES
Aids in finding a temporary or permanent out-of-town refuge; encourages an eco-friendly lifestyle; creates contentment within yourself.

MYTHOLOGY AND HISTORY
Seriphos Green Quartz is mined only on the Greek island of Seriphos (named after the angelic Seraphim) in the Aegean Sea in a cave at low tide. Once known as prasius, by Roman naturalist Pliny the Elder, prase, or, more recently prasem quartz, this crystal grows to resemble leaves or leafy stalks in plant-like clusters.

Serpentine

COLORS: Shades of green, yellow; sometimes veined or spotted with red or brown inclusions; distinguished by its oily feel; rarely silver and fibrous
CRYSTAL TYPE: Hydrous magnesium iron phyllosilicate in twenty varieties (see Atlantisite, Bowenite or New Jade, and Williamsite, pages 42, 89, and 505)
ZODIAC SIGN: Scorpio (October 24–November 22)
CANDLE COLOR: Olive green

PHYSICAL: Addresses issues relating to the stomach, bowels, Alzheimer's, senile dementia, stings, blood sugar, eczema, rashes, varicose veins, warts, skin or hair parasites; directs energies to the root of illness.
EMOTIONAL: Sheds old sorrows, unresolvable injustices, and burdens from the past.
HOME: Ensures privacy from complaining neighbors and school playground parental factions.
WORKPLACE: Discourages rivalry and backstabbing; enables you to take over and turn around a failed business.
CHILDREN: Helps overcome fears of insects and snakes.
ANIMALS: Deters fleas, ticks, and mites.
PROTECTION: Guards against spite, jealousy, lies, and gossip,

MAGICKAL AND PSYCHIC USES
Dowsing and Earth energies at ancient sites; aligning with the Earth; working with mythical creatures, such as dragons.

SPECIAL PROPERTIES
Said to contain the power of creation, fertility, and the life force.

MYTHOLOGY AND HISTORY
Named after its snake-like coloring and resemblance to snakeskin (some Serpentine is scaly) and valued since ancient times as a protective amulet against snake and other venomous bites, disease, and the dark arts. Sacred to the ancient snake goddesses, for example the ancient Egyptian goddess Uadjet, spitting poison at anyone who would do the pharaoh harm, it is still used in Indigenous serpent goddess rituals. In modern times, Serpentine is linked with computer fantasy games involving serpentine creatures.

Sesame Stone or Kiwi Jasper

COLORS: Light sea-green with black and clear speckles; sometimes the lighter, almost white, variety is given the name *sesame jasper*

CRYSTAL TYPE: Jasper, containing tourmaline, quartz, and amazonite

ZODIAC SIGN: Cancer (June 22–July 22)

CANDLE COLOR: Pale green

PHYSICAL: Alleviates colds, persistent coughs, influenza and other highly contagious viral conditions; addresses children's illnesses.

EMOTIONAL: Curbs addictions, phobias, and compulsions.

HOME: Creates, restores, and maintains a sense of fun on family outings and vacations; for happy times spent by the ocean.

WORKPLACE: For counseling or mentoring professionally or within the workplace to support less experienced colleagues; aids in displaying leadership when others are panicking.

CHILDREN: Useful for those who find it hard to share toys or take turns; for times when extra nurturing is needed.

ANIMALS: For pets who are overly possessive about their food if anyone comes near while they are eating.

PROTECTION: Acts as a shield against negative atmospheres and psychological or psychic attacks.

MAGICKAL AND PSYCHIC USES

Premonitions and prophecy; sea rituals; communicating with water essences; ability to return to a dream and change the ending.

SPECIAL PROPERTIES

Many people find that Sesame Stone feels warm when used in healing or meditation; regulates the natural inner ebbs and flows to avoid high and low mood swings.

MYTHOLOGY AND HISTORY

Named *sesame* after the seed-like black inclusions, a seed that magickally reflects abundance and prosperity. The small, brave kiwi, the national bird of New Zealand, has fought to survive and succeeded. This stone, which comes from New Zealand, reflects the same unquenchable dynamic action to overcome all difficulties and express the true self.

Shaman Dow Phantom Quartz

COLORS: Usually colorless; may be other clear colors with a white ghostly shape inside or occasionally a black phantom (smoky quartz)

CRYSTAL TYPE: Clear crystal quartz; may be formed of other quartzes, including yellow citrine; defined as Shaman Dow because of the phantom within; Dows have three seven-sided faces that alternate with three triangular faces (see Dow crystal, page 165)

ZODIAC SIGN: Aquarius (January 21–February 18)

CANDLE COLOR: White

PHYSICAL: Resolves deep-seated conditions or those hidden behind or within major organs or orifices of the body; ensures successful scans, ultrasound, biopsies, endoscopy, and other investigative probing procedures.

EMOTIONAL: Keeps you from hiding your true self out of fear of being rejected.

HOME: Aids in moving home after long, unavoidable delays in a home sale or purchase; reaps an unexpected financial gain through an investment or extra source of income.

WORKPLACE: For wise authority and respect in whatever work you do, not necessarily linked with worldly status or reaching the top.

CHILDREN: Helps adopted children to discover their birth origins without pain.

ANIMALS: For a pet not expected to thrive, who exceeds all expectations.

PROTECTION: Guards against being overshadowed by those who push for recognition, regardless of merit.

MAGICKAL AND PSYCHIC USES

A Shaman Dow draws out existing, undeveloped psychic talents; using new psychic insights to improve daily life.

SPECIAL PROPERTIES

Over time, Phantom Quartzes become a treasure trove of your personal spiritual blueprint, its gifts strengthened by the amplified healing and wisdom within it.

MYTHOLOGY AND HISTORY

A crystal of transformation as the inner spiritual and creative self is manifest in continuing growth. Some believe we have owned our Phantom Dow in previous lifetimes as a repository of what we have learned as personal insights from these older worlds.

Shantilite

COLORS: Gray and white

CRYSTAL TYPE: An unusual form of banded agate; silicon dioxide

ZODIAC SIGN: Pisces (February 19–March 20)

CANDLE COLOR: Gray

PHYSICAL: For recovery after a serious or prolonged illness; for stress-related conditions or those made worse by anxiety, such as high blood pressure and a racing heart.

EMOTIONAL: Keeps you from becoming too involved in the lives and problems of others; for feeling constantly out of step with the world.

HOME: A calm center to any home; filters out the worries of the day.

WORKPLACE: For all who manage or work in therapy centers, crystal or magick stores to create a financially secure business; for integrating a fractious workplace where your efforts are unrewarded.

CHILDREN: Valuable for those who sense that they are different from their family or peers.

ANIMALS: For tranquil pets who instantly soothe and know when extra affection is needed.

PROTECTION: Guards against the world spinning out of control.

MAGICKAL AND PSYCHIC USES

Chanting, drumming, sacred dance, prayer, deep trance meditation; angelic energies and healing.

SPECIAL PROPERTIES

Shanti is Sanskrit for "peace" or "divine peace." Shantilite brings freedom from stress and the frantic world, spiritual peace, and universal silence.

MYTHOLOGY AND HISTORY

Shantilite comes from Madagascar, home of many highly spiritually attuned crystals and often associated with Lemurian wisdom. For students of Buddhism, Hinduism, yoga, tai chi, and transcendental meditation to gain freedom from earthly concerns.

Shark Tooth—Fossilized

COLORS: Variety of colors, depending on the sediment in which the tooth became fossilized; usually with black root and gray/cream/brown crown

CRYSTAL TYPE: Organic, some shark teeth fossils between 50 million and 100 million years old, composed of calcium phosphate

ZODIAC SIGN: Capricorn (December 22–January 20)

CANDLE COLOR: Cream

PHYSICAL: Alleviates issues involving the teeth, jaw, bones, cartilage, osteoporosis, aging, genetic and hereditary conditions, mobility, slow-healing wounds; relieves pain.

EMOTIONAL: Counters repetition of old mistakes; keeps you from remaining locked in adulthood in dependent roles with parents or authority figures; addresses issues with alcohol.

HOME: Attracts abundance and resources; keeps debt at bay; traditionally brings long life and health.

WORKPLACE: Cultivates business where there is fierce competition; for negotiating with ruthless people; aids in earning a living from ocean- or water-based activities; generates successful international business interests.

CHILDREN: Promotes safety on school trips or adventure vacations, particularly involving water sports; allays fears of being immersed in water.

ANIMALS: Protects cruelly and illegally hunted sea mammals.

PROTECTION: Guards against tricksters, scams, computer hacking, identity theft, loss when traveling overseas.

MAGICKAL AND PSYCHIC USES

Rituals to overcome betrayal by those with close access to past worlds of seafaring communities.

SPECIAL PROPERTIES

A symbol of animus power, confidence, and courage for men and women alike, transforming hesitation into decisive action.

MYTHOLOGY AND HISTORY

In Hawaii, Shark Teeth represent the power and protection of the shark god Kāmohoali, who guided to safety boats in danger and the original inhabitants to their new island home.

Shattuckite

COLORS: Deep blue, turquoise blue, sometimes with azure, red, or brown streaks

CRYSTAL TYPE: Copper silicate hydroxide

ZODIAC SIGN: Aquarius (January 21–February 18)

CANDLE COLOR: Blue

PHYSICAL: Addresses issues stemming from diabetes, calcium absorption, parathyroid, ear, nose, throat, mouth, teeth, gums, blood, arthritis, rheumatism.

EMOTIONAL: Releases what is gone or can never be in love; assists reconciliation of old wrongs.

HOME: For clearing clutter and delegating instead of doing everything yourself; increases family quality time.

WORKPLACE: For processing and accurate recall of information; for detectives, customs officers, security services, air traffic controllers, scientific researchers, medical personnel, lecturers, and compilers of dictionaries, encyclopedias, and quizzes.

CHILDREN: Focuses those with unsettled minds; for those who find it hard to answer questions in class.

ANIMALS: For canine obedience training; dressage with horses.

PROTECTION: Prevents mediums and anyone dabbling with spirits from being manipulated, deceived, or taken over by trickster entities.

MAGICKAL AND PSYCHIC USES

For enhanced claircognizance, telepathy, healing past lives, and interpreting wisdom from angels, guides, and one's higher self (especially through automatic writing).

SPECIAL PROPERTIES

For communication of deep feelings, fears, and vulnerability in a love relationship after previous hurt or betrayal; forgiving yourself for past mistakes.

MYTHOLOGY AND HISTORY

Shattuckite is a traditional magickal healing and love charm among Indigenous people in Arizona and parts of Africa; still regarded as a lucky charm in the modern world, especially for manifesting money; known for synthesizing all the psychic senses, so spiritual awareness becomes a multisensory experience.

Shell Marble or Shell Jasper

COLORS: Mottled black, white, and gray patterns

CRYSTAL TYPE: White fossil brachiopods, comprising a group within a matrix of cementing black limestone, creating marble

ZODIAC SIGN: Pisces (February 19–March 20)

CANDLE COLOR: White

PHYSICAL: Alleviates issues involving the liver, gallbladder, stomach lining, stomach ulcers, digestive disorders; promotes long life.

EMOTIONAL: Curbs excesses of all kinds; counters arrested emotional development with dependence on or ruled by parents throughout adulthood.

HOME: A stone if you are setting up home with a new partner later in life; for anyone buying a second home overseas or near the ocean.

WORKPLACE: For business negotiations that will prosper over time; overseas or out-of-state networking.

CHILDREN: Soothes children who are cared for full time by grandparents while their parents work.

ANIMALS: For older pets to settle after a move to a new home; for telepathy with pets.

PROTECTION: Guards against malicious magick, curses, hexes, and ill-wishing.

MAGICKAL AND PSYCHIC USES

Linked with ancient times, when life began under the seas; Atlantean wisdom through meditation and visualization; dolphin healing using dolphin calls, set to music; telepathic communication with Star Beings.

SPECIAL PROPERTIES

A stone of balancing the whole person, not seeking to eradicate or suppress the shadow side but using it as a catalyst for positive change.

MYTHOLOGY AND HISTORY

Also called shell obsidian or marbled shell jasper, Shell Marble has been formed over millions of years; as the shells became buried on the sea floor, black mud entered the bottom of the shells, the rest filling with white crystalline calcite and the mud turning to stone through the millennia.

Shiva Lingam

COLORS: Earth tones, especially tan

CRYSTAL TYPE: Cryptocrystalline quartz; inclusions of basalt, feldspar, and iron oxide; some naturally formed, others crafted into a phallic shape and hand-polished

ZODIAC SIGN: Scorpio (October 24– November 22)

CANDLE COLOR: Indigo

PHYSICAL: Promotes fertility; relieves impotence, premature ejaculation, prostate issues, vaginismus; increases libido; for easy childbirth; fosters healthy menstruation and eases the transition to menopause; enhances health.

EMOTIONAL: Counters uncertainty about sexuality, sexual partners, or gender; keeps you from acting out an ultra-macho or super-feminine role, due to pressure from others.

HOME: Shiva Lingam directs the free, steady flow of life-force energies; strengthens loving relationships.

WORKPLACE: Prevents inappropriate sexual behavior in the workplace; aids in overcoming sexism; for a couple working together in the same department if there is resentment.

CHILDREN: Connects with as-yet-unborn children preconception or in the womb during sleep or waking visions.

ANIMALS: For a breeding animal who has problems becoming pregnant.

PROTECTION: Guards against those who try to manipulate you through guilt.

MAGICKAL AND PSYCHIC USES

For sacred or tantric sex; full moon fertility rituals.

SPECIAL PROPERTIES

If a single sex or gender-fluid couple are trying for a baby; stimulates the kundalini within the base of the spine; for reconciliation between a couple when others have caused divisions.

MYTHOLOGY AND HISTORY

An ancient symbol, traditionally found at Onkar Manadhata, one of the sacred sites of India, Shiva Lingam is gathered from the riverbed of the Narmada in the dry season. It represents the cosmic egg, the creation and uniting of both divine male and female energies.

Shiva Shell, Pacific Cat's Eye, or Eye of Shiva

COLORS: White with a brown or black swirl, forming an eye

CRYSTAL TYPE: Calcium carbonate

ZODIAC SIGN: Pisces (February 19–March 20)

CANDLE COLOR: White or silver

PHYSICAL: Brings the body back into natural rhythm; for kidneys, pancreas, gallbladder, liver, lymph nodes, spleen, and white blood cells.

EMOTIONAL: Counters sleep disturbances caused by an overactive mind and 2:00 a.m. angst.

HOME: Suspend a Shiva Shell over the front door to deter intruders and unpleasant visitors.

WORKPLACE: Enables you to discover hidden rivals who resent your success.

CHILDREN: Allays fears of the water and swimming.

ANIMALS: For the well-being of fish in ponds or aquariums.

PROTECTION: The eye formation guards against the evil eye of jealousy and envy.

MAGICKAL AND PSYCHIC USES

Used in water rituals as an offering to the deities of the ocean in different cultures to grant wishes; also used in blessing newborn children, so that the children will be watched over even when their parents are not present.

SPECIAL PROPERTIES

Called mermaids' money, brings luck both to fisherfolk and for accumulating and keeping wealth.

MYTHOLOGY AND HISTORY

Found on the seabed of the shallow seas of Thailand, Indonesia, and those north of Australia; as the detached door of the turban snail's shell, Shiva Shell signifies the soul's doorway via the third eye (seen on statues on the brow of Shiva the Hindu transformer father god); brings knowledge of the future.

Shungite

COLOR: Silvery black

CRYSTAL TYPE: Almost entirely carbon

ZODIAC SIGN: Virgo (August 24–September 22)

CANDLE COLOR: Silver

PHYSICAL: A whole-body healer, detoxifier, and antibacterial as the Crystal Elixir (see page 145); relieves headaches, back pain, insomnia.

EMOTIONAL: Helps overcome the repetition of self-sabotaging patterns in life and relationships, replacing them with positive new approaches.

HOME: Set Shungite in each room to absorb any overactive, subterranean, Earth energies and gently release blocked energies; good if you live near a cell phone tower.

WORKPLACE: Near technological equipment and Wi-Fi routers as a shield from excessive technological pollution.

CHILDREN: Helps children who are easily led to be less influenced; for accident-prone children.

ANIMALS: Calms overly excitable animals and those who react badly to noise.

PROTECTION: Absorbs and protects from negativity of all kinds; guards against misfortune.

MAGICKAL AND PSYCHIC USES

An amulet against psychic and psychological attack, curses, and hexes.

SPECIAL PROPERTIES

In love relationships, shields against outside interference and jealous rivals.

MYTHOLOGY AND HISTORY

Around two billion years old, it is found mainly in the Lake Onega, Karelia area, in Russia. Here the late-seventeenth-early-eighteenth-century Russian czar Peter the Great created the first Russian spa, where people bathed (and still do) in water purified by the Shungite through which it naturally flows.

Siberian Blue Quartz

COLORS: Deep blue and clear, the blue caused by the addition of cobalt to the mix

CRYSTAL TYPE: Natural quartz, broken down and regrown with cobalt in the laboratory, mirroring and speeding the natural process of crystal formation

ZODIAC SIGN: Sagittarius (November 23–December 21)

CANDLE COLOR: Blue

PHYSICAL: Alleviates issues concerning the throat, neck and neck glands, glandular fever, ears, eyes, teeth, gum infections, fevers, skin inflammation, sunburn, stomach problems exacerbated by stress.

EMOTIONAL: Keeps you from dealing with problems by creating distractions through a constant whirl of activity; helps you find inner peace.

HOME: Asserting or reasserting the way you wish to live and commanding respect from those who disregard you.

WORKPLACE: Propels you to a position of leadership, authority, and major promotion; cobalt attracts lasting prosperity.

CHILDREN: Comforts Star Children who sometimes feel as if they do not fit with their peers.

ANIMALS: For special pets who protect and show exceptional patience toward young children.

PROTECTION: Guards against the evil eye of envy.

MAGICKAL AND PSYCHIC USES

A stone of communication on a spiritual level, with each of the senses attuned to its psychic form; clairvoyance, clairaudience, clairsentience, prophecy, psychokinesis, communicating with the departed.

SPECIAL PROPERTIES

Assists in finding lost objects, missing animals, and calling estranged family members home, with insights coming in dreams.

MYTHOLOGY AND HISTORY

Grown in Russia, Siberian Blue Quartz possesses the same chemical composition as a naturally grown crystal, but has additional purity, so it encourages altruism and the highest ethics. Said to be a true alchemical mixture of human endeavor and natural materials, Siberian Blue Quartz creates greater energy, radiating power generated by the intensity of its creation.

Siberian Golden Quartz

COLORS: Golden, yellow-gold, and pure in color

CRYSTAL TYPE: Different from Gold-Included Quartz because Siberian Golden Quartz is laboratory-grown and the gold added to the liquid quartz as part of the mix; makes beautiful jewelry as well as polished stones

ZODIAC SIGN: Leo (July 23–August 23)

CANDLE COLOR: Gold

PHYSICAL: Boosts stamina, health, strength, vitality to overcome malaise, sickness, and exhaustion; for transplants, transfusions, and implants, especially bone marrow and liver; eases seasonal affective disorder, psychosomatic conditions; promotes fertility, potency.

EMOTIONAL: Curbs depression; inertia, dependency and codependency; keeps you from inducing guilt in others.

HOME: Fills even the gloomiest property with sunshine and light, fun and laughter; for success in sports, particularly endurance and extreme sports.

WORKPLACE: Attracts leadership and promotion opportunities, plus fame and fortune in creative and performing endeavors.

CHILDREN: Increases confidence in shy children so they will make friends more easily; for invitations to other children's parties, social events, and being asked to join teams.

ANIMALS: For winning prizes in shows and competitions.

PROTECTION: Guards against overly loud people who steal the limelight.

MAGICKAL AND PSYCHIC USES

Sun and solstice magick; prosperity spells; appearing in the media or at major new-age festivals and shows with mediumship or psychic skills; starting a psychic phone line; gaining demonstrable proof of your psychic gifts.

SPECIAL PROPERTIES

The golden crystal to attract success and prosperity to whatever you try; finding happiness with your soul twin and engaging in joint ventures.

MYTHOLOGY AND HISTORY

The crystal of making your own luck because it is an alchemical stone created by the combination of human and natural endeavor; the most proactive and dynamic of the Siberian quartzes, always involving sharing that good fortune.

Siberian Purple Quartz

COLORS: violet and clear

CRYSTAL TYPE: Like the other Siberian quartzes, grown from natural quartz in the laboratory with the addition of iron and manganese to incorporate the color as part of the crystal

ZODIAC SIGN: Pisces (February 19–March 20)

CANDLE COLOR: Purple

PHYSICAL: Enhances short-term memory; alleviates migraines with visual disturbances; counters malfunctioning of the autoimmune system and nerve endings; valuable with Reiki, angel, crystal, and energy therapies under many names, both therapeutically and as chances to enable recall from past worlds.

EMOTIONAL: Mitigates alienation from others; counters disillusion with life, cynicism; keeps you from excessive consumption of food, alcohol, tobacco, and prescription or recreational drugs.

HOME: Makes your present home a sanctuary, even if it's not ideal or in the place you would wish to be.

WORKPLACE: Aids in maintaining dignity and high ethics, no matter what difficulties you are experiencing; a chance to consider a spiritual career, at least part time.

CHILDREN: For Indigo Children who are having psychic experiences that may trouble them.

ANIMALS: Helps discover your shamanic or totem protective animals, one of which may be an old-soul present pet.

PROTECTION: Guards against false gurus who resent your gifts.

MAGICKAL AND PSYCHIC USES

Transmits the violet healing flame of truth, forgiveness, and transformation of the ascended master St. Germain and the Archangel Zadkiel; for clairvoyance, clairaudience, and communication with archangels and access to the Akashic records.

SPECIAL PROPERTIES

The ongoing purification crystal of the aura, chakra energy centers, the present environment, and negative energies from others.

MYTHOLOGY AND HISTORY

The most highly evolved spiritually of the Siberian quartzes, helpful for those already on their spiritual journey to perfect techniques and begin to teach others healing, divination, and the psychic arts.

Sichuan Quartz

COLORS: Mainly clear, usually containing white or black spot-like inclusions; may be cloudy

CRYSTAL TYPE: Quartz, silicon dioxide, small, thick double-terminated points; much more proactive than Tibetan Quartz; contains carbon where there are black spots

ZODIAC SIGN: Aquarius (January 21–February 18).

CANDLE COLOR: White

PHYSICAL: Draws out pain and illness with one pointed end, followed by energizing and restoring health with the other; alleviates chronic fatigue, recurring illnesses; for older people, with slowly deteriorating conditions, to slow or reverse their progress.

EMOTIONAL: Curbs eating disorders, which may be linked with past-world starvation; counters immovable belief patterns established earlier in this life.

HOME: Use Sichuan Quartz to cleanse inherited artifacts of unhappy memories or gifts from those who do not always have good intentions.

WORKPLACE: Brings together different talents and factors when a complete overview is needed.

CHILDREN: Useful if you dream of your unborn or as-yet-unconceived child to communicate with them in meditation.

ANIMALS: For being psychically drawn to a particular place or information where your new pet is waiting to be rehoused.

PROTECTION: Keeps away negative thought forms and lower-level spirits.

MAGICKAL AND PSYCHIC USES

For accessing ancient Chinese wisdom; understanding the *I Ching* intuitively; increases psychic abilities.

SPECIAL PROPERTIES

A gift for an adult child leaving home for the first time to carry the love of the family and enable them to enjoy freedom knowing that they always have a place back home.

MYTHOLOGY AND HISTORY

From the Chinese province of Sichuan, an area where new quartz is constantly being found, such as Evolight crystal with its etched faces in 2016 (see Etched Quartz); like other Himalayan quartzes, Sichuan Quartz was traditionally believed by Indigenous people to be the eyes of the gods.

Siderite

COLORS: Brown, tan, pale or brownish-yellow, greenish- or reddish-brown, occasionally blue; sometimes pearly

CRYSTAL TYPE: Iron carbonate, magnetic when heated

ZODIAC SIGN: Aries (March 21–April 20)

CANDLE COLOR: Yellow

PHYSICAL: Bolsters strength; addresses chronic digestive and bowel disorders affected by food allergies, balance, plus assimilation of calcium, magnesium, and iron; alleviates osteoporosis, anemia; strengthens the elimination system.

EMOTIONAL: Resists pressure from controlling, critical relatives or your partner; aligns every aspect of yourself if your life is chaotic.

HOME: For backseat drivers who keep up a commentary of unwanted advice; calms fear of strange noises or shadows at night if you live alone.

WORKPLACE: Promotes fairer working conditions; aids in obtaining a permanent position if you are not on contract; helps stabilize your employment.

CHILDREN: For those who are clumsy or accident-prone.

ANIMALS: Inspires affection for abandoned or abused pets from rescue centers.

PROTECTION: Traditionally protective against mischievous fairies, elves, or nature spirits; an amulet against bad luck, breakage, breakdown of vehicles or equipment, and accidents.

MAGICKAL AND PSYCHIC USES

Fire rituals, defensive magick, psychokinesis to discover by psychic touch hidden information about people and situations.

SPECIAL PROPERTIES

For joy and enthusiasm in life, work, and relationships; for all who are restricted from living freely and those who care for them.

MYTHOLOGY AND HISTORY

Formed on seabeds millions of years ago, Siderite granules were used extensively in early European and North American iron industries. Siderite combines dynamic innovative action with proven experience, especially in a career.

Sieber or Sieber Agate

COLORS: Swirls of pale gray-green/blue within a deeper blue/gray base, similar to patterns found in natural agates; deep blue and shiny; may include rainbows

CRYSTAL TYPE: Not an agate, formed when copper is extracted from copper ore under heat by an ancient process; best as tumbled stones for healing and magick

ZODIAC SIGN: Libra (September 23–October 23)

CANDLE COLOR: Blue

PHYSICAL: Relieves pain; alleviates conditions involving impaired short-term memory and vision; eases painful joints and muscles, arthritis and rheumatism, prostate issues; useful for transplants, especially involving artificial implants, such as mechanical heart valves, pacemakers, or stents.

EMOTIONAL: Mitigates personality disorders, claustrophobia; keeps you from falling prey to hard-luck stories and too-good-to-be-true offers.

HOME: Aids in finding your own role and boundaries if you move into a new partner's home, formerly shared with an ex.

WORKPLACE: Brings security in employment in uncertain times; for confidence to express your views when colleagues or management dominate brainstorming sessions.

CHILDREN: Encourages children to speak the truth without fear of punishment; helps hesitant children gain confidence in small social or educational settings.

ANIMALS: For pets who hate noise and crowds.

PROTECTION: Guards against being sold fake designer goods, substandard products, or romance frauds online.

MAGICKAL AND PSYCHIC USES

Telepathy, clairvoyance; aura cleansing; all forms of divination to overcome blocks because of fears of your interpretation being wrong.

SPECIAL PROPERTIES

For clear communication, where there have been misunderstandings; when honesty is needed in a relationship if there has been deception.

MYTHOLOGY AND HISTORY

Sieber Agate is found in Siebertal, Harz, Germany and is quite rare. Useful for learning new languages.

Sillimanite

COLORS: Green, grayish-blue, blue, yellow, brown, white, black, striated, silky; may be found totally transparent in Myanmar, where there are also violet-blue specimens; often opaque

CRYSTAL TYPE: Aluminum silicate; shares the same chemistry as andalusite and kyanite, but with a different structure; because it is brittle, it is hard to facet and therefore much prized as jewelry in clear form

ZODIAC SIGN: Virgo (August 24–September 22)

CANDLE COLOR: Green or blue

PHYSICAL: Valuable for breast implants, stents, pacemakers, heart-valve replacements, bypass surgery.

EMOTIONAL: Keeps you from overthinking and -analyzing every situation; counters distrust of your instincts; enables you to express emotions; keeps you from losing your joie de vivre.

HOME: For loans, grants, or mortgages previously declined; protects the home from natural disasters.

WORKPLACE: If you have to multitask, aids in prioritizing and completing one step at a time.

CHILDREN: For starting day care or school if they find socializing hard; for changing schools mid-year with the least disruption because of relocation of family; for those with a short attention span.

ANIMALS: Soothes pets who can anticipate danger; seen in guide, therapy, and particularly tuned-in pets.

PROTECTION: Guards against obstacles when situations or people are preventing you from moving forward.

MAGICKAL AND PSYCHIC USES

The stone of trusting instincts, especially maternal telepathy or premonitions at any age between parent and child.

SPECIAL PROPERTIES

An amulet against accidents while traveling, for yourself, for your loved ones, for documents and possessions.

MYTHOLOGY AND HISTORY

Discovered in Andalusia, Spain, in 1824 by scientist and mineralogist Benjamin Silliman, and since found in Madagascar, France, Myanmar, Kenya, and the eastern United States. A highly prized gemstone often treasured by those involved in physically hazardous occupations and competitors partaking in extreme sports or team games. Also called fibrolite with a cat's eye effect, frequently blue.

Silver

COLOR: Silver
CRYSTAL TYPE: Metal, element
ZODIAC SIGN: Cancer (June 22–July 22)
CANDLE COLOR: Silver

PHYSICAL: Promotes detoxification, digestion of essential minerals, fertility; alleviates issues involving PMS, menstruation, pregnancy, hormones, hepatitis, visual disturbances, headaches, fluid retention, circulation blockages, pineal and pituitary glands.
EMOTIONAL: Enables women to value and care for their body; for men forced unwillingly into a macho role; for those inadequately mothered or who lost their mother when they were young.
HOME: Attracts money and health; for all issues concerned with mothers and mothering.
WORKPLACE: Encourages patience and perseverance in the face of complex or tedious tasks; for night workers; aids in avoiding having your energy drained while dealing with the public.
CHILDREN: Protects children from nightmares and frightening ghosts at night; improves clarity of speech.
ANIMALS: For dogs who howl when left alone.
PROTECTION: Guards against emotional and psychological vampires; reflects back ill-wishing; guards travelers at night and overseas, especially as a silver St. Christopher medallion.

MAGICKAL AND PSYCHIC USES
For good fortune as silver lucky charms; wish magick turning silver over three times facing the crescent moon; full moon fertility magick; astral travel, full moon ceremonies; Wicca; sea spells; scrying in moonlit water on a full moon.

SPECIAL PROPERTIES
Silver jewelry attracts love, fertility, and prosperity; silver doubles the powers of crystal jewelry; for love, especially new and young love, or after betrayal.

MYTHOLOGY AND HISTORY
Silver is sacred to the moon and the pre-Christian Moon Goddesses, such as the Greco-Roman Artemis and Diana. According to legend, Silver bullets kill vampires and werewolves.

Silver Aura Actinolite or Actinolite in Talc

COLOR: Silvery
CRYSTAL TYPE: Actinolite, amphibole silicate, talc. Hydrated magnesium silicate; actinolite is often found in talc deposits
ZODIAC SIGN: Taurus (April 21–May 21)
CANDLE COLOR: Silver

PHYSICAL: Promotes absorption of nutrients; alleviates issues stemming from the kidneys, liver, intestines, bowels, rashes and adverse reactions caused by plant allergies and additives, heartburn, mercury and lead poisoning.
EMOTIONAL: Counters lack of self-worth if you have been denigrated throughout your life or during the formative years; opens emotional blockages if you come from an undemonstrative family.
HOME: Silver Aura Actinolite creates a sense of contentment and being blessed; encourages praise, rather than criticism.
WORKPLACE: For training apprentices and students in vocational courses, especially disaffected teenagers; repels those who block healing or psychic energies through fear.
CHILDREN: Useful for those with behavioral difficulties at school who are easily influenced by others.
ANIMALS: For clumsy, large animals in confined spaces.
PROTECTION: Protects against seeing life in terms of victims and villains, and seeking rescue by others.

MAGICKAL AND PSYCHIC USES
Silver Aura Actinolite expands the boundaries of possibility, offering proof of psychic powers to doubters; a counterbalance to Mercury retrograde and planets in opposition or adversely positioned in your current chart.

SPECIAL PROPERTIES
For attracting lasting love with a soul mate or kindred spirit, not an ideal or dream lover, but a real partner who will care for you in good times and bad.

MYTHOLOGY AND HISTORY
Also called argent aura, Silver Aura Actinolite should not be confused with Silver Aura Quartz, where quartz is coated with silver. Silver Aura Actinolite restores faith in people and in good fortune.

Silver Aventurine

COLORS: Pale gray or white with silvery sparkles

CRYSTAL TYPE: Microcrystalline quartz, with inclusions of mica that give it the silvery sheen

ZODIAC SIGN: Cancer (June 22–July 22)

CANDLE COLOR: Silver

PHYSICAL: Alleviates psoriasis, acne, rosacea, PMS, menstrual irregularities, symptoms of menopause, blurred vision, vertigo, migraines, glandular fever, cataracts, glaucoma; regulates hormones.

EMOTIONAL: Aids in overcoming the trauma of sexual abuse or rape; counters insomnia, disturbed sleep, and nightmares due to an inability to switch off from the day.

HOME: Unlocks a treasure trove from attics or inheritances.

WORKPLACE: Promotes the financial viability of healing, therapeutic, and spiritual businesses without sacrificing integrity.

CHILDREN: Protects young ones from online attacks, predators, and trolls.

ANIMALS: For all nocturnal creatures—pets and wildlife, especially owls in sanctuaries.

PROTECTION: Guards against incubi and succubi, paranormal sexual predators and spirits in séances and ouija board sessions pretending to be celebrities or deceased royalty.

MAGICKAL AND PSYCHIC USES

For moon magick, especially at full moon, clairvoyance; scrying in moonlight; meeting a present or future lover on the dream plane; opens doorways to other dimensions.

SPECIAL PROPERTIES

The crystal of secret love and lovers parted by circumstances, distance, or existing relationships; aids in keeping secrets when pressured to reveal them.

MYTHOLOGY AND HISTORY

The most magickal and mystical aventurine linked with manifesting wishes; relieves loneliness far from home; attracts a soul twin on or offline, called the mirror of the soul because it allows the true self to shine through.

Silver-Bearing or Silver-Included Quartz

COLORS: Silver, silvery gray

CRYSTAL TYPE: Silver found within quartz host rock (see also Silver-Rutilated Quartz and Silver-Light Quartz, pages 440 and 439); silver may appear as flakes within the quartz or as spider veins

ZODIAC SIGN: Cancer (June 22–July 22)

CANDLE COLOR: Silver

PHYSICAL: Promotes fertility, pregnancy (both spontaneously and after medical or surgical intervention), IVF using donated sperm and eggs from known donors; regulates menstrual cycles.

EMOTIONAL: Allays fears of childbirth; curbs acute anxiety about dying when children are still young, especially if you are a single parent.

HOME: Enhances the life-force flow through the home; beneficial for all-female households.

WORKPLACE: Helps overcome limitations in worldview and personal expansion; for those working for cultural organizations, especially Indigenous ones.

CHILDREN: Teaches children to discover and value their total cultural heritage.

ANIMALS: For breeding and conserving rare and endangered species; guards against poaching creatures in danger of becoming extinct.

PROTECTION: Guards against being categorized or experiencing any form of prejudice and intolerance.

MAGICKAL AND PSYCHIC USES

Moon magick on the different phases of the moon, money spells, goddess rituals for both sexes; connects with the wisdom of ancient alchemists for revealing the hidden properties of minerals.

SPECIAL PROPERTIES

Pure silver in quartz is an alchemist's transformation stone, as the quartz amplifies the natural powers of silver.

MYTHOLOGY AND HISTORY

Very rare, as much Silver-Bearing Quartz has been crushed through the years to release the silver; jewelry still exists from the Comstock Lode in Nevada in the 1840s.

Silver Leaf Agate

COLORS: Cream to silver, bluish-gray to black, with distinctive silvery translucent swirls

CRYSTAL TYPE: Chalcedony, microcrystalline quartz; in opaque darker form, sometimes called silver leaf jasper, with similar properties

ZODIAC SIGN: Gemini (May 22–June 21)

CANDLE COLOR: Silver

PHYSICAL: Eases sleep disturbances, migraines, neurological conditions, MS, Parkinson's disease, bipolar disorder, autism, Asperger's syndrome; strengthens veins, arteries, cells.

EMOTIONAL: Allays fears of being persecuted or watched; counters overreliance on clairvoyants and mediums for every decision.

HOME: Encourages generosity among siblings of any age who play favorites.

WORKPLACE: Aids in making safe business decisions when complete information is not available.

CHILDREN: Keeps little ones safe near water; reassures reluctant young swimmers; comforts small children afraid of darkness or ghosts.

ANIMALS: Safeguards koi and other ornamental fish.

PROTECTION: For those who sail or practice water sports; curbs fears of traveling by boat.

MAGICKAL AND PSYCHIC USES

A moon crystal for all phases—wish magick on the crescent and waxing moon, success or love at full moon, releasing pain on the wane; dream recall and magickal dreaming.

SPECIAL PROPERTIES

Attracts abundance into life in practical ways most needed, but not anticipated.

MYTHOLOGY AND HISTORY

Associated with Nyx, ancient Greek goddess of night, whose daughter Hemera, goddess of morning, replaced her mother each dawn with the early silver light. Silver Lace Agate is associated with the silver birch tree, signifying in many cultures new beginnings, independence, and returning to former enthusiasm and dreams.

Silver-Light Quartz or Silver Quartz

COLORS: Very clear without inclusions, with a high luster that makes the crystal shine silver with rainbows

CRYSTAL TYPE: Clear quartz in different kinds; may be wand shape. The silver brilliance distinguishes it as Silver-Light Quartz

ZODIAC SIGN: Cancer (June 22–July 22)

CANDLE COLOR: Silver

PHYSICAL: Repairs cells; rejuvenates the body; eases migraines, visual disturbances; repels infections and viruses.

EMOTIONAL: Counteracts a tendency to self-harm; helps overcome poor self-image, leading to eating disorders; keeps you from reflecting the views of whoever is currently present.

HOME: For an overcrowded home or accommodations to create a sense of space; removes stagnant energies.

WORKPLACE: Aids in finding the right employment that reflects your core ideas, ambitions, and ethics; creates an undisturbed space if colleagues constantly interrupt you.

CHILDREN: Teaches children to care about others less fortunate than they are and to offer help in small ways; protects young ones from online grooming.

ANIMALS: For pets who have been hurt in an accident or attack.

PROTECTION: Reflects back harm or ill-wishing from any source.

MAGICKAL AND PSYCHIC USES

Mirror magick to connect with ancestors and spirit guides; scrying by moonlight; offers understanding of present fears through past life regression. A Master Crystal to empower other crystals.

SPECIAL PROPERTIES

A crystal to fill every occasion with joy and light and raise the level of communication if people are being petty, spiteful, or overly critical.

MYTHOLOGY AND HISTORY

Found in Brazil, Colombia, and Arkansas, Silver-Light Quartz is said to have the highest vibration of all quartzes; the crystal of light in the darkness, transforming doubt into certainty, despair into hope, and sorrow into joy.

Silver-Rutilated Quartz

COLORS: Clear, containing silver, the amount depending on the number of rutiles

CRYSTAL TYPE: Quartz with titanium dioxide rutiles or needles within, sometimes with gold rutiles in the same quartz

ZODIAC SIGN: Cancer (June 22–July 22)

CANDLE COLOR: Silver

PHYSICAL: Alleviates issues involving the uterus, ovaries, cervix, early-onset menopause, hysterectomy, optic nerves, glaucoma, minor and same-day surgery.

EMOTIONAL: Allays fears of aging and losing your looks, especially for women; counters an emotionally suffocating partner and children, agoraphobia.

HOME: For finding a home where you have space to develop your creativity or spirituality; for gardening by the moon phases.

WORKPLACE: Enables you to start a spiritual or creative business in the second half of life; for an unexpected increase in salary or perks.

CHILDREN: Encourages youngsters to spend quality time with their grandparents, when grandparents are their main caregivers.

ANIMALS: For an older mother animal struggling with a new litter.

PROTECTION: Guards against premonitions of disaster that cannot be prevented, random spirit messages or threats from beyond.

MAGICKAL AND PSYCHIC USES

Most powerful when the full moon appears from behind the clouds; for lunar eclipse rituals, women's mysteries, intuition, prophecy, and scrying in water by moonlight.

SPECIAL PROPERTIES

For women wanting to have children later in life, especially if they intend to become single parents; for finding lasting love late in life.

MYTHOLOGY AND HISTORY

Linked with Arianrhod, Welsh Celtic goddess of the full moon, time, and destiny, who turned the silver wheel of the stars; under the sway of the silver-haired Moon Goddesses who rule the days after full moon and guide a woman to the next phase of her life.

Silver Sheen Obsidian

COLORS: Dark brown or black with a silver-gray iridescent sheen caused by small air bubbles during fast cooling as lava meets water

CRYSTAL TYPE: Natural silica-rich volcanic glass

ZODIAC SIGNS: Cancer (June 22–July 22) and Scorpio (October 24–November 22)

CANDLE COLOR: Silver

PHYSICAL: Addresses migraines, visual disturbances, posture defects, burns, skin grafts, plastic surgery, skin cell abnormalities, conditions requiring emergency intervention; relieves pain.

EMOTIONAL: Releases hidden traumas connected with neglectful or absent mothering; helps to mother ourselves instead of seeking substitutes.

HOME: Enables you to host safe teenage parties at home to avoid damage, excessive noise, and gate-crashers.

WORKPLACE: For successful advertising. publicity, marketing, graphic design; useful for astronomers, astrologers, clairvoyants, and meteorologists.

CHILDREN: Calms behavioral issues causing educational or social problems.

ANIMALS: Assists older pregnant animals.

PROTECTION: Shields against manipulation and over-possessiveness by family or a partner.

MAGICKAL AND PSYCHIC USES

Hold a Silver Sheen sphere to full moonlight for inner visions of your future path; all moon rituals.

SPECIAL PROPERTIES

Called the stone of the galaxy, Silver Sheen Obsidian soothes those adversely affected by full moon energies; brings fertility into alignment with moon cycles.

MYTHOLOGY AND HISTORY

Found mainly in Mexico and the remote Glass Buttes region of central Oregon, Silver Sheen Obsidian has been prized and traded by Native North Americans for many centuries.

Simbercite or Simbircite Pyrite Agate

COLORS: Amber, green, red, black, brown, and white stripes with sparkling pyrite veins throughout; a silky sheen

CRYSTAL TYPE: Agatized mineral that fills the chambers of the ammonite Lamberticeras and other ancient sea creatures, made up of a mixture of magnesium-rich calcite, aragonite, pyrite, marl, chabazite, hematite, golden marble onyx, and quartz; often made into cabochons or jewelry

ZODIAC SIGN: Leo (July 23–August 23)

CANDLE COLOR: Gold

PHYSICAL: Eases headaches (including migraines), digestion, arthritis, rheumatism; generates small miracles and unexpected improvements.

EMOTIONAL: Counters indecision, suspicion of the motives of others, expecting and so attracting the worst outcome.

HOME: Attracts lasting prosperity through home-based enterprises.

WORKPLACE: Removes limits to what is possible in career and creativity; for making a business your sole future source of income.

CHILDREN: For teens who live in a state of chaos to gain structure and order in their lives; for gifted children who are excluded by less motivated peers.

ANIMALS: Consoles a grieving pet whose owner has recently died.

PROTECTION: Guards against fear, despair, and doubt.

MAGICKAL AND PSYCHIC USES

A magickal alchemical stone for wish magick; absorbs negative energies and transforms them into light and life; protective during rituals.

SPECIAL PROPERTIES

The beauty of the stone fills the heart, body, mind, and soul with love, confidence, and clarity to turn life around and find ongoing joy in small daily pleasures.

MYTHOLOGY AND HISTORY

The many minerals comprising Simbercite formed into an alloy 130–160 million years ago. This remarkable natural creation is both a gemstone and fossil. Simbercite's only source is the area around the Russian city of Simbirsk, now called Ulyanovsk. Simbercite is also known as volzhsky amber.

Singing Quartz

COLORS: Varies, usually clear quartz but can be found as smoky quartz, citrine, or other quartzes

CRYSTAL TYPE: Small laser crystals bought in pairs; some with spiral formations; different singing crystals have different sounds

ZODIAC SIGN: Aquarius (January 21–February 18)

CANDLE COLOR: Silver

PHYSICAL: Strengthens bones; straightens skeletal misalignment; addresses whole-body healing, restless legs syndrome, Parkinson's; alleviates issues involving the throat, mouth, jaw, ears, and teeth; promotes fertility, especially before IVF or fertility treatment.

EMOTIONAL: Curbs excessive workaholic tendencies; enables you to relax or switch off.

HOME: Useful if played gently before the family returns or challenging visitors arrive.

WORKPLACE: For noisy workplaces to create your own peaceful workspace and deter colleagues from intruding.

CHILDREN: Keeps teens from playing their music too loud or always shouting.

ANIMALS: For calming neighborhood barking dogs and yowling cats.

PROTECTION: Use the sound to surround your aura energy before a potentially challenging day.

MAGICKAL AND PSYCHIC USES

Singing Quartz resonates with *Om* or *Aum* as the first, the primal, or the sacred sound that brought the universe into being; for working with crystal singing bowls, sound healing.

SPECIAL PROPERTIES

True Singing Quartz produces a soft, sweet, resonant, musical sound, as opposed to when two pieces of ordinary quartz are rubbed together.

MYTHOLOGY AND HISTORY

Singing Quartzes are associated with extraterrestrial communication; believed to have been created by beings from other planets to act as a link and guide to UFOs; they resonate extra powerfully in areas of high UFO sightings and around crop circles. First discovered in Brazil.

Single-Point or Terminated Quartz

COLORS: Usually clear, especially if polished; varies according to the kind and purity of the quartz; Single-Point Quartz is milkier or cloudier near the base, no matter what form the quartz

CRYSTAL TYPE: Clear crystal quartz, also in amethyst, smoky quartz, and citrine, with a single six-sided or six-faced termination or point at one end (see page 164 for double-terminated crystals and page 155 for wands)

ZODIAC SIGN: Sagittarius (November 23–December 21)

CANDLE COLOR: According to the quartz

PHYSICAL: Single-Terminated Quartz channels healing energy directly to the patient via the point.

EMOTIONAL: Eases panic attacks, obsessive thoughts.

HOME: A crystal point layout, seven for the days of the week or twelve for the months of the year, facing alternately inward and outward, keeps fresh energies flowing.

WORKPLACE: Citrine, the merchant's crystal, and clear quartz, points facing inward, close to the door of a business or store, attracts new business.

CHILDREN: Attach amethyst points to a dream catcher for peaceful sleep.

ANIMALS: Energize or infuse calm into the water bowl with a clear quartz or amethyst point before use.

PROTECTION: Smoky or amethyst points facing outward in the bedroom keep away bad dreams.

MAGICKAL AND PSYCHIC USES
Use a clear quartz as a pendulum, pointed downward, or as a wand, spiraling it clockwise, pointed outward to call what you want to manifest; smoky quartz, pointing outward and spiraled counterclockwise, banishes what you do not want in your life.

SPECIAL PROPERTIES
Display different crystal points for daily use, vibrant shades for ongoing energy and softer shades for calmer energy.

MYTHOLOGY AND HISTORY
A most versatile crystal tool. Every morning, without looking, pick a crystal point from a mixed collection to act as a lucky, inspiring talisman or protective amulet.

Sinhalite

COLORS: Green-brown, brown, green, and golden yellow; yellow-brown, light pink, brownish-pink

CRYSTAL TYPE: Gem; rough pebbles may be polished smooth by water from flowing or dried-up streams; contains aluminum, magnesium, oxygen, and boron silicate

ZODIAC SIGN: Gemini (May 22–June 21)

CANDLE COLOR: Yellow or green

PHYSICAL: Addresses rare conditions; useful in medical trials to test promising new treatments; mitigates epidemics and pandemics where little is initially known about treatment.

EMOTIONAL: Keeps you from living in a cult that forbids individual thinking, being obsessed with a person and becoming locked in unrequited love.

HOME: Encourages new activities and new places; for a major clean and declutter, repairing what can be fixed, throwing away what cannot.

WORKPLACE: For an inventor and innovator to patent and market original and useful products; for launching an unusual business.

CHILDREN: Enables a child who is being teased for being different in any way to value their uniqueness; keep the gem in the family treasure box to be given to the child as jewelry on their eighteenth birthday.

ANIMALS: For exotic pets to have the right habitat where they feel at home.

PROTECTION: Guards against refusal to compromise or relax rigid rules that affect well-being and freedom.

MAGICKAL AND PSYCHIC USES
Reveals the source and remedies of hard-to-diagnose illnesses in dreams or meditation by taking you astrally to the ancient Aesculapian Greco-Roman dream temples.

SPECIAL PROPERTIES
Teaches the difference between being alone and loneliness; encourages walking in your own light of inspiration.

MYTHOLOGY AND HISTORY
Originally thought to be brown peridot before it was recognized in 1952 as a new mineral species; gems may occur in large sizes in the Sri Lankan gravels, occasionally up to 100 carats; named after Sinhala, the Sanskrit name for Sri Lanka; also found in Madagascar, Tanzania, and Myanmar as gems.

Skye Marble

COLORS: White, gray, pink, yellow, different shades of green, black with distinctive and varying markings and color mix

CRYSTAL TYPE: Created by pressure on marine sediments over 500 million years ago; may contain fossils; calcium carbonate or crystallized dolomite; hand-mined and sometimes found by divers

ZODIAC SIGN: Taurus (April 21–May 21)

CANDLE COLOR: Pink or green

PHYSICAL: Alleviates viruses, slow-to-clear bacterial infections, lower back pain, slipped or damaged disks; useful in bone marrow transfusions; promotes mobility, skin clarity.

EMOTIONAL: Counters cynicism; keeps you from dismissing out of hand what cannot be physically seen or heard; encourages you to have fun or be spontaneous.

HOME: For preparing organic foods; exploring natural remedies and alternative medical therapies, such as homeopathy, herbalism, and naturopathy.

WORKPLACE: Supports creative projects involving imagination, fantasy, and writing or making a historical fictional television series; for starting or transferring a business from the city to a rural or ocean location.

CHILDREN: Connects younger children with the fey and magickal worlds.

ANIMALS: For dragon and unicorn magick and other semi-mythical or maybe extinct mystical power icons.

PROTECTION: Guards against those who denigrate psychic and spiritual experiences that cannot be scientifically verified.

MAGICKAL AND PSYCHIC USES
For visions in meditation and dreams of remote Scottish shores, battles, and the fabulous rainbows of the Isle of Skye and other Scottish islands.

SPECIAL PROPERTIES
A stone for developing mediumship skills or feeling closer to recently departed relatives or more distant ancestors.

MYTHOLOGY AND HISTORY
Skye Marble has been produced for hundreds of years in the same place, Strath Suardal, Torrin, on the Isle of Skye. A stone with romantic associations when on June 28, 1746, the defeated Bonnie Prince Charlie escaped in a boat to Skye, aided by Flora Macdonald. The stone has become a symbol of all far from home.

Sleeping Beauty Turquoise

COLORS: Pale to bright blue, usually sky blue; pure clear colors

CRYSTAL TYPE: Hydrated aluminum phosphate with copper and iron traces; very little veining or webbing

ZODIAC SIGN: Sagittarius (November 23–December 21)

CANDLE COLOR: Turquoise

PHYSICAL: Strengthens the immune system, vision; helps overcome sensitivity to sunlight, throat conditions made worse by stress, communication difficulties, sleep apnea, sleep disturbances.

EMOTIONAL: Opens you to awareness of life and opportunities; keeps you from waiting for a rescuer to fix your problems.

HOME: Creates a home of beauty and a sanctuary whether for one, a family, or opening your home as a spiritual retreat.

WORKPLACE: For rekindling ideas once dismissed as impractical that, with the passage of time, have become workable; for those in the creative and performing arts, media, and communication field.

CHILDREN: Aids in learning the difference between beauty and merely expensive beauty products.

ANIMALS: Empowers aristocratic pets; horses in dressage competitions or best-of-breed dogs and cats.

PROTECTION: Guards against harm by those motivated by jealousy of others' success; protects you from physical danger.

MAGICKAL AND PSYCHIC USES
Connection with Air spirits, especially sylphs, the archetypal swan-like maidens who protect mountains. A good luck charm to bring prosperity, fame, and fortune.

SPECIAL PROPERTIES
A stone for storytellers and illustrators, those who follow the art for pleasure or who publish fantasy fiction especially for children.

MYTHOLOGY AND HISTORY
Sleeping Beauty Turquoise is so named because the mountain where it is mined resembles a sleeping woman resting on her back with crossed arms; first discovered forty years ago. Originally, miners sought copper and gold there; however, Sleeping Beauty Turquoise has been known and prized by Native North Americans for hundreds of years; crafted by them into beautiful jewelry and sacred artifacts.

Smithsonite

COLORS: Pink, mauve, lavender to purple, white, aqua or paler blue, apple green, yellow or brown; lustrous

CRYSTAL TYPE: A form of calcite, a minor ore of zinc, often found growing naturally with Hemimorphite (see page 240)

ZODIAC SIGN: Pisces (February 19–March 20)

CANDLE COLOR: Same as crystal

PHYSICAL: Pink, aqua, or mauve Smithsonite balances excesses or deficiencies; boosts your immune system.

EMOTIONAL: Pink, purple, or green Smithsonite soothes distress, sadness, or hurt.

HOME: Brings moderation during or after separation or divorce.

WORKPLACE: In aqua or pale blue, confers authority where others may resent your position or expertise.

CHILDREN: For children in the hospital, especially if treatment is prolonged or invasive; calms restless babies.

ANIMALS: Comforts baby animals who have experienced a traumatic birth.

PROTECTION: Keep yellow Smithsonite with official or legal dispute papers to forge compromise.

MAGICKAL AND PSYCHIC USES

Using pastel or white Smithsonite and the same color candle, hold it up to the candlelight, making a wish. Blow out the candle.

SPECIAL PROPERTIES

Keep purple Smithsonite with tarot cards, runes, or crystal ball; hold before energy healing.

MYTHOLOGY AND HISTORY

Smithsonite was first used by the Romans to make brass. It is named after the British mineralogist James Smithson (1754–1829) who founded the Smithsonian Institute in Washington.

Smoky Amethyst

COLORS: Varies according to the proportion and blending of purplish and smoky brown, one sometimes forming an inner phantom

CRYSTAL TYPE: Combination of amethyst and smoky quartz; also occasionally amethysts banded with white and smoky quartz

ZODIAC SIGN: Aquarius (January 21–February 18)

CANDLE COLOR: Purple

PHYSICAL: Strengthens the endocrine system, metabolism; cleanses the body of toxins; alleviates complex illnesses, where one part of the body adversely affects another, as well as psychological problems.

EMOTIONAL: Curbs a major addiction to alcohol, when treatment has failed several times; keeps you from remaining in a destructive relationship.

HOME: Releases negative Earth energies from beneath the home, balancing them so they flow freely but not too fiercely.

WORKPLACE: Releases redundant and outdated work practices; for takeovers and major management changes.

CHILDREN: Shields little ones from nightmares, especially about ghosts and monsters.

ANIMALS: For unpredictable pets who may suddenly snap or scratch.

PROTECTION: Guards against psychic attack, negative spirit entities, and alien intrusions.

MAGICKAL AND PSYCHIC USES

To remove from past worlds unwise soul commitments that are holding an individual back from moving to a new loving relationship.

SPECIAL PROPERTIES

Smoky Amethyst combines the protection of Smoky Quartz with the harmonizing energies of amethyst to create transformation, whereby what is removed or lost is replaced with positive powers.

MYTHOLOGY AND HISTORY

A crystal that brings spiritual ideas and practices into everyday life in a practical way. Choose one with smoky coloring if you need protection, or more purple to restore or create balance in your life.

Smoky Quartz

COLORS: Tinted by natural radiation, smoky brown, usually transparent (see also Morion Quartz, page 307)
CRYSTAL TYPE: Quartz, silicon dioxide
ZODIAC SIGN: Capricorn (December 22–January 20)
CANDLE COLOR: Indigo

PHYSICAL: Melts energy blocks; assists in toxin elimination from adrenal glands, kidneys, and pancreas; relieves chronic pain; shields against invasive treatments.
EMOTIONAL: Restores optimism after prolonged illness or depression; calms anxiety; releases psychological sexual blocks; eases insomnia, self-harming, and panic attacks.
HOME: Protects home and possessions from thieves, natural disasters, accidents, malicious ghosts, and negative Earth energies.
WORKPLACE: Absorbs negativity from your workplace; deflects online attacks.
CHILDREN: Banishes nightmares, fears of the dark; protects teens who secretly dabble in the occult.
ANIMALS: Soothes old, chronically unwell animals in pain.
PROTECTION: Guards against electromagnetic energies, from workplace technology to cell phone towers and power lines; repels curses and paranormal attack.

MAGICKAL AND PSYCHIC USES
Astral travel, Mother Earth rituals; channels Earth spirits at ancient sites; holding a downward-pointing Smoky Quartz in each hand drains misfortune or sorrows.

SPECIAL PROPERTIES
In a vehicle, protects you from aggressive drivers, stressful commuting, accidents, and mechanical breakdown.

MYTHOLOGY AND HISTORY
Guardian against bad luck, especially in Alpine regions, Smoky Quartz was traditionally made into crucifixes, set on bedroom walls to deter evil, especially at night; in Celtic spirituality, sacred to Earth deities and in many lands a talisman for the afterlife.

Snakeskin Agate

COLORS: White, cream, or yellowish, with a wrinkled, cracked surface resembling snakeskin
CRYSTAL TYPE: Agate, chalcedony, cryptocrystalline quartz
ZODIAC SIGN: Scorpio (October 24–November 22)
CANDLE COLOR: Cream

PHYSICAL: Alleviates skin disorders, warts, verrucae, bites, stings, hearing problems, stomach disorders; useful for cosmetic and reconstructive surgery; promotes healthy weight loss, cell regrowth.
EMOTIONAL: Aids in shedding sorrow and pain, reducing cravings when you're quitting smoking, calming whirling thoughts.
HOME: Helps you find the right home and location if you are not settled.
WORKPLACE: Useful if you are pressured to reach targets; for heavy physical work, especially construction; for work-life balance.
CHILDREN: Allays fears of snakes; replaces online with outdoor activities.
ANIMALS: For keeping healthy snakes, lizards, or other reptiles.
PROTECTION: Guards against human snakes, spite, criticism, false friends, and bad influences; for those who are too trusting.

MAGICKAL AND PSYCHIC USES
Deep meditation and trance work; awaking kundalini serpent power in chakra healing and balancing; Mother Goddess rituals; creating a protective web around the aura to lower your profile in unsafe situations.

SPECIAL PROPERTIES
Offers extra stamina for challenges, marathons, intensive sports training, multitasking, missing out on sleep or rest.

MYTHOLOGY AND HISTORY
White Snakeskin Agate, found in Oregon, is sacred to the wise power serpent in Native North American tradition. These serpentine energies are reflected in ancient sacred sites, like the Great Serpent Mound in southwest Ohio; aids in finding lost items, reconnecting with people who have disappeared from your life.

Snowflake Epidote

COLORS: Green with white; mottled

CRYSTAL TYPE: A mix of epidote (green) and a considerable proportion of quartz (white)

ZODIAC SIGN: Virgo (August 24–September 22)

CANDLE COLOR: Green

PHYSICAL: Accelerates a slow-beating heart; for successful pacemaker surgery; alleviates issues stemming from the nervous system, thyroid, liver, gallbladder, digestive disorders caused by rushing meals or grazing, skin; promotes natural resistance to illnesses, especially viruses.

EMOTIONAL: Keeps you from having unrealistic goals and not settling for what is possible and practical; curbs a tendency to be overly critical of others; counters workaholic tendencies.

HOME: For outdoor family activities whatever the time of year or weather; increases awareness of healthy eating; preparing meals and eating together as a family or with roommates.

WORKPLACE: Removes obstacles to prosperity and success faster than anticipated; for winning people to your point of view.

CHILDREN: For those who hate getting wet, muddy, or messy.

ANIMALS: Useful for pets who prefer human food.

PROTECTION: Guards against self-defeating thought patterns.

MAGICKAL AND PSYCHIC USES

Natural magick; seasonal celebrations, especially winter and spring; rituals where the manifestation of the spell purpose is urgently needed; weather magick; druidry; dowsing with a wooden forked rod found in situ.

SPECIAL PROPERTIES

Resembles snow that has fallen and is melting on springtime grass, indicating that new beginnings and better times are just around the corner.

MYTHOLOGY AND HISTORY

Discovered recently in South Africa, Snowflake Epidote blends the best of both minerals; epidote, a powerful manifestation and achievement crystal works gradually and sometimes behind the scenes; combined with white quartz, matters are strengthened, accelerated, and brought to the fore; together this deceptively gentle-looking crystal brings what is most needed at the right time, place, and manner without disruption or undue stress.

Snowflake Obsidian

COLORS: Black with inclusions of small, white, snowflake-like shapes; smooth and shiny

CRYSTAL TYPE: Volcanic glass/magma formed with crystobalite inclusions as obsidian began to crystallize

ZODIAC SIGN: Capricorn (December 22–January 20)

CANDLE COLOR: White

PHYSICAL: Addresses issues relating to the veins, arteries, cholesterol, skeletal structure, circulation, skin, eyes, migraines, influenza, sinusitis, rhinitis, diarrhea.

EMOTIONAL: Helps overcome accepting the victim role; alleviates isolation if your emotions are frozen; promotes acceptance of who you are rather than what others want you to be.

HOME: Prevents loss of money or love; attracts warm family feelings and abundance; spring-cleaning your home and mind of clutter.

WORKPLACE: Clears stagnation, inertia, and underlying tensions; encourages mutual cooperation between people with differing viewpoints.

CHILDREN: Fosters understanding between stepparents and stepchildren.

ANIMALS: For healing animals, especially horses.

PROTECTION: Protects against excessive anger triggered by buried unrelated feelings.

MAGICKAL AND PSYCHIC USES

Drawing together medicine wheel and magick circle elements; a charm against hard winters and difficult times; healing magick; clairaudience; divining the true intentions of someone new.

SPECIAL PROPERTIES

For transitions of all kinds, replacing what is destructive or outworn with new beginnings; reconciling estrangements and coldness in relationships; balancing head with heart.

MYTHOLOGY AND HISTORY

Like the Chinese yin-yang symbol, uniting anima and animus, god and goddess energies; combining fire and ice, Snowflake Obsidian reconciles life-change conflicts, such as children and a new partner or a high-flying career with family demands.

Snow Quartz

COLORS: Polar white and opaque as Snow Quartz; microscopic gas bubbles trapped within cause the whiteness; called milky quartz if cloudier and less opaque
CRYSTAL TYPE: Silicon dioxide
ZODIAC SIGN: Capricorn (December 22-January 20)
CANDLE COLOR: White

PHYSICAL: Strengthens bones; alleviates issues stemming from osteoporosis, bone marrow, breasts, teeth, absorption of calcium, anemia, fevers, hot flashes, early-onset menopause, hysterectomy, resistance to winter ills; in hot climates, keeps you cool.
EMOTIONAL: Mitigates major estrangement from family; curbs an inability to control excessive emotions; helps overcome a tendency to freeze into inaction in crises.
HOME: Protects your home against winter hazards; for safe driving through ice or snow.
WORKPLACE: Aids in completing tedious tasks and paperwork; to survive a temporary financial downturn.
CHILDREN: Eases lactation in nursing mothers; for colicky, fretful, or teething infants.
ANIMALS: Strengthens sick or weak baby animals and those abandoned by their mother.
PROTECTION: Guards against those who use silence and coldness as emotional blackmail.

MAGICKAL AND PSYCHIC USES
Ice rituals to end coldness between lovers, family members, or close friends; rune divination; full moon magick; a lucky charm for the gradual return of luck, love, and opportunity.
SPECIAL PROPERTIES
A stone for clearing the mind, to study, revise, or identify the true nature of a problem and therefore its solution; if frequently provoked or teased, prevents overreaction.
MYTHOLOGY AND HISTORY
Snow Quartz is the crystal of the snow moon, the full moon in January or early February that, among the Algonquian nation, was called Hunger Moon because of food shortages; Snow Quartz likewise represents weathering hard times.

Soapstone or Steatite

COLORS: White, cream, green, gray, pink, and brown
CRYSTAL TYPE: Highly concentrated form of talc schist—harder than pure talc—magnesium silicate; contains impurities of chloride, magnesite, dolomite, and serpentine
ZODIAC SIGN: Sagittarius (November 23-December 21)
CANDLE COLOR: Cream

PHYSICAL: Salves wounds; alleviates food and chemical allergies that affect the stomach and skin; absorbs fat; balances chemical and electrical impulses in the brain and body; eases hyperventilation.
EMOTIONAL: Curbs panic attacks, oversensitivity to underlying tensions and the emotions of others; counters rigid attitudes and intolerance toward anyone or anything outside your own narrow definitions of how life should be.
HOME: An antidote to harsh or sarcastic words and inconsiderate behavior; Soapstone statues around the home create tranquility.
WORKPLACE: Translates original ideas and plans into practical, workable form; for meeting deadlines.
CHILDREN: Soapstone animals and birds calm anxious or overactive children and act as sleep guardians.
ANIMALS: Choose appropriate Soapstone animals or deities to stand at the four quarters of a personal altar or ritual circle.
PROTECTION: Guards against fears and panic in an unfamiliar situation or if you get lost; choose a fierce creature to guard your home.

MAGICKAL AND PSYCHIC USES
For power animal and deity statues, especially Kuan Yin, protectress of women, and the lucky Buddha given daily offerings, in a sacred place in the home or the center of the home to attract blessings.
SPECIAL PROPERTIES
Buy a matching pair of Soapstone animals, birds, mandarin ducks, cranes, or swans facing each other to attract a lifelong, faithful, loving partner. Set as many smaller creatures of the same species as the number of children you want.
MYTHOLOGY AND HISTORY
An antidote to the modern world as jewelry, bowls for petals or herbs in your workspace if your work is technologically based; a favorite bedside animal if a teen spends excessive time on electronic devices.

Sodalite

COLORS: Deep blue with white flecks of calcite, sometimes with purplish or gray markings; indigo

CRYSTAL TYPE: Tectosilicate: sodium silicate with chlorine and aluminum (see also Hackmanite, page 234)

ZODIAC SIGN: Cancer (June 22–July 22)

CANDLE COLOR: Indigo

PHYSICAL: Addresses fevers, racing pulse or heart, high blood pressure, menopause, inflammation, burns; alleviates issues involving the ears, throat, sinuses, mouth, thyroid, pituitary and lymph glands; regulates blood sugar levels.

EMOTIONAL: Keeps you from trying to control adult children's lives; tempers aging issues, such as loss of fertility, worries about sexuality, or when adult children finally leave home.

HOME: Aids in converting deconsecrated religious buildings or former warehouses into homes; helps you handle the dual responsibility of caring for grandchildren and older parents.

WORKPLACE: Useful for unsought retirement or redundancy; to sell your expertise or ideas at a presentation or interview if you are naturally reticent; for becoming a published author.

CHILDREN: Helps maintain connection with grandparents living far away, and overcome the death of a grandparent.

ANIMALS: For mother animals if their young are taken away too soon.

PROTECTION: Guards against fears of flying, especially takeoff and landing; shields from small-minded or hot-tempered individuals.

MAGICKAL AND PSYCHIC USES

For croning/wise-woman ceremonies to mark a powerful new phase of life; before healing to understand the true source of an illness.

SPECIAL PROPERTIES

For having children later in life or a second family; cooperation in group and team ventures.

MYTHOLOGY AND HISTORY

In modern spirituality, Sodalite has, like amethyst, become a stone of empowerment for women in their middle years and beyond. The early advanced Caral civilization from North-Central Peru prized and traded Sodalite over four thousand years ago.

Sonora Sunrise or Sunset

COLORS: Red, turquoise/bluish-green, and black tints

CRYSTAL TYPE: Cuprite with chrysocolla; a mixture of copper minerals

ZODIAC SIGN: Gemini (May 22–June 21)

CANDLE COLOR: Turquoise

PHYSICAL: Soothes inflammation, cramps, menstrual pain; promotes fertility following natural cycles, oxygenation of heart and blood; regulates hormones; for end-of-life preparation and care.

EMOTIONAL: Deflects the stifling influence of controlling gurus, teachers, officials, or father figures; keeps you from engaging in self-destructive patterns of behavior.

HOME: Infuses the home with beauty and harmony.

WORKPLACE: Valuable for independent ventures involving color and practical creation in crafts, weaving, tapestry, collage, pottery, and art using natural materials.

CHILDREN: Teaches children to appreciate natural beauty and natural materials as playthings to stimulate imagination.

ANIMALS: For allowing older pets to slow down and eventually pass on without distress.

PROTECTION: Guards against envy, jealousy, and anger within yourself and by others directed your way.

MAGICKAL AND PSYCHIC USES

For spiritual retreats and solitary sacred journeys; encourages learning through contact with the natural world.

SPECIAL PROPERTIES

The fusion of cuprite and chrysocolla creates a unique energy; as the name suggests, the crystal incorporates natural mini endings followed by beginnings as part of a natural cycle, with each day replaced by night and then day again, and each life phase flows into the next.

MYTHOLOGY AND HISTORY

Sometimes called the Christmas stone because of its festive coloring; found in Northwest Mexico in 2006, a Mother Earth crystal to bring joy and healing to counteract the ills of the modern age.

Spectrolite

COLORS: Darker background, but more colorful and iridescent than Labradorite (page 267), with aqua, golden yellow, peacock blue, reddish-orange, green, and red; often found in gem quality

CRYSTAL TYPE: Plagioclase feldspar, sodium calcium aluminum silicate; metallic sheen

ZODIAC SIGN: Aquarius (January 21–February 18)

CANDLE COLOR: Purple

PHYSICAL: Alleviates issues involving vision, migraines with visual disturbances, memory, concentration, metabolism, hormones, fluid imbalances, PMS, menstruation, menopause, endometriosis.

EMOTIONAL: Allays irrational fears; counters obsession with conspiracy theories; curbs nightmares involving ghosts and evil spirits.

HOME: At the entrance to the home, attracts abundance and blessings; encourages social interactions.

WORKPLACE: Creates a positive impression in situations where personality predominates over ability.

CHILDREN: Protective against fears of monsters in the bedroom, insomnia, and night terrors.

ANIMALS: Placed in the window, calls a lost pet home.

PROTECTION: Useful in haunted places where there has been tragedy.

MAGICKAL AND PSYCHIC USES
Called elven rainbows, Spectrolite is beloved by Finnish shamans; the surface provides a doorway for meditation.

SPECIAL PROPERTIES
Spectrolite spans the everyday and spiritual worlds, allowing clear communication with spiritual guardians.

MYTHOLOGY AND HISTORY
Spectrolite, also called Finnish labradorite, was traditionally buried in fields as an offering to the land guardians in Finland. Spectrolite was discovered in 1941, during the Second World War, while antitank defense lines were being built on Finland's eastern border. It was later named *Spectrolite* by Professor Aarne Laitakari, former director of the Geological Survey of Finland, because of its spectrum of rainbow colors and those of the natural beauty of Finland.

Specular Hematite, Hematite, or Specularite

COLORS: Shiny black or silver

CRYSTAL TYPE: Crystallized iron oxide with metallic sheen, caused by sparkling hematite flakes and mica inclusions during formation

ZODIAC SIGN: Aries (March 21–April 20)

CANDLE COLOR: Silver or red

PHYSICAL: Addresses circulation, anemia, and red blood cell disorders; oxygenates the blood; alleviates motion sickness, jet lag, headaches caused by digestive problems.

EMOTIONAL: Allays fear of the judgment of others if you think, act, or speak independently; keeps you from hiding your strengths behind the helplessness of little boy/little girl–lost behavior.

HOME: A high-vibration super version of Hematite; protects against harmful electromagnetic energies in the home, radiating over the surrounding area; attracts friends, prosperity, successful property deals.

WORKPLACE: For the manifestation of creative dreams and plans in the working world through single-mindedness.

CHILDREN: Kept in the home, Specular Hematite encourages talented teens to persevere with necessary practice and hard work when they want to have fun.

ANIMALS: Helps win money prizes and trophies through dedicated training.

PROTECTION: Guards against attempts to sabotage efforts to succeed; sends malice back on the perpetrator.

MAGICKAL AND PSYCHIC USES
Defensive magick; chaos rituals; becoming aware of significant dreams, signs, and symbols to transmit messages from guides.

SPECIAL PROPERTIES
Assists those who are physically uncoordinated and find sequencing hard to gain skills and dexterity in martial arts, yoga, and tai chi; promotes justice.

MYTHOLOGY AND HISTORY
Hematite, especially the shimmering kind, represents the shed blood of Uranus, consort of the primal creatrix goddess Gaia; from this blood sprang the Giants, the avenging Erinyes or Furies' sisters, the Meliae Nymphs of the healing ash tree and Aphrodite, goddess of love.

Spessartine Garnet

COLORS: Yellowish-orange to brownish- or deep red; pale yellow if nearly pure; mandarin Spessartines may be pure orange
CRYSTAL TYPE: Manganese aluminum silicate, usually some of the manganese replaced by ferrous oxide
ZODIAC SIGNS: Sagittarius (November 23–December 21) and Capricorn (December 22–January 20)
CANDLE COLOR: Orange

PHYSICAL: Promotes a healthy reproductive system, fertility, and libido in both sexes; alleviates issues stemming from the kidneys, bladder, circulation, chilblains, Raynaud's disease, food intolerances to wheat and dairy products, inefficient fat processing.
EMOTIONAL: Curbs cravings for comfort food.
HOME: Useful if people use your home as a drop-in center and don't return the hospitality.
WORKPLACE: Encourages creativity in art, fashion, textiles, jewelry design and making, weaving, embroidery, interior decoration, architecture, graphic design, photography, and landscaping.
CHILDREN: Persuades teens to abandon their gadgets to enjoy outdoor activities and develop creative hobbies.
ANIMALS: For dressage horses, sheep and cattle-dog shows, and carriage driving.
PROTECTION: Shields you from those who befriend your partner or a family member to cause dissension between you.

MAGICKAL AND PSYCHIC USES
Guards against nighttime malevolent spirits and psychic and emotional vampires, masquerading as friendly entities; clairvoyance, sun rituals.
SPECIAL PROPERTIES
The garnet of the sun, for vacations or relocation to exotic or sunny places; building happiness and fun into your everyday world.
MYTHOLOGY AND HISTORY
Spessartine, one of the lesser-known varieties of garnet, takes its name from the Spessart district of Bavaria. A stone of raising your profile at work and increasing your popularity socially, Spessartine also boosts your sexual magnetism to attract someone special.

Sphalerite

COLORS: Red, black, brown, yellow, yellowish-brown, greenish-gray, white, sometimes colorless; some are faceted into gems
CRYSTAL TYPE: Zinc sulfide in crystalline form
ZODIAC SIGN: Gemini (May 22–June 21)
CANDLE COLOR: Yellow

PHYSICAL: Oxygenates the blood; strengthens vision; promotes fitness, good nutrition and vitality, libido, women's reproductive system; useful for male genitals; boosts sperm count, immunity.
EMOTIONAL: Curbs food cravings; helps overcome addictions, such as those involving alcohol, excessive smoking, and recreational drugs.
HOME: Establishes regular hours and undisturbed times if you are working from home.
WORKPLACE: Eases the transition during career changes, particularly if you must manage two jobs for a time or there is ill feeling during the period before you leave your old position.
CHILDREN: Encourages children to enjoy sports and outdoor activities; for teens pressured over gender.
ANIMALS: For hyperactive, clumsy pets.
PROTECTION: Guards against deception, fraud, and scams on- and offline.

MAGICKAL AND PSYCHIC USES
Among Indigenous peoples in Africa, Australia, and Native America, Sphalerite was used in fire ceremonies; generates an orange flame, and draws power, physical strength, and protection.
SPECIAL PROPERTIES
Regarded as a stone of wise choice, to convey intuitive knowledge as words, images, or impressions.
MYTHOLOGY AND HISTORY
As the chief source of zinc ore, Sphalerite carries the properties of the planet and god of change Uranus, whose sacred metal is zinc. The dark variety, black jack, with a higher iron content than other colors, is very protective. Red Sphalerite, known as ruby jack, contains very little or no iron content and will bring change and independence.

Sphene or Titanite

COLORS: Green, yellow, brown, black, and white, also sometimes orange; occasionally red or with red and orange tinge (may be heat-treated)

CRYSTAL TYPE: Calcium titanium silicate

ZODIAC SIGN: Virgo (August 24–September 22)

CANDLE COLOR: Green

PHYSICAL: Alleviates issues stemming from the eyes, inner ear, bone fractures, osteoporosis, red and white blood cells, gingivitis; preserves teeth.

EMOTIONAL: Counters an unwillingness to learn from your mistakes; curbs a butterfly mind that has trouble focusing.

HOME: Placed in the garden, promotes healthy plant growth.

WORKPLACE: Aids in adapting to new systems of technology and online conferencing, retraining after unemployment.

CHILDREN: Helps youngsters learn new languages and mathematics, study if this proves hard or tedious; for valuing their heritage.

ANIMALS: For training dogs and horses to carry out complex tasks or maneuvers.

PROTECTION: Guards against fear of sudden or unsought change.

MAGICKAL AND PSYCHIC USES

Study and understanding of ancient wisdom, assisted by the Wise Ones, encountered on astral or dream travel; softens the intensity of crystal therapy if a client is vulnerable.

SPECIAL PROPERTIES

A light-bringer that floods every aspect of your being with optimism and joy; for those who enjoy detective novels or television series.

MYTHOLOGY AND HISTORY

Sphene is also named Titanite, due to its titanium content. For many years, it has been a source of titanium dioxide; used as a pigment in artists' oil paints; an inspiration to painters. Called the stone of ancient wisdom, Sphene is linked with the legendary Lemurian Wise Ones who were believed to store their wisdom in crystals (see also Lemurian Seed Crystal and Lemurian Golden Opal, pages 275 and 274).

Spiderweb Jasper

COLORS: Black, web-like markings on grayish-white, earthy browns with white or dark spiderweb markings, ochre patterns on brown or red

CRYSTAL TYPE: Silicate, microcrystalline quartz, often with organic matter or other minerals as inclusions

ZODIAC SIGN: Scorpio (October 24–November 22)

CANDLE COLOR: Brown

PHYSICAL: Addresses issues involving the veins, arteries, blood vessels, nerve connections, chronic fatigue, microsurgery, skin grafts, heart valves, bypass and pacemaker operations; aids in recovering mobility.

EMOTIONAL: Combats manipulation by others, lies, or secrecy surrounding your birth or early life; curbs emotional abuse; allays fear of spiders and crawling insects.

HOME: For lively, harmonious celebrations, parties, and family gatherings; weaving together two separate families.

WORKPLACE: Helps you network on- and offline; valuable for establishing or expanding websites, bartering, making money from garage sales, successful market stalls.

CHILDREN: For shy or solitary children joining group activities at school or on the playground.

ANIMALS: Repels fleas, ticks, and mites.

PROTECTION: Deters those playing favorites or setting one person against another.

MAGICKAL AND PSYCHIC USES

Divination of all kinds; deflects bad dreams; for finding answers in dreams.

SPECIAL PROPERTIES

Reviving old connections through friendship reunion sites and social media; picking up threads of a relationship that never developed.

MYTHOLOGY AND HISTORY

Spiderweb Jasper is associated with the mythological tradition of weaver and creatrix goddesses in many ages and cultures, such as the ancient Egyptian Neith who wove the fabric of the world. The Native North American goddess Grandmother Spider created people from four different clays as the nations of the Earth; a crystal of choosing the right future pathway.

Spiderweb Obsidian

COLORS: Dark blue or gray with spiderweb patterns in lighter gray, green, or blue
CRYSTAL TYPE: Volcanic glass
ZODIAC SIGN: Cancer (June 22–July 22)
CANDLE COLOR: Gray

PHYSICAL: Clears blockages in arteries and veins; opens constrictions within the intestines; helps overcome failure of nerve endings to connect; ensures successful microsurgery; alleviates misalignments of back, neck, and spine.
EMOTIONAL: For those caught in webs of deceit of their own making; keeps you from holding others back through guilt and obligation.
HOME: Prevents breakages in the home through rushing or carelessness; for family celebrations.
WORKPLACE: Aids in developing new talents and starting new internet businesses; for organizing or participating in a franchise.
CHILDREN: Transforms those who are careless with their own and others' possessions.
ANIMALS: Useful if your dog runs away when off the leash.
PROTECTION: Guards against falling prey to manipulation.

MAGICKAL AND PSYCHIC USES

Empowering dream catchers to drive away nightmares; making a desired love into more than a friend.

SPECIAL PROPERTIES

A recent discovery in Chihuahua, Mexico, a symbol of uniting faiths, cultures, and nations in humanitarian causes.

MYTHOLOGY AND HISTORY

Obsidian links with the creative energies of the Native North American goddess Grandmother Spider who taught the people, crafts such as weaving, food cultivation, use of herbs, and making dream catchers. She returned as the Navajo White Shell or Changing Woman who controlled the seasons, and the Lakota White Buffalo Calf Woman who taught healing ceremonies and promised that, after suffering, their wisdom would be spread to many nations; Spiderweb Obsidian breaks through barriers to release your full potential.

Spiralite Gemshells

COLORS: Tan, brown, gray, white, yellow, or purple
CRYSTAL TYPE: Formed into agate through the petrification of ancient spiral seashells with hollow areas in which drusy crystals have formed
ZODIAC SIGN: Pisces (February 19–March 20)
CANDLE COLOR: Purple

PHYSICAL: Promotes a long and happy life; for recovery after illness or injury, especially after sports accidents.
EMOTIONAL: Allays fears of mortality; calms anxiety that a relationship will not last.
HOME: Helps you find a permanent home if you have moved a great deal or are temporarily living with friends or relatives.
WORKPLACE: Strengthens well-established or inherited businesses; for all who work in marine or water-based businesses; for paleontologists, marine biologists, and all concerned with the preservation of the oceans.
CHILDREN: For premature babies or those with a traumatic start to life.
ANIMALS: Encourages telepathic communication with whales, dolphins, and their healing powers.
PROTECTION: For safety near or while on or in water.

MAGICKAL AND PSYCHIC USES

For intuitive medicine and healing channeling, recalling ancient lives before humans walked the Earth; earth energies and spiral dances.

SPECIAL PROPERTIES

Forms a bridge between organic and crystalline life; therefore, brings a deep understanding of crystal healing and wisdom.

MYTHOLOGY AND HISTORY

Associated with the Hindu preserver god Vishnu, Spiralite Gemshells, found in Central India, link with the ancient sacred spiral symbol. The symbol is based on spirals found in nature that became associated with the power and fertility of the Earth and Sea Mothers. The spiral was adopted as a protective symbol by early humans and appears on cave walls in the Pyrenees and Siberia.

Spirit or Cactus Quartz

COLORS: Clear/white (called fairy spirit quartz), shades of purple amethyst, rich orange or yellow as citrine, grayish-brown smoky quartz

CRYSTAL TYPE: Quartz forming multiple-terminated points emerging from the main crystal

ZODIAC SIGN: Libra (September 23–October 23)

CANDLE COLOR: Purple

PHYSICAL: Alleviates skin allergies, melanomas, scars, internal growths; promotes fertility; mitigates issues involving the fallopian tubes, ovaries, testes, pregnancy, after caesarean section, cleft palate; for end-of-life care.

EMOTIONAL: Keeps you from feeling out of place; counters rejection by your family as a scapegoat; addresses adoption issues in adulthood, unexpected bereavement.

HOME: Reduces rivalries caused by relatives; for older people who move in with relatives; for completing successful home extensions.

WORKPLACE: Encourages team building within a company or sports team; prevents one person from dominating proceedings.

CHILDREN: Aids when a child moves to a larger school or to college; for welcoming a foster/adopted child or stepchildren if siblings are resistant.

ANIMALS: Fosters harmony among creatures of different species, living together in sanctuaries, rescue centers, or conservation areas.

PROTECTION: A shield against vulnerability or during intensive spiritual work.

MAGICKAL AND PSYCHIC USES

For remote healing through a healing circle; mediumship groups and safe séances; connection with higher realms and fey; enhances crystal layouts; rebirthing.

SPECIAL PROPERTIES

Promotes cooperation socially, in community, sporting, or charity ventures; helps an unsociable partner relax in company.

MYTHOLOGY AND HISTORY

The more crystals growing on Spirit Quartz, the more powerful its energies. Spirit Quartz with distinctive mini-crystals growing from it is a powerful fertility charm. Though there are different kinds of Spirit Quartz, its distinctive properties are shared by every variety.

Spodumene

COLORS: Colorless, white, or gray; the yellow kind, called Triphane (page 483); Pink or Lilac Kunzite (pages 357 and 279); Hiddenite or Green Kunzite (page 242)

CRYSTAL TYPE: Lithium aluminum silicate

ZODIAC SIGN: Aquarius (January 21–February 18)

CANDLE COLOR: Gray

PHYSICAL: Alleviates issues stemming from epilepsy, hearing, blurred vision, trapped nerves, joint problems, bones, spinal cord; for low sperm count, sexually related conditions.

EMOTIONAL: Curbs addictions, particularly gambling, shopaholic tendencies, and running up debt through overspending.

HOME: Promotes house clearing or cleansing for a clutter clear, home moving, or to remove unhappy memories.

WORKPLACE: Clear or white Spodumene, as a bowl of crystal chips in your workspace, spreads its energies to raise the level of honesty and integrity; clears away secrecy and uncertainty.

CHILDREN: Helps teens approaching a major educational turning point to find what is right for them and not just what is expected.

ANIMALS: For rescuing an animal too old for racing, breeding, or show purposes, who is in danger of being abandoned.

PROTECTION: Gray Spodumene offers an ongoing shield against manipulation, guilt, obligation, or bullying.

MAGICKAL AND PSYCHIC USES

The gray crystalline form aids spiritual learning where there are hidden aspects that become clearer with deeper study; particularly helpful for understanding of the Kabbalah, Buddhism, and Golden Dawn ritual magick.

SPECIAL PROPERTIES

Spodumene encourages seeing a task through when enthusiasm wanes, particularly for people who are constantly starting projects or taking up new interests and abandoning them.

MYTHOLOGY AND HISTORY

Found in the United States, Brazil, Afghanistan, Madagascar, and Pakistan, Spodumene in its clear or opaque, white or gray color, is regarded by many healers and crystal practitioners as of an even higher spiritual vibrational level than its colorful cousins, such as kunzite.

Starburst or Starry Jasper

COLORS: Brown/black background with tan/creamy/orange starry sprays

CRYSTAL TYPE: Jasper/rhyolite with sparkling pyrite stars; often found as tumbled stones or made into cabochons

ZODIAC SIGN: Aries (March 21–April 20).

CANDLE COLOR: Red

PHYSICAL: For prolonged stays in hospital or an ongoing series of invasive treatments or necessary lifelong medications; enables conception of a child after hope was lost.

EMOTIONAL: Curbs a tendency to misinterpret the words and intentions of others to always hear a negative message; counters an unwillingness to accept that a particular path or relationship has run its course.

HOME: Encourages you to set up a music studio at home, or attend theater, dancing, or music classes at any age; for joining an amateur theater company, an orchestra, jazz band, or establishing a music group.

WORKPLACE: Brings about a sudden promotion or an unexpected job offer that may involve a change of location and role; for developing and launching a franchise idea.

CHILDREN: A lucky charm for children attending auditions or making videos/You Tube presentations to gain admission to the stage as performers, in modeling, or in television advertising.

ANIMALS: For winning competitions and shows by persevering with an animal others dismissed as second rate.

PROTECTION: Shields you in times of danger or sudden disruption or against delays in travel or finances; guards against social media malice.

MAGICKAL AND PSYCHIC USES

Star magick and wishes; extraterrestrial encounters in out-of-body momentary experiences; visions, meditation, or vivid dream recall.

SPECIAL PROPERTIES

A stone to help overcome injustice in any area of life, but especially when your reputation or business is under attack.

MYTHOLOGY AND HISTORY

Found in Mexico, a stone for those alone, to avoid feeling lonely; for doing good for others by raising the profile of an existing charity or to address your chosen cause and publicize it.

Star Garnet

COLORS: Deep brownish-red, burgundy, or reddish-black

CRYSTAL TYPE: Unusual form of garnet; the star effect is caused by inclusions of rutiles reflecting light in the pattern of a four- or six-rayed star

ZODIAC SIGN: Aries (March 21–April 20)

CANDLE COLOR: Red

PHYSICAL: Addresses issues involving the spine, lumbar punctures, amniocentesis, bones, cells, heart, lungs, blood, impotence, vaginismus, candida, sexually transmitted diseases.

EMOTIONAL: Keeps you from living and thinking chaotically; counters a tendency to drain emotional energies, money, and resources from others.

HOME: Keeps your personal space and possessions private and untouched.

WORKPLACE: Encourages major success in business or a promotion; aids in turning around a failing business; for success in media or the performing arts.

CHILDREN: Valuable if your child is unconventionally talented but has problems in the education system.

ANIMALS: For winning a place for a pet to appear in advertisements or to shine in the show ring.

PROTECTION: Guards against dangers at night, when traveling or working night shifts.

MAGICKAL AND PSYCHIC USES

Makes connections with other worlds, especially distant galaxies, for those who believe they originally came from the stars; for banishing psychic vampires, poltergeists, and sexual demons.

SPECIAL PROPERTIES

A special token of love—less ostentatious than Star Ruby—given to a love met later in life, a childhood sweetheart who has returned to your life, or a love that must be kept secret.

MYTHOLOGY AND HISTORY

Star Garnet is the state gemstone of Idaho, where it is mined; also found in India and in small quantities in Brazil, Russia, and North Carolina; best seen in sunlight or the beam of a flashlight, standing above the stone looking down.

Star Hollandite Quartz

COLORS: Clear, containing tiny black or grayish six-pointed stars

CRYSTAL TYPE: Quartz crystal points, silicon dioxide with inclusions of hollandite, barium manganese oxide with goethite

ZODIAC SIGN: Pisces (February 19–March 20)

CANDLE COLOR: White

PHYSICAL: A crystal of self-regeneration, manifest as better health; offers gentle weight regulation by listening to hunger signals.

EMOTIONAL: Keeps you from becoming what others have dictated through the years is the right path and losing contact with the true self.

HOME: For a first home or a new one that reflects your own preferences and personality after a relationship breakup.

WORKPLACE: Musters the courage to leave a family business or multigenerational land management if it is not right for you.

CHILDREN: Helps children pressured at school to find their own level.

ANIMALS: For linking psychically with pets.

PROTECTION: Reflects back physical, psychological, and psychic threats.

MAGICKAL AND PSYCHIC USES

For contacting Star Beings and discovering a personal star guardian; astrology, clairaudience.

SPECIAL PROPERTIES

Star Hollandite allows the expression of the inner star, the unique spiritual self and earthly talents that can be manifest in many ways.

MYTHOLOGY AND HISTORY

Found in India and Africa, Star Hollandite Quartz has close links with past worlds in ancient Egypt; it is believed that Star People from Sirius B brought knowledge of the advanced Egyptian civilization; shown in the later artistic representations of the sun boat of Ra the sun god, sailing through the sky, filled with gods and goddesses.

Star Mica

COLORS: Mainly found in yellow; also brown and white

CRYSTAL TYPE: A form of muscovite mica, Star Mica forms where two crystals grow at the same time, creating an interlocking star shape; very fragile; may be found in quartz, which is easier to handle

ZODIAC SIGN: Cancer (June 22–July 22)

CANDLE COLOR: Silver

PHYSICAL: Addresses issues involving the arteries, liver, digestion, blood sugar, colds, viruses, skin elasticity; for candida and sexually transmitted infections.

EMOTIONAL: Curbs an obsession with becoming or marrying a celebrity; keeps you from trying to imitate someone you admire, leading to a loss of individuality; counters a tendency to judge people purely on the basis of status or beauty.

HOME: As a centerpiece, draws in energies of abundance, prosperity, the granting of wishes, and ongoing good fortune.

WORKPLACE: Fosters fame and fortune due to a lucky break; protects against harmful rays from electronic equipment; for advancement in a new setting after being head-hunted.

CHILDREN: For Star Children, keep Star Mica where they can see it daily, as a form of reassurance and to help them to settle into everyday life; for developing an exceptional talent from the early years.

ANIMALS: Promotes champion animals, whether in breeding, shows, or competitions.

PROTECTION: Guards against giving up if the road to recognition is slow or hard; deflects psychic attack.

MAGICKAL AND PSYCHIC USES

Astrology, for Star Souls to find their kindred spirit; for night magick; clairvoyance; astral travel in dreams and meditation to other realms and galaxies.

SPECIAL PROPERTIES

Attracts love and friendship by radiating optimism, confidence, and charisma; creates opportunities to make contact with a desired future partner and develop that relationship.

MYTHOLOGY AND HISTORY

Found in Brazil, Star Mica is a creative stone for artists, authors, musicians, craftspersons, and performers to attract the attention and approval of the right people to gain recognition.

Star Rose Quartz

COLORS: Pale to deep pink

CRYSTAL TYPE: Quartz, silicon dioxide with manganese impurities; three rays, or lines of light, intersecting to create a six-ray star; sometimes there is a four-pointed star; appears when rose quartz is polished and shaped into a sphere or crystal skull; rare

ZODIAC SIGN: Taurus (April 21–May 21)

CANDLE COLOR: Pink

PHYSICAL: Alleviates heart conditions in young people; aids in successful heart transplants in all ages; addresses endometriosis, ectopic pregnancy, problems with ovulation, twin or multiple births.

EMOTIONAL: Keeps you from dreaming of marrying celebrities or millionaires; counters a tendency to put a love interest on a pedestal and then become disillusioned; curbs eating disorders.

HOME: For a parent with several children who combines childcare with a high-flying career; for fulfilling a talent set aside until the children are older.

WORKPLACE: Supports those who work with fertility, pregnancy, childbirth, and care of parent and infant in the early months.

CHILDREN: Encourages a special talent to be developed, from an early age.

ANIMALS: For a pet who nurtures orphan animals of any species.

PROTECTION: Guards against becoming caught up in others' dramas.

MAGICKAL AND PSYCHIC USES

For scrying with a Star Rose Quartz sphere; working with rose crystal skulls; rituals for couples when a second child does not follow the first.

SPECIAL PROPERTIES

The ultimate soul-twin symbol, linked with Star Souls who have been together in many lifetimes.

MYTHOLOGY AND HISTORY

Star Rose Quartz represents the unity of the three kinds of love: *philos*, mental, earthly love, friendships and family ties; erotic and romantic love; and *agape*, divine love and the love of all humanity.

Star Ruby

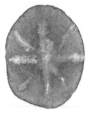

COLORS: Pinkish-red, purple-red, dark red, rich red with a hint of blue

CRYSTAL TYPE: Corundum, aluminum oxide silicate, displaying a six- or, more rarely, twelve-ray star-shaped light effect across the surface

ZODIAC SIGNS: Aries (March 21–April 20) and Sagittarius (November 23–December 21)

CANDLE COLOR: Dark red.

PHYSICAL: Helps overcome sexual dysfunction; promotes fertility, particularly in older couples; useful for vasectomy reversal, IVF, artificial insemination, menstruation, migraines; helps with heart valves, stents, bypasses, plus healthy weight regulation.

EMOTIONAL: Counters self-harm, the effects of childhood sexual abuse, domestic violence, suppressed anger.

HOME: Guards against misfortune; attracts money, health, and abundance.

WORKPLACE: Brings about fame and fortune; for major interviews, examinations, or auditions; for profitable contracts and sales of products.

CHILDREN: Useful for winning prizes in competitions or talent shows.

ANIMALS: For best-of-breed and prestigious awards.

PROTECTION: The star deflects all harm to sender and attacks from sexual demons.

MAGICKAL AND PSYCHIC USES

Most powerful at full moon, scrying to access Akashic records; for Star Souls; calling a soul twin; attracting spirit guides; sex magick.

SPECIAL PROPERTIES

Each Star Ruby is said to contain three angels; overcomes personal doubts and shakes off poor self-esteem.

MYTHOLOGY AND HISTORY

One of the world's finest star rubies is said to be the Rosser Reeves Ruby, weighing 137.5 carats, donated to the Smithsonian Museum in Washington, DC in 1965. The largest Star Ruby is the De Long Star Ruby, given to the American Museum of Natural History in New York City in 1938. It was stolen in October 1964 with other famous stones, returned only after a ransom payment of $25,000.

Star Sapphire

COLORS: The star effect, especially prized in deep blue sapphires, is also distinctive in light silver-gray, blue-gray, grayish-white, blue-white, or yellowy-white sapphires; found also in darker-colored sapphires, most black Star Sapphires are actually dark brown

CRYSTAL TYPE: Corundum, aluminum oxide, a six-rayed star, cut as cabochons or faceted gems; occasionally with twelve rays

ZODIAC SIGN: Gemini (May 22–June 21)

CANDLE COLOR: Silver

PHYSICAL: Amplifies the healing properties of sapphires, including alleviating issues with blood, bone marrow, rare viruses, glands, Alzheimer's, ears, eyes, menopausal hot flashes, nausea.

EMOTIONAL: Eases a sense of inferiority because of denigration in early life.

HOME: A family heirloom, the twelve-rayed star accumulates good fortune throughout generations.

WORKPLACE: For altruistic female entrepreneurs; black sapphires help ambitious men achieve success with integrity.

CHILDREN: Supports gifted children in their quest to be admitted to theater school, sports academy, or winning early admission to college.

ANIMALS: Useful for animals in films, advertising, or television.

PROTECTION: Promotes safety for nighttime travelers; keeps you from feeling second best in remarriages.

MAGICKAL AND PSYCHIC USES

The three crossbars in six-ray sapphires represent angels of faith, hope, and destiny. Black Star Sapphires assist men in becoming professional mediums.

SPECIAL PROPERTIES

Achieving the seemingly impossible, especially stardom. White Star Sapphires bring lasting love for those seeking a permanent relationship.

MYTHOLOGY AND HISTORY

The most famous Star Sapphire is the blue Star of Asia in the Smithsonian Institute, in Washington, DC, flawless and more than 330 carats. Star Sapphires form when titanium atoms become trapped within corundum. As the crystal cools, they form rutile needles, orienting in three directions.

Staurolite

COLORS: Black, dark reddish- or yellowy-brown, streaked with white, gradually weathering gray

CRYSTAL TYPE: Twinned crystals of iron aluminum silicate, forming equal-armed crosses or cross formations

ZODIAC SIGN: Scorpio (October 24–November 22)

CANDLE COLOR: Burgundy

PHYSICAL: Strengthens muscles, blood; counters the signs of aging; combats tropical diseases; aids in adapting to individual health needs; realigns body, mind, and spirit after illness or stress overload.

EMOTIONAL: Helps you give up smoking; overcomes compulsive behavior and depression.

HOME: Useful if you are caring for a seriously ill or disabled relative or you cannot leave an unhappy situation because of dependents.

WORKPLACE: Reduces stress caused by traveling long distances for work or working away from home; for peace campaigners and aid workers.

CHILDREN: Promotes a good quality of life for those with chronic or degenerative conditions.

ANIMALS: For donkeys and all working animals.

PROTECTION: A gentle shield against negativity from a vulnerable relative.

MAGICKAL AND PSYCHIC USES

The cross shape, the meeting of the four elements, creating the fifth element Akasha, provides a powerful focus for elemental magick; connecting with nature essences, extraterrestrials, and ancient Middle Eastern wisdom.

SPECIAL PROPERTIES

A magickal crystal, bringing good fortune and connections beyond the mundane to the wonders of life and infinite spiritual possibilities.

MYTHOLOGY AND HISTORY

Called fairy crosses, said to be crystallized tears fairies wept when they heard of the crucifixion; carried by Crusaders, believed to have cured Richard the Lionhearted of malaria; a traditional charm, used by former US president Theodore Roosevelt.

Stellar Beam Calcite

COLORS: Golden to pale yellow and rich yellow amber

CRYSTAL TYPE: Calcium carbonate, double-terminated with distinctive sharp points, suggesting its alternative name, dogtooth calcite

ZODIAC SIGN: Pisces (February 19–March 20)

CANDLE COLOR: Yellow

PHYSICAL: Clears neural pathways, creating new ones after brain injury or damage; addresses autoimmune conditions, rare illnesses; promotes remission.

EMOTIONAL: Breaks patterns causing mistakes to be repeated; offers hope after you've given up on life and people.

HOME: Brings peace if you are where you don't want to be.

WORKPLACE: Assists memory and understanding of new technology, especially later in life; for spiritual counselors, clergy, students of comparative religions, and those working for interfaith organizations.

CHILDREN: For Crystal and Indigo Children and any wrongly labeled by society.

ANIMALS: Supports dogs involved in rescue work.

PROTECTION: For escaping from cults or spiritual brainwashing and for relatives trying to free loved ones; guards against religious intolerance, cruelty, or violence in the name of faith.

MAGICKAL AND PSYCHIC USES

Connection with extraterrestrials, evolved Beings of Light, UFOs, and otherworlds, creating pathways from everyday perception to higher spiritual awareness; deep meditation, even for beginners; past lives linked with ancient Egypt, Lemuria, and Atlantis; mediumship.

SPECIAL PROPERTIES

A high-vibration stone integrating people meeting for business, major international charity initiatives, interfaith organizations, or world peace to focus on similarities, not differences.

MYTHOLOGY AND HISTORY

Rare, mainly from Tennessee; believed to help Star Souls feel more at home in the world; for guiding you to your cosmic twin.

Stellerite

COLORS: Colorless, white, pink, salmon, orange

CRYSTAL TYPE: Zeolite in the stilbite subgroup. Pearly orange, pink, and salmon are formed by small inclusions of hematite or celadonite

ZODIAC SIGN: Gemini (May 22–June 21)

CANDLE COLOR: Yellow

PHYSICAL: Alleviates blood disorders, muscle weakness, bone thinning, stress-related illnesses; prompts breakthrough research into an existing problem.

EMOTIONAL: Curbs emotional outbursts; keeps you from feeling resentment at the unfairness of life and other people without accepting any responsibility for events or seeking to resolve them.

HOME: For major alterations in your life, whether property renovations, children leaving the nest, new people joining the family, for example, a baby or step-relative.

WORKPLACE: For logic-based jobs involving precision, measurements, and calculations; for mastering new technology and teaching it to others.

CHILDREN: Helps those on the autism spectrum to cope with unexpected change or disruption to routine.

ANIMALS: Aids in moving a pet who has been in the same home since first weaned.

PROTECTION: Guards against harmful effects not caused by you; shields you from drama kings and queens.

MAGICKAL AND PSYCHIC USES

Connection with angels and higher beings who have personal links with you and messages to offer; encountering for the first time a spirit guide who will function as a protector if you are new to mediumship or healing; for meditation if circumstances are less than ideal for stillness and silence.

SPECIAL PROPERTIES

For travel if you have always said, "One day," and suddenly the chance arises; likewise, encourages opportunities to try exciting if slightly risky activities.

MYTHOLOGY AND HISTORY

The reality check crystal to clear lofty illusions and dreams standing in the way of what is attainable and will be far more rewarding than the "someday" ideas; ideal for inventors, innovators, and pioneers exploring the world beyond the comfort zone.

Stepped or Step Quartz

COLORS: Colorless in clear quartz; may occur in other quartzes, such as citrine and rose quartz, also different crystals, like purple or green fluorite

CRYSTAL TYPE: Stepped or Step Quartz crystals, most common in clear quartz, have distinct physical steps or ridges etched into at least one of their termination faces; the number of stepped faces you choose on your selected crystal represents and aids steps needed in different aspects of your life.

ZODIAC SIGN: Aquarius (January 21–February 18)

CANDLE COLOR: White

PHYSICAL: For progressing through different stages of recovery or treatment toward health; alleviates chronic or progressive conditions; aids in starting a step-by-step exercise and nutrition program.

EMOTIONAL: Encourages those who begin detoxing from addictions, to complete the program; keeps you from refusing to take steps toward mending quarrels or coldness, right or wrong.

HOME: Offers support to family members in need, while encouraging independent efforts and solutions; assists in successfully applying for grants, loans, and mortgages.

WORKPLACE: For a career that involves specific stages, time frames, and assessments to achieve accreditation.

CHILDREN: Prompts a child to reach milestones in development at their own pace.

ANIMALS: Useful for careers in animal training and rehabilitation after neglect or trauma.

PROTECTION: Keeps you from allowing others to diminish your achievements or block your way to the next stage.

MAGICKAL AND PSYCHIC USES

Opens the way to the next spiritual level, whether that is the beginning of the journey, to practicing healing or counseling others through divination.

SPECIAL PROPERTIES

Balancing your own needs for progress and to compete for success and assisting and mentoring others on their journey.

MYTHOLOGY AND HISTORY

Identify, touch, and focus on each step on your crystal, representing the current area of your life that needs the most attention and the steps ahead will become clear.

Stichtite

COLORS: Lilac to bright purple, light to rose pink; occasionally containing yellowish-green

CRYSTAL TYPE: Hydrated magnesium chromium carbonate

ZODIAC SIGN: Virgo (August 24–September 22)

CANDLE COLOR: Deep pink

PHYSICAL: Addresses physical problems with roots in emotions, such as eating disorders, high blood pressure, and tension headaches; alleviates issues stemming from the teeth, gums, skin elasticity after pregnancy or major weight loss, mucous membranes, hernia, dementia.

EMOTIONAL: Counters acute anxiety about what may never happen; for those who carry others' guilt.

HOME: A gentle stone for reducing irritability and hyperactivity; creates a calm, loving environment; for those who live alone, whether by choice or necessity.

WORKPLACE: Before making speeches, presentations, or chairing meetings for calm, coherent, and authoritative words.

CHILDREN: Aids in developing friendships at a new school or activity; calms overexcitability and spontaneous aggression; eases ADHD.

ANIMALS: For making anxious pets more sociable in human and animal company.

PROTECTION: Guards against lies and those who constantly break promises.

MAGICKAL AND PSYCHIC USES

For inner stillness; contacting ancient guides from traditional cultures; clairaudience; clearing old karma through past-life dreams.

SPECIAL PROPERTIES

A stone of forgiveness and reconciliation within the family; building positive relationships in the workplace; forging friendships or finding a significant other.

MYTHOLOGY AND HISTORY

Stichtite is usually attached in small clusters to other crystals, in particular serpentine (see Atlantisite, page 42, which is stichtite and serpentine combined). Called the stone of rescue and recovery, Stichtite overcomes illness, depression, and old wounds, even from childhood, that shut out new love and friendship.

Stilbite

COLORS: Pink, creamy pink, peach, white, orange, reddish-brown, yellow, or gray

CRYSTAL TYPE: Sodium calcium hydrous aluminum silicate; a member of the zeolite family

ZODIAC SIGNS: Aries (March 21–April 20) and Taurus (April 21–May 21)

CANDLE COLOR: Pink

PHYSICAL: Alleviates brain disorders, melanomas, skin pigmentation problems, torn or strained ligaments; cleanses the body of toxins; counters loss of taste, sunburn, tanning-bed damage.

EMOTIONAL: Stems relationship breakdown; salves you at the loss of a parent, especially the mother, through death or divorce during childhood.

HOME: Aids in beginning and persisting with long-overdue home improvements or repairs.

WORKPLACE: For fast authoritative decision making if matters are complicated or there are conflicting opinions.

CHILDREN: Curbs sleep disturbances, nightmares, and sleepwalking; reestablishes bonds if you work long hours or after a distressing visit with an estranged parent.

ANIMALS: For pets who inflict damage because they hate being alone.

PROTECTION: Guards against remaining in destructive situations through guilt or obligation.

MAGICKAL AND PSYCHIC USES

For communication with angelic realms, guardian angels, and totem animals; psychic dreaming, healing dreams, dream interpretation, and astral travel during sleep.

SPECIAL PROPERTIES

Slows a whirling mind after working late or bringing work home; encourages leaving business worries at the door and focusing on domestic problems at home.

MYTHOLOGY AND HISTORY

Stilbite is often joined to or as inclusion within Apophyllite crystals (page 35). Its name comes from the Greek word *stilbein* meaning "to shine," referring to its pearly luster.

Strawberry Quartz

COLORS: Natural Strawberry Quartz is usually medium pink, with lighter pink markings; may be pale pink or strawberry-colored

CRYSTAL TYPE: Silicon dioxide, quartz; often mottled

ZODIAC SIGN: Taurus (April 21–May 21)

CANDLE COLOR: Pink

PHYSICAL: Addresses skin rashes, rosacea, food allergies, pigmentation birthmarks, scars, burns, blisters, heart irregularities, issues concerning the breasts.

EMOTIONAL: Counters low self-esteem brought on by overly critical family members or a controlling partner; keeps you from blushing, stammering; allays fear of loneliness.

HOME: For spontaneous day or weekend trips, barbecues, picnics, and outdoor parties; promotes domestic contentment.

WORKPLACE: Valuable when studying or working in day care, as a nanny, an au pair, a Steiner or Montessori teacher, or in the field of child psychology.

CHILDREN: Reassures them that they are safe sleeping away from home, especially without parents; for teens newly rooming at college.

ANIMALS: For the runt of the litter to thrive.

PROTECTION: Keeps you from becoming entangled in others' dramas; insulates the young or vulnerable from unpleasant experiences.

MAGICKAL AND PSYCHIC USES

Past-life journeying to ancient worlds; Mother Goddess rituals; spiritual quests to places of natural beauty; increases the power of other stones and the healing powers of those using them.

SPECIAL PROPERTIES

For long journeys by plane, car, bus, or train; making hotel rooms feel welcoming; nurtures the self; keeps you from envying those on social media with beauty, glamour, and celebrity.

MYTHOLOGY AND HISTORY

In the folk traditions of a number of cultures, the Mother Goddess, including the Virgin Mary, consumed strawberries, which contain nutrients such as vitamin C, potassium, iron, and folic acid, all of which are essential for pregnant women. So Strawberry Quartz offers hope to those anxious to be parents who fear they will never have a child.

Stromatolite

COLORS: Golden and deep brown; may include gray, beige, reddish-brown, tan, yellow, white, and sand-colored

CRYSTAL TYPE: Micro fossils, cyanobacteria, dating back over 3.5 billion years, formed by huge colonies of blue-green algae (see also Kambaba Jasper and Mary Ellen Stromatolite Jasper)

ZODIAC SIGN: Capricorn (December 22–January 20)

CANDLE COLOR: Gold

PHYSICAL: Strengthens memory; alleviates issues stemming from the throat, teeth, bones, brain stem, emphysema, asbestosis, and progressive lung conditions; aids in maintaining health in older people, oxygenation of the blood.

EMOTIONAL: Keeps you from disregarding tradition and convention; curbs a tendency to accrue debt.

HOME: For resisting family pressure in planning your retirement, especially if there is a hidden financial agenda concerning inheritance.

WORKPLACE: Fosters perseverance in taking a project from conception to completion; for fighting against agism.

CHILDREN: Teaches children family history and maintains communication between the generations.

ANIMALS: For settling into your home an older pet who belonged to a recently deceased relative.

PROTECTION: Guards against those who denigrate your opinions as out of date.

MAGICKAL AND PSYCHIC USES

For past worlds extending long before human life through connection with a stone that has survived billions of years; receiving automatic writing messages of the unknown past from the Akashic records.

SPECIAL PROPERTIES

Finding missing family links due to adoption, colonization, or emigration; for adopted adults and children discovering their birth roots.

MYTHOLOGY AND HISTORY

Stromatolites may have been the earliest life-form and the original building blocks of life; therefore, they contain the Earth and our own historic core; for finding compromise where family, cultural, and religious values differ from those of the wider community.

Strontianite

COLORS: Gray, white, light yellow, green, brown or colorless; fragile; almost always fluorescent

CRYSTAL TYPE: Aragonite, rare strontium-rich carbonate, may be found in geodes and concretions

ZODIAC SIGN: Aries (March 21–April 20)

CANDLE COLOR: Red

PHYSICAL: Addresses sexual dysfunction, especially impotence and vaginismus; balances left- and right-brain hemispheres, and establishes new neural pathways after accident or illness; strengthens red blood cells, veins, vision, vitality in the face of chronic disease; alleviates calcification.

EMOTIONAL: Counters hysteria; mitigates fight-or-flight reactions; bolsters your empathy, sympathy, and love.

HOME: Promotes economizing and counters a tendency to incur debt; aids in feeling at home anywhere; for pleasurable vacations; fosters healthy plants and pest-free gardens.

WORKPLACE: Ensures safe long-distance business travel; helps you adjust to different locations, time zones, and climates; helps overcome jet lag.

CHILDREN: Assists in making friendships in new situations or environments.

ANIMALS: For introducing an older animal to established pets.

PROTECTION: Clears inner emotional and psychic debris before healing sessions, counseling, or therapy.

MAGICKAL AND PSYCHIC USES

For martial arts, tai chi, qi gong, and yoga; awakening spiritual energies; connecting with kindred planetary beings in this world and beyond.

SPECIAL PROPERTIES

A storm crystal that brings strength, power, and confidence; enables recognition of past-life connections, explaining dislikes and attractions.

MYTHOLOGY AND HISTORY

Named in 1791 after Strontian, Argyllshire, Scotland, where it was first discovered, a principal source of strontium, it has become a collector's piece in its finer, lustrous, waxy form and, as tumbled stones, a powerful stone for claiming or reclaiming your unique place and space in the world.

Sugar Blade Quartz

COLORS: Usually clear and colorless, though it can be found in other colored quartzes

CRYSTAL TYPE: Silicon dioxide; quartz, sugar-like coating around the outside with rainbows in tiny terminations, like frost on snow; may have a point like a blade

ZODIAC SIGN: Pisces (February 19–March 20)

CANDLE COLOR: White

PHYSICAL: Alleviates issues stemming from blood circulation, veins and arteries, heart-valve stenosis, deep vein thrombosis; cleanses the body of toxins.

EMOTIONAL: Tempers codependency; keeps you from trying to fit in with others to the point of losing your personal identity; allays fear of surgery, medical treatments.

HOME: Cuts through inertia and procrastination to set in motion definite renovation or redecorating plans.

WORKPLACE: For evaluations or interviews to show yourself at your best; for moving up within the same company or applying for extra training or study to climb the corporate ladder.

CHILDREN: Calms fears of those with invisible friends who can sometimes seem frightening.

ANIMALS: For pets who are terrified of vets and being handled by strangers.

PROTECTION: Guards against psychic and psychological attack whose source you do not know.

MAGICKAL AND PSYCHIC USES

Connection with extraterrestrials; some believe that Sugar Blade Quartz psychically guides spacecraft to Earth; psychic surgery, using the blade to cut through negative attachments.

SPECIAL PROPERTIES

For Star Beings and very old souls who do not feel at home in the world or in their skin, to find their true soul purpose.

MYTHOLOGY AND HISTORY

The stone of balancing the need for friendship and love and retaining your independence within relationships to follow your own star.

Suleiman Agate

COLORS: Blue-gray or red-brown, with black and white color bands

CRYSTAL TYPE: Fibrous chalcedony

ZODIAC SIGN: Aries (March 21–April 20)

CANDLE COLOR: Red

PHYSICAL: A whole-body healer; alleviates chronic illnesses involving ongoing psychosomatic or stress factors; addresses dry or scaly skin, IBS, celiac disease; constipation; enhances faith healing.

EMOTIONAL: Allays fears of being cursed or harmed by magick; calms acute anxiety when you want to express an opinion or argue because of ridicule earlier in life, resulting in a sense of inferiority.

HOME: In Southeast Asia, Nepalese people call the stones' medicine Buddha beads; sometimes made as an offering in the Western world to the Laughing Buddha to bring health, good fortune, and happiness to the home.

WORKPLACE: Aids in achieving status, authority, and leadership positions; for making your positive mark in a new position within a company.

CHILDREN: Deeply protective as a circlet of beads hung high in a youngster's room; helps parents to make wise decisions.

ANIMALS: For noble, altruistic pets who anticipate your needs and moods.

PROTECTION: In Vedic astrology, Suleiman Agate shields you from the negative effects of the shadow planets Rahu and Ketu, and also Saturn, as well as from the evil eye.

MAGICKAL AND PSYCHIC USES

Connects with higher realms; used by shamans and healers over many centuries and recently rediscovered; for wish magick; overcoming past-life trauma.

SPECIAL PROPERTIES

Suleiman Agates encourage the acquisition and sharing of spiritual knowledge for its own sake; for healers, mediums, and diviners constantly needing to seek verification.

MYTHOLOGY AND HISTORY

Suleiman Agate, also called Solomon's Agate, is named after Suleiman the Magnificent, sultan of the Ottoman Empire from 1520 to 1566. According to legend, the stones were originally found in a secret location known only to King Solomon and contained power over the Djinn, the Middle Eastern genies.

Sunset Orange Labradorite

COLORS: Predominantly shimmering, flame-like, golden orange, often with pink, blue, and purple; yellow and red flashes in an iridescent play of colors

CRYSTAL TYPE: Feldspar, a mixture of silica and aluminum; polished or as jewelry

ZODIAC SIGN: Leo (July 23–August 23)

CANDLE COLOR: Orange

PHYSICAL: Alleviates visual disturbances accompanied by migraines, breathing difficulties, persistent coughs without apparent cause, PMS, women's reproductive problems; helps with recovery from a hysterectomy.

EMOTIONAL: Curbs a sense that getting older is the beginning of the end; keeps you from trying to recapture lost youth, especially for women who feel life has passed them by.

HOME: Useful when relocating for work, at retirement, or for early retirement; planning a long road trip or a once-in-a-lifetime boating or backpacking adventure at any age.

WORKPLACE: Prompts you to move on to a new position or company if there is no further advancement potential; for those who retire early or start a new business in their golden years.

CHILDREN: If young children are reluctant to go to bed when the sun sets late, the magickal sunset stone brought out by the parent can herald the transition between day and night.

ANIMALS: An amulet to ease the later months of an aging pet.

PROTECTION: Provides a sunset shield to reflect back negativity sent toward the aura from human malice or paranormal sources, especially after dark

MAGICKAL AND PSYCHIC USES

Lucid dreaming, shamanism; fire magick; psychic artistry; contact with the ancestors; prophecy, nature-based witchcraft.

SPECIAL PROPERTIES

The stone of transformation in any area of life that, even if not chosen, brings longer-term advantage if embraced.

MYTHOLOGY AND HISTORY

Shimmering orange crystals are often named after the sunset because, in many lands and ages, according to legend, sunset crystals were pieces of the sun discarded at the end of the day, representing unfulfilled hopes and dreams; the sun and new chances would be reborn in the morning.

Sunset Sodalite

COLORS: Blue, with white veins and orangey-rust bands

CRYSTAL TYPE: Mixture of sodalite and iron rich feldspar, a form of Sunstone (see page 465)

ZODIAC SIGN: Aquarius (January 21–February 18)

CANDLE COLOR: Orange

PHYSICAL: Alleviates issues relating to the pineal gland, throat, digestion, wheat and dairy allergies; addresses problems with aging, sexual difficulties for women after a period of celibacy.

EMOTIONAL: Eases panic attacks, fears during long-distance air travel or flying in small planes or helicopters, extreme anxiety when speaking to strangers.

HOME: Increases savings; promotes moneymaking through wise property sales.

WORKPLACE: Aids in overcoming writers' block; asking for and receiving financial and practical support for a new business venture from older relatives.

CHILDREN: Enables youngsters to keep in contact with and spend regular time with grandparents if they live far away.

ANIMALS: For a continuing breeding line for good-natured pets.

PROTECTION: Guards against being financially and emotionally drained by overly demanding younger family members.

MAGICKAL AND PSYCHIC USES

For wise woman rites of passage ceremonies where there are plans for major life changes; organizing and leading a psychic development group or healing circle.

SPECIAL PROPERTIES

For all who study, research, or teach, combining traditional and new information with independent interpretation.

MYTHOLOGY AND HISTORY

Recently found in Canada, the combination of harmony and enthusiasm, experience and new approaches makes Sunset Sodalite an exciting stone; especially powerful in the second half of life for regeneration of health; wakes up sleepy partners of both sexes to realize their other half is ready for adventure with or without them.

Sunshine Aura Quartz

COLOR: Bright yellow; like all aura quartzes, has iridescent gleam
CRYSTAL TYPE: Clear quartz infused with gold and platinum
ZODIAC SIGN: Leo (July 23–August 23)
CANDLE COLOR: Yellow

PHYSICAL: Cleanses the body of toxins; addresses issues relating to digestion, pancreas, liver, spleen, gallbladder; constipation, nervous system, seasonal affective disorder; promotes absorption of vitamins A, D, and E.
EMOTIONAL: Helps overcome depression, pessimism, disappointment with life or bitterness at lack of opportunities, as well as OCD.
HOME: Sunshine Aura Quartz brings light to dark or gloomy rooms or negative Earth energies; radiates brightness in lands with long winters and dark days.
WORKPLACE: Attracts fulfillment as well as success; for positive recognition of proposals, applications, and projects; for comedians and entertainers.
CHILDREN: Helps overly serious children have fun; for those worried about going outdoors in bad weather.
ANIMALS: For an older pet coping with younger boisterous ones.
PROTECTION: Guards against sarcasm and spiteful humor at your expense.

MAGICKAL AND PSYCHIC USES

In the center of healing layouts, infuses the body with health and well-being; psychometry, information from family treasures and ancient places; solstice magick; resisting spirit possession; good weather spells.

SPECIAL PROPERTIES

A power crystal, even the smallest piece radiating happiness on social and business occasions; attracting positive experiences and people.

MYTHOLOGY AND HISTORY

Called crystalline sunshine, variants are also called sunshine aura, all characterized by a light glow as if illuminated by sunlight. For example, orange-gold imperial gold sunshine aura, is created by bonding titanium and silver onto clear quartz.

Sunshine Optical Calcite

COLORS: Clear, shades of golden yellow
CRYSTAL TYPE: Calcium carbonate; may be cube-like; it is possible to see double viewing writing looking through the Sunshine Optical Calcite (see also Optical Calcite or Iceland Spar, page 326)
ZODIAC SIGN: Gemini (May 22–June 21)
CANDLE COLOR: Yellow

PHYSICAL: Addresses vision, seasonal affective disorder, disorientation; sports injuries (especially during competitions), treatments involving a dual approach, such as medicine and surgery.
EMOTIONAL: Keeps you from continually changing home or location because none ever feels right, as well as trying to live a double life or secretly maintaining two love relationships; curbs chronic pessimism.
HOME: If separated or divorced with children, aids in dividing time amicably between the former and present relationship where there is joint custody.
WORKPLACE: Ideal for multitasking and for any advocacy or mediation work for which it is necessary to understand both points of view and reach resolution.
CHILDREN: Helps overcome study and examination difficulties, dyslexia, learning or physical difficulties not adequately recognized or compensated for, panic during an examination or oral test.
ANIMALS: For horses panicked by traffic and cats who frequently cannot find their way home; Sunshine Optical Calcite guides back pets missing after a location move.
PROTECTION: Guards against those whose words and actions have a hidden, less positive meaning and agenda, while radiating friendliness.

MAGICKAL AND PSYCHIC USES

For scrying within the crystal or in water in rippling sunlight; seeing the hidden world of the fey and nature spirits; meeting your soul twin on the dream plane.

SPECIAL PROPERTIES

For meeting new people and making new friends; enhancing charisma and ease at parties and in social settings.

MYTHOLOGY AND HISTORY

Found in Mexico in this gentle golden shade, Sunshine Optical Calcite brings new beginnings after loss in any part of life, building on the best of the old world and experience gained; for the growth of self-confidence and self-esteem.

Sunstone

COLORS: Gentle to golden or tangerine orange, with iridescent flashes or a sparkly red or golden sheen

CRYSTAL TYPE: Plagioclase feldspar, with tiny particles of hematite, sometimes called the Oregon sunstone or heliolite

ZODIAC SIGN: Leo (July 23–August 23)

CANDLE COLOR: Gold

PHYSICAL: Boosts energy; promotes cell regeneration, male sexual potency, women's reproductive organs and cycles; addresses seasonal affective disorder, digestive and prostate issues.

EMOTIONAL: Counters lack of motivation; reduces phobic reaction in presence of a trigger; allays fears of darkness and enclosed spaces.

HOME: Restores happiness after sorrow or misfortune.

WORKPLACE: For leadership and major promotion; prevents petty rivalries; fosters successful advertising online.

CHILDREN: Aids in setting boundaries for teens who are easily influenced; increases popularity of shy children.

ANIMALS: For tropical birds, fish, and reptiles.

PROTECTION: Removes psychic and emotional hooks; reduces the power of strong-minded people determined to override your wishes; banishes emotional and financial vampires.

MAGICKAL AND PSYCHIC USES

Paired with Moonstone for soul-twin love, sex and god/goddess rituals; weather magick; a lucky charm for competitions, lotteries, auditions, talent, or reality shows and fame.

SPECIAL PROPERTIES

Reveals talents; attracts prosperity; for new sports or exercise regimens; brings about fun travel, improves your social life; leads to relocation to the sun.

MYTHOLOGY AND HISTORY

Associated with Ra, ancient Egyptian sun god, and Helios the ancient Greek sun god; in folklore, Sunstone is said to be pieces of the sun falling to Earth during a solar eclipse; highly prized by magicians; linked also with the legendary golden phoenix. The Vikings wore Sunstone as an amulet while traveling.

Super Five

COLORS: The most colorful of the Super crystals, often with a crystalline orangey tip, clear patches, and a gray base, or orange and yellow, depending on the proportions of each mineral within the individual crystal

CRYSTAL TYPE: Differs from Super Six (page 466) and Super Seven (page 466) in that it usually contains chlorite and hematite, along with amethyst, citrine, and clear quartz; the combination effect is especially powerful in healing and protection

ZODIAC SIGN: Gemini (May 22–June 21)

CANDLE COLOR: Yellow

PHYSICAL: Alleviates blood sugar fluctuations, viruses, blood disorders, exhaustion; brings the system back into balance; relieves pain; replaces health problems with energy and good growth.

EMOTIONAL: Curbs irregular health care, swinging between obsessive fitness and indulgent excesses or inertia; counters feast-or-famine dieting.

HOME: Spreads health-promoting energies throughout the home if there is a current epidemic or seasonal illnesses.

WORKPLACE: For dealing calmly with those who get their own way by shouting others down or using sarcasm.

CHILDREN: Protects against potential threats of bullying if a child is gentle and bullying is a problem in the school.

ANIMALS: Useful when household pets fight.

PROTECTION: Guards against those who take advantage of others' good nature.

MAGICKAL AND PSYCHIC USES

Clairaudience and automatic writing with messages from guides and angels; manifesting wishes; psychic defense; angel and crystal Reiki.

SPECIAL PROPERTIES

Citrine brings ease of learning, logic, and the potential for travel; amethyst the avoidance of excesses; clear quartz enthusiasm and innovation; chlorite healing and cleansing; and hematite power and protection. All dynamically combine and are transformed to unite inner well-being with success in the way most needed and desired.

MYTHOLOGY AND HISTORY

Recently found in Canada as well as after the flooding of the Super Seven Brazilian Espirito mine from two mines in Bahia in northern Brazil and another in India; all are producing Super Six (page 466) and Super Five minerals.

Super Seven, Sacred Seven, or Melody Stone

COLOR: Dark purple with gold and misty gray within

CRYSTAL TYPE: The fusion of seven minerals—amethyst, cacoxenite, goethite, lepidocrocite, clear quartz, rutilated quartz, and smoky quartz

ZODIAC SIGN: Aquarius (January 21-February 18)

CANDLE COLOR: Gold

PHYSICAL: A whole-body healer; addresses allergies and illnesses connected with modern living, hereditary conditions, as well as illnesses where the cure or prognosis is uncertain.

EMOTIONAL: Brings confident expression of the unique self, rather than fitting in with others' expectations.

HOME: For home and meal blessings and to integrate disparate family members.

WORKPLACE: For staying on target without becoming obsessed with work; keeps you from taking work worries home or home worries to work.

CHILDREN: Boosts self-esteem when it has been shattered by bullying or abuse.

ANIMALS: Toward the end of life, especially if an owner faces a difficult decision.

PROTECTION: Guards against despair when life is bleak.

MAGICKAL AND PSYCHIC USES

Psychokinesis, connection with ancient Egyptian (especially Isis), Inca, Mayan, and Aztec worlds, Sta systems and angels; seeing auras.

SPECIAL PROPERTIES

The combined minerals give Super Seven its all-embracing healing and transformative powers· amethyst balance; cacoxenite infinite possibility; goethite overcoming old karma; lepidocrocite synchronizing mind, body, and spirit; rutile hidden gifts; smoky quartz protection; and clear quartz pure life force.

MYTHOLOGY AND HISTORY

Super Seven was introduced to the healing community by Melody, the US crystal expert, and was found in the Brazilian tiny southeastern coastal state Espírito Santo; other sources may contain five or six minerals, but work just as well; occasionally reddish hematite is present for extra fire.

Super Six

COLORS: Golden orangey brown, cream and brown mix; colors depend on the mineral proportions

CRYSTAL TYPE: Contains six of the seven minerals in the original Super Seven stone: amethyst, cacoxenite, goethite, clear quartz, rutilated quartz, and smoky quartz; as with Super Seven, the other minerals are enclosed in clear quartz; may be sold as tumbled or cut stones

ZODIAC SIGN: Cancer (June 22-July 22)

CANDLE COLOR: Silver

PHYSICAL: A whole-body healer; alleviates illnesses and allergies caused or made worse by modern living and pollutants; useful if needing rest and quiet after illness.

EMOTIONAL: Curbs a tendency to regret what cannot be achieved instead of rejoicing in existing blessings.

HOME: Aids in accepting that the home is not a showpiece, and the perceived expectations of others are of no importance.

WORKPLACE: Aids in avoiding burnout.

CHILDREN: Encourages relatives living together to feel valued and responsible for the others' well-being.

ANIMALS: For those working in a busy rescue center where there never seems to be enough time to spend with each animal.

PROTECTION: Guards against becoming overwhelmed by psychic impressions.

MAGICKAL AND PSYCHIC USES

For aura cleansing and chakra energy center healing and empowerments; opens the gateway to other dimensions; brings enhanced psychic awareness for those who are nervous about or new to spiritual exploration.

SPECIAL PROPERTIES

The six minerals form an alchemist's stone in which each energizes and transforms the others to create a power greater than the separate components—amethyst bringing balance, cacoxenite infinite possibility, goethite overcoming past karma, rutile revealing hidden gifts, smoky quartz protection, and clear quartz unrestrained energy and new beginnings.

MYTHOLOGY AND HISTORY

Lepidocrocite from the Super Seven is not included in Super Six. The original Brazilian Espirito Super Seven mine is flooded; two new mines—one in Bahia in northern Brazil and another in India—are producing Super Six and Super Five (page 465) minerals.

Taaffeite

COLORS: Mauve, pinkish-clear, lilac, violet, blue, green, red, red being extremely rare; transparent

CRYSTAL TYPE: Beryllium, magnesium, and aluminum; mixture of chrysoberyl and spinel in a unique formula; among the ten rarest stones in the world; generally sold only as a gemstone

ZODIAC SIGN: Aquarius (January 21–February 18)

CANDLE COLOR: Purple

PHYSICAL: Boosts iron in blood cells; regulates alkali/acid balance in body; relieves deep-seated pain; alleviates migraines with visual disturbances.

EMOTIONAL: Counters intense psychic experiences that cause distress; curbs a sense of being watched, even when alone.

HOME: Should you be able to obtain Taaffeite, it gives even the most active home a sense of sanctity and piece; liberates the mind from inhibitions and so the naturally impulsive may find that contact leads to bad dreams and excesses.

WORKPLACE: Enables you to have clear judgment at times when you must make decisions that affect others' careers.

CHILDREN: Put a Taaffeite crystal on the photo of a child who has suffered a traumatic experience and for whom conventional counseling is not helping.

ANIMALS: Place Taaffeite near a missing pet's bed for news if you fear they have died or have been taken and sold.

PROTECTION: Protects against deception.

MAGICKAL AND PSYCHIC USES

Connection with higher realms in deep meditation to learn psychic gifts from spirit teachers; telepathy with absent family members; healing through angelic or higher guidance.

SPECIAL PROPERTIES

The crystal of love, soul-twin love, the love of family and friends, and, above all, the love of humanity that inspires altruistic actions; opens the mind to opportunity and sudden intense joy.

MYTHOLOGY AND HISTORY

Originally found in a small jewelry store in Dublin, Ireland, in 1946 by Count Richard Taaffe; thought mistakenly to be Purple Spinel; until the 1980s there were only three known Taaffeite specimens worldwide; by 2002, fifty were in circulation. Taaffeite is found in Sri Lanka and more recently in Tanzania. Russia, China, South Australia, and Myanmar, especially in lower-grade gem pebbles.

Tabby or Tabular Quartz

COLORS: White or clear

CRYSTAL TYPE: Quartz with two large flat sides, usually more than twice as wide as the other sides, forming a crystalline tablet with striations or notches on one or both opposing flat sides; may be found in clusters

ZODIAC SIGN: Leo (July 23–August 23)

CANDLE COLOR: Gold

PHYSICAL: Naturally transmits healing from your personal immune system, and from angels and healing guides; brings the body into alignment for balanced health.

EMOTIONAL: Counters an unwillingness to meet others halfway; keeps you from ignoring the feelings of others out of a determination to show that you're right.

HOME: Resolves misunderstandings due to poor communication between family members; fills the home with light, health, and joy.

WORKPLACE: For tackling underlying disputes or seething resentment through positive discussion and compromise.

CHILDREN: Placed in the center of the home, Tabby Quartz encourages young people who are left out or misunderstood to feel valued.

ANIMALS: Encourages another person's pet to fit in with your animals if you adopt or temporarily care for that pet.

PROTECTION: Guards against those who twist your words.

MAGICKAL AND PSYCHIC USES

Spontaneous communication between the everyday and spiritual world, with angels, guides, and ancient wisdom; enables you to access the Akashic records by opening the stored crystalline files by means of rubbing a fingernail down a striation (upward to close the records) during meditation or quiet moments.

SPECIAL PROPERTIES

Activates other crystals, oils, and essences if you hold Tabby Quartz in the power or dominant hand and the crystals, oils, or essences to be empowered in the nondominant hand, again rubbing the notches downward.

MYTHOLOGY AND HISTORY

Associated with ancient Greece and prayer offerings and rites to deities by priests and priestesses. Tabular Quartz crystals are considered mentor crystals, holding for the owner the key to spiritual experiences and pathways.

Tangerine Lemurian Quartz

COLORS: Tangerine, between golden-orange, red, and orange-red, the brightness depending on the presence of iron

CRYSTAL TYPE: Silicon dioxide with iron oxide impurities; varying striations on alternate sides marking it as Lemurian

ZODIAC SIGN: Sagittarius (November 23–December 21)

CANDLE COLOR: Orange

PHYSICAL: Addresses issues involving blood circulation, veins and arteries, spinal alignment; promotes fertility, especially if you're trying for a first child later in life; bolsters the reproductive system in both sexes; alleviates sexual dysfunction.

EMOTIONAL: Keeps you from repeating problems because of unresolved inner issues; curbs a resistance to counseling or therapy out of an unwillingness to embrace change.

HOME: Brings connection with the ancestors if you are hitting genealogical blanks or trails leading nowhere.

WORKPLACE: Increases awareness of new ways to improve your career or business, resulting in growing prosperity through opening yourself up to wider perspectives and opportunities.

CHILDREN: For old-soul children confused by past-life memories.

ANIMALS: Allays an illogical fear of animals, rooted in past-world attacks.

PROTECTION: Guards against allowing past mistakes and failures to choke off new beginnings.

MAGICKAL AND PSYCHIC USES

A crystal aphrodisiac; removing present and future misfortune due to past bad karma; access to ancient wisdom of the Earth and divine realms.

SPECIAL PROPERTIES

Each Tangerine Lemurian Quartz has unique guiding energies to move your life forward in ways most needed, especially if you feel stuck or static.

MYTHOLOGY AND HISTORY

While all crystals contain wisdom from the ancient land of Mu or Lemuria, certain Lemurian crystals contain codes to unlock deeper cosmic understanding. Tangerine Lemurian Quartz opens the way to sacred sexuality between couples; associated with the divine uniting of gods and goddesses in past cultures to bring fertility to land, animals, and people.

Tangerine Quartz

COLOR: Tangerine, rusty orange to red, with the clear crystal seen within

CRYSTAL TYPE: Silicon dioxide; naturally occurring quartz permanently coated with hematite or iron that has rusted in water

ZODIAC SIGN: Sagittarius (November 23–December 21)

CANDLE COLOR: Orange

PHYSICAL: Promotes healthy weight loss, assimilation of iron and minerals; addresses reproductive problems, sexual dysfunction, recovery after accident or trauma; alleviates issues stemming from the abdomen, seasonal affective disorder; counters resistance to colds, influenza, and winter viruses.

EMOTIONAL: Keeps you from loving the wrong person too much and too long; curbs sex and pornography addiction; allays fears of lovemaking or close physical contact after a bad sexual experience.

HOME: Balances the budget and moneymaking ideas to boost your finances; for pleasurable short breaks and fun days out; prompts you to stay in touch with unsociable relatives.

WORKPLACE: Fosters useful brainstorming sessions to come up with original solutions; valuable for leisure or hospitality personnel and performers or teachers of dance, sports, gymnastics, martial arts, yoga, or tai chi.

CHILDREN: Helps depressed or solitary teens.

ANIMALS: For exotic cats.

PROTECTION: Protects against self-sabotage and harmful thoughts.

MAGICKAL AND PSYCHIC USES

For rituals to increase passion; fertility and sex magick; past-life healing to shed karma long repaid.

SPECIAL PROPERTIES

For abundance and happiness in present life, abandoning regrets from the past, including past lives or dreaming of an ideal future.

MYTHOLOGY AND HISTORY

Tangerine Quartz, called the fruit of the Earth, is said to grow only in enriched soil; brings inner growth and increases prosperity though creativity and unique enterprise; offers new opportunities each day.

Tantalite

COLORS: Deep black, brown, brownish-black, red, orange-red, and reddish-brown; metallic, especially when polished or tumbled

CRYSTAL TYPE: A mineral and major source of the metal tantalum; chemically similar to Columbite (a radioactive mineral from Mozambique); found both in a manganese-rich and an iron-rich format

ZODIAC SIGN: Aquarius (January 21–February 18)

CANDLE COLOR: Orange

PHYSICAL: Addresses hard-to-solve health issues, arthritis, adrenal glands, back pain, vision, heart, fertility, skin; useful after radiation.

EMOTIONAL: Curbs constant cravings for nicotine, gambling, sexual thrills, excess food, alcohol, or drugs.

HOME: Counteracts environmental pollution if you're living near a major highway or industrial plant; aids in obtaining a fair price when buying or selling a home.

WORKPLACE: Rekindles enthusiasm for a project or blocked creativity; steers back to your original direction if you've gone off track.

CHILDREN: Keep with a picture of your teen if they're threatening to quit school or college.

ANIMALS: For old pets who have lost their enthusiasm for life.

PROTECTION: Blocks negative spells against you or malevolent thought forms; any psychic or psychological ill-wishing.

MAGICKAL AND PSYCHIC USES

Removes hooks and negative attachments in present destructive relationships, those earlier in life, or those from past worlds; counters psychic and emotional vampires.

SPECIAL PROPERTIES

A mineral that grounds and calms any place, person, or situation, replacing impulsive behavior with wise decision making.

MYTHOLOGY AND HISTORY

A stone that counters excess and offers resistance to temptations. Aptly named after Tantalus, a son of Zeus, who was punished after death by standing in a pool of shallow water with a fruit tree hanging just above him—unable to reach either the fruit or the water—so he was locked in a position of unfulfilled temptation.

Tanzanite

COLOR: Blue-purple gem with flashing violet lights

CRYSTAL TYPE: Rare form of zoisite, calcium aluminum silicate

ZODIAC SIGN: Sagittarius (November 23–December 21)

CANDLE COLOR: Purple

PHYSICAL: Addresses issues involving cells, skin, hair, vitality, ears, eyes, throat, lungs, side effects of medical treatments; boosts immunity; counters the effects of aging.

EMOTIONAL: Restores belief after losing confidence; alleviates psychological disorders, stress.

HOME: Releases redundant patterns of reacting to a partner or your family as a result of past traumas or karma.

WORKPLACE: For a second or alternative career using untapped talents; promotes clear decision making.

CHILDREN: For psychic children recalling past worlds; encourages imagination in logical children.

ANIMALS: Consoles pets grieving for a family member who moved away or died.

PROTECTION: Guards against secrets or deceit between lovers.

MAGICKAL AND PSYCHIC USES

Connects with ancient Indigenous wisdom; aids in visualization of other dimensions; contacting spirit guides; moon magick; clairvoyance, clairaudience.

SPECIAL PROPERTIES

In its rough state, almost always purple-brown, heat-treated to reveal clear blue-violet. Once treated, it changes color, from blue to violet, yellow, or burgundy in different lights. Occasionally, clear-blue crystals are found naturally when exposed to intense heat underground. All grades of Tanzanite have the same healing and magickal properties.

MYTHOLOGY AND HISTORY

Masai cattle herders discovered blue Tanzanite after brown zoisite crystals on the ground were seared by a lightning fire at the foot of Mount Kilimanjaro, Tanzania; regarded as a gift from the gods and a peace-bringer, commercialized in 1967 after Manuel de Souza, a gold prospector, found similar Tanzanite on a ridge near the mountain.

Tanzine or Tanzan Aura Quartz

COLORS: Indigo blue to indigo violet, with a soft metallic sheen

CRYSTAL TYPE: Clear quartz, bonded with gold and the rare metal indium

ZODIAC SIGN: Pisces (February 19–March 20)

CANDLE COLOR: Indigo

PHYSICAL: Alleviates issues stemming from the pituitary and pineal glands, plus the hypothalamus; addresses fibromyalgia, diabetes, vision, blood pressure, metabolic and hormone imbalance.

EMOTIONAL: Eases out-of-proportion reactions to certain people and situations; keeps you from using excess weight to insulate yourself from facing painful feelings.

HOME: Aids in living by spiritual values in a materialistic, success-oriented society; for communal or self-sufficient living.

WORKPLACE: For brainstorming, leading think tanks, and inspirational seminars; establishing a viable spiritual business where there is fierce competition.

CHILDREN: Assists Indigo Children who find the everyday world hard to deal with; for children to resist peer pressure.

ANIMALS: Keeps connection with a soul-mate animal who has departed this life.

PROTECTION: Shields against lower-vibration and malevolent spirits and against false gurus.

MAGICKAL AND PSYCHIC USES

For connection with ascended masters, extraterrestrials, and higher spiritual guides and energies.

SPECIAL PROPERTIES

Tanzine Aura Quartz draws cosmic energies into the individual that, combined with a healthy diet and gentle energy program—such as yoga or tai chi—realigns the body, mind, and spirit into a state of health.

MYTHOLOGY AND HISTORY

Also called indigo aura quartz, this newly created aura quartz links with the higher indigo ray of enlightenment and with dolphin energies; while playing whale or dolphin sounds, Tanzine Aura Quartz allows the self to momentarily merge with the peace and healing of the universe.

Tektite

COLOR: Black or dark gray; smooth, shiny on the outside

CRYSTAL TYPE: Natural glass (see Moldavite, page 304) created from the immense heat of meteorite impact with the Earth, melting together to form Tektite, which does not have a crystalline structure

ZODIAC SIGN: Aries (March 21–April 20)

CANDLE COLOR: Gray

PHYSICAL: A whole-body healer; alleviates issues relating to the skin, autoimmune system, chronic fatigue syndrome, glandular fever, HIV, hard-to-diagnose conditions, tropical diseases, psychic surgery.

EMOTIONAL: When life lacks meaning, Tektite triggers the inner impetus, rather than seeking support from external sources.

HOME: Protects property from fire, lightning and storms; also useful for air travel.

WORKPLACE: Fosters good fortune, increased sales, rapid promotion, and opportunities for actual travel and successful online networking.

CHILDREN: For Star Children and those who talk about other worlds.

ANIMALS: Aids in studying cryptozoology or dreaming of encounters with creatures from other worlds.

PROTECTION: Guards against alien abduction dreams and negative extraterrestrial experiences.

MAGICKAL AND PSYCHIC USES

Telepathy with loved ones or someone you cannot forget; out-of-body experiences, lucid dreaming, past-life regression to rediscover forgotten strengths; star magick, dream recall.

SPECIAL PROPERTIES

Positive connection with extraterrestrial beings and UFOs to receive messages concerning the future of the world.

MYTHOLOGY AND HISTORY

Tektites were associated with the gods of thunder and lightning; for example, the Roman father god Jupiter. Associated with channeling energies from Guardians of the Pleiades, myths recount that the Mayans came from the Pleiades and thereby inherited guardianship of the solar system. Tektite is a traditional talisman of power, wealth, and fertility.

Terraluminite

COLORS: White, pink, and black, mixed together
CRYSTAL TYPE: Mixture of quartz (white), feldspar (pink), and biotite mica (black); speckled, granular and granitic
ZODIAC SIGN: Aquarius (January 21–February 18)
CANDLE COLOR: White

PHYSICAL: Brings imbalances in the body and its separate parts into harmony, health, and smooth functioning; curbs autoimmune problems; promotes healthy circulation and a healthy nervous system.
EMOTIONAL: Counters childhood wounds in this and previous lives that have closed off responsiveness to those in need.
HOME: Empowers other crystals, plants, and precious artifacts, and transfers its healing light to all who live there or visit.
WORKPLACE: For making a difference through working for an ethical company that is not just concerned with profit; for establishing or becoming involved professionally in a charitable venture; for volunteer work or fund-raising.
CHILDREN: Helps those who have haloes of light or rainbows around them, who see and hear what others cannot, and who may feel isolated.
ANIMALS: Aids in developing animal mediumship skills to connect owners with deceased pets; for psychic artistry, drawing power animals around clients.
PROTECTION: Guards against making the same mistakes time and again and wondering why identical problems recur.

MAGICKAL AND PSYCHIC USES
Earth healing; deep meditation to connect with the source of divine light, full moon rituals, seasonal change point celebrations, and full and partial lunar eclipses.
SPECIAL PROPERTIES
Fills the body with light and well-being upward from the Earth (the anima/female energies) and downward from the cosmos (the animus/male energies), combining them within the individual in a calm yet joyous mix to animate your own life and that of others for the better.
MYTHOLOGY AND HISTORY
Found in Vermont and the northeastern United States, a crystal of divine love whose name means "light of the Earth." One of the cosmic crystals believed to be placed on Earth by cosmic beings as teachers and way-openers.

Texas Red Plume Agate

COLORS: Reddish-brown, with inclusions of black bush or fern patterns; plume-like forms when cut horizontally
CRYSTAL TYPE: Biscuit-shaped nodules, growing in reddish-gray basalt beds; iron/manganese (the fern shapes) covered with agate (microcrystalline quartz, chalcedony); about 10 percent is gem-quality, beautiful tumbled stones, and jewelry
ZODIAC SIGN: Aries (March 21–April 20)
CANDLE COLOR: Red

PHYSICAL: Eases blood flow through arteries, veins, and capillaries; alleviates broken or veined skin; useful for blood tests and transfusions; stabilizes blood pressure and heart rate.
EMOTIONAL: Keeps you from being inflexible; counters a tendency to expect loved ones to follow strict religious and cultural beliefs, then cutting them off if they refuse or question.
HOME: For returning to an area where you lived as a child; moving back into the family home either because of a financial or emotional setback or inheriting a family property.
WORKPLACE: Aids in networking to attract new business, especially overseas; being alert to promotion or better work opportunities.
CHILDREN: Helps find a field in which the child can succeed if they have experienced setbacks or lack confidence.
ANIMALS: For breeding cattle and horses or taking part in rodeos.
PROTECTION: Guards against becoming too tangled up in the problems of others.

MAGICKAL AND PSYCHIC USES
Collective rituals, especially outdoors; for psychometry or psychic touch; for learning to distinguish between the voices of different guides in channeling.
SPECIAL PROPERTIES
An agate of the pioneer for adventuring; for prospectors of minerals, metals, gas, and oil; for explorers—both professional and those who challenge themselves.
MYTHOLOGY AND HISTORY
Also called Woodward Ranch agate after the only place it is found in Alpine, Texas, highly prized Texas Red Plume Agate is found in dense grassland; until 2018 this rich site for agates and jaspers was open to amateur prospectors.

Thetis Hair Stone

COLORS: Light to dark green, grayish-green; may be yellowish-brown

CRYSTAL TYPE: Actinolite (page 12) or Hornblende (page 247) enclosed in clear quartz, with the interior crystal resembling tangled hair so dense that the stone may appear opaque. Actinolite is hydrous calcium magnesium iron silicate; since actinolite may occasionally contain asbestos, the enclosing quartz is a particularly safe precaution for all Actinolite

ZODIAC SIGN: Scorpio (October 24–November 22)

CANDLE COLOR: Green

PHYSICAL: Counters hair loss; strengthens nails; builds up cells and connective tissues; removes toxins.

EMOTIONAL: Aids in sorting out confused and confusing feelings about your mother if she died or left when you were young or, in later life, still acts as a controlling force.

HOME: Enhances the growth of indoor and outdoor plants; helps you save for special purchases or to buy a first home.

WORKPLACE: Offers a shield if colleagues are hostile.

CHILDREN: Keep a Thetis Hair Stone with a photo so your child will arrive safely home whether from school, vacation, or summer camp.

ANIMALS: Maintains the bond if you leave your pet in a cattery or kennel while you are on vacation.

PROTECTION: Guards against rivalry between older children and fathers or stepfathers.

MAGICKAL AND PSYCHIC USES

As an amulet for safe travel; especially overseas or by boat.

SPECIAL PROPERTIES

Thetis Hair Stone links with the universal life force and promises growth in every way, especially money.

MYTHOLOGY AND HISTORY

Thetis was a sea goddess and the leader of the fifty sea nymphs, the Nereids. Rejected in marriage by Zeus and Poseidon because it was prophesied that her son would be greater than his father, she married the mortal Peleus and their son Achilles became a mighty warrior. She immersed him as a babe in the waters of Hades to make him immortal, but the heel by which she held him did not touch the water; this was the weak spot where he was eventually killed by an arrow during the Trojan War.

Thomsonite-CA

COLORS: White, beige, cream, light shades of yellow, gray, brown, orange, and pink; may appear porcelain-like

CRYSTAL TYPE: Hydrous sodium calcium aluminum silicate; a rare zeolite. Common Thomsonite, called Thomsonite-CA, does not contain strontium (which Thomsonite-SR does); the calcium-dominated form is safer, more easily obtainable, and effective for magick and healing

ZODIAC SIGN: Gemini (May 22–June 21)

CANDLE COLOR: White

PHYSICAL: Releases physical blockages, sometimes caused by emotional blocks, fevers, fungal infections of the mouth, connective tissue, cysts.

EMOTIONAL: Useful for those who suffer from muddled thinking; counters inertia and an unwillingness to take action involving effort.

HOME: Aids in organizing neighborhood opposition to landfill sites, toxic waste dumps, and fracking for gas, mineral, or oil exploration.

WORKPLACE: Promotes problem solving, motivating employees or colleagues; for horticulture, irrigation, and agriculture.

CHILDREN: For teens reluctant to do chores.

ANIMALS: Motivates overfed, overindulged pets, who resist going for walks.

PROTECTION: Guards against discouragement by those who find fault with everything; shields you from treachery.

MAGICKAL AND PSYCHIC USES

For Earth-healing rituals; prayer and chant cycles during meditation using Thomsonite-CA beads to count prayers; love and sex rituals.

SPECIAL PROPERTIES

Thomsonite-CA boosts youthfulness and fosters new lifestyles after retirement; for grandparents and great-grandparents used as babysitters to make time for their own priorities.

MYTHOLOGY AND HISTORY

Created from lava flows over 600 million years ago, Thomsonite-CA was first identified in 1820 in Scotland in the Kilpatrick Hills in Dunbartonshire and named after the chemist and mineralogist Thomas Thomson. Thomsonite-CA stones are found on the shoreline of Lake Superior, Minnesota; Thomsonite-CA brings awareness of all the factors involved in making a decision.

Thulite or Rosaline

COLORS: Pale pink to deep rose or dark red, depending on the amount of manganese; may also contain black, gray, or white

CRYSTAL TYPE: Calcium aluminum silicate hydroxide mineral, the pink variety of Zoisite

ZODIAC SIGNS: Taurus (April 21–May 21) and Gemini (May 22–June 21)

CANDLE COLOR: Deep pink

PHYSICAL: Alleviates issues stemming from the digestive system, calcium deficiency, sexual and reproductive disorders.

EMOTIONAL: Counters acute shyness, fears of speaking or eating in public; curbs eating disorders, self-harm.

HOME: Encourages harmonious gatherings to reconcile family differences.

WORKPLACE: Enables entertainers, actors, lecturers, teachers, public speakers to develop a powerful presence.

CHILDREN: For acute shyness; reduces stress about school plays, performances, and exams.

ANIMALS: Helps animals entering shows or competitions to appear at their best.

PROTECTION: Shields against bad habits or influences; guards against financial deception.

MAGICKAL AND PSYCHIC USES

For love and reconciliation rituals; sex magick; as a charm to increase popularity.

SPECIAL PROPERTIES

A strong stone of the heart chakra energy center; heals past abuse, neglect; creates positive love relationships and aids in rearing happy children.

MYTHOLOGY AND HISTORY

Named after the fabled isle of Thule, described by the ancient Greek explorer Pythias, where it was said there were no nights. The national stone of Norway where it was first discovered; also found in Australia, Italy, Japan, Russia, Sweden, and South Africa.

Thunder Egg

COLORS: Hardened brown, black, or gray matrix, the inner cavity filled with patterned agate, chalcedony, jasper, clear quartz, amethyst, or occasionally opal

CRYSTAL TYPE: Spherical siliceous volcanic rock masses from less than two or three centimeters in diameter to more than a hundred centimeters internally, with star- or flower-like formations

ZODIAC SIGNS: Scorpio (October 24–November 22) and Capricorn (December 22–January 20)

CANDLE COLOR: Indigo

PHYSICAL: Relieves pain; diminishes growths; promotes fertility and potency in later life; useful in reconstructive surgery; counters energy-depleting conditions.

EMOTIONAL: Curbs poor body image; allays fears of revealing your true self.

HOME: Thunder Egg creates beauty despite untidy family or roommates; promotes neighborhood and community activities.

WORKPLACE: Valuable for backroom staff, copywriters, publicity agents, editors, and those supporting others in the public eye.

CHILDREN: For imaginative play of treasure caves and hidden worlds; attracts friends to introspective children.

ANIMALS: Empowers nocturnal and secretive creatures.

PROTECTION: For keeping necessary secrets; straightens out misaligned Earth energies causing sick-building syndrome; staves off overwhelming energy directed your way by others.

MAGICKAL AND PSYCHIC USES

For guided group visualization or meditation of other realms; shamanism; recognizing Kindred Star People in this life; Earth rituals; seeing auras.

SPECIAL PROPERTIES

Encourages the expression of creative talents professionally and for pleasure.

MYTHOLOGY AND HISTORY

Thunder Eggs are protective luck-bringers among Indigenous people, including some Australian Aboriginal tribes. One account of their origin in Native North America describes two warring mountain spirits throwing thunderbolts at each other. Some, like those formed in rhyolite lava flows in Oregon, whose state rock is the Thunder Egg, are estimated to be sixty million years old.

Tibetan Quartz or Black Spot Quartz

COLORS: Varies between water clear with rainbows, cloudy, smoky, clear with black spot inclusions, or almost totally black

CRYSTAL TYPE: Quartz with varying amounts of carbon and manganese included that determine the darkness or other color(s) of the crystals; often as single- or double-terminated points; silicon dioxide; some have enhydro bubbles

ZODIAC SIGN: Pisces (February 19–March 20)

CANDLE COLOR: Silver

PHYSICAL: A gentler energizer than conventional clear quartz, minimizing side effects for any treatment or intervention.

EMOTIONAL: Counters self-destructive or destructive tendencies; enables you to move past guilt for past misdeeds.

HOME: For inducing quiet times and winding down at the end of the day; fosters clear divisions if work and home life overlap.

WORKPLACE: Promotes ongoing harmony if you teach spiritual arts by avoiding petty in-class rivalry or overemphasis on achievement by students; fends off constant interruptions when working from home.

CHILDREN: Tibetan Quartz stimulates children's imagination and storytelling abilities.

ANIMALS: Enables psychic pets to remain alert to possible hazards for owners.

PROTECTION: Guards against intrusion on your personal space and boundaries—actual, psychic, and psychological.

MAGICKAL AND PSYCHIC USES

Attaining deep, trance-like levels during meditation; practicing Asian healing arts, such as Reiki, shiatsu, Ayurveda, or traditional Chinese medicine.

SPECIAL PROPERTIES

Attracts money for any positive purpose; eases fasting and reduces cravings when dieting.

MYTHOLOGY AND HISTORY

Himalayan or Nepalese Quartz is considered sacred. It is found high in the mountains, hand-mined by monks, and carried down in packs. Indeed, the mystical home of immortality, called Shambhala—the land of peace, harmony, and enlightenment—lies north of the Himalayas and its healings are linked with Tibetan Quartz.

Tibetan Turquoise

COLORS: Light to deep blue, greenish-blue or apple green, with black veins

CRYSTAL TYPE: Hydrous aluminum phosphate, colored by copper (blue) and iron (green)

ZODIAC SIGN: Sagittarius (November 23–December 21)

CANDLE COLOR: Green

PHYSICAL: Alleviates issues stemming from the liver, anemia, nerve endings, ears, eyes, throat, bladder, stomach, viral infections, inflammation, rashes.

EMOTIONAL: Curbs a tendency to be a drama king or queen; encourages narcissistic people to acknowledge needs in others.

HOME: Attracts prosperity, luck, health, and happiness; for uniting stepfamilies; for house and apartment sharing with relative strangers.

WORKPLACE: Fosters promotion and leadership; useful in establishing a business; aids in standing up to corruption in the corporate world.

CHILDREN: Protects babies and small children parted from the birth mother; given to children to keep them from falling.

ANIMALS: Sewn on fabric on a horse's bridle for luck in racing or competitive sports.

PROTECTION: Guards against those who would divide lovers.

MAGICKAL AND PSYCHIC USES

A personal stone, each unique, whose color becomes paler to warn of ill health, infidelity, or burnout and brighter for opportunity and lasting love; a master healer, enhancing other crystals, natural remedies, and healers; promotes psychic dreams, love, and fidelity spells.

SPECIAL PROPERTIES

For empowering and protecting the wearer from childhood to old age; regularly upgraded by individuals to reflect different life stages.

MYTHOLOGY AND HISTORY

Tibetan Turquoise has been sacred in the Himalayas since 1000 BCE, as jewelry, prayer beads, musical instruments, prayer wheels, and bells. It is believed that Tibetan Turquoise was brought to Earth from heaven.

Tiffany Stone

COLORS: Mainly blue, purple, and white, with pink, orange, red, white, black, clear, and green; has dendrites (fern-like patterns) and plumes

CRYSTAL TYPE: Silica and/or calcium carbonate base; predominantly opalized fluorite, purple opal, and agate (chalcedony); may include jasper, quartzite, bertrandite, and dolomite

ZODIAC SIGN: Sagittarius (November 23–December 21)

CANDLE COLOR: Purple

PHYSICAL: Regulates hormones; eases childbirth; addresses issues relating to blood thinning, kidneys, nausea linked with headaches or migraines due to food intolerances.

EMOTIONAL: Counters an inability to acknowledge negative as well as positive feelings; for men told that big boys don't cry.

HOME: For decluttering your home and your life.

WORKPLACE: Encourages successful youth enterprise schemes and apprenticeships, individual ventures; aids in applying for business grants and loans.

CHILDREN: Empowers those who find study uninspiring to consider alternative future paths involving practical or creative skills.

ANIMALS: For pets reluctant to go on unfamiliar walks; allays fear of traveling in a car.

PROTECTION: Guards against consequences of displeasing those you care for if they do not approve of your plans.

MAGICKAL AND PSYCHIC USES
Clairaudience, clairvoyance, mediumship; for increased accuracy with tarot cards, runes, and other forms of divination; sex magick, tantra.

SPECIAL PROPERTIES
A stone representing freedom from old restrictions; brings joy and shares that joy with others.

MYTHOLOGY AND HISTORY
Popularly called the ice cream stone, as well as opalized fluorite; Tiffany Stone is rare; mined only at the Brush Wellman mine in western Utah. Tiffany Stone enables you to strive for happiness now.

Tiger Iron or Mugglestone

COLOR: Banded black, gold, silver, and red

CRYSTAL TYPE: Banded ironstone (combining black hematite, red jasper, and golden tiger's eye)

ZODIAC SIGNS: Aries (March 21–April 20) and Leo (July 23–August 23)

CANDLE COLOR: Red

PHYSICAL: Strengthens blood cells; oxygenates the blood; relieves fatigue from illnesses; increases stamina; addresses issues involving the liver, nervous system, muscles, legs, sexual organs.

EMOTIONAL: Helps overcome illnesses, depression, and addictions; eases panic attacks and obsessive-compulsive disorder.

HOME: Guards against fears of ghosts at night, in old houses, and with overly imaginative or psychic children.

WORKPLACE: For salable creations by artists, sculptors, potters, wood- and metalworkers, and other artisans; in planning offices and government departments for realistic, tangible, people-centered results.

CHILDREN: Ensures the safety of children who lack manual dexterity or are accident-prone.

ANIMALS: For cattle and sheepdogs and horses used for work or competitions; prevents fear of traffic and sudden noises in sensitive animals.

PROTECTION: Guards against physical danger and in extreme sports.

MAGICKAL AND PSYCHIC USES
Fends off psychic attack by malevolent ghosts, succubi, incubi, and poltergeists; counters against curses and hexes; amplifies release of magickal power in spells.

SPECIAL PROPERTIES
The amplification of three powerful crystals as one: hematite for clear thinking, jasper for determination, and tiger's eye for courage.

MYTHOLOGY AND HISTORY
The fix-all Mugglestone, recalling, for Harry Potter devotees, the earthbound Muggles, is named after Moclestone or Mucklstone (an Anglo-Saxon word) on the boundaries of Shropshire/Staffordshire in the English Midlands, where it was first found; reflecting also the pioneering spirit of Western Australia, a major source; some tiger iron may date back 2.2 billion years.

Tiger's Eye

COLORS: Brown and gold stripes; gleaming (see also Falcon, Hawk, or Blue Tiger's Eye, page 184, and Red Tiger's Eye, page 403)
CRYSTAL TYPE: Chalcedony quartz
ZODIAC SIGN: Leo (July 23–August 23)
CANDLE COLOR: Gold

PHYSICAL: Alleviates issues dealing with the stomach, gallbladder, digestion; slows an overloaded system; energizes weakness or exhaustion; warms aching joints; aids in detoxification, healthy eating, or exercise plans.
EMOTIONAL: Reduces food cravings, binges; keeps you from in indulging in excess smoking, prescription drugs, or alcohol; allays fears.
HOME: Promotes money flowing into the home; preventing extravagance; enables longer-term wealth.
WORKPLACE: For entrepreneurial ventures, new businesses, acquiring skills for major career changes; to shine creatively in competitions, exhibitions, performances, or on- and offline sales; careers in stocks, real estate, banking, and insurance.
CHILDREN: Supports young entrepreneurs starting businesses while still at school or college.
ANIMALS: Prevents a pet from trying to dominate humans or other animals; for conservation of tigers and other endangered big cats.
PROTECTION: Reflects back envy, verbal, emotional, or psychic attacks; guards travelers.

MAGICKAL AND PSYCHIC USES
Prosperity rituals; scrying by candlelight or sunlight to access past worlds; shields against mind control, paranormal presences, psychological or psychic vampires.
SPECIAL PROPERTIES
Called the all-knowing eye, allows the possessor to know if a person or offer is trustworthy.
MYTHOLOGY AND HISTORY
A power crystal, associated with the tiger; to ancient Egyptians, Tiger's Eye offered dual protection from sun and Earth. Roman soldiers carried Tiger's Eye for courage in battle and to be alert to danger. In ancient China, it was considered a good luck charm.

Tinguaite

COLORS: Pale, grass, moss, dark green to almost black with tortoise or turtle-like markings or striations; may be fluorescent; the most intense colors used in jewelry
CRYSTAL TYPE: Volcanic rock, containing feldspar, nepheline, aegirine, plus small amounts of cancrinite, sphene, and hackmanite
ZODIAC SIGN: Virgo (August 24–September 22)
CANDLE COLOR: Green

PHYSICAL: Alleviates illnesses caused or made worse by an unhealthy lifestyle, aging worries, memory lapses; addresses issues concerning the back and spine, including scoliosis.
EMOTIONAL: Eases burdens and attachments that weigh heavy, but that you are unwilling or unable to shed.
HOME: For self-sufficiency and stability within yourself if you relocate frequently or are traveling long term on a boat or in a camper.
WORKPLACE: Restores the work-life balance if work dominates evenings, weekends, and vacations; keeps you from doing more than your share.
CHILDREN: Calms those who do not like staying away from home or are not settling in after a relocation or a move to a new school.
ANIMALS: Calls domestic cats who wander and are hard to track down.
PROTECTION: Guards against codependency and blurring the boundaries between self and others.

MAGICKAL AND PSYCHIC USES
A shamanic stone for healing, astral travel, and psychic flight; breaks ties with undesirable influences and hooks of guilt.
SPECIAL PROPERTIES
Encourages healthy eating and a pleasurable exercise regimen; the stone of self-sufficiency and establishing personal identity if this has been eroded by domineering people.
MYTHOLOGY AND HISTORY
Tinguaite is mined in the Khibiny Mountains of the Kola Peninsula in Russia, an area rich in natural energies, and in Brazil, where it was first discovered in Sierra de Tinguá (hence the name). Based on its tortoise or turtle-like markings, Tinguaite is symbolically associated with tortoises, among the oldest of creatures, who acted as icons of wisdom and protection for traditional societies. In Native American lore, Mother Turtle brought the Earth from the primordial waters.

Tinkasite

COLORS: Gold, yellow, orangish-brown, creamy brown; may be colored by purple charoite inclusions or be enclosed and mixed with charoite, a mineral with which it often is joined (see Charoite with Tinkasite, page 115)

CRYSTAL TYPE: Titanium, sodium, potassium, and silicon; best for healing and magick as a tumbled stone

ZODIAC SIGN: Gemini (May 22–June 21)

CANDLE COLOR: Yellow

PHYSICAL: Alleviates infections, bacterial and viral conditions, mineral deficiency (especially calcium and potassium), sodium excesses, dehydration, swollen and painful limbs.

EMOTIONAL: Allays fears of failure; curbs an inability to leave past mistakes and injustices behind.

HOME: Brings privacy against overly curious neighbors about your past and your family life; place Tinkasite at the corners around the boundaries indoors or out to keep your property safe from burglary when you are away from home.

WORKPLACE: Establishes your role in a new career or when setting up an innovative business; aids you in promoting original, inspirational ideas and putting them into practice.

CHILDREN: If teens are obsessed with looking and acting like a particular celebrity or the alpha male or female at college.

ANIMALS: For previously abused pets who need extra attention.

PROTECTION: Guards against stalkers, malicious phone calls and texts, and social media trolling.

MAGICKAL AND PSYCHIC USES

Past-life therapy to understand and leave behind trauma and guilt from old worlds; Buddhism, Daoism, and faiths without emphasis on sin and punishment.

SPECIAL PROPERTIES

The stone of justice, countering personal unfair treatment and accusations; fosters success in official or court matters, whether you are opposed by or seeking damages from a powerful organization, a vindictive ex-partner, or a dishonest witness.

MYTHOLOGY AND HISTORY

Tinkasite is found only in Siberia; traditionally used in ceremonies in Eurasia for personal purification, the removal of illness and evil entities, and for healing the Earth; a powerful crystal for defining or redefining the self.

Tisbury Starred Agate

COLORS: Cream with brown, star-like markings all over or brown with cream stars

CRYSTAL TYPE: A fossil agate found only in Tisbury, Wiltshire in the southwest of England; silicified, preserved in quartz, of the species *Isastraea oblonga*, a Jurassic fossil coral agate; may be polished, tumbled, or used for jewelry

ZODIAC SIGN: Capricorn (December 22–January 20)

CANDLE COLOR: Cream

PHYSICAL: Addresses issues relating to hormones, water retention; alleviates problems with and worries about aging, skin, cosmetic surgery, emphysema, asthma, bronchitis, and lung allergies caused by pollen, fur, or dust mites.

EMOTIONAL: Counters an overreliance on astrology to explain and dictate destiny; curbs a sense of the world being out of step and sharing no common ground with others.

HOME: Aids in preserving older homes to combine modern-day comfort with tradition; protection against floods, lightning strikes, and bad weather cycles.

WORKPLACE: Keeps faith with your own ideas and approaches, even if they differ from the majority view.

CHILDREN: For sensitive, dreamy children to cope in the everyday world while retaining their unique magick.

ANIMALS: For the conservation of whales, dolphins, and other endangered sea creatures, associated with the Sirius star realms.

PROTECTION: Guards against fears of water and drowning, perhaps a result of past-world memories.

MAGICKAL AND PSYCHIC USES

Calls up past-world memories of life by the ocean, whether personal or more universal recall of early oceans that once covered much of the world; for sea wishes.

SPECIAL PROPERTIES

For Star People to meet and recognize other Star Souls.

MYTHOLOGY AND HISTORY

The first known finding of Tisbury Starred Agate was in a 100,000-year-old grave of a young woman in Kent in southeast England. This would suggest that early humans traveled to Tisbury, perhaps for the agates; the stone was buried with the girl as a protective amulet for the afterlife.

Titanite in Quartz

COLORS: Brown, green, or yellow; sparkling; golden brown within smoky quartz

CRYSTAL TYPE: Titanite, calcium titanium silicate, also known as Sphene (page 451), found naturally as inclusions or growing on clear quartz, occasionally smoky quartz; also on minerals such as albite or calcite

ZODIAC SIGN: Pisces (February 19–March 20)

CANDLE COLOR: White

PHYSICAL: Curbs out-of-control cell reproduction; addresses autoimmune system problems, lupus, strokes, hip and knee replacements.

EMOTIONAL: Alleviates psychological disorders or phobias resistant to treatment; helps overcome repeating self-destructive patterns.

HOME: For making separate financial and practical arrangements if you're sharing a home with relatives or jointly inheriting a property.

WORKPLACE: Combines conventional medical or psychological training with energy and natural therapies to create a successful holistic practice; brings order out of chaos.

CHILDREN: Helps children whose families are relocating if the youngsters are reluctant to leave their friends and schools.

ANIMALS: Comforts a pet you are giving to a new owner because of relocation.

PROTECTION: Guards against leaving the future to chance.

MAGICKAL AND PSYCHIC USES

For accurate professional or informal parapsychological research; restores spontaneity to divination or mediumship if you feel blocked by rules.

SPECIAL PROPERTIES

Ensures safe backpacking, trekking, camping, and exploration of remote areas; for research trips to locations threatened by climate change.

MYTHOLOGY AND HISTORY

Titanite in Quartz is different from Titanium Aura Quartz, where quartz is bombarded with titanium and becomes multicolored and iridescent. The crystal of setting life in order, whether clearing clutter before a house move, writing wills, filling in planning applications, or checking the small print on contracts.

Titanium Aura Quartz, Rainbow Aura Quartz, or Flame Aura Quartz

COLORS: Rainbow, iridescent

CRYSTAL TYPE: Bonded crystal, quartz fused with a fine layer of titanium and niobium

ZODIAC SIGN: Pisces (February 19–March 20)

CANDLE COLOR: Rainbow or gold

PHYSICAL: Addresses hard-to-diagnose conditions; fevers; water retention; issues involving cells, bones, and blood; multiple sclerosis; life-changing degenerative conditions.

EMOTIONAL: For consolation in life's darkest hours; helps overcome a tendency not to forgive and move on.

HOME: Brings joy wherever you are living or staying if you cannot be where you consider home.

WORKPLACE: Brightens your workplace and workspace; for inspiring creative and lateral thinking; for those in advertising, publicity, design, website work, children's television, book illustrations, journals, or animation.

CHILDREN: Restores magick to young children after being told by peers that Santa Claus and fairies aren't real.

ANIMALS: Helps abused animals re-establish their faith in humanity.

PROTECTION: Guards against making bad financial decisions.

MAGICKAL AND PSYCHIC USES

Scrying the iridescent surface by candlelight; tai chi, yoga, and all spiritual energy-transference arts; astral travel, especially in dreams, meditation, automatic writing.

SPECIAL PROPERTIES

Seeing your own and others' auras; a Titanium Aura point energizes the aura when passed through and around the hair in spirals; for chakra balance with a piece above your head and one below your feet.

MYTHOLOGY AND HISTORY

A transmitter of universal light, and an alchemist stone combining two high-vibration crystals to create something greater, Titanium Aura Quartz melds the strength and bonding powers of titanium and the pure energy of quartz; diffuses rainbows to raise awareness, joy, and creativity to new levels.

Topazolite

COLORS: Yellow, golden, yellowish-green, or brownish; sparkling
CRYSTAL TYPE: A form of Andradite Garnet (page 241), so called because of its resemblance to topaz; calcium iron silicate
ZODIAC SIGN: Gemini (May 22–June 21)
CANDLE COLOR: Yellow

PHYSICAL: Boosts the immune system, absorption of iron and calcium, mobility; alleviates rheumatism, arthritis, bone weakness, sluggish metabolism.
EMOTIONAL: Keeps you from putting no effort into life and resenting those who have succeeded through working hard; for those who blame others for their own failings.
HOME: Spreads happiness and sunshine to dispel the gloomiest mood or on the darkest day.
WORKPLACE: The salesperson's garnet, Topazolite brings dynamic energies to increase persuasive powers for selling products and ideas.
CHILDREN: For teens who do not get invited to social events; for those who have studied insufficiently for examinations to remember what is most relevant.
ANIMALS: Useful for pets who perform in the media or appear in advertisements.
PROTECTION: Guards against others' jealousy and attempts to sabotage your achievements.

MAGICKAL AND PSYCHIC USES
Healing through light; crystal and angel Reiki; aura interpretation and healing; color therapies and divination; for heightened intuition and spontaneous predictions.

SPECIAL PROPERTIES
Warms and cheers; a stone of early summer, especially in northern climes in lands where the sun is slow to return and departs early.

MYTHOLOGY AND HISTORY
A powerful form of andradite garnet, Topazolite strengthens willpower, determination to succeed, and the ability to shine by spreading radiance and charisma so others open the way.

Topaz—White or Clear

COLOR: The purest form of topaz, clear and sparkling; also called silver topaz (see also Golden or Imperial Topaz and Blue Topaz, pages 209 and 83)
CRYSTAL TYPE: Hydrous aluminum silicate
ZODIAC SIGNS: Leo (July 23–August 23) and Cancer (June 22–July 22)
CANDLE COLOR: Silver

PHYSICAL: Strengthens the endocrine system; alleviates cystic fibrosis, emphysema, asthma, dust allergies, colds, bronchitis, influenza, pleurisy, pneumonia; promotes healthy weight, vision.
EMOTIONAL: Calms whirling minds; balances excessive emotional reactions to crises.
HOME: Radiates energy, health, happiness, and infinite possibility.
WORKPLACE: Aids in integrating different sources of information and viewpoints; for teachers, lecturers, those creating training manuals or programs; coordinating meetings to achieve desired results.
CHILDREN: Reduces the influences of advertising and desire for material possessions.
ANIMALS: For assessing reliability in new pets; communicating telepathically with pets and wildlife.
PROTECTION: Guards against false friends and those who would mislead.

MAGICKAL AND PSYCHIC USES
Clairaudience, clairvoyance, psychometry, full moon scrying; detecting the presence of evil spirits (becomes cloudy); connects with power animals.

SPECIAL PROPERTIES
Gentle and lunar-inspired, Topaz is a commitment token for first or new love or love after betrayal.

MYTHOLOGY AND HISTORY
The ancient Greeks prized clear Topaz to prevent negative enchantment and bring invisibility if in danger. Increasing in luster with the waxing moon, clear Topaz becomes most powerful at full moon; often mistaken for diamonds or white sapphire, the huge seventeenth-century Braganza diamond, as it was called, was part of the Portuguese crown jewels.

Topaz with Hematite

COLORS: Generally blue or yellow (topaz) with black/dark gray/reddish-brown or silvery-metallic (hematite) included; as yellow/blue within black or as a yellow/blue matrix with black/dark gray/dark silver attached

CRYSTAL TYPE: Silicate mineral of aluminum and fluorine (topaz) and iron oxide (hematite); may be found as a tumbled stone

ZODIAC SIGN: Aries (March 21–April 20)

CANDLE COLOR: Gold

PHYSICAL: Aids in recovery from major surgery or prolonged medical treatment; alleviates blood, lung, and digestive disorders that may result from a whole-body infection or virus.

EMOTIONAL: Curbs impulsive and excessive reactions to minor irritations; helps overcome a sense that the world and those in it are unfair; keeps you from adopting a blind belief in conspiracy theories without considering facts.

HOME: Protects against domestic abuse—psychological as well as physical—and musters the courage to walk away.

WORKPLACE: For manifesting the right opportunities and offering the strength to carry them through in the face of opposition or indifference; for asserting authority if you're temporarily promoted, owing to an illness or the temporary absence of the usual holder of the position.

CHILDREN: Useful for those who find following rules hard.

ANIMALS: Valuable for protective pets if you live in a dangerous neighborhood or work with a trained guard dog.

PROTECTION: Blocks psychic attacks by earthly perpetrators and malevolent spirits summoned mistakenly during a séance.

MAGICKAL AND PSYCHIC USES

An alchemical stone; the separate properties of the crystals create energies for manifesting dreams and desires in tangible ways through ritual, and then generate an unexpected earthly solution; for psychic defense.

SPECIAL PROPERTIES

Two stones of justice and authority, Topaz with Hematite confers power against corruption.

MYTHOLOGY AND HISTORY

Mined in Brazil, Topaz with Hematite makes the seemingly impossible attainable; to allow a secret or forbidden love to be safely expressed; breaks through and reveals dishonesty.

Tourmalated or Tourmalinated Quartz

COLOR: Clear with sparkling black; the proportion of black to white varies according to the number of rutiles within

CRYSTAL TYPE: Needles of black tourmaline embedded in crystal quartz; occasionally has green or pink tourmaline inclusions

ZODIAC SIGNS: Scorpio (October 24–November 22) and Gemini (May 22–June 21)

CANDLE COLOR: White

PHYSICAL: Alleviates blocked arteries, heart valves, veins, scars, lesions; addresses deep vein thrombosis, sinuses, digestion; useful after traffic accidents or a traumatic injury.

EMOTIONAL: Eases bipolar disorder; counters Asperger's syndrome, autism, in adults and children; curbs self-sabotage, self-harm, addiction to painkillers or prescription drugs.

HOME: Clears unfriendly ghosts or poltergeists and negativity from previous occupants; insulates the home from a noisy household.

WORKPLACE: Disperses pettiness; encourages resolution of long-standing resentments; for temporary, short-term contract and supply work.

CHILDREN: Helps sensitive children cope with group activities, such as day care or social gatherings.

ANIMALS: Prevents horses and dogs from overreacting to sudden noise or traffic.

PROTECTION: Shields against negativity from others and deliberate psychic or psychological attack; guards against harmful electromagnetic energies at home and at work.

MAGICKAL AND PSYCHIC USES

Astral projection, traditional Chinese medicine, acupuncture, astral travel, remote viewing, knot rituals; a charm for specific good luck; walking meditation.

SPECIAL PROPERTIES

For traveling safely alone, working vacations involving conservation or charity work overseas.

MYTHOLOGY AND HISTORY

Protective black tourmaline, combined with proactive quartz, offers a doorway into hidden realms of ancestors and totem animals; balances polarities—yin and yang, active and receptive, challenging and defensive.

Transmitter Quartz

COLORS: Colorless but may appear in other colored quartzes, especially those regarded as Master Crystals (page 297) in their own right, including Amethyst, Citrine, Rose Quartz, and Smoky Quartz

CRYSTAL TYPE: Clear quartz crystal with two symmetrical, seven-sided faces, separated by a large, perfectly triangular main front face

ZODIAC SIGN: Gemini (May 22–June 21)

CANDLE COLOR: White

PHYSICAL: Useful in treatments involving heat, lasers, and light, plus heart-valve replacement.

EMOTIONAL: Enables you to open up to counseling or cognitive behavioral therapy; counters mistrust of those suspected of invading your personal privacy, even with good intentions.

HOME: For speaking spontaneously, clearly, and wisely, no matter what needs to be said or written; keep Transmitter Quartz near computers, smartphones, tablets.

WORKPLACE: Useful in customer service, producing and communicating in writing, visually, and verbally.

CHILDREN: Teaches children to pray or talk to their guardian angels.

ANIMALS: Reassures pets telepathically, when they need to stay overnight at the vet or in a kennel or cattery.

PROTECTION: Guards against those who try to silence you.

MAGICKAL AND PSYCHIC USES

Asking questions through the crystal to guides, guardian angels, and deceased relatives, and receiving answers clairaudiently through the inner voice, automatic writing, or a pendulum.

SPECIAL PROPERTIES

Asking for help through the crystal if you cannot cope or see your way through a crisis. Practical solutions may appear in your mind and in some cases online resources or the appearance of a human guardian angel follows.

MYTHOLOGY AND HISTORY

Receiver Quartz (page 392) is ideal paired with Transmitter Quartz, asking questions holding your transmitter and then being given the answer via the receiver crystal; aids in calling telepathically people to contact you with whom you have lost touch or are estranged.

Treasure Agate

COLORS: Varies according to the composition; often deep brown and blue with spots of gold and darker ones of manganese, plus white (quartz)

CRYSTAL TYPE: Not actually an agate, but a combination of gold, silver, platinum alloys; may include cuprite, copper, azurite, pyrite, malachite, and manganese within the quartz

ZODIAC SIGN: Leo (July 23–August 23)

CANDLE COLOR: Gold

PHYSICAL: Addresses issues with the throat (especially swallowing caused by or made worse by stress or the inability or fear to speak your mind), chronic cough without obvious physiological cause, whole-body healing.

EMOTIONAL: Curbs extreme introversion; keeps you from shunning others considered less knowledgeable or worthy of attention.

HOME: Treasure Agate, with the center filled with minerals, attracts abundance and good fortune.

WORKPLACE: Aids in progressing toward your ultimate goal, pushing through obstacles, and refusing to give up.

CHILDREN: If they are challenging authority, provides the patience to see life from their point of view.

ANIMALS: Helps you discover your spirit familiars and power creatures who have guided you through many lifetimes.

PROTECTION: Guards against those who are stingy with their time and resources and never pay their share.

MAGICKAL AND PSYCHIC USES

Meditation to access higher realms, planetary, stellar, angelic worlds and evolved teachers; for visions of wise beings.

SPECIAL PROPERTIES

To communicate without bitterness or anger what you really want to say to loved ones and others who may have wronged you; opening channels enabling you to reveal your authentic self.

MYTHOLOGY AND HISTORY

A rare and expensive stone, although it can be purchased in small raw pieces and is a wonderful collector's item. Found only in Arizona in the Harquahala Mountains, whose name was given by the Native North Americans meaning "water that is high up because of the many springs in the area."

Trigonal or Trigonic Quartz

COLORS: Often clear or milky white, but depends on the crystal

CRYSTAL TYPE: Extremely rare, found in clear quartz, amethyst, citrine, or smoky quartz; with the inclusion of one or sometimes many inverted triangles etched by nature on the crystal

ZODIAC SIGN: Leo (July 23–August 23)

CANDLE COLOR: Gold

PHYSICAL: Bolsters the immune system, brain, circulation, lymph nodes; addresses fluid imbalance, swollen joints; for end-of-life care and transiting peacefully to the next world.

EMOTIONAL: Allays fear of childbirth; curbs obsession with future serious illnesses and dying.

HOME: Helps settle neighborhood and community disputes; aids in living amicably alongside those whose lifestyles and beliefs are very different from your own.

WORKPLACE: The inverted triangle is the magickal symbol for the Water element, so Trigonal Quartz creates calm times so business flows steadily in and obstacles naturally clear.

CHILDREN: Ensures safe delivery of healthy newborn babies.

ANIMALS: For a first-time mother struggling to care for her litter; for another motherly pet adopting different orphaned species.

PROTECTION: Guards against losing valuable data, results, or paperwork.

MAGICKAL AND PSYCHIC USES

Accessing dream-like, semihypnotic states in meditation; for shamans and hedge witches who astrally walk between the worlds and dimensions.

SPECIAL PROPERTIES

Trigonic Record Keepers point directly downward from the apex of the crystal termination toward the base. They offer insights into future possibilities in order to choose the way ahead; traditional Record Keepers (page 392) reveal the wisdom of the past.

MYTHOLOGY AND HISTORY

A powerful soul-retrieval crystal if trauma has caused a wound in the soul in past worlds, or earlier in this incarnation; if childbirth or bereavement has changed your world or is imminent, enables you to accept birth, death, and rebirth or immortality as part of a necessary continuing cycle; the crystal leads some to Buddhism.

Trilobite

COLORS: Gray, also sometimes black or brown

CRYSTAL TYPE: Trilobites were hard-shelled, segmented creatures that existed over 540 million years ago. Segmented creatures have organs that are repeated throughout the body, such as arthropods and annelids

ZODIAC SIGN: Cancer (June 22–July 22)

CANDLE COLOR: White

PHYSICAL: Alleviates difficulties with vision, headaches, bone thinning; age-related memory loss, psoriasis and skin eruptions, growths and swellings, degenerative disorders.

EMOTIONAL: Keeps you from being stuck in the past; allays fears of aging and mortality.

HOME: For tough love when a family member or close friend abuses your trust or generosity.

WORKPLACE: Encourages leadership and management skills, especially if you lack experience; because of the Trilobite's ability to transfer shells, it is considered a talisman for changing jobs or companies for a similar but more advantageous position.

CHILDREN: Teaches children patience, perseverance, and an awareness of long-term time frames.

ANIMALS: For keeping rare insects, lizards, or snakes.

PROTECTION: Guards against staying in a situation when it becomes destructive or hopeless.

MAGICKAL AND PSYCHIC USES

Rebirthing to overcome problems linked with traumatic prebirth and birth experiences; for past-life recall, especially in dreams.

SPECIAL PROPERTIES

Helps to stay the course on a long-term creative project or training that requires sustained effort; for writers, artists, musicians, and poets if recognition is slow in coming.

MYTHOLOGY AND HISTORY

Some seventeen thousand species of Trilobites have been recorded, so their fossilized remains are common. Many are found in the northern Sahara Desert, once a prehistoric ocean, so combining the power of water and Earth. As one of the Earth's earliest complex life-forms that became extinct before the age of the dinosaurs, Trilobites represent the need to adapt to changing stages in relationships and career like the Trilobite changing shell.

Triphane

COLORS: Pale to bright yellow; transparent with inclusions; vertically striated; the yellow caused by iron impurities

CRYSTAL TYPE: Pyroxene, lithium aluminum silicate; though not often of gem quality, its clarity and color do make it a source of gem-like jewelry

ZODIAC SIGN: Gemini (May 22–June 21)

CANDLE COLOR: Pale yellow

PHYSICAL: Addresses issues stemming from the lymphatic system; addresses blood sugar balance, water retention, indigestion, gallstones, constipation, IBS, skin eruptions, eczema.

EMOTIONAL: Curbs ongoing sadness about what cannot or who cannot return to your life; keeps you from maintaining secrecy and trying to lead a double life.

HOME: In the center of a room, acts as an ongoing cleanser and purifier of the aura energy field of the house.

WORKPLACE: For combining two jobs; promotes intuitive speculation if all the facts are not known; helps you succeed at professional gambling, especially horse racing using computers and calculated risk assessment.

CHILDREN: Aids in retaining facts for tests; fosters fluency in oral examinations if nerves tend to cause the mind to seize up.

ANIMALS: For discerning genuine sales of pedigreed puppies or kittens and avoiding online pet sale scams.

PROTECTION: Guards against harmful rays from domestic and office equipment, continual background noise, or music loops.

MAGICKAL AND PSYCHIC USES

Heals through learning ancient methods, such as traditional Chinese medicine, herbalism, and Ayurveda; enhances premonitions and predictions, especially applied to speculation.

SPECIAL PROPERTIES

The stone of fixing what is needed to make your life happier, whether a new job, a new relationship, a new location, or a change of lifestyle within your present environment.

MYTHOLOGY AND HISTORY

Sometimes clear Spodumene (page 453) is called Triphane, but generally its properties are closer to white or gray Spodumene, its close cousin. Yellow Triphane continuously brings recycling of what has been learned and is of advantage and what should be left behind and replaced with reworked or original ideas.

Trolleite

COLORS: Light green, greenish-blue, or colorless; may be colored by included minerals, notably lazulite and scorzalite, which make Trolleite celestial blue; may be grayish-blue; may have a yellow or golden stripe

CRYSTAL TYPE: Aluminum phosphate, usually contained within quartz, as tumbled stones or occasionally as jewelry

ZODIAC SIGN: Sagittarius (November 23–December 21)

CANDLE COLOR: Turquoise

PHYSICAL: Addresses stress-related illnesses, predispositions to hereditary conditions, issues relating to glands, headaches, migraines, tunnel vision or reduced night vision.

EMOTIONAL: Eases hypochondria; curbs a refusal to change your lifestyle to improve your health; keeps you from frequently changing direction in life without following through on anything.

HOME: Brings a sense of peace to the most hectic lifestyle; the double-terminated crystal absorbs overactivity and irritability, and recycles it as a relaxed atmosphere.

WORKPLACE: Clarifies matters that are being concealed or misrepresented; aids in finding or creating your unique niche.

CHILDREN: Helps youngsters understand the history of the area they live in and their birthplace or root culture, if different.

ANIMALS: Keeps you from overdomesticating your pet.

PROTECTION: As a single termination, repels those who would confine you to a box.

MAGICKAL AND PSYCHIC USES

Deep meditation to connect with guides, angels, and evolved spiritual teachers; for increasing healing powers by spontaneously recalling knowledge from earlier lives; clairaudience to transmit messages from higher planes; clairsentience to increase intuition.

SPECIAL PROPERTIES

Quiets a restless mind that may prevent relaxation and sleep and interfere with meditation.

MYTHOLOGY AND HISTORY

Trolleite was originally found in Skåne, in southern Sweden, in 1868, but now has been discovered in Brazil, Australia, and Virginia. A stone of spiritual enlightenment that reveals the beauty of the world once we slow down, look, and listen.

Truffle Chalcedony or Womb Stone

COLORS: White, tan, deep brown with a burned appearance; colors may be mixed within the same nodule

CRYSTAL TYPE: Botryoidal crystalline chalcedony clusters

ZODIAC SIGN: Cancer (June 22–July 22)

CANDLE COLOR: Silver

PHYSICAL: Promotes fertility whether you're trying for a baby for the first time, a subsequent child if nothing is happening, or you're undergoing fertility treatment after years of not conceiving; strengthens the uterus, ovaries, and fallopian tubes; eases the transition to menopause.

EMOTIONAL: Curbs acute anxiety stemming from not conceiving that is blocking conception; allays constant fears of harm occurring to children or obsessive fears of your dying while they are still dependent; mitigates empty nest syndrome.

HOME: For transitions such as relocation, a new partner moving in, marriage and acquiring stepchildren, giving up work.

WORKPLACE: Useful for combining motherhood with a career if there are childcare problems; for mentoring younger colleagues, generating new ideas and carrying them through.

CHILDREN: Moderates mutual dependency between parents and children of any age that makes it hard to let go; enables you to bond with a hard-to-like child.

ANIMALS: For pet mothers who become aggressive if anyone approaches the litter.

PROTECTION: Guards against unjustified fears of abandonment by loved ones.

MAGICKAL AND PSYCHIC USES

Fertility magick; Mother Earth healing rituals; full moon spells; rebirthing; rituals and initiations in caves and enclosed tree groves.

SPECIAL PROPERTIES

For taking up new hobbies and activities involving attending classes, going to a fitness center, or joining clubs to make new friends.

MYTHOLOGY AND HISTORY

Found recently in Morocco, Truffle Chalcedony is a major stress buster and relaxant that enables meditation anywhere without formal techniques; aligns mind, body, and spirit in spontaneous harmony and well-being; can bring money through treasure hidden beneath dust or rust or buried in junk.

Trulite Silica

COLORS: Greens and blues mixed in complex patterns, mirroring swirling subterranean Earth energy streams

CRYSTAL TYPE: A recently discovered, quartz-based gemstone, some say a crystalline form of malachite; has affinities to ajoite, chrysocolla, and gem silica

ZODIAC SIGN: Taurus (April 21–May 21)

CANDLE COLOR: Turquoise

PHYSICAL: Counters allergies caused by modern pollutants, chemicals, and additives; aids in finding cures for modern ills using forgotten plant remedies.

EMOTIONAL: Helps you stop and reflect on words and actions before making judgments.

HOME: Aids in introducing or reintroducing board games and traditional ways of entertainment, plus creating a small wildflower area in gardens and local open spaces.

WORKPLACE: For imposing high standards of ethics in your own working practices, even if your ability to persuade others not to engage in petty pervasive corruption is limited.

CHILDREN: Encourages honesty in words and deeds; teaches children to care for those less fortunate.

ANIMALS: For pets who may never win prizes for appearance.

PROTECTION: Guards against those who trivialize spiritual experiences or feelings in others.

MAGICKAL AND PSYCHIC USES

The study of ancient wisdom, especially traditional healing practices (such as herbalism, traditional Chinese medicine, and Ayurveda) that link physical ills with environmental lifestyle; finding healing teacher guides from past worlds in dreams, regression, automatic writing, psychic artistry, and meditation to transmit to self and others.

SPECIAL PROPERTIES

Appreciating blessings in hard times; shedding an image and expressing the real you without fear of disapproval.

MYTHOLOGY AND HISTORY

Recently discovered in South Africa, a stone believed to be released by Mother Earth to reconnect people with their deep awareness from the universal well of wisdom and with responsibility for the Earth and all her creatures.

Tsavorite or Tsavolite

COLOR: Shimmering pale to emerald-green
CRYSTAL TYPE: Calcium aluminum silicate, Grossular Garnet containing vanadium and chromium (see Grossular Garnet, page 231)
ZODIAC SIGN: Virgo (August 24–September 22)
CANDLE COLOR: Green

PHYSICAL: Strengthens the immune system, heart, pituitary and thyroid glands; alleviates blood sugar disorders, skin irritation, influenza, allergies affecting the lungs, frequent colds, rhinitis, issues affecting the breasts; boosts female libido; acts as an anti-inflammatory.
EMOTIONAL: Keeps you from being manipulated by others using guilt and obligation; helps overcome a tendency to complain but never change your behavior.
HOME: Helps if a neighbor visits too regularly and overstays their welcome.
WORKPLACE: Counters a situation in which colleagues or managers become overly involved in the emotional lives of staff; reduces factions and rivalries at work.
CHILDREN: Diminishes sibling rivalry and accusations of favoritism.
ANIMALS: For pets to coexist peacefully if a new animal is bullied.
PROTECTION: Guards against emotional and psychic vampires.

MAGICKAL AND PSYCHIC USES
Meditation to communicate with our inner divinity; increases psychic awareness and intuition.
SPECIAL PROPERTIES
An anti-envy crystal if others seem more fortunate or possess more, valuing instead your own inner worth and talents.
MYTHOLOGY AND HISTORY
In 1967, Scottish geologist Campbell Bridges discovered the first green Grossular Garnets inside rock nodules in East African bushland along the border between Kenya and Tanzania near Tsavo National Park, after which the gem was named. On his second foray, in 1971, Bridges rediscovered Tsavorite in the Tsavo region of Kenya. In true adventurer style, he lived in a tree house, a python guarding his finds. Non-gem Tsavorite possesses the same properties as the gem.

Tsesit or Tsesite

COLOR: Brownish black
CRYSTAL TYPE: Oxide, Goethite (see page 204); rounded nuggets resembling stony meteorites, iron ore with weathered desert varnish
ZODIAC SIGN: Aries (March 21–April 20)
CANDLE COLOR: Red

PHYSICAL: Alleviates breathing difficulties, irregular sleep patterns, issues involving red blood cells; promotes blood circulation, stamina; eases muscle weakness, chronic exhaustion conditions made worse by aging.
EMOTIONAL: Buries primal fears of lack of food and shelter, represented by the constant need for money or physical over-indulgence; allays fears of being attacked, manifest as aggression, timidity, or elaborate domestic security measures.
HOME: Aids in resisting bullying tactics, law enforcement officers, and loan sharks if your home is under threat because of potential repossession or eviction.
WORKPLACE: Useful for physically demanding work, long hours, security services.
CHILDREN: Motivates teens who stay in their rooms, refusing to socialize face-to-face.
ANIMALS: For small pets who bite without warning.
PROTECTION: Guards against an obsession with extreme bodybuilding.

MAGICKAL AND PSYCHIC USES
Earth-based spirituality, meditation, dowsing, sand divination; promotes visions and dreams of times before the dawn of civilization.
SPECIAL PROPERTIES
Helps overcome challenges and obstacles through persistence; acting rather than waiting for others to make decisions.
MYTHOLOGY AND HISTORY
Tsesit is named after the village of Tses in the Karas region of Namibia, near where the stone is found. The area has been inhabited by Indigenous hunter-gatherer San people for twenty thousand years; the San believe that each stone contains its own soul; each acts as a repository of ancient wisdom.

Tugtupite or Reindeer Stone

COLORS: Usually pink to deep red; fluorescent; increases and even changes color in warmth and sunlight

CRYSTAL TYPE: Sodium aluminum beryllium silicate

ZODIAC SIGN: Leo (July 23–August 23)

CANDLE COLOR: Deep pink

PHYSICAL: Promotes fertility and healthy childbirth, long life; addresses issues stemming from blood pressure, heart, hormones.

EMOTIONAL: Releases the pain of lost or unrequited love, alleviates grief; helps overcome sexual inhibitions.

HOME: Encourages an emotionally repressed partner to show affection.

WORKPLACE: Frees you from the need for the praise and approval of others to measure your success.

CHILDREN: Makes a self-pitying child cheerful and emotionally robust.

ANIMALS: For abused rescue animals or whose owner has died.

PROTECTION: Shields you from emotional manipulation and codependency.

MAGICKAL AND PSYCHIC USES

For love and sex magick; said to turn brighter red the deeper the passion.

SPECIAL PROPERTIES

Stimulates the heart chakra to attract romance and lasting love and a strong sense of self-love so we love from choice not from need.

MYTHOLOGY AND HISTORY

Found near the town of Narsaq in Greenland, its main source; also in St. Hilaire, Canada and the Kola Peninsula in Russia; named after a young woman who lived with the reindeer, who gave birth in the mountains at Tugtup (which means "reindeer"). The life-bringing blood stained the stones pink or red.

Tugtupite with Nuumite

COLORS: Black, pink, and red flares in a pale yellow or cream matrix; mottled; may be predominantly pink with black and also colored flashes

CRYSTAL TYPE: Sodium aluminum beryllium silicate (tugtupite) and metamorphosed igneous rock composed of anthophyllite and gedrite (nuumite)

ZODIAC SIGN: Cancer (June 22–July 22)

CANDLE COLOR: Silver

PHYSICAL: Promotes fertility (especially for single parents), safe childbirth, long life; boosts libido; enhances all-purpose healing.

EMOTIONAL: Allays fears of abandonment and being alone in the world that may cause clinging to an unsatisfactory relationship or situation.

HOME: For moving to an old property with character that can be restored to its former glory; rediscovering family roots.

WORKPLACE: Enables you to obtain a job where there are few openings or difficult criteria to enter; aids in pursuing a career where qualifying takes time and great resources but eventually yields good rewards.

CHILDREN: Useful if you have mothering or fathering issues from childhood that make you doubt your own parenting skills.

ANIMALS: For mothers who reject their litter or show indifference.

PROTECTION: Guards against outside interference, intrusion, and emotional blackmail.

MAGICKAL AND PSYCHIC USES

Breaks curses, hexes, and jinxes from the present or earlier lifetimes and prevents them from returning.

SPECIAL PROPERTIES

Transforms the role of victim to victor at home or at work, with an infusion of self-respect, confidence, and assertiveness. If you cannot obtain this or any other combined crystals, work with the two separate minerals, one in each hand.

MYTHOLOGY AND HISTORY

Tugtupite and Nuumite are stones from the magickal Greenland source of minerals and amplify the power of the land that was once green; the Norse voyager Erik the Red founded the first colony in Greenland during exile in 983; he was the inspiration for his son, who discovered coastal North America five hundred years before Christopher Columbus.

Turquoise

COLOR: Blue-green; sometimes mottled
CRYSTAL TYPE: Hydrated aluminum phosphate with copper and iron traces
ZODIAC SIGN: Sagittarius (November 23–December 21)
CANDLE COLOR: Turquoise

PHYSICAL: Alleviates issues involving headaches, ears, eyes, throat, asthma, hay fever, arthritis, cramps, viruses; a detoxifier.
EMOTIONAL: Keeps you from feeling like a victim of circumstance; helps you recover from emotional burnout; overcomes jet lag and fear of flying.
HOME: Prevents falls and accidents, especially in children or older people; repels intruders.
WORKPLACE: Achieves justice in disputes; promotes leadership; aids in overcoming writers' and creative blocks; for careers in law or government, human rights campaigners, those seeking fame.
CHILDREN: For taking the lead and starring roles; protects youngsters from bullying.
ANIMALS: Prevents pets from straying, being stolen, or being injured.
PROTECTION: Guards against paranormal and human attacks; encourages safe horseback riding.

MAGICKAL AND PSYCHIC USES
Ancient Egyptian magick; ancient wisdom; leading a coven or healing circle; psychic protection, curse breaking, purification rituals; a talisman for good luck, creative success and prosperity.
SPECIAL PROPERTIES
The ultimate travel crystal for long and short trips, adventures and commuting; protects self and luggage, vehicles, and keeps you from air, traffic, and water hazards.
MYTHOLOGY AND HISTORY
Turquoise has been prized for thousands of years among ancient Egyptians, Aztecs, Native North Americans, and in China. The death mask of Tutankhamen was studded with turquoise. Hathor, ancient Egyptian Mother Goddess, was called Lady of Turquoise, and turquoise was sacred to the sun gods. Turquoise adorned the inlaid skulls, shields, and power statues of Moctezuma, the early sixteenth-century Aztec ruler (the last one). Above all, turquoise is a crystal of justice in every area of life.

Turritella Agate

COLOR: Brown or black and brown, with black or white circular patterns
CRYSTAL TYPE: Chalcedony with a thick coating of fossilized seashells, sea creatures, and fossil snail patterns
ZODIAC SIGN: Capricorn (December 22–January 20)
CANDLE COLOR: Brown

PHYSICAL: Addresses exhaustion, rashes, lesions, varicose veins, sexual dysfunction, aging, gastroenteritis, gallstones; strengthens hands, feet; eases abdominal swelling; promotes absorption of zinc, magnesium, and vitamin A.
EMOTIONAL: Counters deep-seated trauma, manifest as physical symptoms and phobias; mitigates unresolved grievances that cloud present harmony.
HOME: A unifying family crystal or, if you're living alone, it creates roots, especially in a new home or temporary accommodations.
WORKPLACE: Keeps you from allowing personal issues to override your professionalism; for hypnotists, psychotherapists, genealogists, anthropologists, archaeologists, and mineralogists.
CHILDREN: For those who constantly play victim.
ANIMALS: Useful for tortoises, lizards, and long-living pets.
PROTECTION: Guards those who travel overseas; prevents you from becoming overwhelmed by seemingly impossible odds.

MAGICKAL AND PSYCHIC USES
A Record Keeper transmitting wisdom from ancient worlds through past lives and dreams; studying or practicing traditional healing; meditation, Earth healing rituals.
SPECIAL PROPERTIES
For fertility if conception is slow, when using IVF, artificial insemination, and/or other fertility treatments; promotes twin births; for those wanting to become parents later in life.
MYTHOLOGY AND HISTORY
Linked with Star Souls, Turritella Agate is associated with the lost city of Atlantis; helps you to learn more about your ancestors and the lands where they originated.

Twin Soul, Twin Flame, or Gemini Quartz

COLORS: Depends on the quartz; mainly in clear quartz

CRYSTAL TYPE: Two very similar quartz crystals, usually growing from the same base, joined at one side, but with separate terminations

ZODIAC SIGN: Gemini (May 22–June 21)

CANDLE COLOR: White

PHYSICAL: Promotes twin and multiple pregnancies and births; addresses concerns with the ears, eyes, ovaries, breasts, and kidneys, even if only one is affected; aids in successful breast reconstruction, regrowth of bones after fractures, cosmetic surgery.

EMOTIONAL: Eases loss of a soul mate through bereavement or divorce; comforts when lovers are parted through circumstances, distance, or existing commitments.

HOME: Useful when a couple maintain separate homes; valuable when two households with children come together.

WORKPLACE: For a couple or close relatives who work together; for workplace relationships if they're discouraged by management; for juggling childcare with a partner.

CHILDREN: Enables twins or siblings very close in age to maintain separate identity; for siblings of twins not to feel excluded.

ANIMALS: For puppies or kittens from the same litter growing up together.

PROTECTION: Guards against those who interfere with happy relationships.

MAGICKAL AND PSYCHIC USES
Fertility rituals for conceiving twins; to attract a soul twin; telepathy with close family members; meeting a dream lover during sleep; tantric sex.

SPECIAL PROPERTIES
Twin crystals are a good luck charm for business partnerships and mergers, commitment and marriages.

MYTHOLOGY AND HISTORY
Named after the heavenly twins of the Zodiac, Castor and Pollux, who were taken into the heavens as the constellation Gemini because they could not bear to be parted in death.

Twisted or Gwindel Quartz

COLORS: Usually clear quartz; also found in smoky and other colored quartzes

CRYSTAL TYPE: Twisted double-terminated quartz, stacked, growing sideways with bent crystal faces; the thicker the crystal the more twisted

ZODIAC SIGN: Scorpio (October 24–November 22)

CANDLE COLOR: White

PHYSICAL: Eases all sprains, torn muscles or tendons, scoliosis, misalignment of skeletal structure, cerebral palsy, mobility in the later years.

EMOTIONAL: Keeps you from overreacting to constructive criticism or advice; curbs a tendency to deliberately misconstrue or twist the words of others.

HOME: Aids in creating a unique home to reflect your personality if your community is ultra-conventional; for high-rise apartment living.

WORKPLACE: For seeing unusual new angles or perspectives to resolve existing problems; for adapting to sudden or unexpected changes; for those who work in ski resorts.

CHILDREN: Encourages children to try new activities outside their comfort zone.

ANIMALS: For pets reluctant to change their routine or normal routes on walks.

PROTECTION: Guards against those who try to enforce conformity at odds with your beliefs; against fears of flying or long-distance traveling.

MAGICKAL AND PSYCHIC USES
Communication with mountain and hill spirits; for clairvoyance and remote viewing over long distances; developing personal methods of spirituality or healing, or starting your own psychic school.

SPECIAL PROPERTIES
A stone of loving yourself as you are and not seeking the approval or permission of others to live your own way; for solo vacations away from crowds.

MYTHOLOGY AND HISTORY
Extremely rare, found at high altitudes, for example in Switzerland or Austria, the term *Gwindel* comes from the German word *gewunden*, which means "twisted"; for uncovering hidden wonders in nature.

Ulexite

COLOR: White or colorless

CRYSTAL TYPE: Hydrous sodium calcium borate

ZODIAC SIGN: Gemini (May 22–June 21)

CANDLE COLOR: White

PHYSICAL: Alleviates issues with the eyes, nerve endings, headaches, memory illnesses hard to detect or diagnose.

EMOTIONAL: Restores creativity if suppressed by insensitive adults during childhood; aids in recovering from brainwashing by cults or overly rigid political or religious organizations; calms you after exposure to black magick and demonology.

HOME: Useful if your partner is leading a double life.

WORKPLACE: Set a Ulexite crystal on top of contracts and official documents to avoid missing vital information; helps in learning technology, complex skills, and languages.

CHILDREN: Aids those in long-term foster care to settle with a new family but maintain their roots.

ANIMALS: For pets with visual impairment.

PROTECTION: Guards against hidden enemies and false friends.

MAGICKAL AND PSYCHIC USES

Clairvoyance, telepathy, premonitions, visualization, rituals to attract or increase abundance; palmistry, numerology, graphology; dream interpretation; dowsing.

SPECIAL PROPERTIES

The crystal of truth and clarity, for uncovering family secrets and lies; finding birth parents if adopted; locating missing persons and pets; discovering solutions where facts are hazy and people uncooperative.

MYTHOLOGY AND HISTORY

Ulexite is known as TV rock or television stone. This is because when Ulexite is about one inch thick and polished on both sides, the fibers act like optical fibers, transmitting an image from one side of the crystal to the other. If placed on top of a book or newspaper, writing appears on top of the crystal without any distortion.

Unakite

COLOR: Moss or olive green, blended with salmon pink or red

CRYSTAL TYPE: An amalgamation of epidote and feldspar

ZODIAC SIGN: Scorpio (October 24–November 22)

CANDLE COLOR: Green

PHYSICAL: Promotes conception, fetal health, healthy childbirth; restores ovulation cycles after prolonged artificial contraception; regulates bodily fluids; useful for healthy weight gain (especially among those with anorexia).

EMOTIONAL: Counters obsessions and compulsions based in childhood trauma; curbs emotionally triggered physical illness; mitigates cigarette cravings.

HOME: Aids in avoiding panic when overwhelmed with chores or conflicting family demands; for beautiful gardens.

WORKPLACE: For couples with a joint business; for calculated risks and wise investments; for all artisans.

CHILDREN: Encourages children to talk about problems; for parents to communicate with a child in utero.

ANIMALS: Promotes successful breeding programs.

PROTECTION: Shields you in uncertain times or when undertaking risky activities or occupations.

MAGICKAL AND PSYCHIC USES

For rebirthing, uncovering prebirth memories and past-life healing; wish spells; dowsing for missing items.

SPECIAL PROPERTIES

Unakite, associated with the union of Mars and Venus, is a token of fidelity between married couples or long-term partners; keep one in a bag with yarrow, the herb of marriage, over the bed for seven years, then replace it.

MYTHOLOGY AND HISTORY

First discovered in the Unaka Mountains in the Southeast United States in 1874, Unakite was carried in glacial drifts of the Ice Age, so it contains a storehouse of potential; now is the time to speak out, seize opportunity, and act without hesitation.

Ussingite

COLORS: Pink, pinkish-beige, deep red, purples, lilac, and violet; mottled

CRYSTAL TYPE: Sodium silicate that forms in igneous rock; sometimes associated or growing with sodalite

ZODIAC SIGN: Pisces (February 19–March 20)

CANDLE COLOR: Pink or purple

PHYSICAL: Addresses issues stemming from the liver, blood purification, anemia, excess white-cell production, hypertension.

EMOTIONAL: For overdependency and codependency; curbs an addiction to gambling.

HOME: In pinks and pinkish-beige to end every day peacefully, with any disagreements mended or set aside.

WORKPLACE: For careers involving the arts, science, and mathematics; keeps you from setting too high a standard for yourself and constantly rechecking your work.

CHILDREN: In the gentler shades, helps children to avoid continuing playground feuds; to forgive after quarrels.

ANIMALS: For gentle pets to not be bullied by other animals.

PROTECTION: Guards against angry people, volatile situations, and personal anger that holds back relationships (as deep red).

MAGICKAL AND PSYCHIC USES

For connecting with angels, spirit guides, and the violet healing flame associated with the archangel Zadkiel and the ascended master St. Germain, as violet or deep purple; for cutting old ties (red).

SPECIAL PROPERTIES

The higher-spectrum colors violet and deeper purple open connection with spiritual realms; the softer pinks focus on more earthly matters and red deals with powerful emotions.

MYTHOLOGY AND HISTORY

Ussingite was first discovered in 1915 in southwestern Greenland, considered to be Mother Earth's reminder that, despite the horrors of war, peace would one day return; found mainly in Greenland, but also in Russia and Canada.

Uvarovite Garnet

COLOR: Emerald green

CRYSTAL TYPE: Calcium chromium silicate; tiny sparkling crystals, often coating a natural surface

ZODIAC SIGN: Taurus (April 21–May 21).

CANDLE COLOR: Bright green

PHYSICAL: An antiinflammatory; alleviates issues stemming from emphysema, asbestosis, cystic fibrosis, heart problems, plant allergies, bladder weakness, sexual dysfunction and libido in both sexes, fertility in older women, repetitive strain injury; counters a gradual buildup of mercury or lead poisoning; addresses slow-growing conditions in older people.

EMOTIONAL: Helps you overcome a sense of inadequacy if you're scapegoated by your family; eases a crisis of confidence, loneliness, grief after bereavement among older women; allays fears of poverty.

HOME: Protective for rural homes; aids in moving from city to countryside.

WORKPLACE: Lessens office politicking; enhances good luck and prosperity through individual enterprise; helps with being in the right place at the right time.

CHILDREN: A fairy wish crystal; for children who feel ignored.

ANIMALS: For tracking down a rare breed or unusual pet.

PROTECTION: Guards against emotional or psychic vampires and those who flaunt wealth.

MAGICKAL AND PSYCHIC USES

Rituals for soul twins and secret love; manifesting wealth; telepathic communication between family, friends, and pets; becoming an animal whisperer or healer; increases effectiveness of herbal remedies.

SPECIAL PROPERTIES

Attracting and keeping prosperity and spiritual wealth in the form of blessings; for renewing wedding vows.

MYTHOLOGY AND HISTORY

Uvarovite was used by the Russian Carl Fabergé to decorate his jeweled eggs; most common of the green garnets (see also green Andradite Garnet, page 29; Demantoid Garnet, page 158; and Tsavorite or Tsavolite, page 485); even the smallest piece of Uvarovite releases healing and magickal properties.

Uvite

COLORS: Dark green to almost black, the two most usual colors; also yellow-brown, light to dark brown, reddish and red; may be colorless; in its brown forms, Uvite may be mistaken for its sister Dravite or Brown Tourmaline (page 166), but mineralogically it is different
CRYSTAL TYPE: Magnesium and iron-rich member of the tourmaline family
ZODIAC SIGN: Virgo (August 24–September 22)
CANDLE COLOR: Dark green

PHYSICAL: Strengthens the immune system; addresses digestive disorders, post-colostomy or -ileostomy care, stomach stapling.
EMOTIONAL: Keeps you from feeling inferior if you have been undermined or scapegoated by your family for years.
HOME: Aids in fitting in to a tightly knit neighborhood or community; for marrying into a new culture.
WORKPLACE: A crystal of ambition and high achievement.
CHILDREN: Helps youngsters become part of a team or other group activities, such as a dance troupe, choir, or theater group.
ANIMALS: Useful when taking pets as visitors into long-term-care facilities and organizing horseback-riding sessions for challenged children.
PROTECTION: Guards against avoiding new activities because of fear of failure.

MAGICKAL AND PSYCHIC USES
As a fertility charm, empowered on the full moon to move into harmony and flow with the natural cycles; rituals for healing the Earth.
SPECIAL PROPERTIES
The ultimate environmental and environmentalists' crystal; assists any form of practical green activity, including making a climate-friendly home using wind and solar power; recycling waste.
MYTHOLOGY AND HISTORY
Uvite is named after the Uva district in Sri Lanka where it was first discovered in 1929. The difference between the other tourmalines, such as Dravite or Brown Tourmaline (page 166), Black Tourmaline or Schorl (page 67), or Multicolored Tourmaline or (page 312), and Uvite is that one of the aluminum elements has been replaced by magnesium. It has stubby crystals, rather than the typical longer prismatic tourmalines. Uvite offers grounding energies to make you feel secure within yourself.

Variscite

COLORS: Light, apple or bright green, bluish-green or turquoise, often with patterned brown veins
CRYSTAL TYPE: Hydrated aluminum phosphate
ZODIAC SIGN: Taurus (April 21–May 21)
CANDLE COLOR: Green

PHYSICAL: Addresses arteries, veins, ulcers, gout, nerve networks, energy pathways, the male reproductive system; a crystalline form of Viagra; alleviates ongoing illnesses if you're despairing of getting any relief.
EMOTIONAL: Eases stress and depression; increases awareness of the cause of problems, whether from present or past lives; reduces the effects of unfair criticism.
HOME: As carved ornaments, Variscite acts as a background filter against lingering work worries or external problems; attracts abundance.
WORKPLACE: For those caring for the elderly, chronically sick, or disabled; promotes business networking; stabilizes uncertain situations; for redeployment or relocation.
CHILDREN: Attracts friends to lonely children or those who are different.
ANIMALS: For pets who overreact to people and animals out of their natural habitat.
PROTECTION: Guards against fears of unfamiliar situations, places, or meeting new people.

MAGICKAL AND PSYCHIC USES
For healing circles and group meditation; connecting with guardians and energies of sacred Earth sites, ley lines, megaliths, and labyrinths; dowsing, vision quests, and pilgrimages.
SPECIAL PROPERTIES
Variscite absorbs free-floating anxiety, inspiring practical solutions to realistic fears and worries; increases social confidence.
MYTHOLOGY AND HISTORY
Variscite is named after the Latin for Vogtland in Saxony, where its color matched the costumes of dancers at the spring festivals. Traditionally used in sacred Earth ceremonies by Native Americans and Australian Aboriginals, Variscite grounds those who live in their heads.

Vatican Stone or Frosterley Marble

COLORS: Black with gray/white inclusions

CRYSTAL TYPE: Limestone containing fossilized remains of stag's horn coral

ZODIAC SIGN: Aquarius (January 21–February 18)

CANDLE COLOR: White

PHYSICAL: Addresses issues associated with aging, hearing, carpal tunnel syndrome, muscular problems, fertility.

EMOTIONAL: During change restores equilibrium when it is necessary to leave our comfort zone; alleviates sexual problems rooted in emotional issues.

HOME: Transforms a home into a sanctuary from the 24/7-frantic world.

WORKPLACE: Anticipates future problems; brings difficult people together as a team.

CHILDREN: Helps children do their best if they give up at the first obstacle.

ANIMALS: Creates a telepathic link with your pet; links you to your totem animals.

PROTECTION: Guards against despair, revealing light at the end of the tunnel.

MAGICKAL AND PSYCHIC USES

Opens doors to half-forgotten psychic abilities; enhances prayer, telepathic powers, and foreknowledge.

SPECIAL PROPERTIES

The stone of discrimination, knowing what is right, thinking and acting peacefully but independent of popular opinion.

MYTHOLOGY AND HISTORY

Vatican Stone is 325 million years old, found only in Frosterley, County Durham, in England. In medieval times, a feature of churches and cathedrals, notably the Chapel of Nine Altars in Durham Cathedral and in the Vatican.

Vera Cruz Amethyst

COLORS: Pale mauve, pale lavender, pale purple, pale violet, rarely deep violet, with color deepest around the tip of the terminations

CRYSTAL TYPE: Amethyst found only in Vera Cruz, Mexico; small, usually with double-terminated points, a single point at each end, through which energy flows both ways; alternatively, forms phantoms, single points, and clusters

ZODIAC SIGN: Pisces (February 19–March 20)

CANDLE COLOR: Lilac

PHYSICAL: Promotes healing on the deepest level; alleviates issues stemming from the pineal gland, pituitary gland, left and right hemispheres of the brain, autoimmune conditions, genetic diseases, persistent exhaustion, laser treatments.

EMOTIONAL: Curbs addictions, especially to alcohol; helps overcome self-sabotage; aids in mustering the courage to leave an abusive situation.

HOME: Useful if you move into a home where there has been sorrow, sickness, violence, or tragedy.

WORKPLACE: Supports all following a spiritual or religious path to guide others.

CHILDREN: Comforts extremely sick children or those with progressive conditions.

ANIMALS: For helper animals, acting as hands, eyes, and ears for owners; for large creatures gentle with children.

PROTECTION: Absorbs and transforms negativity and destructiveness into love and creativity.

MAGICKAL AND PSYCHIC USES

For healing, especially Reiki, continually replenishing the healer; in the center of crystal grids; as a wand with a single or double termination; deep meditation.

SPECIAL PROPERTIES

Of higher vibration than ordinary purple amethyst, Vera Cruz Amethyst invokes angels and guides and calls from within our personal divinity and higher self.

MYTHOLOGY AND HISTORY

The compassionate crystal, continuously in its double-terminated form, transforms harshness into gentleness and careless words and thoughtless actions into wise, restrained responses, even when you're provoked.

Verdite or Buddstone

COLORS: Deep rich green to lighter green
CRYSTAL TYPE: Silicate; fuchsite mica, often found close to deposits of gold
ZODIAC SIGN: Virgo (August 24–September 22)
CANDLE COLOR: Deep green

PHYSICAL: Enhances potency and fertility; relieves genitourinary problems and sexual dysfunction; addresses issues relating to the prostate, hernia, dizziness, vertigo, heart, genetic conditions, sunstroke and sunburn; cleanses blood.
EMOTIONAL: Alleviates the effects of hereditary illnesses on sufferers and caregivers; for people who worry all the time.
HOME: Keep Verdite statues around the home for a sense of tradition and roots, even in a new house or apartment.
WORKPLACE: Counteracts rumors, misinformation; helps you discover whom you can trust; enables you to choose the right business deals.
CHILDREN: Encourages children in multicultural homes or adopted from another culture to connect with their roots.
ANIMALS: For breeding healthy, trustworthy, pedigreed animals.
PROTECTION: Teaches an impatient, irritable partner tolerance; guards against negative Earth energies beneath the home or workplace.

MAGICKAL AND PSYCHIC USES
For ghost hunting; connecting with family spirits and totem animals; past-life recall.
SPECIAL PROPERTIES
The bargain hunter's stone, for sales, auctions, markets, and successful bidding online.
MYTHOLOGY AND HISTORY
Verdite, which comes from South Africa and Zimbabwe, is the oldest form of exposed rock, from 3.5 million years ago. From time immemorial, local craftspeople created Verdite animals, ancestral statues, and fertility and abundance charms.

Vesuvianite, Cyprine, or Idocrase

COLORS: Pale to olive green, yellowish-green as Vesuvianite; yellow, brown, red, blue, and purple as Idocrase; blue as Cyprine and apple or lime green gem-quality as Californite (found in California)
CRYSTAL TYPE: Calcium magnesium aluminum silicate; good to handle as tumbled stones
ZODIAC SIGN: Sagittarius (November 23–December 21)
CANDLE COLOR: Red

PHYSICAL: Alleviates diverticulitis, gingivitis, skin rashes, allergies; eases loss of sense of smell and taste; promotes digestion.
EMOTIONAL: Calms free-floating anger and irritability, fears, depression, unwarranted guilt; curbs overeating, feast-and-famine eating with emotional roots.
HOME: Promotes loyalty to family, partner, and friends in good times and bad; keeps links with home if you're living or working overseas.
WORKPLACE: Enables you to risk your job security by following or changing to the career where your true passion lies.
CHILDREN: Keeps youngsters from envying others their gifts, popularity, or prowess, but valuing and developing their own personal talents.
ANIMALS: Protects pets who are frequently threatened or attacked by other animals.
PROTECTION: Guards against being threatened or intimidated.

MAGICKAL AND PSYCHIC USES
Fire magick; mountain magick; cleanses and energizes the aura, enables you to see auras more clearly; keeps contact with your spiritual nature when earthly matters demand attention.
SPECIAL PROPERTIES
For family members in the armed forces, especially in combat; to set a love relationship going wrong back on track.
MYTHOLOGY AND HISTORY
The name *Vesuvianite* was given to the mineral because it was originally found on Mount Vesuvius in Italy in 1795 by German mineralogist Abraham Werner. Renowned for its qualities in releasing anger and dispelling negativity, Vesuvianite releases a sense of being stifled, whether in work or relationships; Vesuvianite also removes creative blocks, allowing inspiration to find fresh outward expression.

Victorite

COLORS: Red or purple mixed with black and white, speckled when in a matrix

CRYSTAL TYPE: Spinel (red or purple) a magnesium aluminum oxide, mixed with biotite (black), mica and snow quartz (white), silicon dioxide

ZODIAC SIGN: Aries (March 21–April 20)

CANDLE COLOR: Red

PHYSICAL: Helps overcome chronic exhaustion, oversensitivity to chemicals, additives, and excess electromagnetic energies; alleviates allergies and breathing difficulties; promotes recovery from acute illnesses, especially long-term viral effects; eases speech difficulties.

EMOTIONAL: Curbs a tendency toward defeatism leading to an unwillingness to try to improve your circumstances; keeps you from blaming others for your misfortune.

HOME: For starting over alone or as a single parent and creating the life you want, despite any pressures.

WORKPLACE: Rebuilds a business in a more viable way after a major setback; creates a new image and makeover in a new job.

CHILDREN: Gives a child with emotional or physical difficulties the courage to overcome hurdles; for confidence when starting a new school or relocating.

ANIMALS: For winning prizes for breeding or competing with animals.

PROTECTION: Guards against giving up when, with one more push, you can achieve your goals.

MAGICKAL AND PSYCHIC USES

A breakthrough if you have been lacking inspiration; learning spirit rescue to move restless spirits to the light; unblocking Earth energies beneath the home that cause inertia and poor plant growth, preventing the flow of good fortune and health.

SPECIAL PROPERTIES

For finding your soul's purpose and life path; a revitalization of purpose if life is stagnant; overcoming opposition in love.

MYTHOLOGY AND HISTORY

A remarkable stone found in South India that combines the powers of three very powerful stones—red spinel for winning through under difficulty; biotite, the birthing stone, for determination to create that new beginning; and snow quartz for a fresh approach and revived enthusiasm.

Viking Balls

COLOR: Gray

CRYSTAL TYPE: Algae and fossil remains, formed more than 65 million years ago in the Cretaceous Age; rough surface and spherical

ZODIAC SIGN: Aries (March 21–April 20)

CANDLE COLOR: Red

PHYSICAL: Strengthens red blood cells; controls hemorrhages; boosts slow blood clotting; addresses fractures, sprains (especially of feet, ankles, and legs); dissolves excessive calcification.

EMOTIONAL: Keeps you from living an image and never revealing true self; curbs extreme loneliness; allays fears of confrontation and controversy.

HOME: Creates a psychic exclusion zone to deter complaining neighbors and those who threaten children and pets.

WORKPLACE: Valuable where there is a combative, overly competitive atmosphere and covert intimidation; for standing up to bullies, especially those in authority.

CHILDREN: Encourages fantasy play; gives courage to ignore teasing; deters play-ground bullies.

ANIMALS: For taking pets out in all weathers if they are reluctant.

PROTECTION: against physical harm, attack and dangers, especially when traveling.

MAGICKAL AND PSYCHIC USES

Viking Balls align with the magnetic energies of the Earth, wherever they are, and therefore bring the whole self into alignment; for reading runes, Ásatrú (Norse) magick.

SPECIAL PROPERTIES

Increases physical fitness and prowess; for winning at athletics, marathon running, aerobics, and bodybuilding.

MYTHOLOGY AND HISTORY

Found in the Mons Klint chalk cliffs along the Baltic coast of Denmark, Viking Balls were created fifteen thousand years ago, after the last Ice Age. Until 1960, Viking Balls were mined to crush gold; since then, the cliffs have been designated part of a national park and the balls are found washed ashore during storms. Viking Balls contain memoires of the long bloody campaigns between the Vikings from Sweden and Norway who fought to rule Denmark and often succeeded. Viking Balls are considered to offer great courage and persistence no matter how great the odds.

Violan

COLORS: Light blue, streaked with white and silver rutiles; also lavender to pink, red, purple, and violet

CRYSTAL TYPE: Silicate, rare form of diopside, colored by manganese

ZODIAC SIGN: Libra (September 23–October 23)

CANDLE COLOR: Light blue

PHYSICAL: A whole-body healer; addresses issues involving the throat, choking, reflux, genitals and the reproductive system, genetic disorders, blushing; helps overcome excessive consumption of tobacco, alcohol, junk food, and exposure to harmful rays or chemicals.

EMOTIONAL: Releases stifled emotions connected with buried tragedy, humiliation, loss, or abuse; enables you to break the hold of taboos imposed by repressive regimes, families, or communities.

HOME: Offers sanctuary from the world if the family has busy or scattered lives; heads off potential confrontations.

WORKPLACE: Counteracts an overemphasis on profit and ruthless competition; for charity workers fighting famine, poverty, abuse, or child labor.

CHILDREN: A bedtime anti-worry stone to ease problems of the day; prevents sibling quarrels and rivalries.

ANIMALS: For dolphins, whales, and captive performing sea creatures; for pets stressed by children's teasing.

PROTECTION: Shields against overreliance on computers, tablets, smartphones, and online games.

MAGICKAL AND PSYCHIC USES

Channeling angels, Star Beings and dolphin energies; enhances angel healing and angel Reiki; awakens psychic awareness.

SPECIAL PROPERTIES

Slows effects of the 24/7 rush of life and inability to switch off; an anti-shopaholic stone; deters partners from thoughts of straying.

MYTHOLOGY AND HISTORY

Discovered in the 1830s in Italy, Violan is believed to have been brought by travelers from Sirius B, resonating with dolphin song and radiating Sirian healing; valuable to incarnated Star Souls and those with Down syndrome.

Violet Flame Opal

COLORS: White and purple, from pale lilac through medium purple to deep, rich violet purple; the purple is caused by small inclusions of fluorite and silica

CRYSTAL TYPE: Non-precious opal without iridescent fire, but with beautiful swirling patterns; occasionally made into tumbled stones as well as jewelry

ZODIAC SIGN: Pisces (February 19–March 20)

CANDLE COLOR: Purple

PHYSICAL: Alleviates migraines and other headaches, visual disturbances, sinus issues, autoimmune diseases, plus Alzheimer's, dementia, and gradual reduction of brain cells and functions.

EMOTIONAL: Eases free-floating anger that can flare any time; allays fears of evil spirits and spirit possession; keeps you from feeling jealousy of those who seem to have it all.

HOME: Takes away the stresses of the day and replaces them with harmony; removes old rivalries and accusations of favoritism toward certain family members.

WORKPLACE: For artistic or creative ventures involving color and color coordination; for beginning a spiritual or therapeutic business or sanctuary on a budget.

CHILDREN: Enables Indigo Children to move into harmony with a world they do not always understand without losing their purity of spirit.

ANIMALS: For pets who have been with us in many lifetimes as spirit guardians.

PROTECTION: Guards against malicious spirits and spirit attack if you are a medium or healer and work in spirit rescue.

MAGICKAL AND PSYCHIC USES

Messages from spirit guides and guardian angels through dreams, deep meditation, and waking visions.

SPECIAL PROPERTIES

Linked with the violet flame of transformation, freedom from fear, divine blessings, and access to higher self and soul energies.

MYTHOLOGY AND HISTORY

Discovered in Central Mexico in 2011 and also called violet or Morado opal, the Spanish word for purple. A stone of spiritual transformation into positive emotions of all that is destructive or self-destructive; releases generosity of spirit, and the potential to show altruism towards strangers as well as kin.

Violet Hypersthene

COLORS: A very dark purple

CRYSTAL TYPE: Pyrozene family, magnesium iron silicate; best as tumbled stones and jewelry

ZODIAC SIGN: Pisces (February 19-March 20)

CANDLE COLOR: Purple

PHYSICAL: migraines, headaches, growth or regrowth of neural pathways after a brain injury or illness; confusion; inherited conditions.

EMOTIONAL: repressed anger and resentment projected as toxic words attached to unrelated causes.

HOME: Brings calm discussion and defusing simmering injustices or concealed feelings of favoritism or being scapegoated; for physically as well as emotionally cleansing the home of bad atmospheres.

WORKPLACE: Promotes a peaceful workplace; taken to staff meetings, negotiations, and disputes to allow the real issues to be expressed and resolved calmly without personal vendettas or rivalries emerging.

CHILDREN: Keep Violet Hypersthene in a treasure box with photos and mementoes of spiritual events in the child's life, including christening, naming, welcoming into a religion, dedication ceremonies, marriage or handfasting, the birth of their first child, to be given at a signature milestone.

ANIMALS: To be buried with the remains of a very special pet who has shared family life for many years.

PROTECTION: Surrounds you with a shield of violet light.

MAGICKAL AND PSYCHIC USES

Strongly linked with the purple healing and inspirational violet flame of the ascended master St. Germain and often used to make healing and empowering wands; brings inner silence for meditation in less-than-ideal circumstances.

SPECIAL PROPERTIES

Removes deep-seated fears pushed deep out of consciousness from earlier in life or in past lives; deepens any religious or spiritual study or participation; for pilgrimages and retreats.

MYTHOLOGY AND HISTORY

Sometimes called velvet labradorite, because of its velvety feel, especially where the iridescence is strongly purple in labradite. Many crystal experts insist they are two different stones, though both have the same calming spiritual energies and both are found in Labrador, Canada.

Vitalite

COLORS: White, red, black and silver/glittery

CRYSTAL TYPE: Layers of quartz (white), piedmontite (red), biotite (black), often covered with small muscovite crystals (silver)

ZODIAC SIGN: Aquarius (January 21-February 18)

CANDLE COLOR: White

PHYSICAL: Alleviates issues stemming from the heart, circulation of blood, anemia, veins and arteries, bypass surgery, breathing difficulties worsened by stress, gallstones, pancreas, and spleen.

EMOTIONAL: Eases chronic irritability without cause, bipolar conditions, overreliance on relatives or therapists for sympathy.

HOME: Fills the home with the prana life force to sweep away inertia, sickness, and misfortune.

WORKPLACE: Awakens an underproductive workforce; for starting a one-person business where there is a gap in market.

CHILDREN: For teens who spend a lot of their time asleep in their bedrooms or on smartphones, doing online gaming.

ANIMALS: Restores energy to a pet who has been injured or suffered a debilitating illness.

PROTECTION: Guards against those who take unfair advantage of your willingness to help.

MAGICKAL AND PSYCHIC USES

Enhances all forms of energy and touch therapies; promotes crystal healing through light, angels, and spirit guides; cleanses the body, mind, aura, and spirit of stagnation and unhelpful repetitive patterns.

SPECIAL PROPERTIES

A stone of generosity of time and resources where these are needed and deserved; aids in expressing feelings of love, sorrow, regret, or reconciliation.

MYTHOLOGY AND HISTORY

From New Zealand, source of many light-bringing and spiritual vibration–raising crystals because the land's pure energies were for so many millennia undisturbed by human footprints, Vitalite was named for its ability to foster lightheartedness, enthusiasm, and well-being.

Vivianite

COLORS: Shades of blue, green, blue-green, and colorless; darkens on exposure to light to deep blue, purple or more usually black; may crack
CRYSTAL TYPE: Hydrated iron phosphate
ZODIAC SIGN: Capricorn (December 22–January 20)
CANDLE COLOR: Blue or green

PHYSICAL: Addresses issues involving the teeth, bones, fractures slow to heal, eye conditions (especially relating to the iris and cataracts); relieves pain.
EMOTIONAL: Counters a lack of ease in the body; allays fears of aging and mental as well as physical deterioration.
HOME: Useful for caregivers of sick or disabled children or adults and elderly relatives, so they receive the necessary support from official agencies; retaining an independent home if younger relatives are pressuring you to sell.
WORKPLACE: Implements gradual, necessary modernization and upgrading of out-of-date practices in a business you are taking over; counters ageism against women.
CHILDREN: Introducing children of all ages to museums, ancient sites, and family and local history.
ANIMALS: Helps when inheriting an aging pet from a deceased relative.
PROTECTION: Shields you if you cannot immediately walk away from a destructive home or workplace situation.

MAGICKAL AND PSYCHIC USES
Connects with visions of ancient worlds through visualization and meditation; dreams and flashes of insight into personal past lives in prehistory; ceremonies to heal the Earth.
SPECIAL PROPERTIES
For solo journeys in the later years, relocating to a new state or overseas or starting a new career after retirement.
MYTHOLOGY AND HISTORY
Originally Vivianite was thought to be identical with odontolite (page 322), the fossilized blue-stained teeth of mastodons, and that it developed from changes within the bone itself during fossilization. Certainly, Vivianite is often found in or attached to fossil bones and fossilized clam or snail shells, but it is a distinct mineral. Vivianite should not be exposed to light, especially sunlight, which will dramatically darken it.

Voegesite or Vogesite

COLORS: Golden yellow, peach, orange, olive, maroon, brown, black, and ivory; mottled, with bands, stripes, swirls, or spots of different color
CRYSTAL TYPE: Jasper
ZODIAC SIGN: Leo (July 23–August 23)
CANDLE COLOR: Gold

PHYSICAL: Addresses illnesses and disabilities not externally visible; alleviates issues involving the reproductive organs, conception, pregnancy, and childbirth (especially if previous pregnancies or births have proven problematic), psychosomatic conditions; mitigates kidney problems.
EMOTIONAL: Curbs an unwillingness to give up the comfort of bad habits, especially cigarette smoking; keeps you from blaming others for your present failures and fears, even if the trauma occurred many years earlier; for unresolved sexual abuse in childhood.
HOME: Useful for spontaneous parties, outings, and last-minute days away or vacations.
WORKPLACE: Valuable if colleagues or managers are hard to get along with; transforms outdated working practices.
CHILDREN: For happiness and spontaneous play if there has been sorrow; avoiding growing up too quickly; happy dreams.
ANIMALS: For contented pets no longer physically active.
PROTECTION: Shields against resisting necessary change because others will disapprove.

MAGICKAL AND PSYCHIC USES
Past-life healing of issues that may have continued over many lifetimes; rebirthing; color magick; meditation following pathways within the stone.
SPECIAL PROPERTIES

Promotes awareness of the interconnection of past, present, and future; keeps what is of value and sheds what rightly belongs in the past.
MYTHOLOGY AND HISTORY
Found in South Africa, a stone of joy and sunshine any time of the year; rediscovering and expressing the true essential self, sometimes called the inner child that brings spontaneity and opens doorways to what was dismissed as impractical or unrealistic, but which is the way to freedom.

Vogel Wands and Vogel Crystals

COLORS: Usually clear with an inner luminescence, visible to the clairvoyant eye; may be made of other transparent quartzes

CRYSTAL TYPE: Double-terminated quartz, either existing naturally or carved to form the terminations

ZODIAC SIGN: Leo (July 23–August 23)

CANDLE COLOR: Gold

PHYSICAL: Draws on the universal life force for healing self and others; assisted by the spirit beings and healer angels who amplify the power of the crystal, raising the vibrations of the healer and the person being healed.

EMOTIONAL: Realigns those whose body, mind, and spirit are out of synchronicity.

HOME: Use the Vogel Wand to cleanse the home by spiraling it around every room if there have been quarrels or misfortune.

WORKPLACE: A four-faceted, pocket-sized Vogel Crystal spreads light and energy around your workspace.

CHILDREN: Pass the wand around the children's bedrooms regularly in their absence to fill them with light and healing.

ANIMALS: Spiral a Vogel Wand around pets' beds, stables, and aviaries if there is an epidemic affecting the species.

PROTECTION: Guards against those who drain your energy.

MAGICKAL AND PSYCHIC USES

Vogels Wands, being precisely aligned with the great Pyramid of Giza with its psychic and healing powers, grant in meditation visions of the ancient Egyptian world, enhancing clairvoyance.

SPECIAL PROPERTIES

Vogels are created from quartz by craftspeople who aim to make them receptacles, amplifiers, and transmitters of universal energy that pours from the proactive termination; the receptive end of the crystal is faceted to form an internal angle of fifty-one degrees to correspond with the angles of the sides of the Giza Great Pyramid; true Vogels each possess at least four and up to twenty or more facets on their sides.

MYTHOLOGY AND HISTORY

Vogel Wands and points were created by the researcher Marcel Vogel to absorb, enhance, and transmit the life force for healing.

Vortexite

COLORS: Black-gray orbs on deep red background

CRYSTAL TYPE: Combines spherulitic rhyolite (black-gray) and quartz (red)

ZODIAC SIGN: Aquarius (January 21–February 18)

CANDLE COLOR: White

PHYSICAL: Brings body, mind, and spirit into alignment; promotes cell regrowth and regeneration.

EMOTIONAL: Keeps you from being out of touch with yourself; curbs disconnection with life and people except on a superficial level.

HOME: Useful when a home is built on a place of human suffering, such as a converted prison or an orphanage where children were badly treated.

WORKPLACE: Counters frequent industrial or interoffice disputes, disciplinary hearings, or the company is part of a large, impersonal, profit-driven organization.

CHILDREN: Comforts those who believe they come from another place.

ANIMALS: For cryptozoological creatures, such as Bigfoot, sighted in remote forests in all fifty US states and may wander between worlds.

PROTECTION: Guards against reputedly harmful energies, such as cell phone towers or power lines.

MAGICKAL AND PSYCHIC USES

Especially powerful if carried while journeying to one of the major Earth vortices or a sacred place with strong vibrational energies.

SPECIAL PROPERTIES

For connecting the inner Earth vortex of energy we all possess with the universal sources of vortex energies, such as Mother Earth.

MYTHOLOGY AND HISTORY

Discovered in 2014, Vortexite was created during volcanic activity on New Zealand's North Island millions of years earlier. Vortexite links you with Earth vortices, such as Sedona in Arizona, the pyramids at Giza in Cairo, Stonehenge in the UK, Uluru in Australia's Northern Territory, and Coromandel Peninsula, New Zealand, location of the Vortexite stone.

Waterfall Quartz

COLORS: Clear, smoky gray, pink, or a combination of colors

CRYSTAL TYPE: Crystal quartz (clear), smoky quartz, rose quartz, cascading with crystals all over the surface; dome-shaped, resembling a waterfall tumbling down over rocks

ZODIAC SIGN: Pisces (February 19–March 20).

CANDLE COLOR: Silver

PHYSICAL: Useful for water therapies; curbs dehydration; regulates hormonal and blood sugar fluctuations; counters obstructions in veins and arteries, especially in the lower limbs.

EMOTIONAL: Releases blocked emotions; keeps you from using sentiment to manipulate others; helps overcome erratic behavior, the effects of institutionalization.

HOME: Valuable as the center of a small indoor water feature; Waterfall Quartz comes in all sizes, from ornamental to pocket-size, but all contain the same flowing, refreshing chi energies.

WORKPLACE: Ensures the continual increasing inflow of new and existing customers; for taking an expansion or financial risk that, if successful, will be advantageous.

CHILDREN: Encourages musical and artistic children to develop their talents and gain pleasure from their creativity.

ANIMALS: Works well for animals being safely released into the wild or into wide-ranging conservation areas.

PROTECTION: Shields against self-imposed restrictions to reveal your talents or expertise; guards against those who block your progress.

MAGICKAL AND PSYCHIC USES

For communication with waterfall and flowing water spirits; clairaudience to hear their voices singing in the water.

SPECIAL PROPERTIES

For washing away dependency and the need for approval; travel to experience local customs and discover the true heart of the host country, not just tourist spots.

MYTHOLOGY AND HISTORY

Waterfall Quartz was once used for magickal and religious rites in Peru, associated with the Incas. El Vero de la Nova waterfall, which means the "veil of the bride," in the Cajamarca Region of Peru, is known for sightings of a white lady in the water; other ghostly sightings in waterfalls worldwide endow this stone with its otherworldly properties.

Watermelon Tourmaline

COLOR: A green outer core melting into inner red or pink, striated in natural form; some Watermelon Tourmalines have two or three colors in the same crystal

CRYSTAL TYPE: Aluminum boron silicate

ZODIAC SIGNS: Libra (September 23–October 23) and Scorpio (October 24–November 22)

CANDLE COLOR: Green

PHYSICAL: Alleviates autoimmune diseases; strengthens the immune system; addresses fertility, heart, and mobility issues, Meniere's, coordination difficulties.

EMOTIONAL: Removes stress manifesting as physical illness; helps overcome personality disorders, especially bipolar disorder and paranoia.

HOME: For harmonious family celebrations; aids in reconciling opposing personalities within the family.

WORKPLACE: Promotes successful team-building exercises, conferences and seminars, progress assessments and career reviews.

CHILDREN: Useful at times of family upheaval or major relocations; for infants or young children adversely affected by changes in routine.

ANIMALS: Comforts a pet when they are temporarily or permanently separated from their owner.

PROTECTION: Guards against unwise behavior at social gatherings that later may be regretted; diminishes unreasonable jealousy.

MAGICKAL AND PSYCHIC USES

The fey wish crystal, as wands or double-terminated; for healers to direct accurate energy flow in Reiki, Bowen therapy, kinesiology, and other energy-balancing modalities.

SPECIAL PROPERTIES

For relationships going through a bad patch; moving on from unrequited love, impossible love dreams, and disillusion when love proves fallible.

MYTHOLOGY AND HISTORY

Watermelon Tourmaline appears transparent, when viewed from the side, and almost opaque down the long axis from either end, a phenomenon called pleochroic. Containing gentle color blending of new growth, Watermelon Tourmaline restores joy after upheaval or disillusion; encourages a more fulfilling, less driven lifestyle.

Watermelon Tourmaline in Citrine

COLORS: Yellow (citrine) and green, pink, and red (tourmaline)

CRYSTAL TYPE: Natural quartz citrine with inclusions of watermelon tourmaline aluminum boron silicate, like tiny jewels studded throughout or through the top part of the citrine

ZODIAC SIGN: Libra (September 23–October 23)

CANDLE COLOR: Yellow

PHYSICAL: Fosters a breakthrough in illnesses slow to clear or treat, including autoimmune disorders; alleviates motion sickness, gallstones, small benign skin growths, polyps.

EMOTIONAL: Curbs resentment of the success and good fortune of others; keeps you from maintaining an unrequited love.

HOME: For celebrations any time of the year; starting a family-based sideline business.

WORKPLACE: Aids in moving from the back room to a more visible role at work; propels study in midlife onward that will open a new career path lasting beyond retirement.

CHILDREN: The ultimate fairy treasure crystal, for bedtime stories; restores faith in a young child, disillusioned by siblings or peers, to continue to believe in the world of magick.

ANIMALS: For pets with unusual talents to appear in advertisements or talent shows; for show or carriage horses not originally expected to succeed.

PROTECTION: Guards against those who steal credit for your ideas or work; recognizes charismatic potential lovers or business advisers who operate scams.

MAGICKAL AND PSYCHIC USES

Combining psychic skills to become a holistic practitioner or spiritual life coach; for past-life hypnotherapy to understand the roots or phobias of clients first manifest in previous worlds.

SPECIAL PROPERTIES

Brings money through natural as-yet-undeveloped talents; attracts bonuses and inheritances.

MYTHOLOGY AND HISTORY

Watermelon Tourmaline in Citrine is rare, as it combines the logic and focus of citrine with the gentle, restorative, intuitive abilities of watermelon tourmaline; repels earthly ill-wishers and spirits masquerading as deceased relatives.

Wavellite

COLORS: Pale green to dark emerald; occasionally white, yellow, or brown

CRYSTAL TYPE: Hydrated aluminum phosphate; fibrous

ZODIAC SIGN: Aquarius (January 21–February 18)

CANDLE COLOR: Green

PHYSICAL: Assists recovery from illness; stimulates resistance to infection; detoxifies; eases post-traumatic stress disorder.

EMOTIONAL: Heals rifts between birth parents, stepparents, and adoptive, step- and foster children.

HOME: Welcomes new family members, especially those with different lifestyles or in less than ideal circumstances.

WORKPLACE: For 20/20 overview in decisions; increases motivation for tedious tasks; for counselors, astrologers, and hypnotherapists.

CHILDREN: Helps youngsters understand the relevance and importance of learning.

ANIMALS: Rehabilitates domestic and wild animals, mistreated in sanctuaries.

PROTECTION: Guards against misunderstandings due to an inability to express your true feelings and needs.

MAGICKAL AND PSYCHIC USES

A gift from Earth spirits; increases intuition from the crescent moon onward to clairvoyant insight at the full moon; aids lucid and psychic dreaming; shields you from past-life recall trauma.

SPECIAL PROPERTIES

Overcomes prejudice, inequalities, and intolerance between communities, religions, cultures, and nations.

MYTHOLOGY AND HISTORY

Radial (wheel-like) clusters of Wavellite, often found embedded in limestone or chert, reflect light to produce a sparkling pinwheel star effect. In Native American lore, these are considered stars that fell to Earth, enclosed in rock to keep them safe; helpful for medicine wheel rituals, drumming, and meditations for people not indigenous to the spirituality.

White Chalcedony

COLOR: Milky, creamy white
CRYSTAL TYPE: Cryptocrystalline quartz
ZODIAC SIGN: Cancer (June 22–July 22)
CANDLE COLOR: White

PHYSICAL: Addresses issues concerning breasts, lactation, headaches, lactose intolerance, wounds, milk teeth, healthy growth of second and wisdom teeth, protection of teeth during pregnancy, fertility and fertility treatments.
EMOTIONAL: Counters insomnia, nightmares, and sleep disturbances during pregnancy; allays fears of dentists, childbirth, and surgery.
HOME: Useful for partners or children who find it hard accepting a new baby.
WORKPLACE: For shift workers, particularly those working at night.
CHILDREN: Comforts constantly crying, colicky, insomniac, or teething babies.
ANIMALS: For mothers of big litters or who initially reject their young.
PROTECTION: From Roman times considered, protective against the evil eye, black magick, and curses.

MAGICKAL AND PSYCHIC USES
Finding answers in dreams; moon magick, fertility spells.

SPECIAL PROPERTIES
The purest form of chalcedony, white chalcedony is credited with granting miracles; connection through prayer to divinity; among Native North Americans, a holy stone offered to Mother Earth.

MYTHOLOGY AND HISTORY
The first White Chalcedony was, it is said, formed from spilled drops from the Virgin Mary's breast as she fed baby Jesus and so called the milk stone. The stones were worn by nuns as a sign of their vow of chastity. Used around 4000 BCE as a seal by the Assyrians and Babylonians and in Minoan Crete from around 1800 BCE; sometimes linked to Clota the Celtic River goddess of the River Clyde in Scotland, originally ruled by the Welsh-speaking Damnonii people.

White Coral

COLORS: Pure or creamy white or in a rare form as angel skin because of its slight pink or peach tinge
CRYSTAL TYPE: Organic, branching calcareous skeletons of sea creatures
ZODIAC SIGN: Cancer (June 22–July 22)
CANDLE COLOR: Silver

PHYSICAL: Addresses respiratory tract infections, children's illnesses at any age; arthritis in women; promotes fertility, safe pregnancies if there have previously been difficulties; useful for female reproductive organs.
EMOTIONAL: Curbs overwhelming unfounded worries about the future; keeps you from thinking the worst of people, total estrangement after a quarrel.
HOME: Allays older people's fears of aging and lack of mobility or failing memory; resolves mothering issues, either with your own mother or with your children.
WORKPLACE: Valuable for those in the beauty, fashion, or hairdressing field; aids in upgrading your workplace image to create the right impression needed for promotion or a front-of-house position.
CHILDREN: Considered protective of the young, a White Coral and silver teething ring or other coral and silver mementos is often given to a new child at the christening or naming ceremony.
ANIMALS: For adopting a pet taken from its mother too young.
PROTECTION: Guards against feeling jinxed if you have broken a superstition.

MAGICKAL AND PSYCHIC USES
Brings awareness of water essences and spirits, especially those of the oceans; associated in modern magick and spirituality with Isis the ancient Egyptian goddess of magick and hidden mysteries.

SPECIAL PROPERTIES
White Coral should be kept in a red bag beneath the bed while lovemaking to conceive a child or increase passion.

MYTHOLOGY AND HISTORY
White Coral traditionally protected sea monsters. In ancient Egypt it was used against evil spirits and in ancient Greece worn on swords to ensure victory. It is illegal in several lands to harvest White Coral; it is possible, however, to find ecologically sustainable coral.

White Howlite

COLORS: White or white with gray or black web-like veins (also dyed Blue Howlite, page 75, and sometimes mistaken for Magnesite, page 286)

CRYSTAL TYPE: Calcium borosilicate hydroxide

ZODIAC SIGN: Virgo (August 24–September 22)

CANDLE COLOR: White

PHYSICAL: Strengthens bones, teeth, hair; relieves pain; aids in lactation; alleviates osteoporosis; promotes health care and fitness, healthy weight loss.

EMOTIONAL: An antistress crystal; calms a whirling mind; counters insomnia, agoraphobia, expectations that others will fix your problems.

HOME: The home blessing stone, traditionally buried around house boundaries; useful for harmonious extended-family gatherings, peaceful mealtimes.

WORKPLACE: For high ethics; defuses factions or cliques; bolsters brainstorming; encourages attention to detail.

CHILDREN: Discourages children from telling lies; allays fear of the dark; boosts concentration on necessary study.

ANIMALS: Prevents pets from straying at night; deters hostile animals from your garden.

PROTECTION: Shields against unfriendly phantoms; protects healers from absorbing clients' pain.

MAGICKAL AND PSYCHIC USES

Yoga, meditation; valuable in a health charm bag; brings healing from angels and divine light.

SPECIAL PROPERTIES

Leads to success in art or music; relieves frustration from lack of support among physically, educationally, or emotionally challenged adults and children; defuses irritability when traveling.

MYTHOLOGY AND HISTORY

Howlite, as symbol of purity and nobility of heart and soul, is sometimes called the snow leopard or white buffalo stone. White Buffalo Calf Woman or Wophe the Creator Woman of the Lakota and other Plains' nations taught the people healing ceremonies, promising when the first rare white buffalo calf, a form she took, returned, Native North American wisdom would spread throughout the world.

White Onyx

COLORS: Pure white, cream, sometimes streaked with cream, black, or gray; often found naturally as broad bands with black onyx

CRYSTAL TYPE: Chalcedony, microcrystalline quartz; White Onyx is less prone to heat-treating than other colors

ZODIAC SIGN: Pisces (February 19–March 20)

CANDLE COLOR: White

PHYSICAL: Strengthens white blood cells, bone marrow, lymph glands, brittle bones, ears, memory, breasts; addresses vaginal infections, cleft palate, osteoporosis; useful during a difficult pregnancy or after gynecological surgery, including breast surgery.

EMOTIONAL: Curbs lack of trust, depression, pessimism; keeps you from setting impossibly high standards; counters excessive sexual ardor.

HOME: Mends quarrels between partners; aids in avoiding flashpoints.

WORKPLACE: Reduces self-interest and excessive competition; for athletes while competing.

CHILDREN: Helps overcome teasing toward and by other children; encourages youngsters to help those less fortunate.

ANIMALS: For animal mothers defensive about letting humans near their kittens or puppies.

PROTECTION: Guards against dishonest dealings by officials.

MAGICKAL AND PSYCHIC USES

As a vessel for mixing herbs, making healing remedies, cleansing crystals kept in them; as candleholders to redouble the power of the flame; for prayer and sacred rituals; repels black magick.

SPECIAL PROPERTIES

Guards against fickleness and temptation to stray when a relationship has passed the honeymoon period; if a partner denigrates you in company.

MYTHOLOGY AND HISTORY

On cameos a protective deity figure would traditionally be etched on White Onyx against a black background; White Onyx signifies purity of intent, words, and actions; an amulet for working or socializing in an environment where sexual innuendo and inappropriate touching is tolerated or encouraged.

White or Clear Sapphire

COLORS: Clear, colorless, free from trace elements, often substituted for diamonds (see also Blue Sapphire, page 81)
CRYSTAL TYPE: Corundum, aluminum oxide
ZODIAC SIGN: Gemini (May 22–June 21)
CANDLE COLOR: White

PHYSICAL: Alleviates issues stemming from blood cells, bone marrow, brain, nervous system, pineal and pituitary glands; promotes fertility; strengthens the female reproductive system.
EMOTIONAL: Counters an unwillingness to accept the truth; eases your way following relationship betrayal; keeps you from constant procrastination; helps overcome an inferiority complex rooted in childhood.
HOME: Valuable if you fear that family members or a partner are concealing the truth about some aspect of their lives.
WORKPLACE: Boosts success in business through honest dealings; focuses on the essentials amid distractions or conflicting opinions.
CHILDREN: Aids in teaching children to do what is right, rather than living by externally imposed rules and prohibitions.
ANIMALS: For guide and therapy dogs.
PROTECTION: Guards against deception, illusion, and those who deliberately mislead, as well as potential partners who declare their love to extract money from you.

MAGICKAL AND PSYCHIC USES
Clairvoyance, remote viewing, discovering causes for seemingly inexplicable scars or illnesses in past lives; intuition of others' true motives.

SPECIAL PROPERTIES
For justice where you are the victim of lies or are being unfairly accused.

MYTHOLOGY AND HISTORY
White Sapphire was discovered in ancient Greece on the island of Naxos and dedicated to Apollo, god of light, medicine, and music. The stone of purity, without the material connotations of diamonds, White Sapphire became an amulet against infidelity, although until the nineteenth century blue sapphires were more highly regarded. In modern times, White Sapphire is a symbol of world peace and wise leadership by fairly elected leaders.

White or Creamy Moonstone

COLORS: Cloudy, resembles the full moon's glow, creamy or white; sometimes with a light bluish tinge and a moving light beam
CRYSTAL TYPE: Feldspar
ZODIAC SIGN: Cancer (June 22–July 22)
CANDLE COLOR: White

PHYSICAL: For women's gynecological issues; regulates hormones; addresses irregular menstrual cycles; eases PMS, menopause; strengthens ovaries and womb; promotes fertility.
EMOTIONAL: Keeps you from being out of touch with your own bodily needs.
HOME: Creates a welcoming sanctuary for all who enter; for family meals and shared cooking.
WORKPLACE: Reduces confrontational, competitive energies when immediate results are required; for shift workers and those who work irregular hours.
CHILDREN: Useful for older children entering early puberty; comforts children who are fretful traveling because they are awake after their bedtime.
ANIMALS: White Moonstone suspended from a hutch or a pen keeps pets who sleep outdoors safe from predators.
PROTECTION: Guards against dangers while traveling overseas; reduces the effects of jet lag.

MAGICKAL AND PSYCHIC USES
To call full moon energies into yourself on full moon night; full moon rituals for fertility; rites of passage ceremonies for women and girls.

SPECIAL PROPERTIES
The moonstone most connected with mothers-to-be and mothers, beginning with conception by harmonizing the body into natural lunar cycles, even if medical intervention is required; valuable for a healthy pregnancy, easy childbirth and lactation, parent/child bonding.

MYTHOLOGY AND HISTORY
The ultimate woman's stone, White Moonstone was sacred to the Greco-Roman moon goddess Diana and symbol of the Divine Feminine; love symbol of female radiance, beauty, and magick.

White or Peace Agate

COLORS: Finely banded, unlike white chalcedony, which is sometimes mistaken for White Agate

CRYSTAL TYPE: Microcrystalline quartz

ZODIAC SIGN: Virgo (August 24–September 22)

CANDLE COLOR: White

PHYSICAL: Alleviates morning sickness; ensures a safe pregnancy and delivery for mother and baby; eases lactation; addresses abdominal problems.

EMOTIONAL: Curbs lack of trust in others; tempers intense frustration at daily challenges; keeps you from being habitually confrontational even when compromise is offered; prevents you from holding on to grudges.

HOME: Balances yin-yang energies in the home if the atmosphere is too frantic and assertive or lethargic and overly emotional.

WORKPLACE: For gaining confidence in your own abilities to apply for promotion or move to another company in a higher-profile or paid position; for working in human resources.

CHILDREN: Useful for teens uncertain of their sexuality if they are being pressured by peers to conform to stereotypes.

ANIMALS: For pets who are territorial toward other pets or aggressive when another animal approaches their food.

PROTECTION: Guards against those who cause trouble behind the scenes and shift the blame.

MAGICKAL AND PSYCHIC USES

Attracts angelic guides and spirit helpers; as a worry stone (see Palm or Worry Stones, page 336), absorbs fears and anxiety (wash the crystal well) and prevents them from returning; because White Agate is so pure in color, it can be imprinted with a symbol or written wish in incense stick smoke drawn in the air above it.

SPECIAL PROPERTIES

White Agate brings good fortune; enables you to discriminate between those who will be helpful and those who are harmful.

MYTHOLOGY AND HISTORY

White Agate was first used by the ancient Egyptians more than three thousand years ago in cooking to introduce health-giving powers to the food and keep it pure, and as an amulet of protection against evil and restless spirits around tombs. It has become a symbol of world peace and reconciliation between nations.

White Plume or Stinking Water Plume Agate

COLORS: Blue to yellow with white to yellowish plumes

CRYSTAL TYPE: Agate, chalcedony, with inclusions of manganese or iron oxide; may be covered with sparkling druzy crystals

ZODIAC SIGN: Pisces (February 19–March 20)

CANDLE COLOR: White

PHYSICAL: Addresses issues stemming from the colon, prostate, skin aging, psoriasis, rosacea, eczema, dermatitis.

EMOTIONAL: Enables you to accept necessary endings when a relationship has run its course; keeps you from acknowledging only what is superficially beautiful and harmonious, while allowing problems to fester beneath the surface.

HOME: Enables you to proceed with necessary structural renovations, and ignore accumulating chores or necessary family discussions and decisions if these may be confrontational.

WORKPLACE: Promotes networking via social media, Zoom, and conference calls; revives ailing businesses with new personnel, equipment, and methods; helps you make hard decisions to reduce the labor force when necessary.

CHILDREN: Aids in making time for children to talk over worries; watching for signs with teens that they are concealing problems.

ANIMALS: For normally domesticated animals living wild, including Australian Brumby horses, US wild horses found near Stinking Water Creek, cattle, buffalo and moorland ponies.

PROTECTION: Continuously purifies stagnant or hostile energies and restores freshness and positive vibes.

MAGICKAL AND PSYCHIC USES

Connecting with spirit guides and guardian angels; mediumship with personal ancestors; for water magick; rebirthing.

SPECIAL PROPERTIES

For speechmaking, oral examinations, dissertations, and addressing meetings; encourages wise, unhurried words and prevents impulsive decision making if you're under pressure.

MYTHOLOGY AND HISTORY

Stinking Water Plume Agate was named by the Indigenous Native North Americans after the creek in eastern Oregon where White Plume Agate is found and where salmon returned to spawn in large numbers and then died. Often the whiter kind of Water Plume Agate is carved into ghost shapes for Halloween.

White Selenite

COLORS: Glows with luminescence, spontaneous emission of white light

CRYSTAL TYPE: Fiber gypsum, hydrous calcium sulfate, with pearl-like luster, often striated or growing as wands (see also Satin Spar, page 419)

ZODIAC SIGN: Cancer (June 22–July 22)

CANDLE COLOR: Silver or white

PHYSICAL: Strengthens blood cells, hormones, vitality, youthfulness; counters attention deficit disorder, hyperactivity, osteoporosis, fluid retention, PMS, menstrual and menopausal problems.

EMOTIONAL: Brings peace from fears of disaster or rejection; cleanses aura overload.

HOME: Clears rooms of stress and artifacts of bad energies; spreads calm.

WORKPLACE: Encourages harmonious business partnerships, especially between love partners; blocks distractions; attracts helpful opportunities and people.

CHILDREN: Prevents fears of darkness and nightmares; helps infants when breastfeeding.

ANIMALS: For nocturnal wandering cats; animal mothers who reject their young; telepathic connection with pets.

PROTECTION: Alerts you to deception, lies, and scams; deters bad spirits or earthly intruders at night.

MAGICKAL AND PSYCHIC USES
Selenite is the ultimate magic wand for moon rituals, full moon love, and fertility magick; connects with wise ancestors, angels and spirit guides, deceased loved ones, and Akashic records.

SPECIAL PROPERTIES
Most powerful in the three days before and full moon; draws love; increases commitment, passion, reconciliation, fidelity; enhances fertility, especially after having difficulty conceiving.

MYTHOLOGY AND HISTORY
Named after Selene, ancient Greek full moon goddess; Selene was a prolific mother, producing fifty-three daughters.

Williamsite

COLORS: Light to intense green with black inclusions or spots of chromite or magnetite; also bluish-green

CRYSTAL TYPE: Phyllosilicates, antigorite variety of serpentine; oily feel

ZODIAC SIGNS: Virgo (August 24–September 22) and Scorpio (October 24–November 22)

CANDLE COLOR: Green

PHYSICAL: Alleviates inflammation, emphysema, coughs, plant allergies, multiple sclerosis, kidney stones, stomach cramps, PMS, pain from bites and stings, diabetes, heart irregularities, toxicity from the environment and food; aids in realigning the spine.

EMOTIONAL: Restores routine when life is chaotic; assists moving away from negative influences, habits, and people.

HOME: For budgeting after a major outlay or expenditure; improves memory if you or others continually lose or misplace possessions.

WORKPLACE: For attainment of short and long-term goals through hard work rather than good luck or opportunism; creating realistic targets and budgets.

CHILDREN: Useful when life has been suddenly disrupted by one parent leaving, family bereavement, or eviction.

ANIMALS: Valuable for snakes, lizards, and other reptiles in tanks.

PROTECTION: Guards against psychic and psychological attack, particularly by those who lead the vulnerable into unnecessary risk; shields against marriage wreckers.

MAGICKAL AND PSYCHIC USES
For meditation, prayer, or contemplation; best in open-air beautiful places; for natural magick, empowering natural remedies; telepathy.

SPECIAL PROPERTIES
Williamsite attracts people who make us happy; helps to rediscover the authentic self if other people or life have controlled freedom.

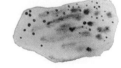

MYTHOLOGY AND HISTORY
Williamsite is often used for sacred objects, such as rosaries or prayer beads, or in adorning beautiful artifacts; called precious serpentine when it resembles translucent emerald-green jade.

Witch's Finger

COLORS: Clear to smoky quartz; varying colors depending on mineral inclusions

CRYSTAL TYPE: Resembles a gnarled, knobbly finger; quartz with inclusions of actinolite, calcite, feldspar, hematite, iron, magnetite, sparkling mica, muscovite, sphalerite, or zircon; sometimes double-terminated (a point at each end)

ZODIAC SIGN: Pisces (February 19–March 20)

CANDLE COLOR: Brown

PHYSICAL: Regulates blood sugar; alleviates dehydration; increases metabolic rate for healthy weight loss; curbs insomnia; addresses issues stemming from the pancreas.

EMOTIONAL: Allays fears of being authentic; overcomes old voices in your head.

HOME: Heals lingering quarrels, illness, or misfortune; moves unhappy ghosts to the light.

WORKPLACE: For planning and achieving your destiny; crystal of lateral thinking.

CHILDREN: Helps children overcome disappointments and try again.

ANIMALS: For physically unappealing pets in an animal shelter or litter to be adopted.

PROTECTION: Guards against ill intent, curses, paranormal attack.

MAGICKAL AND PSYCHIC USES

As a wand in Wiccan rituals and nature spirituality; brings the spirit guides you need.

SPECIAL PROPERTIES

For tact to stay silent in the face of provocation; shields the aura and maintains chakra balance; keeps you from anticipating problems in a new relationship because of past pain.

MYTHOLOGY AND HISTORY

Found in Zambia, Witch's Finger is hard to obtain; assists cooks, chefs, winemakers, and brewers; as tumbled stones, it is called the Magdalena stone and, when containing gold rutiles or needles, Venus hair; helps women develop spiritual power; aids men encountering their anima, rather than projecting it onto their wives, mothers, and daughters.

Wonderstone or Wonderstone Jasper

COLORS: Beautiful, colorful, wave-like bands, pale tan or yellow, maroon, red, violet, or pink, within an off-white to gray matrix

CRYSTAL TYPE: Silicon dioxide, microcrystalline quartz, or chalcedony

ZODIAC SIGN: Sagittarius (November 23–December 21)

CANDLE COLOR: Orange

PHYSICAL: Addresses infections, bites, stings from mosquitoes and other disease-carrying insects, regeneration of cells and tissues, sciatica, skin disorders.

EMOTIONAL: Alleviates stress, anxiety, depression, constant worrying about future (especially worries that relationships or good fortune will not last).

HOME: Revives family finances through moneymaking ideas as well as budgeting.

WORKPLACE: Translates imaginative ideas into viable products; for setting up unusual businesses, developing a niche market.

CHILDREN: Calms children who are easily hyped by others or noise and overstimulation.

ANIMALS: For dogs who bark at the slightest sound.

PROTECTION: Guards against being caught in past-life issues or repeating earlier patterns from this lifetime.

MAGICKAL AND PSYCHIC USES

Deep meditation, astral travel, direct contact with deceased relatives.

SPECIAL PROPERTIES

Balances the animus and anima, male and female energies, within the individual and within a relationship; for unresolved gender issues and same-sex or transgender marriages where there is family opposition.

MYTHOLOGY AND HISTORY

Surprisingly similar in appearance to its Australian counterpart Mookaite (page 306), Wonderstone, found in Utah and Nevada, has a place in ongoing modern myth with Dungeons and Dragons devotees; it is said that it's activated when in contact with a magickal item or enchanted being, glowing blue.

Yellow Apatite

COLOR: Pale yellow-green, bright yellow to golden
CRYSTAL TYPE: Calcium phosphate
ZODIAC SIGN: Sagittarius (November 23-December 21)
CANDLE COLOR: Yellow

PHYSICAL: Addresses seasonal affective disorder, brittle bones, teeth, Raynaud's disease, chilblains; promotes healthy weight loss; enhances fitness regimens, spleen, gallbladder, liver, digestion.

EMOTIONAL: Keeps you from living on other people's terms, feeling overshadowed by talented or successful family members; curbs a victim mentality.

HOME: Ushers in prosperity; for buying a vacation vehicle or a vacation home; reintroduces light after illness, unhappiness, or misfortune; encourages happy family parties.

WORKPLACE: Enables rapid decision making in competitive business situations; boosts the fortunes of a team trying for the big leagues; for turning a sideline into a business, successful bargaining, online selling and buying.

CHILDREN: Helps making new friends on vacation; encourages healthy growth.

ANIMALS: Promotes animal conservation, especially for horned and hoofed species.

PROTECTION: Guards against false friends, spirits masquerading as deceased relatives, or celebrities during séances.

MAGICKAL AND PSYCHIC USES

For midsummer and solstice celebrations; awareness of spirits near the site of a massacre or battle anniversary; creating an aura power shield of gold; connecting with archangels, especially Michael, archangel of the sun.

SPECIAL PROPERTIES

A stone of the sun, also called golden apatite, brings self-confidence, optimism, draws like-minded friends; encourages harmony for community events; generates brilliant ideas and the means to manifest them.

MYTHOLOGY AND HISTORY

The stone of the sun promises happy vacations, days out, or moving to a sunnier clime if you hate the cold; studying to advance your career and for pleasure; an instant dispeller of gloom and grumpiness.

Yellow Aragonite

COLORS: Yellow/honey, also colorless, white (page 127), and orange or reddish-brown (pages 327 and 95)
CRYSTAL TYPE: Calcium carbonate usually growing as twin crystals in clusters
ZODIAC SIGN: Virgo (August 24-September 22)
CANDLE COLOR: Yellow

PHYSICAL: Strengthens bones, spine, teeth, hair; aids in absorbing necessary nutrients, notably calcium; addresses chilblains and poor circulation in winter, SAD, colds, flu and viral infections (especially respiratory), super bugs; curbs the overprescribing of antibiotics.

EMOTIONAL: Eases agoraphobia, inability to switch off the mind leading to burnout; keeps you from focusing on drawbacks and constantly complaining.

HOME: For effective recycling and minimizing waste in your home and neighborhood.

WORKPLACE: A stressbuster; an antidote to constant air conditioning, artificial lighting, and overillumination in natural daylight; for artists and cosmetologists and beauticians.

CHILDREN: Banishes nightmares; reduces mood swings in hormonal teenagers; for cheerleaders and team supporters.

ANIMALS: For city pets living in high-rise buildings; encourages kindness toward all creatures; for beekeepers.

PROTECTION: Guards against becoming overwhelmed by responsibilities and the unreasonable demands of others.

MAGICKAL AND PSYCHIC USES

Herbalism, natural magick in urban settings, tarot reading, water scrying in rippling sunlight, solar ceremonies.

SPECIAL PROPERTIES

For winter vacations or relocating to warm, sunny places; avoids overreacting and speaking without thinking.

MYTHOLOGY AND HISTORY

Yellow and honey Aragonite is like the warm winter sun in Spain (named after Aragon where it was discovered). It is also found as a deposit from hot springs and so a stone of the Earth Mother from whose womb the warm waters flow.

Yellow Brucite

COLORS: Lemon or canary yellow

CRYSTAL TYPE: Magnesium hydroxide, botryoidal, grape-like in yellow

ZODIAC SIGN: Gemini (May 22–June 21)

CANDLE COLOR: Yellow

PHYSICAL: Counters nausea, motion sickness, and morning sickness; alleviates issues stemming from gallstones, pancreas, spleen, digestion of fats, arteries, stomach ulcers.

EMOTIONAL: Keeps you from emotionally draining others; fends off a victim mentality as a means of control; curbs a tendency to instigate gossip to deflect negative comments away from yourself.

HOME: For family, friends, and neighbors who borrow money, tools, or food supplies and never return them; for passing driving tests and getting planning permits for alterations or extensions.

WORKPLACE: Establishes new goals and situations to make the right decisions; aids in thinking on your feet and gaining the necessary information as you go along; for speculation combining knowledge, logic, and instinct; helps you decide when you are ready to move on at your own time and on your terms.

CHILDREN: For those who constantly misplace their possessions; helping teens to recognize and avoid online grooming.

ANIMALS: Trains bad-tempered pets to become more amenable.

PROTECTION: Shields yourself, your home, your loved ones, and your possessions; works as a safe travel stone; for all who are in dangerous jobs or hazardous places carrying out duties.

MAGICKAL AND PSYCHIC USES

Psychic self-defense; repels the evil eye of envy; for attending or organizing psychic events, festivals, spiritual classes, and celebrations to welcome the equinoxes and solstices.

SPECIAL PROPERTIES

The stone of self-confidence and self-esteem so you no longer accept responsibility for what is not your fault; stepping back and politely declining if you are drowning in others' guilt and offloaded blame.

MYTHOLOGY AND HISTORY

Found only in Killarney, Saifullah District, Baluchistan, Pakistan, this is the stone of pure sunshine; increases your natural charisma, draws people to you socially; for fun vacations and group activities.

Yellow Diamond

COLORS: Light yellow, canary yellow, greenish-yellow, and orangey or brownish-yellow; most valuable as pure bright yellow

CRYSTAL TYPE: Carbon with replacement of some carbon atoms with nitrogen during formation

ZODIAC SIGN: Leo (July 23–August 23)

CANDLE COLOR: Yellow

PHYSICAL: Addresses seasonal affective disorder; promotes absorption of vitamin D; curbs intolerance to sunlight; aids following liver transplants or when a patient has given up hope.

EMOTIONAL: Counters deep depression; for those who have witnessed horrific incidents or suffer burnout after working with human tragedy; for recluses.

HOME: As a betrothal or eternity ring when a couple live together if they cannot marry because of particular circumstances.

WORKPLACE: For fame, celebrity status, the manifestation of seemingly impossible dreams.

CHILDREN: A birth gift to ensure the child will always be joyous and spread sunshine.

ANIMALS: The stone of the magickal golden phoenix, said to rise anew from the ashes of her funeral fire every five hundred years.

PROTECTION: Guards against personal weakness, greed, and envy in self and others.

MAGICKAL AND PSYCHIC USES

Magick on the solstices; protective at séances, in mediumship circles; for gifted psychics, healers, and humanitarians.

SPECIAL PROPERTIES

Radiates pure life force and creativity; brings fulfillment where material gain is a secondary purpose.

MYTHOLOGY AND HISTORY

Yellow Diamond contains the life essence of the sun. The most famous Yellow Diamond is the Florentine Yellow Diamond from India, a 127-facet stone, weighing 137.27 carats, first appearing in legends of Charles the Bold, duke of Burgundy in 1467.

Yellow Fluorite

COLORS: From light to dark or amber yellow
CRYSTAL TYPE: Halide/calcium fluoride
ZODIAC SIGN: Gemini (May 22–June 21)
CANDLE COLOR: Yellow

PHYSICAL: Alleviates issues stemming from high cholesterol, liver, pancreas, stomach stapling or gastric-band operations, cosmetic surgery, arthritis; addresses bones, teeth, gums, shingles.
EMOTIONAL: Curbs self-defeating behavior, comparing yourself unfavorably with others; keeps you from feeling unfounded jealousy as a result of insecurity, causing fears of betrayal.
HOME: Limits the number of people who make no worthwhile contribution or those with hard-luck stories from taking up residence in your home.
WORKPLACE: For those with spiritual businesses to combine a desire to help with sound business acumen; persuades workplace despots and fledgling stars to do their fair share; aids in setting up a viable, self-employed venture, as well as meeting deadlines.
CHILDREN: Encourages young people with grandiose plans of instant celebrity status to study or embrace apprenticeships.
ANIMALS: Useful for training unwilling dogs and horses.
PROTECTION: For adults and children who are too generous and trusting.

MAGICKAL AND PSYCHIC USES
For objective paranormal investigations or experiments; if you are easily spooked when ghost hunting or attending séanc to keep away malevolent spirits.

SPECIAL PROPERTIES
The crystal of the persuader and quicksilver mind who can sell any idea or product; when you need to come up with a plausible excuse or talk your way out of trouble fast.

MYTHOLOGY AND HISTORY
Also called golden fluorite, yellow is a rarer form of fluorite. Yellow Fluorite identifies what is obtainable through logic and by stages, rather than waiting for the ideal opportunity or big break that may never come.

Yellow Jade

COLOR: Lemon, bright, or golden yellow
CRYSTAL TYPE: A mix of silicate, iron, calcium, and magnesium
ZODIAC SIGN: Gemini (May 22–June 21)
CANDLE COLOR: Yellow

PHYSICAL: Addresses issues relating to the digestive system, bladder, kidneys, bowels, liver, gallbladder, pancreas, spleen, bone calcification, ulcers, impetigo, ringworm.
EMOTIONAL: Helps overcome self-consciousness at parties or events where you don't know anyone; keeps you from letting abrasive, sarcastic people make you feel inadequate, if you must see them frequently.
HOME: For good relationships with adult children, especially ones still at home; attracts happiness.
WORKPLACE: Guards against gossip, factions, and hidden agendas; for professionalism if others treat the workplace like a social club; assimilating new material and techniques.
CHILDREN: Protects children and teenagers from peer pressure and classroom spite, as well as social media abuse and trolling.
ANIMALS: Helps a new pet to be accepted by existing ones.
PROTECTION: Repels ill-wishing, psychological attacks, and false accusations; ensures safety on long journeys to remote or unfamiliar places.

MAGICKAL AND PSYCHIC USE
A good luck talisman for career, travel, and wealth through speculation; an intuitive radar guiding you to what is genuine; healing and lucid dreams.

SPECIAL PROPERTIES
The stone of friendship and sociability for new and growing friendships, maintaining long-standing ones, increasing popularity; successful parties and social gatherings.

MYTHOLOGY AND HISTORY
Used from Neolithic times, the most valuable of jades, Yellow Jade became popular, especially among Imperial rulers during the Chinese Ming dynasty, which ruled from 1368 until 1644 and the following Qing dynasty.

Yellow Jasper

COLORS: Single-colored mustard, sandy, or burnished yellow

CRYSTAL TYPE: Microcrystalline quartz

ZODIAC SIGNS: Gemini (May 22–June 21) and Capricorn (December 22–January 20)

CANDLE COLOR: Yellow

PHYSICAL: Addresses issues stemming from the liver, gallbladder (including gallstones, bile duct), large intestine, nausea, fat and lactose intolerance, chronic indigestion; absorbs pain, especially back pain.

EMOTIONAL: Curbs chronic anxiety and self-consciousness about the opinions others hold about you; helps overcome embarrassment about eating in public.

HOME: Guards against nasty neighbors; prevents relatives from using blatant favoritism or divisive tactics at family gatherings.

WORKPLACE: For a competitive workplace where unrealistic targets and rivalry are encouraged by management; aids in clearing a backlog of work and avoiding business scams.

CHILDREN: Reduces sibling rivalry; encourages outdoor play and respect for the environment; helps youngsters make friends if they find communication hard.

ANIMALS: For exotic pets, such as lizards or snakes.

PROTECTION: Guards against spite, gossip, jealousy, those who would deceive, and spreaders of misinformation.

MAGICKAL AND PSYCHIC USES

For Native American rituals and local Indigenous traditions; totem animals, sand divination and magick, connection with urban Earth energies, dowsing, Mother Earth preservation rites.

SPECIAL PROPERTIES

Ensures safety traveling to remote countries, backpacking, doing volunteer work overseas or emergency relief aid; helps avoid stomach upset from eating unfamiliar food.

MYTHOLOGY AND HISTORY

Earth-colored jaspers are revered among Indigenous peoples, entering the modern spiritual world as icons of Earth awareness and the interconnectedness of all life; they promote tolerance and unity where different ethnic or religious communities live and work in close proximity.

Yellow or Agni Gold Danburite

COLORS: Pale to golden yellow; also in rare and powerful form, Agni Gold Danburite, which is bright yellow-gold

CRYSTAL TYPE: Calcium borosilicate

ZODIAC SIGN: Leo (July 23–August 23)

CANDLE COLOR: Gold

PHYSICAL: Addresses issues involving digestion, slow metabolism, allergies to additives; promotes fertility, healthy childbirth; enhances brain function in the face of memory loss.

EMOTIONAL: Counters depression, profound pessimism, agoraphobia, suicidal thoughts, self-harm, postnatal depression.

HOME: The sunshine crystal, any Yellow Danburite radiates joy and optimism; neutralizes negative Earth energies or spooky atmospheres.

WORKPLACE: Offers clarity to convincingly express ideas and proposals; Agni Gold brings power and leadership opportunities without sacrificing ethics.

CHILDREN: Restores happiness after family loss; confers confidence to help young ones defend themselves against school or social media bullying.

ANIMALS: Encourages a timid animal to stand their ground without aggression.

PROTECTION: Guards against those who try to shake your faith in your abilities.

MAGICKAL AND PSYCHIC USES

Agni Gold, called the golden healer, is said to flow with inner fire solar power; any Yellow Danburite brings enhanced clairvoyance, angelic wisdom; links with the music of the spheres, so it brings gifts for sound healing.

SPECIAL PROPERTIES

Offers the discovery of one's true soul purpose and leaving behind redundant karma; aids in approaching driving tests, examinations (written or oral), presentations, or interviews with confident authority.

MYTHOLOGY AND HISTORY

Agni Gold was discovered in a mine in the southern part of Africa in 2006; Yellow Danburite is found mainly in Myanmar, Madagascar, and Mexico, originally discovered as yellowy-brown crystals in the 1830s in Danbury, Connecticut, after which the crystal is named.

Yellow or Golden Mica

COLORS: Pale yellow to golden, the yellow caused by iron oxide; found also in yellow as Star Mica (page 256)
CRYSTAL TYPE: Crystallizes as flakes, scales, and sheets; usually on a matrix, often clear quartz.
ZODIAC SIGN: Leo (July 23–August 23)
CANDLE COLOR: Gold

PHYSICAL: Alleviates inflammation of the skin, as well as jaundice, liver and pancreatic problems; addresses issues stemming from the bone marrow, glands, perimenopausal symptoms, dizziness.
EMOTIONAL: Curbs an unwillingness to learn anything new; keeps you from staying in the same comfort zone.
HOME: Promotes good fortune that benefits others and helps turn your own life around; ensures that you nurture yourself as well as caring for others.
WORKPLACE: Aids in suddenly finding that a difficult new concept of working makes perfect sense; helps you rapidly analyze and memorize data, facts, and figures.
CHILDREN: Place a tiny piece of Yellow Mica with a child's books or by a computer or flash drive overnight to guard against spite in school, college, or on the way to and from an educational institution.
ANIMALS: Protects pets from unfriendly animals they encounter during exercise or when visiting a home with their owners.
PROTECTION: Guards against psychic attack by ill-wishers and those seeking to put psychological and emotional hooks into your aura.

MAGICKAL AND PSYCHIC USES
Deep meditation to become momentarily one with the universe and experience a state of bliss outside conscious awareness; telepathy with a loved one far away.
SPECIAL PROPERTIES
For awakening the inner warrior if others take you for granted or take advantage of you; balances the animus and anima in a way that accords with your chosen lifestyle.
MYTHOLOGY AND HISTORY
Mainly found in Brazil, this is the stone of bringing out dormant or abandoned talents, fitting in study with other commitments, and developing mental acuity to maximize every opportunity and shine in the way most desired; balances achievement and pleasure.

Yellow or Gold Zircon

COLORS: Pale yellow, greenish-yellow, canary yellow to gold; sometimes heat-treated; sparkly. Some natural yellow zircons display tenebrescence, so when kept in darkness they become brownish-yellow or orangey-yellow, but, once exposed to the light, turn yellow again
CRYSTAL TYPE: Zirconium silicate
ZODIAC SIGN: Sagittarius (November 23–December 21)
CANDLE COLOR: Yellow

PHYSICAL: Addresses issues stemming from the liver, pancreas, spleen, stomach ulcers (and successful surgery on these), IBS, celiac disease, lactose intolerance, hepatitis, nausea; relieves pain.
EMOTIONAL: Curbs envy of others' possessions, family, or lifestyle; helps those who are bullied verbally or constantly undermined at work or at home.
HOME: Yellow or Gold Zircon encourages good humor and spontaneity if you have an unenthusiastic partner or family.
WORKPLACE: Promotes prosperity through developing moneymaking ideas, starting or developing a home-based business on a small scale, or making money from a hobby.
CHILDREN: Protects children or teens suffering schoolyard spite or social media trolling.
ANIMALS: Useful if you feel intimidated by an animal with an aggressive owner on walks with your pet.
PROTECTION: Guards against unpleasant or gossiping neighbors; shields you from nightmares, particularly those involving paranormal forces.

MAGICKAL AND PSYCHIC USES
Banishes poltergeists and spirits called up carelessly as a result of dabbling with demons summoned using medieval formulas from the internet; for sex magick.
SPECIAL PROPERTIES
Traditionally associated with the planet Pluto, Yellow or Gold Zircon assists in replacing what is redundant in any part of your life with a minimum of hurt and disruption.
MYTHOLOGY AND HISTORY
The name *zircon* comes from the Persian word *zargun*, which means "yellow-hued." The noblest of zircons, in its more golden shades zircon is associated with supporting and participating in humanitarian projects.

Yellow Quartz

COLORS: Medium to bright yellow; may vary from light yellow to pinkish-yellow when it is coated with chabazite; milky and opaque

CRYSTAL TYPE: Quartz, silicon dioxide, different in appearance from clear yellow citrine, the transparent, golden gem variety of macrocrystalline quartz that is heated naturally in the Earth or artificially. Yellow quartz is often found as tumbled stones or jewelry

ZODIAC SIGN: Sagittarius (November 23–December 21)

CANDLE COLOR: Yellow

PHYSICAL: Addresses issues involving digestion, gallbladder and gallstones, intolerance to fat and lactose, skin allergies, memory, hyperactivity due to additives (especially in children and teenagers).

EMOTIONAL: Counters pessimism, emotional burnout, panic attacks; keeps you from overthinking.

HOME: Attracts prosperity and blessings to the home and all within; for happy mealtimes if some family members are picky or prefer to graze.

WORKPLACE: Combines friendliness with the need to focus on essential tasks if colleagues treat the office like a social club; boosts confidence to apply for promotion.

CHILDREN: For those who find it hard to settle into a structured school environment or to read signals to avoid getting into trouble.

ANIMALS: Trains pets to wait at home in your absence, without barking or becoming destructive.

PROTECTION: Guards against those who spread doom and gloom.

MAGICKAL AND PSYCHIC USES

Seasonal magick on the solar festivals; learning new psychic skills that require study and practice as well as intuition; researching parapsychology; ghost hunting.

SPECIAL PROPERTIES

For optimism in hard times that happiness and success are just around the corner.

MYTHOLOGY AND HISTORY

Yellow Quartz is mainly found in China, but also in Brazil and India. The sunshine crystal spreads happiness and confidence even on the gloomiest day or situation; for making a good impression socially, in the workplace and succeeding in examinations and other tests (especially driving tests).

Yellow Sapphire

COLORS: Yellow, lemon, greenish-yellow, orangish-yellow, and canary yellow; brightness according to amount of included iron; sparkling

CRYSTAL TYPE: Corundum, aluminum oxide, yellow trace-element iron, with feather-like inclusions in untreated stones

ZODIAC SIGN: Sagittarius (November 23–December 21)

CANDLE COLOR: Bright yellow

PHYSICAL: Alleviates issues stemming from jaundice, stomach, spleen, gallbladder, liver, nausea, SAD; promotes fertility and healthy pregnancy.

EMOTIONAL: Curbs obsessive jealousy and a need to constantly seek reassurance; enables you to resist temptations.

HOME: Brings blessings and abundance, ensuring that there are always sufficient resources and love.

WORKPLACE: Promotes the acquisition of formal knowledge, including long training or study programs for professional qualifications; encourages lucky breaks in pursuit of fame; for teachers, spiritual counselors, and all involved in higher education.

CHILDREN: Welcomes the birth of a child after difficulties in conception and pregnancy or when parents have their first child late in life.

ANIMALS: For the revival of a species on the brink of extinction.

PROTECTION: Guards against poverty; shields you from snakebite and venomous humans.

MAGICKAL AND PSYCHIC USES

For fire and candle magick; defensive and angel magick; creating auric boundaries against gossipers and disruptors; for discovering past worlds of warrior priests and priestesses.

SPECIAL PROPERTIES

For a happy marriage or committed relationship, healthy children, and a harmonious family life through the generations, especially if there are initial obstacles; favorable for women searching for the right partner.

MYTHOLOGY AND HISTORY

Symbol of wealth in India, associated with Ganesha, god of prosperity, worn by merchants in Asia since ancient times. In Vedic astrology Yellow Sapphire, called *pukhraj*, represents good fortune; linked with the planet Jupiter, it is a symbol of authority, success, and expansion in every aspect of life.

Yellow Spinel

COLORS: From pale to golden yellow; sometimes in the untreated stone brownish-yellow, orangey-yellow, or greenish-yellow

CRYSTAL TYPE: Magnesium aluminum oxide; rare in natural yellow; spinels colored yellow through heat treatment should be empowered regularly

ZODIAC SIGN: Sagittarius (November 23–December 21)

CANDLE COLOR: Yellow

PHYSICAL: Boosts energy; clears toxins (especially mercury or lead) from the body; removes digestive blockages; eases problems with the liver, pancreas, and gallbladder.

EMOTIONAL: Curbs pessimism, depression, lethargy without physical cause, jealousy of others.

HOME: Cheers up family members during rainy days and holidays; for creative cooking; reassures you in the face of social occasions or family events you are dreading.

WORKPLACE: Helps you master difficult material for assessments, tests, or where there is fierce competition at interviews; for learning languages.

CHILDREN: Boosts enthusiasm for new experiences or adventures.

ANIMALS: For species from sunny or desert places, such as lizards, to thrive in an artificial habitat.

PROTECTION: Guards against people who automatically dismiss any suggested ideas or plans; defuses potential conflict.

MAGICKAL AND PSYCHIC USES

For upbeat clairvoyant or therapeutic sessions with clients who block energies; psychic spring-cleaning rituals any time of the year.

SPECIAL PROPERTIES

Yellow Spinels attract beautiful things, happy people, and chances for spontaneous fun and laughter.

MYTHOLOGY AND HISTORY

Yellow Spinel is a crystal of personal power and determination to fulfill our destiny in a way that will bring happiness rather than just material success. It is the antidote to a boring, routine-filled existence.

Yellow Turquoise

COLORS: Yellow with black or gray web patterns in its most authentic form; sometimes greenish

CRYSTAL TYPE: Not a turquoise at all, but serpentine/jasper with hematite webbing; called turquoise because it is found in turquoise mines and has a similar webbed matrix pattern to conventional turquoise; quartz inclusions; may be laboratory made, but this will have very bright artificial colors

ZODIAC SIGN: Sagittarius (November 23–December 21)

CANDLE COLOR: Yellow

PHYSICAL: Reduces toxicity and increases immunity; counters frequent stomach upsets, gallstones, pancreatitis. fluid retention (especially in the feet, ankles, and abdomen).

EMOTIONAL: Keeps you from inflexibility and closed emotions; helps overcome issues with mothers living and deceased.

HOME: Aids in making friendships with newly arrived neighbors or if you move to a different area to attract like-minded friends.

WORKPLACE: For starting a new job or changing a career; to make a positive initial impression; for leadership and major promotion.

CHILDREN: Enables you to gain confidence in yourself if you struggle with mothering or fathering and have challenging children.

ANIMALS: Assists reluctant animal mothers to nurture a large litter.

PROTECTION: Guards against energy drains by emotional and psychic vampires when worn as protective beads.

MAGICKAL AND PSYCHIC USES

For empaths to gain heightened awareness of clients' deepest memories and feelings; for continuing automatic aura cleansing and chakra energy center balancing.

SPECIAL PROPERTIES

Yellow Turquoise brings insights through bad as well as good experiences; a travel crystal to protect and open the way for exciting new experiences; promotes a sense of adventure.

MYTHOLOGY AND HISTORY

Worn as jewelry or tumbled stones, Yellow Turquoise is highly portable to bring confidence to any situation with people of whom you feel uncertain or have met for the first time; automatically radiates charisma from your aura energy field; helps in getting to know someone better as a friend or lover.

Yin-Yang Quartz

COLORS: Half cloudy (yin receptive energies), half clear (yang active energies); this 50/50 division defines a true Yin-Yang crystal

CRYSTAL TYPE: Clear quartz, the base either milky with Fairy Frost (page 182) and the top part of the tip clear, sometimes with a few inner wisps, merging in the middle; Yin-Yang crystals may have other characteristics, such as Empath Wounded Warrior (page 173) or Time Link or Timeline (page 195)

ZODIAC SIGN: Gemini (May 22–June 21)

CANDLE COLOR: White

PHYSICAL: Alleviates breathing difficulties, chronic lung problems, gender-related issues (especially during puberty), excessive or insufficient testosterone or progesterone in either sex.

EMOTIONAL: Keeps you from alternating between fight or flight, excessive assertiveness or passivity.

HOME: Balances the energies in the home so the chi life force flows freely, bringing health, prosperity, and good fortune.

WORKPLACE: For harmony in an all-male or all-female workplace; aids in overcoming homophobia.

CHILDREN: Helps teens to feel comfortable with their sexuality.

ANIMALS: Helps an unneutered pet to be naturally sociable.

PROTECTION: Guards against excessive reactions by others.

MAGICKAL AND PSYCHIC USES

Useful in working with the *I Ching*, Taoism, feng shui, tai chi, yoga, qi gong, spiritual energy, and breath therapies; community and world peace rituals.

SPECIAL PROPERTIES

For balanced numbers and status in currently male- or female-dominated institutions; equality of women in lands where this does not exist.

MYTHOLOGY AND HISTORY

A Master healer and teacher. Life, natural forces, people, even food—all are made up of *yang*, the original directly focused sun concept, balanced by *yin*, the cyclical moon concept. Yang represents heaven and all things active—light, animus, assertiveness, logic, and power. Yin controls the Earth and passive, dark, soft, still, receptive, and intuitive energies. Each contains elements of the other. The perfect-balance crystal.

Yooperlite

COLORS: Grays, black, white, speckled, polished; orange and yellow glow under UV light from the inside out; flame-like and resembling galaxies in the night sky

CRYSTAL TYPE: Granite-like alkaline feldspar syenite with fluorescent sodalite, sodium silicate with chlorine and aluminum; the ultimate glow-in-the-dark crystal

ZODIAC SIGN: Sagittarius (November 23–December 21)

CANDLE COLOR: Orange

PHYSICAL: Addresses water retention; regulates blood pressure and heart rate; alleviates inflammation, fever, headache, throat issues.

EMOTIONAL: Curbs fears, phobias, eating disorders, self-anger and -dislike, panic attacks; counters a tendency not to show yourself in the best light so as not to become the center of attention.

HOME: Draws the family together in love. First, illuminate Yooperlites representing those absent or estranged to call them home; an ideal moving-in gift for a first home to send continuing love to the person leaving the family home.

WORKPLACE: The ultimate communication and persuasion stone that, in its plain form, serves as a repository of confidence and charisma to win any discussion or make a good sale or contract.

CHILDREN: For creating a light display on special occasions in the child's life.

ANIMALS: As the plain rock for soothing overactive or sensitive pets before a known change in routine.

PROTECTION: Guards against those who flatter for personal gain and control.

MAGICKAL AND PSYCHIC USES

For connecting with the fey, especially water spirits; making contact with extraterrestrials if illuminated outdoors on a starry night.

SPECIAL PROPERTIES

To speak the truth kindly, not to diminish but to uplift others and cut through uncertainty and damaging misconceptions.

MYTHOLOGY AND HISTORY

Discovered on the shores of Lake Superior in the Upper Peninsula of Michigan by Erik Rintamaki in the summer of 2018 (some accounts date this discovery to 2017); at the time of writing, it is still possible to go Yooperlite hunting on the shore at night with a filtered UV light.

Youngite

COLORS: Orange, brown, salmon-pink, light tan, beige, and white

CRYSTAL TYPE: Brecciated (colored) jasper, coated with tiny, colorless microcrystalline druzy quartz

ZODIAC SIGN: Gemini (May 22–June 21)

CANDLE COLOR: White

PHYSICAL: Relieves pain in teeth, jaw and gums, mouth ulcers; addresses issues involving the lungs, large intestine, spleen; counters a malfunctioning nervous system, affecting mobility and speech.

EMOTIONAL: Tempers false memory syndrome; mitigates stress that makes everyday living hard; curbs lethargy.

HOME: A stone of fun and joy for birthdays, holidays, religious celebratory festivals, and spontaneous outings if family or friends are somewhat restrained; lets the inner child out to play.

WORKPLACE: Aids in asserting authority if you're newly promoted or temporarily acting as a team leader for colleagues during an absence of the regular person in charge; for mastering new techniques.

CHILDREN: Builds happy family memories and recalls family legends and customs.

ANIMALS: For a pet who has lost a lifetime mate.

PROTECTION: Guards against those who use status, wealth, and positions of authority to intimidate you into silence.

MAGICKAL AND PSYCHIC USES

For shamanistic dance, drumming, trance dance, and rattle; for trance mediumship; meditation if time is short or you lack a quiet space.

SPECIAL PROPERTIES

Fluoresces under a black/ultraviolet light, pastel blue to green; for dealing with grief when it is necessary to carry on life as normal.

MYTHOLOGY AND HISTORY

An Indigenous shamanic stone from eastern Wyoming; for all who feel they have lost part of themselves as a result of fulfilling the needs of others.

Yttrium, Yttrian, or Lavender Fluorite

COLORS: Pale or pinkish-lavender, violet, gray or reddish-brown. lustrous; may be lightly banded

CRYSTAL TYPE: A highly unusual fluorite variant where up to 20 percent of calcium is replaced by the rare element yttrium, forming masses rather than crystals, best as a tumbled stone

ZODIAC SIGN: Gemini (May 22–June 21)

CANDLE COLOR: Lavender

PHYSICAL: Creates new neural pathways; addresses chronic and acute lung conditions, sinuses, spinal injuries, nerve pain and damage, external growths.

EMOTIONAL: Curbs acute shyness, free-floating fear, debilitating anxiety about the future.

HOME: For decluttering home and life; keep the crystal wrapped in soft cloth when not in use.

WORKPLACE: Brings prosperity; aids in carrying plans through from concept to completion; helps with learning and teaching complex techniques and new technology; promotes success in driving tests and career evaluations.

CHILDREN: Place Yttrium with a photo of an older teen before major examinations or intense study when success is crucial.

ANIMALS: For establishing an animal sanctuary or rescue center.

PROTECTION: Guards against reactivating redundant karma at times of crisis.

MAGICKAL AND PSYCHIC USES

For mediumship, clairvoyance, channeling spirit guides and ancestors through automatic writing, psychic life coaching; developing psychic gifts; dream recall, psychic dreaming.

SPECIAL PROPERTIES

Knowing when to speak and when to remain silent, when to act or wait, when stay or go.

MYTHOLOGY AND HISTORY

From Mexico, Yttrium Fluorite, a high-vibration stone, is beloved by teachers, healers, and all who serve or guide humankind; brings intellectual achievement, incorporation of the higher self, universal wisdom, and light into the daily world.

Zebra Calcite

COLORS: Banded pale yellow, smoky gray/brown/black, and white, resembling zebra stripes

CRYSTAL TYPE: Calcium carbonate, also known as raw phantom calcite, though it is found as tumbled stones; may contain aragonite traces

ZODIAC SIGN: Gemini (May 22–June 21)

CANDLE COLOR: Yellow

PHYSICAL: Strengthens vision, hearing, sense of taste and smell; works as an insect bite repellent; propels pollutants and waste products from the body; addresses eczema.

EMOTIONAL: Keeps you from holding on to negative experiences and feelings; alleviates a sense of isolation; allays fear of crowds or crowded elevators.

HOME: Helps you accept others' idiosyncrasies without sacrificing your own lifestyle if you share multi-occupancy accommodations; for college reunions.

WORKPLACE: Balances sociability with the need to concentrate if you share a large, open-plan workspace; for professional athletes.

CHILDREN: Encourages children to join teams and participate in summer school and group activities.

ANIMALS: For the safety of herd animals—farm and wild; for socializing a pet to live with others if the pet is used to living just with you.

PROTECTION: Guards against being swept along by others' enthusiasm you do not share.

MAGICKAL AND PSYCHIC USES

For organizing a healing or mediumship circle; group meditations and visualizations; increasing telepathy with loved ones.

SPECIAL PROPERTIES

Promotes unique strengths and pride in one's own individuality, just as each zebra's markings are slightly different; finding fulfilling community organizations.

MYTHOLOGY AND HISTORY

Recently discovered in Mexico and different from the Western Australian Zebra Stone or Rock; Zebra Calcite is a symbol of the untamable spirit that needs freedom even in the busiest, most-people filled world.

Zebra Stone or Rock

COLORS: Black and white stripes; also reddish-brown bands on white to pale brown clay-rich matrix; gray, yellow, brown, red, or pinkish-brown; always characterized by stripes

CRYSTAL TYPE: Sedimentary siltstone formed over 600 million years ago; the black and white kind, found in Africa and Brazil, contains quartz and basinite

ZODIAC SIGN: Virgo (August 24–September 22)

CANDLE COLOR: Brown

PHYSICAL: Alleviates osteoporosis, chronic fatigue, post-viral weakness, palpitations, spasms; address issues stemming from the teeth, gums, bladder, skin, IBS; relieves pain.

EMOTIONAL: Controls addictions and habits adversely affecting health; dampens excessive sentimentality.

HOME: As ornaments, counteracts sluggish Earth energies beneath the home.

WORKPLACE: Aids in expressing creativity tangibly; for marathon runners, sports coaches, athletes, fitness instructors, gymnasts, weightlifters.

CHILDREN: Enables teens with gender issues to discover their true nature; for competing in sports.

ANIMALS: Makes hesitant pets adventurous.

PROTECTION: Shields against mind games; indicates whether it's better to persevere or quit.

MAGICKAL AND PSYCHIC USES

Black and white Zebra Stones are associated with yin and yang in feng shui, Taoist philosophy, energy balancing, moving meditation, grounding during astral travel, power animals, connecting with Indigenous cultures.

SPECIAL PROPERTIES

Success in sports, manifesting realistic plans through practical action; persevering in hard times.

MYTHOLOGY AND HISTORY

Several striped Earth Mother stones with similar properties are given the generic name zebra stone: zebra rock, zebra jasper, zebra marble, and zebra agate. Australian Zebra Stone was the first one discovered, in 1924, in Western Australia.

Zincite

COLORS: Dark red, deep orange, red-orange, orange-yellow, yellow-green, deep brown; sometimes more than one color
CRYSTAL TYPE: Zinc oxide, zinc ore (see also Schalenblende, page 422)
ZODIAC SIGN: Taurus (April 21–May 21)
CANDLE COLOR: Orange

PHYSICAL: Alleviates issues involving wounds, prostate, genitalia and reproductive organs of both sexes, libido, fertility, menopause, HIV, blockages, autoimmune diseases; addresses bronchitis, colds, influenza, hair, skin.
EMOTIONAL: Counters worries about keeping relationships from developing; allays fears of change; for when children leave home.
HOME: Aids in finding the right home, and achieving a profitable sale of the one you are leaving.
WORKPLACE: For teamwork, team leadership, combining two businesses, couples setting up home enterprises; an anti-computer virus amulet.
CHILDREN: Kept with a photo of your children playing, encourages sociability when meeting new children.
ANIMALS: For animals living together in stables, kennels, or rescue centers.
PROTECTION: Blocks harmful environmental energies; slows progress of infections and diseases.

MAGICKAL AND PSYCHIC USES
Dragon magick; candle or fire magick for good fortune, prosperity, and fertility; group meditation.
SPECIAL PROPERTIES
The problem solver's crystal for a detached overview of what is right for you; enhances well-being even in those less responsive to crystals.
MYTHOLOGY AND HISTORY
Called among Indigenous peoples the lifeblood of Mother Earth, natural Zincite is found in zinc and manganese mines in New Jersey, and rarely elsewhere. It is also grown artificially as a result of Zincite produced in a fire at a Polish zinc-smelting works a hundred years ago. Enhances creativity; attracts like-minded people; increases physical attraction.

Zoisite

COLOR: Green, yellowish-green, white, or gray
CRYSTAL TYPE: Calcium aluminum silicate hydroxide, obtaining its green color from the presence of chromium and vanadium (see also Ruby in Zoisite, Thulite or Rosaline, and Tanzanite, pages 414, 473, and 469)
ZODIAC SIGN: Gemini (May 22–June 21), Aries (March 21–April 20), and Taurus (April 21–May 21)
CANDLE COLOR: Green

PHYSICAL: Boosts energy; strengthens reproductive organs from puberty throughout life, plus cells, heart, spleen, pancreas, lungs, immune system; promotes fertility (especially linked with anxiety).
EMOTIONAL: Allays deep-seated fears, lack of trust, chronic pessimism.
HOME: For decorating and furnishing a home the way you want; ideal for starting over after loss of home due to divorce or bereavement.
WORKPLACE: Awakens dormant creativity; propels you to follow a life path different from one imposed on you through family pressures or chosen as a safe option.
CHILDREN: Reduces lethargy; for teens afraid of or discouraged from expressing their true sexuality or gender fluidity.
ANIMALS: Prompts overweight pets to exercise more.
PROTECTION: Transforms negative energies into greater positive power.

MAGICKAL AND PSYCHIC USES
Brings profound spiritual insights, especially during the zodiac periods Gemini, Taurus, and Aries, their full moons, and those born under those signs.
SPECIAL PROPERTIES
Encourages discovery and expression of the authentic self that may differ from the image shown to or imposed on you by the world.
MYTHOLOGY AND HISTORY
Though less exotic than its other forms, such as dazzling blue tanzanite, green Zoisite is a gentle healer after intrusive medical or surgical treatment; for end-of-life care spiritually as well as physically, easing the passage to the afterlife.

Z Stone

COLORS: Dark gray to black

CRYSTAL TYPE: Rare concretions found in the Sahara Desert, often in amazing sculpture-like shapes; some may have embedded fossils

ZODIAC SIGN: Aquarius (January 21–February 18)

CANDLE COLOR: Yellow

PHYSICAL: Clears neurological pathways; alleviates autoimmune conditions, migraines with distorted vision, frozen limbs, scoliosis.

EMOTIONAL: Enables you to live in the everyday world; keeps you from creating fantasies and more exciting alternative lives.

HOME: Brings happiness through a sense of security; aids in finding practical solutions if there are threats of eviction or repossession.

WORKPLACE: Offers answers and untapped sources of income that have been overlooked because they seem too obvious; helps persuade a workplace ghost to move on.

CHILDREN: Insulates psychic children from frightening experiences; for adolescents who are troubled by premonitions of unpreventable disasters.

ANIMALS: For pets who become distressed by their human companions' moods.

PROTECTION: Shields you from paranormal attack, especially tulpas or thought forms created by people dabbling with dark forces.

MAGICKAL AND PSYCHIC USES
Astral travel to other dimensions; connection with Fire and Earth elemental energies; wish magick.

SPECIAL PROPERTIES
For exploring spirituality through rocks and unpolished crystals.

MYTHOLOGY AND HISTORY
Associated with the mysteries of the Sahara Desert, this exceedingly rare stone is worth seeking, as it offers visions of other worlds, distant times, and alternative realities. At the same time, it maintains a secure connection with the Earth; in ancient magickal terms, provides the hedge or wall to allow magickal practitioners to keep one foot in the everyday world.

Zunyite

COLORS: White, shades of gray to pink, pale beige or tan, sometimes with small colorless sections embedded in matrix; fluoresces under UV light

CRYSTAL TYPE: Sorosilicate composed of aluminum, silicon, hydrogen, chlorine, oxygen, and fluorine

ZODIAC SIGN: Sagittarius (November 23–December 21)

CANDLE COLOR: White

PHYSICAL: Relieves pain; eases lasting problems or disability caused by accidents, natural disasters, war, or terrorism; alleviates progressive conditions where communication powers are gradually lost.

EMOTIONAL: Counters acute distress, unresolved grief over the loss of a child at any age or a parent in early childhood, post-traumatic stress disorder, postnatal depression.

HOME: For communication if families no longer share experiences, mealtimes, and outings.

WORKPLACE: A crystal of the arts, for those who create and those working in art colleges, galleries, or organizing exhibitions; encourages new talent.

CHILDREN: Fosters the expression of childhood imagination through art and literature.

ANIMALS: For litters struggling to thrive.

PROTECTION: Guards against those who use sulking and silence as weapons.

MAGICKAL AND PSYCHIC USES
Communication with the spirit world, both deceased relatives and spirit teachers.

SPECIAL PROPERTIES
Alleviates ongoing guilt because of a preventable accident or unwise actions; takes away insoluble sorrows that must be left behind.

MYTHOLOGY AND HISTORY
An extremely rare mineral that strengthens links between people and with other dimensions; through the years its energies will enhance your unique personality. Named after its discovery in 1884 at the Zuni mine in San Juan County, Colorado, gem-quality crystals are found near quartzite in Arizona.

Appendices

Crystals and Colors

Blue through Black

Color is one of the easiest ways to identify the best crystal for any purpose. If a crystal is vibrant or sparkling, it releases more active immediate energies than a softer hue. Hold two crystals of the same color in different hands—for example, a soft Blue Lace Agate and a rich gold and blue Lapis Lazuli—to feel the different sensations.

CRYSTAL COLOR	USES	HEALING	SUGGESTED CRYSTALS
BLUE	Leadership, justice, career, promotion, authority, marriage, partnerships of all kinds, prosperity, business expansion, peace	Thyroid gland, throat, fevers, inflammation, teeth, childhood rashes, cuts, bruises, scalds, burns; high blood pressure, vision, communication disorders	Chrysocolla, Turquoise, Lapis Lazuli, Andean Opal, Sodalite, Blue Topaz, Angelite, Celestine, Kyanite, Blue Lace Agate
PURPLE	Spirituality, imagination, dreams, psychic powers, intuition, teaching, counseling, healing from higher sources such as angels, energy healing like Reiki, banishing past sorrow or present troublesome influences; psychic protection	Headaches (including migraines), ears, hair, sinusitis, childbirth, addictions, neuroses, phobias, nerve endings and connections, allergies to chemicals and modern living, hyperactivity, insomnia.	Amethyst, Charoite, Lepidolite, Purple Fluorite, Chevron Amethyst, Kunzite, Sugilite
PINK	Reconciliation, happy family relationships, friendship, kindness, children and teenagers, girls entering puberty, young or new love, trust after betrayal	Glands, ears, PMS, skin, ulcers, psychosomatic and stress-induced illnesses, insomnia, nightmares; family ills, babies, children; abuse and self-hatred	Rose Quartz, Mangano and Pink Calcite, Andean Opal, Rhodonite, Rhodochrosite, Pink Chalcedony

(continued)

CRYSTAL COLOR	USES	HEALING	SUGGESTED CRYSTALS
BROWN	Practical matters, security, gradual accumulation of money, learning new skills in later years; home, property, financial institutions, officialdom (also blue), older people, animals, finding what is lost or stolen, perseverance, patience	Feet, legs, bowels, hernia, anus, prostate, chronic conditions, relief of chronic pain; growths, degenerative conditions in old age, panic attacks	Golden Tiger's Eye, Petrified Wood, Jasper, Banded Agate, Desert Rose, Chiastolite, Zircon
GRAY	Compromise, adaptability, ability to merge into the background, neutralizing unfriendly energies, negotiations, keeping secrets, shielding from psychic attack	Lesions, wounds, burns, tissue and nerve connections, obsessions and acute anxiety, persistent pain	Smoky Quartz, Hematite, Laboradite, Iron Pyrites, Banded Agate, Cat's Eye
BLACK	Transformation; peaceful endings; grief; banishing sorrow, guilt, and destructive influences; acceptance of what cannot be changed; working within restrictions, blocking a negative or harmful force; psychic protection	Pain relief, constipation, IBS, side effects of invasive treatments such as x-rays or chemotherapy	Obsidian, Snowflake Obsidian, Jet, Tourmaline, Onyx, Apache Tear, Obsidian Arrows

White through Green

Color is one of the easiest ways to choose a crystal for a particular purpose, including for healing, empowerment, or protection, if you do not have time to search the book or you are choosing from your personal collection of special crystals (see also Crystals and Colors, Blue through Black, page 520). I would suggest you keep one of each of the main colors in a bowl. I have listed popular crystals for each color.

CRYSTAL COLOR	USES	HEALING	SUGGESTED CRYSTALS
WHITE SOLIDUS COLORLESS	Originality, new beginnings, developing talents, ambitions, innovations, good health, contact with angels and spirit guides; can be substituted for any other color	Whole-body healing; integration of mind, body, and soul; neurological disorders; autoimmune system; acute pain relief	Aragonite, Clear and Optical Calcite, Fluorite, Herkimer Diamond, Crystal Quartz, Topaz
WHITE SOLIDUS CLOUDY (translucent) or OPAQUE (solid color)	Nurturing; slower new beginnings, unfolding potential; protection against negativity, mothers and babies; granting wishes, calling love from the past or from afar	Hormones; fluid balance; fertility, pregnancy; gradual recovery from illness, depression, or exhaustion; bone marrow, cells	Calcite, Chalcedony, Howlite, Magnesite, Milky or Snow Quartz, Moonstone, Selenite
RED	Movement, courage, positive change, strength, action, determination, assertiveness, power, sexual passion, male potency, taking the initiative, competitiveness, protecting loved ones, overcoming obstacles	Energy, muscles, low blood pressure, poor circulation, anemia; feet, hands, skeleton, reproductive organs	Aventurine, Blood or Fire Agate, Garnet, Jasper, Mahogany Obsidian, Poppy Jasper, Ruby, Red Tiger's Eye
ORANGE	Confidence, joy, creativity, female fertility (also red), abundance, independence; self-esteem and image, happiness, media, self-employment	Ovaries, intestines, pulse rate, kidneys, bladder, menstruation, menopause, food allergies, arthritis, rheumatism, immune system, food-related addictions	Amber, Aragonite, Peach Aventurine, Calcite, Carnelian, Mookaite

(continued)

CRYSTAL COLOR	USES	HEALING	SUGGESTED CRYSTALS
YELLOW	Logic, memory, determination, concentration, study, examinations, tests, new technology, clear communication (also blue); job changes, moneymaking ventures, speculation, conventional healing, repelling envy, malice, spite, deception	Lymphatic system, metabolism, blood sugar (also green and blue), digestion, liver, gallbladder, pancreas, spleen, nervous system, eczema, skin problems, nausea	Yellow and Honey Calcite, Citrine, Lemon Chrysoprase, Jade, Jasper, Mookaite, Golden Topaz
GREEN	Love, fidelity, commitment, beauty, horticulture, environment; healing through nature, crystal healing, gradual growth in every way, health, wealth, luck-bringer, winning competitions	Heart, lungs, respiratory system, infections and viruses, especially colds and influenza (also blue), pollen and fur allergies, addictions and obsessions (also blue)	Amazonite, Aventurine, Calcite, Chrysoprase, Fluorite, Jade, Nephrite and Jadeite, Malachite, Serpentine, Tree Agate

Crystal Grids or Layouts

COLORS: Choose a mix of colored crystals (see pages 520 and 523 for color meanings) or the same crystal color to represent any physical, emotional, or spiritual purpose, or a combination

CRYSTAL TYPE: Crystal layouts or grids are tumbled stone crystal pattens, as elaborate or simple as you wish, usually with a larger central crystal, clear quartz or amethyst as a Master Crystal, wand, sphere, or pyramid; from a single, seven-, or eight-crystal ring to radiating wheels; many-armed stars and/or interlocking circles (see diagram). There are no correct layouts, only what feels right for different purposes; if uncertain, copy a simple mandala design.

ZODIAC SIGN: Leo (July 23–August 23)

CANDLE COLOR: White

PHYSICAL: Grids may be placed around a bed, under a chair, around a room, or around a home if there are frequent recurring illnesses, or encircling the photo of someone sick who is absent.

EMOTIONAL: Addresses scattered, chaotic energies, plus total uncertainty because of ever-changing needs.

HOME: Crystal layouts attract ongoing healing, as well as empowering and protective energies; draw good fortune, health, love, and wealth; a bowl of mixed tumbled stones enables family and visitors, or you alone, to add or change the evolving layout, generating unity and harmony.

WORKPLACE: A small layout—on your desk, around a computer, phone, or workspace—creates a private space or invites appreciation and orders, according to the mix.

CHILDREN: Supervised if young, even active children become tranquil, instinctively adding the most needed crystals to heal secret worries.

ANIMALS: Secure crystals to the underside of a sick animal's bed, where a pet will not swallow them.

PROTECTION: Every layout, even the smallest, radiates protection; buried near a boundary or arranged among plants, the layout deters intrusive neighbors and thieves.

MAGICKAL AND PSYCHIC USES

Whatever its purpose, the grid becomes an increasing repository of whatever is most needed; trust your instincts as to the right crystal choices and arrangements.

SPECIAL PROPERTIES

Odd numbers of crystals increase health, money, career prospects, love, and happiness; even numbers of crystals bring stability, guard against ill health, bad luck, or negativity; round crystals call love, fertility, happy families, children, and animals; elongated crystals attract prosperity, change, career success, and travel; points are dynamic, facing inward for power and outward to repel negativity.

MYTHOLOGY AND HISTORY

Traditionally, touch each crystal clockwise from the center, using a clear crystal wand or Master Crystal (page 297), asking the blessing of your special guardians; reempower the grid monthly, lighting a silver candle on full moon, if needed adding or changing the purpose and grid. For a permanent grid, fix the grid on wood with organic glue. Whenever you have an urgent need or worry, light a candle, writing the wish on white paper in green ink (the angel color); fold your written request beneath the central crystal.

Gem and Crystal Jewelry

Each zodiac sign possesses an affinity with certain gems and crystals, as you will have seen in each crystal entry under Symbolic Associations. Wearing a crystal or gemstone compatible with your zodiac sign is the most powerful and protective gem or crystal you can wear. You may also have special gems given for a birthday, graduation, engagement, your wedding day, or the birth of a child, filled with the love of the giver.

Some relatives buy a pearl or small diamond for a newborn each year on their birthday, and, for their eighteenth birthday, set them in jewelry.

You can collect crystal bracelets and pendants for different purposes. As each metal has significance, check the entries for the most appropriate.

CLEANSING AND EMPOWERING YOUR SPECIAL JEWELRY

If a crystal is pointed or angular, gently stroke it, base to tip, down again to the base and up again to create a rhythmic movement.

For a round or oval crystal, hold it in your nondominant hand and with the index figure of your dominant hand, spiral over the crystal surface until you connect with its inner pulse.

Empower each crystal, blowing softly three times on it and between each breath saying, "Be—[breath in] for—[breath out]—me [breath in]. Afterward, dedicate it to the current purpose.

THE MAGICKAL SIGNIFICANCE OF JEWELRY

Necklaces or pendants protect your inner throat energy center from spiteful words and give you the power to say what you want or need to express (see Crystals and Chakras, page 147).

Earrings guard your third or psychic eye in the center of your brow above and between your eyes, where nasty thoughts from others enter; this also keeps you safe from malicious paranormal experiences.

Bracelets shield your sensitive loving heart and also send out *love me* vibes because your inner wrist pulse points are connected to the heart.

A necklace or pendant that covers your heart does the same thing. A ring worn on your wedding finger attracts a soul twin.

A belly button ring protects your inner sun center, your solar plexus chakra, at the base and center of your rib cage to give you power and confidence. It also guards your invisible center of fears, feelings, and cravings around your navel or sacral chakra.

Ankle bracelets and toe rings offer defense through your root kundalini center, covering your lower spine, against physical threats or danger, if you are intimidated by verbal bullying, if you travel alone late at night, or if you have abuse issues in a relationship, also if you have a tendency to panic.

Toxic Crystals

Tumbled stones or minerals included in quartz are generally safe to handle. Crystals that contain sulfur, aluminum, lead, and traces of asbestos in tumbled-stone form are also safe to use in Reiki, meditation, healing grids, etc., although I personally prefer not to, to be totally cautious. However, the amount of aluminum is very small in a single tumbled stone.

Children and Pets

Of course, you won't let young children or pets swallow or lick crystals, which they might ingest. Tumbled clear and rose quartz, amethyst, and most calcites and agates are safe for children under supervision.

Raw Crystals

Raw or unpolished crystals, if they are soft or porous, can easily start to dissolve, flake, or give off dust and should be handled with care. Wash hands after handling, as absorbing the dust, even from nontoxic crystals can, if you are sensitive, be hazardous.

  Never drink or eat powdered homemade crystal remedies. Some people keep a clear quartz tumbled stone in a bottle of water they sip throughout the day or to empower a glass of water overnight, which is perfectly fine.

Crystal Elixirs
(see also page 145)

I have suggested an indirect method of using crystals to make crystal elixirs or waters, if you are not certain of your crystal composition; this method is just as effective as soaking a crystal in water, without any worries. Raw crystals should not be soaked directly.

I have given mineral compositions for many of the crystals throughout the book and, where possible, have avoided listing toxic ones containing lead, asbestos, etc. Some do contain copper or aluminum and are excellent tumbled for healing, but not suitable for direct elixirs. If in doubt, check the mineral content on the internet and use the indirect elixir method.

For example, while tumbled Tiger's Eye is quite safe, raw Tiger's Eye may contain asbestos, as may some fibrous Serpentine.

Most quartzes are safe to soak, including Clear Quartz and Amethyst (these two will meet most elixir needs), Rose Quartz, most agates, most calcites (though not for prolonged periods) and some but not all jaspers (for example, bumblebee jasper, not in the book, contains arsenic and sulfur).

Master Crystals

Accepted Master Crystals include:
Bridge Quartz, Cathedral, Channeling Quartz, Devic Temple Quartz, Dolphin/Mother and Child Quartz, all forms of Dow and Elestial, Fenster or Window Quartz, Future Time Link or Timeline Quartz), Generator or Projector Quartz, Golden Healer Quartz, Isis Quartz, Key or Keyhold Quartz, Lemurian Seed Crystal, Manifestation Quartz Past Time Link or Timeline Quartz, Record Keeper Quartz, Tabby or Tabular Quartz, Transmitter Quartz, Twin Soul, Twin Flame, or Gemini Quartz Crystal, Yin Yang quartz.

Crystal Care

These are some crystals you should avoid soaking directly in water to make elixirs (I have noted some in the section on elixirs), and instead use them as tumbled stones, cabochons, or polished for healing whenever possible. It is not a comprehensive list.

- Actinolite
- Adamite
- Ajoite
- Alexandrite
- Amazonite
- Aquamarine
- Aragonite
- Atacamite
- Aventurine
- Azurite
- Beryls
- Black Tourmaline
- Boji
- Brochnantite
- Cavansite
- Celestite
- Chalcopyrite
- Chrysocolla
- Cinnabar

- Copper in any form
- Covellite
- Crocoite
- Dalmation Jasper
- Dioptase
- Dumortierite
- Emerald
- Erithyrite
- Feldspar
- Fluorite
- Fuchsite
- Garnets (all)
- Gem Silica
- Halite
- Hematite Iolite
- Kunzite
- Labradorite
- Lapis
- Lepidolite

- Malachite
- Marcasite
- Meteorite
- Mica
- Moldavite
- Moonstones
- Morganite
- Pietersite
- Prehnite
- Pyrite
- Realgar
- Ruby
- Selenite
- Serpentine (some)
- Smithsonite
- Sodalite
- Spinels
- Staurolite
- Stibnite

- Stilbite
- Sugilite
- Sulfur
- Sunstone
- Tanzanite
- Topaz
- Tourmaline
- Tremolite
- Turquoise
- Vandanite
- Variscite
- Vesuvianite
- Wavellite
- Wulfenite
- Zircon
- Zoisite

Index of Crystals

General Index